Ratio	Computation of Ratio	Indicates
9. Number of times preferred dividends earned (Chapter 15)	$\dfrac{\text{Net income}}{\text{Annual preferred dividends}}$	The primary measure of the safety of an investment in preferred stock—the ability of a firm to meet its preferred dividend requirement
10. Creditors' equity ratio (Chapter 2)	$\dfrac{\text{Total liabilities}}{\text{Total assets}}$	The percent of creditor sources of total assets
11. Stockholders' equity ratio (Chapter 2)	$\dfrac{\text{Stockholders' equity}}{\text{Total assets}}$	The percent of owner sources of total assets

Earning power and growth potential measurements

Ratio	Computation of Ratio	Indicates
12. Earnings yield rate (Chapter 15)	$\dfrac{\text{Earnings per share}}{\text{Market price per share}}$	Earnings as related to market value of the shares
13. Dividends yield rate (Chapter 15)	$\dfrac{\text{Dividends per share}}{\text{Market price per share}}$	Dividend payout as related to market value of the shares
14. Earnings per share of common[a] stock for a corporation with a simple capital structure (Chapters 3, 13)	$\dfrac{\text{Net income} - \text{Annual preferred dividend}}{\text{Average outstanding common shares}}$	The company's earning power as related to common stockholders' equity
15. Price-earnings ratio (Chapter 3)	$\dfrac{\text{Market price per share}}{\text{Earnings per share}}$	Market value per share as related to profitability of the firm
16. Rate of return on total investment (Chapter 3)	$\dfrac{\text{Net income} + \text{Interest expense}}{\text{Average total assets}}$	The profitability of the firm expressed as a rate of return on total investments by both owners and creditors
17. Rate of return on stockholders' equity (Chapter 3)	$\dfrac{\text{Net income}}{\text{Average stockholders' equity}}$	The profitability of the firm expressed as a rate of return on stockholders' equity
18. Book value per share (Chapter 13)	$\dfrac{\text{Common stockholders' equity}}{\text{Outstanding common shares}}$	The amount of net assets available for each share of common stock

Other measurements

Financial structure measurements: These measurements can be determined from a common-size balance sheet that shows the composition of items on the balance sheet.

Asset utilization ratios: These are measures of asset turnover or the dollars of sales generated by each dollar of investment in total assets or in each individual asset.

Operating performance ratios: These are measures that show the relationship of each income statement item or groups of items to sales.

[a] See Chapter 13.

Financial Accounting

Second Edition

Isaac N. Reynolds *University of North Carolina at Chapel Hill*
Allen B. Sanders *Elon College*
A. Douglas Hillman *Drake University*

The Dryden Press
Chicago   New York   Philadelphia   San Francisco   Montreal   Toronto
London   Sydney   Tokyo   Mexico City   Rio de Janeiro   Madrid

Acquisitions Editor: Larry Armstrong
Project Editors: Nancy Shanahan, Anne Knowles
Managing Editor: Jane Perkins
Design Director: Alan Wendt
Production Manager: Claire Roth
Cover Photo: Sharon Cooper
Copy Editor: Michele Heinz
Indexer: Lois Oster
Compositor: The Clarinda Company
Text Type: 10/12 ITC Garamond Light

Library of Congress Cataloging in Publication Data

Reynolds, Isaac N.
   Financial accounting.

   Rev. ed. of: Financial accounting/Albert Slavin,
Isaac N. Reynolds, Allen B. Sanders. c1980.
   Includes bibliographical references and index.
   1. Accounting. I. Sanders, Allen B. II. Hillman,
A. Douglas. III. Slavin, Albert. Financial accounting.
IV. Title.
HF5635.R43   1986   657   85-4432
ISBN 0-03-001384-4

Printed in the United States of America
678-016-98765432

Copyright 1986 CBS College Publishing
Copyright 1980 The Dryden Press
All rights reserved

Address orders:
383 Madison Avenue
New York, NY 10017

Address editorial correspondence:
One Salt Creek Lane
Hinsdale, IL 60521

CBS COLLEGE PUBLISHING
The Dryden Press
Holt, Rinehart and Winston
Saunders College Publishing

Acknowledgments for use of extracts and logos:
El-9, p. 36, The Goodyear Tire and Rubber Company; P1-2A, p. 38, with permission from Ford Motor Company; P1-2B, p. 42, with permission from General Motors Corporation; P9-7A, p. 407, CBS Inc.; P9-7B, p. 411, with permission from Dennison Manufacturing; P16-5B, p. 684, with permission from Varlen Corporation.

To our esteemed colleague
Albert Slavin
who has retired from active participation in this edition.

The Dryden Press Series in Accounting

Belkaoui
Cost Accounting: A Multidimensional Emphasis

Davidson, Stickney, and Weil
**Financial Accounting:
An Introduction to Concepts, Methods, and Uses**
Fourth Edition

Davidson, Hanouille, Stickney, and Weil
**Intermediate Accounting:
Concepts, Methods, and Uses**
Fourth Edition

Davidson, Maher, Stickney, and Weil
**Managerial Accounting:
An Introduction to Concepts, Methods, and Uses**
Second Edition

Huefner and Largay
Advanced Financial Accounting
Second Edition

Lee
Elementary Accounting

Mueller and Smith
Accounting: A Book of Readings
Second Edition

Reynolds, Sanders, and Hillman
Principles of Accounting
Third Edition

Reynolds, Sanders, and Hillman
Financial Accounting
Second Edition

Titard
Managerial Accounting: An Introduction

Preface

Financial Accounting, second edition, is designed for an undergraduate first semester financial accounting course or for the first financial accounting course in a graduate program. It is built on the assumption that the student has had no previous accounting education and little, if any, introduction to business. Thus, every effort has been made to provide thorough and simple explanations and illustrations of financial accounting concepts and procedures.

Today, a person is surrounded by media output regarding the corporate form of business. The first actual financial reports that a person encounters are likely to be corporate annual reports.

This book emphasizes the corporate approach to accounting. Beginning in Chapter 1, this text provides sufficient corporate accounting concepts to allow that form of business to serve as a model throughout the book. The text material is up to date with the current Financial Accounting Standards Board pronouncements and contains frequent references to authoritative sources.

Revising a book offers an opportunity for the authors to refine the textual material and illustrations. This has been accomplished with the aid of recommendations from many reviewers, whose names are listed in the Acknowledgments section of this preface.

General Organization of the Book

The book is organized in four parts:

1. The Basic Accounting Model
2. Income Measurement and Valuation Issues
3. Sources and Uses of Capital
4. Financial Reporting.

Preface

Part One—The Basic Accounting Model (Chapters 1 through 6)

In Part One, the basic accounting model is developed with a corporate orientation. Because the student will need to understand certain generally accepted accounting standards, a short appendix to Chapter 1 explains such basic principles as consistency, materiality, and matching of revenues and expenses. These concepts are more fully developed as they arise in individual chapters, where the student is better prepared to handle them.

Part Two—Income Measurement and Valuation Issues (Chapters 7 through 11)

Part Two begins in Chapter 7 with a discussion of compound interest techniques. The voucher system and payroll procedures are appended to Chapter 8, "Control of Cash," and can be included at the discretion of the instructor. In Chapter 9, current payables and receivables are combined so that the student can study the features these concepts have in common. Contrary to tradition, payables are presented first because they provide a better opportunity for the student to obtain a good understanding of bank discount where the maturity value of notes is the same as face value. Inventory coverage includes both the periodic and perpetual systems, methods of estimating inventories, and the lower of cost or market concept.

Part Three—Sources and Uses of Capital (Chapters 12 through 15)

Part Three contains an in-depth study of owners' equity issues for single proprietorships and partnerships, and corporations. Debt structures are illustrated in detail. Because the accounting for short-term and long-term investments involves concepts that parallel accounting for debt, this material is included here. The illustrations of investment in bonds in Chapter 15 use the same debt illustrations that are covered in Chapter 14.

Part Four—Financial Reporting (Chapters 16 and 17)

Part Four opens with a new chapter that explains consolidated statements and international accounting. Chapter 17 introduces the statement of changes in financial position with the simple analytical approach. Two appendixes then illustrate the work sheet and T account methods.

End-of-Book Appendixes

Three appendixes are included at the end of the book. Appendix A discusses the impact of the computer on accounting, emphasizing the role of microcomputers. Appendix B briefly discusses price-level accounting, incorporating the changes brought about by FASB 82. Appendix C contains compound interest tables for the four basic compound interest techniques.

Highlights of the Second Edition

Financial Accounting, second edition, contains many changes that strengthen and make it a more teachable book. These include the following:

1. Real-life references and examples now appear in most chapters. Real-life examples are also included in the end-of-chapter material.
2. The end-of-chapter material in each chapter contains 8 to 14 single-concept exercises that cover each important new concept introduced in the chap-

Preface

ter. There are also 12 to 14 problems, divided equally into A and B sections, each of which integrates several accounting concepts. Newly included in the integrative problems are two *thought-provoking problems* for each chapter. Some of these are taken from real-life situations in which actual U.S. firms are identified.

3. Managerial analysis (ratio analysis) is included in almost every chapter at a spot that makes it more meaningful. In addition, a summary of the key ratios with the method of calculation and meaning is shown in the inside front cover of the book.

4. Internal control issues are also included in virtually every chapter. A summary of the key internal control principles and procedures appears on the inside back cover of the book.

5. Included in Chapter 1 is a complete set of financial statements with boxed explanations of the major sections they contain. These statements provide a comprehensive illustration of the conceptual framework explained in this chapter, and they give students a handy reference to check against later discussions of financial statements and their relationships.

6. The basic accounting model for a service organization has been spread over five chapters rather than four. This makes the opening chapters more even in length and level of difficulty.

7. The discussion of payroll accounting has been condensed and is included in Chapter 8 as an appendix. Also included as an appendix to Chapter 8 is a brief illustration of the voucher system.

8. Capital leases are included as an appendix to Chapter 11.

9. Equity issues related to proprietorships and partnerships are briefly discussed and illustrated in a new Chapter 12.

10. Chapter 13 contains a new appendix illustrating two methods of preparing the stockholders' equity section of the balance sheet.

11. Chapter 16, "Consolidated Statements and International Accounting," is new. The common theme among the topics in this chapter is the concept of reciprocal accounts. A brief appendix to Chapter 16 covers the basic concepts of international accounting.

12. Chapter 17, "Statement of Changes in Financial Position," has been completely rewritten to make the area more teachable. The chapter now emphasizes the simple analytical approach to the development of information for the statement. In two appendixes, both the work sheet and T account method of accumulating the information for the statement are presented.

13. Computers, especially microcomputers, have revolutionized the processing of accounting information. Appendix A, new to this edition, describes the use of computers in processing routine accounting information. It also describes the use of such software packages as electronic spreadsheets and data base management in the production of accounting information by managers.

14. Price-level accounting is covered in Appendix B, which briefly discusses both general price level and current cost issues.

Key Teaching Features of the Book

Financial Accounting, second edition, contains many features that will enhance the teaching of accounting to students who have had no business experience.

1. Learning goals are listed after each chapter introduction. Students are told what major concepts they are expected to understand when they have completed the chapter.

2. As key terms are introduced and defined in the book, they are shown in color. A glossary at the end of each chapter defines each key term for that chapter.

3. The T form of the ledger account is emphasized throughout the book; the debit-credit-balance form is illustrated for subsidiary ledgers.

4. The totality of accounting is emphasized in the early chapters. This will enable the student to see its broad influence and the sequence of accounting procedures, which should aid in learning specific techniques and relationships.

5. Many of the key concepts are highlighted for easy recognition.

6. The book contains many new teaching diagrams and flow charts.

7. Some optional topics are discussed in appendixes to chapters. Any or all of the appendixes may be taught or omitted with no loss of continuity.

8. The end-of-chapter material includes exercises suitable for classroom laboratory situations or homework, as well as questions and problems for in-class or out-of-class assignments. Each exercise and problem has a side head that describes its aim or content.

For the Student

Why Study Accounting?

A forward-thinking group of accounting educators joined together in 1971 to study the approach to teaching introductory college courses in accounting. This group was sponsored by a national accounting firm, Price Waterhouse. Its report said: "The purpose of accounting is to provide information that is useful in decision making affecting resource allocation . . . at all levels in society."[1] Each of us must make financial decisions daily. Those decisions will be much better if the person who makes them understands how the information upon which he or she relies was developed. In business and in personal transactions, the person with a knowledge of accounting will have a distinct advantage.

Use of the Textbook Assignments in the text can best be read by first scanning the material to acquire a general idea of the content. The material should then be studied carefully, with particular attention devoted to difficult portions. Special attention should be given to charts, diagrams, and model forms and statements. Headings, indentations, and captions should be ob-

---

[1] *A New Introduction to Accounting: Report of the Study Group on Introductory Accounting* (New York: Price Waterhouse Foundation, 1971), p. 11.

served carefully, and the origin or derivation of all amounts should be determined. Ample marginal notations and underlining by the student will highlight the significant data for later review, class discussion, and examinations.

Answering Questions and Problems   To answer questions and problems, it is most important to read them with great care in order to assimilate the facts and, particularly, the requirements. Most accounting problems require some kind of schedule, statement, exhibit, work sheet, journal entry, or T account. Statements should always include a heading that gives the name of the business, the name of the statement, and the date or period covered. The derivation of computed totals should be shown in the solution. Answers to essay questions should be based on logical reasoning and should be well written.

If a problem allows for two or more solutions, an assumption should be made and the problem should be solved on the basis of that assumption. If time permits, alternative solutions should be furnished to correspond with alternative assumptions. This is especially desirable if the problem is intentionally vague or, because of its content, is open to several possible interpretations. The main purpose of homework problems and exercises is to achieve practice in applying concepts from the chapter. The correct answer, while important, is not the primary aim. It is the "hands-on" experience that comes only from putting concepts to use that is most effective in preparing for examinations. It is therefore helpful to rework problems and then to compare the reworked solutions with the original corrected solutions. Solved problems should be filed systematically for future use.

Study Guide

The *Study Guide*, written by **A. Douglas Hillman, Drake University,** differs from the usual workbook of exercises found with most accounting texts. This learning aid is in a programmed learning format, which requires students to make sure they know the structure and derivation of amounts in the illustrations of accounting techniques and reports. It leads the student through some of the more difficult concepts in the book, and provides great help in determining whether he or she understands the important ideas and concepts in each chapter. Each chapter also contains a self-test of learning goal achievement, with answers to check test results.

Working Papers

The single volume of *Working Papers* contains the proper form for each exercise and for each pair of A and B problems. Some of the working papers for earlier chapters are partially completed; in later chapters, the working papers contain less help for the student.

Practice Set

The learning package contains one practice set, **Foster Furniture, Inc.** written by **Donald R. Davis, St. Louis Community College,** specifically for this edition. The package is designed for both manual solution and solution using a microcomputer.

Preface

In addition, instructors may want to adapt one or more of the three practice sets written by Davis for use with *Principles of Accounting,* third edition, by Isaac N. Reynolds, Allen B. Sanders, and A. Douglas Hillman. These sets, described below, are available in manual and computerized versions. The anticipated solution time for the manual version of each set is 10 to 15 hours.

Francis and Daughter A single proprietorship practice set with documents, this set is designed for use after completion of Chapter 6. This set uses only the general journal, general ledger, and subsidiary ledgers.

MEE-High Furniture Store This set features a wholesale business operated as a single proprietorship using special journals. It is designed for use anytime after completion of Chapter 6.

Catalina Island Corporation This is a corporate practice set that is designed to be used after completion of Chapter 13. The main focus is on analyzing and recording transactions that directly affect the capital structure.

For the Instructor

In addition to the text, this package includes the instructor's manual, solutions manual, test banks A and B, transparency acetates of chapter concepts for classroom use, a computerized practice set (along with three others from *Principles of Accounting,* third edition, by the same authors, that may be adapted for use with this book), a study guide, and working papers.

Instructor's Manual

This manual contains the following elements:

1. Suggested assignments
2. Chapter organizers for each chapter
   a. Summary of major concepts
   b. Behavioral objectives
   c. Lecture notes
   d. Content analysis of exercises and problems
3. Suggested uses for the teaching transparencies

Solutions Manual

This manual contains solutions to all questions, exercises, and problems. It is an oversize format that also serves as transparency masters.

Test Banks A and B

The test banks are bound together in one volume. Each test bank contains two parts: (1) a set of 30 true-false and multiple choice questions for each chapter (these are suitable for computer scoring); and (2) a set of achievement tests for each semester, consisting of (a) periodic tests for logical chapter groupings, (b) a midterm examination, and (c) a comprehensive final examination. Test banks A and B have the same depth of coverage and level of difficulty. Solutions are included with the test banks. Achievement tests are readily reproducible on any copying machine. If the chapter groupings of the achievement test do not suit an individual professor's syllabus, they can be cut and pasted to create new examinations.

Preface

Acknowledgments

Sincere thanks are extended to those dedicated professors, practicing accountants, other professionals, and students whose suggestions for improvement have been significant:

Stevie Glass Champion
Chapel Hill, North Carolina

Gail Robinson
Burlington, North Carolina

Hobart W. Adams
University of Akron

Allan B. Afterman
Univ. of Illinois at Chicago

Enzo V. Allegretti
Westchester Community College

Lana Bone
West Valley College

M. Robert Carver, Jr.
Southern Illinois University

Charles F. Chanter
Grand Rapids Junior College

Joe J. Cramer, Jr.
Howard University

Donald R. Davis
St. Louis Community College at Meramec

Carol Dobitz
Moorhead State University

John W. Durham
Northern Arizona University

William G. Engelbret
Pennsylvania State University

David F. Fetyko
Kent State University

Joseph L. Ford
Mesa Community College

William S. Jensen
Lewis & Clark College

Robert P. Kenny
St. Michael's College

Richard F. Kochanek
University of Connecticut

Charles A. Konkol
Univ. of Wisconsin at Milwaukee

Larry F. Konrath
University of Toledo

Frank Korman
Mountain View College

James M. Krueger
Univ. of Missouri at St. Louis

Marshall K. Pitman
Univ. of Texas at San Antonio

George D. Sanders
University of Alabama

Robert Trezevant
College of Marin

Richard E. Veazey
Grand Valley State College

Ara G. Volkan
Syracuse University

Bea L. Wallace
Univ. of Texas at San Antonio

Dick Wasson
Central Washington University

Finally, we would like to thank the staff of The Dryden Press—Bill Schoof, Jane Perkins, Larry Armstrong, Anne Knowles, Nancy Shanahan, Alan Wendt, and Diane Tenzi—as well as Michele Heinz, copy editor, for their help in turning the manuscript into a bound book.

Isaac N. Reynolds
Chapel Hill, North Carolina

Allen B. Sanders
Elon College, North Carolina

A. Douglas Hillman
West Des Moines, Iowa

Contents

Part One The Basic Accounting Model / 1

Chapter 1 The Nature and Function of Accounting / 3

Nature of Accounting / 4
Definition of Accounting / 4
History of Accounting / 5
Why Study Accounting? / 6
Who Uses Accounting Information? / 7
  External Users / Internal Users

What Accountants Do / 8
The Entity Concept / 9

The Basic Financial Statements / 10
The Income Statement / 10
The Balance Sheet / 12
Statement of Retained Earnings / 13
Statement of Changes in Financial Position / 14
Interrelationship of Financial Statements / 15

Financial Statements Illustrated and Explained / 15
Significance of Financial Statements / 21
  Significance of the Income Statement / Significance of the Statement of Retained Earnings / Significance of the Balance Sheet / Significance of Statement of Changes in Financial Position / Significance of Notes to Financial Statements

Appendix 1.1   Generally Accepted Accounting Principles (GAAP) / 24
Sources of Generally Accepted Accounting Principles (GAAP) / 25
  American Institute of Certified Public Accountants (AICPA) / Financial Accounting Standards Board (FASB) / Securities and Exchange Commission (SEC)

Generally Accepted Accounting Principles / 27
  Entity / Going Concern / Consistency / Conservatism / Periodicity / Objective Evidence / Materiality / Full Disclosure / Historical Cost / Stable Dollar / Revenue Realization / Matching Expense and Revenue / Other Concepts

Chapter 2 The Development of the Basic Accounting Model / 47
The Entity Concept / 48
Assets / 48
Equities: Liabilities and Owners' Equity / 49

Contents

Forms of Business Organization / 49
  Corporation / Single Proprietorship / Partnership
The Accounting Equation / 52
The Balance Sheet / 52
Need for Classification in a Financial Statement / 54
  Classification of Assets—Current Assets / Classification of Assets—Property, Plant, and Equipment / Classification of Liabilities—Current Liabilities / Classification of Liabilities—Long-Term Liabilities / Classification of Ownership Claims—Stockholders' Equity

Developing the Accounting System / 58
Objective Evidence—The Business Document / 58
Transactions of the Modern Realty Corporation / 59
  Analysis of Transactions—Effect on Balance Sheet
Expansion of the Accounting Equation / 63
Accumulation of Transaction Data / 65
  A Separate Page for Each Item / Division of Each Accounting Page into Columns—Creation of Accounts
Tools of Accounting / 70
  The T Account / Debits and Credits / The Formal Account / The Ledger
Managerial Analysis of Financial Position / 72
  Debt-Equity Ratios / Common-Size Balance Sheet
Internal Control / 74

Chapter 3

A Simple Accounting System; Dynamic Measurement Accounts / 89

Capturing and Processing Financial Data / 90
A Simple Accounting System / 90
Illustration of Journalizing and Posting / 91

The Modern Realty Corporation Illustration / 94
Journalizing and Posting / 94
  Trial Balance / Balance Sheet

Recording Changes in Stockholders' Equity / 98
Revenues / 98
Gains / 100
Expenses / 100
Losses / 101
Operational Terms / 102
Operating Results / 102
Authorized Withdrawals by Stockholders—Dividends / 103
Expanding Rules for Debits and Credits / 104
The General Ledger and Subsidiary Ledgers / 106
  Accounts Receivable Subsidiary Ledger / Accounts Payable Subsidiary Ledger / Posting to the General Ledger and Subsidiary Ledgers
An Overview of the Accounting Sequence / 109

An Illustration—Data Equipment Repair Shop / 112

Selecting a Chart of Accounts / 113
  Analyzing Transactions and Journalizing
Introduction to Adjustments / 117
Posting to the Ledgers / 117
Preparing a Trial Balance / 120
Preparing a Schedule of Accounts Receivable / 120
Preparing a Schedule of Accounts Payable / 121
Preparing the Financial Statements from the Trial Balance / 121
  The Income Statement / The Statement of Retained Earnings / Balance Sheet
Managerial Analysis of Operations—Common-Size Income Statement and Earning Power Measurements / 124
  Common-Size Income Statement / Earning Power Measurements for Centel Corporation

Chapter 4 End-of-Period Process without a Work Sheet / 145

The Accounting System—Another Look / 146

The Data Equipment Repair Shop Example—Remaining End-of-Period Steps / 147

Closing and Ruling the Revenue, Expense, and Dividend Accounts / 147
The Closing Procedure / 148
  Ruling the Closed Nominal Accounts
Real Accounts after Closing / 150
  Taking a Postclosing Trial Balance
Statement of Retained Earnings with Beginning Balance / 151
Interrelationship of the Financial Statements / 152

More about Adjustments: Accruals and Deferrals / 154

The Accounting Bases / 154
  Cash Basis of Accounting / Accrual Basis of Accounting / Comparison of Cash and Accrual Bases of Accounting
Adjusting Entries / 156
Adjustment Classification / 156
An Accounting Illustration—The Electronics Consulting Service / 157
Short-Term Cost Apportionments—A Type of Deferral / 159
  Adjustment of Prepaid Rent / Adjustment of Prepaid Insurance / Adjustment of Office Supplies
Short-Term Revenue Apportionment—A Second Type of Deferral / 163
  Adjustment of Unearned Rent
Long-Term Cost Apportionments—A Third Type of Deferral / 165
  Adjustment for Depreciation of Office Equipment / Adjustment for Depreciation of Automobiles
Accrued Revenues—The First of Two Types of Accruals / 169
  Adjustment for Unrecorded Interest Revenue
Accrued Expenses—The Second Type of Accrual / 171
  Adjustment for Unrecorded Wages Expense / Adjustment for Unrecorded Interest Expense / Income Tax Expense Adjustment

Contents

Summary of Adjustments / 174
Application of the Materiality Concept to Adjustments / 175
Alternative Adjustment Methods for Deferrals / 176
A Note on Reversing Entries / 177
   Illustrations / Which Adjusting Entries May be Reversed / Guideline for Reversal

Chapter 5 — End-of-Period Process with a Work Sheet / 197

Review of the Accounting Process / 197

An Accounting Example—Electronics Consulting Service / 199

The Work Sheet / 199
   Overview of the Work Sheet / Four Steps in Preparing the Work Sheet of Electronics Consulting Service / Completing the Work Sheet / Preparation of Financial Statements from the Work Sheet

Recording Adjustments in the General Journal / 207
   The Result of Adjusting Entries

Recording Closing Entries Directly from the Work Sheet / 209
The Postclosing Trial Balance / 210
Subsequent Period Entries Related to Accruals / 212
   Receiving the Accrued Interest Receivable / Paying the Accrued Wages Payable

The Accounting Cycle—Review / 214
Managerial Analysis—Revenue Dollar Statement / 215

Chapter 6 — Merchandising: Measuring and Reporting the Results of Operations / 237

Merchandising: An Overview / 238
Sales Revenue Accounts / 239
   The Sales Account / The Sales Returns and Allowances Account / The Sales Discounts Account

Cost of Goods Sold Accounts / 241
   Net Cost of Purchases / The Purchases Returns and Allowances Account / The Purchases Discounts Account / The Net Cost of Purchases Disclosed / The Merchandise Inventory Account

Cost of Goods Sold / 245
Gross Margin on Sales / 245
Functions of the Merchandise Accounts / 246
The Operating Expense Accounts / 250
Net Operating Margin / 250
Other Revenue and Other Expenses / 251
   Other Revenue / Other Expenses

Income Tax Expense / 251
Work Sheet for a Merchandising Business / 251
   Trial Balance Columns / Adjustments Columns / Adjusted Trial Balance Columns / Income Statement Columns / Balance Sheet Columns

Statements Prepared from the Work Sheet / 253
Closing Entries / 256

Management Control—The Exception Principle / 257
   Purchases Discounts Lost Method

Trade Discounts / 258
Internal Control over Inventory / 259
Sales Taxes Payable / 260

Appendix 6.1   Special Journals / 261

Design of a Record System / 261
Expansion of the General Journal: Evolution of a Simple Manual System / 264
Special Journals / 265
   Sales Journal / Purchases Journal / Cash Receipts Journal / Cash Payments Journal /
   Result of Posting / Combined Cash Receipts and Payments Journal / Other Special
   Journals / Entries in the General Journal

Direct Posting from Business Documents to Subsidiary Ledgers / 282

Part Two   Income Measurement and Valuation Issues / 299

Chapter 7   Compound Interest Concepts / 301

A Comparison of Simple Interest and Compound Interest / 302
Compound Interest Techniques / 303
Future Amount of a Single Sum at Compound Interest / 303
   The Idea / The Arithmetic Approach / The Formula Approach /
   The Table Approach

Present Value of Single Given Sum / 307
   The Idea / The Table Approach

Interrelationship of Future Amount of 1 and Present Value of 1 / 308
Future Amounts of an Ordinary Annuity / 309
   Introduction / The Idea / The Table Approach / Example: Determining the Value
   of Rents When Future Amount Is Known

Present Value of an Ordinary Annuity / 312
   Introduction / The Idea / The Table Approach / Example: Determining the Value
   of Period Rents When the Present Value Is Known

Chapter 8   Control of Cash / 321

Cash Management Systems / 322

Internal Control / 322
Cash Flows / 323
Analysis of Cash Needs: Cash Forecast / 324
Petty Cash / 325
   Cash Over and Short

The Bank Statement / 327
   Reconciliation Procedure / Recording the Adjustments

The Voucher System / 335

The Voucher / 335

Voucher Register and Check Register / 336
Advantages and Limitations of Vouchers / 337

Appendix 8.1 Payroll Systems / 337

Gross Pay / 337
Payroll Deductions / 338
Employer Payroll Taxes / 338
Wage Bases and Tax Rates / 339
Recording the Payroll / 340
Recording the Employer's Payroll Tax Expense / 341
Accrual of Salaries and Wages / 341
Liabilities for Compensated Absences / 341
Managerial Control of Payroll / 343

Appendix 8.2 The Voucher System Illustrated / 343

The Voucher Register / 344
The Check Register / 346
Control of Unpaid Vouchers / 347
Recording and Paying Vouchers / 347
Cancelling and Replacing Vouchers / 348
Posting from the Voucher Register and the Check Register / 349
Elimination of the Accounts Payable Subsidiary Ledger / 349

Chapter 9

Current Receivables and Payables / 363

Sources and Classification of Receivables / 364
Trade Receivables / Nontrade Receivables / Classification of Receivables

Bad Debts Expense: Allowance Method / 365
Recording the Bad Debts Adjustment / Writing Off Uncollectible Accounts / Estimating the Amount of Bad Debts Expense / Writing off Uncollectible Accounts / Recovery of Bad Debts

Bad Debts Expense: Direct Write-Off Method / 375
Comparison of the Two Recording Procedures / 376
Valuation Accounts for Returns and Allowances and Cash Discounts / 377
Credit Card Sales / 377
Opposite Balances in Accounts Receivable and Accounts Payable / 379
Internal Control: Accounts Receivable / 380
Receivables Turnover and Average Collection Period

Accounts Payable / 381

Accounting for Notes / 381

The Short-Term Financing Climate / 381
Notes Payable / 382
Maturity Dates of Notes / Recording Procedures Involving Notes Payable / End-of-Period Adjusting Entries for Interest on Notes Payable

Notes Receivable / 388
Recording Procedures Involving Notes Receivable / Dishonor of a Note Receivable by the Maker / End-of-Period Adjusting Entries for Interest on Notes Receivable

Discounting Customers' Notes Receivable / 391
Internal Control: Notes Receivable / 395

Chapter 10   Measurement and Control of Inventory / 413

Basis of Inventory Valuation: Cost / 414
Two Inventory Systems / 415
Assigning Inventory Cost / 416
Periodic Inventory System / 417
   Specific Identification Costing / First-In, First-Out (FIFO) Costing / Last-In, First-Out (LIFO) Costing / Weighted Average Costing

Perpetual Inventory System / 420
   First-In, First-Out (FIFO) Costing / Last-In, First-Out (LIFO) Costing / Moving Average Costing

Two Systems Compared and Analyzed / 424
Lower of Cost or Market (LCM) / 426
Estimation of Inventory / 428
   Gross Margin Method / Retail Method

Evaluation of Estimating Procedures / 431
Consistency in the Application of Inventory Valuation Procedures / 431
Internal Control over Inventory / 431
Managerial Analyses Enhancing Internal Control / 432
   Inventory Turnover / Ratio of Inventory to Working Capital

A Real-Life Example / 434
Financial Statement Disclosure / 435

Chapter 11   Long-Lived Assets / 447

Definition of Terms / 448

Tangible Plant Assets / 448

Valuation of Tangible Plant Assets / 448
   Subsidiary Records

Depreciation of Tangible Plant Assets / 451
   Estimated Useful Life (EUL) / Estimated Salvage Value / Methods of Computing Depreciation / Comparison of Methods / Depreciation for Partial Accounting Periods / Accelerated Cost Recovery System (ACRS) / Guidelines for Depreciation Methods

Recording and Financial Reporting / 459
Capital and Revenue Expenditures / 460
Changing of Depreciation Expense / 461
Disposal of Tangible Plant Assets / 462
   Sale or Discard of Tangible Plant Assets

Trade-in of Tangible Plant Assets / 464
   Trade-in of Tangible Plant Assets—Dissimilar Items / Trade-in of Tangible Plant Assets—Similar Items

Natural Resources or Wasting Assets / 468

Depletion of Wasting Assets / 468

Intangible Assets / 469

Contents

Patents / 470
Other Intangible Assets / 471

Internal Control over Plant and Intangible Assets and Financial Statement Reporting / 472
Internal Control Measures / 472
Ratios for Investment in Property, Plant, and Equipment / 473
Financial Statement Disclosure: A Real life Example / 473

Appendix 11.1   Accounting for Lessee's Capital Leases / 476
Identifying Capital Leases / 476
   Terminology / Criteria for Identifying Capital Leases
Accounting for Capital Leases / 478
   Recording the Lease
Recording Lease Payments / 479
   Recording Amortization / Balance Sheet Presentation / Other Issues

Part Three — Sources and Uses of Capital / 493

Chapter 12 — Single Proprietorship and Partnership Accounting / 495

The Single Proprietorship and Partnership Forms of Business Organization / 496
   Characteristics
Owners' Equity Accounts for the Three Basic Forms of Business Organization / 497
Formation of a Single Proprietorship / 498
   Withdrawals by Proprietor
The Closing of the Income Summary Account / 500
Statement of Owner's Equity / 500
Formation of a Partnership / 501
Withdrawals by Partners / 501
Division of Partnership Profits and Losses / 503
Partnership Financial Statements / 505
Changes in Capital Structure / 506
   Admission of a New Partner / Retirement or Death of an Existing Partner / Liquidation of a Partnership
Internal Control and Ratio Analysis / 508

Chapter 13 — Accounting for Corporate Equity / 519

The Corporation as a Form of Business Organization / 520
   Deciding to Incorporate / Preparing the Corporation for Operations

Paid-in Capital / 521
Sources of Capital / 521
   Capital Stock / Key Terms
Recording Capital Stock Transactions / 527
   Illustration Group A / Capital Stock Issued at a Discount / Illustration Group B / Donations

Contents

Disclosure of Paid-in Capital on the Balance Sheet / 534

Retained Earnings / 535

Net Income and Net Loss / 535
Retained Earnings—Restricted or Appropriated / 536
Prior Period Adjustments / 537
Dividends / 538
   Cash Dividends / Stock Dividends / Stock Split

Treasury Stock and Other Corporate Capital Concepts / 545

Treasury Stock / 545
   Recording the Purchase of Treasury Stock / Recording Reissuance of Treasury Stock / Recording Treasury Stock Donations / Taxation of Income

Managerial Analysis—Book Value and Earnings per Share / 548

Book Value of Common Stock / 548
   When Only One Class of Stock Is Outstanding / When More than One Class of Stock Is Outstanding

Earnings per Share (EPS) / 550
Internal Control Issues / 551

Appendix 13.1 Two Methods of Illustrating Stockholders' Equity / 552

Stockholders' Equity Illustrated / 553

Chapter 14

Long-Term Liabilities / 573

Definitions and Types of Long-Term Liabilities / 574
Bonds Payable / 574
Classification of Bonds / 575
   Registered and Coupon Bonds / Secured Bonds / Unsecured Bonds / Other Bonds

Bonds Compared to Capital Stock / 576
   Reasons for Issuing Bonds instead of Capital Stock

The Bond Issue / 578
   Authorizing the Bond Issue / Recording Issuance and Interest

Why Bonds Sell at a Premium or Discount / 580
Calculation of the Exact Price of Bonds to Yield a Given Rate / 582
Methods of Amortization of Premium and Discount / 583
   Examples Using Straight Line Amortization / Examples Using the Interest Method of Amortization

The Issuance of Bonds between Interest Dates / 596
Retirement of Bonds Payable / 599
   Retirement of Bonds before Maturity / Conversion of Bonds into Common Stock / Bond Sinking Fund

Restriction of Retained Earnings for Bond Redemption / 603
Long-Term Notes Payable / 603
Current Liabilities (Short-Term Debt) Expected to Be Refinanced / 604
Managerial Analysis—Number of Times Bond Interest Earned / 604
Internal Control Measures / 605

Chapter 15 — Temporary and Long-Term Investments / 617

Temporary Investments / 618
Nature of Temporary Investments / 618
Bonds as Temporary Investments / 618
Stocks as Temporary Investments / 621
  Valuation of Temporary Investments / Valuation of Temporary Investments at Cost / Valuation of Temporary Investments in Marketable Equity Securities at Lower of Cost or Market

Long-Term Investments / 626
Long-Term Investments in Stocks / 627
  The Cost Method of Recording and Valuation / Recording and Valuation of Long-Term Investments in Marketable Equity Securities at Lower of Cost or Market / The Equity Method of Accounting for an Investment in Stock

Long-Term Investments in Bonds / 633
  Example A: Bonds Purchased at Face Value on an Interest Date / Methods of Amortization / Examples B and C Using Straight Line and Interest Methods of Amortization / Example D: Bonds Purchased between Interest Dates

Other Long-Term Investment Items / 641
Managerial Analysis / 642
Internal Control of Investments / 643

Part Four — Financial Reporting / 655

Chapter 16 — Consolidated Statements and International Accounting / 657
Parent-Subsidiary Relationships / 659
  Exercise of Control / Economic versus Legal Entity / Reciprocal Accounts and Their Elimination
Acquisition at a Price in Excess of Fair Market Value / 670
Minority Interest / 670
Importance of Acquisition Information / 671
Managerial Analysis: Segment Reporting / 671
Foreign Operations / 672

Appendix 16.1 International Accounting / 673
Currency Fluctuations / 673
Financial Reporting Issues / 674
  Translation for Specific Transactions / Translation for Consolidated Statements

Chapter 17 — Statement of Changes in Financial Position / 687
Broad Objectives and Content of the Statement / 688
  Broad Objectives / Evolution and Content of the Statement / All Financial Resources on a Working Capital Basis / Working Capital Provided by Operations
Preparation of Statements by Simple Analytical Method / 697

Example 1: The Simple Analytical Approach, Year 1987 /
Example 2: The Simple Analytical Approach, Year 1988

All Financial Resources: Cash Basis / 708
Generalized Approach to Cash Basis Statement /
Example: Cash Basis Statement

Extraordinary Income Statement Items / 713

Managerial Analysis of Statement of Changes in Financial Position—Working Capital Basis / 715

Appendix 17.1   Illustration Using Work Sheet Method / 716
Work Sheet Illustration—Working Capital Basis / 716
Adaptation of the Work Sheet for Cash Basis / 722

Appendix 17.2   Illustration Using T Account Method / 722
Basic Steps in the T Account Method—Working Capital Basis / 723
Applying the T Account Method to the CHL Company for 1988—Working Capital Basis / 724
Adaptation of T Account Work Sheet for Cash Basis / 729

Appendix A

Use of Computers in Accounting / 749

Computerization of the General Accounting Function / 750
Functional Parts of a Computer Accounting System / 750
The Basic Computerized Accounting System / 751
Functioning of a Computerized Accounting System / 752

Managerial Information with Personal Computing / 755
Electronic Spreadsheet Software / 755
Cash Forecast / Bond Amortization Table

Generation of Graphs for Accounting Information / 758
Application of Data Base Management Software / 759
Benefits of Computerization in Accounting / 761

Appendix B

Price-Level Accounting / 765

Historical Cost Reporting / 766
Alternative Methods to Historical Cost / 767
General Price-Level Adjusted Accounting / Current Cost Accounting

Basic Concepts in General Price-Level Accounting / 769
Use of Index Numbers to Adjust Costs / Monetary vs. Nonmonetary Items

Illustration of Price-Level Information in an Annual Report / 770

Appendix C

Compound Interest Tables / 777

Index / 784
Check List of Key Figures for Exercises and Problems / CL-1

Part One

The Basic Accounting Model

1 The Nature and Function of Accounting

Introduction

Although United Airlines, Ford Motor Company, and CBS Inc. are in different industries, they share many common needs. A major need of all of these firms is for the management personnel of each to have information that enables them to evaluate their firm's past performance and to make decisions about future directions. This chapter explains how financial statements prepared from accounting records provide that information. It also explains what accounting is and what accountants do. After a brief description of each of the four basic financial reports, an illustrative set of statements is presented complete with footnotes. Explanatory comments on these statements discuss major items in general terms. Appendix 1.1 then provides an explanation of some of the major generally accepted accounting principles.

Learning Goals

1. To be able to define accounting.

2. To understand that accounting as a profession has a history that extends back for centuries.

3. To know who uses accounting information and to appreciate the role of accounting in the decision-making process.

4. To be acquainted with the four basic accounting statements and how they relate to each other.

5. To understand the meaning and usefulness of accounting statements and to whom they are useful for various purposes.

6. To understand the type of detailed information that is available in financial statements.

7. To understand the use of footnote disclosure in financial statements to make them more useful.

Nature of Accounting

Accounting information is used in making decisions about how wealth is to be distributed all over the world. How many loaves of bread to put on a supermarket shelf in New York or in Paris is decided by looking at records that show how many are usually sold in that store each day. The price of a loaf of bread in Los Angeles depends in part upon the costs of making the dough, baking it, wrapping it, and transporting it to the shelf of a store. To know these costs every group in the chain from the farmer to the merchant needs accounting information. What people buy depends upon the amount of income they have. Salaries and wages, unemployment benefits, social security payments, interest on savings, and many other sources of income are all based on accounting records. The same is true of large companies; management decides to build new buildings or purchase new equipment if accounting information indicates that money can be made available and that these actions will be profitable. The term **profit** (net income) is used to describe the reward to an organization for bringing together people and resources to render services, to make and sell products, or to accomplish another objective. Because accounting is so important to society, this book is intended to provide a basic understanding of how accounting information is developed and used. Decision making will be shown to be the primary reason for accounting records and reports.

Definition of Accounting

Accounting consists of the gathering of financial and other economic data. In the metric system the basic physical unit of measure is the meter. In accounting in the United States and Canada the basic financial unit of measure is the dollar. Just as physical measurements are provided by the metric system, economic measurements are provided by the accounting system and are stated in financial terms. These economic measurements are put together in reports that carry the information essential for planning activities, for control of operations, and for decision making by managers of business units.

Accounting also provides financial reports that are needed by outside persons who invest in business units, lend money to them, or extend credit to them. Accounting also furnishes reports to be used by government agencies that regulate business and by tax authorities such as the Internal Revenue Service that must determine that the correct amount of tax is collected. When the unit accounted for is a *not-for-profit organization* (such as a school, hospital, church, or other charitable group), its members and those who contribute to it need to know for what purposes and in what proportions their money is being used. Accounting reports tell them.

Accounting

In summary, **accounting** *is the process of using a set of rules and methods by which financial and economic data are collected, processed, and summarized into reports that can be used in making decisions.*

Figure 1–1 Where a Typical Sales Dollar Goes

Informative financial reports and the accounting records from which they are prepared are developed and extensively illustrated in Chapters 1 through 6. Often these reports are accompanied by graphics, such as Figure 1–1, that show how one company divides each dollar of sales.

The next sections of this part provide a brief history of accounting, present a discussion of the uses of accounting in decision making, and describe the types of work that accountants do.

History of Accounting

Some of the world's first documents date from 5000 B.C.; even then the need to account for holdings of wealth prompted the development of a form of writing referred to as script.[1] The temple priests of Sumer operated a tax system that brought under their control vast stocks of grain, animals, and estates. It was necessary for these priests to develop accounting methods to (1) maintain managerial control of collections, loans, repayments, and other transactions and (2) give an account of their management over these holdings.

The Egyptian civilization, covering a broad span from about 5000 B.C. to 525 B.C., is described as one in which great construction projects were completed involving the labor of thousands of people, the operation of large stone quarries, and the large-scale transportation of building materials. Out of these operations arose a need for an information system to keep details of

---

[1]Claude S. George, *The History of Management Thought,* 2d ed. (Englewood Cliffs, N.J.: Prentice-Hall, 1972), p. 4.

transactions in both business and government affairs. In Babylonian textile mills in existence about 600 B.C., production control records were kept, and workers were paid based upon the amount of their production. In 1494, an Italian monk named Luca Pacioli included a section on bookkeeping in a mathematics textbook. This was the first known printed description of double-entry bookkeeping, described later.

In early America, accounting generally served to maintain a firm's records of business dealings with its customers. As the United States moved toward an industrial economy, the appearance of large companies created requirements for more accounting information. New inventions brought forth new products, and rapid population growth helped create a demand for them. Accounting methods and techniques had to be developed to meet these changes. Today almost every large commercial firm prepares an annual report. Annual reports in booklet form contain financial information useful to a great variety of readers.

Why Study Accounting?

Early in the 1970s, a forward-thinking group of accounting educators joined together to study the approach to teaching the introductory college course in accounting. This group was sponsored by a national accounting firm, Price Waterhouse. Its report said: "The purpose of accounting is to provide information that is useful in decision making affecting resource allocation . . . at all levels in society. . . ."[2] The major private source of accounting guidance in the United States reinforced this purpose when it stated ". . . their [investors' and creditors'] decisions significantly affect the allocation of resources in the economy."[3] Each of us must make financial decisions daily. Those decisions will be much better if the person who makes them understands how the information upon which he or she relies was developed. In business and in personal transactions, the person with a knowledge of accounting will have a distinct advantage.

Another reason to study accounting is that many persons work directly in the field of accounting. They may record purchases and sales, compute payrolls, or obtain cost and expense information in business firms. Others may work in not-for-profit organizations or in government. Some work as accountants; others in tasks involving sales, production management, personnel, and many other functions. They all need record systems to show how money of the organization was used, and they need to be able to read and understand financial reports.

---

[2] *A New Introduction to Accounting: Report of the Study Group on Introductory Accounting* (New York: Price Waterhouse Foundation, 1971), p. 11.

[3] Financial Accounting Standards Board, *Statement of Accounting Concepts No. 1,* "Objectives of Financial Reporting by Business Enterprises" (Stamford, Conn.: 1978), paragraph 30.

Many persons work in public accounting. Some keep records for organizations that are too small to afford their own accounting departments. Others perform a function known as *auditing*—the independent review of the financial records of an organization. Public accountants also perform management services such as the design of accounting systems, or help businesses prepare their tax returns. No matter what job a person holds in the accounting field, he or she will benefit from a complete understanding of accounting.

Perhaps the most important reason of all to study accounting is that most people must use accounting information in their personal and business lives. The next section gives examples of people not in accounting jobs who depend upon accounting information. These persons need to know how to interpret the information available to them. If they understand accounting, their interpretations will more likely lead to sound choices among the many possible courses of action that may be open to them.

Who Uses Accounting Information?

External Users

External users are persons or groups outside an organization who need and use accounting information about that organization. Following are some examples of external users.

Investors seek information that will allow them to study and compare the financial health and earning ability of business firms. Sometimes they lend money to a business firm, thus becoming **creditors**. Individuals or institutions (for example, large insurance companies) with excess funds on hand may lend those funds to large corporations. In such a case, the lenders (or creditors) receive interest in payment for the use of their money.

Sometimes investors would rather invest as owners than as creditors in order to receive a portion of the profits. Owner investors may be individuals, insurance companies, large universities, or other organizations that have accumulated more cash than they need for day-to-day expenditures.

As a basis for their investment decisions, all investors depend upon accounting information included in financial reports. In deciding whether or not to invest in a particular company, investors ask questions such as: Does this company have a history of profitable operations? How does its rate of profit compare with that of other companies?

Contributors to not-for-profit organizations, such as community funds, churches, colleges, service clubs, and similar organizations, need accounting reports. They want to know how their funds are being used so they can determine whether or not the organization deserves continued support and what the amount of such support should be. They ask questions such as: What percentage of each contributed dollar actually serves the purpose of the organization? What percentage is used for administrative expenses? They look to accounting reports for the answers.

Taxing authorities, regulatory agencies, and other governmental institutions use accounting information. Income tax returns are prepared with information taken directly from accounting records of individuals and businesses.

The reports accompanying payment of taxes to fund federal social security programs or to fund unemployment compensation payments are based upon payroll records.

Important to consumers is the use of accounting reports by governmental regulatory commissions. Some of these commissions have the legal authority to set the rates that may be charged for services to the public. Rates that public utilities such as gas or electric producers are allowed to charge usually are based on the concept of allowing those companies to earn a fair, but not excessive, profit. Thus, decisions involving setting of rates are based on accounting information.

Internal Users

Internal users of accounting information are those users in an organization who must make managerial decisions regarding operations.

Planning is the management function that defines the goals and objectives of the operation. Budget preparation is an important part of the planning function. A **budget** is simply a financial plan for a future period. The starting point in preparing a budget is the accounting records of the current and prior years.

Controlling is the management function of checking on operations of an enterprise and acting when necessary to redirect them. The accounting system provides special reports to each responsible manager. An example is a report to the sales manager, showing planned sales of merchandise to date compared with actual sales to date.

Cost determination is another management function. Many internal decisions require information about costs of operation. A firm may have to bid competitively against others for a specific job; if the price it bids exceeds cost plus a reasonable profit, it probably will not be awarded the contract. On the other hand, if the firm bids less than its cost to perform the job, it may be awarded the contract but will also incur a loss.

What Accountants Do

More than 200,000 accountants in the United States have passed a uniform national examination and are designated by state laws as **Certified Public Accountants (CPAs)**. One of the major jobs of a CPA is auditing. After reviewing the organization's records, the CPA issues an audit report, which contains an opinion as to the fairness with which the organization's accounting reports reflect its financial condition and operating results. This professional role is referred to as the *attest function* of accounting. CPAs perform other types of work besides auditing. They do tax work for clients, help design accounting systems, and render other managerial services. The size of public accounting firms ranges from local one-person or two-person offices to huge firms with offices all over the world. A majority of the companies whose stock is listed on stock exchanges in the United States have their financial statements audited by one of the "Big Eight" firms, as the eight largest accounting firms are known. In alphabetical sequence, the "Big Eight" firms are:

- Arthur Andersen & Co.
- Arthur Young & Co.
- Coopers & Lybrand
- Deloitte Haskins & Sells
- Ernst & Whinney
- Peat, Marwick, Mitchell & Co.
- Price Waterhouse
- Touche Ross & Co.

In addition to the CPAs, accountants work in every type of institution in society. They work at various levels in business, government, government-related, and not-for-profit organizations. Some hold certificates attesting to their professional competence. A **Certified Management Accountant (CMA)** is a person who demonstrates ability in management accounting by passing a national examination. Other accountants are **Certified Internal Auditors (CIAs)**. These internal auditors perform a review function but work solely on the records of the firm by which they are employed.

Although much of accounting work is highly specialized and is performed in many types of organizations, the greatest number of accountants work at keeping the records of commercial enterprises. For this reason, illustrations and problems in this book focus mostly upon private business.

The Entity Concept

Accounting entity

To understand accounting, one must clearly understand the meaning of an accounting entity.

An accounting entity is any organizational unit for which financial and economic data are gathered and processed. This is referred to as the **entity concept**.

For example, the Tyler Corporation headquartered in Dallas, Texas, provides services and products to industrial customers through four operating companies, shown here in graphic form:

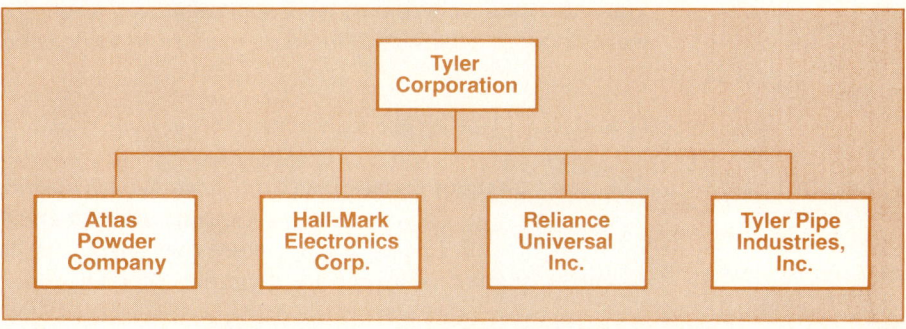

For purposes of making annual public financial reports to external users, a single set of consolidated financial statements is prepared by Tyler Corporation. However, accounting information for the total group lumped together is not satisfactory for making decisions about any single company. A separate set of records must be maintained for each of the individual companies so that information appropriate to the planning and controlling decisions that must be made within each of the companies will be available. Each unit for which a separate set of accounting records is kept is known as an *accounting entity*. Thus, to keep one set of accounting records for Tyler Corporation would mean that managers of Reliance Universal would not have information specific to their company. By keeping a separate set of records for each of the companies, managers of each business will have information pertaining strictly to their business.

In a corporate group, each separate company is both an accounting entity and a *legal entity* (an organizational unit endowed with certain legally recognized characteristics). The entity concept applies in the same way to a group of unincorporated businesses owned by one person. Assume that Lucy Genova owns and operates a laundromat, a hardware store, and a framing shop. Because she needs separate details about each of them to be a successful operator, each is a separate accounting entity with a separate group of records. Against this background, the next section describes the four basic types of financial reports.

The Basic Financial Statements

One end product of an accountant's work is a set of financial statements containing useful financial information. The four statements that are usually prepared periodically are: (1) the income statement, (2) the balance sheet, (3) the statement of retained earnings, and (4) the statement of changes in financial position. Each of these statements has a unique function, but they are all designed to communicate information to individuals for the overriding purpose of making decisions. The statements are here described briefly and their interrelationship is shown. Later in this chapter, a complete set of financial statements is illustrated with explanatory notes about their content. Although the statements look complex at first sight, the organization of the details they contain will soon become clear. It is most important at this early stage to grasp the basic function of each statement as a finished product before one learns how to accumulate the data that are incorporated in the statement.

The Income Statement

The first statement usually prepared from the accounting records is the income statement. The **income statement** is the financial report that shows how much profit or loss was incurred over a specific period of time—a month, a quarter, or a year, for example. To comprehend the basic function of the income statement, one must understand two basic accounting concepts—revenues and expenses.

Revenues

The sources of the inflows of items of value to an entity that result from carrying out the basic purpose of the business are called **revenues**.

These inflows usually result from the performance of a service or the production and sale of a good. In a service business, the fees charged for providing its service are revenues. In a firm dealing in a product, the sources of inflows coming from the sale of the product are called *revenues*. A business enterprise usually has a major or primary source of revenue—ticket sales by an airline are an example—and one or more secondary sources such as interest earned.

Expenses

The costs that are expended to produce revenues in a period are called **expenses**.

A typical business enterprise has many types of expenses, such as employee wages and salaries, advertising, cost of supplies used, rental cost of buildings and equipment, heat, light, power, and many other things that cause outflows of items of value. Expenses are incurred because they are necessary to generate revenues.[4] In a specified period of time, revenues are matched with expenses to determine whether a business has an income or a loss. The basic information provided by the income statement is diagrammed in Figure 1–2.

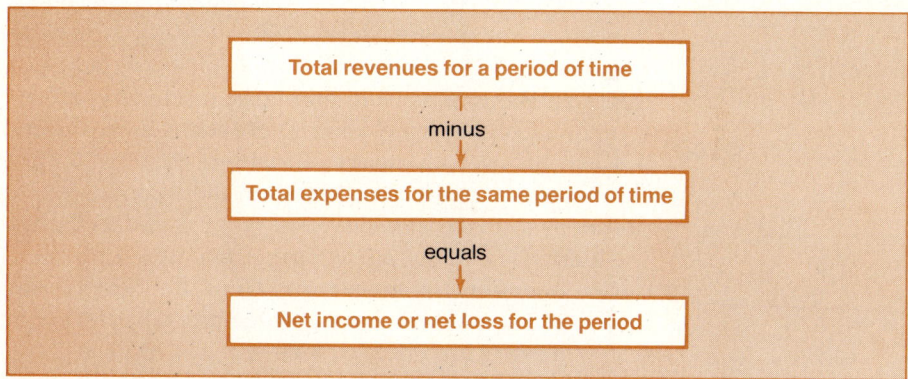

Figure 1–2   **Conceptual Diagram of the Income Statement**

---

[4]The Financial Accounting Standards Board, in its *Statement of Financial Accounting Concepts No. 3,* "Elements of Financial Statements of a Business Enterprise" (Stamford, Conn.: FASB, 1980), includes definitions of gains and losses. At this point, it is sufficient simply to recognize that gains are shown on the income statement with the same effect as revenues, and losses with the same effect as expenses.

If total revenues are greater than total expenses, the difference is called **net income** for the period. If expenses are greater than revenues during a period, the difference is a **net loss**. Obviously, a business that remains in existence over a period of years must generate net income. In 1981 and 1982, Ford Motor Company had net losses of $1,060.1 million and $658.7 million respectively. In 1983, however, the company regained profitability with a net income of $1,866.9 million.

The income statement's primary purpose is to provide information about the operating success of an enterprise over a period of time. These operating results are also shown in the next statement usually prepared, the statement of retained earnings. Its description is delayed in this discussion to introduce some terms that apply to the balance sheet.

The Balance Sheet

The **balance sheet** displays the financial condition of an enterprise at a specific moment in time. It shows the things of value that are held by an enterprise to be used in carrying out its stated purpose—for a business enterprise, to earn income. These items of value are called **assets** of the enterprise. They are described in more detail later in this chapter and in Chapter 2, but it is useful to know at this point that they fall into two broad categories, *current assets* and *long-lived assets*. Generally speaking, **current assets** are those with a relatively short useful life. Such items as cash, supplies, prepaid insurance, and inventories expire or are consumed in the revenue-producing process in a short period of time. For this reason, they are classified as current. Long-lived assets consist of both *long-term investments* (usually whole or partial ownership of another company to ensure availability of supplies, control, or for other purposes) and a classification called *property, plant, and equipment*. **Property, plant, and equipment** held by most enterprises includes such things as land, buildings, machinery, office equipment, sales equipment, and delivery vans. These items have a useful life to the enterprise that extends over a number of years, in contrast to the short useful lives of current assets. Assets are divided on the balance sheet into the foregoing classifications to make this statement more useful to the user.

All things of value (assets) are claimed by someone. The claims against assets of an enterprise are also shown on the balance sheet and are known as **equities**. Because all things of value are subject to equity claims, it is logical that total assets are equal to total equities. Thus, we say that the balance sheet is "in balance," and use the title *balance sheet*. There are two types of equities: (1) creditors' claims, called *liabilities,* and (2) ownership claims called *owners' equity*.

Liabilities are the amounts owed to individuals, financial institutions, other enterprises, or to government. Those of a short-term nature—for example, accounts payable to vendors or notes payable due in less than one year—are classified on the balance sheet as **current liabilities**. Other liabilities, such as bonds payable or notes payable that are not due to be paid until years in the future, are classified as **long-term liabilities**. As in the case of

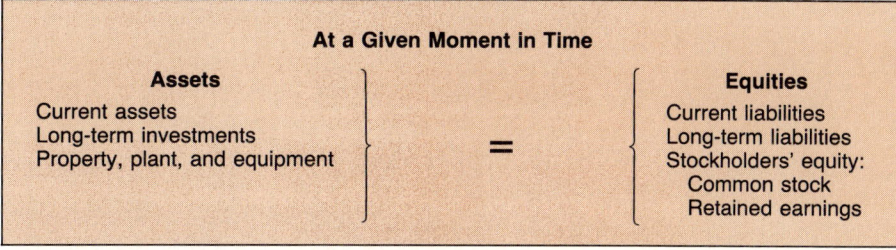

Figure 1–3   **Conceptual Diagram of the Balance Sheet**

assets, the grouping of liabilities into classes makes a balance sheet more useful to its readers because the information is made comparable.

Owners' equity is the amount of residual claims of owners against the assets of an enterprise.[5] In a corporation, since the owners are stockholders, their equity is described as **stockholders' equity**. There are two major sources of stockholders' equity: (1) investment of personal assets of the owners (usually in exchange for shares of common stock) and (2) profitable operations that increase the assets and produce a special type of owners' equity called *retained earnings* (discussed in the next section).

The balance sheet protrays a picture of the financial status of a business as diagrammed in Figure 1–3.

Along with the other basic financial statements, balance sheets provide decision-making information. Primarily, they give an indication of the financial strength of the enterprise at a given date. The link between the income statement and the balance sheet is the statement of retained earnings.

Statement of Retained Earnings

Retained earnings is the amount of ownership equity in a business that results from profitable operations. As a business earns net income, the inflows of assets are greater than the outflows. This causes an increase in total assets; this increase belongs to the owners (or stockholders, for a corporation). Since the increase is caused by a source other than personal investment, retained earnings has increased. The increased assets can be retained in the corporation to allow for further growth and expansion, or they may be paid out to the stockholders periodically in cash as a reward for their willingness to invest and accept the risks involved. Periodic payouts to stockholders by corporations of a proportionate share of income are called **dividends**. Since payments made to stockholders cause a reduction in assets, retained earnings must decrease. Thus, just as periodic net income increases retained earnings, periodic dividend payments reduce retained earnings. So that readers of financial statements can know the effects of these actions, a **statement of retained earnings** is prepared along with the other financial statements. Its basic purpose and concept are diagrammed in Figure 1–4 on page 14.

---

[5]Owners' equity is equal to *net assets* because the amount is total assets minus total creditors' claims (liabilities).

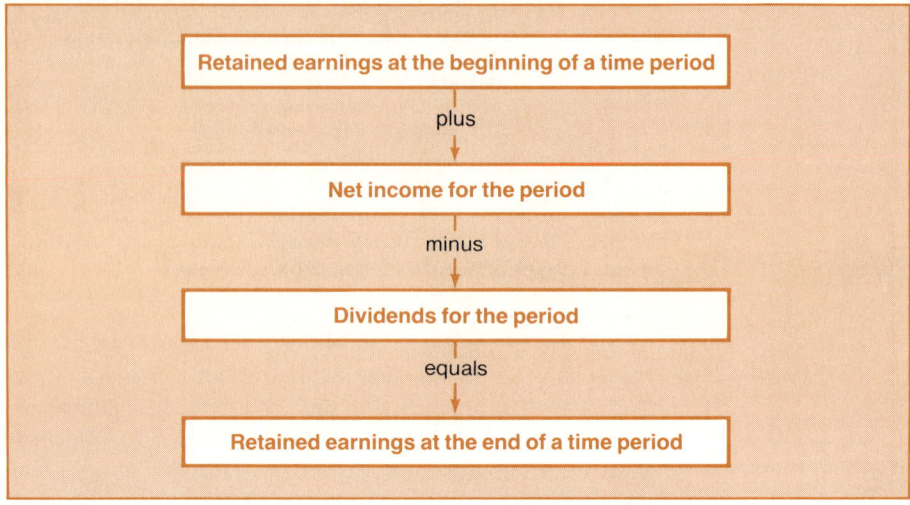

Figure 1–4   **Conceptual Diagram of the Statement of Retained Earnings**

This statement shows how the retained earnings portion of total stockholders' equity changed across the same period of time as the income statement; it reconciles the beginning balance to the ending balance. Accordingly, it serves as the link between the income statement and the balance sheet. The fourth major statement, the statement of changes in financial position, completes the picture.

Statement of Changes in Financial Position

During a period of operations, the composition or mix of financial resources of a business will change. Some resources—perhaps cash or accounts receivable—may increase; others—perhaps supplies or inventories—may decrease. There usually are changes in the total amount of long-term items such as machinery, equipment, or long-term debt. The summarized result of all these increases and decreases during an accounting period is the net change in financial resources. It is important to users of statements to know what changes in financial resources occurred and what caused them. For example, a business may have a profitable year and end up with a severe shortage of cash. The natural question is, where did the cash go? The reverse possibility is an unprofitable year with an increase in cash or other financial resources. Here, the question is: where did the increase come from? It is the function of the **statement of changes in financial position** to answer such questions. The statement is diagrammed in Figure 1–5.

Such a statement has been in use for many years, but it has become much more important in the last decade. With high rates of inflation and high interest rates, the timing and types of flows into and out of a company need to be monitored very carefully. The statement of changes in financial position provides information to do this.

> **Sources of financial resources:**
> Operations
> Issuance of stock (additional investment by owners)
> Issuance of bonds (long-term borrowing)
> Sale of long-lived assets
> Others
>
> **Uses of financial resources:**
> Repurchase of own previously issued stock
> Repayment of bonds
> Purchase of long-lived assets
> Payment of dividends
> Others
>
> Difference in totals of above is the net increase or decrease in financial resources over the same time period used for income statement.[a]
>
> [a] In essence, the information contained in this statement reconciles the beginning balance of financial resources with the ending balance.

Figure 1–5   Conceptual Diagram of Statement of Changes in Financial Position

Inter-relationship of Financial Statements

Each of the four basic financial statements provides a different type of information to decision makers. Balance sheets are static statements that show the financial position of an entity as of a specific date. They are usually published annually by corporations. Balance sheets from one date to the next are linked together by the three other major statements. These three statements—the income statement, statement of retained earnings, and statement of changes in financial position—are dynamic statements. They reflect the changes that affected items in the latest balance sheet.

With the foregoing discussion of the types and roles of financial statements as a background, we can now move in for a close-up view of a set of financial statements. This is done in Figure 1–6 for a fictitious firm, Bradensota Chemical Company.

Financial Statements Illustrated and Explained

Note to Readers: The following section is intended to expose you to a complete and realistic set of financial statements. The boxed references added to the statements show how the concepts presented in the previous sections are implemented by accountants. It is not expected at this point in your study that you will master details of the statements but you should get an overview of the content of financial statements. This provides a background for a more thorough understanding of the material in later chapters.

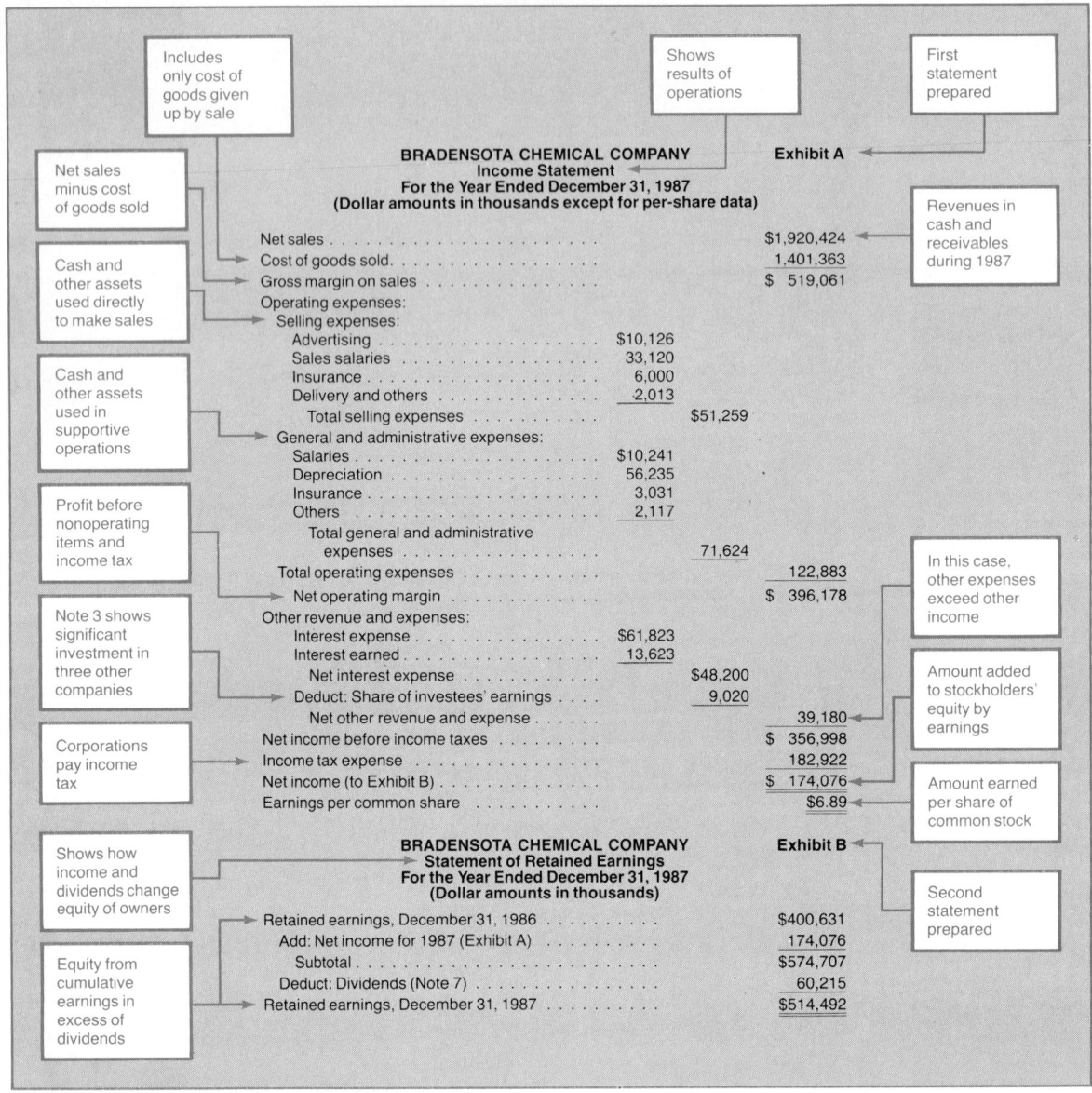

Figure 1–6   **Typical Financial Statements**

(continued on next page)

Figure 1–6 contains a complete set of financial statements for a fictional but typical corporation named the Bradensota Chemical Company. In a typical annual report, a corporation includes the four basic statements accompanied by a number of notes. The notes to financial statements are an integral part of the statements and serve to disclose nonquantitative information (see Notes 8 and 9 on page 19) or provide quantitative information in more detail than

Figure 1–6 (Continued)

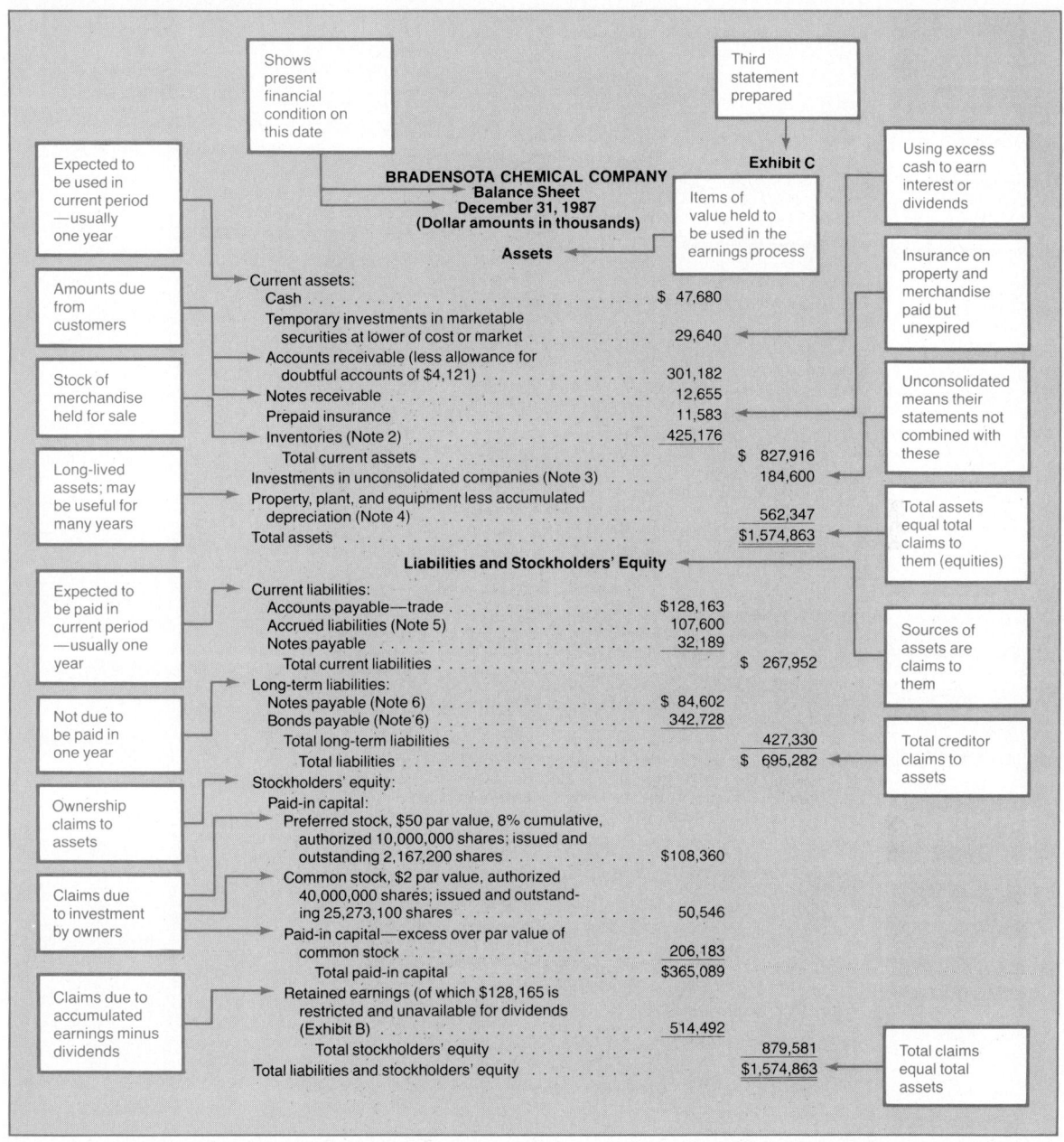

presented in the body of the statements (see Notes 3, 4, and 5 on page 19). The information in the notes is very important to a statement reader and, unless indicated as unaudited, is covered by the opinion in the report of the independent accountants who performed the annual audit.

(continued on next page)

Figure 1–6 (*Continued*)

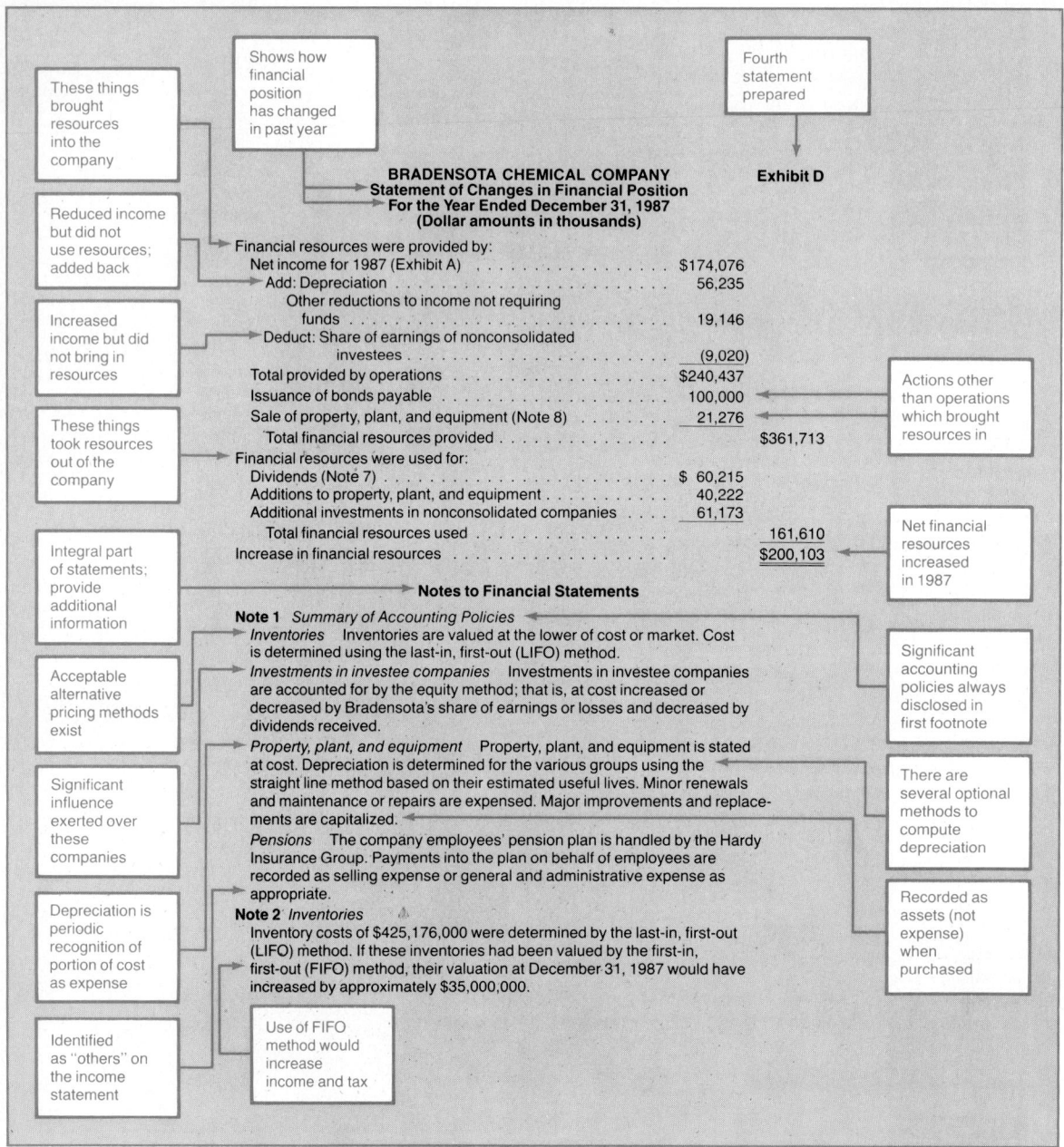

(*continued on next page*)

Figure 1–6 (*Continued*)

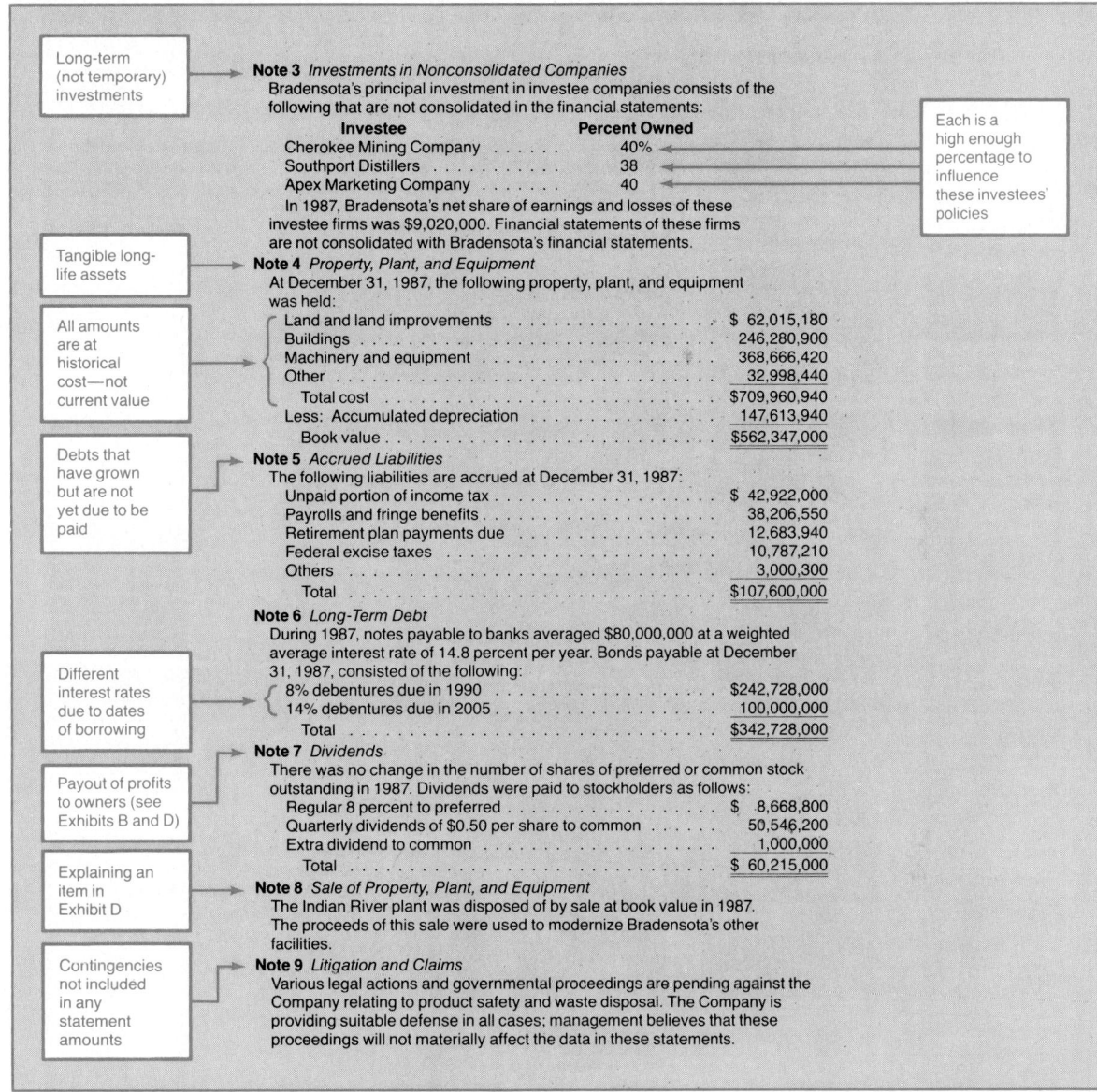

Long-term (not temporary) investments →

Note 3 *Investments in Nonconsolidated Companies*
Bradensota's principal investment in investee companies consists of the following that are not consolidated in the financial statements:

Investee	Percent Owned
Cherokee Mining Company	40%
Southport Distillers	38
Apex Marketing Company	40

← Each is a high enough percentage to influence these investees' policies

In 1987, Bradensota's net share of earnings and losses of these investee firms was $9,020,000. Financial statements of these firms are not consolidated with Bradensota's financial statements.

Tangible long-life assets →

Note 4 *Property, Plant, and Equipment*
At December 31, 1987, the following property, plant, and equipment was held:

All amounts are at historical cost—not current value →

Land and land improvements	$ 62,015,180
Buildings	246,280,900
Machinery and equipment	368,666,420
Other	32,998,440
Total cost	$709,960,940
Less: Accumulated depreciation	147,613,940
Book value	$562,347,000

Debts that have grown but are not yet due to be paid →

Note 5 *Accrued Liabilities*
The following liabilities are accrued at December 31, 1987:

Unpaid portion of income tax	$ 42,922,000
Payrolls and fringe benefits	38,206,550
Retirement plan payments due	12,683,940
Federal excise taxes	10,787,210
Others	3,000,300
Total	$107,600,000

Note 6 *Long-Term Debt*
During 1987, notes payable to banks averaged $80,000,000 at a weighted average interest rate of 14.8 percent per year. Bonds payable at December 31, 1987, consisted of the following:

Different interest rates due to dates of borrowing →

8% debentures due in 1990	$242,728,000
14% debentures due in 2005	100,000,000
Total	$342,728,000

Payout of profits to owners (see Exhibits B and D) →

Note 7 *Dividends*
There was no change in the number of shares of preferred or common stock outstanding in 1987. Dividends were paid to stockholders as follows:

Regular 8 percent to preferred	$ 8,668,800
Quarterly dividends of $0.50 per share to common	50,546,200
Extra dividend to common	1,000,000
Total	$ 60,215,000

Explaining an item in Exhibit D →

Note 8 *Sale of Property, Plant, and Equipment*
The Indian River plant was disposed of by sale at book value in 1987. The proceeds of this sale were used to modernize Bradensota's other facilities.

Contingencies not included in any statement amounts →

Note 9 *Litigation and Claims*
Various legal actions and governmental proceedings are pending against the Company relating to product safety and waste disposal. The Company is providing suitable defense in all cases; management believes that these proceedings will not materially affect the data in these statements.

(*continued on next page*)

20 Part One / The Basic Accounting Model

Figure 1–6 (*Continued*)

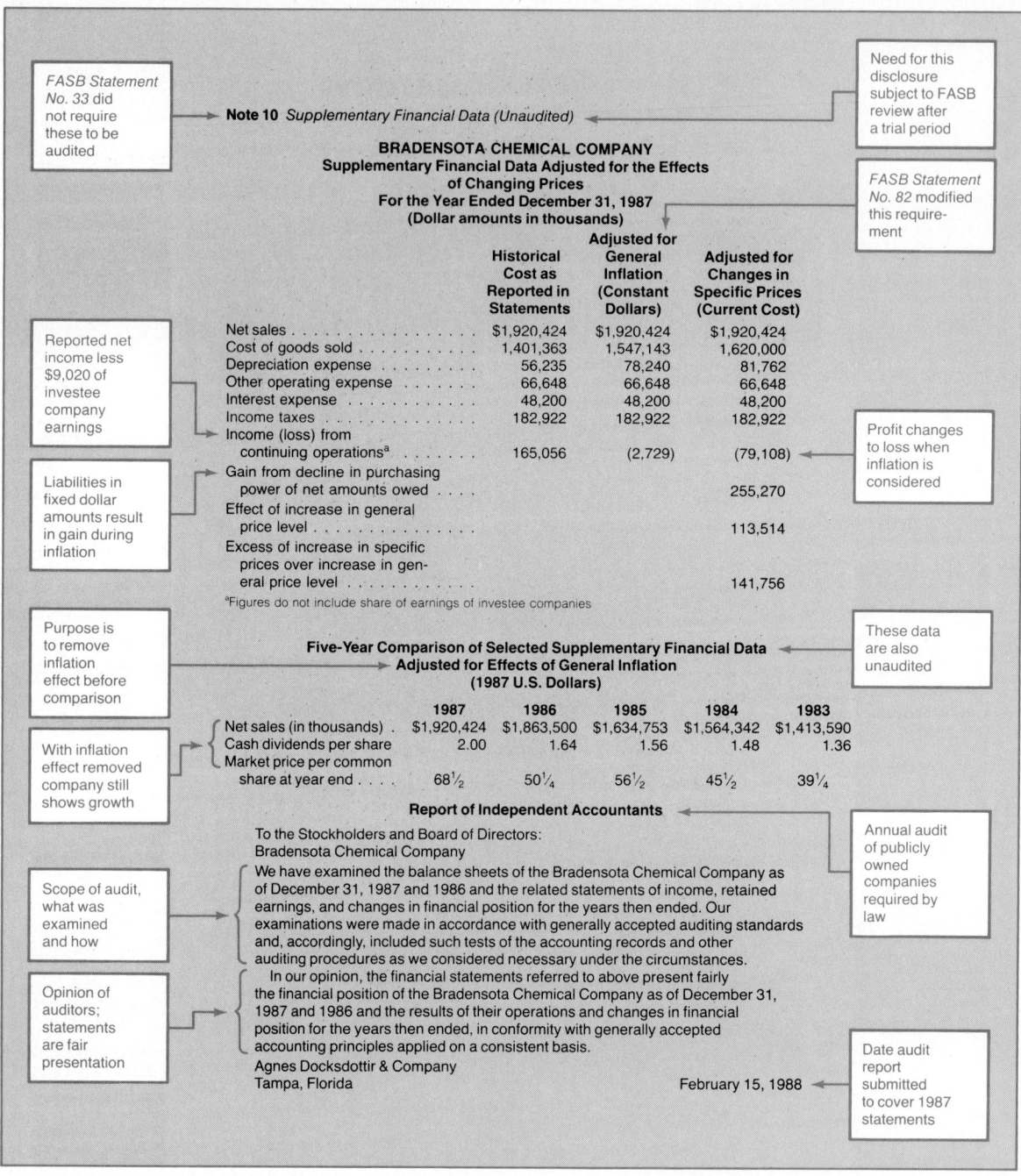

The statements in Figure 1–6 are presented in a complete unit as found in the annual reports of corporations. They are referred to by name in the discussions and explanations of them. Each part of every statement is not discussed in detail; the explanations at this point are intended to give the reader an overview and a general understanding of the types of information generated by accounting records. The usefulness of these data to various groups will become apparent as the dollar figures are studied in detail.

Significance of Financial Statements

The discussion which follows presents very general comments to illustrate the nature of the basic financial statements and the information they convey. In the Bradensota Chemical Company's statements, dollar information is given in the thousands (000 omitted). This is typical of annual and quarterly reports of large corporations whose data are rounded to the nearest $1,000.

Significance of the Income Statement

From the income statement, the reader can determine total revenues from sales and the cost to the company of the goods that were sold. The difference, called *gross margin on sales,* is the amount available to cover expenses (including income tax expense) and to provide a profit. It is customary to divide *operating expenses* (those associated with production of major sources of revenue) into the two major categories shown in Bradensota's income statement. Details of major items are provided under each category. A great number of different expenses are identified in the accounting records for the attention of management; it is not feasible to show them in such detail in the income statement.

An important figure in the income statement is the earnings per share amount of $6.89. This means that the company earned $6.89 per weighted average share of common stock outstanding after providing for dividends to preferred stockholders in 1987.[6] Investors compare this figure with the price of a share of the company's common stock on the market in making decisions to hold, increase, or reduce their investments in this corporation.

Significance of the Statement of Retained Earnings

In Exhibit B, the net income figure for 1987 is brought forward to show how the stockholders' equity was increased by the company's operations. Then the deduction of dividends to stockholders yields the current retained earnings amount to be carried to the new balance sheet at the end of the year. In some corporations, this statement is enlarged to show the changes that took place in other types of owners' equity; such a statement is called a *statement of changes in stockholders' equity.*

---

[6]Weighted average shares are determined by weighting the shares for the length of time they are outstanding. For example, if 2,000 additional shares were issued on July 1, 1987, they would be included in the weighted average for the year as 1,000 shares.

Part One / The Basic Accounting Model

Significance of the Balance Sheet

While the first two statements covered a period of time (the year ended December 31, 1987), the balance sheet does not. It shows the financial condition at the end of the year. At that time, total assets of Bradensota Chemical Company were $1,574,863,000; this is equal to total equities of the same amount. Thus, the balance sheet is said to be in balance. Note that the items on the balance sheet are grouped into various classifications. These classification subtotals are useful to the readers of statements, and are explained in more detail in Chapter 2.

A more complete understanding of all financial statements can be gained by the calculation of certain ratios.

Ratio

*A **ratio** is one number stated in relation to another.*

Some ratios are used to determine important relationships between balance sheet items. For example, one would observe that total current assets are three times greater than current liabilities. One of the ratios frequently computed by accountants is the ratio of current assets to current liabilities, called the **current ratio**. It is computed by dividing total current assets by total current liabilities. For Bradensota, it is 3.09 to 1 = ($827,916 ÷ $267,952). This would confirm the observation that Bradensota is in a good position to pay short-term debts. A more rigorous test of the ability to pay short-term debts is the **acid-test ratio**. It is the ratio of cash, temporary investments, and receivables to total current liabilities. For Bradensota, this ratio is 1.46 to 1 = [($47,680 + $29,640 + $301,182 + $12,655) ÷ $267,952]. That this ratio is greater than 1 to 1 indicates a favorable position with respect to ability to pay current debts. Many other ratios are described in other sections of this book. They are summarized on the inside front cover.

Another figure of significance in a company is the amount of working capital. **Working capital** is the sum of current assets minus the sum of current liabilities. For Bradensota, this amount is $559,964 = ($827,916 − $267,952). That this is a positive and not a negative figure is another indicator of the firm's favorable short-term liquidity. Users of financial statements use this absolute measure along with the current and acid-test ratios to help make credit and investment decisions.

Significance of Statement of Changes in Financial Position

Financial resources consist of items of value used in an enterprise to achieve its purposes. The method of preparation of the statement of changes in financial position is covered in Chapter 17, but it is appropriate here to observe certain aspects of this financial report. It has already been noted that net income increases stockholders' equity. In Exhibit D, Bradensota's net income of $174,076,000 is cited as a source of financial resources. Among the expenses in the income statement (Exhibit A) are depreciation expense of $56,235,000 and $19,146,000 of other expenses that were of such a nature that *they did not require the use of financial resources.* Since they were subtracted on the income statement, they are added back to net income in determining the financial resources generated by business operations. There is also an item added into Bradensota's income in Exhibit A that did not actually bring financial resources into the company. Bradensota's share ($9,020,000) of earnings of *investee corporations* (companies over which Bradensota's management can exercise significant influence) was added in because the value of these investments has increased. This increase, however, was not actually realized as an increase in financial resources that Bradensota can use to produce operational earnings; accordingly, it is deducted in determining resources generated by business operations. The actual financial resources generated by Bradensota's operations in 1987 amounted to $240,437,000. This statement shows other sources and uses of financial resources. For example, the company issued $1,000,000 in long-term bonds, bringing financial resources into the company that can be used in operating the business. Thus, it is shown as an increase. Also, Bradensota purchased $40,222,000 in property, plant, and equipment. Since this purchase required the use of financial resources, it is shown as a decrease on the statement. The net result of the activities that provided and used financial resources was an increase of $200,103,000 during the year.

Significance of Notes to Financial Statements

Throughout this set of financial statements, there are parenthetical references to the notes to financial statements (called footnotes). Some of the notes serve to disclose which of the acceptable accounting methods for recording events have been used. Note 1, for example, tells the reader which of the alternative inventory costing methods were used. Note 2 reveals that the valuation would have differed by $35,000,000 if another acceptable method had been used. (The methods that could have been used to place a cost valuation on inventory are described in Chapter 10.) If the statement reader is aware of the accounting policies and methods followed by the company, he or she can interpret the statements in a more informed manner. Because the footnotes provide valuable data with details and explanations of the summarized statement amounts, they are an integral part of the financial statements of any entity.

Two special types of notes deserve separate attention. These notes describe *contingencies* and the *impact of inflation*.

Contingencies

A **contingency** is a situation that may arise if certain events occur. Because such future events could have an impact on the financial position of the company, the reader should be made aware of the possibility of their occurring. Note 9 is an example of a contingency disclosure. Although Bradensota could incur some expenses (and the related asset reduction or liabilities increase), these are not shown in the income statement or balance sheet for two reasons. First, they have not occurred—and may not—so they are not recordable accounting events. Second, their amounts cannot be known with reasonable accuracy (a requirement for recording an item in the accounting records). But, for the statements to make a presentation of a company's condition with fairness, the existence and the nature of contingencies is disclosed in the footnotes.

Impact of Price-Level Changes   A second type of footnote that merits special attention is the disclosure of the effects of changing prices. The dollar amounts in the financial statements are actual (historical cost) figures that do not reflect the effect of inflation or other shifts in costs. Since 1975, major public companies have been required to estimate and provide data to show what management believes would be the effect of price-level changes. Note 10 to Bradensota's financial statements contains such a disclosure. This type of note is usually accompanied by an explanation in detail of management's assumptions and philosophy in developing such estimates. These explanations are sometimes lengthy and are not illustrated in Figure 1–6. The disclosure of effects of changing prices is discussed in Appendix B.

Obviously, the presentation of a complete set of financial statements at the beginning of an accounting textbook leaves the reader with unanswered questions. The statements are introduced at this point to provide a broad picture of what the accounting process does and how the information it produces is used. As the methods and techniques of recording accounting information unfold throughout this book, it may be useful to refer back to these statements to view some special topic in its overall context.

Appendix 1.1
Generally Accepted Accounting Principles (GAAP)[7]

Introduction

In Figure 1–6, there were references to acceptable alternative procedures available to record accounting information. Who decides what procedures are acceptable, and what guidance does an accountant follow in applying such procedures? This appendix covers briefly the authoritative bodies for accounting standards in the United States and describes some guidelines that will be useful in the study of the early chapters of this book.

Learning Goals

1. To recognize the major sources of authoritative guidance in accounting.
2. To understand the commonly used generally accepted accounting principles (GAAP).

---

[7]The material in this appendix could be delayed and taught after Chapter 6.

Sources of Generally Accepted Accounting Principles (GAAP)

Accounting has been performed for thousands of years. In England, the industrial revolution had advanced in 1845 to the point that a national corporation act was enacted that year. This act legally established the corporation as a form of business in England, but it had other important consequences. It required an audit of the records of a corporation and a separate report on the fairness of financial statements by persons who were not connected with its management. The result was a need for some type of standards so that evaluations made by various independent accountants would be consistent. To meet this need, the Institute of Chartered Accountants was founded in Scotland in 1854 and a similar group in England in 1880. As these groups became more active, a set of accounting guidelines emerged that gradually became accepted as standard practice by the members of the two organizations.

In the United States, some corporations were established before 1800 by the English Crown, and a few states adopted general incorporation acts in the early 1800s. Until the mid-1880s, however, the United States was primarily an agricultural country with accounting needs of a business focused mainly on records of dealings with its customers. It was the move toward an industrial economy that made the corporate form of business attractive and caused an increase in the number of states with laws allowing them to issue charters to corporations. As in England, this change brought about a need for standardization of accounting practices.

American accountants formed societies and sponsored state legislation that later led to the formation of some of the authoritative bodies described in the next sections. Although reference is made to several sources throughout this book, three major authoritative bodies are described here. They are: (1) the American Institute of Certified Public Accountants (AICPA), (2) the Financial Accounting Standards Board (FASB), and (3) the Securities and Exchange Commission (SEC). The first two are private sector organizations; the SEC is a federal government agency.

American Institute of Certified Public Accountants (AICPA)

The **American Institute of Certified Public Accountants (AICPA)**—formerly named the American Institute of Accountants—was created in 1936 by the merger of the two national accounting organizations then in existence. Its formation created the basic authoritative body for certified public accountants in the United States.[8] The AICPA played a very active role in the development of guidelines for accountants from 1937 to 1973. These years saw many changes in the form of business; each change created new accounting problems.

In 1937, the AICPA created the Committee on Accounting Procedure, which issued a series of **Accounting Research Bulletins (ARBs)**. These bulletins—the last of which was issued in 1957—were issued in the interest of standardizing accounting practices. In 1959, this committee was replaced

---
[8] CPAs are described earlier in Chapter 1.

by the **Accounting Principles Board (APB)**. The APB—also an arm of the AICPA—continued the series of ARBs in effect, but began to publish a new set of pronouncements, entitled **Opinions of the Accounting Principles Board (APB Opinions)**. They are in a numbered series starting with number 1 in 1962. By the time the APB was replaced in 1973, it had issued 31 opinions. Each *APB Opinion* provides guidelines in a specific area—for example, accounting for investments in other companies. They carry authority because they are widely accepted by CPAs in auditing the financial records of enterprises.

In mid-1973, an independent private body, the **Financial Accounting Standards Board (FASB)**, replaced the APB and assumed responsibility for the issuance of financial accounting standards. The AICPA, having yielded the determination of accounting standards to the FASB, remains the primary source today for auditing standards for CPAs.

Financial Accounting Standards Board (FASB)

The FASB began to issue standards in 1973 and is now the independent nongovernmental body that develops and issues standards for financial accounting. The seven members of the FASB serve full time and are paid for their services. A technical staff assists FASB members in their work on a continuing agenda of projects. As it began to issue **Statements of Financial Accounting Standards (SFAS)**, some earlier issuances were replaced or modified.[9] The FASB also issues *Statements of Financial Accounting Concepts.* These constitute the basic conceptual framework for all accounting. By mid-1985, the FASB had issued 85 standard statements and five concept statements, so that today accountants must look to a mixture of *ARBs, APB Opinions,* and *FASB Statements* for authoritative guidance.

Securities and Exchange Commission (SEC)

The **Securities and Exchange Commission (SEC)** was created by the Securities Exchange Act of 1934. The SEC has the legal authority to prescribe accounting methods for firms whose shares of stock are sold to the investing public on the stock exchanges. The law requires that such companies make reports to the SEC giving detailed information about their operations. The SEC has broad powers as to the amount and type of information to be included in these reports and the methods used to develop the information that they contain. Since its creation in 1934, the SEC has concentrated on protection of investors. It has given high priority to the public disclosure of financial information in a fair and accurate manner. In doing so, it has left the task of issuing detailed accounting rules to the accounting profession. However, the SEC has kept a watchful eye on the private rule-making bodies and has not hesitated to exercise its influence where deemed necessary.

---

[9]Although the formal title is *Statements of Financial Accounting Standards,* these guidelines are commonly referred to as *FASB Statements.*

Today, **accounting standards** are the fundamental guidelines that determine whether a specific accounting method is acceptable. These include the set of generally accepted accounting principles that have stood the test of time over many years.

Generally Accepted Accounting Principles

Over the years the accounting profession has developed a set of standards which are called **generally accepted accounting principles (GAAP)** from their widespread usage. Some of the basic generally accepted accounting principles are presented in this section.

Entity

The **entity** concept dictates that a separate set of records must be kept for each business enterprise of an owner. Owners will be required to make decisions regarding the operation of each of the businesses in which they have an interest. Therefore, the financial reports concerning a business must report only the resources of that business, claims to those resources, and changes in those resources. The accountant must guard against intermingling the transactions of the several businesses which may be owned by a single owner or the personal transactions of the owner with any one of the businesses.

Going Concern

It is assumed that an entity is a **going concern**—that is, that it will continue in operation indefinitely—unless there is evidence to the contrary. Because of the going concern assumption, the accountant records prepaid insurance at the value of its unexpired fraction of cost and not at its cash surrender value. Long-term debts are reported at their face value and not at the amount it is estimated that creditors would receive if the company were to go out of business. This concept also supports reporting of plant items at historical cost.

Consistency

In some instances, acceptable alternative methods can be used in accounting records. Once a choice has been made, the principle of **consistency** requires that the same procedure be followed in all future entries so that statements covering different time periods will be comparable. This principle does not mean that a change to a better procedure cannot be made. If there is sufficient reason to change an accounting method, the accountant may do so as long as adequate disclosure is made.

Conservatism

Where acceptable alternatives exist, the one normally chosen is that which produces the least favorable immediate result. The principle of **conservatism** aims to avoid favorable exaggeration in accounting reports. Reporting inventories at lower of cost or market is an example of this standard.

Periodicity

Financial statements are prepared at regular specified time periods during the lifetime of a firm. The principle of **periodicity** holds that items of expense and revenue can be allocated to such time periods so that expenses and revenues can be properly matched for income determination. It is for this reason that adjusting entries are made. The accrual concept is essential to this standard. Items of expense and revenue should be recognized at the time of the occurrence of the economic events that produced them without regard to the timing of the related collection or payment of cash.

Objective Evidence

To the greatest extent possible, the amounts used in recording events are based upon **objective evidence** rather than subjective judgment. Sales invoices, receiver's reports, and other source documents provide such evidence. It should follow that two separate accountants independently recording transactions from such documents would arrive at the same result. This does not mean that certain items are not to be estimated. For example, in calculating depreciation expense, it is necessary to estimate useful life and salvage value. When such estimates are necessary, however, they should be based upon past experience or upon some other logical base that is used consistently from year to year.

Materiality

An item small enough that it would not influence a decision based upon the statement in which it is used is immaterial. The accounting treatment thereof need not follow prescribed accounting standards. (For example, the inventory value of unused stationery in the typing pool or paper clips in the office would not be counted as part of the supplies inventory at the end of a period since it would not have a material effect on income or assets.) **Materiality** depends upon the size and the nature of the item relative to the size of the business. In a very small business, an inventory error of $300 may definitely be large enough to influence the decision of the user of the financial statement in which it is made. On the other hand, an error of $300 in valuation of inventories of a multimillion-dollar company would be unlikely to be considered material.

Full Disclosure

Financial statements should report all significant financial and economic information relating to an entity. If the accounting system does not automatically capture some specific item of significance, it should be included in a footnote to the accounting statements. As indicated earlier in this appendix, the SEC has placed primary emphasis on **full disclosure**.

Historical Cost

The **historical cost** principle states that actual incurred cost—arrived at through agreement by two independent entities—is the appropriate amount to be used to record the value of a newly acquired asset. There is little argument that historical cost is the only objective value at which an asset can be recorded at the time of its purchase. There are reasons (illustrated in Chapter 1) to believe that the historical cost of some assets becomes less useful as the asset grows older.

Stable Dollar

The **stable dollar concept** assumes that the dollar is sufficiently free from changes in purchasing power to be used as the basic unit of measure in accounting without adjustment for price-level changes. Many accountants challenge the general use of this principle on the grounds that it simply is not true.

Revenue Realization

Under the assumptions of accrual accounting, revenue is said to be realized when it is "earned." But, when is revenue earned? Is it earned when we do something to the product which adds value? Is it earned when the product changes hands? Or is it earned when the cash is collected?

With certain exceptions, generally accepted accounting principles require that revenue be realized at the *point of sale* (the method used in this text). For a business that deals with a product, the point of sale is commonly defined to be the delivery of the merchandise. For a service business, the point in time that the service is rendered is normally agreed to be the point of sale. Thus, revenue is earned in the accounting period in which the sale is construed to have taken place. Two other revenue realization methods are acceptable under specific circumstances: the collection method and the percentage of completion method.

Under the **collection method**, the realization of revenue is deferred until the cash is collected. This may be applied using either the cost recovery basis or the installment basis. With the **cost recovery basis**, all collections are first construed to be a recovery of the cost of the product sold. After the total cost is recovered, then the gross margin on the product is recognized. This method is appropriate when there is a high probability that total payment will never be received. It is considered to be a very conservative method.

Under the **installment basis**, each dollar collected is considered to be a proportionate return of the cost of the merchandise and a realization of the gross margin. For example, assume that a television set which cost $300 was sold for $400. Each dollar collected by the company would be construed to be a return of $0.75 = ($300 ÷ $400) of the cost of the set and a $0.25 = [($400 − $300) ÷ $400] realization of the gross margin from the sale. If in a given month the customer made a $100 installment payment, the company would consider $25 in gross margin realized. The installment basis should be used when the company has no reasonable basis for estimating the extent of uncollectability of the receivable.

The other alternative to point of sale, the **percentage of completion method**, is appropriate for large construction projects requiring more than one accounting period to complete, such as a high-rise office building. Under these circumstances, use of the point of sale method of revenue realization could significantly distort income reporting, since several periods might go by with no expense or revenue shown. Then in the period that the project was completed, a large amount of expense or revenue would be recorded. This distortion can be counteracted by realizing a portion of the gross margin from the project during each period in which the work on the project was done. The gross margin is allocated to each accounting period based upon the proportion of the project estimated to be complete. This estimated percentage of completion is the ratio of the current year's actual costs to the total estimated costs. In the final period, the remaining actual gross margin is recognized.

For example, assume that a construction company entered into a contract to build a high-rise condominium building at a price of $4 million. Also assume that it was estimated that the total cost of the building would be $3 million, giving a gross margin of $1 million on the project. If the actual incurred costs year by year were as shown in the schedule below, the gross margin recognized by the company would have been as shown in the schedule. If at the end of an accounting period a loss on the project becomes apparent, the loss should be recognized in that period.

Year	Actual Incurred Cost	Percentage of Completion	×	Total Gross Margin	Gross Margin Recognized
1	$ 900,000	900,000/3,000,000		$1,000,000	$300,000
2	$1,200,000	1,200,000/3,000,000		$1,000,000	$400,000
3	$1,000,000				$200,000[a]
	$3,100,000				$900,000

[a] Balance of gross margin: ($4,000,000 − $3,100,000) − ($300,000 + $400,000) = $200,000.

Matching Expense and Revenue

The **matching principle** states that the expenses incurred in the generation of revenues should be matched against those revenues in the determination of income. As explained in Chapter 4, income is properly measured only when the expenses which were incurred to produce revenues are recorded in the same period as the revenues. This requires the accrual of expenses incurred or revenues earned because of the passage of time, for example, interest on a note. It also requires adjustment of deferrals to assign expenses associated with the sale of a product or the performance of a service to the period that revenues are recorded. Examples are recording of advertising expense in the period the advertisement to produce the sale appeared, or the proper determination of ending inventory to calculate accurately the cost of goods sold. Proper matching of revenue and expense is achieved through adherence to accrual accounting methods.

Other Concepts

Many other concepts and assumptions might be included in the list. As research and study continue, certain standards will be revised and new ones will be issued. Accounting systems are designed to meet changing user needs. These needs continue to increase in scope and complexity as changes occur in the environment in which users make economic decisions. It is the ongoing task of the authoritative bodies to develop and publish new and revised accounting standards that will keep pace with these changes.

Glossary

Accounting The set of rules and methods by which financial and economic data are collected, processed, and summarized into reports that can be used in making decisions.

Accounting Principles Board (APB) A committee of the American Institute of Certified Public Accountants that was the basic source of accounting guidance from 1959 to 1973.

Accounting Research Bulletin (ARB) Issuance of the Committee on Accounting Procedure of the American Institute of Certified Public Accountants that gave the opinion of the committee on specific controversial methods of accounting.

Accounting standard A fundamental guideline that helps determine whether or not a specific accounting method is acceptable.

Acid-test ratio The ratio of cash, temporary investments, and receivables to current liabilities.

American Institute of Certified Public Accountants (AICPA) The national organization of certified public accountants that is the major source of auditing standards.

Assets Things of value held in an enterprise.

Balance sheet The financial report that displays the financial condition of a business at a specific time.

Budget A financial plan for a future period usually developed in organizational detail.

Certified Internal Auditor (CIA) An accountant who has passed a national examination and met the requirements for the certificate issued by the Institute of Internal Auditors; these persons perform the review function for a single enterprise, by which they are employed.

Certified Management Accountant (CMA) Holder of a certificate granted for demonstrated ability in management accounting by passing a national examination and completing two years of management accounting.

Certified Public Accountant (CPA) An accountant who has passed a national examination and is licensed by the state to perform independent audits.

Collection method (of revenue recognition) The realization of revenue is deferred until cash is collected.

Conservatism Where acceptable alternatives exist, the one that produces the least favorable immediate result is chosen.

Consistency Once a method of recording is chosen over an alternative, the chosen method must be used consistently from year to year.

Contingencies Situations that would arise if certain events occur.

Controlling The management function of checking on day-to-day operations of an enterprise and taking action where necessary to redirect operations.

Cost recovery basis (of revenue recognition) All collections are first construed to be a recovery of cost before income is recognized.

CPA See *Certified Public Accountant*.

Current assets Assets with a relatively short useful life, usually a year or less.

Current liabilities Liabilities of a short-term nature, such as accounts payable to creditors or notes payable due in less than a year.

Current ratio The ratio of current assets to current liabilities.

Creditors Persons who lend money to a firm.

Dividends Payments to stockholders of a share of profits of a corporation.

Entity concept The concept that the focus of a set of accounting records must be on a single enterprise.

Equities Claims against the assets of an enterprise.

Expenses Expired costs of earning revenues in a business.

Financial Accounting Standards Board (FASB) The current independent private body that issues accounting concepts and standards statements.

Full disclosure The accounting standard that requires an organization to reveal in its financial reports all significant economic and financial information relating to it.

Generally Accepted Accounting Principles (GAAP) Accounting principles (standards) that have arisen from wide acceptance in the past or are contained in authoritative pronouncements..

Going concern The concept that an enterprise will continue to operate indefinitely unless there is evidence to the contrary.

Historical cost The actual cost arrived at through arm's-length bargaining of an item or service.

Income statement A financial statement that matches revenue and expenses to show the net income (or loss) of a business.

Installment basis (of revenue recognition) Each dollar collected is considered to be a proportionate return of cost and the realization of gross margin.

Liabilities Debts of an enterprise; creditors' claims against the assets.

Long-term liabilities Liabilities such as bonds payable that are not due to be paid until years in the future.

Matching principle Expenses incurred in generating revenue should be matched against that revenue to determine income.

Materiality The concept that an item must be given prescribed accounting treatment only if it is significant enough to influence a decision by a user of the accounting information.

Net income An excess of revenue over expenses in an accounting period.

Net loss An excess of expenses over revenue in an accounting period.

Objective evidence The concept that recording accounting events is based upon some type of document that supports the amount and method of recording.

Opinions of the Accounting Principles Board (APB Opinions) A numbered series of statements that provide accounting guidelines.

Owner's (or) **Owners' equity** The sum of all ownership claims against assets of an enterprise.

Percentage of completion basis (of revenue recognition) The amount of estimated gross margin earned is proportional to percentage of completion of a long-term contract.

Periodicity The concept that items of revenue and expense can be allocated to a time period to determine net income for that period.

Planning The management function that determines the goals and objectives of an organization.

Profit See *Net income*.

Property, plant, and equipment This classification consists of such things as land, buildings, machinery, office equipment, and sales equipment; these items have a long useful life to the enterprise.

Ratio One number in relation to another number.

Retained earnings Stockholders' equity that has grown from net income not paid out to stockholders as dividends.

Revenues Inflows of things of value in exchange for providing products or services.

Securities and Exchange Commission (SEC) The federal government agency with legal authority to prescribe accounting methods for firms whose stock or bonds are sold to the public on the exchanges.

Stable dollar assumption The concept that historical cost dollars of different years are comparable.

Statement of changes in financial position A financial statement that shows sources and uses of financial resources during a period.

Statement of Financial Accounting Standards (SFAS) The basic issuance of the FASB to provide accounting guidance.

Statement of retained earnings A financial statement showing changes in retained earnings over a period.

Stockholders' equity The name for total owners' equity in a corporation.

Working capital The excess of current assets over current liabilities.

Questions

Q1–1   What is the primary reason for recording accounting information?

Q1–2   What is the difference between external users and internal users of accounting information? Discuss the purposes for which each group uses accounting information.

Q1–3   What is the role of a certified public accountant (CPA)? What are some services that CPAs provide?

Q1–4   What are the four basic financial reports? What is the primary function of each?

Q1–5   What dollar amount is the same on the income statement and the statement of retained earnings? On the statement of retained earnings and the balance sheet?

Q1–6   How would you describe an asset? A liability? An expense? A revenue?

Q1–7   What types of items are included in the balance sheet caption "property, plant, and equipment"?

Q1–8   What is the basic purpose of the statement of changes in financial position? How does this purpose differ from that of the income statement?

Q1–9   What is the meaning of the concept of an accounting entity?

Q1–10 What is a current ratio? An acid-test ratio? What does each reveal about a corporation?

Q1–11 (Appendix) What is the purpose of the Financial Accounting Standards Board?

Q1–12 (Appendix) How does the Securities and Exchange Commission affect the work of an accountant?

Q1–13 (Appendix) What was the role of the American Institute of Certified Public Accountants (AICPA) in providing accounting guidance prior to the formation of the FASB? What is the AICPA's major role today?

Q1–14 (Appendix) What is a *generally accepted accounting principle* (GAAP)? Explain the importance of GAAP to users of financial statements.

Exercises

E1–1
Users of accounting information

The persons or groups listed below use the financial reports or accounting records of Sunbelt Excursions, Incorporated. Identify each as an external or an internal user.

1. The loan manager of a bank to which Sunbelt has applied for a 90-day loan.
2. Brenda Weiss who owns 100 shares of Sunbelt common stock.
3. The vice-president for operations of Sunbelt.
4. The regional director of the Internal Revenue Service.
5. Shane Kelly, the corporation's capital budgeting manager.
6. Van Mantoya, the corporation's budget director.
7. Audrey Josey, who has a sum of money to invest in bonds.
8. Dawn Denby, tour director of Sunbelt.

E1–2
Financial terms

Column A contains descriptions of items listed in column B. For each item in column A, show the appropriate letter from column B.

Column A
1. Persons who own shares of common stock in a corporation. ____
2. Persons who lend money to a company. ____
3. Formal written promises to pay a debt. ____
4. Payments of a portion of a corporation's profits to its owners. ____
5. Items of value held in an enterprise. ____
6. The general term for overall debts of an enterprise. ____
7. The excess of revenues over expenses. ____
8. The supply of goods or products that a firm has for sale. ____
9. The excess of total assets over total liabilities. ____
10. Claims against the assets of an enterprise. ____

Column B
a. Assets
b. Dividends
c. Liabilities
d. Equities
e. Stockholders
f. Bonds
g. Net income
h. Creditors
i. Owners' equity
j. Inventory

E1–3
Content of financial statements

Each of the items listed below appears in one or more of the four basic financial statements. Using the following code, indicate all statements in which each is found:

IS—Income statement
RE—Statement of retained earnings
BS—Balance sheet
FP—Statement of changes in financial position

1. Property, plant, and equipment. ____
2. Net income. ____
3. Net sales. ____
4. Retained earnings. ____
5. Proceeds from sale of property, plant, and equipment. ____
6. Total liabilities. ____
7. Income tax expense. ____
8. Depreciation expense. ____
9. Dividends. ____
10. Total assets. ____

E1–4
Nature of financial statements

Using the codes for financial statements given in E1–3, show which statements would be most useful for each purpose listed below:

1. Determination of ability to pay a loan due in 90 days. _____
2. Deciding whether it is feasible to pay a dividend to stockholders. _____
3. Learning the reason for increase in property, plant, and equipment. _____
4. Determining the amount of inventory on hand. _____
5. Deciding whether last quarter's operating results were satisfactory. _____
6. Comparing selling expenses with general and administrative expenses. _____
7. Computing the cost of goods sold as a percent of sales. _____
8. Learning the number of shares of common stock outstanding. _____
9. Learning the amount of dividends paid. _____
10. Computing the percentage of total assets provided by debt financing. _____

E1–5
Financial statement content

After preparing financial statements for 1987 for the Caravati Company, it was determined that two major errors had been made, as follows:

a. A sale of $125,000 to a customer in late December had been overlooked and not recorded. The sale was on credit with payment to be made in 30 days.
b. The last payroll was recorded on December 24, 1987. Employees who worked on December 28–31, 1987, had earned $30,000, but this fact was unrecognized in any of the accounting records.

Compute the effect of these errors on:

1. Net income.
2. Total assets.
3. Total liabilities.

E1–6
Gross margin on sales

Solar Products Company sold 132,000 thermal energy units in 1987 at a sales price of $20 per unit. Each unit cost the company $14 per unit. Total selling expenses were $210,000; total general and administrative expenses were $240,000. Compute the gross margin on sales.

E1–7
Earnings per share

Chula Vista Air Couriers reported a net income of $3,654,000 in 1987. The earnings per share of common stock was $6.00. There was no preferred stock outstanding. Compute the weighted average number of common shares outstanding during 1987.

E1–8
Computation of dividends

Alpha Corporation had 100,000 shares of 9 percent preferred stock with a par value of $50 per share outstanding all during 1987. The company also had 2,000,000 shares of common stock oustanding during the same period. The directors of the corporation declared all dividends due to preferred stockholders at the contract rate of 9 percent of par. They also declared dividends on common stock as follows:

> First quarter—30 cents per share.
> Second quarter—20 cents per share.
> Third quarter—10 cents per share.
> Fourth quarter—none.

Julia Klein held 100 shares of preferred stock and 1,200 shares of common stock all through 1987. All dividends were paid by December 31, 1987. Compute:

1. Total dividends paid by Alpha Corporation.
2. The amount received by Julia Klein.

E1–9
Current and acid-test ratios

The following data are reproduced from the 1983 *Annual Report* of The Goodyear Tire and Rubber Company:

CONSOLIDATED BALANCE SHEET
The Goodyear Tire & Rubber Company and Subsidiaries

(Dollars in millions)	December 31, 1983	1982
ASSETS		
Current Assets:		
Cash and short term securities	$ 111.1	$ 102.2
Accounts and notes receivable	1,527.4	1,431.7
Inventories	1,218.9	1,305.0
Prepaid expenses	63.0	103.3
Total Current Assets	2,920.4	2,942.2
Other Assets:		
Investments in nonconsolidated subsidiaries and affiliates, at equity	151.5	147.8
Long term accounts and notes receivable	50.7	34.5
Investments and miscellaneous assets, at cost	24.2	30.9
Deferred charges	19.5	12.3
	245.9	225.5
Properties and Plants	2,819.2	2,718.2
	$5,985.5	$5,885.9
LIABILITIES AND SHAREHOLDERS' EQUITY		
Current Liabilities:		
Accounts payable—trade	$ 593.4	$ 538.9
Accrued payrolls and other compensation	281.1	257.0
Other current liabilities	204.0	168.7
United States and foreign taxes:		
Current	178.8	213.1
Deferred	78.6	106.5
Notes payable to banks and overdrafts	154.6	4.8
Long term debt due within one year	41.7	10.3
Total Current Liabilities	1,532.2	1,299.3
Long Term Debt and Capital Leases	665.2	1,174.5
Other Long Term Liabilities	296.5	256.4

Compute for 1983 and 1982:

1. The current ratio.
2. The acid-test ratio.
3. Working capital.

E1–10 *Computation of net income*

In 1983, Duke Power Company included the following items in its *Annual Report* (dollars in thousands):

Electric revenues	$2,420,252
Other income	213,001
Electric expenses (includes taxes)	1,971,038
Interest expense	230,938
Dividends on preferred and preference stocks	62,600
Dividends on common stock	226,964

Compute the net income for 1983.

1 / The Nature and Function of Accounting

E1–11
Generally accepted accounting principles (GAAP)

(Appendix) Refer to the Notes to Financial Statements of the Bradensota Chemical Company in Figure 1–6. What generally accepted accounting principle is probably the basis for:

1. The continued use of a specific method of costing inventories as indicated in Note 2.
2. Separate accounting records for the investee companies described in Note 3.
3. Reporting of plant items at the valuations shown in Note 4.
4. The information in Note 9.

E1–12
Percentage of completion method of revenue recognition

(Appendix) Delta Contractors, using the percentage of completion method of revenue recognition, has a contract to build a dormitory for State University at a price of $12,000,000. Total costs to build the dormitory are expected to be $10,500,000. By the end of 1987, the first year of construction, construction costs of $7,665,000 had been incurred. Compute the amount of gross margin on this contract to be recognized in 1987.

E1–13
Financial statements

Select the best answer for each of the following items:

1. The financial statement that summarizes the financial position of the company is the
    a. Income statement.
    b. Balance sheet.
    c. Statement of changes in financial position.
    d. Retained earnings statement.

2. If a company issues both a balance sheet and an income statement with comparative figures from last year, a statement of changes in financial position
    a. Is no longer necessary; but may be issued at the company's option.
    b. Should not be issued.
    c. Should be issued for each period for which an income statement is presented.
    d. Should be issued for the current year only.

E1–14
Objectivity standard

Select the best answer to the following item:

1. Objectivity is assumed to be achieved when an accounting transaction
    a. Is recorded in a fixed amount of dollars.
    b. Involves payment or receipt of cash.
    c. Involves an arm's-length transaction between two independent parties.
    d. Allocates revenue and expense in a rational and systematic manner.

A Problems

P1–1A
Computation of net income and earnings per common share

The following information is taken from the 1983 *Annual Report* of Utah Power and Light Company (dollars in thousands) for the year ended December 31, 1983:

Operating revenues	$854,898
Other income	20,660
Fuel generation expenses	197,772
Power purchases (from others)	29,539
Maintenance expense	69,658
Depreciation expense	63,328
Other operating expenses	147,332
Income tax expense	88,851
Other tax expense	33,902
Interest expense	100,714
Preferred stock dividend requirements	20,937

The average number of shares of common stock outstanding in 1983 was 51,681,716.

Part One / The Basic Accounting Model

Required:

1. Compute the net income for 1983.
2. Compute the net income applicable to common stock and the earnings per common share (rounded to the nearest cent).

P1–2A
Computing and using current and acid-test ratios.

The following data are selected amounts shown on the balance sheet of Ford Motor Company and are reproduced from Ford's 1983 *Annual Report*:

CONSOLIDATED BALANCE SHEET — Ford

December 31, 1983 and 1982 (in millions)
Ford Motor Company and Consolidated Subsidiaries

Assets	1983	1982
Current Assets		
Cash and cash items	$ 2,185.4	$ 943.7
Marketable securities, at cost and accrued interest (approximates market)	966.7	611.7
Receivables (including $519.8 and $215.3 from unconsolidated subsidiaries)	2,767.6	2,376.5
Inventories	4,111.7	4,123.3
Other current assets (Note 5)	787.7	743.7
Total current assets	10,819.1	8,798.9
Equity in Net Assets of Unconsolidated Subsidiaries and Affiliates	2,582.7	2,413.4
Property:		
Land, plant, and equipment, at cost (Note 8)	17,410.4	17,014.9
Less accumulated depreciation	10,119.0	9,546.9
Net land, plant, and equipment	7,291.4	7,468.0
Unamortized special tools	2,510.5	2,668.3
Net property	9,801.9	10,136.3
Other Assets	665.2	613.1
Total Assets	$23,868.9	$21,961.7
Liabilities and Stockholders' Equity		
Current Liabilities		
Accounts payable		
Trade	$ 4,097.6	$ 3,117.5
Other	1,149.5	1,002.1
Total accounts payable	5,247.1	4,119.6
Income taxes	362.1	383.0
Short-term debt	832.8	1,949.1
Long-term debt payable within one year	109.2	315.9
Accrued liabilities (Note 9)	3,764.7	3,656.4
Total current liabilities	10,315.9	10,424.0
Long-Term Debt	2,712.9	2,353.3
Other Liabilities	2,054.4	1,922.7

1 / The Nature and Function of Accounting

Required:

1. Compute the current ratios for 1983 and 1982.
2. Compute the acid-test ratios for 1983 and 1982.
3. Was Ford in a better position to meet its current obligations at the end of 1983 than at the end of 1982? Explain your answer.

P1–3A
Use of income statement

The following are summary data from the income statements for Treasure Land, Incorporated, for two years:

	Year Ended December 31	
	1987	**1986**
Net admissions revenue	$688,500	$542,450
Operating expenses:		
Promotion and advertising	$ 88,590	$ 50,208
Commissions to travel agencies	68,850	54,245
Salaries expense	172,125	108,490
Other expenses	34,425	27,123
Total operating expenses	$363,990	$240,066
Net operating margin	$324,510	$302,384
Income tax expense	129,804	120,954
Net income	$194,706	$181,430

Required:

1. For each year, compute net income as a percentage of net admissions revenue.
2. What items appear to need management's attention? Support your answers with computations.

P1–4A
Use of balance sheet

The following are summarized data from the balance sheet of Obachi Steak House at December 31, 1987:

Assets

Current assets	$ 262,650
Long-term investments (at cost)	300,000
Property, plant, and equipment (less accumulated depreciation of $128,600)	478,350
Total assets	$1,041,000

Liabilities and Stockholders' Equity

Current liabilities	$ 112,230
Long-term liabilities	275,000
Stockholders' equity:	
Common stock, 200,000 shares	400,000
Retained earnings	253,770
Total liabilities and stockholders' equity	$1,041,000

There is more than $100,000 in cash included in the current assets. Also, footnotes to the financial statements include the following information:

a. Cost of investments approximates their current market value. They do not represent a controlling interest in another company; average income from investments is 14 percent per year.

b. Current replacement value of property, plant, and equipment after deducting accumulated depreciation is $650,000.

c. The long-term debt consists of 30-year bonds due in 1999 that carry annual interest at the rate of 6 percent.

Required: (Round answers to nearest tenth of a percent where appropriate.)

1. Compute the percentage of total assets claimed by owners.
2. Compute the percentage of total assets claimed by creditors.
3. The year ended December 31, 1987, was profitable, and a 50¢ per share dividend has been suggested. Would you vote in favor of this dividend if you were a director? Explain.
4. It has been suggested that the investments be sold and the proceeds used to pay the long-term debt early. Make a recommendation to management as to whether to adopt this suggestion; support your recommendation with computations.

P1–5A
Evaluation of operating results

Southern Catfish Farm, Incorporated, had a profitable year in 1987 but paid only a small dividend to its stockholders. Debra Fogleman holds 10 percent of the company's common stock, and is disappointed to have received only $5,000 in dividends. In early 1988, she is considering the sale of her stock to invest the cash proceeds elsewhere. The following financial statement appeared in the 1987 *Annual Report:*

SOUTHERN CATFISH FARM, INCORPORATED   Exhibit D
Statement of Changes in Financial Position
For the Year Ended December 31, 1987

Financial resources were provided by:		
Net income (from Exhibit A)	$300,000	
Add: Items charged to net income that did not use financial resources:		
Depreciation	50,000	
Total provided by operations	$350,000	
Sale of obsolete equipment	10,000	
Total financial resources provided		$360,000
Financial resources were used for:		
Dividends.	$ 50,000	
Payment of long-term, 20½ percent notes payable (due in 1990)	300,000	
Total financial resources used		350,000
Increase in financial resources.		$ 10,000

In a letter to stockholders at the beginning of the *Annual Report,* the chief operating officer of the company indicated that 1988 operating income is expected to exceed that of 1987. The balance sheet shows no other long-term debt outstanding; average stockholders' equity in 1987 was $2,000,000.

Required:

1. Evaluate (with supporting computations) the decision to make early repayment of long-term debt in 1987.
2. Indicate whether you believe that decision improved or worsened Fogleman's chances for greater dividends in 1988. Explain.
3. Should Fogleman sell her stock and reinvest elsewhere?

P1–6A
Preparation of income statement and statement of retained earnings

On December 31, 1987, the following balances are extracted from the accounting records of Northeastern Bus Lines (some items have been omitted):

Item	Amount
Cash	$102,500
Accounts receivable	262,500
Accounts payable	103,200
Bonds payable (due 2001).	600,000

(continued on next page)

Item	Amount
Common stock, 100,000 shares	250,000
Retained earnings, December 31, 1986	382,500
Passenger revenues	987,575
Advertising and promotion expense	122,850
Sales salaries expense	86,300
Other selling expense	26,360
Depreciation expense	132,350
General and administrative salaries expense	260,000
Other general and administrative expense	62,380
Interest expense	90,000
Dividends	80,000

Assume an income tax rate for 1987 of 40 percent.

Required:

1. Prepare an income statement for the year ended December 31, 1987.
2. Prepare a statement of retained earnings for the same period.

P1–7A
Thought-provoking problem: Using financial reports

Selected data from *Annual Reports* of three companies are provided as follows:

	Earnings (Loss) per Share	Dividends per Share	Market Price at Year-End
General Motors Corp.	$11.84	$2.80	$74.375
Ford Motor Company	10.29	0.50	63.00
Republic Airlines	(4.28)	0	3.75

Required: Comment as to the desirability of investing in each of the above companies if the criterion to be used is:

1. Earnings as a percentage of market price.
2. Dividend payout as a percentage of market price.
3. Number of shares of stock that can be purchased with the $20,000 of investable funds that you have.

B Problems

P1–1B
Computation of net income and earnings per common share

The following information is taken from the 1983 *Annual Report* of Utah Power and Light Company (dollars in thousands) for the year ended December 31, 1982:

Operating revenues	$782,070
Other income	27,513
Fuel generation expenses	209,317
Power purchased (from others)	49,962
Maintenance expense	55,167
Depreciation expense	52,492
Other operating expenses	132,736
Income tax expense	56,339
Other tax expense	30,808
Interest expense	89,319
Preferred stock dividend requirements	20,936

The average number of shares of common stock outstanding in 1982 was 47,204,277.

Required:

1. Compute the net income for 1982.
2. Compute the net income applicable to common stock and the earnings per common share (rounded to the nearest cent).

P1–2B
Computing and using current and acid-test ratios

The following data are reproduced from the 1983 *Annual Report* of General Motors Corporation:

CONSOLIDATED BALANCE SHEET GM

December 31, 1983 and 1982
(Dollars in Millions Except Per Share Amounts)

ASSETS	1983	1982
Current Assets		
Cash	$ 369.5	$ 279.6
United States Government and other marketable securities and time deposits—at cost, which approximates market of $5,834.6 and $2,835.5	5,847.4	2,846.6
Total cash and marketable securities	6,216.9	3,126.2
Accounts and notes receivable (including GMAC and its subsidiaries—$3,560.7 and $312.0)—less allowances (Note 8)	6,964.2	2,864.5
Inventories (less allowances) (Note 1)	6,621.5	6,184.2
Prepaid expenses and deferred income taxes	997.2	1,868.2
Total Current Assets	20,799.8	14,043.1
Equity in Net Assets of Nonconsolidated Subsidiaries and Associates (principally GMAC and its subsidiaries—Note 8)	4,450.8	4,231.1
Other Investments and Miscellaneous Assets—at cost (less allowances)	1,222.5	1,550.0
Common Stock Held for the Incentive Program (Note 3)	56.3	35.2
Property:		
Real estate, plants and equipment—at cost (Note 9)	37,777.8	37,687.2
Less accumulated depreciation (Note 9)	20,116.8	18,148.9
Net real estate, plants and equipment	17,661.0	19,538.3
Special tools—at cost (less amortization)	1,504.1	2,000.1
Total Property	19,165.1	21,538.4
Total Assets	$45,694.5	$41,397.8
LIABILITIES AND STOCKHOLDERS' EQUITY		
Current Liabilities		
Accounts payable (principally trade)	$ 4,642.3	$ 3,600.7
Loans payable (principally overseas) (Note 11)	1,255.2	1,182.5
Accrued liabilities (Note 10)	9,011.5	7,601.8
Total Current Liabilities	14,909.0	12,385.0
Long-Term Debt (Note 11)	3,137.2	4,452.0
Capitalized Leases	384.6	293.1
Other Liabilities (including GMAC and its subsidiaries—$300.0 and $876.0)	4,698.2	4,259.8

1 / The Nature and Function of Accounting

Required:

1. Compute the current ratios for 1983 and 1982.
2. Compute the acid-test ratios for 1983 and 1982.
3. Was General Motors in a better position to meet its current obligations at the end of 1983 than at the end of 1982? Explain your answer.

P1–3B
Use of income statement

The following are summary data from the income statements of the Seattle Sizzlers of the Universal Basketball Conference for two years:

	Year Ended December 31	
	1987	1986
Net admissions revenue	$2,065,500	$1,627,350
Operating expenses:		
Promotion and advertising	$ 265,770	$ 150,624
Travel expense	206,550	162,735
Salaries expense	516,375	325,470
Other expenses	103,275	81,369
Total operating expense	$1,091,970	$ 720,198
Net operating margin	$ 973,530	$ 907,152
Income tax expense	389,412	362,862
Net income	$ 584,118	$ 544,290

Required:

1. For each year, compute net income as a percent of net admissions revenue.
2. What items appear to need management's attention? Support your answers with computations.

P1–4B
Use of balance sheet

The following are summarized data from Radford Air Freight, Incorporated, at December 31, 1987:

Assets

Current assets	$ 656,625
Long-term investments (at cost)	750,000
Property, plant, and equipment (less accumulated depreciation of $321,500)	1,195,875
Total assets	$2,602,500

Liabilities and Stockholders' Equity

Current liabilities	$ 280,575
Long-term liabilities	687,500
Stockholders' equity:	
Common stock, 500,000 shares	1,000,000
Retained earnings	634,425
Total liabilities and stockholders' equity	$2,602,500

There is more than $250,000 in cash included in the current assets. Also, footnotes to the financial statements include the following information:

a. Cost of investments approximates their current market value. They do not represent a controlling interest in another company; average income from investments is 15 percent per year.
b. Current replacement value of property, plant, and equipment after deducting accumulated depreciation is $1,625,000.
c. The long-term debt consists of 30-year bonds due in 1999 that carry annual interest at the rate of 6½ percent.

Required: (Round to the nearest tenth of a percent where appropriate.)

1. Compute the percentage of total assets claimed by owners.
2. Compute the percentage of total assets claimed by creditors.
3. The year ended December 31, 1987, was profitable, and a 50¢ per share dividend has been suggested. Would you vote in favor of the dividend if you were a director? Explain.
4. It has been suggested that the investments be sold and the proceeds used to pay the long-term debt early. Make a recommendation to management as to whether to adopt this suggestion; support your recommendation with computations.

P1–5B
Evaluation of operating results

Winona State Corporation had a profitable year in 1987, but paid only a relatively small dividend to its stockholders. John Toloupos holds 15 percent of the company's common stock, and is disappointed to have received only $12,000 in dividends. In early 1988 he is considering the sale of his stock to invest the cash proceeds elsewhere. The following financial report appeared in the 1987 *Annual Report*:

WINONA STATE CORPORATION
Statement of Changes in Financial Position
For the Year Ended December 31, 1987   **Exhibit D**

Financial resources were provided by:		
Net income (from Exhibit A)	$480,000	
Add: Items charged to net income that did not use financial resources:		
Depreciation	80,000	
Total provided by operations	$560,000	
Sale of obsolete equipment	16,000	
Total financial resources provided		$576,000
Financial resources were used for:		
Dividends.	$ 80,000	
Payment of long-term 21 percent notes payable (due in 1990). . .	480,000	
Total financial resources used		$560,000
Increase in financial resources.		$ 16,000

In a letter to the stockholders at the beginning of the *Annual Report,* the chief operating officer of the company indicated that 1988 operating income is expected to exceed that of 1987. The balance sheet shows no other long-term debt outstanding. Average stockholders' equity in 1987 was $3,000,000.

Required:

1. Evaluate (with supporting computations) the decision to make early repayment of long-term debt in 1987.
2. Indicate whether you believe that decision improved or worsened Toloupos's chances for greater dividends in 1988. Explain.
3. Should Toloupos sell his stock and invest elsewhere? Explain.

P1–6B
Preparation of income statement and statement of retained earnings

On December 31, 1987, the following balances were extracted from the accounting records of Boomer Airlines (some items have been omitted):

Item	Amount
Cash	$ 225,500
Accounts receivable	577,500
Accounts payable	227,040
Bonds payable (due 2001).	1,320,000

(continued on next page)

Item	Amount
Common stock, 100,000 shares	550,000
Retained earnings, December 31, 1986	841,500
Passenger revenues	2,172,665
Advertising and promotion expense	270,270
Sales salaries expense	189,860
Other selling expense	57,992
Depreciation expense	291,170
General and administrative salaries expense	572,000
Other general and administrative expense	137,236
Interest expense	198,000
Dividends	176,000

Assume an income tax rate for 1987 of 40 percent.

Required:

1. Prepare an income statement for the year ended December 31, 1987.
2. Prepare a statement of retained earnings for the same period.

P1–7B
Thought-provoking problem: Using financial data

Standard and Poor's Corporation, an independent financial rating service, provided the following financial data (dollars in millions except for stock prices) in April 1984:

Company	Cash and Equivalents	Current Assets	Current Liabilities	Closing February Stock Price
Delta Air Lines	$ 10.3	$ 441.0	$ 718.0	$34.50
Eastern Air Lines	299.0	823.0	852.0	6.375
Pan Am World Airway	284.0	687.0	932.0	6.875
Piedmont Aviation	49.5	194.0	190.0	31.25
Trans World Airlines	191.0	908.0	1,015.0	8.625
UAL Inc.	161.0	1,165.0	1,671.0	30.00
USAir Group	204.0	438.0	288.0	28.125

Required:

1. Compute for each airline:
   a. The current ratio
   b. The acid-test ratio (using cash and equivalents only)
2. Rank the above airlines in descending sequence by:
   a. Current assets
   b. Current ratio
   c. Acid-test ratio
   d. Closing stock price
3. Is there any relation between stock prices and current balance sheet strength? Why or why not? What other factors do you think the public considered in determining the prices to pay for airline stocks in early 1984?

2 The Development of the Basic Accounting Model

Introduction

Chapter 1 shows that an end product of financial accounting is a set of financial statements containing useful information from which decisions are made. The complete set of statements presented in Chapter 1 had only brief explanations of key terms. This chapter, after a short description of the forms of business organizations, begins to develop in a simple and logical style the structure of accounting and of financial reports. To proceed from the simple to the complex, Chapter 2 describes several possible approaches to developing accounting systems (some means of recording and summarizing business events). To simplify the learning process, this chapter uses only those business activities that affect the balance sheet. The structure of accounting for other financial statements is developed similarly in Chapters 3, 4, and 5. The objective of these early chapters is to provide an understanding of the means of preparing a set of statements similar to three of those illustrated in the opening chapter: the balance sheet, the income statement, and the statement of retained earnings. The fourth statement, the statement of changes in financial position, is described more fully in Chapter 17.

In the initial development of an accounting system (as described in Chapters 2 through 5), service businesses (such as real estate offices, accounting firms, and consulting firms), selling services rather than merchandise, are used. The corporate form of organization is used to illustrate the basic concepts. The differences found in a single proprietorship and a partnership are discussed in Chapter 12.

Learning Goals

1. To be able to describe the entity concept.

2. To be acquainted with the common forms of business organization.

3. To know and understand the basic accounting equation and to recognize assets, liabilities, and stockholders' equity.

4. To be able to read a balance sheet and to know its classifications.

5. To be able to make practical application of the accounting equation.

6. To understand the transactions approach in entering the accounting information in ledger accounts.

7. To know the function of the basic accounting records (specifically, the ledger).

8. To prepare end-of-period trial balances and balance sheets.

9. To calculate and understand the meaning of the debt-equity ratios.

10. To be able to prepare and to understand the basic significance of a common-size balance sheet.

The Entity Concept

To understand accounting, one must first clearly understand the meaning of an **accounting entity**. This term refers to the business organizational unit for which financial and economic data are gathered and processed. Since a corporation by law is a legal entity separate and apart from its owners (the stockholders), the legal unit and the accounting unit are the same. This topic is covered thoroughly in Chapter 1. The introduction of accounting with a discussion of the corporation enhances the reader's understanding of the entity concept.

Before considering the forms of business organizations, the major elements contained in a balance sheet of these organizations are discussed.

Assets

The **assets** of a business are everything of value held by the business.[1] The word value as used here means future usefulness to a continuing business enterprise. Cash, notes and accounts receivable (amounts owed to the business by customers), land, buildings, and high-grade, readily marketable stocks or bonds of other companies are examples of assets in a business.[2] An asset is recorded on the books of the acquiring entity at its actual full cost (historical cost), even though it has not been fully paid for in cash (referred to as the *cost principle*). The amount of any debt or claim against the asset is included in the liabilities.

---

[1]The Financial Accounting Standards Board defines assets as ". . . probable future economic benefits obtained or controlled by a particular entity as a result of past transactions or events." *Statement of Financial Accounting Concepts No. 3* (Stamford, Conn.: 1980), paragraph 19.

[2]Some items of value—for example, the loyalty of a work force—cannot be stated in dollar terms. Such items are not currently listed in the accounting records. Much research in this area, usually referred to as *human resources accounting,* is underway now.

Equities: Liabilities and Owners' Equity

Equities are claims against the assets of a business. The two major classifications of individuals who have equities in a business are the **creditors** (liability holders) and the *owners*.

The business's liabilities are owed to creditors. **Liabilities** (debts) are claims of the creditors against the assets of the business unit.[3] Accounts payable and notes payable—amounts owed by the business through purchases on credit—are some liabilities that a business may have. Wages owed to employees, referred to as accrued wages payable, is another example.

Owners' equity[4] (net worth) involves ownership claims against a business's assets. It is the excess of total assets over total liabilities. Because creditor claims (debts) have priority over claims of the owner or owners, owners' equity claims are secondary (or residual). Specifically, the owners' equity of a corporation is called **stockholders' equity**; of a partnership, partners' equity; and of a single proprietorship, simply owner's equity. In all chapters of this book except Chapter 12, the corporate form of organization is presented. However, since all forms of business are equally concerned with most accounting concepts, a brief description of forms of business organization follows.

Forms of Business Organization

In its long history, accounting has served a variety of organizational entities. The forms of these entities changed as the centers of power and wealth changed. In early economic history, the entity was the central bureaucracy, the temple, or the household of the nobleman. During the Middle Ages, the partnership form was popular; later came the corporations. An outgrowth of the early household organization is the small individual proprietorship, which still exists in large numbers.

The owner's, partners', or stockholders' equity of a business results from assets contributed by the proprietor, partners, or stockholders, respectively, and from earnings retained in the business. Considered below is a brief description of the three common forms of business.

Corporation

A **corporation** is a separate legal entity, created by a *charter* from the state in which it is organized. Most have more than one owner; the owners are called **stockholders** or **shareholders**. Each stockholder owns a certain portion of the corporation, expressed in shares of stock. Figure 2–1 shows a

---

[3]Liabilities, according to *Statement of Financial Accounting Concepts No. 3*, paragraph 28, ". . . are probable future sacrifices of economic benefits arising from present obligations of a particular entity to transfer assets or provide services to other entities in the future as a result of past transactions or events."

[4]Owners' equity, according to *Statement of Financial Accounting Concepts No. 3*, paragraph 43, is ". . . the residual interest in the assets of an entity that remains after deducting its liabilities. In a business enterprise, the [owners'] equity is the ownership interest."

Figure 2–1   **Face of a Stock Certificate**

stock certificate. **Stock certificates** are issued to owners as evidence of their ownership. Common stock is a term describing the basic investments by stockholders. Shares may be issued at *par* (for example, the common stock of CBS Inc. has a $2.50 par), which is an amount agreed upon by the organizers; it is usually shown on the stock certificate and is stated in the charter. Some stock certificates do not have any stated certificate amount—these are referred to as *no-par shares*.

The primary advantage of the corporate form to its owners is that the stockholders' personal assets cannot be taken by creditors to satisfy the debts of the business; only the assets of the business itself can be taken. Since the corporation is a legal entity separate from its owners, the law has bestowed this characteristic called **limited liability** on shareholders. There are also other significant legal advantages, which will be studied in later chapters. In turn, a corporation is subject to special government regulation and to an income tax on its earnings. Because the corporate form is the most important form of business ownership today, it is stressed throughout this text. Moreover, the use of the simple form of corporate ownership accentuates the entity concept of accounting.

The income, or profits, of the corporation may be paid out to the stockholders in the form of **dividends** or may be retained in the corporation to increase stockholders' equity. Stockholders' equity arising from such retention is referred to as **retained earnings**. Retained earnings, therefore, are equity from the accumulated undistributed earnings of the corporation—that is, the total net income of the business from the date it was organized less the total dividends paid and the total losses sustained during the same period. Although they are a part of the total stockholders' equity, retained earnings must be accounted for separately from the common stock because of legal restrictions placed on the basic investments.

Single Proprietorship

A business owned by a single individual and not incorporated is referred to as a **single proprietorship**. If a business is small and its operations are comparatively simple, the single-proprietorship form of ownership offers several advantages over the corporate form: The owner has a more direct control of the business; he or she does not have to report to several stockholders; and the business is not subject to the special regulations and income tax on earnings as are corporations. Instead, the owner must include profit from the business in his or her personal income tax return. Also, the personal assets of the proprietor can be taken as payment of the debts of the business. This concept is referred to as **unlimited liability**. Careful management will, of course, minimize the chances of such an event.

Partnership

"A **partnership** is an association of two or more persons to carry on as co-owners a business for profit."[5] The association described in this definition may be based upon an oral or a written agreement. Partnerships have multiple owners and tend to be larger than single proprietorships. Although many partnerships have only two partners, some have many. For example, some of the nationally known certified public accounting firms have a hundred or more partners. The original capital investment for a partnership must come from the personal wealth and borrowing power of the partners. Since many partnerships have only two or three partners, this form of business is not generally found among the larger firms in the United States, except in large certified public accounting firms. Of the three basic forms of business in the United States, the partnership form is least used.

The partnership is relatively easy to form, but like the single proprietor of a proprietorship, most partners (except limited partners—see Chapter 12) are liable jointly and individually for the debts of the partnership if the partnership assets are not sufficient to meet these debts. A partnership must file an informational income tax return, but the organization as such does not pay a separate income tax. Rather, each partner must include in his or her tax re-

---

[5]*Uniform Partnership Act,* Part II, Section 6 (emphasis added).

turn the appropriate share of revenue, expenses, and other tax-related items of the partnership.

Most of the concepts discussed in this book are equally applicable to all forms of business organizations. The main differences in accounting for the different organizational forms occur mainly in accounting for owners' equity. Thus, when the single proprietorship and partnership forms are discussed in Chapter 12, the accounting for owner's and partners' equity is emphasized.

The Accounting Equation

Because equities represent the total claims against assets, *assets must equal equities*. This relationship is shown in Figure 2–2.

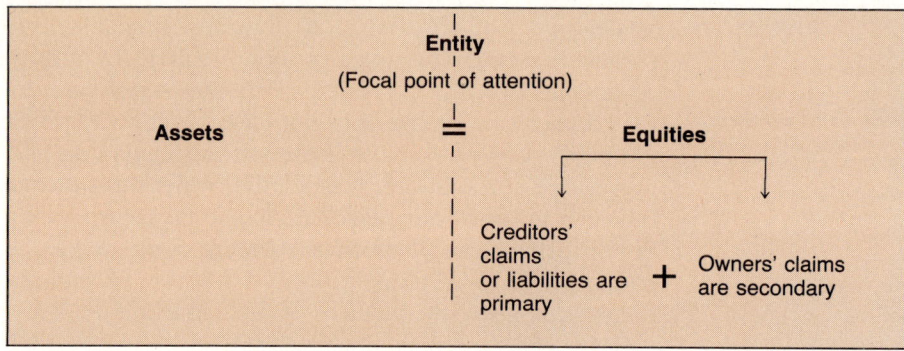

Figure 2–2   The Accounting Equation and the Entity Concept

As illustrated, the equities of the unit are broken down into primary claims—those of the creditors, and secondary claims—those of the owners. Since assets are derived from these two sources, the following is true for a corporation[6]:

$$\text{Assets} = \text{Liabilities} + \text{Stockholders' equity, or } A = L + SE.$$

This is the *basic accounting equation,* which expresses the financial position of any business entity at all times. *Net assets,* a term often used in business, may be found as follows:

$$\text{Assets} - \text{Liabilities} = \text{Net assets (equal to stockholders' equity)}.$$

The Balance Sheet

The **balance sheet** is an expanded expression of the accounting equation. It summarizes the assets, liabilities, and stockholders' equity of a business entity as of a specific point in time. This statement is also called a *statement of financial position.* A common form of balance sheet, the **account form**, for

---

[6]The equation for other forms of organizations would be modified slightly by changing the name of the owners' equity.

Assets = Liabilities + Stockholders' Equity

SUPER ELECTRONICS COMPANY
Balance Sheet
December 31, 1987

Assets			Liabilities and Stockholders' Equity		
Current assets:			Current liabilities:		
Cash	$ 325		Accounts payable	$12,060	
Temporary investments	1,900		Notes payable	2,060	
Accounts receivable	11,025		Accrued wages payable	970	
Notes receivable	2,520		Total current liabilities		$15,090
Merchandise inventory	14,750		Long-term liabilities:		
Prepaid insurance	275		Bank loan payable (due		
Office supplies	26		June 1, 1990)	$ 4,000	
Store supplies	89		Mortgage payable	10,000	
Total current assets		$30,910	Total long-term liabilities		14,000
Property, plant, and equipment:			Total liabilities		$29,090
Land	$ 3,000		Stockholders' equity:		
Building	10,000		Common stock	$15,000	
Store equipment	2,500		Retained earnings	5,570	
Delivery equipment	3,250		Total stockholders'		
Total property, plant, and			equity		20,570
equipment		18,750			
			Total liabilities and		
Total assets		$49,660	stockholders' equity		$49,660

Figure 2–3   Balance Sheet—Account Form

the Super Electronics Company with the accounting equation superimposed is shown in Figure 2–3. Another form of the same statement, the **report form**, is shown in Figure 2–4.[7] Both are acceptable. They express the basic accounting equation in detail by showing amounts of specific asset, liability, and stockholders' equity items. The balance sheet is a snapshot of the status of assets, liabilities, and stockholders' equity at any specific moment. Operations that take place later will make changes, but at any point in time the basic equation is always true.

The heading of *any* financial statement usually contains three lines of information:

1. Name of the business.
2. Name of the statement.
3. Date of the statement or period of time covered.

The date given in the balance sheets illustrated here shows that they present the financial position of the firm as of the close of business on December 31, 1987.

Dollar signs are used on formal statements at the top of each column of figures. A new column is created whenever a line is drawn for addition, subtraction, or other reasons. A double line is drawn under any amount that is

---

[7]This version is called the *report form* because it is in the form of a typical one-page report.

**Figure 2–4
Balance Sheet—
Report Form**

SUPER ELECTRONICS COMPANY
Balance Sheet
December 31, 1987

Assets

Current assets:
Cash	$ 325	
Temporary investments	1,900	
Accounts receivable	11,025	
Notes receivable	2,520	
Merchandise inventory	14,750	
Prepaid insurance	275	
Office supplies	26	
Store supplies	89	
Total current assets		$30,910

Property, plant, and equipment:
Land	$ 3,000	
Building	10,000	
Store equipment	2,500	
Delivery equipment	3,250	
Total property, plant, and equipment		18,750
Total assets		$49,660

Liabilities and Stockholders' Equity

Current liabilities:
Accounts payable	$12,060	
Notes payable	2,060	
Accrued wages payable	970	
Total current liabilities		$15,090

Long-term liabilities:
Bank loan payable (due June 1, 1990)	$ 4,000	
Mortgage payable	10,000	
Total long-term liabilities		14,000
Total liabilities		$29,090

Stockholders' equity:
Common stock	$15,000	
Retained earnings	5,570	
Total stockholders' equity		20,570
Total liabilities and stockholders' equity		$49,660

the final result of a series of calculations. Each specific element of the balance sheet is explained in the next section.

Need for Classification in a Financial Statement

To be of maximum value to an analyst, banker, creditor, employee, or other interested person, a financial statement should be classified. The kind of classification and the order of arrangement to be shown in the statement depend on tradition, the nature of the business activity, and the expected use of the statement. These classifications aid in the communication of information to readers. In Figure 2–4, assets and liabilities of the Super Electronics Company are classified as to their nature.

2 / The Development of the Basic Accounting Model

Statement classification

Classification *is the arrangement of financial statement items into groupings that have some common basis or similarity.*

Classification of Assets— Current Assets

Current assets consist of cash and other assets that are expected to be converted into cash or to be used in the operation of the business within one year.[8] Current assets are usually listed in descending order of their expected conversion into cash (liquidity). The current assets of the Super Electronics Company in order of liquidity are the following:

Cash Any item that a bank will accept as a deposit and that is immediately available and acceptable as a means of payment is *cash*. It includes coins, currency, traveler's checks, checks, money orders, and the amount on deposit in the entity's checking account.

Temporary Investments Businesses that have a temporary excess of cash on hand and want to earn interest on it may buy promises to pay issued by other companies (usually referred to as commercial paper) or by governmental agencies or institutions (notes or bonds).

Accounts Receivable Amounts due from customers for services rendered, for merchandise, or for any asset sold on credit are *accounts receivable*. A simple sales ticket is prepared for merchandise sold on credit, describing a source of accounts receivable. These credit arrangements are called *open accounts* because they are not backed by a formal promissory note and are open to receive additional purchases by customers.

Notes Receivable Notes receivable are formal written promises to pay a fixed amount of money at a future date. Most notes can usually be exchanged for cash at a bank (a practice called discounting).

Merchandise Inventory Businesses that offer products for sale must have them readily available. All the merchandise on hand at any given time is called *merchandise inventory*. Merchandise inventory items are found on retail store shelves and in stockrooms or warehouses.

Prepaid Items Services and supplies acquired to be consumed during the next 12 months are *prepaid items*. They are assets because they are items of value that have future usefulness in business operations. Some examples of prepaid items are:

Prepaid Insurance Every business must protect itself against hazards. Consequently, businesses take out insurance policies for protection. The cost

---

[8]If the period required to convert noncash short-life assets into cash (the operating cycle) is longer than one year, this longer operating cycle is the period used to determine whether an asset is current.

of this type of protection, an insurance premium, is paid in advance. Insurance policies commonly are issued against such hazards as fire, burglary, personal injury, business interruption, and injury to employees (workmen's compensation). The unexpired portion is an asset.

Office Supplies   Supplies such as stamps, stationery, and business forms required in an office are grouped under the title office supplies and are current assets of the business.

Store Supplies   Store supplies include wrapping paper, twine, paper bags, and similar items used in a store. They are also classified as current assets. Office supplies and store supplies to be used in the general operation of the business should not be included in merchandise inventory.

Classification of Assets—Property, Plant, and Equipment

Property, plant, and equipment comprises assets used over a long period in the operation of a business. They are customarily listed on the balance sheet according to their degree of permanence; the most permanent item is listed first. Some typical property, plant, and equipment assets are:

Land   Land is shown separately. Although land and the buildings on the land are usually sold together, they are classified separately because the buildings will deteriorate through usage, whereas the land will not. Land is considered the most permanent asset.

Buildings   Buildings owned by the business appear on the balance sheet. Rented buildings are not owned and are, therefore, not assets.

Store Equipment   Cash registers, showcases, counters, and shelves are typical permanent items of store equipment used in selling the merchandise inventory.

Delivery Equipment   Delivery equipment consists of trucks, cars, vans, and other types of equipment owned and used for the delivery of products to customers.

Classification of Liabilities—Current Liabilities

The term **current liabilities** designates obligations whose liquidation (payment or settlement) is reasonably expected to require the use of current assets or the creation (substitution) of other current liabilities. All liabilities to be paid within a one-year period are classified as current. In general, they are listed in their probable order of liquidation; those that are expected to be paid first are shown first, those to be paid next follow, and so on. Some typical current liabilities are:

Accounts Payable   Purchases on credit result in *accounts payable* to the buyer. They are the unpaid amounts owed to creditors from purchases on an account arrangement. They are usually due to be paid within 30 days and are also called open accounts, because no specific written promise is presented to the creditors and they are open for additional purchases.

Notes Payable The opposite of notes receivable, **notes payable** are formal written promises by the entity to pay money to creditors. Trade notes payable arise from the purchases of merchandise or services used in the course of business. Notes payable to a bank arise when a company borrows money for business use. Notes payable are classified as current liabilities unless the date for payment is more than one year in the future.

Accrued Liabilities **Accrue** means to increase by growth or to accumulate in a uniform manner. Accrued wages payable and accrued interest payable are typical accrued liabilities. These are debts that have accumulated because of the passage of time and that are not yet due for payment. These items are customarily placed last among the current liabilities.

Classification of Liabilities— Long-Term Liabilities

Debts that are not due for at least a year are called **long-term liabilities**. They may appear on the balance sheet in any sequence.

Mortgage Payable A *mortgage payable* is a debt owed by the business for which specific assets are pledged as security. The borrower issues a legal document that is secured by a pledge of specific assets and is called a *mortgage*.

Bonds Payable As a means of raising funds, some businesses borrow money by issuing bonds. *Bonds* are long-term promises to repay funds that are borrowed; they usually extend over a period of 10 to 30 years.

Classification of Ownership Claims— Stockholders' Equity

Since it is not unusual for a corporation to have thousands of stockholders, it would not be feasible to show their individual amounts of ownership on a balance sheet. The emphasis in corporations is on the sources of **stockholders' equity**. Classifications show how elements of equity were provided. In this chapter, only two classifications are considered: (1) **common stock**, which represents a portion of the invested capital, and (2) **retained earnings**, which is that part of owners' equity generated by profits and not paid out to the stockholders as dividends. In Figures 2–3 and 2–4, these two amounts as of December 31, 1987, are:

Stockholders' equity:	
Common stock.	$15,000[9]
Retained earnings.	5,570
Total stockholders' equity.	$20,570

---

[9]Recall that shares of stock have a par value, which is a certificate amount agreed upon by the incorporators. The significance of this par value is explained in Chapter 13.

58 Part One / The Basic Accounting Model

The form of business organization determines the manner of reporting owners' equity on the balance sheet. For the single proprietorship and partnership, this accounting is discussed in Chapter 12.

The foregoing discussion concerns the balance sheet, the detailed statement based on the accounting equation. As the accounting system is developed in this book, it begins with those business activities that affect only the balance sheet. Hence as this chapter moves in the direction of developing a means of recording business events, first consider how an accountant knows that a business activity has taken place.

Developing the Accounting System

Objective Evidence— The Business Document

Business firms are initially created by investments by stockholders. The firms then buy and sell assets, collect receivables, pay debts, and engage in other operating activities. In accounting, these activities are referred to as **transactions**. Before an accountant can record or process a transaction, he or she must be made aware that the transaction has taken place. In other words, there must be some objective evidence of the transaction—usually in the

			INVOICE		INVOICE NO. **04101**	

Jones Company
1512 Main Street
Everytown, Any State 28556

SOLD TO
Modern Realty Corporation
211 Main Street
Anytown, Any State 27555

SHIP TO
Mr. Penn James, Modern Realty Corporation
211 Main Street
Anytown, Any State 27555

CUSTOMER'S ORDER	SALESMAN	TERMS	SHIPPED VIA	F.O.B.	DATE	
101	Goluck	$5,000 due $3,000 due	in 10 days in 30 days	Anytown, AS	7-11-87	
4	Executive desks			367	31	1,469	24
4	Executive chairs			172	00	688	00
4	Secretary's chairs			127	00	508	00
4	Regular desks			310	00	1,240	00
10	Filing cabinets			205	63	2,056	30
1	Painting -- Classic					1,730	77
	Total before sales tax					7,692	31
	Sales tax at 4%					307	69
	Total					8,000	00

Figure 2–5   A Typical Invoice

form of a *business document*. For example, an accountant can learn that cash has been paid out of the firm by viewing either a copy of a check, the check stub of a checkbook, or a receipt for payment of cash. A copy of the supplier's invoice (the description of the item shipped in terms of quantity and price) could be used to indicate that supplies, furniture, or merchandise had been purchased. Figure 2–5 shows a supplier's invoice for a shipment of furniture. Other accounting forms also indicate that transactions have occurred.

These business documents flow across the accountant's desk. They are first used in developing accounting information as described in this chapter. These documents are then filed for future reference and for review by the independent certified public accountant. In this section, the effect of some transactions on the financial position of the Modern Realty Corporation are illustrated.

Transactions of the Modern Realty Corporation

All businesses go through an initial cycle in which the owner makes an investment and acquires various assets prior to opening the doors to start regular operations. The transactions involved in the organization of the Modern Realty Corporation illustrate this cycle.

1987		
Jul.	1	(Transaction 1) The Modern Realty Corporation was organized by Penn James, Joseph Hewes, and William Hooper. The charter (proper legal authorization) was received from the secretary of state, and common stock in the amount of $50,000 was issued at par (sold for face amount) for cash; that is, the stockholders—James, Hewes, and Hooper—made an investment of $50,000 in the business. James invested $40,000; Hewes, $6,000; and Hooper, $4,000. Issued stock certificates numbered 1001, 1002, and 1003.
	5	(Transaction 2) Purchased land and building for $30,000 in cash. The land was valued at $5,000; the building, at $25,000. Issued check no. 1.
	11	(Transaction 3) Received furniture and painting purchased on open charge account from the Jones Company for $8,000; supplier's invoice dated July 11, 1987 (see Figure 2–5).
	20	(Transaction 4) Paid the Jones Company $5,000 on amount owed to it. Issued check no. 2.
	25	(Transaction 5) The company found that one of the items classified as furniture was not what it wanted, so it sold the classic painting which had cost $1,800 = ($1,730.77 + sales tax of $69.23) to James Hill for $1,800 on account. Hill promised to pay this amount in 30 days; issued invoice no. 1.
	29	(Transaction 6) Collected $1,000 from James Hill on amount he owed to Modern Realty Corporation for the classic painting sold to him on July 25.

The following discussion is based on these transactions.

Analysis of Transactions—Effect on Balance Sheet

Since the balance sheet is an expanded variation of the accounting equation, it stands to reason that the total of the two sides should always be equal. A possible solution to the problem of accumulating data is the preparation of a balance sheet immediately after each transaction. To illustrate their effect on the balance sheet, consider the six transactions of Modern Realty Corporation.

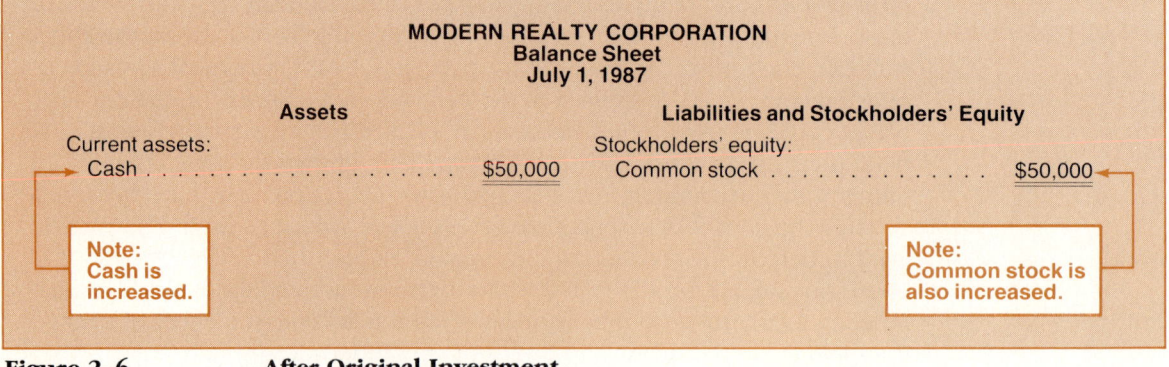

Figure 2–6   After Original Investment

Transaction 1   *Investment by stockholders of $50,000 on July 1; that is, common stock is issued.* Using the basic accounting equation of

Assets = Liabilities + Stockholders' equity,

the *balance sheet* shown in Figure 2–6 can be prepared after the three stockholders incorporate their business and the common stock of $50,000 has been issued (that is, the stockholders invest $50,000 in the business). (In this chapter, the traditional or *account form* of the balance sheet—information presented on two sides—is used to show the effect of each transaction on each side of the accounting equation.) The asset cash has increased from zero to $50,000. The investment also creates stockholders' equity of $50,000; common stock has increased from zero to that amount. The balance sheet is in balance.

Transaction 2   *Purchase of land and building for $30,000.* After this transaction on July 5, the balance sheet elements appear in Figure 2–7. The asset, cash, has decreased from $50,000 to $20,000 because $30,000 of it was exchanged for two new assets, land and building, at a cost of $5,000 and $25,000, respectively. Total assets remain at $50,000. Since no equities are changed, the balance sheet remains in balance.

Transaction 3   *Purchase of furniture on account for $8,000.* The July 11 purchase on credit has created a debt to the Jones Company of $8,000. This liability increase is accompanied by an increase in total assets because the new asset, furniture, was added at a cost of $8,000. The balance sheet after this transaction appears in Figure 2–8. This transaction has caused an increase in total assets, but the corresponding increase in total liabilities keeps the balance sheet in balance at $58,000 = $8,000 + $50,000.

Transaction 4   *Payment of accounts payable of $5,000.* On July 20, a check for $5,000 was sent to the Jones Company in partial payment of the debt created by the purchase of furniture. Since the entire debt was not paid,

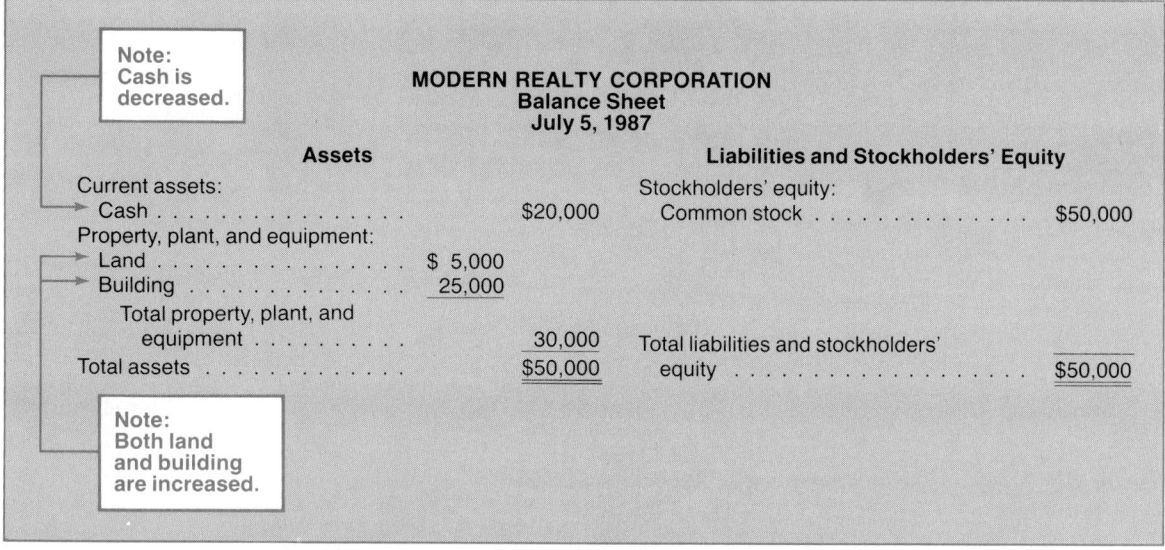

Figure 2–7   After Purchase of Land and Building

a balance of $3,000 is still owed to the Jones Company. The balance sheet after this transaction is shown in Figure 2–9. In this transaction, the cash reduction is accompanied by a reduction in liabilities in the same amount. The balance sheet remains in balance at $53,000 = $3,000 + $50,000.

Transaction 5   *Sale of furniture on account for $1,800.* On July 25, the classic painting classified as furniture was found to be unsuitable and was sold to James Hill at its cost price of $1,800. Hill did not pay the Modern Realty Corporation at the time of the transaction but promised to complete

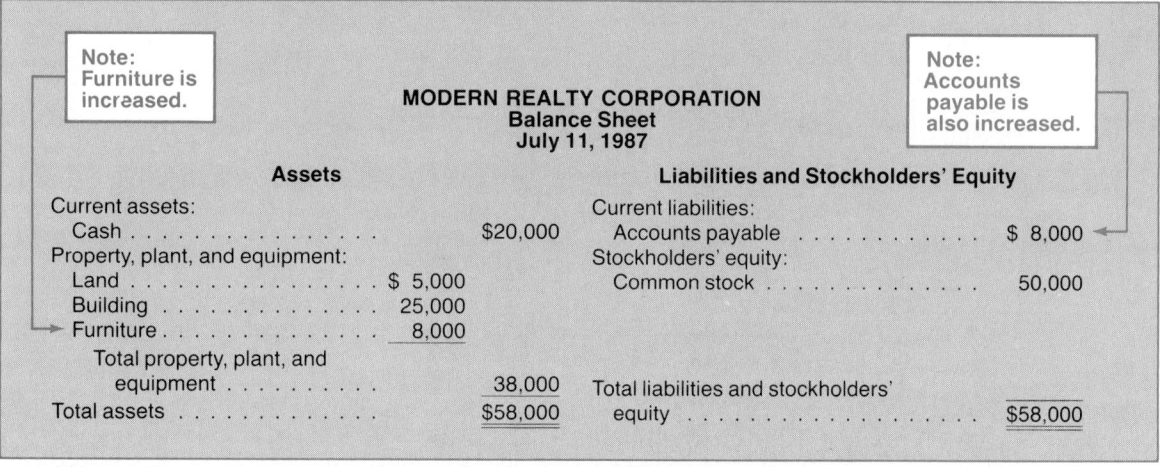

Figure 2–8   After Purchase of Furniture on Account

MODERN REALTY CORPORATION
Balance Sheet
July 20, 1987

Assets		Liabilities and Stockholders' Equity	
Current assets:		Current liabilities:	
Cash	$15,000	Accounts payable	$ 3,000
Property, plant, and equipment:		Stockholders' equity:	
Land	$ 5,000	Common stock	50,000
Building	25,000		
Furniture	8,000		
Total property, plant, and equipment	38,000	Total liabilities and stockholders'	
Total assets	$53,000	equity	$53,000

Note: Cash is decreased.
Note: Accounts payable is decreased.

Figure 2–9   After Payment of Accounts Payable

payment in 30 days. The balance sheet shown in Figure 2–10 could be prepared after the sale of the furniture. Four points should be noted:

1. The amount of money yet to be received from James Hill is reflected as an asset, accounts receivable. It is a current asset because it is expected to be collected within a year.

2. Transaction 5 involves an increase of an asset, accounts receivable, accompanied by a decrease of an asset, furniture. It is similar to the transaction of July 5 in that it consists of an exchange of one asset for another (see Figure 2–7).

MODERN REALTY CORPORATION
Balance Sheet
July 25, 1987

Assets		Liabilities and Stockholders' Equity	
Current assets:		Current liabilities:	
Cash	$15,000	Accounts payable	$ 3,000
Accounts receivable	1,800	Stockholders' equity:	
Total current assets	$16,800	Common stock	50,000
Property, plant, and equipment:			
Land	$ 5,000		
Building	25,000		
Furniture	6,200		
Total property, plant, and equipment	36,200	Total liabilities and stockholders'	
Total assets	$53,000	equity	$53,000

Note: Furniture is decreased.
Note: Accounts receivable is increased.

Figure 2–10   After Sale of Furniture on Account

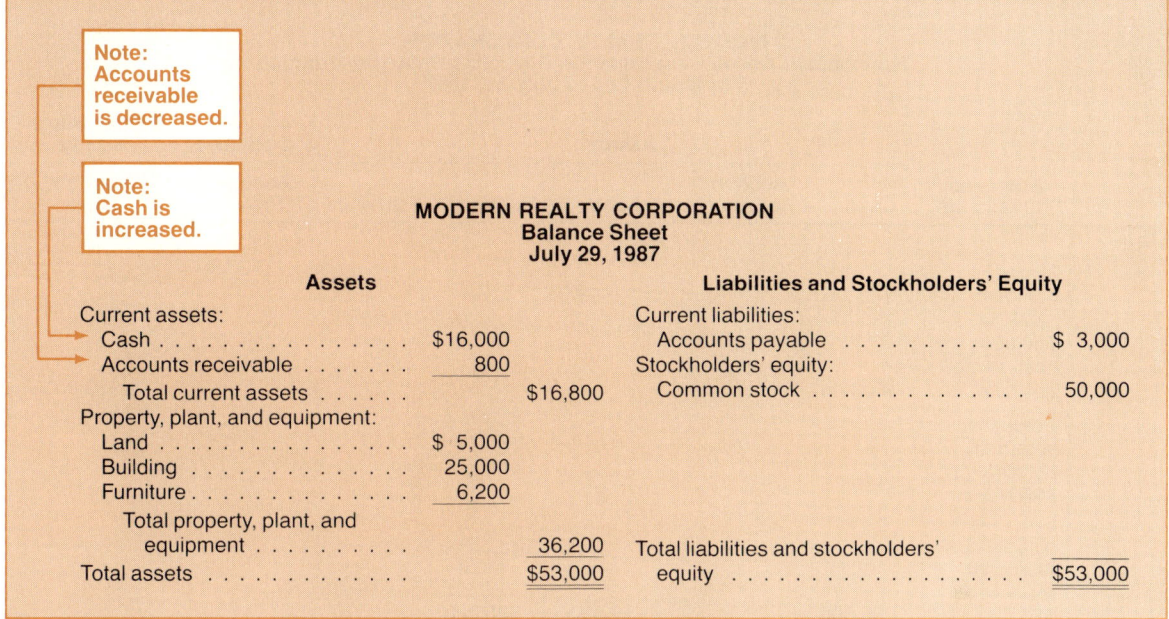

Figure 2–11   After Collection of Accounts Receivable

3. The classic painting was sold at cost. If it had been sold at a price other than at its cost, the stockholders' equity item, retained earnings, would ultimately have been increased by the amount of the gain or decreased by the amount of the loss.

4. The balance sheet totals did not change. The sum of the assets ($53,000) equals the sum of the liabilities ($3,000) plus common stock ($50,000).

Transaction 6 *Collection of accounts receivable of $1,000.* After James Hill made a payment of $1,000 on the amount owed for the classic painting, the balance sheet on July 29, 1987, is as shown in Figure 2–11. As in Transaction 5, the July 29 transaction is an exchange of one asset for another. Cash is increased by $1,000, and the asset, accounts receivable, is decreased by $1,000. All totals remain the same, with the balance sheet in balance at $53,000 = $3,000 + $50,000. No more transactions occurred during July.

Expansion of the Accounting Equation

The method of accumulating accounting data illustrated thus far in most instances is time-consuming and costly. Moreover, those who use accounting information do not need a balance sheet prepared after each transaction. Using the basic accounting equation, it is possible to show how each transaction will affect the balance sheet and yet have all six transactions combined in one end-of-month statement. In Figure 2–12, the balances are brought down after each transaction and form an equation, from which a formal balance sheet can be prepared. For example, a balance sheet could be prepared at the end of July. Such a balance sheet is shown in Figure 2–13. Since no transactions

MODERN REALTY CORPORATION
Summarized Accounting Equation Revealing Financial Position
For Month Ended July 31, 1987

Date	Business Transaction	Assets					=	Liabilities	+	Stockholders' Equity
		Cash	+ Accounts Receivable +	Land	+ Building +	Furniture	=	Accounts Payable	+	Common Stock
1987 Jul. 1	Issued common stock for $50,000 cash to start business...	+$50,000					=			+$50,000
5	Purchased land and building for $30,000 in cash. Land is appraised at $5,000; building at $25,000...	−30,000		+$5,000	+$25,000					
	Balances	$20,000 +		$5,000 +	$25,000		=			$50,000
11	Purchased furniture on account from the Jones Company for $8,000					+$8,000		+$8,000		
	Balances	$20,000 +		$5,000 +	$25,000 +	$8,000	=	$8,000	+	$50,000
20	Paid the Jones Company $5,000 on account...	−5,000						−5,000		
	Balances	$15,000 +		$5,000 +	$25,000 +	$8,000	=	$3,000	+	$50,000
25	Sold classic painting at cost to James Hill for $1,800 on account		+$1,800					−1,800		
	Balances	$15,000 +	$1,800 +	$5,000 +	$25,000 +	$6,200	=	$3,000	+	$50,000
29	Collected $1,000 from James Hill on account	+1,000	−1,000							
	Balances	$16,000 +	$ 800 +	$5,000 +	$25,000 +	$6,200	=	$3,000	+	$50,000

Figure 2–12   **Summarized Accounting Equation**

MODERN REALTY CORPORATION
Balance Sheet
July 31, 1987

Assets			Liabilities and Stockholders' Equity	
Current assets:			Current liabilities:	
Cash	$16,000		Accounts payable	$ 3,000
Accounts receivable	800		Stockholders' equity:	
Total current assets		$16,800	Common stock	50,000
Property, plant, and equipment:				
Land	$ 5,000			
Building	25,000			
Furniture	6,200			
Total property, plant, and equipment		36,200	Total liabilities and	
Total assets		$53,000	stockholders' equity	$53,000

Figure 2–13 Balance Sheet as of July 31, 1987

occurred on July 30 and 31, the July 31 balance sheet is the same as the one shown in Figure 2–11 on July 29, except for the date.

Although this method tends to shorten the accounting process, it is unsuitable for most companies that use a manual accounting system because it cannot easily be expanded to provide for a large number of asset and liability items. For example, it would be virtually impossible to use this procedure in a business that has 50 assets and 25 liabilities. Some other method is needed to accumulate transaction data. The next sections begin the development of the double-entry accounting system.

Accumulation of Transaction Data

A Separate Page for Each Item

A possible solution to the problem of data accumulation for an expanded number of assets and liabilities is to designate a separate page for each asset, liability, and stockholders' equity item, and to record the increases and decreases in the accounting equation elements directly into these separate pages. Using the transactions of Modern Realty Corporation, this method may be illustrated:

ASSET PAGES

	Cash		Page 101
1987			
Jul. 1	Investment by stockholders		+$50,000
5	Purchase of land and building		− 30,000
20	Payment to Jones Company on account		− 5,000
29	Collection from James Hill		+ 1,000
	(Cash on hand $16,000)		

(continued on next page)

Accounts Receivable		Page 111
1987		
Jul. 25	Sale of classic painting on account	+$1,800
29	Collection on account	− 1,000
	(Balance receivable $800)	

Land		Page 151
1987		
Jul. 5	Purchase of land	+$5,000

Building		Page 152
1987		
Jul. 5	Purchase of building	+$25,000

Furniture		Page 157
1987		
Jul. 11	Purchase of furniture on account	+$8,000
25	Sale of furniture at cost	− 1,800
	(Furniture on hand $6,200)	

LIABILITY PAGES

Accounts Payable		Page 201
1987		
Jul. 11	Purchase of furniture on account	+$8,000
20	Payment on account	− 5,000
	(Balance payable $3,000)	

STOCKHOLDERS' EQUITY PAGES

Common Stock		Page 301
1987		
Jul. 1	Investment by stockholders; common stock is issued	+$50,000

A comment should be made about the page numbering system. The pages could be numbered 1, 2, 3, 4, 5, 6, 7. It would be better if the numbers used have a specific meaning—for example, 100–199 for assets, 200–299 for liabilities, and 300–399 for stockholders' equity items—especially with unassigned numbers left for expansion.

At the end of a designated period, the **balance**, or final amount, of each page may be obtained by adding the plus and minus items and subtracting the total of the minus items from the total of the plus items. These balances can then be arranged as a classified balance sheet similar to the one shown in Figure 2–13.

Although this procedure permits unlimited expansion, it is still inadequate. Use of the plus and minus signs contributes to arithmetic errors, and there is no economical way to run a mathematical check on the accuracy of the items contained in the accounting equation. Something else needs to be done to the system.

Division of Each Accounting Page into Columns—Creation of Accounts

A possible solution is to divide each page, referred to in accounting as an **account**, into two sections by drawing a line down the middle of the page and using both sides to record financial information. The accounting equation

$$\text{Assets} = \text{Liabilities} + \text{Stockholders' equity}$$

suggests the following possible arrangement: Assets appear on the left side of the equation; therefore, the left side of the account is used to record increases of assets, and the opposite side, the right side, is used to record decreases. Similarly, since liabilities and stockholders' equity appear on the right side of the accounting equation, the right side of the account is used to record increases in liability and stockholders' equity accounts, and the opposite side, the left side, is used to record decreases. An account number replaces the page number. An example of this kind of account is shown here.

		Account Title			Account Number
Date	Explanation	Amount	Date	Explanation	Amount
	Use this side to record increases in assets and decreases in liability and stockholders' equity items.			Use this side to record decreases in assets and increases in liability and stockholders' equity items.	

Again using the same six transactions of Modern Realty Corporation, the "account" feature of the accounting system is demonstrated. Before information is recorded in the accounts (see Figure 2–13), each transaction is analyzed in the light of the procedure just described for recording the information.

1987

Jul. 1 The Modern Realty Corporation was organized, and common stock was issued for cash of $50,000, to start the business. Cash, an asset, is increased by $50,000, and common stock, a stockholders' equity item, is likewise increased. The $50,000 is placed on the left side of the asset account Cash to indicate that it has been increased, and the same figure is placed on the right side of the Common Stock account to indicate that it also has been increased.

5 Purchased land and building for $30,000 in cash. The cost of the land was determined to be $5,000; the building, $25,000. Both land and building are assets and are increased; thus, the $5,000 and the $25,000 are placed on the left sides of the Land and Building accounts, respectively. The Cash account is decreased by $30,000; thus, this amount is placed on the right side of the Cash account.

11 Purchased furniture on account from the Jones Company for $8,000. The asset furniture is increased by $8,000; this amount is placed on the left side of the Furniture account. A liability account Accounts Payable is increased by the amount due the Jones Company; $8,000 is placed on the right side of the Accounts Payable account to indicate that it has been increased.

20 Paid the Jones Company $5,000 on account. The liability accounts payable is decreased and the asset cash is also decreased. The $5,000 is placed on the left side of the Accounts Payable account to record the decrease; the same figure is placed on the right side of the asset account Cash to reflect the decrease.

25 Sold the classic painting that cost $1,800 to James Hill for $1,800 on account. The asset accounts receivable is increased by $1,800 and the asset furniture is decreased by $1,800. The increase in the asset accounts receivable is shown by placing the amount on the left side of the Accounts Receivable account; and the decrease in the asset furniture is shown by placing the amount on the right side of the Furniture account.

29 Collected $1,000 from James Hill on account. The asset cash is increased by $1,000; the asset accounts receivable is decreased by $1,000. The increase of the asset cash is shown by placing the $1,000 on the left side of the Cash account; the decrease of the asset accounts receivable is shown by placing the $1,000 on the right side of the Accounts Receivable account.

These transactions would appear in the accounts as shown in Figure 2–14. After all transactions are recorded, the accounts are **footed**; that is, each amount column containing more than one entry is totaled in small figures (in practice this is usually done in pencil) under the last amount on each side (see the Cash account, for example). Then the balance of each account is determined by subtracting the smaller amount from the larger. The balance is placed in the Explanation column of the side with the larger amount. As a check on the accuracy of the work, a listing of the account balances is made. The total of the balances on the left side of the accounts is compared to the total of the balances on the right side. Since the left-hand balances represent the left side and the right-hand balances the right side of the accounting equation items, their totals should be equal. As this is a test or a trial of the equality of the balances, it is called a **trial balance** (see Figure 2–15 on p. 70).

If the totals agree, it is presumed that the accounting is accurate up to this point. This presumption may not be correct, for the equality shows only that the sum of the left-hand balances equals the sum of the right-hand balances. Yet the accountant, acting as if it is correct, proceeds to complete the remaining steps in the accounting process. After the trial balance is prepared, a classified balance sheet is prepared from it. This balance sheet is the same as that shown in Figure 2–13; therefore it is not repeated here.

2 / The Development of the Basic Accounting Model

Cash — Acct. No. 101

Date		Explanation	Amount	Date		Explanation	Amount
1987 Jul.	1	Investment by stockholders[a]	50,000	1987 Jul.	5	Purchased land and building	30,000
	29	Collection from Hill	1,000		20	Payment to Jones Co.	5,000
			16,000				35,000
			51,000				

Accounts Receivable — Acct. No. 111

Date		Explanation	Amount	Date		Explanation	Amount
1987 Jul.	25	Sold classic painting on account 800	1,800	1987 Jul.	29	Collection from Hill	1,000

Land — Acct. No. 151

Date		Explanation	Amount	Date		Explanation	Amount
1987 Jul.	5	Purchased land	5,000				

Building — Acct. No. 152

Date		Explanation	Amount	Date		Explanation	Amount
1987 Jul.	5	Purchased building	25,000				

Furniture — Acct. No. 157

Date		Explanation	Amount	Date		Explanation	Amount
1987 Jul.	11	Purchased furniture on account 6,200	8,000	1987 Jul.	25	Sold furniture on account	1,800

Accounts Payable — Acct. No. 201

Date		Explanation	Amount	Date		Explanation	Amount
1987 Jul.	20	Payment to Jones Co.	5,000	1987 Jul.	11	Purchased furniture on account 3,000	8,000

Common Stock — Acct. No. 301

Date		Explanation	Amount	Date		Explanation	Amount
				1987 Jul.	1	Investment by stockholders	50,000

[a]After the accounting system is more fully developed, it will be evident that explanations in the accounts are rarely needed.

Figure 2–14   Accounts of Modern Realty Corporation on July 31, 1987

```
                    MODERN REALTY CORPORATION
                            Trial Balance
                            July 31, 1987
   Account                                          Left-Side    Right-Side
   Number          Account Title                    Balances     Balances
     101      Cash.......................           $16,000
     111      Accounts Receivable........               800
     151      Land.......................             5,000
     152      Building...................            25,000
     157      Furniture..................             6,200
     201      Accounts Payable...........                         $ 3,000
     301      Common Stock...............                          50,000
              Totals.....................           $53,000       $53,000
```

Figure 2–15 Trial Balance

Tools of Accounting

Before the remainder of the basic accounting model is discussed, the following accounting tools are considered: (1) the T account, (2) debits and credits, and (3) the formal account.

The T Account

A T account is so named because of its shape. Owing to its simplicity, this form makes it easy to understand the effects of transactions on a given account. Each **T account** consists of a left side and a right side, with the title of the account written across the top.

```
              Account Title
         ─────────────────────
          Left side  │  Right side
        (the debit side) │ (the credit side)
```

Debits and Credits

Although originally the terms debit and credit had a specific meaning related to debtor and creditor accounts, today they are used as nouns, verbs, or adjectives depending on whether one is talking about an amount on the left side (a **debit**) or the right side (a **credit**), or the process of placing an amount on the left side *(to debit)* or the right side *(to credit),* or the characteristics of information on the left side (a *debit entry*) or the right side (a *credit entry*).

Debit and credit *The left side of the T form of an account is called the* **debit** *side, and the right side is called the* **credit** *side.*

Substituting the terms debit and credit for the words left side and right side, the following rules may be stated:

Any Account	
Debit an account to record:	**Credit an account to record:**
An increase of an asset	A decrease of an asset
A decrease of a liability	An increase of a liability
A decrease in the stockholders' equity	An increase in the stockholders' equity

The relationship of the rules of debit and credit to the balance sheet and to the accounting equation may be illustrated as follows:

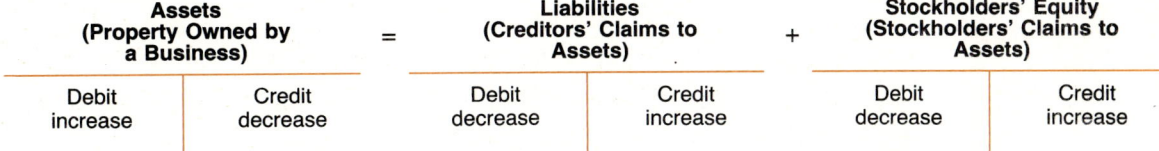

The abbreviation for debit is *Dr.;* for credit is *Cr.* For any account in the above illustration, the side marked "increase" is the *normal balance* side, since increases will normally exceed decreases.

The Formal Account

In actual business practice, the T account is expanded to a formal account. An **account** is a recording device used for sorting accounting information into similar groupings. It often consists of two sides with four columns on each side: the date, an explanation, the page number of the source from which the amount was transferred (called the *folio column*), and the debit or credit amount.[10] A standard form for the account for Cash is shown in Figure 2–16. Note that the folio column is indicated by an F.

			Cash				Acct. No. 101
Date	Explanation	F	Debit	Date	Explanation	F	Credit

Figure 2–16   T Form of Account

A variation of the T form is the three-amount-column form, with debit, credit, and balance columns. After each entry, the balance of the account may be computed and entered in the balance column. This form is useful when frequent reference is made to the balance of an account, as, for example, in individual customer's and creditor's accounts; it is extremely popular in the

---

[10]The folio column is also called a posting reference (P.R.).

general practice of accounting. A three-amount-column account form is shown in Figure 2–17.

Cash				Acct. No. 101
Date	Explanation	F	Debit	Credit	Balance

Figure 2–17   Three-Amount-Column Form of Account

Other variations of accounts are found in practice. One of these variations is a four-column account where the last two columns provide space to show whether the balance is a debit or credit.

The Ledger

The collection of all the accounts is called a **ledger**. It may be a book or other storage medium. Larger businesses that have electronic data processing use magnetic disks or some other form of record for accounts in the ledger. In all cases, the basic concepts are the same as in the preceding model.

The above tools of accounting are expanded and illustrated in Chapter 3, first with the Modern Realty Corporation, then with other more complex examples. Additional balance sheet analyses and internal control issues are presented next.

Managerial Analysis of Financial Position

The use of ratio analysis was introduced in Chapter 1 with the computation of the current ratio and the acid-test ratio. Two other important balance sheet ratios are the debt-equity ratios, that is, the ratios of stockholders' equity and liabilities to assets. These ratios and a compositional percentage analysis referred to as a common-size balance sheet are now considered.

Debt-Equity Ratios

A significant measure of the stability of a business is the percentage relationship of the equities of the creditors and of the stockholders in the total assets, popularly known as **debt-equity ratios**. These ratios for the Super Electronics Company (Figure 2–3 shown on page 53) at the end of 1987 are computed as follows:

1. Creditors' interest in assets (creditors' equity ratio):

$$\frac{\text{Total liabilities}}{\text{Total assets}} = \frac{\$29,090}{\$49,660} = 58.6\%.$$

2. Stockholders' interest in assets (stockholders' equity ratio):

$$\frac{\text{Total stockholders' equity}}{\text{Total assets}} = \frac{\$20,570}{\$49,660} = 41.4\%.$$

The sum of these two ratios must always be 100 percent, because they equal total claims against assets. These ratios are considered by many analysts to be equal in importance to the current ratio as indicators of credit strength and sound management. There are no universally accepted percentage relationships to serve as guides for the equity ratios, but it is generally felt that when interest rates are high, the larger the stockholders' equity ratio, the stronger is the financial condition of the business. A company may, for example, borrow money on a long-term note for working capital purposes. The loan increases the current assets and creates a more favorable current ratio, but it also reduces the stockholders' equity ratio, signaling a possible overdependence on outside sources for financial needs.

The pursuit of a favorable stockholders' equity ratio has its disadvantages. The long-term debt may be reduced to a point where the company is forgoing the tax deduction for interest expense and the opportunity to use borrowed funds to generate a higher rate of return than the borrowing rate.

Common-Size Balance Sheet

A percentage analysis of the balance sheet where each asset item is expressed as a percentage of total assets and each equity item is expressed as a percentage of total liabilities and stockholders' equity is referred to as a **common-size balance sheet**. A common-size balance sheet for the Super Electronics Company (Figure 2–3) as of December 31, 1987, is shown in Figure 2–18.

This form of the balance sheet is useful in making comparisons within a company, with other companies in the same industry, or with the entire

---

SUPER ELECTRONICS COMPANY
Common-Size Balance Sheet
December 31, 1987

Current assets:			Current liabilities:		
Cash	0.7%		Accounts payable	24.3%	
Temporary investments	3.8		Notes payable	4.1	
Accounts receivable	22.2		Accrued wages payable	2.0	
Notes receivable	5.1		Total current liabilities		30.4%
Merchandise inventory	29.7		Long-term liabilities:		
Prepaid insurance	0.6		Bank loan payable (due June 1, 1992)	8.1%	
Office supplies	0.1		Mortgage payable	20.1	
Store supplies	0.2		Total long-term liabilities		28.2
Total current assets		62.4%[a]	Total liabilities		58.6%
Property, plant, and equipment:			Stockholders' equity:		
Land	6.0%		Common stock	30.2%	
Building	20.1		Retained earnings	11.2	
Store equipment	5.0		Total stockholders' equity		41.4
Delivery equipment	6.5				
Total property, plant, and equipment		37.6	Total liabilities and stockholders' equity		100.0%
Total assets		100.0%			

[a]Computed by summing individual percentages. The ratio of total current assets to total assets is slightly less than 62.4%.

Figure 2–18   **Common-Size Balance Sheet of Super Electronics Company**

industry. The common-size nature permits the spotting of important relationship differences with companies of unlike size. In addition, the analysis of the composition of individual asset items helps to make other ratios more meaningful. For example, an analyst interpreting the meaning of a current ratio or acid-test ratio would certainly like to see the percentage relationship of the individual assets and liabilities making up the numerator and the denominator of the ratio. In the case of the Super Electronics Company, the two debt-equity ratios can be read from the common-size balance sheet: the ratio of total liabilities to the total of liabilities and stockholders' equity (the same as total assets) of 58.6 percent, and the similar percentage for stockholders' equity of 41.4 percent.

Internal Control

The basic double-entry system has been introduced in this chapter.

Internal control *One tangential aspect of an accounting system is a self-policing mechanism that helps to prevent errors, helps to prevent misappropriation of assets, and establishes responsibility for activities that occur. This mechanism is referred to as* internal control; *the accounting system is an essential element of it.*

A good system of internal control requires an integration of the accounting system with a company's organizational structure that will accomplish the preceding objectives. Each person who is employed should be well-trained, and his or her duties, responsibilities, and authority should be well-defined. The business documents issued and received by a business—see the invoice illustrated in Figure 2–5—are of paramount importance to a good system of internal control. Examples of business forms mentioned in the transactions of the Modern Realty Corporation are the stock certificate, checks, and invoices. These documents and related forms have two important functions: (1) they tell the accountant that a transaction has occurred, and (2) they establish the responsibility of the person signing, initialing, or approving the document for the event. This latter function is one element of internal control because a properly signed business form permits the tracing of the transaction for error detection and for any possible misappropriation.

An adequate system of internal control must be tailored to a particular business. Throughout this book, suggestions for implementing a system of internal control are emphasized.

Glossary

Account A recording device used for sorting accounting information into similar groupings.

Account form of balance sheet A form of the balance sheet that shows the assets on the left side of the statement and the liabilities and stockholders' equity on the right side.

Accounting entity The focal point of attention of accounting records; an organization such as a corporation is both a legal entity and an accounting entity.

Accrue To accumulate or grow over a period of time.

Asset A thing of value owned by an entity.

Balance The difference between the total of the debit amounts in an account and the total of the credit amounts in an account.

Balance sheet The statement that summarizes the assets, liabilities, and owners' equity of a business unit as of a specific date.

Classification Arrangement of financial statement items into groupings that have a common basis of similarity.

Common stock Share representing fractional elements of the ownership of a corporation; also the title of an account in which is recorded the par value of stock issued.

Common-size balance sheet A balance sheet in which each element is shown as a percentage of either total assets or total liabilities and stockholders' equity.

Corporation A form of business authorized by a state as a legal entity; in the eyes of the law, it is an artificial being with the rights and responsibilities of an individual.

Credit The right-hand side of an account, the amount shown on the right side of an account, or the process of placing an amount on the right side of an account.

Creditors Persons or groups to whom debts are owed.

Current assets Cash and other assets that will be consumed or converted into cash within one year.

Current liabilities Liabilities to be paid within one year.

Debit The left-hand side of an account, the amount shown on the left side of an account, or the process of placing an amount on the left side of an account.

Debt-equity ratios The relationship of total liabilities and total stockholders' equity to total assets.

Dividends Cash or other asset distributions made by a corporation to its stockholders; dividends reduce retained earnings.

Footing Showing the total of a column of figures in small pencil figures under the last amount in the column, or the total derived from this procedure.

Internal control A self-policing interaction of the organizational structure of a business with the accounting system that helps to prevent errors, helps to prevent misappropriation of assets, and establishes responsibility for business actions.

Ledger The book that contains all the ledger accounts; or a collection of ledger accounts in any form.

Liability An obligation of a business, or a creditor's claim against the assets of a business.

Limited liability A liability restricted by law. A characteristic of a corporation whereby the stockholders have no personal liability for debts of the business.

Long-term liabilities Liabilities that fall due for payment more than a year from date.

Owners' equity Residual claims of owners against the assets of a partnership or a corporation; owner's equity refers to residual claims of an owner against assets of a single proprietorship.

Partnership An association of two or more persons to carry on, as co-owners, a business for profit.

Property, plant, and equipment The long-lived assets of a firm that are used in the operations of the firm and are not held for resale.

Report form of balance sheet A form of the balance sheet that shows the assets at the top of the statement with the liabilities and stockholders' equity appearing immediately below.

Retained earnings Owners' equity in a corporation represented by profits earned but not paid out to the stockholders.

Shareholders Persons who own shares of capital stock in a corporation.

Single proprietorship An unincorporated business that is owned entirely by one individual.

Stock certificate A printed or engraved, serially numbered document issued to the stock purchaser as evidence of ownership of shares of stock in a corporation.

Stockholders See *Shareholders*.

Stockholders' equity Ownership claims against corporate assets.

T account A simple form of ledger account in the shape of a T used for analyzing transactions and for teaching purposes.

Transaction A business activity or event which has taken place.

Trial balance A statement that shows the name and balance of all ledger accounts arranged according to whether they are debits or credits. The total of the debits must equal the total of the credits in this statement.

Unlimited liability A characteristic of single proprietorships and partnerships; an owner has personal liability for the debts of the business.

Questions

Q2–1 Discuss briefly the three basic forms of business organizations. In what major area is the accounting different for each form?

Q2–2 What determines when an asset is classified as a current asset? Give three examples.

Q2–3 What is the basic accounting equation? Explain the nature of a balance sheet in terms of the elements of the accounting equation.

Q2–4 What is the basic difference between the account form and report form of the balance sheet?

Q2–5 What is a business transaction? Give six examples. What type of document could serve as objective evidence for each of your examples?

Q2–6 What is the difference between the terms *debit* and *credit*?

Q2–7 Is it ever possible for a liability account to have a debit balance? An asset account to have a credit balance? Explain and give examples of each.

Q2–8 Discuss the following statement: A balanced trial balance is a correct trial balance.

Q2–9 Why is a trial balance prepared? If it does not balance, how can errors be located?

Q2–10 The Kay Roberta Corporation purchased furniture on account from the Campbell Company. The accountant debited the Furniture account for $600 and erroneously credited the Accounts Receivable account for $600. (a) What effect would the error have on the debit and credit totals of the trial balance taken at the end of the period? (b) What accounts in the trial balance would be incorrectly stated?

Q2–11 What does the term *general ledger account* mean? Describe two forms of the account. State the reasons and circumstances for using each form.

Q2–12 Give an example of a transaction that would result in (a) an increase of an asset accompanied by an increase in the stockholders' equity; (b) an increase of an asset accompanied by an increase of a liability; (c) an increase of an asset accompanied by a decrease of an asset; (d) a decrease of an asset accompanied by a decrease of a liability.

Q2–13 State how each of the debt-equity ratios should be computed. What is a common-size balance sheet? What is the major purpose of each of these managerial analyses?

Q2–14 On December 31, 1987, the Agel Company had a current ratio of 3 to 1 and a stockholders' interest in assets of 60 percent; the Boston Company had a current ratio of 2 to 1 and a stockholders' interest in assets of 45 percent. Is the Agel Company in a better financial position to pay its accounts payable when they are due than the Boston Company is? Discuss.

Q2–15 What is the importance of business documents to (a) recording transactions and (b) internal control?

Exercises

E2–1
Normal balance of accounts

Indicate the normal balance (debit/credit) of the following accounts:

a. Accounts Payable Credit
b. Cash Debit
c. Machinery
d. Accrued Wages Payable Credit
e. Notes Payable Credit
f. Temporary Investments
g. Prepaid Insurance Debit
h. Common Stock Credit
i. Accounts Receivable debit
j. Supplies debit
k. Mortgage Payable credit
l. Land debit
m. Income Taxes Payable credit
n. Merchandise Inventory debit

E2–2
Calculating current liabilities

Assume that the Chapel Village Corporation has the following items at the end of the year:

Total assets	$405,000
Total long-term liabilities	50,500
Common stock	150,000
Retained earnings	135,000
Current assets	80,000

Compute the amount of current liabilities.

E2–3
Current asset section of balance sheet

The books of the Armour Company contain the following items on December 31, 1987:

Retained earnings	$ 75,000
Cash	45,000
Common stock	150,000
Accounts receivable	9,000
Accounts payable	6,400
Prepaid insurance	1,600

Select the current assets and prepare in good form the current assets section of the balance sheet.

E2–4
Property, plant, and equipment section of balance sheet

The books of the Bunker Company contain the following items on December 31, 1987:

Cash	$ 10,500
Land	20,000
Common stock	150,000
Building	320,000
Long-term notes payable (due July 1, 2006)	100,000
Delivery equipment	20,000
Office supplies	2,000
Retained earnings	50,000

Select the property, plant, and equipment items, and prepare in good form the property, plant, and equipment section of the balance sheet.

$A = L + OE$

E2–5
Current liabilities section of balance sheet

The books of the Canyon Company contain the following items on December 31, 1987:

Accounts receivable	$ 3,500
Accounts payable	12,000
Notes receivable (due in four months)	2,000
Notes payable (due in six months)	4,000
Accrued wages payable	1,500
Retained earnings	45,000
Bonds payable (due July 1, 2009)	35,000

Select the current liabilities, and prepare in good form the current liabilities section of the balance sheet.

E2–6
Effect of transactions on accounting equation

Indicate the effect of each of the following transactions on the accounting equation. Follow the format used for item *a,* which is answered below.

a. Purchased furniture on account.

Assets = Liabilities + Stockholders' equity

+	+	no effect

b. Received a cash investment from the stockholders.
c. Paid for the furniture purchased on account.
d. Purchased supplies on account.
e. Returned the supplies purchased in *d* above.
f. Purchased merchandise for cash.
g. Borrowed money from a bank.

E2–7
Determining property, plant, and equipment total

Assume that a firm has current assets of $65,000; current liabilities of $36,000; long-term liabilities of $55,000; and stockholders' equity of $278,000 at the end of the year. Compute the amount of property, plant, and equipment.

E2–8
Account form balance sheet and computing ratios

The following financial information is available for the Rowse Company as of December 31, 1987:

Temporary investments	$ 50,000
Accounts receivable	110,000
Wages payable	100,000
Buildings	120,000
Prepaid insurance	3,000
Merchandise inventory	100,000
Common stock	150,000
Accounts payable	85,000
Cash on hand	6,500
Cash in bank	205,000
Retained earnings	?
Land	50,000
Bonds payable	260,000

1. Prepare an account form balance sheet for the Rowse Company as of December 31, 1987.
2. Compute (a) current ratio, (b) acid-test ratio, and (c) working capital.
3. Compute (a) creditors' equity ratio and (b) stockholders' equity ratio.
4. Explain the significance to management of each of the ratios.

E2–9
Balance sheet errors

The following balance sheet was prepared by the bookkeeper of the World Electronics Company:

WORLD ELECTRONICS COMPANY
Balance Sheet
For the Year Ended December 31, 1987

Assets

Current assets:		
Cash	$ 3,500	
Accounts receivable	15,000	
Building	28,000	
Merchandise inventory	9,500	
Total current assets		$ 56,000
Property, plant, and equipment:		
Temporary investments	$ 6,000	
Land	2,500	
Store equipment	24,300	
Office supplies	225	
Delivery equipment	23,100	
Total property, plant, and equipment		56,125
Total assets		$112,125

Liabilities and Stockholders' Equity

Current liabilities:		
Accounts payable	$15,600	
Notes payable (due June 1, 1988)	6,000	
Notes payable (due July 1, 2009)	1,500	
Total current liabilities		$ 23,100
Long-term liabilities:		
Mortgage payable (due May 1, 2003)	$18,000	
Accrued wages and salaries payable	430	
Total long-term liabilities		18,430
Total liabilities		$ 41,530
Stockholders' equity:		
Common stock	$60,000	
Retained earnings	10,595	
Total stockholders' equity		70,595
Total liabilities and stockholders' equity		$112,125

List the errors in this statement.

E2–10
Entering accounting information in ledger accounts and performing other end-of-period processes

The following transactions were engaged in by the Super Circuit Corporation during the month of March 1987:

1987

Mar. 1 Received a charter and issued all authorized common stock at par for $400,000 in cash.
    4 Purchased land and building for $80,000 in cash and a 20-year mortgage payable for $70,000. The land was appraised at $45,000; the building, at $105,000.
   12 Purchased service supplies from the Cox Company for $1,600 on account.
   31 Sold a portion of the lot purchased on March 4 for its cost of $10,000. The buyer, the Williams Company, paid $8,000 in cash and issued a ninety-day note for $2,000.

1. Analyze the transactions, enter in formal general ledger accounts, and determine account balances. (Assign appropriate numbers to accounts.)
2. Prepare a trial balance.
3. Prepare a classified account form balance sheet.

E2–11
Balance sheets prepared after each transaction

The Nolta Cable Corporation engaged in the following transactions during the first week of operations:

1987

Jun. 1 Issued common stock at par to the four incorporators for $80,000 in cash.
    3 Purchased office equipment from Bleu Supply for $8,200 on account.
    5 Purchased land for a future building site at a cost of $60,000; paid $10,000 down and issued a mortgage note payable in ten years for the balance.

Prepare a classified account form balance sheet after each transaction.

E2–12
Analyzing transactions

The following T accounts contain data from the general ledger of the Redford Corporation:

Cash			
1987		1987	
Sep. 20	100,000	Sep. 23	6,300
		29	5,500
		30	35,000

Temporary Investments (U.S. Treasury Notes)	
1987	
Sep. 29	5,500

Office Supplies	
1987	
Sep. 23	6,300

Land	
1987	
Sep. 30	22,500

Building	
1987	
Sep. 30	32,500

Mortgage Payable	
	1987
	Sep. 30 20,000

Common Stock	
	1987
	Sep. 20 100,000

Describe each of the four transactions that caused these amounts to be recorded.

2 / The Development of the Basic Accounting Model

E2–13
Missing figures from incomplete data

The following lists show selected statement totals for four different corporations: Wee, Xee, Yee, and Zee. In each case, the amount is omitted for one total.

	Wee	Xee	Yee	Zee
Current assets.	$100,000	$ 72,000	$?	$ 20,000
Property, plant, and equipment	200,000	130,000	71,500	200,000
Current liabilities.	50,000	10,000	5,000	10,750
Long-term liabilities	75,000	?	25,500	61,400
Common stock.	175,000	50,000	100,000	?
Retained earnings.	?	20,000	6,500	10,850

In each case, compute the missing figure.

E2–14
Entity decisions

James Johnson, who owns 100 percent of the common stock of the Johnson Corporation, engaged in the following transactions:

1987

Aug. 2 Purchased a freezer for his home and recorded it on the corporate set of books as Equipment.
    15 Purchased a truck that is to be used 100 percent for pleasure. It was paid for by the corporation, and the entire cost was recorded on the corporate set of books as Trucks.
    30 Purchased a motorcycle for his son and recorded it as Supplies on the corporation books.

1. Discuss the entity implications of each of these transactions.
2. Without entering the information in accounts, describe how each of these items should be recorded on the books of the corporation assuming that a Johnson Corporation check was written in each case.

A Problems

P2–1A
Calculating statement totals from balance sheet data and computing ratios

The loan officer of a bank is considering a request from the Inner City Laundry, Inc., for a 60-day loan. She obtained the following balance sheet figures by telephone:

Cash	$ 14,000
Accounts receivable	62,000
Laundry supplies	65,000
Laundry equipment	92,000
Accounts payable	25,000
Notes payable	?
Equipment mortgage payable	40,000
Common stock	100,000
Retained earnings	26,000

After hanging up the phone, she realized that she had failed to write down the amount of notes payable.

Required:

1. Supply the missing figure for notes payable.
2. Compute the amount of total assets.
3. Compute the amount of total liabilities.
4. Compute the current ratio, acid-test ratio, and working capital.
5. Compute the creditors' equity ratio and the stockholders' equity ratio.

P2–2A
Preparing a balance sheet, computing ratios, and explaining significance

The following information is available for Thelma's Drug Store as of December 31, 1987:

Temporary investments	$ 30,000
Accounts receivable	70,000
Wages payable	3,500
Building	210,000
Prepaid insurance	3,400
Inventories	125,000
Common stock	250,000
Retained earnings	?
Accounts payable	55,000
Cash on hand	12,000
Cash in bank	30,000
Land	50,000
Mortgage payable	170,000

Required:

1. Prepare a report form balance sheet for Thelma's Drug Store as of December 31, 1987.
2. Compute the current ratio, acid-test ratio, and working capital.
3. Compute the creditors' equity ratio and the stockholders' equity ratio.
4. Explain the significance to management of each item in requirements 2 and 3.

P2–3A
Selecting correct balances to accounts and preparing a balance sheet

The Electronic Chips Repair Corporation was started on April 21, 1987. During the first several days of operations, its part-time bookkeeper (a high school student who had a few months' instruction in bookkeeping) recorded the transactions and rendered the following unbalanced trial balance as of April 30, 1987:

ELECTRONIC CHIPS REPAIR CORPORATION
Trial Balance
April 30, 1987

Account Title	Debits	Credits
Accounts Payable	$ 14,275	
Accounts Receivable		$15,000
Building	35,000	
Common Stock	47,500	
Cash	17,750	
Furniture	13,000	
Land		6,000
Mortgage Payable		20,000
Notes Payable	15,175	
Notes Receivable		4,000
Service Supplies	1,400	
Temporary Investments		4,800
Total	$144,100	$49,800

Required:

1. Assuming that the amounts are correct but that the bookkeeper did not understand the proper debit-credit position of some accounts, prepare a corrected trial balance showing the accounts in correct balance sheet order.
2. Prepare a report form balance sheet.
3. Prepare a common-size balance sheet.

P2–4A

Accounting sequence steps

The following transactions were engaged in by the newly created corporation to be called the Hill Camera Services during May 1987:

1987

May 3	The corporation received its charter and issued common stock at par value (the amount to be recorded), $100,000 to 20 stockholders.
6	Purchased land and building for $90,000 in cash and a 20-year mortgage payable for $60,000. The land was appraised at $15,000 and the building at $135,000.
7	Purchased repair supplies from the Klob Company for $6,000 on account.
31	Sold for $5,000 one-third of the lot purchased on May 6. The buyer, the Serf Sands Company, paid $2,500 in cash and issued a 90-day note for $2,500.

Required:

1. Record these transactions directly in general ledger accounts and determine account balances. (Assign appropriate numbers to accounts.)
2. Prepare a trial balance.
3. Prepare an account form balance sheet as of May 31, 1987.

P2–5A

Accounting sequence steps

The following account numbers and titles were designed for the Lanson Car Rental System, Inc.:

101	Cash		150	Office Equipment
111	Accounts Receivable		201	Accounts Payable
120	Land		205	Notes Payable
130	Building		301	Common Stock
140	Automobiles		302	Retained Earnings

During the first month of operation the following transactions occurred:

1987

Jun. 4	The newly formed corporation received its charter and issued common stock at par value (the amount to be recorded) for $200,000 to five individuals.
5	Purchased land for $20,000 and a building on the lot for $50,000. A cash payment of $25,000 was made, and a 20-year promissory note was issued for the balance.
6	Purchased 20 new automobiles at $7,200 each from the Liefson Motor Company. A down payment of $30,000 in cash was made; the balance was promised in 60 days.
12	Sold one automobile to a company employee at cost. The employee paid $2,000 in cash and agreed to pay the balance within 30 days.
14	One automobile proved defective and was returned to the Liefson Motor Company. The amount due was reduced by $7,200.
15	Purchased a cash register and office desks for $3,400 in cash.
28	Paid $22,800 in cash to the Liefson Motor Company on account and gave a 60-day note payable for the balance due.

Required:

1. Record these transactions directly in general ledger accounts.
2. Prepare a trial balance.
3. Prepare an account form balance sheet as of June 30, 1987.

P2–6A

Thought-provoking problem: analysis of business opportunity

Carl Shadrow wanted to go into business for himself for some time. One day he saw the following advertisement in a newspaper:

> **BUSINESS OPPORTUNITIES**
>
> Chance of a lifetime! Owner must sell now. Dry cleaning shop and laundromat. Buyer take over building, equipment, receivables, and payables. Own your own business for $12,000!
>
> Call Mr. Dole
> 555-6071

This looked like a good opportunity to become his own boss. Things looked even better after he called Dole and went to look at the business. The building was new, and the equipment appeared to be in good condition. Only a few customers showed up while he was there, but Dole explained that it was the off-season. Dole also told him that the total fair market value of the building and equipment was $25,000. (For details, see newspaper ad above.) Shadrow, upon the advice of a certified public accountant, asked to see the latest balance sheet. After receiving it, he discovered that total assets were $25,000, just as Dole had told him. But he also noticed that current liabilities added to $7,200 and that there was an item entitled Mortgage Payable of $12,500 under long-term liabilities.

Required: What decision seems to be indicated and why?

B Problems

P2–1B

Calculating statement totals from balance sheet data and computing ratios

The Joppa Corporation is considering the purchase of a small corporation, owned by the Alonzo family. An executive of the Joppa Corporation copied the balance sheet figures and went home to consider how much to offer. Later the executive noted that she had failed to include the amount of notes payable. She does have the following data:

Cash	$21,000
Accounts receivable	23,000
Delivery supplies	46,250
Delivery equipment	53,000
Accounts payable	23,750
Notes payable	?
Equipment mortgage payable	20,000
Common stock	70,000
Retained earnings	22,500

Required:

1. Supply the missing figure for notes payable.
2. Compute the amount of total assets.
3. Compute the amount of total liabilities.
4. Compute the current ratio, acid-test ratio, and working capital.
5. Compute the creditors' equity ratio and the stockholders' equity ratio.

P2–2B

Preparing a balance sheet, computing ratios, and explaining significance

The following information is available from Hudson Bike Repair Corporation as of October 31, 1987:

Temporary investments	$ 28,000
Accounts receivable	44,000
Wages payable	10,000
Building	110,000
Prepaid insurance	1,920
Repair parts inventory	146,000
Common stock	150,000
Retained earnings	?
Accounts payable	38,000
Cash on hand	2,000
Cash in bank	16,000
Land	40,000
Mortgage payable	82,000

Required:

1. Prepare a report form balance sheet for Hudson Bike Repair Corporation as of October 31, 1987.
2. Compute the current ratio, acid-test ratio, and working capital.
3. Compute the creditors' equity ratio and the stockholders' equity ratio.
4. Explain the significance to management of each item in requirements 2 and 3.

P2–3B

Selecting correct balances to accounts and preparing a balance sheet

Quebec Repair Shop was opened for business on March 7, 1987. During the first 3 weeks of operations, its part-time bookkeeper recorded the transactions and prepared the following unbalanced trial balance as of March 31, 1987:

QUEBEC REPAIR SHOP
Trial Balance
March 31, 1987

Account Title	Debits	Credits
Accounts Payable	$ 18,550	
Accounts Receivable		$ 20,000
Building	60,000	
Common Stock	115,300	
Cash	25,500	
Furniture	16,000	
Land		22,000
Mortgage Payable		30,000
Notes Payable (due in 30 days)	20,350	
Notes Receivable (due in 60 days)		18,000
Repair Supplies	3,100	
Temporary Investments		19,600
Totals	$258,800	$109,600

Required:

1. Assuming that the amounts are correct but that the inexperienced bookkeeper did not understand the proper debit-credit position of some accounts, prepare a trial balance showing the accounts in correct balance sheet order.
2. Prepare a report form balance sheet.
3. Prepare a common-size balance sheet.

P2–4B
Accounting sequence steps

The Pica Photo Service, a corporation owned by the Pica family, engaged in the following transactions during April, 1987:

1987

Apr. 1 The corporation was chartered and issued common stock at par value (the amount to be recorded) for $200,000 to create the Pica Photo Service.
2 Purchased land and building for $80,000 in cash and a 20-year mortgage payable for $100,000. The land was appraised at $50,000 and the building at $130,000.
5 Purchased photo supplies from the Camera Corner for $6,500 on account.
30 Sold for $10,000 one-fifth of the lot purchased on April 2. The buyer, Action Company, paid $4,000 in cash and issued a 90-day note for $6,000.

Required:

1. Record these transactions directly in general ledger accounts and determine account balances. (Assign appropriate numbers to accounts.)
2. Prepare a trial balance.
3. Prepare an account form balance sheet as of April 30, 1987.

P2–5B
Accounting sequence steps

The following account numbers and titles were designed for Terrence Rentals, Inc.:

101 Cash
111 Accounts Receivable
120 Land
130 Building
140 Rental Equipment
150 Office Equipment
201 Accounts Payable
205 Notes Payable
301 Common Stock
302 Retained Earnings

During the first month of operations, the following transactions occurred:

1987

Aug. 1 The newly formed corporation received its charter from the state and issued common stock at par value (the amount to be recorded) for $180,000.
5 Purchased land for $20,000 and a building on the lot for $60,000. A cash payment of $15,000 was made, and a three-year promissory note was issued for the balance.
6 Purchased rental equipment for $50,500 from the Franklin Street Company. A down payment of $17,000 was made; the balance was promised to be paid in 30 days.
7 Sold a lawn mower to an employee at its cost of $300. The employee paid $100 in cash and agreed to pay the balance in 30 days.
8 A chain saw proved to be defective and was returned to the Franklin Street Company. The amount due was reduced by $450.
11 Purchased a typewriter and an office desk for $1,450 in cash.
29 Paid $10,000 in cash to the Franklin Street Company and gave a 90-day note payable for the balance due.

Required:

1. Record these transactions directly in general ledger accounts.
2. Prepare a trial balance.
3. Prepare an account form balance sheet as of August 31, 1987.

P2–6B
Thought-provoking problem: accounting policy decisions and analysis of financial strength

The Barton Corporation has been operating for some years. In November 1987 the accountant of the company disappeared, taking the records with him. You are hired to reconstruct the accounting records and to determine the basic condition of the corporation. With this in mind, you make an inventory of all company assets. By checking with banks, counting the materials on hand, investigating the ownership of buildings and equipment, and so on, you develop the following information as of December 31, 1987:

Account Title	Balance	Account Title	Balance
Land	$30,000	Temporary Investments	$ 10,000
Equipment	50,000	Inventories	28,000
Buildings	60,000	Cash on Hand	6,000
Accounts Receivable	20,000	Cash in Banks	106,000

Statements from creditors and unpaid invoices found in the office indicate that $80,000 is owed to trade creditors, all due on open accounts. A $20,000 long-term mortgage (30 years) is outstanding. Interviews with the board of directors and a check of the common stock record book indicate that 2,000 shares of capital stock are outstanding and that the stockholders have contributed $60,000 to the corporation. No record is available regarding past retained earnings.

Required:

1. Prepare a trial balance, a report form balance sheet, and a common-size balance sheet as of December 31, 1987.
2. Write a report to management indicating a simple accounting system that could be used and why you recommend such a system. Include in the report the kinds of records and overall system you recommend.
3. Calculate (a) the amount of working capital, (b) the current ratio, (c) the acid-test ratio, (d) the creditors' equity ratio, and (e) the stockholders' equity ratio.
4. Write a second report to management evaluating the financial strength of the corporation.

3

A Simple Accounting System; Dynamic Measurement Accounts

Introduction

In Chapter 2, the accounting system was partially developed using only financial-type transactions. This chapter completes the simple accounting system and introduces changes in stockholders' equity other than from the issuance of common stock illustrated in Chapter 2. Specifically, the major changes in stockholders' equity discussed are caused by: (1) revenues, (2) gains, (3) expenses, (4) losses, and (5) dividends to stockholders. For Warner Lambert Company in 1983, the combination of these items brought an increase of $86,987,000 to stockholders' equity. In the same year, they brought a decrease of $80,745,000 to Republic Airlines. These changes and the statements on which they are reflected are explained in this chapter. The fundamentals of the steps in the accounting sequence are illustrated with a specific corporate example—Data Equipment Repair Shop, started in this chapter and completed in Chapter 4.

Learning Goals

1. To know the function of the basic accounting records (journal and ledger).

2. To apply a basic method of processing data: the journalizing of simple transactions and posting to ledger accounts.

3. To be able to identify changes in stockholders' equity brought about by operations (net income and net loss).

4. To understand the nature and use of nominal accounts (revenue, gains, expense, losses, and dividends).

5. To know the rules for use of debit and credit for both nominal and real accounts.

6. To recognize the need for and be able to use subsidiary ledgers and know their relationship to controlling accounts.

7. To be able to prepare and use a chart of accounts.

8. To know how to use the routine steps in the accounting sequence.

9. To be able to explain the nature of an extended simple accounting system.

10. To prepare the income statement, statement of retained earnings, and balance sheet.

11. To be able to compute and explain the importance of the basic operating ratios of a business.

Capturing and Processing Financial Data

A Simple Accounting System

Before completing the Modern Realty Corporation illustration introduced in Chapter 2, it is important to see a simple overall accounting system. The steps in a simple accounting system are presented in pictorial form as shown in Figure 3–1.

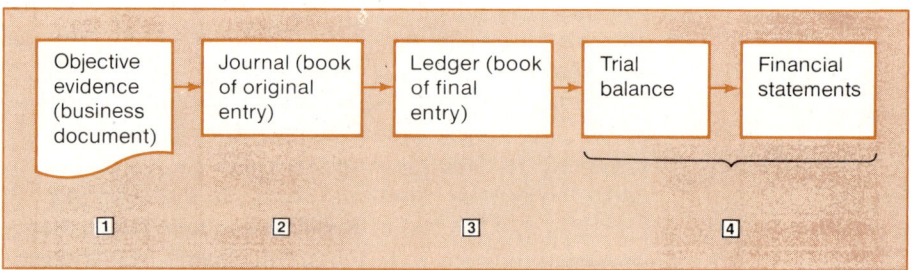

Figure 3–1   **A Simple Accounting System**

[1] Every entry made in an accounting system must have objective evidence, usually a business document, to justify the entry.

[2] Every business needs a chronological record of transactions and a complete history of all transactions recorded in the order they occurred and in one place. It is often necessary to view a transaction in its entirety in terms of the specific business unit. Since every transaction consists of at least one debit and one credit, the entry is necessarily recorded on different ledger pages. If the ledger contains many accounts, it may be difficult to reconstruct the debit and credit for any single transaction. Therefore, all entries must be first recorded in the **general journal** (or journal), a book of original entry.

[3] To have information available for later summarization and classification, it is necessary to sort it into homogeneous groups. To do so, it is necessary to transfer the information—a process called posting—from the journal to

the ledger accounts. All journal entries, therefore, must be *posted* to the ledger. Absolutely no entries are made in a ledger except those posted from a journal. There is no other source for ledger entries.

4. A test check is made of the accounting system in the form of a trial balance. Financial statements are then prepared from the information presented in the trial balance.

Illustration of Journalizing and Posting

As a means of introducing the basic accounting sequence, two of the steps introduced in Figure 3–1—that of journalizing and posting—are reviewed and expanded:

Journalizing

1. **Journalizing** *is recording transactions in a book called a* **journal**, *a book of original entry. The record of a transaction in the journal is called a journal entry.*

Posting

2. **Posting** *is transferring amounts in the journal to the correct accounts in the* **ledger**, *a book of final entry.*

To illustrate, consider the July 1 transaction of Modern Realty Corporation in which three stockholders invested $50,000 to start the Modern Realty Corporation. This transaction is first recorded in the journal as shown in Figure 3–2. The form of the journal in this figure is referred to as the *general journal*.

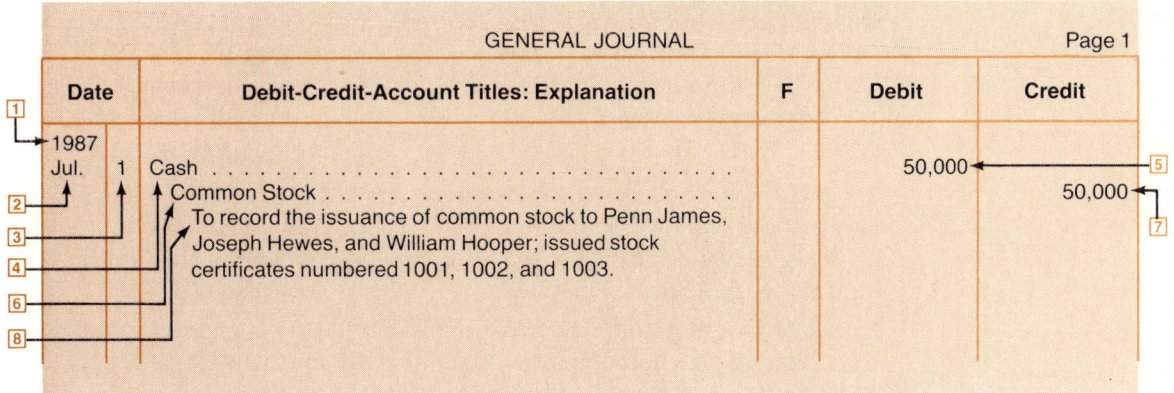

Figure 3–2   **The Journalizing Process in the General Journal**

Explanations of numbered items in Figure 3–2 are as follows:

1. The year is written in small figures at the top of the Date column. It should be written in that position on every page of the journal.
2. The month of the first transaction recorded on this page is entered. It is not necessary to write the month again on this page unless it changes.

[3] The date of each transaction is entered.

[4] The title of the account debited is placed in the Debit-Credit-Account Titles: Explanation column against the date line. In order to eliminate confusion, it is important that *the account title written in the journal entry should be the exact title of the account as it appears in the ledger*.

[5] The amount of the debit is entered in the Debit amount column.

[6] The title of the account credited should be indented approximately one inch from the Date column.

[7] The amount of the credit is entered in the Credit column.

[8] The explanation is entered on the next line, indented an additional one inch. It should contain all the essential information as well as a reference to the relevant source document from which the information was obtained—check number, cash receipt date or number, and so on.

In journals, ledger accounts, and trial balances, the use of two zeros or a dash in the cents column to indicate that the cents are zero is a matter of choice. Thus, an amount may be written 2,375.00 or 2,375.—. In a balance sheet and other statements containing a mixture of items with and without cents, it is preferable, for the sake of appearance, to use zeros for those items having no cents. In this book, most examples contain whole dollar amounts; thus the cents column is often omitted in statements, journals, and ledgers. Dollar signs should *not* be written in journals and ledger accounts. They should be used in the balance sheet and all other formal statements.

Notice that the journal does not *replace* the ledger account. The journal is called a book of *original entry*. It is necessary first to journalize the transaction and then to post to the proper accounts in the ledger.

Figure 3–3 illustrates the posting of the Modern Realty Corporation July 1 entry from the general journal to the ledger. Posting normally should be done daily. Explanations of numbered items in Figure 3–3 follow:

[1] The debit amount ($50,000), the journal page (1), and the date (Jul. 1) are entered on the debit side of the Cash account in the ledger. The year (1987) is written at the top of the Date column. Remember that dollar signs are not used in journals or ledgers.

[2] The ledger account number for the debit entry (101) is entered in the folio (F) column of the journal to cross-reference the journal and the ledger. *The presence of the account number here indicates that the item has been posted; so it must not be inserted until after the posting has been made.*

[3] The credit amount ($50,000), the journal page (1), and the date (Jul. 1) are entered on the credit side of the common stock account in the ledger. The year (1987) is written at the top of the Date column.

[4] The ledger account number for the credit entry (301) is entered in the folio column of the journal to complete the cross-referencing. It follows again that the cross-reference in the journal indicates that the posting to the ledger has been completed.

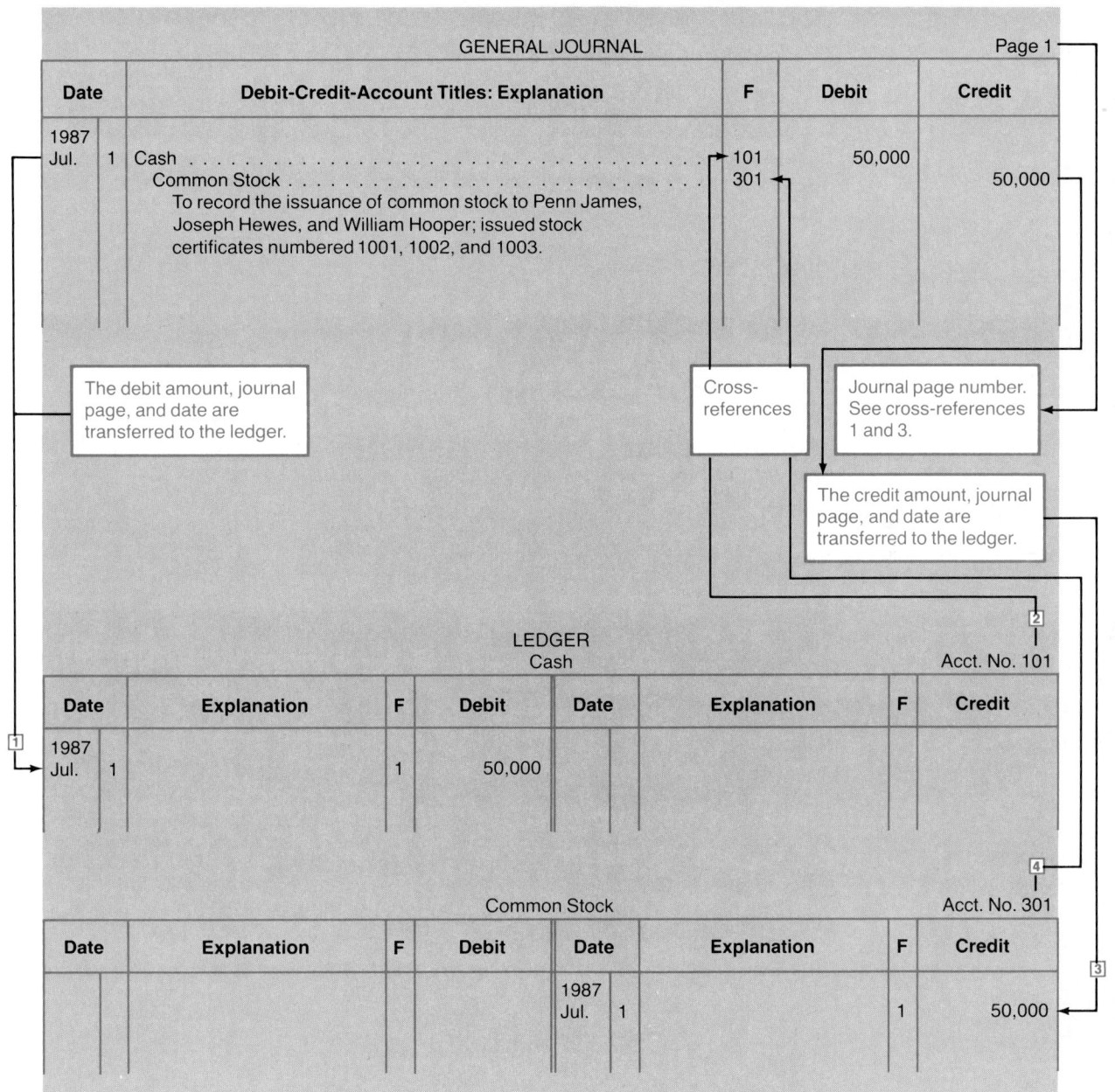

Figure 3–3   **Posting Flow Chart**

Part One / The Basic Accounting Model

Explanations are not usually given in the Explanation columns of the ledger accounts. The cross-reference to the journal page from which the information was recorded permits any interested person to find quickly a complete story of the transaction in the journal. Short explanations are used in the ledger accounts only when deemed especially useful in particular transactions. The total journalizing and posting sequence for the Modern Realty Corporation is described and illustrated next.

The Modern Realty Corporation Illustration

The Modern Realty Corporation introduced in Chapter 2 will illustrate the accounting sequence steps discussed so far. Assuming that objective evidence indicates that the transactions have taken place, the six transactions are first journalized, including repeating the July 1 transaction; then the amounts are posted to traditional ledger accounts; and last, a trial balance and financial statements are prepared.

As a starting point, the six transactions of Modern Realty Corporation discussed in Chapter 2 are repeated below:

1987

Jul. 1 The Modern Realty Corporation was organized by Penn James, Joseph Hewes, and William Hooper. The charter (proper legal authorization) was received from the secretary of state, and common stock in the amount of $50,000 was issued at par (sold common stock for $50,000).

5 Purchased land and building for $30,000 in cash. The land was valued at $5,000; the building at $25,000. Issued check no. 1.

11 Received furniture purchased on open charge account from the Jones Company for $8,000; supplier's invoice dated July 11, 1987.

20 Paid the Jones Company $5,000 on amount owed to it. Issued check no. 2.

25 The company found that the classic painting item classified as furniture was not what it wanted, so it sold the painting, which had cost $1,800, to James Hill for $1,800 on account. Hill promised to pay this amount in 30 days; issued invoice no. 1.

29 Collected $1,000 from James Hill on amount he owed to Modern Realty Corporation for the classic painting sold to him on July 25.

Journalizing and Posting

These transactions are first journalized as shown in Figure 3–4. Although cross-reference figures are shown in the folio column, they would *not* be entered until after posting to the ledger. *Note also that a blank space is left to separate each journal entry.*

The transactions are posted from page 1 of the general journal to the ledger accounts shown in Figure 3–5. The cross-references are entered in both the journal and the accounts.

After all journal entries are posted, the accountant foots each account as shown in the ledger that follows the journal.

		GENERAL JOURNAL			Page 1
Date		Debit-Credit-Account Titles: Explanation	F	Debit	Credit
1987 Jul.	1	Cash.. Common stock.................................... To record the issuance of common stock to Penn James, Joseph Hewes, and William Hooper; issued stock certificates numbered 1001, 1002, and 1003.	101 301	50,000	50,000
	5	Land... Building.. Cash... To record purchase of land and building for cash; issued check no. 1.	151 152 101	5,000 25,000	30,000
	11	Furniture....................................... Accounts Payable................................ To record purchase of furniture on account; supplier's invoice is dated July 11, 1987. Jones Company............................ $8,000	157 201	8,000	8,000
	20	Accounts Payable................................ Cash... To record payment on account; issued check no. 2: Jones Company............................ $5,000	201 101	5,000	5,000
	25	Accounts Receivable............................. Furniture....................................... To record credit sale of furniture at cost; invoice no. 1: James Hill................................ $1,800	111 157	1,800	1,800
	29	Cash... Accounts Receivable............................. To record collection on account: James Hill................................ $1,000	101 111	1,000	1,000

Figure 3–4 **General Journal of Modern Realty Corporation**

This accounting system is called **double-entry accounting** because it requires that each record of a transaction have debits and credits with total debits equal to total credits. Every transaction does not necessarily have a single debit and a single credit. For example, the July 5 entry of the business involves two debits totaling $30,000 and one credit of $30,000. A journal entry that has more than one debit or credit is called a **compound entry**. Regardless of the number of accounts debited and credited in a single transaction, the total amount of all debits must equal the total amount of all credits in each transaction It follows that the total of the debit balances and the total of the credit balances in the ledger of all the accounts must also be equal.

Trial Balance As stated in Chapter 2, it is customary to prepare a trial balance to test the equality of the debit and credit balances in the ledger before a formal balance sheet is prepared. The accountant could prepare a balance sheet directly

LEDGER

Cash — Acct. No. 101

Date	Explanation	F	Debit	Date	Explanation	F	Credit
1987 Jul. 1		1	50,000	1987 Jul. 5		1	30,000
29	16,000	1	1,000	20		1	5,000
			51,000				35,000

Accounts Receivable — Acct. No. 111

Date	Explanation	F	Debit	Date	Explanation	F	Credit
1987 Jul. 25	800	1	1,800	1987 Jul. 29		1	1,000

Land — Acct. No. 151

Date	Explanation	F	Debit	Date	Explanation	F	Credit
1987 Jul. 5		1	5,000				

Building — Acct. No. 152

Date	Explanation	F	Debit	Date	Explanation	F	Credit
1987 Jul. 5		1	25,000				

Furniture — Acct. No. 157

Date	Explanation	F	Debit	Date	Explanation	F	Credit
1987 Jul. 11	6,200	1	8,000	1987 Jul. 25		1	1,800

Accounts Payable — Acct. No. 201

Date	Explanation	F	Debit	Date	Explanation	F	Credit
1987 Jul. 20		1	5,000	1987 Jul. 11	3,000	1	8,000

Common Stock — Acct. No. 301

Date	Explanation	F	Debit	Date	Explanation	F	Credit
				1987 Jul. 1		1	50,000

Figure 3–5   General Ledger of Modern Realty Corporation

MODERN REALTY CORPORATION
Trial Balance
July 31, 1987

Acct. No.	Account Title	Debits	Credits
101	Cash	$16,000	
111	Accounts Receivable	800	
151	Land	5,000	
152	Building	25,000	
157	Furniture	6,200	
201	Accounts Payable		$ 3,000
301	Common Stock		50,000
	Totals	$53,000	$53,000

Figure 3–6   Trial Balance of Modern Realty

from the accounts, but the trial balance furnishes a convenient summary of the information for the preparation of the balance sheet. The July 31, 1987, trial balance of Modern Realty Corporation is shown in Figure 3–6. The trial balance proves the equality of debits and credits but not the accuracy of the accounts. For example, an entire transaction could be omitted, the debit and credit amounts of an entry could be identically incorrect, a wrong account could be debited or credited, or both the debit and credit amounts for a given transaction could be posted twice. If the trial balance is in balance, however, the accountant considers this reasonable evidence of accuracy and proceeds from that point.

Balance Sheet

The next step in the illustrated accounting sequence is the preparation of the formal balance sheet for Modern Realty Corporation, Figure 3–7, which is the same as Figure 2–13. This form of the balance sheet is referred to as the account form, because information is placed on the left and right sides of the statement, as accounting information is placed in the traditional account (the T form).

As indicated previously, dollar signs are used on formal statements. They should be placed at the beginning of each column of figures. Note, however, that a new column of figures is started whenever a line is drawn for addition or subtraction, as can be seen in Figure 3–7.

In the preceding illustration, the transactions of Modern Realty Corporation were journalized. The information in the journal was posted to appropriate accounts. Account balances were determined, and a trial balance was prepared. A balance sheet was prepared from the information summarized in the trial balance. Only balance sheet accounts, referred to as real accounts, were used in these illustrations.

MODERN REALTY CORPORATION
Balance Sheet
July 31, 1987

Assets			Liabilities and Stockholders' Equity	
Current assets:			Current liabilities:	
Cash	$16,000		Accounts payable	$ 3,000
Accounts receivable	800		Stockholders' equity:	
Total current assets		$16,800	Common stock	50,000
Property, plant, and equipment:				
Land	$ 5,000			
Building	25,000			
Furniture	6,200			
Total property, plant, and equipment		36,200	Total liabilities and	
Total assets		$53,000	stockholders' equity	$53,000

Figure 3–7   The Account Form of the Balance Sheet

Recording Changes in Stockholders' Equity

The expansion of the accounting system beyond the simple illustration creating the Modern Realty Corporation requires that the transactions that change stockholders' equity other than investment be examined. These are: revenues, gains, expenses, losses, and dividends.

Revenues

The term **revenue** describes the source of the inflows of assets; it involves a process that generates new assets in exchange for (1) services rendered, (2) sales of merchandise, (3) earnings from investments in stocks and bonds, and (4) advantageous settlement of liabilities at less than the amount of the debt.[1] Since revenue involves an earnings process, the term does not include increases in assets arising from stockholders' investments or from borrowed funds. For revenue to be earned, it does not have to be collected immediately in cash; it is sufficient that claims for cash on customers or clients exist. Although revenue items are first recorded in separate accounts, they ultimately increase Retained Earnings because this account reflects the retention of the accumulation of all past net earnings (past revenues less expenses). In other words, it represents the accumulation of all past net earnings less dividends declared.

A distinction must be made between revenues and assets. As learned in Chapter 2, *assets* are things of value (resources) held in a firm. *Revenues* rep-

---

[1] The Financial Accounting Standards Board defines revenue as "... inflows or other enhancements of assets of an entity or settlement of its liabilities (or a combination of both) during a period from delivering or producing goods, rendering services, or other activities that constitute the entity's ongoing major or central operations." *Statement of Financial Accounting Concepts No. 3* (Stamford, Conn.: 1980).

resent one *source* of the inflow of assets. In other words, in the double entry process both the assets flowing in and the source (often revenues) of the assets must be accounted for.

Revenue accounts are created to accumulate the amounts earned during a specified period—usually one year; for teaching purposes, however, a shorter period of one month will often be used. The title of a revenue account should indicate the nature of the source of revenue; examples are Commissions Earned, Sales, Interest Earned, Dividends Earned, Accounting Fees Earned, and Shop Repair Revenue.

Since revenues ultimately act to increase the Retained Earnings account, the rules for increasing and decreasing stockholders' equity apply. Revenue accounts, therefore, are *credited when they are increased,* and the particular asset that is increased is *debited*. Revenue accounts are debited to reflect decreases. The normal balance of a revenue account is therefore a credit balance. To illustrate the journalizing of revenue transactions, several companies that earned different kinds of revenue are considered. At the end of a period, these revenue accounts are closed out, and the excess of revenues over expenses is transferred to the Retained Earnings account. (This process is illustrated in Chapter 4.)

First, suppose that on August 3, 1987, the Modern Realty Corporation sells a house and lot and receives a commission of $500 in cash; this can be recorded in its journal as follows:

GENERAL JOURNAL   Page 29

1987					
Aug.	3	Cash....................		500	
		Commissions Earned...........			500
		To record receipt of commission earned on sale of house and lot.			

Note that the account representing the cash received was increased, and the account representing the source of the cash—the revenue—was also increased. Next, assume that on July 30, 1987, Lameica Miller, CPA, bills the Baker Company for $1,000 for an annual audit that she has made; her journal entry might look like this:

GENERAL JOURNAL   Page 42

1987					
Jul.	30	Accounts Receivable		1,000	
		Accounting Fees Earned.........			1,000
		To record billing of following client for audit:			
		Baker Company........$1,000.00			

The recording of revenue in the period that it is earned prior to its being collected is adhering to a concept referred to as the accrual basis of accounting (discussed more fully in Chapter 4).

Gains

Gains are similar to revenues in that they represent an inflow of assets from incidental transactions of an entity, and they have the same debit and credit rules as revenues for increasing and decreasing their accounts.[2] The most common source of gains is the sale or trade-in of assets other than merchandise inventory. As a usual rule, the gain element is only the excess of the selling price over the cost of the item sold or exchanged. In the introductory chapters of this book, gains are *not* emphasized; only revenues are considered.

Expenses

The next cause of change in retained earnings is **expenses**, the expired cost of the *assets consumed* and *services received* during a specified period and used in the production of revenue during that same period.[3] Expense accounts are created to accumulate the amounts incurred during a specific period. The title of the account should indicate the cause of the expense. Since expenses ultimately act to decrease the Retained Earnings account, the rules for increases and decreases to stockholders' equity apply. Therefore, an expense account is debited when it is increased because it ultimately will decrease retained earnings. An expense is credited when it is decreased; the normal balance is a debit. When an expense is recorded by a debit, the offsetting credit is to Cash, to a liability account, or to some other asset account. The recording process for expenses is illustrated by the following five transactions that took place at Modern Realty Corporation in August 1987:

1987

Aug. 2 Paid $900 in rent for the month of August.
    10 Purchased an advertisement in the local newspaper for $75 in cash.
    15 Paid semimonthly salaries of $2,000.
    20 Had some office equipment repaired by Able Company at a cost of $45 to be paid in September.
    31 Determined that $185 of office supplies had been consumed in August. The amount of the office supplies originally purchased was debited to an asset account, Office Supplies.[4]

---

[2]The FASB, in its *Statement of Financial Accounting Concepts No. 3*, "Elements of Financial Statements of Business Enterprises," defines gains as ". . . increases in equity (net assets) from peripheral or incidental transactions of an entity and from all other transactions and other events and circumstances affecting the entity during a period except those that result from revenues or investments by owners."
[3]In its *Statement of Financial Accounting Concepts No. 3*, the FASB defined expenses as ". . . outflows or other using up of assets or incurrences of liabilities (or a combination of both) during a period from delivering or producing goods, rendering services, or carrying out other activities that constitute the entity's ongoing major or central operations."
[4]This transaction is illustrated at this point to demonstrate that expenses consist of assets consumed as well as cost of services received. It is normally treated as an end-of-period adjusting entry. Adjustments are introduced in this chapter and then discussed more in depth in Chapter 4.

These transactions are recorded in the general journal as follows:

		GENERAL JOURNAL			Page 10

1987
Aug.
	2	Rent Expense[a]................................
		    Cash ....
		      To record payment of rent for month of January 1987.
				900	900

	10	Advertising Expense..............................
		    Cash ....
		      To record payment for advertising.
				75	75

	15	Salaries Expense[b]...............................
		    Cash ....
		      To record payment of semimonthly salaries.
				2,000	2,000

	20	Repairs Expense—Office Equipment....................
		    Accounts Payable..............................
		      To record repairs to office equipment on account from:
		        Able Company $45
				45	45

	31	Office Supplies Expense............................
		    Office Supplies ....
		      To record consumption of office supplies for month.
				185	185

[a]For a more complete explanation of why expenses are recorded as debits, see Figure 3–9.
[b]As discussed in Appendix 8.1, both state and federal income taxes and social security taxes will have to be withheld from salaries paid to employees; thus, pending payment of those items to the appropriate governmental units, liability accounts would be credited. In the interest of simplicity and teachability, these are ignored at this time.

In the preceding journal entries recording expenses, note that the first three involve immediate payments for expenses where credits to Cash are made. The fourth one involves the creation of an accounts payable liability. The fifth records the use of supplies during a period: in this case, the credit is to the asset account, Office Supplies. The recording of the use of supplies is made as an adjusting entry; adjustments are introduced in this chapter and developed more completely in the next chapter. For each expense account the normal balance is a debit balance.

Losses

Losses are similar to expenses in that they represent an expiration of costs—the using up of assets. They differ from expenses, however, since losses do not usually help to produce revenues.[5] Neither gains nor losses are emphasized in the introductory chapters of this book. Revenues and expenses are the primary components involved in measuring the results from operations.

---

[5]The FASB, in its *Statement of Financial Accounting Concepts No. 3*, "Elements of Financial Statements of Business Enterprises," defines losses as ". . . decreases in equity (net assets) from peripheral or incidental transactions of an entity and from all other transactions and other events and circumstances affecting the entity during a period except those that result from expenses or distributions to owners."

Before the remaining cause of change in stockholders' equity (dividends) is discussed, the relationship of revenues to expenses in the determination of net income or net earnings—the measuring of the results of operations for a period of time—is considered. Broadly speaking, the excess of revenues over expenses is called *net income;* it is defined more specifically later.

Operational Terms

To determine the results of operations, it is important to understand the meaning of certain operational terms.

Cost and expense

Cost, *the amount to purchase an asset, becomes an* **expense** *when the purchased item is no longer an asset; that is, when it can no longer produce future revenue.*

It is necessary to distinguish between an expense and a cost. A *cost* is the amount paid or payable in either cash or the equivalent for goods, services, or other assets purchased. Thus a cost of a resource that benefits the future is recorded as an asset. When a cost no longer has asset status—that is, when its potential to produce future revenue is lost—it is said to be expired and thus to have become typically an *expense*. From this statement the following conclusions are warranted:

Expenses = Expired costs (used up in *producing* this period's revenue).
Assets = Unexpired costs (to be used to produce future revenue).

For example, rent paid in advance for three months is an asset, prepaid rent. As time passes, this becomes rent expense.

A **disbursement** is a payment in cash or by check. Hence, a machine may be acquired at a cost of $10,000; the transaction is completed by a disbursement in the form of a check for $10,000. As the machine is used in operations, it loses part of its service value, or depreciates. The original purchase is not an expense. However, the expiration of service potential is a depreciation expense, another adjusting entry that is discussed in detail in Chapter 4.

Operating Results

Most businesses cannot keep the detailed records necessary to indicate the expense of each service rendered and therefore cannot determine the net income or net loss from each transaction. Even when it is possible, the clerical costs involved in getting the information would not justify the end result. For example, a law firm bills its client $1,000 for services performed. How much did it cost the law firm to perform the service and how much net income did it make on this one transaction? The firm might total the number of hours devoted to the case and arrive at an expense in terms of time spent. But how about the rent for the office? The secretary's salary? The telephone bill? The electricity bill? Since the determination of the exact expense involved in rendering service for a particular client would require a considerable amount of record keeping, accounting has evolved another and easier method for ac-

Matching concept; Income statement

complishing an acceptable result. Attempts are seldom made to determine the cost of each service; instead, records of revenue and expense are kept for a period, perhaps a year or a shorter period of time.

At the end of the period, the period's expenses are matched *against the period's revenue to determine the net income or net loss for that period, a principle referred to as the* matching concept. *This information is contained in a financial statement called an* income statement, *discussed and illustrated later in this chapter.*

In measuring the results of operations for a period of time, the accountant compares revenues and expenses to determine operating results. Depending upon whether the expenses or the revenues are greater, a business may have a net income or a net loss for the period. Net income (also called comprehensive income,[6] net earnings, or profit) for any period is measured by deducting total expenses from total revenues for that period.[7] It shows the change in stockholders' equity resulting from business operations. The operations information shown on the income statement that results in an increase in stockholders' equity may be generally expressed in equation form as

$$\text{Total revenues} - \text{Total expenses} = \text{Net income.}$$

If revenues exceed expenses, the right-hand figure is *net income*. If the total expenses for a period exceed the revenues for that period, however, a net loss results, and the stockholders' equity is decreased. The equation now becomes

$$\text{Total expenses} - \text{Total revenues} = \text{Net loss.}$$

Net loss; Losses

The term net loss *should not be confused with the term* losses. *Net loss is equivalent to a negative net income; whereas losses are gross expirations of costs that do not make a contribution to the production of revenue.*

Authorized Withdrawals by Stockholders —Dividends

Dividends, the fifth cause of changes in stockholders' equity, are distributions of assets resulting from net income regardless of whether that income is earned in the current period or in past periods. A dividend must be declared by a corporation's board of directors (the executive group representing all shareholders) before it can be paid. Although dividends reduce the stockholders' equity, they are *not* expenses; they are not declared and paid for the

---

[6] The FASB in *Statement of Financial Accounting Concepts No. 3* defines comprehensive income as "... the change in equity (net assets) of an entity during a period from transactions and other events and circumstances from non-owner sources. It includes all changes in equity during a period except those resulting from investments by owners and distributions to owners."

[7] Even though gains and losses are ignored initially, it should be understood that net income = (total revenues + total gains) − (total expenses + total losses).

purpose of producing revenue. A dividend may be recorded by a debit to a special Dividends account and a credit to Cash, or a credit to a liability account if it is to be paid at a date subsequent to the date of declaration. For example, suppose that on November 10, 1987, the Johanna Corporation declared a regular quarterly cash dividend of $2,000 to its stockholders and paid it on December 15, 1987. These transactions would be recorded in the general journal of the Johanna Corporation as follows:

GENERAL JOURNAL   Page 84

1987				
Nov.	10	Dividends..	2,000	
		Dividends Payable		2,000
		To record declaration of fourth quarterly dividend.		
Dec.	15	Dividends Payable...	2,000	
		Cash		2,000
		To record payment of fourth quarterly dividend.		

Expanding Rules for Debits and Credits

Since new types of accounts have been introduced, the rules for debiting and crediting accounts can now be expanded and restated as follows:

Debit to record:

1. An increase of an asset account
2. An increase of an expense account
3. An increase of a dividends account
4. A decrease of a liability account
5. A decrease in a stockholders' equity account
6. A decrease in a revenue account.

Credit to record:

1. A decrease of an asset account
2. A decrease of an expense account
3. A decrease of a dividends account
4. An increase of a liability account
5. An increase in a stockholders' equity account
6. An increase in a revenue account.

The relationship of the rules of debits and credits to the accounting equation is diagramed in T account form in Figure 3–8. Although the debit-credit processing rules for expenses and dividends are the same, it should be emphasized again that the Dividends account is not an expense account. *The payment made to the stockholders in the form of dividends does not produce revenue.* Another important basic accounting concept shown in Figure 3–8 is the normal balance of the accounts. Asset, dividends, and expense accounts normally have a debit balance, whereas liability, stockholders' equity, and revenue accounts normally have a credit balance.

It is evident from the expanded accounting equation that a *decrease* in stockholders' equity results in a debit entry. When the decrease in stockhold-

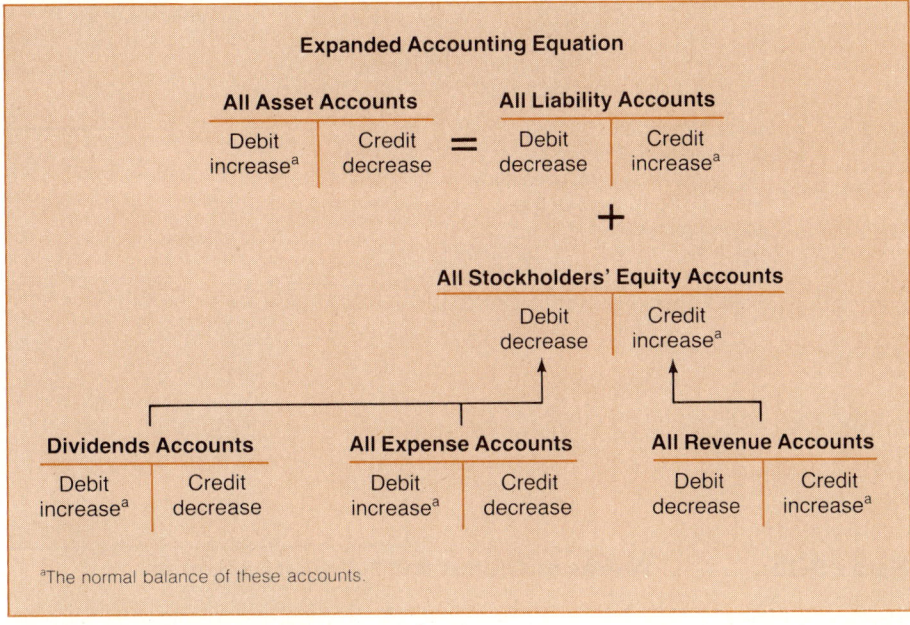

Figure 3–8   **Expanded Accounting Equation**

ers' equity is temporarily entered in an expense account, the expense account is *increased* (debited). All expense accounts are designed to *accumulate* expired costs, which are later transferred as reductions to the Retained Earnings account. The specific relationship between the expense accounts and stockholders' equity is further illustrated in Figure 3–9.

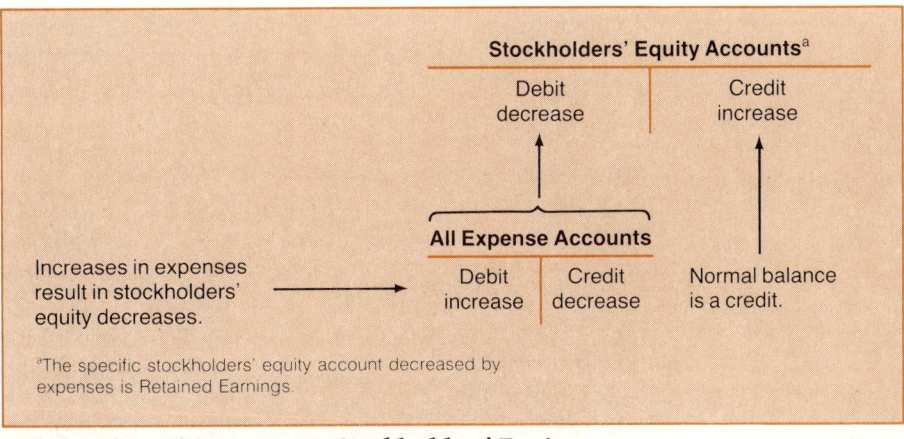

Figure 3–9   **Relationship of Expenses to Stockholders' Equity**

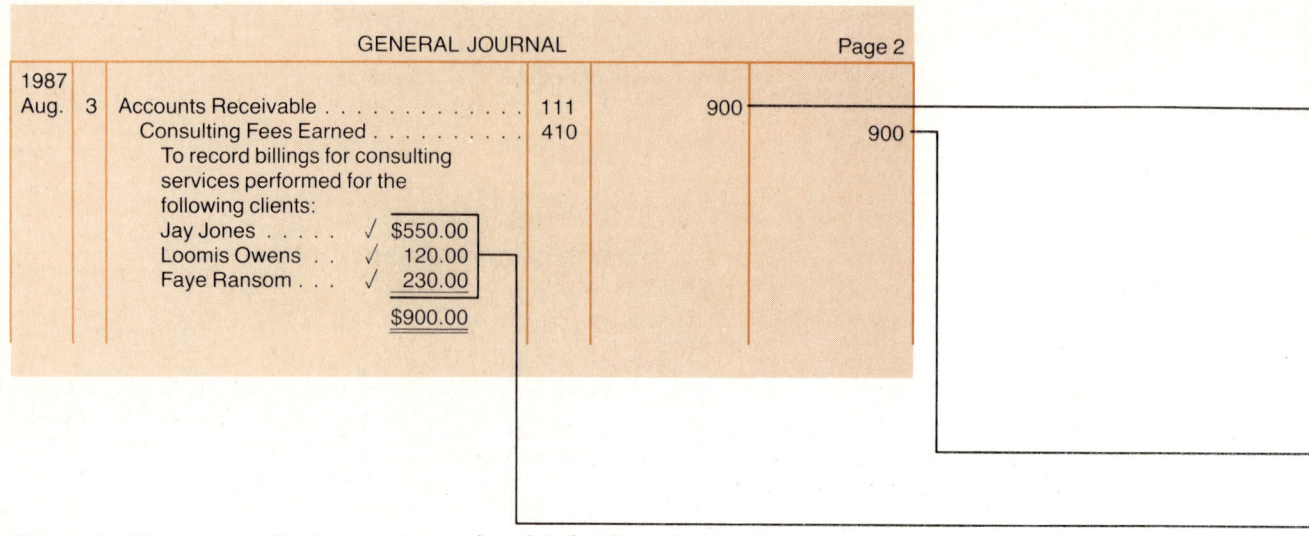

Figure 3–10   Posting to Control and Subsidiary Accounts

It naturally follows that dividends reduce stockholders' equity. As they occur (increase), they are also recorded as debits.

The General Ledger and Subsidiary Ledgers

Asset, liability, common stock, retained earnings revenue, expense, and dividends accounts have now been introduced. These accounts that are incorporated in the regular end-of-period financial statements are kept in a separate book or collection, called the **general ledger**. Other ledgers that are supplementary, subordinate, or supporting to the general ledger are referred to as **subsidiary ledgers**. The general ledger may actually be a loose-leaf binder, a bound book, cards in open trays, punched cards, or one of several types of computer data storage devices. General ledger accounts are usually arranged in the sequence in which they will appear in the financial statements—that is, assets, liabilities, stockholders' equity, revenues, and expenses.

Accounts Receivable Subsidiary Ledger

Many businesses have a large number of customers, and detailed information must be kept of transactions with each one. A separate account thus is required for each. If the general ledger were to include each customer's account, it would become too large and unwieldy. Consequently, a summary account, Accounts Receivable, is maintained in the general ledger showing the combined increases and decreases in the amounts due from all customers. The individual customer accounts are kept in a separate, or subsidiary, ledger called the **accounts receivable subsidiary ledger**. The Accounts Receivable account in the general ledger, referred to as a **controlling account** summarizes those individual customers' accounts that are assigned to the subsidiary ledger. After all transactions for the period have been entered,

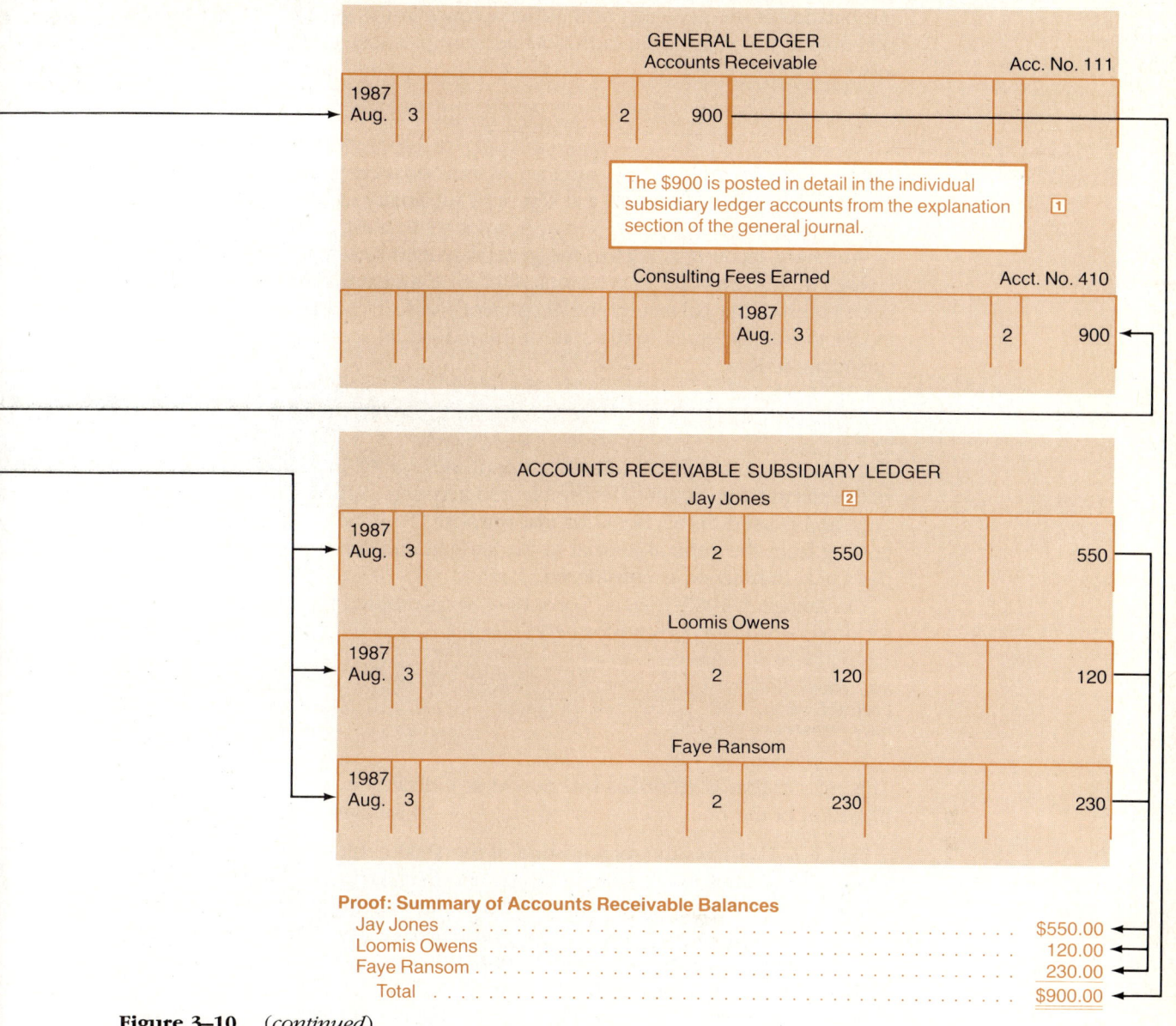

Figure 3–10 *(continued)*

the balance of the Accounts Receivable account in the general ledger should be equal to the sum of the individual account balances in the subsidiary ledger.

Accounts Payable Subsidiary Ledger

Many businesses have a large number of individual creditors. Consequently, individual creditors' accounts are kept in a subsidiary ledger called the **accounts payable subsidiary ledger**; Accounts Payable, another controlling or summary account, is kept in the general ledger showing increases and decreases in amounts due to creditors. After all transactions for the period have been entered, the balance of the Accounts Payable account in the general ledger should be equal to the sum of the individual account balances in the subsidiary ledger.

Posting to the General Ledger and Subsidiary Ledgers

The three-amount-column form of account introduced in Chapter 2 is especially effective for accounts receivable and accounts payable subsidiary ledgers, and is used in this book for that purpose. To illustrate the method of posting from the general journal to the general and subsidiary ledgers, a hypothetical transaction is considered.

On August 3, 1987, Rogers' Consulting Service billed the following clients for professional services performed:

Jay Jones	$550
Loomis Owens	120
Faye Ransom	230

This information is recorded and posted as indicated in Figure 3–10. An explanation of the numbered items in Figure 3–10 follows:

[1] Figure 3–10 shows the total posting of the $900 debit to the Accounts Receivable account in the general ledger and detailed posting to the subsidiary ledger accounts. Each customer's account is debited for the amount shown in the explanation of the general journal entry. The balance is extended then to the Balance column of the three-amount-column ledger account. The journal page number is entered in the folio (F) column. Last, the date is entered. After each posting has been completed, a check mark (√) is entered to the left of each amount in the Explanation column of the general journal to indicate that the amount has been posted to the proper subsidiary ledger account. A check mark is used rather than a page number because subsidiary accounts in the illustration are not numbered but are kept in alphabetical order. (Most large businesses use account numbers; that clerical procedure is avoided in this book to concentrate on concepts.)

[2] The three-amount-column form of ledger account is most often used for the accounts receivable and accounts payable subsidiary ledgers for two

reasons: (a) the balances have to be referred to quite often, and (b) the form is adaptable to noncomputerized machine accounting, which is frequently employed for subsidiary ledger accounting. As noted in Chapter 2, the three-amount-column form of ledger account may also be used for general ledger accounts as well as for subsidiary accounts. As a matter of fact, it is *the* common form of ledger accounts found in practice for *both* general ledger and subsidiary ledger use when the ledgers are not computerized. It is easy to prepare and extremely convenient in the preparation of the trial balance. The authors of this book, however, consider the T form of ledger account to be the most useful for *teaching* most accounting concepts. The T form, therefore, is used throughout the book when the general ledger is used. Since the three-amount-column form is virtually the only form used in accounts receivable and accounts payable subsidiary ledgers, that form is the typical form used in this book to illustrate the subsidiary ledger recording. In the typical three-amount-column ledger account, the balance column does not indicate whether it is a debit or credit balance. The preparer must know the type of normal balance for each account. The normal balance, for instance, in the customers' accounts in the accounts receivable subsidiary ledger is a debit. Should there be an opposite-from-normal balance in this type of account, it should be encircled.

A business such as a department store that makes hundreds of credit sales daily does not list each one in the journal entry explanation; instead, posting to the subsidiary ledger accounts are made from the copies of the sales tickets (this option is described in Appendix 6.1). The principle, however, is the same as illustrated in Figure 3–10.

At first it may seem that this dual accounting for accounts receivable would result in double debits that would be incorrectly reflected in the trial balance. Note carefully, however, that only one debit goes into the Accounts Receivable controlling account for later use in the trial balance. The amounts entered in the accounts receivable subsidiary ledger will *not* go in the trial balance, but the total of the uncollected balances at the end of a period will be compared with the single balance of the Accounts Receivable controlling account as a check on the accuracy of both the accounts receivable subsidiary ledger and the Accounts Receivable controlling account in the general ledger. Entries to the Accounts Payable controlling account and the accounts payable subsidiary ledger are handled similarly.

An Overview of the Accounting Sequence

It is important to take a look at the steps in the accounting sequence that is illustrated by the example presented in this and the next chapter. Figure 3–11 shows an overview of the following 11 steps in the accounting sequence: (1) selecting a chart of accounts, (2) journalizing the transactions, (3) posting to the general and subsidiary ledgers, (4) preparing a trial balance, (5) preparing a schedule of accounts receivable, (6) preparing a schedule of accounts payable, (7) preparing the financial statements, (8) journalizing and

Figure 3–11   An Overview of the Accounting Sequence

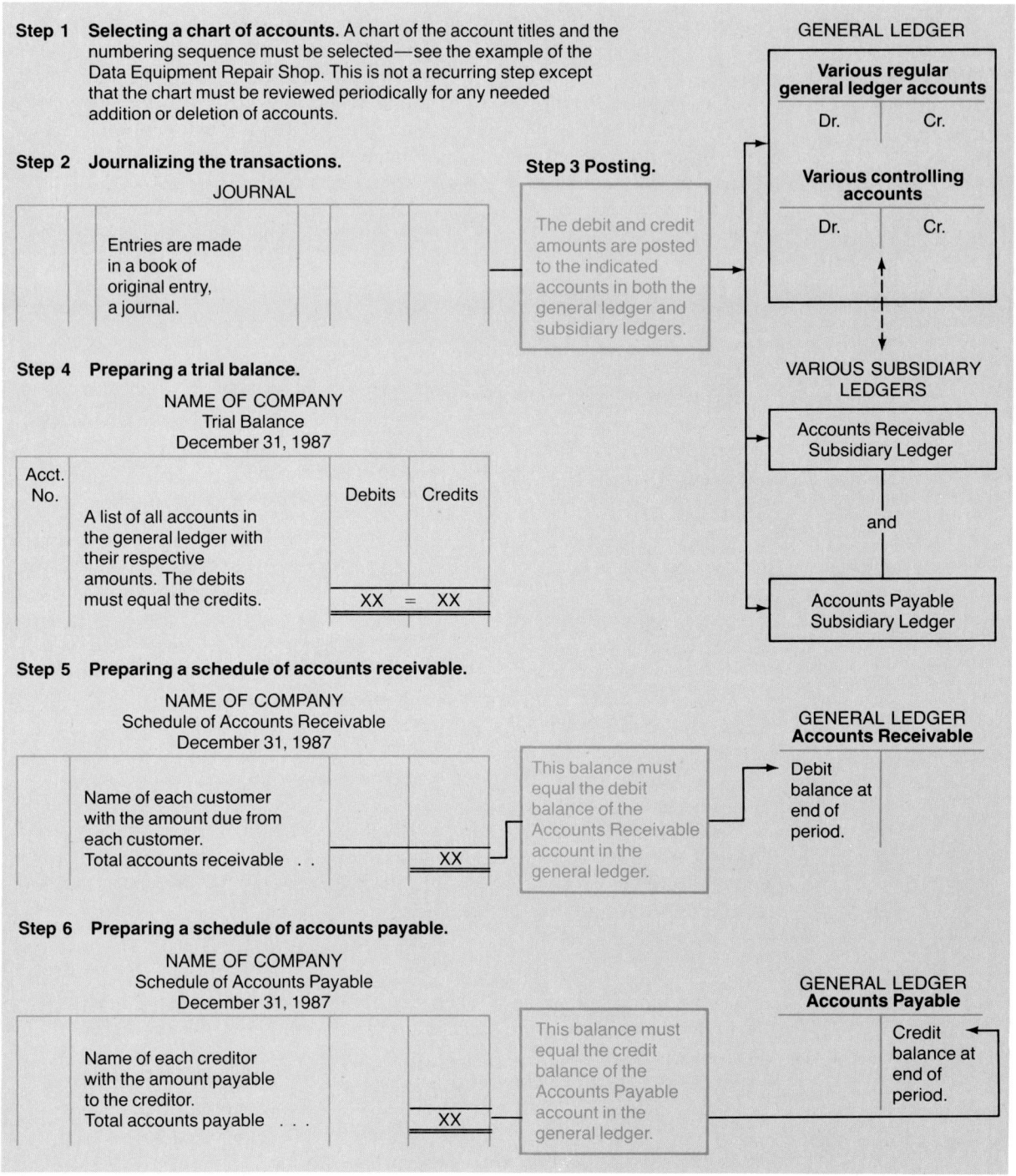

Figure 3–11 (*continued*)

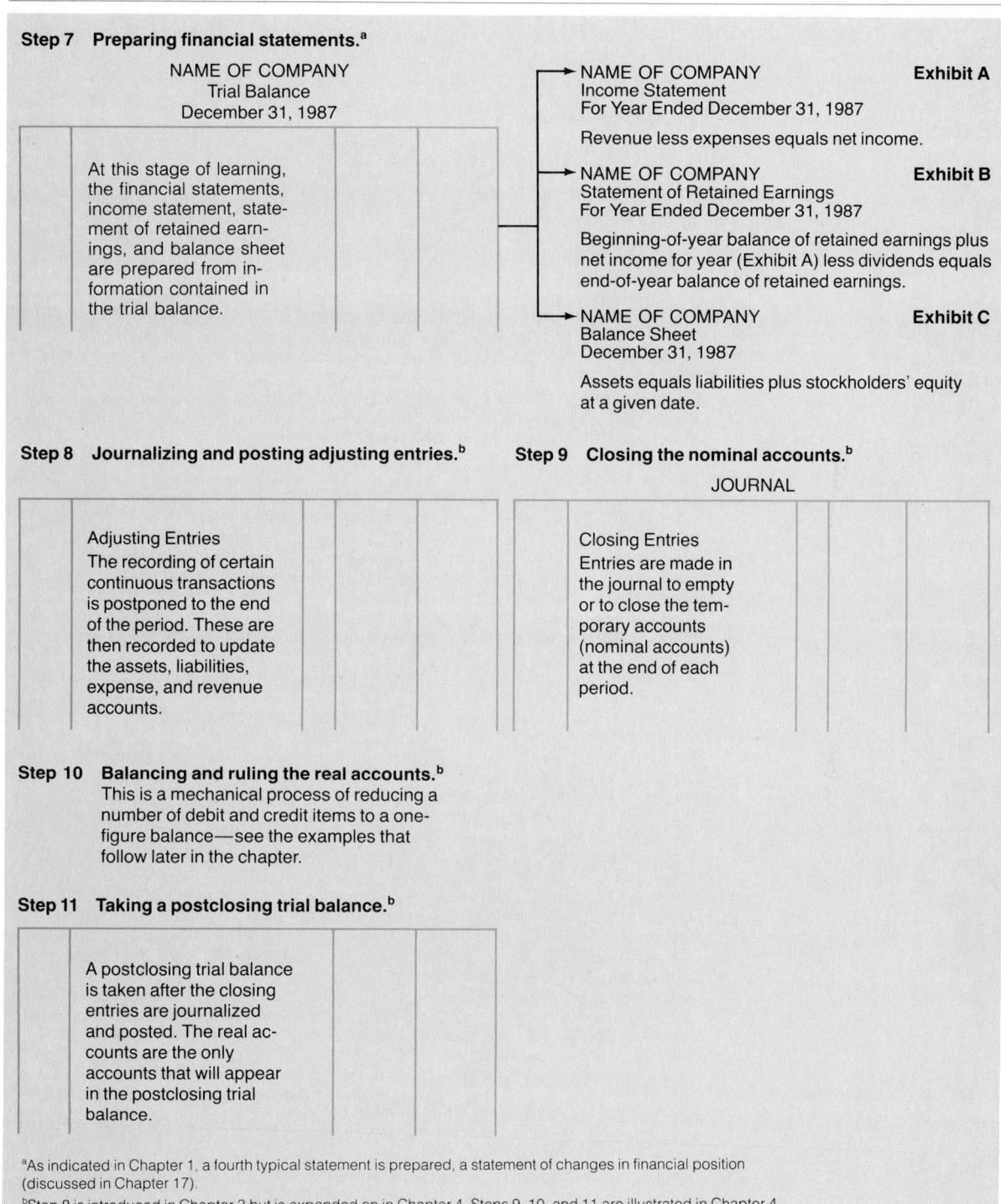

[a]As indicated in Chapter 1, a fourth typical statement is prepared, a statement of changes in financial position (discussed in Chapter 17).
[b]Step 8 is introduced in Chapter 3 but is expanded on in Chapter 4. Steps 9, 10, and 11 are illustrated in Chapter 4.

posting adjusting entries, (9) closing and ruling the revenue, expense, and dividends accounts, (10) balancing and ruling the real accounts, and (11) taking a postclosing trial balance. This figure, on pages 110 and 111, should be studied carefully before proceeding further.

An Illustration— Data Equipment Repair Shop

The example of the Data Equipment Repair Shop illustrates the 11 steps in the accounting sequence. The transactions for the month of January 1987 follow:

1987

Jan. 2 The corporate charter for the Data Equipment Repair Shop was received on this date, and the 3,000 shares of authorized common stock were issued to three stockholders at par (the amount to be recorded in the Common Stock account) for $30,000 in cash.
   3 Rented a temporary shop and paid $300 for the January rent; issued check no. 1.
   5 Rented tools and equipment pending purchase of the firm's own. Rent in the amount of $80 was paid for January; issued check no. 2.
   5 Purchased repair parts and supplies on invoice no. 306 from Southern Supply Company for $400 on account.
   10 Purchased land as a prospective building site for $10,000. Paid $4,000 in cash (check no. 3) and issued a one-year note payable for the balance. By agreement interest at 10 percent per year does not begin until February 1, 1987.
   12 Made repairs on George Shipman's data processing equipment for $40. Shipman asked that a charge account be opened in his name; he promises to settle the account within thirty days. This open account arrangement was authorized by the service manager.
   26 Made repairs on Jay Munson's data processing equipment for $180. A charge account was opened in his name.
   29 Purchased repair parts and supplies from the Delco Supply House for $250 on account (invoice no. 1004).
   30 Paid the Southern Supply Company $300 on account (check no. 4).
   31 Paid electricity and water bills for January, $80 (check no. 5).
   31 Made data processing equipment repairs for various cash customers for $4,800.
   31 Paid $1,700 in salaries for the month (check no. 6 issued to obtain payroll cash).
   31 Paid a $300 cash dividend to the three stockholders (checks no. 7, 8, and 9).
   31 Purchased tools and equipment for cash, $4,000 (check no. 10). The list price was $5,000.
   31 Paid a premium of $600 (check no. 11) on a 12-month comprehensive insurance policy; the policy becomes effective on February 1, 1987.
   31 Received a check for $10 from George Shipman as part payment of his account.
   31 Took a physical inventory of repair parts and supplies; it showed that parts and supplies costing $375 were on hand, thus indicating that $275 (January 5 purchase, $400 + January 29 purchase, $250 − inventory, $375) worth of repair parts and supplies had been used, becoming an expense. As parts and supplies were purchased, they were debited to an asset account. Now, as the amount used becomes known, an entry is made debiting an expense account, Repair Parts and Supplies Expense, to show that the expense account has been increased, and crediting the asset account, Repair Parts and Supplies, to show that the asset account has been decreased. This type of cost apportionment transaction is normally recorded in an *adjusting entry*. It is presented here to introduce adjustments and to broaden the scope of this illustration. The discussion of adjustments is further expanded in Chapter 4.

The steps involved in this illustration are presented below. The various accounting elements are shown in Figures 3–12 through 3–22 and 4–2.

Selecting a Chart of Accounts

The first step in establishing an efficient accounting system that will satisfy the needs of management, government agencies, and other interested users is the construction of a *chart of accounts*.

Chart of accounts

A separate account should be set up for each item that appears in the financial statements to make the statements easier to prepare. The chart of accounts *is the complete listing of account titles to be used by the entity.*

The classification and the sequence of the items in the chart of accounts corresponds to those in the statements. Figure 3–12 shows a suggested chart of accounts for the Data Equipment Repair Shop.

DATA EQUIPMENT REPAIR SHOP
Chart of Accounts

Asset Accounts (100–199)

Current Assets (100–150)
- 101 Cash
- 121 Accounts Receivable
- 131 Repair Parts and Supplies
- 141 Prepaid Insurance

Property, Plant, and Equipment (151–199)
- 151 Land
- 161 Tools and Equipment

Liability and Stockholders' Equity Accounts (200–399)

Current Liabilities (200–250)
- 201 Accounts Payable
- 202 Notes Payable

Long-Term Liabilities (251–299)

Stockholders' Equity (300–399)
- 301 Common Stock
- 311 Retained Earnings
- 321 Dividends

Income Statement Accounts (400–599)

Revenue (400–499)
- 401 Shop Repair Revenue

Expenses (500–599)
- 501 Rent Expense—Shop Building
- 502 Rent Expense—Tools and Equipment
- 504 Salaries Expense
- 508 Electricity and Water Expense
- 509 Repair Parts and Supplies Expense

Clearing and Summary Accounts (600–699)
- 601 Income Summary

Figure 3–12
Chart of Accounts, Data Equipment Repair Shop

Account titles should be carefully selected to suit the needs of the business and should indicate clearly and precisely the nature of the accounts to ensure proper recording of transactions. However, titles are not standardized; for example, one business may use Unexpired Insurance and another Prepaid Insurance to describe the same asset.

In Figure 3–12, a three-digit system is used to number the accounts; a larger business with a number of departments or branches may use four or more digits. In this illustration accounts 100–199 represent assets; accounts 200–399 represent liabilities and stockholders' equity; and accounts 400–599 represent *income statement* accounts (revenue and expense accounts that are incorporated in the income statement). The numbers in the 600 range are designated for clearing and summary accounts. The more detailed breakdown for property, plant, and equipment, and current liabilities, for example, can be seen in the chart. As stated previously, the gaps between the assigned account numbers allow for additional accounts as they are needed by the business.

Analyzing Transactions and Journalizing

After a chart of accounts is prepared, the accountant must analyze each of the transactions in terms of increases and decreases in the accounting equation by using the basic system of debits and credits that has already been outlined. The first four transactions are repeated below *accompanied by a description of the analytical thinking that must precede journalizing.* These and the remaining transactions are then journalized. Note that, in the journal, space is left between entries to ensure that they are separate and distinct.

A Detailed Analysis of First Four Transactions

(use these as a guide to future action):

1987

Jan. 2 The corporate charter for the Data Equipment Repair Shop was received on this date, and the 3,000 shares of authorized common stock were issued to three stockholders at par for $30,000 in cash. An asset, cash, is received; to record an increase of an asset, it must be debited; therefore, the Cash account is debited for $30,000. The stockholders have a claim against the business; the increase in the stockholders' equity account, Common Stock, is shown by a credit to that account.

3 Rented a temporary shop and paid $300 for the January rent; issued check no. 1. Since all the rent will have expired by the time the financial statements are prepared, it is considered an expense of the month of January. An increase of an expense account is recorded by a debit; therefore, the Rent Expense—Shop Building account is debited. The decrease of the asset, cash, is recorded by a credit to Cash. A single rent account may be sufficient for all rented buildings and equipment. In this case, the accountant felt that managerial analyses required a separate rent expense account for the shop building.

5 Rented tools and equipment pending purchase of the firm's own. Rent in the amount of $80 was paid for January; issued check no. 2. As in the preceding transaction, all this rent will have expired before the financial statements are prepared; therefore it is considered an expense of January. An increase of an expense account is recorded by a debit—in this case to Rent Expense—Tools and Equipment. The decrease of the asset cash is recorded by a credit to Cash. Again, a single rent expense account may have been sufficient.

5 Purchased repair parts and supplies described on invoice no. 306 from the Southern Supply Company for $400 on account. The Repair Parts and Supplies account is an asset and is increased by the transaction; the increase in the asset is shown by a debit to Repair Parts and Supplies. Since the purchase was not paid in cash, a liability is created. To record the increase in the liability, the Accounts Payable account is credited. The amount payable to the particular creditor, the Southern Supply Company, must be shown in the books. A note should be made in the Explanation column of the journal to the effect that the creditor is the Southern Supply Company, so that the amount can be posted to the accounts payable subsidiary ledger.

Transactions Are Journalized The transactions of the Data Equipment Repair Shop are journalized in the general journal shown in Figure 3–13. Account numbers appear in the folio column of the journal in Figure 3–13. These should *not* be entered while journalizing. In this example, they were entered *after posting* to indicate that the item had been posted.

GENERAL JOURNAL   Page 1

1987 Jan.	2	Cash.. Common Stock.. To record issuance of common stock for cash.	101 301	30,000	30,000
	3	Rent Expense—Shop Building.......................... Cash.. To record payment of rent on shop building for month of January, 1987; issued check no. 1.	501 101	300	300
	5	Rent Expense—Tools and Equipment................... Cash.. To record payment of rent for tools and equipment for month of January, 1987; issued check no. 2.	502 101	80	80
	5	Repair Parts and Supplies............................. Accounts Payable..................................... To record purchase of parts and supplies on account on invoice no. 306: Southern Supply Company................. ✓ $400	131 201	400	400
	10	Land... Cash.. Notes Payable.. To record purchase of land; issued check no. 3.	151 101 202	10,000	4,000 6,000
	12	Accounts Receivable.................................. Shop Repair Revenue................................. To record billing for repairs rendered: George Shipman............................. ✓ $40	121 401	40	40

(continued on next page)

Figure 3–13 **General Journal, Data Equipment Repair Shop**

Figure 3–13 (continued)

Page 2

1987 Jan.	26	Accounts Receivable . . . . Shop Repair Revenue . . . . To record billing for repair services rendered: Jay Munson. . . . . ✓ $180	121 401	180	180
	29	Repair Parts and Supplies . . . . Accounts Payable. . . . . To record purchase of parts and supplies on account on invoice no. 1004: Delco Supply House . . . . ✓ $250	131 201	250	250
	30	Accounts Payable . . . . Cash . . . . To record payment; issued check no. 4: Southern Supply Company . . . . ✓ $300	201 101	300	300
	31	Electricity and Water Expense. . . . . Cash . . . . To record payment of electricity and water bills for month of January; issued check no. 5.	508 101	80	80
	31	Cash. . . . . Shop Repair Revenue . . . . To record collections from cash customers for services rendered.	101 401	4,800	4,800
	31	Salaries Expense[a] . . . . Cash . . . . To record payment of salaries for month of January; issued check no. 6 to obtain payroll cash.	504 101	1,700	1,700
	31	Dividends . . . . Cash . . . . To record payment of dividends to stockholders; issued checks no. 7, 8, and 9.	321 101	300	300

[a]As indicated previously, the company would have to withhold certain payroll taxes (discussed in Appendix 8.1).

Page 3

1987 Jan.	31	Tools and Equipment . . . . Cash . . . . To record purchase of tools and equipment at a cost of $4,000 (list price, $5,000); issued check no. 10.	161 101	4,000	4,000
	31	Prepaid Insurance . . . . Cash . . . . To record payment of insurance premium for 12 months. Insurance is effective February 1, 1987; issued check no. 11.	141 101	600	600
	31	Cash. . . . . Accounts Receivable . . . . To record collection to apply on account: George Shipman . . . . ✓ $10	101 121	10	10
		Adjustments			
	31	Repair Parts and Supplies Expense . . . . Repair Parts and Supplies. . . . . To record cost of parts and supplies used during month of January.	509 131	275	275

Introduction to Adjustments

Accrual accounting and the resultant income determination dictate that all earned revenue and incurred expenses be recorded in the period earned and incurred. Some transactions are postponed to the end of the period because it is not convenient for the accountant to record them on a day-by-day basis. For example, repair parts and supplies are used each day and could be recorded on a daily basis. This procedure, however, requires a great deal of time and expense. Since statements are prepared only at the end of designated periods, it is acceptable to record the supplies used at the end of that period before the statements are prepared. The recording at the end of a period of expired cost, other earned but unrecorded revenue and expenses, and other postponed transactions necessary to measure properly earned revenue and incurred expenses is referred to as preparing **adjusting entries**. As a typical rule, the accountant would take a trial balance to test the equality of debits and credits up to that point in time *before the adjustments are made*. After the adjusting entries are made, an adjusted trial balance then may be taken. Since there is only one adjustment in the Data Equipment Repair Shop example, only one trial balance is prepared and that is taken after the one adjustment. The subject of adjusting entries is discussed in depth in Chapter 4.

Posting to the Ledgers

As the transactions are posted to the ledger, the account numbers are entered in the general journal folio (F) column. At the same time, the number of the journal page from which the entry is posted is entered in the folio (F) column of the ledger account.

The timing of the posting process is a matter of personal preference and expediency. All postings, however, must be completed before financial statements can be prepared. It is advisable to keep accounts with customers and creditors up to date, so that the account balances are readily available. Because of this, it is best to post from the journal to the subsidiary ledgers on a daily basis. The three posted ledgers are shown in Figures 3–14 (general ledger), 3–15 (accounts receivable subsidiary ledger), and 3–16 (accounts payable subsidiary ledger).

GENERAL LEDGER

Cash   Acct. No. 101

Date		F	Amount	Date		F			F	Amount
1987 Jan.	2	1	30,000	1987 Jan.	3				1	300
	31	2	4,800		5				1	80
	31	3	10 23,450		10				1	4,000
			34,810		30				2	300
					31				2	80
					31				2	1,700
					31				2	300
					31				3	4,000
					31				3	600
										11,360

Figure 3–14   General Ledger, Data Equipment Repair Shop   *(continued on next page)*

Figure 3–14 (*continued*)

		Accounts Receivable			Acct. No. 121
1987 Jan. 12		1 40	1987 Jan. 31		3 10
26	210	2 180			
		220			

		Repair Parts and Supplies			Acct. No. 131
1987 Jan. 5		1 400	1987 Jan. 31		3 275
29	375	2 250			
		650			

		Prepaid Insurance			Acct. No. 141
1987 Jan. 31		3 600			

		Land			Acct. No. 151
1987 Jan. 10		1 10,000			

		Tools and Equipment			Acct. No. 161
1987 Jan. 31		3 4,000			

		Accounts Payable			Acct. No. 201
1987 Jan. 30		2 300	1987 Jan. 5	350	1 400
			29		2 250
					650

		Notes Payable			Acct. No. 202
			1987 Jan. 10		1 6,000

		Common Stock			Acct. No. 301
			1987 Jan. 2		1 30,000

		Retained Earnings			Acct. No. 311

		Dividends			Acct. No. 321
1987 Jan. 31		2 300			

(*continued on next page*)

Accounts Receivable controlling account in the general ledger. A schedule of accounts receivable is usually prepared to check this agreement. The one taken from the Data Equipment Repair Shop's accounts receivable subsidiary ledger shows that the total of all customers' accounts is $210, which agrees with the balance of the Accounts Receivable account that is also $210 (see Figure 3–18).

DATA EQUIPMENT REPAIR SHOP
Schedule of Accounts Receivable
January 31, 1987

Jay Munson	$180
George Shipman	30
Total accounts receivable	$210

Figure 3–18   Schedule of Accounts Receivable, Data Equipment Repair Shop

Preparing a Schedule of Accounts Payable

The next step is similar to the preceding one; it involves the preparation of a **schedule of accounts payable**. At the end of the accounting period, the total of the balances of the individual creditors' accounts should equal the balance of the Accounts Payable controlling account. The schedule of accounts payable taken from the Data Equipment Repair Shop's accounts payable subsidiary ledger shows that the total of the creditors' accounts is $350, which agrees with the balance of the Accounts Payable account, which is also $350 (see Figure 3–19).

DATA EQUIPMENT REPAIR SHOP
Schedule of Accounts Payable
January 31, 1987

Delco Supply House	$250
Southern Supply Company	100
Total accounts payable	$350

Figure 3–19   Schedule of Accounts Payable, Data Equipment Repair Shop

Preparing the Financial Statements from the Trial Balance

The income statement, the statement of retained earnings, and the balance sheet are usually prepared at the end of the accounting period. They are marked with an exhibit letter or number that can be used for cross-referencing remarks. In this book, they are marked as follows:

☐ Income statement: Exhibit A

☐ Statement of retained earnings: Exhibit B

☐ Balance sheet: Exhibit C

The Income Statement

The income statement shown in Figure 3–20 was prepared from the trial balance of the Data Equipment Repair Shop. Its heading shows the following:

1. Name of the business
2. Name of the statement
3. Period covered by the statement.

It is important that the period covered be specified clearly. The date, January 31, 1987, is not sufficient; it alone does not indicate whether the net income of $2,585 was earned in one day, one month, or one year ended January 31, 1987. The analyst must know how long a period it took for the firm to earn the $2,585.

```
                    DATA EQUIPMENT REPAIR SHOP                Exhibit A
                          Income Statement
                    For the Month Ended January 31, 1987
    Revenue:
        Shop repair revenue.....................................    $5,020
    Expenses:
        Rent expense—shop building .................      $  300
        Rent expense—tools and equipment ..........          80
        Salaries expense ...........................       1,700
        Electricity and water expense ..............          80
        Repair parts and supplies expense..........         275
            Total expenses ........................................     2,435
    Net income......................................................    $2,585
        Earnings per share .........................     $0.86
```

Figure 3–20   Income Statement, Data Equipment Repair Shop

The determination of net income for the Data Equipment Repair Shop at this level should not be interpreted as being complete. For example, a corporation is subject to income taxes; the accounting for income taxes and certain other more complex problems is deferred to later chapters.

There is no standard order for listing accounts in the income statement. Size of each revenue and expense item may be one criterion, or the sequence of the accounts in the general ledger may be used as the basis for establishing the order used.

In today's corporate accounting, an **earnings per share** figure is usually disclosed at the bottom of the income statement. For the Data Equipment Repair Shop, it is $0.86. It is determined by dividing the weighted average number of shares of common stock outstanding (the shares in the hands of stockholders—3,000 shares in the case of the Data Equipment Repair Shop) into the net income of $2,585 ($2,585 ÷ 3,000 = $0.86). Earnings per share is generally considered to be an excellent indicator of future profitability.[8]

---

[8] See Chapter 13 for an expanded explanation of earnings per share.

The Statement of Retained Earnings

Since the corporation is a creature of the law, there are certain legal restrictions on it, including a requirement that the net income retained in a business be recorded separately from the Common Stock account. The typical title of the account used to accumulate this information is Retained Earnings. The **statement of retained earnings**, which should cover the same period as the income statement, shows the changes in that part of the stockholders' equity designated as retained earnings. Since by definition, retained earnings is the accumulation of all past net income less any dividends paid out, it follows that net income and dividends for a period must be reflected in the statement. The first end-of-period statement of retained earnings of the Data Equipment Repair Shop is shown in Figure 3–21.

DATA EQUIPMENT REPAIR SHOP Statement of Retained Earnings For the Month Ended January 31, 1987	Exhibit B
Retained earnings, January 1, 1987.	$ 0
Add: Net income for January 1987	2,585
Subtotal	$2,585
Deduct: Dividends.	300
Retained earnings, January 31, 1987.	$2,285

Figure 3–21   Statement of Retained Earnings for a New Business, Data Equipment Repair Shop

Its heading is similar to that of the income statement. The opening figure is the balance of retained earnings as of the beginning of the current period. In the case of the Data Equipment Repair Shop, it is zero, since the business was started in January 1987. This zero amount could be omitted from the statement, but it is included to show the reader a generalized format of a statement of retained earnings.

Balance Sheet

Since the retained earnings of the Data Equipment Repair Shop as of January 31, 1987, have now been determined, it is possible to prepare the formal balance sheet, as shown in Figure 3–22 (on page 124). The heading of the balance sheet contains the single date *January 31, 1987*. This statement is like a still photograph, revealing the financial position as of the close of business on that day, whereas the income statement and statement of retained earnings are like moving pictures—they show the changes that have taken place during a specific period.

The next step in the accounting sequence is that of closing the temporary accounts. Chapter 4 opens with a discussion of closing entries using the Data Equipment Repair Shop example. Before leaving the financial statement part of this illustration, it is important again to consider applicable managerial analyses.

```
                        DATA EQUIPMENT REPAIR SHOP                            Exhibit C
                                 Balance Sheet
                                January 31, 1987

              Assets                            Liabilities and Stockholders' Equity
Current assets:                          Current liabilities:
  Cash . . . . . . . . . . . . .  $23,450   Accounts payable . . . . . . . . . $   350
  Accounts receivable . . . . . .     210   Notes payable . . . . . . . . . .   6,000
  Repair parts and supplies . . .     375     Total current liabilities . . . .          $ 6,350
  Prepaid insurance . . . . . . .     600  Stockholders' equity:
    Total current assets . . . . .         $24,635    Common stock . . . . . . . . . $30,000
Property, plant, and equipment:            Retained earnings . . . . . . .    2,285
  Land . . . . . . . . . . . . .  $10,000    Total stockholders' equity . . .           32,285
  Tools and equipment . . . . . .    4,000
    Total property, plant, and
      equipment . . . . . . . . .          14,000  Total liabilities and stockholders'
Total assets . . . . . . . . . . .         $38,635   equity . . . . . . . . . . . . .           $38,635
```

Figure 3–22 Account Form of Balance Sheet for Data Equipment Repair Shop

Managerial Analysis of Operations—Common-Size Income Statement and Earning Power Measurements

Ratio analysis involving the income statements of corporations is extremely popular and meaningful to readers of these statements—particularly to investors. These users like to see a common-size income statement and various earning power measurements such as earnings per share, the price-earnings ratio, the rate of return on total investments, and the rate of return on stockholders' equity. A common-size income statement for the Data Equipment Repair Shop for the month of January 1987 is presented below followed by the calculation and discussion of four earning power measurements for a real-life company, the Centel Corporation.

Common-Size Income Statement

A common-size income statement is constructed in a manner similar to the common-size balance sheet: for this statement, all the items are stated as a percentage of total revenue. The information contained in Figure 1–1 showing where the typical sales dollar goes is a variation of a common-size income statement. All that is necessary to convert this information into common-size percentages is to drop the decimal and add a percent sign to each of the items. To convert the Data Equipment Repair Shop (see Figure 3–20) income statement data for January 1987 into common-size percentages, it is necessary to divide each item—expense and net income—by the shop repair revenue amount. An example of the conversion of the rent expense—shop building dollar amount into a common-size percentage is shown below:

$$\frac{\text{Rent expense—shop building}}{\text{Shop repair revenue}} = \frac{\$300}{\$5,020} = 6.0\%.$$

Thus 6 percent of each sales dollar or six cents out of each sales dollar is used to rent a shop building during the month of January. The calculation of the remaining items is done in a similar manner. The full common-size income statement is shown in Figure 3–23.

DATA EQUIPMENT REPAIR SHOP
Common-Size Income Statement
For the Month Ended January 31, 1987

Revenue:	
Shop repair revenue............................	100.0%
Expenses:	
Rent expense—shop building.....................	6.0%
Rent expense—tools and equipment...............	1.6
Salaries expense..............................	33.9
Electricity and water expense...................	1.6
Repair parts and supplies expense...............	5.5
Total expenses............................	48.6
Net income.....................................	51.4%[a]

[a]This percent is the result of addition and subtraction of expenses from revenue rounded to the nearest tenth of a percent. Net income as a percent of sales is 51.5% = ($2,585 ÷ $5,000).

Figure 3–23   Common-Size Income Statement, Data Equipment Repair Shop

The usefulness of the common-size statement is enhanced when prepared in comparative statement form involving several periods. Then trends can be noted. The relationship of net income to total revenue is viewed as one indication of earning power. A net income of 51.4 percent of revenue would be considered outstanding for almost any company. Other earning power measurements are discussed next.

Earning Power Measurements for Centel Corporation

Of considerable significance and usefulness to investors are the following four measures of earning power: (1) earnings per share, (2) the price-earnings ratio, (3) the rate of return on total investments, and (4) the rate of return on stockholders' equity.

Earnings Per Share   As indicated earlier in this chapter, the earnings per share figure is calculated by dividing the net income available for common shareholders by the weighted average common shares outstanding. Although this figure is placed on the income statement, it is a form of ratio analysis. Investors use this figure as an indicator of earning power and future profitability; they also use it with other related ratios such as the price-earnings ratio discussed later in this section. In its unaudited summary of earnings (net income) for the years ended December 31, 1983 and 1982, the Centel Corporation's statements revealed the following:

Line		Year Ended December 31 1983	1982
1	Earnings available for common shareholders (in thousands)	$112,052	$106,952
2	Weighted average common shares outstanding (in thousands)	27,197	26,986
3	Earnings per share (1 ÷ 2)	$4.12	$3.96

The earnings per share figure for 1983 of $4.12 showed an increase of $0.16 over the 1982 figure of $3.96. This represents a 4 percent improvement.

Price-Earnings Ratio The **price-earnings ratio**, another earning power measurement, is calculated by the following formula:

$$\frac{\text{Market value per share}}{\text{Earnings per share}} = \text{Price-earnings ratio.}$$

This ratio uses the earnings per share figure discussed previously. The market price of the Centel Corporation common stock was $35.125 as of December 31, 1983. Thus the price-earnings ratio at this time would be

$$\frac{\$35.125}{\$4.12} = 8.5.$$

This measure is watched carefully by investors. They study what happens to the price-earnings ratio for companies such as Centel to determine the price that they would be willing to pay for a share of common stock of a given corporation. This ratio, sometimes known as *times earnings,* varies greatly; many of the better known companies' stock sold for six to twelve times earnings in 1984 and 1985, but Ford Motor Company stock was selling at about four times earnings in early 1985. The 8.5 times for Centel was about the average for such companies at that time.

Rate of Return on Total Investment The relationship of the earnings of a business to its total resources is an important indicator of the effectiveness of management in generating a return to suppliers of capital; it is also a method of predicting future earnings. The **rate of return on total investment** is:

(Net income for year + Interest expense) ÷ Average total assets = Rate of return on total investment.

Excerpts from the financial statements of the Centel Corporation follow:

1. From the consolidated balance sheet (in thousands of dollars):

	December 31 1983	1982
Total assets.	$2,352,018	$2,199,397
Total stockholders' equity.	$ 768,712	$ 699,351

2. From the consolidated income statement (in thousands of dollars):

	For the Year Ended December 31, 1983
Net income.	$113,259
Interest expense.	$ 80,398

Using the preceding information and the stated formula, Centel Corporation's rate of return on total investment is calculated as follows:

$$(\$113{,}259 + \$80{,}398) \div \left(\frac{\$2{,}352{,}018 + \$2{,}199{,}397}{2}\right) = 8.5\%.$$

This rate shows the degree of profitability measured against *total investment* by creditors and stockholders combined (thus, interest expense should be added back to net income).

Rate of Return on Stockholders' Equity
The relationship between earnings and the average stockholders' investment is a significant measure of the profitability of a business and is of particular interest to the corporate shareholders. The 1983 **rate of return on stockholders' equity** for the Centel Corporation is:

$$\frac{\text{Net income}}{\text{Average stockholders' equity}} = \frac{\$113{,}259}{(\$768{,}712 + \$699{,}351) \div 2} = 15.4\%.$$

In this case, interest expense is part of the cost to stockholders of earning the net income and is not added back. Since this rate is significantly higher than the rate of return on total investments, by 76.5% = [(15.4% − 8.5%) ÷ 8.5%], it appears that the Centel Corporation is using the assets acquired from creditors in a manner that is beneficial to the stockholders. That is to say, the return to stockholders is greater than the interest rate on money borrowed.

Other earning power measurements are used by investors, but these are the key ones. Again, as indicated in Chapters 1 and 2, the reader should be cautioned: ratios are *indicators of fact* and not a fact in themselves. Also, no one ratio should be considered to be the answer to any particular question.

One ratio should be considered in the light of another or several other ratios and with careful consideration being given to nonfinancial information before a decision is to be made.

Glossary

Accounts payable subsidiary ledger The collection of individual creditors' accounts. (See *Subsidiary ledger*.)

Accounts receivable subsidiary ledger The collection of individual customers' accounts. (See *Subsidiary ledger*.)

Adjusting entries End-of-period entries made to update assets, liabilities, expenses, and revenue accounts to attain a proper matching for the period.

Chart of accounts A list of all accounts in the general ledger which the entity anticipates using. Their numbering system indicates the types of accounts by subgroups.

Compound entry A journal entry with more than one debit or credit account.

Controlling account One account in the general ledger that controls and is supported by a group of accounts in a separate subsidiary ledger.

Cost The amount paid or payable in either cash or its equivalent for goods, services, or other assets purchased.

Disbursement A payment in cash or by check.

Double-entry accounting A system of accounting requiring that each transaction be recorded in such a way that the natural equality of the debit and credit characteristics is recognized.

Earnings per share Net income divided by average outstanding shares of stock; it is considered to be an excellent indicator of future profitability.

Expense Expired cost; the material used and service utilized in the production of revenue during a specific period.

Gains Increases in net assets of an entity from incidental transactions other than revenue transactions; these amounts are usually the amount of the selling price over the cost of items sold or exchanged.

General journal Where there is only one journal used, it is referred to as the general journal. When more than one journal is used, the general journal is used to record all transactions that cannot be recorded in a special journal. (See *Journal*.)

General ledger The collection of accounts incorporated in the regular end-of-period financial statements.

Income statement A statement showing all revenue and expense items for a given period, arranged in such a manner that the total of the expenses is subtracted from the total of the revenues, thus revealing the net income earned during that period.

Journal The book of original entry for all transactions.

Journalizing The process of recording a transaction, analyzed in terms of its debits and credits, in a record of original entry referred to as a journal.

Losses Expired costs that do not produce any revenue to match with their expiration.

Matching concept The matching of incurred expenses and earned revenue identified for a given time period in order to determine net income for that period.

Net income Excess of revenue over expenses for a given period.

Net loss Excess of expenses over revenue for a given period.

Posting The process of transferring an amount recorded in the journal to the indicated account in the ledger.

Price-earnings ratio Market value per share of common stock divided by the earnings per share.

Rate of return on stockholders' equity Net income as a percentage of average stockholders' equity.

Rate of return on total investment Net income plus interest expense as a percentage of average total assets.

Revenue A term describing the source of inflows of assets received in exchange for services rendered, sales of products or merchandise, advantageous settlement of liabilities, and earnings from interest and dividends on investments.

Schedule of accounts payable A listing of individual creditors, with amount owed to each and the total owed to all creditors at a given moment in time.

Schedule of accounts receivable A listing of individual customers (debtors), with the amount owed by each and the total amounts receivable from all customers at a given moment in time.

Statement of retained earnings A statement showing the changes that occurred in retained earnings of a corporation during a given period.

Subsidiary ledger A group of accounts in a separate ledger that provides information in detail about one controlling account in the general ledger.

Questions

Q3–1 What is the function (a) of the general journal? (b) of the general ledger?

Q3–2 Transactions are recorded in a journal and then posted to the appropriate accounts. Why is this two-step procedure followed instead of entering the transaction directly in the ledger?

Q3–3 Define the term *revenue*. Does the receipt of cash by a business indicate that revenue has been earned? Explain. List 10 types of businesses or professions, and name the major source of revenue for each.

Q3–4 Define the term *expense*. Does the payment of cash by a business indicate that an expense has been incurred? Explain. Distinguish between a dividend and an expense.

Q3–5 Distinguish between a revenue and a gain.

Q3–6 Distinguish between an expense and a loss.

Q3–7 The accountant for Samuel Tyler, Inc., a parking lot company, listed the parking lot at a cost of $20,000 on the balance sheet. The president of the corporation argues that this amount should be $28,000, because the corporation has recently been offered $28,000 for the lot. Discuss.

Q3–8 The Greer Corporation purchased electrical supplies on account from the O'Neal Company for $350 and from Lewis, Inc. for $200. Greer debited Electrical Supplies for $550, and erroneously credited Accounts Receivable for $550 in the general ledger. The credit postings to the accounts payable subsidiary ledger were properly made.

1. What effect would the error have on the debit and credit totals of the trial balance taken at the end of the month?
2. What accounts in the trial balance would be incorrectly stated?
3. How would the error be discovered?

Q3–9 List the advantages to management of keeping separate general and subsidiary ledgers and using controlling accounts. Is it equally advantageous to exclude the individual items included in the schedules of accounts receivable and accounts payable from the general ledger trial balance? Explain.

Q3–10   The following transaction occurred on April 15, 1987: Received bills representing charges for truck maintenance and repairs as follows: Becon Hill Garage, $150; Ray's Garage, $225. Showing the proper general journal and general and subsidiary ledger accounts, prepare flow diagrams as shown in Figure 3–10 to illustrate posting from the general journal to the general ledger and the accounts payable subsidiary ledger.

Q3–11   Assume that your firm has 2,000 customers who buy on credit.

a. Why would you want to keep your posting up to date?
b. Is it true that posting depends on previous journalizing?
c. Does journalizing, in turn, depend on earlier procedures in the complete accounting system? Explain.

Q3–12   The sale of a used cash register by a clothing dry cleaners was recorded as follows:

```
Cash .........................................................  XX
    Dry Cleaning Revenue......................................      XX
```

Is this a correct entry? Why or why not?

Q3–13   Would the amount paid to purchase a machine that has an estimated 10-year life qualify as an expense in the year of purchase? Explain.

Q3–14   What is the difference between real accounts and nominal accounts? List five examples of each.

Q3–15   State the debit/credit rule for increasing and decreasing the following types of accounts: assets, liabilities, revenues, gains, expenses, losses, and dividends.

Q3–16   How would the following ratios be determined: price-earnings ratio, rate of return on total investment, and rate of return on stockholders' equity. Explain the importance of each.

Exercises

E3–1   Place the following activities in the correct sequence:

Sequence of accounting steps

_____ Recording the transactions in a journal.
_____ Preparing the financial statements.
_____ Gathering objective evidence of the transactions.
_____ Preparing a trial balance.
_____ Transferring the amounts in the journal to the ledger.

E3–2   Some of the possible effects of a transaction are listed:

Effect of transactions on accounting elements

1. An asset increase accompanied by an asset decrease.
2. An asset increase accompanied by a stockholders' equity increase.
3. An asset increase accompanied by a liability increase.
4. An asset increase accompanied by a revenue increase.
5. An asset decrease accompanied by a liability decrease.
6. An asset decrease accompanied by a stockholders' equity decrease.
7. An asset decrease accompanied by an expense increase.
8. An expense increase accompanied by a liability increase.

Using the identifying numbers to the left of the listed combinations, indicate the effect of each of the following transactions, as done in the example.

Example: Issued common stock for cash. Answer: (2).

a. Collected a commission on a sale made today.
b. Borrowed money from a bank and issued a note.
c. Collected an account receivable.
d. Paid an account payable.
e. Paid for an ad in a magazine.

E3–3
Impact of errors on accounts

A new accountant began work on January 2, 1987. Unfortunately, he made several errors that were discovered by the auditor during the year-end review. Indicate the effect of each error described below by completing the following solution form. Treat each error separately; do not attempt to relate them to one another.

	Suggested Solution Form				
Error	Would the December 31, 1987 Trial Balance Be Out of Balance?		If Yes, by How Much?	Which Would Be Larger?	
	Yes	No		Debit Total	Credit Total
a					
b					
etc.					

a. A cash register was purchased for $2,000 and cash was paid and credited. The debit was entered twice in the Asset account.
b. A credit to the Cash account of $3,121 was posted as $3,211.
c. Cash collections of $4,475 from customers in settlement of their accounts were not posted to the Accounts Receivable account but were posted correctly to the Cash account and to accounts in the accounts receivable subsidiary ledger.
d. A purchase of office supplies of $410 was recorded as a credit to Cash and also as a credit to Office Supplies.

E3–4
Journalizing, posting, and end-of-period statements

The following transactions were engaged in by the Village Circuit Corporation during the month of August 1987:

1987

Aug. 1 Received a charter and issued all authorized common stock at par for $400,000 in cash.
   4 Purchased land and building for $80,000 in cash and a twenty-year mortgage payable for $70,000. The land was appraised at $45,000; the building, at $105,000.
  12 Purchased service supplies from the Cox Company for $1,600 on account.
  31 Sold a portion of the lot purchased on August 12 for its cost of $10,000. The buyer, the Williams Company, paid $8,000 in cash and issued a ninety-day note for $2,000.

1. Journalize the transactions.
2. Post to formal general ledger accounts and determine account balances. Do not post to subsidiary ledger accounts. (Assign appropriate numbers to accounts.)
3. Prepare a trial balance.
4. Prepare a classified account form balance sheet.

132 Part One / The Basic Accounting Model

E3–5
Recording cash transactions

The following cash receipts and cash payment transactions involving different companies occurred during a period:

a. A realty company received a commission of $5,000 on the sale of land for a client. This commission had not previously been recorded.
b. A corporation received semiannual interest of $70,500 on its temporary investments.
c. Landard Corporation received monthly rentals of $50,000; the entire amount was for property rented during the current month.
d. A company paid salaries of $10,200 for the month.
e. A company purchased for $250 an advertisement in the local newspaper.

Record the foregoing transactions in a general journal using *a, b, c, d,* or *e* instead of dates.

E3–6
Recording revenue transactions

The following cash receipt transactions occurred at the Delores Realty Corporation during the month of August 1987:

1987

Aug.	1	Issued additional stock for $60,000 in cash.
	7	Received a commission of $4,500 from the sale of a house and lot; no receivable had been previously recorded.
	8	Received $8,100 in cash from the issuance of a note payable to a bank.
	31	Received $400 in interest from U.S. government bonds.
	31	Received $600 in cash for August rent of part of the corporation's building.

Journalize the *revenue* transactions only. State why the ones not recorded are not revenue items.

E3–7
Recording expense transactions

The following were among the cash payment transactions at the Houston Garage during the month of May 1987:

1987

May	3	Paid $12,000 for a truck.
	7	Paid $4,000 in salaries for the week.
	9	Paid $9,300 in settlement of an open account.
	12	Paid $700 for a typewriter.
	16	Declared and paid a $3,600 cash dividend to stockholders.
	22	Paid $580 for rent of the office for May.

Journalize the *expense* transactions only. State why the ones not recorded are not expense items.

E3–8
Analysis of transactions

The August 1987 transactions of the Continental Travel Service are given below:

1987

Aug.	1	Paid $450 for an advertisement in the travel section of the *Durham Tribune*.
	2	Arranged a round-the-world trip for Mr. and Mrs. Franklin Pepard. Collected a commission of $380 in cash from the steamship company.
	3	Arranged fly-now, pay-later Asian trips for several clients. The Great Circle Airway System agreed to a commission of $980 for services rendered, payment to be made at the end of the month.
	4	Another advertisement was placed in the *Durham Tribune* for $370, payment to be made in 10 days.
	16	A dividend was declared and paid to stockholders, $3,500.
	19	Collected $980 from the Great Circle Airway System.

Following the example given below for the August 1 transaction, analyze each transaction and prepare the necessary journal entry.

Example:
Aug. 1 **a.** Advertising is an operating expense. Increases in expenses are recorded by debits. Debit Advertising Expense for $450.
b. The asset Cash was decreased. Decreases of assets are recorded by credits. Credit Cash for $450.
c. Journal entry:
  Advertising Expense 450
  Cash   450

E3–9
Accounts Receivable controlling and subsidiary accounting

The following transactions occurred at the Dutens Dog Grooming Clinic:

1987

Nov. 1 Billed the following customers for $280 for dog grooming:
  Timothy Amal . . . . $ 60
  John Carson.   80
  Thomas Queens 140
    Total $280

30 Received $210 on account from the following customers:
  Timothy Amal . . . . $ 50
  John Carson.   60
  Thomas Queens 100
    Total $210

1. Prepare general journal entries to record the transactions.
2. Post to general ledger and accounts receivable subsidiary ledger accounts. (Assign appropriate numbers to general ledger accounts.)
3. Prepare a schedule of accounts receivable.

E3–10
Income statement and managerial analysis

The trial balance of Sparrow Brick Mason, Inc., as of September 30, 1987, follows:

SPARROW BRICK MASON, INC.
Trial Balance
September 30, 1987

Account Title	Debits	Credits
Cash	$30,500	
Masonry Supplies.	4,500	
Equipment	15,000	
Accounts Payable.		$ 490
Common Stock (5,000 shares)		10,000
Retained Earnings, September 1, 1987		9,320
Bricklaying Fees.		51,440
Salaries Expense	20,000	
Advertising Expense	160	
Rent Expense	340	
Masonry Supplies Expense	410	
Utilities Expense.	140	
Dividends.	200	
Totals.	$71,250	$71,250

(continued on next page)

1. Prepare an income statement for the month of September.
2. Assume that the market price of the common stock is $31.50 as of September 30, 1987; calculate the price-earnings ratio.

E3–11
Preparing statement of retained earnings from transactions

Spence Dance Studios, Unlimited, recorded the following transactions for the month of February 1987:

1987

Feb.	2	Issued 20 shares of common stock, $300.
	6	Paid the rent for February, $400.
	9	Paid for an advertisement in *The Globe,* $200.
	14	Collected fees for dance instruction not previously recorded, $950.
	17	Declared and paid a cash dividend of $1 per share of stock (200 shares are now currently outstanding).
	20	Paid monthly wages, $770.
	28	Purchased supplies on account, $120.
	28	Paid the March rent in advance, $400.
	28	Collected fees for dance instruction not previously recorded, $1,200.

Prepare a statement of retained earnings for the month of February, assuming that the February 1 balance of retained earnings was $2,450.

E3–12
End-of-period statements and earning power measurements

The following trial balance was prepared for Timothy's Bookkeeping Services, Inc. on December 31, 1987, the end of its accounting year.

TIMOTHY'S BOOKKEEPING SERVICES, INC.
Trial Balance
December 31, 1987

Account Title	Debits	Credits
Cash	$ 64,550	
Supplies	10,500	
Equipment	30,000	
Land	25,000	
Building	205,000	
Notes Payable		$ 10,000
Mortgage Payable		50,000
Common Stock (50,000 shares)		100,000
Retained Earnings, January 1, 1987		95,000
Dividends	8,750	
Bookkeeping Fees Earned		504,000
Rent Revenue		48,000
Supplies Expense	168,000	
Salary Expense	198,000	
Insurance Expense	66,000	
Miscellaneous Expenses	31,200	
Totals	$807,000	$807,000

1. Prepare an income statement, a statement of retained earnings, and a report form balance sheet.
2. Assume that the total assets and stockholders' equity on January 1, 1987, were $260,000 and $195,000, respectively, and that the market price of the common stock as of December 31, 1987, was $17.75. Calculate the price-earnings ratio, the rate of return on total investments, and the rate of return on stockholders' equity.
3. Write a brief report to management evaluating these earning power measurements.

Use of three-amount-column account

E3-13 An account in the accounts receivable subsidiary ledger of the Zoom Corporation showed the following entries:

Victor Zaharia & Co.

1987					1987				
Jan.	1	Balance	✓	85,400	Jan.	3		49	85,400
Feb.	4		50	40,000	Feb.	15		51	38,000
May	5		55	20,400	May	16		55	20,400
June	9		60	36,200	Jul.	1		61	18,000

Using a three-amount-column account, recast the foregoing entries in that account.

Journal entry errors

E3-14 Errors have been made in the following page of a general journal:

1987				
Oct.	17	Office Supplies..................................	8,000	
		Accounts Payable.............................		8,000
		To record the purchase of supplies on account.		
Oct.	19	Cash..	2,800	
		Accounts Receivable...........................		280
		To record the collection of an account for $2,800.		

Ignoring subsidiary accounts, describe the errors and prepare corrected journal entries.

A Problems

Accounting sequence steps

P3-1A The following transactions were engaged in by the newly created corporation to be called the Varina Camera Services during July 1987:

1987

Jul. 3   The corporation received its charter and issued common stock at par value (the amount to be recorded), $150,000 to 20 stockholders.
    6   Purchased land and building for $90,000 in cash and a 20-year mortgage payable for $60,000. The land was appraised at $18,000 and the building at $132,000.
    7   Purchased repair supplies from the Nobb Company for $6,000 on account.
   31   Sold one-third of the lot purchased on May 6 for $6,000. The buyer, the Silver Sands Company, paid $2,500 in cash and issued a 90-day note for $3,500.

Required:

1. Journalize the transactions.
2. Post to formal general ledger accounts and determine account balances. Do not post to subsidiary ledger accounts. (Assign appropriate numbers to accounts.)
3. Prepare a trial balance.
4. Prepare an account form balance sheet as of July 31, 1987.

P3–2A

Accounting sequence steps

Accounts included in the trial balance of the Bethel Corporation as of November 30, 1987, were as follows (the corporation was organized on November 21, 1987, and has not started to render any service to customers as of the current date although several receivables and payables result from getting the proper plant items in place):

Acct. No.	Account Title	Balance
101	Cash	$ 48,430
111	Accounts Receivable	23,570
120	Office Supplies	2,440
150	Land	?
151	Building	?
153	Furniture and Fixtures	16,000
155	Machines	120,000
157	Delivery Equipment	24,000
201	Accounts Payable	7,706
251	Notes Payable (due in two years)	50,000
301	Common Stock	?
302	Retained Earnings	0

Land and building were acquired at a cost of $120,000. It was determined that one-third of the total cost should be applied to the cost of land.

The following transactions were completed during the month of December 1987:

1987

Dec. 3 Paid in full a liability of $220 to the Allison Company.
  3 Collected in full an account receivable of $1,340 from the Parkison Supply Company.
  4 Purchased office supplies from the Billison Company for $800 on account.
  7 Additional common stock was issued at par value (the amount to be recorded) for $32,000.
  10 Collected $2,000 from the Jones Company on account.
  11 Purchased a machine from the International Office Machine Company for $12,400; a cash payment of $4,000 was made, the balance to be paid within 30 days.
  14 Paid in full a liability of $800 to the Peace Company.
  20 Paid $4,400 in cash to the International Office Machine Company in partial settlement of the liability of December 11. Issued a 30-day note payable for the balance.
  31 Collected in full an account receivable of $600 from the Wilson Company.

Required:

1. Journalize these transactions.
2. Enter the balances of November 30, 1987, in general ledger accounts, post the December entries to the general ledger, and determine the new balances. Do not post to subsidiary ledger accounts.
3. Prepare a trial balance as of December 31, 1987.
4. Prepare a report form balance sheet.

P3–3A

Accounts Payable controlling and subsidiary ledger accounting

On July 1, 1987, the Supro Electronics Repair Company purchased electronic supplies on account as follows:

Baker Company	$ 4,050
Goodson Company	6,710
Lawson Corporation	2,040
Total	$12,800

On July 14, 1987, the Supro Electronics Repair Company paid its creditors on account as follows:

Baker Company	$2,000
Goodson Company	3,000
Lawson Corporation	1,000
Total	$6,000

Required:

1. Prepare general journal entries to record the transactions.
2. Post to general ledger and accounts payable subsidiary ledger accounts. (Assign appropriate numbers to general ledger accounts.)
3. Prepare a schedule of accounts payable.

P3–4A
Accounting sequence

Village Electrical Corporation completed the following transactions during the month of August 1987:

1987

Aug. 1 The corporation received its charter and issued common stock for $16,500.
    1 Paid $250 for shop rent for the month.
    1 Pending the purchase of store equipment, the corporation rented store equipment and paid August rent of $510.
    1 Purchased electrical supplies for $1,500 on account, as follows:

Burnett Supply Company	$ 100
Mystic Wire Company	300
Ray Electrical Supply Company	1,100

    4 Rented a truck for $600 from Bennett Motor Company, paying August rent.
    8 Received $800 in cash for a completed wiring job.
   12 Paid the following creditors:

Burnett Supply Company	$ 50
Mystic Wire Company	200
Ray Electrical Supply Company	400

   15 Additional common stock of $2,000 was issued.
   20 Paid $50 for cleaning the shop.
   23 Received $400 in cash for a completed wiring job.
   26 Paid $30 for telephone service.
   27 Paid $165 for gas, oil, and other truck expenses.
   28 Dividends of $250 were declared and paid.
   28 Received $2,000 in cash for a completed wiring job.
   30 Paid the *Weekly Mercury* $25 for advertising space.
   30 Paid $100 for electrical service.
   30 Billed customers for completed work, as follows:

Arlex Company	$120
James Phillips	45
Raymond Wills	60

   31 Paid a $200 premium on a one-year comprehensive insurance policy, effective September 1, 1987.
   31 Purchased store equipment costing $2,000 and paid this amount to Best Equipment Company.
   31 Purchased a truck for $8,100 from Bennett Motor Company, paying $2,000 and giving a 60-day note for the balance.
   31 Received a promissory note from Arlex Company for balance due on its account.

Required:

1. Open the following accounts in the general ledger: Cash, 101; Accounts Receivable, 111; Notes Receivable, 115; Electrical Supplies, 136; Prepaid Insurance, 140; Trucks, 162; Store Equipment, 166; Accounts Payable, 201; Notes Payable, 204; Common Stock, 301; Dividends, 303; Electrical Service Revenue, 401; Advertising Expense,

501; Rent Expense—Shop, 503; Rent Expense—Store Equipment, 504; Rent Expense—Trucks, 505; Heat and Light Expense, 506; Telephone and Telegraph Expense, 509; Truck Expense, 510; Miscellaneous General Expense, 512.
2. Open customers' accounts in the accounts receivable subsidiary ledger.
3. Open creditors' accounts in the accounts payable subsidiary ledger.
4. Journalize all the transactions in the general journal.
5. Post from the general journal to the appropriate ledgers.
6. Prepare a trial balance from the general ledger.
7. Prepare a schedule of accounts receivable.
8. Prepare a schedule of accounts payable.

P3–5A
End-of-period statement preparation from trial balance data and earning power measurements

The trial balance of the Cuthin Company on December 31, 1987, follows:

THE CUTHIN COMPANY
Trial Balance
December 31, 1987

Acct. No.	Account Title	Debits	Credits
101	Cash	$ 93,000	
111	Accounts Receivable	6,640	
121	Supplies	2,988	
131	Equipment	33,200	
201	Accounts Payable		$ 6,640
301	Common Stock (10,000 shares)		100,000
302	Retained Earnings, January 1, 1987		17,651
311	Dividends	3,320	
401	Commissions Earned		24,900
411	Rent Earned		8,300
501	Salaries Expense	11,122	
502	Advertising Expense	1,660	
503	Supplies Expense	2,656	
504	Miscellaneous Expense	2,905	
	Totals	$157,491	$157,491

Required:

1. Prepare an income statement for 1987.
2. Assume that the total assets and stockholders' equity on January 1, 1987, were $125,800 and $117,651, respectively, and that the market price of the common stock as of December 31, 1987, was $15.75. Calculate the price-earnings ratio, rate of return on total investment, and rate of return on stockholders' equity.
3. Write a brief report to management evaluating these earning-power measurements.

P3–6A
Thought-provoking problem: public utility compared to an industrial firm

The following data for a three-year period are provided for a public utility and for a major manufacturer of home appliances:

	Utah Power and Light Company		
	1983	1982	1981
Stockholders' equity (000 omitted)	$1,210,899	$1,096,059	$1,011,232
Total assets (000 omitted)	2,837,949	2,736,488	2,432,646
Earnings per common share	$2.39	$2.38	$2.29
Dividends per common share	2.29	2.26	2.15

	White Consolidated Industries, Inc.		
	1983	1982	1981
Stockholders' equity (000 omitted)	$ 625,385	$ 531,045	$ 530,536
Total assets (000 omitted)	1,314,857	1,200,088	1,268,300
Earnings per common share	$3.20	$2.06	$4.26
Dividends per common share	1.50	1.50	1.475

Required:

1. Compute for each year (a) stockholders' equity ratio, (b) creditors' equity ratio, and (c) dividend payment ratio (dividends in ratio to earnings per share).
2. If these two companies are typical of their respective industries, what conclusions would you draw about industry capitalization and dividend patterns?
3. What information would you like to have to try to determine if these firms are typical?

B Problems

P3–1B
Accounting sequence steps

The Gold Photo Service, a corporation owned by the Gold family, engaged in the following transactions during June 1987:

1987

Jun. 1 The corporation was chartered and issued common stock at par value (the amount to be recorded) for $225,000 to create the Gold Photo Service.
2 Purchased land and building for $80,000 in cash and a 20-year mortgage payable for $100,000. The land was appraised at $60,000 and the building at $120,000.
5 Purchased photo supplies from the Camera Corner for $6,500 on account.
30 Sold one-fifth of the lot purchased on April 2 for $12,000. The buyer, Action Company, paid $4,000 in cash and issued a 90-day note for $8,000.

Required:

1. Journalize the transactions.
2. Post to formal general ledger accounts and determine account balances. Do not post to subsidiary ledger accounts. (Assign appropriate numbers to accounts.)
3. Prepare a trial balance.
4. Prepare an account form balance sheet as of June 30, 1987.

P3–2B
Accounting sequence steps

Accounts included in the trial balance of Barbara Corporation as of January 31, 1987, were as follows (the corporation was organized on January 25, 1987, and has not started to render any services to customers as of the current date although several receivables and payables result from getting the proper plant items in place):

Acct. No.	Account Title	Balance
101	Cash	$172,985
111	Accounts Receivable	25,355
120	Office Supplies	4,660
150	Land	?
151	Building	?
153	Furniture and Fixtures	44,000
155	Machines	150,000
157	Delivery Equipment	45,000
201	Accounts Payable	12,000
251	Notes Payable (due in two years)	80,000
301	Common Stock	?
302	Retained Earnings	0

Land and building were acquired at a cost of $210,000. It was determined that one-third of the total cost should be applied to the cost of land.

The following transactions were completed during the month of February:

1987

Feb. 2 Paid in full a liability of $500 to Taylor Company.
3 Collected in full an account receivable of $4,000 from Doby Company.
4 Purchased office supplies from the Sampson Company for $1,500 on account.
5 The corporation issued additional common stock at par value (the amount to be recorded) for $50,000.
8 Collected $3,500 from the Champion Company on account.
10 Purchased a machine from the National Office Machine Company for $15,400; a cash payment of $5,400 was made, the balance to be paid within 30 days.
12 Paid in full a liability of $1,200 to the Peace Company.
25 Paid $5,000 in cash to the National Office Machine Company in partial settlement of the liability of February 10. Issued a 30-day note payable for the balance.
28 Collected in full an account receivable of $800 from the Wilson Company.

Required:

1. Journalize these transactions.
2 Enter the balances of January 31, 1987, in general ledger accounts, post the February entries to the general ledger, and determine the new balances. Do not post to subsidiary ledger accounts.
3. Prepare a trial balance as of February 28, 1987.
4. Prepare a report form balance sheet.

P3–3B
Accounts receivable and subsidiary accounting

The following transactions occurred at the Adden Rug Cleaning Company:

1987

Sep. 1 Billed customers for $285 for rug cleaning work, as follows:

Charles Abbott	$ 75
Morgan Hooley	120
Arthur Rogers	90
Total	$285

30 Received $135 on account from the following customers:

Charles Abbott	$ 25
Morgan Hooley	60
Arthur Rogers	50
Total	$135

Required:

1. Prepare general journal entries to record the transactions.
2. Post to general ledger and accounts receivable subsidiary ledger accounts. (Assign appropriate numbers to general ledger accounts.)
3. Prepare a schedule of accounts receivable.

P3–4B
Accounting sequence

The Adams Welding Shop was incorporated on July 1, 1987, and during the month of July, the corporation completed the following transactions:

1987

Jul. 1 Issued for cash common stock, $50,000.
1 Paid $810 for July shop rent.
2 Pending the purchase of shop equipment, the company rented equipment and paid $650 for the July rent.
2 Purchased shop supplies on account as follows:

(continued on next page)

	Phillips Supply House	$ 900
	Saunders Supply Company	2,100
	Venable Tool Company	400

5   Rented an automobile for July for $680 from Peter's Motor Company and paid cash for this rent.
9   Received $2,200 in cash for welding services not previously billed.
10   Paid $250 in cash for advertising space in the *Las Vegas Herald*.
15   Paid cash for gas, oil, and other automobile expenses for two weeks, $75.
15   Paid $2,500 to the following creditors:

Phillips Supply House	$ 600
Saunders Supply Company	1,600
Venable Tool Company	300

18   Received $800 in cash for welding services.
21   Declared and paid a $1,000 dividend.
22   Paid $65 for telephone service.
23   Paid $40 for a new battery for the automobile (debit Automobile Expense).
24   Billed customers $1,310 for welding services:

Hamilton Industries	$500
James, Inc.	400
Jordan Company	410

25   Paid $45 for cleaning the shop.
25   Received $750 in cash for welding services.
26   Purchased additional shop supplies on account:

Phillips Supply House	$200
Saunders Supply Company	420

27   Paid $90 for electric service.
29   Received $970 on account from the following customers:

Hamilton Industries	$350
James, Inc.	250
Jordan Company	370

30   Paid $47 for gas, oil, and other automobile expenses for two weeks.
30   Purchased shop equipment costing $3,000 and paid this amount to Goode Equipment Company.
30   Received $660 from customers for welding work not previously billed.
30   Paid $330 in cash for advertising space in a local magazine.
31   Received a promissory note from Hamilton Industries for the balance due on its account.
31   Paid a $400 premium on a one-year comprehensive insurance policy, effective August 1, 1987.
31   Purchased an automobile for $12,000 from Ray Motor Company, paying $4,000 in cash and giving a 90-day note for the balance.

Required:

1. Open the following accounts in the general ledger: Cash, 101; Accounts Receivable, 111; Notes Receivable, 115; Shop Supplies, 136; Prepaid Insurance, 140; Automobile, 162; Shop Equipment, 166; Accounts Payable, 201; Notes Payable, 204; Common Stock, 301; Dividends, 303; Welding Revenue, 401; Advertising Expense, 501; Rent Expense—Shop, 503; Rent Expense—Shop Equipment, 504; Rent Expense—Automobiles, 505; Heat and Light Expense, 506; Telephone and Telegraph Expense, 509; Automobile Expense, 510; Miscellaneous General Expense, 512.
2. Open customers' accounts in the accounts receivable subsidiary ledger.
3. Open creditors' accounts in the accounts payable subsidiary ledger.
4. Journalize all the transactions in the general journal, including the issuance of common stock.

5. Post to the appropriate ledgers.
6. Prepare a trial balance.
7. Prepare a schedule of accounts receivable.
8. Prepare a schedule of accounts payable.

P3–5B
End-of-period statements prepared from trial balance data and earning power measurements

The trial balance of the Champion Company on December 31, 1987, follows:

THE CHAMPION COMPANY
Trial Balance
December 31, 1987

Acct. No.	Account Title	Debits	Credits
101	Cash	$110,000	
111	Accounts Receivable	23,280	
121	Supplies	5,976	
131	Equipment	76,400	
201	Accounts Payable		$ 23,280
301	Common Stock (10,000 shares)		100,000
302	Retained Earnings, January 1, 1987		69,302
311	Dividends	6,640	
401	Commissions Earned		49,800
411	Rent Earned		16,600
501	Salaries Expense	22,244	
502	Advertising Expense	3,320	
503	Supplies Expense	5,312	
504	Miscellaneous Expense	5,810	
	Totals	$258,982	$258,982

Required:

1. Prepare an income statement for 1987.
2. Assume that the total assets and stockholders' equity on January 1, 1987, were $205,400 and $169,302, respectively, and that the market price of the common stock as of December 31, 1987, was $24.25. Calculate the price-earnings ratio, rate of return on total investment, and rate of return on stockholders' equity.
3. Write a brief report to management evaluating these earnings power measurements.

P3–6B
Thought-provoking problem: measuring accounting elements not stated in money[9]

Once upon a time many, many years ago, there lived a feudal landlord in a small province of Central Europe. The landlord, called the Red-Bearded Baron, lived in a castle high on a hill, and this benevolent fellow was responsible for the well-being of many peasants who occupied the lands surrounding his castle. Each spring, as the snow began to melt and thoughts of other, less influential men turned to matters other than business, the Baron would decide how to provide for all his serf-dependents during the coming year.

One spring, the Baron was thinking about the wheat crop of the coming growing season. "I believe that 30 acres of my land, being worth 5 bushels of wheat per acre, will produce enough wheat for next winter," he mused, "but who should do the farming? I believe I'll give Ivan the Indefatigable and Igor the Immutable the task of growing the wheat." Whereupon Ivan and Igor, two gentry noted for their hard work and not overly active minds, were summoned for an audience with the landlord.

---

[9] This problem was written by Professor W. T. Andrews, Jr., of Florida Atlantic University, and was published in *The Accounting Review,* April 1974, under the title of "Another Improbable Occurrence." It is used by permission of the author and of the editor of *The Accounting Review.*

"Ivan, you will farm on the 20-acre plot of ground and Igor will farm the 10-acre plot," the Baron began. "I will give Ivan 20 bushels of wheat for seed and 20 pounds of fertilizer. (Twenty pounds of fertilizer are worth 2 bushels of wheat.) Igor will get 10 bushels of wheat for seed and 10 pounds of fertilizer. I will give each of you an ox to pull a plow but you will have to make arrangements with Feyador, the Plowmaker, for a plow. The oxen, incidentally, are only three years old and have never been used for farming, so they should have a good 10 years of farming ahead of them. Take good care of them, because an ox is worth 40 bushels of wheat. Come back next fall and return the oxen and the plows along with your harvest."

Ivan and Igor genuflected and withdrew from the Great Hall, taking with them the things provided by the Baron.

The summer came and went, and after the harvest Ivan and Igor returned to the Great Hall to account to their master for the things given them in the spring. Ivan, pouring 223 bushels of wheat onto the floor, said, "My Lord, I present you with a slightly used ox, a plow broken beyond repair, and 223 bushels of wheat. I, unfortunately, owe Feyador, the Plowmaker, 3 bushels of wheat for the plow I got from him last fall. And, as you might expect, I used all the fertilizer and seed you gave me last spring. You will also remember, my Lord, that you took 20 bushels of my harvest for your own personal use."

Igor, who had been given 10 acres of land, 10 bushels of wheat, and 10 pounds of fertilizer, spoke next. "Here, my Lord, is a partially used ox, the plow for which I gave Feyador, the Plowmaker, 3 bushels of wheat from my harvest, and 105 bushels of wheat. I, too, used all my seed and fertilizer last spring. Also, my Lord, you took 30 bushels of wheat several days ago for your own table. I believe the plow is good for two more seasons."

"Knaves, you did well," said the Red-Bearded Baron. Blessed with this benediction and not wishing to press their luck further, the two serfs departed hastily.

After the servants had taken their leave, the Red-Bearded Baron, watching the two hungry oxen slowly eating the wheat piled on the floor, began to contemplate what had happened. "Yes," he thought, "they did well, but I wonder which one did better?"

Required: Assume that the Red-Bearded Baron was willing to give the peasant who achieved the greater gain a bonus of 1 bushel of wheat. Which peasant would receive the bonus? Support your answer with carefully identified calculations.

4 End-of-Period Process without a Work Sheet

Introduction

Chapter 3 started the Data Equipment Repair Shop example involving a simple service company with transactions. Chapter 4 completes this illustration after first taking another broad look at the accounting system. Emphasized in the remainder of the Data Equipment Repair Shop example are closing entries, postclosing trial balance, and the ledger after closing. How to obtain a more accurate net income or loss figure is presented in another illustration, the Electronic Consulting Service. This complex illustration expands the concept of adjustments by introducing five different types of adjustments that are recorded at the end of the accounting period. The remaining steps in the end-of-period process—emphasizing the work sheet—for this company are then completed in Chapter 5. Also discussed in Chapter 4 are an alternative approach to the accounting for deferrals and the use of reversing entries to facilitate the subsequent accounting for certain adjustments for deferrals and accruals.

Learning Goals

1. To be able to explain the nature of an extended simple accounting system.

2. To understand the closing process and to journalize closing entries in the general journal, post these to the general ledger accounts, and rule the closed accounts.

3. To be able to state the interrelationship between financial statements.

4. To be able to compare the accrual basis of accounting with the cash basis of accounting.

5. To understand the need for adjusting entries and the specific point in the accounting cycle at which adjusting entries are made.

6. To be able to classify adjustments into two broad groups—accruals and deferrals.

7. To be able to explain the reasons for the different types of adjusting entries.

8. To prepare and journalize five types of adjusting entries for a corporation.

9. To explain how reversing entries could be used in the accounting cycle and when they are advantageous.

The Accounting System—Another Look

The Data Equipment Repair Shop example illustrates the basic steps in the accounting cycle.[1] Before returning to this example, let us take another look at the overall accounting system being developed. It is important to always have an overview in mind and not to get bogged down with the mechanics of any individual step. The way the various parts are related to each other is graphically presented in Figure 4–1.

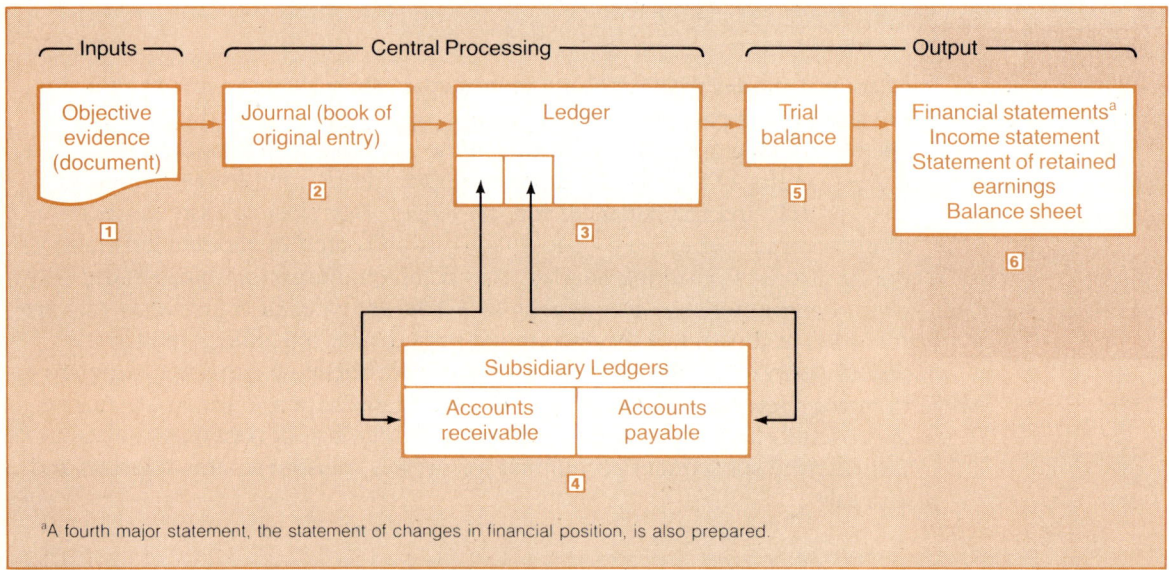

ᵃA fourth major statement, the statement of changes in financial position, is also prepared.

Figure 4–1   **The Accounting System**

Explanations for numbered items follow:

[1] Every entry in an accounting system must be justified by objective evidence, usually a document such as a receipt for payment of cash. These business documents are referred to as inputs into the accounting system because

---

[1]The work sheet step is reserved for Chapter 5.

they are the method by which data are introduced into the accounting system.

[2] All transactions are analyzed and recorded first in a journal, a book of original entry. The journalizing and posting process is referred to as central processing.

[3] All journal entries must be posted to the ledger. Absolutely no transaction entries can be made in a ledger except those posted from a journal. There is no other source for ledger entries.

[4] Various subsidiary ledgers—represented here by accounts receivable and accounts payable ledgers—are used to present a detailed breakdown of a single account in the general ledger, referred to as a controlling account.

[5] As a test check of the equality of debits and credits, a trial balance is taken.

[6] The final output of central processing is the financial statements prepared from the information taken from the ledgers.

The Data Equipment Repair Shop Example—Remaining End-of-Period Steps

Returning to the Data Equipment Repair Shop example started in Chapter 3, let us now complete the end-of-period process. The one adjusting entry recognizing the use of repair parts has been journalized and posted. A trial balance has been taken—this trial balance was an adjusted trial balance (prepared after the adjusting entry was made). End-of-period financial statements have been prepared. Now it is time to empty, or close, the temporary accounts.

Closing and Ruling the Revenue, Expense, and Dividend Accounts

Revenue, expense, and dividend accounts are used to measure changes that take place in the Retained Earnings account. At the end of an accounting period, these temporary or *nominal accounts* are closed (balances are reduced to zero) so that they may be used to accumulate changes for the Retained Earnings account for the next period. Therefore, closing entries are made to transfer the final effects of the temporary stockholders' equity accounts to the Retained Earnings account—a permanent or *real account*.

Nominal accounts

The revenue, expense, and dividends accounts are closed at the end of a specified period. For this reason, these accounts are often called temporary Retained Earnings accounts, or **nominal accounts**.

Real accounts

The term **real accounts** *is applied to the accounts that appear in the balance sheet; these accounts are not closed at the end of a period. They carry amounts forward from one period to the next.*

The Closing Procedure

To simplify the transfer of revenue and expense account balances, a *clearing and summary account* called Income Summary is used. The balances of all revenue and expense accounts are transferred to the Income Summary account, the balance of which reveals the net income or loss for the period; it is then closed by transferring its balance to the Retained Earnings account, a part of the stockholders' equity. This action, termed **closing the books**, is justified because net income or net loss accrues to the stockholders. Since the Dividends account is not an expense account, it is not closed to Income Summary; rather, it is closed directly to Retained Earnings. After the revenue and expense accounts are closed, they are ruled to indicate that they have zero balances and that they are now available to accumulate information for measuring the changes in retained earnings in the next accounting period. The closing procedure is diagrammed in Figure 4–2.

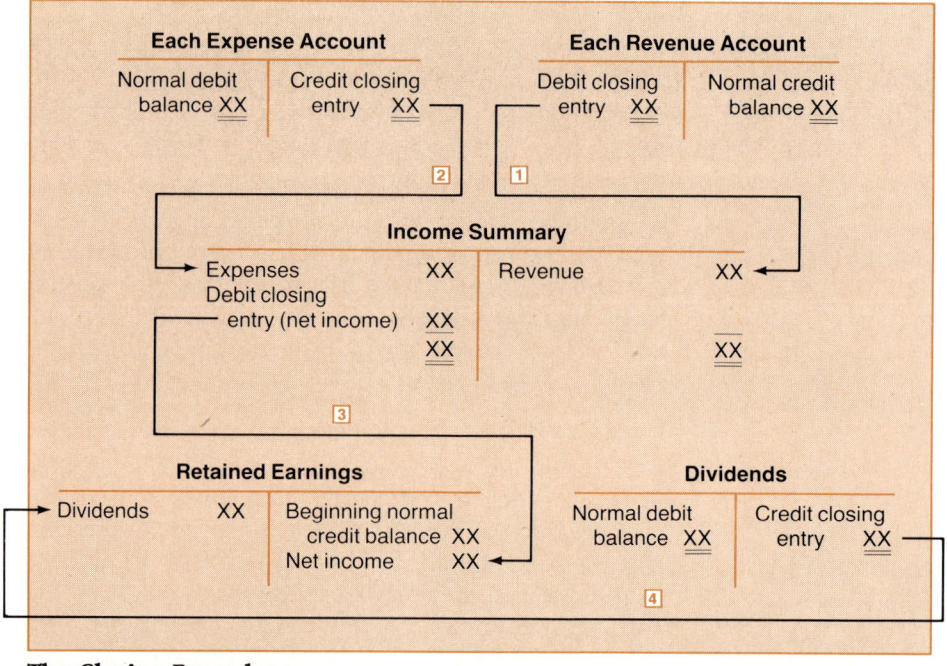

Figure 4–2   **The Closing Procedure**

To identify the particular type of events, the caption Closing Entries may be written in the middle of the first unused line in the general journal under the adjusting entries. Then the **closing entries** are begun directly under that. They are posted immediately to the general ledger and are made in the following sequence, as shown in Figure 4–2:

1 Each revenue account is debited in one compound entry, and the sum of the revenue items is credited to the Income Summary account.

[2] Each expense account is credited in a second compound entry, and the sum of the expense items is debited to the Income Summary account.

[3] After entries 1 and 2 are posted, a credit balance in the Income Summary account represents net income; a debit balance, net loss. The balance of the account is transferred to the Retained Earnings account.

[4] The Dividends account is closed directly to the Retained Earnings account by a debit to Retained Earnings and a credit to Dividends.

The closing process is a simple but very important phase of accounting. In summary, it involves shifting and summarizing previously determined amounts. The closing journal entries of the Data Equipment Repair Shop on January 31, 1987, are shown in Figure 4–3 and are identified by the numbered steps in Figure 4–2. The presence of account numbers in the folio column of the journal indicates that the closing journal entries have been posted to the ledger accounts indicated in the folio column.

GENERAL JOURNAL — Page 4

Closing Entries

Date		Description	Folio	Debit	Credit
1987 Jan.	31	[1]ª Shop Repair Revenue	401	5,020	
		Income Summary	601		5,020
		To close revenue to summary account.			
	31	[2] Income Summary	601	2,435	
		Rent Expense—Shop Building	501		300
		Rent Expense—Tools and Equipment	502		80
		Salaries Expense	504		1,700
		Electricity and Water Expense	508		80
		Repair Parts and Supplies Expense	509		275
		To close expenses to summary account.			
	31	[3] Income Summary	601	2,585	
		Retained Earnings	311		2,585
		To transfer net income to retained earnings.			
	31	[4] Retained Earnings	311	300	
		Dividends	321		300
		To close dividends to retained earnings.			

ªThese boxed numbers do not actually appear in the journal. They are shown here to emphasize the four-step closing sequence.

Figure 4–3   **Closing Entries, Data Equipment Repair Shop**

Ruling the Closed Nominal Accounts

After the closing entries have been posted, the temporary stockholders' equity accounts consist of equal debit and credit totals; that is, they have zero balances. These nominal accounts are then ruled to show that they are emptied or closed. This procedure is the same for all the nominal accounts. It is illustrated only for the Shop Repair Revenue account. After the closing entry is posted to Shop Repair Revenue, it will be ruled as indicated below. The double rule shows that the account is closed and clearly separates the information of the current period from that of the next period.

				Shop Repair Revenue						Acct. No. 401
1987					1987					
Jan.	31	Closing entry	4	5,020	Jan.	12			1	40
						26			2	180
						31			2	4,800
				5,020[a]						5,020

[a] With the debit and credit sides being equal, the balance is zero.

The other remaining nominal accounts would be accounted for in a similar manner. With zero balances, they are now ready to receive entries to record business events in February.

Real Accounts after Closing

After the closing entries have been posted, the only real account that is affected is Retained Earnings. This account as updated is shown in Figure 4–4. Net income is reflected in this account by a credit entry of $2,585. Also, the Dividends account has been closed directly to Retained Earnings and is reflected as a decrease in Retained Earnings of $300. The ending balance of Retained Earnings ($2,285) must appear on *both* the statement of retained earnings and the balance sheet.

				Retained Earnings						Acct. No. 311
1987					1987					
Jan.	31	Dividends[a]	4	300	Jan.	31	Net income[a]		4	2,585
	31	Balance	√	2,285						
				2,585						2,585
					1987					
					Jan.	31	Balance		√	2,285

[a] These explanations are not required to be placed in the account; they are shown here for teaching purposes.

Figure 4–4 **Updated Retained Earnings Account, Data Equipment Repair Shop**

When the T form of account is used, it is not unusual to rule the real accounts and to bring down the balance as indicated by the ruling of Retained Earnings in Figure 4–4. A similar process would be carried out for the remaining real accounts that have more than one entry.

Taking a Postclosing Trial Balance

After the closing entries have been posted and the accounts are ruled and balanced, a **postclosing trial balance** is taken from the general ledger. Since the only accounts with open balances are the real accounts, the accounts and amounts in the postclosing trial balance are the same as those in the balance sheet. This procedure tests the debit and credit equality of the general ledger before the accounts receive postings of the next accounting period. It is absolutely essential to start a new period with the accounts in proper balance. Failure to take a postclosing trial balance could carry over errors into a new period. These prior-period errors would be difficult to trace because the accountant would likely look for them in the current period entries.

The postclosing trial balance of the Data Equipment Repair Shop (shown in Figure 4–5) is taken from the real accounts in Figure 3–17 (page 120) and the updated Retained Earnings account shown in Figure 4–4.

Figure 4–5 Postclosing Trial Balance, Data Equipment Repair Shop

DATA EQUIPMENT REPAIR SHOP
Postclosing Trial Balance
January 31, 1987

Acct. No.	Account Title	Debits	Credits
101	Cash	$23,450	
121	Accounts Receivable	210	
131	Repair Parts and Supplies	375	
141	Prepaid Insurance	600	
151	Land	10,000	
161	Tools and Equipment	4,000	
201	Accounts Payable		$ 350
202	Notes Payable		6,000
301	Common Stock		30,000
311	Retained Earnings		2,285
	Totals	$38,635	$38,635

Statement of Retained Earnings with Beginning Balance

In the example given in Figure 3–21, the statement of retained earnings of the Data Equipment Repair Shop had a zero beginning balance in Retained Earnings. Suppose this company had the following for February 1987:

Net income	$5,000
Dividends	1,000

Then its statement of retained earnings for February 1987 would appear as presented in Figure 4–6.

Figure 4–6
Statement of Retained Earnings for Second Month of Operations, Data Equipment Repair Shop

DATA EQUIPMENT REPAIR SHOP Statement of Retained Earnings For the Month Ended February 28, 1987	Exhibit B
Retained earnings, February 1, 1987	$2,285
Add: Net income for February	5,000
Subtotal	$7,285
Deduct: Dividends	1,000
Retained earnings, February 28, 1987	$6,285

The basic steps in the accounting sequence are essentially the same for all forms of business organizations. Differences appear in accounting for the initial investment by owners and in the closing process. These differences are illustrated in Chapter 12, when accounting for single proprietorships and partnerships is discussed.

Interrelationship of the Financial Statements

Chapter 1 presents a general overview of the way financial statements relate to each other. Abbreviated end-of-February statements now are used to demonstrate the interrelationship between the January and February statements for Data Equipment Repair Shop. In addition to the statement of retained earnings in Figure 4–6, assume the condensed data as presented in Figure 4–7. With these data and the January statements, the interrelationship is shown in Figure 4–8.

Figure 4–7
February Summary Statements for Data Equipment Repair Shop

DATA EQUIPMENT REPAIR SHOP
Balance Sheet Data[a]
February 28, 1987

Total assets		$48,635
Total liabilities		$12,350
Stockholders' equity:		
Common stock	$30,000	
Retained earnings	6,285	
Total stockholders' equity		36,285
Total liabilities and stockholders' equity		$48,635

DATA EQUIPMENT REPAIR SHOP
Income Statement Data[a]
For the Month Ended February 28, 1987

Revenues (totals)	$9,420
Expenses (totals)	4,420
Net income	$5,000

[a]Summary totals are given. This procedure is not acceptable for solving end-of-chapter material.

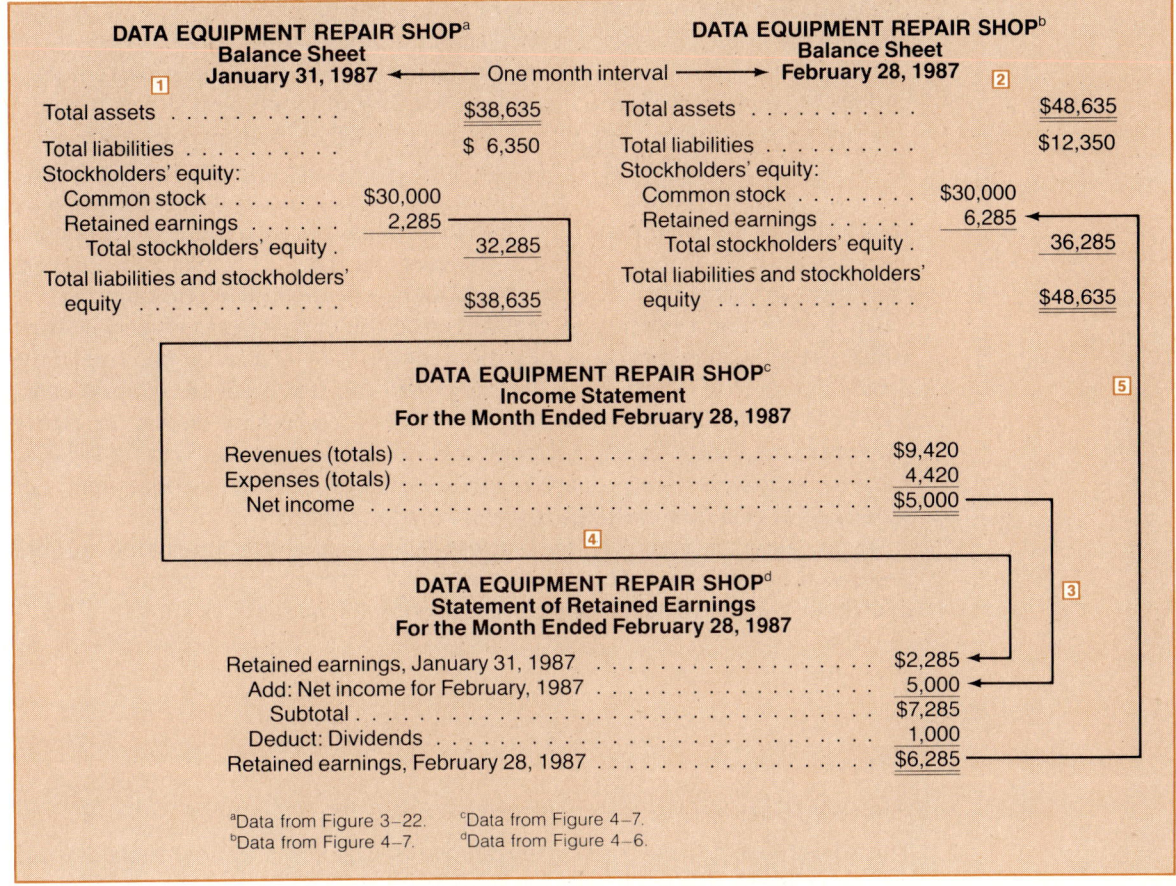

Figure 4–8   **The Interrelationship of Financial Statements**

The explanation of the boxed figures in Figure 4–8 follows:

[1] The information on the January 31, 1987, balance sheet becomes the beginning amounts for February. Therefore, the date of the first balance sheet is also the beginning date of the income statement and the statement of retained earnings. (*For the Month Ended February 28, 1987,* means the period beginning immediately after January 31.)

[2] The date of the second balance sheet (February 28, 1987) is also the ending date of the statement of retained earnings and the income statement.

[3] The net income for February ($5,000) is transferred from the income statement to the statement of retained earnings.

[4] The retained earnings balance in the first balance sheet ($2,285) is the same as the beginning amount in the statement of retained earnings.

[5] The end-of-period retained earnings balance ($6,285) is transferred from the statement of retained earnings to the balance sheet dated February 28, 1987.

Figure 4–8 shows a comparison of statements prepared at the end of January with those for February for the Data Equipment Repair Shop. There is a significant interrelationship among the balance sheet, the income statement, and the statement of retained earnings. The income statement shows the net amount remaining after revenues have been matched with expenses for a given period. This amount, the net income, shows the change that has taken place in retained earnings as a result of the operations for the period. It is transferred to the statement of retained earnings. The statement of retained earnings must also show additional changes that have taken place in retained earnings—in this particular case, the dividend payment. The end-of-period balance of retained earnings is transferred to the end-of-period balance sheet, which presents information as of a moment of time—that is, at the end of the accounting period. The income statement and the statement of retained earnings help to explain the changes in the stockholders' equity during the interval between balance sheets. Although it is not absolutely necessary, it is helpful if the statements are prepared in this sequence: (1) income statement, (2) statement of retained earnings, and (3) balance sheet.

Again, summary totals are used in the figure so that the illustration can be presented on one page. This procedure is not acceptable for solving the end-of-chapter materials; details should be given on all statements shown in Figure 4–8.

More about Adjustments: Accruals and Deferrals

The adjustment process, briefly introduced in Chapter 3, is now looked at in more detail.

The Accounting Bases

Two accounting bases are used in practice: (1) the accrual basis and (2) the cash basis. Generally accepted accounting principles typically require the use of the accrual basis; it is the only basis that is emphasized in this book. A concept, however, often can be better understood when it is compared with its opposite. Therefore, a beginning look at the cash basis should provide a means of better grasping the meaning of the accrual basis.

Cash Basis of Accounting

Under the **cash basis of accounting**, revenue is recognized and recorded only when the cash is received. Expenses are recognized in the period when payment is made. Recording of revenues and expenses during an accounting period is based on an inflow and outflow of cash. A matching of cash receipts and cash disbursements is done to determine operating results during the period. This method is simple in application but in most cases does not produce information that permits an acceptable measurement of net income. For example, it does not recognize revenues earned but uncollected as being earned and does not recognize expenses incurred but unpaid. Hence, it matches only some revenues and expenses for a given period. From a theoretical viewpoint, an *expense is incurred* when the effort is expended (the asset status is lost) in attempting to create revenue. **Earned Revenue** *is said to be earned* in a given period when the service has been performed or the product delivered (the necessary efforts, except cash collection, are made to bring the revenue into being).

There are instances, particularly in small businesses, in which the cash basis of accounting is used with acceptable results. For example, if a firm has no receivables and no payables, it can use the cash basis of accounting and still get an adequate matching of expired costs (expenses) against earned revenue of a given period. Mixed systems—combinations of the cash basis and the accrual basis (often referred to as the modified cash basis)—are found in practice, but in many of these cases an independent accountant is engaged to convert the end-of-year financial reports to an accrual basis.

Accrual Basis of Accounting

The **accrual basis of accounting** is based on the principle that all revenue earned during a period and all the related incurred expenses of earning that revenue assignable to the period must be determined. These then are matched against each other to determine net income or net loss. Revenues are recognized at the time of sale of the services or merchandise, and expenses are usually recognized at the time the services are received and used in the production of revenue. This is the concept, discussed earlier, of matching revenue and expenses for a given period.

Matching revenues and expenses

The central goal of the accrual basis of accounting is to achieve a better **matching** *of the earned revenue of a period with the incurred expenses of that period, regardless of when, whether, or how much cash has been received or paid.*

Comparison of Cash and Accrual Bases of Accounting

The cash and accrual bases may produce different net income figures, as the following example will show. The Mount Pilot Company, which does landscape gardening, performed work during August for which it charged $1,000. It received $600 on August 15 and $400 on September 11. Wages of $550 (the only expense) were paid on August 31. No work was performed during September.

	Cash Basis		Accrual Basis	
	August	September	August	September
Revenue	$600	$400	$1,000	$0
Expense	550	0	550	0
Net income	$ 50	$400	$ 450	$0

The accrual basis of accounting presents a more useful picture of operating results because revenue is reflected in the period to which it properly belongs—the period in which it was earned. Net income is the difference between revenue earned and expenses incurred during the accounting period. The accrual method, by matching expenses incurred with revenue earned for the period, presents the better measurement of net income. Since it results in more useful financial statements, most businesses keep their books on the accrual basis.

During the accounting period, regular business transactions are recorded as they occur. At the end of a period, the accountant will find the ledger accounts incomplete; some new accounts must be brought onto the books, and others must be brought up to date. This is called the adjustment process, and the journal entries necessary to accomplish it are referred to as adjusting entries. This process is required if the financial statements are to reflect the company's position realistically—its assets and equities—as of the end of the period and the results of its operations—revenue earned and expenses incurred—during the period.

Adjusting Entries

At the end of each period, the accountant must make **adjusting entries** to bring the accounts up to date. This process identifies and records revenues that have been earned and expenses that have been incurred but not yet recorded (accruals) because certain business transactions have not yet been completed or are continuous over two or more periods. The adjustment process must also update previously recorded assets, liabilities, revenues, and expenses (deferrals). Income for the period can be measured accurately only if the effects of these transactions are recorded in the accounts. In addition the financial position at this given point in time is more accurately stated.

Adjustment Classification

It is impractical and sometimes impossible to record the day-to-day changes in certain accounts. For example, when the premium payment is made on an insurance policy, the asset account, Prepaid Insurance, is usually debited. At the end of the accounting period, however, only part of the balance of the Prepaid Insurance account represents an asset. The amount that has expired with the passage of time is an expense representing the cost of insurance protection received. At the end of the accounting period, therefore, Prepaid Insurance contains both an asset and an expense element. A **short-term cost apportionment adjustment** is necessary to record the correct amount of Insurance Expense and to reduce Prepaid Insurance. A similar situation exists with revenue received in advance—a **short-term revenue apportionment**; for example, rent may be collected a year in advance. As used here as well as in other adjustments, **apportionment** simply means dividing among two or more periods a cost or revenue that has already been paid or received (and recorded). Both of these apportionments are called **deferrals** because the recognition of expense or revenue has been postponed. Such apportionment could be either short-term or long-term.

Another type of adjusting entry may be required to record an **accrual**—for both expenses and revenue—(previously unrecorded data). Assume, for example, that a company paid wages on March 28 for the two-week period that ended on that date. However, the employees worked on March 29, 30, and 31. If March 31 is the end of the accounting period, recognition must be given to this unrecorded but incurred wages expense as well as to the corresponding increase in the liability. In addition, a corporation has to pay an income tax on its net income. The accrual basis of accounting would dictate that the income tax expense—a special application of an accrued expense adjustment—be recorded on the books of the corporation in an adjusting-type entry. An **accrued expense** *adjustment* is needed so that the financial statements may show the liability and the proper assignment of the expense to the period. In a similar manner, an **accrued revenue** *adjustment* is needed to record such items as unrecorded interest that has been earned but is not yet due to be collected. In this context the term **accrued** means accumulated, built up, or grown.

Adjusting entries have a different goal than entries that record regular business transactions. Regular business transactions start and complete their cycles within an accounting period. Adjusting entries deal with continuous transactions. The adjusting entry for wages, for example, records a change that has been occurring daily—the increase in a liability incurred—but is unrecorded. The adjusting entry for insurance expense, on the other hand, recognizes the amount of day-to-day expiration of an item that was recorded in an asset account at the time of acquisition. Both items, whether originally recorded or not, undergo continuous change. Accounts must be updated to reflect that change any time financial statements are to be prepared.[2] Three types of deferrals (short-term cost apportionments, short-term revenue apportionments, and long-term cost apportionments) and two types of accruals (accrued revenue and accrued expenses) are discussed and illustrated in the next section of this chapter.

An Accounting Illustration— The Electronics Consulting Service

The adjusting process is illustrated through an example for the Electronics Consulting Service. The Electronics Consulting Service was incorporated with 2,500 shares of stock issued; and it started operations on June 1, 1987. It plans to close its books at the end of each month. The transactions for June 1987 *have been recorded and posted*. The preclosing trial balance has been prepared and is shown in Figure 4–9. This approach is different from the Chapter 3 illustration. For this more complex situation, a trial balance should be taken *before* adjusting entries are prepared and posted. By so doing the

---

[2]An adjustment not discussed here is *bad debts expense*. It is covered in Chapter 9.

accountant can test the accuracy of debits and credits up to this point. Then if errors are detected later, the accountant likely will *not* have to review the journalizing and posting of the regular transactions to find the error.

ELECTRONICS CONSULTING SERVICE
Trial Balance
June 30, 1987

Acct. No.[a]	Account Title[a]	Debits	Credits
101	Cash	$ 5,250	
111	Accounts Receivable	550	
112	Notes Receivable	1,440	
131	Office Supplies	230	
141	Prepaid Insurance	2,160	
142	Prepaid Rent	1,500	
201	Office Equipment	1,400	
211	Automobiles	26,000	
301	Accounts Payable		$ 200
302	Notes Payable		8,000
321	Unearned Rent		600
401	Common Stock (2,500 shares)		25,000
404	Dividends	500	
501	Consulting Revenue		7,465
601	Heat and Light Expense	40	
602	Maintenance and Repairs Expense	375	
603	Telephone and Telegraph Expense	95	
604	Gas and Oil Expense	525	
605	Wages Expense	1,200	
	Totals	$41,265	$41,265

[a]Account number 403, Retained Earnings, is not listed here because it still has a zero balance.

Figure 4–9   **Trial Balance for Electronics Consulting Service**

Other information required for adjustments is as follows:

a. Rent in the amount of $1,500 was prepaid for three months on June 1.

b. Insurance premium of $2,160 for a comprehensive three-year insurance policy was prepaid on June 1.

c. By physical count, the June 30, 1987, inventory of office supplies was determined to be $60.

d. The company rented out one of its automobiles for off-hours use and collected rent of $600 in advance for six months starting June 1.

e. The office equipment purchased on June 1, 1987, has an estimated life of 10 years and a salvage value of $200 at the end of that period; this is to be depreciated by the straight line method.

f. The two automobiles purchased on June 1, 1987, have an estimated life of five years, and each has a salvage value of $1,000 at the end of that period; they are to be depreciated by the straight line method.

g. The company received a $1,440, 15 percent, 30-day note on June 10.

h. Wages of $150 for June 28, 29, and 30 have not been paid or recorded.

i. The company borrowed money from a bank on June 12 and issued a 45-day, 16 percent note for $8,000.

j. The estimated income tax for June is $1,900.

Using the data in Figure 4–9 and the added information in items a through j, the end-of-period adjusting process can now be illustrated in Chapter 4. The remaining end-of-period process is discussed in Chapter 5. At various spots, new data for use in the process are presented or assumed.

Short-Term Cost Apportionments— A Type of Deferral

At the *end of the period,* certain accounts contain mixtures of asset and expense elements. In the Electronics Consulting Service example, there are three such accounts that require short-term cost apportionment adjustments. The accountant follows three steps in adjusting the accounts involving a short-term cost apportionment between asset and expense elements:[3]

1. Determine the balance of each account to be adjusted.
2. Determine the amount of the asset and expense elements in each account.
3. Record the adjusting entries to bring the accounts into agreement with the amounts determined in step 2.

Adjustment of Prepaid Rent

On June 1, the Electronics Consulting Service paid $1,500 in cash for *three months' rent.*

Step 1. The general ledger shows the following balance in the account:

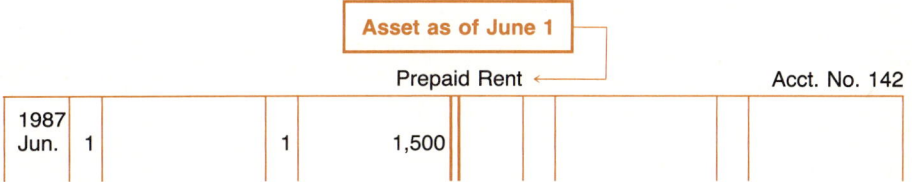

The information in the foregoing ledger account (and other similar illustrations in this chapter) is reproduced from the original ledger and includes folio references for the original data. Note that the Prepaid Rent account is definitely an asset as of June 1.

---

[3]Each of the three costs to be illustrated was originally recorded as an asset. If originally recorded as an expense, the adjustment would be different (see "Alternative Adjustment Methods for Deferrals" later in this chapter).

Step 2. The amount of expense applicable to June is $500 = (\$1,500 \div 3$ months). By June 30, therefore, Prepaid Rent before adjustment has become a mixed account consisting of an expense element of $500 and an asset element of $1,000. The $500 expense element relates to the rent cost which has expired in June. The $1,000 asset element relates to the rent cost that will benefit July and August. (Since the nature of accounts used in short-term apportionments adjustment changes, the time when it has the specific characteristic is indicated in the appropriate box.)

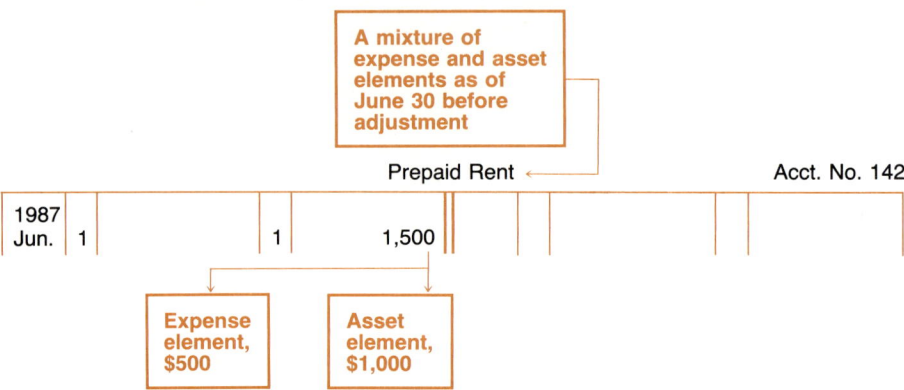

Step 3. For teaching purposes the adjusting entries for the Electronics Consulting Service are made and posted as each adjustment is explained. The timing of journalizing the adjustments is optional; it may be delayed until the formal financial statements have been prepared from the work sheet discussed later in Chapter 5. The required adjusting entry is shown below with the folio references indicating that posting has been done.

GENERAL JOURNAL Page 4

1987				
Jun.	30	Rent Expense 606	500	
		Prepaid Rent 142		500
		To record rent expense for June.		

By crediting the asset account for $500, the expense element is removed from the asset account; debiting the expense account inserts the $500 into Rent Expense. This is shown by the following posting in the ledger accounts:

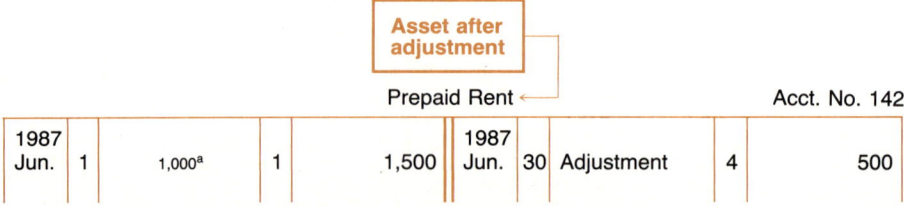

[a]The 1,000 figure is the balance of the Prepaid Rent account after adjustment.

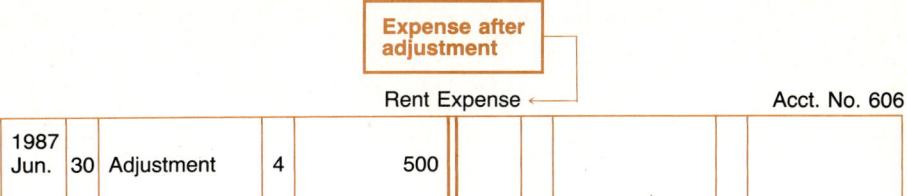

Prepaid rent ($1,000) is classified in the balance sheet as a current asset, and rent expense ($500) appears in the income statement as an expense.

Adjustment of Prepaid Insurance

The Electronics Consulting Service paid a premium of $2,160 for a comprehensive three-year insurance policy, effective June 1.

Step 1. Prepaid Insurance, before adjustment, shows a balance of $2,160. The title Prepaid Insurance identifies that the account is an asset account, but on June 30, 1987, it is in fact a mixture of an asset and an expense element.

Step 2. By computation we can determine that the expense element for the month of June is $60 = ($2,160 ÷ 36 months) and that the unused portion of $2,100 is the asset prepayment benefiting future periods.

Step 3. The following adjusting entry is made:

		GENERAL JOURNAL			Page 4
1987 Jun.	30	Insurance Expense . . . . Prepaid Insurance. . . . . To record insurance expense for June.	607 141	60	60

The information is shown in the following ledger accounts after posting:

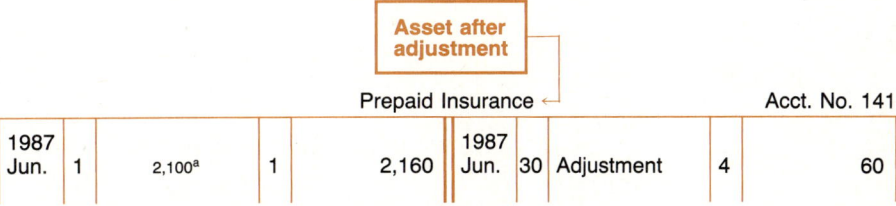

^aThe 2,100 figure is the balance of the Prepaid Insurance account after adjustment.

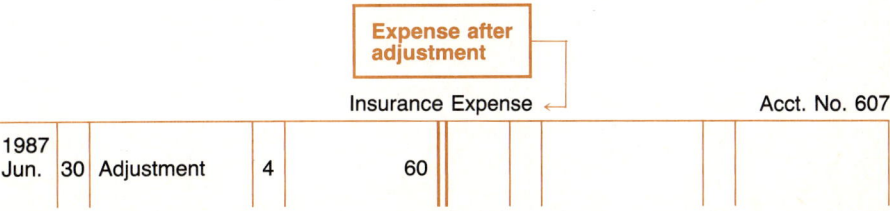

Prepaid insurance ($2,100) is typically classified in the balance sheet as a current asset, although in this case part of it technically could be disclosed in some noncurrent asset caption of the balance sheet since the remaining life of the policy is two years and eleven months. The classification of the item as a current asset is justified on the basis that the average life of the several business insurance policies a business would normally own would be one year or less. Insurance expense ($60) appears in the income statement as an expense.

Adjustment of Office Supplies

Step 1. On the trial balance (Figure 4–9), Office Supplies has a debit balance of $230, representing a purchase made on June 6. Again, the title, Office Supplies, indicates that the account is an asset; but on June 30, 1987, it contains a mixture of asset and expense elements because some of the supplies have been used.

Step 2. An inventory (a physical count) taken on June 30 showed $60 worth of unused supplies; therefore, the expense element is $170 = ($230 − $60) of supplies used.

Step 3. The expense of $170 is removed from the mixed account by the following adjusting entry, and the adjustment information is posted to the accounts shown below the journal entry:

		GENERAL JOURNAL			Page 4
1987 Jun.	30	Office Supplies Expense . . . . Office Supplies . . . . To record supplies used during June.	608 131	170	170

Asset after adjustment

Office Supplies   Acct. No. 131

| 1987 Jun. | 6 | 60[a] | 1 | 230 | 1987 Jun. | 30 | Adjustment | 4 | 170 |

[a] The 60 figure is the balance of the Office Supplies account after adjustment.

Expense after adjustment

Office Supplies Expense   Acct. No. 608

| 1987 Jun. | 30 | Adjustment | 4 | 170 |

Office supplies ($60 balance after adjustment) is classified in the balance sheet as a current asset, and office supplies expense ($170) appears in the income statement as an expense.

Short-Term Revenue Apportionment—A Second Type of Deferral

At the end of the period, some accounts contain mixtures of liability and revenue elements. The same three steps are followed in making short-term revenue apportionments of amounts originally recorded in liability accounts.[4] Applicable to short-term revenue apportionment, these steps are:

1. Determine the balance of each account to be adjusted.

2. Determine the amount of the liability and revenue elements in each account.

3. Record the adjusting entries to bring the accounts into agreement with the amounts determined in step 2.

Adjustment of Unearned Rent

The Electronics Consulting Service had only one short-term revenue adjustment. On June 1, the company signed a contract for the use of one of its automobiles on a part-time basis and received an advance payment of $600 for *six months' rent*. At that time, Cash was debited and a liability account, Unearned Rent, was credited for $600. By June 30, 1987, the Unearned Rent account represents a mixture of liability and revenue elements. Therefore, on June 30, the portion earned in the month of June must be transferred from the liability account Unearned Rent to the revenue account Rent Earned. The unearned portion must remain in Unearned Rent as a liability because the Electronics Consulting Service must provide the use of its automobile on a part-time basis for another five months.

Step 1. The amount of the unearned rent liability as of June 1, 1987, in the ledger account is shown below:

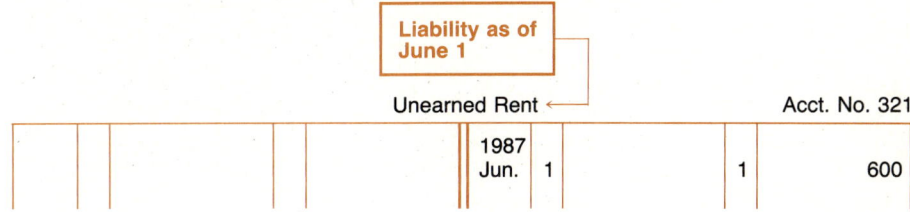

Note that the Unearned Rent account is definitely a liability as of June 1.

---

[4]Again, the reader is referred to the section found later in this chapter, "Alternative Adjustment Methods for Deferrals." The way a deferral adjustment is made depends on how the original entry was recorded.

Step 2. The rent actually earned in June is $100 = (\$600 \div 6$ months); therefore, by June 30 the Unearned Rent account consists of revenue and liability elements.

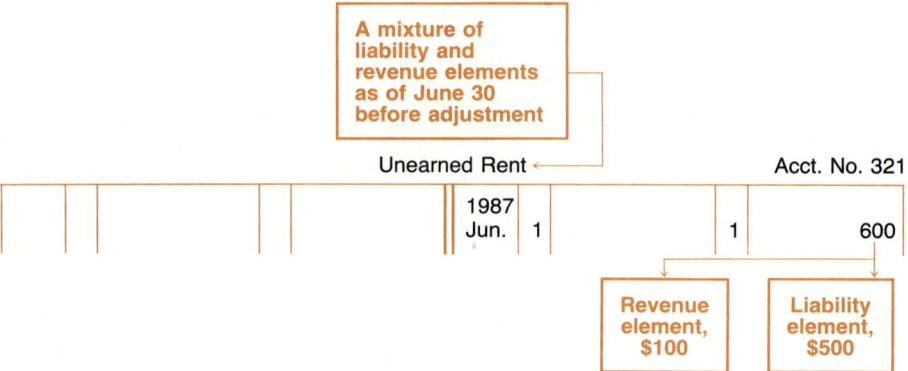

Step 3. The following adjusting entry is made:

		GENERAL JOURNAL			Page 4
1987					
Jun.	30	Unearned Rent................	321	100	
		Rent Earned................	511		100
		To record revenue earned from rental of automobile during June.			

By debiting the liability account Unearned Rent, the revenue element of $100 is removed from the liability account. Crediting the revenue account inserts the $100 into Rent Earned. This is shown by the following posting:

ªThe 500 figure is the balance of the Unearned Rent account after adjustment.

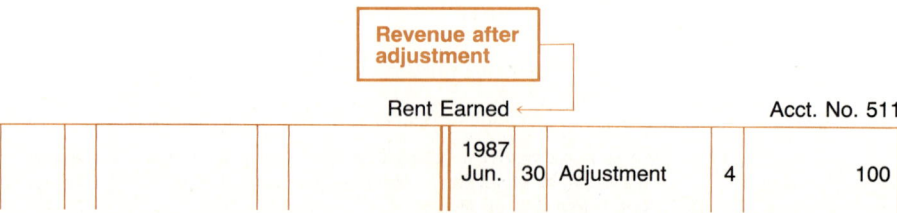

Rent earned ($100) appears in the income statement as a revenue item, and unearned rent ($500 balance after adjustment) appears in the balance sheet as a current liability.

Long-Term Cost Apportionments—A Third Type of Deferral

Two of Electronics Consulting Service's adjusting entries involve the recording of long-term asset cost expiration, or **long-term cost apportionment**. In general practice, three steps similar to the short-term cost apportionments are followed in analyzing the adjustment.

Adjustment for Depreciation of Office Equipment

Step 1. The trial balance in Figure 4–9 shows a balance of $1,400 in the Office Equipment account. This is the original cost of the asset as recorded in the ledger account.

Step 2. The equipment, acquired on June 1 for $1,400, is estimated to have a useful life of 10 years, or 120 months, and a salvage value of $200 at the end of that period. **Salvage** or **residual value** is the estimated price for which an asset may be sold when it is no longer serviceable to the business. In effect, the use of office equipment for 10 years has a net cost of $1,200 = ($1,400 − $200). A portion of this cost expires in each accounting period during the useful life of the equipment. This periodic expired cost, called depreciation expense, requires no periodic cash outlay, but nevertheless is a continuous expense of operating the business.

Depreciation expense

The portion of the cost of a property, plant, and equipment asset assigned to the accounting period is called **depreciation expense**.

A number of methods may be used in calculating the periodic depreciation expense. Depreciation for the month of June is computed in this case by using the **straight line method**, in which a uniform portion of the cost is assigned to each period. Other depreciation methods used in practice are discussed in Chapter 11. The straight line method is a popular method mainly because of its simplicity of calculation:

$$\frac{\text{Cost} - \text{Salvage value}}{\text{Estimated months of useful life}} = \text{Depreciation per month.}$$

The depreciation expense for the office equipment in June is computed as:

$$\frac{\$1,400 - \$200}{120} = \$10.$$

Step 3. The following adjusting entry is made:

GENERAL JOURNAL				Page 4
1987 Jun. 30	Depreciation Expense—Office Equipment	609	10	
	Accumulated Depreciation—Office Equipment	201A		10
	To record depreciation for June.			

Both of the foregoing accounts are new. The account credited, Accumulated Depreciation—Office Equipment, is called a **contra account**—specifically, a contra asset account—because its balance is deducted from Office Equipment to show the book value, or carrying value, of the asset. In other words, the **book value** of a plant asset is its cost less accumulated depreciation. Other contra or negative-type accounts are established to measure separately specific deductions from parent-type accounts whose amounts need to be preserved. For instance, contra liability, contra revenue, or even contra expense accounts are used; but none of these is used as frequently as the contra asset accounts described here. Office Equipment is not credited directly because depreciation is an estimate, and it is informative to keep asset cost separate from the estimated expiration of cost. When separate accounts are used, the original cost and the accumulated depreciation can be determined readily. The June 30 adjusting information is shown in the following ledger accounts:

Expense

Depreciation Expense—Office Equipment — Acct. No. 609

| 1987 Jun. | 30 | Adjustment | 4 | 10 | | | | |

Office Equipment[a] — Acct. No. 201

| 1987 Jun. | 1 | | 1 | 1,400 | | | | |

[a]The asset account is not debited or credited by the adjusting entry.

Contra asset account

Accumulated Depreciation—Office Equipment — Acct. No. 201A

| | | | | | 1987 Jun. | 30 | Adjustment | 4 | 10 |

In the balance sheet (see Figure 5–6), the contra asset account, Accumulated Depreciation—Office Equipment, is deducted from Office Equipment; the remainder is the **undepreciated cost** (or book value) of the asset, that is, the portion of the cost of the asset that is not yet charged to expense. Depreciation Expense—Office equipment ($10) is shown in the income statement as an expense.

Adjustment for Depreciation of Automobiles

Step 1. On June 1, the Electronics Consulting Service purchased two automobiles for business use, each costing $13,000. Because the useful life of automobiles is limited, a portion of the cost is allocable to each month (June in this case) the automobiles are used. It is estimated that their useful life is five years, or 60 months, at the end of which time each automobile will have a salvage value of $1,000.

Step 2. The computation and recording of the depreciation expense for the automobiles is similar to that for the office equipment. The depreciation expense for June for the two automobiles is calculated by the straight line method as follows:

$$\frac{\text{Cost of } \$13{,}000 - \text{Salvage value of } \$1{,}000}{60 \text{ months}} = \$200 \text{ per month per automobile.}$$

Thus the total depreciation for the two automobiles is $400 for the month of June.

Step 3. The following adjusting entry is made on June 30 and posted to the accounts shown after the journal entry:

GENERAL JOURNAL   Page 4

1987					
Jun.	30	Depreciation Expense—Automobiles	610	400	
		Accumulated Depreciation—			
		Automobiles	211A		400
		To record depreciation for June.			

Depreciation Expense—Automobiles   Acct. No. 610

1987					
Jun.	30		4	400	

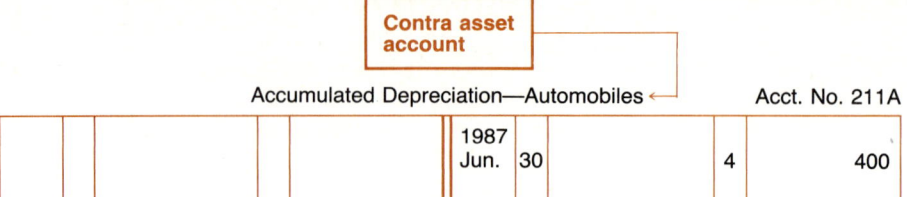

Depreciation expense—automobiles and accumulated depreciation—automobiles are classified in the financial statements in the same manner as depreciation expense—office equipment and accumulated depreciation—office equipment. Depreciation expense—automobiles is shown in the income statement as an expense, and accumulated depreciation—automobiles is deducted from the automobiles amount in the balance sheet (see Figures 5–4 and 5–6).

Accumulated Depreciation accounts are used to accumulate the current and all the past periodic charges made to expense and to set up in one account the amount of the deduction for asset valuation. Depreciation Expense shows the expired cost for the accounting period and is closed along with the other expense accounts in an entry that transfers the total expense to Income Summary. Assume that the same adjusting entry for automobiles is made on July 31. After it is posted, the general ledger accounts for Automobiles, Depreciation Expense—Automobiles, and Accumulated Depreciation—Automobiles appear as follows:

			Automobiles				Acct. No. 211
1987 Jun.	1	1	26,000				

			Accumulated Depreciation—Automobiles				Acct. No. 211A
			1987 Jun.	30	Adjustment	4	400
			Jul.	31	Adjustment	8	400
					800ª		

ªThe 800 figure is the balance of the Accumulated Depreciation—Automobiles account.

			Depreciation Expense—Automobiles				Acct. No. 610
1987 Jun.	30	Adjustment	4	400	1987 Jun.	30 Closing	5	400
1987 Jul.	31	Adjustment	8	400				

The cost of the automobiles and the accumulated depreciation are shown in the balance sheet on July 31 as follows:

```
Property, plant, and equipment:
    Automobiles ................................ $26,000
    Deduct: Accumulated depreciation—automobiles ....    800    $25,200
```

The $25,200 figure is referred to as the book value of the automobiles, that is, original cost less accumulated depreciation. In the next sections, adjustments for accruals are illustrated. Both revenues and expenses accrue continuously during the period and must be recorded to update the accounts before financial statements can be prepared.

Accrued Revenues—The First of Two Types of Accruals

Accrued revenues include items that have accumulated and have been earned in a given period but not recorded in the accounts because it is not feasible to record them on a daily basis. At the end of the accounting period, the accountant records the revenue in the period in which it is earned and also records the accompanying receivable, an asset. The accrued revenue adjustment described in the example is that of unrecorded interest.

Adjustment for Unrecorded Interest Revenue

Step 1. The Electronics Consulting Service made a loan of $1,440 to one of its suppliers, who signed a 30-day, 15 percent, interest-bearing note dated June 10. An entry was made on June 10 debiting Notes Receivable and crediting Cash for $1,440.

Step 2. The company earned interest on the loan for 20 days in June (observe that in counting days for accrual of interest, the date of the note is not counted; hence the time in this case is calculated for June 11–June 30 inclusive). The interest will be received on the maturity date, July 10, when the amount due (principal plus total interest) is paid by the supplier. Interest earned accrues with the passage of time. The 20 days' interest earned by June 30 means that Interest Earned (a revenue account) should be $12, and Electronics Consulting has an asset (accrued interest receivable) of $12.

The formula for computing simple interest (interest on the original principal only) is shown in Figure 4–10.[5]

---

[5]A more detailed presentation of the calculation of interest is found in Chapter 9.

**Figure 4–10
Interest Formula**

$$\text{Interest} = \text{Principal} \times \text{Interest rate} \times \frac{\text{Elapsed time in days}}{360}.$$

The uncollected interest accrued on the note held by Electronics Consulting for 20 days through June 30 is computed as follows:

$$\text{Interest} = \$1{,}440 \times 0.15 \times \frac{20}{360} = \$12.$$

In the calculation we can see that when the principal is multiplied by the interest rate, the interest for one year, $216 = (\$1{,}440 \times 0.15)$, is determined. Thus the interest for one year ($216) must be multiplied by the elapsed fraction of a year (20/360 or 1/18) to determine the interest for 20 days, which is $12. The use of 360 days in the formula is consistent with commercial practice. The primary reason for its use is the simplicity of calculation.

Step 3. In order to reflect this unrecorded information in the accounts, the formal adjusting entry made on June 30 debiting Accrued Interest Receivable and crediting Interest Earned records the asset amount of $12 and establishes the revenue amount of $12 in the Interest Earned account. The adjusting journal entry and the posting to the accounts are shown below.

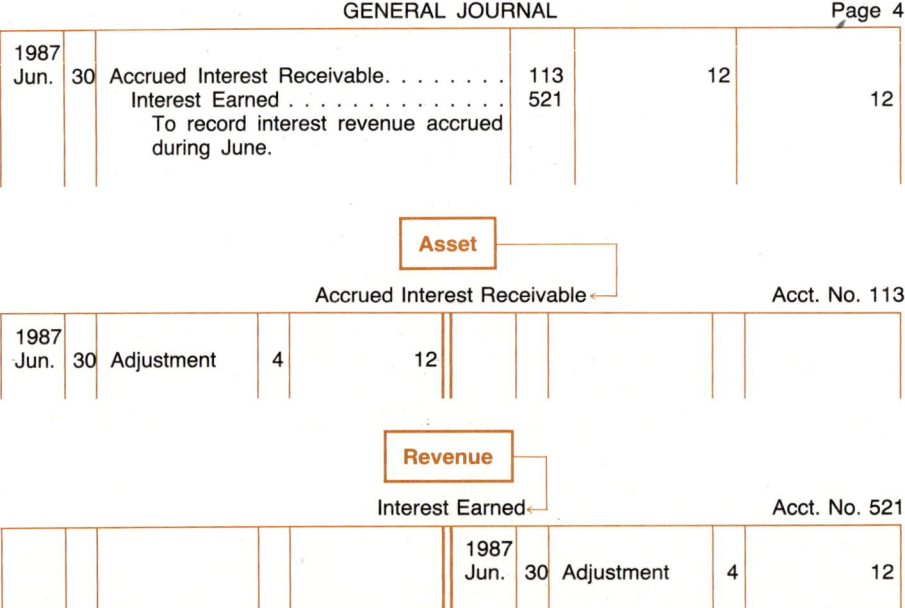

Accrued interest receivable ($12) is a current asset in the balance sheet. Interest earned is a revenue in the income statement. In all accrual adjustments, accrued revenues will be found to cause assets to increase.

Accrued Expenses—The Second Type of Accrual

Accrued expenses are expenses that have been incurred or have accumulated in a given period but have not yet been recorded. An expense is said to be incurred in the period when the effort to produce revenue is made. At the end of the accounting period the accountant must record the expense in the proper period of incurrence and must record the accompanying liability. The first accrued expense adjustment described here involves unrecorded wages expense.

Adjustment for Unrecorded Wages Expense

Step 1. The Wages Expense ledger account contains two debits of $600 each, representing gross wages earned every two weeks by employees through June 27.

Step 2. The employees earned wages of $150 for work on June 28, 29, and 30, the last three days of the accounting period. Although the company will not pay the employees again until July 11, it has nevertheless incurred $150 of wages expense for these three days, and a $150 liability exists as of June 30.

Step 3. An adjusting entry is made to record the $150 in wages expense incurred for the last three days of June and to reflect the liability amount of $150. It is then posted to the accounts shown after the journal entry.

GENERAL JOURNAL   Page 4

1987					
Jun.	30	Wages Expense	605	150	
		Accrued Wages Payable	311		150
		To record wages expense accrued during June.			

Expense

Wages Expense   Acct. No. 605

1987					
Jun.	13	From cash payment	2	600	
	27	From cash payment	3	600	
	30	Adjustment	4	150	
		1,350[a]			

[a]The 1,350 figure is the balance of the Wages Expense account.

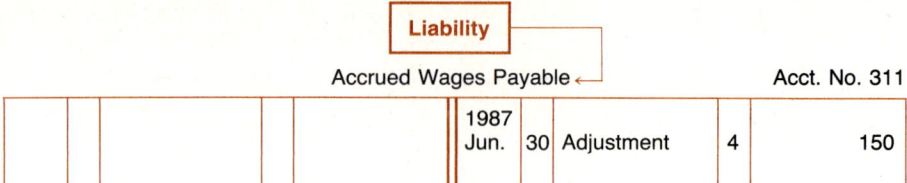

Wages expense ($1,350 balance after adjustment) is shown in the income statement as an expense; accrued wages payable ($150) is shown in the balance sheet as a current liability (see Figures 5–4 and 5–6). Just the opposite of an accrual of a revenue, all accruals of expenses cause increases in liabilities instead of assets.

Adjustment for Unrecorded Interest Expense

Step 1. On June 12, the Electronics Consulting Service borrowed $8,000 from the bank and signed a 45-day, 16 percent interest-bearing note payable. This transaction was recorded in the general journal by debiting Cash and crediting Notes Payable for $8,000.

Step 2. The cost of the use of the $8,000—interest expense—continues throughout the 45 days because interest expense accumulates with the passage of time. The total interest expense plus the $8,000 principal amount will be paid to the bank on July 27, the maturity, or due, date. However, unpaid interest expense on an interest-bearing note payable for the period from the day after June 12 through June 30 inclusive (18 days—the date of the note is not counted, but June 30 is) must be recognized by an adjusting entry reflecting Interest Expense and Accrued Interest Payable.

Using the formula shown in Figure 4–10, the unpaid interest expense accrued on June 30 is computed as follows:

$$\text{Interest} = \$8{,}000 \times 0.16 \times \frac{18}{360} = \$64.$$

Step 3. The adjusting entry records the interest expense incurred to date of $64 and the resulting liability of the same amount; the entry is made on June 30 and posted to the accounts indicated below:

				GENERAL JOURNAL			Page 5
1987 Jun.	30	Interest Expense............ Accrued Interest Payable .... To record interest expense accrued during June.			611 303	64	64

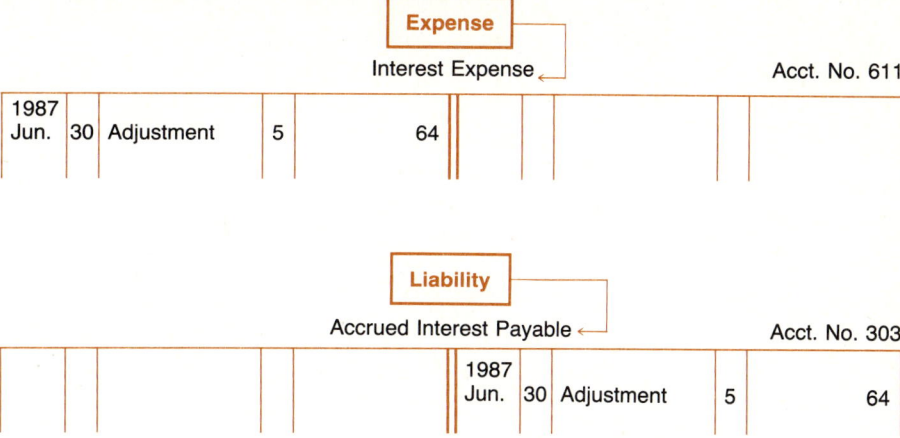

Interest expense ($64) is reported as an expense in the income statement. Accrued interest payable ($64) appears as a current liability in the balance sheet; it is actually an **accrued liability** (liability for an expense accumulated and incurred during one accounting period but not payable until a future accounting period). Expenses incurred for which invoices have not yet been received—telephone, heat, light, water, and so on—are also in this category. These may be estimated and recorded by debits to appropriate expense accounts and a credit to Accrued Utilities Payable or a similarly named account.

Income Tax Expense Adjustment

The income tax expense adjustment is a special example of an accrued expense adjustment. It is accrued since it is an incurred but not yet recorded expense. The word *accrued,* however, is often eliminated from the name of the liability that is recorded.

A single proprietor or a partner combines the net income from the proprietorship or partnership interest with the income from other sources and computes income tax as an individual taxpayer. A corporation, however, is taxed as a separate entity, and its financial statements must show the corporate income tax expense and the liability for the tax.

Step 1. It is difficult to determine precisely the tax related to the taxable income for the month of June, because the annual taxable income, on which the tax is based, is not yet known. Nevertheless, the business must make the best possible estimate.

Step 2. The Electronics Consulting Service estimates its income taxes for the month of June to be $1,900. This amount must be recorded in both the expense and liability accounts. Since this is the first month of operations, there are no balances in the Income Tax Expense or liability accounts.

Step 3. The income tax estimate is journalized on June 30 and posted to the accounts indicated below the general journal:

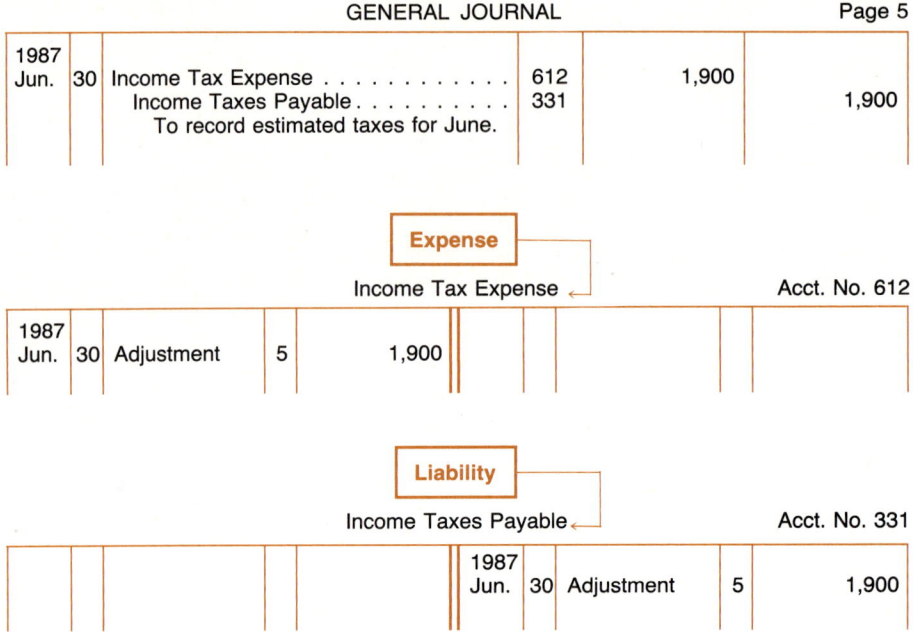

The income tax expense of $1,900 appears in the income statement; it is deducted from net income before income taxes to determine net income (see Figure 5–4). Income taxes payable appears in the balance sheet as a current liability.

Before moving to Chapter 5 and continuing our illustration, this seems to be an appropriate time to stop and to review the types of adjustments, to look at a threshold limitation on the requirement for adjustments (that of materiality) to consider a possible alternative approach to the adjustment of deferrals, and to introduce a note on reversing entries.

Summary of Adjustments

As stated previously, the adjustments are classified into two broad groups, deferrals and accruals. Figure 4–11 summarizes five types of adjustments into these classifications and gives brief summary entries for each type of adjustment.

As noted previously, the way a deferral adjustment is made depends on how the original entry was recorded. Because the reader will encounter deferrals that have been debited to expense or credited to a revenue, this idea is expanded in a later section, Alternative Adjustment Methods for Deferrals.

Broad Classification	No.	Kind of Adjustment	Brief Definition	Pro Forma Adjusting Entry[a]
Deferrals	1	Short-term cost apportionment. Assumption: The original debit is made to an asset account.	A prepaid item that benefits two or more periods; if the original amount is debited to an asset, it is necessary to apportion expense to appropriate periods.	Dr. Appropriate Expense (E) Cr. Prepaid Asset (A)
	2	Short-term revenue apportionment. Assumption: The original credit is made to a liability account.	A revenue item that is collected in advance of the period(s) earned; if the amount is credited to a liability account, it is necessary to apportion the revenue to the appropriate period in which it is earned.	Dr. Unearned _____ (L) Cr. Appropriate Revenue (R)
	3	Long-term cost apportionment. (Note: this is always originally debited to an asset.)	A prepaid item that benefits the present and several future periods; the amount must be apportioned to the periods benefited by the prepayment.	For a depreciable property, plant, and equipment item: Dr. Depreciation Expense (E) Cr. Accumulated Depreciation (Contra A)
Accruals	4	Accrued revenue.	Revenue earned in a given period but not yet collected or recorded.	Dr. Accrued _____ Receivable (A) Cr. Appropriate Revenue (R)
	5	Accrued expense.	Expense incurred in a given period but not yet paid or recorded.	Dr. Appropriate Expense (E) Cr. Accrued _____ Payable (L)

[a]Codes used: A, asset; R, revenue; E, expense; L, liability; Contra A, contra asset or valuation account.

Figure 4–11   **Summary of Deferrals and Accruals**

Application of the Materiality Concept to Adjustments

The preceding adjustments were made to update the assets, liabilities, expenses, and revenues of the Electronics Consulting Service. After they are made, a correctly stated income statement and balance sheet can be prepared. No exceptions were mentioned to the general rule that all adjustments should be made.

One exception (usually referred to as the materiality concept) generally accepted in practice is that adjustments do not have to be made for insignificant, immaterial, or trivial items.[6] For example, the box of paper clips in someone's desk as of the balance sheet date is an asset of the company, although its cost has been debited to expense. It is possible but not practical to make an adjusting entry for the asset value of the unused clips. Because of

---

[6]This is one of the generally accepted accounting principles (GAAP) described in Appendix 1.1.

the item's small cost, failure to make the adjustment will have no material effect on the financial statements and cannot mislead the user of such statements. A similar situation exists with respect to other minor items of supply or services.

Materiality concept

The need for adjustment and the need for full disclosure do not apply to insignificant, immaterial, or trivial matters, a standard called the **materiality concept**.

The accountant is faced with the problem of determining what is material and what is immaterial. For instance, an item costing $100 may be material in a small business, whereas an item costing $1,000 may be insignificant in a multimillion-dollar business. *The decision hinges on whether the failure to disclose a given item separately will affect the decision of an informed statement user.* For example, it may not be misleading to combine several insignificant items of expense or revenue into one account. However, the cumulative effect of many separate items which are immaterial individually may become material and thus require recognition in the adjustment process. Regardless of the amount, it may be necessary to disclose an item separately because it may be an essential component in a business decision or because of its very nature. For example, even a small bribe to an official of a foreign government may have far-reaching implications. And, it may be very misleading to combine a significant loss from a lawsuit with a regular expense account.

Alternative Adjustment Methods for Deferrals

Accountants may record deferrals in two different ways. For instance, prepaid insurance (or other short-term costs) may be initially recorded as an asset and then adjusted as shown on page 161. Alternatively, the accountant might originally record the prepaid amount in an Insurance Expense account (that is, debit Insurance Expense and credit Cash). At the end of the period, the accountant would then remove from the expense account the amount still unexpired or prepaid for the future. Had the Electronics Consulting Service originally recorded the insurance premium in the Insurance Expense account, the adjusting entry as of June 30, 1987, would be a debit to Prepaid Insurance, $2,100, and a credit to Insurance Expense, $2,100. Thus, after the adjusting entry is journalized and posted, the asset element ($2,100) would be recorded in the asset account, leaving the expense element ($60) in the Insurance Expense account.

Similarly, unearned rent revenue (or other short-term revenues) may be initially recorded as a liability and then adjusted as shown on page 164. The accountant alternatively might record the unearned amount upon receipt in a Rent Earned account (debit Cash and credit Rent Earned). At the end of the period, the accountant then would have to remove from the revenue account the amount still unearned at that time. Had the Electronics Consulting Service originally recorded the advance receipt of rent in the Rent Earned account, the adjusting entry as of June 30, 1987, would be a debit to Rent Earned, $500, and a credit to Unearned Rent, $500. Thus after the adjusting entries are journalized and posted, the correct amount of the liability element ($500) would be recorded in the liability account, and the revenue element ($100) would be properly adjusted in the revenue account. Normally, when the alternative adjustment method is used, the accountant will employ a technique referred to as reversing entries, briefly discussed next.

A Note on Reversing Entries

In some situations, it is possible to save time and to reduce the cost of performing the accounting function by the use of a specially designed procedure. One such procedure involves the use of reversing entries. **Reversing entries** are made at the beginning of the next accounting period and are the reverse of certain previous year adjusting entries. The preparation of these entries is not a required step in the accounting process, and they should be prepared only when they are beneficial to the accountant. This section contains an explanation of reversing procedures.

Illustrations

Assume a small company with a five-day work week pays its employees each Friday. The payroll is $500 a day, or $2,500 for a five-day work week. Throughout the period, year 1, the company's accountant makes a journal entry each Friday as follows:

	Salaries and Wage Expense...................................	2,500	
	Cash		2,500
	To record payment of salaries for the week.		

Next, assume that the last day of the period is December 31 and that it falls on a Wednesday. All expenses of this year must be recorded before the expense accounts are closed and financial statements as of December 31 are prepared. An adjusting entry, therefore, must be made to record the salaries expense and the related liability to the employees for Monday, Tuesday, and Wednesday of year 1, the days that they have worked since the preceding payday on Friday. The adjusting entry for the $1,500 = (3 × $500) is journalized as follows:

Year	1			
Dec.	31	Salaries and Wages Expense	1,500	
		Accrued Salaries and Wages Payable		1,500
		To record the accrued salaries for the last three days of December.		

When closing entries are made, the Salaries and Wages Expense account is reduced to zero. The liability account, Accrued Salaries and Wages Payable, remains open with its $1,500 balance at the beginning of the new period, year 2. On the next regular payday, Friday, January 2, the company's accountant may elect not to follow the reversing procedure and to record the $2,500 weekly payroll by a debit of $1,500 to Accrued Salaries and Wages Payable, a debit of $1,000 to Salaries and Wages Expense (for Thursday and Friday), and a credit of $2,500 to Cash. However, analyzing the payment into the amount applicable to a liability ($1,500) and to an expense ($1,000) requires more knowledge and accounting experience than if the entry were identical to the other weekly payroll entries made during the year.

Making a reversing entry on the first day of the new accounting period simplifies the recording of routine transactions and removes the need for reference back to previous adjustments. The reversing entry for the $1,500 year-end accrual of salaries should be dated January 1, year 2 and is:

| Year 2 Jan. 1 | Accrued Salaries and Wages Payable.................. Salaries and Wages Expense........................ To reverse the accrual made on December 31, year 1. | 1,500 | 1,500 |

The reversing entry reduces the Accrued Salaries and Wages Payable account to zero by transferring the $1,500 liability to the credit column of the Salaries and Wages Expense account. Thus, this expense account will have a credit balance of $1,500 before the first payroll is paid. On Friday, January 2, year 2, the normal payroll entry for $2,500 is made in the same way as on every other Friday during the year, as follows:

| Year 2 Jan. 2 | Salaries and Wages Expense...................... Cash .... To record the salaries for the week ended January 2, year 2. | 2,500 | 2,500 |

After this January 2 entry has been posted, the expense account shows a debit balance of only $1,000, the result of the January 1 reversing entry and the January 2 payroll entry. The end results are exactly the same as if no reversing entry had been used and the company's accountant had split the debit side of the January 2 payroll entry between Accrued Salaries and Wages Payable and Salaries and Wages Expense.

The two accounts are shown below to illustrate the effect of posting the adjusting entry on December 31, year 1, and the reversing entry on January 1, year 2.

Salaries and Wages Expense							Acct. No. 605
Year 1 (Various)		Balance—51 entries of 2,500	127,500	Year 1 Dec. 31		Closing	129,000
Dec. 31		Adjusting	1,500				
			129,000				129,000
Year 2 Jan. 2		Weekly payroll 1,000ᵃ	2,500	Year 2 Jan. 1		Reversing	1,500

ᵃThe 1,000 figure is the balance of the Salaries and Wages Expense account.

Accrued Salaries and Wages Payable							Acct. No. 311
Year 2 Jan. 1		Reversing	1,500	Year 1 Dec. 31		Adjusting	1,500

Which Adjusting Entries May be Reversed

Any accrual adjustment may be reversed; the reversal is optional. Examples are accrued interest expense, accrued interest revenue, and accrued salaries expense. Accrued adjustments bring expenses and revenues and the accompanying liability or asset into the records and are followed by payment or receipt of cash in the next period.

Adjusting entries for both short-term and long-term cost apportionments originally recorded as assets are not reversed. If deferrals originally are recorded in an expense account or revenue account (see Alternative Adjustment Methods for Deferrals section), the subsequent adjusting entries are reversed.

Guideline for Reversal

Again, reversing entries are devices which can be helpful under some circumstances. They should be used *only* when they are beneficial to the accountant. If a particular optional adjustment procedure requiring reversing entries is helpful in some way to a firm, it should be used. If some beneficial results—ease of recording or saving in time and effort—are not achieved, it should not be used. Adjustments for deferrals originally set up as assets and liabilities are never reversed. Adjustments for long-term cost apportionments are never reversed.

The remaining steps in the accounting cycle for the Electronics Consulting Service are completed in Chapter 5. Related managerial analyses also are postponed to the end of Chapter 5.

Glossary

Accrual basis of accounting The basis that assumes that revenue is realized at the time of the sale of goods or services, regardless of when the cash is received; expenses are recognized at the time the services are received and utilized or an asset is consumed in the production of revenue, regardless of when payment for these services or assets is made.

Accruals A classification of adjustments that is required to update unrecorded accumulated revenues and expenses.

Accrued Accumulated or built onto.

Accrued expenses Expenses that have been incurred in a given period—for example, services received and used—but that have not yet been paid or recorded.

Accrued liability The liability for an expense that has been accumulated but not yet paid or recorded.

Accrued revenues Revenues that have been earned in a given period but that have not yet been collected or recorded.

Accumulated Depreciation An account which reveals all past depreciation that has been recorded on a depreciable property, plant, and equipment item and charged against revenue; it is in essence a postponed credit to the applicable property, plant, and equipment account.

Adjusting entries Entries for regular continuous transactions whose recording has been postponed to the end of an accounting period for the convenience of the accountant; they are made to update revenue, expense, asset, liability, and stockholders' equity accounts as required by the accrual basis of accounting.

Apportionment The dividing of a cost or revenue among two or more periods.

Book value The difference between the original cost of a depreciable property, plant, and equipment item and its related accumulated depreciation.

Cash basis of accounting The basis that reflects the recognition of revenue at the time that cash is received for the sale of goods and services and the recognition of expenses in the period of the payment for the expense.

Closing entries Those journal entries that close the nominal accounts at the end of a period—that is, reduce these accounts to a zero balance. In the closing process, the net effect of this closing is transferred to the Retained Earnings account.

Closing the books The process of clearing the temporary or the nominal accounts at the end of a period; this process requires preparation of closing journal entries, posting of these entries, and ruling of the nominal accounts that are closed.

Contra account A negative element of (offset to) a related account that is shown in a separate account; the contra account should always be shown in the ledger immediately following the account of which it is a reduction. Both assets and liabilities may have contra accounts.

Deferrals A classification of adjustments that includes short-term revenue apportionments, short-term cost apportionments, and long-term cost apportionments. They are called deferrals because the recognition of expense or revenue is deferred until adjusting entries are made.

Depreciation expense The amount of property, plant, and equipment cost that is assigned to a given period.

Earned revenue Revenue is said to be earned when substantially all efforts to bring it into existence have been expended except the collection of the revenue in the form of cash.

Long-term cost apportionment adjustment An adjustment requiring the apportioning of the cost of a long-lived asset between the current period and a future time span of two or more years.

Matching The standard involving the matching of earned revenue of a period against incurred expenses of the same period to determine net income.

Materiality concept An accounting concept that requires an item that is large enough and significant enough to influence decisions by statement users to be separately identified in accounting statements.

Nominal accounts Temporary accounts that are set up to collect and to measure part of the change that takes place in retained earnings or other applicable owners' equity accounts. They are closed at the end of each accounting period.

Postclosing trial balance A trial balance taken of the ledger accounts that have any balances in them (the real accounts) after closing entries have been recorded and posted.

Real accounts The accounts that appear in the balance sheet and are not closed at the end of the period.

Reversing entries Entries made on the first day of a new fiscal period that are reversals of adjusting entries.

Salvage value The estimated scrap value, resale value, or trade-in value that a property, plant, and equipment item should have at the end of its estimated useful life. Also called residual value.

Short-term cost apportionment adjustment An adjustment that requires that a previously recorded prepaid item be apportioned between the current period and a future short period (usually a year). The prepayment may be originally debited to an asset or to an expense account.

Short-term revenue apportionment adjustment An adjustment that requires that a previously recorded advance collection of a revenue be apportioned between the current period and a future short period (usually one year). The advance collection may be originally credited to a liability or to a revenue account.

Straight line method of depreciation A method that allocates the cost of a depreciable asset over the estimated useful life of the asset in equal amounts for each time period.

Undepreciated cost The remaining property, plant, and equipment cost to be charged as depreciation in the future; mathematically, it is the original cost of a property, plant, and equipment item less the sum of the accumulated depreciation and any salvage value.

Questions

Q4–1   What is the purpose of closing the books? Using T accounts for Revenues, Expenses, Dividends, Income Summary, and Retained Earnings, diagram the closing process.

Q4–2   Draw a diagram showing the interrelationship of the balance sheet, the statement of retained earnings, and the income statement.

Q4–3   What item is common in each of the following pairs of statements of a corporation?

a. The income statement and statement of retained earnings.
b. The statement of retained earnings and the balance sheet prepared at the end of an accounting period.

Q4–4   Retained earnings on the Beach Company's balance sheet on December 31, 1987, was $2,000 less than on December 31, 1986. Give two possible reasons for the decrease.

Q4–5   The adjustment process is really a question of measuring net income first and balance sheet items second. From an income measurement point of view, why is it important to match all incurred expenses against all earned revenue to determine net income?

Q4–6   (a) What are the essential differences between the cash basis of accounting and the accrual basis of accounting? (b) Since the accrual basis is the only one that satisfies the basic accounting needs, how can a firm justify the use of the cash basis? Discuss.

Q4–7   (a) What purpose is served by adjusting entries? (b) What types of events make adjusting entries necessary?

Q4–8   Most adjustments are grouped into two categories—deferrals and accruals. Discuss these terms and indicate what kinds of adjustments would fall in each group.

Part One / The Basic Accounting Model

Q4–9 There are two methods of recording and adjusting for deferrals. Discuss these methods. Do you see any problems with alternative methods?

Q4–10 Does the need to make adjusting entries at the end of a period mean that errors were made in the accounts during the period? Discuss.

Q4–11 Define the following terms: (a) accrued revenues, (b) accrued expenses, (c) short-term cost apportionments, (d) long-term cost apportionments, (e) short-term revenue apportionments.

Q4–12 (a) What is a contra account? (b) Name one contra account involved in adjusting entries. (c) What is the specific purpose served by the contra account you just named?

Q4–13 On the balance sheet, where do you classify the following: (a) prepaid insurance, (b) unearned rent, (c) accrued interest receivable, (d) accrued wages payable.

Q4–14 During 1987, the Elfland Company made prepayments of premiums on one-year, two-year, and three-year property insurance policies. The company recorded the premium payments in an account that it calls Prepaid Property Insurance.

1. At the close of 1987, will the necessary adjusting entry be a deferral or an accrual?
2. Which of the following types of accounts will be affected by the related adjusting entry required at the end of the year?
   a. Asset.
   b. Liability.
   c. Revenue.
   d. Expense.

Q4–15 At the end of the fiscal year, a company has a 150-day interest-bearing note payable that had been issued to a supplier 90 days earlier.

1. Will the interest on the note as of the end of the current year represent a deferral or an accrual?
2. Which of the following types of accounts will be affected by the related adjusting entry at the end of the current year? a. Asset. b. Liability. c. Revenue. d. Expense.
3. Assuming that the note is not paid until maturity, what fraction of the total interest should be allocated to the year in which the note is paid?

Q4–16 (a) Do you agree with the statement that "items of little or no consequence may be dealt with as expediency may suggest"? (b) Do you agree with the statement that "problems of materiality are easily resolved and, in any case, are not very important"?

Q4–17 When earned but uncollected revenue is not recorded until the end of the year—for example, interest earned—the reversing entry on January 1 of the next year is optional. Explain what account is affected when the revenue is collected, depending on whether or not a reversing entry is made.

Q4–18 (a) Define long-term cost apportionment and give an example of a transaction that would require such an apportionment. (b) Would the adjustment for long-term cost apportionment ever be reversed?

Q4–19 (a) List two kinds of adjustments in which the reversing entry is optional. (b) Give an example of the reversing entry for each type of adjustment.

Q4–20 (a) What is the purpose of reversing entries? (b) Under what conditions would the reversing procedure be advantageous?

Exercises

Final closing entry

E4–1 The Mini-Electronics Corporation finished its first year of operations on December 31, 1987. After all of its revenue and expense accounts had been closed, its Income Summary account showed the following:

4 / End-of-Period Process without a Work Sheet

	Income Summary		
Total expenses	740,000	Total revenues	610,000

Prepare the journal entry to close the Income Summary account.

E4–2 As of December 31, 1987, the ledger of the Parks Company contained the following accounts and account balances, among others: Cash, $85,000; Accounts Receivable, $38,000; Retained Earnings, $91,900; Commissions Earned, $69,000; Rent Earned, $9,000; Salaries Expense, $47,000; Office Expense, $6,250; Miscellaneous Expense, $16,750; Dividends, $6,000. (All the nominal accounts are included.) Journalize the closing entries.

Journalizing closing entries

E4–3 The trial balance of the Greene Brick Mason, Inc., as of September 30, 1987, follows:

Income statement and closing entries

GREENE BRICK MASON, INC.
Trial Balance
September 30, 1987

Account Title	Debits	Credits
Cash	$35,500	
Masonry Supplies	4,500	
Equipment	15,000	
Accounts Payable		$ 490
Common Stock (5,000 shares)		10,000
Retained Earnings, September 1, 1987		9,320
Dividends	200	
Bricklaying Fees		61,440
Salaries Expense	25,000	
Advertising Expense	160	
Rent Expense	340	
Masonry Supplies Expense	410	
Utilities Expense	140	
Totals	$81,250	$81,250

1. Prepare an income statement for the month of September.
2. Prepare closing journal entries to close the nominal accounts.

E4–4 Make the additional closing journal entries indicated by the following accounts (adjustments have been recorded):

Preparing closing entries for a corporation

Retained Earnings		Dividends	
	75,000	3,500	

Income Summary	
305,000	280,000

E4–5 Because of a quarrel with his boss, the company's accountant quite unexpectedly quit; he took off for parts unknown just before the close of the company's accounting year. In his haste to leave, he did not have a chance to discuss what adjusting entries would be

Adjusting entries from incomplete data

necessary at the end of the year, December 31. Fortunately, however, he did jot down a few notes on his memo pad that provide some leads:

a. Depreciation on furniture and equipment for the year is $3,200.
b. Charge off $750 of expired insurance from prepaid account for the year.
c. Accrued interest at end of year on notes payable to bank is $2,350; make sure to pick up when adjusting entries are made.
d. No bill received yet from car rental agency for sales staff cars—should be about $2,600 for December.
e. Two days' salaries will be unpaid at year-end; weekly (five days) total salary is $26,400.

Answer the following:

1. On the basis of the available information given above, prepare for each adjustment that should be recorded a general journal entry with brief explanation.
2. What other normal or usual adjustments may have to be recorded in addition to the ones above? Briefly explain each one.

E4–6
Calculating information from adjustment data

The balances of the Prepaid Insurance account of the Owens Company were:

December 31, 1986	$2,560
December 31, 1987	1,340

The income statement for 1987 showed insurance expense of $2,950. What was the amount of expenditures for insurance premiums during 1987?

E4–7
Adjustments for deferrals

The trial balance of the Westerhoff Company on December 31, 1987, the end of its fiscal year, included the following account balances before adjustments:

Prepaid Insurance	$3,600
Prepaid Advertising Supplies	2,840
Prepaid Rent	3,870
Office Supplies	5,200
Office Equipment	9,500

Data for end-of-year adjustments on December 31, 1987, were:

a. On November 1, 1987, the company purchased a three-year comprehensive insurance policy for $3,600.
b. Advertising supplies on hand totaled $1,250 on December 31, 1987.
c. On September 1, 1987, the company paid one year's rent in advance.
d. The office supplies inventory was $2,650 on December 31, 1987.
e. The office equipment was purchased on July 1, 1987, and has an estimated useful life of 8 years and an estimated salvage value of $1,500.

Make the adjusting journal entries as of December 31, 1987.

E4–8
Adjusting entry: alternative recording of a deferral

Arts Publications, Inc., credited Subscription Revenue for $72,000 received from subscribers to its new monthly magazine. All subscriptions were for 12 issues. The initial issue was mailed during October 1987. Journalize the end-of-year adjusting entry on December 31, 1987.

E4–9
Adjusting entry for tax

The income statement of the Moffie Company for the three-month period ended March 31, 1987, shows net income before income taxes of $334,000. Assuming an income tax rate of 35 percent, journalize the necessary adjusting entry.

E4–10
Transaction and adjusting entry accrual and next year payment

On October 2, 1987, Taylor Corporation borrowed $20,000 from a local savings and loan association and issued a note. The terms of the loan are as follows:

Principal and interest due	March 31, 1988
Interest rate	18 percent

4 / End-of-Period Process without a Work Sheet

Assuming Taylor Corporation closes its books on December 31, 1987, prepare the following journal entries:

1. The entry on October 2, 1987, to record the loan.
2. The adjusting entry on December 31, 1987.
3. The entry on March 31, 1988, to record repayment of the loan.

E4–11
Various adjustments reconstructed

From the account balances given below, prepare the adjusting journal entries.

Account	Account in Trial Balance	Balance after Adjustment
Prepaid Insurance	$ 5,500	$ 1,200
Unearned Rent	3,600	1,100
Accumulated Depreciation—Building	20,000	30,000
Accrued Salaries and Wages Payable	0	2,500
Accrued Interest Receivable	0	550
Accrued Interest Payable	0	400

E4–12
Adjusting entries with reasons

Upon examining the books and records of the Riggsbee Company on December 31, 1987, you find the following:

a. The inventory of office supplies on hand is $680; some partially filled cans of duplicating fluid valued at $4.50 were not inventoried. All purchases of office supplies were debited to Office Supplies Expense.
b. Included in Miscellaneous Expense was a charge of $1,250 for uninsured losses from a fire. (Hint: The item is large enough to be recorded in a separate loss account.)

Required: Indicate the adjustment, if any, that should be made and state why.

E4–13
Transaction and adjusting entries; interest accrual and payment

On September 15 the Ritchie Company received a 30-day, 14 percent note for $900 from a customer. On September 20 the company borrowed $4,000 from the bank on its own 30-day, 14 percent note. Make entries to adjust the books on September 30 and entries to record the collection and payment of the notes on their respective due dates.

E4–14
Errors, effect, and adjusting entries

Noreen Murphy, the accountant of the Singer Corporation, had been ill, and the company's bookkeeper prepared the annual adjusting and closing journal entries on December 31, 1987. Upon her return, Murphy noticed that adjusting entries had not been made for the following:

a. The Prepaid Insurance account had a balance of $2,400 on January 1, 1987. No entry had been made to this account in 1987. During 1987, the insurance premiums paid in advance in the amount of $3,600 were debited to Insurance Expense. The correct amount of the Prepaid Insurance account was $1,600 on December 31, 1987.
b. Depreciation expense on the building has not been recorded. The building cost $90,000 and has an estimated useful life of 20 years with no salvage value. The building had been acquired on December 31, 1986.
c. Wages earned by employees for December 29, 30, and 31 have not been recorded. Weekly wages (five days) amount to $2,000.
d. Interest earned on investments but not received, $720.

Journalize the preceding adjusting entries and for each separate case indicate the effect (overstated/understated) of omitting the above items on

1. total assets,
2. total liabilities and stockholders' equity, and
3. net income.

Part One / The Basic Accounting Model

E4–15
Transaction, adjusting, and reversing entries

The Sexton Company incurred the following transactions during 1987:

1987

Nov. 1   Received 12 percent, 90-day note receivable in the amount of $6,000 in exchange for an account receivable.
Dec. 1   Issued a 14 percent, 60-day note payable in the amount of $2,400 to eliminate an account payable.
     31 The year ended on a Wednesday. Weekly wages are $1,500, and Sexton has a 5-day workweek.

1. Journalize the transactions, adjusting entries, and closing of the nominal accounts created.
2. Prepare reversing entries.
3. Record collection of the note receivable, payment of the note payable, and payment of the weekly wages. (Wages are paid each Friday.)

E4–16
Various issues involving adjusting and reversing process

On February 28, 1987, Brussells paid insurance premiums for a one-year period beginning March 1. It recorded the payment as follows:

Prepaid Insurance   9,600
   Cash 9,600

1. What adjustment is required on December 31, 1987?
2. What reversing entry, if any, would you make?
3. What nominal account could be debited instead of Prepaid Insurance?
4. What adjustment would then be necessary?
5. What reversing entry, if any, would you make?

A Problems

P4–1A
End-of-period process from trial balance data in alphabetical order

The trial balance of the Highland Parking Lot, Inc., shows the following accounts, arranged in alphabetical order:

HIGHLAND PARKING LOT, INC.
Adjusted Trial Balance
December 31, 1987

Account Title	Debits	Credits
Accounts Payable		$ 16,000
Accounts Receivable	$ 39,500	
Cash	140,300	
Common Stock (8,000 shares issued and outstanding)		120,000
Dividends	5,700	
Equipment Maintenance Expense	7,200	
Heat and Light Expense	4,800	
Interest Earned		3,600
Land	30,000	
Notes Payable		12,000
Notes Receivable	19,000	
Parking Fees Earned		117,900
Retained Earnings, January 1, 1987		17,500
Salaries Expense	27,000	
Supplies on Hand	4,200	
Supplies Expense	8,700	
Telephone Expense	600	
Totals	$287,000	$287,000

Required:

1. Prepare an adjusted trial balance in proper chart-of-accounts sequence.
2. Prepare an income statement, a statement of retained earnings, and a balance sheet.
3. Journalize the closing entries.
4. Set up ledger accounts for Retained Earnings, Income Summary, and all nominal accounts. Enter the balances that are in the trial balance in these accounts under the date December 31, 1987. Then post the closing entries to these accounts. Rule the accounts that are closed.

P4–2A
Cash and accrual bases

Selected cash transactions of the Eason Sales Company for 1987 are given:

1987

Apr.	1	Purchased a one-year insurance policy for $3,600.
Jul.	1	Bought two trucks for a total of $41,500. The trucks are expected to last five years, at the end of which time their salvage value will be $2,000 each.
Dec.	31	Paid $900 rent for the three-month period ending March 31, 1988.
	31	Purchased office supplies for $350.

Required:

1. Make journal entries to record the transactions using the accrual basis.
2. Make the adjusting journal entries as of December 31, 1987, using the accrual basis. The company closes its books annually on December 31.
3. Make the journal entries to record the transactions using the cash basis.
4. What adjusting journal entries would be made if the Eason Sales Company were on the cash basis?

P4–3A
Adjustments and effect on statements

Certain unadjusted account balances from the trial balance of Darrell Noblitt's Consulting Firm for the year ended December 31, 1987, are given:

DARRELL NOBLITT'S CONSULTING FIRM
Partial Trial Balance
December 31, 1987

Account Title	Debits	Credits
Accounts Receivable	$50,000	
Notes Receivable	21,000	
Prepaid Insurance	4,320	
Office Supplies	3,480	
Automobiles	30,000	
Accumulated Depreciation—Automobiles		$ 6,000
Notes Payable		9,000
Revenue—Consulting Fees		490,000
Interest Earned		1,000
Rent Earned		2,400
Advertising Expense	2,200	
Rent Expense	50,000	
Salaries Expense	51,000	
Property Taxes Expense	3,450	
Heat and Light Expense	2,600	

Adjustment data on December 31 are as follows:

a. Office supplies on hand totaled $750.
b. Depreciation for the year was $3,000.
c. Estimated heat and light expense not recorded was $410.

d. Of the amount shown for Interest Earned, $300 was unearned as of December 31, 1987.

e. The balance of the Prepaid Insurance account consists of $1,440 for the premium on a three-year policy dated July 1, 1987, and $2,880 for premiums on a three-year policy dated January 1, 1987.

f. Advertising supplies on hand were $280.

g. The balance of the Notes Payable account represents a 12 percent interest-bearing note dated January 1, 1987, due July 1, 1988.

h. The rent expense is $5,000 a month.

i. Salaries earned by employees but not paid were $2,500.

j. Property taxes accrued were $280.

k. On January 1, 1987, the Noblitt firm subleased a section of its rented space. The lease with the tenant specifies the minimum yearly rental fee to be the greater of $2,400, payable at the beginning of each month, or 5 percent of gross sales. The amount of the adjustment in rent, if there is any adjustment, is due on January 15, 1988. The tenant reported sales of $53,000 for 1987.

l. Included in the Revenue—Consulting Fees account are advance payments of $15,500 by clients for services to be rendered early in 1988.

Required: For each of the foregoing events, do the following three things, using the format shown below:

1. Record adjusting journal entries.
2. Indicate the financial statement classification of each account in each entry.
3. Show the amount reported on the financial statements.

Example: Item a.

Item	Adjusting Journal Entries December 31, 1987	Dr.	Cr.	Financial Statement Classification	Amount Reported on Financial Statement
a	Office Supplies Expense Office Supplies	2,730	2,730	Expense Current Asset	2,730 750

P4–4A
Various adjusting entries

After an analysis of the accounts and the other records of Rumpkin Company, the following information is made available for the year ended December 31, 1987:

a. The Office Supplies account has a debit balance of $2,500. Office supplies on hand at December 31 total $810.

b. The Prepaid Rent account has a debit balance of $16,400. Included in this amount is $1,500 paid in December for the succeeding January; $14,900 has expired.

c. The Prepaid Insurance account has a debit balance of $5,760. It consists of the following policies purchased during 1987:

Policy No.	Date of Policy	Life of Policy	Premium
XY-462	January 1	3 years	$3,600
C3PX	April 1	2 years	1,440
Y206	October 1	1 year	720

d. The Prepaid Advertising account has a debit balance of $5,400. Included in this amount is $900 paid to a local monthly magazine for advertising space in its January and February 1988 issues.

e. At the close of the year, three notes receivable were on hand:

Date	Face Value	Total Time of Note in Days	Interest Rate
November 1	$15,000	90	16%
December 1	18,000	60	18
December 16	9,000	30	20

f. At the close of the year, two notes payable were outstanding:

Date	Face Value	Total Time of Note in Days	Interest Rate
September 2	$18,000	180	15%
November 1	21,000	90	18

g. Salaries and wages accrued totaled $4,800.
h. The Rent Earned account has a credit balance of $28,800 representing receipt of payment on a one-year lease effective May 1, 1987.
i. The Store Equipment account has a debit balance of $40,500. The equipment has an estimated useful life of 10 years and a salvage value of $4,500. All store equipment was acquired prior to January 1, 1987, and has a remaining life of five years.
j. The Vans account has a debit balance of $13,000. The van was purchased on June 1, 1986, and has an estimated life of 5 years and a salvage value of approximately $1,500.
k. Property taxes accrued were $3,100.
l. Estimated income taxes for the year were $10,400.

Required: Prepare the adjusting journal entries required at December 31, 1987.

P4–5A
Adjusting and closing entries from a trial balance and added data

The unadjusted trial balance of the Hight Company contained the following accounts as of December 31, 1987.

HIGHT COMPANY
Partial Trial Balance
December 31, 1987

Acct. No.	Account Title	Debits	Credits
121	Accrued Interest Receivable	$ 0	
131	Office Supplies	2,800	
132	Prepaid Insurance	6,940	
133	Prepaid Advertising	0	
205	Accrued Wages Payable		$ 0
212	Unearned Rent		0
406	Rent Earned		136,000
410	Interest Earned		2,800
503	Wages Expense	110,000	
504	Advertising Expense	18,000	
505	Insurance Expense	0	
506	Office Supplies Expense	0	
601	Income Summary		0

Additional information is given below:

a. Interest that had accrued on notes receivable at December 31, 1987, amounted to $970.
b. The inventory of office supplies at December 31, 1987, was $785.

(continued on next page)

c. The insurance records show that $4,000 of insurance has expired during 1987.
d. Included in Advertising Expense is a prepayment of a $3,400 contract for advertising space in a regional magazine; 30 percent of this contract has been used, and the remainder will be used in the following year.
e. Wages due to employees of $3,800 had accrued as of December 31, 1987.
f. Rent collected in advance that will not be earned until 1988 amounted to $18,000.

Required:

1. Open the accounts listed in the trial balance, and record the balance in the appropriate column as of December 31, 1987.
2. Journalize the adjusting entries and post to the appropriate account. In the accounts, identify the postings by writing "Adjusting" in the explanation columns.
3. Prepare journal entries to close the revenue and expense accounts. Do *not* transfer the net income (or net loss) to the Retained Earnings account.
4. Post the closing entries. In the accounts, identify the postings by writing "Closing" in the explanation columns.

P4–6A
Thought-provoking problem: treating interest on stockholders' equity as an expense

The closing entries and postclosing trial balance of the Fulton Realty Company, as of December 31, 1987, are given below. A yearly accounting period is used. Tyson Fulton, the stockholder who owned all of the stock of the corporation, had an equity of $18,050 on January 1, 1987. No additional common stock was issued during 1987.

GENERAL JOURNAL

Page 12

Closing Entries

1987				
Dec. 31	Rental Revenue		5,500	
	Commission Revenue		21,600	
	Income Summary			27,100
31	Income Summary		20,050	
	Rent Expense			1,800
	Insurance Expense			400
	Supplies Expense			150
	Commission Expense			16,500
	Depreciation Expense—Office Equipment			1,000
	Miscellaneous Expense			200
31	Income Summary		7,050	
	Retained Earnings			7,050
31	Retained Earnings		2,050	
	Dividends			2,050

FULTON REALTY COMPANY
Postclosing Trial Balance
December 31, 1987

Account Title	Debits	Credits
Cash	$ 8,300	
Office Supplies	150	
Prepaid Insurance	1,600	
Office Equipment	16,000	
Accumulated Depreciation—Office Equipment		$ 2,000
Notes Payable to Banks		1,000
Common Stock (1,700 shares)		17,000
Retained Earnings		6,050
Totals	$26,050	$26,050

Required:

1. Prepare an income statement for 1987.
2. Prepare a common size income statement.
3. Prepare a statement of retained earnings.
4. Fulton believes that the income statement should show a deduction of an interest expense based on the average bank prime rate (the rate that banks charge their most creditworthy customers) multiplied by the average stockholders' equity. Assuming that you are the accountant for Fulton, should you do this? Why? Why not?

B Problems

P4-1B
End-of-period process from trial balance data in alphabetical order

The trial balance of the P. P. Fairgrounds Corporation shows the following accounts, arranged in alphabetical order:

P. P. FAIRGROUNDS CORPORATION
Adjusted Trial Balance
December 31, 1987

Account Title	Debits	Credits
Accounts Payable		$ 13,000
Accounts Receivable	$ 39,500	
Cash	83,900	
Common Stock (8,000 shares issued and outstanding)		80,000
Dividends	3,350	
Equipment Maintenance Expense	4,100	
Heat and Light Expense	2,900	
Interest Earned		2,000
Land	25,000	
Notes Payable		7,000
Notes Receivable	4,500	
Parking Fees Earned		78,950
Retained Earnings, January 1, 1987		13,750
Salaries Expense	24,500	
Supplies Expense	4,550	
Supplies on Hand	2,100	
Telephone Expense	300	
Totals	$194,700	$194,700

Required:

1. Prepare an adjusted trial balance in proper chart-of-accounts sequence.
2. Prepare an income statement, a statement of retained earnings, and a balance sheet.
3. Journalize the closing entries.
4. Set up ledger accounts for Retained Earnings, Income Summary, and all nominal accounts. Enter the balances that are in the trial balance in these accounts under the date of December 31, 1987. Then post the closing entries to these accounts. Rule the accounts that are closed.

P4-2B
Cash and accrual bases

Selected cash transactions of the Raison Consulting Service for 1987 are given:

1987

Jan. 1 Purchased a three-year insurance policy for $2,700.
Jul. 1 Bought 2 vans for $19,000. The vans are expected to last 5 years, at the end of which time their salvage value will be $1,000 each.
Dec. 31 Paid $1,200 rent for the four-month period ending April 30, 1988.
31 Purchased office supplies for $710.

(continued on next page)

Required:

1. Make journal entries to record the transactions using the accrual basis.
2. Make the adjusting journal entries as of December 31, 1987, using the accrual basis. The company closes its books annually on December 31.
3. Make the journal entries to record the transactions using the cash basis.
4. What adjusting journal entries would be made if the Raison Consulting Service were on the cash basis?

P4–3B
Adjustments and effect on statements

Certain unadjusted account balances from the trial balance of Rex Davidson's Accounting Service for the year ended December 31, 1987, are given:

REX DAVIDSON'S ACCOUNTING SERVICE
Partial Trial Balance
December 31, 1987

Account Title	Debits	Credits
Accounts Receivable	$74,000	
Notes Receivable	38,800	
Prepaid Insurance	5,184	
Office Supplies	2,084	
Vans	34,000	
Accumulated Depreciation—Vans		$ 7,200
Notes Payable		10,600
Revenue—Accounting Fees		768,000
Interest Earned		1,960
Rent Earned		3,840
Advertising Expense	3,880	
Rent Expense	64,000	
Salaries Expense	78,400	
Property Taxes Expense	5,360	
Heat and Light Expense	3,840	

Adjustment data on December 31 are as follows:

a. Office supplies on hand totaled $250.
b. Depreciation for the year was $3,600.
c. Estimated heat and light expense not recorded was $510.
d. Of the amount shown for Interest Earned, $500 was unearned as of December 31, 1987.
e. The balance of the Prepaid Insurance account consists of $1,728 for the premium on a three-year policy dated July 1, 1987, and $3,456 for premiums on a three-year policy dated January 1, 1987.
f. Advertising supplies on hand were $280.
g. The balance of the Notes Payable account represents a 13 percent interest-bearing note dated January 1, 1987, due July 1, 1988.
h. The rent expense is $6,400 a month.
i. Salaries earned by employees but not paid were $2,300.
j. Property taxes accrued were $325.
k. On January 1, 1987, the Davidson Accounting Service subleased a section of its rented space. The lease with the tenant specifies the minimum yearly fee to be the greater of $3,840, payable at the beginning of each month, or 5 percent of gross sales. The amount of the adjustment in rent, if there is any adjustment, is due on January 15, 1988. The tenant reported sales of $84,800 for 1987.
l. Included in the Revenue—Accounting Fees account are advance payments of $24,000 by clients for services to be rendered early in 1988.

4 / End-of-Period Process without a Work Sheet

Required: For each of the foregoing events, do the following three things, using the format shown below:

1. Record adjusting journal entries.
2. Indicate the financial statement classification of each account in each entry.
3. Show the amount reported on the financial statements.

Example: Item a.

Item	Adjusting Journal Entries December 31, 1987	Dr.	Cr.	Financial Statement Classification	Amount Reported on Financial Statement
a	Office Supplies Expense Office Supplies	1,834	1,834	Expense Current Asset	1,834 250

P4–4B
Various adjusting entries

After an analysis of the accounts and the other records of Dunbar, Inc., the following information is made available for the year ended December 31, 1987:

a. The Office Supplies account has a debit balance of $3,595. Office supplies on hand at December 31 total $950.

b. The Prepaid Rent account has a debit balance of $27,920. Included in this amount is $2,460 paid in December for the succeeding January; $25,460 has expired.

c. The Prepaid Insurance account has a debit balance of $9,058. It consists of the following policies purchased during 1987:

Policy No.	Date of Policy	Life of Policy	Premium
NCC-1702	January 1	3 years	$5,184
2004	April 1	2 years	2,074
DV-19	October 1	1 year	1,800

d. The Prepaid Advertising account has a debit balance of $9,750. Included in this amount is $1,560 paid to a local monthly magazine for advertising space in its January and February 1988 issues.

e. At the close of the year, three notes receivable were on hand:

Date	Face Value	Total Time of Note in Days	Interest Rate
November 1	$22,600	90	12%
December 1	24,920	60	13
December 16	15,440	30	14

f. At the close of the year, two notes payable were outstanding:

Date	Face Value	Total Time of Note in Days	Interest Rate
September 2	$24,760	180	12%
November 1	38,000	90	14

g. Salaries and wages accrued totaled $8,500.

h. The Rent Earned account has a credit balance of $41,472 representing receipt of payment on a one-year lease effective May 1, 1987.

(continued on next page)

i. The Store Equipment account has a debit balance of $60,750. The equipment has an estimated useful life of 10 years and a salvage value of $5,750. All store equipment was acquired prior to January 1, 1987, and has a remaining life of five years.

j. The Vans account has a debit balance of $22,700. The vans were purchased on June 1, 1986, and have an estimated life of five years and a salvage value of approximately $3,700.

k. Property taxes accrued were $5,550.

l. Estimated income taxes for the year were $12,750.

Required: Prepare the adjusting journal entries required at December 31, 1987.

P4–5B
Adjusting and closing entries from a trial balance and added data

The unadjusted trial balance of the Wise Company contained the following accounts as of December 31, 1987.

WISE COMPANY
Partial Trial Balance
December 31, 1987

Acct. No.	Account Title	Debits	Credits
121	Accrued Interest Receivable	$ 0	
131	Office Supplies	950	
132	Prepaid Insurance	3,920	
133	Prepaid Advertising	0	
205	Accrued Wages Payable		$ 0
212	Unearned Rent		0
406	Rent Earned		222,000
410	Interest Earned		1,950
503	Wages Expense	51,000	
504	Advertising Expense	9,000	
505	Insurance Expense	0	
506	Office Supplies Expense	0	
601	Income Summary		0

Additional information includes the following:

a. Interest that had accrued on notes receivable at December 31, 1987, amounted to $420.

b. The inventory of office supplies at December 31, 1987, was $620.

c. The insurance records show that $2,000 of insurance has expired during 1987.

d. Included in Advertising Expense is a prepayment of a $1,500 contract for advertising space in a regional magazine; 60 percent of this contract has been used, and the remainder will be used in the following year.

e. Wages due to employees of $1,800 had accrued as of December 31, 1987.

f. Rent collected in advance that will not be earned until 1988 amounted to $9,500.

Required:

1. Open the accounts listed in the trial balance and record the balance in the appropriate column as of December 31, 1987.

2. Journalize the adjusting entries and post to the appropriate accounts. In the accounts, identify the postings by writing "Adjusting" in the explanation columns.

3. Prepare journal entries to close the revenue and expense accounts. Do *not* transfer net income to the Retained Earnings account.

4. Post the closing entries. In the accounts, identify the postings by writing "Closing" in the explanation columns.

P4–6B
Thought-provoking problem: selection of an accounting basis and related adjusting entries

A new accountant for the Hot Springs Corporation prepared the following condensed income statement for the year ended December 31, 1987, and the condensed balance sheet as of the same date:

HOT SPRINGS CORPORATION Exhibit A
Income Statement
For the Year Ended December 31, 1987

Revenue from services		$142,850
Operating expenses:		
Insurance expense	$ 4,095	
Miscellaneous expense	14,820	
Office supplies expense	1,365	
Wages expense	46,800	67,080
Net income		$ 75,770

HOT SPRINGS CORPORATION Exhibit B
Balance Sheet
December 31, 1987

Assets

Cash	$ 33,650
Accounts receivable	32,760
Equipment	118,950
Total assets	$185,360

Liabilities and Stockholders' Equity

Accounts payable	$ 32,760
Stockholders' equity (common stock, $50,000)	152,600
Total liabilities and stockholders' equity	$185,360

The new accountant argued that the net income would better approximate reality if the modified cash basis were used; hence she had not recorded any of the following:

a. Depreciation of equipment (acquired January 1, 1987): usually with an estimated life of 10 years, with no salvage value.
b. Wages earned by employees that have not been paid, $2,550.
c. Office supplies on hand, $525 (purchases during 1985 were debited to Office Supplies Expense).
d. Unexpired insurance premiums, $1,650; all premiums were debited to Insurance Expense.
e. Estimated federal income taxes of $20,000.

Required:

1. Do you agree with the accountant? Why? If not, how would you reply to her argument?
2. If you do not agree with the accountant, what adjusting entries would you make? Prepare these in general journal form.
3. Prepare revised *classified* statements giving effect to the adjustments prepared in requirement 2 and any other classification improvements.

5

End-of-Period Process with a Work Sheet

Introduction

In Chapter 4, the end-of-period adjustment process was illustrated with the Electronics Consulting Service example without the use of a work sheet. This chapter first presents a broad overview of the complete accounting process so that the reader can see both the individual components and the panoramic sweep of the process. Then using the Electronics Consulting service example, it illustrates the additional end-of-period steps in the accounting cycle other than those discussed in Chapter 4. The major new concept in these steps is the work sheet.

Learning Goals

1. To explain the steps in the accounting cycle.

2. To be able to prepare a work sheet.

3. To prepare from the work sheet an income statement, a statement of retained earnings, and a balance sheet.

4. To journalize adjusting and closing entries in the general journal using data from the work sheet and to post those entries.

5. To be capable of preparing a postclosing trial balance.

6. To journalize, in the period following adjustments, transactions that are related to those adjustments.

7. To be able to prepare and interpret a revenue-dollar statement.

Review of the Accounting Process

Before the illustration of the Electronics Consulting Service is resumed, the overall accounting process is reviewed to see what has been covered, and what the example now will cover. Figure 5–1 shows the individual phases of the accounting process. Chapters 1 through 3 illustrated the various steps that must be taken *during the accounting period:* (1) selecting a proper chart of

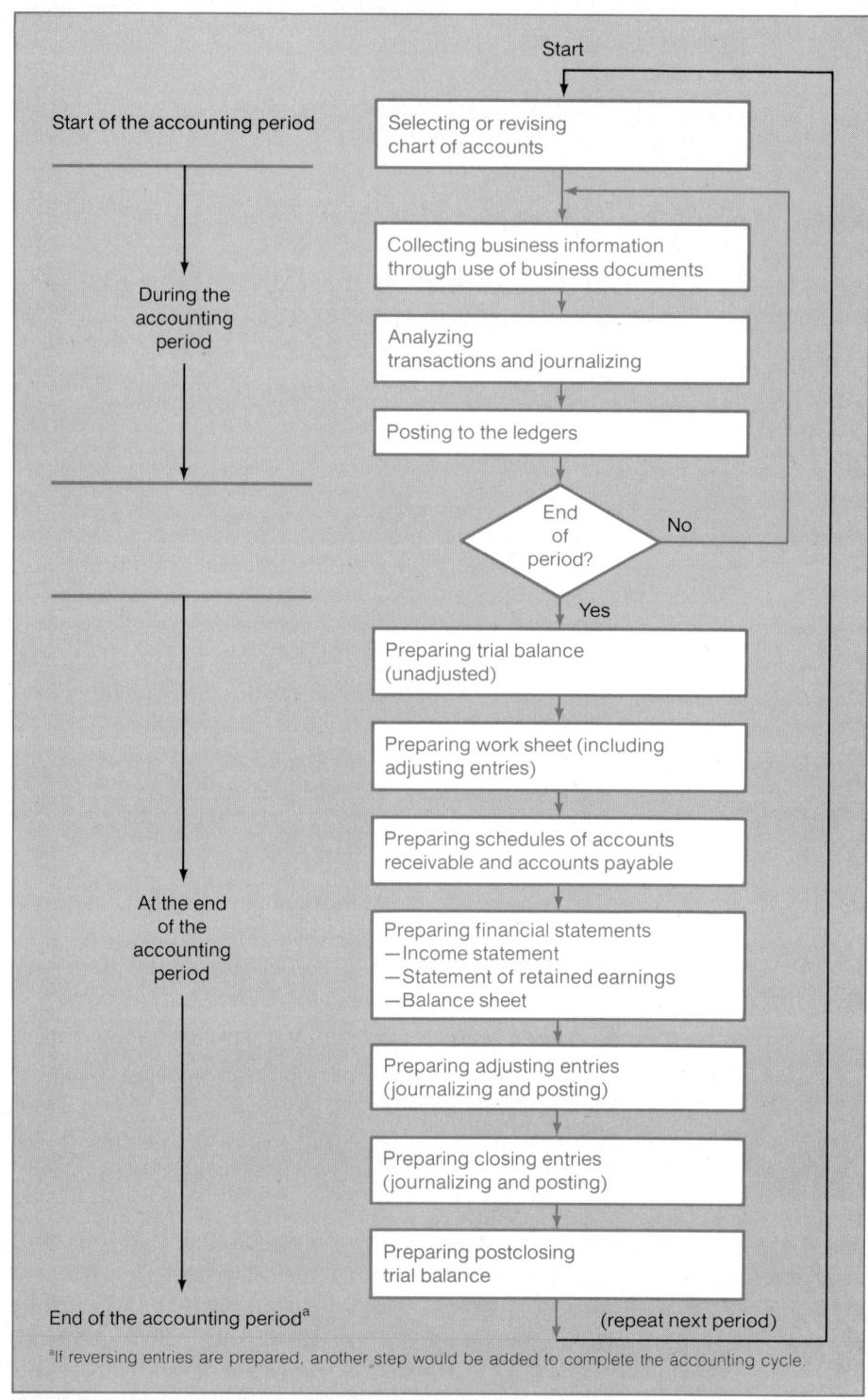

Figure 5–1 Diagram of the Accounting Process

accounts; (2) collecting business information through the use of business documents, analyzing transactions, and journalizing; and (3) posting the journal entries to the appropriate ledgers. Chapter 4 emphasized the closing and adjusting procedures that are made at the end of the period.

In this chapter, certain steps illustrated in Chapters 1 through 4 are reinforced, and some new dimensions are added to the accounting process through completing the Electronics Consulting Service example. As can be seen from Figure 5–1, the accounting phases that must be accomplished at the end of the accounting period are: (1) preparing the unadjusted trial balance; (2) collecting the adjustment information, placing the adjustment data on the work sheet, and completing the work sheet; (3) preparing the schedules of accounts receivable and accounts payable; (4) preparing the financial statements; (5) journalizing and posting the adjustments; (6) journalizing and posting the closing entries; and (7) preparing a postclosing trial balance.[1]

An Accounting Example—Electronics Consulting Service

Resuming the illustration of the Electronics Consulting Service, the next phase of the accounting process—that of preparing a work sheet—is discussed. (The reader should turn back to Figure 4–9 and also review the initial information needed for adjustments presented in reference to this example.) In this illustration, an accounting period is assumed to consist of one month. While this simplifies the learning process, most major corporations use an annual reporting period.

The Work Sheet

The end-of-period **work sheet** is a tool used by the accountant to bring together information necessary in the preparation of the formal financial statements. It is not a substitute for the financial statements but is the document from which they are prepared. Although the work sheet is not absolutely essential, it would be difficult in most instances to prepare the statements directly from the journals and ledgers since that approach would often require consolidating material from books, cards, and other documents. The work sheet bridges the gap between the accounting records and the formal statements. It permits the calculation of the effect of the adjustments in the determination of net income or net loss before the adjustments are formally

---

[1] In these early chapters, one month is typically used to represent the accounting period. This is done to simplify the learning process. In actual practice, statements prepared on a monthly or quarterly basis are interim statements. For interim statement periods, the books are not formally closed with journal entries; rather a work sheet is often used to accumulate the necessary information for these reports.

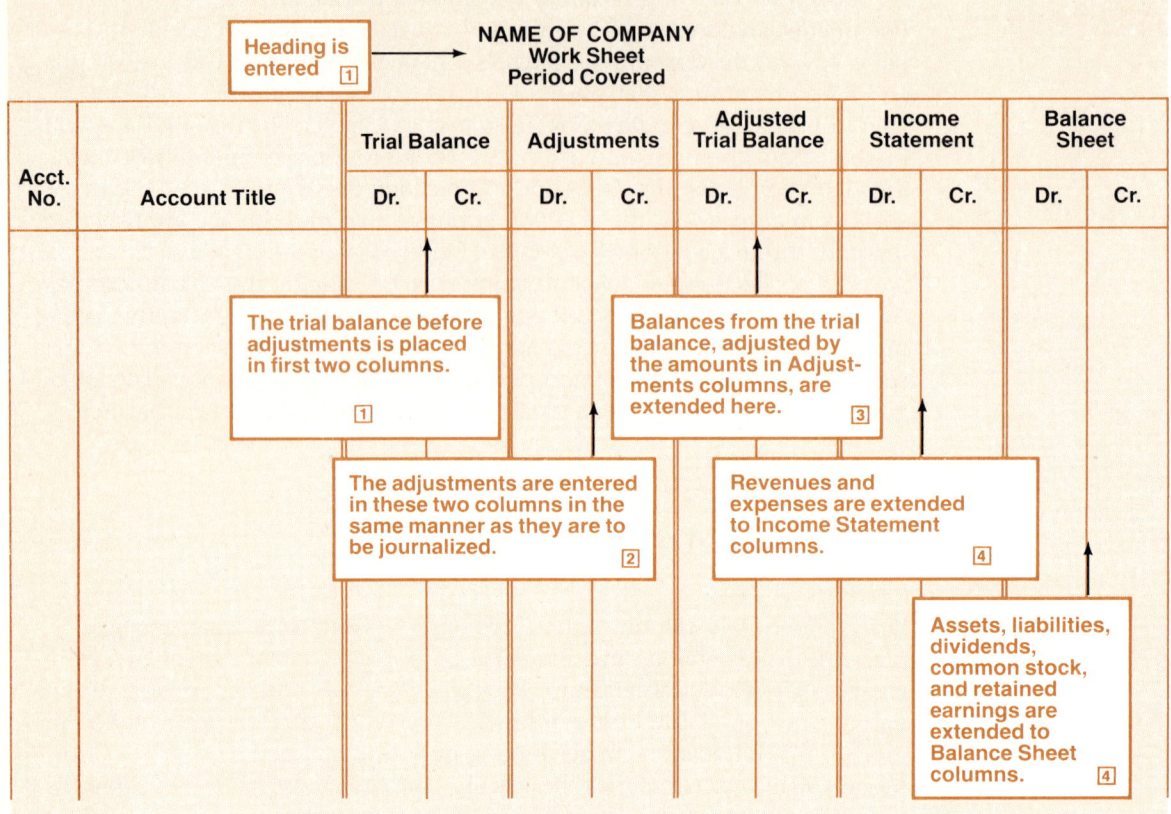

Figure 5–2 Pictorial View of a Work Sheet

journalized and posted to the ledger. It does not, however, eliminate the necessity for journalizing and posting these adjusting entries and the closing entries at the end of the accounting period.[2]

Overview of the Work Sheet

Before the work sheet for the Electronics Consulting Service is prepared step by step, the basic format of a work sheet is presented (see Figure 5–2). The heading is entered first; it shows the name of the company, the title *Work Sheet,* and the period covered. Then the trial balance before adjustments and closing is entered in the first two columns (instead of in a separate statement). The adjustments are then entered in the Adjustments columns in the same manner as they will be journalized. If an account to be debited or cred-

---

[2]While the work sheet does not eliminate journalizing adjusting and closing entries *at the end of the accounting period* (usually a year), it does provide a means for preparation of financial statements for shorter periods without going through the formal journalizing process.

ited is not listed in the trial balance before closing, its title is added below the trial balance totals. Next, the information in the first four columns for each account is combined or netted to determine the adjusted trial balance figures; these are extended to the Adjusted Trial Balance columns. These figures are then extended to either the Income Statement columns (revenues and expenses) or the Balance Sheet columns (assets, liabilities, dividends, common stock, and beginning balance of retained earnings). The net income or net loss is the difference between the two Income Statement subtotals. When it is entered to balance these columns and in the appropriate debit or credit Balance Sheet column, it should cause the two Balance Sheet columns to balance.

Four Steps in Preparing the Work Sheet of Electronics Consulting Service

The concepts presented in the preceding overview (Figure 5–2) now can be summarized in four distinct steps as the work sheet is completed for the Electronic Consulting Service (Figure 5–3, page 202). These steps are now considered and additional comments are presented relative to each of the following four steps.

Step 1. The heading and trial balance before adjustments are entered.

Step 2. Adjustments are entered.

Step 3. Adjusted trial balance is determined.

Step 4. Amounts in adjusted trial balance are extended.

[1] The heading for our illustrative company as shown in Figure 5–3 is:

ELECTRONICS CONSULTING SERVICE
Work Sheet
For the Month Ended June 30, 1987

The trial balance is next entered; the trial balance account numbers, titles, and amounts are entered either directly from the general ledger or from a prepared listing, if available. The account titles are entered in the space provided, and the amounts are entered in the first pair of money columns (see the first two dollar columns of Figure 5–3).

[2] The adjustments are generally entered on the work sheet before they are formally journalized in order to help speed up preparation of the formal financial statements. Ten adjustments for the Electronics Consulting Service, discussed in detail in Chapter 4, are entered on the work sheet (see the Adjustments columns of Figure 5–3):

Adjustment a: To adjust for expired rent.

Adjustment b: To adjust for expired insurance.

ELECTRONICS CONSULTING SERVICE
Work Sheet
For Month Ended June 30, 1987

Acct.[a] No.	Account Title[a]	Trial Balance Dr.	Trial Balance Cr.	Adjustments Dr.	Adjustments Cr.	Adjusted Trial Balance Dr.	Adjusted Trial Balance Cr.	Income Statement Dr.	Income Statement Cr.	Balance Sheet Dr.	Balance Sheet Cr.
101	Cash	5,250				5,250				5,250	
111	Accounts Receivable	550				550				550	
112	Notes Receivable	1,440				1,440				1,440	
131	Office Supplies	230			(c) 170	60				60	
141	Prepaid Insurance	2,160			(b) 60	2,100				2,100	
142	Prepaid Rent	1,500			(a) 500	1,000				1,000	
201	Office Equipment	1,400				1,400				1,400	
211	Automobiles	26,000				26,000				26,000	
301	Accounts Payable		200				200				200
302	Notes Payable		8,000				8,000				8,000
321	Unearned Rent		600	(d) 100			500				500
401	Common Stock (2,500 shares outstanding)		25,000				25,000				25,000
404	Dividends	500				500				500	
501	Consulting Revenue		7,465				7,465		7,465		
601	Heat and Light Expense	40				40		40			
602	Maintenance and Repairs Expense	375				375		375			
603	Telephone and Telegraph Expense	95				95		95			
604	Gas and Oil Expense	525				525		525			
605	Wages Expense	1,200		(h) 150		1,350		1,350			
	Totals	41,265	41,265								
606	Rent Expense			(a) 500		500		500			
607	Insurance Expense			(b) 60		60		60			
608	Office Supplies Expense			(c) 170		170		170			
511	Rent Earned				(d) 100		100		100		
609	Depreciation Expense— Office Equipment			(e) 10		10		10			
201A	Accumulated Depreciation— Office Equipment				(e) 10		10				10
610	Depreciation Expense— Automobiles			(f) 400		400		400			
211A	Accumulated Depreciation— Automobiles				(f) 400		400				400
311	Accrued Wages Payable				(h) 150		150				150
113	Accrued Interest Receivable			(g) 12		12				12	
521	Interest Earned				(g) 12		12		12		
611	Interest Expense			(i) 64		64		64			
303	Accrued Interest Payable				(i) 64		64				64
612	Income Tax Expense			(j) 1,900		1,900		1,900			
331	Income Taxes Payable				(j) 1,900		1,900				1,900
	Totals			3,366	3,366	43,801	43,801	5,489	7,577	38,312	36,224
	Net income for month							2,088			2,088
	Totals							7,577	7,577	38,312	38,312

[a] Account number 403, Retained Earnings, is not listed here because it still has a zero balance.

The difference between the Income Statement columns is net income.

Net income is transferred to the Balance Sheet Credit column.

Figure 5–3   Completed Work Sheet for Electronics Consulting Service

Adjustment c: To adjust for office supplies used.

Adjustment d: To adjust for the rent that is earned.

Adjustment e: To adjust for depreciation of the office equipment.

Adjustment f: To adjust for depreciation of the automobiles.

Adjustment g: To adjust for the accrued interest revenue.

Adjustment h: To adjust for the accrued wages expense.

Adjustment i: To adjust for the accrued interest expense.

Adjustment j: To adjust for estimated income taxes expense.

The **keying of adjustments** by letter for identification (cross-referencing) is done as they are entered in the Adjustments columns. Any additional accounts required by the adjusting entries are written in below the trial balance. (Another way would be to list them without amounts in sequence with the other accounts in the Trial Balance columns.) In Entry *a,* for example, Rent Expense is debited for $500. Since this account does not appear in the trial balance, the title is written on the line immediately below the trial balance totals and the amount is entered directly in the Adjustments Debit column on the same line; the $500 is also entered in the Adjustments Credit column opposite Prepaid Rent. In this adjustment, only one of the accounts involved had to be written in below the trial balance. In Entry *e,* however, both the debited and the credited accounts had to be written in. After all the adjustments are entered, the Adjustments columns are added as a proof of their equality.

3 Computations in this step result in the **adjusted trial balance** figure. The amounts extended to the Adjusted Trial Balance columns result from combining the amounts in the Trial Balance columns with the amounts in the Adjustments columns as follows:

- ☐ If there are no adjustments to an account, extend a debit trial balance amount to the debit column of the Adjusted Trial Balance, and extend a credit trial balance amount to the credit column of the Adjusted Trial Balance.

- ☐ If the account in the trial balance has a debit balance, add its debit adjustments and subtract its credit adjustments. The result, if a debit, is extended to the Adjusted Trial Balance Debit column; if a credit, it is extended to the Credit column.

- ☐ If the account in the trial balance has a credit balance, add its credit adjustments, and subtract its debit adjustments. The adjusted balance is extended to the proper Adjusted Trial Balance column.

- ☐ For the accounts listed below the trial balance totals, extend the adjustment amounts directly to the appropriate Adjusted Trial Balance column.

The amount in the Adjusted Trial Balance columns will be the same as the balances in the general ledger accounts after adjusting entries have been journalized and posted. Each line on the work sheet essentially represents a general ledger account and functions in the same manner as to the debit and credit position. For example, after the adjusting entries are journalized and posted, the Prepaid Rent account appears in the general ledger as shown below:

Prepaid Rent						Acct. No. 142
1987 Jun.	1	1,000[a]	1	1,500	1987 Jun. 30 Adjustment	4	500

[a] The 1,000 figure is the balance of the account.

The new balance is a debit of $1,000, which is the amount shown opposite Prepaid Rent in the Adjusted Trial Balance Debit column of the work sheet. Refer to Figure 5–3 to observe how the adjusted trial balance is prepared.

[4] The amounts in the Adjusted Trial Balance columns are extended either to the Income Statement columns or to the Balance Sheet columns, depending on their statement classification. Each amount must be extended to only one column; *no figure is ever extended to more than one place.* Expense and revenue accounts are entered in the Income Statement columns; asset, liability, and common stock and dividends (and, if present, the beginning balance of retained earnings) are entered in the Balance Sheet columns.

The last four columns are then subtotaled.

Completing the Work Sheet

The difference between the subtotals of the Income Statement columns is the net income or net loss for the period. A net income is indicated if the subtotal of the credit column exceeds the subtotal of the debit column. The excess is entered in the Income Statement Debit column and in the Balance Sheet Credit column just below the column subtotals. This procedure records on the work sheet the increase in the stockholders' equity resulting from an excess of revenue over expenses during the period. A net loss is indicated if the subtotal of the Income Statement Debit column exceeds that of the Income Statement Credit column. A loss is shown on the work sheet in the Income Statement Credit column and the Balance Sheet Debit column just below the column subtotals. The designation "Net income (or loss) for the month," whichever is pertinent, is entered in the Account Title column on the same line. Note, however, that net income or net loss is the result of a calculation and is not an account title.

The work sheet is now completed (see Figure 5–3). In this figure, note particularly the method of subtotaling the columns. After the net income is extended to the Balance Sheet Credit column, the final debit and credit totals should be equal.

If the differences between the Income Statement Debit and Credit columns (net income) and the Balance Sheet Debit and Credit columns are not the same, an error has definitely been made. Balancing the last four columns provides only a limited proof of the accuracy of the work sheet—proof that the equality of debits and credits has been maintained throughout its preparation. The extension of the Cash account debit into the Income Statement Debit column, for example, would not destroy the debit-credit relationship of the work sheet, although statements prepared from that work sheet would be inaccurate. Also, the total of the Balance Sheet Debit column need not correspond with the total assets reported in the statement. Accumulated Depreciation—Automobiles, for example, is extended to the Balance Sheet Credit column because it represents a balance sheet account with a credit balance. It is neither an asset nor a liability but rather a deduction from Automobiles, and is referred to as a contra asset account.

The work sheet may vary in form—particularly with respect to the number of columns—to meet specific needs of the user. Two examples are: (1) the Adjusted Trial Balance columns may be omitted, and (2) an extra pair of columns could be created for statement of retained earnings. If both of the foregoing alternatives are present, it would be necessary to combine the initial trial balance amounts with any adjustment amounts as the extensions are made to the appropriate statement pair of columns.

Preparation of Financial Statements from the Work Sheet

With the work sheet prepared as indicated in Figure 5–3, (1) the income statement is prepared from the amounts in the Income Statement columns of the work sheet, and (2) the statement of retained earnings and the balance sheet are prepared from the amounts in the Balance Sheet columns. In the preparation of financial statements, care should be taken to use each amount just once and in its proper debit and credit relation. The debit-credit relationship is not shown in the statements, but it is present. In the balance sheet, for example, Accumulated Depreciation—Automobiles, with a credit balance of $400, is deducted from Automobiles, which has a debit balance. Net income (or loss) appears in both the income statement and the statement of retained earnings. Also, the ending balance of retained earnings appears in both the statement of retained earnings and the balance sheet.

The financial statements of the Electronics Consulting Service for June are shown in Figures 5–4, 5–5, and 5–6. As indicated in previous chapters, some form of designation should be used to identify and cross-reference the financial statements; here the income statement, statement of retained earnings, and balance sheet are designated Exhibits A, B, and C, respectively.

ELECTRONICS CONSULTING SERVICE — Exhibit A
Income Statement
For the Month Ended June 30, 1987

Revenues:		
Consulting revenue		$7,465
Interest earned[a]		12
Rent earned[a]		100
Total revenues		$7,577
Expenses:		
Heat and light expense	$ 40	
Maintenance and repairs expense	375	
Telephone and telegraph expense	95	
Gas and oil expense	525	
Wages expense	1,350	
Rent expense	500	
Insurance expense	60	
Office supplies expense	170	
Depreciation expense—office equipment	10	
Depreciation expense—automobiles	400	
Interest expense	64	
Total expenses		3,589
Net income before income taxes		$3,988
Income tax expense		1,900
Net income after income taxes—to Exhibit B		$2,088
Earnings per share: $0.84		

[a]These two items are usually shown in a separate section of the income statement entitled "other revenues and expenses." They are shown in this statement with the major revenue sources to emphasize the fact that they are revenues.

Figure 5–4   **Income Statement**

Because there were 2,500 shares of common stock outstanding during the month, the earnings per share would be $0.84 = ($2,088 ÷ 2,500). Corporate income statements typically show this figure rounded to the nearest cent. Since the company was organized on June 1, 1987, its beginning balance in the Retained Earnings account is zero.

ELECTRONICS CONSULTING SERVICE — Exhibit B
Statement of Retained Earnings
For the Month Ended June 30, 1987

Retained earnings, June 1, 1987	$ 0
Add: Net income for month of June, 1987—Exhibit A	2,088
Subtotal	$2,088
Deduct: Dividends	500
Retained earnings, June 30, 1987—to Exhibit C	$1,588

Figure 5–5   **Statement of Retained Earnings**

Exhibit C

ELECTRONICS CONSULTING SERVICE
Balance Sheet
June 30, 1987

Assets

Current assets:
Cash		$ 5,250
Accounts receivable		550
Notes receivable		1,440
Accrued interest receivable		12
Office supplies		60
Prepaid insurance		2,100
Prepaid rent		1,000
Total current assets:		$10,412

Property, plant, and equipment:
Office equipment	$ 1,400		
Deduct: Accumulated depreciation	10	$ 1,390	
Automobiles	$26,000		
Deduct: Accumulated depreciation	400	25,600	
Total property, plant, and equipment			26,990
Total assets			$37,402

Liabilities and Stockholders' Equity

Current liabilities:
Accounts payable		$ 200
Notes payable		8,000
Accrued interest payable		64
Accrued wages payable		150
Unearned rent		500
Income taxes payable		1,900
Total current liabilities		$10,814

Stockholders' equity:
Common stock, 2,500 shares outstanding	$25,000	
Retained earnings—Exhibit B	1,588	
Total stockholders' equity		26,588
Total liabilities and stockholders' equity		$37,402

Figure 5–6   **Balance Sheet**

Recording Adjustments in the General Journal

Formal adjusting entries are usually not recorded in the general journal until after the financial statements have been prepared.[3] The adjusting entries then may be taken directly from the Adjustments columns of the work sheet, dated as of the last day of the accounting period, and journalized following the last regular journal entry. After the adjusting entries have been posted, the general ledger account balances will correspond with the amounts in the Ad-

---

[3] Remember that formal journal entries are typically recorded only at the end of an annual accounting period. A month is used here for the sake of simplicity.

justed Trial Balance columns of the work sheet. Although the adjusting journal entries for the Electronics Consulting Service *have already been made* as they were introduced, they are collected and repeated in Figure 5–7 in order to emphasize the recommended timing of the recording process and to add realism to the model illustration. The account numbers in the folio column indicate that they have been posted.

		GENERAL JOURNAL			Page 4
		Adjusting Entries			
1987 Jun.	30	Rent Expense . . . . Prepaid Rent. . . . . To record rent expense for June.	606 142	500	500
	30	Insurance Expense . . . . Prepaid Insurance. . . . . To record insurance expense for June.	607 141	60	60

	30	Office Supplies Expense . . . .
		  Office Supplies . . . .
		    To record office supplies used during June.
			608
			131
				170	170

	30	Unearned Rent. . . . . Rent Earned . . . . To record revenue earned from rental of automobile during June.	321 511	100	100

	30	Depreciation Expense—Office Equipment . . . .
		  Accumulated Depreciation—Office Equipment . . . .
		    To record depreciation for June.
			609
			201A
				10	10

	30	Depreciation Expense—Automobiles . . . .
		  Accumulated Depreciation—Automobiles . . . .
		    To record the depreciation of automobiles for June.
			610
			211A
				400	400

	30	Accrued Interest Receivable . . . .
		  Interest Earned . . . .
		    To record interest revenue accrued during June.
			113
			521
				12	12

	30	Wages Expense . . . . Accrued Wages Payable. . . . . To record wages expense accrued during June 28–30, 1987.	605 311	150	150

		GENERAL JOURNAL			Page 5
1987 Jun.	30	Interest Expense. . . . . Accrued Interest Payable . . . . To record interest expense accrued during June.	611 303	64	64
	30	Income Tax Expense . . . . Income Taxes Payable. . . . . To record estimated taxes for June.	612 331	1,900	1,900

Figure 5–7   Adjusting Entries

The Result of Adjusting Entries

When all the adjusting entries are recorded in the journal and posted to the general ledger, the mixed elements will have been eliminated. Accounts consisting of asset and expense elements and accounts containing liability and revenue elements now have been apportioned so that each element is recorded in a separate account—revenue elements are recorded in revenue accounts and expense elements are recorded in expense accounts. Advance payments for goods and services to be consumed in the future are shown in the appropriate asset accounts. Advance receipts for future revenue are shown in liability accounts. All other supplementary data not previously recorded but necessary for the preparation of financial statements (that is, the data for accrual types of adjustments) are available in the appropriate ledger accounts. The general ledger should contain all the accounts and amounts—expenses, revenues, assets, liabilities, and stockholders' equity items—necessary for the presentation of the financial position of the company as of the end of the accounting period as well as the results of its operations for the period then ended. Failure to adjust for deferrals or for accruals will result in incorrect financial statements at the end of either an interim or an annual accounting period. Recall, however, that the need for adjustment and full disclosure does not apply to insignificant or immaterial matters.

Recording Closing Entries Directly from the Work Sheet

The closing entries are recorded (see Figure 5–8) and then posted to the T accounts shown in Figure 5–9. As shown in Chapter 4, **closing entries** are made to empty (close or reduce to zero balance) those *nominal accounts* that are set up to measure some of the changes in the Retained Earnings account during a given period of time. In the closing process, the net effect reflected in these temporary accounts (the net income or net loss) is transferred to the Retained Earnings account; the Dividends account balance is transferred to the Retained Earnings account. The closing entries can be made directly from the work sheet in the following sequence:

Step 1. Each account in the Income Statement Credit column is debited, and their sum is credited to the Income Summary account.

Step 2. Each account in the Income Statement Debit column is credited, and their sum is debited to the Income Summary account.

Step 3. The balance of Income Summary, which after posting entries 1 and 2 represents the net income or the net loss as shown on the work sheet, is transferred to Retained Earnings.

Step 4. The balance of the Dividends account is closed into Retained Earnings; the amount of this entry is the amount on the Dividends account line in the Balance Sheet Debit column of the work sheet.

GENERAL JOURNAL Page 5

Closing Entries

Date		Description		Debit	Credit
1987 Jun.	30	[1]ᵃ Consulting Revenue	501	7,465	
		Rent Earned	511	100	
		Interest Earned	521	12	
		Income Summary	902		7,577
		To close revenue accounts.			
	30	[2]ᵃ Income Summary	902	5,489	
		Heat and Light Expense	601		40
		Maintenance and Repairs Expense	602		375
		Telephone and Telegraph Expense	603		95
		Gas and Oil Expense	604		525
		Wages Expense	605		1,350
		Rent Expense	606		500
		Insurance Expense	607		60
		Office Supplies Expense	608		170
		Depreciation Expense—Office Equipment	609		10
		Depreciation Expense—Automobiles	610		400
		Interest Expense	611		64
		Income Tax Expense	612		1,900
		To close the expense accounts.			
	30	[3]ᵃ Income Summary	902	2,088	
		Retained Earnings	403		2,088
		To close net income to Retained Earnings.			
	30	[4]ᵃ Retained Earnings	403	500	
		Dividends	404		500
		To close Dividends directly to Retained Earnings.			

ᵃThese boxed numbers are not actually entered in the journal. They are shown here to identify the entries with text explanations and the flow in Figure 5–9.

Figure 5–8   **Closing Entries**

These closing entries are posted to the indicated accounts. Figure 5–9 shows the posting to formal ledger accounts for Income Summary and Retained Earnings and to T accounts (without any dates or posting references shown) for the nominal accounts: Dividends, Expenses, and Revenues. Also, indicated in Figure 5–9 is a posting flow. The reader should trace the closing journal entries to these T accounts as a means of reviewing the closing process.

The Postclosing Trial Balance

The postclosing trial balance of the Electronics Consulting Service would normally be taken from the general ledger after the closing entries had been posted and the nominal accounts ruled. Since the entire general ledger is not reproduced in this example, the postclosing trial balance shown in Figure 5–10 can be traced to the work sheet (Figure 5–3), except for Retained Earnings, which is shown in Figure 5–9.

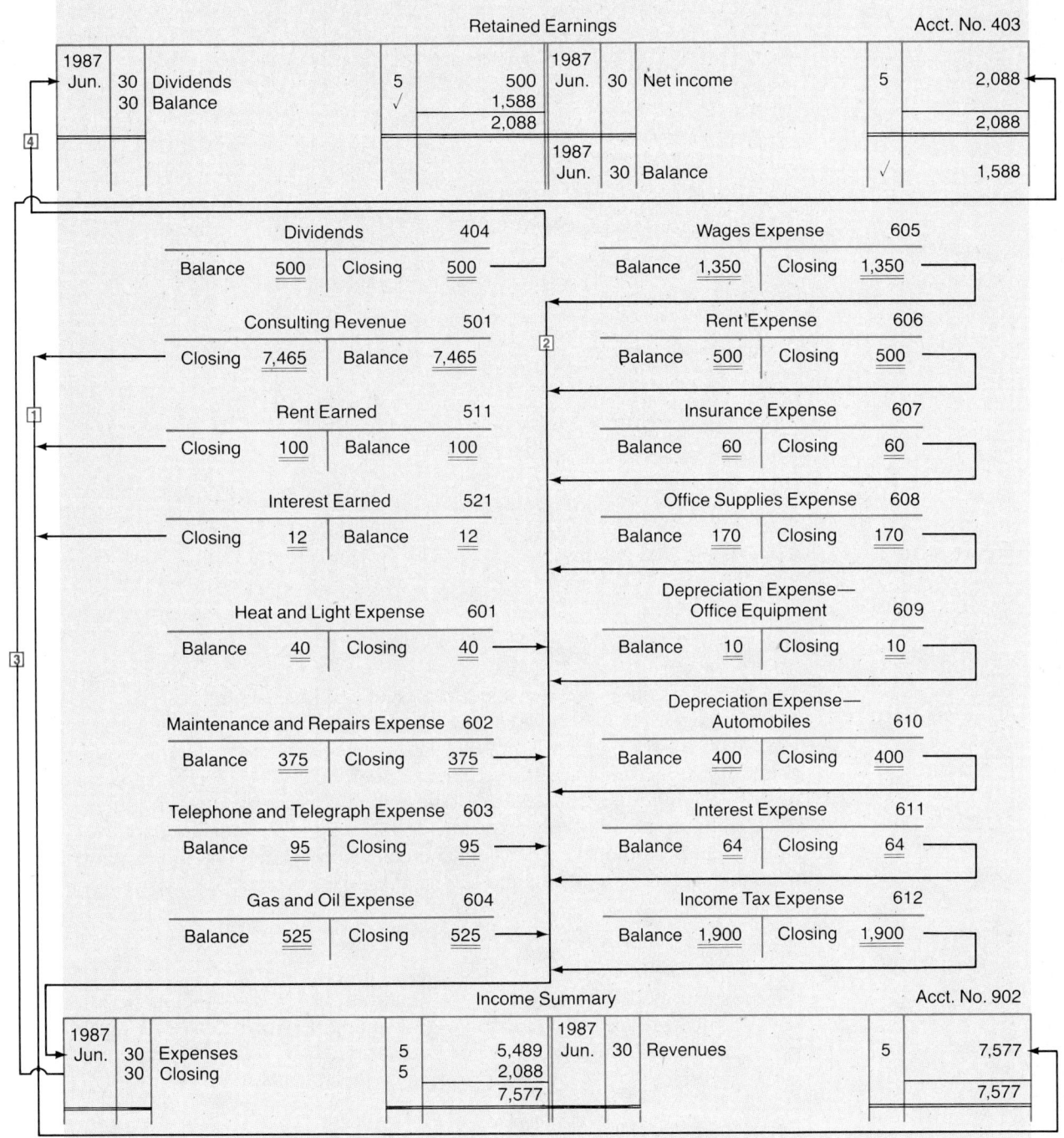

Figure 5-9 General Ledger Accounts Affected by Closing Process

Figure 5–10 Postclosing Trial Balance

ELECTRONICS CONSULTING SERVICE
Postclosing Trial Balance
June 30, 1987

Acct. No.	Account Title	Debits	Credits
101	Cash	$ 5,250	
111	Accounts Receivable	550	
112	Notes Receivable	1,440	
113	Accrued Interest Receivable	12	
131	Office Supplies	60	
141	Prepaid Insurance	2,100	
142	Prepaid Rent	1,000	
201	Office Equipment	1,400	
201A	Accumulated Depreciation—Office Equipment		$ 10
211	Automobiles	26,000	
211A	Accumulated Depreciation—Automobiles		400
301	Accounts Payable		200
302	Notes Payable		8,000
303	Accrued Interest Payable		64
311	Accued Wages Payable		150
321	Unearned Rent		500
331	Income Taxes Payable		1,900
401	Common Stock		25,000
403	Retained Earnings		1,588
	Totals	$37,812	$37,812

Subsequent Period Entries Related to Accruals

The adjusting entries are recorded in the general journal and posted to the general ledger. Four of the adjusting entries—g, h, i, and j (see Figure 5–3)—involve accrual of previously unrecorded revenue or expense items assignable to June. If reversing entries have not been made, the receipt or payment of cash in July must be analyzed to determine the respective effect of the transaction on June and July accounts. To illustrate two examples of these subsequent period entries, consider the collection of the note and interest from the supplier on July 10 and the next regular payment of the payroll on July 11.

Receiving the Accrued Interest Receivable

On the maturity date of the note receivable July 10 (30 days, including 20 days accrued in June), the Electronics Consulting Service receives the maturity value, $1,458. The maturity value is determined by adding 30 days' interest at 15 percent, or $18, to the principal of $1,440, computed as follows:

$$\text{Interest} = \$1,440 \times 0.15 \times \frac{30}{360} = \$18.$$

The entry to record the receipt from the supplier is:

		GENERAL JOURNAL			Page 5
1987 Jul.	10	Cash... Notes Receivable............................... Accrued Interest Receivable.................. Interest Earned.................................. To record the collection of a note and interest.	101 112 113 521	1,458	1,440 12 6

On June 30, the adjusting entry accrued 20 days' interest earned on the note, or $12, in June. The Accrued Interest Receivable and Interest Earned accounts again show that the total interest earned of $18 is split by the July entry in such a way that the $12 asset, Accrued Interest Receivable, is cancelled (reduced to zero) and the balance of $6 = ($18 − $12) is entered as interest earned in July.

GENERAL LEDGER

Accrued Interest Receivable   Acct. No. 113

1987 Jun.	30	Adjustment	5	12	1987 Jul.	10		5	12

Interest Earned   Acct. No. 521

1987 Jun.	30	Closing entry	5	12	1987 Jun.	30	Adjustment	5	12
					1987 Jul.	10		5	6

Ruling the asset account Accrued Interest Receivable would not normally be done during the month. It is ruled in the foregoing illustration and in similar cases that follow to emphasize that the account has a zero balance.

Paying the Accrued Wages Payable

The next regular pay day at the Electronics Consulting Service is on July 11. On July 1, Wages Expense had a zero balance as a result of the closing entries on June 30, but the Accrued Wages Payable account had a credit balance of $150 as a result of the adjusting entries. Assuming that the biweekly wages again amounted to $600, the entry on July 11 to record this payment is:

		GENERAL JOURNAL			Page 5
1987 Jul.	11	Accrued Wages Payable........................ Wages Expense................................. Cash... To record the payment of biweekly wages.	311 605 101	150 450	600

In the Accrued Wages Payable and Wages Expense accounts, reproduced below, these results have been achieved: the biweekly wages of $600 is divided so that $150, which was recognized as a June expense, is debited to Accrued Wages Payable, and $450 is recorded as an expense in July. Accrued Wages Payable now has a zero balance.

GENERAL LEDGER
Accrued Wages Payable — Acct. No. 311

1987 Jul.	11		5	150	1987 Jun.	30	Adjustment	4	150

Wages Expense — Acct. No. 605

1987 Jun.	13		2	600	1987 Jun.	30	Closing entry	5	1,350
	27		3	600					
	30	Adjustment	4	150					
				1,350					1,350
1987 Jul.	11		5	450					

The Accounting Cycle—Review

In this chapter and the preceding ones, the complete **accounting cycle** of a service business has been presented. The cycle—the total picture—consists of eleven steps, which are reviewed below (see Figure 5–1 for an overview).[4]

1. *Selecting an appropriate chart of accounts,* which consists of selecting the accounts that are likely to be needed for financial statements and designating a numerical index system for them. Once this is done, in subsequent periods the accountant merely uses the correct accounts contained in the original chart of accounts or adds any new accounts that may be created by expansion or shifts of business for a given firm.

2. *Collecting business information through the use of business documents, analyzing the transactions, and journalizing,* which consists of capturing the information, analyzing, and recording transactions in chronological order in the journal.

3. *Posting,* which consists of transferring debits and credits to the appropriate ledgers and to the proper accounts in the ledgers.

---

[4] If reversing entries are prepared, a twelfth step would be added to complete the accounting cycle.

4. *Preparing a trial balance,* or summarizing the general ledger accounts to test the equality of debits and credits; this can be prepared as a part of the work sheet.

5. *Preparing the work sheet,* or assembling and classifying information in columnar form to facilitate the preparation of financial statements.

6. *Preparing a schedule of accounts receivable,* which is summarizing the accounts receivable subsidiary ledger accounts and reconciling the total with the balance of the Accounts Receivable controlling account in the general ledger.

7. *Preparing a schedule of accounts payable,* which is summarizing the accounts payable subsidiary ledger accounts and reconciling the total with the balance of the Accounts Payable controlling account in the general ledger.

8. *Preparing the financial statements* from the work sheet; these are the income statement, statement of retained earnings, and balance sheet.

9. *Adjusting the books,* or recording and posting the adjusting entries from the work sheet.

10. *Closing the books,* which consists of recording and posting the closing entries from the Income Statement columns of the work sheet.

11. *Taking a postclosing trial balance,* or totaling the open-account balances to prove the equality of the debits and credits in the general ledger.

As explained at the beginning, to keep the Electronics Consulting Service example simple, steps 9, 10, and 11 were illustrated for a period of only one month. Most businesses use a yearly accounting period; the adjusting and closing entries are actually recorded in the journals and ledgers at the end of this period. However, those businesses sometimes *do* prepare monthly work sheets and monthly financial statements—called **interim statements**—for the management's use. Quarterly interim statements are mailed to stockholders and released to the public. These interim statements are in themselves forms of analysis. This subject is now expanded in the next section.

Managerial Analysis—Revenue Dollar Statement

In addition to such graphic presentations as that shown in Figure 1–1 and the common-size income statement shown in Figure 3–23, annual reports often include a type of analysis referred to as a **revenue-dollar statement**. This analysis shows the disposition of each sales dollar.

A revenue-dollar statement for a real life company, R. J. Reynolds Industries, is shown on page 216.[5] Each sales dollar for the years 1981 through 1983 was allocated as follows:

---

[5]Based on data in R. J. Reynolds Industries 1983 *Annual Report.*

	1983	1982	1981
Net sales	$1.00	$1.00	$1.00
Cost of products sold	0.68	0.68	0.70
Gross margin on sales	$0.32	$0.32	$0.30
Selling, advertising, general, and administrative expenses	0.20	0.19	0.16
Net operating income from continuing operations	$0.12	$0.13	$0.14
Other income (expense)	(0.01)	a	a
Net income from continuing operations before income tax	$0.11	$0.13	$0.14
Income tax expense	0.05	0.06	0.06
Net earnings from continuing operations	$0.06	$0.07	$0.08
Net earnings from discontinued operations	a	0.01	a
Net income	$0.06	$0.08	$0.08

[a]Less than ½ of 1 cent.

In the foregoing analysis, the disposition is shown in cents. If the decimals were dropped and the figures converted into percentages, the resulting statement would be referred to as a *common-size statement*. Both forms of this analysis are useful to management and external users in making comparisons within a company, with other companies in the same industry, or with the entire industry. The common-size nature permits the spotting of trends for the company and of important relationships even with companies of unlike size. Any significant trends or differences discovered in these comparisons may indicate that further investigation and analyses are required.

Glossary

Accounting cycle The steps that must be followed to process and record information, summarize and classify this information, and prepare the books to accomplish these steps during the next period.

Adjusted trial balance A trial balance prepared after the adjusting entries are made.

Closing entries These journal entries that close the nominal accounts at the end of a period—that is, reduce these accounts to a zero balance. In the closing process, the net effect of this closing is transferred to the Retained Earnings account.

Interim statements Any statements that are made during the period but not including those statements made at the end of the period.

Keying of adjustments The method of cross-referencing the debit amount(s) of an adjustment to the credit amount(s); letters a, b, c, and so on are often used for the keying of adjustments.

Revenue-dollar statement A statement showing the disposition of each sales dollar.

Work sheet An orderly and systematic method of collecting information needed for the preparation of financial statements.

Questions

Q5–1 Identify the steps an accountant would take at the end of an annual accounting period. Why is each step taken?

Q5–2 (a) What is the purpose of the work sheet? (b) Can the work of the accountant be completed without the use of the work sheet? Explain.

Q5–3 (a) Why are the parts of each entry in the adjustment columns cross-referenced with either letters or numbers? (b) How is the amount to be extended into another column determined?

Q5–4 (a) What determines the column into which an amount is to be extended? (b) Is the work sheet foolproof? Explain.

Q5–5 Student A argues that since the work sheet has columns headed Income Statement and Balance Sheet, there is no need to prepare any end-of-period statement except the statement of retained earnings. Student B counters that formal statements for balance sheet, income statement, and statement of retained earnings should be prepared. With which student do you agree? Why?

Q5–6 Since adjustments are entered on the work sheet, does this step eliminate the need for journalizing the adjustments and posting them to the ledger accounts at the end of an annual period? Why or why not?

Q5–7 Is it possible to prepare the formal financial statements from a four-column work sheet consisting of the trial balance amounts and all the necessary adjustments? Explain.

Q5–8 (a) When would the amounts for Depreciation Expense and for Accumulated Depreciation be the same in the adjusted trial balance column of the work sheet? (b) When would these amounts be different?

Exercises

E5–1

Effect of errors in adjustments on statements

The inexperienced accountant for the San Diego Company prepared the following condensed income statement for the year ended December 31, 1987, and the condensed balance sheet as of the same date:

SAN DIEGO COMPANY Exhibit A
Income Statement
For the Year Ended December 31, 1987

Revenue from services		$73,575
Operating expenses:		
Insurance expense	$ 2,048	
Miscellaneous expense	7,410	
Office supplies expense	682	
Wages expense	23,400	33,540
Net income		$40,035

SAN DIEGO COMPANY Exhibit C
Balance Sheet
December 31, 1987

Assets

Cash	$ 6,825
Accounts receivable	16,380
Equipment	59,475
Total assets	$82,680

Liabilities and Stockholders Equity

Accounts payable	$16,380
Common stock	25,000
Retained earnings	41,300
Total liabilities and stockholders' equity	$82,680

(continued on next page)

The following items were overlooked by the accountant in the preparation of the statements:

a. Depreciation of equipment (acquired January 1, 1987); estimated life, 10 years; no salvage value.
b. Wages earned by employees that have not been paid, $1,170.
c. Office supplies on hand, $275 (purchases during 1987 were debited to Office Supplies Expense).
d. Unexpired insurance premiums, $710.
e. Income tax for year, $5,950.

1. Journalize all necessary adjusting entries.
2. Prepare revised *classified* financial statements after all adjustments have been made.

E5–2
Simple work sheet

The Ringo Company's adjusted trial balance, taken from the work sheet for the year ended December 31, 1987, was as follows:

RINGO COMPANY
Adjusted Trial Balance
December 31, 1987

Account Title	Debits	Credits
Cash	$ 33,450	
Accounts Receivable	27,100	
Equipment	59,350	
Accumulated Depreciation		$ 20,000
Accounts Payable		11,560
Notes Payable		16,400
Common Stock		30,000
Retained Earnings, January 1, 1987		34,440
Dividends	12,500	
Service Revenue		95,000
Heat and Light Expense	4,500	
Wages Expense	57,500	
Depreciation Expense	8,000	
Income Tax Expense	5,000	
Totals	$207,400	$207,400

1. Enter the adjusted trial balance on a work sheet.
2. Complete the work sheet.
3. Prepare an income statement, a statement of retained earnings, and the closing journal entries.

E5–3
Adjusting, closing, and future-year entries for accruals

The Saint John Company incurred the following transactions during 1987:

1987

Nov. 1 Received 16 percent, 90-day note receivable in the amount of $8,000 in exchange for an account receivable.
Dec. 1 Issued a 15 percent, 60-day note payable in the amount of $2,500 to eliminate an account payable.
    31 The year ended on Wednesday. Weekly wages are $1,500, and Saint John has a five-day work week that ends on Friday.

1. Journalize the transactions, adjusting entries, and closing of the nominal accounts created.
2. Prepare journal entries to record collection of the note receivable, payment of the note payable, and payment of the weekly wages. (Wages are paid each Friday.)

E5–4
Analyzing adjusting entries and determining statement effect

The following information is taken from Raymondorff Company's work sheet as of December 31, 1987, and from additional records:

Unadjusted Trial Balance Amount		Adjustment Data	
1. Prepaid Insurance	$ 3,600	Expired insurance	$1,800
2. Rent Expense	12,000	Rent paid in advance as of end of year	3,000
3. Wages Expense	18,000	Accrued wages	950
4. Interest Expense	900	Accrued interest	180
5. Unearned Rent	7,200	Rent earned	2,400
6. Interest Earned	3,150	Interest unearned at end of year	1,120

For each account:

1. prepare the adjusting journal entry;
2. state the amount to be shown in the income statement;
3. state the amount to be shown in the balance sheet.

E5–5
Work sheet, accrual basis income statement, and determining cash basis income

Following is the trial balance of Bahama Lawn Mower Service for the month of July, the *first month* of operations:

BAHAMA LAWN MOWER SERVICE
Trial Balance
July 31, 1987

Account Title	Debits	Credits
Cash	$ 8,000	
Accounts Receivable	2,700	
Service Supplies	900	
Prepaid Insurance	650	
Accounts Payable		$ 900
Common Stock		10,470
Dividends	900	
Service Revenue		3,200
Advertising Expense	350	
Miscellaneous Expense	460	
Telephone and Telegraph Expense	250	
Wages Expense	360	
Totals	$14,570	$14,570

Supplementary data on July 31 were as follows:

a. Service supplies on hand were $720.
b. Expired insurance was $610.
c. Wages earned by employees but not paid were $208.
d. The income tax expense was $200.

1. Enter the trial balance on a work sheet.
2. Complete the work sheet for the month of July.
3. Prepare an income statement for the month.
4. How much would net income be if the cash basis of accounting were used?

E5–6
Partial work sheet

Column totals for the partially completed work sheet of the Lyle Corporation are shown below:

	Income Statement		Balance Sheet	
	Dr.	Cr.	Dr.	Cr.
Totals	46,950	60,600	129,300	115,650

Complete the work sheet.

E5–7
Work sheet with adjustments and reason for certain information being common to income statement and balance sheet columns

The books of the Alligator Movie Theater are closed annually on December 31. The company obtains revenue from admission fees and from a refreshment stand that is leased on a concession basis. Its general ledger showed the following balances on December 31, 1987:

Cash	$31,000
Theater Supplies	6,400
Prepaid Insurance	6,000
Prepaid Rent	8,400
Projection Equipment	76,000
Accumulated Depreciation	18,000
Mortgage Payable	25,000
Common Stock	40,000
Retained Earnings, January 1, 1987	19,500
Dividends	6,500
Admissions Revenue	43,500
Concession Revenue	17,500
Wages Expense	21,500
Repair Expense	4,100
Heat and Light Expense	1,900
Telephone and Telegraph Expense	500
Miscellaneous Expense	1,200

Supplementary data:

a. Theater supplies on hand, based on a physical count, total $900.
b. The balance of the Prepaid Insurance account represents the premium on a four-year insurance policy, effective January 1, 1987.
c. Rent expense for the year was $5,400.
d. The projection equipment has an expected useful life of 12 years and an estimated salvage value of $4,000. No equipment was acquired during the year.
e. Salaries earned by employees but unpaid on December 31 were $800.

Answer the following:

1. Enter the trial balance on a work sheet.
2. Complete the work sheet.
3. Why is the difference between the totals of the Income Statement columns and of the Balance Sheet columns the same amount?

E5–8

Completion of a work sheet

The following data for a new corporation are given at the end of its first year of operation:

Acct. No.	Account Title	Trial Balance Dr.	Trial Balance Cr.	Adjustments Dr.	Adjustments Cr.	Adjusted Trial Balance Dr.	Adjusted Trial Balance Cr.	Income Statement Dr.	Income Statement Cr.	Balance Sheet Dr.	Balance Sheet Cr.
101	Cash	34,000								34,000	
111	Accounts Receivable	16,000								16,000	
131	Office Supplies	7,500								1,500	
141	Prepaid Insurance	8,400								2,400	
142	Prepaid Rent	12,000								3,000	
201	Office Equipment	31,000								31,000	
301	Accounts Payable		8,700								8,700
321	Unearned Rent		9,800								1,800
401	Common Stock (10,000 shares)		70,000								70,000
404	Dividends	5,000								5,000	
501	Revenue		43,700								
601	Heat and Light Expense	300									
605	Wages Expense	18,000									
	Totals	132,200	132,200								
606	Rent Expense										
607	Insurance Expense										
608	Office Supplies Expense										
511	Rent Earned										
609	Depreciation Expense—Office Equipment										
201-A	Accumulated Depreciation—Office Equipment										
311	Accrued Wages Payable										
610	Income Tax Expense										
331	Income Taxes Payable										
	Totals										
	Net Income										
	Totals										

Additional data follow:

a. The office equipment has a 10-year life and a $6,100 salvage value and was purchased on January 1, 1987.
b. Wages earned but unpaid at year-end are $750.
c. Estimated income taxes are $4,700.

Complete the foregoing work sheet. Other adjustment data are to be determined from information on the work sheet.

A Problems

P5–1A
Work sheet and end-of-period statements

Addie's Bake Shop's *adjusted trial balance,* taken from the work sheet for the month ended July 31, 1987, was as follows:

ADDIE'S BAKE SHOP
Adjusted Trial Balance
July 31, 1987

Account Title	Debits	Credits
Cash	$12,195	
Accounts Receivable	3,340	
Baking Supplies	6,200	
Prepaid Insurance	4,120	
Building	36,000	
Accumulated Depreciation—Building		$14,820
Land	8,800	
Accounts Payable		5,200
Notes Payable		3,120
Notes Payable to Banks (due July 31, 1990)		9,360
Common Stock		10,000
Retained Earnings, July 1, 1987		19,129
Dividends	2,235	
Baking Revenue		25,670
Heat and Light Expense	412	
Telephone and Telegraph Expense	204	
Wages Expense	3,180	
Baking Supplies Expense	9,420	
Insurance Expense	516	
Depreciation Expense—Building	724	
Property Tax Expense	2,050	
Accrued Wages Payable		182
Interest Expense	165	
Accrued Interest Payable		130
Property Taxes Payable		1,950
Totals	$89,561	$89,561

Required:

1. Enter the *adjusted trial balance* on a work sheet using the appropriate two columns.
2. Complete the work sheet.
3. Prepare an income statement, a statement of retained earnings, and a balance sheet.

P5–2A
Completion of a work sheet

The general ledger of Nicholas's Golfing Green showed the following balances at December 31, 1987. The company obtains revenue from its driving ranges and from a concession stand.

Account Title	Debits	Credits
Cash	$ 35,200	
Golfing Supplies	12,960	
Prepaid Insurance	10,800	
Prepaid Rent	11,700	
Golfing Equipment	85,000	
Accumulated Depreciation—Golfing Equipment		$ 22,050
Mortgage Payable		50,400
Common Stock		15,000
Retained Earnings, January 1, 1987		21,796
Dividends	12,960	

(continued on next page)

Account Title	Debits	Credits
Golf Driving Revenue		76,080
Concession Revenue		10,350
Wages Expense	18,400	
Maintenance Expense	3,725	
Utilities Expense	2,780	
Telephone and Telegraph Expense	495	
Miscellaneous Expense	1,656	
Totals	$195,676	$195,676

Supplementary data include the following:

a. Golfing supplies on hand, based on a physical count, totaled $850.
b. The balance of the Prepaid Insurance account represents the premium on a four-year insurance policy, effective January 1, 1987.
c. Rent expense for the year was $8,100.
d. The golfing equipment has an expected life of 10 years and a salvage value of $1,500. No equipment was acquired during the year.
e. Salaries earned by employees but unpaid on December 31 were $205.

Required:

1. Enter the trial balance on a work sheet.
2. Complete the work sheet.
3. Why do the totals of the Income Statement columns and the totals of the Balance Sheet columns have the same difference?

P5–3A
Work sheet, financial statements, and revenue-dollar statement

The Country Biscuit Shop's *adjusted trial balance* taken from the work sheet for the month ended August 31, 1987, was as follows:

COUNTRY BISCUIT SHOP
Adjusted Trial Balance
August 31, 1987

Account Title	Debits	Credits
Cash	$ 9,560	
Accounts Receivable	8,340	
Baking Supplies	5,200	
Prepaid Insurance	3,120	
Land	20,206	
Building	26,000	
Accumulated Depreciation—Building		$14,820
Accounts Payable		5,200
Notes Payable		3,120
Bank Loan Payable (due July 31, 1989)		9,360
Common Stock		20,000
Retained Earnings, August 1, 1987		5,500
Dividends	2,235	
Baking Revenue		30,670
Heat and Light Expense	412	
Telephone and Telegraph Expense	204	
Wages Expense	4,080	
Baking Supplies Expense	8,320	
Insurance Expense	716	
Depreciation Expense—Building	624	
Property Tax Expense	1,950	
Accrued Wages Payable		282
Interest Expense	65	
Accrued Interest Payable		130
Property Taxes Payable		1,950
Totals	$91,032	$91,032

(continued on next page)

Required:

1. Record the *adjusted trial balance* on a work sheet.
2. Complete the work sheet.
3. Prepare an income statement, a balance sheet, and a statement of retained earnings.
4. Prepare a revenue-dollar statement.

P5–4A
End-of-period process

The *Hill Weekly,* a small-town weekly newspaper, began operations on August 1, 1986. The date is now July 31, 1987, and the company bookkeeper wishes to adjust and close the books in order to prepare end-of-year statements. As a local certified public accountant, you have been asked to offer recommendations as to what adjusting and closing entries are necessary.

After talking with the corporate president, Henry Wilcoxen, about your very limited responsibilities, you ask the bookkeeper to let you see the company balance sheet as of the close of business on August 1, 1986 (the opening day), and the unadjusted trial balance as of today (July 31, 1987, the end of the first year's operations). He shows you the balance sheet given below and the trial balance that follows.

THE HILL WEEKLY
Balance Sheet
August 1, 1986
(After one day's operation)

Exhibit C

Assets			Liabilities and Stockholders' Equity		
Current assets:			Current liabilities:		
Cash	$ 15,000		Accounts payable	$4,000	
Accounts receivable—advertisers	2,400		Notes payable	4,800	
Accounts receivable— subscribers	1,600		Unearned advertising	2,400	
Supplies inventory	5,000		Unearned subscriptions	1,600	
Total current assets		$ 24,000	Total current liabilities		$ 12,800
Land and depreciable assets:			Long-term liabilities:		
Land	$ 35,000		Mortgage payable		100,000
Building	120,000				
Printing equipment	40,000		Stockholders' equity:		
Office equipment	6,000		Common stock		112,200
Total land and depreciable assets		201,000	Total liabilities and stockholders' equity		$225,000
Total assets		$225,000			

Assume that you had been asked when the company started operations to suggest what general ledger account titles were needed. You now notice that the bookkeeper has placed all these titles on the trial balance, including the accounts with a zero balance. During a talk with Wilcoxen and his bookkeeper, you make the following notes:

a. The supplies inventory consists of items that cost $5,700. You note that some items had been debited to Supplies Inventory and some to Supplies Expenses.
b. The building has an estimated useful life of 50 years and no salvage value.
c. The printing equipment has an estimated useful life of 11 years and an estimated salvage value of $4,800.
d. The office equipment has an estimated useful life of 10 years and an estimated salvage value of $600.
e. Interest of $36 for the month of July 1987 on the note payable will be paid on August 1, 1987, when the regular $200 installment payment will be made.

f. Unearned advertising as of July 31 is determined to be $900.
g. Unearned subscriptions as of July 31 are determined to be $5,600.
h. Salaries and wages that have been earned by employees but that are not due to be paid until the next payday (in August) amount to $675.
i. Interest of $792 on the mortgage payable for the month of July will be paid on August 1, 1987, when the regular $800 principal payment is made.
j. The company's insurance coverage is provided by a single comprehensive 24-month policy that began on August 1, 1986.
k. The trial balance prepared as of July 31, 1987, is given as follows:

THE HILL WEEKLY
Trial Balance
July 31, 1987

Account Title	Debits	Credits
Cash	$ 32,000	
Accounts Receivable—Advertisers	5,000	
Accounts Receivable—Subscribers	2,200	
Unexpired Insurance	0	
Supplies Inventory	5,000	
Land	30,000	
Building	120,000	
Accumulated Depreciation—Building		$ 0
Printing Equipment	40,000	
Accumulated Depreciation—Printing Equipment		0
Office Equipment	6,000	
Accumulated Depreciation—Office Equipment		0
Accounts Payable		5,200
Notes Payable		3,600
Unearned Advertising		2,400
Unearned Subscriptions		1,600
Accrued Salaries and Wages Payable		0
Accrued Interest Payable		0
Mortgage Payable		95,200
Common Stock		112,200
Retained Earnings		0
Dividends	0	
Advertising Revenue		75,800
Subscriptions Revenue		65,400
Depreciation Expense—Building	0	
Depreciation Expense—Printing Equipment	0	
Depreciation Expense—Office Equipment	0	
Interest Expense	4,730	
Insurance Expense	3,600	
Promotional Expense	8,600	
Salaries and Wages Expense	66,950	
Supplies Expense	31,600	
Utilities Expense	5,720	
Totals	$361,400	$361,400

Required:

1. Enter the trial balance on a work sheet.
2. Complete the work sheet.
3. Prepare an income statement, a statement of retained earnings, and a balance sheet.
4. Journalize all needed adjusting entries.
5. Journalize the closing entries.

P5–5A

Work sheet with adjustments and reason for certain information being common to income statement and balance sheet columns

The general ledger of Shawnee Putterer showed the following balances at December 31, 1987. The books are closed annually on December 31. The company obtains revenue from its putting courses and from a concession stand.

Cash.	$ 44,200	
Putting Supplies	12,960	
Prepaid Insurance	10,800	
Prepaid Rent	11,700	
Putting Equipment	100,000	
Accumulated Depreciation—Putting Equipment		$ 22,050
Mortgage Payable		60,400
Common Stock, 3,340 shares issued and outstanding		33,400
Retained Earnings		18,396
Dividends	12,960	
Putting Revenue		82,080
Concession Revenue		10,350
Wages Expense	23,400	
Maintenance Expense	4,725	
Utilities Expense	3,780	
Telephone and Telegraph Expense	495	
Miscellaneous Expense	1,656	
Totals	$226,676	$226,676

Supplementary data include the following:

a. Putting supplies on hand, based on a physical count, totaled $980.
b. The balance of the Prepaid Insurance account represents the premium on a three-year insurance policy, effective January 1, 1987.
c. Rent expense for the year was $9,800.
d. The putting equipment has an expected life of 10 years and a salvage value of $2,000. No equipment was acquired during the year.
e. Salaries earned by employees but unpaid on December 31 were $350.

Required:

1. Enter the trial balance on a work sheet.
2. Complete the work sheet.
3. Why do the totals of the Income Statement columns and the totals of the Balance Sheet columns have the same difference?

P5–6A

The complete accounting cycle, assuming monthly closing

On March 1, 1987, Davido Corporation received its charter and completed the following transactions during the month of March:

1987

Mar.	1	Issued common stock at par for $8,000 cash.
	2	Paid $300 for office supplies.
	3	Purchased second-hand office equipment for $900 in cash.
	4	Issued a check for $300 for March rent.
	5	Paid a premium of $192 for an insurance policy on the equipment, effective March 1.
	9	Purchased supplies on account to be used in repair work, as follows:

Fisher, Inc.	$ 240
Harrison Supply Company	280
Isaacs Company	160
Rex Supplies Unlimited	480
Total	$1,160

15 Received $5,200 for repair work completed but not previously billed.
19 Additional repair work was completed, and bills were sent out, as follows:

Baker and Sons.	$ 840
Able Jacobs.	480
Harvey Walters.	280
Yonton Younts.	224
Total.	$1,824

21 Paid $170 for the telephone service for the month.
24 Paid the following creditors:

Fisher, Inc.	$ 80
Harrison Supply Company	160
Isaacs Company.	80
Rex Supplies Unlimited.	240
Total.	$560

28 Received cash from customers to apply on account, as follows:

Baker and Sons.	$200
Able Jacobs.	80
Harvey Walters.	40
Yonton Younts.	40
Total.	$360

30 Dividends of $500 were declared and paid.

Supplementary data as of March 31, 1987, were as follows:

a. The insurance premium paid on March 5 is for one year.
b. A physical count shows that office supplies on hand total $150, and repair supplies on hand total $270.
c. The office equipment has an estimated useful life of six years with no salvage value.

Required:

1. Open the following accounts in the general ledger: Cash, 101; Accounts Receivable, 111; Office Supplies, 136; Repair Supplies, 137; Prepaid Insurance, 140; Office Equipment, 163; Accumulated Depreciation—Office Equipment, 163A; Accounts Payable, 201; Common Stock, 301; Retained Earnings, 302; Dividends, 303; Repair Revenue, 401; Insurance Expense, 502; Rent Expense, 503; Office Supplies Expense, 508; Telephone and Telegraph Expense, 509; Repair Supplies Expense, 512; Depreciation Expense—Office Equipment, 517; Income Summary, 601.
2. Open accounts in the accounts receivable subsidiary ledger for Baker and Sons, Able Jacobs, Harvey Walters, and Yonton Younts.
3. Open accounts in the accounts payable subsidiary ledger for Fisher, Inc., Harrison Supply Company, Isaacs Company, and Rex Supplies Unlimited.
4. Prepare general journal entries to record all the transactions, post to the appropriate ledgers, and enter the general ledger account balances directly in the Trial Balance columns of the work sheet.
5. Enter the adjustment data in the Adjustments columns of the work sheet.
6. Complete the work sheet.
7. Prepare an income statement, a balance sheet, and a statement of retained earnings.
8. Prepare a schedule of accounts receivable.
9. Prepare a schedule of accounts payable.

(continued on next page)

10. Prepare adjusting journal entries in the general journal.
11. Post the adjusting journal entries from the general journal to the general ledger.
12. Prepare closing journal entries in the general journal and post to the general ledger.
13. Prepare a postclosing trial balance.

P5–7A
Thought-provoking problem: interpreting adjusting and reversing entries

The unadjusted and adjusted trial balance taken from the work sheet of the Fulton Realty Company along with a portion of the general journal is given below.

FULTON REALTY COMPANY
Trial Balances
December 31, 1987

Account Title	Unadjusted Debits	Unadjusted Credits	Adjusted Debits	Adjusted Credits
Cash	$ 50,000		$ 50,000	
Notes Receivable	10,500		10,500	
Accrued Interest Receivable	0		420	
Office Supplies	4,250		3,750	
Prepaid Insurance	1,270		960	
Office Equipment	25,200		25,200	
Accumulated Depreciation—Office Equipment		$ 7,560		$ 10,080
Notes Payable to Banks		20,000		20,000
Accrued Interest Payable		0		126
Common Stock		25,000		25,000
Retained Earnings, January 1, 1987		26,970		26,970
Dividends	7,000		7,000	
Commissions Earned		62,000		62,000
Salaries Expense	33,000		33,000	
Other Expenses	8,000		11,330	
Interest Expense	3,150		3,276	
Interest Earned		840		1,260
Totals	$142,370	$142,370	$145,436	$145,436

GENERAL JOURNAL

1988					
Jan.	1	Interest Earned		420	
		Accrued Interest Receivable			420
		To reverse.			
	1	Accrued Interest Payable		126	
		Interest Expense			126
		To reverse.			

Required:

1. Prepare an income statement for 1987.
2. Prepare a statement of retained earnings.
3. Did the accountant make only two adjusting entries: (a) for accrued interest receivable and (b) for accrued interest payable? If others were made, indicate what entries

were made and the amounts of the adjustments—you do not need to make the adjusting entries.

4. Why would the accountant choose to make reversing entries for the two accrued interest adjustments?

B Problems

P5–1B
Work sheet and end-of-period statements

Mama's Cake Shop's *adjusted trial balance*, taken from the work sheet for the month ended July 31, 1987, was as follows:

MAMA'S CAKE SHOP
Adjusted Trial Balance
July 31, 1987

Account Title	Debits	Credits
Cash	$ 4,150	
Accounts Receivable	5,210	
Baking Supplies	11,500	
Prepaid Insurance	7,340	
Building	54,000	
Accumulated Depreciation—Building		$ 29,940
Land	16,800	
Accounts Payable		10,900
Notes Payable		6,340
Notes Payable to Banks (due December 31, 1989)		18,820
Common Stock		10,000
Retained Earnings, July 1, 1987		8,748
Dividends	2,580	
Baking Revenue		43,340
Heat and Light Expense	715	
Telephone and Telegraph Expense	260	
Wages Expense	5,210	
Baking Supplies Expense	18,650	
Insurance Expense	838	
Depreciation Expense—Building	1,350	
Property Tax Expense	3,950	
Accrued Wages Payable		385
Interest Expense	180	
Accrued Interest Payable		310
Property Taxes Payable		3,950
Totals	$132,733	$132,733

Required:

1. Enter the adjusted trial balance on a work sheet using the appropriate columns.
2. Complete the work sheet.
3. Prepare an income statement, a statement of retained earnings, and a balance sheet.

P5–2B
Completion of a work sheet

The general ledger of Putt-A-Rama, showed the following balances at December 31, 1987. The books are closed annually on December 31. Putt-A-Rama obtains revenue from its putting courses and from a concession stand.

(continued on next page)

Account Title	Debits	Credits
Cash	$ 18,500	
Putting Supplies	6,780	
Prepaid Insurance	5,750	
Prepaid Rent	5,950	
Putting Equipment	46,000	
Accumulated Depreciation—Putting Equipment		$ 11,050
Mortgage Payable		25,500
Common Stock		15,000
Retained Earnings, January 1, 1987		7,270
Dividends	6,550	
Putting Revenue		42,040
Concession Revenue		6,150
Wages Expense	11,900	
Maintenance Expense	2,365	
Utilities Expense	2,010	
Telephone and Telegraph Expense	265	
Miscellaneous Expense	940	
Totals	$107,010	$107,010

Supplementary data include the following:

a. Putting supplies on hand, based on a physical count, totaled $475.
b. The balance of the Prepaid Insurance account represents the premium on a two-year insurance policy, effective January 1, 1987.
c. Rent expense for the year was $2,975.
d. The putting equipment has an expected life of 10 years and a salvage value of $1,000. No equipment was acquired during the year.
e. Salaries earned by employees, but unpaid on December 31, were $115.

Required:

1. Enter the trial balance on a work sheet.
2. Complete the work sheet.
3. Why do the totals of the Income Statement columns and the totals of the Balance Sheet columns have the same difference?

P5–3B
Work sheet, financial statements, and revenue-dollar statement

The Candyman Shop's *adjusted trial balance,* taken from the work sheet for the month ended January 31, 1987, was as follows:

THE CANDYMAN SHOP
Adjusted Trial Balance
January 31, 1987

Account Title	Debits	Credits
Cash	$ 6,120	
Accounts Receivable	5,680	
Baking Supplies	11,400	
Prepaid Insurance	6,240	
Land	17,600	
Building	52,000	
Accumulated Depreciation—Building		$ 29,640
Accounts Payable		10,400
Notes Payable		7,500
Bank Loan Payable (due December 31, 1990)		18,900
Common Stock		12,000
Retained Earnings, January 1, 1987		1,388
Dividends	3,000	
Baking Revenue		45,340

(continued on next page)

Account Title	Debits	Credits
Heat and Light Expense	650	
Telephone and Telegraph Expense	210	
Wages Expense	4,200	
Baking Supplies Expense	16,650	
Insurance Expense	850	
Depreciation Expense—Building	1,248	
Property Tax Expense	3,800	
Accrued Wages Payable		460
Interest Expense	250	
Accrued Interest Payable		370
Property Taxes Payable		3,900
Total	$129,898	$129,898

Required:

1. Enter the *adjusted trial balance* on a work sheet.
2. Complete the work sheet.
3. Prepare an income statement, a balance sheet, and a statement of retained earnings.
4. Prepare a revenue-dollar statement.

P5–4B
End-of-period process

The *Chapel Ledger,* a small-town biweekly newspaper, began operations on May 1, 1986. The date is now April 30, 1987, and the company bookkeeper wishes to adjust and close the books in order to prepare end-of-year statements. As a local certified public accountant, you have been asked to offer recommendations as to what adjusting and closing entries are necessary.

After talking with the corporate president, Renee Marquis, about your very limited responsibilities, you ask the bookkeeper to let you see the company balance sheets as of the close of business on May 1, 1986 (the opening day), and the unadjusted trial balance as of today (April 30, 1987, the end of the first year's operations). She shows you the balance sheet given below and the trial balance that follows.

THE CHAPEL LEDGER　　　　　　　　　　　　　　　　　　　Exhibit C
Balance Sheet
May 1, 1986
(After one day's operations)

Assets			Liabilities and Stockholders' Equity		
Current assets:			Current liabilities:		
Cash	$ 23,200		Accounts payable	$4,800	
Accounts receivable—			Notes payable	5,760	
advertisers	3,880		Unearned advertising	3,880	
Accounts receivable—			Unearned subscriptions	2,920	
subscribers	2,920		Total current liabilities		$ 17,360
Supplies inventory	6,000				
Total current assets		$ 36,000	Long-term liabilities:		
			Mortgage payable		120,000
Land and depreciable assets:					
Land	$ 36,000		Stockholders' equity:		
Building	144,000		Common stock		133,840
Printing equipment	48,000				
Office equipment	7,200				
Total land and depreciable assets		235,200			
			Total liabilities and stockholders equity		$271,200
Total assets		$271,200			

(continued on next page)

Assume that you had been asked when the company started operations to suggest what general ledger account titles were needed. Now you notice that the bookkeeper has placed all these titles on the trial balance, including the accounts with a zero balance. During a talk with the corporate president and her bookkeeper, you make the following notes:

a. The April 30, 1987, supplies inventory consists of items that cost $6,840. You note that some items had been debited to Supplies Inventory and some to Supplies Expense.
b. The building has an estimated useful life of 50 years and no salvage value.
c. The printing equipment has an estimated useful life of 11 years and an estimated salvage value of $5,760.
d. The office equipment has an estimated useful life of 10 years and an estimated salvage value of $720.
e. Interest of $43 for the month of April 1987 on the note payable will be paid on May 1, 1987, when the regular $240 installment payment will be made.
f. Unearned advertising as of April 30 is determined to be $1,100.
g. Unearned subscriptions as of April 30 are determined to be $6,820.
h. Salaries and wages that have been earned by employees but that are not due to be paid until the next payday (in May) amount to $790.
i. Interest of $597 on the mortgage payable for the month of April will be paid on May 1, when the regular $600 principal payment is made.
j. The company's insurance coverage is provided by a single comprehensive 24-month policy that began on May 1, 1986.
k. The trial balance prepared as of April 30, 1987, is given as follows:

THE CHAPEL LEDGER
Trial Balance
April 30, 1987

Account Title	Debits	Credits
Cash	$ 35,600	
Accounts Receivable—Advertisers	6,000	
Accounts Receivable—Subscribers	2,640	
Unexpired Insurance	0	
Supplies Inventory	6,000	
Land	38,000	
Building	144,000	
Accumulated Depreciation—Building		$ 0
Printing Equipment	48,000	
Accumulated Depreciation—Printing Equipment		0
Office Equipment	7,200	
Accumulated Depreciation—Office Equipment		0
Accounts Payable		6,240
Notes Payable		4,320
Unearned Advertising		2,880
Unearned Subscriptions		1,920
Accrued Salaries and Wages Payable		0
Accrued Interest Payable		0
Mortgage Payable		114,240
Common Stock		133,840
Retained Earnings		0
Dividends	0	
Advertising Revenue		90,960
Subscriptions Revenue		78,480
Depreciation Expense—Building	0	
Depreciation Expense—Printing Equipment	0	
Depreciation Expense—Office Equipment	0	

(continued on next page)

Account Title	Debits	Credits
Interest Expense	5,676	
Insurance Expense	4,320	
Promotional Expense	10,320	
Salaries and Wages Expense	80,340	
Supplies Expense	37,920	
Utilities Expense	6,864	
Totals	$432,880	$432,880

Required:

1. Enter the trial balance on a work sheet.
2. Complete the work sheet.
3. Prepare an income statement, a statement of retained earnings, and a balance sheet.
4. Journalize all needed adjusting entries.
5. Journalize the closing entries.

P5–5B

Work sheet with adjustments and reason for certain information being common to income statement and balance sheet columns

The general ledger of Pure Putting Place showed the following balances at December 31, 1987. The books are closed annually on December 31. The company obtains revenue from its putting courses and from a concession stand.

Cash	$ 35,100	
Putting Supplies	8,480	
Prepaid Insurance	5,400	
Prepaid Rent	5,850	
Putting Equipment	45,000	
Accumulated Depreciation—Putting Equipment		$ 11,025
Mortgage Payable		35,200
Common Stock, 2,170 shares issued and outstanding		21,700
Retained Earnings, January 1, 1987		9,198
Dividends	6,480	
Putting Revenue		41,040
Concession Revenue		5,175
Wages Expense	11,700	
Maintenance Expense	2,363	
Utilities Expense	1,890	
Telephone and Telegraph Expense	247	
Miscellaneous Expense	828	
Totals	$123,338	$123,338

Supplementary data include the following:

a. Putting supplies on hand, based on a physical count, totaled $940.
b. The balance of the Prepaid Insurance account represents the premium on a three-year insurance policy, effective January 1, 1987.
c. Rent expense for the year was $5,400.
d. The putting equipment has an expected life of 10 years and a salvage value of $900. No equipment was acquired during the year.
e. Salaries earned by employees, but unpaid on December 31, were $180.

Required:

1. Enter the trial balance on a work sheet.
2. Complete the work sheet.
3. Why do the totals of the Income Statement columns and the totals of the Balance Sheet columns have the same difference?

P5–6B

The complete accounting cycle assuming monthly closing

On July 1, 1987, Janie Corporation was incorporated to operate a repair shop. During July the following transactions were completed:

1987

Jul.		
1	Issued common stock at par value for $16,000 in cash.	
2	Paid $500 for office supplies.	
3	Purchased second-hand office equipment for $2,500 in cash.	
4	Issued a check for $600 for July rent.	
7	Paid a premium of $384 for an insurance policy on the equipment, effective July 1.	
10	Purchased supplies on account to be used in repair work, as follows:	

Ames Manufacturers	$ 960
Elmer and Associates	480
Sanders Company	560
Thomas' Supply Company	320
Total	$2,320

14	Received $10,400 for repair work completed and not previously billed.	
18	Additional repair work was completed, and bills were sent out as follows:	

James Baker	$ 960
Melissa Lawson	1,680
Roger Sutton	560
Thomas Tutterow	448
Total	$3,648

22	Paid $320 for telephone service for the month.	
26	Paid the following creditors:	

Ames Manufacturers	$ 480
Elmer and Associates	160
Sanders Company	320
Thomas' Supply Company	160
Total	$1,120

29	Received cash from customers to apply on account, as follows:	

James Baker	$160
Melissa Lawson	400
Roger Sutton	80
Thomas Tutterow	80
Total	$720

31	A dividend of $800 was declared and paid.	

Supplementary data as of July 31, 1987, were as follows:

a. The insurance premium paid on July 7 is for one year.
b. A physical count shows that office supplies on hand total $250, and repair supplies on hand total $450.
c. The office equipment has an estimated useful life of six years with no salvage value.

Required:

1. Open the following accounts in the general ledger: Cash, 101; Accounts Receivable, 111; Office Supplies, 136; Repair Supplies, 137; Prepaid Insurance, 140; Office Equipment, 163; Accumulated Depreciation—Office Equipment, 163A; Accounts Payable, 201; Common Stock, 301; Retained Earnings, 302; Dividends, 303; Repair Revenue, 401; Insurance Expense, 502; Rent Expense, 503; Office Supplies Expense,

508; Telephone and Telegraph Expense, 509; Repair Supplies Expense, 512; Depreciation Expense—Office Equipment, 517; Income Summary, 601.

2. Open accounts in the accounts receivable subsidiary ledger for James Baker, Melissa Lawson, Roger Sutton, and Thomas Tutterow.

3. Open accounts in the accounts payable subsidiary ledger for the Ames Manufacturers, Elmer and Associates, Sanders Company, and Thomas' Supply Company.

4. Prepare general journal entries to record all the transactions, post to the appropriate ledgers, and enter the general ledger account balances directly in the Trial Balance columns of the work sheet.

5. Enter the adjustment data in the Adjustments columns of the work sheet.

6. Complete the work sheet.

7. Prepare an income statement, a balance sheet, and a statement of retained earnings.

8. Prepare a schedule of accounts receivable.

9. Prepare a schedule of accounts payable.

10. Prepare adjusting journal entries in the general journal.

11. Post the adjusting journal entries from the general journal to the general ledger.

12. Prepare closing journal entries in the general journal and post to the general ledger.

13. Prepare a postclosing trial balance.

P5–7B
Thought-provoking problem: issue of interest on invested capital

The closing entries of the Thomas Realty Company as of December 31, 1987, are given below. A yearly accounting period is used. The stockholders had a capital stock balance of $15,000 on January 1, 1987; they purchased additional stock for $5,000 during the year. The Retained Earnings balance on January 1, 1987, was $8,500.

GENERAL JOURNAL

Closing Entries

1987				
Dec. 31	Rental Revenue		5,500	
	Commission Revenue		21,600	
	Income Summary			27,100
31	Income Summary		20,050	
	Rent Expense			1,800
	Insurance Expense			400
	Supplies Expense			150
	Commission Expense			16,500
	Depreciation Expense—Office Equipment			1,000
	Miscellaneous Expense			200
31	Income Summary		7,050	
	Retained Earnings			7,050
31	Retained Earnings		2,050	
	Dividends			2,050

Required:

1. Prepare an income statement for 1987.
2. Prepare a statement of retained earnings for 1987.
3. The major stockholder, Tyson Thomas, argues that the corporate income statement should show a deduction for interest on the invested capital—$20,000 of common stock. Do you agree or disagree? Comment.

6

Merchandising: Measuring and Reporting the Results of Operations

Introduction

In all previous chapters, the businesses for which records are maintained have earned revenue from providing a service. Their income statements—limited to revenues and operating expenses—have been relatively easy to prepare. However, a great number of businesses earn revenue from selling merchandise to customers. Examples include Sears, Roebuck and Company, Kmart, and JCPenney. In these merchandising businesses, there is an additional cost—the cost of merchandise sold. Since a merchandising business is involved in the purchase of goods, their handling, and their sale, additional accounts are needed to record these transactions. Also, the income statements are more complex.

This chapter examines the functions and the financial statement classifications of the accounts needed for a merchandising business and shows how to complete the work sheet and financial statements for this type of business. The chapter closes with a discussion of the "management by exception" principle, especially as it relates to the managerial control of cash discounts.

Learning Goals

1. To understand the concept of cost of goods sold.

2. To identify the functions and financial statement classifications of merchandising accounts.

3. To compute the cost of goods sold.

4. To prepare and complete a work sheet for a merchandising business.

5. To be able to explain the difference between the income statements for nonmerchandising and merchandising businesses.

6. To journalize and post to the merchandise accounts in the closing process.

7. To journalize transactions involving cash discounts using both the net and gross price methods.

8. To be able to distinguish between cash discounts and trade discounts and to compute both.

Merchandising: An Overview

The principal difference between a merchandising firm and a service firm is the need to include in computing net income the cost of merchandise that was sold during the period. In general terms, the cost of goods sold is the cost, to the merchandising firm, of the merchandise that was sold to customers during the accounting period. There are alternative approaches to determining cost of goods sold. One of these, the **periodic inventory system**, determines inventory and cost of goods sold only at the end of each accounting period. (This is the method used in this chapter.) The other, the **perpetual inventory system** produces a continuous record of goods on hand and cost of goods sold.

Under the periodic inventory system cost of goods sold can be calculated only after a cost is determined for the merchandise remaining on hand at the end of the period (usually done by physical count and tracing to cost records). To simplify the discussion and to focus on the important merchandising concepts in this chapter, it will be assumed that the end-of-period inventory valuations have already been determined. In Chapter 10, the determination of the periodic inventory valuation is discussed, and the perpetual inventory system is explained.

In broad terms the income statement of a merchandising firm takes on the preceding form.[1] The next several sections contain discussions of the various accounts needed to develop *net sales revenue* and *cost of goods sold*.

---

[1] The amounts used in this illustration come from the example used later in the chapter—Tarrant Wholesale Company. As will be seen later, there are other expenses including income tax expense to be deducted in determining final net income.

Sales Revenue Accounts

The Sales Account

Sales are transactions involving the transfer of goods or services in exchange for cash or a promise to pay at a later date. A sale of merchandise is recorded by a credit to the revenue account, **Sales**. Suppose, for example, that the Tarrant Wholesale Company sold merchandise on credit to John Roundtree. This transaction would be recorded as shown below:

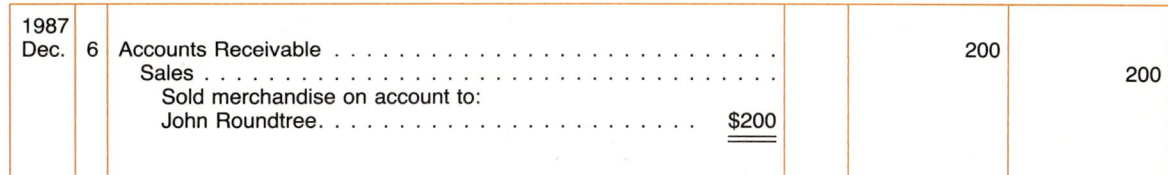

The debit to Accounts Receivable (or to Cash if the sale is for cash) records an increase in an asset. The credit to Sales, a revenue account, records the gross increase in the stockholders' equity. This credit constitutes a recovery of the cost of the merchandise sold as well as a profit. However, many businesses would find it next to impossible to divide each sale into a return of cost and a profit. Therefore, the entire sale price of the goods is recorded as revenue. The total cost of goods sold for the year becomes a deduction from the year's total revenue in the income statement. The calculation of the cost of goods sold is explained later in the chapter.

A copy of the invoice showing the sale to John Roundtree appears in Figure 6–1.

DATE SOLD		TARRANT WHOLESALE COMPANY Sherbourne, Mass. 02666					OUR INVOICE No. 10032	
12/6/87	No. X00137			SALESMAN	JB			
TERMS	SOLD TO	John Roundtree					CUSTOMER ORDER No. A232	
F.O.B. Destination	TOWN AND STATE	Cambridge, Ma. 12115					LEDGER FOLIO	
2/10, n/30	SHIP BY	Allen Motor Freight		WHEN TO SHIP	12/6/87		S10006	
ITEM No.	SHIPPER'S CHECK	QUANTITY	DESCRIPTION	UNIT	PRICE	AMOUNT		
67181	✔	84	Relzohn, Semi-cut	Lb.	$1.00	$ 84	00	
4979	✔	10	Keg, 10 gal. Hearthstone	Ea.	8.50	85	00	
347	✔	2	Jar, 1 qt. Acrolyx	Ea.	15.50	31	00	
			Total			$200	00	

Note: Although most states have sales taxes, they are omitted here for simplicity.

Figure 6–1 Sales Invoice

The Sales Returns and Allowances Account

A customer may return merchandise because it is not exactly as ordered, or the customer may be entitled to an allowance, or a reduction of the amount owed, for defective or broken goods not worth returning. The effect of the entry to record a return or allowance is the opposite of a sale. However, when Cash or the customer's account is credited, an account entitled **Sales Returns and Allowances**, a contra account to Sales, is debited. This contra account is used, rather than Sales, so that a record may be available of the amount of returns and allowances. If John Roundtree returned 10 pounds of Relzohn, item number 67181, as defective, the journal entry would be:

1987 Dec.	9	Sales Returns and Allowances...............................		10	
		Accounts Receivable			10
		Defective merchandise was returned by:			
		John Roundtree.....................	$10		

A business form called a **credit memorandum** is issued to Roundtree to advise that his account has been credited for the return. It is not necessary to change the inventory amount. The loss of defective units is automatically included in the cost of the goods sold computation (discussed later).

The Sales Discounts Account

The customer who pays within a stated discount period may be allowed a **cash discount**, or reduction in price. If the buyer pays within the discount period, the seller has the cash available during the interval between the end of the discount period and the end of the credit period for reinvestment in the business. The balance in the uncollected accounts receivable for that interval has also been reduced.

Sales discounts are computed on the invoice price; the conditions of payment are stated on the invoice. Two examples of cash discount terms are 2/10, n/30, and 1/10, n/60. The first of these terms, *2/10, n/30* (read two ten, net thirty), means that if the buyer pays within 10 days from the date shown on the invoice, two percent may be deducted from the invoice price, or the buyer may take 30 days before paying the total invoice price.

It is important to recognize the magnitude of the discount offered. This can be done best if the discount is converted into its equivalent annual interest rate. Assuming terms of 2/10, n/30, the cost of the additional 20 days is high, because the loss of the two percent discount amounts to one-tenth of one percent per day = (2 percent ÷ 20), or 36 percent per 360-day year = (0.1 percent × 360). The prudent buyer should compare carefully the cost of the failure to take a cash discount with current interest rates.

Since the effect of a discount is to reduce the amount actually received from the sale, Sales Discounts is debited for the amount of the discount. **Sales Discounts** is a contra account to Sales and is also used to supply management with valuable information about the business. When discounts are offered, the customer is in fact being offered the choice of paying (1) the full amount of the invoice or (2) the full amount reduced by the amount of the discount. The seller does not know at the time of the sale whether the customer is going to take the discount, so the customer is charged the full amount of the sale. If payment is received within the discount period, the collection is recorded as follows:

1987					
Dec. 16	Cash....................................			186.20	
	Sales Discounts........................			3.80	
	Accounts Receivable.................				190.00
	Received payment from John Roundtree for the sale of December 6 less the 2% cash discount:				
	Gross sale price.....................	$200.00			
	Merchandise returned...............	10.00			
	Accounts receivable balance.......	$190.00			
	2% discount[a]........................	3.80			
	Cash received.......................	$186.20			
	John Roundtree......................	$190.00			

[a] Discount is allowed only on the $190 of merchandise actually retained.

It is not necessary to place the details of returns and discount computations in the journal entry explanations. In this chapter, it is done only so the reader can see the source of debits and credits.

The following partial income statement of Tarrant Wholesale Company, whose accounts are used for illustrative purposes throughout this chapter, shows the classification of the Sales and its contra accounts to derive net sales revenue.

TARRANT WHOLESALE COMPANY
Income Statement
For the Year Ended December 31, 1987

Exhibit A

Gross sales revenue...............................		$124,200
Deduct: Sales returns and allowances..........	$2,400	
Sales discounts.......................	1,800	4,200
Net sales revenue.................................		$120,000

Cost of Goods Sold Accounts

In the diagram at the beginning of this chapter, cost of goods sold is shown as a deduction from net sales revenue to determine gross margin on sales. It is now logical to examine the accounts used to collect information about cost of goods sold.

Net Cost of Purchases

The Purchases Account Under the periodic inventory system, merchandising businesses use a separate **Purchases** account for all merchandise bought for resale. The account is not used for the purchase of operating supplies, for example, or for store equipment. It is debited for the cost of the goods bought for resale as shown on the seller's invoice. It therefore provides a record of the cost of the goods purchased during the period—not a record of the goods on hand. During the year, the Purchases account is debited with each receipt of merchandise. This account is increased as each purchase is recorded. Credits to the account are made to close the account or to correct errors. A typical entry to record a purchase of merchandise of $800 from Jay Stores is:

1987 Dec.	5	Purchases.. Accounts Payable................................... Purchased merchandise on account, terms 1/10, n/30: Jay Stores......................... $800	800	800

The Transportation In Account The invoice price of goods may include the cost of transporting the goods from the seller's place of business to that of the buyer. If so, no separation is made, and the entire purchase price is debited to Purchases. If the cost of transportation is not included, the freight cost may be borne by the buyer, who debits the amount to **Transportation In** (or Freight In). This account balance is added to Purchases in the income statement to determine the delivered cost of merchandise. The buyer makes an entry as follows:

1987 Dec.	7	Transportation In.................................... Cash .... Paid for freight charges on merchandise purchased F.O.B. shipping point.	50	50

The following terms are used in connection with the transportation of merchandise:

Transportation terms

1. *The term* **F.O.B.** *(free on board)* **shipping point** *indicates that title (ownership of the goods) passes to the buyer when the seller turns the shipment over to a common carrier. The owner of the merchandise while it is in transit (the buyer) bears the freight cost from the point of shipment to the destination.*

2. *The term* **F.O.B. destination** *indicates that title passes to the buyer at the destination. The owner of the merchandise while it is*

in transit (the seller) bears the freight cost to the buyer's location. (Sometimes the buyer pays the cost and deducts the amount from the payment to the seller.)

The Purchases Returns and Allowances Account Goods bought for resale may be defective, broken, or not of the quality or quantity ordered. Either they may be returned for credit, or the seller may make an adjustment by reducing the original price. The buyer makes an entry as follows:

1987				
Dec.	8	Accounts Payable	100	
		Purchases Returns and Allowances		100
		Returned defective merchandise to vendor:		
		Jay Stores $100		

Purchases Returns and Allowances is a contra account to Purchases. The same result could be accomplished by crediting Purchases, but it is useful to management to have the books show total purchases as well as total purchases returns and allowances. Analysis of the Purchases Returns and Allowances account may indicate the need for changes in the procedures for ordering and handling merchandise.

The Purchases Discounts Account The **Purchases Discounts** account, a contra account to Purchases, is used to record cash discounts on the purchase price of goods for payments that are made within the discount period specified by the seller. A typical payment entry within the discount period is:

1987				
Dec.	13	Accounts Payable	700	
		Cash		693
		Purchases Discounts		7
		Paid for merchandise purchased on December 5 less discount:		
		Gross purchase $800		
		Merchandise returned 100		
		Accounts payable balance $700		
		1% discount 7		
		Cash paid $693		
		Jay Stores $700		

The Net Cost of Purchases Disclosed

The **net cost of purchases**, then, is the total cost of purchases plus transportation in, minus purchases returns and allowances and purchases discounts. The amounts for Tarrant Wholesale Company are as follows:

Purchases		$63,580
Transportation in		4,800
Gross delivered cost of purchases		$68,380
Deduct: Purchases returns and allowances	$1,500	
Purchases discounts	3,600	5,100
Net cost of purchases		$63,280

The Merchandise Inventory Account

Illustrated in this chapter is the periodic inventory system. Under the periodic inventory system, merchandise purchased is recorded at *cost* in the Purchases account; merchandise sold is recorded at *selling price* in the Sales account. Therefore, an account called **Merchandise Inventory** is needed to show the cost of merchandise actually on hand at the end of each accounting period. The amount is determined by making a list of the goods on hand, with an actual count of each showing physical quantities and cost. This *ending inventory* is entered in the books and becomes the *beginning inventory* of the next period. This new amount in the ledger account will not be changed until the end of the next accounting period because the Merchandise Inventory account is not used during the period. Since the account remains open, its balance—the beginning inventory—appears in the trial balance at the end of the period and is charged against income by a debit to Income Summary and a credit to Merchandise Inventory when the books are closed. Concurrently, in the closing entries, the new ending merchandise inventory is entered as a debit to Merchandise Inventory and a credit to Income Summary. Thus the amount of the beginning inventory has been eliminated and replaced by the amount of the ending inventory. After the closing entries are posted, the Merchandise Inventory account in the general ledger of the Tarrant Wholesale Company appears as shown below:[2]

Merchandise Inventory   Acct. No. 121

1986 Dec. 31	[1]	12	15,400	1987 Dec. 31	[2]	20	15,400
1987 Dec. 31	[3]	20	11,480				

[1] The debit amount of $15,400 is the cost of the merchandise inventory on hand as of December 31, 1986 (the beginning inventory).

[2] The credit posting of $15,400 closes the account temporarily and transfers the balance to Income Summary.

---

[2] Some accountants prefer to use an adjusting entry to record the change in inventory valuation. If this is done, two adjusting entries are normally made: (1) a debit to Income Summary and a credit to Merchandise Inventory—for the beginning inventory—and (2) a debit to Merchandise Inventory—for the ending inventory—and a credit to Income Summary. With either method, the result in the Merchandise Inventory account must be the same.

[3] The debit posting of $11,480 is the cost of the merchandise inventory on hand as of December 31, 1987 (the ending inventory); this amount will remain unchanged in the account until the books are closed again on December 31, 1988.

Items 2 and 3 came from the 1987 closing entries. Footnote 2 explains an alternative procedure.

Cost of Goods Sold

The cost of goods sold section of the Tarrant Wholesale Company income statement can now be presented in full. The net cost of purchases, illustrated earlier, is repeated here to show that when using the periodic inventory system it is necessary to add the beginning inventory to the net cost of purchases to arrive at the cost of merchandise available for sale, and then to deduct the ending inventory to arrive at the **cost of goods sold**. (Note how major amounts are kept in the right-hand column with computations of subtotals moved left as necessary.)

Cost of goods sold:			
Merchandise inventory, January 1, 1987			$15,400
Purchases		$63,580	
Transportation in		4,800	
Gross delivered cost of purchases		$68,380	
Deduct: Purchases returns and allowances	$1,500		
Purchases discounts	3,600	5,100	
Net cost of purchases			63,280
Cost of merchandise available for sale			$78,680
Deduct: Merchandise inventory, December 31, 1987			11,480
Cost of goods sold			$67,200

This type of computation to determine the cost of goods sold is necessary because sales are recorded only at selling price under the periodic system. A continuous record of the *cost* of each individual sale is not recorded under the periodic method.

Gross Margin on Sales

The **gross margin on sales** is the difference between net sales revenue and cost of goods sold. The term *gross* indicates that the expenses necessary to operate the business must still be deducted to arrive at the net operating margin. If the gross margin on sales is less than the operating expenses, the difference is a net operating loss for the period. The amounts for Tarrant are as follows (the detailed computations of net sales revenue and cost of goods sold have already been illustrated and are not repeated here):

Net sales revenue	$120,000
Cost of goods sold	67,200
Gross margin on sales	$ 52,800

Part One / The Basic Accounting Model

Functions of the Merchandise Accounts

The following T accounts summarize the functions of the merchandise accounts described in this chapter and their locations in the financial statements. The description *Balance* in each account refers to the balance before the closing entries have been posted. After the closing entries are posted, all the merchandise accounts except Merchandise Inventory have zero balances.

Sales

Debited	Credited
At the end of the accounting period to close the account.	During the accounting period for the sales price of goods sold.
	Balance before closing A credit representing cumulative sales for the period to date.
	Statement classification In the income statement as the first item on the statement.

Sales Returns and Allowances

Debited	Credited
During the accounting period for unwanted merchandise returned by customers and allowances granted for defective or broken goods.	At the end of the accounting period to close the account.
Balance before closing A debit representing cumulative sales returns and allowances for the period to date.	
Statement classification In the income statement, a deduction from sales revenue.	

Sales Discounts

Debited	Credited
During the accounting period for the amounts that the customers deduct from the gross sales price when payment is made within the period established by the seller.	At the end of the accounting period to close the account.
Balance before closing A debit representing cumulative sales discounts taken by customers for the period to date.	
Statement classification In the income statement, a deduction from sales revenue.	

Purchases

Debited	Credited
During the accounting period for the purchase price of goods bought for resale.	At the end of the accounting period to close the account.

Balance before closing
A debit representing cumulative purchases for the period to date.

Statement classification
In the income statement, added to the beginning inventory under cost of goods sold.

Transportation In

Debited	Credited
During the accounting period for delivery costs—freight or cartage—on merchandise purchases.	At the end of the accounting period to close the account.

Balance before closing
A debit representing cumulative costs for the period to date incurred by the buyer for the delivery of merchandise.

Statement classification
In the income statement, in the cost of goods sold section, added to purchases.

Purchases Returns and Allowances

Debited	Credited
At the end of the accounting period to close the account.	During the accounting period for unwanted merchandise returned to the vendor or allowances received for defective or broken merchandise.

Balance before closing
A credit representing cumulative purchases returns and allowances for the period to date.

Statement classification
In the income statement, in the cost of goods sold section, as a deduction from the gross cost of merchandise purchased.

Purchases Discounts	
Debited At the end of the accounting period to close the account.	*Credited* During the accounting period for the amounts of discount from the gross purchase price of merchandise when payment was made within the period established by the seller. *Balance before closing* A credit representing cumulative purchases discounts taken for the period to date. *Statement classification* In the income statement, in the cost of goods sold section, as a deduction from the gross cost of merchandise purchased.

Merchandise Inventory	
Beginning balance A debit representing the cost of goods on hand at the beginning of the period. This was the ending inventory of the previous period. *Debited* At the end of each accounting period in a closing entry for the merchandise actually on hand (the ending balance of the account). *Statement classification* 1. In the balance sheet the ending inventory under current assets. 2. In the income statement, in the cost of goods sold section, the beginning inventory is added to purchases and the ending inventory is deducted from the cost of merchandise available for sale.	*Credited* At the end of each accounting period in a closing entry to remove the beginning inventory from the account.

The balances in the merchandising accounts are brought together with other temporary accounts to prepare an income statement. The income statement for Tarrant Wholesale Company is shown below in Figure 6–2.

TARRANT WHOLESALE COMPANY
Income Statement
For the Year Ended December 31, 1987

Exhibit A

Gross sales revenue			$124,200
Deduct: Sales returns and allowances		$ 2,400	
Sales discounts		1,800	4,200
Net sales revenue			$120,000
Cost of goods sold:			
Merchandise inventory, January 1, 1987		$15,400	
Purchases	$63,580		
Transportation in	4,800		
Gross delivered cost of purchases	$68,380		
Deduct: Purchases returns and allowances	$1,500		
Purchases discounts	3,600	5,100	
Net cost of purchases		63,280	
Cost of merchandise available for sale		$78,680	
Deduct: Merchandise inventory, December 31, 1987		11,480	
Cost of goods sold			67,200
Gross margin on sales			$ 52,800
Deduct: Operating expenses:			
Selling expenses:			
Sales salaries expense		$12,000	
Transportation out expense		2,400	
Advertising expense		3,000	
Total selling expenses		$17,400	
General and administrative expenses:			
Rent expense		$ 6,000	
Property tax expense		7,800	
Heat and light expense		2,160	
Miscellaneous general expense		480	
Insurance expense		1,920	
Supplies expense		2,040	
Depreciation expense—machinery and equipment		3,600	
Total general and administrative expenses		24,000	
Total operating expenses			41,400
Net operating margin			$ 11,400
Other revenue:			
Interest earned	$ 125		
Rent earned	300	$ 425	
Other expenses:			
Interest expense	$ 75		
Loss on sale of equipment	100	175	250
Income before income taxes			$ 11,650
Income tax expense			4,660
Net income			$ 6,990
Earnings per share		$0.70[a]	

[a]Based on average of 10,000 shares.

Figure 6–2 Income Statement

The Operating Expense Accounts

Operating expenses include salaries, postage, telephone and telegraph, computer services, heat and light, insurance, advertising, and any other expired costs incurred for goods or services used in operating the business. The breakdown of operating expenses into a detailed account for each type facilitates analyses and comparisons that aid in cost control. The amount of detail shown depends on the size and type of the business and on the needs and wishes of management.

The operating expenses are often classified into selling or general and administrative. Those incurred in packaging, advertising, selling, and delivering the product are classified as **selling expenses**. Sales salaries, commissions, and supplies used in the sales department are examples of expenses incurred in making the sale. Expenses of delivering the product include freight paid by the seller (transportation out expense—not to be confused with transportation in) and the expense of operating delivery vehicles. Expenses such as rent, taxes, and insurance, to the extent that they are incurred in selling the product, are also classified as selling expenses. Other operating expenses are classified as **general and administrative expenses**, including office expenses, computer services, executive salaries, and the portion of rent, taxes, and insurance applicable to the administrative function of the business.

Expenses that are common to both selling and administrative functions may be apportioned on some equitable basis. If an apportionment is not practicable, the account should be classified under the function it serves most. In Figure 6–2, the operating expense accounts that are entirely related to selling are classified as such; all the others are classified as general and administrative.

If the operating expense accounts in the general ledger are too numerous, it is advisable to remove them to subsidiary selling expense and general and administrative expense ledgers. Two controlling accounts are substituted in the general ledger—Selling Expense Control and General and Administrative Expense Control—in place of the accounts that have been removed. (The function of controlling accounts was explained in Chapter 3 and diagrammed in Figure 3–10.)

Net Operating Margin

Net operating margin measures the net revenue from the major operating function of the business. In Figure 6–2, the total operating expenses of $41,400 are deducted from the gross margin on sales of $52,800 to arrive at the net operating margin of $11,400.[3]

---

[3]Some accountants prefer to list the expenses in decreasing order of size of these amounts. However, the relative sizes of amounts change over the years. Once an account number has been assigned, there is less possibility of error if expenses are listed in account number order from the work sheet.

Other Revenue and Other Expenses

Revenue and expenses that are generated by transactions not related to the principal activity of the business are classified as **other revenue and other expenses**. These sections of the income statement serve a valuable function; they permit calculation of the net operating margin without its being distorted by nonoperating items and link the net operating margin for the period with the net income for that period.

Other Revenue

In Figure 6–2, Tarrant Wholesale Company shows $125 in interest earned and $300 in rent earned under other revenue. These additional examples are included under other revenue because they arose from a source other than the sale of merchandise, the basic business purpose of Tarrant. Other examples of items classified as other revenue are gains from the sale of temporary investments, dividends received on shares of stock owned, and gains from the sale of property, plant, and equipment.

Other Expenses

Nonoperating expenses, such as interest on money borrowed from the bank or on notes given to creditors for the purchase of merchandise or losses from the sale of property, plant, and equipment, are shown under other expenses. In Figure 6–2, there are $75 in interest expense and $100 from a loss on a sale of equipment under this heading. The loss is the excess of the undepreciated cost of the equipment over the sales price.

The accountant added $250, the excess of other revenue over other expenses, to the net operating margin. If other expenses exceed other revenue, the expenses are listed first and the excess is deducted from the net operating margin. In the absence of other revenue or other expenses, net operating margin becomes net income and net operating loss becomes net loss.

Income Tax Expense

Because it is a corporation, the earnings of Tarrant Wholesale Company are subject to federal and state income tax. While the exact amount is not known until the tax returns for 1987 are filed in 1988, it is estimated that combined federal and state taxes will be 40 percent of taxable income. For Tarrant, this is $4,660 = (0.40 \times \$11,650)$.

The complete income statement for the Tarrant Wholesale Company for the year ended December 31, 1987 (Figure 6–2) was prepared from the work sheet shown later (Figure 6–5).

Work Sheet for a Merchandising Business

The procedure for completing the work sheet of a merchandising business is similar to that of a service business, with the exception of the account for merchandise inventory. At the end of the period, the balance of the Merchandise Inventory account, the beginning inventory of $15,400, is extended to

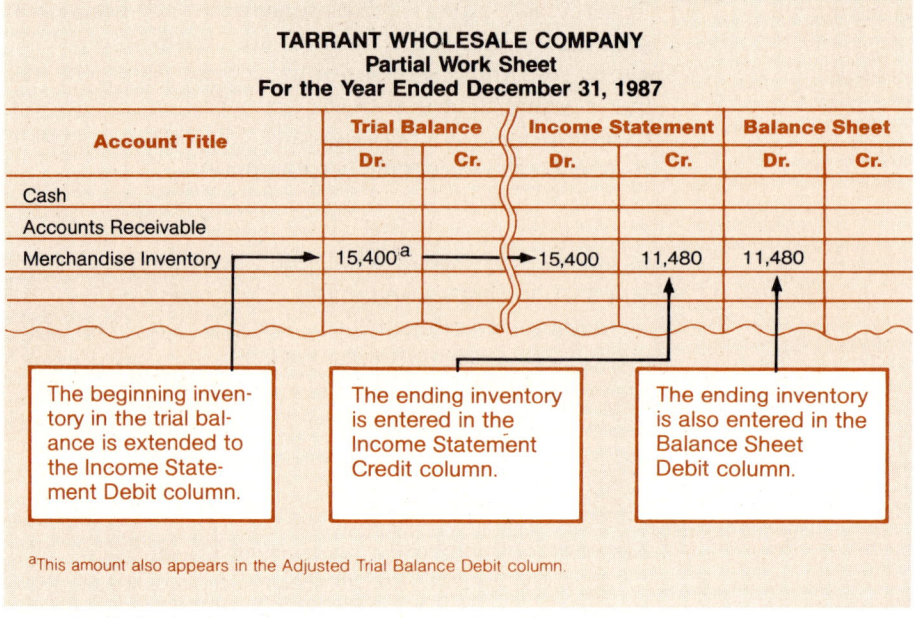

Figure 6–3   **Partial Work Sheet**

the Income Statement Debit column of the work sheet because it is part of the cost of merchandise available for sale. The ending inventory, $11,480, is entered in the Income Statement Credit column because it is an offset or deduction from the accounts comprising the total cost of goods available for sale that will have been extended into the income statement debit column.[4] The ending inventory amount is also entered in the Balance Sheet Debit column because it is a balance sheet asset. Note that the ending inventory amounts are always entered on the same horizontal line as the beginning inventory. Entering an income statement credit and a balance sheet debit maintains the essential debit/credit equality of the work sheet as illustrated in Figure 6–3. (The complete work sheet is shown in Figure 6–5.)

Trial Balance Columns

The account balances in the trial balance are taken from the general ledger of the Tarrant Wholesale Company as of December 31, 1987.

Adjustments Columns

The adjustments are entered in the Adjustments columns of the work sheet in the same manner as illustrated in Chapter 5. No entry is made in these columns for the change in the Merchandise Inventory account. That change is accomplished directly through the Income Statement and the Balance Sheet columns, as shown in Figure 6–3.

---

[4] Some accountants prefer to handle the end-of-period inventory change as an adjustment on the worksheet and in the adjusting entries. When this is done, the end result remains the same.

Adjusted Trial Balance Columns

The combined Trial Balance and Adjustments column amounts are extended to the Adjusted Trial Balance columns.

Income Statement Columns

All the account balances that enter into the measurement of net income are extended to the Income Statement columns. The income statement accounts that enter into the determination of gross margin on sales are shown in Figure 6–4.

Acct. No.	Account Title	Income Statement Dr.	Income Statement Cr.
121	Merchandise Inventory	15,400	11,480
401	Sales		124,200
402	Sales Returns and Allowances	2,400	
403	Sales Discounts	1,800	
501	Purchases	63,580	
502	Transportation In	4,800	
503	Purchases Returns and Allowances		1,500
504	Purchases Discounts		3,600
	(Totals of the foregoing items)	87,980	140,780

Figure 6–4 Abstract from the Work Sheet

The difference between the column totals in Figure 6–4 is $52,800 = ($140,780 − $87,980). It is the same as the gross margin on sales in the formal income statement (Figure 6–2) because all the accounts that enter into the determination of the gross margin are present. Similar examples could be shown using all the other sections of the income statement and balance sheet.

Balance Sheet Columns

All the amounts used to prepare the balance sheet and statement of retained earnings are extended to the Balance Sheet columns.

Statements Prepared from the Work Sheet

The income statement illustrated in Figure 6–2, the statement of retained earnings illustrated in Figure 6–6, and the classified balance sheet shown in Figure 6–7 are prepared directly from the work sheet (Figure 6–5), not from the ledger accounts or other sources. Information for all sections except the

TARRANT WHOLESALE COMPANY
Work Sheet
For the Year Ended December 31, 1987

Acct. No.	Account Title	Trial Balance Dr.	Trial Balance Cr.	Adjustments Dr.	Adjustments Cr.	Adjusted Trial Balance Dr.	Adjusted Trial Balance Cr.	Income Statement Dr.	Income Statement Cr.	Balance Sheet Dr.	Balance Sheet Cr.
101	Cash	7,200				7,200				7,200	
111	Accounts Receivable	39,800				39,800				39,800	
121	Merchandise Inventory	15,400				15,400		15,400	11,480	11,480	
131	Office Supplies	3,240			(b) 2,040	1,200				1,200	
141	Prepaid Insurance	3,740			(a) 1,920	1,820				1,820	
151	Machinery and Equipment	70,100				70,100				70,100	
151A	Accumulated Depreciation—Machinery and Equipment		7,200		(c) 3,600		10,800				10,800
201	Accounts Payable		17,700				17,700				17,700
202	Notes Payable		7,300				7,300				7,300
221	Mortgage Payable		20,000				20,000				20,000
301	Common Stock		60,000				60,000				60,000
302	Retained Earnings		5,150				5,150				5,150
303	Dividends	1,000				1,000				1,000	
401	Sales		124,200				124,200		124,200		
402	Sales Returns and Allowances	2,400				2,400		2,400			
403	Sales Discounts	1,800				1,800		1,800			
501	Purchases	63,580				63,580		63,580			
502	Transportation In	4,800				4,800		4,800			
503	Purchases Returns and Allowances		1,500				1,500		1,500		
504	Purchases Discounts		3,600				3,600		3,600		
601	Sales Salaries Expense	12,000				12,000		12,000			
602	Transportation Out Expense	2,400				2,400		2,400			
603	Advertising Expense	3,000				3,000		3,000			
701	Rent Expense	6,000				6,000		6,000			
702	Property Tax Expense	7,800				7,800		7,800			
703	Heat and Light Expense	2,160				2,160		2,160			
704	Miscellaneous General Expense	480				480		480			
801	Interest Earned		125				125		125		
802	Rent Earned		300				300		300		
821	Interest Expense	75				75		75			
822	Loss on Sale of Equipment	100				100		100			
	Totals	247,075	247,075								
705	Insurance Expense			(a) 1,920		1,920		1,920			
706	Office Supplies Expense			(b) 2,040		2,040		2,040			
707	Depreciation Expense—Machinery and Equipment			(c) 3,600		3,600		3,600			
708	Income Tax Expense			(d) 4,660		4,660		4,660			
203	Income Taxes Payable				(d) 4,660		4,660				4,660
	Totals			12,220	12,220	255,335	255,335	134,215	141,205	132,600	125,610
	Net income for the year							6,990			6,990
	Totals							141,205	141,205	132,600	132,600

Figure 6–5   Work Sheet

TARRANT WHOLESALE COMPANY
Statement of Retained Earnings
For the Year Ended December 31, 1987

Exhibit B

Retained earnings, January 1, 1987	$ 5,150
Add: Net income for the year (Exhibit A)	6,990
Subtotal	$12,140
Deduct: Dividends	1,000
Retained earnings, December 31, 1987	$11,140

Figure 6–6
Statement of Retained Earnings

TARRANT WHOLESALE COMPANY
Balance Sheet
December 31, 1987

Exhibit C

Assets

Current assets:		
Cash		$ 7,200
Accounts receivable		39,800
Merchandise inventory		11,480
Office supplies		1,200
Prepaid insurance		1,820
Total current assets		$ 61,500
Property, plant, and equipment:		
Machinery and equipment	$70,100	
Deduct: Accumulated depreciation	10,800	
Total property, plant, and equipment		59,300
Total assets		$120,800

Liabilities and Stockholder's Equity

Current liabilities:		
Accounts payable	$17,700	
Notes payable	7,300	
Income taxes payable	4,660	
Total current liabilities		$ 29,660
Long-term liabilities:		
Mortgage payable		20,000
Total liabilities		$ 49,660
Stockholders' equity:		
Common stock	$60,000	
Retained earnings	11,140	
Total stockholders' equity		71,140
Total liabilities and stockholders' equity		$120,800

Figure 6–7
Balance Sheet

---

retained earnings amount is taken directly from the work sheet. The new retained earnings amount, however, must be taken from the statement of retained earnings or computed as the work sheet beginning-of-year balance plus net income minus dividends.

		GENERAL JOURNAL			Page 20
1987		**Closing Entries**			
Dec.	31	**Merchandise Inventory**	121	**11,480**	
		Sales	401		124,200
		Purchases Returns and Allowances	503		**1,500**
		Purchases Discounts	504		**3,600**
		Interest Earned	801		125
		Rent Earned	802		300
		Income Summary	901		141,205
		To record the ending inventory and to close the revenue and the credit balance merchandising accounts.			
	31	Income Summary	901	134,215	
		Merchandise Inventory	121		**15,400**
		Sales Returns and Allowances	402		2,400
		Sales Discounts	403		1,800
		Purchases	501		**63,580**
		Transportation In	502		**4,800**
		Sales Salaries Expense	601		12,000
		Transportation Out Expense	602		2,400
		Advertising Expense	603		3,000
		Rent Expense	701		6,000
		Property Tax Expense	702		7,800
		Heat and Light Expense	703		2,160
		Miscellaneous General Expense	704		480
		Interest Expense	821		75
		Loss on Sale of Equipment	822		100
		Insurance Expense	705		1,920
		Office Supplies Expense	706		2,040
		Depreciation Expense—Machinery and Equipment	707		3,600
		Income Tax Expense	708		4,660
		To close the beginning inventory, the expense, and the debit balance merchandising accounts.			
	31	Income Summary	901	6,990	
		Retained Earnings	302		6,990
		To transfer net income.			
	31	Retained Earnings	302	1,000	
		Dividends	303		1,000
		To close the Dividends account.			

Figure 6–8   **Closing Entries**

Closing Entries

The procedure for recording the closing entries in a merchandising business is essentially the same as that in a service business (illustrated in Chapter 4).[5] The only difference involves the accounts introduced in this chapter. The

---

[5] Adjusting entries are journalized from the work sheet as explained in Chapter 5 and are not illustrated again here.

closing entries, including the closing of the beginning merchandise inventory and the recording of the ending inventory, are also prepared from the work sheet. They are shown in Figure 6–8. The accounts that enter into the determination of the cost of goods sold under the periodic system are in boldface type. After the closing entries are posted, all the revenue and expense accounts have zero balances. The remaining accounts—the open balance sheet accounts—are used to prepare a postclosing trial balance.

Management Control— The Exception Principle

The control principle of **management by exception** involves isolating those amounts or accounts that indicate operating inefficiencies and focusing attention on the areas that might require corrective action. Since only exceptions from the norm require such corrective action, management's task is simplified and expedited by separating from the mass of data the exceptional items for further study. The alternative method for recording cash discounts, the discounts lost method, is an application of the principle of management by exception.

Purchases Discounts Lost Method

Under the **gross price method**, the dollar amount of discounts granted or taken is accumulated in the Sales Discounts and Purchases Discounts accounts, as was shown earlier in this chapter. Management is interested primarily, however, not in the amount of discounts taken, but rather in the exceptions—that is, the *discounts not taken*.

The alternative procedure for recording purchase discounts is called the **purchases discounts lost method** or the **net price method**. Purchases are recorded at net—invoice price minus discount—and discounts lost are entered in a special account. The Purchases Discounts account would not then be required.

To illustrate the accounting for discounts lost, assume that a purchase of $5,000 in merchandise is received on July 5, with terms of 2/10, n/30, and that the invoice is paid July 15. The entries for the purchase and payment are:

1987				
Jul.	5	Purchases.	4,900	
		Accounts Payable.		4,900
		Purchased merchandise on account ($5,000 less 2%):		
		Ace Company. $4,900		
	15	Accounts Payable	4,900	
		Cash		4,900
		Paid for merchandise purchased on July 5:		
		Ace Company. $4,900		

If the invoice were not paid until July 30, the entries would be:

1987					
Jul.	5	Purchases..		4,900	
		Accounts Payable..................................			4,900
		Purchased merchandise on account:			
		Ace company....................... $4,900			
	30	Accounts Payable...................................		4,900	
		Purchases Discounts Lost.......................		100	
		Cash...			5,000
		Paid for merchandise purchased on July 5:			
		Ace Company....................... $4,900			

Under the discounts lost procedure, the debit to Purchases is $4,900 whether or not the discount is lost, and the lost discount of $100 appears in a separate account, isolating the amount for the detection of possible laxities in procedures. The loss of available discounts may indicate a weakness in the organization, such as lack of bank credit or slowness in processing invoices for payment. The Purchases Discounts Lost account balance is classified under other expenses in the income statement.

There are some disadvantages to recording purchases at the net price: (1) the amount of discounts taken is not reported separately in the income statement; (2) statements from creditors do not agree with net of discount amounts recorded in the accounts payable ledger; (3) there are increased clerical costs and inconveniences; and (4) an adjusting entry is needed at the end of the period to record the lapsed discount portion of unpaid invoices by debiting Purchases Discounts Lost and crediting Accounts Payable. However, for many firms, the strengthened internal control gained from using the net price method outweighs these disadvantages. If there is a need for management to monitor sales discounts, the net price method could also be used to record sales. Under the net price method, sales discounts lost would be credited to the Sales Discounts Not Taken account. They would be reported as other revenue in the income statement.

Trade Discounts

Another class of discount is the trade discount, which, unlike the cash discount, is not related to the prompt payment of the invoice. A **trade discount** is a percentage reduction from a list price; the list price is not recorded in the accounts. The seller prints a catalog in which the prices of the various articles are shown. The actual price charged may differ from the list price because of the class of buyer (wholesalers, retailers, and so on), the quantity ordered, or changes in the catalog. The granting of trade discounts eliminates the need for frequent reprinting of catalogs or printing different lists for different classes of buyers.

If more than one discount is given—a so-called **chain discount**—each discount is applied successively to the declining balance to arrive at the invoice price. Thus, the invoice price of an item listed at $300 less trade discounts of 20 percent, 10 percent, and 5 percent is $205.20, computed as follows:

List price.	$300.00
Less discount of 20% × $300.	60.00
Remainder.	$240.00
Less discount of 10% × $240.	24.00
Remainder.	$216.00
Less discount of 5% × $216.	10.80
Invoice price.	$205.20

Another way to compute the actual price is to multiply the list price by the complements of the discounts: for example, $300 × 0.80 × 0.90 × 0.95 = $205.20. The journal entry on the buyer's books to record such a purchase is:

1987				
Nov.	4	Purchases.	205.20	
		Accounts Payable.		205.20
		To record merchandise purchased.		

Note that the purchase is recorded at the billing price. There is no need, therefore, for an accountant to record trade discounts.

Internal Control over Inventory

The presence of an inventory in a merchandising firm raises an internal control problem that is not present in service enterprises. Internal control over inventory is discussed in Chapter 10, but one aspect—the efficiency of inventory use—is appropriate for discussion here. A company that has too much inventory is incurring unnecessary interest expense or is losing the opportunity to make temporary investments. On the other hand, a company that has too little inventory will constantly experience shortages of goods to sell and probably the loss of customers. A ratio used to evaluate the amount of inventory is called the inventory turnover.

Inventory turnover is the number of times the inventory is purchased, sold, and repurchased (turned over) during the year. This ratio is computed as the cost of goods sold in ratio to average inventory.[6] For the Tarrant Wholesale Company, this ratio is 4.45 (or approximately 4½ times) computed as

$$\frac{\$67,200}{\frac{(\$15,400 + \$14,800)}{2}}$$

The inventory turnover is compared with experience of previous years and with the same ratio for other wholesalers to evaluate Tarrant's performance in inventory management.

Sales Taxes Payable

Most states have a law that levies a sales tax on the purchase of certain types of merchandise by customers. The typical law levies a tax on the customer buying the merchandise but requires the seller to collect the tax and to remit it to the appropriate governmental unit. To illustrate, assume that a retail sales tax of 4 percent is levied on all sales in a given state. If Saleo Company sells merchandise for cash with a retail sales price of $10,000, it would have to collect $10,400. This transaction is recorded as follows:

1987				
Jun.	30	Cash..	10,400	
		Sales...		10,000
		Sales Taxes Payable...............................		400
		To record cash sales with a 4 percent sales tax.		

Although Saleo Company collects the sales taxes, the amount belongs to the appropriate government; hence a liability must be created for the amount payable. It is a current liability. The company must file a sales tax return—usually each month. At the time the return is filed, the sales tax is paid. Then an entry is made debiting Sales Taxes Payable and crediting Cash.

---

[6]Average inventory is used to provide a measure that spans the year, as does the cost of goods sold.

Appendix 6.1
Special Journals

Introduction

At this point, the reader should understand the fundamentals of recording transactions in the accounting records and reporting results in financial statements. These fundamental methods and concepts can now be put together into an accounting system (a set of interrelated documents, records, rules, and procedures). In each type of business, certain unique features may present a need to adapt documents or procedures. However, the basic goal is an effective and efficient flow of information to produce accurate and useful accounting records. This appendix describes briefly how an accounting system is designed for a business. After a discussion of record systems design, a simple manual system is illustrated, using the New Generation Shop, a wholesale clothing store. The concepts used in manual accounting systems are the same as those used in computerized systems.

Learning Goals

1. To understand how financial statements and accounting reports depend upon a transaction based record system.

2. To trace the flow of data from source documents into the system and the flow of useful information out.

3. To make journal entries in a manual system with four specialized journals and a general journal.

4. To know when to post column totals when posting from specialized journals into the ledger.

5. To understand that posting column totals from specialized journals to the ledger produces the same result as posting individual entries.

Design of a Record System

The transaction is the basic source of accounting information; it is central to the data collection process. Before data processing by any system can begin, some evidence must exist that a transaction has occurred. A set of procedures and standard forms must require employees to make a record each time a transaction occurs. A general name for these business papers is **source documents**.

A typical flow of source documents through a business for the purchase and payment of merchandise or materials is diagrammed in Figure A6–1. Explanatory remarks are keyed to the numbers in the diagram.

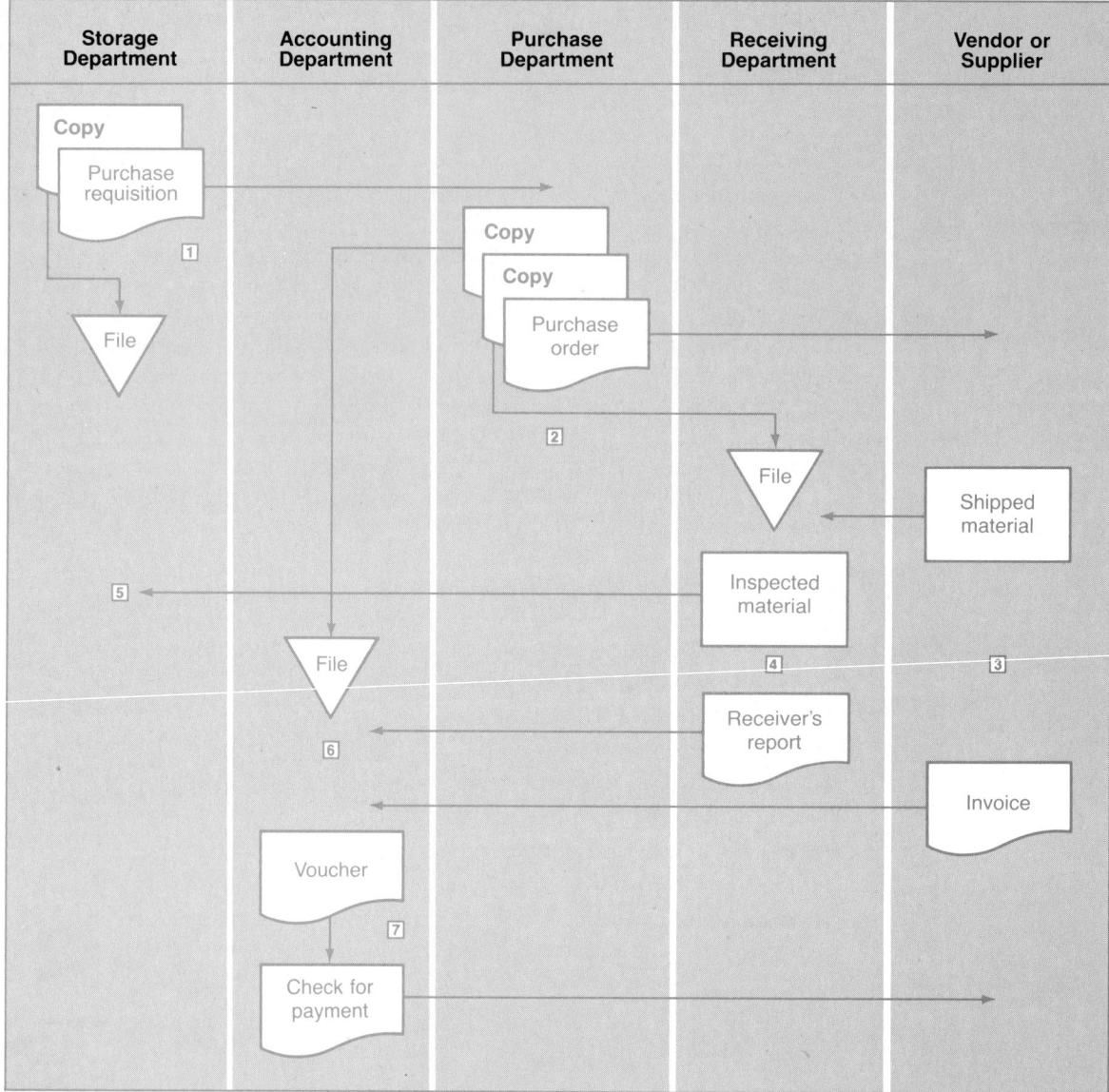

Figure A6–1 **Purchase and Payment Procedure**

[1] Since the Storage Department requires some material, a purchase requisition is sent to the Purchase Department. A copy is retained in the Storage Department file for follow-up if the material is not received in time.

[2] The Purchasing Department negotiates a purchase and sends a purchase order to the supplier. A copy sent to the Receiving Department is to be used

to check for receipt of proper items and quantities. Another copy sent to the Accounting Department will be used to check the accuracy of billed prices and discount terms on the invoice.

3. The supplier (or vendor) ships the material to the buyer's Receiving Department and mails an invoice directly to the buyer's Accounting Department.

4. When the material is received, the Receiving Department checks the material against its filed copy of the purchase order, inspects the material for quality, and forwards accepted items to the Storage Department. A receiver's report, sent to the Accounting Department, shows what was received and notes any shortage or damage.

5. The Storage Department checks off items received against its file copy of the original purchase requisition and stores the material.

6. The Accounting Department matches the purchase order copy, the vendor's invoice, and the receiver's report. After the accuracy of prices, extensions, and discount is checked (with any adjustment for damage or shortage), a voucher (explained in Appendix 8.2) is prepared approving payment of the invoice.

7. The approved invoice is sent to the disbursing section of the Accounting Department, where a check is prepared to mail to the vendor.

These are examples of the many source documents on which details of each transaction are recorded. Now the data must be introduced into the system. Data can be processed from these documents by handwritten procedures, accounting machines, electronic equipment, or a combination of these. As volume and variety of information become larger, the accounting system must become more sophisticated. Figure A6–2 shows that these means of data collection all lead to the same results. The information flow is from input to output. Source documents provide input data describing and measuring in dollars each transaction. **Processing** consists of a series of steps, such as classifying or summarizing, which will change the original data to a useful form. The output is in the form of reports.

Development of the system is generally in four stages: (1) study and design, (2) implementation, (3) operation, and (4) audit as to efficiency. The company's work is studied and a method of data collection is proposed for adoption. Once adopted, it is put into operation for verification, for review for improvements and redesign, and for testing for effectiveness of the controls. The flow of information from the source of input to the disposition of the output is examined with the following considerations:

☐ Where will the information be found and stored?
☐ Who will use the information?
☐ How will the information be used?
☐ When will the information be needed?

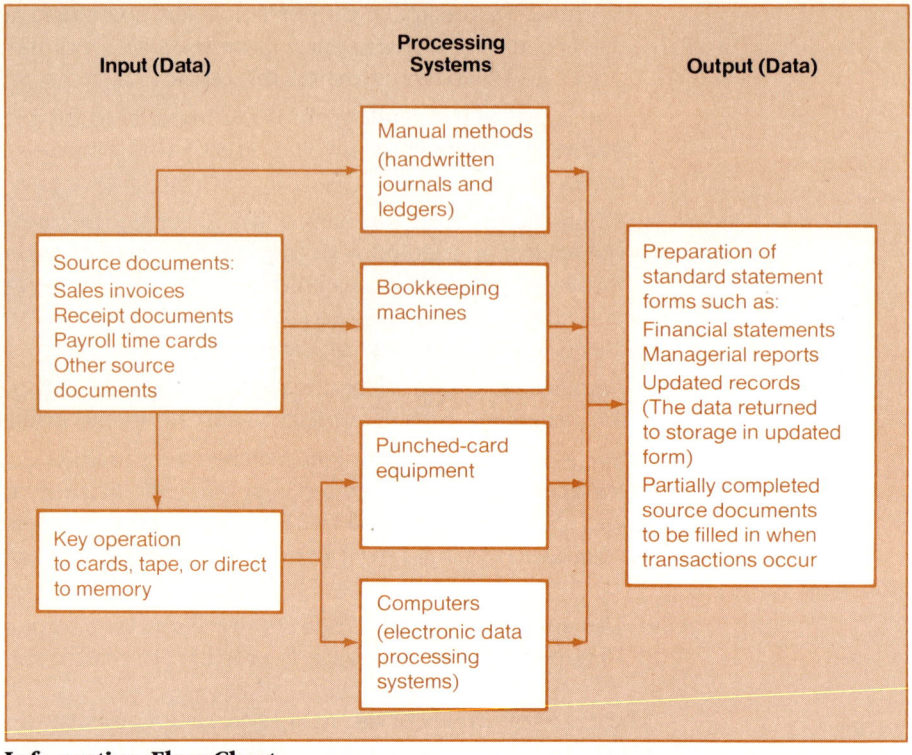

Figure A6–2 **Information Flow Chart**

Thus, setting up a system for collecting and processing data in a business requires a total examination of the business and its environment. In view of all this, the evolution of a simple manual system is now illustrated by expanding the journal with no change to the ledgers.

Expansion of the General Journal: Evolution of a Simple Manual System

As the frequency of similar transactions increases, a means of processing data that is more efficient than the two-column general journal must be devised. Time and effort must be saved. With use of the two-column journal, each entry must be posted individually to its general ledger accounts, and in subsidiary ledger accounts each entry must be posted a second time. In essence, the data in the journal are repeated in detail in the ledgers. In a large business, thousands of transactions occur each day.

Accounting records and procedures should meet the needs of the individual business firm. For example, for a small firm where one accountant records all the transactions, additional columns (each representing an account that receives repeated entries) may be added to the general journal. As the number of transactions increases and the processing becomes too much for one accountant, similar transactions can be grouped into classes, with a special journal used to record each class of transactions. The combination of accounting records and procedures designed for an entity is known as its **accounting system**. An important feature of any accounting system is its ability to strengthen internal control.

Special Journals

The manual system illustrated in the following pages saves time in recording the transactions and in posting. It also enables a business to divide the work among several employees. Modifying some of the journals and subsidiary ledgers for use with computers makes the system even more useful.

The procedures in the preceding chapters can be modified by creating several **special journals**, each of which carries a special class of transactions. The number and kinds of journals used are influenced by the type of business and the information desired. The model used in Appendix 6.1 is shown in the following chart:

Journal	Class of Transaction	Symbol
Sales journal	Sale of *merchandise* on account	S
Purchases journal	Purchase of *merchandise* on account	P
Cash receipts journal	Receipt of cash from *all* sources	CR
Cash payments journal	Payment of cash for *all* purposes	CP
General journal	All other transactions that are not grouped in the four classes above—for example, closing or adjusting entries or purchase of equipment or supplies on credit	J

Special journals bring two primary advantages to an accounting system: (1) they increase efficiency of processing, and (2) they strengthen internal control. Examples of increased efficiency of processing include:

☐ Similar transactions are grouped in chronological sequence in one place. All credit sales of merchandise, for example, are entered in the sales journal.

☐ The repeated writing of many account titles—Sales, Purchases, Cash, and so on—is eliminated.

☐ Postings to the general ledger are made from column totals rather than item by item, thereby reducing the volume of work.

☐ The responsibility of recording transactions can be divided among several individuals to speed up the work of journalizing.

Examples of strengthened internal control are:

☐ The general ledger has fewer entries and is therefore more compact and less likely to contain errors.

- ☐ The division of duties separates recording of credit sales from recording of collections for them and the recording of purchases from the recording of payment for them.
- ☐ The cash receipts and payments journals provide daily and monthly information that can be compared to bank deposit slips and to checkbook stubs as a further control over cash.

This appendix emphasizes the sales/cash receipts cycle and the purchases/cash payments cycle. The information in these two cycles flows from source documents through the special journals into both the general ledger and the subsidiary ledger accounts. Figure A6–3 diagrams this flow. The individual journals for the New Generation Shop are illustrated throughout this chapter. They should be studied in the context of the overall information flow shown in Figure A6–3.

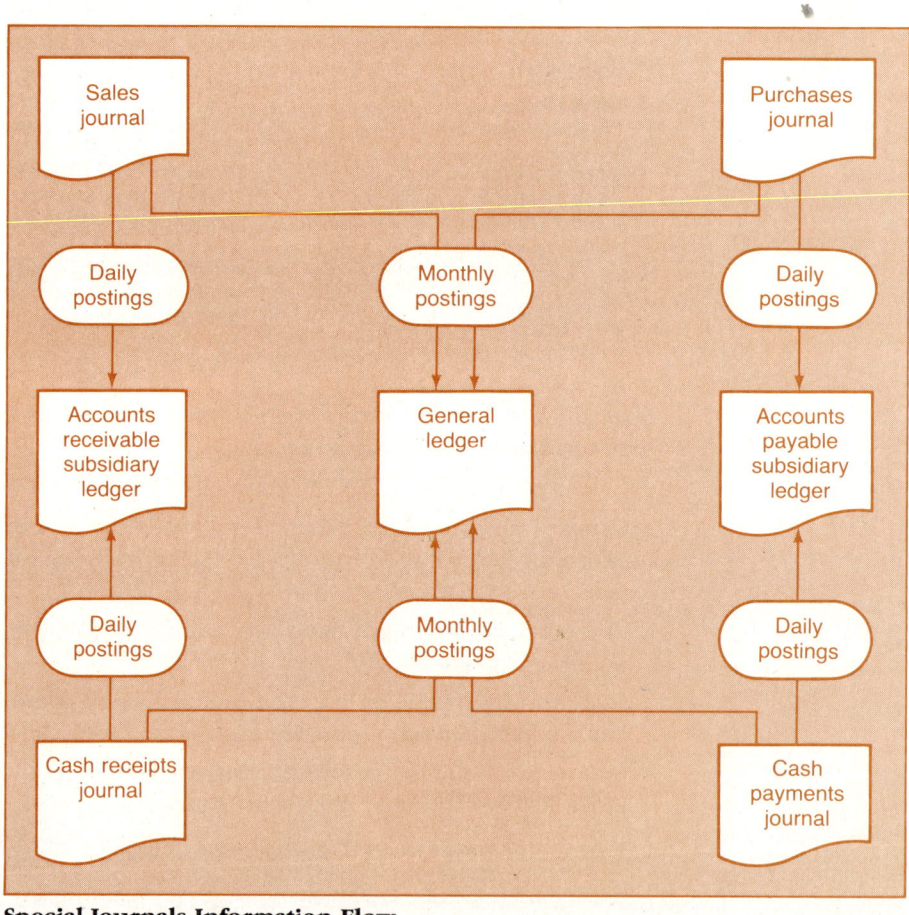

Figure A6–3   **Special Journals Information Flow**

6 / Merchandising: Measuring and Reporting the Results of Operations

Sales Journal All sales of merchandise on account are recorded in the **sales journal**. The following transactions at the New Generation Shop, which began to use special journals in June 1987 illustrate the use of the sales journal.

1987

Jun. 7	Sold merchandise to Shirley Lloyd, $400, terms 2/10, n/30, invoice no. 1.
8	Sold merchandise to Frank P. Allen, $600, terms 2/10, n/30, invoice no. 2.
8	Sold merchandise to Linda Weavil, $300, terms 2/10, n/30, invoice no. 3.
30	Sold merchandise to Earl Menova, $800, terms 2/10, n/30, invoice no. 4.

When merchandise is sold on account, the transaction is recorded in the sales journal as follows:

1. The date of the transaction is entered in the Date column.

2. Sales invoices are numbered in sequence; the numbers are entered in chronological order in the Sales Invoice No. column.

3. The name of the customer to whom the sale was made is entered in the Account Debited column.

4. The terms of the sale are listed in the Terms column.

5. If the subsidiary ledger account has a customer number, it is entered in the folio (F) column when posting is complete; otherwise, a check mark is entered.

6. The amount of the sale is entered in the Amount column.

The sales journal illustrated in Figure A6–4 shows the entries for sales of merchandise on account. Each will result in a debit to the Accounts Receivable account and to the customer's account in the accounts receivable subsid-

SALES JOURNAL   Page 1

Date	Sales Invoice No.	Account Debited	Terms	F	Amount
1987					
Jun. 7	1	Shirley Lloyd	2/10, n/30	√	400
8	2	Frank P. Allen	2/10, n/30	√	600
8	3	Linda Weavil	2/10, n/30	√	300
30	4	Earl Menova	2/10, n/30	√	800
		Total			2,100

Accounts Receivable debit and Sales credit

Figure A6–4 **Sales Journal**

iary ledger and a credit to the Sales account. The effect is the same as if they were entered in a two-column general journal. These transactions are *not* recorded in the general journal.

As indicated in Figure A6–3, postings are made as described in the following sections.

Daily Postings The daily posting in the subsidiary ledger is usually done in the following sequence:

1. The amount of the sale is posted to the Debit column of the customer's account and is added to the balance, if any, in the Balance column.

2. The journal symbol and page number (in this case, S1, "S" for sales journal and "1" for page number) are written in the folio (F) column.

3. The date of the sale is recorded in the Date column.

4. A check mark (or the customer account number) is placed in the folio (F) column of the sales journal to indicate that the entry has been posted.

Monthly Postings At the end of the month, the Amount column of the sales journal is totaled. The total, the date of the posting, and the sales journal page number are then posted as a debit in the Accounts Receivable controlling account and as a credit in the Sales account in the general ledger. The general ledger account numbers are recorded in the sales journal immediately below the footing. To minimize errors, a systematic procedure should be followed in posting. The following sequence is suggested:

Debit Posting

1. The amount is posted to the Debit money column of the Accounts Receivable account in the general ledger.

2. The journal symbol (S1) is written in the folio (F) column of the account.

3. The end-of-month date is recorded in the Date column; in this case it is June 30, 1987.

4. The Accounts Receivable account number is written in parentheses below and to the left of the double rule in the Amount column of the sales journal.

Credit Posting

5. The same amount as the debit posting is posted to the Credit money column of the Sales account in the general ledger.

6. The journal symbol (S1) is written in the folio (F) column of the account.

7. The date is recorded in the Date column.

8. The Sales account number is written in parentheses below the double rule in the Amount column of the journal, to the right of the debit posting reference number.

Postings from the sales journal of the New Generation Shop for June 1987 are shown in Figure A6–5.

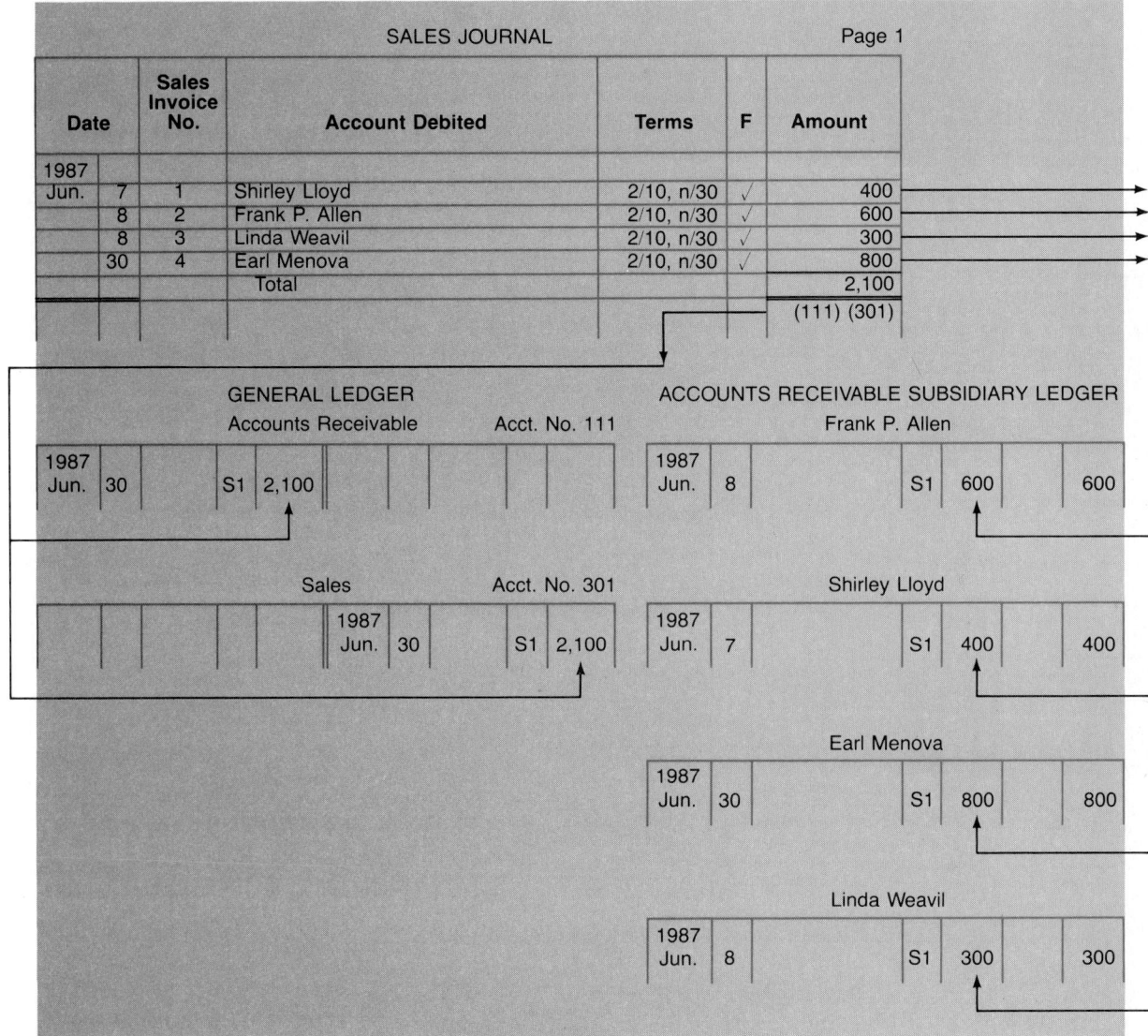

Figure A6–5 Posting Flow from the Sales Journal

Purchases Journal

All purchases of merchandise on account are recorded in the **purchases journal**. The relationship of the purchases journal and the accounts payable subsidiary ledger is similar to that of the sales journal and the accounts receivable subsidiary ledger. The transactions of the New Generation Shop during June 1987 illustrate the use of this journal.

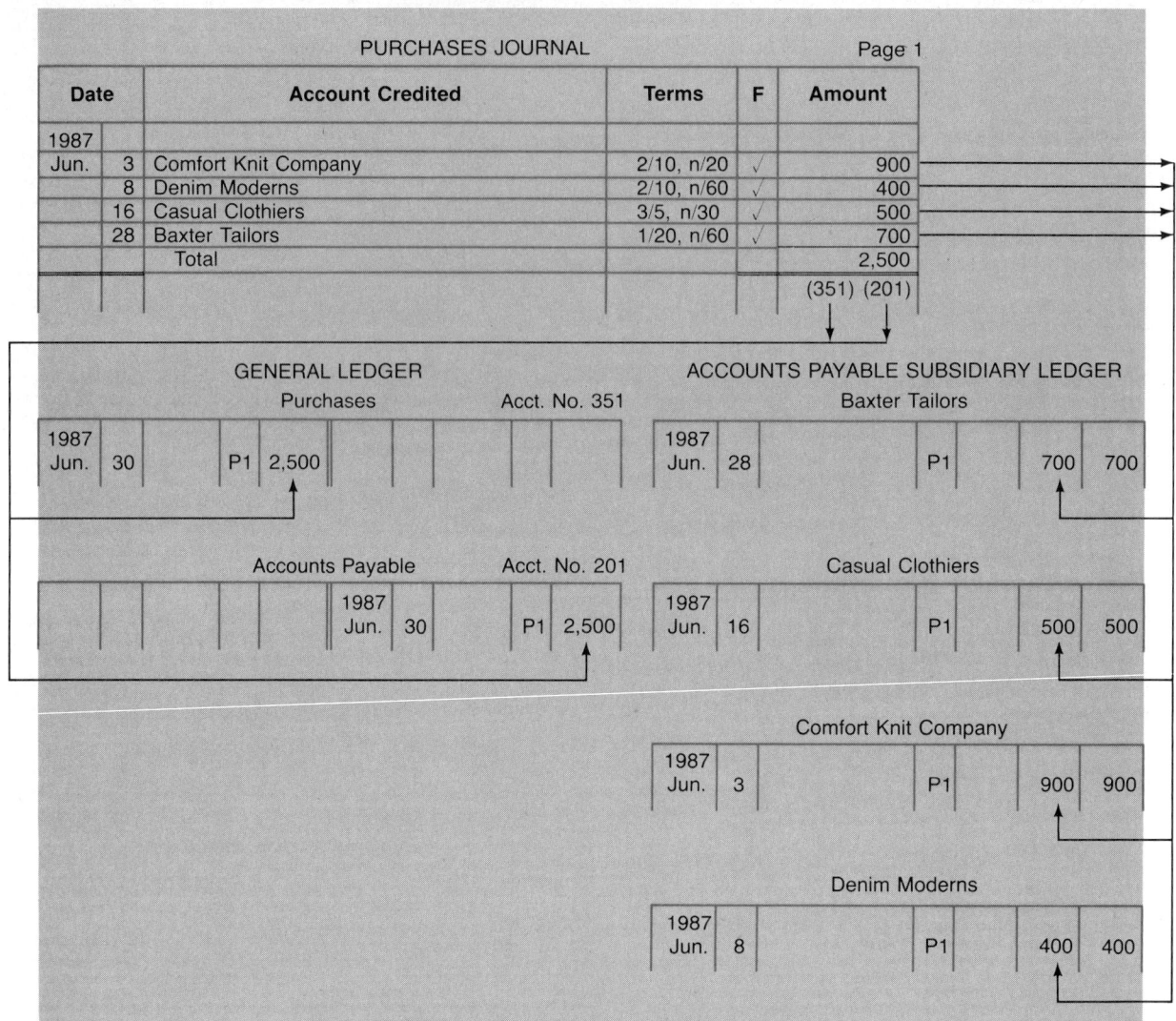

Figure A6–6   **Posting Flow from the Purchases Journal**

1987

Jun. 3   Purchased merchandise on account from Comfort Knit Company, $900, terms 2/10, n/20.
     8   Purchased merchandise on account from Denim Moderns, $400, terms 2/10, n/60.
    16   Purchased merchandise on account from Casual Clothiers, $500, terms 3/5, n/30.
    28   Purchased merchandise on account from the Baxter Tailors, $700, terms 1/20, n/60.

Figure A6–6 shows how these transactions are recorded in the purchases journal and posted to the general and subsidiary ledger accounts. Each transaction is posted separately as a credit to the accounts payable subsidiary ledger to support the credit posted at the end of the month to the Accounts Payable controlling account in the general ledger. Transactions are usually posted to the subsidiary ledger daily. The date of the entry in the subsidiary ledger account is the invoice date. At the end of the month, the Amount column of the purchases journal is footed. This total is posted to the Purchases account in the general ledger as a debit. The same total is posted to the Accounts Payable controlling account in the general ledger as a credit.

Cash Receipts Journal

All transactions involving the receipt of cash are entered in the **cash receipts journal**. The column headings typically provide the flexibility necessary to record cash receipts from customers or any other source and to record sales discounts. The form may be varied, particularly in the number and headings of the columns, to meet the needs of the individual business. Using the cash receipts of the New Generation Shop, an explanation of the various columns in the cash receipts journal (illustrated in Figure A6–7) follows:

CASH RECEIPTS JOURNAL — Page 1

		Debits					Credits					
			Sales	Other Accounts			Account	Accounts Receivable			Other Accounts	
Date	Explanation	Cash	Discounts	Account Title	F	Amt.	Credited	√	Amt.	Sales	F	Amt.
1987												
Jun. 1	Invested in business	2,500					Common Stock					2,500
10	Payment in full	588	12				F. P. Allen	√	600			
15	Cash sales	1,000					Sales			1,000		
17	Payment in full	392	8				S. Lloyd	√	400			
22	Borrowed from bank	600					Notes Payable					600
30	Cash sales	950					Sales			950		
30	Payment on account	100		Notes Receivable		200	Linda Weavil	√	300			
	Totals	6,130	20			200			1,300	1,950		3,100

Figure A6–7   Cash Receipts Journal

1. The date of the transaction is entered in the Date column.
2. The explanation of the transaction is written in the Explanation column.
3. There are three Debit columns. Cash debits are entered in the first Debit column. Every transaction entered in this journal includes a debit to Cash.

4. The Sales Discounts Debit column is used for recording discounts granted to customers for paying within the discount period. (Throughout this appendix, the gross price method is used.)

5. The Other Accounts Debit column is for debits to general ledger accounts for which no special columns have been provided.

6. The name of the general ledger or subsidiary ledger account to be credited is written in the Account Credited column.

7. When a charge customer makes a payment on account, an entry is made in the Accounts Receivable Credit column, the first of three Credit columns. The amount entered is the actual amount of credit to Accounts Receivable despite discounts properly taken by the customer.

8. Sales of *merchandise* for cash are entered in the Sales Credit column.

9. The Other Accounts Credit column is for credits to general ledger accounts for which no special columns have been provided.

10. There are three folio columns—two labeled (F) and one labeled ($\checkmark$); a posting symbol indicating that the amount has been posted to the general ledger or to the accounts receivable subsidiary ledger is placed in the folio columns.

In previous chapters, transactions involving the receipt of cash were recorded in a simple two-column general journal. Similar transactions are recorded in the cash receipts journal in Figure A6–7. Although transactions may be entered on a single line, the equality of debits and credits is still maintained through the use of multiple columns. The cash receipts transactions of the New Generation Shop are presented below; immediately following each transaction is an analysis of the debit-credit relationship of the entries in Figure A6–7 to indicate their effect on the accounts. These transactions, however, are actually recorded *only* in the cash receipts journal, not in the general journal.

Transaction:

| Jun. 1 | Incorporators invested $2,500 in the New Generation Shop. |

In the cash receipts journal, Cash is debited by entering the amount in the Cash Debit column. Since there is no special column for Common Stock, the account title is written in and the amount is entered in the Other Accounts Credit column.

Transaction:

| Jun. 10 | Received payment in full from Frank P. Allen. |

The sales journal shows that on June 8, merchandise with an invoice price of $600 was sold to Frank P. Allen, terms 2/10, n/30. Since payment was made within 10 days, Allen deducted $12 from the invoice price and paid $588. Entering the three amounts in the special columns as shown has the same effect on the general ledger as entering them in a general journal entry. The customer's name is entered in the Account Credited column for posting to the accounts receivable subsidiary ledger. If cash receipts from charge customers are numerous, a daily total may be entered from an adding machine tape; in that event, posting to the subsidiary ledger is done from supporting documents.

Transaction:

> Jun. 15   Cash sales for the first half of the month were $1,000.

The word *Sales* is written in the Account Credited column to fill the space. However, it could be omitted since both the debit and credit amounts are entered in the special columns. Although a one-half month summary amount is used to simplify the illustration, cash sales should be recorded during each business day.

Transaction:

> Jun. 17   Received full payment from Shirley Lloyd.

The sales journal shows that on June 7 merchandise with an invoice price of $400 was sold to Shirley Lloyd, terms 2/10, n/30. Since payment was made within 10 days, she deducted $8 from the invoice amount and paid $392.

Transaction:

> Jun. 22   Borrowed $600 from the bank on a note payable.

Since there is no special column for the Notes Payable account, the amount is entered in the Other Accounts Credit column, and the name of the account is written in the Account Credited column.

Transaction:

> Jun. 30   Cash sales for the last half of the month were $950.

This transaction is recorded in the same manner as the June 15 cash sales.

Transaction:

> Jun. 30   Received $100 from Linda Weavil on account and a promissory note payable in 30 days for the balance in her account.

The sales journal shows that on June 8 merchandise with an invoice price of $300 was sold to Linda Weavil, terms 2/10, n/30. The Sales Discounts account is not involved in this partial payment because the discount period has expired.

At the end of the month, the columns in the cash receipts journal are footed. Since each entry contains equal debits and credits, it follows that the total of the Debit column footings should equal the total of the Credit column footings. This equality should be proved for each special journal before the column totals are posted to the general ledger. Otherwise, errors in the special journals may not be detected, the ledger will not have equal total debit and credit balances, and the trial balance will not balance. Moreover, the controlling accounts may not agree with their corresponding subsidiary ledgers. The cash receipts journal of the New Generation Shop is proved by cross-footing it. This procedure involves a comparison of the sum of the debit totals with the sum of the credit totals. For this cash receipts journal, the debit totals are ($6,130 + $20 + $200) = $6,350; the credit totals are ($1,300 + $1,950 + $3,100) = $6,350. Postings from the cash receipts journal are shown in Figure A6–8. Individual credit postings made to the accounts receivable subsidiary ledger support the $1,300 credit posting to the Accounts Receivable controlling account in the general ledger. A check mark is entered in the folio ($\checkmark$) column on the line of the entry to indicate that the item has been posted to the customer's account in the subsidiary ledger. Any positive balance in a customer's account would normally be a debit. Transactions have already been posted to these accounts from the sales journal.[7]

The totals of the Cash Debit column ($6,130) and the Sales Discounts Debit column ($20) are posted to the respective general ledger accounts. The regular sequence for transferring an amount from a journal to a ledger is followed. The general ledger account number entered in parentheses below the double rule in each column shows that the total has been posted to that account.

The (X) below the Other Accounts Debit column means that the column total has not been posted to the general ledger. The $200 debit to Notes Receivable was posted individually during the month. The account number of Notes Receivable (112) was entered in the folio (F) column of the journal at the time the posting was done.

The Accounts Receivable account is credited for $1,300, and the Sales account is credited for $1,950. These postings are also dated June 30. No posting symbol is used in the folio (F) column on the line of the entry for a cash sale because the item does not require individual posting.

The (X) below the double rule in the Other Accounts Credit column indicates that the column total is not to be posted to the general ledger. The total is not posted because the $2,500 credit to Common Stock and the $600 credit to Notes Payable were posted separately during the month. The ledger page numbers of these accounts were entered in the folio (F) column of the journal when the posting was done. Note that account numbers 251 and 205 are

---

[7]Earl Menova's account is shown out of sequence in Figure A6–8 to simplify illustration of the posting flow. His unpaid balance of $800 is a debit and is equal to the balance in the Accounts Receivable account in the general ledger.

6 / Merchandising: Measuring and Reporting the Results of Operations

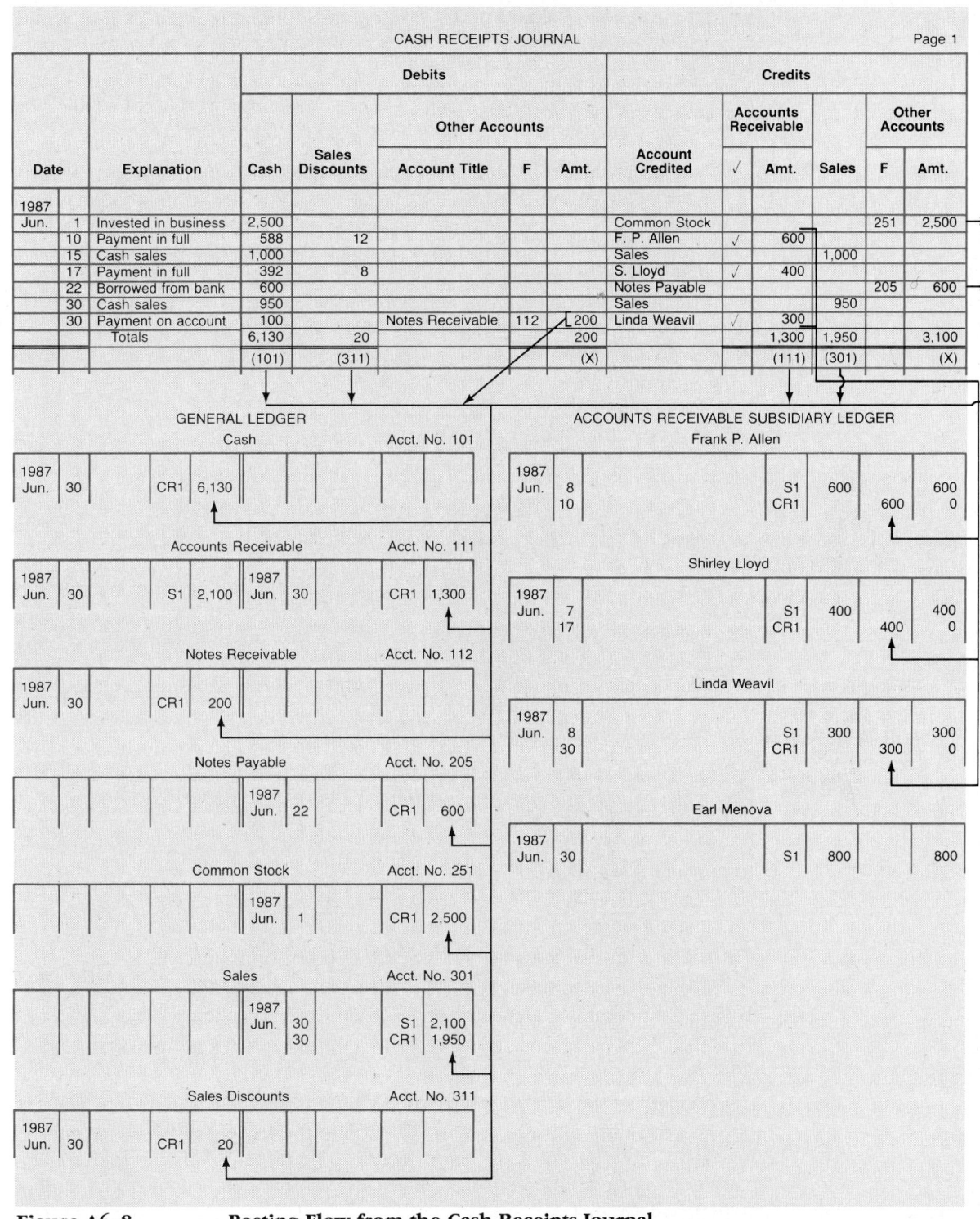

Figure A6–8   **Posting Flow from the Cash Receipts Journal**

written in the folio column of the cash receipts journal in Figure A6–8. Postings from the Other Accounts Credit column are dated as of the date of the entry.

Cash Payments Journal

Cash payments should be made by check, and all check payments are entered in the **cash payments journal**. Small payments in currency may be made from a petty cash fund, procedures for which are discussed in Chapter 8. The check to establish the fund, however, is entered in the cash payments journal.

A typical cash payments journal is illustrated in Figure A6–9. The columns provide for recording cash payments, either to creditors or for any other purpose, and for recording purchases discounts. Explanation of the various columns follows:

CASH PAYMENTS JOURNAL — Page 1

Date	Check No.	Explanation	Credits					Debits					
			Cash	Purchases Discounts	Other Accounts			Account Debited	Accounts Payable		Purchases	Other Accounts	
					Account Title	F	Amt.		✓	Amt.		F	Amt.
1987													
Jun. 1	1	Scuba Realty	150					Rent Expense					150
10	2	Payment in full	882	18				Comfort Knit Co.	✓	900			
14	3	Payment in full	392	8				Denim Moderns	✓	400			
15	4	Cash purchases	200					Purchases			200		
30	5	Partial payment	300		Notes Payable		200	Casual Clothiers	✓	500			
30	6	Dividend paid	400					Dividends					400
30	7	Various exp. items	100					Misc. General Exp.					100
		Totals	2,424	26			200			1,800	200		650

Figure A6–9   **Cash Payments Journal**

1. The date of the disbursement of cash is entered in the Date column.

2. Detailed information is initially recorded on the check stub, which bears the same number as the check. Entries in the cash payments journal are then made from the check stub, and the check number is listed in the Check No. column.

3. An explanation of the transaction is entered in the Explanation column.

4. There are three Credit columns located to the left of the Debit columns. In a special journal, the sequence of columns need not follow the traditional placement. Cash will be used in each transaction entered in this journal and is therefore the first column.

5. The Purchases Discounts Credit column is used for recording discounts taken on invoices paid within the discount period.

6. Credits to general ledger accounts other than those for which a special column has been provided, such as Cash and Purchases Discounts, are recorded in the Other Accounts Credit column.

7. The name of the general ledger or subsidiary ledger account to be debited is written in the Account Debited column.

8. When a creditor is paid, the amount is entered in the Accounts Payable Debit column. The amount entered is the actual amount of the check plus any purchases discounts taken.

9. The purchase of merchandise for cash is entered in the Purchases Debit column.

10. The other Accounts Debit column is used for entries to general ledger accounts that have no special column.

11. There are three folio columns, two labeled (F) and one labled ($\sqrt{}$); a posting symbol indicating that the amount has been posted to the general ledger or to the accounts payable subsidiary ledger is placed in the appropriate folio column.

Although most transactions may be entered on a single line, some may require more than one line. Each *new* transaction entry should begin on a vacant line. The equality of debits and credits is maintained through the use of multiple columns.

The cash payments of the New Generation Shop (see Figure A6–9) are presented on this and the next few pages. Each is analyzed in terms of debits and credits to indicate their effect on the accounts. They represent cash payments made by the New Generation Shop in June 1987.

Transaction:

> Jun. 1   Issued check no. 1 in the amount of $150 for the June rent.

The $150 decrease in cash is entered in the Cash column on the same line as the explanation. Since there is not a special debit column for Rent Expense, the account title is written in the Account Debited column, and the $150 debit amount to Rent Expense is shown in the Other Accounts column. Note that this entire transaction appears on a single line.

Transaction:

> Jun. 10   Paid Comfort Knit Co. in full; check no. 2.

The purchases journal shows that on June 3, merchandise with an invoice price of $900 was purchased from Comfort Knit Company, terms 2/10, n/20. Since payment was made within 10 days, a two percent discount of $18 is taken and a check for $882 is issued. Entering the three amounts in the special columns has the same effect on the general ledger as recording them in a general journal entry. The creditor's name is entered in the Account Debited column for posting to the accounts payable subsidiary ledger.

Transaction:

> Jun. 14 Paid Denim Moderns in full; check no. 3.

The explanation for this entry is similar to that for the entry of June 10.

Transaction:

> Jun. 15 Purchased merchandise and issued a check for the full amount of the invoice; check no. 4.

Purchases of merchandise on account are entered in the purchases journal. A company may occasionally purchase merchandise for cash, probably from another company with which no credit relationship exists. These cash purchases are recorded directly in the cash payments journal. If cash purchases of merchandise occur frequently, a special Purchases Debit column may be provided in the cash payments journal.

Transaction:

> Jun. 30 Paid Casual Clothiers $300 on account (check no. 5) and issued a promissory note for the balance, to be paid in 30 additional days.

Reference to the purchases journal shows that on June 16 merchandise with an invoice price of $500 was purchased from the Casual Clothiers, terms 3/5, n/30. Since the discount period has expired, no discount is taken.

Transaction:

> Jun. 30 A dividend of $400 was declared and paid.

Since there is no special column for Dividends, the amount paid is entered in the Other Accounts Debit column. Since dividends are not expected to be paid oftener than quarterly, there is no need for a special column for the Dividends account.

Transaction:

> Jun. 30 Issued check no. 7 in the amount of $100 for miscellaneous general expenses.

The expense account is debited for various items purchased and consumed during the month.

Before the end-of-the-month postings are made, the columns of the cash payments journal should be cross-footed. For this cash payments journal, the debit totals are ($1,800 + $200 + $650) = $2,650; the credit totals are ($2,424 + $26 + $200) = $2,650. The total debit and total credit postings from this journal to the general ledger are equal. Posting from the cash payments journal of the New Generation Shop is shown in Figure A6–10.

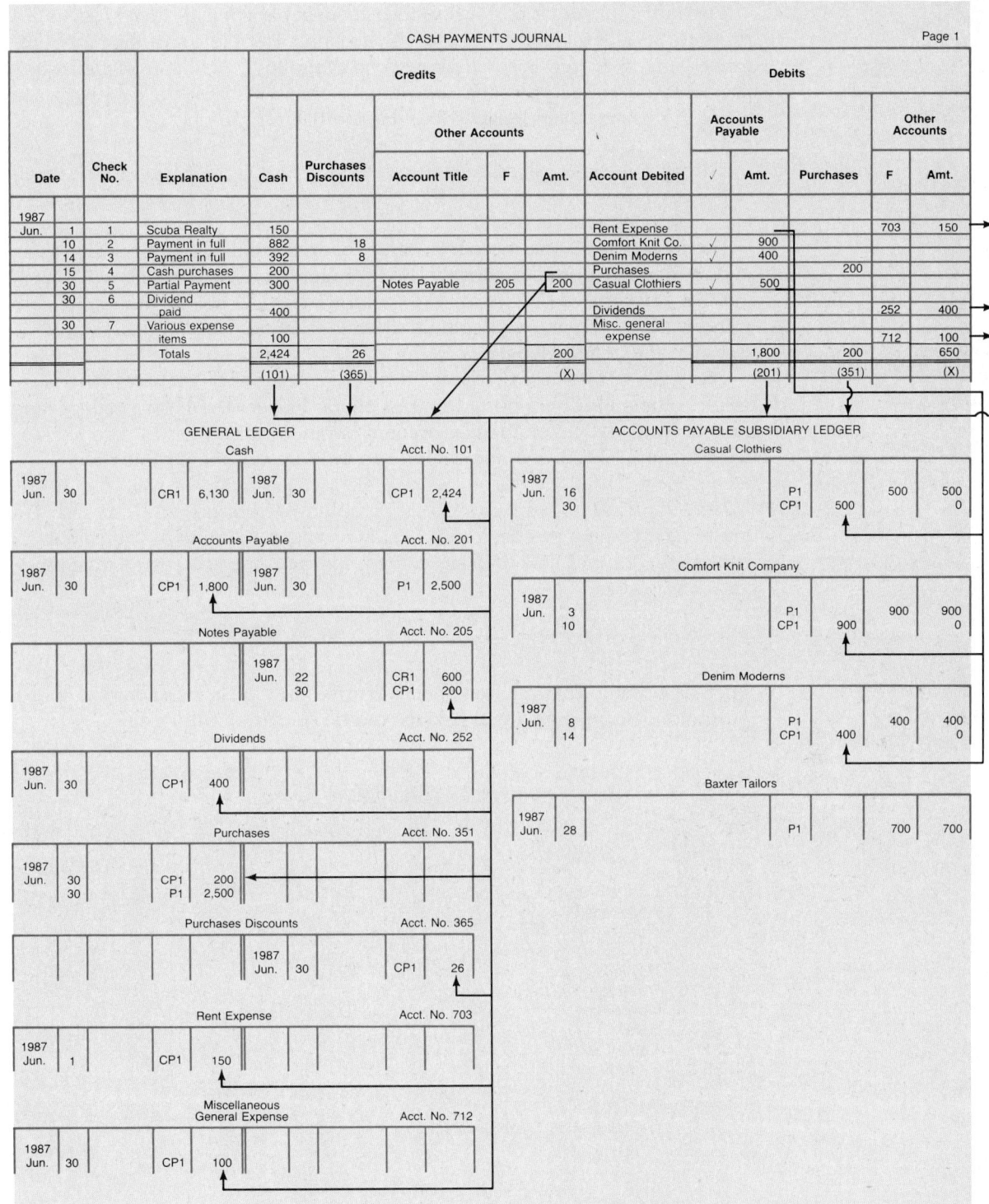

Figure A6–10 Posting Flow from the Cash Payments Journal

The individual debit postings to the accounts payable subsidiary ledger support the $1,800 debit posting to the Accounts Payable controlling account in the general ledger. Each check mark in the folio (√) column of the cash payments journal indicates that a posting has been made to the supplier's account in the subsidiary ledger. Note that the balance of each account is either a credit or zero.

The Accounts Payable account is debited for $1,800 as of June 30. The total of the Purchases Debit column, $200, is posted to the Purchases account in the general ledger.

The total of the Other Accounts Debit column is not posted because each amount must be posted separately. The numbers of these accounts—703, 252, and 712—are entered in the folio (F) column. The (X) below the double rule in the Other Accounts Debit column indicates that the column total is not posted to the general ledger.

The totals of the Cash Credit column ($2,424) and the Purchases Discounts Credit column ($26) are posted to the general ledger. The basic posting steps are followed. The general ledger account numbers are placed in parentheses below the double rules in the columns to indicate that the postings have been done.

The total of the Other Accounts Credit column is not posted since each entry in the column has been individually posted at the time the entry was made in the journal. The folio (F) column indicates the account to which the entry was posted.

Result of Posting

When all posting from the four special journals in the New Generation Shop illustration is complete, a trial balance can be prepared as follows:

NEW GENERATION SHOP
Trial Balance
June 30, 1987

Acct. No.	Account Title	Debits	Credits
101	Cash	$3,706	
111	Accounts Receivable	800	
112	Notes Receivable	200	
201	Accounts Payable		$ 700
205	Notes Payable		800
251	Common Stock		2,500
252	Dividends	400	
301	Sales		4,050
311	Sales Discounts	20	
351	Purchases	2,700	
365	Purchases Discounts		26
703	Rent Expense	150	
712	Miscellaneous General Expense	100	
	Totals	$8,076	$8,076

To enhance understanding of the posting procedures from special journals, the reader is encouraged to draw T accounts, post from the journals in this appendix, and verify this trial balance.

Combined Cash Receipts and Payments Journal

Many small businesses use a combined cash receipts and cash payments journal, sometimes called a **cashbook**. This journal is simply a combination of the cash receipts journal and the cash payments journal described earlier. The specialized debit and credit columns (except for cash) are unique to the needs of the particular entity using it. Such a journal is appropriate not only to small commercial enterprises but to many not-for-profit organizations such as fraternities and sororities, civic clubs, and professional service organizations.

Other Special Journals

Other special journals may be adopted as the need for them becomes apparent. Such a need is indicated if labor may be saved or if the special journal provides an element of flexibility or strengthens internal control in the accounting system. Examples of other special journals are sales returns and allowances journal, purchases returns and allowances journal, notes receivable register, notes payable register, and voucher register.

Entries in the General Journal

Although special journals provide for recording frequently recurring transactions, a need remains for recording (1) unusual current transactions, (2) correcting entries, and (3) adjusting and closing entries. For these purposes, a two-column general journal is used in conjunction with the special journals.

Unusual Current Transactions All the transactions that cannot be entered in the special journals are recorded in the general journal. Sales returns and allowances and purchases returns and allowances, for example, are entered in the general journal if special journals for these transactions are not maintained. Other typical current transactions recorded in the general journal include credit purchases of assets other than merchandise inventory, the incurrence of liabilities for services, notes received from customers to apply toward accounts receivable, and notes issued to creditors to apply toward accounts payable.

Correcting Entries If it is discovered that an error has been made in the process of journalizing and posting, it can be corrected by a general journal entry. Erasures should be avoided because they may create doubt about the reason for the erasures in the minds of persons who examine the records. This becomes particularly important when the records are audited and when they are offered as evidence in cases of litigation.

Assume that a $15 entry, recording the payment of an invoice for repairs to machinery, has been journalized in the cash payments journal with a debit to the Machinery account. The debit should have been to an expense account; the error may be corrected by the following entry in the general journal:

1987				
Jul.	26	Maintenance and Repairs Expense....................	15	
		Machinery		15
		To correct entry of July 19 in cash payments journal.		

If an error in a journal entry is discovered before it is posted, it may be corrected by drawing a line through the incorrect account or amount and entering the correction immediately above it.

Adjusting and Closing Entries Adjusting and closing entries are always recorded in the general journal.

Direct Posting from Business Documents to Subsidiary Ledgers

In many business firms, data can be processed more efficiently and rapidly by posting from the original documents—sales invoices, sales slips, purchase invoices, and so on—directly to the *subsidiary ledgers* instead of first copying the information in special journals and then posting to the accounts. For example, if sales slips are serially numbered, a binder file of duplicate slips arranged in numerical order can take the place of a more formal sales journal. Amounts from the individual slips are posted daily to the accounts receivable subsidiary ledger; at the end of a designated period—a week or a month—the sales slips in the binder file are totaled and the following general journal entry is made:

1987				
Aug.	31	Accounts Receivable	120,000	
		Sales		120,000
		To record charge sales for the month of August.		

A similar procedure may be used to record purchases on account.

If postings are made from sales slips to the accounts receivable subsidiary ledger, and if for any reason a special sales journal is still desired, a streamlined journal can be constructed by simply eliminating the Account Debited and Terms columns, as shown below. Entries to such a sales journal may be made in batches; for example, a single line may read:

SALES JOURNAL

Date	Sales Invoice Numbers	F	Amount
1987 Aug. 12	13,500–13,599		18,329.21

A batch could represent a day's credit sales, or simply a predetermined quantity of invoices or sales slips. The use of *batch totals* is one means of checking the accuracy of posting to subsidiary ledgers.

These changes in procedure and the increasing use of direct posting from original documents are discussed here to add emphasis to a statement made earlier in the chapter. Accounting records and procedures should be designed to meet the needs of the particular business firm.

In many firms, business documents are keyed directly into and processed by a computer. Appendix A to this book develops the concepts and techniques of computerization of the accounting function.

Glossary

Accounting system The various processing steps, equipment, personnel, and procedures that change original data to useful form.

Cashbook A simplified combination of the cash receipts journal and the cash payments journal.

Cash discount A reduction in price offered by terms of sale to encourage payment within a shorter period.

Cash payments journal A special journal in which *all* cash payments are recorded.

Cash receipts journal A special journal in which *all* cash receipts are recorded.

Chain discount A multiple percentage reduction from a list price with each discount in the chain applied successively to the declining balance to arrive at the billing price.

Cost of goods sold A computation that appears on the income statement in a separate section. It is calculated by adding net purchases to the beginning inventory to derive the cost of goods available for sale and then deducting from this sum the ending inventory.

Credit memorandum A business form issued to a customer to advise that his or her account has been credited for a return of merchandise or an allowance for defective merchandise.

F.O.B. destination A term indicating the point at which the title to merchandise passes to the buyer; here the title would pass when the goods arrive at their destination. The owner (the seller) of the goods while they are in transit should bear the cost of freight.

F.O.B. shipping point A term indicating the point at which the title to merchandise passes to the buyer; here the title would pass when the seller placed the goods on the common carrier (railroad or truck). The owner (the buyer) of the goods while they are in transit should bear the cost of the freight.

General and administrative expenses Expired cost of goods or services generally reflecting the cost of operating expenses other than the direct marketing cost.

Gross margin on sales The excess of net sales revenue over the cost of goods sold.

Gross price method Accounting for cash discounts by accumulating the amount of the discount in Sales Discounts and in Purchases Discounts accounts.

Inventory turnover The ratio of cost of goods sold to average inventory; a measure of the efficiency of inventory management.

Management by exception Isolating accounts and amounts that may indicate operating inefficiencies and focusing attention on areas that require corrective action.

Merchandise Inventory An account which shows merchandise on hand (at cost price) at the end of the accounting period. The ending inventory of one period becomes the beginning inventory of the next period.

Net cost of purchases The cost of all merchandise bought for sale, including transportation in but reduced by purchases returns and allowances and purchases discounts.

Net price method Procedures that apply the principle of management by exception by requiring that purchases be recorded at net of discount prices in anticipation of qualifying for the discount (purchases discounts lost method).

Operating expenses The cost of goods or services expired or used in operating the business, excluding cost of goods sold.

Other revenue and other expenses Items of ordinary revenue and expense that arise from a source other than the basic business purpose of the company.

Periodic inventory system Means of determining the amount of merchandise actually on hand at the end of each accounting period by making a list of the goods on hand, with an actual count of each, showing physical quantities and cost.

Perpetual inventory system A method in which a continuous record of merchandise on hand is maintained.

Processing A series of activities that make data useful. Classifying and summarizing are examples.

Purchases An account debited for the cost of merchandise bought for resale.

Purchases Discounts An account credited with amounts of deductions from invoice price that are allowed for payment within the stated discount period.

Purchases discounts lost method Purchases are recorded at net; the discounts lost are recorded in a special account.

Purchases journal A special journal in which credit purchases of merchandise are recorded.

Purchases Returns and Allowances An account credited for cost of merchandise returned to a vendor or for allowances for defective merchandise purchases received.

Sales An account credited for the selling price of merchandise sold.

Sales Discounts An account debited for the amounts that customers deduct from the invoice price when payment is made within the stated discount period.

Sales journal A special journal in which credit sales of merchandise are recorded.

Sales Returns and Allowances An account debited for selling price of merchandise returned by customers or allowances for defective merchandise returned to them.

Selling expenses Direct expenses incurred in marketing a product.

Source documents Business papers on which each individual transaction is recorded. They provide objective evidence of transactions.

Special journals Books of original entry that have been designed so that each receives the initial recording of specialized classifications of transactions.

Trade discount A percentage reduction in a list price that results in the net price or billing price. Unlike the cash discounts, it is not recorded in the accounts.

Transportation In An account debited for various delivery costs of merchandise purchases.

Questions

Q6-1   Why is the income statement for a merchandising business more complicated than for a service business?

Q6-2   Student A says that because cost of goods sold is an item that can't be controlled by management, there is little need to be concerned with it. Do you agree? Give examples to support your answer.

Q6-3   Sales discounts cause a business to collect less cash from sales. Why, then, would a company offer them to its customers? Does management really want customers to take advantage of sales discounts? Why or why not?

Q6-4   Why not debit the Purchases account for all purchases, including store supplies, advertising supplies, and postage stamps, for example?

Q6-5   How does the use of contra accounts for purchases returns and allowances and for purchases discounts strengthen internal control in a business?

Q6-6   How can the use of management by exception be applied to strengthen internal control over purchases discounts?

Q6-7   It has been estimated that billions of dollars are lost in the United States each year because of shoplifting. How does this loss affect the cost of goods sold in businesses that use the periodic inventory system?

Q6-8   If a seller in Pittsburgh, Pennsylvania sells to a buyer in Williamsport, Pennsylvania would you expect the invoice price to be higher if terms were F.O.B. destination or F.O.B. shipping point? Why?

Q6-9   Does a work sheet for a merchandising business need a column for adjustments? Why or why not?

Q6-10   In what columns of the work sheet are the elements that make up cost of goods sold found? How is cost of goods sold treated in the closing entries when a periodic inventory system is used?

Q6-11   What is the difference between selling expenses and general and administrative expenses? Between operating expenses and other expenses?

Q6-12   How does a trade discount differ from a cash discount?

Q6-13   Could interim financial statements be made from the work sheet without journalizing adjusting and closing entries? Do you think this is done frequently? Why or why not?

Q6-14   What is the significance of inventory turnover? How does knowledge of this figure add to the strength of internal control?

Q6-15   (Appendix) How do special journals strengthen internal control? Promote efficiency?

Q6-16   (Appendix) Do special journals eliminate the need for a general journal? Explain.

Q6-17   (Appendix) How do special journals reduce postings to the general ledger? Do you feel that this is an advantage of special journals? Why or why not?

Q6-18   (Appendix) When are postings from special journals made to the subsidiary ledgers? To the general ledgers? Why is such timing of postings desirable?

Q6–19 (Appendix) When is a special column for an account provided in the cash receipts and cash payments journal?

Q6–20 (Appendix) What are the special columns in a cash receipts journal? In a cash payments journal?

Exercises

E6–1
Calculation of total merchandise available and cost of goods sold

During the year, the Towson Company purchased merchandise costing $45,000. In each of the following cases, calculate (1) the total merchandise available for sale and (2) the cost of goods sold for the year.

Case	Beginning Inventory	Ending Inventory
1	$ 0	$ 0
2	9,000	0
3	12,000	15,000
4	0	3,000

E6–2
Computation of net sales, net purchases, cost of goods sold, and gross margin on sales

The following information is taken from the books of Galax Company:

Merchandise inventory, January 1, 1987	$ 1,800
Merchandise inventory, January 31, 1987	1,300
Sales	12,900
Transportation in	400
Purchases discounts	330
Sales returns and allowances	210
Purchases	5,600
Sales discounts	120
Purchases returns and allowances	100

Compute for the month of January: (1) net sales, (2) net purchases, (3) cost of goods sold, (4) gross margin on sales.

E6–3
Calculation of gross sales

The following information was taken from the books of the Dominion Company:

Merchandise inventory, beginning	$ 6,500
Net cost of purchases	31,200
Total operating expenses	15,600
Other expenses	650
Merchandise inventory, ending	5,200
Net income	3,250

Calculate the gross sales for the period.

6 / Merchandising: Measuring and Reporting the Results of Operations

E6–4
Income statement from work sheet

The following account balances were taken from the Income Statement columns of Sawyer Company work sheet for the year ended December 31, 1987:

Account Title	Income Statement Dr.	Income Statement Cr.
Merchandise Inventory	23,760	25,650
Sales		62,370
Sales Returns and Allowances	745	
Sales Discounts	1,215	
Purchases	19,210	
Transportation In	1,015	
Purchases Returns and Allowances		610
Purchases Discounts		1,730
Selling Expenses	4,590	
General and Administrative Expenses	9,720	
Totals	60,255	90,360
Net Income	30,105	
Totals	90,360	90,360

The Balance Sheet Debit column showed a balance of $3,500 for the Dividends account. Prepare an income statement.

E6–5
Sales and purchases discounts—gross price method

Using the gross price procedures, prepare general journal entries to record the following transactions: (1) on the books of the Welch Company, (2) on the books of the Raven Company, and (3) on the books of each company, assuming that the terms were F.O.B. shipping point.

1987

Oct. 4   Welch Company sold merchandise to the Raven Company for $9,600, terms 2/10, n/30; F.O.B. destination.
  7   The Raven Company paid $275 freight on receipt of the shipment.
  8   The Raven Company returned some unsatisfactory merchandise and received credit for $300.
  14 The Raven Company mailed a check to the Welch Company for the net amount due.

E6–6
Recording a purchase—net price method

On June 5, 1987, VTS Company, which uses the net price procedure, purchased merchandise for $7,000, terms 2/10, n/30. The invoice was paid on July 1, 1987.

1. Journalize the purchase and the payment of the invoice.
2. Is the net cost of purchases the same under both the gross and the net procedures? Show your computations.

(continued on next page)

288　Part One / The Basic Accounting Model

3. Assume that VTS desires to take advantage of all purchases discounts. Is there any advantage in using the gross price method of recording the purchase of merchandise?

E6–7
Closing entries

The following amounts are found in the Income Statement columns of the work sheet of the Newberry Company for the year ended June 30, 1987:

Account Title	Debit	Credit
Merchandise Inventory	$ 47,520	$ 51,300
Sales		124,740
Sales Returns and Allowances	1,490	
Sales Discounts	2,430	
Purchases	38,420	
Transportation In	2,030	
Purchases Returns and Allowances		1,220
Purchases Discounts		3,460
Selling Expenses Control	9,180	
General and Administrative Expenses Control	19,440	
Totals	$120,510	$180,720
Net Income	60,210	
Totals	$180,720	$180,720

The Dividends account has a debit balance of $18,700. Journalize the closing entries.

E6–8
Thought-provoking discount exercise: (partial payment)

Juan's, Inc. grants customer discounts on partial payments made within the discount period. On June 10, 1987, the company sold merchandise to Jean Glick for $20,000, terms 2/10, n/30. On June 20, 1987, the company received a check in the amount of $10,000. On July 8, 1987, it received a check for the balance due. Journalize the sale and both collection entries using the gross price method on Juan's books. Then journalize the transactions using the net price method on Jean Glick's books.

E6–9
Trade discounts

Mesa Company purchased merchandise from Grant Stores with a list price of $12,000 and a trade discount of 20, 10, and 5 percent. Cash discount terms were 2/10, n/30. The invoice date was April 8, 1987. Journalize the purchase and payment on April 17, 1987.

E6–10
Sales taxes

Naosuke Company records cash sales in a daily summary entry. On July 5, 1987, total cash sales were $18,200. The state sales tax rate is 4 percent. Record the July 5 sales in a general journal entry.

E6–11
Use of sales journal

(Appendix) Alabama Merchandisers uses an accounting system with the special journals described in the appendix. From the following list of selected transactions, journalize *only* those that belong in the sales journal:

1987

Sep. 2　Sold merchandise to Tom Hamilton on account, $500, terms 2/10, n/30.
　　 5　Sold merchandise to Susan Sexton for cash, $825.
　　 9　Sold land to Jay Garbarino in amount of $20,000; accepted 30-day, 15 percent note receivable from Garbarino.
　　12　Sold a piece of excess furniture to June Mesta on account, $980.

E6–12
Use of purchases journal

(Appendix) Scottish Woolen Goods Company uses the special journals described in the appendix. From the following list of selected transactions, journalize *only* those that belong in the purchases journal:

1987		
Jul.	5	Purchased merchandise from the Glasgow Sales Company for $1,875. Issued check no. 586 in payment.
	11	Purchased merchandise from Edinburgh Company for $2,275 on account. Terms were 2/10, n/30; Scottish Woolen Goods Company expects to pay in 10 days.
	15	Purchased merchandise from Dumfries Wholesalers on account for $9,345. Terms are 1/10, n/30; it is doubtful that this discount can be taken.
	19	Purchased store supplies from Moffat Company for $320 on account. Terms are 2/10, n/30.
	26	Purchased office supplies from Dundee Company for $250. Issued check no. 658 in payment.

E6–13
Use of cash receipts journal

(Appendix) Tampa Company uses a cash receipts journal. Journalize the following transactions:

1987		
Apr.	4	Received a check from Tarpon Springs Corporation in amount of $2,352 in payment of a $2,400 account receivable less discount.
	5	Borrowed $10,000 from Bank of Mullet Key on a 90-day, 18 percent note.
	8	Made total cash sales of merchandise for the day in amount of $3,720.
	9	Sold for cash to Largo Used Furniture Company a piece of excess office equipment for $800. (The equipment was sold at book value, so there was no gain or loss on the sale.)
	11	Collected a total of $3,090 in payment of $3,000 note plus interest by Bellaire Company.
	12	Received a check for $500 from George Ozoha plus a 90-day, 16 percent note for $500 in settlement of an overdue $1,000 account receivable.

E6–14
Use of cash payments journal

(Appendix) The Houston Corporation uses a cash payments journal. Journalize the following selected transactions:

1987		
Jan.	3	Paid with check no. 832 to Crosby Company an account payable of $4,000 less two percent discount.
	4	Purchased merchandise for cash from Alvino Sales, issuing check no. 841 for $6,240.
	7	Purchased a tract of land from Sugar Land Realty for $20,000. Issued check no. 855 for $5,000 and a mortgage note payable for the balance.
	8	Paid to the Bank of Needville a $6,000 note plus $210 interest, using check no. 862.
	10	Paid the Newgulf Sales Company for a $5,000 merchandise purchase made on January 3, terms 2/10, n/30. Issued check no. 890 for the proper amount.

E6–15
Sales journal with batch numbers

(Appendix) The Muhlenberg Company uses a sales journal but posts to customer accounts in the accounts receivable subsidiary ledger from copies of sales invoices. Sales are entered daily by batch totals. The following sales were made during the first week of June 1987:

Date	Invoice Numbers	Total Amount
Jun. 3	2,851–2,972	$6,820
4	2,973–3,113	7,256
5	3,114–3,243	5,082
6	3,244–3,366	6,117
7	3,367–3,518	8,546

Journalize the sales for the week in a sales journal.

E6–16
Posting from cash receipts journal

(Appendix) The cash receipts journal of GT Stores is shown below. Create account numbers, post to the general ledger and to any subsidiary ledger(s) involved, and show all posting references. Disregard account balances.

CASH RECEIPTS JOURNAL — Page 1

Date		Explanation	Debits					Credits					
			Cash	Sales Disc.	Other Accounts			Account Credited	Accounts Receivable		Sales	Other Accounts	
					Account Title	F	Amount		✓	Amount		F	Amount
1987													
Jun.	3	Invested in											
		business	2,500					Common Stock					2,500
	10	Payment in											
		full	588	12				William Ramey		600			
	15	Cash sales	1,000					Sales			1,000		
	18	Payment in											
		full	396	4				Ella Gray		400			
	21	Borrowed											
		from bank	600					Notes Payable					600
	28	Cash sales	950					Sales			950		
	28	Payment on			Notes								
		account	100		Receivable		200	Arthur James		300			
		Totals	6,134	16			200			1,300	1,950		3,100

A Problems

P6–1A
Use of merchandise accounts

Itasca Company had the following transactions:

1987

Feb. 4 Purchased merchandise from St. Paul Company at an invoice price of $8,000; terms n/30, F.O.B. shipping point.
     6 Paid Overnight Express $20 for delivery cost of the purchase of February 4.
     6 Upon inspection, noted that merchandise invoiced at $1,200 in the St. Paul shipment was the wrong model. Returned the incorrect merchandise by Overnight Express collect as authorized by St. Paul Company.
     8 Sold merchandise to Susan Sexton in amount of $1,620; terms 2/10, n/30, F.O.B. shipping point.
    18 Received a check from Susan Sexton in total payment of her purchase of February 8.
    19 Sold merchandise to Dale Page in amount of $1,500; terms 2/10, n/30, F.O.B. destination.

19	Paid $225 to Overnight Express for delivery of merchandise to Page.
20	Page reported that an item in the shipment was defective; it was agreed that Page would retain the item and receive a credit of $100.
28	Received a check from Dale Page for amount due.
Mar. 4	Paid the St. Paul Company the amount due on the purchase of February 4.

Required:

1. Journalize the above transactions using the gross price method. Assign journal page numbers.

2. Open general ledger accounts and post the journal entries. Assign account numbers to all accounts and place a beginning balance of $12,200 in the Cash account as of February 4.

P6–2A
Income statement from data given

The adjusted trial balance of the Buckeye Company on December 31, 1987 included the following accounts:

Account Title	Debits	Credits
Merchandise Inventory	$ 27,100	
Sales		$652,800
Sales Returns and Allowances	6,250	
Sales Discounts	6,500	
Purchases	398,000	
Transportation In	6,250	
Purchases Returns and Allowances		7,020
Transportation Out Expense	2,210	
Advertising Expense	12,400	
Sales Salaries Expense	160,000	
Administrative Salaries Expense	32,000	
Office Supplies Expense	4,800	
Depreciation Expense—Office Equipment	1,200	
Interest Expense	8,600	

The merchandise inventory on December 31, 1987 was determined to be $24,600.

Required: Prepare an income statement for 1987 assuming a 40 percent income tax rate.

P6–3A
Completion of a work sheet, preparation of statements, adjusting and closing entries

Following is the trial balance of Zumbro Company on December 31, 1987 (the end of the fiscal year):

Account Title	Debits	Credits
Cash	$ 55,200	
Temporary Investments	145,200	
Accounts Receivable	319,800	
Notes Receivable	54,600	
Accrued Interest Receivable	0	
Merchandise Inventory	390,000	
Store Supplies	60,900	
Advertising Supplies	38,100	
Prepaid Insurance	19,500	
Store Equipment	315,900	
Accumulated Depreciation—Store Equipment		$ 78,000
Accounts Payable		171,600
Notes Payable (due 1988)		180,000
Accrued Interest Payable		0
Accrued Wages Payable		0

(continued on next page)

Account Title	Debits	Credits
Unearned Rent.		2,400
Common Stock (100,000 shares)		300,000
Retained Earnings		324,000
Dividends	42,900	
Sales		1,950,000
Purchases.	1,103,700	
Transportation In.	19,500	
Advertising Expense.	0	
Store Supplies Expense	0	
Depreciation Expense—Store Equipment	0	
Heat, Light, and Power Expense[a]	39,000	
Miscellaneous General Expense.	66,300	
Rent Expense[a]	37,500	
Sales Salaries Expense.	199,700	
Office Salaries Expense	96,700	
Interest Expense.	11,700	
Interest Earned.		3,000
Rent Earned		7,200
Totals	$3,016,200	$3,016,200

[a]Classified as general and administrative expense.

The merchandise inventory at December 31, 1987, has been determined to be $293,000.

Data for adjustments are as follows:

a. Accrued interest receivable is $546.
b. Store supplies on hand are determined to have a valuation of $2,400.
c. Advertising supplies on hand are determined to have a valuation of $9,300.
d. Depreciation of store equipment for 1987 is $22,425.
e. Interest of $3,420 is accrued on notes payable.
f. Wages earned as of December 31 but not due to be paid until January are $3,000; they are equally divided between sales salaries and office salaries.
g. The last quarterly rent collection for October, November, and December was credited to Unearned Rent when collected on October 1, 1987.
h. The insurance policy is new; none expired in 1987.

Required (excluding income taxes):

1. Enter the above balances in a work sheet and complete the work sheet.
2. Prepare (a) an income statement, (b) a statement of retained earnings, and (c) a balance sheet.
3. Journalize the adjusting and the closing entries.

P6–4A
Recording purchases net of discount

The following transactions were completed by the Iowa Company during July 1987:

1987

Jul. 2 Purchased merchandise from the Cornell Company for $500, terms 3/10, n/30, F.O.B. destination.
   3 Purchased merchandise on account from the Kirkwood Company for $425, terms 1/10, n/30, F.O.B. shipping point.
   4 Paid freight charges of $10 on the merchandise purchased from the Kirkwood Company.
   5 Received a $50 credit (gross amount) for defective merchandise returned to the Kirkwood Company.
   11 Paid the Cornell Company.
   31 Paid the Kirkwood Company.

Required:

1a. Journalize the transactions using the gross price method.
1b. Prepare the cost of goods sold section of the income statement. Assume the following inventories: July 1, $250; July 31, $425.
2a. Journalize the transactions using the net price procedure.
2b. Prepare the cost of goods sold section of the income statement. Assume inventories are identical to those in Part 1b.
3. Under the net price procedure, how are purchases discounts lost classified in the income statement?

P6–5A
Sales and collection transactions

(Appendix) University City Sales had the following selected transactions in April 1987:

1987

Apr.	1	Sold merchandise to Clayton Company on account; invoice price $2,000; terms 2/10, n/30; invoice no. 0117.
	3	Sold merchandise to Wellston Company on account; invoice price $3,600; terms 2/10, n/30; invoice no. 0118.
	4	Received a check from Maplewood, Inc., in payment of a sale made March 27; invoice price $1,400; terms 2/10, n/30.
	5	Authorized an allowance of $200 to be credited to the account of Clayton Company, who reported that merchandise in the sale of April 1 was defective.
	5	Sold merchandise to Richmond Heights Company on account; invoice price $1,800; terms 2/10, n/30; invoice no. 0119.
	8	Recorded cash sales for the day amounting to $6,200.
	10	Sold excess store supplies to Kirkwood Company on account; invoice price $195; terms n/15.
	12	Received a check from Wellston Company for the amount due.
	15	Received a check from Richmond Heights Company for the amount due.
	15	Recorded cash sales for the day amounting to $6,560.
	19	Sold merchandise to Maplewood, Inc., on account; invoice price $1,500; terms 2/10, n/30; invoice no. 0120.
	25	Received a check from Kirkwood Company for the amount due.
	29	Sold merchandise to Wellston Company on account; invoice price $2,600; terms 2/10, n/30; invoice no. 0121.
	29	Received a check from Maplewood, Inc., for the amount due.
	30	Received a check from Clayton Company for the amount due.

Required:

1. Journalize the April transactions in the appropriate journals using the gross price method.
2. Open the necessary accounts in the general ledger and accounts receivable subsidiary ledger; enter a debit balance in the account of Maplewood, Inc., and in the Accounts Receivable account of $1,400 representing a sale recorded on March 27, 1987. Also enter a $500 debit balance in the Store Supplies account.
3. Post the April transactions to both ledgers (provide account numbers for the general ledger accounts).

P6–6A
Purchases and payment transactions

(Appendix) The Auburn Company had the following selected transactions in October 1987:

1987

Oct. 2 Purchased merchandise from Lee Company on account; invoice price $3,700; terms 1/10, n/30.
 3 Purchased office supplies from Beulah Company on account; invoice price $300; terms n/15.
 4 Purchased merchandise from Opelika, Inc., on account; invoice price $1,850; terms 2/10, n/30.
 7 Paid Gold Hill Company for a purchase made on September 28; invoice price $3,200, terms 2/10, n/30; check no. 870.
 12 Purchased merchandise for cash from the Pepperell Company; invoice price $825; check no. 871.
 14 Paid Opelika, Inc., the amount due; check no. 872.
 15 Purchased merchandise from Gold Hill Company on account; invoice price $3,600; terms 2/10, n/30.
 18 Paid Beulah Company the amount due; check no. 873.
 18 Returned merchandise that was the wrong size to Gold Hill Company; invoice price $600.
 24 Paid Gold Hill Company the amount due; check no. 874.
 28 Purchased merchandise from Opelika, Inc., on account; invoice price $2,750; terms 2/10, n/30.
 30 Paid Lee Company the amount due; check no. 875.

Required:

1. Journalize the October transactions in the appropriate journals using the gross price method.
2. Open the necessary accounts in the general ledger and the accounts payable subsidiary ledger; enter a credit balance in the account of Gold Hill Company and in the Accounts Payable account in the amount of $3,200 representing a purchase made on September 28, 1987. Also enter a debit of $25,600 in the Cash account.
3. Post the October transactions to both ledgers (provide account numbers for the general ledger accounts).

P6–7A
Thought-provoking problem: sales and inventory changes

White Consolidated Industries, Inc. reported the following in its *First Quarter Report* for 1984 (dollars in thousands):

Three Months Ended March 31

	1984	1983
Net sales	$514,542	$493,748
Inventories	463,390	456,617

Required:

1. Compute the dollar amount and percentage of change in net sales and in inventories.
2. Using the data you have computed (this is a form of horizontal analysis), comment on the company's performance in 1984 compared to the same quarter in 1983.

B Problems

P6–1B
Use of merchandise accounts

Lander Company had the following transactions:

1987

Apr. 1 Purchased merchandise from Winthrop Company at an invoice price of $11,200; terms n/30, F.O.B. shipping point.
 2 Paid Fastair Express $728 for delivery cost of the purchase of April 1.

(continued on next page)

2 Upon inspection, noted that merchandise invoiced at $1,680 in the Winthrop shipment was the wrong size. Returned the incorrect merchandise by Fastair Express collect as authorized by Winthrop Company.
5 Sold merchandise to Lester Raines in amount of $2,260; terms 2/10, n/30, F.O.B. shipping point.
15 Received a check from Lester Raines in total payment of the purchase of April 5.
19 Sold merchandise to Susan Wilhelm in amount of $2,100; terms 2/10, n/30, F.O.B. destination.
19 Paid $315 to Fastair Express for delivery of merchandise to Wilhelm.
22 Wilhelm reported that an item in the shipment was defective; it was agreed that Wilhelm would retain the item and receive a credit of $140.
29 Received a check from Susan Wilhelm for the amount due.
May 4 Paid the Winthrop Company the amount due on the purchase of April 1.

Required:

1. Journalize the above transactions using the gross price method. Assign journal page numbers.

2. Open general ledger accounts and post from the journal entries. Assign account numbers to all accounts, and place a beginning balance of $17,080 in the Cash account as of April 1.

P6–2B
Income statement from data given

The adjusted trial balance of the Keystone Company on December 31, 1987, included the following accounts:

Account Title	Debits	Credits
Merchandise Inventory	$ 24,390	
Sales		$587,520
Sales Returns and Allowances	5,625	
Sales Discounts	5,850	
Purchases	358,200	
Transportation In	5,625	
Purchases Returns and Allowances		6,318
Purchases Discounts		5,373
Transportation Out Expense	1,989	
Advertising Expense	11,160	
Sales Salaries Expense	144,000	
Administrative Salaries Expense	25,600	
Office Supplies Expense	4,320	
Depreciation Expense—Office Equipment	1,080	
Interest Expense	7,740	

The merchandise inventory on December 31, 1987, was determined to be $22,140.

Required: Prepare an income statement for 1987 assuming a 40 percent income tax rate.

P6–3B
Completion of a work sheet, preparation of statements, adjusting and closing entries

Following is the trial balance of Walbusser Company on December 31, 1987 (the end of the fiscal year):

Account Title	Debits	Credits
Cash	$ 49,680	
Temporary Investments	130,680	
Accounts Receivable	287,820	
Notes Receivable	49,140	
Accrued Interest Receivable	0	
Merchandise Inventory	351,000	
Store Supplies	54,810	
Advertising Supplies	34,290	

(continued on next page)

Account Title	Debits	Credits
Prepaid Insurance	17,549	
Store Equipment	284,310	
Accumulated Depreciation—Store Equipment		$ 70,201
Accounts Payable		154,440
Notes Payable (due 1988)		162,000
Accrued Interest Payable		0
Accrued Wages Payable		0
Unearned Rent		2,160
Common Stock (200,000 shares)		400,000
Retained Earnings		161,598
Dividends	38,610	
Sales		1,755,000
Purchases	993,330	
Transportation In	17,550	
Advertising Expense	0	
Store Supplies Expense	0	
Depreciation Expense—Store Equipment	0	
Heat, Light, and Power Expense[a]	35,100	
Miscellaneous General Expense	59,670	
Rent Expense[a]	33,750	
Sales Salaries Expense	179,730	
Office Salaries Expense	87,030	
Interest Expense	10,530	
Interest Earned		2,700
Rent Earned		6,480
Totals	$2,714,579	$2,714,579

The merchandise inventory at December 31, 1987 has been determined to be $282,700. Data for adjustments are as follows:

a. Accrued interest receivable is $492.
b. Store supplies on hand are determined to have a valuation of $2,160.
c. Advertising supplies on hand are determined to have a valuation of $8,370.
d. Depreciation of store equipment for 1987 is $20,182.
e. Interest of $3,078 is accrued on notes payable.
f. Wages earned as of December 31 but not due to be paid until January are $2,700; they are equally divided between sales salaries and office salaries.
g. The last quarterly rent collection for October, November, and December was credited to Unearned Rent when collected on October 1, 1987.
h. The insurance policy is new; none expired in 1987.

Required (excluding income taxes):

1. Enter the above balances in a work sheet and complete the work sheet.
2. Prepare (a) an income statement, (b) a statement of retained earnings, and (c) a balance sheet.
3. Journalize the adjusting and the closing entries.

P6–4B
Recording purchases net of discount

The following transactions were completed by the Massasoit Company during November 1987:

1987

Nov. 6 Purchased merchandise from the Bay Path Company for $1,000, terms 3/10, n/30, F.O.B. destination.
  8 Purchased merchandise on account from the Stonehill Company for $950, terms 1/10, n/30, F.O.B. shipping point.

(continued on next page)

	11	Paid freight charges of $10 on the merchandise purchased from the Stonehill Company.
	13	Received a $50 credit (gross amount) for defective merchandise returned to the Stonehill Company.
	15	Paid the Bay Path Company.
	26	Paid the Stonehill Company.

Required:

1a. Journalize the transactions using the gross price method.
1b. Prepare the cost of goods sold section of the income statement. Assume the following inventories: November 1, $500; November 30, $950.
2a. Journalize the transactions using the net price procedure.
2b. Prepare the cost of goods sold section of the income statement. Assume inventories are identical to those in Part 1b.
3. Under the net price procedure, how are purchases discounts lost classified in the income statement?

P6–5B
Sales and collection transactions

(Appendix) Texas Sales had the following selected transactions in July 1987:

1987

Jul.	1	Sold merchandise to Saginaw Company on account; invoice price $3,400; terms 2/10, n/30; invoice no. 0205.
	3	Sold merchandise to Watauga, Inc., on account; invoice price $6,120; terms 2/10, n/30; invoice no. 0206.
	4	Received a check from Carswell Company in payment of a sale made June 27; invoice price $2,380; terms 2/10, n/30.
	5	Authorized an allowance of $340 to be credited to the account of Saginaw Company.
	5	Sold merchandise to Arlington Company on account; invoice price $3,060; terms 2/10, n/30; invoice no. 0207.
	8	Recorded cash sales for the day amounting to $10,540.
	10	Sold excess office supplies to Fort Worth Company on account; invoice price $332; terms n/15.
	12	Received a check from Watauga, Inc., for the amount due.
	15	Received a check from Arlington Company for the amount due.
	19	Sold merchandise to Carswell Company on account; invoice price $2,550; terms 2/10, n/30; invoice no. 0208.
	25	Received a check from Fort Worth Company for the amount due.
	29	Sold merchandise to Watauga, Inc., on account; invoice price $4,420; terms 2/10, n/30; invoice no. 0209.
	29	Received a check from Carswell Company for the amount due.
	30	Received a check from Saginaw Company for the amount due.

Required:

1. Journalize the July transactions in the appropriate journal using the gross price method.
2. Open the necessary accounts in the general ledger and the accounts receivable subsidiary ledger; enter a debit balance in the account of Carswell Company and in the Accounts Receivable account in the amount of $2,380 representing a sale recorded on June 27, 1987. Also enter a debit balance of $950 in the Office Supplies account.
3. Post the July transactions to both ledgers (provide account numbers for the general ledger accounts).

P6–6B

Purchases and payment transactions

(Appendix) The Pensacola Company had the following selected transactions in January 1987:

1987		
Jan.	2	Purchased merchandise from Warrington Company on account; invoice price $5,920; terms 1/10, n/30.
	3	Purchased office supplies from Gull Point Company on account; invoice price $480; terms n/15.
	4	Purchased merchandise from Santa Rosa Company on account; invoice price $2,960; terms 2/10, n/30.
	7	Paid Milton Company for a purchase made on December 30, 1986; invoice price $5,120; terms 2/10, n/30; check no. 970.
	12	Purchased merchandise for cash from Yellow River Sales; invoice price $1,320; check no. 971.
	14	Paid Santa Rosa Company the amount due; check no. 972.
	15	Purchased merchandise from Milton Company on account; invoice price $5,760; terms 2/10, n/30.
	18	Paid Gull Point Company the amount due; check no. 973.
	18	Returned merchandise that was the wrong model to Milton Company; invoice price $360.
	24	Paid Milton Company the amount due; check no. 974.
	28	Purchased merchandise from Santa Rosa Company on account; invoice price $4,400; terms 2/10, n/30.
	30	Paid Warrington Company the amount due; check no. 975.

Required:

1. Journalize the January transactions in the appropriate journals using the gross price method.

2. Open the necessary accounts in the general ledger and the accounts payable subsidiary ledger; enter a credit balance in the account of Milton Company and the Accounts Payable account in the amount of $5,120 representing a purchase made on December 30, 1986. Also enter a debit balance of $42,120 in the Cash account.

3. Post the January transactions to both ledgers (provide account numbers for general ledger accounts).

P6–7B

Thought-provoking problem: inventory turnover and changes in sales and inventory

Fleming Companies, Inc. is a major wholesale food distributor based in Oklahoma City that serves stores, restaurants, and other food-service institutions in 31 states. The following data were reported in the 1983 *Annual Report* (dollars in thousands):

	1983	1982
Sales	$4,898,175	$3,688,011
Cost of goods sold	4,654,214	3,508,601
Inventories (end-of-year)	273,165	221,547

Required:

1. Compute the dollar amount and percentage of change in sales and cost of goods sold.

2. Compute inventory turnover for 1983 and 1982; end-of-year inventories for 1981 were $169,479.

3. Using the information computed in 1 and 2, comment on the favorable or unfavorable aspects of the company's operations.

Part Two

Income Measurement and Valuation Issues

7 Compound Interest Concepts

Note: The exact point in a financial course for this chapter to be taught is optional with the instructor. It may be omitted entirely; if it is, the instructor should note that certain exercises and problems in Chapters 9, 11, 14, and 15 require a knowledge of present value concepts. It may be taught as sequenced, or after Chapter 8 or Chapter 13. The interest rates used in this chapter and throughout the book usually range from 15 to 20 percent. These rates are not meant to be representative of what will be in effect in 1987, the year date used most prevalently in this book.

Introduction

In periods of high interest rates, it is extremely important for managers to understand how interest is calculated because it is such a material expense in the measurement of net income. For example, two large corporations reported these interest expense figures for 1983: American Brands, $101,721,000; Eaton Corporation, $48,461,000. This chapter discusses means of calculating compound interest, including present and future value, because they are significant elements not only in the accounting for borrowing and lending money but also in solving complex management problems and in determining the value of assets and liabilities. This information will be used extensively in Chapters 9, 11, 14, and 15 and referred to in other chapters to help explain certain valuation issues. Specifically, these interest concepts are used in:

1. Accounting for notes used for purchase of equipment.
2. Accounting for capital leases.
3. Accounting for installment receivables and payables.
4. Determining the issue price and the resale/purchase price of bonds.

5. Measuring the carrying value of bonds payable or book value of investments in bonds; that is, measuring the amortization of bond premium and discount in each case.

Learning Goals

1. To know how to determine and to use the future compound amount of a single sum.

2. To know how to determine and to use the present value of a single sum due in the future.

3. To know how to determine and to use the future compound amount of an ordinary annuity.

4. To know how to determine and to use the present value of an ordinary annuity.

A Comparison of Simple Interest and Compound Interest

A better understanding of compound interest may be gained by comparing it with simple interest. As indicated in Figure 4–10, simple interest is interest computed on the original principal (face value) of a note or time draft (a written order to pay). Compound interest, on the other hand, is interest that accrues on unpaid interest of the past periods as well as on the principal. In other words, **compound interest** is interest earned on a principal sum that is increased at the end of each period by the interest for that period. To contrast the difference between simple interest, compare the simple *annual* interest of $1,600 on a $10,000, 16 percent, one-year note with compound interest. Suppose the 16 percent interest were to be compounded *quarterly for one year*. The total compound interest would then be $1,698.59, as shown in Figure 7–1.

Period	Accumulated Amount at Beginning of Quarter (Principal)	×	Rate	×	Time	=	Compound Interest	Future Accumulated Amount at End of Quarter
1st quarter	$10,000.00		0.16		¼		$ 400.00	$10,400.00
2nd quarter	10,400.00		0.16		¼		416.00	10,816.00
3rd quarter	10,816.00		0.16		¼		432.64	11,248.64
4th quarter	11,248.64		0.16		¼		449.95	11,698.59
Compound interest on $10,000 at 16 percent compounded quarterly for one year.							$1,698.59	

Figure 7–1 **Compound Interest Computation**

In Figure 7–1, note that the future accumulated amount at the *end* of each quarter becomes the principal sum for *purposes of computing* the interest for the next period.

Compound Interest Techniques

For the purpose of computing the information needed in helping to solve many modern business problems, the accounting student should be familiar with the following four basic types of compound interest computations.

1. Future amount of a single given sum at compound interest.
2. Present value of a single given sum due in the future.
3. Future amount of an ordinary annuity.
4. Present value of an ordinary annuity.

The following discussion of these basic types attempts to present them in as clear and straightforward a manner as possible. To help the reader discover how these computations are related to each other, the approach stated below is used to develop a logical thought pattern that is necessary for an understanding of the first compound interest technique, that of the future amount of a single sum at compound interest.

1. The idea or concept is graphically illustrated.
2. The computation is accomplished by a laborious, successive, longhand calculation.
3. The computation is accomplished by the use of formulas.
4. The method of constructing and using tables is discussed.
5. Finally, the use of the tables to solve various compound interest problems quickly is illustrated.

Although these steps are only used with the future amount of a single sum at compound interest presentation, the reader could develop a similar approach with each of the other three methods.

Future Amount of a Single Sum at Compound Interest

The first of these compound interest techniques, the **future amount of a single sum at compound interest**, is the original sum plus the compound interest which has been earned and added on up to a specific future date. It is also referred to as the future value of a single sum or sometimes simply as the amount of a single investment at compound interest. For example, suppose that a single amount of $10,000 is invested in a fund on January 1, 1987.

The Idea

What will be the future amount in the fund on December 31, 1990, if interest at 16 percent is *compounded annually*? The problem can be shown graphically as follows:

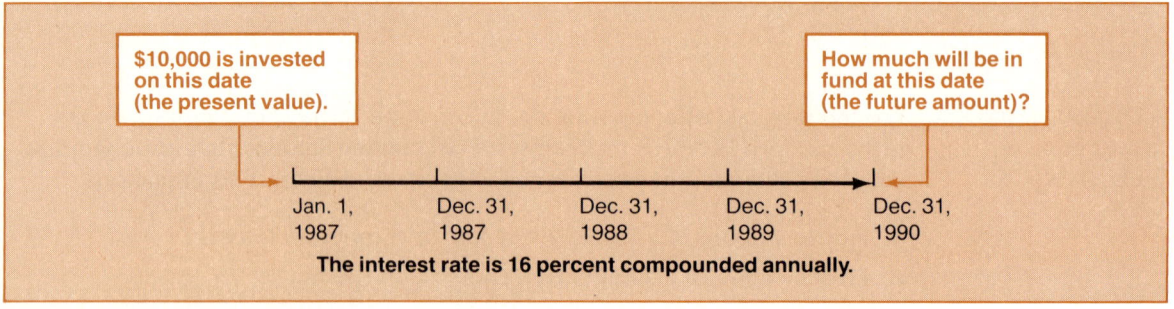

The Arithmetic Approach

With very few exceptions, compound interest calculations can be made by applying longhand arithmetic in a laborious, successive manner. To illustrate, the future amount of $10,000 for four years at 16 percent compounded annually is calculated in Figure 7–2.

The single sum of $10,000 invested on January 1, 1987, has by December 31, 1990, grown to $18,106.39, known as the *future compound amount, future value,* or in this book simply as the *future amount*. The total interest for the four years ($8,106.39) is referred to as **compound interest**.

Another slight variation of a longhand arithmetic approach is to determine what $1 invested at January 1, 1987, would amount to by December 31, 1990, if interest at 16 percent is compounded annually. Then multiply this amount by the principal sum to find the future amount. In solving this problem, an individual *must not round* the intermediate figures to the nearest cent or else the final results will contain a significant rounding error. For example, $1 would amount to $1.810639 in four years. Given this fact, the future amount of an investment of 10,000 individual dollars for four years can be calculated by multiplying the 10,000 dollars by $1.810639. Thus:

$$10,000 \times \$1.810639 = \$18,106.39.$$

This particular variation leads to the table approach that is used later.

Figure 7–2
Calculation of Future Amount of a Single Sum at Compound Interest

(1) Year	(2) Amount at Beginning of Year	+	(3) Annual Amount of Compound Interest (Col. 2 × 0.16)	=	(4) Future Accumulated Amount at End of Year (Col. 2 + Col. 3)
1987	$10,000.00		$1,600.00		$11,600.00
1988	11,600.00		1,856.00		13,456.00
1989	13,456.00		2,152.96		15,608.96
1990	15,608.96		2,497.43		18,106.39

The Formula Approach

Each amount in Column 4 of Figure 7–2 is 116 percent of the corresponding amount in Column 2. The final future amount is:

$$\$10,000 \times 1.16 \times 1.16 \times 1.16 \times 1.16 = \$18,106.39.$$

This means that 116 percent, or 1.16, has been used as a multiplier four times; thus 1.16 has been raised to the fourth power. The future amount is therefore, $10,000 multiplied by 1.16 to the fourth power, as shown below:

$$\text{Future amount} = \$10,000\,(1.16)^4 = \$18,106.39.$$

From the foregoing, we can state a formula for the future amount of a single sum at compound interest as follows:

$$a = p\,(1 + i)^n$$

where

a = Future amount at compound interest i for n periods.
p = Principal sum (present value).
n = Number of time periods.
i = Interest rate for each of the stated time periods.

It is important to observe that the interest rate i must be *the* rate of interest applicable for each time period that interest is compounded. For example, a nominal *annual* rate of interest of 16 percent means that i is equal to:

- 16 percent if interest is compounded annually.
- 8 percent if interest is compounded semiannually.
- 4 percent if interest is compounded quarterly.
- 1⅓ percent if interest is compounded monthly.

Mathematicians, to obtain the future value calculation of $1 or 1 of any monetary unit, have derived a formula for the future amount of 1 as follows:

$$a_{n,i} = 1\,(1 + i)^n.$$

Because 1 multiplied by another number or factor is that number or that factor, the foregoing formula is usually presented without the principal amount of 1 being stated:

$$a_{n,i} = (1 + i)^n$$

where

$a_{n,\,i}$ = Future amount of 1 ($1 or 1 of any other monetary unit) at interest rate i for n periods.
n = Number of time periods.
i = Interest rate per time period.

In this description of compound interest, the 1 usually appears in front of the formula to remind the reader that that is the given sum for which the future amount is to be determined. Using the foregoing formula for the future amount of a given sum of 1, we can restate the formula for the future compound amount of *any* single sum of compound interest as follows:

$$a = p(a_{n,i}).$$

Our example of the future amount of $10,000 invested at 16 percent with interest compounded annually can now be calculated in two steps by using the foregoing two formulas:

Step 1: $\quad a_{n=4, i=16\%} = 1(1.16)^4 = 1.810639.$

Step 2: $\quad a = \$10,000(1.810639) = \$18,106.39.$

Recall that this approach is exactly the same as the variation that was used in the successive, arithmetic method described above.

The Table Approach

As a means of further developing shortcuts to the solution of the compound interest problem, tables for the future amount of 1 have been constructed. These tables are nothing more than a precalculation of the future amount of $1(1 + i)^n$ for varying amounts of i and n. For example, suppose that tables of the future amount of 1 at 9 and 16 percent for time periods 1, 2, 3, 4, and 40 are needed. The information for these could be calculated as follows:

$a_{n=1, i=9\%} = 1(1.09)^1 = 1.090000.\quad a_{n=1, i=16\%} = 1(1.16)^1 = 1.160000.$
$a_{n=2, i=9\%} = 1(1.09)^2 = 1.188100.\quad a_{n=2, i=16\%} = 1(1.16)^2 = 1.345600.$
$a_{n=3, i=9\%} = 1(1.09)^3 = 1.295029.\quad a_{n=3, i=16\%} = 1(1.16)^3 = 1.560896.$
$a_{n=4, i=9\%} = 1(1.09)^4 = 1.411582.\quad a_{n=4, i=16\%} = 1(1.16)^4 = 1.810639.$
$a_{n=40, i=9\%} = 1(1.09)^{40} = 31.409420.\quad a_{n=40, i=16\%} = 1(1.16)^{40} = 378.721158.$

The foregoing information could then be accumulated in a partial table as indicated in Figure 7–3. In this kind of table, the amounts are shown without dollar signs. Again, they could be the future amount of 1 of any monetary unit. More complete tables are given in Appendix C.

Periods (n)	9%	16%
1	1.090000	1.160000
2	1.188100	1.345600
3	1.295029	1.560896
4	1.411582	1.810639
40	31.409420	378.721158

**Figure 7–3
Future Amount of
$1 = 1(1 + i)^n$**

Since the table factors in Figure 7–3 and Table C–1 of the Compound Interest Tables (Appendix C) are reflections of the formula $1(1 + i)^n$, the table approach for a, the future amount of a single sum, can be expressed in this manner:

$$a = p(\text{Table factor for } a_{n,i}).$$

If tables for $a_{n,i}$ are available, it thus becomes a simple matter to calculate what an investment of $10,000 will accumulate to in four years at 16 percent compounded annually. First, look up the table factor for $a_{n=4, i=16\%}$ (that is, the table factor for the future amount of 1 for four time periods at 16 percent), which is 1.810639 (from Figure 7–3). Then multiply the $10,000 times this factor, as follows:

$$a = \$10,000(1.810639) = \$18,106.39.$$

Present Value of Single Given Sum

The Idea

If $10,000 is worth $18,106.39 when it is left at 16 percent compound interest each year for four years, then it follows that cash of $18,106.39 four years from now should be worth $10,000 at the present time, **time period zero** with an interest rate of 16 percent compounded annually; that is, $10,000 is the present value of $18,106.39 discounted backward in time for four years at 16 percent. Thus, the present value is the amount that must be invested at time period zero to produce the known future value. The difference between these two amounts is referred to as the **compound discount**.

In the discussion which follows, this amount is confirmed by calculating the present value of $18,106.39 discounted for four years at 16 percent compounded annually. This problem can be shown graphically as follows:

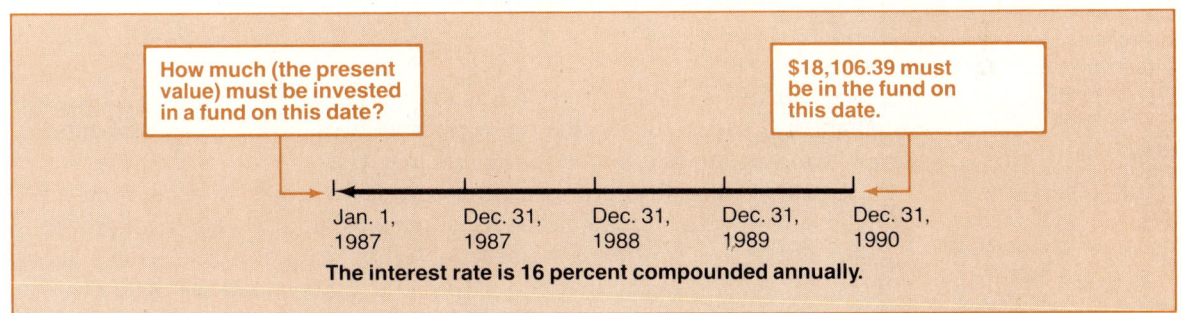

The Table Approach

Since the shortcut table approach is emphasized in this book, this concept will be rapidly developed with this and the next two techniques. Using the approach illustrated with the future amount of a single sum and the general formula for the present value of a single given sum of

$$p = a\left[\frac{1}{(1 + i)^n}\right],$$

mathematicians have developed tables for different interest rates (i) and for different numbers of time periods (n) for the present value of a single sum of 1 (p value of 1). The formula for these table values ($p_{n,i}$) is:[1]

$$p_{n,i} = 1\left[\frac{1}{(1+i)^n}\right].$$

Table factors for selected interest rates for time periods of 1 through 40 have been precalculated and are given in compound interest Table C–2. Turn to this table and note that the table factors are carried out to only six decimal places.

Rounding errors would thus creep into a calculation where the present value of large numbers is determined. These figures, however, will serve reasonably well as a means of understanding the concept of present value.

Since Table C–2 reflects the precalculation of

$$1\left[\frac{1}{(1+i)^n}\right],$$

the generalized table approach can be stated in this manner:

$$p = a(\text{Table factor for } p_{n,i}).$$

To calculate the present value of $18,106.39 discounted at 16 percent for four years, first look up the $p_{n=4, i=16\%}$ value in the present-value-of-1 table; it is 0.552291. Then the $18,106.39 needed future amount must be multiplied by the table factor for $p_{n=4, i=16\%}$ to determine the present value amount of $10,000, as shown below:

$$p = \$18{,}106.39 \times 0.552291 = \$10{,}000 \text{ (rounded)}.$$

Interrelationship of Future Amount of 1 and Present Value of 1

If present-value-of-1 tables are *not* available and future-amount-of-1 tables *are* available, it is easy to determine the applicable present-value-of-1 amounts by simply dividing the future amount figures into 1.

It should also be observed that $a_{n,i}$ should grow larger for increasing rates of interest and for increasing numbers of periods. In a reverse manner, the $p_{n,i}$ should become smaller as 1 is discounted by using increasing rates of interest and for increasing numbers of periods. A knowledge of this fact should help an individual to test intuitively the answer to future amount and present value problems. For instance, an individual must instantly realize that all future-amount-of-1 table factors must be greater than 1 and that all pres-

---

[1]Since 1 multiplied by another mathematical number is that number, this formula usually drops the 1 and is expressed as:

$$p_{n,i} = \left[\frac{1}{(1+i)^n}\right].$$

ent-value-of-1 table factors must be less than 1. Assume that you look up the $a_{n=4, i=16\%}$ value and write down 0.552291; you should realize that this is wrong and that you are looking at the values in the wrong table, because the amount is less than 1. Upon rechecking the tables, you would find that you had looked up the value in the present-value-of-1 tables instead of the future-amount-of-1 tables.

Future Amount of an Ordinary Annuity

Introduction

An **annuity** is a series of equal payments (deposits, receipts, or withdrawals), often referred to as **rents**, made at regular intervals with interest compounded at a certain rate. The regular intervals between payments may be any time period: a year, a month, six months, or three months. In the simple case, the calculation of the future amount of an ordinary annuity, (1) the periodic rents must be equal in amount, (2) the time periods between rents must be of the same length, (3) the interest rate for each time period must be constant, and (4) the interest rate must be compounded at the end of each time period.

The Idea

If the future amount of a series of deposits (rents) is determined *immediately* after the last deposit in the series is made, the future amount calculation is referred to as that of an **ordinary annuity**. For the first example, assume that the requirement is to determine the future amount of four rents of $10,000 each with interest compounded annually at 16 percent, assuming that the first deposit is made on December 31, 1987, and the last deposit on December 31, 1990. This information is graphically presented[2] as follows:

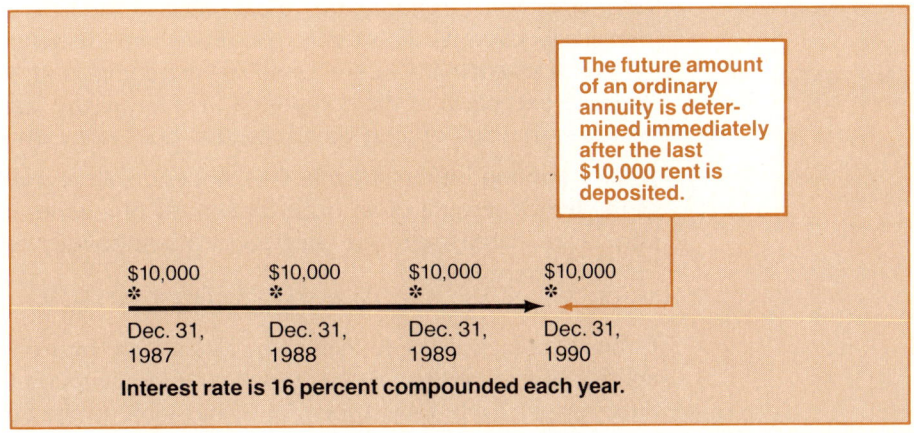

---

[2]The time graphs presented from this point in the chapter deal with annuities and use asterisks rather than vertical lines. The lines in earlier graphs represented time periods, whereas the asterisks here represent *rents*.

The Table Approach

As with the two preceding compound interest techniques, mathematicians start with the general formula for the future amount of an ordinary annuity of

$$A_o = R\left[\frac{(1+i)^n - 1}{i}\right]$$

where

A_o = The future amount of an ordinary annuity of a series of rents of *any* amount.
R = The value of each rent.
n = The number of rents (*not time periods;* remember that for an ordinary annuity there is always one more rent than there are time periods).
i = The interest rate per time period.

Then they develop tables for different interest rates and for different numbers of rents of 1 each. The formula for these table values ($A_{on,i}$) is:[3]

$$A_{On,i} = 1\left[\frac{(1+i)^n - 1}{i}\right].$$

Table factors for selected interest rates and for rents of 1 each for 1 through 40 rents have been precalculated and are presented in Table C–3, Compound Interest Tables. Turn to this table and note the following from these precalculations:

1. The numbers in the first column (n) represent the number of rents, not the number of time periods.

2. The future amount values are always equal to or greater than the number of rents of 1; for example, the future value of three rents of 1 unit each at 14 percent is 3.439600. This figure comprises two elements: (1) the three rents of 1 each *without* any interest, and (b) the compound interest on the rents with the exception of the compound interest on the last rent in the series, which in the case of an ordinary annuity does *not* earn any interest.

Since compound interest Table C–3, Appendix C, reveals the precalculation of the future amount of an ordinary annuity of a series of rents of 1 each, a generalized table approach can be stated as follows:

$$A_o = R(\text{Table factor for } A_{on,i}).$$

It thus becomes a simple matter to calculate the future amount of an ordinary annuity of four rents of $10,000 each at 16 percent compounded annually. First, turn to Table C–3, Appendix C, and look up the table factor for

---

[3]This formula for the future amount of an ordinary annuity of rents of 1 each is usually stated as:

$$A_{On,i} = \left[\frac{(1+i)^n - 1}{i}\right].$$

$A_{On=4, i=16\%}$. That table factor is 5.066496. Second, multiply the $10,000 by this table factor as follows:

$$A_o = \$10,000 \ (5.066496) = \$50,664.96.$$

Two typical kinds of future-amount-of-an-annuity problems are: (1) given a known amount of each rent and known compound interest rate, calculate the future amount at compound interest—this is the example that has just been illustrated, and (2) given a known future amount of an ordinary annuity and known compound interest rate, calculate the amount or value of each rent. This second kind is now illustrated.

Example: Determining the Value of Rents When Future Amount Is Known

At the beginning of 1987, the Lasley Company issued a 10-year note with a principal amount of $1,000,000 due on December 31, 1996. The company desires to accumulate a fund to retire this note at maturity. It wants to make annual deposits to the fund beginning with December 31, 1987. How much must the company deposit each year, assuming that the fund will earn 20 percent interest compounded annually?

The facts of the problem can be seen from the following diagram:

Ten rents are unknown

R R R R R R R R R R

Dec. 31, 1987 | Dec. 31, 1988 | Dec. 31, 1989 | Dec. 31, 1990 | Dec. 31, 1991 | Dec. 31, 1992 | Dec. 31, 1993 | Dec. 31, 1994 | Dec. 31, 1995 | Dec. 31, 1996

$1,000,000 is needed in fund on this date.

Interest rate is 20 percent compounded annually.

Solution The future amount, the number of rents, and the compound interest rate are known; the value of each of the ten rents is the unknown factor. Expressing the formula for A_o as

$$R(\text{Table factor for } A_{On,i}) = A_o,$$

then we could divide both sides of the equation by table factor for $A_{On,i}$ and derive this formula:

$$R = \frac{A_o}{\text{Table factor for } A_{On,i}}.$$

Substituting the known amounts and the appropriate table values in this formula gives

$$R = \frac{\$1,000,000}{25.958682} = \$38,522.76.$$

Present Value of an Ordinary Annuity

Introduction

The **present value of an annuity** is the present value of a series of withdrawals or payments (rents) discounted at compound interest. In other words, it is the amount that must be invested now and, if left at compound interest, will provide for a withdrawal of a series of equal rents at regular intervals, the last withdrawal to be made on the final date. Over time, the present value balance is increased periodically for interest and decreased periodically for the withdrawal of each rent. Thus the last withdrawal (rent) in the series exhausts the balance on deposit.

The present value of an annuity concept is frequently used in the measuring and reporting of (1) notes payable and notes receivable when the interest rate differs from the current market rate, (2) the carrying value of investment in bonds and the bonds payable liability, (3) the receivable or debt under installment contracts, and (4) the desirability of capital investment projects.

The Idea

If the present value of the series of rents is determined one period *before* the withdrawal of the first rent, the series of rents is known as the **present value of an ordinary annuity**. For the illustrative problem, assume that the following is to be determined: the present value on January 1, 1987, of four withdrawals of $10,000 discounted at 16 percent, with the first withdrawal being made on December 31, 1987, one year after the determination of the present value.

This information is graphically presented below:

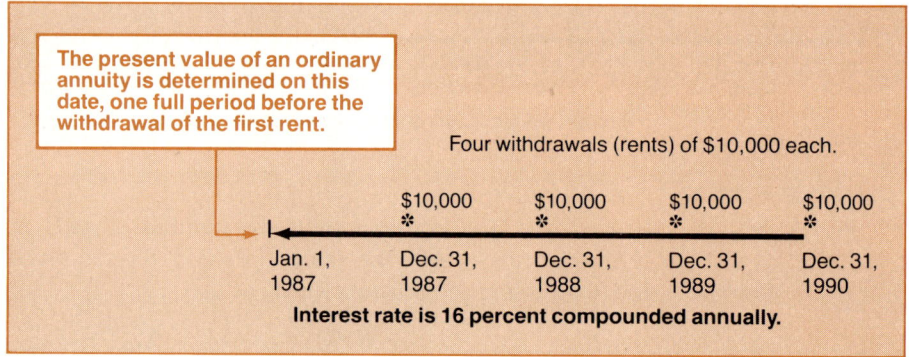

The Table Approach

Again, mathematicians start with the general formula for the present value of an ordinary annuity of

$$P_o = R \left[\frac{1 - \frac{1}{(1+i)^n}}{i} \right]$$

where

P_o = The present value of an ordinary annuity of a series of rents of *any* amount.
R = The value of each rent.
n = The number of rents.
i = The interest rate per period.

They then develop tables for different interest rates and for different numbers of rents of 1 each. The formula for these table values ($P_{On,i}$) is:[4]

$$P_{On,i} = 1\left[\frac{1 - \frac{1}{(1+i)^n}}{i}\right].$$

Table factors for selected interest rates and for rents of 1 each for 1 through 40 rents have been precalculated and are presented in Table C–4, Compound Interest Tables. Turn to this table and observe that:

1. The numbers in the first column (n) represent the number of rents of 1 each.

2. The present value amounts are *always smaller* than the number of rents of 1; for example, the present value of three rents of 1 at 14 percent is 2.321632. A user of compound interest tables should realize this fact and use this knowledge to test quickly whether the correct tables are being selected. If $P_{On=4, i=16\%}$ is looked up and the table value is 5.066496, then the user should realize that the wrong table value has been obtained. Upon investigating, the user would see that the future-amount-of-an-ordinary-annuity table value had been picked up rather than the present-value-of-an-ordinary-annuity table value.

Since Table C–4 reveals the precalculation of $P_{On,i}$ values, it is possible to express a generalized table approach as follows:

$$P_o = R \text{ (Table factor for } P_{On,i}\text{)}.$$

Thus, to calculate the present value on January 1, 1987, of four rents of $10,000 discounted at 16 percent, with the first rent being withdrawn on December 31, 1987, first look up the $P_{On=4, i=16\%}$ value in the table for present value of an ordinary annuity of 1. This value is 2.798181. Then multiply this

---

[4]This formula for the present value of an ordinary annuity of rents of 1 each is usually stated as:

$$P_{On,i} = \left[\frac{1 - \frac{1}{(1+i)^n}}{i}\right].$$

factor by $10,000 to determine the present value figure of $27,981.81, as shown below:

$$P_o = \$10,000 (2.798181) = \$27,981.81.$$

This calculated amount, $27,981.81, can be proven to be true by reference to the schedule below.

Period	Amount on Deposit at Beginning of Period	+	Interest Earned	−	Withdrawal	=	Amount on Deposit at End of Period
1	$27,981.81		$4,477.09		$10,000.00		$22,458.90
2	22,458.90		3,593.42		10,000.00		16,052.32
3	16,052.32		2,568.37		10,000.00		8,620.69
4	8,620.69		1,379.31		10,000.00		0

Two typical kinds of present-value-of-an-ordinary-annuity problems can be solved by the use of these table factors: (1) for known amount of each rent and known compound interest rate, calculate the present value of the ordinary annuity—this is the example already illustrated, and (2) for known present value of an ordinary annuity and known compound interest rate, calculate the amount of each rent. The latter problem is now illustrated.

Example: Determining the Value of Period Rents When the Present Value Is Known

On January 1, 1987, Jan Owens Corporation borrows $100,000 to finance a plant expansion project. Owens plans to pay this amount back with interest at 14 percent on the beginning of the year balance over a 10-year period, with the first annual payment being due on December 31, 1987. What is the amount of each of the installment payments, provided that each is to be of an equal amount and to include both interest and a partial retirement of the principal of the debt?

The facts of the problem can be seen from the following diagram:

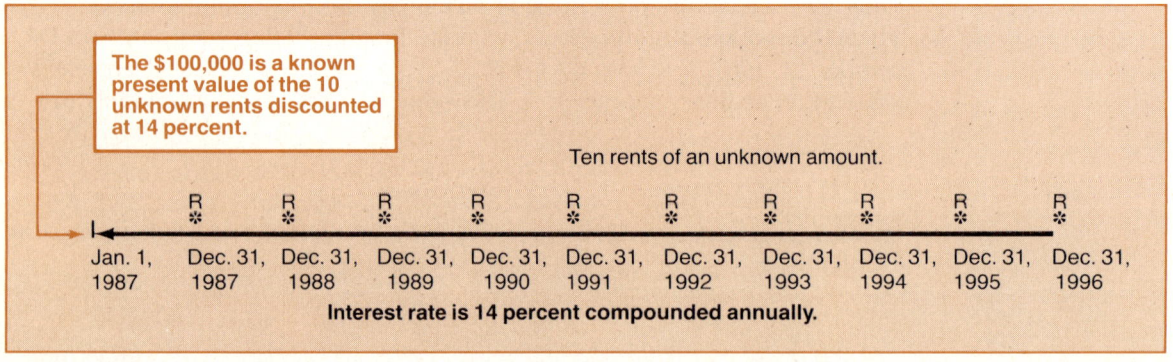

7 / Compound Interest Concepts

Solution The present value amount and the compound interest rate are known; the value of each of the ten rents is the unknown factor. We can use this formula for P_o:

$$R \text{ (Table factor for } P_{On,i}) = P_o.$$

Then, dividing both sides of the equation by table factor for $P_{On,i}$,

$$R = \frac{P_o}{\text{Table factor for } P_{On,i}}.$$

It is possible to solve for the amount of each payment (the R value) by looking up the $P_{On=10, i=14\%}$ value in Table C–4, Appendix C, and dividing this factor into the $100,000 present value figure, as shown below:

$$R = \frac{\$100,000}{5.216116} = \$19,171.35.$$

It should be remembered that each of these payments of $19,171.35 constitutes: (1) a payment of annual interest, and (2) a retirement of debt principal. For example, the interest for 1987 is $14,000 = (14 percent × $100,000); thus the amount of the payment on principal is $5,171.35 = ($19,171.35 − $14,000). For the year 1988, the interest is $13,276.01 = 14 percent × [($100,000 − $5,171.35)], and the retirement of principal is $5,895.34 = ($19,171.35 − $13,276.01). The *last* payment of $19,171.35, which will be made on December 31, 1996, should be sufficient to retire the remaining principal and to pay the interest for the tenth year.

Glossary

Annuity A series of equal payments—deposits, receipts, or withdrawals—made at regular intervals with interest compounded at a certain rate.

Compound discount The difference between the future amount of a sum of money and the present value of the sum.

Compound interest Interest computed not only on the principal but also on any interest that has been earned in the past but not yet paid. This term also refers to the difference between the future compound amount and the original principal.

Future amount of an ordinary annuity The future amount of a series of equal rents at equal intervals plus interest compounded at a certain rate, with the future amount being determined immediately after the last rent in the series is made.

Future amount of a single sum at compound interest This is also called future compound amount or amount of a single sum; the amount of a single investment plus compound interest for a given number of periods thereon.

Ordinary annuity A series of equal rents made at regular intervals with interest compounded at a certain rate and with the calculation of the present value or the future amount being determined as described by these two terms elsewhere in this glossary.

Present value In general, a future sum discounted back to the present time by the use of an interest factor. Present value is used in connection with two approaches: (1) the present value of a single sum due in the future and (2) the present value of a series of equal withdrawals or rents made in the future.

Present value of an annuity The present worth of a series of equal withdrawals or rents discounted at a given rate of interest.

Present value of an ordinary annuity Present value at time period zero of a series of equal rents made at equal intervals of time in the future. The present value of an ordinary annuity is determined one interest period before the withdrawal of the first rent.

Present value of a sum due in the future Present value at time period zero of a single future investment.

Rent The amount of each of a series of equal annuity deposits made or receipts.

Time period zero The date at which the present value is determined.

Time value of money The concept that money earns interest over time periods; the term is used to include the future amount of a given sum or annuity or the present value of these two.

Questions

Q7–1 Assume that you have a favorite aunt who has made you three offers as to methods of sharing her estate with you:

   a. A gift of $10,000 made at the present time.
   b. A gift of $12,000 to be made five years from now.
   c. A bequest in her will of $18,000.

   Assume that time value of money is a constant at 16 percent per year and that for this calculation the estimate of the remaining length of life of the aunt is 12 years. Discuss the method that you should use to determine which offer is the most beneficial to you.

Q7–2 Distinguish between simple interest and compound interest.

Q7–3 Distinguish between the future amount of 1 and the present value of 1.

Q7–4 Distinguish between the present value of 1 and the present value of an ordinary annuity of 1.

Q7–5 Distinguish between the future amount of 1 and the future amount of an ordinary annuity of 1.

Q7–6 What is the interest rate per period and the frequency of compounding per year in each of the following: **a.** 20 percent compounded semiannually. **b.** 16 percent compounded quarterly. **c.** 18 percent compounded monthly.

Q7–7 Timothy wishes to deposit a sum that at 16 percent interest compounded semiannually will permit two withdrawals: $10,000 at the end of five years, and $20,000 at the end of 10 years. Analyze the problem to determine the required deposit, stating the procedure to be followed and the tables to be used in developing the solution.

Q7–8 If a student looks up a table factor for the present value of a single sum and writes down 1.810639, what should common sense tell him or her? Explain.

Exercises

E7–1 *Various compound interest issues*

Fill in the correct response to complete the sentences below: **a.** greater than (>) **b.** less than (<) **c.** equal to (=)

1. The present value of an amount on date zero should be _____ the amount desired on future date X.
2. The future value of an amount should be _____ the amount invested on date zero.
3. The table factor for the future amount of a single sum should be _____ 1.
4. The table factor for the present value of a single sum should be _____ 1.

7 / Compound Interest Concepts

E7–2
Future amount of a single investment issues

Using the future-amount-of-a-single-sum tables, solve the following problems:

1. What is the future amount on January 1, 1992, of $9,000 invested on January 1, 1987, to earn interest at 16 percent compounded annually?
2. What is the future amount on January 1, 1990, of $7,250 invested on July 1, 1987, to earn interest at 9 percent compounded semiannually?
3. What is the future amount on January 1, 1993, of $6,000 invested on January 1, 1987, to earn interest at 16 percent compounded annually?

E7–3
Present value of a single sum issues

Using the present-value-of-a-single-sum tables, solve the following problems:

1. What is the present value on January 1, 1987, of $20,550 due to be paid on January 1, 1992, discounted at 16 percent compounded annually?
2. What is the present value on January 1, 1987, of $4,000 due to be paid on July 1, 1989, discounted at 20 percent compounded quarterly?
3. What is the present value on July 1, 1987, of $10,000 due to be paid on July 1, 1997, discounted at 20 percent compounded annually?

E7–4
Present value of an annuity

What is the present value on January 1, 1987, of five equal annual rents of $2,000 beginning on January 1, 1988, compounded annually at 16 percent?

E7–5
Present value of an annuity

What is the present value on July 1, 1987, of eight equal semiannual rents of $500 beginning on January 1, 1988, compounded semiannually at an annual rate of 18 percent?

E7–6
Future amount of an annuity

What is the future amount on January 1, 1990, of four equal annual rents of $6,600 beginning on January 1, 1987, compounded annually at 16 percent?

E7–7
Future amount of an annuity

What is the future amount on April 1, 1992, of 20 equal quarterly rents of $400 beginning on July 1, 1987, compounded quarterly at a 16 percent annual rate?

E7–8
Future amount issue

Ben West deposited $20,000 in a special investment that provides for interest at the annual rate of 18 percent compounded monthly if the investment is maintained for three years. Using the future amount tables, calculate the balance of the savings account at the end of the three-year period.

E7–9
Determining amount of rent of an annuity

Five equal annual contributions are to be made to a fund, the first deposit to be made on December 31, 1987. Using the future amount tables, determine the equal contributions that, if invested at 16 percent compounded annually, will produce a fund of $50,000, assuming that this sum is desired on December 31, 1991.

E7–10
Determining amount of equal payments of a loan

Charlene Murphy borrows $9,000 that is to be repaid in 18 equal monthly installments with interest at the rate of 2½ percent a month. Using the tables, calculate the equal installments.

E7–11
Various compound interest issues

On January 1, 1987, Carl Bledsoe borrows $40,000 from his father to open a business. The son is the beneficiary of a trust created by his favorite uncle, from which he will receive $15,000 on January 1, 1995. He signs an agreement to make this amount payable to his father and further to pay his father equal annual amounts from January 1, 1988, to January 1, 1994, inclusive, in retirement of the debt. Interest is to be charged at 16 percent. What are the annual payments?

E7–12
Future amount of a debt

On September 1, 1987, Jo Jackson puts her hotel bill of $210 on a charge account. The stipulated annual interest rate is 18 percent compounded monthly. How much will she owe in three months? Six months? One year?

E7–13

Converting future amount of a single sum factors to other factors

While taking a test, Jane Tottingham, a student, realizes that she has failed to bring her present-value-of-a-single-sum tables, although she does have her future-amount-of-a-single-sum tables. She needs to answer the following: How much needs to be invested now in order to have $6,000 at the end of three years at 2½ percent monthly interest?

1. Can the student use the future-amount-of-a-single-sum tables to solve this problem? Explain.
2. If the future-amount-of-a-single-sum table factor for 2½ percent for 36 months is 2.432535, how much needs to be invested now in order to have $5,000 at the end of three years?

A Problems

P7–1A

Future amount of an annuity

Theo Owens is depositing his Christmas bonus in a special fund. Owens receives an $8,000 bonus each year. Assume that he will continue to receive this amount and that he deposits these bonuses each December 31 in a fund that will earn 14 percent compounded annually. Also assume that the first deposit was made on December 31, 1987.

Required: What amount will be in the fund after the deposit on December 31, 1991?

P7–2A

Calculating amount of equal payments of a debt

On July 1, 1987, the Rose Corporation purchased real estate for $180,000 to be paid in 20 equal annual installments, including interest of 16 percent on any unpaid balance. The first installment is due on July 1, 1988.

Required: What is the amount of each equal payment?

P7–3A

Calculating amount of withdrawals of an annuity

Ten equal semiannual withdrawals are to be made beginning January 1, 1988. On July 1, 1987, $50,000 is invested at 18 percent interest compounded semiannually.

Required: Using the proper table, determine the equal semiannual withdrawals.

P7–4A

Calculating amount of deposits for a given future amount

Joseph Cotten desires to accumulate $16,000 in his savings account by December 31, 1993. His savings account earns 16 percent compounded annually. Cotten will begin making equal annual deposits on December 31, 1987, and will continue to make deposits through December 31, 1993.

Required: What is the amount of each equal annual payment?

P7–5A

Various compound interest issues

On January 1, 1987, June Joyce borrows $70,000 from her father to open a business. The daughter is the beneficiary of a trust created by her favorite uncle from which she will receive $30,000 on January 1, 1996. She signs an agreement to make this amount payable to her father and further to pay her father equal annual amounts from January 1, 1988, to January 1, 1995, inclusive, in retirement of the debt. Interest is to be charged at 16 percent.

Required: What is the amount of the annual payment?

P7–6A

Thought-provoking problem: deciding by which plan to acquire a computer

The president of the Roxboro Corporation has consulted you, the controller, as to which of the following plans you would recommend in acquiring a computer:

a. Purchase the equipment and pay immediately a cash price of $55,000.
b. Rent (lease) the computer at the rate of $2,500 per month, payable at the end of each month.

The estimated useful life of the computer is three years, with a resale value at the end of that time of zero.

Required: Assume that the approximate time value of money is 2½ percent per month. Disregard all factors other than those stated above. Evaluate the two alternatives and indicate which plan you would recommend to the president; state the amount of savings that would be made.

B Problems

P7–1B
Future amount of an annuity

Jan Benson is depositing her Christmas bonus in a special fund. Benson receives a $7,000 bonus each year. Assume that she will continue to receive this amount and that she deposits these bonuses each December 31 in an account that will earn 16 percent compounded annually. Also assume that the first deposit was made on December 31, 1987.

Required: What amount will be in the fund after the deposit on December 31, 1994?

P7–2B
Calculating amount of equal payments of a debt

On April 16, 1987, Jean Ormany purchased real estate for $120,000 to be paid in 12 equal installments, including interest of 14 percent on any unpaid balance. The first installment is due on April 16, 1988.

Required: What is the amount of each equal payment?

P7–3B
Calculating amount of withdrawals of an annuity

Twenty equal annual withdrawals are to be made beginning December 31, 1987. On December 31, 1986, $80,000 is invested at 14 percent interest compounded annually.

Required: Using the proper table, determine the equal annual withdrawals.

P7–4B
Calculating amount of deposits for a given future amount

Robert Bailey desires to accumulate $9,800 in his investment account by December 31, 1990. His account earns 14 percent compounded annually. Bailey will begin making equal annual deposits on December 31, 1987, and will continue to make deposits through December 31, 1990.

Required: What is the amount of each equal annual payment?

P7–5B
Various compound interest issues

On January 1, 1987, Hammer Hunter borrows $60,000 from his father to open a business. The son is the beneficiary of a trust created by his favorite aunt from which he will receive $15,000 on January 1, 2000. He signs an agreement to make this amount payable to his father and further to pay his father equal annual amounts from January 1, 1988, to January 1, 1999, inclusive, in retirement of the debt. Interest is to be charged at 14 percent.

Required: What is the amount of the annual payment?

P7–6B
Thought-provoking problem: deciding on which source of funds is the least expensive

Because of a severe cash crunch, the Illinois Company finds itself needing sources of short-term funds. After investigating all possibilities, the controller lists these alternatives:

a. To forgo discounts on the purchases of merchandise and pay the full invoice price at the latest possible date. These discounts are generally on a 2/10, n/30 basis.
b. To borrow money from the local bank at 18 percent; the local bank requires that a minimum balance of 10 percent of the amount borrowed be maintained throughout the period of the loan.
c. To borrow money from the Brady Finance Company and pay a monthly fee of 2½ percent of the unpaid balance at the beginning of each month.

(continued on next page)

d. To borrow money from Judson Funds Company on a year's contract basis, agreeing to pay 15 percent of the original amount and to add this interest to the amount borrowed, then to repay the loan and interest in equal monthly installments.

Required: Assuming that two or more of these sources will be needed to provide adequate short-term funds, indicate the order of the desirability of the sources, from most desirable to least desirable, by calculating an approximation of the annual effective simple interest rates for each alternative.

8 Control of Cash

Introduction

In a recent year, a major airline in the United States received what is known as a *qualified opinion* in the report of its annual audit. The auditors' opinion stated that the financial statements were a fair presentation of the airline's financial position and results of operations only if it were able to continue in business as a going concern. Among the factors creating doubt as to the company's continuation as a going concern was the fact that it had used cash of $73,821,000 in excess of receipts in its operations for the year just ended. Effective management and control of cash are very important to a firm because cash represents instantly available purchasing power and nearly every transaction ultimately involves the exchange of cash. Good cash management requires (1) that an adequate cash balance be maintained at all times, and (2) that sufficient safeguards be established to prevent theft or misappropriation.

Cash includes any item that a bank customarily accepts for deposit—coins, currency, savings accounts, bank drafts, cashier's checks, money orders, bank credit card sales invoices, traveler's checks, and foreign and domestic checking account balances.

This chapter examines internal control concepts, petty cash fund operation, the use of a checking account, and monthly bank reconciliation procedures. It then describes a system of internal control—the voucher system. The aspect of a voucher system as an aid to the internal control of cash payments is stressed.

Learning Goals

1. To know the concepts of internal control of cash.

2. To record entries using an imprest petty cash system.

3. To read and interpret monthly bank statements and to prepare a bank reconciliation.

4. To make the journal entries required after the bank reconciliation.

5. To understand the use of vouchers to achieve internal control of disbursements.

6. To describe the relationship between the voucher files and cash payments.

Cash Management Systems

Internal Control

Cash is naturally vulnerable to theft or misuse. If it is handled and controlled properly, both the employer and the employee benefit—the employer safeguards the asset and the employee avoids suspicion of inaccuracy or dishonesty. Safeguards must be designed to prevent the following:

- Theft of cash receipts covered by failure to record the transaction in the cash receipts journal. For example, scrap and waste material may be sold by an employee for cash and not reported.
- Delay in recording the receipt of cash (the cash being withheld during the interval) or recording false entries. For example, cash may be pocketed on receipt of a payment from a customer and his or her accounts receivable subsidiary ledger account credited. The general ledger debit, however, may be made to an account such as Sales Returns and Allowances.
- The recording of false debits to expense accounts or other accounts to cover fraudulent cash withdrawals. For example, a branch supervisor may carry a terminated employee's name on the payroll for several additional pay periods, forging the endorsement of the former employee on payroll checks that continue to be issued.
- Theft of cash by computer. For example, cash may be transferred to an unauthorized account by changing the computer program.

Certain basic controls must be instituted to prevent the misuse of funds. Individual responsibility for each step in the flow of cash must be clearly established. On receipt, all checks should be endorsed and rubber-stamped *For deposit only* to prevent their misuse. Total cash receipts should be deposited intact daily; payments should be made by company check and not out of cash receipts. Automated accounting control devices should be used wherever possible.

The protection of cash against losses through fraud, error, and carelessness requires certain fundamental steps, including:

- Clear separation of duties and responsibilities.
- Provision of the necessary facilities, such as cash registers.

- ☐ Definite written instructions that control authorization for payment of cash.
- ☐ Organization of the flow and recording of documents so that, whenever possible, the work of one employee is subject to automatic verification by another. The handling of cash should be separated from the record keeping, so that no one person both receives or disburses cash and also records it in the cash journals.
- ☐ Periodic testing to see if internal controls are operating effectively. For example, at unannounced times, recorded cash receipts should be compared with cash on hand and deposits that have been made.
- ☐ Establishing controls over access to computers and computer programs.

Cash Flows

A business depends on inflows of cash to cover and hopefully to exceed its outflows of cash. One class of cash flow causes is operating transactions. **Operating transactions** are transactions to produce income and to distribute a portion of it to the stockholders. They include net income (adjusted for certain items affecting income that do not affect cash), investment in revenue-producing properties and vehicles, and payment of dividends to stockholders. A second class of events affecting cash flow is known as **financing transactions**. These are transactions to secure the necessary financial resources and to repay the resultant debts. They include short-term and long-term borrowing, repayments, and issuance of stock.

Household International, Inc. is a large United States corporation with assets of $8,446,000,000 at the end of 1983. Its many subsidiary companies include HFC (consumer finance), Ben Franklin (variety stores), U.S. Brass (plumbing fittings), King-Seely (cooking appliance controls), Alexander Hamilton Life Insurance Company of America (insurance), and National Car Rental (rental and leasing). The consolidated cash flows for Household International, Inc. in 1983 are shown in Figure 8–1. In this diagram beginning and ending cash balances for the year that would be disclosed on the balance sheets do not really give any idea of the huge inflows and outflows of cash that the company experienced. The balance on January 1 was increased by a net amount of $117,400,000 from operating transactions and decreased by a net amount of $152,100,000 from financing transactions. Broad classifications of these transactions on the left of the diagram represent sources of cash flowing into the company, and those on the right represent uses of cash outflows. It is not the balance sheet cash amounts that represent the cash control problem in a business. The challenge for management is to exercise control over these relatively large cash inflows and outflows that occur between balance sheet dates. A tool used in cash planning—the cash forecast—is discussed next.

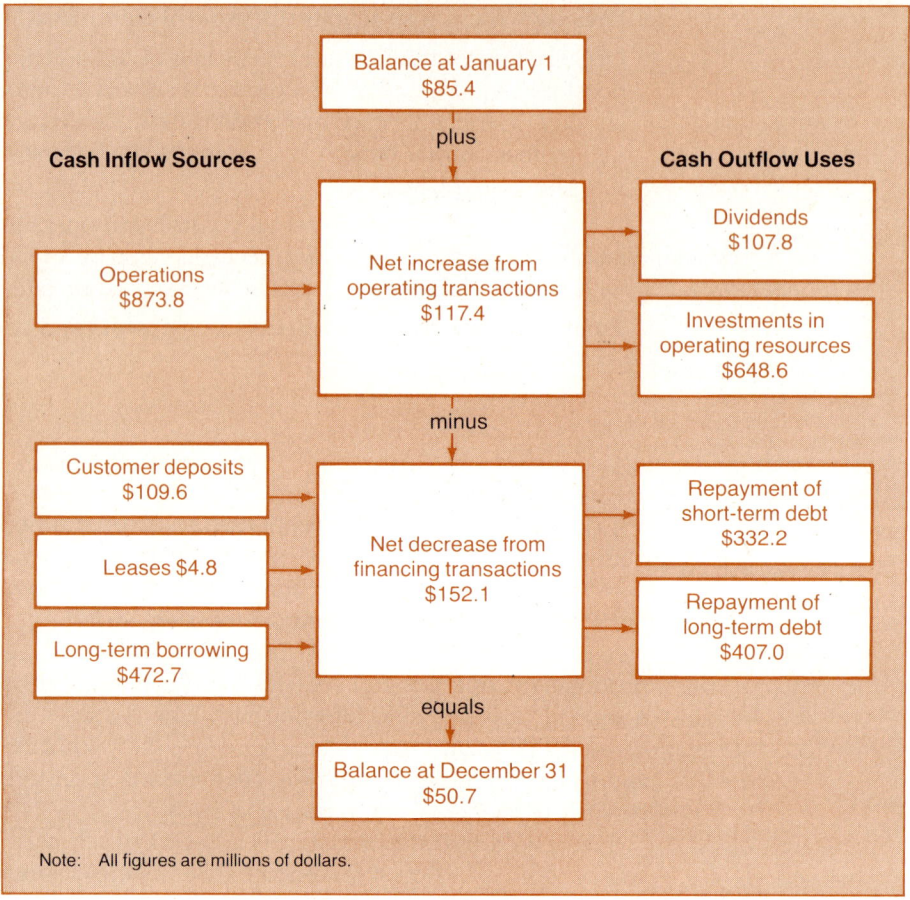

Figure 8–1   **Household International, Inc. 1983 Cash Flows**

Analysis of Cash Needs: Cash Forecast

The managers of a business must make certain that adequate cash funds are available at all times. Sufficient cash must be available to meet payrolls, take advantage of discounts, and maintain a good credit rating. Excessive cash balances, particularly during inflationary periods when cash suffers a loss in purchasing power or when interest rates are high, indicate ineffective management.

    To maintain an adequate cash balance requires a projected cash plan, called a **cash forecast**, for a number of months in advance. The period covered by a forecast may be a month, a quarter, or a longer period. If cash flows are erratic, weekly forecasts may be desirable. In the end-of-chapter problems for this chapter, problem P8–5B gives a form for a cash forecast. Recognizing that the end-of-month cash balance is the beginning balance of the next month, anticipated receipts are added and anticipated payments are deducted. This device gives advance warning of cash shortages or excesses, and is an important part of overall cash control.

Petty Cash

For adequate internal control, total cash receipts should be *deposited intact daily* and disbursements normally should be made by check. There are occasions, however, when payment by check is impractical, such as for postage, small contributions, express charges, taxi fares, and minor supplies. A special **petty cash fund** should be set up for these purposes. The fund is placed in custody of one person. Each payment should be supported by a receipt signed by the person receiving the cash (a **petty cash voucher**) that shows the purpose of the expenditure, the date, and the amount (see Figure 8–2).

To establish the petty cash fund, a check for the amount to be placed in the fund is drawn to the order of the fund custodian and cashed. The journal entry to record the establishment of a petty cash fund of $500 by the High Company is:

1987 Aug.	3	Petty Cash . . . . Cash . . . . Established petty cash fund.	500	500

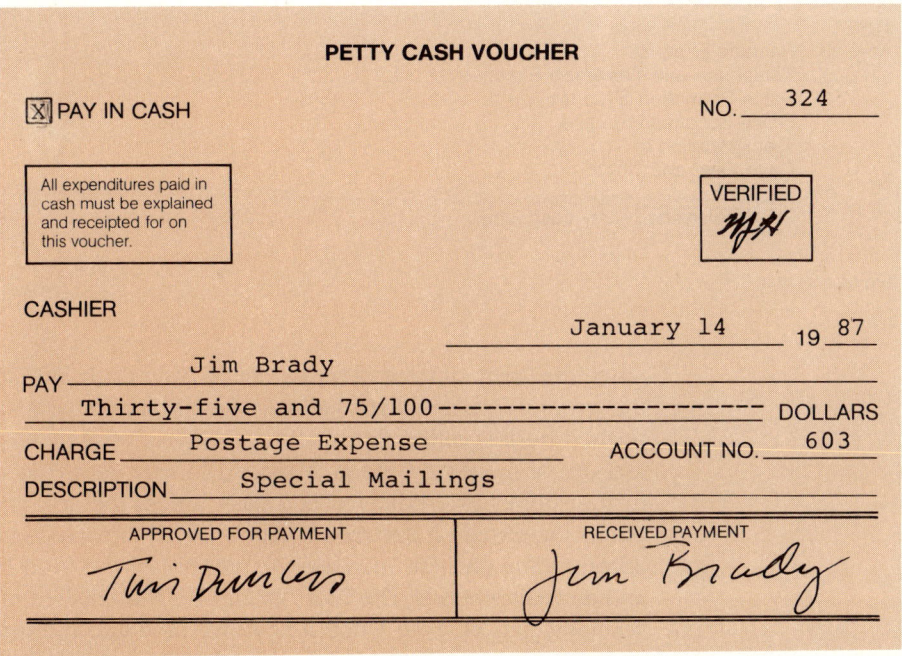

Figure 8–2 **Petty Cash Voucher**

Safekeeping of the money and the signed vouchers is the responsibility of the custodian, who should be provided with a secure petty cash box or cash register.

When the cash in the fund approaches a stated minimum, or at the end of each accounting period, the fund is replenished; the signed petty cash vouchers serve as evidence of the disbursements. Assume that on August 31, 1987, the High Company petty cash fund consisted of cash and signed receipts for expenditures as shown:

Cash	$ 47.00
Postage stamps and parcel post	112.00
Telegrams and outside telephone calls	54.00
Supplies for exhibition booth at regional sales meeting	114.50
Blank form pads	12.75
Truck delivery expenses on purchases	158.25
Total	$498.50
Shortage	1.50
Total to be accounted for	$500.00

The custodian is issued a check for $453 = ($500 − $47) to replenish the fund to its original cash balance of $500. The entry to record this check is:

1987				
Aug.	31	Postage Expense	112.00	
		Telephone and Telegraph Expense	54.00	
		Sales Promotion Expense	114.50	
		Office Supplies Expense	12.75	
		Transportation In	158.25	
		Cash Over and Short[a]	1.50	
		Cash		453.00
		Replenished petty cash fund.		

[a]See next section.

Since the entry did not debit or credit Petty Cash, the Petty Cash account in the general ledger remains at its original balance of $500. The method described here is called the **imprest petty cash system** because a fixed amount of money has been advanced in trust to a custodian. There are no further debits or credits to Petty Cash unless the amount of the fund itself is either increased or decreased. Thus, the $500 balance is imprest upon the account. The entry to increase the amount of the fund is a debit to Petty Cash and a credit to Cash. The fund should be replenished at the end of each accounting period, even when it is above its stated minimum cash balance, to record all the expenses incurred during the period and to bring the amount of currency and coins on hand in the fund up to the balance of the Petty

Cash Over and Short

In the foregoing illustration, a cash shortage of $1.50 was found when the petty cash fund was replenished. It is also true that the daily count of cash in the cash registers may differ from the cash register readings. If the records do not disclose a clerical error, it may be assumed that the overage or shortage was caused by an error in making change. The discrepancy should be entered in the books as a debit or a credit to the Cash Over and Short account. To illustrate, assume that a cash register tape shows cash sales for the day of $1,000, but the count shows the cash on hand to be $1,003.13. The journal entry to record the cash sales based on the cash register tape total, the cash based on the actual count, and the cash overage is:

1987			
Nov. 30	Cash...	1,003.13	
	Sales..		1,000.00
	Cash Over and Short..............................		3.13
	To record cash sales and cash overage.		

If the cash count showed $996.87, the Cash Over and Short account would be debited instead of credited.

Cash over and short is classified on the income statement as a general and administrative expense if a debit, or other revenue if a credit. Overages and shortages considered unreasonable should be investigated.

The Bank Statement

Most transactions ultimately involve the receipt or payment of cash, often in the form of a **check**—a written order directing a bank to pay a specified amount of money to the order of a payee. When opening an account with a bank, the person or persons who will sign checks must fill out signature card forms, an essential part of the internal control system. New cards must be completed whenever there is a change in authority to sign checks.

A carbon copy of the check is one way of communicating the payment information to the accounting department for recording. Banks customarily send depositors a monthly statement together with the cancelled checks and notices of bank charges and credits. The bank statement shows the activities for the month; it should list, at a minimum:

☐ Beginning balance.
☐ Deposits received.
☐ Checks paid.

☐ Other charges and credits to the account.
☐ Ending balance.

The September 1987 bank statement of Clearwater Company is shown in Figure 8–3. The letter codes in its upper section identify entries on the statement other than checks paid by the bank and deposits credited. Certain letter codes commonly used in this statement are explained as follows:

Cost of service (CS): (Service Charge) Unless depositors keep a specified minimum balance in the bank, a *service charge* is imposed by the bank for its costs of handling the account.

Debit memo (DM): This memo is a deduction from the depositor's account. Typical is a customer's check previously deposited but uncollectible (NSF) reported in a debit memo. It is a debit memo to the bank because the bank's liability to the depositor for the amount on deposit is reduced. From the de-

Wachovia
Wachovia Bank & Trust Company, N.A.

Account 1239-876-543
Period Ending 09-30-87
Page 1

CLEARWATER COMPANY
403 Engleman Avenue
Burlington, NC 27215

Balance From Last Statement	Deposits Received a Number	Amount	Checks Paid Number	Amount	Cost of Service	Exchange
586.50	8	765.08	14	1,418.58	5.40	

Average balance this statement	Transaction symbols:			Balance this statement
186.22	CS Cost of Service DM Debit Memo EX Exchange	IN Interest Credit L List post M Miscellaneous OD Overdraft Charge PD Payroll Deposit	RC Reverse OD Charge RF Return Check Fee SM Sav-O-Matic TX Intangibles Tax T2 Teller II	204.24

Date 1987	Checks and Other Debits		Deposits and Credits	Balance
09 02			82.20	468.70
09 03	49.00	238.60	56.72	237.82
09 04	200.16	118.37	102.54	21.83
09 05	86.50	25.75	108.72	18.30
09 06	21.20DM	18.30	112.30	91.10
09 16	67.60		497.00CM	520.50
09 18	138.20	300.00L	86.80	169.10
09 27	9.80	100.00CC	103.62	162.92
09 30	15.68	50.62	112.18	208.80
09 30	5.40CS		0.84IN	204.24

[a] As indicated earlier, effective internal control requires daily deposit of cash receipts intact. To shorten the illustration, this practice is not followed after the deposit of September 6.

Source: Courtesy Wachovia Bank and Trust Company, N.A.

Figure 8–3   **Bank Statement**

positor's point of view, it is a reduction in the bank balance and a credit—*not a debit*—to the Cash account in the ledger.

Credit Memo (CM): This memo is a credit, usually shown in the Deposits column, for items collected; for example, the collection of a note receivable left at the bank by a depositor. It is a credit memo to the bank because the bank's liability to the depositor is increased. From the depositor point of view, it is an increase in the bank balance and a debit—*not* a credit—to the Cash account in the ledger.

Certified Check (CC): When the depositor requests a certified check, the bank immediately deducts the amount of the check from the depositor's balance. This procedure assures the payee that the check will be paid upon presentation.

Interest (IN): Some banks pay interest based on daily balances in checking accounts.

List (LS or L): A list is a tape enclosed with the bank statement listing two or more amounts to support the coded entry on the bank statement.

Reconciliation Procedure

The use of a business checking account is essential to control of cash. Total receipts should be deposited intact daily and all payments should be made by check, as emphasized earlier. This means that for each entry in the depositor's books, there should be a counterpart in the bank's books. Each total daily debit to Cash in the depositor's books should be matched by a credit entry to the depositor's account in the bank's books. All credit entries to Cash in the depositor's books should be matched by debit entries at the bank to the depositor's account. For instance, daily cash received from customers is recorded in the company's books by debiting Cash and crediting Accounts Receivable or Sales; the bank, on receiving the daily deposit, increases the depositor's account. The company records a check written in payment to a creditor by debiting Accounts Payable and crediting Cash; the bank decreases the depositor's account when the check arrives at the bank. Thus, although the bank is making entries later than the firm, a separate record of cash is being kept by an outside organization.

The records of the depositor and of the bank normally will not agree at the end of the month. Items will appear on one record but not on the other because of the time lag in recording deposits and checks, special charges and credits of which the depositor is unaware, or errors or irregularities. The two balances must be reconciled and the true or **adjusted cash balance** determined. The **bank reconciliation** is a statement that shows the items that account for the difference between the Cash account balance and the bank statement balance. One of its primary purposes is to strengthen internal control over cash. It is prepared as follows:

1. Deposits shown on the bank statement are compared with daily entries in the cash receipts journal. Deposits made too late in the month to be credited

by the bank on the current statement are referred to as **deposits in transit**. The bank reconciliation for the previous month should be inspected for any deposits in transit at the end of that period; they should appear as the early deposits of the current period. Any such items not on the statement should be investigated.

2. Checks paid and returned by the bank (cancelled checks) should be arranged in numerical order and compared with the entries in the cash payments journal. Checks that have not yet been presented by the payees to the bank for payment are called **outstanding checks**. The previous bank reconciliation should be inspected to see that outstanding checks from that reconciliation have now cleared through the bank on this statement.

NAME
Bank Reconciliation
Date

Per Books			Per Bank		
Cash balance per ledger, date......		$XXX	Cash balance per bank statement, date		$XXX
Add:			Add:		
(1) Any proper increases in cash already recorded by the bank that have not been recorded as yet by the firm			(1) Any proper increases in cash already recorded by the firm that have not been recorded as yet by the bank		
Example: Collection of note by bank..........	$XX		*Example:* Deposits in transit ..	$XX	
(2) Any error in the firm's books that failed to reveal a proper increase in cash or that improperly decreased cash			(2) Any error by the bank that failed to reveal a proper increase in cash or that improperly decreased cash		
Example: Check from customer for $90 entered as $70....	XX	XX	*Example:* Another depositor's check incorrectly charged to this depositor's account .	XX	XX
Subtotal.............		$XXX	Subtotal.............		$XXX
Deduct:			Deduct:		
(1) Any proper decreases in cash already recorded by the bank that have not been recorded as yet by the firm			(1) Any proper decreases in cash already recorded by the firm that have not been recorded as yet by the bank		
Example: Bank service charges	$XX		*Example:* Outstanding checks .	$XX	
(2) Any error in the firm's books that failed to reveal a proper decrease in cash or that improperly increased cash			(2) Any error by the bank that failed to reveal a proper decrease in cash or that improperly increased cash		
Example: Check issued in payment to a creditor for $462 entered as $426..........	XX	XX	*Example:* Firm's deposit of $679 entered by bank as $697.....	XX	XX
Adjusted cash balance, date		$XXX	Adjusted cash balance, date		$XXX

Figure 8–4   **Format for a Bank Reconciliation**

3. Special debits and credits made by the bank—usually reported in debit or credit memos—are compared with the depositor's books to see if they have already been recorded.

4. Any errors in the bank's or the depositor's records that become apparent during completion of the prior steps are listed. The chance of bank errors is small unless there is an error in coding a document.

A format for bank reconciliation is given in Figure 8–4. Errors and adjustments in the *Per Books* section require entries in the general journal or special cash journals to correct the books. Adjustments in the *Per Bank* section do not require entries in the depositor's books, but action may be necessary to see that they are recorded in the bank's books.

Preparation of a bank reconciliation is illustrated here using the Clearwater Company's bank statement for September, shown in Figure 8–3. In the Clearwater Company's August 1987 bank reconciliation, a deposit of $82.20 made on August 30 was listed as a *deposit in transit*. Outstanding checks on August 31 were:

Check No.	Amount	Check No.	Amount
637	$ 49.00	641	$ 86.50
638	238.60	642	25.75
639	15.00	643	5.00
640	201.06	644	118.37

The Cash account of Clearwater Company showed activity in September as follows:

	Deposits[a]		Checks	
Date		Amount	Check No.	Amount
Sep. 2		$ 56.72	645	$ 18.30
3		102.54	646	110.00
4		108.72	647	10.00
5		112.30	648	180.00
17		86.80	649	138.20
26		103.62	650	67.60
27		112.18	651	100.00
30		421.50	652	30.20
			653	9.80
			654	21.50
			655	15.68
			656	50.62
			657	9.85
			658	3.72
			659	13.80
			660	12.95

[a] As indicated earlier, effective internal control requires daily deposit of cash receipts intact. To shorten the illustration, this practice is not followed after the deposit of September 5 (recorded September 6 on the bank statement).

The balance in the Cash account on September 30, 1987, is $41.58. The balance for September 30 shown on the bank statement (Figure 8–3) is $204.24. The following are noted by Clearwater's accountant in studying the bank statement:

1. The debit memorandum dated September 6 for $21.20 represented a customer's check included in an earlier deposit and returned marked **"NSF" (not sufficient funds)**. This check has not yet been charged back to the customer's account on Clearwater's books.

2. The credit memorandum for $497.00 dated September 16 represented a $500.00 credit and a $3.00 collection fee for a note receivable collected by the bank for Clearwater. There was no interest on the face value of this note.

3. The $300.00 debit marked L (List) on September 18 was a list that recorded the charging of check nos. 646, 647, and 648. This information is needed to determine the checks that are outstanding.

4. The $100.00 debit marked CC (Certified Check) on September 27 was for check no. 651 certified for Clearwater Company on that date. It was among the checks returned as paid by the bank; even if it were not, it would *not* be included as an outstanding check on September 30 because it was deducted from Clearwater's balance on the date of certification—not on the date it was paid by the bank.

Noting these facts, Clearwater's accountant then verifies that the deposit in transit on August 31 is credited on the September bank statement. The next task is to trace the August 31 outstanding checks and checks written in September to the bank statement. All that are not debited thereon are listed as outstanding checks. Then a bank reconciliation, as shown in Figure 8–5, is prepared.

CLEARWATER COMPANY
Bank Reconciliation
September 30, 1987

Cash balance per ledger, September 30.			$ 41.58	Cash balance per bank statement, September 30		$204.24
Add: Customer note collected by bank . . . . [1]	$500.00			Add: Deposit in transit . . . . . . [6]		421.50
Less: Collection charge . .	3.00	$497.00		Subtotal		$625.74
Interest earned on account . . . . [2]		0.84		Deduct: Outstanding checks:[a] [7]		
Error in check no. 640 . . . [3]		0.90	498.74	No. 639	$15.00	
Subtotal			$540.32	643	5.00	
Deduct: Customer's NSF check . . . . [4]		$ 21.20		652	30.20	
Bank service charge . . . [5]		5.40	26.60	654	21.50	
				657	9.85	
				658	3.72	
				659	13.80	
				660	12.95	112.02
Adjusted cash balance, September 30			$513.72	Adjusted cash balance, September 30		$513.72

[a] A lengthy list of outstanding checks is usually shown in a separate schedule, with only the total shown here.

Figure 8–5   **Bank Reconciliation**

The following comments are made about the numbered items on the reconciliation in Figure 8–5:

1. Clearwater Company had a note receivable from a customer made out for its maturity value due on September 16. Since the customer had an account at the same bank, the note was delivered to the bank with a request that it be collected. The bank, after securing permission from the customer, debited his account on September 16 for $500.00 and credited Clearwater's. There was a $3.00 service charge for this service. Neither the $500.00 credit nor the $3.00 charge has been recorded in Clearwater's books, so the note proceeds is added to the balance per books and the service charge is deducted in the reconciliation.

2. The interest earned on this checking account has been credited by the bank but is not on the company's records. It is added to the balance per books.

3. When the checks were traced to the bank statement, it was discovered that check no. 640 in payment for equipment repairs had been recorded in error as $201.06. The correct amount, as shown on the bank statement and the cancelled check, is $200.16. Since the credit to the Cash account was $0.90 greater than it should have been, this amount is added to the balance per books.

4. As indicated earlier, a customer's check for $21.20 had been returned marked "NSF." Since it was rejected for deposit by the bank, it must be deducted from the balance per books.

5. The monthly bank service charge has not been entered in the company's books and must be deducted from the balance per books.

6. The deposit of September 30 in amount of $421.50 was received at the bank too late to be included in this bank statement. It is added to the balance per bank statement and should appear as the first deposit on the October statement.

7. A comparison of the checks previously outstanding and those paid in September with the debits on the statement shows that two checks listed on the bank reconciliation had not yet reached the bank. Check nos. 639 and 643 were outstanding on August 31 and still did not clear through the bank in September. It is not unusual (although not a sound financial practice) for some recipients of checks to be negligent in depositing them. If these two checks continue to be outstanding, there is a possibility that they have been lost; correspondence to verify their receipt may be in order.

Recording the Adjustments

The adjustments made to the cash balance per ledger (often called the *Per Books* section) in the bank reconciliation require journal entries to update Clearwater Company's accounts so that the Cash account balance will be in agreement with the adjusted balance in the reconciliation. Other ledger account balances are also affected; the entries could be made in the cash receipts journal and cash payments journal because they are in effect receipts and payments of cash. If those journals have been balanced and posted as of September 30, the adjustments can be recorded in the general journal. All adjustments can be made in one compound entry or in separate entries as follows:

1987			
Sep. 30	Cash	497.00	
	Collection Fees Expense	3.00	
	Notes Receivable		500.00
	Collection of customer note made out for face value.		
30	Cash	0.84	
	Interest Earned		0.84
	Credit of interest on checking account from September bank statement.		
30	Cash	0.90	
	Repairs Expense		0.90
	Error in check no. 604 written for $200.16 but recorded at $201.06.		
30	Accounts Receivable	21.20	
	Cash		21.20
	Customer's NSF check deducted on September bank statement:		
	Ann Lanier $21.20		
30	Bank Service Charge Expense	5.40	
	Cash		5.40
	Cost of checking account service in September.		

After the entries are posted, the Cash account will have a new balance of $513.72 and will be up to date with unrecorded bank transactions as of the date of the bank statement. The other affected accounts are also updated.

Only the items from the reconciliation that either increase or decrease the balance per books need to be entered in the journal. The items that increase or decrease the balance per bank already have been recorded on the depositor's books and therefore require *no adjusting entry*. Any errors made by the bank should be brought to the bank's attention. If a running cash balance is maintained in the checkbook, the necessary adjustments must be made there also. Other forms of bank reconciliation, which reconcile from a bank statement balance to a balance per checkbook, are often found in blank on the reverse side of the monthly bank statement. However, the form used in Figures 8–4 and 8–5 strengthens internal control over cash by highlighting all differences between the accounts and the bank's records. It also shows that the balances for both the bank and the Cash account are reconciled to the adjusted cash figure at the end of each month.

To this point, the emphasis in this chapter has been on internal control in cash management practices. A second important emphasis is cash *expenditure control*. An essential ingredient in a system that strengthens control over cash expenditures is the voucher system, discussed in the following sections.

The Voucher System

The accounting system must be designed not only to record transactions and prepare financial statements but also to achieve other managerial objectives. An important objective of management is to strengthen internal control to protect the assets of the business against loss through errors or fraud. The achievement of this objective goes hand in hand with the achievement of maximum operating efficiency and maximum earnings. A properly functioning voucher system plays a key role in establishing and maintaining effective internal control.

The **voucher system** is a method of verifying the accuracy of creditor claims and authorizing payment. The system covers any transaction that will require the payment of cash (except for payments out of petty cash). These include the payment of expenses or the purchase of merchandise, services, supplies, and plant items. Expenditures are verified, classified, and recorded; when authorized, they are paid by check. The duties of reporting the receipt of goods or services, authorizing expenditures, and signing checks are distributed. This helps prevent cash from being disbursed from the business without proper approval by permitting disbursement only after verifications have been made by several members of the organization.

The voucher system is strengthened when a firm uses a set of carefully designed business documents; a typical procedure for purchase and payment is illustrated in Figure A6–1. Each document in that diagram serves a specific useful purpose. Control of payments is centralized in the voucher, discussed next.

The Voucher

The **voucher** is a serially numbered form giving written authorization for recognizing an obligation and later authorizing the payment. It is prepared from the seller's invoice or group of invoices and from other documents that serve as evidence of the liability. It is sometimes called a *check request* or a *request for check*.

The voucher, not the invoice, is the basis for the accounting entry. A typical voucher is shown in Figure 8–6. The invoice, the purchase order, and other supporting documents are the evidence for the voucher. The voucher form, tailored to meet the needs of a particular business, should provide space for such things as:

☐ Summary of the invoice data.

☐ Account number(s) and amounts to be debited.

☐ Details of payment.

☐ Initials of persons who have checked accuracy of quantities, unit prices, extensions, and discount terms.

☐ Signature of the person who authorizes the payment.

☐ Signature of the person who records the voucher.

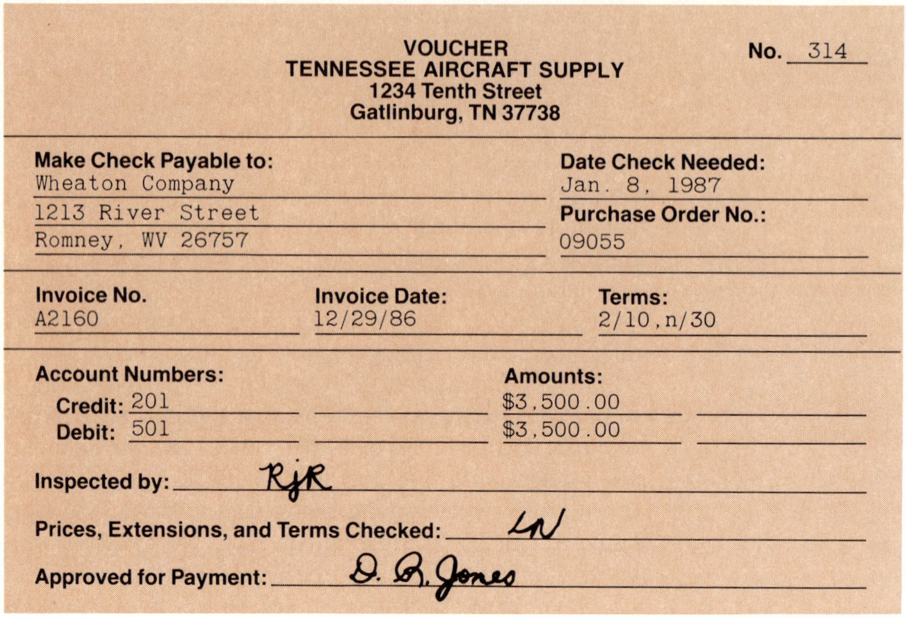

```
                    VOUCHER                           No. 314
              TENNESSEE AIRCRAFT SUPPLY
                   1234 Tenth Street
                   Gatlinburg, TN 37738
```

Make Check Payable to:
Wheaton Company
1213 River Street
Romney, WV 26757

Date Check Needed:
Jan. 8, 1987

Purchase Order No.:
09055

Invoice No. A2160
Invoice Date: 12/29/86
Terms: 2/10, n/30

Account Numbers:
Credit: 201
Debit: 501

Amounts:
$3,500.00
$3,500.00

Inspected by: RjR
Prices, Extensions, and Terms Checked: LN
Approved for Payment: D. R. Jones

Figure 8–6 Voucher

In Figure 8–6 voucher 314 has been prepared to authorize payment to Wheaton Company for a shipment of merchandise. The voucher shows that the Purchases account (501) will be debited for $3,500. Vouchers Payable (201) will be credited.[1] Payment has been authorized by the manager, D. R. Jones, whose signature appears in the approval block. Initials of persons who verified count, price, and so on are also on the voucher.

The invoice for this merchandise carries cash discount terms of 2/10, n/30. In this example, it will be recorded using the gross price procedure. However, the net price procedure can be used with a voucher system.

Voucher Register and Check Register

In addition to the internal control strengths provided by the voucher system, some firms find that creating special journals to be used with the vouchers increases efficiency. Such journals are called a *voucher register* and a *check register*. Their use is explained in Appendix 8.2.

---

[1] For details of recording vouchers and their payment see Appendix 8.2.

Advantages and Limitations of Vouchers

In a properly functioning voucher system, all invoices must be verified and approved for payment. As a result, responsibility is fixed and the possibility of error or fraud is reduced. The maintenance of a chronological unpaid voucher file organized by due date facilitates the payment of invoices without loss of discounts and also enables management to determine its future cash needs for the settlement of liabilities. The vendor's file of paid vouchers provides a ready reference source for data and underlying documents for audit of disbursements. On the other hand, the voucher system has certain limitations. The need for the preparation of separate vouchers involves extra clerical and accounting work. The internal control advantages, however, outweigh the disadvantages in most cases.

Appendix 8.1
Payroll Systems

Introduction

In a recent *Annual Report,* Ingersoll-Rand Company reported that 33.1 percent of its total sales revenue was used to pay employees. This is typical of today's large enterprises; costs of having the services of a group of employees are second only to payments to suppliers. Payroll taxes are a major source of revenue to both the federal and state governments. Accordingly, it is important for the accountant to understand the many aspects of payroll computation and to record payroll information accurately. This appendix describes the accounting for payrolls. It covers computation of gross pay, payroll deductions, and net pay (take-home pay). The recording of income taxes, Social Security taxes, and other deductions withheld from employees' gross pay is explained. Also discussed are the calculation and recording of employers' Social Security tax and unemployment compensation taxes.

Learning Goals

1. To be able to identify and calculate the various payroll deductions and payroll taxes that apply to business.
2. To compute net pay due.
3. To record a periodic payroll and the employer's payroll taxes.
4. To understand accrual of vacation pay liability.
5. To describe effective control of payroll.

Gross Pay

The total earnings of an employee before any deductions are applied is known as **gross pay**. It is computed in several ways. For some employees, periodic gross pay is a fractional amount of an annual salary. For example, a person with an annual salary of $36,000 would have a gross pay of $3,000 per monthly pay period. Another popular method of determining an employee's gross pay is to use an hourly wage rate—sometimes coupled with an incentive bonus for good production—for weekly or semimonthly pay periods. If Cynthia Winters worked at the rate of $12 per hour for a 40-hour week, her gross pay would be $480 = ($12 × 40). However, if she were to work 45 hours, she would receive *time and one half* for her overtime hours and her gross pay would then be calculated as follows:[2]

Regular pay for 40 hours ($12 × 40)	$480
Regular pay for overtime hours ($12 × 5)	60
Premium pay for overtime hours ($12 × 1/2 × 5)	30
Gross pay earned	$570

Payroll Deductions

The periodic total wage or salary earned by an employee is not the amount the employee will take home. From the total or gross pay, a number of **payroll deductions** may be withheld for many purposes. The amount remaining after deductions is **net pay**.

The deductions may be grouped into two broad classes:

1. Payroll taxes
   a. Social Security program taxes referred to as the *Federal Insurance Contributions Act* (FICA) taxes
   b. Federal income tax withholdings
   c. State and local income tax withholdings
2. Voluntary deductions[3]
   a. Pension and retirement plans
   b. Group health and life insurance
   c. Charitable contributions
   d. Union dues
   e. Other miscellaneous deductions

Employer Payroll Taxes

Certain payroll taxes are levied on the *employer* in addition to those deducted from employees' wages. They are discussed in the following sections.

---

[2] It is desirable to compute any overtime premium separately from regular and overtime pay because the premium is often debited to a different account.
[3] The number of voluntary deductions has increased in recent years as employees have taken advantage of plans such as Individual Retirement Arrangements (IRAs) to defer payment of income tax to later years.

8 / Control of Cash

Federal Insurance Contributions Act (FICA) The **Federal Insurance Contributions Act (FICA)** tax is levied in equal amounts on employees and employers. Thus, an employer must pay a matching sum for all FICA deductions from employee pay.

Federal Unemployment Tax Act (FUTA) The **Federal Unemployment Tax Act (FUTA)** establishes a program administered locally by the states for payments to persons who become unemployed. Under it, a tax is levied on employers only. There is no withholding for this purpose. The current tax rate is applied to taxable wages until the wages reach the current **taxable wage base**. There is no further tax liability on the employer for wages paid beyond the maximum taxable base during the remainder of that calendar year.

State Unemployment Compensation Tax All the states have laws requiring the payment of unemployment compensation taxes. The state unemployment compensation systems are tied in to the federal unemployment system, which pays part of the administration costs of the state systems. Funds are provided by a payroll tax levy on the employer and, in three states (Alabama, Alaska, and New Jersey), on both employer and employees. Unemployed persons who qualify for benefits are paid by a state agency from funds acquired through the tax.

State unemployment tax laws vary in their detail and application. There are maximum rates which may be reduced on a merit basis if the employer's annual contributions are sufficiently in excess of withdrawals for unemployment payments made to discharged employees. The merit-rating plan provides an incentive to employers to maintain steady employment. Employers who maintain a stable work force and whose employees experience relatively little unemployment will pay a lower rate than employers with a less favorable unemployment experience and unemployment expenditures. Both the amount of unemployment benefits and the number of weeks payable to an unemployed worker depend on wages earned and amount of time worked during a base period.

Wage Bases and Tax Rates

The FICA and the FUTA wage bases and tax rates may be changed by Congress at any time. They have been increased steadily over the years. *To simplify the computations in all illustrations and problems in this textbook (except for illustrations of some actual forms), the following assumed wage bases and tax rates are used* (the accounting principles and recording procedures are the same regardless of the bases and the rates used):

1. For FICA computations—an assumed tax rate of 14 percent; 7 percent each on employer and on employee, limited to a taxable wage base of $40,000 during a calendar year.

2. For FUTA computations—an assumed tax rate only on employers of 5 percent, limited to a taxable wage base of $10,000 with a maximum of 4 percent payable to the state and 1 percent payable to the federal government.

Recording the Payroll

Accurate payroll records are necessary to determine operating expenses and to report earnings information to employees and to federal, state, and other agencies. A *payroll register* must show the names, earnings, and payroll deductions of all employees for each pay period. A *yearly individual compensation record* for each employee showing his or her earnings and deductions must also be kept. In most large businesses these records are maintained by computer; some smaller organizations keep manual records.

To illustrate the accounting entries required for a payroll, assume the following data for the Orbit Company (which has five employees) for the week ended May 31, 1987:

Gross pay of salespersons	$1,529.50	
Gross pay of executives	750.00	
Gross pay of office personnel	645.00	
Total gross pay		$2,924.50
Deductions:		
Employee FICA taxes	$ 204.72	
Federal income tax	630.40	
State income tax	49.74	
Group health insurance premiums	150.00	
Total deductions		1,034.86
Net pay		$1,889.64

The entry to record the payroll is as follows:[4]

1987				
May	31	Sales Salaries Expense	1,529.50	
		Executive Salaries Expense	750.00	
		Office Salaries Expense	645.00	
		FICA Taxes Payable		204.72
		Federal Income Tax Withholding Payable		630.40
		State Income Tax Withholding Payable		49.74
		Group Health Insurance Premiums Payable		150.00
		Salaries and Wages Payable		1,889.64
		Payroll for the week ended May 31, 1987, with assumed FICA rate of 7.0 percent.		

The entry to record the payment of the payroll (or any other of the liabilities) is simply a debit to the liability and a credit to Cash.

---

[4]Since a full 7 percent of gross pay has been deducted for FICA, the reader should note that none of the employees has yet earned the $40,000 base amount in 1987.

Recording the Employer's Payroll Tax Expense

The employer's payroll tax expense may be recorded at the end of each payroll period or at the end of each month. Assume that the Orbit Company records the payroll tax expense for each payroll and that, because of its merit-rating record, it is subject to a state unemployment tax rate of only 2 percent (reduced for merit from assumed 4 percent maximum). If no employee has reached the taxable wage base of $10,000, Orbit's payroll tax entry to match the May 31 payroll is:

1987 May	31	Payroll Tax Expense	292.47	
		FICA Taxes Payable		204.72
		State Unemployment Taxes Payable		58.50
		Federal Unemployment Taxes Payable		29.25
		To record payroll taxes for week ended May 31, computed as follows: FICA tax ($2,924.50 × 0.07); State unemployment compensation tax ($2,924.50 × 0.02); and Federal unemployment compensation tax ($2,924.50 × 0.01).		

Accrual of Salaries and Wages

If the end of the payroll period does not coincide with the end of the accounting period, an adjusting entry is made for salaries and wages earned but not paid. The several salary and expense accounts are debited and Accrued Salaries and Wages Payable is credited. The employer's payroll tax expense on the accrued payroll for the partial pay period should be recognized, although there is no legal liability for the tax until the wages are actually paid. The reason for this recognition is that under the accrual basis all expense items applicable to the salaries and wages of the period should be measured and recorded. An employer is liable for payroll taxes in the calendar year in which the payment for services was made. The time of payment rather than the time the services were performed establishes the legal existence of the liability. The expense associated with the accrued liability, however, is the amount that should be matched with the revenues of a period for proper determination of income. For better matching of expenses with revenues, the FASB specifies another accrual of payroll expense—pay for compensated absences.

Liabilities for Compensated Absences

The FASB has concluded that an employee's right to receive compensation for future absences should be accrued during the time the employee renders services leading to that benefit.[5] The board has indicated that such accruals should be made only if the future right to receive pay is attributable to services already rendered, the payment of such compensation is probable, and

---

[5]*Statement of Financial Accounting Standards No. 43*, "Accounting for Compensated Absences" (Stamford, Conn.: November 1980), paragraph 1.

the amount can be reasonably estimated.[6] While such conditions may not always be present for sick leave, they usually do exist in the case of vacation pay. Such absences for which employees are paid are called **compensated absences**. To illustrate, assume that the LeBlanc Company has 50 employees who are paid an average of $500 per week and has a policy of allowing each employee a two-week paid vacation per year. The total cost of the paid vacations (a form of compensated absence) is $50,000 = (50 employees × $500 × 2 weeks). Since this cost is actually earned as employees work, it should be accrued during their 50 working weeks; it will be paid during the time they are on vacation. Further, assume that one-half the employees are in the sales force; the remainder are employed in various administrative departments. The entry to accrue the liability for the week ended February 8, 1987, is as follows:

1987				
Feb.	8	Vacation Pay Expense—Selling........................	500	
		Vacation Pay Expense—General and Administrative...........	500	
		Liability for Vacation Pay............................		1,000
		Accrual of liability for 1/50 of annual vacation pay.		

If 15 employees take a week of vacation during the week ended July 12, the entry to record payment of their compensated absence is:[7]

1987				
Jul.	12	Liability for Vacation Pay............................	7,500	
		FICA Taxes Payable...............................		525
		Federal Income Tax Withholdings Payable...............		1,278
		State Income Tax Withholdings Payable................		175
		Cash..		5,522
		Payment to 15 employees for one week's vacation.		

The liability account balance should be shown as a current liability on the balance sheet. Conceivably, if a large number of employees take paid vacations early in the year—for example, during slack periods of business—the liability account could have a debit balance due to payments made faster than the liability is accrued. Such a debit balance should be shown as a current asset with a caption such as "prepaid vacation pay." A debit balance would be a temporary situation as the account should clear to a zero balance at year end if all employees have taken their two-week vacations.

Similar accruals should be made for sick pay and other forms of compensated absences if the conditions of *FASB Statement No. 43* are met. A primary

---

[6]Ibid., paragraph 6.

[7]No employee has reached the $40,000 FICA base; income tax amounts are assumed. Employer payroll taxes are also applicable but are not illustrated in this example.

purpose of such accruals is to adhere more closely to the matching standard. Expenses to be matched with revenues are recorded in the period in which the act that causes the expense occurs—in this case, use of employee services. A similar situation exists with company costs of pension plans and other post-retirement benefits. These are complex issues and are left for a later course in accounting.

Managerial Control of Payroll

The payroll of a firm is a significant part of total expense, making continuous management control essential. The availability of machines and high-speed electronic equipment has facilitated the processing of payroll data and the establishment of effective controls at a reasonable cost. But the use of an electronic data processing system for the payroll does not lessen the need for built-in self-policing control devices and procedures as part of the payroll system. Computer programs and data processing systems can be manipulated to defraud the firm.

Effective managerial control of payroll requires that:

- ☐ Management has properly authorized the payroll payment.
- ☐ Wages paid be correct and have been received by authorized employees; that is, for example, that no fictitious names or names of persons no longer employed have been listed on the payroll.
- ☐ The numerous reports based on payroll information that are made to governmental agencies, union organizations, and employees be reliable.
- ☐ Adequate security systems are in effect to prevent unauthorized access to computer programs for the payroll.

Appendix 8.2
The Voucher System Illustrated

Introduction

Some companies find that greater efficiency results from the use of a voucher system with special journals in which to record liabilities approved for payment and their subsequent payment. Such journals are called a voucher register and a check register. Their use is explained and illustrated in this appendix.

Learning Goals

1. To record transactions in the voucher register and check register.
2. To know when to post individual transaction entries or column totals from the voucher register to the ledger accounts.

				VOUCHER		
					Paid	Credit
Date		Voucher Number	Name	Date	Check No.	Vouchers Payable
1987						
Jan.	3	314	Wheaton Company	1/8	709	3,500
	3	315	Dover Furniture Company	1/5	708	800
	6	316	L. Kett			90
	10	317	Palmer Company	1/24	731	1,212
	10	318[a]	Payroll	1/10	711	1,575
	10	319	Petty Cash	1/10	712	80
	10	320	Helene Ellis Company	Canc.	333–334	4,000
	31	333	Helene Ellis Company			2,000
	31	334	Helene Ellis Company			2,000
	31	335	Internal Revenue Service	1/31	732	850
	31	336	State Division of Employment Security	1/31	733	297
	31	337	Internal Revenue Service	1/31	734	315
			Totals			22,324
						(201)

[a]Note that each new voucher is entered on the next totally vacant line.

Figure A8–1   **Voucher Register**

The Voucher Register

The **voucher register**, a special journal for recording all liabilities approved for payment, is ruled in Debit and Credit columns for frequently used accounts. It must be tailored to meet the needs of a particular enterprise. The register provides columns for each general class of expenditure and Other General Ledger Accounts column with space for the number of the specific account to be debited. It combines almost unlimited flexibility with economy of space. The voucher register for Tennessee Aircraft Supply is shown in Figure A8–1. The voucher register is used for recording all authorized payments except from the petty cash fund. Each transaction is entered in the voucher

REGISTER					Page 8
Debit			**Other General Ledger Accounts**		
Purchases	Miscellaneous Selling Expense	Miscellaneous General Expense	Other Accounts Debit	F	Amount Debit
3,500					
			Office Equipment	163	800
		90			
			Notes Payable	203	1,200
			Interest Expense	851	12
			Salaries and Wages Payable	211	1,575
30	25	25			
4,000					
			Vouchers Payable	201	4,000
			FICA Taxes Payable	212	280
			Income Tax Withholding Payable	215	570
			State Unemployment Taxes Payable	213	297
			Federal Unemployment Taxes Payable	214	315
9,780	475	243			11,826
(351)	(600)	(700)			(X)

Figure A8–1 (*continued*)

register first, followed by an entry in the check register *when payment is made.*

Vouchers are entered in the voucher register in numerical order. An entry is made in the Credit Vouchers Payable column for the amount due on each voucher.[8] The account or accounts to be debited are indicated on the voucher, and entries are made in one of the special debit columns. If no special column applies, the Other General Ledger Accounts column provides

---

[8]The Vouchers Payable account is a recognition that a liability is ready for payment. The liability may have existed—for example, as a note payable—before it is approved for payment with a voucher.

space for the name of the account to be debited, a ledger folio (F) column, and an Amount Debit column. Entries in this column may be posted to the ledger daily; *all the other columns are posted in total only at the end of the month* to the general ledger account indicated in the column heading. Ledger folio references are shown beneath the double ruling for the items. The posting procedure is the same as for other special journals. Some of the entries in Figure A8–1 are explained in a later section.

Transactions involving liabilities that are not initially credited to Vouchers Payable—notes payable and accrued expenses, for example—are usually not entered in the voucher register until liability for payment is recognized. Vouchers are not prepared for accrued expenses because the amounts as accrued do not represent the amounts for which a check will be written. When payment is authorized and vouchers are prepared, any accrued liabilities are debited and the Vouchers Payable credit is entered (see vouchers 335, 336, and 337 in Figure A8–1).

The function of the Vouchers Payable account is the same as that of the Accounts Payable account. It is a controlling account—its balance represents the total of the unpaid vouchers recorded in the voucher register. Unpaid vouchers may, therefore, be readily determined to be those without entries on the corresponding line of the Paid column or those in the unpaid voucher file. At the end of the period, a list of the unpaid vouchers in the file should be prepared for reconciliation with the balance of the Vouchers Payable account in the general ledger.

The Check Register

All check payments must be recorded in the book of original entry called the **check register**. No payment is made until a specific voucher has been prepared, recorded, and approved. Hence, each entry is a debit to Vouchers Payable, a credit to Cash, and a credit to Purchases Discounts, if any. No other debit and credit columns are needed because the transaction already has been classified under an appropriate heading in the voucher register. Checks are entered in the check register in numerical sequence, one line to each check. At the time the check is entered, a notation must also be made in the Paid column of the voucher register showing the date of payment and the check number.

The check register will include a Purchases Discounts column only if the vouchers are recorded in the voucher register at gross invoice amounts. Also, this register shows the serial number of the check and the number of the voucher being paid.

Companies that use the net price method (discussed in Chapter 6) prepare each voucher for the net amount due. This means that if payment is not made within the discount period, an additional voucher will be required, underscoring the expense for lost discounts. The entry in the voucher register for the additional voucher is a debit to Purchases Discounts Lost and a credit to Vouchers Payable. One check is made out for the full amount due, as shown by the two vouchers. The check register for Tennessee Aircraft Supply is illustrated in Figure A8–2 and discussed below.

Control of Unpaid Vouchers

A schedule of unpaid vouchers—the ones that have not been marked either "Paid" or "Cancelled" in the Paid Column—is prepared at the end of the month. Its total should correspond to the balance of the Vouchers Payable account in the general ledger. Thus the unpaid vouchers file is a subsidiary record supporting the Vouchers Payable account. It is often maintained by payment due date to gain better control of discounts.

Recording and Paying Vouchers

The first entry in the voucher register is for approved voucher 314, payable to the Wheaton Company for $3,500 worth of merchandise received, terms 2/10, n/30. On January 8, check 709 is issued to the Wheaton Company for $3,430. An entry is made in the check register, dated that day, debiting Vouchers Payable for $3,500 and crediting Purchases Discounts and Cash for $70 and $3,430, respectively. The number 314 entered in the Voucher Number column cross-references the check with the paid voucher. After this entry is made, the date of the entry and the check number are entered in the Paid column of the voucher register on the line for voucher 314. The voucher with its supporting documents is removed from the unpaid voucher file and filed in the vendor's file, a file of paid copies of all vouchers arranged in chronological order.

When a note payable becomes due, a voucher is prepared for the maturity value of the note and entered in the voucher register. In Figure A8–1, voucher 317 was issued to authorize payment of a 30-day, 12 percent note to Palmer Company. Two lines are required for the amounts debited in the Other Accounts column: Notes Payable ($1,200) and Interest Expense ($12). The payment of the voucher then is recorded in the check register in the usual manner.

Under the voucher system, the payroll for the period is recorded as usual in the payroll records. The liability is entered in the general journal by debiting the payroll expense accounts and crediting Salaries and Wages Payable and the accounts for the deductions. A voucher is prepared for the amount of the net payroll, and a check is issued to transfer cash to the payroll account. In Figure A8–1 the payroll of January 10 is covered by voucher 318; check 711 was issued.

At the end of the month, payment of the tax liabilities is recorded in the voucher register. Voucher 335 and check 732 are made payable to the Internal Revenue Service.

CHECK REGISTER   Page 6

Date		Voucher No.	Name	Check No.	Vouchers Payable Dr.	Purchases Discounts Cr.	Cash Cr.
1987 Jan.	5	315	Dover Furniture Company	708	800		800
	8	314	Wheaton Company	709	3,500	70	3,430
	9	302	Johnson and Son	710	305		305
	10	318	Payroll	711	1,575		1,575
	10	319	Petty Cash	712	80		80
	24	317	Palmer Company	731	1,212		1,212
	31	335	Internal Revenue Service	732	850		850
	31	336	State Div. of Employ. Sec.	733	297		297
	31	337	Internal Revenue Service	734	315		315
			Totals		13,154	113	13,041
					(201)	(365)	(101)

Figure A8–2 **Check Register**

January 31 is also the last day for filing the state unemployment tax form for the last quarter (October through December). Voucher 336 and check 733 were made payable to the State Division of Employment Security.

Assuming that the total payroll subject to the federal unemployment compensation tax was $31,500 in 1986, voucher 337 records the yearly liability for $315 = ($31,500 × 0.01).

Cancelling and Replacing Vouchers

Certain transactions do not fall into the routine pattern of the voucher system. For effective internal control, the voucher system requires that the amount of the voucher be exactly the same as the amount of the check to be issued when payment is due, except for purchases subject to discount. Provision must be made, however, for cancelling and replacing vouchers. In Figure A8–1, voucher 320 was prepared on January 10 with the assumption that it will be paid in full when due, but it is later paid in two installments. The original voucher is cancelled and a new voucher is issued for *each installment* (vouchers 333 and 334). The entry in the voucher register contains a debit to Vouchers Payable in the Other General Ledger Accounts Debit column for the amount of the original voucher. The credits to Vouchers Payable are entered on two lines and numbered consecutively. A notation is made in the Paid column opposite the entry for the original voucher indicating its cancellation and referring to the new voucher numbers.

Posting from the Voucher Register and the Check Register

All voucher register money columns are totaled at the end of the month. The totals of the debit columns and of the credit columns should be equal. The totals of all the special columns are posted to the proper accounts in the general ledger; the amounts in the Other General Ledger Accounts Debit column have been posted individually. A posting symbol reference is entered in the ledger account folio (F) columns to cross-reference postings from the voucher register—VR8, for example, represents page 8 from the voucher register.

The check register columns are totaled at the end of the month. The total of the Vouchers Payable Debit column should equal the totals of the two credit columns, Purchases Discounts and Cash. Postings are made at the end of the month to the three general ledger accounts. The symbol CkR and the page number is used in the ledgers to cross-reference postings from the check register.

Elimination of the Accounts Payable Subsidiary Ledger

When the voucher system is used, the accounts payable subsidiary ledger can be eliminated. Each numbered voucher is entered on a separate line in the voucher register and may be considered as a credit to a creditor's account. When the liability is settled and a notation is made in the Paid column, it is equivalent to a debit to that same creditor's account. The file of unpaid vouchers replaces the accounts payable subsidiary ledger. When all posting is up to date, the total of the unpaid vouchers in the file must agree with the total of the Vouchers Payable controlling account.

Glossary

Adjusted cash balance The true cash balance resulting from reconciling the difference between the balance reported by the bank and the amount shown on the depositor's books.

Bank reconciliation A statement which shows the specific items that account for the differences between the balance reported by the bank and the amount shown on the depositor's books.

Cash forecast A plan projecting cash needs for a future period.

Certified check (CC) A depositor's check, payment of which is guaranteed by a bank by endorsement on the face of the check, the bank having previously deducted the amount of the check from the depositor's balance.

Check An order written by a depositor directing a bank to pay a specified amount of money to the order of the payee.

Check register A book of original entry for all cash disbursements except petty cash.

Compensated absences Absences such as vacations or sick leave for which employees are paid.

Cost of service (CS) A monthly service charge which may be imposed by the bank to cover its costs of handling an account.

Credit memo (CM) A form explaining an addition to the bank balance not caused by a deposit.

Debit memo (DM) A form explaining a deduction from the depositor's account.

Deposits in transit Deposits made too late in the month to be credited by the bank on the current statement.

Federal Insurance Contributions Act (FICA) A federal law requiring both employers and employees to contribute equal amounts based on a stated percentage of taxable wages paid; it provides funds to the Social Security program.

Federal Unemployment Tax Act (FUTA) A federal law that levies a tax on the employer at a specified rate up to a limited amount of wages paid; it provides for payment to persons who became unemployed.

FICA tax See *Federal Insurance Contributions Act (FICA)*.

Financing transactions Transactions to secure the necessary financial resources and pay any resultant debts.

FUTA tax See *Federal Unemployment Tax Act (FUTA)*.

Gross pay Total wages before any deductions; this amount is the salaries and wages expense.

Imprest petty cash fund A petty cash fund system in which the balance of the petty cash account remains unchanged because a specified amount is advanced to a custodian in trust.

List (L) A code on the bank statement to indicate that a tape is enclosed with the bank statement listing two or more amounts.

Net pay Wages after all deductions; this is referred to as take-home pay.

NSF (not sufficient funds) A customer's check that has been deposited but does not clear on presentation for payment is marked "NSF" because of "not sufficient funds"—the customer's bank balance is less than the amount of the check.

Operating transactions Transactions involving the earning of income and distributions to the stockholders.

Outstanding checks Checks sent to payees but not yet presented to the depositor's bank for payment.

Payroll deductions Amounts withheld from gross pay by the employer; these include federal and state taxes, union dues, and medical insurance.

Petty cash fund A separate cash fund when payment by check is impractical for relatively minor items.

Petty cash voucher A signed receipt that shows the purpose of a petty cash expenditure, the date, and the amount.

Service charge See *Cost of service (CS)*.

Taxable wage base The amount of employee earnings that are subject to FICA and FUTA taxes.

Voucher A serially numbered form that is the written authorization for each expenditure. It is prepared from the documents that serve as evidence of the liability.

Voucher register A columnar journal for recording and summarizing all liabilities approved for payment.

Voucher system A method of accumulating, verifying, recording, and disbursing all the expenditures of a business. It covers all payments except those from the petty cash fund.

Questions

Q8–1   What specific items qualify to be included in the term cash? What is a basic rule to determine whether or not an item is part of cash?

Q8–2   The extent of an auditor's examination of a client's accounts and records is influenced to a large extent by the auditor's evaluation of the adequacy of the existing internal controls. Why is this so? Do you believe this to be an acceptable practice?

Q8–3   Why is it important to involve two or more persons in the handling and recording of cash receipts?

Q8–4   Why is it advantageous to deposit total cash receipts intact and to make all disbursements by check?

Q8–5   (a) What is a petty cash fund? (b) How does it operate? (c) Why should the petty cash fund always be replenished at the end of each accounting period?

Q8–6   Explain the matching relationships between the cash records of the bank and those of the depositor.

Q8–7   Explain the following terms: certified check, total of listed checks, cost of service, NSF, debit memo, credit memo.

Q8–8   (a) How often should bank reconciliations be prepared? (b) What are the steps to be followed when preparing the bank reconciliation? (c) Which items must be entered on the books? (d) What do you think is the most important function of a bank reconciliation?

Q8–9   What is the primary purpose of a voucher system? How does a properly functioning voucher system achieve that purpose?

Q8–10   (Appendix 8.1) What is gross pay? Net pay? Why should total gross pay be debited to expense when it is not all paid to employees?

Q8–11   (Appendix 8.1) What are three common payroll taxes levied on an employer?

Q8–12   (Appendix 8.1) (a) What is a state unemployment merit-rating plan? (b) Do you believe that the use of merit-rating plans is justified? Why or why not?

Q8–13   (Appendix 8.1) What are some requirements of effective internal control of payroll?

Q8–14   (Appendix 8.1) What deductions are required by law? What are some other deductions that may be withheld by the employer?

Q8–15   (Appendix 8.1) Why should an employer begin to recognize the expense of vacation pay before the vacations are taken? Does such recognition provide a cash fund to pay for vacations?

Q8–16   (Appendix 8.2) (a) What is a voucher? (b) What is a voucher register? (c) What are the advantages of the voucher system? (d) What are the disadvantages?

Q8–17   (Appendix 8.2) (a) What is a check register? (b) What column headings are needed for the check register?

Q8–18   (Appendix 8.2) What procedures should be followed to control unpaid vouchers?

Q8–19   (Appendix 8.2) Do you believe that basic internal control concepts apply to assets other than cash (for example, supplies, inventory, or receivables)? If so, should there be a separate internal control system for each, or one company-wide internal control system?

Exercises

E8–1
Establishing a petty cash fund

On May 1, 1987, the Aiken Company established a petty cash fund in the amount of $1,250. Prepare a general journal entry for establishment of the fund.

E8–2
Replenishment of petty cash fund

Newberry, Inc., has an imprest petty cash fund of $1,000. On October 31, 1987, the fund consisted of cash and other items as follows:

Currency and coins		$ 98.10
Petty cash vouchers for:		
Transportation in	$316.70	
Telephone	24.30	
Postage expense	418.42	
Stationery	137.58	897.00
Total		$995.10

Assuming that the petty cash fund was replenished, make the necessary entry at October 31, 1987, in general journal form.

E8–3
Cash over and short

Saluda Company has a change fund of $50 in the cash register to start each day. At the end of the day on September 4, 1987, the cash register tape showed cash sales of $968.72. The total amount of cash and checks in the register was $1,017.10. Is there a cash shortage or overage? Compute it and prepare a general journal entry to record cash sales for the day.

E8–4
Handling items on the bank reconciliation

From the following information pertaining to the banking activities of the Cardinal Company, indicate which of the following items should be (a) added to the balance per bank statement, (b) deducted from the balance per bank statement, (c) added to the balance per books, or (d) deducted from the balance per books:

1. Bank service charges (cost of service).
2. Deposits in transit.
3. Outstanding checks.
4. Credit for a customer note collected by the bank.
5. A customer's check returned marked NSF
6. Check for $68 entered in the cash payments journal as $86.
7. Check for $86 entered in the cash payments journal as $68.
8. Deposit of Forest Company credited in error to the Cardinal Company.
9. A check made out by the Avery Company charged in error to the Cardinal Company's account.
10. Interest earned on an interest checking account.

E8–5
Simple bank reconciliation

Westwego Company's Cash account shows a balance of $20,818.37 as of January 31, 1987. The balance on the bank statement on that date is $23,334.17. Checks for $750.00, $533.46, and $126.54 are outstanding. The bank statement shows a charge for $75, with a cancelled check enclosed, that belongs to another company. The statement shows a credit of $1,200 for maturity value of a note receivable that was left with the bank for collection; no collection fee is charged by the bank. A customer's NSF check for $19.20 was returned with a debit memo. What is the true cash balance as of January 31?

8 / Control of Cash

E8–6
Recording reconciliation adjustments

Following is a bank reconciliation for Greenstein Company:

GREENSTEIN COMPANY
Bank Reconciliation
October 31, 1987

Cash balance per ledger, October 31		$644.37	Cash balance per bank, October 31		$1,082.20
Add: Error in check number 407 for office rent	$ 5.00		Add: Deposit in transit . .		210.50
Note collected by bank	100.00		Subtotal		$1,292.70
Interest on account	3.39	108.39	Deduct: Outstanding checks		618.54
Subtotal		$752.76			
Deduct: NSF customer check.	$ 75.60				
Cost of service .	3.00	78.60			
Adjusted cash balance, October 31		$674.16	Adjusted cash balance, October 31		$ 674.16

In general journal form, make all entries required by this reconciliation.

E8–7
Challenging bank reconciliation and journal entries

The accountant for the Estes Drive Hotel has the following data for the bank reconciliation of February 28, 1987:

Balance per bank statement	$8,719.63
Balance per Cash account	8,721.60
NSF check from overnight guest returned by bank	57.50
Deposit made on February 28 not credited by bank	1,625.70
Check number 790 for $618 entered in the books as $681	63.00
Outstanding checks total	2,122.73
Debit memo for note payable of $500 plus interest that bank collected for holder of note.	522.50
Credit memo to cancel January service charge	18.00

Prepare a bank reconciliation and the entries (in general journal form) to adjust the accounts.

E8–8
Computing gross and net pay

(Appendix 8.1) Joy Rogowski works at Tallahassee Corporation at an hourly wage rate of $13.50. At the end of a typical week, she had worked 46 hours. Federal income tax withheld is $137.10 and state income tax withheld for this week is $34.15. Her only nontax deductions are $16.70 for medical insurance and $9.50 for union dues. Compute her gross pay and net pay for the week.

E8–9
Recording payroll and employer taxes

(Appendix 8.1) Mankato Company had the following payroll data for the week ended January 31, 1987:

		Tax Withholdings			
Department	**Gross Pay**	**FICA**	**Federal Income**	**State Income**	**Union Dues**
Sales	$3,497.80	$244.85	$516.70	$112.50	$34.98
Office	1,034.30	72.40	173.75	34.80	10.34
Executive	1,500.00	105.00	201.65	45.80	0

(continued on next page)

Assuming that no employee has yet earned $10,000 in the current year, and using maximum assumed FUTA rates, prepare the general journal entries to record (a) the payroll and (b) the employer's payroll taxes.

E8–10
Recognizing expense and payment of vacation pay

(Appendix 8.1) Auburn Corporation has 100 employees who earn an average of $700 per week and receive a two-week paid vacation each year. Expenses of the paid vacations are recognized evenly over the first 50 weeks of the year. Prepare general journal entries for the following:

a. Recording of vacation pay expense in the week ended January 11, 1987.
b. Recording of the payment of vacation pay on January 11 to six employees who went on a cruise to Bermuda during the second week in January. Federal and state taxes withheld were $947.40 and $127.00 respectively.

E8–11
Simple voucher and check register transactions

(Appendix 8.2) M and W Stores uses a voucher system. During June 1987, the following selected transactions were completed:

1987

Jun.	3	Purchased merchandise from the Debbie Company, $2,000; terms 2/10, n/30. Prepared voucher no. 675 approving payment to be made on June 13.
	6	Purchased merchandise from the Mollie Company, $3,200; terms, 2/10, n/30. Prepared voucher no. 676 authorizing payment on June 15.
	13	Paid the Debbie Company the total amount due; check no. 0207.
	15	Paid the Mollie Company the amount due; check no. 0208.
	17	Prepared voucher no. 677 for a $675 purchase of office equipment, to be paid in 30 days.
	19	Purchased merchandise from the Judy Company, $1,800; terms, 1/10, n/60. Decided not to take discount and prepared voucher no. 678 to be paid August 19.
	28	Prepared voucher no. 679 for June rent, $950.
	28	Paid June rent; check no. 0209.

Enter the above transactions in a voucher register and a check register using the gross price procedure.

E8–12
Vouchers and payments—net price procedure

(Appendix 8.2) New Bern Company uses a voucher system and records all vouchers at the net amount. The following transactions occurred during October and November 1987:

1987

Oct.	3	Issued a voucher payable to the Gray Company for $2,400 of merchandise; terms 2/10, n/30.
	7	Issued a voucher payable to Greene, Inc., for $3,000 of merchandise; terms, 1/10, n/30.
	12	Issued a check to the Gray Company in payment of the October 3 voucher.
Nov.	7	Issued a voucher payable to Greene, Inc., for the discount not taken on the transaction of October 7.
	8	Issued a check payable to Greene, Inc., for the amount due.

Record the transactions in the voucher register and check register (assign voucher and check numbers).

E8–13
Partial payment—discount allowed

(Appendix 8.2) On July 1, 1987, Stepson Company received $8,000 of merchandise with an invoice offering terms of 2/10, n/30. Unsure of the method of settlement of the bill, management did not authorize a voucher and did not record the purchase on that date. On July 10, learning that the supplier would allow discounts on partial payments,

8 / Control of Cash

management authorized voucher no. 584 for which check no. 1670 was written for $6,321. Record that voucher (using the gross price procedure) and the payment on July 10.

E8–14
Voucher cancellation

(Appendix 8.2) Purewater Company prepared voucher no. 381 for a $5,000 purchase of merchandise on September 4, 1987. Terms were 2/10, n/30. On September 13, voucher no. 381 was cancelled and replaced with voucher no. 398 for $4,000, to be paid that date taking the discount, and voucher no. 399 for $1,000, to be paid on October 4. Record all transactions using the gross price method including both payments. Provide check numbers.

A Problems

P8–1A
Petty cash fund

Lihue Company established a petty cash fund of $1,500 by issuing a check to the custodian on November 1, 1987. On November 30, management desired to prepare financial statements for internal use and replenished the fund in order to record the expenditures. The content of the fund on November 30 was as follows:

Currency and coins.		$ 518.65
Receipted petty cash vouchers for:		
Repairs to office equipment.	$132.75	
Transportation in for merchandise.	362.30	
Sales promotion at Aloha Fair	256.70	
Postage paid on outgoing mail.	118.80	
Emergency payments for interisland sales travel	111.65	982.20
Total.		$1,500.85

On December 31, the fund was again replenished. On that date, the contents were:

Currency and coins.		$ 618.75
Receipted petty cash vouchers for:		
Repairs to office equipment.	$162.80	
Transportation in for merchandise.	375.82	
Christmas sales promotion	132.40	
Postage paid on outgoing mail.	208.70	879.72
Total.		$1,498.47

After two months of experience with the fund, management has decided to reduce the fund to about 30 days requirements; a reduction to $1,000 was ordered on December 31.

Required:

1. A general journal entry to establish the fund.
2. A general journal entry to replenish the fund on November 30.
3. A general journal entry to replenish and reduce the fund on December 31.

P8–2A
Bank reconciliation—routine items

The Cash account of the Winnebago Company showed a balance of $7,410.60 on May 31, 1987. The bank statement showed a balance of $7,173.00. Other differences between the firm's Cash account and the bank's records are as follows:

  a. A deposit of $630.00 made on May 31 was not included on the bank statement.
  b. The following items were included with the bank statement:
      i. A debit memo for $60.00 with a customer's NSF check that the firm had included in its deposit of May 30.

(continued on next page)

  ii. A debit memo for $30.00 for safe deposit box rental.
  iii. A cancelled check for $690.00 drawn by another company charged against Winnebago by mistake.
 c. Check number 607 was made out correctly for $61.74 in payment for office supplies but was entered in the cash payments journal as $62.34; it was returned with the statement.
 d. Outstanding checks on May 31 totaled $1,171.80.

Required:

1. Prepare a bank reconciliation as of May 31, 1987.
2. Prepare entries in general journal form as required by the reconciliation.

P8–3A
Bank reconciliation—tracing items to statements

Nussbaum Company had a Cash account balance of $9,934.31 on April 12, 1987. A special bank statement requested by the auditors for that date showed a balance of $12,011.77. At the end of March there were no deposits in transit. There were three checks outstanding on March 31 as follows:

Number	Amount
620	$ 12.00
621	462.40
622	397.60

Deposits made and checks written in the first 12 days of April were as follows:

Deposits		Checks	
Date	Amount	Number	Amount
Apr. 1	$346.25	623	$ 115.80
2	438.75	624	99.20
3	98.75	625	1,110.00
4	96.25	626	143.50
5	986.50	627	682.21
8	483.50	628	49.90
9	421.30	629	20.00
10	359.50	630	760.00
11	251.27	631	62.23
12	248.73	632	198.50

On the bank statement of April 12, the deposit of neither April 11 nor April 12 had yet been credited. Cancelled checks of the Nussbaum Company returned with the bank statement were in the amounts of $12.00, $462.40, $397.60, $115.80, $99.20, $1,110.00, $62.23, and $198.50. Also returned with the bank statement were the following:

 a. A credit memo for $1,030.00 representing a customer note receivable for $1,000 plus interest collected by the bank for Nussbaum.
 b. A debit memo for $2.75 for the note collection fee.
 c. A $90.00 customer check marked NSF.
 d. A $15.40 cancelled check made out by another company and charged to Nussbaum's account.

Required:

1. Prepare a bank reconciliation as of April 12, 1987.
2. Prepare the entries needed to adjust the books (use general journal form).

P8–4A
Voucher register and check register

(Appendix 8.2) Fox Inc. used a voucher system in July 1987 and prepared its vouchers at gross amounts. The following transactions were completed during July:

1987

Jul. 3 Established a petty cash fund of $500 by the issuance of voucher no. 362; issued check no. 357 in payment of this voucher.
3 Purchased a one-year insurance policy from Liberty Insurance Company for $720. Issued voucher no. 363, and check no. 358 in payment of the voucher.
4 Issued voucher no. 364 payable to Kay Realty for $600 for the July rent; issued check no. 359 in payment of the voucher.
5 Issued voucher no. 365 payable to R. Kelly, Inc., for $1,200 of merchandise, terms 2/10, n/30.
10 Issued voucher no. 366 payable to L. Scotch Company for $3,600 of merchandise, terms n/10.
11 Issued voucher no. 367 payable to Danvers Supply Company for $200 of office supplies; issued check no. 360 in payment of the voucher.
17 Issued voucher no. 368 payable to J. Waitt Company for $1,800 of merchandise, terms 2/10, n/30.
18 Recorded the following payroll data in the general journal:

Gross salaries:	Sales	$ 750	
	Office	450	
	Executive	1,000	$2,200
Deductions:	FICA tax	$ 154	
	Federal income tax	378	
	U.S. bonds	75	
	Employee loan	20	
	Community fund	10	637
Net amount due			$1,563

Issued voucher no. 369 payable to Payroll for the net amount due to employees. Issued check no. 361 in payment of the voucher.
20 The L. Scotch Company agreed to an extension of time on its invoice due today, as follows: $1,800 payment due in 20 days, and another $1,800 payment due in 30 days. Cancelled voucher no. 366 and issued vouchers no. 370 and 371.
24 Purchased two electric typewriters from Atlas Office Company for $1,500. Issued voucher no. 372 for $500, and check no. 362, in partial payment. Issued voucher no. 373 for $1,000 for the balance, payable in 30 days.
25 Issued voucher no. 374 payable to the S. Furry Company for $800 of merchandise, terms 1/10, n/60.
26 Issued check no. 363 in payment of voucher no. 370.
27 Issued voucher no. 375 to the *Salem Sun* for $75 for advertising. Issued check no. 364 in payment of the voucher.

Required:

1. Prepare a voucher register, a check register, and a two-column general journal similar to the illustrations in the text, and record the July transactions.
2. Open a Vouchers Payable account and post all entries affecting that account.
3. Prove the end-of-month balance of the Vouchers Payable account by preparing a schedule of unpaid vouchers.

P8–5A
Thought-provoking problem: internal control system (based on an actual occurrence)

At the Capital City public swimming pool, lockers are rented from the locker room attendant for $0.75 per visit. Several popular brands of candy bars are kept at the locker room entrance for sale to the pool patrons. All cash collected is placed in a metal cash box that is locked in the locker room when the pool is closed. When the locker room attendant is absent, she turns the box over to one of the lifeguards to collect cash and make change for locker rentals or candy sales. An assistant city recreation supervisor stops by every few days to deliver more candy and to take out cash for deposit to the

(continued on next page)

city's bank account. There are no signatures for receipt of candy or for cash taken out for deposit.

One day in August, the city recreation supervisor noticed a full box of candy on the back seat of a lifeguard's car. Becoming suspicious, she compared total swimming pool operations with the same period to date last year. Although the number of swimmers had increased by about 20 percent, cash receipts were several hundred dollars less than for the same period last year. Obviously, someone was stealing candy or cash (or both), but who?

Required:

1. Point out the internal control weaknesses in the present system.
2. Suggest some steps that the city recreation supervisor might take to correct this situation. She cannot hire additional employees.

B Problems

P8–1B
Petty cash fund

San Jose Company established a petty cash fund by issuing a check to the custodian for $2,000 on March 1, 1987. On March 31, management desired to prepare financial statements for internal use and replenished the fund in order to record the expenditures. The content of the fund on March 31 was as follows:

Currency and coins.		$ 721.35
Receipted petty cash vouchers for:		
Word processor and computer repairs	$325.35	
Transportation in on merchandise	262.50	
Postage paid on outgoing mail.	336.40	
Employee transportation (bus tickets).	132.60	
Office supplies purchased and used	218.40	1,275.25
Total.		$1,996.60

On April 30, the fund was again replenished. On that date, the contents were:

Currency and coins.		$ 742.50
Receipted petty cash vouchers for:		
Word processor and computer repairs	$342.50	
Transportation in on merchandise	240.10	
Postage paid on outgoing mail.	330.70	
Employee transportation (bus tickets).	108.20	
Office supplies purchased and used	237.15	1,258.65
Total.		$2,001.15

After two months experience with the fund, management has decided to reduce the fund to about 30 days requirements; a reduction to $1,250 was ordered on April 30.

Required:

1. A general journal entry to establish the fund.
2. A general journal entry to replenish the fund on March 31.
3. A general journal entry to replenish and reduce the fund on April 30.

P8–2B
Bank reconciliation—routine items

The Cash account of the Oshkosh Company showed a balance of $3,705.30 on September 30, 1987. The bank statement showed a balance of $3,586.50. Other differences between the firm's Cash account and the bank's records are as follows:

a. A deposit of $315.00 made on September 30 was not included on bank statement.
b. The following items were included with the bank statement:

8 / Control of Cash

i. A debit memo for $30.00 with a customer's NSF check that had been included in the deposit of September 27.
ii. A debit memo for $15.00 for safe deposit box rental.
iii. A cancelled check for $345.00 drawn by another company and charged against Oshkosh by mistake.

c. Check no. 515 was made out correctly for $30.87 in payment for office supplies but was entered in the cash payments journal as $31.17.
d. Outstanding checks on September 30 totaled $585.90.

Required:

1. Prepare a bank reconciliation as of September 30, 1987.
2. Prepare entries in general journal form as required by the reconciliation.

P8–3B
Bank reconciliation—tracing items to statement

Shapiro Company had a Cash account balance of $19,868.62 on October 11, 1987. A special bank statement requested by the auditors for that date showed a balance of $24,023.54. At the end of September there were no deposits in transit. There were three checks outstanding on September 30 as follows:

Number	Amount
862	$ 24.00
863	924.80
864	795.20

Deposits made and checks written in the first 11 days of October were as follows:

Deposits		**Checks**	
Date	Amount	Number	Amount
Oct. 1	$ 692.50	865	$ 231.60
2	877.50	866	198.40
3	197.50	867	2,220.00
4	192.50	868	287.00
7	1,973.00	869	1,364.42
8	967.00	870	99.80
9	842.60	871	40.00
10	719.00	872	1,520.00
11	1,000.00	873	124.60
		874	397.00

On the bank statement of October 11, the deposit of October 11 had not been credited. Cancelled checks of the Shapiro Company returned with the bank statement were in the amounts of $24.00, $924.80, $795.20, $231.60, $198.40, $2,220.00, $124.60, and $397.00. Also returned with the bank statement were the following:

a. A credit memo for $2,060.00 representing a customer note receivable for $2,000 plus interest collected by the bank for Shapiro.
b. A debit memo for $5.50 for the note collection fee.
c. A $180.00 customer check marked NSF.
d. A $30.80 cancelled check made out by another company and charged to Shapiro's account.

Required:

1. Prepare a bank reconciliation as of October 11, 1987.
2. Prepare the entries needed to adjust the books (use general journal form).

P8–4B

Voucher register and check register

(Appendix 8.2) East Lansing Company used a voucher system in May 1987 and prepared its vouchers at gross amounts. The following transactions were completed during May:

1987

May 3   Established a petty cash fund of $850 by issuance of voucher no. 472; issued check no. 467 in payment of this voucher.

3   Purchased a one-year insurance policy from Downs Insurance Agency for $500. Issued voucher no. 473, and check no. 468 in payment of the voucher.

4   Issued voucher no. 474 payable to Glynn Realty for $735 for the May rent; issued check no. 469 in payment of the voucher.

6   Issued voucher no. 475 payable to J. Powell, Inc., for $3,210 of merchandise, terms 2/10, n/30.

10   Issued voucher no. 476 payable to B. Childs Company for $4,150 of merchandise, terms 2/10, n/30.

11   Issued voucher no. 477 payable to Burlington Office Supply Company for $300 of office supplies; issued check no. 470 in payment of the voucher.

17   Issued voucher no. 478 payable to K. Wald Company for $3,100 of merchandise, terms 1/10, n/30.

17   Recorded the following payroll data in the general journal:

Gross salaries:	Sales	$1,500	
	Office	900	
	Executive	2,000	$4,400
Deductions:	FICA tax	$ 308	
	Federal income tax	850	
	U.S. bonds	150	
	Employee loan	50	
	Community fund	75	1,433
Net amount due			$2,967

Issued voucher no. 479 payable to Payroll for the net amount due to employees. Issued check no. 471 in payment of the voucher.

20   The B. Childs Company agreed to an extension of time on its invoice due today, as follows: $2,150 payment due in 20 days and another $2,000 payment due in 30 days. Cancelled voucher no. 476 and issued vouchers no. 480 and 481.

24   Purchased copying equipment from Dover Supply Company for $3,000. Issued voucher no. 482 for $1,500, and check no. 472 in partial payment. Issued voucher no. 483 for $1,500 for the balance, payable in 30 days.

25   Issued voucher no. 484 payable to the G. Floray Company for $1,620 of merchandise, terms 2/10, n/60.

27   Issued check no. 473 in payment of voucher no. 480.

28   Issued voucher no. 485 to the *Norwood Times* for $150 for advertising. Issued check no. 474 in payment of the voucher.

Required:

1. Prepare a voucher register, a check register, and a two-column general journal similar to the illustrations in the text, and record the May transactions.

2. Open a Vouchers Payable account and post all entries affecting that account.

3. Prove the end-of-month balance of the Vouchers Payable account by preparing a schedule of unpaid vouchers.

P8–5B

Thought-provoking problem: cash forecast

An important part of cash management systems is a cash forecast. It is usually prepared on a quarterly basis with the following format:

	First Quarter 1987		
	January	February	March
Beginning cash balance	$XXX	$XXX	$XXX
Add: Collections	XXX	XXX	XXX
Total cash available	$XXX	$XXX	$XXX
Deduct: Cash payments (list them)	$XXX	$XXX	$XXX
Cash balance forward	$XXX	$XXX	$XXX

Pensacola Company's accountant has gathered the following data for the first calendar quarter of 1987:

a. Estimated sales (collected 60 percent during month of sale and 40 percent in month following):

December 1986	$23,400
January 1987	23,400
February 1987	31,200
March 1987	45,500

b. Materials purchases (90 percent paid in month of purchase and 10 percent in month following):

December 1986	$15,600
January 1987	10,400
February 1987	19,500
March 1987	26,000

c. Wages paid in cash:

January 1987	$ 7,800
February 1987	7,800
March 1987	7,800

d. Other cash expenses:

January 1987	$ 5,850
February 1987	4,160
March 1987	6,500

e. Expected cash balance on January 1, 1987 .... $11,219

Required:

1. Prepare a cash forecast for the first three months of 1987.
2. Comment on the results of the forecast with regard to plans for temporary investment or borrowing, assuming that the company needs a minimum balance of $10,000 at the beginning of the month.

9 Current Receivables and Payables

Introduction

In Chapter 8, the cash flows of a major United States corporation, Household International, Inc., were diagrammed (Figure 8–1). To add to the dimensions of that diagram, we could note that Household International, Inc. had $4,887,700,000 in short-term receivables at the end of the year. At the same time, there were short-term payables of $2,661,800,000. A portion of these short-term payables were interest-bearing; interest expense for the year was $492,000,000. These amounts are significant and it is important to manage and account for them properly.

Sources of short-term receivables and payables include sales on open account (accounts receivable), sales of merchandise for notes (notes receivable), purchases on open account (accounts payable), and borrowing (notes payable). This chapter explains and illustrates the basic accounting for accounts receivable and for notes payable and receivable. Related topics include the recognition of bad debts expense, interest expense on notes payable, and interest earned on notes receivable. In the illustrations and explanations, internal control aspects of short-term payables and receivables are emphasized.

Learning Goals

1. To identify the sources and classification of receivables.
2. To understand the nature of bad debts expense and determine bad debts expense by the balance sheet and income statement approaches.
3. To record the bad debts adjustment, write-off, and recovery.
4. To describe the uses of the aging schedule of accounts receivable.
5. To distinguish between the direct write-off and the estimating method of accounting for bad debts expense.

6. To explain the balance sheet classification of an opposite balance in accounts receivable or accounts payable.

7. To understand the recording of credit card sales.

8. To recognize the importance of the internal control of accounts receivable.

9. To compute receivables turnover and number of days sales uncollected and use them in evaluation of the management of accounts receivable.

10. To know the characteristics of promissory notes and the method of transferring them.

11. To record transactions dealing with issuance of notes payable.

12. To record notes receivable transactions.

13. To calculate the proceeds of notes discounted at banks and to record the discounting of these notes.

14. To account for dishonored notes.

Sources and Classification of Receivables

A receivable represents a claim against individuals or companies for cash or other assets. Two broad categories of receivables are:

1. Those arising out of a trade or a sale of goods or services, referred to as **trade receivables**.

2. All the other receivables arising out of a variety of claims of a source other than trade, referred to as **nontrade receivables**.

Trade Receivables

Trade receivables are of three classes: accounts receivable, notes receivable, and credit card receivables. *Accounts receivable* are claims against customers (either individual or business) for sales made on account with the credit terms determined in advance. For individuals, these are usually 30-day charge accounts with a finance charge assessed on balances more than 30 days old. Generally these are shown in a ledger account entitled Accounts Receivable.

Notes receivable are claims supported by written formal promises to pay; that is, promissory notes from customers. Both categories represent the same legal claims against customers. One major advantage to a firm of holding a note receivable is that it is a written acknowledgment that the debt exists. The note also is a negotiable instrument; this permits the firm to endorse (sign the firm's name on the back of the instrument possibly with some type of specific instruction) and transfer it for cash or use it as collateral for a loan from a bank. Notes can arise from either a trade or a nontrade situation. For a note to be a trade receivable, it must arise from a sale of goods or services.

Credit card receivables are claims arising from sales made by the acceptance of credit cards where the resulting invoices are not accepted by banks for deposit—for example, oil company credit cards. These are trade receivables but require a special type of accounting discussed later in this chapter.

Nontrade Receivables

Other types of receivables arise from nontrade sources, giving rise to a wide variety of nontrade receivable accounts. *Accounts Receivable, Employees* arises from sales to employees—usually at a discount—to be deducted from the next paycheck. *Accrued Interest Receivable* represents the accrual of interest on notes receivable or other interest-bearing instruments. *Investment in Bonds* represents claims against companies for money loaned to them for interest-yielding bonds. *Refundable Deposits* are made by companies as good-faith indications for such business events as contract bids with government agencies or others. *Notes Receivable, Officers and Employees* results from loans made by the company to officers and employees.

Classification of Receivables

Receivables that are due and collectible within a year (or one operating cycle if it is longer than a year) should be shown in the current assets section of the balance sheet. The terms *accounts receivable, receivables from credit card companies,* and *notes receivable,* if unqualified, should be understood to represent trade receivables collectible within one year or one operating cycle if it is longer than a year. Receivables that are not due or are not collectible within a year (or after an operating cycle that is longer than a year) should be shown in a balance sheet category between current assets and property, plant, and equipment called long-term investments. Accounting issues involved in trade accounts receivable are discussed first in the next sections.

Bad Debts Expense: Allowance Method

Matching standard

The cost of the goods sold and all other expenses incurred during the period should be related to or should be deducted from the revenue of that period.

A basic principle in accounting, the* matching standard, *is that in any accounting period the earned revenue and the actual expense incurred in realizing that revenue should be assigned to that period and used in calculating net income.

The balance in the Accounts Receivable account normally represents uncollected amounts included in revenue. Accordingly, losses that may arise through failure to collect any of these receivables should be recognized as an expense (**bad debts expense**) during the period when the sales were made. Thus, accounts receivable originating from 1987 credit sales estimated to be uncollectible in 1988 represent a bad debts expense of the year 1987.

It also follows that, in the balance sheet, accounts receivable should be shown at the amount expected to be realized through actual cash collections from customers (**net realizable value**). Only in this way will the amount satisfy the definition of an asset. If accounts receivable were shown at their gross amount without any accompanying adjustment for the estimated uncollectible portion, the total assets and the total stockholders' equity would be overstated to the extent of the failure to recognize an expense that arises out of the uncollectible sale of goods on account. Accordingly, the Financial Accounting Standards Board has indicated that losses from uncollectible accounts shall be accrued and recognized as an expense even though the specific receivables that will become uncollectible are not known.[1]

Recording the Bad Debts Adjustment

Bad debts expense is estimated and recorded in an end-of-period adjusting entry. Assume that on December 31, 1987, after its first year of operations, the credit department of the Gadson Company, having analyzed 1987 sales and past-due accounts, determines that out of the current year's sales, $650 will be uncollectible. This amount represents a bad debts expense to be shown in the general and administrative expenses section of the income statement. The expense pertains to accounts receivable resulting from sales of the current period; therefore, in accordance with the principle of periodic matching of expenses and revenue, the estimated amount of bad debts expense should be charged against current revenue. The adjusting general journal entry recorded on December 31, 1987, and the posting of the entry to the general ledger are:

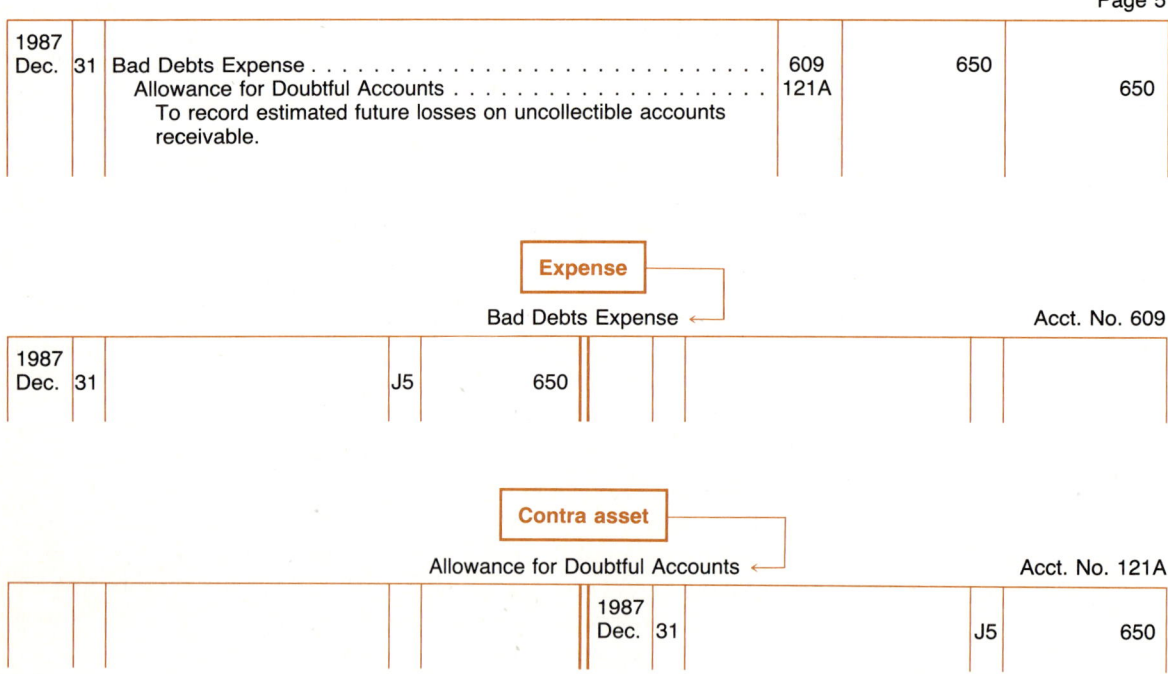

---

[1]*Statement of Financial Accounting Standards No. 5,* "Accounting for Contingencies" (Stamford, Conn.: FASB, March 1975), paragraph 22.

This method is called the *allowance method*. The Bad Debts Expense account is closed into Income Summary and represents an operating expense on the income statement. **Allowance for Doubtful Accounts** is a contra asset or a valuation account to Accounts Receivable. A contra or **valuation account** is subtracted from another account to arrive at the book value or carrying value. As a contra to Accounts Receivable, the Allowance for Doubtful Accounts will cause accounts receivable to be shown on the balance sheet at their estimated collectible or net realizable value. In this first year, there was no previous balance before adjustment in Allowance for Doubtful Accounts and no account receivable was written off during the year 1987. These complications are discussed in more detail later in the chapter.

Since the amount of $650 is an estimate not related to specific customers' accounts, the credit must be made to the contra or valuation account. If the credit were to be made directly to Accounts Receivable without corresponding credits to subsidiary accounts, the equality of the controlling account and the subsidiary accounts would no longer exist. Using the Allowance for Doubtful Accounts account permits a reduction in the asset carrying value without destroying this essential equality between the controlling account and subsidiary ledger. Its effect on the balance sheet as a deduction from the related asset account is as follows:

GADSON COMPANY
Partial Balance Sheet
December 31, 1987

Assets

Current assets:		
Cash		$1,210
Accounts receivable	$6,945	
Deduct: Allowance for doubtful accounts	650	6,295
Notes receivable		1,000

The amount of $6,295 represents the net cash expected to be received when the accounts receivable are collected (net realizable value).

Writing Off Uncollectible Accounts

As actual accounts receivable are determined to be uncollectible during subsequent accounting periods, Allowance for Doubtful Accounts is debited instead of Bad Debts Expense, with offsetting credits to the Accounts Receivable account in the general ledger and to the specific customers' accounts in the accounts receivable subsidiary ledger. This contra account is debited because the expense already has been recognized by the bad debts adjusting entry. A debit to Bad Debts Expense at the time of write-off would cause the expense associated with the uncollectible item to be recorded twice: when the expense was estimated and again when written off.

Assume that, on January 15, 1988, the Gadson Company decides that a claim of $80 against Thomas Lee for a sale made on September 1, 1987, is uncollectible. The entry to record the write-off of this account is:

1988				
Jan.	15	Allowance for Doubtful Accounts	80	
		Accounts Receivable		80
		To write off an uncollectible account:		
		Thomas Lee. $80		

Estimating the Amount of Bad Debts Expense

Management must make a careful estimate, based on judgment and past experience, of the amount of its uncollectible accounts. Accurate records must be kept and overdue accounts must be carefully analyzed. Two alternative approaches are commonly used in estimating bad debts expense. They are referred to as (1) the **income statement approach**, based on the dollar volume of sales, and (2) the **balance sheet approach**, based on the amount of receivables. The income statement approach is often referred to as the *percentage of sales* approach. The balance sheet approach is sometimes referred to as the *percentage of receivables (trade)* approach.

The Income Statement Approach

The income statement approach answers the question: How much bad debts expense is associated with this year's sales? Thus, in associating the bad debts expense directly with dollar volume of sales, the estimate is based on a percentage of an income statement item. Typically, it is based on a percentage of sales less sales returns and allowances. The percentage is determined from information derived from the company's past experience. Even though it is not usually done, it may be desirable to establish the percentage on the basis of credit sales only, excluding cash sales, particularly if the ratio of cash sales to total sales changes substantially from year to year. The method is simple to apply and furnishes an equitable basis for distributing bad debts expense. Since the computation used in this method yields the total estimated amount of the bad debts expense for the year directly, any existing balance in the Allowance for Doubtful Accounts is ignored. Thus, a small error in the same direction over the years could accumulate to a large amount in the Allowance for Doubtful Accounts, since its balance is ignored in the adjustment process. This would cause the amount of net realizable receivables to be distorted; a restudy of the percentage figure used would then be in order.

To illustrate the adjustment by this approach using the credit sales variation, assume that an examination of the accounts of a given company for the preceding five years shows that approximately ½ of 1 percent of credit sales have proven to be uncollectible. Assume further that credit sales for a particular year are $200,000 and that there is a credit balance of $105 in Allowance for Doubtful Accounts before adjustments are made. The bad debts expense for the year is $1,000 = (0.005 \times \$200,000)$. In recording the adjustment, the $105 balance in the Allowance for Doubtful Accounts is ignored because it represents a carryover of potential losses from sales of prior years. Also, the $1,000 amount is the estimate of bad debts expense for the year and hence the amount of the adjustment. The adjusting journal entry to record the expense is:

Page 5

1987					
Dec.	31	Bad Debts Expense....................................	609	1,000	
		Allowance for Doubtful Accounts.....................	121A		1,000
		To record the bad debts expense for the year based on credit sales.			

Once the foregoing information is posted, the Allowance for Doubtful Accounts and Bad Debts Expense would appear as indicated below:

Allowance for Doubtful Accounts — Acct. No. 121A

				1987				
				Dec.	31	Balance	✓	105
					31		J5	1,000

Bad Debts Expense — Acct. No. 609

1987					
Dec.	31		J5	1,000	

After the adjusting entry is posted to the Allowance for Doubtful Accounts, its balance is $1,105. Notice that this amount is different from the $1,000 amount of Bad Debts Expense for the year. This does not represent an error, since the two accounts measure different things:

1. The Allowance for Doubtful Accounts measures the estimated uncollectible accounts receivable regardless of what year's sales gave rise to the receivables.

2. Bad Debts Expense measures the uncollectible portion of the current year's sales on account.

The Balance Sheet Approach The balance sheet approach requires an adjustment of the existing balance of Allowance for Doubtful Accounts to an amount that, when deducted from accounts receivable on the balance sheet, will show accounts receivable at their net realizable value. This approach seeks an answer to the question: How large a valuation allowance is needed to disclose our receivables at the net cash to be realized from those items? Thus the amount of the balance sheet item, accounts receivable, rather than the income statement item, sales, is used as the base for the adjustment.

The amount of bad debts expense is determined indirectly. The necessary balance of Allowance for Doubtful Accounts is determined by either of two procedures: (1) **aging** the accounts receivable (that is, analyzing them by the amount of time they have remained unpaid), or (2) by computing an amount equal to an estimated blanket percentage of current accounts receivable. The expense adjustment is the amount needed to produce the desired balance.

Aging the Accounts Receivable to Obtain Allowance for Doubtful Accounts Aging the accounts receivable involves consideration of the date on which payment was due, the number of days that have elapsed *since the due date,* and any other available data of a financial nature that give some clue to collectibility of the accounts. A columnar work sheet similar to the one shown in Figure 9–1 is often used to facilitate the analysis. It is sometimes referred to as an **aging schedule**. Computerized accounting systems produce an aging schedule as a standard procedure.

All accounts in the accounts receivable subsidiary ledger and their corresponding balances are listed in the Customer's Name and Total Balance columns. The amounts that make up each balance in the Total Balance column are then extended to the appropriate columns, after being analyzed into age classifications.

The aging method yields a more satisfactory Allowance for Doubtful Accounts than does any other method because the estimate is based on a study

ROGERS COMPANY
Analysis of Accounts Receivable by Age
December 31, 1987

Customer's Name	Total Balance	Not Yet Due	Items Past Due			
			1–30 Days	31–60 Days	61–90 Days	Over 90 Days
Walter G. Arnold	$ 880	$ 800	$ 80			
Allan Conlon	1,800	1,000	500	$ 300		
Charles Peacock	50				$ 50	
Richard C. Smith	320	100	200	20		
Jerome Werther	960				900	$ 60
Others	51,990	27,220	15,460	5,280	730	3,300
Totals	$56,000	$29,120	$16,240	$5,600	$1,680	$3,360
Percent of total	100	52	29	10	3	6

Figure 9–1 Analysis of Accounts Receivable by Age

of individual customer accounts rather than on a blanket percentage of a single general ledger account balance. The bad debts expense, however, of a given year could be greatly distorted by the use of this method. For instance, if recoveries of accounts receivable previously written off or the write-off in the current year of accounts receivable arising from prior years' sales are credited or debited to the Allowance for Doubtful Accounts without any designation as to which of these items affect prior years' net income—which is the usual practice—the bad debts expense of the current year will be distorted.

The analysis of accounts receivable aids management not only in the accounting for uncollectible accounts but also in making credit decisions. In interpreting this information for credit decisions, management should also compare the current analysis of accounts receivable by age with those of earlier periods, especially the age-group percentages. In Figure 9–1, 52 percent of the total accounts receivable are not yet due, 29 percent are past due from 1 to 30 days, and so on. When compared with earlier years, percentage increases in the lower age classifications with offsetting decreases in the older classes are favorable.

The analysis in Figure 9–1 is also used to determine the proper balance to be established in Allowance for Doubtful Accounts. To make this determination, companies may apply a sliding scale of percents based on previous experience to the total amount shown in each column. The computation to determine expected uncollectible items for the Rogers Company is as follows:

	Amount	Estimated Percent Uncollectible	Allowance for Doubtful Accounts
Not yet due	$29,120	3	$ 873.60
Past due			
1–30 days	16,240	4	649.60
31–60 days	5,600	10	560.00
61–90 days	1,680	20	336.00
Over 90 days	3,360	50	1,680.00
Total accounts receivable	$56,000		
Total balance needed in allowance. .			$4,099.20

On the basis of this summary, it is estimated that $4,099.20 of the outstanding accounts receivable on December 31 will become uncollectible. Consequently, an Allowance for Doubtful Accounts with a balance of $4,099.20 is required. Before the adjusting entry is made, the existing balance in the account must be considered to measure the balance that is needed in the Allowance for Doubtful Accounts. The Rogers Company has a present credit balance in Allowance for Doubtful Accounts of $150 remaining from earlier periods. The adjusting entry amount will be for $3,949.20 = ($4,099.20 − $150); when this amount is posted to the allowance account, it will bring that account up to $4,099.20, the amount estimated to be uncollectible. The adjusting journal entry is:

Page 9

1987					
Dec.	31	Bad Debts Expense		3,949.20	
		Allowance for Doubtful Accounts			3,949.20
		To increase the asset valuation account by the estimated expense.			

Assume that in 1987 before an adjusting entry is made, the Allowance for Doubtful Accounts had a debit balance of $300 before adjustment rather than a credit balance of $150. The adjusting entry and thus the bad debts expense recognized in 1987 would then be $4,399.20 = ($4,099.20 + $300). After this entry is posted, the allowance account contains the desired credit balance of $4,099.20. The ledger account would then appear as follows:

Allowance for Doubtful Accounts   Acct. No. 121A

1987						1987				
Dec.	31	Balance	✓	300.00		Dec.	31	A.E.	J9	4,399.20
								Bal. 4,099.20		

Use of Blanket Percentage to Obtain Allowance for Doubtful Accounts

Unless the subsidiary ledger is processed by computer, an analysis of accounts receivable by age is time consuming. If there is a reliable pattern, the estimate of Allowance for Doubtful Accounts may be based on a single blanket percentage of accounts receivable, computed as follows for the Garu Company:

End of Year	Balance of Accounts Receivable	Total Losses from Uncollectible Accounts
1984	$20,000	$ 800
1985	24,000	480
1986	22,000	700
Totals	$66,000	$1,980

The average loss of the past three years has been 3 percent = ($1,980 ÷ $66,000). Assume that at the end of 1987, total accounts receivable are $30,000 and a credit balance of $150 is in the allowance account. Estimated uncollectible accounts at 3 percent of accounts receivable are $900 = ($30,000 × 0.03). The following adjusting entry on the books of the Garu

Company at the end of 1987 increases the Allowance for Doubtful Accounts to the desired amount of $900:

1987				
Dec.	31	Bad Debts Expense.................................	750	
		Allowance for Doubtful Accounts		750
		To increase the asset valuation account by the estimated expense.		

A portion of the information for the following partial balance sheet is taken from the preceding data.

GARU COMPANY
Partial Balance Sheet
December 31, 1987

Assets

Current assets:		
Cash..		$ 3,200
Accounts receivable	$30,000	
Deduct: Allowance for doubtful accounts	900	29,100
Notes receivable		18,000

Promissory notes receivable arising from the sale of merchandise may also prove to be uncollectible. When notes receivable specifically arise from the sale of merchandise, the current allowance for estimated bad debts losses should be adequate to cover outstanding notes receivable and accounts receivable. This is accomplished by including trade notes receivable in the aging schedule, including their total if a blanket percentage approach is used, or by separate analysis of trade notes receivable. The following partial balance sheet presentation shows that the allowance covers notes receivable and accounts receivable jointly:

GARU COMPANY
Partial Balance Sheet
December 31, 1987

Assets

Current assets:		
Cash..		$ 3,200
Accounts receivable	$30,000	
Notes receivable	18,000	
Total...	$48,000	
Deduct: Allowance for doubtful accounts and notes........	900	47,100

Writing Off Uncollectible Accounts

When it is decided that a specific customer's account is definitely uncollectible, the amount due should be written off. Assuming that on February 15, 1988, the Garu Company definitely determined that the account of a customer, Joseph Nykerk, is uncollectible, the entry to record the write-off is:

1988			
Feb. 15	Allowance for Doubtful Accounts	75	
	Accounts Receivable		75
	To write off uncollectible account:		
	Joseph Nykerk $75		

This entry has no effect on the net realizable value of the receivables; it only adjusts the balance of Accounts Receivable and its contra. The entry does not affect expenses, because no expense was incurred on February 15, 1988. The expense was recorded by the adjusting entry of December 31, 1987. Assume that immediately before this entry was made, the books of the Garu Company showed the following account balances:

Accounts Receivable...	$30,000
Allowance for Doubtful Accounts (credit)	900

When the entry to write off Nykerk's account is posted, the result is:

	Balances before Write-Off	Write-Off	Balances after Write-Off
Accounts receivable	$30,000	$75	$29,925
Deduct: Allowance for doubtful accounts	900	75	825
Net realizable value................	$29,100		$29,100

This calculation points up the fact that since the expense was recorded in the period when the sale was made, the subsequent write-off does not change net realizable value of assets, and since there was no net change in assets, there would likewise be no change in liabilities or stockholders' equity.

Recovery of Bad Debts

An account that is written off as uncollectible may later be recovered in part or in full. In that event, the entry that was made to write off the account is reversed to the extent of the amount recovered or expected to be recovered. Assuming that Joseph Nykerk settles with his creditors for 50 cents on the dollar and that a check for $37.50 is received, the required journal entires are:

1988 Nov.	15	Accounts Receivable .... Allowance for Doubtful Accounts .... To restore the collectible portion of the account previously written off: Joseph Nykerk $37.50	37.50	37.50
	15	Cash .... Accounts Receivable .... To record payment received: Joseph Nykerk $37.50	37.50	37.50

The debit and the credit to Accounts Receivable cancel each other, but they are necessary if a complete record of all transactions with the customer is to be maintained. Such a record may be of considerable aid if further extension of credit to Joseph Nykerk is considered at some future date.

Bad Debts Expense: Direct Write-Off Method

If the amount of bad debts expense cannot be reasonably estimated, a company must use the direct write-off method for recognition of bad debts expense.[2] This method postpones recording the expense until the specific receivable is definitely determined to be uncollectible. In this case, an Allowance for Doubtful Accounts is *not* used, and no end-of-period adjusting entry for estimated expense is made. The February 15, 1988, entry on the books of the Garu Company to remove Joseph Nykerk's account in full under the direct write-off method is:

1988 Feb.	15	Bad Debts Expense .... Accounts Receivable .... To write off uncollectible account: Joseph Nykerk $75	75	75

The expense is recognized in the *period of write-off* rather than in the period when the sale is made. The direct write-off method, as well as the allowance method previously illustrated, is acceptable for federal income tax reporting

---

[2]*FASB Statement No. 5,* paragraph 8. This statement provides for accrual of loss contingencies only if the loss is probable and its amount can be reasonably estimated.

purposes. However, it does not assign to each accounting period the expenses arising out of sales made in that period and therefore violates the principle of matching expenses and revenue in each accounting period. Thus the error in matching causes the net income shown in the income statement to be in error. It also causes the net receivables as shown in the balance sheet to be overstated. Such a departure from the matching principle is justified if the amount of losses cannot be reasonably estimated.

Assume again that on November 15, 1988, Nykerk makes a settlement of 50 cents on the dollar and issues a check for $37.50. The required journal entries are:

1988				
Nov.	15	Accounts Receivable	37.50	
		Bad Debts Recovered		37.50
		To restore the collectible portion of the account previously written off:		
		Joseph Nykerk $37.50		
	15	Cash	37.50	
		Accounts Receivable		37.50
		To record payment received:		
		Joseph Nykerk $37.50		

The **Bad Debts Recovered** account reflects cost recoveries (in this case, expense cancellations); its balance often is reported in the other revenue section of the income statement.[3]

Comparison of the Two Recording Procedures

The two methods of recording bad debts expense are compared in Figure 9–2 assuming the following data:

Allowance for doubtful accounts (credit balance, January 1)	$ 4,200
All sales on account	510,000
Cash collections on account	495,000
Sales returns and allowances	4,000
Accounts receivable written off as uncollectible	3,950
Bad debts recovered	250

The basis for estimating bad debt expenses is 1 percent × (Sales − Sales returns and allowances).

---

[3]Theoretically, this account is a contra account to Bad Debts Expense and, in the normal case, it would be acceptable to credit that account. In some cases, however, the elements of such a decision involve complexities beyond the scope of this book.

Transactions (Jan. 1– Dec. 31, 1987)	Estimating Bad Debts Expense			Direct Write-Off		
All sales on account	Accounts Receivable............ Sales.................	510,000	510,000	Accounts Receivable............ Sales.................	510,000	510,000
Cash received on account	Cash.................. Accounts Receivable.........	495,000	495,000	Cash.................. Accounts Receivable.........	495,000	495,000
Sales returns and allowances	Sales Returns and Allowances.............. Accounts Receivable.........	4,000	4,000	Sales Returns and Allowances.............. Accounts Receivable.........	4,000	4,000
Accounts receivable determined to be uncollectible	Allowance for Doubtful Accounts.............. Accounts Receivable.........	3,950	3,950	Bad Debts Expense............ Accounts Receivable.........	3,950	3,950
Bad debts recovered	Accounts Receivable............ Allowance for Doubtful Accounts............... Cash.................. Accounts Receivable.........	250 250	 250 250	Accounts Receivable............ Bad Debts Recovered......... Cash.................. Accounts Receivable.........	250 250	 250 250
Adjusting entry, December 31, 1987: ($510,000 − $4,000 = $506,000; $506,000 × 0.01 = $5,060)	Bad Debts Expense............ Allowance for Doubtful Accounts...............	5,060	5,060	(No entry is made.)		
Closing entry, December 31, 1987	Sales.................. Sales Returns and Allowances............... Bad Debts Expense............ Income Summary............	510,000	4,000 5,060 500,940	Sales.................. Bad Debts Recovered.......... Bad Debts Expense........... Sales Returns and Allowances................ Income Summary............	510,000 250	3,950 4,000 502,300

Figure 9–2   Two Methods of Accounting for Bad Debts Expense

Valuation Accounts for Returns and Allowances and Cash Discounts

The net realizable amount of receivables on the balance sheet indicates the amount of collections available to the firm after allowing for bad debts expense. For example, accounts receivable of $30,000 and a corresponding allowance for doubtful accounts of $2,000 should result in a company's collecting approximately $28,000. In reality, other deductions may be made that will decrease this amount. Typical deductions are sales returns, sales allowances, cash discounts granted to customers for prompt payments, and collection expenses. Theoretically, all these additional deductions should have corresponding valuation accounts, so that accounts receivable will be stated in the balance sheet at an amount closer to the net amount that will be collected. However, such valuation accounts as *Allowance for Sales Returns* and *Allowance for Sales Discounts* are rarely used because the items carried over from one year and recognized during the next year are usually immaterial and counterbalance each other. Moreover, these adjustments are not recognizable for income tax purposes.

Credit Card Sales

At least four kinds of credit cards have become extremely popular during the last two decades: (1) those issued by banks (referred to as bank credit cards) such as VISA and MasterCard, (2) those issued by other financial institutions (referred to as nonbank credit cards) such as the green American Express card, (3) those issued by oil companies, such as Gulf Oil and Exxon, and (4) those issued by department stores and certain airlines such as the Wings card issued by Eastern Airlines.

The first three of the issuing institutions usually charge the retailer a fee ranging from 3 to 7 percent for accepting and collecting the credit card receivable. This credit card fee represents an expense that is a combination of cash discount, bad debts expense, collection fee, and certain accounting expense for recording a receivable and later recording the collection in two or more installments.

Credit cards issued by oil companies are similar to nonbank credit cards such as the green American Express. They are classified separately because of the restriction on their use. Exxon cards are typically accepted (with some exceptions) only by Exxon service stations, while the American Express card is accepted by many different merchandizing and service entities. Credit cards issued by department stores such as Sears, Roebuck & Company are basically a means of identifying their own customers. When these cards are presented and a credit sale is made, the issuing store will debit Accounts Receivable, credit Sales, and do its own billing.[4] Only two types of credit card sales require additional explanations of their accounting: sales made on bank credit cards and sales made on nonbank credit cards.

The signed **credit card sales slips** received by a company upon making sales with bank credit cards are accepted for deposit by banks and hence are treated as cash items. To illustrate, assume that a typical day's bank credit card sales of a company amounted to $10,000 with a 5 percent credit card fee. These sales would be recorded as follows:

1987				
Apr.	3	Cash...	9,500	
		Credit Card Fees Expense........................	500	
		Sales.......................................		10,000
		To record bank credit card sales.		

Sales slips recording sales on certain nonbank financial and other institutions are not usually accepted by banks for deposit. Rather, they must be sent to the issuing institution where a check will be written for the gross sales *less* the credit card fee. For these credit card sales, the company making the sale should record a special trade receivable for the net amount to be received from the credit card issuer since the credit card fee is a known amount. This

---

[4]Many of these receivables result in installment-type receivables. Often these stores place a finance charge of 1½ percent per month on any unpaid balance at the beginning of each month, which is an annual rate of 18 percent (some state laws allow higher rates).

receivable can be entitled Accounts Receivable, Credit Cards. It should not be merged with the other trade receivables that require a measurement of bad debts expense, discussed earlier in this chapter. A typical day's credit card sales of $3,000 with a 6 percent card fee may be recorded as follows:

1987 Apr.	4	Accounts Receivable, Credit Cards................... Credit Card Fees Expense........................ Sales.. To record sales made and billed this date to credit card companies.	2,820 180	3,000

Opposite Balances in Accounts Receivable and Accounts Payable

In the accounts receivable subsidiary ledger, the customer's accounts normally have debit balances. Sometimes an overpayment, a sales return or allowance after a customer has paid an account, or an advance payment may convert the balance into a credit. Assume that there is a net debit balance of $29,600 in an accounts receivable subsidiary ledger consisting of 100 accounts, as follows:

98 accounts with a debit balance........................	$30,000
2 accounts with a credit balance.......................	400
Net debit balance of 100 accounts receivable................	$29,600

The debit amount of $30,000 and the credit amount of $400 would appear on the balance sheet as follows:

Current assets:		Current liabilities:	
Accounts receivable.....	$30,000	Credit balances in customer accounts.......	$400

The controlling account balance of $29,600 should not be used in the balance sheet because it would conceal the current liability of $400, which should be shown with the caption **"credit balances in customer accounts."** Similarly, if the accounts payable subsidiary ledger contains creditors' accounts with debit balances, the balance sheet should show the debit-balance accounts as a current asset. For example, a net balance in the Accounts Payable controlling account of $88,600 (with certain subsidiary ledger accounts having debit balances that total $1,400) would appear in the balance sheet as follows:

Current assets:		Current liabilities:	
Debit balances in creditor accounts	$1,400	Accounts payable	$90,000

Internal Control: Accounts Receivable

As in the use of cash, adequate safeguards must be established for accounts receivable. Among needed internal control features are the following:

- ☐ Separation of duties so that the work of one employee can be verified by another employee.
- ☐ Authorization by a supervisor of recording returns and allowances, discounts, and bad debt write-offs.
- ☐ Checking and mailing of statements of account by persons who do not make entries into the accounts receivable subsidiary ledger.
- ☐ Review of delinquent accounts periodically.

Adequate control of receivables begins with the credit authorization and continues through the remaining stages of the cycle to collection.

Receivables Turnover and Average Collection Period

Two guides to the overall condition of the accounts receivable are the average collection period and the annual **receivables turnover**. If goods are sold on terms of 2/10, n/30, the amount of accounts receivable outstanding at any time should be less than the credit sales for the last 30 days because many of the sales will have been paid within the discount period. If allowance is made for slow-paying accounts, the receivables may represent 30 to 35 days' sales. If the receivables exceed this limitation, a careful analysis of all the accounts should be made.

Average collection periods vary with the industry and with the firm's credit policy. Wholesalers of shoes may average 45 days, while grocery wholesalers may average 15 days. For a standard of comparison, the preceding year's rate or the industry rate may be used. Using assumed data for two years for a company, the computations are as follows:

		1987	1986
1.	Net credit sales	$197,000	$151,000
2.	Days in year	365	365[a]
3.	Net credit sales per day (Line 1 ÷ Line 2)	$540	$414
4.	Average trade receivables (balance at beginning of year + balance at end of year) ÷ 2	$30,000	$28,000
5.	Average collection period (Line 4 ÷ Line 3)	56 days	68 days
6.	Receivables turnover per year (Line 1 ÷ Line 4)	6.6 times	5.4 times

[a]Although a 360-day year has been used previously for such things as interest calculations, a 365-day year is used for this ratio analysis.

If line 1 covered sales for a period of less than one year, then Line 2 would be changed accordingly. Thus, if the sales were for a three-month period, Line 2 would show 91 days (one-fourth of 365 days).

Using the previous year for comparison, there is an improvement in 1987. The turnover has increased from 5.4 times to 6.6 times resulting in a shorter collection period. The average collection period has decreased by 12 days indicating that customers are paying more quickly. This should be evaluated in light of industry changes and the company's credit terms.

Accounts Payable

Accounting for accounts payable does not involve issues such as recognition of bad debts expense. Other issues such as cash discounts are present with accounts payable. Therefore, an important internal control issue is the establishment of a system to ensure that discounts will be taken. Use of the net price procedure for recording accounts payable as described in Chapter 6 will strengthen internal control in this regard.

Accounting for Notes

The next sections present a discussion of accounting for notes. Notes payable are discussed first because the concepts related to discounting of notes payable are easier to understand than those related to discounting of notes receivable.

The Short-Term Financing Climate

Business firms often find it more economical to use some means of short-term financing than to pay cash for various purchases; for example, many purchase merchandise, supplies, and equipment on 30-day or 60-day open charge accounts. As previously indicated, an open charge account is an extension of credit without a formal written promise to pay. It often includes a cash discount to encourage early payment (see Chapter 6). Other businesses may use promissory notes to acquire assets or borrow money to take advantage of discounts.

When various financing methods—both long-term and short-term—are available to a company, the financial manager must consider (1) the cost of the interest of each method, (2) whether the financing method will continue to be available to the firm, and (3) the possible effect that short-term financing will have on long-term borrowing; or the reverse, the effect that committing the organization for 10 to 20 years will have on short-term borrowing. In regard to short-term financing, the financial manager should choose the method that will produce consistently the desired short-term funds at the lowest possible cost. The rate of interest that an organization must pay depends on its ability to pledge assets as security, its record of financial integrity, and its prospects for the future. When the instrument used for financing is a short-term note, some new accounting issues arise. They are discussed in the following sections beginning with notes payable.

Notes Payable

A negotiable **promissory note** may be defined as an unconditional written promise to pay a specified sum of money to the order of a designated payee or to bearer at a fixed or determinable future time or on demand. It is negotiable by simple transfer (if payable to bearer) or by endorsement and transfer (if payable to a designated payee).

Maturity Dates of Notes

The term of a note may be expressed in years, months, or days. A note expressed in years or months, matures on the corresponding date in the maturity year or month. For example, a two-year note dated April 3, 1987, is due on April 3, 1989, and a two-month note dated April 3, 1987, is due on June 3, 1987. Occasionally, when time is expressed in months, there may be no corresponding date in the maturity month, in which case the last day of the month of maturity is used. A three-month note dated March 31 is due on June 30, and a one-month note dated January 29, 30, or 31 is due on the last day of February. If the term of the note is expressed in days, the maturity date is found by counting forward the specified number of days *after* the date of the note, excluding the date of the note but including the maturity date. Assume that a 90-day note has an issuance date of April 19; the due date of July 18 is determined as follows:

Total days in April	30
Deduct: Date of note in April	19
Number of days note runs in April (excluding April 19)	11
Add: Total days in May and June	61
Total number of days note has run through May 31	72
Add: Due date in July (90 days minus 72 days)	18
Term of note	90

For short-term credit instruments, simple interest (interest on the original principal only) is computed by using the *ordinary interest at exact time* approach (a 360-day denominator with the numerator containing exact days). Thus, a three-month note dated April 19 is due 91 days later, on July 19. The interest amount by the ordinary interest at exact time method is computed for 91 days. This usual commercial practice is used here for short-term interest calculations.[5]

---

[5] Another approach is *accurate interest* (exact days in the numerator and a 365-day year in the denominator). This method is used by government and many banks. A third approach is *30-day month time* with the assumption that every month has 30 days (used in Chapters 14 and 15 for bonds).

Recording Procedures Involving Notes Payable

All obligations backed up by promissory notes **(notes payable)** issued to others may be recorded in a single Notes Payable account in the general ledger. Supplementary details including name of payee, interest rate, and terms of the note, are indicated in the explanation column as follows:

		Notes Payable			Acct. No. 205
1987 Dec. 24	B. T. Arnold (paid)	CP40	450	1987 Nov. 15	B. B. Baker, 16%, 60 days	J62	2,000
				24	B. T. Arnold, 15%, 30 days	J65	450
				Dec. 3	J. L. Jones, 14%, 90 days	J70	800
				10	F. T. Merrick, 16%, 60 days	J74	1,000
				18	P. O. Paulson, 16%, 90 days	J76	95

Issuance of Notes for Property, Plant, and Equipment The following example illustrates the recording of notes payable in the acquisition of property, plant, and equipment.

Assume that on July 10, 1987, the Ace Company buys from the Triangle Machine Company a bookkeeping machine at a cost of $4,000; the creditor agrees to take a 90-day, 16 percent note for the purchase price.[6] This transaction is recorded as follows:

1987 Jul.	10	Office Equipment..................................	4,000	
		Notes Payable..................................		4,000
		To record the purchase of a bookkeeping machine and the issuance of a 16%, 90-day note to the Triangle Machine Company.		

On October 8, 1987, the payment of the note and interest to the Triangle Machine Company is recorded as follows:[7]

1987 Oct.	8	Notes Payable..................................	4,000	
		Interest Expense..................................	160	
		Cash..................................		4,160
		To record payment of a 16%, 90-day note and interest to the Triangle Machine Company.		

---

[6]Sometimes plant assets are purchased with a note having no interest rate. In this case, the face of the note unquestionably includes an element of interest. *APB Opinion No. 21* requires that such notes be discounted to their present value using a current realistic borrowing rate of interest.

[7]To simplify illustrations, the general journal form of entry is used, even though most companies would actually use special journals. The amount of interest is calculated as $4,000 × 0.16 × 90/360 = $160 (see Figure 4–10).

Issuance of Notes for Merchandise
When interest rates are high, a business may be required to use notes if payment for merchandise purchased is delayed. These transactions may be recorded as were those in the preceding section. However, since the volume of business done with a particular supplier or customer must be known for managerial purposes, such as applying for any available discounts based upon quantity purchased, the accounts payable subsidiary ledger account should show the total history of all transactions with a particular firm. To supply this information, the accountant should record all merchandise purchases involving notes through the Accounts Payable account and the individual creditors' accounts in the accounts payable subsidiary ledger. For example, assume that on October 11, 1987, the Ace Company purchases merchandise costing $3,600 from the Boone Company and issues a 16 percent, 45-day note to the creditor. The note and interest are paid on November 25, 1987. These transactions are recorded as follows:

1987				
Oct.	11	Purchases..	3,600	
		Accounts Payable....................................		3,600
		To record merchandise purchased:		
		Boone Company....................... $3,600		
	11	Accounts Payable..	3,600	
		Notes Payable...		3,600
		To record the issuance of a 16%, 45-day note:		
		Boone Company....................... $3,600		
Nov.	25	Notes Payable...	3,600	
		Interest Expense..	72	
		Cash..		3,672
		To record payment of note and interest to Boone Company.		

Issuance of Notes in Settlement of Open Accounts
A firm may issue a note to an open-account creditor as a means of further postponing payment, or a creditor may require a debtor to give a note if the account is past due. The entry for the issuance of a note in settlement of an open account payable is similar to the second entry above, dated October 11.

Issuance of Notes to Borrow from Banks
A business faced with the possibility of losing cash discounts may find it advantageous to borrow money from a bank to pay the open accounts within the discount periods. A 2/10, n/30 cash discount, for example, represents an annual cost saving of 36 percent, as was illustrated in Chapter 6. It is a sound financial decision to borrow money at the interest rate of 16 percent, for example, to prevent the loss of a 36 percent cost saving.

Banks and other grantors of credit handle notes in two ways:

1. Money may be borrowed on a note *bearing interest on face value,* in which case the borrower receives the face value of the note and pays the face value plus the accumulated interest on the maturity date.

2. Money may be advanced on a note issued for maturity value (the amount to be paid) which includes interest. This type of note is referred to by bankers as a note discounted to maturity. In this book, it is called a *note payable discounted on face value.* This kind of note is sometimes erroneously called a noninterest-bearing note. This seems to be a misleading description since interest, or *discount,* is deducted in advance, and the borrower receives only the discounted value. At the maturity date, the borrower pays the face value of the note, which includes the interest. The element of interest is present in either case; the difference is primarily one of form.

The amount of the discount on a note is the difference between its value on the date of discount and its value at maturity. **Maturity value**, the amount that will be paid at maturity, is the principal plus total interest for the life of the note. Since discount and interest are similar in that each represents the charge for the use of money, the Interest Expense account is used in this text to record the *incurred* portion of expense for each of these items.

Bank discount

Bank discount *may be defined as a deduction made from a gross future sum (the discount is computed on maturity value) to arrive at the current present value of that sum.*

Issuance of Note Bearing Interest on Face Value   On March 1, 1987, the Ace Company borrowed $12,000 from the First National Bank, issuing a 16 percent, 60-day note, and on April 30 paid the bank for the note and interest. The issuance and payment of the note are recorded in the Ace Company's books as follows.[8]

1987				
Mar.	1	Cash..	12,000	
		Notes Payable..		12,000
		To record a 16%, 60-day note issued to the First National Bank.		
Apr.	30	Notes Payable.......................................	12,000	
		Interest Expense.....................................	320	
		Cash		12,320
		To record payment of a 16%, 60-day note issued to the First National Bank.		

Issuance of Note Payable Discounted on Face Value   Also on May 1, 1987, the Ace Company borrowed money from the City National Bank, discounting on face value its own $12,000, 60-day note at the discount rate of 16 percent. The amount of cash received in this case is $11,680, or $12,000 minus a discount of $320. The amount of bank discount is computed by applying the discount rate to the maturity value (the face value for this type of

---

[8]From Figure 4–10, $I = PRT$, and $\$12,000 \times 0.16 \times \dfrac{60}{360} = \$320$.

note) for the discount period of 60 days. The following entry is made in the Ace Company's books to record the initial borrowing:

| 1987
May | 1 | Cash.................................
Discount on Notes Payable..................
    Notes Payable...........................
      To record a note issued to City National Bank discounted on
      face value at 16% for 60 days. | 11,680
320 |

12,000 |

The $320 discount is debited to Discount on Notes Payable because the note is written for the maturity value.[9] The interest element is deducted when the borrowing takes place. Since this is a form of discounting, the account is properly called Discount on Notes Payable. It should *not* be called Prepaid Interest, because the interest is not paid until the note matures. At that time, the net amount borrowed of $11,680 plus interest of $320 is paid as is now illustrated.

At the maturity date, June 30, 1987, a journal entry could be made recognizing that the interest element of $320 has now become an incurred expense in the following manner:

| 1987
Jun. | 30 | Interest Expense.........................
    Discount on Notes Payable................
      To recognize the incurrence of interest expense. | 320 |
320 |

The foregoing entry is an adjusting entry and *could be postponed* to the end of the period and made when regular adjusting entries are made. It is made

---

[9]If the maturity date of the note falls within the current accounting period and thus all of the discount will be an expense by the time the books are closed, an acceptable alternative to the May 1, 1987, entry would be:

| 1987
May | 1 | Cash.....................
Interest Expense.............
    Notes Payable...............
      To record a note issued to City National
      Bank discounted on face value at 16% for
      60 days. | 11,680
320 |

12,000 |

In this case, no adjustment is required. The payment is simply recorded at face value as illustrated above.

here to reinforce the nature of the expense item. After this entry is made, the only remaining entry is the one to record the payment of the principal amount of the note. It is:

1987				
Jun.	30	Notes Payable	12,000	
		Cash		12,000
		To record payment of a discounted note to the City National Bank.		

If the Ace Company had issued the note on December 16, 1987, and the books were closed on December 31, 1987, an adjusting entry would have to be made transferring 15/60, or 1/4, of the discount amount to interest expense. Then at maturity in 1988, the remaining part of the discount could be recognized as an expense at the time the principal amount of the note is paid. (Alternatively, the remaining 45/60, or 3/4, of the discount could be transferred to Interest Expense as a regular adjusting entry at the end of the year.)

Discount on notes payable should be shown in the balance sheet as a contra account to (subtracted from) notes payable under current liabilities. Thus, on the date of issuance of the note, the carrying value indicates the net amount of funds received from creditors on the note. Later, as adjustments are made to the Discount on Notes Payable account, the difference between the Notes Payable account and the balance of the Discount on Notes Payable account shows the net amount borrowed plus accrued interest on that amount.

Effective Interest Calculation   In both the March 1 and May 1 bank loans, the amount paid at maturity was $320 more than the amount received from the bank by the borrower. However, the borrower had the use of $12,000, or the full face value of the note bearing interest on face value (March 1 bank loan), whereas only $11,680 was available from the discounted note. The **annual effective interest rate** (i in the following equation) on a discounted note may be computed by the following formula:

$$i = \frac{D}{P} \times \frac{360}{T}$$

where

D = The amount of the discount.
P = The net proceeds.
360 = Days in the year.
T = The term of the note in days.

The annual effective interest rate in the example thus is not 16 percent; rather it is 16.44 percent, calculated as follows:[10]

$$i = \frac{\$320}{\$11,680} \times \frac{360}{60} = 0.1643836 \text{ or } 16.44\%.$$

The annual effective interest rate is also called the annual percentage rate or APR. Accountants should carefully determine the APR of a loan, since this is relevant to making any short-term financial decision.

End-of-Period Adjusting Entries for Interest on Notes Payable

Since interest is incurred daily throughout the life of a note payable, it is necessary to make adjusting entries for the interest expense on those notes payable that are written in one accounting period and mature in a later accounting period. Two kinds of adjustments can arise: (1) the accrual of interest on a note payable bearing interest on its face, and (2) the expense apportionment on a discounted note payable. The first type of adjustment, accrual of interest on a note payable bearing interest on its face is explained and illustrated in Chapter 4 on page 172. The second type of adjustment, expense apportionment on a discounted note payable, is discussed in this chapter on page 386. It is important that both types of adjustments be carefully made for all notes outstanding at the end of an accounting period to cause expense realization in the appropriate accounting period. Discussed next is the topic Notes Receivable, which uses many of the same concepts developed in this section.

Notes Receivable

Many firms accept promissory notes from customers; these are recorded in an account entitled **Notes Receivable**. They may then discount these notes at (same as selling to) financial institutions as a means of obtaining short-term funds. The accounting for notes receivable is similar to that for notes payable. Hence, a pattern similar to that used in the foregoing section to describe notes payable is followed in the discussion of notes receivable.

Recording Procedures Involving Notes Receivable

Many businesses require promissory notes in sales of merchandise on credit. These businesses include firms selling high-priced durable goods such as furniture, farm machinery, and automobiles. Notes receivable are also received by a financial institution when it lends money.

It is perhaps even more important to keep good accounting records for notes receivable than it is for notes payable. The payee of a note payable will send a statement to the maker that a note is due, so there is little danger that

---

[10]Under the *Truth in Lending Law,* this rate would probably be stated as 16.5 percent since the law permits the credit grantor to round the APR to the nearest quarter of a percent.

the maker will overlook the due date. The holder of notes receivable must have the records arranged so that he or she can notify the debtor that the note is due.

All notes receivable are usually recorded in a single general ledger account. In a business that accepts only a few notes, the name of the maker, the term, and the interest rate can be displayed in the explanation column of the account. If a business accepts a large number of notes, a file of notes receivable serves as a subsidiary notes receivable ledger. The Notes Receivable account of the Travis Armour Company is shown here.

Notes Receivable — Acct. No. 111

1987					1987				
Nov.	1	C. Anson, 45 days, 16%	J51	775	Dec.	16	C. Anson (paid)	CR20	775
Dec.	20	B. Barker, 90 days, 17%	J60	425					
	20	L. Watts, 60 days, 16%	J60	500					

Each debit posting indicates that an asset, Notes Receivable, has been acquired from a customer. The credit entry indicates that a particular note has been settled by payment. Credits will also be recorded if a note has been dishonored (not paid) or renewed (matured and replaced by a new note).

If the information is not provided in the Explanation column of the Notes Receivable account, then it must be provided in some supplementary records for use in later accounting, such as adjustments. For example, if the volume of transactions warrants it, a special notes receivable register could be created. Debit and credit money columns could be inserted, along with memorandum columns for supplementary information. Such a file is easily stored on computer media. This register could serve as both a journal and a subsidiary record of notes receivable. Some specific types of notes receivable transactions are discussed next.

Receipt of a Note for a Sale   Assume that on March 3, 1987, the Potter Company sells merchandise to John Rawson and receives a 16 percent, 90-day note for $1,300. The following entries are made:

1987				
Mar.	3	Accounts Receivable	1,300	
		Sales		1,300
		To record sale of merchandise:		
		John Rawson $1,300		
	3	Notes Receivable	1,300	
		Accounts Receivable		1,300
		To record the receipt of a 16%, 90-day note:		
		John Rawson $1,300		

The first entry is made so that the customer's account in the accounts receivable subsidiary ledger will contain a complete record of all credit sales transactions. This information is useful to management in making decisions about collection efforts and further extension of credit.

On June 1, 1987, when the Potter Company receives payment in full from John Rawson, the following entry is made:

1987				
Jun.	1	Cash..	1,352	
		Notes Receivable....................................		1,300
		Interest Earned......................................		52
		To record receipt of payment from John Rawson for note and interest due today.		

The amount of interest earned is $52 = (\$1,300 \times 0.16 \times 90/360)$. The Interest Earned account is a revenue account. Its balance is closed to the Income Summary account at the end of the accounting period.

Receipt of a Note in Settlement of an Open Account Because of the interest cost of money to replace inventories, it is normal to require customers to give notes if open accounts are not paid on time. The entry for such notes is in the same form as the second journal entry on March 3 in the Potter Company illustration in the previous section.

Dishonor of a Note Receivable by the Maker

If a note cannot be collected at maturity, it is said to be a **dishonored note**, or the maker is said to have **defaulted** on the note. If the maturity date of a note passes without the note being collected, an entry should be made transferring the face value of the note plus any uncollected accrued interest to the Accounts Receivable account.

Assume that on June 1, 1987, Ronald Raymond issued a 16 percent, 90-day note for $4,000 to the Potter Company. At the maturity date, August 30, 1987, Raymond fails to pay the amount of the note and interest, at which time the following entry is made on the books of the Potter Company:

1987				
Aug.	30	Accounts Receivable................................	4,160	
		Notes Receivable....................................		4,000
		Interest Earned......................................		160
		To record the dishonor of a 16%, 90-day note: Ronald Raymond.................... $4,160		

Two questions arise in connection with this entry: (1) Why should $160 be recognized as revenue and credited to the Interest Earned account? (2) Why should the item be allowed to remain as a valid account receivable?

Under the accrual concept, the interest has been earned. It represents a valid claim against the maker of the note; if the face of the note is collectible, then so is the interest. This leads to the answer to the second question. The fact that a note is not collected at its maturity is not a definite indication that it will never be collected. In the absence of evidence to the contrary most business firms assume that notes will ultimately be collected. If the amounts involved are material, all possible steps, including legal action, will certainly be taken to collect both accounts and notes receivable, and only after such steps have failed will an account be considered to be written off as a loss.

End-of-Period Adjusting Entries for Interest on Notes Receivable

The adjusting entries for interest on notes receivable parallel the adjusting entries for interest on notes payable. The primary purpose is accurate measurement of the revenue, Interest Earned, and the asset, Accrued Interest Receivable. The end-of-period accrual of interest on notes receivable is explained and illustrated in Chapter 4 on page 170. The payee of a note receivable discounted to maturity at face value usually uses an Unearned Interest account to record discount withheld but not earned. To ensure the proper revenue recognition at the end of the accounting period, this account must be apportioned between unearned interest and interest earned. The journal entry follows the pattern for adjustment described earlier in this chapter for the Discount on Notes Payable account.

The negotiability of notes raises an additional accounting issue, the discounting of customers' notes receivable. This topic is discussed next.

Discounting Customers' Notes Receivable

For a business that receives a large number of notes from customers and may need to obtain cash to continue operations, it may be economically advantageous to obtain this cash by *discounting its notes receivable* at a bank rather than holding them to maturity. The bank purchases the notes for cash less a discount. If the credit rating of the firm is good, most banks will usually discount customers' notes receivable. The firm that has discounted the note—having previously endorsed it—must make payment to the bank if the maker fails to pay.

Contingent liability

A potential obligation on the part of the endorser such as the one described above requiring the endorser to pay a dishonored note is an example of a **contingent liability**

Determining the Cash Proceeds
As far as the bank is concerned, it is making a loan to the discounter based on the maturity value of the note (which includes interest) because that is the amount the bank will collect from the maker at the maturity date. The discount the bank deducts is based on a bank discount rate applied to maturity value for the remaining period the note has to run. The discount subtracted from the maturity value yields a

balance representing **cash proceeds** to be received by the discounter. To compute the proceeds of a discounted note:

1. Determine the maturity value (the principal plus the total interest to maturity).

2. Find the discount period (the number of days the note still has to run after the date of the discount).

3. Compute the discount on the maturity value at the stipulated bank discount rate for the discount period.

4. Deduct the discount from the maturity value to find the cash proceeds.

This approach may be stated as:

$$P = MV - (MV \times d \times RL)$$

where

P = The cash proceeds.
MV = The maturity value.
d = The rate of discount.
RL = The remaining life of the note

Assume that on April 19, 1987, the Fuller Company receives from Edward Grande a 16 percent, 60-day note for $6,000 in settlement of a past-due open account. This transaction is recorded as follows:

1987				
Apr.	19	Notes Receivable	6,000.00	
		Accounts Receivable		6,000.00
		To record receipt of a 16%, 60-day note in settlement of a past-due open account:		
		Edward Grande $6,000		

On May 1, 1987, the Fuller Company, needing short-term funds, decides to discount Grande's note at the bank's rate of 15 percent. Calculation of the proceeds follows:

1. Maturity value of note:
    Face value $6,000
    Total interest to maturity 160 $6,160.00
2. Due date . . . . June 18
3. Period of discount:
    May 1–May 31 (not counting May 1) . . . . . . 30 days
    June 1–June 18 (including June 18) . . . . . . 18 days
                                                    48 days
4. Discount at 15% for 48 days on the maturity value:
    $6,160 × 0.15 × 48/360 . . . .   123.20
    Net cash proceeds $6,036.80

Recording the Proceeds The entry on the Fuller Company's books to record the discounting of the Grande note is:

1987 May	1	Cash...
		  Notes Receivable Discounted....................
		  Interest Earned...............................
		    To record the discounting of Edward Grande's 16%, 60-day
		    note at the bank at 15%.
			6,036.80	6,000.00
				36.80

The **Notes Receivable Discounted** account is used to indicate that the Fuller Company, having endorsed the note before turning it over to the bank, is now obligated to pay the bank if Grande fails to do so. That is, the Fuller Company must pay the $6,000 contingent liability plus the $160 interest at 16 percent for 60 days, plus any **protest fee** (the charge made by the bank for notifying the last endorser that the maker has failed to pay the amount of the note and interest). The obligation assumed by the Fuller Company is contingent on Grande's failure to pay and the account is therefore referred to as a **contingent liability account**. The Notes Receivable Discounted account brings the existence of the contingent liability to the attention of the reader of the balance sheet. Grande does not need to be informed that the note has been discounted, and no entry is required on his books. His obligation to pay the maturity value of the note on its presentation by the legal owner remains unchanged.

Full disclosure

In preparing financial statements, **full disclosure** *of all essential facts such as contingent liabilities is of paramount importance.*

Presentation on the Balance Sheet Assume that on May 31 the Notes Receivable account shows a balance of $17,500 (including the $6,000 note discounted on May 1). The balance sheet prepared on that date may disclose the existence of the contingent liability on the balance sheet, as follows:

FULLER COMPANY
Partial Balance Sheet
May 31, 1987

Assets

Current assets:		
Notes receivable................................	$17,500	
Deduct: Notes receivable discounted...............	6,000	
Net notes receivable...........................		$11,500

An alternative method of disclosure is to show only the undiscounted amount on the face of the balance sheet with a footnote to describe the contingent liability. If the alternative is chosen, the financial statements would appear as follows:

FULLER COMPANY
Partial Balance Sheet
May 31, 1987

Assets

Current assets:
  Notes receivable (see Note 6) $11,500

Note 6: The company is contingently liable for notes receivable discounted in the amount of $6,000.

Elimination of Contingent Liability On the maturity date, an entry is made to eliminate the contingent liability as follows:

1987				
Jun.	18	Notes Receivable Discounted	6,000	
		Notes Receivable		6,000
		To eliminate the contingent liability on Grande's note, which was discounted on May 1, 1987.		

As of this date, the contingent liability is eliminated because payment has been made by the maker of the note, or the contingent liability becomes a real liability as described below. Also, as of this date a valid negotiable instrument—a note receivable—ceases to exist.

Payment of a Discounted Note The bank normally does not notify the discounter of payment by the maker. Therefore, if notification of dishonor is not received from the bank, it is assumed that the maker has paid the note at the maturity date, and the discounter is released from the contingent liability. Since an entry recording the elimination of the contingent liability was made on the maturity date, no further accounting is required.

Nonpayment of a Discounted Note If Edward Grande dishonors the note at the maturity date, the bank must follow a certain formal procedure involving the preparation of notarized protest documents to establish the legal basis for the collection of the full amount from the Fuller Company. Since this procedure usually requires a few days and technically a negotiable instrument ceases to exist on the maturity date (whether it is paid or not), the entry to eliminate the contingent liability as of the maturity date should be made as described above.

On June 21, 1987, assume that the bank advises that Grande has defaulted and charges a protest fee of $8. The following entries are made on the Fuller

Company's books when the company pays the bank the face value of the note, the interest, and the protest fee:

1987				
Jun.	21	Accounts Receivable	6,168	
		Cash		6,168
		To record payment of Edward Grande's note, which was discounted and is now dishonored:		
		Protest fee . . . . $ 8		
		Interest 160		
		Face value 6,000		
		Total debited in subsidiary ledger to:		
		Edward Grande $6,168		

Observe that *Accounts Receivable,* instead of Notes Receivable Discounted, is debited in the entry recording the cash payment. The Notes Receivable Discounted account was debited when the contingent liability was removed on June 18, 1987.

The fact that a note is dishonored does not mean that it will be definitely uncollectible or that it should be written off as a loss. Grande, in this case, may pay at a later date, either voluntarily or on a court order. The account remains open in the general ledger and the accounts receivable subsidiary ledger until it is settled or definitely determined to be uncollectible and written off.

Internal Control: Notes Receivable

Notes receivable are negotiable instruments; the term **negotiable** indicates that ownership can be transferred to a person or corporation other than the original payee. If the note is payable to bearer, ownership can be transferred simply by delivery. If payable to a specific payee, ownership is transferred by endorsement and delivery. Types of endorsements include: (1) **blank endorsement** (signature on reverse by payee), (2) **full endorsement** ("Pay to the order of . . . "), or (3) **qualified endorsement** (signature of payee and phrase "without recourse" on reverse).[11] Because of their negotiability, notes receivable should be the focus of internal control measures similar to those used for checks.

Among the important internal control measures in the corporation are the following:

☐ Written procedures for receipt, recording, and physical security of notes receivable. These should provide for separation of duties.

---

[11] A note endorsed "without recourse" leaves the endorser with no liability to pay upon dishonor by the maker.

- Written instructions that clearly delineate who has authority to endorse notes receivable.
- A filing/records system to ensure that action is taken to collect notes when they reach maturity.
- Unannounced examinations of notes receivable records and comparison with the actual file of notes to verify that they agree. This is often a part of the function known as *internal auditing*.
- Proper security to prevent unauthorized access to computerized records of notes receivable. This involves the use of special passwords to gain access to the file and periodic changing of those passwords.

Glossary

Aging A method of classifying individual receivables by age groups, according to time elapsed from due date.

Aging schedule A columnar work sheet showing the individual receivables by age groups, according to time elapsed from due date. The individual age groups are also totaled, and a percentage analysis is computed to aid in determining the allowance for doubtful accounts.

Allowance for Doubtful Accounts A valuation account contra to accounts receivable showing the amount of estimated uncollectible accounts as of a given date.

Annual effective interest rate The correct interest rate computed on only the remaining balance of an unpaid debt for the specific time period, usually stated as an annual fraction.

Bad Debts Expense An expense account showing the estimated uncollectible credit sales made in a given time period (for one year if the accounting period is a year) or actual write-offs if the direct write-off method is used.

Bad Debts Recovered A revenue account that is credited for the recovery of an account receivable previously written off under the direct write-off method.

Balance sheet approach A method of estimating the adjusted amount that is needed in the Allowance for Doubtful Accounts; the estimate is based on the balance sheet item, accounts receivable.

Bank discount An amount subtracted from a maturity value to determine net cash proceeds as of the present time.

Blank endorsement The signature of the owner on the back of a negotiable instrument; the endorsement guarantees the validity of the instrument and warrants its payment in case of dishonor by the maker at maturity.

Cash proceeds The amount of cash that is received when a firm discounts a note at a bank.

Contingent liability An amount that may become a liability in the future *if* certain events occur.

Contingent liability account An account in which a contingent liability is recorded. (See *Contingent liability*.)

Credit balances in customer accounts A liability item representing the amounts due customers because of overpayment or a sales return made after payment had been made.

Credit card sales slip A signed voucher prepared from a sale on a credit card. The item substantiates the sale and serves as an invoice.

Defaulted Having failed to pay the amount owed on a negotiable instrument at its maturity. (See *Dishonored note.*)

Dishonored note A note that has not been paid by the maker at the maturity date.

Full disclosure A concept requiring that all essential facts about an item (or activity) be shown in applicable financial statements. An example is the disclosure of contingent liabilities.

Income statement approach A method of estimating the bad debts expense for a given period; the estimate is based on an income statement item, sales.

Matching standard A basic standard in accounting which requires that incurred expenses of a given period be offset against earned revenue of that same period to determine net income.

Maturity value The amount payable (or receivable) on a negotiable instrument at its maturity date; it includes face value plus any stated interest.

Negotiable A characteristic of a document that permits it to be transferred for value received by endorsement to another person.

Net realizable value The estimated collectible amount of accounts receivable.

Nontrade receivable A receivable arising from a source other than sales of merchandise or sales of ordinary services.

Note bearing interest on face value A note with a specified interest rate with interest to be paid at maturity in addition to the face value of the note.

Notes payable Amount payable to creditors supported by formal written promises to pay.

Notes receivable Claims against individuals or companies supported by formal written promises to pay; a note receivable may be either a trade note or a nontrade note.

Notes Receivable Discounted An account that discloses the contingent liability for customers' notes which have been discounted.

Promissory note An unconditional written promise to pay a specified sum of money to the order of a designated person, or to bearer, at a fixed or determinable future time or on demand.

Protest fee A fee charged by a bank or financial institution for a note which is dishonored (not paid) at maturity.

Qualified endorsement An endorsement accompanied by the phrase "without recourse" that tends to relieve the endorser of any further liability.

Receivables turnover A ratio of the net credit sales to the average accounts receivable.

Simple interest Interest on the original principal only.

Trade receivable Claim against a customer arising from sale of merchandise or sale of ordinary services.

Valuation account A contra account—one that is related to and offsets, in whole or in part, one or more other accounts. A contra asset account should be deducted from the asset to which it is related to determine a carrying or book value.

Questions

Q9–1 (a) What is the function of the Allowance for Doubtful Accounts account? (b) What methods may be used to estimate its amount? (c) How is this account shown on the balance sheet?

Q9–2 What is the difference between the income statement approach and the balance sheet approach in estimating bad debts expense? What are the advantages and disadvantages of each?

Q9–3 What kind of account (asset, liability, expense, and so on) is Allowance for Doubtful Accounts? Is its normal balance a debit or a credit? What action is taken if its normal balance becomes negative?

Q9–4 The Rockwood Company, which had Accounts Receivable of $75,822 and an Allowance for Doubtful Accounts of $3,814 on January 1, 1987, wrote off a past due account of Mark Slater in 1987 for $680.
a. What effect will the write-off have on the total current assets of the company? Why?
b. What effect will the write-off have on 1987 net income? Why?

Q9–5 A company systematically adjusts its Allowance for Doubtful Accounts at the end of each year by adding a fixed percent of the year's sales minus sales returns and allowances. After five years, the credit balance of the Allowance for Doubtful Accounts has become disproportionately large in relationship to the balance in Accounts Receivable. What are two possible explanations for the large balance?

Q9–6 Credit card sales on other than bank credit cards basically result in two different types of accounting. Why?

Q9–7 How does the valuation of receivables arising from nonbank credit card sales differ from the valuation of other trade receivables?

Q9–8 (a) What are some reasons for credit balances occurring in individual accounts receivable accounts? (b) How are such balances presented in the balance sheet?

Q9–9 Discuss the internal control procedures applicable to accounts receivable.

Q9–10 The Jamison Company had a debit balance in its Allowance for Doubtful Accounts account before adjustments. Does this mean an error has been made? Discuss.

Q9–11 Define interest. How is interest similar to rent?

Q9–12 What is the meaning of APR? Why is APR significant?

Q9–13 What is a negotiable promissory note? What does the term "negotiable" indicate?

Q9–14 Discuss the managerial factors that a company must consider in determining what method of short-term financing should be used.

Q9–15 Describe briefly how a person can calculate the effective annual interest rate (APR) on a note discounted at the bank. Give an example.

Q9–16 Is it better for a company to borrow money on a note discounted at a bank at 16 percent or on a note bearing interest on the face at 16 percent? Explain.

Q9–17 Explain the following terms:
a. Discounting a note
b. Bank discount rate
c. Contingent liability
d. Proceeds
e. Maturity value
f. A dishonored note.

Q9–18 The following account balances appear in the general ledger of the Hardison Company:

Notes Receivable		Notes Payable	
87,500			50,000

Notes Receivable Discounted	
	37,500

a. What is the amount of customers' notes outstanding?
b. What amount of customers' notes are in the Hardison Company's possession?
c. What amount of customers' notes have been discounted?
d. What is the Hardison Company's contingent liability on discounted notes?
e. How would these accounts be shown in the balance sheet?

Q9–19 Why should the Notes Receivable Discounted account and the Notes Receivable account be eliminated at maturity date regardless of whether a discounted note is paid or not?

Q9–20 (a) What is a contingent liability? (b) Can there be more than one person contingently liable on a particular note? Explain. (c) What amounts must a person who is contingently liable on an interest-bearing note pay if the maker dishonors the note on its due date?

Exercises

E9–1
Balance sheet classification of receivables

The Abelson Company had the following items in its adjusted trial balance as of December 31, 1987:

Account Title	Debits	Credits
Accounts Receivable	$60,000	
Accounts Receivable, Credit Cards	10,000	
Mortgage Notes Receivable	52,000	
Allowance for Doubtful Accounts		$1,250
Accrued Interest on Mortgage Notes Receivable[a]	1,750	
Notes Receivable, Officers[b]	18,500	

[a]The mortgage notes receivable mature on October 1, 1995. The interest, however, is paid each April 1 and October 1.

[b]These three-year-old notes are demand notes but they are expected to remain outstanding indefinitely.

1. Prepare a partial balance sheet showing how you recommend that the foregoing should be reported using generally accepted accounting principles.
2. Explain why you classified each item as you did.

E9–2
Journalizing accounts written off and bad debts expense

The Stallion Company, which uses an Allowance for Doubtful Accounts, had the following transactions involving worthless accounts in 1987 and 1988:

1987

Dec. 31 Recorded bad debts expense of $12,600.

1988

Apr. 23 Wrote off Fran Noody's account of $6,300 as uncollectible.
Jun. 12 Wrote off Marsh Toms's account of $1,320 as uncollectible.
Aug. 1 Recovered 50 cents on the dollar from Marsh Toms.

Journalize the transactions.

E9–3
Recording bad debts expense by use of allowance method

The Youngsville Company had sales on credit of $965,000 during 1987 with accounts receivable of $97,800 and a credit balance of $300 in Allowance for Doubtful Accounts at the end of the year. Record the bad debts expense for the year, using each of the following methods for the estimate:

1. Allowance for doubtful accounts is to be increased to 4 percent of accounts receivable.

(continued on next page)

2. Bad debts expense is estimated to be 0.48 percent of sales on credit.
3. Allowance for doubtful accounts is to be increased to $6,058, as indicated by an aging schedule.

E9–4
Recording bad debts expense, write-off, and balance sheet presentation

The trial balance of the Levin Company included the following accounts on June 30, 1987, the end of the company's fiscal year:

Accounts Receivable	$ 95,800
Allowance for Doubtful Accounts (credit)	450
Sales	624,500

Uncollectible accounts are estimated at 4.8 percent of accounts receivable.

1. Make the adjusting entry to record the bad debts expense.
2. Show the presentation of accounts receivable and allowance for doubtful accounts in the June 30, 1987, balance sheet.
3. Give the entry to write off the account of an insolvent customer, Samuel David, for $1,310 on July 3, 1987.
4. Determine the net realizable value of accounts receivable immediately before and after the write-off of David's account.

E9–5
Computing cash received from customers

The Cash account page in the general ledger of the Xanadu Company has been temporarily misplaced. The following account data are available:

	December 31 1988	1987	Year 1988
Accounts Receivable, Trade	$68,400	$57,200	
Allowance for Doubtful Accounts	5,015	3,945	
Sales			$585,000
Sales Discounts			9,750

During 1988 accounts receivable of $3,850 were written off as uncollectible, and one account of $700, written off in 1987, was collected and recorded in the following manner:

Accounts Receivable	700	
Allowance for Doubtful Accounts		700
Cash	700	
Accounts Receivable		700

Compute the cash received from customers during 1988.

E9–6
Interpreting various receivable accounting (using special journals)

The JR Company uses a cash receipts journal, a cash payments journal, a single-column purchases journal, a single-column sales journal, and a two-column general journal. The Accounts Receivable account in the general ledger at June 30, 1987, is given below (posting references have been omitted):

Accounts Receivable

1987					1987			
Jun.	1	Balance	✓	47,000	Jun.	5		3,000
	25			3,030		10		250
	30			54,400		28		3,030
						30		39,500

During the month, the general journal was used to record transactions with only two customers. The subsidiary ledger accounts of these customers are shown below:

William Asserman

1987 Jun.	1	Credit balance				(600)
	6		S2	1,400		800
	10		J4		250	550

Tenneson Rhu

1987 Jun.	1	Debit balance	✓			3,000
	5	(20-day note)	J4		3,000	0
	25		CP6	3,030		3,030
	28		J4		3,030	0

1. Explain the $600 credit balance on June 1 in William Asserman's account.
2. What would the posting references (without page numbers) for the June 30 entries in the Accounts Receivable controlling account be?
3. What should be the total of the schedule of accounts receivable on June 30?
4. Explain the transaction that resulted in the debit of $3,030 on June 25 in Tenneson Rhu's account.
5. State in narrative form the transactions that resulted in each of the following credits to the Accounts Receivable controlling account: June 5, $3,000; June 10, $250; June 28, $3,030; and June 30, $39,500.

E9–7

Applying direct write-off method

The Humphrey Company uses the direct write-off method of accounting for bad debts expense. The company had the following transactions involving worthless accounts in 1987:

1987

Apr. 18 Wrote off Thomas Emmerson's account of $930 as uncollectible. The merchandise had been sold in 1986.
Jul. 25 Wrote off Darrell Damson's account of $850 as uncollectible.
Nov. 28 Recovered $650 from Thomas Emmerson.

Journalize the transactions in general journal form.

E9–8

Accounting for credit card sales

The Davidson Corporation makes sales on account only to customers who charged purchases on credit cards from the Supercard Company (a bank credit card) and the Marksman Card Company (a nonbank credit card). These two credit card companies charge a fee of 4½ and 5½ percent, respectively, for paying for these sales and collecting from the credit customers. On December 12, 1987, customers of the Davidson Corporation charged merchandise to these credit cards that totaled the following:

Supercard Company $21,200
Marksman Card Company 11,400

Journalize these sales on the books of the Davidson Corporation.

Part Two / Income Measurement and Valuation Issues

E9–9
Determining maturity value of notes

Information regarding five notes is given below:

Date of Note	Term of Note	Interest Rate	Principal
March 1, 1987	150 days	16%	$3,000
April 5, 1987	60	15	4,000
August 24, 1987	45	17	5,000
September 13, 1987	120	18	2,500
November 3, 1987	90	14	4,860

Determine the maturity date and maturity value of each note.

E9–10
Calculating and recording accrued interest

Information regarding four notes receivable held by the Cowen Company follows:

Date of Note	Term of Note	Interest Rate	Principal
November 1, 1987	150 days	16%	$3,000
November 16, 1987	90	17	3,600
December 1, 1987	45	15	3,300
December 16, 1987	60	16	4,800

Assume that the books are closed on December 31, 1987. Compute and journalize the total amount of simple interest that should be debited to the Accrued Interest Receivable account.

E9–11
Recording notes payable discounted

The following were among the transactions of the Stephen Company for 1987 and 1988:

1987

Aug. 3   Issued its own 90-day note, made out to the Bank of Winthrop in the maturity amount of $12,000, and discounted it at a rate of 16 percent.
Nov. 1   Paid the Bank of Winthrop the amount due.
Dec. 1   Issued its own 90-day note, made out to the Bank of Jamestown in the maturity amount of $15,000, and discounted it at a rate of 15 percent.

1988

Feb. 29   Paid the amount due the Bank of Jamestown.

1. Journalize the transactions, including all necessary adjusting entries. Assume books are closed each December 31.
2. Prepare a partial balance sheet as of December 31, 1987 reflecting the account balances related to the note issued to the Bank of Jamestown.

E9–12
Recording notes payable transactions with interest on face value

The following were among the transactions of the Elfland Company for 1987 and 1988:

1987

Jan. 2   Purchased $6,000 of merchandise from the Emmerson Company and issued a 16 percent, 45-day note.
Feb. 16   Paid note and interest due the Emmerson Company.
Mar. 15   Issued a 15 percent, 90-day note to the Franks Company in settlement of an open account of $9,000.
Jun. 13   Paid the Franks Company $4,000 on principal and all the interest for the preceding 90 days; issued a new 16 percent, 60-day note for the balance of the principal.
Aug. 12   Paid the remaining amount due the Franks Company.
Dec. 1   Issued a 17 percent, 90-day note to the Zelda Company in settlement of an open account of $12,000.

9 / Current Receivables and Payables

1988

Feb. 29 Paid the amount due the Zelda Company.

1. Journalize the transactions, including any necessary adjusting entries on December 31, 1987.
2. Prepare a partial balance sheet as of December 31, 1987, reflecting the account balances related to the Zelda Company note.

E9–13
Recording notes receivable transactions

The following were among the transactions of the Haw River Corporation for 1987 and 1988:

1987

Apr. 19	Sold merchandise for $3,000 to René Burstaw and received a 16 percent, 60-day note.
Jun. 18	Collected the amount due from Burstaw.
21	Received a 17 percent, 120-day note from Roger Camero in settlement of an open account for $4,500.
Oct. 19	Roger Camero dishonored his note.
Nov. 15	Received a 15 percent, 90-day note from Lilly Dulane in settlement of an open account of $3,600.

1988

Feb. 13 Collected the note and interest frum Dulane.

Journalize the transactions, including any necessary adjusting entries on December 31, 1987.

E9–14
Discounting a customer's note receivable: paid by customer

Gupta Company completed the following transactions in 1987 and 1988:

1987

Aug. 1	Sold $1,200 of merchandise on account to the Owens Company.
Oct. 8	Received a 90-day, 16 percent note in full settlement of the Owens account.
Dec. 5	Discounted the above note at 15 percent at the Bank of Andover.

1988

Jan. 6 The October 8 note was paid at maturity.

Journalize the transactions on the books of Gupta Company and Owens Company, including any necessary adjusting entries on December 31, 1987.

E9–15
Discounting a customer's note receivable: dishonored by customer

On September 5, 1987, the Dunstan Company sold $5,400 of merchandise on account to Berne Company and received a 16 percent, 90-day note. This note was discounted at 15 percent on October 20, 1987, at the Foxhall Bank. At maturity date, the note was dishonored by Berne Company, and the Dunstan Company paid the maturity value plus a $10 protest fee. Journalize the transactions on the books of the Dunstan Company.

A Problems

P9–1A
Recording over a three-year period

The Allowance for Doubtful Accounts account at the St. Paul Company shows a credit balance of $950 on December 31, 1986, before adjustments are made. The bad debts expense for 1986 is estimated to be 3 percent of the sales on credit of $435,200 for the year. The following transactions occurred during the next two years:

1987

May	1	Wrote off Mendota Company's account of $8,600 as uncollectible.
Oct.	15	Wrote off Fort Snelling Company's account of $4,950 as uncollectible.
Nov.	30	Bankruptcy proceedings in Mendota Company's case were completed; received a check for 20 cents on the dollar for the account written off.
Dec.	31	An analysis of accounts receivable by aging indicated that accounts doubtful of collection amounted to $12,236. (Note that the method of estimating bad debts expense is changed.)

1988

Aug.	21	Wrote off the Falcon Heights Corporation account of $11,105 as uncollectible.
Dec.	31	Estimated that uncollectible accounts receivable totaled $13,025.

Required:

1. Record in general journal form the transactions and events (including adjusting entries) for 1986, 1987, and 1988.
2. Post to a general ledger account for Allowance for Doubtful Accounts.
3. What generally accepted accounting principle was violated when the method of estimating bad debts expense was changed? Explain.

P9–2A
Recording various accounts receivable transactions

During November and early December 1987, the Waco Corporation had the following sales and receivable transactions (all sales were made on account and, except on credit cards, carried terms of 2/10, n/30):

1987

Nov.	2	Sold merchandise to Mart, Inc. for $9,400 on invoice no. 2161.
	7	Credited Mart, Inc. for returned merchandise with an invoice price of $1,400.
	10	Sold merchandise to Bosque River Mills for $3,200 on invoice no. 2162.
	13	Received a check for $862.40 from Bosque River Mills in partial payment of invoice no. 2162. Discounts are allowed on partial payments.
	23	Received a check for the amount due from Mart, Inc.
	30	Sold merchandise to Mount Calm Sellers for $27,600 on invoice no. 2163.
	30	Summary bank credit card sales for November were $12,800; nonbank credit card sales were $14,200 (these both are normally recorded daily). A fee of 4 percent is charged for each of these sales.
	30	Estimated the bad debts expense for November to be 3.6 percent of credit sales less sales returns and allowances (excluding credit card amounts).
Dec.	8	Received a notice that Bosque River Mills had filed for bankruptcy; the balance of its account was judged to be uncollectible.

Required:

1. Journalize the transactions in general journal form.
2. Post all entries (excluding credit card sales) to the Accounts Receivable controlling account and to the accounts receivable subsidiary ledger accounts. Post credit card sales to the appropriate accounts.
3. Prepare a schedule of accounts receivable after the December 8 transaction has been posted.

P9–3A
Aging accounts receivable and recording bad debts expense

The accounts receivable subsidiary ledger of the Mobile Corporation shows the following data on December 31, 1987 (the general ledger shows a $450 credit balance in Allowance for Doubtful Accounts before adjustment):

Name of Customer	Invoice Date	Amount
Dauphin Island, Inc.	May 2, 1987	$ 2,560
Brookley Distributors	August 15, 1987	1,200
Spring Hills Company	October 20, 1987	4,300
Prichard Stores	December 8, 1987	3,900
	March 3, 1987	3,440
Satsuma Corporation	November 11, 1987	760
	November 20, 1987	480
Bon Secour, Incorporated	September 15, 1987	1,930
	July 10, 1987	1,440
Others	December 5, 1987	46,440

Terms of sale are n/30.

Required:

1. Prepare an aging schedule for accounts receivable using the categories in requirement 2.

2. Compute the estimated uncollectible accounts receivable based on the following fixed percentages:

	Estimated Percent Uncollectible
Accounts not due	1.0
Amounts past due:	
1–30 days	2.5
31–60 days	4.0
61–90 days	5.5
91–120 days	10.0
More than 120 days	35.0

3. Record the bad debts expense in general journal form.

P9–4A

Recording notes payable transactions

The Columbia Retail Store completed the following transactions during 1987 and 1988 (the fiscal year ends December 31):

1987

Jan. 2   Purchased $4,800 of merchandise from Huntsdale Wholesalers; issued a 15 percent, 60-day note.
Mar. 3   Paid the Huntsdale Wholesalers the amount due.
      3   Issued a 16 percent, 45-day note to Browns Station Company in settlement of a past-due account of $4,800.
Apr. 17   Paid Browns Station Company $3,800 on the March 3 note plus all the interest due; issued a new 15 percent, 30-day note for the balance of the principal.
May 17   Paid Browns Station Company for the April 17 note.
Jun. 1   Discounted at 16 percent its own $7,200, 30-day note payable made out to the McBaine Bank for the maturity value.
Jul. 1   Paid the McBaine Bank the amount due.
Dec. 1   Issued to the Rockport Corporation a 14 percent, 90-day note in settlement of a past-due account of $6,000.
      16   Discounted at 16 percent its own $18,000, 60-day note made out to the Englewood Bank for the maturity value.

(continued on next page)

1988

Feb.	14	Paid the Englewood Bank the amount due.
	29	Paid the amount due to Rockport Corporation for the note issued December 1, 1987.

Required: Journalize the transactions including all adjusting entries. Assume that the books are closed each December 31.

P9–5A
Recording various note transactions

During 1987, the Akron Sales Corporation completed the following transactions, among others:

1987

Jan.	3	Purchased merchandise for $6,000 from Summit Company giving a 16 percent, 30-day note, payable at the Ohio State Bank.
	4	Sold $3,000 of merchandise on account to Munroe Falls, Inc.
	6	Sold $1,500 of merchandise on account to Sawyer Company.
	8	Purchased on account merchandise for $1,800 from Cuyahoga Falls Sellers.
	10	Gave Cuyahoga Falls Sellers a 15 percent, 30-day note in settlement of the (January 8 purchase) open account, payable at the Ohio State Bank.
	12	Sawyer Company gave a 17 percent, 20-day note payable at the Buckeye Bank in settlement of its open account.
	15	Munroe Falls, Inc. gave a 16 percent, 30-day note, payable at the Ohio State Bank, in full settlement of the purchase on January 4.
	24	Sold $9,000 of merchandise to Ghent Company and received a 17 percent, 30-day note, payable at the Akron Bank.
Feb.	1	Sawyer Company's note of January 12 was dishonored.
	2	Paid Summit Company for the note due today.
	9	Paid Cuyahoga Falls Sellers for the note due today.
	14	Received payment from Munroe Falls, Inc. in settlement of their note due today.
	23	Received a check from Ghent Company for $5,000 plus interest, and accepted a new 17 percent, 30-day note, payable at the Akron Bank for the balance of the principal.
	28	Discounted at 15 percent at the Ohio State Bank, Ghent Company's note of February 23.
Mar.	25	Received notice that Ghent Company had dishonored its note of February 23. Paid the bank the maturity value of the note plus a $9 protest fee.

Required: Record the transactions in general journal form.

P9–6A
Effective interest rate and choice between alternatives

Vermillion Company needs between $95,000 and $100,000 for a 90-day period to finance a short-term project. The First National Bank has offered to extend to Vermillion a $100,000, 90-day loan on a note payable at one percentage point over the prime interest rate. (The prime rate is the rate charged by banks for loans to the most creditworthy customers; at the time of this loan, it is 13 percent). As an alternative, the First National Bank has agreed to accept a note payable with a face value of $100,000 discounted to maturity date at a bank discount rate of 13.4 percent.

Required:

1. Compute the effective interest rate in each case.
2. Which alternative is Vermillion Company's better choice assuming that the sole criterion in the choice is the cost of borrowing?
3. Assume that the bank discount rate required by the bank were 13.6 percent instead of 13.4 percent. Would you choose the same alternative as you did in 2 above? Support your answer with computations.

P9–7A

Thought-provoking problem: receivables turnover

The current assets section of the 1983 *Annual Report* of CBS Inc. is reproduced below (dollars are in thousands). Sales for the comparable years (dollars in thousands) were:

	1983	1982	1981
Broadcasting	$2,380,198	$2,158,232	$1,916,519
Products	2,078,161	1,894,039	1,942,709

CONSOLIDATED BALANCE SHEETS
CBS Inc. and subsidiaries

ASSETS

	1983	December 31 1982	1981
Current assets:			
Cash and cash equivalents:			
Cash and cash items	$ 24,150	$ 12,643	$ 1,745
Short-term marketable securities, at cost plus accrued interest (approximates market)	18,698	15,292	26,275
	42,848	27,935	28,020
Notes and accounts receivable, less allowances for doubtful accounts, returns and discounts: 1983, $146,887; 1982, $153,663; 1981, $166,567	829,604	733,521	713,331
Inventories (note 8)	295,338	306,955	306,845
Program rights and feature film productions	490,861	439,004	391,570
Prepaid expenses and other	150,885	172,084	111,393
Total current assets	**1,809,536**	**1,679,499**	**1,551,159**

Required:

1. Compute the number of days in the average collection period and the receivables turnover for 1983 and 1982. Should you add back the allowances for doubtful accounts, returns, and discounts before making this computation? Explain.

2. Comment on the differences in the two years with specific reasons as to whether they are favorable or unfavorable.

B Problems

P9–1B

Recording over a three-year period

The Allowance for Doubtful Accounts account at the Annapolis Company shows a credit balance of $2,090 on December 31, 1986, before adjustments are made. An aging analysis of accounts receivable indicates that accounts in the amount of $28,875 are doubtful of collection on December 31, 1986. The following transactions occurred during the next two years:

1987

Jun. 1	Wrote off Anne Arundel Company's account of $18,920 as uncollectible.
Oct. 21	Wrote off Severn River Corporation's account of $12,250 as uncollectible.
Nov. 30	Bankruptcy proceedings in Anne Arundel Company's case were completed; received a check for 10 cents on the dollar for the account written off.
Dec. 31	An analysis of accounts receivable indicated that accounts doubtful of collection amounted to $27,430.

1988

Aug. 27 Wrote off the Eastport Corporation account of $24,830 as uncollectible.
Dec. 31 Estimated that bad debts expense for 1988 is equal to 4 percent of credit sales of $650,000. (Note that the method of estimating bad debts expense is changed.)

Required:

1. Record in general journal form the transactions and events including adjusting entries for 1986, 1987, and 1988.
2. Post to a general ledger account for Allowance for Doubtful Accounts.
3. What generally accepted principle was violated when the method of estimating bad debts expense was changed? Explain.

P9–2B
Recording various accounts receivable transactions

During November and early December, 1987, the St. Louis Corporation had the following sales and receivable transactions (all sales were made on account and, except on credit cards, carried terms of 2/10, n/30):

1987

Nov. 3 Sold merchandise to Clayton Corporation for $20,680 on invoice no. 3561.
5 Credited Clayton Corporation for returned merchandise with an invoice price of $3,080.
12 Sold merchandise to Webster Grove Stores for $7,040 on invoice no. 3562.
13 Received a check from Webster Grove Stores for $1,176 in partial payment of invoice no. 3562. Discounts are allowed on partial payments.
23 Received a check for the amount due from Clayton Corporation.
30 Sold merchandise to Valley Park Sales for $60,720 on invoice no. 3563.
30 Summary bank credit card sales for November were $28,160; nonbank credit card sales were $31,240 (these both are recorded daily). A fee of 3.5 percent is charged for each of these sales.
30 Estimated bad debts expense for November is 4 percent of credit sales less sales returns and allowances (excluding credit card amounts).
Dec. 10 Received a notice that Webster Grove Stores had filed for bankruptcy; the balance of its account was judged to be uncollectible.

Required:

1. Journalize the transactions in general journal form.
2. Post all entries (excluding credit card sales) to the Accounts Receivable controlling account and to the accounts receivable subsidiary ledger accounts. Post credit card sales to the appropriate accounts.
3. Prepare a schedule of accounts receivable after the December 10 transaction has been posted.

P9–3B
Aging accounts receivable and recording bad debts expense

The accounts receivable subsidiary ledger of Muncie Company shows the following data on December 31, 1987 (the general ledger shows a $990 credit balance in Allowance for Doubtful Accounts before adjustment):

Name of Customer	Invoice Date	Amount
White River, Inc..	May 15, 1987	$ 5,630
Delaware Sales Shop.	August 17, 1987	2,640
Selma Company.	October 20, 1987	9,460
Daleville Company	November 10, 1987	8,580
	October 12, 1987	7,570
Cammack Energy, Inc..	November 18, 1987	1,670

Name of Customer	Invoice Date	Amount
Desoto Sales Group	November 20, 1987 September 23, 1987 August 20, 1987	1,056 4,240 3,170
Others	December 3–31, 1987 November 6–26, 1987	44,000 16,400

Terms of sale are n/30.

Required:

1. Prepare an aging schedule for accounts receivable using the categories in requirement 2.

2. Compute the estimated uncollectible accounts receivable based on the following percentages:

	Estimated Percent Uncollectible
Accounts not due	1.2
Amounts past due:	
1–30 days	2.6
31–60 days	4.5
61–90 days	5.8
91–120 days	11.5
More than 120 days	34.0

3. Record the bad debts expense in general journal form.

P9–4B
Recording notes payable transactions

The Los Angeles Mart completed the following transactions during 1987 and 1988 (the fiscal year ends on December 31):

1987

Jan. 13	Purchased $15,360 of merchandise from Orange County, Inc.; issued a 14 percent, 60-day note.
Mar. 14	Paid Orange County, Inc. the amount due.
14	Issued a 15 percent, 45-day note to Santa Monica Company in settlement of a past-due account of $15,360.
Apr. 28	Paid Santa Monica Company $10,360 on the March 14 note plus all the interest due; issued a new 14 percent, 30-day note for the balance of the principal.
May 28	Paid Santa Monica Company for the April 28 note.
Jun. 4	Discounted at a bank discount rate of 13 percent its own $24,000, 60-day note made out to the Hollywood Bank for the maturity value.
Aug. 3	Paid the Hollywood Bank the amount due.
Nov. 1	Issued to the Burbank Corporation a 13 percent, 90-day note in settlement of a past-due account of $19,200.
16	Discounted at a bank discount rate of 14 percent its own $57,600, 60-day note made out to the Beverly Hills Bank for the maturity value.

1988

Jan. 15	Paid the Beverly Hills Bank the amount due.
30	Paid the Burbank Corporation the amount due for the note issued November 1, 1987.

Required: Journalize the transactions including all adjusting entries. Assume that the books are closed each December 31.

P9–5B
Recording various note transactions

During 1987, the Southcaro Company completed the following transactions, among others:

1987

Mar. 3 Purchased merchandise from the Columbia Company for $19,200 giving a 12 percent, 30-day note payable at the Richland Bank.
   4 Sold $9,600 of merchandise to Eau Claire Corporation on account.
   6 Sold $4,800 of merchandise to College Place Shop on account.
   9 Purchased on account merchandise for $5,760 from Forest Acres Company.
   10 Gave Forest Acres Company a 13 percent, 30-day note in settlement of the (March 9 purchase) open account, payable at the Richland Bank.
   12 College Place Shop gave a 14 percent, 20-day note payable at the South Carolina National Bank in settlement of its open account (purchase of March 6).
   16 Eau Claire Corporation gave a 16 percent, 30-day note, payable at the South Carolina National Bank in full settlement of its purchase of March 4.
   25 Sold $28,800 of merchandise to White Rock Company and received a 14 percent, 30-day note, payable at the Richland Bank.
Apr. 1 College Place Shop's note of March 12 was dishonored.
   2 Paid Columbia Company for the note due today.
   9 Paid Forest Acres Company for the note due today.
   15 Received payment from Eau Claire Corporation in settlement of their note due today.
   24 Received a check from White Rock Company for $18,800 plus interest and accepted a new 15 percent, 30-day note, payable at the Richland Bank for the balance of the principal.
   30 Discounted at 15 percent at the Richland Bank, White Rock Company's note of April 24.
May 24 Received notice that White Rock Company had dishonored its note of April 24. Paid the bank the maturity value of the note plus a $12 protest fee.

Required: Record the transactions in general journal form.

P9–6B
Effective interest rate and choice between alternatives

Northern Arizona Company needs between $195,000 and $200,000 to finance a short-term project that will return enough cash to pay off the loan in 45 days. The Traders Bank has offered to extend to Northern Arizona Company a $200,000, 45-day loan at one percentage point over the prime interest rate. (The prime rate is the rate that the bank charges its most creditworthy customers; at the time of this loan, it is 12 percent). As an alternative, the Traders Bank has offered to accept a note payable with a face value of $200,000 discounted to maturity at a bank discount rate of 12.5 percent.

Required:

1. Compute the effective interest rate in each case.
2. Which alternative is Northern Arizona's better choice assuming that the sole criterion in the choice is the cost of borrowing?
3. Assume that the bank discount rate required by the bank were 12.6 percent instead of 12.5 percent. Would you choose the same alternative as in 2 above? Support your answer with computations.

P9–7B

Thought-provoking problem: allowance as a percent of accounts receivable

Reproduced below is the current assets section of the 1983 *Annual Report* of Dennison Manufacturing Company (dollars in thousands). Sales for 1983 and 1982 respectively (in thousands) were $628,659 and $577,281.

Consolidated Balance Sheet
Dennison Manufacturing Company and Subsidiaries

(in thousands) December 31	1983	1982
Assets		
Current Assets		
Cash and marketable securities	$ 27,765	$ 24,618
Trade accounts receivable, less allowance of $3,235 ($3,147 in 1982) for doubtful accounts	111,252	94,147
Inventories:		
Finished products	36,614	35,039
In process	24,618	25,747
Raw materials and supplies	28,460	32,559
	89,692	93,345
Prepaid expenses and other current assets	2,879	3,110
Total Current Assets	**231,588**	**215,220**

Required:

1. For each year, compute the allowance for doubtful accounts as a percent of accounts receivable. Do you consider the 1983 ratio to be more or less favorable than 1982?
2. Do you think these ratios were influenced by the increase in sales? Explain.

10 Measurement and Control of Inventory

Introduction

In a nonmanufacturing business, **inventory** is generally understood to mean goods owned by the business for sale to customers. Other acceptable terms are merchandise inventory or simply merchandise. Up to this point in the text, the valuation of the merchandise inventory has been specified. In Chapter 10, the journal entries for a periodic inventory system and a perpetual inventory system are compared. Then, the basis for placing a valuation on inventory is explained. This discussion leads to the development of an inventory figure necessary in the calculation of cost of goods sold on the income statement. Cost of goods sold is a significant charge against sales in determination of net income. For Dennison Manufacturing Company in 1984, it was more than 65 percent of net sales. Therefore, the determination of an inventory valuation and subsequent calculation of cost of goods sold is vital to income measurement.

Learning Goals

1. To distinguish between periodic and perpetual inventory systems.
2. To make journal entries recording transactions under each system.
3. To be able to use FIFO, LIFO, and average costing assumptions under both the periodic and the perpetual systems.
4. To record transactions on inventory record cards.
5. To compute cost of goods sold under the periodic and perpetual systems.
6. To explain the effect of various cost flow assumptions on financial statements.

7. To apply the lower-of-cost-or-market concept to the inventory valuation.

8. To use both the gross margin method and the retail method of estimating inventory valuation.

Basis of Inventory Valuation: Cost

Inventories are originally recorded at cost. The AICPA has defined **cost of an inventory item** to include all expenditures "incurred in bringing an article to its existing condition and location."[1] Cost consists of the invoice price of the merchandise (less purchases discounts) plus transportation in, insurance while in transit, and any other expenditures made by the buyer to get the merchandise to the place of business.

The determination of total cost valuation of an inventory is relatively simple when each stock item acquired can be marked and identified permanently with its specific cost. This procedure, the **specific identification method**, is possible in certain businesses—for example, with automobiles on a dealer's lot. In most businesses—say with gasoline in a service station—specific identification is not feasible. When it is not feasible, one of three cost-flow assumptions is used to assign costs. Being *assumptions* regarding flow of costs through the business, they do *not* necessarily represent the actual flow of the goods.

1. **First-in, first-out (FIFO)**. FIFO is an assumption that the cost of the oldest goods on hand is the cost of the asset given up each time a sale is made. Thus, ending inventory is composed of the cost of the newest batches of goods acquired.

2. **Last-in, first-out (LIFO)**. LIFO is an opposite assumption that the cost of the newest goods on hand is the cost of the asset given up each time a sale is made. Thus, ending inventory is composed of the cost of the oldest batches of goods.

3. **Average**. The cost of any items sold can be assumed to be a weighted average of the cost prices of that item. Ending inventory is assumed to have the same weighted average cost per item.

Each of these three cost-flow assumptions is developed in more detail in later sections of the chapter.

The method used to determine cost should be the one that "most clearly reflects periodic income."[2] In other words, the method used should provide the most reliable figure for cost of goods sold on the income statement, thus providing a more acceptable income statement and balance sheet amount. Regardless of the method used, the cost standard set by AICPA (also referred

---

[1]*Accounting Research Bulletin No. 43*, "Restatement and Revision of Accounting Research Bulletins" (New York: AICPA, 1953), Chapter 4, statement 3.

[2]Ibid., statement 4.

to as **historical cost**) restricts the proper uses of the word **valuation** in inventory accounting to the statement of items at cost or at modifications of cost.[3]

Two Inventory Systems

Two systems of accounting for inventory and determination of cost of goods sold are in use. The *periodic inventory system,* which depends on end-of-period determination of inventory valuation, was explained in Chapter 6. A second system, in which a continuous record of quantities (and sometimes valuation) of items on hand is maintained, is called the *perpetual inventory system.* Journal entries for the perpetual system are compared in this chapter to those for a periodic system. The method of assigning a cost valuation to items under both systems is also explained and illustrated.

Under the periodic system, cost of goods sold is determined by an end-of-period computation; thus no general ledger account is created for it. Under the perpetual system, however, Cost of Goods Sold becomes a general ledger account that is used to record the cost of the items sold at the time of the sale. Similar in nature to an expense account, it should be numbered in the chart of accounts as if it were an expense. Under the *periodic* system, entries to the Merchandise Inventory account are made only at the end of the accounting period to close out the old inventory and establish the new inventory as the current asset valuation both for income statement (computing the cost of goods sold) and balance sheet purposes. Under the *perpetual* system, the Merchandise Inventory account is constantly updated by journal entries to record receipts, cost of goods sold, and returns to vendors of merchandise. To compare the entries to record transactions under the two systems, assume the following data for Saint Josephs Company for April 1987:

1987

Apr. 1	Total inventory on hand at cost.	$100,000
4	Sales on account (cost $6,000)	10,000
5	Purchases on account from Ojata Company	2,000
6	Transportation charges paid on purchase of April 5.	80
8	Return to Ojata Company of an incorrect item. Since it was Ojata's error, the company agreed to allow credit for the invoice price of $200 plus $8 of transportation cost that applied to this item	208

The entries to record the above transactions are shown in general journal form in Figure 10–1. As this comparison shows, the periodic system's Purchases, Purchases Discounts, Purchases Returns and Allowances, and Transportation In accounts are replaced, in the perpetual system, by debits and credits direct to the Merchandise Inventory account. A second major difference is in the closing process. Under the periodic inventory system, all

---

[3] In all illustrations in this chapter, the cost figures will be assumed to include such elements as freight, discounts, and allowances.

Date	Periodic System		Perpetual System	

1987
Apr. 4
	Accounts Receivable 10,000
	  Sales ....
		10,000	Accounts Receivable 10,000
			  Sales ....
				10,000

	(Note: The cost of goods sold is not determined at this time but is determined at the end of the period.)		Cost of Goods Sold .... 6,000 Merchandise Inventory	6,000

5	Purchases............. 2,000
	  Accounts Payable........
		2,000	Merchandise Inventory 2,000
			  Accounts Payable........
				2,000

6	Transportation in.......... 80
	  Cash ....
		80	Merchandise Inventory 80
			  Cash ....
				80

8	Accounts Payable 208
	  Transportation in ....
	  Purchases Returns and
	    Allowances ....
		8
		
		200
			Accounts Payable 208
			  Merchandise Inventory ....
				208

Figure 10–1   Entries for Periodic and Perpetual Inventory Systems Compared

merchandising accounts are closed to Income Summary (see Chapter 6). Cost of goods sold is automatically a part of the determination of net income because the beginning and ending inventory amounts are a part of the closing process. Under the perpetual system, the only closing entry required for merchandise accounts is as follows (amount and end-of-fiscal-year dates are assumed):

1987
Dec. 31
	Income Summary ....
	  Cost of Goods Sold ....
	    To close the Cost of Goods Sold account.
		497,620	497,620

Since the Merchandise Inventory account has been kept up to date with continuous entries under the perpetual system, it does not enter into the closing process. However, it is necessary to adjust the account if the physical inventory count (equally important for internal control under either system) finds items out of agreement with stock record quantities. The real-life example at the end of this chapter contains such an adjustment.

Assigning Inventory Cost

To illustrate both systems of assigning cost to inventories, the following information about a single inventory item, a stapler (stock number 802A), is given:

1987	
Apr. 1	Inventory on hand consisted of 40 units (or staplers) that were purchased in March at $2.20 each.
5	Purchased 120 staplers at $2.60 each.
12	Sold 110 staplers.
16	Purchased 70 staplers at $2.80 each.
28	Sold 60 staplers.

The number on hand on April 30, 1987, determined by physical count, is 60 staplers. This on-hand amount is verified below. Presented with the calculation is a rearrangement of cost information to be used in later illustrations.

	Units	Unit Cost	Total Cost	Specific Identification of April 30 Inventory
Inventory, April 1......	40	$2.20	$ 88	10
Purchases:				
April 5..........	120	2.60	312	30
April 16..........	70	2.80	196	20
Total units available for sale.........	230		$596	60
Sales:				
April 12.......... 110				
April 28.......... 60				
Total sales.......	170			
Inventory, April 30.....	60			

Periodic Inventory System

With the **periodic inventory system**, the valuation of the inventory for the balance sheet and for computing the cost of goods sold is determined at the end of each annual accounting period by a complete physical count and costing of all inventory items. Acquired goods not on hand are assumed to have been sold. This causes losses due to theft, breakage, or other causes to be automatically included in the cost of goods sold as a deduction from revenue.

Specific Identification Costing

As previously mentioned, the specific identification method requires that inventory items be marked with a specific identity and cost. For example, using the foregoing data, the specific identification cost of the 60 items in stock on April 30 is known from tracing them back to their original invoices as follows:

Lot	Units	Unit Cost	Total Cost
April 1	10	$2.20	$ 22
5	30	2.60	78
16	20	2.80	56
	60		$156

This method cannot be used for inventory items whose specific identity is lost. Even in those situations in which identity is possible, use of this method is costly. Its use is restricted to special inventory situations where the unit

First-In, First-Out (FIFO) Costing

cost is high and inventory turnover is low, such as automobiles on a dealer's lot. Therefore, cost flow assumptions are usually substituted for this method and are the only ones discussed in the remainder of this chapter.

The periodic FIFO method of determining the cost of goods on hand and the cost of goods sold is based on the *assumption* that the cost flow follows the idea that units are sold in the order in which they were acquired; that is, the oldest units on hand are sold first, the units acquired next are sold next, and so on. *Cost flow assumptions relate only to the method of accounting and not to the actual physical movement of the goods. They may or may not approximate the actual physical flow.* The unsold units on hand at the date of the inventory are assumed to be the units acquired most recently. Consequently, for income measurement, earlier costs are matched with revenue and the most current costs are used for balance sheet valuation.

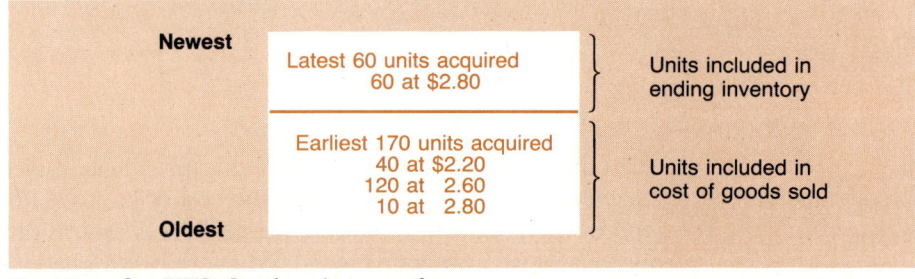

Figure 10–2   **Cost Lots for FIFO Costing Assumption**

The cost groupings for the FIFO assumption are presented in Figure 10–2. Under the periodic FIFO assumption, the 60 staplers on hand April 30, 1987, are part of the lot purchased on April 16. Since the last purchase made was large enough to make up the entire ending inventory, all 60 units are valued at $2.80. Therefore the cost assigned to the inventory is:

60 units at $2.80 . . . . $168

Using this inventory cost and assuming that the firm stocks only this one stapler, the cost of goods sold section of the income statement appears as follows:

Beginning inventory	$ 88
Add: Purchases	508
Cost of goods available for sale	$596
Deduct: Ending inventory (at FIFO)	168
Cost of goods sold	$428

10 / Measurement and Control of Inventory

The assumption that oldest goods are sold first leads to the following verification of cost of goods sold:

Date of Sale	Units Sold	Sales Made from	Units	Unit Cost	Total Cost
Apr. 12	110	Beginning inventory	40	$2.20	$ 88
		Purchase of April 5	70	2.60	182
28	60	Purchase of April 5	50	2.60	130
		Purchase of April 16	10	2.80	28
			170		$428

Last-In, First-Out (LIFO) Costing

Periodic LIFO costing *assumes* that the cost of goods sold should be based on prices paid for the most recently acquired units and *the inventory consists of the oldest units on hand.*

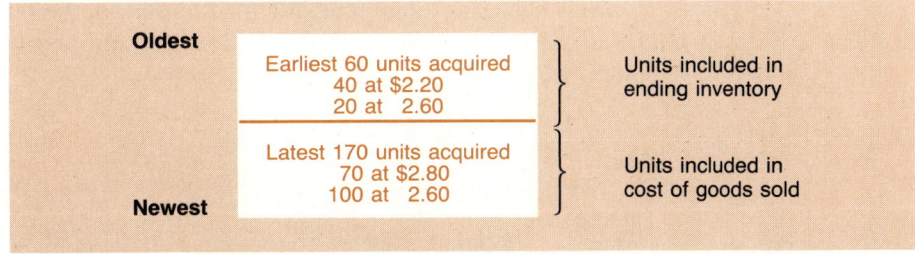

Figure 10–3 **Cost Lots for LIFO Costing Assumption**

The cost groupings for the LIFO assumption are presented in Figure 10–3. Since the oldest cost lot, beginning inventory, is not large enough to make up the entire ending inventory, sufficient units from the first April purchase have to be included. The cost assigned to inventory is:

Ending inventory (60 units):	
From beginning inventory, 40 units at $2.20	$ 88
From purchase of April 5, 20 units at $2.60	52
Cost assigned to April 30 inventory	$140

The two cost layers that result in inventory must be kept separate in future periods for proper valuation; they are not averaged together as one layer. The assumption that newest goods are the first sold leads to the following method of verification of cost of goods sold for the one inventory item.[4]

---

[4]Note that the sale of April 12 could not actually contain units from a purchase of April 16, but periodic LIFO causes us to make the *assumption* that it did.

Date of Sale	Units Sold	Sales Made from	Units	Unit Cost	Total Cost
Apr. 28	60	Purchase of April 16	60	$2.80	$168
12	110	Purchase of April 16	10	2.80	28
		Purchase of April 5	100	2.60	260
			170		$456

Weighted Average Costing

Under **weighted average costing** the ending inventory is priced at the end of each accounting period at a unit cost computed by dividing the total cost of all goods available for sale by the total physical units available for sale. Similarly, all quantities sold are stated at a uniform cost—the computed weighted average unit cost for the period (typically one month). Under the periodic system, cost of goods sold must be a computed amount. For any assumption, this amount can be computed only at the end of the period.

The weighted average unit cost for the period, the ending inventory valuation in the income statement, and the verification of cost of goods sold are computed as follows:

Date		Units	Unit Cost	Total
1987				
Apr. 1	Beginning inventory.	40	$2.20	$ 88
5	Purchase.	120	2.60	312
16	Purchase.	70	2.80	196
	Total available for sale	230		$596

$$\text{Weighted average unit cost} = \frac{\text{Cost of goods available for sale}}{\text{Units available for sale}} = \frac{\$596}{230} = \$2.5913.$$

Units on hand, April 30	60
Inventory valuation = (60 × $2.5913)	$155.48
Units sold	170
Cost of goods sold = (170 × $2.5913).	$440.52

Perpetual Inventory System

The **perpetual inventory system** provides for a continuous book inventory of items on hand. An inventory record card (often called a **stock record card**) or a record in a computer file is kept for each inventory item. When units are purchased or sold, the inventory record for the item must be adjusted to show the updated quantity on hand.

The maintenance of continuous inventory records does not eliminate the need for a complete annual physical inventory. Companies that use the perpetual inventory system should take physical counts of portions of the inventory during the course of the year to test whether the records are in agreement with quantities actually on hand, or they should take a single end-of-year count. Only by physical count will shrinkage such as evaporation losses, theft, or duplicate shipments be discovered. During the course of a year, all inventory items should be physically verified at least once. Proper control of the inventory will not be exercised unless this is done.

Perpetual inventory records are costly to maintain, especially when the inventory includes numerous items of small value. A company may want to maintain continuous records for only certain classifications of its inventory. A hardware supply company, for example, may find it better to use the perpetual inventory system only for items with a high unit selling price and the periodic inventory system for all other items. Perpetual inventory concepts are always appropriate when the specific identification method is used.

Computerization of the inventory control system will greatly ease the burden of maintaining the records. All of the data necessary to maintain the perpetual records can be obtained from the purchases and sales data. The data-gathering process is further enhanced by using input devices at the point that merchandise is received and on the sales floor where sales data are initially recorded. Having data captured in machine readable form at the earliest point will result in more up-to-date records, leading to better control over the inventory.

First-In, First-Out (FIFO) Costing

A perpetual inventory card using the FIFO costing method is illustrated in Figure 10–4. As each shipment of goods is received, its quantity, unit cost, and total cost are recorded as a separate batch or lot. When goods are sold, the oldest goods on hand are assumed to make up the sale. The balance on hand, unit cost, and total cost *for each batch from which units are assumed to remain* are recorded in the Balance columns. Note that these batches are kept in chronological sequence.

Utilizing the FIFO cost flow assumption, the cost of the 110 units sold on April 12 is assumed to consist of the 40 units on hand on April 1 and 70 units from the April 5 purchase. The cost of the 60 units sold on April 28 is assumed to consist of the remaining 50 units from the April 5 purchase and 10 units from the April 16 purchase. When a sale or the balance on hand consists of units from more than one batch (see sale of April 12 in Figure 10–4), brackets are used to indicate that the sets of figures should be combined. The 60 units on hand on April 30 are all assumed to be from the batch purchased on April 16. The cost of goods sold for an item is the sum of the Total Cost

Figure 10–4 Perpetual Inventory Card (FIFO)

Item: Stapler, Stock Number 802A, Location L-7

Date		Ref.	Purchased (or Received)			Sold (or Issued)			Balance		
			Quantity	Unit Cost	Total Cost	Quantity	Unit Cost	Total Cost	Quantity	Unit Cost	Total Cost
1987											
Apr.	1	Balance							40	2.20	88.00
	5	P.O.[a] 673	120	2.60	312.00				40	2.20	
									120	2.60	400.00[c]
	12	S.T.[b] 401				40	2.20	88.00			
						70	2.60	182.00	50	2.60	130.00
	16	P.O. 690	70	2.80	196.00				50	2.60	
									70	2.80	326.00
	28	S.T. 409				50	2.60	130.00			
						10	2.80	28.00	60	2.80	168.00

[a] Purchase order: the document placing the order with the supplier.
[b] Shipping ticket: the internal document reporting a sale.
[c] The total cost has been computed for the convenience of the user as 40 × $2.20 plus 120 × $2.60.

column in the Sold (or Issued) section of the card. For this stapler the cost of goods sold is:

Sale of April 12 ($88 + $182)	$270
Sale of April 28 ($130 + $28)	158
Cost of goods sold	$428

Last-In, First-Out (LIFO) Costing

When LIFO is used with a perpetual system each sale is listed at the unit cost of the latest acquisitions. For instance, in Figure 10–5, the 110 units sold on April 12 are assumed to have come from the units received on April 5. The balance on hand, unit cost, *and total cost for each batch from which units are assumed to be on hand* are recorded in the Balance columns.

The inventory on April 30 is verified as follows:

40 units at $2.20	$ 88
10 units at 2.60	26
10 units at 2.80	28
60 units	$142

Figure 10–5 Perpetual Inventory Card (LIFO)

Item: Stapler, Stock Number 802A, Location L-7

Date		Ref.	Purchased (or Received)			Sold (or Issued)			Balance		
			Quantity	Unit Cost	Total Cost	Quantity	Unit Cost	Total Cost	Quantity	Unit Cost	Total Cost
1987											
Apr.	1	Balance							40	2.20	88.00
	5	P.O. 673	120	2.60	312.00				40	2.20	
									120	2.60	400.00
	12	S.T. 401				110	2.60	286.00	40	2.20	
									10	2.60	114.00
	16	P.O. 690	70	2.80	196.00				40	2.20	
									10	2.60	
									70	2.80	310.00
	28	S.T. 409				60	2.80	168.00	40	2.20	
									10	2.60	
									10	2.80	142.00

The cost of goods sold for this item is obtained by adding the Total Cost column of the Sold (or Issued) section of the inventory card: $286 + $168 = $454.

Moving Average Costing

In the moving average costing method (illustrated in Figure 10–6), units are priced at a continuous weighted average cost—that is, the total cost of units on hand divided by quantity on hand. This average unit cost is used for sales until additional units are purchased at a different cost. Then a new average unit cost must be computed. For example, the receipt of 120 units on April 5 required computation (a) in Figure 10–6. Also, the purchase of April 16 required that a new unit cost again be computed (illustrated in computation (b) in Figure 10–6).

This method is called **moving average costing** because a new average unit cost must be computed and used after each receipt of goods at a unit cost that is different from the current one. It is not necessary to compute a new unit cost after each sale because sales do *not* change the unit cost of the balance.

As in the other perpetual methods, the cost of goods sold is the sum of the amounts in the Total Cost column of the Sold (or Issued) section; under

Figure 10–6 Perpetual Inventory Card (Moving Average)

Item: Stapler, Stock Number 802A, Location L–7

Date		Ref.	Purchased (or Received)			Sold (or Issued)			Balance			
			Quantity	Unit Cost	Total Cost	Quantity	Unit Cost	Total Cost	Quantity	Unit Cost	Total Cost	
1987												
Apr.	1	Balance							40	2.20	88.00	
	5	P.O. 673	120	2.60	312.00				160	2.50	400.00	(a)
	12	S.T. 401				110	2.50	275.00	50	2.50	125.00	
	16	P.O. 690	70	2.80	196.00				120	2.675	321.00	(b)
	28	S.T. 409				60	2.675	160.50	60	2.675	160.50	

(a)
40 at $2.20 = $ 88
120 at 2.60 = 312
160 . . . . . . $400
Average = $2.50 = ($400 ÷ 160)

(b)
50 at $2.50 = $125
70 at 2.80 = 196
120 . . . . . . $321
Average = $2.675 = ($321 ÷ 120)

the moving average method, it is $435.50 = ($275.00 + $160.50). However, it is not necessary to separate batches, and brackets are not required. Receipts and issues (sales) are added to or deducted from the balance.

Two Systems Compared and Analyzed

The amount of the ending inventory as well as the amount of the cost of goods sold is identical under the periodic and the perpetual inventory systems when FIFO costing is used. This is because in each instance the goods on hand are assumed to consist of the most recently acquired units.

Under LIFO costing, however, the valuations of the cost of goods sold and ending inventory may differ under the two systems. Costs at the beginning of the period are assumed to be in the ending valuation with the periodic inventory system, whereas they may have been dropped from the running balance as sales or issues are recorded with the perpetual system. When the inventory is given a valuation only at the end of the period (as is the case in the periodic system), *the dates of sales are ignored.* Although the LIFO procedure may be used appropriately with either periodic or perpetual inventories, it is important that the system selected be followed consistently. The following tabulation illustrates the different results of LIFO costing with the perpetual and the periodic inventory systems:

	LIFO Periodic Inventory	LIFO Perpetual Inventory
Inventory, April 1	$ 88[a]	$ 88[a]
Purchases	508	508
Total goods available for sale	$596	$596
Inventory, April 30	140	142
Cost of goods sold	$456	$454

[a] These beginning LIFO inventory amounts are the same for this illustration but are not likely to be the same in the future (see April 30 inventory).

Similarly, the weighted average (periodic system) and the moving average (perpetual system) yield different results. With the same example used to illustrate both, the results were:

	Weighted Average Periodic Inventory	Moving Average Perpetual Inventory
Inventory, April 1	$ 88.00[a]	$ 88.00[a]
Purchases	508.00	508.00
Total goods available for sale	$596.00	$596.00
Inventory, April 30	155.48	160.50
Cost of goods sold	$440.52	$435.50

[a] These beginning average amounts are the same for this illustration but are not likely to be the same in the future (see April 30 inventory).

Regardless of whether the periodic or perpetual system is used, the method used to determine inventory valuation can have a direct effect on the financial statements. In a period of rising or falling prices—especially if the inventory turnover is rapid—the difference in inventory valuation can be significant. In the example used in this chapter the price of a stapler rose from $2.20 to $2.80 in the month of April. To illustrate the comparative effect of rising prices on the financial statements under perpetual FIFO, moving average, and LIFO costing, the basic data for the preceding discussions are used again. Two additional assumptions are made: (1) the selling price of each unit is $5.50, and (2) the operating expenses for the month are $200.

The computations of income in this simple illustration are for a single inventory item. The effect of the different methods on net income would be proportionately increased with increasing volume and number of items. The effect of the three methods of allocating inventory cost and cost of goods sold under the stated assumptions is highlighted in Figure 10–7.

During a period of rising prices, FIFO costing results in the highest ending inventory valuation, gross margin on sales, and net income, while having the

	Perpetual Inventory		
	FIFO	**Moving Average**	**LIFO**
Sales (170 units × $5.50)	$935.00	$935.00	$935.00
Cost of goods sold	428.00	435.50	454.00
Gross margin on sales	$507.00	$499.50	$481.00
Deduct: Operating expenses	200.00	200.00	200.00
Net income	$307.00	$299.50	$281.00
Ending Inventory	$168.00	$160.50	$142.00

Figure 10–7 **Summary Tabulation**

lowest cost of goods sold.[5] Given the same rising market conditions, the LIFO inventory method gives the opposite results: lowest ending inventory valuation, gross margin on sales, and net income, while having the highest cost of goods sold. During a period of falling prices, FIFO results in the lowest ending inventory valuation, gross margin on sales, and net income and the highest cost of goods sold; LIFO gives the opposite results.

LIFO's purpose is to match revenue with cost of last purchases rather than with earliest cost, as is done under FIFO costing. Also, during a prolonged period of generally rising prices, lower year-to-year earnings are reported under LIFO, resulting in a lower taxable income for a corporation. However, during inflationary periods LIFO costing results in a significant understatement of current assets, which limits the significance and usefulness of the balance sheet.

Figure 10–7 shows that the amounts for the income statement items listed under moving average costing fall between the corresponding amounts for FIFO and LIFO costing. The same position would be maintained in a falling market. Moving average costing reduces the effect of widely fluctuating prices.

Ending inventory appears in the balance sheet as a current asset. Consequently, this statement as well as the income statement is affected by the method of inventory valuation used. Because inventory is often the largest single item in the current assets section, the method of assigning cost may have a significant effect on the results of statement analysis (discussed later in this chapter).

Lower of Cost or Market (LCM)

The various methods of inventory valuation discussed thus far in this chapter are means of arriving at the cost of the inventory. In some industries, conditions may develop that diminish the utility (ability of the product to produce

---

[5]This leads to a condition that accountants call *phantom profits* because units sold must be replaced at a cost greater than cost of goods sold. Hence, more cash is used than the income statement showed as a potential inflow from operations.

a consistent amount of revenue) of some of the items in the inventory. When this occurs, the loss of utility should be reflected as a charge against current income and a reduction of the valuation of the inventory. To effect these results, a long-standing convention in accounting requires that inventories may be valued at the **lower of cost or market (LCM)**.[6] The term **market** broadly means the cost of replacing the goods as of the balance sheet date; this is also referred to as **replacement cost**. Cost is first determined by any of the methods already discussed in this chapter.

						[1]	Basis for LCM [2]	[3]
Item	Quantity	Unit Cost	Unit Market Price	Total Cost	Total Market	Item	Major Category	Total Inventory
Category X:								
Item A	100	$10	$9.00	$1,000	$ 900	$ 900		
Item B	200	4	6.00	800	1,200	800		
Subtotal				$1,800	$2,100		$1,800	
Category Y:								
Item C	400	1	1.25	$ 400	$ 500	400		
Item D	600	6	5.00	3,600	3,000	3,000		
Item E	250	3	2.50	750	625	625		
Subtotal				$4,750	$4,125		4,125	
Totals				$6,550	$6,225			$6,225
Inventory at lower cost or market						$5,725	$5,925	$6,225

Figure 10–8   **Application of LCM**

The process of valuing the inventory at LCM occurs at the end of the accounting period, when financial statements are prepared. It may be applied (1) to each item individually, (2) to each major inventory category, or (3) to the entire inventory. On the basis of the inventory tabulations in Figure 10–8 (FIFO costing is assumed), the valuation under each procedure is as follows:

[1] If each item is valued individually, the inventory is reported as $5,725. This basis for LCM always produces the smallest possible inventory valuation.

[2] If the inventory is valued by major categories, it is reported as $5,925. This basis for LCM produces an inventory valuation that is equal to or greater than in [1] and equal to or smaller than [3].

[3] If the inventory is valued in total, it is reported as $6,225. This basis for LCM always produces the greatest possible LCM inventory valuation.

---

[6]*Accounting Research Bulletin No. 43,* Chapter 4, Statement 5 authorizes the use of LCM. Statement 6 of that chapter places an upper and lower limit on the *market value* used here. The rules for applying the limits to the term *market* are covered thoroughly in most intermediate accounting textbooks.

Estimation of Inventory

Gross Margin Method

The accounting procedures for recording the chosen LCM valuation may involve a direct reduction to the inventory account or the use of a valuation account. They are normally covered in a more advanced accounting course.

Taking a physical inventory or maintaining perpetual inventory records is often costly and time consuming. For some purposes an estimate is needed. To prepare monthly financial statements, check the accuracy of a physical inventory, or estimate inventory valuation when an accurate valuation cannot be made (as in the case of a fire loss) the **gross margin method** of estimating inventory valuation may be used. This method consists of deducting the estimated cost of goods sold from the total cost of goods available for sale.

Assume that during the previous three years the Lander Company has averaged a gross margin rate on sales of 30 percent. Since gross margin as a percent of sales is 30 percent, cost of goods sold as a percent of sales must be 70 percent = (100% − 30%). For the current year, the following data are available from the records of the company:

Inventory, January 1, 1987	$ 20,000
Purchases during 1987	110,000
Sales during 1987	160,000

Under the gross margin method, the estimated inventory on December 31, 1987, would be computed as follows:[7]

a. Sales × Cost percent = Cost of goods sold:
$160,000 × 0.70 = $112,000.
b. Beginning inventory + Net cost of purchases − Cost of goods sold = Ending inventory:
$20,000 + $110,000 − $112,000 = $18,000.

---

[7]In both the gross margin method and the retail method (discussed next), transportation in should be added to purchases; discounts and returns and allowances should be deducted. With the cost percent determined, an alternative computation is:

Beginning inventory	$ 20,000
Add: Net purchases	110,000
Cost of goods available for sale	$130,000
Deduct: Cost of goods sold	112,000
Ending inventory	$ 18,000

On the basis of the foregoing computation, the partial income statement is as follows:

LANDER COMPANY
Partial Income Statement
For the Year Ended December 31, 1987

Exhibit A

Sales		$160,000
Cost of goods sold:		
Inventory, January 1, 1987 (given)	$ 20,000	
Purchases (given)	110,000	
Total goods available for sale	$130,000	
Estimated inventory, December 31, 1987 (item b)	18,000	
Cost of goods sold (item a)		112,000
Gross margin (sales − cost of goods sold)		$ 48,000

This method is based on the assumption that the rate of gross margin on sales is substantially the same in every period. It is accurate, therefore, only to the extent that the assumed gross margin rate is accurate. A careful study should be made of possible differences between the past data from which the assumed rate is derived and the corresponding current data. Appropriate adjustments should be made for significant differences. A recent change in the mix of products sold may add items with different *markons* (addition to cost to establish selling price). In such a case, the gross margin rate of the most recent year could be a more accurate estimate of the current rate than an average of several prior years.

Retail Method

Another method of estimating the ending inventory at cost when its retail valuation is known is the retail inventory method. Its value is twofold: (1) it serves as a means of computing the ending inventory without a physical count, and (2) it provides a method of centrally controlling inventories that consist of a variety of items dispersed over several departments or several branch stores.

Goods are charged to the departments or branches at their selling price, records of both cost and selling price of goods purchased are kept centrally, and records of sales are kept in the usual manner. From these records, the inventory valuation may be prepared at any time. Under the **retail inventory method** the estimated inventory at retail is derived by deducting the sales during the period from the total goods available for sale priced at retail. This amount is then converted to cost by applying the cost percent (the ratio of the cost of goods available for sale to the retail price of those goods).

Example 1: No Changes in Price Consider the data on page 430.

	Cost	Retail
Inventory at beginning of period	$ 20,000	$ 30,000
Purchases during period	180,000	270,000
Total goods available for sale	$200,000	$300,000

Cost percent (ratio of cost to retail)
$$\frac{\$200,000}{\$300,000} = 66.667\%$$

Sales during period		258,000
Inventory at retail		$ 42,000
Estimated inventory at cost (66.667% of $42,000)	$ 28,000	

This simple example is in a situation where there are no changes in price during the period. Presented next is an example of estimation of inventory valuation after price changes have occurred.

Example 2: Traditional Method—Price Changes Pricing goods for sale requires an addition to the cost of the merchandise (a *markon*) to cover operating expenses and profit; markons determine the original retail (or selling) price. A company may find it necessary to increase or decrease these previously established prices. Increases in the original retail prices are called *markups;* decreases below original retail are called *markdowns.* Traditionally, markups are added to the total retail valuation in determining the cost percentage. This results in a lower cost percentage and a lower estimated inventory cost valuation when that percentage is applied to the retail inventory valuation. Markdowns are excluded in arriving at the cost percentage but added to sales for determination of the ending retail inventory valuation. This procedure approximates the inventory valued at LCM as a result of applying the smaller LCM cost percent as described above.

Consider the following change to the previous illustration:

	Cost	Retail
Inventory at beginning of period	$ 20,000	$ 30,000
Purchases during period	179,000	270,000
Transportation in during period	1,000	
Markups during period		10,000
Total goods available for sale	$200,000	$310,000

LCM cost percent (ratio of cost to retail)
$$\frac{\$200,000}{\$310,000} = 64.516\%$$

Sales during period	$258,000	
Markdowns during period	10,000	268,000
Inventory at retail		$ 42,000
Estimated inventory at LCM (64.516% of $42,000)	$ 27,097	

10 / Measurement and Control of Inventory

Evaluation of Estimating Procedures

Both the gross margin and retail inventory methods are based on a calculation of the cost-of-goods-sold rate. The gross margin method uses past experience as a basis; the retail inventory method uses current experience. The gross margin method may be less reliable because past experience may be different from current experience.

Both methods are useful because they enable the accountant to prepare frequent financial statements without the cost of a physical count each period or of maintaining perpetual inventory records. However, they do not eliminate the need for a careful physical count at least once a year. The physical count will disclose losses due to thefts or shrinkage and serves as the basis for an adjustment to the inventory records and the Merchandise Inventory account. Such an adjustment is illustrated in the real-life example at the end of this chapter.

Consistency in the Application of Inventory Valuation Procedures

Different procedures may be used to place a valuation on various classes of the inventory. It is most important, therefore, that the selected method should be followed consistently from year to year in each class. Inconsistency in inventory pricing, cost allocations, and financial statement presentation would make year-to-year comparisons of operating results and financial position meaningless. Since such comparisons often serve as the basis for managerial decisions and decisions of external users of accounting information, the importance of consistency becomes evident.

Consistency

Whatever the method of inventory valuation chosen, a company should exhibit consistency ***in following it from year to year.***

The principle of consistency does not preclude required changes to a better interpretation of GAAP properly made and fully disclosed. A change from FIFO to average inventory costing, for example, requires an explanation accompanying the financial statements of the year of change, giving the nature of the change and its cumulative effect. In the annual report, financial statements of prior periods would be shown as they were previously reported. Then the cumulative effect of the change will be reflected in the income of the period in which the change is made.[8]

Internal Control over Inventory

Control of inventory through separation of duties is as applicable to merchandise as it is to control of cash. Other internal controls must be established to protect against loss, theft, and misappropriation of inventory. The system for receiving, storing, issuing, and paying for merchandise must provide for records and supporting documents and for the assignment of individual respon-

---

[8]*Opinions of the Accounting Principles Board No. 20,* "Accounting Changes" (New York: AICPA, July 1971), paragraph 19.

sibility and accountability to safeguard the assets. Recording of purchases discounts lost associated with the net price method (see Chapter 6) focuses attention on the losses. Thus, the likelihood of lost discounts is reduced.

Absence of control over inventories can seriously damage a business. An excessive inventory is expensive to carry. Studies indicate that the costs of carrying an inventory—taxes, insurance, warehousing, handling, and inventory taking—may be as high as 25 percent of the original purchase price. This is exclusive of potential lost earnings (interest) on funds tied up in inventories. On the other hand, sufficient items and quantities must be stocked to provide customers with good service.

Maintaining a proper balance to avoid both shortages and excesses of inventory requires organization and planning. Control plans must provide for day-to-day comparisons of projected inventory acquisitions with current sales volume. A reduction in sales volume will result in excess inventories unless purchasing adjustments are made. A firm's success in inventory management can be evaluated by two ratios discussed in the next sections.

Managerial Analyses Enhancing Internal Control

Inventory Turnover

One of the ratios used in inventory analysis is the **inventory turnover**—the relationship between inventory and the cost of goods sold. It is computed by dividing the cost of goods sold by the average inventory. The figure used may be the average of the beginning and ending inventories of the period or, preferably, the average of the end-of-month inventories to minimize the effect of seasonal fluctuations. Although high turnover is usually a sign of good management, the ratio varies widely from one industry to another. A wholesaler of automobile parts and accessories may average five inventory turnovers per year, while a wholesaler of perishables such as meat and poultry may average 35 or more. Also, a high-volume, low-margin business such as a fast-food chain would have to turn over its inventory more often than a business having a low-volume, high-margin policy, such as an art gallery.

Using assumed data, the inventory turnover computation is:

		1987	1986
1.	Cost of goods sold.	$123,000	$92,000
	Average merchandise inventory:		
2.	January 1.	$ 36,000	$29,700
3.	December 31	45,000	36,000
4.	Total	$ 81,000	$65,700
5.	Average (Line 4 ÷ 2)	$ 40,500	$32,850
	Inventory turnover (Line 1 ÷ Line 5)	3.0	2.8

This firm sold and replaced its merchandise inventory three times during the year 1987; that is, the cost of merchandise sold was three times greater than the average cost of merchandise on hand. This is an improvement over 1986. The rate may be computed for major categories or for individual items in order to establish item-by-item control. In making comparisons of companies with this ratio, the method of inventory costing should be considered. Remember that LIFO produces a higher cost of goods sold and a lower inventory valuation than FIFO during periods of rising prices. This can cause a company using LIFO to have a greater inventory turnover rate than a company using FIFO.

Ratio of Inventory to Working Capital

Working capital is equal to total current assets minus total current liabilities. The *ratio of inventory to working capital* is an indication of the amount of working capital represented by inventory. Again, using assumed data, it is computed as:

$$\frac{\text{Ending inventory}}{\text{Working capital}} = \frac{\$45,000}{\$54,450} = 82.6\%.$$

This ratio, being less than 100 percent, indicates that the current debt can be paid in full from quick current assets (cash plus receivables), assuming that all receivables can be collected. For the ratio to be less than 100 percent, the quick current assets must be greater than current liabilities. Otherwise, when the inventory is removed from current assets the computed acid-test ratio will be less than 1 to 1. To show this, assume the following:

Current assets:	
Cash and receivables	$15,000
Merchandise inventory	20,000
Total current assets	$35,000
Current liabilities	$16,000

Working capital is $19,000 = ($35,000 − $16,000), and the ratio of inventory to working capital is 105.3 percent = ($20,000 ÷ $19,000). The acid-test ratio is 0.9375 to 1 = ($15,000 ÷ $16,000). By reversing the current asset dollar amounts, we have:

Cash and receivables	$20,000
Merchandise inventory	15,000
Total current assets	$35,000

With the same current liabilities, working capital remains at $19,000; the ratio of inventory to working capital now is 93.75 percent = ($15,000 ÷ $16,000). The acid-test ratio now becomes 1.25 to 1 = ($20,000 ÷ $16,000). In spite of the best internal control efforts, errors do occur. Correction of the records is illustrated in the example that follows.

A Real-Life Example

The Shaw Paint Company used its perpetual inventory records to determine the inventory at the end of each month in 1987. These records enabled the accountant to prepare monthly financial statements for management. At the end of 1987, a physical count costed by moving average unit prices was taken and recorded on inventory sheets. After the physical count had been completed on December 31, 1987, the inventory supervisor had recounts made on all items in which she suspected there could be errors. All inventory tickets are now considered to be correct and have been listed on 37 inventory sheets. Each item has been priced and extended. The last sheet and the latest general ledger account page for inventory are as follows:

SHAW PAINT COMPANY
Physical Inventory Sheet   Sheet No. 37

Stock Number	Description	Quantity	Unit Price	Amount
16 × 207	Enamel, Inside, Almond	210	$6.80	$ 1,428.00
17 × 503	Enamel, Outside, Yellow	108	6.50	702.00
17 × 519	Enamel, Outside, Green	27	6.25	168.75
	Grand total			$27,602.83

Merchandise Inventory   Acct. No. 132

| 1987 Dec. 31 | Balance | ✓ | 28,001.18 | | |

The general ledger account Merchandise Inventory shows a balance ($28,001.18) that does not agree with the value of the physical count

($27,602.83). Since the priced count sheets are the best evidence of the correct valuation, an entry to adjust the account will be made as follows:

1987				
Dec.	31	Loss from Inventory Shrinkage....................	398.35	
		Merchandise Inventory.........................		398.35
		To adjust account for merchandise evaporated, lost, stolen, or otherwise missing.		

The accounting task is not yet completed. Since the individual stock records are a subsidiary ledger for Merchandise Inventory, these individual records must be changed to reflect the correct physical counts. This will then give management the accurate details with which to control the inventory effectively.

Financial Statement Disclosure

If financial statement data are to be useful to readers, the figures must be comparable from period to period within a firm *and among different firms in an industry.* As noted in Figure 10–7, the use of alternative acceptable methods of costing inventory can make a significant difference in cost of goods sold, ending inventory, and net income. To help overcome this lack of comparability, the existing accounting guidance requires that financial statements disclose the methods and policies used to develop certain pieces of information. In its *Opinion No. 22,* the Accounting Principles Board provided for disclosure in the financial statements of the principles followed and the methods used to apply them if changes in financial position or results of operations are materially affected by the amounts reported.[9] Among examples of areas where such disclosure would be commonly required, the APB specifically included inventory pricing.[10] Typical of such disclosure is that of American Brands, Inc.; two segments of the company's 1983 *Annual Report* are reproduced in Figure 10–9. Note that American Brands discloses certain segments of its inventory valuations in the balance sheet and the pricing methods in the first footnote entitled "Summary of Significant Accounting Policies." Thus the reader has a better basis for comparison with other firms.

---

[9]*Opinions of the Accounting Principles Board No. 22,* "Disclosure of Accounting Policies" (New York: AICPA, 1972), paragraph 12.

[10]Ibid., paragraph 13.

Consolidated Balance Sheet
(in thousands)

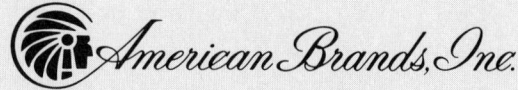

December 31	1983	1982
Current assets		
Cash	$ 31,320	$ 24,420
Accounts receivable, customers, less allowances for discounts, doubtful accounts and returns, 1983, $19,129; 1982, $17,927	641,402	560,687
Inventories		
Leaf tobacco	692,247	675,104
Bulk whiskey	113,661	109,163
Other raw materials, supplies and work in process	228,570	239,832
Finished products	347,308	376,631
	1,381,786	1,400,730
Other current assets	88,191	62,797
Total current assets	2,142,699	2,048,634

Summary of Significant Accounting Policies

Inventories
Inventories are priced at the lower of cost (average; first-in, first-out; and minor amounts at last-in, first-out) or market. In accordance with generally recognized trade practice, the leaf tobacco and bulk whiskey inventories are classified as current assets, although part of such inventories, due to the duration of aging processes, ordinarily will not be sold within one year.

The last-in, first-out inventory included in the consolidated balance sheet is $1,690,000 in excess of the valuation reported by a subsidiary for federal income tax purposes, resulting from a revaluation of this asset to fair value at the date the subsidiary was purchased.

Figure 10–9 Selected Portions of 1983 *Annual Report*; Courtesy, American Brands, Inc.

Glossary

Average (cost flow assumption) The cost of items sold and ending inventory items is assumed to consist of weighted average unit costs.

Consistency The concept that uniformity—with full disclosure for any departures—from year to year, especially in inventory pricing, cost allocation, and financial statement presentation, is essential to make comparisons meaningful.

Cost of an inventory item The expenditures incurred in bringing an inventory item to its existing condition and location.

FIFO (first-in, first-out) inventory costing A method of determining the cost of goods on hand and the cost of goods sold based on the assumption that the cost flows of the units sold are in the order in which they were acquired.

Gross margin method A method of estimating inventory value by deducting the cost of goods sold from the total cost of goods available for sale. The cost of goods sold is the result of the average gross margin percent for prior periods applied to sales for the current period.

Historical cost See *Cost of an inventory item*.

Inventory Goods owned by the business for sale to customers.

Inventory Turnover Cost of goods sold in ratio to average inventory.

LIFO (last-in, first-out) inventory costing A costing method based on the assumption that the cost of goods sold should be calculated on prices paid for the most recently acquired units and that the units on hand consist of the oldest units acquired.

Lower of cost or market (LCM) An inventory valuation method by which units are valued at the lower of either original acquisition cost or replacement cost (market).

Market In LCM, the cost of replacing an item at the balance sheet date.

Moving average costing A perpetual inventory costing method by which the cost of each purchase is added to the cost of units on hand, and the total cost is divided by the total quantity on hand to find the new average unit price each time new merchandise is received at a different price.

Periodic inventory system An inventory system by which the valuation of the inventory for balance sheet presentation is determined at the end of each annual period by a complete physical count and pricing of all inventory items. Cost of goods sold must be computed.

Perpetual inventory system An inventory system of record keeping that provides for a continuous book inventory of items on hand.

Replacement cost The current cost of replacing inventory items using the usual sources of supply and in quantities usually bought.

Retail inventory method A method of estimating inventory value in which the ratio of the cost of goods to the selling price is used to convert the inventory valued at retail to cost.

Specific identification method An inventory costing method by which the unit cost is identified specifically with the related supporting acquisition document of the purchase lot from which the inventory item comes.

Stock record card Card on which a perpetual record is kept for an item of inventory.

Valuation (of inventory) The statement of inventory items in accounting records at cost or modifications of cost.

Weighted average costing A costing method by which the ending inventory and the cost of goods sold are priced at the end of each accounting period at a unit cost computed by dividing the total cost of goods available for sale by the physical units available for sale.

Working capital Total current assets minus total current liabilities.

Questions

Q10–1 What specific elements are included in the cost of an item of inventory? For each item you name, explain why it is an inventory cost instead of an expense.

Q10–2 How do the perpetual and the periodic inventory systems differ? Does the perpetual inventory system eliminate the need for a physical inventory count? Explain.

Q10–3 (a) What is the relationship between the actual physical flow of goods in and out of inventory and the method used for inventory valuation? (b) What inventory valuation method should a company use if, as new shipments of inventory items are received, they are commingled with identical items on hand in storage bins?

Q10–4 How would overstatements or understatements of inventory affect net income in the period when the error is made? In the following year?

Q10–5 What effect do the different methods of inventory valuation have on the financial statements?

Q10–6 Explain the effect on the balance sheet valuation and on the income determination of the use of LIFO as compared with FIFO (a) if prices have risen during the year, and (b) if prices have fallen during the year.

Q10–7 Why is it important that the selected method of inventory valuation be applied consistently from year to year? Does strict compliance with the principle of consistency preclude a change from FIFO to LIFO?

Q10–8 Define the term market as used in LCM inventory valuation. What are reasons that a business would price inventory at LCM?

Q10–9 Compare the gross margin method with the retail inventory method.

Q10–10 An audit of the records of the Bates Company showed that the ending inventory on December 31, 1986, was overstated by $7,600. What was the effect of the error on the income statements for 1986 and 1987? What was the overall effect for the two-year period, assuming no further errors were made in inventories?

Q10–11 How does internal control over inventory resemble internal control over cash? Why?

Q10–12 Explain how internal control can be strengthened by ratio analysis. Explain two commonly used inventory ratios, and how they would be applied.

Exercises

E10–1
Income statement using specific identification

In October 1987, the Gaston Company began buying and selling a recently patented stamping machine. Transactions for the month follow:

1987

Oct. 3 Purchased machine no. 1 at $11,800.
   7 Purchased machine no. 2 at $12,600.
  14 Sold machine no. 2 at $25,200.
  21 Purchased machine no. 3 at $14,400.
  28 Sold machine no. 1 at $25,200.

Prepare an income statement for the month of October through gross margin on sales, using the specific identification method of inventory costing.

E10–2
Computing inventory valuation and cost of goods sold assuming FIFO

The beginning inventory, purchases, and sales of an item by Bellvue Company for the month of July 1987 were as follows:

1987

Jul. 1 Inventory on hand consisted of 90 units at $4.00 each.
   10 Sold 50 units.
   15 Purchased 40 units at $4.20 each.
   17 Purchased 60 units at $4.30 each.
   20 Sold 30 units.
   27 Purchased 50 units at $4.50 each.
   29 Sold 40 units.

Compute the July 31 inventory valuation and July cost of goods sold using periodic FIFO.

E10–3
Computing inventory valuation and cost of goods sold assuming LIFO

The Dutchess Company sells a single item. Using periodic LIFO, compute the March 31, 1987, inventory valuation and March cost of goods sold from the following:

1987

Mar. 1	Inventory on hand consisted of 120 units at $3.90.	
4	Sold 70 units.	
14	Purchased 60 units at $4.00 each.	
16	Purchased 90 units at $4.20 each.	
21	Sold 45 units.	
28	Sold 70 units.	

E10–4
Recording on perpetual cards using FIFO and LIFO

The Alaska Machine Company buys and sells dryers. Purchases and sales during June 1987 are shown below:

Date	Purchases	Sales
1987		
Jun. 3	100 units at $300	
11		165 units
14	70 units at 310	
18	90 units at 315	
20		60 units
25	95 units at 325	
28		170 units

The inventory on June 1 consisted of 100 units at $280 each. Enter the beginning inventory on a perpetual inventory card and record the transactions using the FIFO assumption. Repeat the process, changing the assumption to LIFO.

E10–5
Weighted average assumption to compute inventory valuation and cost of goods sold

The following data are from purchase invoices and sales tickets for a notebook at the Gettysburg College bookstore during February 1987:

Purchases			Sales	
Date	Quantity	Cost	Date	Quantity
Feb. 4	400	$1.35	Feb. 8	235
13	200	1.50	11	120
25	200	1.60	19	200
			22	100

The balance on February 1 was 200 notebooks at a cost of $1.30 each. Using the weighted average assumption (periodic system), compute (a) inventory valuation on February 28, and (b) cost of notebooks sold in February.

E10–6
Recording on perpetual inventory card using moving average

Record on a perpetual inventory card the activity of the following item stocked and sold by Bay Path Store during November 1987. Use the moving average cost flow assumption.

1987

Nov. 1	Balance on hand is 165 units at a cost of $3.00 each.
8	Sold 35 units.
11	Purchased 150 units at a total cost of $506.
22	Sold 200 units.
28	Purchased 100 units at $3.56 each.

Part Two / Income Measurement and Valuation Issues

E10–7
Estimating inventory by gross margin method

The entire stock of the York Shop was destroyed by fire on June 22, 1987. The books of the company (kept in a fireproof vault) showed the value of goods on hand on June 1 to be $80,000. Transactions for the period June 1 through June 22 resulted in the following amounts:

Sales	$197,560
Sales returns	4,210
Purchases	159,600
Purchases returns	3,630
Transportation in	2,950

The rate of gross margin on net sales for the previous three years averaged 36 percent. Determine the cost of the inventory destroyed by the fire.

E10–8
Retail method

Iowa Traders estimates its merchandise inventory when preparing monthly financial statements. The following information was available on April 30:

	Cost	Retail
Merchandise inventory, April 1	$ 156,000	$ 176,129
Purchases during April (net)	1,267,500	2,145,000
Transportation in during April	15,600	
Sales during April (net)		1,248,000

Compute the estimated inventory on April 30, using (a) the retail inventory method and (b) the retail method assuming markups of $77,371 and markdowns of $50,000.

E10–9
Possible LCM valuations

Schotzberger Company had the following items in stock on May 31, 1987:

Item	Quantity	Unit Cost	Unit Market Price
Class A:			
Item M	50	$5.00	$4.00
Item N	100	2.50	3.00
Item O	200	7.00	6.50
Class B:			
Item X	200	1.00	1.25
Item Y	400	3.00	2.50
Item Z	800	1.25	1.50

Compute all inventory valuations that could be used in financial statements for lower of cost or market.

E10–10
Correction of inventory errors

The Merchandise Inventory account of Onondoga Traders has a debit balance of $268,152.50 on December 31, 1987. The final tally of inventory sheets shows that the total cost valuation per physical count and pricing is $265,431.25. Prepare a general journal entry to cause the proper balance to be reported in the December 31 balance sheet.

E10–11
Inventory ratios

Neuvotexi Company had the following information in its annual report for 1987:

	1987	1986	1985
Current assets:			
Cash	$565,000	$468,050	$353,200
Temporary investments	234,500	45,900	47,600
Merchandise inventory	672,360	564,670	498,730
Total current liabilities	817,700	719,080	599,687

Cost of goods sold was $3,708,345 in 1987 and $2,124,780 in 1986. Compute the inventory turnover for 1987 and 1986 and the ratio of inventory to working capital for all three years. Comment on the meaning of these ratios and whether or not the trend of each is favorable or unfavorable giving your reasons for conclusions in each case.

A Problems

P10–1A
Journal entries for a perpetual inventory system

Folea Company maintains perpetual inventory records. All purchases are received F.O.B. destination, and returns are made at the supplier's expense. Following are summary data from the records for January 1987, the first month of operations:

Total purchases (on account)	$396,350
Total returns of defective merchandise for credit	6,420
Operation expenses (paid in cash)	141,672
Total sales (on account)	472,240
Cost of goods sold per stock records	283,344

Required:

1. Prepare summary general journal entries dated January 31 to record purchases, purchase returns, sales, and operating expenses.
2. Journalize summary closing entries, including the transfer of net income to the Retained Earnings account.

P10–2A
Computing inventory and cost of goods sold—periodic inventory system

The inventory of Boko Company on January 1 and December 31, 1987, consisted of 42,500 and 12,500 units, respectively, of Commodity X-1. The beginning inventory was priced at $1,700. The following purchases were made during the year:

Date	Quantity	Cost
1987		
Jan. 3	25,000	$1,125.00
Apr. 16	42,500	1,955.00
Jul. 5	60,000	2,850.00
Oct. 3	15,000	750.00
Dec. 16	40,000	2,200.00

Required: Under the periodic inventory system, determine: (1) the ending inventory and (2) cost of goods sold, using (a) the FIFO cost flow assumption, (b) the LIFO cost flow assumption, and (c) the weighted average cost flow assumption.

P10–3A
Recording transactions on a perpetual inventory card

Maple, Inc., uses a perpetual inventory system. During May 1987, the following activity was experienced with a pocket calculator, stock number LT56:

1987

May	1	Balance on hand is 200 units at $9.25 each.
	6	Sold 160 units.
	10	Received 160 units at $9.10 each.
	24	Sold 180 units.
	30	Received 80 units at $9.00 each.

Required: Record the beginning balance and the May activity on perpetual inventory cards, and determine: (1) the ending inventory valuation and (2) the cost of goods sold, using (a) the FIFO cost flow assumption, (b) the LIFO cost flow assumption, and (c) the moving average cost flow assumption.

P10–4A
Three LCM valuations and effect on gross margin

Melba Assemblers has determined the following to be applicable to the inventory of August 31, 1987, the end of the accounting year:

			Unit	
Item		Quantity	Cost	Market
Frames:				
Type F–1		100	$14.75	$15.50
Type F–12		200	26.00	22.50
Type F–15		60	21.50	21.00
Spring (sets):				
Type S–1		500	7.40	8.50
Type S–12		1,000	10.50	11.25
Type S–15		300	8.60	6.00

Required:

1. Compute the ending inventory at the lower of cost or market, applied (a) to each item, (b) to each category, and (c) to the entire inventory.
2. What is the effect of each application of LCM on the gross margin in the current year? In the following year?

P10–5A
Estimating ending inventories—both methods

Data for two companies are provided as follows:

Company A

Inventory, September 1	$ 281,600
Net purchases during September	847,140
Net sales during September	1,470,280

Average gross margin rate for the past three years has been 35 percent of net sales.

Company B

Sales	$203,625
Transportation in	2,700
Purchases at cost	128,250
Purchases at retail	202,500
Inventory—June 1 (cost)	47,250
Inventory—June 1 (retail)	67,500

Required:

1. Estimate the September 30 inventory of Company A using the gross margin method.
2. Estimate the June 30 inventory of Company B using the retail method.
3. Estimate the June 30 inventory of Company B using the retail method assuming markups of $27,000 and markdowns of $20,000.

P10–6A
Inventory ratios

In the 1983 *Annual Report,* Colt Industries Inc. reported the following data (dollars in thousands):

	1983	1982
Cost of sales [cost of goods sold]	$1,205,531	$1,175,962
Total inventories	327,329	343,256
Other current assets (listed)	403,607	433,801
Total current liabilities	320,962	263,926

Required:

1. Compute the inventory turnover for 1983.
2. Compute the ratio of inventory to working capital for both years. Is 1983 an improvement over 1982? Explain.
3. Does the cost flow assumption used to determine inventory valuation affect these ratios? Explain.

P10–7A
Thought-provoking problem: effect of cost flow assumptions on financial statements

On July 1, 1987, three incorporators formed the Policastro Company by receiving a corporate charter and issuing common stock for $80,000 in cash. Purchases and sales of an item during the month are shown below.

1987

Jul.	1	Purchased 2,880 units at $19.20.
	10	Sold 1,680 units at $32.
	13	Purchased 2,400 units at $20.40.
	17	Sold 2,640 units at $32.
	22	Purchased 3,600 units at $21.20.
	29	Sold 2,160 units at $32.

Operating expenses were $22,400. Cash settlements on all transactions were completed by the end of the month.

Required:

1. Prepare perpetual inventory schedules, using (a) FIFO, (b) LIFO, and (c) moving average cost flow assumptions.
2. Prepare income statements and balance sheets based on each of the foregoing methods of inventory valuation.
3. Explain why the different methods yield different results. Which method is correct?
4. What factors should Policastro consider in its choice of method of inventory valuation?
5. Which method would you recommend? Explain.
6. FIFO reflects price increases of goods on hand in net income, but these are not real profits because, as the inventory is depleted, replacement costs will be higher. Do you agree? Explain.

B Problems

P10–1B
Journal entries for a perpetual inventory system

San Juan Company maintains perpetual inventory records. All purchases are received F.O.B. destination, and returns are made at the supplier's expense. Following are summary data from the records for July 1987, the first month of operations:

Total purchases (on account)	$590,200
Total returns of defective merchandise for credit	10,150
Operating expenses (paid in cash)	140,150
Total sales (on account)	705,300
Cost of goods sold per stock records	419,800

Required:

1. Prepare summary general journal entries dated July 31 to record purchases, purchase returns, sales, and operating expenses.
2. Journalize summary closing entries, including the transfer of net income to the Retained Earnings account.

P10–2B
Computing inventory and cost of goods sold—periodic inventory system

The inventory of Ohio Industries on January 1 and December 31, 1987, consisted of 10,625 and 15,625 units, respectively, of stock number L300. The beginning inventory was priced at a cost of $8,500. The following purchases were made during the year:

Date	Quantity	Cost
1987		
Feb. 7	6,250	$ 5,625.00
Apr. 4	10,625	10,093.75
Jun. 8	15,000	14,700.00
Sep. 19	3,750	3,750.00
Nov. 1	10,000	10,500.00

Required: Under the periodic inventory system determine: (1) the ending inventory, and (2) cost of goods sold, using (a) the FIFO cost flow assumption, (b) the LIFO cost flow assumption, and (c) the weighted average cost flow assumption.

P10–3B
Recording transactions on a perpetual card

Mingo Company uses a perpetual inventory system. During August 1987, the following activity was experienced with a fruit crate, stock number 102-XA:

1987

Aug. 1 Balance on hand is 300 units at $5.50.
    5 Sold 240 units.
  12 Received 240 units at $6.00.
  23 Sold 270 units.
  30 Received 120 units at $6.25.

Required: Record the beginning balance and the August activity on perpetual inventory cards, and determine: (1) the ending inventory valuation, and (2) the cost of goods sold, using (a) the FIFO cost flow assumption, (b) the LIFO cost flow assumption, and (c) the moving average cost flow assumption.

P10–4B
Three LCM valuations and effect on gross margin

Blue Mountain Repair Shop has determined the following to be applicable to the inventory of December 31, 1987, the end of the accounting year:

		Unit	
Item	Quantity	Cost	Market
Boxes:			
Size A	300	$2.85	$3.10
Size B	600	5.20	4.50
Size C	180	4.30	4.20
Corner seals:			
Size A	1,200	1.45	1.70
Size B	2,400	2.10	2.30
Size C	720	1.72	1.20

Required:

1. Compute the ending inventory at the lower of cost or market applied (a) to each item, (b) to each category, and (c) to the entire inventory.
2. What is the effect of each application of LCM on the gross margin in the current year? In the following year?

P10–5B
Estimating ending inventories—both methods

Data for two companies are provided as follows:

Company A

Inventory, January 1	$120,600
Net purchases during January	363,060
Net sales during January	630,100

Average gross margin rate for the past three years has been 37 percent of net sales.

Company B

Sales	$407,250
Transportation in	5,400
Purchases at cost	256,500
Purchases at retail	405,000
Inventory—July 1 (cost)	94,500
Inventory—July 1 (retail)	135,000

Required:

1. Estimate the January 31 inventory of Company A using the gross margin method.
2. Estimate the July 31 inventory of Company B using the retail method.
3. Estimate the July 31 inventory of Company B using the retail method assuming markups of $16,875 and markdowns of $12,400.

P10–6B
Inventory ratios

In the 1983 *Annual Report,* White Consolidated Industries, Inc. reported the following data (dollars in thousands):

	1983	1982
Cost of products sold	$1,699,154	$1,663,881
Net inventory	388,390	442,141
Other current assets (listed)	474,397	293,929
Total current liabilities	366,607	329,582

Required:

1. Compute inventory turnover for 1983.
2. Compute the ratio of inventory to working capital for both years. Is 1983 an improvement over 1982? Explain.
3. Does the cost flow assumption used to determine inventory values affect these ratios? Explain.

P10–7B
Thought-provoking problem: effect of inventory errors

At Boiling Springs Company, where a periodic inventory system is used, the December 31, 1987, inventory was undervalued by $120,000 because of a failure to include some merchandise that had been received and debited to the Purchases account. As a result, additional orders were placed at the beginning of 1988 resulting in a duplication of items on hand that was not corrected until return of the merchandise three months later for credit. The company's short-term borrowing rate to finance the unnecessary purchase was 12 percent per year. Boiling Springs Company paid transportation costs of $620 for the return.

Required:

1. What was the effect of the error on the net income for 1987?
2. What was the effect of the error on 1988 net income? Support your answer with assumptions and computations.
3. What was the ultimate effect of the error on retained earnings?

11 Long-Lived Assets

Introduction

When the court-ordered divestiture of AT&T took place on January 1, 1984, the largest of the seven regional holding companies formed was BellSouth Corporation. Its two operating companies had total assets in excess of $20,800,000,000, of which more than $19,000,000,000 (about 92 percent) were plant assets.[1] Industry often requires large expenditures for three groups of long-term assets that are used in the operations of a business:

1. **Tangible plant assets (plant assets)**, such as land, building, machinery, equipment, and trucks.

2. Natural resources or **wasting assets**, such as those found in mining, oil and gas, forestry, and other extractive industries.

3. **Intangible assets**, such as patents, trademarks, and goodwill.

This chapter deals with the determination of and accounting for the costs of these long-lived assets, their allocation as expense (if applicable) to appropriate accounting periods, and their disposal or retirement.

Learning Goals

1. To know which cost elements are included in the original cost of property, plant, and equipment items.

2. To understand the nature of depreciation, depletion, and amortization.

3. To know the acceptable methods of computing depreciation and to make the necessary accounting entries.

4. To differentiate between capital and revenue expenditures.

---

[1] BellSouth *Prospectus,* November 8, 1983, page 37.

5. To account for disposal of plant assets including trade-in transactions.

6. To record depletion of natural resources and to understand the accounting for depletion costs as part of cost of goods sold or as inventory.

7. To identify, define, and account for intangible plant assets.

8. To be familiar with financial statement disclosure requirements for plant assets.

9. To understand and be able to compute the various ratios that are used to evaluate the efficiency of use of property, plant, and equipment.

Definition of Terms

The term **property, plant, and equipment** includes all *tangible* assets including natural resources of a relatively permanent nature, acquired for use in the regular operation of the business, but not for resale, whose use or consumption will cover more than one accounting period. *Long-term intangible assets* are those that have no form or substance but contribute to the operation of a business. These groups of assets are now considered in more detail.

Tangible Plant Assets

Some of the tangible plant assets have been discussed in preceding chapters. Now they are considered in more depth, including a determination of their costs and valuation, allocation of their cost to expense, and their disposal.

Valuation of Tangible Plant Assets

A tangible plant asset is initially recorded in the records at cost, which includes the purchase price (less any cash discount) plus *all other expenditures required to secure title and to get the asset ready for operating use*. The cost of a building includes permit fees, excavation and grading, architectural and engineering fees, and remodeling costs. In October 1979, the FASB issued *Statement No. 34,* "Capitalization of Interest Cost." As amended in 1982 by *FASB Statements No. 58 and 62,* it requires that certain interest paid or accrued during the period of construction, if material, be **capitalized** (that is, debited to the constructed plant asset). The cost of machinery includes transportation, installation, and all other costs incurred in preparing the machinery for operations. These asset acquisition costs are called *initial capital expenditures.*

Assume that a company purchases a machine for $5,000 at terms of 2/10, n/60, with freight to be paid by the buyer. Installation of the machine requires specialized electrical wiring and the construction of a cement foundation. All these expenditures are debited to the asset account. The total asset cost includes the following:

Purchase price	$5,000
Deduct: Cash discount	100
Net purchase price	$4,900
Transportation (including in-transit costs)	125
Cost of wiring	75
Construction of a special foundation	110
Total asset cost	$5,210

The various expenditures could be debited directly to the asset account. However, as explained in Chapter 3, an expense occurs as asset costs expire *while being used to produce revenue.* The expense of using tangible plant assets (depreciation expense) is explained in detail later in this chapter. Frequently a significant period of time passes between the initial purchase of an asset and its readiness to be used in the revenue-producing process. To collect the asset costs during the preparation period, a Construction in Progress account is used.[2] When the asset is ready for service, the debits in that account are transferred to the asset account, and the depreciation process (recognition of expense) is begun. The following entries illustrate the initial purchase and the preparation of the machine in the above illustration:

1987				
Jun.	1	Construction in Progress	4,900	
		Cash		4,900
		Purchased a machine, 2/10, n/30.		

The entry for the freight payment on June 11 is:

1987				
Jun.	11	Construction in Progress	125	
		Cash		125
		Paid freight on delivery of machine.		

The entry to record the payment for installation of the machine on July 24 is:

1987				
Jul.	24	Construction in Progress	185	
		Cash		185
		Paid for installation of machine.		

---

[2]Construction in Progress is the traditional title for this account, even when the asset is a purchased one. Other titles such as Assets Being Readied for Service could be used to show the broad nature of this account.

Other initial capital expenditures would also be debited to the Construction in Progress account. The entry to record the readiness for service of the asset on July 24 is:

1987				
Jul.	24	Machinery....................	5,210	
		Construction in Progress..........		5,210
		To record readiness of machinery for service.		

When these entries are posted, the Machinery account shows a total cost for the machine of $5,210. If the discount of $100 is not taken, it should still be deducted from the purchase price of $5,000 and debited to Discounts Lost—Nonmerchandise Items. Although Construction in Progress is an asset account, the process of depreciation is not applicable until the item is declared ready for use and Construction in Progress is closed into the plant asset account.

A tangible plant asset acquired in some manner other than cash or credit purchase—for example, by gift or in exchange for capital stock—is valued on the basis of the amount of cash that would be required for its acquisition (**fair market value**). When a used plant asset is acquired, all expenditures incurred in getting the asset ready for use—paint, replacement parts, and so on—become debits to the asset account.

The cost of land includes brokers' fees, legal fees, transfer taxes, and costs incurred in preparing the land for use, such as grading, clearing, and the removal of unwanted existing structures less amounts received for scrap and salvage. Land is shown separately on the balance sheet because it is not subject to depreciation. However, improvements to land—lighting, parking areas, fencing—that deteriorate through use are subject to depreciation and should be classified in a separate account, Land Improvements.

Subsidiary Records

Within the accounts, assets are grouped into similar categories. Typewriters, calculators, copying machines, and similar items are usually debited to an account called Office Equipment. Machinery, Buildings, Store Equipment, Delivery Equipment, and many other accounts each contain groups of similar assets. It is usually necessary for management to have specific information about each long-lived asset for purposes of computing depreciation, making disposal and replacement decisions, and sometimes maintaining a repair and maintenance history. To serve this need, a plant ledger contains an equipment record for each item. For a large company, such records are most efficiently maintained by computer. A smaller company may have a card file with a record similar to that shown in Figure 11–1 for each item.

EQUIPMENT RECORD				ASSET NO. 1252	CLASS NO. 14	ACCT. NO. 163
NAME OF ASSET Package Sealer						
Made by	Northern Motors			Manufacturer's Serial No. 1BS50216	Location Packing Department	
Purchased From	Mebane Company		Purchase Guarantee			
Year 1987	Type A	Model Medium	Size	H. P. Generated or Required		
Estimated Life 10 Yrs.	Years	Depreciation Rate 10%	% or $	Per Year	Estimated Residual Value $ $100	
Insurance Carried Under general equipment policy						
Appraised by Kelly O'Ferrell		When Appraised 1/12/87		Appraised Value $ 580	Appraisal Report Reference GA 2012	

ACCUMULATED DEPRECIATION			NET ASSET VALUE	DATE	DESCRIPTION	POSTING REF.	COST		
YEAR	ANNUAL AMT.	TO DATE					DEBIT	CREDIT	BALANCE
1987	48	48	532	12/31		163	580		580

Figure 11–1   **Equipment Record**

Depreciation of Tangible Plant Assets

Depreciation is an allocation of cost. It recognizes that depreciable assets used in the business have a predictable and limited service life, over which asset costs should be allocated for the purpose of income measurement. The emphasis is on the systematic periodic debit to expense rather than the resulting balance sheet valuation. Recording depreciation was introduced along with adjusting entries in Chapter 4. Depreciation theory and practice are treated in more detail in the following sections.

Although the serviceable life of the asset cannot be definitely known at the time of its acquisition, its cost cannot be considered as an expense chargeable entirely either to the period of acquisition or to the period of disposal. It is better to estimate the useful life of the asset for purposes of making periodic debits to expense than to omit the expense debit on the grounds that there is no definitely known period of service life.

Purpose of depreciation

Since most tangible plant assets have a limited useful life, their costs are properly allocable as expenses to the accounting periods in which the assets are used. The purpose of depreciation *is to recognize the expiration of asset cost through use. Its primary purpose is cost allocation.*

Estimated Useful Life (EUL)

It is often difficult to predict the useful service life of an asset. The estimate is important because the amount of cost assigned as expense of each period (depreciation for a period) is deducted from current revenue, thereby affecting net income for the period. Past experience, standard operating policies, and equipment replacement policies may be used in estimating the period during which the asset can or will be used by the business. A machine may be able to withstand wear and tear for 20 years, but it may be used for only 10 years because it has become too slow or too small for current requirements; or it may have become obsolete. The estimated useful service life over which the cost is allocated is called the **estimated useful life (EUL)** of the asset.

Estimated Salvage Value

The amount that is expected to be recovered when the asset is ultimately scrapped, sold, or traded in is called **salvage value** (or residual value). The salvage value is deducted from the cost to determine the **depreciable cost**, the total amount of depreciation to be recorded over the estimated useful life. If an expenditure will be required in dismantling or removing the asset, the estimated gross salvage value is reduced by the anticipated removal cost. It is frequently assumed that the salvage value will be offset by the removal cost, in which case the depreciable cost is the total cost of the asset.

A company may trade in any assets that have a market value. For example, some businesses trade in cars, trucks, and office equipment for new models after a period of use. In such instances, the expected market value at the date of trade-in should be used as the salvage value amount.

Methods of Computing Depreciation

A number of methods are used to calculate periodic depreciation charges; each may give a significantly different result. The method selected in any specific instance should be based on a careful evaluation of all the factors involved, including estimated useful life, intensity of use, speed of changes in the technology of the industry and equipment, and revenue-generating potential. The objective is to debit expense of each period in proportion to the benefits received in that period. Depending upon the method used, the amounts apportioned to each period may be irregular, follow a regularly increasing or decreasing pattern, or be the same.

The depreciation methods described in the following sections include (1) the straight line method, (2) production methods, including the working hours and the production unit methods, and (3) accelerated methods, including the double-declining balance and the sum-of-the-years'-digits methods. The method selected for computing depreciation is crucial because the amount of the expense affects the net income for current and future periods and the carrying value of the asset in the balance sheet.

Straight Line Method Under the **straight line method**, depreciation is considered a function of time, and a uniform portion of the cost is allocated to each accounting period. It is popular because it is simple to use. It assumes, however, uniform levels of operating efficiency, repair and maintenance, and revenue contributions for each period of the asset's EUL.

A formula for the straight line method may be expressed as follows:

$$\frac{\text{Cost} - \text{Salvage value}}{\text{Number of years in estimated useful life of asset}} = \text{Depreciation expense for each year.}$$

Assume that a machine costing $20,000, with an estimated useful life of five years and an estimated net salvage value of $3,500, is purchased on January 3, 1987. The annual depreciation expense is:

$$\frac{\$20,000 - \$3,500}{5 \text{ years}} = \$3,300 \text{ per year.}$$

Straight line depreciation can also be computed by use of a *straight line rate,* calculated by dividing 100 percent by the number of years in EUL (alternatively calculated as $1/n$, where n = EUL). In the foregoing situation:

$$\frac{100\%}{5 \text{ years}} = 20\% \text{ per year, or } \frac{1}{n} = \frac{1}{5} = 0.20 = 20\%.$$

Production Methods Production methods relate depreciation to use or to results rather than to time, recognizing either working hours or units of output. Each hour or unit is charged an equal amount.

The **working hours method** requires an estimate of useful life in service hours instead of years. The depreciation expense for an accounting period is determined as follows:

$$\frac{\text{Cost} - \text{Salvage value}}{\text{Total estimated working hours}} = \text{Depreciation expense per hour, and}$$

$$\begin{bmatrix} \text{Depreciation} \\ \text{expense} \\ \text{per hour} \end{bmatrix} \times \begin{bmatrix} \text{Working hours} \\ \text{for the} \\ \text{period} \end{bmatrix} = \begin{bmatrix} \text{Depreciation} \\ \text{expense for} \\ \text{the period} \end{bmatrix}.$$

Assume, for example, that a machine costing $20,000 with a salvage value of $3,500 is expected to be operated 150,000 hours. If it is operated 10,000 hours during an accounting period, the computation for the period would be:

$$\frac{\$20,000 - \$3,500}{150,000 \text{ hours}} = \$0.11 \text{ per hour, and}$$

$0.11 \times 10,000$ hours = $1,100 depreciation expense for the period.

Under the **production unit method**, depreciation is computed on units of output, and therefore an estimate of total units of output is required. Assume, for example, that the machine costing $20,000 with a salvage value of $3,500 has an estimated productive life of 10,000 units. If 1,500 units were processed during the current period, the debit to depreciation expense for the period would be:

$$\frac{\$20,000 - \$3,500}{10,000 \text{ units}} = \$1.65 \text{ per unit produced, and}$$

$$\$1.65 \times 1,500 \text{ units} = \$2,475 \text{ depreciation expense for the period.}$$

The production methods allocate cost in proportion to the use that is made of the asset, the assumption being that there is a correlation between units of use and revenue generated.

Accelerated Methods The use of **accelerated methods** results in larger depreciation expense during the early years of asset life, with gradually decreasing depreciation expense in later years. Two commonly used forms are (1) the declining balance method, and (2) the sum-of-the-years'-digits method.

Declining Balance Method Under a *declining balance method,* a uniform depreciation rate is applied in each period to the remaining **carrying value** (cost less accumulated depreciation).[3] One form that uses twice the straight line rate is termed the **double-declining balance method (DDB)**. *Salvage value is not deducted under the declining balance method,* although the asset cannot be depreciated below salvage value.

In a period in which the use of DDB reduces the carrying value to an amount less than salvage value, the use of DDB should be discontinued. For that period and future periods of the EUL, the remaining depreciation may be computed by the straight line method.[4] On the other hand, a balance greater than salvage value may remain at the end of the EUL. Such a balance (less salvage value) may be depreciated under the straight line method over a period determined at that time, by an adjustment in the amount of depreciation for the final period, or by the fixed percentage of the carrying value until it is retired from use.

Assume the data used previously (a machine is purchased on January 3, 1987, at a cost of $20,000, salvage value estimated at $3,500, and EUL of five years). Use of DDB results in a 40 percent depreciation rate—twice the straight line rate of 20 percent—which is applied annually to remaining carrying value.

---

[3] *Carrying value* is also known as *book value,* which is discussed later in this chapter.

[4] If planned at the time the depreciation method is adopted, a change to straight line at this point is not required to be reported as a change in accounting principle under *APB Opinion No. 20.*

DDB—Case 1. Since the DDB rate is applied to carrying value, the salvage value is not deducted from cost in computing depreciation. The annual amounts are as follows:

Year	Computation	Annual Depreciation	Accumulated Depreciation	Carrying Value
1987	40% of $20,000	$8,000	$ 8,000	$12,000
1988	40% of 12,000	4,800	12,800	7,200
1989	40% of 7,200	2,880	15,680	4,320
1990	$4,320 − $3,500[a]	820	16,500	3,500
1991	None	None	16,500	3,500

[a]40% of $4,320 is $1,728, which would reduce the carrying value below estimated salvage value. Accordingly, only $820 is recorded in 1990.

Because depreciation was stopped after the fourth year of its useful life, no further depreciation expense is recorded for this asset even though it is kept in service. When the asset is disposed of, the $3,500 carrying value will be used to determine any loss or gain on disposal (discussed later in this chapter). A typical method is to change to straight line in the year that carrying value would fall below salvage value; it is illustrated next.

DDB—Case 2. In the fourth year of EUL, the carrying value would fall below salvage value if DDB is continued. Many companies plan to switch to straight line at this point, as follows:

Year	Computation	Annual Depreciation	Accumulated Depreciation	Carrying Value
1987	40% of $20,000	$8,000	$ 8,000	$12,000
1988	40% of 12,000	4,800	12,800	7,200
1989	40% of 7,200	2,880	15,680	4,320[a]
1990	½ of $820[b]	410	16,090	3,910
1991	½ of $820	410	16,500	3,500

[a]40% of $4,320 is $1,728, which would reduce carrying value below salvage value if recorded in 1990. Hence, the change to straight line.
[b]Carrying value of $4,320 minus salvage value of $3,500 equals $820, the amount to be depreciated by straight line over the last two years.

In the change to straight line in 1990, only the difference between end-1989 carrying value and estimated salvage value is to be depreciated over the remaining EUL.

Sum-of-the-Year's-Digits Method Under the **sum-of-the-year's-digits method (SYD)**, depreciation for any year is determined by multiplying the cost less salvage value by a fraction. The denominator is the sum of the numbers of years of estimated useful life of the asset and the numerator is the number of the specific period applied in reverse order, or the number of years remaining, including the current year. The following steps may be followed in sequence in making the calculations:

1. Calculate the sum of the series of digits represented by the life of the asset, starting with the EUL (n) and going down to 1:

$$5 + 4 + 3 + 2 + 1 = 15.$$

2. The denominator is: The sum of the years' digits from Step 1.
3. The numerators are the digits in the EUL used in reverse order as stated.
4. The annual depreciation expense is: (Cost of asset − Salvage) × Fraction for that year.

On the basis of the same facts as before (cost of $20,000 and salvage value of $3,500), the annual depreciation is computed as follows:

Year	Years' Digits	Fraction Times Depreciable Cost	Annual Depreciation
1987	5	5/15 × $16,500	$ 5,500
1988	4	4/15 × $16,500	$ 4,400
1989	3	3/15 × $16,500	3,300
1990	2	2/15 × $16,500	2,200
1991	1	1/15 × $16,500	1,100
Total depreciation for 5 years			$16,500

For long-lived assets, the sum of the years' digits (S) can be found by using a formula based on arithmetical progression of 1:

$$S = \frac{n(n+1)}{2} = \frac{n}{2}(n+1) = n\left(\frac{n+1}{2}\right)$$

where n = EUL.

For example,

$$S = \frac{5(5+1)}{2} = \frac{5}{2}(5+1) = 5\left(\frac{5+1}{2}\right) = 15.$$

Comparison of Methods

For a machine purchased for $20,000 on January 3, 1987, with a salvage value of $3,500 and an EUL of five years, a comparison of methods shows the following depreciation expense under each method:

Year	Straight Line Only	Pure Double-Declining Balance[a]	DDB with a Switch to Straight Line	Sum-of-the Years'-Digits
1987	$ 3,300	$ 8,000	$ 8,000	$ 5,500
1988	3,300	4,800	4,800	4,400
1989	3,300	2,880	2,880	3,300
1990	3,300	820	410	2,200
1991	3,300	0	410	1,100
Totals	$16,500	$16,500	$16,500	$16,500

[a]Without a switch to straight line.

Double-declining balance results in the highest depreciation in the first year because of the higher rate (40 percent) and higher base ($20,000 as compared with $16,500). The total for both the DDB methods for the five-year period is the same as straight line and SYD because of the change in the fourth year to avoid depreciating the asset below salvage value. If the use of DDB leaves an undepreciated carrying value at the end of the EUL that is greater than estimated salvage value and the machine is kept in service, a changeover to straight line for the remainder of the revised EUL is in order at this point. If the change to straight line is not made and if the item is disposed of at the end of the EUL, there is simply a greater book value to be considered in calculating a gain or loss.

Depreciation for Partial Accounting Periods

A consistent method should be followed for recording depreciation on assets acquired or retired during an accounting period. Since depreciation is an estimate, exact methods such as counting the number of days of use are not commonly used. One often used method that is both simple and relevant is to consider that a tangible plant asset is purchased as of the beginning of the month of acquisition if it is purchased on or before the fifteenth of the month, or as of the first day of the following month if it is purchased on or after the sixteenth of the month. The minimum measurable unit of time for the depreciation expense charge should be one month.

Computation of depreciation for a partial year presents no special problems when the straight line method or a production method is used. For accelerated methods, however, a special problem does arise. In both sum-of-the-years'-digits and declining balance methods, the amount of depreciation is associated with the *asset-life year*. When the asset-life year is not the same as the accounting year, depreciation is recorded based on a combination of fractions of asset-life years. To illustrate, assume that on January 3, 1987, Barber Company bought the $20,000 machine that has been used in the previous illustrations. Assume, however, that Barber's accounting year ends on June 30. Referring to the foregoing tables, the depreciation expense in the fiscal year ended June 30, 1987, would be:

Under DDB: 1/2 × $8,000 = $4,000.
Under SYD: 1/2 × $5,500 = $2,750.

However, for the fiscal year ended June 30, 1988, Barber should record:

$$\text{Under DDB: } (1/2 \times \$8,000) + (1/2 \times \$4,800) = \$6,400.$$
$$\text{Under SYD: } (1/2 \times \$5,500) + (1/2 \times \$4,400) = \$4,950.$$

These figures differ because in the fiscal (or accounting) year ended June 30, 1987, Barber has received the benefits of only one-half the first asset-life year of the machine. In the fiscal year ended June 30, 1988, it is receiving the benefits of the second half of the machine's first asset-life year plus the first half of the machine's second asset-life year.[5]

Accelerated Cost Recovery System (ACRS)

To encourage increased capital investment by business, the *Economic Recovery Tax Act of 1981* revised federal income tax laws relating to depreciation. For tax purposes, businesses are entitled to "cost recovery deductions" at varying rates instead of depreciation deductions for tangible property placed in service after 1980. The methods authorized are called the **accelerated cost recovery system (ACRS)**. Depreciable personal property falls into four cost recovery classes: three-year; five-year; ten-year; and fifteen-year. Automobiles, light-duty trucks, and certain special tools fall into the three-year class, while most machinery and equipment fall into the five-year class. Certain heavy equipment such as railroad tank cars falls into the ten-year class; permanent buildings usually fall into the fifteen-year class. Within each class, statutory percentages of cost can be deducted annually adding up to 100 percent of cost recovery in the class time period.

Assume that the $20,000 machine used in previous examples was placed in service on December 31, 1984. It falls into the five-year property category. At the rates then in effect as stipulated by the Internal Revenue Service, cost recovery tax deductions would be:

Year	%		Amount
1985	15%	=	$ 3,000
1986	22	=	4,400
1987	21	=	4,200
1988	21	=	4,200
1989	21	=	4,200
Total	100%	=	$20,000

The ACRS amounts are for federal income tax purposes only; conventional methods are still used for financial reporting using estimated useful lives that often differ from ACRS recovery periods.

---

[5] Under DDB, this process can be simplified by using only one-half year for 1987 in the amortization table. Thus 1987 depreciation is ½ × 40% × $20,000 = $4,000. The 1988 year begins with a carrying value of $16,000 = $20,000 − $4,000; depreciation for 1988 is 40% × $16,000 = $6,400. In future years, the annual DDB rate can be applied to carrying value. There is no parallel simplification for SYD.

Under ACRS, firms have an option to use the straight line method for tax reporting or certain prescribed accelerated methods that were phased in from 1981 to 1985. At the time of this writing, firms were using a variety of the methods described in this book for reporting to stockholders; the majority appeared to be using straight line in annual reports.

Guidelines for Depreciation Methods

The user should select the depreciation method that is most practical and meaningful. Since the amount of the depreciation deduction has a direct effect on net income and since the alternative methods of calculating depreciation result in different amounts, the method chosen may significantly affect a corporation's income tax liability. Any tax savings become available for investment in new property, plant, and equipment or for any other use management chooses. *Minimization of income taxes by choice of depreciation method is a good management practice.* It is acceptable practice to use one depreciation method for income tax reporting and a different method for financial reporting.

The straight line method is simple to apply and is satisfactory under conditions of fairly uniform usage. The production methods allocate depreciation in proportion to usage or output. This is important if usage is the dominant cause of loss in usefulness of the asset. The accelerated methods are based on the idea that the service rendered by a tangible plant asset is greatest in the early years of use. Hence, depreciation charged under these methods results in a more accurate matching of expense and revenue. These methods also take into account the fact that as an asset gets older, it requires more maintenance. The increasing maintenance expenses in later years are offset by the diminishing depreciation expense, thus equalizing, to some extent, the total expense of the asset and thereby achieving a better matching of expense with revenue.

Recording and Financial Reporting

The basic entries to record depreciation expense and reporting of depreciation on the balance sheet were covered in Chapter 4. They are repeated here briefly for review. Only the straight line amounts are used—recording and reporting for all methods is the same except for dollar amounts. Using the earlier straight line example, the entry to record 1987 depreciation expense is:

1987				
Dec.	31	Depreciation Expense—Machinery	3,300	
		Accumulated Depreciation—Machinery		3,300
		To record depreciation for the year.		

On the balance sheet for December 31, 1987, the figure would be reported as follows:

Assets		
Property, plant, and equipment:		
Machinery	$20,000	
Deduct: Accumulated depreciation	3,300	$16,700

As additional depreciation expense is recorded in subsequent periods and the accumulated depreciation increases, the carrying value continues to decrease. In general, the carrying value will equal the estimated salvage value at the end of EUL.

Up to this point, all debits have been made to an expense account when depreciation is recorded. The debit to an expense account is correct when the depreciation represents an expired cost of the accounting period. In some cases, however—for example, manufacturing—depreciation represents an inventoriable cost rather than an expense. This concept is discussed later with depletion of natural resources and reinforced when patent amortization is illustrated.

Capital and Revenue Expenditures

Capital expenditures are significant payments benefiting two or more periods. They may be (1) initial costs of acquiring tangible plant assets (as previously illustrated), and (2) costs subsequent to the original purchase of these assets (asset alterations, additions or improvements to existing assets, or extraordinary repairs). They prolong the useful life of the asset or make it more valuable or adaptable. Expenditures that improve or enlarge existing assets *should be capitalized by a debit to the asset account.*

Expenditures for extraordinary repairs made to equipment during its life are also classified as capital expenditures if they extend the useful life or capacity of the asset or otherwise make it more serviceable (for example, overhaul of an aircraft engine). Accountants view an extraordinary repair as restoring the effects of previous wear, that is, as a recovery of previous asset services. They record the capitalization by debiting Accumulated Depreciation, thereby canceling past depreciation charges.

Assume that the $20,000 machine used in previous illustrations received a complete overhaul at the end of 1990. The overhaul, at a cost of $2,500, added two years to the original EUL of five years. The general journal entry to record the overhaul is:

1990				
Dec.	30	Accumulated Depreciation—Machinery	2,500	
		Cash		2,500
		To record the overhaul of a machine.		

When any capital expenditure—an enlargement or extraordinary repair—is made on an asset already in service, the carrying value is changed, and a new depreciation schedule is needed. The method for doing this is explained in the next section.

Revenue expenditures benefit a current period and are made for the purpose of maintaining the asset in satisfactory operating condition. A routine repair or the replacement of a minor part that has worn out is an expense of the current accounting period. These expenditures do not increase the serviceability of the asset beyond the original estimate but rather represent normal maintenance costs.

Careful distinction between capital and revenue expenditures is one of the fundamental problems of accounting. It is essential for the matching of expenses and revenue and, therefore, for the proper measurement of net income. A capital expenditure recorded as a revenue expenditure (for example, a purchase of office equipment debited to Office Expense) causes an understatement of net income in that year. If the error is not corrected, net income for the following years will be overstated by the amount of depreciation expense that would otherwise have been recognized. Conversely, a revenue expenditure recorded as a capital expenditure (for example, an office expense debited to Office Equipment) overstates net income for that year. If the error is not corrected, net income for the following years will be understated by the depreciation charge on the overstated portion of the Office Equipment account.

Changing of Depreciation Expense

The periodic depreciation expense may require revision as the result of (1) an additional capital expenditure made on an original asset, or (2) errors in the original EUL or estimated salvage value. In either case, the new depreciable cost is typically allocated over the remaining life of the property on which the expenditure was made. Assume, for example, that an additional wing costing $80,000 is added to a five-year-old factory building. The original cost of the building was $330,000, the estimated salvage value that was not changed by the improvement was $30,000, and the estimated useful life was 25 years. The straight line method of depreciation has been used. The calculation of the revised annual depreciation charge is:

Original cost	$330,000
Deduct: Accumulated depreciation ($300,000 ÷ 25 = $12,000 per year × 5 years)	60,000
Book value	$270,000
Additional cost	80,000
New book value	$350,000
Deduct: Estimated salvage value	30,000
New depreciable cost	$320,000
New annual depreciation charge, based on a remaining useful life of 20 years ($320,000 ÷ 20)	$ 16,000

Part Two / Income Measurement and Valuation Issues

If the improvement prolongs the life of the asset or increases salvage value, the calculations must be altered to show the effect of such changes. For example, if after the addition of the wing the remaining useful life was estimated to be 24 years and the estimated salvage value was $38,000, the revised annual depreciation charge would be determined as follows:

New book value (from above)	$350,000
Deduct: Estimated salvage value	38,000
New depreciable cost	$312,000
New annual depreciation charge, based on a remaining useful life of 24 years ($312,000 ÷ 24)	$13,000

If at any time it is determined that an error has been made in EUL, a new depreciation schedule is prepared. From that point on, the new depreciation amount will be recorded.[6] It will be calculated in the manner just illustrated.

At some point, however, it is necessary to dispose of most items of tangible plant property. Accounting for such disposal of tangible plant property is explained in the next section.

Disposal of Tangible Plant Assets

A tangible plant asset may be disposed of by being discarded, by sale, or by being traded in as part of the purchase price of a replacement. The accounting treatment of sales and discards is similar; that of trade-ins is somewhat different.

Sale or Discard of Tangible Plant Assets

When an asset is sold or discarded, the entry for the transaction must remove the appropriate amounts from the asset and the accumulated depreciation accounts. Assume, for example, that a company acquired a truck with a five-year EUL on January 3, 1987, at a cost of $18,000. It has no salvage value. Depreciation is recorded on a straight line basis at the rate of $3,600 annually. Three situations, together with the methods of accounting for the disposal of the truck, are illustrated.

---

[6]*Opinions of the Accounting Principles Board*, No. 20, "Accounting Changes" (New York: AICPA, July 1971) defines such a change as a change in accounting estimates and requires footnote disclosure in the financial statements.

Example 1: Sale of Asset at a Price Equal to Book Value
The truck is sold on October 1, 1991, for $900. The first entry records the depreciation for the current year up to the date of sale:

1991 Oct. 1	Depreciation Expense—Trucks .... Accumulated Depreciation—Trucks. .... To record depreciation on trucks for the 9-month period 1/1/91 to 10/1/91.	2,700	2,700

The Accumulated Depreciation account now has a credit balance of $17,100 = [(4 years × $3,600) + $2,700 in 1991]. The book value of the truck is $900, computed as follows:

```
Cost at acquisition . . . . . . . . . . . . . . . . . . . . . . . . . . . . . . . $18,000
Deduct: Accumulated depreciation . . . . . . . . . . . . . . . . . . . .  17,100
    Book value . . . . . . . . . . . . . . . . . . . . . . . . . . . . . . . . . . $   900
```

As shown above, the *book value* of an asset—as distinguished from market value and replacement value—is its cost at acquisition reduced by the portion of the accumulated depreciation account applicable to that asset. Other terms commonly used are *carrying value* and *undepreciated cost*. The entry to record the sale is:

1991 Oct. 1	Cash. .... Accumulated Depreciation—Trucks. .... Trucks .... To record sale of truck.	900 17,100	18,000

Its purpose is to record the receipt of cash, eliminate the accumulated charges from the Accumulated Depreciation account, and reduce the asset account by the original cost of the truck.[7]

Example 2: Sale of Asset at a Price Above Book Value
The truck is sold on October 1, 1991, for $1,200—or at a gain of $300 (see calculation in journal entry). The entry to record the depreciation for the current year

---

[7] If this truck had been discarded instead of sold, there would be a loss on disposal of plant assets of $900 (the book value). The loss account would have been debited instead of Cash in the above journal entry.

up to the date of sale is the same as in Example 1. The following entry is made to record the sale:

1991						
Oct.	1	Cash.		1,200		
		Accumulated Depreciation—Trucks.		17,100		
		Trucks				18,000
		Gain on Disposal of Plant Assets.				300
		To record sale of truck at a gain computed as follows:				
		Cost of truck. $18,000				
		Deduct: Accumulated depreciation. 17,100				
		Book value of truck. . . . . $ 900				
		Amount received 1,200				
		Gain on disposal. $ 300				

Gains and losses on disposal of tangible plant assets result from differences between the book value of an asset and the proceeds from its disposal. A gain results when the proceeds are greater than the book value, a loss when they are less. Gain on disposal of plant assets is shown in the income statement under other revenue.

Example 3: Sale of Asset at a Price Below Book Value

The truck is sold on October 1, 1991, for $400 in cash—or at a loss of $500 (see calculation in journal entry). Again, the entry to record the depreciation applicable to the year of sale is the same as in Example 1. The entry to record the sale is:

1991						
Oct.	1	Cash.		400		
		Accumulated Depreciation—Trucks.		17,100		
		Loss on Disposal of Plant Assets		500		
		Trucks				18,000
		To record sale of truck at a loss computed as follows:				
		Cost of truck. $18,000				
		Deduct: Accumulated depreciation. 17,100				
		Book value of truck. . . . . $ 900				
		Amount received 400				
		Loss on disposal . . . . $ 500				

Trade-in of Tangible Plant Assets

When a plant asset is traded in connection with the purchase of a new asset, two situations are possible. Most frequently, the trade-in is on the purchase of a similar plant asset that continues the same stream of earnings function as the old one. Sometimes, however, the trade-in is on a dissimilar asset that discontinues the old stream of earnings function and starts a new and different one. The accounting issue in trade-ins involves recognizing gains and losses on the transactions. In trade-in transactions for dissimilar items, all gains and losses are recognized. These situations are considered first because the authors believe that the accounting procedures involved are easier to understand.

Trade-in of Tangible Plant Assets—Dissimilar Items

If the new property does not perform essentially the same function as the old property, the transaction is a trade-in for a dissimilar item; the earnings generated by the used asset have ended. The new asset will generate new and different earnings. In such cases, the new asset should be recorded at fair market value.[8]

If the trade-in allowance is not arbitrarily excessive (as a partial offset to an unrealistic list price of the new asset), it may be considered the fair market value and therefore the proper selling price of the old asset. The new asset is recorded at its purchase price. If the trade-in allowance *is* excessive, the list price is ignored and the fair market value of the asset traded in is used to compute the cost of the new asset.

In the following discussion, *the fair market value of the old asset is assumed to be equal to the trade-in allowance*. After the accumulated depreciation up to the date of the trade-in is recorded, the book value of the old assets is compared with its trade-in allowance. A gain is recognized if the trade-in allowance is greater than the book value, a loss if it is less. When the book value and the trade-in allowance are equal, there is no recognized gain or loss.

Example 1: Trade-in Allowance the Same as Book Value A lathe that cost $5,000 with accumulated depreciation of $4,500 up to date of the trade-in is exchanged for land with a fair market value of $4,000; the trade-in allowance is $500. Cash given was $3,500. The new asset is recorded at its cash market price—the cash payment plus the fair market value of the old asset. The transaction is recorded as follows:

1991					
Sep.	1	Land...	4,000	
		Accumulated Depreciation—Equipment	4,500	
		Cash..		3,500
		Equipment..		5,000
		To record trade-in of old lathe for land.		

---

[8]*Opinions of the Accounting Principles Board, No. 29,* "Accounting for Nonmonetary Transactions" (New York: AICPA, May 1973), paragraph 18.

The cash payment of $3,500 is calculated as follows:

Selling price—new asset	$4,000
Trade-in allowance—old asset	500
Cash payment	$3,500

There is no gain or loss in this example because the trade-in allowance is the same as the book value.

Example 2: Trade-in Allowance Less Than Book Value

The old asset in Example 1 is traded in for an allowance of $400.

1991					
Sep.	1	Land		4,000	
		Accumulated Depreciation—Equipment		4,500	
		Loss on Disposal of Plant Assets		100	
		Cash			3,600
		Equipment			5,000
		To record trade-in of equipment at a loss, computed as follows:			
		Cost of old asset $5,000			
		Accumulated depreciation to date of trade-in 4,500			
		Book value . . . . $ 500			
		Trade-in allowance 400			
		Loss on trade-in . . . . $ 100			

A loss is recorded because the book value of $500 is greater than the fair market value of $400. Furthermore, the new, dissimilar asset received cannot be recorded at more than its fair market value of $4,000.

Example 3: Trade-in Allowance Greater Than Book Value

The old asset in Example 1 is exchanged for a new one listed at $4,000; the trade-in allowance is $800.

1991					
Sep.	1	Land		4,000	
		Accumulated Depreciation—Equipment		4,500	
		Cash			3,200
		Equipment			5,000
		Gain on Disposal of Plant Assets			300
		To record trade-in of old lathe for land at a gain computed as follows:			
		Cost of old asset $5,000			
		Accumulated depreciation to date of trade-in 4,500			
		Book value . . . . $ 500			
		Trade-in allowance 800			
		Gain on trade-in . . . . $ 300			

A gain is recorded because the fair market value of $800 is greater than the book value of $500.

Trade-in of Tangible Plant Assets— Similar Items

In many cases, a tangible plant item is traded in on a similar asset—one that has essentially the same function as the old asset. The Accounting Principles Board viewed the new similar asset as being used to continue the same stream of earnings as the old one.[9] The board recognized that such an exchange may include a monetary consideration (sometimes called **boot**) and believed that the entity *paying* the monetary consideration should not recognize any gain on a trade-in for a similar asset but should record the asset received at the amount of the *monetary consideration paid plus the book value of the nonmonetary asset surrendered* (emphasis added).[10] A gain is not appropriate because the same stream of earnings is being continued. The board's opinion further states that when a loss is indicated in exchanges of nonmonetary assets, the "entire indicated loss on the transaction should be recognized."[11] If the loss were not recorded, it would be necessary to record the new asset at more than its fair market value, which is inconsistent with generally accepted accounting principles.

At a Loss To examine first the loss situation, refer back to Example 2 in the preceding section. If the new asset received had been a similar asset—a newer model of the lathe in the same shop—the trade-in for a similar asset at a loss would have been recorded by the type of entry used to record the exchange in Example 2. The loss on disposal of $100 would have been recognized. In other words, accounting for the trade-in for a similar asset at a loss is the same as the trade for a dissimilar asset at a loss.

At a Gain In a gain situation, however, the recording differs. In this book, it is assumed that the entity trading in the old asset is the one *paying* the monetary consideration (or boot); it will not recognize a gain.[12] To illustrate, refer back to Example 3. Assume that the old lathe is being traded in on a

---

[9] *APB Opinion No. 29,* paragraph 21.

[10] Ibid., paragraph 22.

[11] Ibid.

[12] *APB Opinion No. 29* addresses another kind of trade-in of a similar tangible plant asset—one where both a new asset and boot are received. In this kind of trade-in transaction, the book value of the old asset is allocated between the sales portion (cash received) and the traded portion in relation to the relative values of the two assets received: the cash amount and the fair market value of the new asset. A gain or loss equal to the difference between the book value assigned and the cash received will be recognized on the sales portion. A gain will not be recognized on the traded portion, but a loss will be recognized.

new lathe for the same shop. The entry to record the trade-in on a similar asset at a gain would be:

1991 Sep. 1	Equipment (new lathe)		3,700	
	Accumulated Depreciation—Equipment (old lathe)		4,500	
	Cash			3,200
	Equipment (old lathe)...................................			5,000
	To record trade-in of old lathe for new lathe. The valuation of the new lathe is computed as follows:			
	Book value of old lathe	$ 500		
	Cash paid	3,200		
	Total given up for new lathe	$3,700		

The cost recorded for the new lathe is equal to the book value of the old lathe plus the cash paid. This is the same as the fair market value of the new lathe ($4,000) less the gain which is not recognized ($300). Federal tax laws do not allow the recognition of gains or losses on the trade-in of similar assets in computing taxes. Note that failure to show the gain in current income is compensated for by having $300 less to depreciate over the EUL of the new asset.

Natural Resources or Wasting Assets

Another property, plant, and equipment class of items, natural resources or wasting assets, includes oil wells, mines, or timber tracts. They are recorded in the asset account at cost. As the resource is extracted, its asset value is reduced. The primary accounting task is to measure the exhaustion or expiration of a natural resource—called its **depletion**. Periodic depletion is recorded on the books by a debit to the Depletion Cost account or an inventory account and a credit to the Accumulated Depletion account. In the balance sheet, accumulated depletion is classified as a contra account to be deducted from the cost of the resource.

Depletion of Wasting Assets

The periodic depletion charge is usually calculated on an output basis similar to the production unit method of recording depreciation. The cost of the wasting asset is divided by the estimated available units of output to arrive at a per-unit depletion charge. The number of units removed during the accounting period multiplied by the per-unit depletion charge represents depletion for that period. For example, if the asset is a mineral measured in tons:

$$\frac{\text{Cost} - \text{Salvage value}}{\text{Estimated tons to be mined}} = \text{Depletion cost per ton.}$$

Assume that a mine costs $180,000 and contains an estimated 400,000 tons of ore. It is estimated that the net salvage value will be $20,000. The per unit depletion charge is:

$$\frac{\$180,000 - \$20,000}{400,000} = \$0.40 \text{ per ton.}$$

There is a basic difference between operations dealing with the depletion of natural resources and the depreciation of a long-lived tangible plant item. The depletion of natural resources is a process that provides an inventory of goods that can be sold. Normally, a merchandising firm buys its inventory, whereas a production firm—for example, a mining company—incurs certain costs to produce an inventory. All costs directly involved in production of inventory (including depletion costs) are referred to as **inventoriable costs**. They are not closed out as expenses of a period but become a part of the cost valuation of inventory. As such, they are carried as assets until they appear in the income statement as cost of goods sold. Continuing with our previous mining example, if 10,000 tons are mined during an accounting period and 8,000 tons sold, the cost of goods sold is calculated as follows:

```
Cost of goods sold:
    Depletion (10,000 tons × $0.40) . . . . . . . . . . . . . . . . . . .    $ 4,000
    Other costs of production (assumed to be $1 per ton) . . . . . . . . . .  10,000
        Total cost of production ($14,000 ÷ 10,000 tons = $1.40 per ton) . . $14,000
    Deduct: Ending inventory (2,000 tons × $1.40 per ton) . . . . . . . . . .  2,800
        Cost of goods sold (8,000 tons × $1.40 per ton). . . . . . . . . . . $11,200
```

The journal entries to record these events depend on whether a perpetual or a periodic inventory system is used. In either case, the inventory valuation of $2,800 would be shown as a current asset in the balance sheet, and the cost of goods sold ($11,200) would appear in the income statement. The mine would appear as a property, plant, and equipment asset in the balance sheet at cost minus accumulated depletion ($180,000 − $4,000 = $176,000). A related but separate class of long-life assets, intangible assets, is discussed in the next section.

Intangible Assets

Intangible assets are long-lived nonmaterial rights that are of future value to a business. Some intangibles, whether purchased or self-developed, such as patents, copyrights, franchises, and leaseholds, can be readily identified and their cost measured. Others, such as goodwill, are not specifically identifiable or measurable.

The process of estimating and recording the periodic charges to operations due to the expiration of an intangible asset is called **amortization**. It is similar to computing and recording depreciation on a property, plant, and equipment item by the straight line method. The amount to be amortized annually is computed by dividing the asset cost by the legal life or the EUL, whichever is shorter. The entry is usually *a debit to an amortization expense account* and *a credit directly to the asset account;* however, theoretically a credit to an Accumulated Amortization account is acceptable. The straight line method is generally used unless another systematic method is clearly more appropriate, that is, will better match revenues and expenses.

Difficulties and uncertainties arise from the uniqueness of intangibles. The EUL may be limited by law (copyright), by contract (franchise), or by the economic factors of demand and competition (patents). Other intangibles (goodwill, trademarks) have an indefinite, almost unlimited, life. Furthermore, some cannot be separately identified because they relate to the total entity (goodwill). Finally, some intangibles are purchased, while others are developed within the firm.

The AICPA Accounting Principles Board has concluded that a company should record as assets the costs of intangible assets acquired from others, including goodwill acquired in a business combination. The board also concluded that the cost of each type of intangible asset should be amortized by systematic charges to income over the period estimated to be benefited. The period of amortization should not, however, exceed 40 years.[13]

Patents

The United States Patent Office grants **patents**—exclusive rights to the owners to produce and sell their inventions or discoveries—for a period of 17 years. All the costs involved in acquiring a patent from others are included in the intangible asset account Patents. In the past, patents that resulted from a company's own research and development expenditures were capitalized as intangible assets and amortized as described above. Under current accounting standards, however, the costs of research and development performed in an entity are usually debited to expense in the period in which they are incurred. The elements of such cost that should be recorded as expenses instead of intangible assets have been carefully defined by the Financial Accounting Standards Board.[14]

The capitalized cost of a patent should be capitalized and amortized over the economic useful life of the asset or 17 years, whichever is shorter. The Patents account is usually credited directly (intangibles usually do not have

---

[13]*Opinions of the Accounting Principles Board, No. 17,* "Intangible Assets" (New York: AICPA, August 1970), paragraphs 24, 26, 28, and 29.

[14]*Statement of Financial Accounting Standards No. 2,* "Accounting for Research and Development Costs" (Stamford, Conn.: FASB, June 1975), paragraph 11.

contra accounts) for the amortized portion; the account debited is Patent Amortization Cost (another form of inventoriable cost in manufacturing). The accounting entry is as follows:

1987 Dec.	31	Patent Amortization Cost^a . . . . Patents . . . . To record amortization of patents for 1987.	1,000	1,000

^{a}If the patent is used in a nonmanufacturing function such as sales, the debit is to an expense account.

Other Intangible Assets

Other types of intangible assets have already been mentioned. Periodic amortization of such assets is computed by the straight line method and recorded in the same form as for patents except that the debit is to an expense account. Some of the intangibles commonly found in business are described in this section.

Goodwill is a general term combining a variety of intangible factors relating to the ability of a firm to realize above-normal net income returns on an investment. Goodwill can be recorded only in connection with purchase of all or part of a business, in which case it is that intangible asset represented by the amount of purchase price that cannot be identified with any other asset. The amount to be paid for goodwill is usually a result of a bargaining process between the buyer and the seller.[15]

A **copyright**, granted by the federal government, is an exclusive right to publish a literary or an artistic work. It is granted for the life of the creator plus 50 years and gives the owner, or heirs, the exclusive rights to reproduce and sell the work. The copyright is recorded at cost and is subject to amortization either over its estimated legal life or its useful economic life.

A **franchise** is a monopolistic right granted by a government or an entity in the private sector to render a service or to produce a good. A right to operate a bus line or a railroad or the exclusive use of a television transmitting channel is a valuable asset to the owner. Franchises are also used in industry when a manufacturer grants a dealer the exclusive privilege to sell the manufacturer's product within a defined geographical area; examples are McDonald's, Dunkin' Donuts, and Holiday Inns. The cost of obtaining the franchise is amortized over its life or 40 years, whichever is shorter.

---

[15]*APB Opinion No. 17*, paragraph 29. In the bargaining process, there are many ways to arrive at the value of goodwill. One popular method is to capitalize excess earnings. A company with annual excess earnings of $15,000 on an expected rate of return of 12 percent would have goodwill of $125,000. It is computed as follows:

$$X = \text{Assets producing excess earnings (goodwill), and}$$
$$0.12X = \$15,000, \text{ so } X = \$15,000 \div 0.12 = \$125,000.$$

Leases are rights to the use of land, buildings, equipment, or other property that belongs to others. Some leases amount to nothing more than simple rental agreements. In those cases, the amount of rent is debited to an expense account as it is incurred, and the lease is not an intangible asset. Other leases are more complex arrangements that are actually a special type of intangible asset. These leases—called *capital leases*—are the subject of Appendix 11.1.

Title to improvements made to leased property, known as **leasehold improvements**, by a lessee reverts to the lessor upon termination of the lease. Accordingly, the lessee should record the cost of such improvements in an intangible asset account, Leasehold Improvements. Leasehold improvements should be amortized over their estimated useful lives or the remaining term of the lease, whichever is the shorter period.

Internal Control over Plant and Intangible Assets and Financial Statement Reporting

Internal Control Measures

Because of their size and bulk in relation to value, one would think that plant assets, unlike cash or inventory, do not need to be the subject of an internal control program. Many types of plant assets, however, are subject to misappropriation by employees (examples are company automobiles, aircraft, and computers). Plant assets may also be used inefficiently resulting in unnecessary expense.

Primary to the internal control system is an individual plant asset record similar to the one pictured in Figure 11–1 for a package sealer. Each plant asset should be tagged to show its plant asset number and organizational responsibility for operation and control. The permanent tag on the package sealer should show that it is asset number 1252 in asset class 14. Assets should be insured for their actual value; this requires a periodic appraisal. An annual physical inventory of the plant assets is also important to verify that they match with the equipment records and to determine their condition. The asset in Figure 11–1 was last appraised on January 12, 1987, by employee Kelly O'Ferrell. If the plant asset equipment records are kept on a computer, it is very important that access codes be known only to authorized personnel and changed often enough to prevent unauthorized persons from having access to the computer file. Other general internal control practices such as written instructions, separation of duties, and careful selection and training of employees who use and record information about plant assets are applicable. Since many intangible assets have no separable value, they present fewer internal control problems than plant assets.

As in the case of cash or inventory, having the right amount of plant assets is important. In the next section, some ratios that can be used to evaluate the adequacy of a company's investment in plant assets are examined.

Ratios for Investment in Property, Plant, and Equipment

The investment by a company in property, plant, and equipment assets may vary considerably, depending on the nature of the business. Manufacturing concerns require a greater investment in machinery and equipment than do retail or wholesale firms. The relationship of the property, plant, and equipment to total assets and sales should be in proper proportion for the industry. If the amount invested in property, plant, and equipment is too high, fewer funds are available for working capital purposes. Depreciation charges will also be high, resulting in either higher prices or lower profits. Finally, the long-term liabilities will be greater, resulting in greater interest costs and the need for funds to pay off debts as they mature.

Three ratios used to determine the suitability of investment in property, plant, and equipment are discussed next.

The *ratio of property, plant, and equipment to long-term liabilities* is obtained by dividing the total book value of the property, plant, and equipment by the long-term liabilities. This comparison is important to the long-term creditors if any of the property, plant, and equipment has been mortgaged as security for loans. The smaller the ratio, the greater the dependence on long-term borrowing to finance property, plant, and equipment acquisitions.

The *ratio of property, plant, and equipment to stockholders' equity* is obtained by dividing the total book value of the property, plant, and equipment by the stockholders' equity. An investment in property, plant, and equipment that is equal to or less than stockholders' equity (a ratio equal to or less than 1.0) indicates that the entire amount of property, plant, and equipment could have been bought by the capital obtained from the owners.

The *ratio of net sales to property, plant, and equipment,* or property, plant, and equipment turnover, is found by dividing net sales by the average total book value of the property, plant, and equipment. A decreasing ratio over a time period shows a possible overinvestment in property, plant, and equipment. For example, an average investment in property, plant, and equipment that exceeds sales (ratio less than 1.0) indicates an overinvestment, which results in higher interest, taxes, maintenance expenses, and depreciation charges and lower working capital. A heavy investment in land, buildings, and machinery greatly restricts the mobility of a company if a change in plant location or type of product manufactured is desirable.

Financial Statement Disclosure: A Real Life Example

Property, plant, and equipment items are reported on the balance sheet at cost less accumulated depreciation, depletion, or amortization. Additional disclosures in the notes to the statements usually include specific asset categories, estimated useful lives, and the method or methods of depreciation applied. The illustration in Figure 11–2 shows how a major worldwide provider of quality health care and consumer products disclosed such information. During periods of inflation the historical cost (and depreciation based

WARNER-LAMBERT COMPANY AND CONSOLIDATED SUBSIDIARIES
Consolidated Balance Sheets

	December 31,	
	1983	1982
	(Thousands of Dollars)	
Assets:		
Cash	$ 35,926	$ 26,755
Short-term investments, at cost which approximates market	213,932	252,692
Receivables, less allowances of $15,532 in 1983 and $22,234 in 1982	474,921	467,093
Inventories	456,431	488,310
Prepaid expenses and other current assets	143,000	128,567
Total current assets	1,324,210	1,363,417
U.S. government guaranteed securities and time deposits	159,437	138,059
Investments and other assets	59,000	74,212
Property, plant and equipment, net	826,232	768,571
Purchased patents, trademarks and other intangibles, net	262,576	231,546
Goodwill, net	287,961	330,552
Total assets	$2,919,416	$2,906,357

Notes to Consolidated Financial Statements

Note 1–Significant Accounting Policies

Property, plant and equipment and depreciation—Property, plant and equipment are recorded at cost, which generally includes interest costs attributable to and incurred during an asset's construction period. The cost of maintenance, repairs, minor renewals and betterments and minor equipment items is charged to income; the cost of major renewals and betterments is capitalized. Depreciation is calculated for financial statement purposes generally by use of the straight-line method based on the estimated useful lives of the assets. These estimated useful lives range from three to fifty years for buildings and building equipment and from three to twenty years for machinery, furniture and fixtures.

Intangible assets—Purchased patents, trademarks, and other intangible assets are recorded at cost. Purchased patents are armortized over their legal lives and purchased trademarks and other intangible assets are amortized over appropriate periods not exceeding 40 years. Goodwill represents the excess of cost over the fair value of the net assets of companies purchased. The value of goodwill arising prior to 1971 is expected to be retained or increased; accordingly, such goodwill is not being amortized unless a diminution in its value becomes apparent. Goodwill arising after 1970 is amortized over appropriate periods not exceeding 40 years.

Figure 11–2   **Extracts from Warner-Lambert Company 1983 Annual Report**

Figure 11–2 (*Continued*)

Note 6–Property, Plant and Equipment:

Major classes of property, plant and equipment at December 31 are summarized below:

	1983	1982
	(In thousands)	
Land	$ 29,602	$ 24,615
Buildings, and building equipment	518,392	476,434
Machinery, furniture and fixtures	735,298	699,905
	1,283,292	1,200,954
Less—accumulated depreciation	(457,060)	(432,383)
	$ 826,232	$ 768,571

Additions to property, plant and equipment include capitalized interest costs of $5.7 million during 1983, $6.8 million during 1982 and $7.6 million during 1981. Depreciation expense for the years 1983, 1982 and 1981 totaled $69.8 million, $67.4 million and $68.7 million, respectively.

Note 7–Intangibles:

The major classes of intangible assets at December 31 are summarized below:

	1983	1982
	(In thousands)	
Purchased patents, trademarks and other intangibles	$324,865	$272,457
Goodwill	303,746	339,728
	628,611	612,185
Less—accumulated amortization	(78,074)	(50,087)
	$550,537	$562,098

Amortization expense for the years 1983, 1982 and 1981 totaled $29.5 million, $19.4 million and $15.8 million, respectively. The increase in amortization expense in 1983 compared to 1982 is primarily due to a full year of amortization in 1983 relative to the intangible assets arising from the acquisition of IMED. In 1983, based upon final determination of the excess total consideration over the fair value of IMED, the values assigned to goodwill and patents, trademarks and other intangibles were adjusted. The change did not have a significant impact on 1983 earnings.

thereon) of long-lived assets tends to become unrealistic in terms of current value. *FASB Statement No. 82* requires that annual reports for fiscal years ended after December 15, 1984, present price-level adjusted historical or current cost amounts of property, plant, and equipment.

Appendix 11.1
Accounting for Lessee's Capital Leases

Introduction

As Chapter 11 noted, long-term leases that meet certain criteria established by the FASB are capitalized as long-lived assets and amortized. This appendix discusses basic accounting for such leases because of the growing importance of leasing as a financing device. The topic is very complex and the discussion here is limited to identifying characteristics of a simple capital lease of personal assets, the recording of the asset, the executory cost, interest and amortization expenses, and financial statement disclosure.

Learning Goals

1. To understand the concept and nature of a capital lease.
2. To understand the criteria that indicate when a capital lease exists.
3. To compute the asset value of a capital lease when it is different from the fair market value.
4. To record the acquisition of a capital lease and the periodic executory, interest, and amortization expenses.
5. To understand the financial statement disclosure of capital lease assets.

Identifying Capital Leases

Leases are rights to use land, buildings, equipment, or other assets that belong to others. Many short-term and long-term leases are simple rental agreements under which the payment represents a periodic expense to the *lessee* (the party using the property and making rental payments to the *lessor,* the owner of the asset). Such simple rental agreements are referred to as **operating leases**. In certain other leases, however, the lessee acquires benefits and assumes responsibilities that are normally associated with ownership to such a degree that the contract is a lease in name only. The economic effect is substantially the equivalent of a purchase. Such leases are called **capital leases**.

As early as 1949, the accounting profession recognized that leases were presenting new accounting issues. To meet the need for accounting guidance required by the increased use of more complex lease financing arrangements, the Accounting Principles Board issued four opinions dealing with leases. Then in November 1976, *FASB Statement No. 13* superseded the *APB Opinions* and consolidated guidance for accounting for leases. As special problems and topics emerged, the FASB issued several additional pronouncements in an effort to reach the original goal of more realistic accounting for and disclosure of leasing arrangements. In May 1980, the FASB issued a revised version of *Statement No. 13* that included in one document its original version plus the later amendments and interpretations.[16]

Terminology

Certain terminology used by the FASB requires further explanation. The **inception of the lease** is the date of the signed written agreement that sets forth the terms of the transaction or the date the property is acquired by the lessor (which sometimes occurs after the lease is signed) whichever is later. This date is important because the lessee's **incremental interest rate** (the rate that the lessee would have to pay to borrow over a similar time period funds to purchase the leased asset) at the inception date usually is used to determine the present value of the lease payments.[17] Also important in determining the amount to be capitalized is the fair market value of the leased property—the price for which the property could be sold in an arm's-length transaction between two unrelated parties.

Many leases contain a **bargain purchase option**. This provision allows the lessee at his or her option to purchase the property for a price sufficiently lower than expected fair market value that purchase by the lessee under this option is reasonably assured. Although all leases require periodic payments, the FASB recognizes a special term called minimum lease payments. The **minimum lease payments** are all the payments that a lessee is obligated to make (or can be required to make) in connection with the leased property. These usually include the periodic rental payments over the life of the lease and the payment called for by a bargain purchase option. In addition to minimum lease payments, the terms of a lease frequently require the lessee to pay routine expenses for upkeep of the property such as insurance, maintenance and repairs, and taxes. These upkeep expenses are known as **executory costs**.

Criteria for Identifying Capital Leases

In the revised *FASB Statement No. 13,* four criteria are listed for identifying a capital lease.[18] If the lease meets *any one* of these four criteria at the date of its inception, the lessee should treat it as a capital lease. The criteria are:

1. The lease transfers ownership of the property to the lessee at the end of the lease term.

2. The lease contains a bargain purchase option (defined in the previous section).

---

[16]*Statement of Financial Accounting Standards No. 13 As Amended and Interpreted through May 1980,* "Accounting for Leases" (Stamford: FASB, May 1980).

[17]If the lessor's rate is also known, the lower of the two is to be used. To simplify the illustration, we will assume that the lessor's rate is unknown.

[18]Paragraph 7.

3. The lease term is equal to 75 percent or more of estimated economic life of the leased property.

4. The present value at the beginning of the lease term of the minimum lease payments (defined in the previous section) equals or exceeds 90 percent of the fair value of the leased property.[19]

Accounting for Capital Leases

Since the capital lease is comparable to a plant asset, it is recorded as such on the books and depreciated or amortized. It also represents the source of the assets as a long-term liability that is being paid by periodic and usually equal payments. Accordingly, the long-term liability is also recorded and the periodic payments are regarded as containing two elements: (1) interest on the unpaid balance of the liability, and (2) reduction of the principal.

Example: Rover Corporation

Assume that the Rover Corporation leases a machine from the National Leasing Company. Basic information regarding the lease agreement and the machine are as follows:

- ☐ Term of lease: Four years beginning January 1, 1987 (inception of the lease).
- ☐ Rental: $4,000 per year payable at the end of each year.[20]
- ☐ Executory costs: $200 per year, paid at the end of each year to a firm that makes all repairs under a fixed fee maintenance agreement, and annual property taxes of $150. These payments are to be made by the lessee.
- ☐ Estimated useful life of machine: Four years.
- ☐ Estimated salvage value: Zero.
- ☐ Bargain purchase agreement: None.
- ☐ Fair market value, which is equal to cost on January 1, 1987: $11,250.
- ☐ Rover Corporation's incremental interest rate: 16 percent per year.

Since there is no mention in the agreement of transfer of ownership and no bargain purchase agreement, the lease does not meet the first or second criterion for identifying capital leases. It does meet criterion 3 and also meets criterion 4 as evidenced by the following computation (see Chapter 7 for a present value discussion):

$$P_{On=4; i=16\%} = \text{Table factor of } 2.798181$$
$$P_o = \$4,000 \times 2.798181$$
$$= \$11,192.72$$

---

[19]This fourth criterion is actually somewhat more complex than stated in that it involves consideration of certain income tax credits in computing the fair value.

[20]Such lease payments are normally due at the beginning of the year. The payment date at the end of the period allows the same illustration using present value of an ordinary annuity rather than the more complex annuity due.

11 / Long-Lived Assets

This present value of $11,192.72 is greater than 90 percent of the fair value to the lessor at the date of inception.

Recording the Lease

The amount to be recorded as an asset and a long-term liability is the lesser of the present value of the minimum lease payments or the fair value—in this illustration, the present value of $11,192.72.[21] The entry to record the lease is:

1987 Jan. 1	Leased Property under Capital Leases.................	11,192.72	
	Obligations under Capital Leases...................		11,192.72
	To record the lease of a machine and the related liability at present value of the minimum lease payments.		

Recording Lease Payments

As indicated earlier, the payments represent an element of interest and the reduction of the principal balance of the obligation. The amount of interest is computed by applying the lessee's incremental borrowing rate to the unpaid balance of the principal.[22] Accordingly, the following **table of payment allocations** would apply:

A	B	C	D	E	F
	Unpaid Principal Balance at Beginning	Interest Expense	Annual Rent	Reduction of Principal	Unpaid Principal at End of Year
Date	of Year	(16% × Col. B)	Payment	(Col. D − Col. C)	(Col. B − Col. E)
1987	$11,192.72	$1,790.84	$4,000	$2,209.16	$8,983.56
1988	8,983.56	1,437.37	4,000	2,562.63	6,420.93
1989	6,420.93	1,027.35	4,000	2,972.65	3,448.28
1990	3,442.28	551.72	4,000	3,448.28	0

Using the data from the above table, the entry for the first lease payment would be:

1987 Dec. 31	Interest Expense (from Column C)	1,790.84	
	Obligations under Capital Leases (from Column E).	2,209.16	
	Cash (from Column D)		4,000.00
	To record 1987 payment.		

---

[21] *FASB Statement No. 13 As Amended and Interpreted,* paragraph 10.

[22] This technique, known as the interest method, is explained in detail in Chapter 14.

The interest expense is calculated as 0.16 × $11,192.72 = $1,790.84. The remainder of the payment is allocated to a reduction of the lease obligation ($4,000.00 − $1,790.84 = $2,209.16). As can be seen from the table of payment allocations, the interest expense (a fixed percent of a declining liability) will be reduced in each of the remaining years of the life of the lease. This causes larger portions of the annual payment to be applied to reduction of the principal, with the final payment reducing it to zero.

In this illustration, Rover Corporation is responsible for the executory costs. Their payment is recorded each year in an entry similar to the following entry:

1987				
Dec.	31	Repairs and Maintenance Expense....................	200.00	
		Property Tax Expense	150.00	
		Cash		350.00
		Payment of annual executory costs for leased machine.		

Recording Amortization

Because the capital lease is a long-lived asset, it is subject to periodic amortization to record the expense of holding it. If the asset meets one of the first two criteria for identifying a capital lease, it should be depreciated in accordance with the lessee's normal depreciation policy for similar owned assets. If it does not meet one of the first two criteria, the lessee's normal depreciation policy must be followed, except that the period of amortization shall be the *term of the lease*.[23] In the Rover Corporation, the leased machine was capitalized under the fourth criterion and must be depreciated over the four-year lease term. Assuming that the Rover Corporation's normal policy is to use straight line depreciation for owned machinery, the depreciation entry for 1987 is:

1987				
Dec.	31	Depreciation Expense—Leased Machinery	2,798.18	
		Accumulated Depreciation—Leased Property.............		2,798.18
		To record depreciation for first year of four-year capital lease using straight line method: $11,192.72 ÷ 4 = $2,798.18.		

Note the following about the above entry:

1. Theoretically speaking, an intangible asset is amortized; the credit could be made to the asset account rather than a contra-asset account.

2. The same entry will be made for 1988, 1989, and 1990, at which time the lease term will have expired.

---

[23]*FASB Statement No. 13 As Amended and Interpreted,* paragraph 11.

3. At the end of the lease term, the book value of the leased property will be equal to its salvage value—in this case, zero.

4. The depreciation expense will be closed to the Income Summary account annually in the usual manner. Both the interest expense and the executory expense will be closed in the same manner; thus the annual matching of expenses and revenues will be more realistic than if the lease payment were expensed at the level rate of $4,000 per year.

Balance Sheet Presentation

In the balance sheet, the asset is shown as "Leased property under capital leases" net of accumulated depreciation along with property, plant, and equipment, and the obligation as a liability. The current portion of the obligation is a current liability; the remainder is a long-term liability. Details of the leasing agreement are shown in footnotes to the financial statements.

Other Issues

This presentation has been held to a simple illustration. Capital leases may involve several complex accounting issues, such as the computation of an implied interest rate if the lease is capitalized at fair market value, or the computation of gain or loss if a bargain purchase option is exercised. Additional accounting issues arise if the leased property includes real estate. These issues and those involving the lessor are left to a higher level accounting course.

Glossary

Accelerated cost recovery system (ACRS) A method of tax deductions to recover cost of depreciable personal property.

Accelerated methods Depreciation methods that result in larger depreciation expense during the early years of asset life, with gradually decreasing expense in later years.

Amortization Often used as a general term to cover write-down of assets; it is most commonly used to describe periodic allocation of costs of intangible assets to expense.

Bargain purchase option A provision allowing a lessee to purchase leased property at a price sufficiently low that purchase is reasonably assured.

Book value See *Carrying value*.

Boot The monetary consideration paid in an exchange of property.

Capital assets See *Property, plant, and equipment.*

Capital expenditures Payments or promises to make future payments for assets that will benefit more than one accounting period. They are carried forward as assets.

Capitalize To increase the property, plant, and equipment book value for expenditures which increase the EUL or the valuation of a property, plant, and equipment asset.

Capital lease A lease whose economic effect is substantially the equivalent of a purchase. Criteria for recognition of a lease as an intangible asset—a capital lease—are strictly provided by the FASB.

Carrying value Cost minus accumulated depreciation.

Copyright An exclusive right granted by the federal government to reproduce and sell a literary or an artistic work.

Depletion The process of estimating and recording periodic charges to operations because of the exhaustion of a natural resource.

Depreciable cost The net cost of an asset to be recorded as expense over the EUL.

Double-declining balance method (DDB) An accelerated depreciation method in which a constant rate—twice that of the straight line rate—is applied to carrying value to compute annual charges.

Estimated useful life (EUL) An estimate, made at the time of acquisition, of the term of usefulness of an asset (may be in years, working hours, or units of output).

Executory costs Routine upkeep expenses for a capital lease such as insurance, maintenance, repairs, or taxes.

Fair market value Value determined by informed buyers and sellers based usually on current invoice or quoted prices.

Franchise A monopolistic right granted by a government or other entity to produce goods or render services.

Goodwill A general term embodying a variety of intangible factors relating to the reputation of a firm and its ability to generate above-normal earnings.

Inception of the lease The date of the signed written agreement that sets forth the terms of a capital lease or the date the leased property is acquired by the lessor whichever is later.

Incremental interest rate The rate that the lessee would have to pay to borrow over a similar time period funds to purchase the leased asset.

Intangible assets Nonphysical assets whose ownership is expected to yield benefits.

Inventoriable costs All costs directly involved in the production of inventory (including depletion costs).

Lease The right to use, over a fixed period of time, property belonging to others.

Leasehold improvements Improvements made to leased property that will revert to the lessor upon termination of the lease.

Minimum lease payments All the payments that a lessee is obligated (or can be required) to make in connection with the leased property.

Operating lease A simple rental agreement to use the property of another.

Patent The exclusive right to exploit a method or a product over a legal life of 17 years.

Plant assets See *Tangible plant assets*.

Production methods Depreciation methods whose charges are based on usage or results (mileage, units of output) rather than time.

Production unit method A method of depreciation based on a fixed rate per unit of output determined by estimating the total units of output.

Property, plant, and equipment Assets whose use will provide benefits over more than one accounting period; these include tangible plant assets (land, buildings, machinery) and wasting assets (oil, gas, minerals).

Revenue expenditures Expenditures that benefit the current period only and are debited to expense.

Salvage value The amount of asset cost that is expected to be recovered when the asset is ultimately scrapped, sold, or traded in; also called *residual value*.

Straight line method A depreciation method that allocates a uniform portion of the depreciable asset cost to each accounting period over the estimated useful life of the asset.

Sum-of-the-years'-digits method (SYD) See *Accelerated methods*.

Table of payment allocations A schedule showing allocation of lease payments between expense and reduction of principal over the life of the lease.

Tangible plant assets Assets with physical forms such as buildings, machinery, or equipment.

Wasting assets Natural resources whose asset value to the firm is diminished through consumption or sale.

Working hours method A method of depreciation based on a fixed rate per hour of use, determined by estimating the number of hours the asset will be used during its useful life.

Questions

Q11–1   Define the term *property, plant, and equipment*. What groups of assets are covered by this term? Give examples of each.

Q11–2   (a) List some expenditures other than the purchase price that make up the cost of tangible plant assets. (b) Why are cash discounts excluded from the cost of tangible plant assets?

Q11–3   (a) What distinguishes a capital expenditure from a revenue expenditure? (b) What is the effect on the financial statements if this distinction is not properly drawn?

Q11–4   Student A maintains that if a tangible plant asset has a fair market value greater than its cost after one year of use, no depreciation need be recorded for the year. Student B insists that the fair market value is irrelevant in this context. Indicate which position you support and give your reasons.

Q11–5   What are some factors that must be considered when the depreciation method to be used is chosen?

Q11–6   Since the total amount to be depreciated cannot exceed the cost of the asset, does it make any difference which method is used in calculating the periodic depreciation charges? Explain.

Q11–7   Does the recording of depreciation have any relation to the accounting standard of matching revenue and expenses? Explain.

Q11–8   Describe the conditions that might lead to the use of each of the following methods of depreciation: (a) straight line, (b) production, (c) accelerated.

Q11–9   What procedures should be followed in computing depreciation on assets held for part of a month?

Q11–10 What is the relationship, if any, between the amount of annual depreciation expense on tangible plant assets and the amount of money available for new plant assets?

Q11–11 What accounting problems result (a) from the trade-in of a tangible plant asset? (b) From the sale of a plant asset?

Q11–12 (a) Distinguish among the terms *depreciation, depletion,* and *amortization.* (b) How is the periodic depletion charge determined?

Q11–13 Is depletion an operating expense? How does depletion cost reduce the net income?

Q11–14 (a) What are intangible assets? (b) What factors must be considered when the acquisition of intangibles is (i) recorded? (ii) amortized? (c) Is a contra account used for accumulated amortization?

Q11–15 Why should intangibles such as goodwill or organization costs be carried on the books as assets and amortized, since they appear to have no separable market value?

Q11–16 Student A says that because tangible plant assets are large and difficult to steal, there is little need for internal control over them. Do you agree? Why or why not?

Q11–17 What three ratios can be used to evaluate whether a company's investment in property, plant, and equipment is adequate? Explain each and what it measures.

Q11–18 (Appendix) What is an operating lease? A capital lease? What is the difference in accounting treatment of the two?

Q11–19 (Appendix) Why is it necessary to depreciate a capital lease when journal entries are already being made to record payments under the lease?

Q11–20 (Appendix) How should capital leases be presented on the balance sheet?

Exercises

E11–1
Accounts to be debited for capital and revenue expenditures

Teaneck Corporation uses a Construction in Progress account for new acquisitions of property, plant, and equipment. For each of the following items, indicate the account to be debited:

a. Expenditure for installing machinery.
b. Expenditure for trial run of new machinery.
c. Expenditure for insurance on machinery after it is in operation.
d. Payment of delinquent taxes on land (taxes were delinquent at the date of purchase of the land).
e. Expenditure for extensive plumbing repairs to make a newly purchased building usable.
f. Sales tax paid on new machinery just purchased.
g. Payment for the right to operate a Holiday Inn.
h. Expenditure for a major overhaul that restores a piece of machinery to its original condition and extends its useful life.
i. Expenditure for an addition to a building leased for 20 years.
j. Amount paid for a purchased business in excess of the appraised value of the net assets.
k. Ordinary repair to machinery after it is in operation.
l. Expenditure for leaflet to advertise new services available because of new machinery.
m. Interest on money borrowed to construct a new building.
n. The determination that the purchased machinery is now ready to be placed in operation.

E11–2
Amount of debit to asset account

The Napa Company made the following expenditures on the acquisition of a new machine:

Invoice cost ($19,000) less 2% cash discount	$18,620
Transportation charges	570
Installation charges	1,250
Help wanted ads for new operators	700
Remodeling to adapt to Napa's needs	2,425
Material and labor used during test runs	285

What is the amount of the debit to the Machinery account for this acquisition?

E11–3
Construction of own plant

The Osaka Company solicited bids for a new wing for its factory building. The lowest bid received was $300,000. The company decided to do the work with its own staff, and the wing was completed for a total cost of $278,000, which was paid in cash. Record the expenditure in one summary entry.

E11–4
Recording depreciation—all methods (full year)

On January 2, 1987, Catawba Airlines bought a new aircraft for $3,000,000. At the end of its EUL, it is expected to have a salvage value of $280,000. Catawba estimates that the aircraft will be used in operations in their company for 16 years. Record, in general journal form, the depreciation adjustment at December 31, 1987, under each of the following assumptions:

a. The straight line method is used.
b. The double-declining balance method is used.
c. The sum-of-the-years'-digits method is used.
d. The working hours method is used. It is estimated that the new aircraft has a useful life of 80,000 flying hours. It was flown 4,800 hours in 1987.

E11–5
Partial year depreciation—three methods (partial year and full year)

Jersey Company began business on July 1, 1987, with three new machines. Data for the machines are as follows:

Machine	Cost	Estimated Salvage Value	EUL (Years)
A	$ 93,000	$15,000	12
B	126,000	16,000	10
C	68,000	12,000	8

Compute the depreciation expense for calendar years 1987 and 1988 by each of the following methods: (a) straight line, (b) sum-of-the-years'-digits, and (c) double-declining balance.

E11–6
Overhaul and new rate

The Fish House acquired a new freezer on October 1, 1987, at an installed cost of $50,000. The freezer had an estimated useful life of eight years and a salvage value of $5,000. Two years later the freezer was completely overhauled at a cost of $10,000. These improvements were expected to increase the total useful life from eight years to twelve years. Salvage value remains at $5,000. Prepare, in general journal form, all entries pertaining to this freezer except closing entries from acquisition through December 31, 1989. The straight line method of depreciation is used.

E11–7
Sale of a used asset

On July 1, 1987, Defiance Corporation sold for $26,500 cash a piece of drilling machinery that had been in use since January 3, 1978. The original cost of the machine was $134,000; straight line depreciation of $12,000 has been recorded annually through December 31, 1986. In general journal form, record the sale.

E11–8
Trade-in on a similar and dissimilar item

On April 2, 1987, Movers, Inc., purchased a new forklift truck for $12,000 cash. It was estimated to have a useful life of five years and a salvage value of $2,000. At the end of 1987, it was concluded that the truck was the wrong model and it was traded in for a similar truck that had a cash price (and fair market value) of $20,000.

1. Record the purchase on April 2, 1987, and the depreciation adjustment on December 31, 1987 (straight line depreciation).
2. Record the trade-in on the following assumptions:
   a. A fair value trade-in allowance of $11,500 was given by the dealer; the balance was paid in cash.
   b. A fair value trade-in allowance of $9,000 was given by the dealer; the balance was paid in cash.
3. Using the assumptions in requirement 2 above, record the trade-in on a parcel of land that had a fair market price of $20,000.

E11–9
Computing depletion cost

Western Mines purchased a piece of land and the mineral rights for $1,200,000. Company engineers estimate that the property contains 500,000 tons of ore and that the land can be sold for $150,000 when mining operations are completed. In the first year, 272,500 tons of ore were mined. Compute depletion cost for the first year.

E11–10
Amortization of franchise

Radio station WSOE received a franchise to transmit on channel 89.0 for a period of seven years. The accounting, legal, clerical, and consultant fees in obtaining this franchise amounted to $21,000. These costs were recorded as an intangible asset, Franchise, on May 1, 1987. Make adjusting entries to record amortization of the franchise in the fiscal years ending December 31, 1987 and 1988.

E11–11
Amortization of patent

On July 1, 1987, Bay Producers purchased a patent for a new process at a cost of $33,600. It is estimated that the patent will give the firm an advantage over its competitors for the next seven years. In general journal form, record the amortization adjustments for the years ended December 31, 1987, and December 31, 1988.

E11–12
Ratio analysis

The following data are from the financial statements of Big Rapids Corporation (dollars in thousands):

	1987	1986
Property, plant, and equipment	$11,592	$10,658
Total long-term liabilities	9,200	9,690
Total stockholders' equity	19,986	16,397
Net sales	42,174	38,970

The property, plant, and equipment at end-1985 was $10,606 (in thousands).
  Rounding to two decimal places where necessary, compute the ratios of property, plant, and equipment to (a) long-term liabilities and (b) stockholders' equity for both years. Also, compute the ratio of net sales to property, plant, and equipment for both years. For each ratio, explain whether 1987 is an improvement over 1986, giving reasons for your conclusions.

E11–13
Capital lease payments.

(Appendix) Laredo Company has agreed to lease from Spartanburg Equipment Company a floating crane for a 10-year period, with annual payments of $24,000 to be paid at the end of each year. The payment for December 31, 1987, the end of the first year, is divided as $17,526.15 as interest and $6,473.85 as principal. Record this first payment in general journal form.

E11–14
Computation and recording of capital lease and amortization

(Appendix) Using the data in E11–13, assume that the lease meets the third criterion of *FASB Statement No. 13* and that the lease is to be recorded at the present value of the lease payments. Laredo's incremental interest rate is 14 percent per year. Give general journal entries to record the lease as of January 1, 1987, and the amortization for 1987 using the straight line method.

A Problems

P11–1A
Depreciation for several years—three methods

Missoula Corporation had the following at the end of 1987:

	Building	Production Equipment	Cleaning Equipment
Date acquired	January 2, 1980	January 2, 1986	January 2, 1986
Cost	$164,000	$600,000	$391,000
Estimated salvage value	14,000	100,000	31,000
EUL in years	30	10	8
Method of depreciation	SL	DDB	SYD

Required:

1. Compute the balance in the Accumulated Depreciation account for each category of plant assets at the beginning of calendar year 1987.
2. Prepare the adjusting entries for depreciation as of December 31, 1987.

P11–2A
Overhaul and new depreciation rate

Buie Motor Freight purchased a delivery truck for $48,000 cash on July 2, 1985. On July 5, 1985, the company paid an additional $3,000 to have a hydraulic lift installed on the truck. Estimating a useful life of six years and a salvage value of $6,000, the company is depreciating this truck on the straight line method. On January 4, 1988, the truck was overhauled at a cost of $16,100; it is estimated that this overhaul will extend the EUL for an additional two years, with the salvage value remaining at $6,000.

Required: In general journal form, prepare entries to record:

1. The purchase on July 2, 1985.
2. The installation of the lift on July 5, 1985.
3. Depreciation for the calendar years 1985, 1986, 1987.
4. The overhaul and the depreciation for 1988.

P11–3A
Entries over the life of a plant asset—SYD

Auburn Corporation purchased a computer system in 1987. Significant events concerning this system were as follows:

1987

Jun.	5	Received equipment at an invoice price of $80,000, terms 2/10, n/30; recorded liability at net amount.
	15	Paid for the equipment in cash.
	19	Paid $8,600 for installation costs.
	28	Paid $5,000 for testing and debugging.
Jul.	1	The computer was placed in full operation. It was estimated that the computer system had an EUL of seven years with a salvage value of $8,000. It is to be depreciated by the sum-of-the-years'-digits method.
Aug.	22	Paid $612 for minor repairs.
Dec.	31	Recorded depreciation for 1987.

1988

Jul.	8	Paid $1,100 for minor repairs.
Dec.	31	Recorded depreciation for 1988.

1989

Jul.	3	Having decided that the system was not required, management sold it for $65,000 cash.

Required: In general journal form, record the above events using a Construction in Progress account until July 1.

P11–4A
Trade-in for similar and dissimilar items

Tulsa Company purchased a drill press on July 1, 1987, at a cost of $65,000. It was estimated to have a useful life of eight years and a salvage value of $5,000. Tulsa uses the double-declining balance method of depreciation. After the depreciation was recorded on December 31, 1987, it was decided that this was not the correct model, so it was traded in on a similar model priced at a fair market value of $92,000 on January 2, 1988.

Required: Record the trade-in under the following independent assumptions:

1. A fair value trade-in allowance of $60,000 is received from the dealer; the balance is paid in cash.

(continued on next page)

2. A fair value trade-in allowance of $52,000 is received from the dealer; the balance is paid in cash.
3. Same as the problem and requirement 1 except that the drill press was traded on a tract of land with a fair market price of $92,000.

P11–5A
Depletion and inventoriable costs

On October 1, 1987, Concordia Oil, Inc., purchased a tract of land and the oil rights to it for $8,000,000. Company engineers estimate that 500,000 barrels of oil will be extracted from this deposit over a period of about two years. It is further estimated that dismantling the drilling rig will cost $100,000, and resale of the land will bring in $300,000. Drilling operations were begun in October, and by December 31, 1987, the well had produced 250,000 barrels of oil; 185,000 barrels of this production were sold in 1985, and 65,000 barrels remained in inventory on December 31, 1985. Labor, materials, depreciation, and other costs in addition to depletion incurred in production operations amounted to $2,580,000. Oil sold in 1987 brought a selling price of $32 per barrel.

Required: For this well, compute:

1. Depletion cost in 1987.
2. Cost of oil sold in 1987.
3. Gross margin on 1987 sales.
4. The valuation to be placed on the December 31, 1987, inventory.

P11–6A
Thought-provoking problem: ratio analysis and evaluation

In its 1984 *Annual Report,* Gearhart Industries, Inc. reported the following data (dollars in thousands):

	1984	1983	1982
Net revenue	$316,872	$345,030	$344,758
Long-term debt	82,709	95,831	87,230
Total stockholders' equity	193,093	192,024	178,439
Property, plant, and equipment	171,761	182,993	165,942

Required:

1. For all three years, compute the ratio of property, plant, and equipment to long-term liabilities (debt) and to stockholders' equity.
2. For 1984 and 1983, compute the ratio of net sales to property, plant, and equipment.
3. Comment on the adequacy of these ratios; explain your conclusions. Is the company improving? Discuss.

P11–7A
Capital lease entries

(Appendix) The Huron Corporation leased a harvesting machine from the Wayne Leasing Company on January 1, 1987. The lease agreement stipulates that Huron will make annual rental payments of $9,500 beginning on December 31, 1987, for a period of six years. It also requires that Huron reimburse the lessor at the end of each year for annual executory costs of $700. The fair market value of the machine on January 1, 1987, was $32,500. The lessor's implicit incremental borrowing rate is unknown and cannot be estimated. Huron's incremental borrowing rate on January 1, 1987, was 20 percent.

Required:

1. Record the lease capitalization on the lessee's books on January 1, 1987.
2. Prepare a table of payment allocations.
3. In general journal form record, (a) the first lease payment, (b) reimbursement for 1987 executory costs, and (c) amortization for 1987 using the straight line method (rounded to the nearest cent).

B Problems

P11–1B
Depreciation for several years—three methods

Megware Corporation had the following at the end of 1987:

	Building	Production Equipment	Cleaning Equipment
Date acquired	January 2, 1984	January 2, 1987	January 2, 1986
Cost	$105,000	$800,000	$275,000
Estimated salvage value	15,000	150,000	15,800
EUL in years	20	10	8
Method of depreciation	SL	DDB	SYD

Required:

1. Compute the balance in the Accumulated Depreciation account for each category of plant assets at the beginning of calendar year 1987.
2. Prepare the adjusting entries for depreciation as of December 31, 1987.

P11–2B
Overhaul and new depreciation rate

Ferris Truckers purchased a delivery truck for $96,000 cash on July 2, 1985. On July 5, 1985, the company paid an additional $6,000 to have a hydraulic lift installed on the truck. Estimating a useful life of six years and a salvage value of $12,000, the company is depreciating this truck on the straight line method. On January 4, 1988, the truck was overhauled at a cost of $32,200; it is estimated that this overhaul will extend the EUL for an additional two years, with the salvage value remaining at $12,000.

Required: In general journal form, prepare entries to record:

1. The purchase on July 2, 1985.
2. The installation of the lift on July 5, 1985.
3. Depreciation for the calendar years 1985, 1986, and 1987.
4. The overhaul and the depreciation for 1988.

P11–3B
Entries over the life of a plant item—straight line

Augusta Airlines purchased a food warmer for in-flight meals in 1987. Significant events concerning this piece of equipment were as follows:

1987

Apr. 4   Received equipment at an invoice price of $72,000, terms 2/10, n/30; recorded liability at net amount.
     14   Paid for the equipment in cash.
     20   Paid $3,600 for installation costs.
     28   Paid $840 for testing and other start-up costs.
     30   The equipment was placed in full operation. It was estimated that the food warmer would have an EUL of 10 years and no salvage value. It is to be depreciated by the straight line method.
Jul. 16   Paid $210 for minor repairs.
Dec. 31   Recorded depreciation for 1987.

1988

Apr. 18   Paid $560 for minor repairs.
Dec. 31   Recorded depreciation for 1988.

1989

Jun. 30   Having decided to have meals delivered to planes by a caterer, management sold the food warmer for $52,500 cash.

Required: In general journal form, record the above events using a Construction in Progress account until April 30.

P11–4B
Trade-in for similar and dissimilar items

El Paso Company purchased a drill press on July 1, 1987, at a cost of $130,000. It was estimated to have a useful life of eight years and a salvage value of $10,000. The company uses the double-declining balance method of depreciation. After the depreciation was recorded on December 31, 1987, it was decided that this was not the correct model, so it was traded in on a similar model priced at a fair market value of $175,000 on January 2, 1988.

Required: Record the trade-in under the following independent assumptions:

1. A fair value trade-in allowance of $117,000 is received from the dealer; the balance is paid in cash.
2. A fair value trade-in allowance of $87,500 is received from the dealer; the balance is paid in cash.
3. Same as the problem and requirement 1, except that the drill press was traded on a sales building with a fair market price of $175,000.

P11–5B
Depletion and inventoriable costs

On October 1, 1987, Towson Oil purchased a tract of land and the oil rights to it for $16,000,000. Company engineers estimate that 1,000,000 barrels of oil will be extracted from this deposit over a period of about two years. It is further estimated that dismantling the drilling rig will cost $250,000, and resale of the land will bring in $500,000. Drilling operations were begun in October, and by December 31, 1987, the well had produced 250,000 barrels of oil; 200,000 barrels of this production were sold in 1987, and 50,000 barrels remained in inventory on December 31, 1987. Labor, materials, depreciation, and other costs in addition to depletion incurred in production operations amounted to $3,000,000. Oil sold in 1987 for $30 per barrel.

Required: For this well, compute:

1. Depletion cost in 1987.
2. Cost of oil sold in 1987.
3. Gross margin on 1987 sales.
4. The valuation to be placed on the December 31, 1987, inventory.

P11–6B
Thought-provoking problem: ratio analysis and evaluation

In its 1983 *Annual Report,* Colt Industries, Inc. reported the following data (dollars in thousands):

	1983	1982	1981
Net revenue	$1,576,183	$1,511,594	$1,765,956
Noncurrent liabilities	389,330	477,337	387,322
Total stockholders' equity	466,831	443,490	735,715
Property, plant, and equipment	332,926	311,165	457,388

Required:

1. For all three years compute the ratio of property, plant, and equipment to long-term (noncurrent) liabilities and to the stockholders' equity.
2. For 1983 and 1982, compute the ratio of net sales to property, plant, and equipment.
3. Comment on the adequacy of these ratios; explain your conclusions. Is the company improving? Discuss.

P11–7B
Capital lease entries

(Appendix) The Anacostia Corporation leased a floating crane from the District Leasing Company on January 1, 1987. The lease agreement stipulates that Anacostia will make annual rental payments of $28,500 beginning on December 31, 1987, for a period of eight years. It also requires that Anacostia reimburse the leasing company at the end of each year for executory costs of $2,100 per year. The fair market value of the crane on

January 1, 1987, was $115,000. The lessor's incremental borrowing rate on January 1, 1987, was unknown and cannot be estimated; Anacostia's rate was 20 percent.

Required:

1. Record the lease capitalization on Anacostia's books on January 1, 1987.
2. Prepare a table of payment allocations.
3. In general journal form, record (a) the first lease payment, (b) reimbursement for the 1987 executory costs, and (c) amortization for 1987 using the straight line method (rounded to the nearest cent).

Part Three

Sources and Uses of Capital

12 Single Proprietorship and Partnership Accounting

Introduction

In the United States today, the dollar volume of business transacted by corporations far exceeds the combined volume of all other forms of business. However, in numbers of business entities, single proprietorships and partnerships outnumber corporations. Some businesses operate as single proprietorships or partnerships because they are the easiest forms of business to start. Others operate as partnerships because they are not legally permitted to incorporate. Some, like CPA firms, although they are permitted to incorporate as professional associations, do not enjoy all the advantages of a regular corporation in most states.

The accounting treatment for operating transactions—incurring expenses and earning revenues—is the same for all forms of business. It is the accounting treatment for the formation of the business, withdrawal of funds, and the closing process that differs. This chapter looks at these aspects of accounting for the single proprietorship and partnership after presenting their distinctive features.

Learning Goals

1. To understand the characteristics of a single proprietorship and a partnership.

2. To compare the accounts for owners' equity of a single proprietorship, a partnership, and a corporation.

3. To understand the accounting methods for recording transactions affecting proprietor's equity.

4. To understand the characteristics of a partnership.

5. To review accounting methods for recording transactions affecting partners' equity.

6. To compute the division of partnership profits and losses using different methods.

The Single Proprietorship and Partnership Forms of Business Organization

Before comparing the equity accounts of a single proprietorship, a partnership, and a corporation, this section looks at the characteristics of the single proprietorship and partnership. A **single proprietorship** is an unincorporated business owned by one person. There are no legal requirements involved in starting such a business other than paying the various state and local license fees.

"A **partnership** is an association of two or more persons to carry on as co-owners a business for profit" (emphasis added).[1] The association described in this definition may be based upon an oral or a written agreement. Although many partnerships have only two partners, some have many. For example, some of the nationally known certified public accounting firms have a hundred or more partners. Of the three basic forms of business in the United States, the partnership is the least used.

Characteristics

Ease of Formation Like single proprietorships, partnerships are relatively easy to form. Although it is desirable that a written agreement form the basis of the association, partnerships may be formed on the basis of a verbal agreement. With a few exceptions, the states have enacted the provisions of the *Uniform Partnership Act* into law. The act contains no special provisions for the formation of a partnership but does contain provisions that regulate the relations of partners with each other and with persons outside the partnership. The written agreement should specify the terms and conditions on all matters that might otherwise lead to controversy. It should contain provisions for the distribution of earnings, investment or withdrawal of funds, the admission of a new partner, the death or withdrawal of a partner, and so on.

Size One measure of size is the amount of capital invested. Because additional owners serve as sources of capital, partnerships tend to be somewhat larger than single proprietorships. However, their original capital investment must come from the personal wealth and borrowing power of the partners. Since many partnerships have only two or three partners, this form of business is not generally found among the larger firms in the United States.

Legal Liability The owner or owners of an unincorporated business are usually liable individually and jointly for the debts of the proprietorship or partnership. This means that the personal assets of the proprietor or partners are available to satisfy creditors' claims against the business entity. In certain states where the law allows it, a limited partnership may be created, and in this form of partnership, under certain circumstances, the liability of some partners may be limited to the amount of their investment. Such a partner, known as a **limited partner**, has restrictions placed upon the business activities in which he or she can engage. There must be at least one **general partner** in each limited partnership. In the common form of partnership, all part-

---

[1]*Uniform Partnership Act,* Part II, Section 6.

ners are general partners. These partners are subject to unlimited liability. Like single proprietors, their assets outside the business entity may be made available to satisfy partnership creditor claims.

Raising of Capital The initial capital of a proprietorship or a partnership must be raised from the personal wealth (or borrowing) of the owners. While the additional persons involved in a partnership would normally provide more capital than a single proprietorship, the partnership form of business does not provide for any special or unique method of bringing additional assets into the business. All property brought into a partnership is **partnership property**. Each partner is a co-owner with the other partners of the partnership's property.

Mutual Agency Another characteristic of a partnership related to the liability of partners is that of **mutual agency**; that is, every partner is an agent of the partnership when performing acts to carry on the business. Thus the act of a single partner is binding on the partnership and on each of the other partners, even though the act may be negligent or wrongful.[2]

Mutual agency

In a partnership, the acts of each partner are binding on all other partners under the concept of mutual agency.

Taxation of Income Neither form of unincorporated business pays income tax as an entity. The owners, however, pay the tax as a part of their individual income taxes. The proprietorship files no income tax return, but the proprietor includes the income or loss on his or her individual tax return on Schedule C, Form 1040.

A partnership must file an income tax return, but it is for information only. The various forms of revenue, expenses, and other tax deductible items are identified with each individual partner on the partnership return. On the partnership federal income tax return, Form 1065, Schedule K shows each partner's share of the taxable items; each partner is then required to include those items in his or her personal income tax return.

Owners' Equity Accounts for the Three Basic Forms of Business Organization

An overview of the owners' equity accounts for the three basic forms of business organization is presented in Figure 12–1, which gives a pictorial view of the owners' equity accounts for a single proprietorship, partnership, and corporation.

The accounting for the equity of partners is very similar to that for the equity of a single proprietor except that a larger number of owners' accounts are involved. A corporation may be formed by receiving a charter from the

---

[2]Ibid., Part III, Section 13.

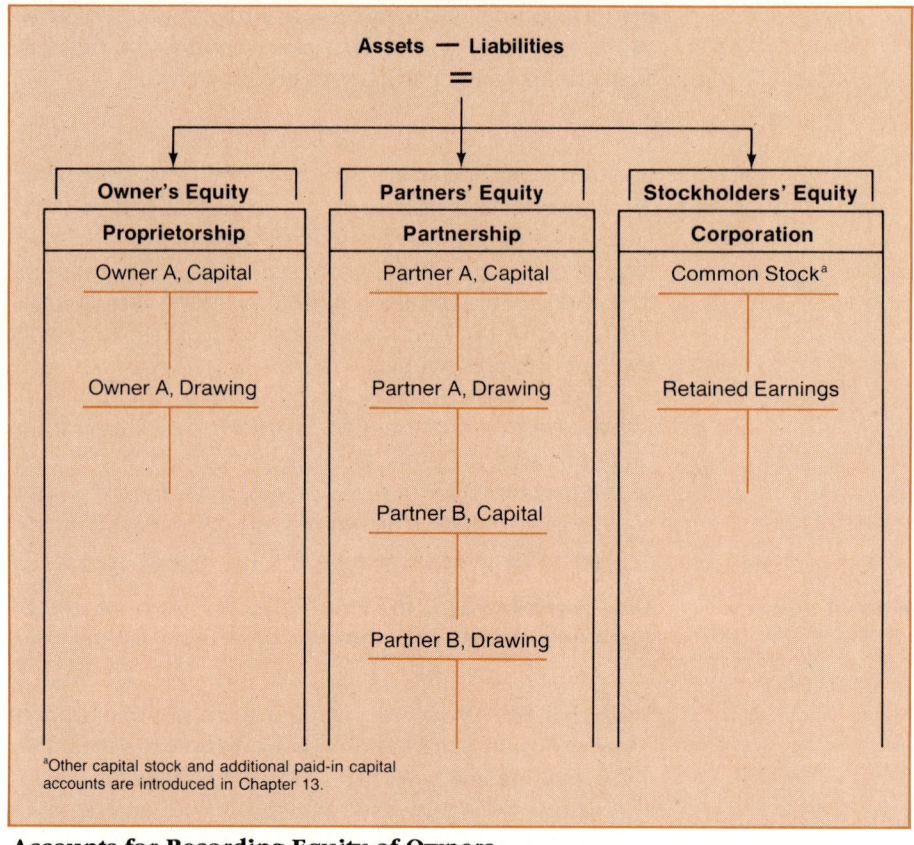

Figure 12–1   **Accounts for Recording Equity of Owners**

state, creating a legal entity. Because state laws may restrict capital changes, a corporation must have special types of capital accounts. The accounting for a simple corporate capital structure uses as a minimum a Common Stock account and a Retained Earnings account. The detailed accounting for corporate equity is discussed in Chapter 13.

Formation of a Single Proprietorship

Accounting for assets, liabilities, revenues, and expenses is the same for all forms of business organization. The primary difference between a corporation, which has been emphasized so far, and a single proprietorship is that owners' equity accounts of a single proprietorship need to show the proprietor's net balance of owner's equity in a single account. On formation of a single proprietorship, the contribution of the owner is recorded in a capital account.

Example 1: Investment of Cash To illustrate, assume that on July 1, 1987, Lucy Genova formed the Good Times Wheels Repair Shop by investing $10,000 in cash. The journal entry to record the initial investment is shown below:

1987				
Jul.	1	Cash..	10,000	
		Lucy Genova, Capital............................		10,000
		To record the investment of Lucy Genova in a new business.		

Example 2: Investment of Cash and Noncash Assets It is not necessary that the original contributions be made only in cash. Assume that Lucy Genova contributed land and a building with a fair market value of $5,000 and $40,000, respectively, plus cash of $10,000. The entry to record the original investment is recorded as follows:

1987				
Jul.	1	Cash..	10,000	
		Land..	5,000	
		Buildings...	40,000	
		Lucy Genova, Capital............................		55,000
		To record the investment of Lucy Genova in a new business.		

Withdrawals by Proprietor

Although there are no restrictions on withdrawals by a proprietor in a single proprietorship, most withdrawals are made in anticipation that net income has been or will be earned. For a single proprietorship, this kind of withdrawal is debited to a special proprietor's or owner's drawing account. The reasons for this accounting are: (1) the earnings of a single proprietorship belong to the owner, (2) it is beneficial for the owner to have a record of periodic withdrawals, and (3) there are no legal restrictions on the withdrawal of earnings by a proprietor. Therefore, the owner of a single proprietorship may withdraw cash or any other asset in expectation of income. Suppose, for example, Lucy Genova, owner of Good Times Wheels Repair Shop withdrew cash of $1,000 on September 2, 1987. This transaction would be recorded in the general journal of the company as follows:

1987				
Sep.	2	Lucy Genova, Drawing...........................	1,000	
		Cash..		1,000
		To record withdrawal by owner in expectation of income.		

The amount of the owner's drawing decreases owner's equity and is shown on the statement of owner's equity (illustrated later in this chapter). Unlike expenses, however, withdrawals by owners do not affect the calculation of net income. For this reason, they are not included in the income statement.

The Closing of the Income Summary Account

The revenue and expense account balances are closed to Income Summary as in the corporation. The balance of the Income Summary account is closed to the owner's capital account. Since the owner's drawing account is *not an expense account,* it is not closed to Income Summary; rather it is closed directly to the owner's capital account.

Assuming that the Good Times Wheels Repair Shop had earned a net income of $5,000 for the year ended December 31, 1987, and that Genova had withdrawn $1,000 from the business during the year (reflected as a debit balance in the Lucy Genova, Drawing account), the last two of the closing entries would appear as follows:

1987			
Dec. 31	Income Summary	5,000	
	Lucy Genova, Capital		5,000
	To transfer net income to the capital account.		
31	Lucy Genova, Capital	1,000	
	Lucy Genova, Drawing		1,000
	To close the amount withdrawn by the proprietor to the capital account.		

Statement of Owner's Equity

Utilizing the data assumed for the closing entries in the preceding section, and assuming a capital balance at the beginning of 1987 of $20,000, the statement of owner's equity for the Good Times Wheels Repair Shop would appear as shown in Figure 12–2. The following sections present the accounting for the partnership form of business organization.

GOOD TIMES WHEELS REPAIR SHOP
Statement of Owner's Equity
For the Year Ended December 31, 1987

Lucy Genova, capital, January 1, 1987	$20,000
Add: Net income for 1987	5,000
Subtotal	$25,000
Deduct: Withdrawals	1,000
Lucy Genova, capital, December 31, 1987	$24,000

Figure 12–2   **Statement of Owner's Equity for a Single Proprietorship**

Formation of a Partnership

The partnership form of business organization also presents no new problems in accounting for assets, liabilities, revenues, and expenses. With the exception of transactions with the owners, they are recorded in the same manner as the other forms of business. The primary difference between a single proprietorship and a partnership is that the equity accounts of the partnership must show the capital and withdrawals of each individual partner of the partnership.

Each partner's share of ownership is recorded in a separate equity account, and its balance is in turn reported on the balance sheet. On formation of a partnership, the contribution of each partner is recorded in that equity account.

Example 1: Equal Investment of Cash To illustrate, assume that on July 1, 1987, Susan Walsh and John Snow form a partnership, each investing $8,000 in cash. The journal entry to record the initial investment by the partners is shown below:

1987 Jul.	1	Cash.	16,000	
		Susan Walsh, Capital.		8,000
		John Snow, Capital.		8,000
		To record the investments of the partners in the Walsh and Snow Company.		

Example 2: Investment of Cash and Noncash Assets It is not necessary that the original contributions be limited to cash. Assume that Walsh contributed land and a building with a fair market value of $3,000 and $20,000 respectively, and merchandise costing $6,200, and that the partnership assumed her mortgage payable of $10,000 and $200 in interest accrued on the mortgage. Snow invested $15,000 in cash. The opening entry is as follows:

1987 Jul.	1	Cash.	15,000	
		Merchandise Inventory (or Purchases).	6,200	
		Land.	3,000	
		Building.	20,000	
		Mortgage Payable.		10,000
		Accrued Mortgage Interest Payable.		200
		Susan Walsh, Capital.		19,000
		John Snow, Capital.		15,000
		To record the investments of the partners in the Walsh and Snow Company.		

Withdrawals by Partners

Withdrawals of assets by a partner in anticipation that profits have been earned are usually at a specified periodic amount as provided for in the partnership agreement. Such withdrawals are accounted for in the same manner as in a proprietorship; the amounts are debited to the respective **partner's drawing** account and the asset withdrawn is credited. To illustrate, assume that Susan Walsh and John Snow agree that each shall withdraw $1,000 per month in anticipation of profits. The entry for their first monthly withdrawal on July 31, 1987, is as follows:

1987				
Jul.	31	Susan Walsh, Drawing	1,000	
		John Snow, Drawing	1,000	
		Cash		2,000
		To record withdrawals in anticipation of profits earned.		

If Walsh and Snow withdraw $1,000 each month for the next five months, their drawing accounts at December 31, 1987, will have a balance of $6,000 each.

Because withdrawals in anticipation of income are routine and fixed by agreement, it follows that any withdrawals of assets by a partner in excess of the agreed amount are permanent reductions to capital. These should be recorded as debits to the partners' capital accounts. For example, suppose that on December 29, 1987, John Snow asks to be allowed to withdraw $5,000 to pay a personal debt and Susan Walsh consents. This is a capital reduction and it should be recorded as follows:

1987				
Dec.	29	John Snow, Capital	5,000	
		Cash		5,000
		To record a capital withdrawal by Snow.		

At the end of the accounting period, the drawing accounts are usually closed to the capital accounts because there is no legal distinction between capital invested and capital earned. The closing of the two drawing accounts with a balance of $6,000 each for the Walsh and Snow Company is illustrated below; this journal entry would normally follow the closing of the Income Summary account to the capital accounts (described in the next section).

1987				
Dec.	31	Susan Walsh, Capital	6,000	
		John Snow, Capital	6,000	
		Susan Walsh, Drawing		6,000
		John Snow, Drawing		6,000
		To close the drawing accounts to the capital accounts.		

Division of Partnership Profits and Losses

Assume that Kay Carter and Ann Foley are partners in the public accounting firm of Carter and Foley. The partners' equity section of the balance sheet at December 31, 1986, appears as follows:

CARTER AND FOLEY
Balance Sheet
December 31, 1986

Liabilities and Partners' Equity

Exhibit C

Partners' equity:		
Kay Carter, capital	$62,500	
Ann Foley, capital	47,500	$110,000

Example 1: Division of Earnings in an Arbitrary Ratio

Profits and losses of a partnership can be divided in any manner that the partners agree upon. If the partners desire to do so, they may adopt a loss-sharing ratio that is different from the method of sharing profits. The method chosen should be contained in the partnership agreement. If a ratio for the division of profits is stated but no ratio for losses is stated, the losses are to be divided in the same ratio as profits. If no articles or other evidence of agreement exist, however, the law assumes that profits and losses are both to be divided equally, even when the factors of investment, ability, or time are unequal. First assume that Carter and Foley share profits and losses equally. The journal entry to close a net income of $67,000 in 1987 would be:

1987				
Dec.	31	Income Summary	67,000	
		Kay Carter, Capital		33,500
		Ann Foley, Capital		33,500
		To transfer net income to capital accounts.		

Example 2: Division of Earnings Based on Salaries, Interest, and Agreed Ratio

A part of the net income may be divided to recognize differences in capital balances, another part to recognize differences in the value of services rendered, and the remainder in an agreed ratio. Although entitled "salary allowances" and "interest allowances," as used here, these are not an expense. They are a mechanism for dividing a portion of the earnings.[3] Assume that Carter and Foley agree to allow interest of 20 percent on

---

[3] A partner may make a loan or advance to the partnership in addition to the capital that he or she has agreed to contribute. This is a different situation, and section 18(c) of the *Uniform Partnership Act* provides that the partner will be paid interest on these loans.

beginning-of-year capital balances, salary allowances of $10,000 and $8,000, respectively, with the remainder to be divided 2:1. Computation is as follows:

	Carter	Foley	Total
Salary allowances	$10,000	$ 8,000	$18,000
Interest on beginning-of-year capital:			
20% of $62,500	12,500		
20% of $47,500		9,500	
Total interest allowances			22,000
Remainder (⅔ and ⅓)	18,000	9,000	27,000
Net income division	$40,500	$26,500	$67,000

The journal entry to record the allocation is:

1987 Dec. 31	Income Summary	67,000	
	Kay Carter, Capital		40,500
	Ann Foley, Capital		26,500
	To allocate the net income for the year divided 2:1 after allowing for salaries and interest on capital balances.		

Example 3: Division of Earnings Based on Salaries, Interest, and Agreed Ratio with Net Income Less Than Salaries and Interest

If there is an agreement for a salary allowance and interest allowance, the salary and interest allocations must be made, even though the net income is less than the total of such allocations. The negative remainder is divided in the same ratio used for dividing an excess of net income over total salaries and interest. To illustrate, assume the same facts as in the previous example, except that the net income for the year is $22,000. The computation is:

		Carter	Foley	Total
Salary allowances		$10,000	$ 8,000	$18,000
Interest on beginning-of-year capital:				
20% of $62,500		12,500		
20% of $47,500			9,500	
Total interest allowances				22,000
Total allowances		$22,500	$17,500	$40,000
Excess of allowances over net income:				
Total allowances	$40,000			
Net income	22,000			
Negative remainder (⅔ and ⅓)		(12,000)[a]	(6,000)[a]	(18,000)[a]
Net income division		$ 10,500	$11,500	$22,000

[a]Negative figures.

The reader should note carefully that a negative remainder does not necessarily indicate that a net loss has occurred. It simply reduces the share of profits allocated to each partner by the salary and interest allowances. The journal entry to record the allocation is:

1987				
Dec.	31	Income Summary	22,000	
		Kay Carter, Capital		10,500
		Ann Foley, Capital		11,500
		To allocate the net income for the year.		

Partnership Financial Statements

The changes in partners' equity accounts during the year are shown in a statement of partners' equity. Its form is similar to the statement of owner's equity for a single proprietorship. It is a supporting statement for the total partners' equities reported in the balance sheet. Assume the facts in Example 3 above. Also, assume that Carter and Foley each withdrew $12,000 in anticipation of income earned (Kay Carter, Drawing had a debit balance of $12,000 and Ann Foley, Drawing had a debit balance of $12,000), and that Carter made an additional investment of $10,000 and Foley, $8,000. The statement of partners' equity would reveal this information as shown in Figure 12–3.

The statement of partners' equity provides an explanation of the changes in partners' capital balances over a period of time. The basic format reconciles the beginning-of-the-period balances to the end-of-the-period balances in the same manner as a statement of owner's equity for a proprietorship. Note, however, in Figure 12–3, a separate column is provided for each partner. Thus, Ann Foley can trace the change in her capital from $47,500 on December 31, 1986, to its new total of $55,000 on December 31, 1987.

CARTER AND FOLEY
Statement of Partners' Equity
For the Year Ended December 31, 1987

Exhibit B

	Carter	Foley	Total
Partners' capital balances, December 31, 1986	$62,500	$47,500	$110,000
Add: Additional investments	10,000	8,000	18,000
Net Income	10,500	11,500	22,000
Subtotals	$83,000	$67,000	$150,000
Deduct: Withdrawals	12,000	12,000	24,000
Partners' capital balances, December 31, 1987	$71,000	$55,000	$126,000

Figure 12–3   **Statement of Partners' Equity**

On December 31, 1987, the balance sheet would disclose the new equity balances as follows:

CARTER AND FOLEY
Balance Sheet
December 31, 1987

Exhibit C

Liabilities and Partners' Equity

Partners' equity:		
Kay Carter, capital	$71,000	
Ann Foley, capital	55,000	$126,000

The financial statements of a partnership are similar to those of a single proprietorship. The allocations of net income to the partners may be shown below the net income line of the income statement or, if they are too numerous, in a supplementary statement. The balance sheet shows the individual capital balances as of the end of the period and their total; or, if they are too numerous, the individual balances are shown in the supplementary statement of partners' equity.

Changes in Capital Structure

Once the partnership has been formed, changes in the capital structure are likely to follow in the future. Such changes result from (1) the admission of a new partner, (2) the death or retirement of an existing partner, or (3) the liquidation of the partnership. The accounting for these changes is discussed in the sections that follow.

Admission of a New Partner

The admission of a new partner technically dissolves the old partnership, although in the absence of complete liquidation or winding up of the business, it continues as before. In this sense, a **dissolution** means the legal end to a specific business. If the business continues, it is in fact a new business organization. A new partner may either (1) *purchase* an interest from one or more of the other partners or (2) be admitted as a partner by making an *investment* in the partnership.

Purchase of an Interest If the new partner buys an interest from one of the original partners, partnership assets are unchanged because the transfer of assets is direct between the persons involved. The only required entry on the partnership books is a transfer of the agreed share from the old partner's capital account to a capital account opened for the new partner. The actual amount paid for all or part of a partner's share of ownership is a private transaction between the two individuals. The cash transaction is not reflected on the books of the partnership.

Investment to Acquire an Interest A new partner may be admitted by making an investment of cash or other assets directly to the firm, thereby increasing partnership assets and total capital. The amount credited to the incoming partner's capital account may be measured by the value of the investment. However, there are several complexities that can be involved in the agreement to admit a new partner. One of these is the recognition of goodwill.

Goodwill

Goodwill *is an intangible asset that represents an expectation of a greater than normal level of earnings of a business in its industry.*

If the old partnership has been successful, the new partner may agree, as a condition, that part of the investment he or she makes be considered a recognition of goodwill in the former partnership. Such goodwill would be attributable to the old partners. On the other hand, if the old partners need additional resources—funds, skills, or both—that the new partner will contribute, they may agree to credit the new partner with an amount greater than his or her investment in the form of goodwill. In other words, the new partner is investing a combination of cash plus goodwill. Under these circumstances, it is assumed that all other assets are valued approximately at current fair market value.

A partner may be admitted by paying in an investment different from the book value of the ownership share of the partnership he or she obtains, with this admission then being recorded by the *bonus method*. Under this method, no new intangible asset is placed on the books. Shifts in amounts are made among the partners' capital accounts to reflect any agreement about the admission.

Retirement or Death of an Existing Partner

The next change in partners' ownership discussed is that caused by death or withdrawal of a partner. The partnership agreement usually contains provisions for determining a deceased partner's current equity and the manner and form of settlement with his or her estate. The partnership agreement should also provide for procedures to be followed when a partner withdraws from the partnership. In both cases, the agreement will *generally* provide for the adjustment of assets to their current fair market value.[4] Resulting increases or decreases are always distributed to the partners' capital accounts in their profit-and-loss-sharing ratios, after which the withdrawing partner receives cash or other assets equal to the adjusted balance in his or her capital account. The entry is a debit to the capital account and a credit to cash or other assets.

---

[4] A bonus method or a goodwill method similar to those in the admission of a partner could be used. They are not illustrated in this book since they are considered to be beyond its scope.

Liquidation of a Partnership

A partnership may be terminated by selling the assets, paying the creditors, and distributing the remaining cash to the partners. This total process is called **liquidation** of a partnership; conversion of assets into cash is called **realization** When a partnership is liquidated, gains and losses resulting from the sale of assets must first be distributed to the capital accounts in profit-and-loss-sharing ratios before cash can be distributed to the partners. If, after all gains and losses are distributed, a partners' capital account shows a debit balance, that partner must pay in the deficiency from personal resources. If that partner has no personal resources, the deficiency must be absorbed by the other partners. This deficiency absorption is on the basis of the solvent partners' profit-and-loss-sharing ratios *to each other*.

The details of accounting for the preceding changes in the capital structure of a partnership are covered in advanced accounting textbooks.

Internal Control and Ratio Analysis

Internal control problems in unincorporated businesses are similar to those in corporations. If the single proprietorship or partnership is relatively small, internal control is less formal and is based primarily on close attention to detail by the owners. In larger unincorporated businesses, formal internal control procedures should be similar to those used in corporations. These procedures are discussed in various chapters throughout the book.

Ratio analysis in single proprietorships and partnerships also parallels that of corporations. Since a large number of small businesses fail through lack of proper control, it is important that the owners evaluate the business financial position and operating results constantly. The current ratio and acid test ratio are very useful in this monitoring. Turnover ratios are also extremely important. Accounts receivable and inventories are more likely to get out of hand unless a continual check of their turnover is made.

Glossary

Dissolution The cessation of a partnership; the legal end of life of a business.

General partner A partner who has unlimited liability for the debts of a partnership.

Goodwill An intangible asset that represents an expected greater than normal level of earnings of a business in its industry.

Interest allowance A mechanism for dividing a portion of the earnings of a partnership by allowing interest on capital balances at a specified interest rate.

Limited partner A partner who has no personal responsibility for the debts of the partnership beyond the amount of his or her investment.

Liquidation The process of terminating a business by selling the assets, paying the creditors, and distributing the remaining cash to the owner(s).

Mutual agency A characteristic of partnerships whereby the act of a single partner is binding on the partnership and on each of the partners.

Partner's drawing The account representing the reduction in the equity of a partner resulting from cash or other assets withdrawn from the business in anticipation of income earned.

Partnership An association of two or more persons who carry on, as co-owners, a business for profit.

Partnership property All assets brought into a partnership; they belong to all partners as co-owners.

Realization The conversion of the noncash assets of a business to cash.

Single Proprietorship An unincorporated business owned by one individual.

Questions

Q12–1 How is the accounting for a partnership similar to that of a single proprietorship? How is it different?

Q12–2 In what ways is the accounting the same for the three basic forms of business organization?

Q12–3 Differentiate between the following: general and limited partners; single proprietorships and partnerships; goodwill account and drawing account.

Q12–4 What is meant by agreed ratio? Mutual agency? Unlimited liability?

Q12–5 Can a partnership exist without any general partners? Explain.

Q12–6 Jones and Smith form a partnership to manufacture microelectronic equipment. Without consulting Jones, Smith buys equipment costing $700,000 to be used in operations. Is this acquisition binding on Jones even though he was not consulted about its purchase? Give your reason.

Q12–7 Does each state have a different set of laws to regulate partnerships? Explain.

Q12–8 B. Wrenn and C. Robin formed a partnership. Wrenn invested $20,000 in cash. Robin invested land and a building with cash market value of $40,000. Five years later they agree to terminate the partnership, and Robin demands the return to her of the land and building. Is she justified in the demand? Explain.

Q12–9 T. Beal and K. Skerry are partners with capital account balances of $40,000 each. They share profits one-third and two-thirds, respectively. (a) Is this an equitable arrangement? (b) Assume that 10 percent interest on beginning balances is agreed upon, with any remainder to be distributed equally to Beal and to Skerry. How will profits of $17,000 be distributed? (c) Should an account be debited for the interest on the capital balances? Explain.

Q12–10 Andrew and Beth formed a partnership. Andrew invested $25,000; Beth invested $75,000. Profits for the first year were $40,000. Beth insisted that her capital account be credited for $30,000. Is her argument valid? Why or why not?

Q12–11 State three ways that a partnership can be dissolved.

Exercises

E12–1
Recording owner's equity transactions by a single proprietor

On June 10, 1987, Joan Rockford formed a new business, Rocky Roads, by contributing $5,000 in cash; land and a building with a fair market value of $10,000 and $45,000, respectively; and a van with a fair market value of $3,000 to be used for deliveries. The business is to assume the $1,000 balance on the note payable due on the van. By the end of 1987, the net income was $27,000 and withdrawals were $7,500.

(continued on next page)

1. Make the general journal entry on the books of the business to record its formation.
2. Prepare a beginning balance sheet for the single proprietorship.
3. Prepare the last two closing entries.

E12-2
Preparing statement of owner's equity

James McQueen, owner of the Quality Store, asks you to determine his equity in the business at December 31, 1987. You determine his net income for the year from the store to be $39,000. In addition, the following transactions occurred during the year:

Original investment.	$45,000
Additional investment.	6,000
Personal withdrawals.	24,000

1. Post the transactions to appropriate T accounts.
2. Prepare a statement of owner's equity.

E12-3
Recording investment by partners and preparing a balance sheet

Burt Barnes and Raymond Strong formed a partnership on May 12, 1987. Barnes contributed $38,000 in cash, land worth $16,000, a building appraised at $131,000, and a truck valued at $10,000. The land and building are encumbered by a mortgage of $30,000, which is assumed by the partnership; interest of $680 has accrued on this mortgage to May 12, 1987. Strong contributed $42,000 in cash.

1. Make the general journal entries on the books of the new partnership to record its formation.
2. Prepare a beginning balance sheet for the partnership, which will do business under the name of B and S Company.

E12-4
Recording investment of cash and noncash assets by partners

Samual David and Elijah Hills are television repairers. They desire to form a partnership to open up a television sales outlet and repair shop. Their attorney prepares a partnership agreement requiring the assets of their respective businesses (operated as single proprietorships) be recorded at current fair market value. These assets that will be invested in the new partnership along with the liabilities to be assumed and their fair market value are as follows:

	David	Hills	Total
Cash	$ 18,000	$ 16,000	$ 34,000
Repair supplies	1,000	900	1,900
Equipment.	34,500	29,200	63,700
Accounts payable.	(14,000)[a]	(12,000)[a]	(26,000)[a]

[a]Credit balance.

Prepare the journal entry to record the original investments on the David and Hills partnership books.

E12-5
Recording transactions by partners

The following selected transactions occurred in the partnership of Whang and Ding:

12 / Single Proprietorship and Partnership Accounting

1987		
Jan. 1		Chi Whang and Pok Ding formed a partnership effective on this date, making the following investments: Whang invested $31,000 in cash. Ding contributed his equity in a building and lot. The partners agreed that the building was worth $49,500 and the land $6,000. There was a mortgage on the land and building with a face value of $12,000 and an interest rate of 14 percent. The interest was last paid on October 1, 1986. The partnership assumed all liabilities relating to the mortgage.
Mar. 2		Whang withdrew $1,200 cash in anticipation of income to be earned.
Apr. 1		Ding withdrew from the business merchandise that cost $800 and had a selling price of $1,200. The firm uses the periodic inventory system, and Purchases must be credited.
Oct. 3		Whang was allowed to withdraw $12,000 in cash to pay a personal debt. The amount exceeds any anticipated income to be earned.

Record the transactions in the general journal.

E12–6
Distribution of income—statements and entries

Jean Ormand, Betsy Peters, and Catherine Queens formed a partnership on May 1, 1987, with investments of $35,000, $27,000, and $30,000, respectively. During the next 12 months, Ormand and Peters made additional investments of $12,000 each. Queens invested an additional $15,000. No withdrawals were made by the partners during this first year of operations. Net income for the period was $60,000. The partnership agreement did not specify the method of dividing profits and losses. Prepare (a) a statement of partners' equity for the year ended April 30, 1988, and (b) an entry to close the Income Summary account.

E12–7
Preparing statement of partners' equity

Robert Hickson and Mary Sipps formed a partnership during their senior year in college to provide tutoring service to new students. After graduation they continued the business, hiring other students to help with much of the actual tutoring. Their account balances in alphabetical sequence on December 31, 1987, are as follows:

Accounts Receivable	$ 2,500
Cash	6,000
Mary Sipps, Capital	4,000
Mary Sipps, Drawing	12,000
Robert Hickson, Capital	15,550
Robert Hickson, Drawing	12,000
Salaries Expense	22,500
Supplies on Hand	3,250
Supplies Expense	5,040
Tutoring Fees Earned	43,740

1. Prepare the December 31, 1987, closing entries. Profits and losses are divided equally.
2. Prepare a statement of partners' equity using three money columns headed Hickson, Sipps, and Total.
3. Explain why the equity of each partner declined in a profitable year.

E12–8
Recording investment by partners and evaluating investment decision

L. Lloyd and M. Minton formed a partnership on September 1, 1987. Lloyd contributed $20,000 in cash, land worth $10,000, a building appraised at $60,000 (the land and the building are encumbered by a mortgage of $10,000, which is assumed by the partnership), and a truck valued at $8,000. Minton contributed $20,000 in cash.

1. Make the general journal entries to record the formation of the partnership.
2. Why may Lloyd be willing to enter into a partnership in which he contributes 4.4 times as much as his partner?

E12-9
Admitting a new partner by purchase of interest from an existing partner

J. Jacobs, K. Kroom, and L. Leuter are partners with capital balances of $40,000, $30,000, and $60,000, respectively. Leuter, with the consent of Jacobs and Kroom, sells one-third of his interest to M. Melson for $25,000. Prepare a journal entry to record the admission of Melson.

E12-10
Adjusting and closing entries from a trial balance and added data

The unadjusted trial balance of the Petrocelli Company contained the following accounts as of December 31, 1987:

PETROCELLI COMPANY
Partial Trial Balance
December 31, 1987

Acct. No.	Account Title	Debits	Credits
121	Accrued Interest Receivable	$ 0	
131	Office Supplies	950	
132	Prepaid Insurance	3,920	
133	Prepaid Advertising	0	
205	Accrued Wages Payable		$ 0
212	Unearned Rent		0
301	A. Petrocelli, Capital		85,000
309	A. Petrocelli, Drawing	34,000	
406	Rent Earned		222,000
410	Interest Earned		1,950
503	Wages Expense	51,000	
504	Advertising Expense	9,000	
505	Insurance Expense	0	
506	Office Supplies Expense	0	
601	Income Summary		0

Additional information includes the following:

a. Interest that had accrued on notes receivable at December 31, 1987, amounted to $420.
b. The inventory of office supplies at December 31, 1987, was $620.
c. The insurance records show that $2,000 of insurance has expired during 1987.
d. Included in Advertising Expense is a prepayment of a $1,500 contract for advertising space in a regional magazine; 60 percent of this contract has been used, and the remainder will be used in the following year.
e. Wages due to employees of $1,800 had accrued as of December 31, 1987.
f. Rent collected in advance that will not be earned until 1988 amounted to $9,500.

Required:

1. Open the accounts listed in the trial balance and record the balance in the appropriate column as of December 31, 1987.
2. Journalize the adjusting entries and post to the appropriate accounts. In the accounts, identify the postings by writing "Adjusting" in the explanation columns.
3. Prepare journal entries for closing.

A Problems

P12-1A
Recording owner's equity transactions and closing for a single proprietorship

E. J. Paul formed a single proprietorship on April 12, 1986. On January 2, 1987, he invested an additional $8,000 in cash and contributed a van to be used as a delivery truck with a fair market value of $3,500. The business assumed the note payable on the van of $1,000. The following adjusted trial balance was available as of December 31, 1987:

PAUL AND COMPANY
Adjusted Trial Balance
December 31, 1987

Account Title	Debits	Credits
Cash	$ 4,000	
Accounts Receivable	12,000	
Prepaid Rent	600	
Store Fixtures	6,000	
Accumulated Depreciation—Store Fixtures		$ 2,000
Delivery Trucks	3,500	
Accumulated Depreciation—Delivery Trucks		700
Accounts Payable		1,500
Notes Payable		1,000
Accrued Interest Payable		160
E. J. Paul, Capital		16,400
E. J. Paul, Drawing	1,800	
Consulting Fees		22,000
Rent Expense	3,600	
Supplies Expense	900	
Depreciation Expense—Store Fixtures	1,000	
Depreciation Expense—Delivery Trucks	700	
Interest Expense	160	
Salaries Expense	9,500	
Totals	$43,760	$43,760

Required:

1. Prepare the general journal entry to record the additional investment by E. J. Paul on January 2, 1987.
2. Prepare general journal entries to close the books on December 31, 1987.
3. Prepare a statement of owner's equity for the year ended December 31, 1987.

P12–2A
Recording partnership transactions

The following selected transactions occurred in the partnership of Collins and Condin:

1987

Jan. 2   Clark Collins and Dan Condin formed a partnership on this date, making the following investments:
Collins invested $55,000 in cash. Condin contributed equity in a building and lot. The partners agreed that the building was worth $90,000 and the land $15,000. There was a mortgage on the land and building with a face value of $27,000; the mortgage carried an interest rate of 9 percent, and the interest was last paid on October 1, 1986. The partnership assumed all liabilities relating to the investment.

Mar. 1   Collins withdrew $800 cash in anticipation of income to be earned.

Apr. 1   Condin withdrew merchandise from the business. The merchandise cost $600 and had a selling price of $800. The firm uses the perpetual inventory system.

Oct. 1   Collins was allowed to withdraw $12,000 in cash to pay a personal debt. This is in excess of anticipated earnings.

Required: Prepare general journal entries to record the transactions.

P12–3A
Recording investments of partners under different situations

Anson Strong and Winston Turner form a partnership.

Required: Journalize their investments on the new partnership books in the general journal on the basis of each of the following independent assumptions:

1. Each partner invests $12,000 in cash.
2. Strong invests $14,000 in cash, and Turner invests $15,000 in cash.
3. Strong invests $5,000 in cash, land worth $18,000, a building worth $40,000, and merchandise worth $6,000. Turner invests $46,000 in cash.

(continued on next page)

4. Strong invests $7,000 in cash, land worth $9,000, and a building worth $50,000. The partnership agrees to assume a mortgage payable of $18,000 on the land and building. Turner invests $6,500 in cash, store equipment worth $12,000, and merchandise worth $6,200.

P12–4A
Preparing financial statements for a partnership

The accountant for Walters and Winston, business information systems consultants, prepared the following adjusted trial balances as of December 31, 1987:

WALTERS AND WINSTON, CONSULTANTS
Adjusted Trial Balance
December 31, 1987

Account Title	Debits	Credits
Cash	$ 9,700	
Accounts Receivable	25,200	
Supplies	7,600	
Prepaid Insurance	5,500	
Land	20,000	
Building	140,000	
Accumulated Depreciation—Building		$ 20,000
Office Equipment	24,000	
Accumulated Depreciation—Office Equipment		7,000
Accounts Payable		9,000
Accrued Salaries Payable		1,000
Mortgage Payable		40,000
Fallon Walters, Capital		40,000
Fallon Walters, Drawing	24,000	
Thomas Winston, Capital		50,000
Thomas Winston, Drawing	30,000	
Professional Fees		170,000
Supplies Expense	6,000	
Depreciation Expense—Office Equipment	2,400	
Depreciation Expense—Building	8,000	
Utilities Expense	2,400	
General Expense	3,000	
Property Tax Expense	2,000	
Interest Expense	3,200	
Salaries Expense	24,000	
Totals	$337,000	$337,000

Required:

1. Prepare an income statement for the year, showing at the bottom of the statement the allocation of net income to each partner. The partners have agreed to divide profits and losses as follows: (a) 20 percent interest on capital balances at the beginning of the year, (b) salaries of $16,000 and $14,000, respectively, and (c) the remainder divided in the ratio of 3:2. Each partner made an additional investment of $4,000 on July 1, 1987.
2. Prepare a statement of partners' equity for the year.
3. Prepare a balance sheet as of December 31, 1987.

P12–5A
Distributing profits and losses

Sarah Gleem and Sandy Hooter formed a partnership on January 1, 1987, with investments of $45,000 and $72,000, respectively. On July 1, 1987, Gleem invested an additional $15,000.

Required: Make the appropriate journal entries to record the distribution of profits and losses on the basis of each of the following independent assumptions:

1. Net income is $24,000, and profits and losses are shared equally.

2. Net loss is $9,000; the partnership agreement provides that profits and losses are to be distributed 60 percent to Gleem and 40 percent to Hooter.

3. Net income is $24,000, to be distributed as follows: salaries of $12,000 to Gleem and $18,000 to Hooter; interest of 12 percent on ending capital balances before the addition of net income; remainder to be distributed equally.

P12–6A
Thought-provoking problem: division of profits

On January 2, 1987, Amram Boheme and Thomas Martin formed a partnership. Boheme invested $70,000 in cash, Martin, $30,000. They wrote a simple partnership agreement, but forgot to mention the division of profits and losses. During 1987, the partners withdrew $24,000 in cash each. At the end of 1987, the Income Summary account showed a net credit balance of $36,000 after all expenses and revenues had been closed. The operating income was $100,000 but there was a loss of $64,000 brought about by a bad decision made by Martin in ordering the wrong kind of property, plant, and equipment. After referring back to the partnership agreement, Boheme argues that his account should be credited with $70,000, particularly since Martin cost the partnership $64,000 in net income because of his unwise decision. Martin disagrees; he says the division should be an equal split.

Required:

1. With which partner do you agree? Why? Does the loss caused by the action of one partner affect the division of net income?

2. Prepare journal entries to record the withdrawals, the proper division of net income, and the closing of the drawing accounts.

B Problems

P12–1B
Recording owner's equity transactions and closing for a single proprietorship

U. Hawk formed a single proprietorship on March 14, 1986. On January 2, 1987, she invested an additional $6,000 in cash and contributed a van to be used as a delivery truck with a fair market value of $6,000. The business assumed the note payable on the van of $3,600. The following adjusted trial balance was available as of December 31, 1987:

HAWK AND COMPANY
Adjusted Trial Balance
December 31, 1987

Account Title	Debits	Credits
Cash	$ 3,000	
Accounts Receivable	8,000	
Prepaid Rent	900	
Store Fixtures	8,000	
Accumulated Depreciation—Store Fixtures		$ 3,000
Delivery Trucks	6,000	
Accumulated Depreciation—Delivery Trucks		1,200
Accounts Payable		2,000
Notes Payable		3,600
Accrued Interest Payable		540
U. Hawk, Capital		18,100
U. Hawk, Drawing	3,000	
Consulting Fees		18,000
Rent Expense	3,600	
Supplies Expense	1,200	
Depreciation Expense—Store Fixtures	1,000	
Depreciation Expense—Delivery Trucks	1,200	
Interest Expense	540	
Salaries Expense	10,000	
Totals	$46,440	$46,440

(continued on next page)

Required:

1. Prepare the general journal entry to record the additional investment by U. Hawk on January 2, 1987.
2. Prepare general journal entries to close the books on December 31, 1987.
3. Prepare a statement of owner's equity for the year ended December 31, 1987.

P12–2B
Recording partnership transactions

The following selected transactions occurred in the partnership of Song and Jung:

1987

Jan. 2 Ann Song and Liz Jung formed a partnership on this date, making the following investments:
Jung invested $60,000 in cash. Song invested the equity in a building and lot. The partners agreed the building was worth $80,000 and the land $20,000. There was a mortgage on the land and building with a face value of $25,000; the mortgage carried an interest rate of 12 percent, and the interest was last paid on November 1, 1986. The partnership agreed to assume all liabilities relating to the investment.

Mar. 1 Jung withdrew $900 cash in anticipation of income to be earned.

Apr. 1 Song withdrew merchandise from the business. The merchandise cost $500 and had a selling price of $800. The firm uses the perpetual inventory system.

Oct. 1 Jung was allowed to withdraw $11,000 in cash to pay a personal debt. This is in excess of anticipated earnings.

Required: Prepare general journal entries to record the transactions.

P12–3B
Recording investments of partners under different situations

Sante Barnard and Leman Trotts form a partnership.

Required: Journalize their investments on the new partnership books in the general journal on the basis of each of the following independent assumptions:

1. Each partner invests $9,200 in cash.
2. Barnard invests $10,800 in cash, and Trotts invests $12,600 in cash.
3. Barnard invests $5,500 in cash, land worth $14,000, a building worth $32,000, and merchandise worth $6,000. Trotts invests $40,500.
4. Barnard invests $5,800 in cash, land worth $9,500, and a building worth $30,500. The partnership agrees to assume a mortgage payable of $10,500 on the land and building. Trotts invests $6,500 in cash, store equipment worth $11,000, and merchandise worth $4,800.

P12–4B
Preparing financial statements for a partnership

The accountants for Barbara and Merton, business information systems consultants, prepared the following adjusted trial balance as of December 31, 1987:

BARBARA AND MERTON, CONSULTANTS
Adjusted Trial Balance
December 31, 1987

Account Title	Debits	Credits
Cash	$ 22,125	
Accounts Receivable	32,500	
Supplies	9,500	
Prepaid Insurance	6,875	
Land	25,000	
Building	175,000	
Accumulated Depreciation—Building		$ 25,000
Office Equipment	30,000	
Accumulated Depreciation—Office Equipment		8,750
Accounts Payable		11,250
Accrued Salaries Payable		1,250

Account Title	Debits	Credits
Mortgage Payable		50,000
Melissa Barbara, Capital		68,000
Melissa Barbara, Drawing	37,500	
Arnold Merton, Capital		55,500
Arnold Merton, Drawing	30,000	
Professional Fees		212,500
Supplies Expense	7,500	
Depreciation Expense—Office Equipment	3,000	
Depreciation Expense—Building.	10,000	
Utilities Expense	3,000	
General Expense	3,750	
Property Tax Expense	2,500	
Interest Expense	4,000	
Salaries Expense	30,000	
Totals	$432,250	$432,250

Required:

1. Prepare an income statement for the year, showing the allocation of net income to each partner. The partners have agreed to divide profits and losses as follows: (a) 15 percent on capital balances at the beginning of the year, (b) salaries of $45,000 and $30,000, respectively, and (c) the remainder divided in the ratio of 3:2. Each partner made an additional investment of $6,000 on July 1, 1987.

2. Prepare a statement of partners' equity for the year.

3. Prepare a balance sheet as of December 31, 1987.

P12–5B
Distributing profits and losses

Oscar Glenn and Robert Greer formed a partnership on January 1, 1987, with investments of $40,000 and $58,000, respectively. On July 1, 1987, Glenn invested an additional $14,000.

Required: Make the appropriate general journal entries to record the distribution of profits and losses on the basis of each of the following independent assumptions:

1. Net income is $20,000, and profits and losses are shared equally.

2. Net loss is $4,000; the partnership agreement provides that profits and losses are to be distributed 60 percent to Glenn and 40 percent to Greer.

3. Net income is $60,000, to be distributed as follows: salaries of $10,000 to Glenn and $15,000 to Greer; interest of 15 percent on ending capital balances before the addition of net income; the remainder to be distributed equally.

P12–6B
Thought-provoking problem: liquidation of a partnership

On July 1, 1987, Laura Greene and Clara Mann formed a partnership. Greene invested land and building with values of $20,000 and $80,000, respectively; Mann invested cash of $40,000. Their attorney prepared a partnership agreement providing for an equal division of profits and losses. The two partners signed the agreement and prepared to take steps to order merchandise, supplies, and fixtures. Before they had a chance to place any orders, a fire destroyed the uninsured building completely. They had planned to wait and take out a comprehensive insurance policy after they had stocked their store. With this misfortune, they agreed to terminate the partnership. Greene said, "I claim the land and all the cash as my share of the liquidation." Mann replied, "Oh! No! I get back my cash of $40,000 and you get back your land."

Required:

1. Which partner is legally correct? Why?

2. Prepare a journal entry or entries to record the investment by Greene and Mann.

3. Prepare a journal entry or entries to record the fire loss and the liquidation of the partnership.

13 Accounting for Corporate Equity

Introduction

The corporate form of business produces the vast majority of the revenue of all companies in the United States. Almost everyone is familiar with corporate giants such as American Telephone and Telegraph Company, General Motors, R. J. Reynolds Industries, and Burlington Industries. Most people, however, do not realize that even the corner grocery store is very likely to be incorporated today to limit the liability of its owners.

The distinctive features of accounting for proprietorships and partnerships are explained in Chapter 12. The detailed accounting for stockholders' equity in corporations is considered in this chapter. Because so many organizations are organized as corporations and because they produce the bulk of revenues of all organizations, this chapter also takes a closer look at the formation of a corporation, sources of corporate capital, the different classes of stock, the terms used to measure capital stock, the recording of the issuance of capital stock, and the source and management of retained earnings.

Learning Goals

1. To understand the essential reasons for a firm to use the corporate form of business organization.

2. To know the sources of paid-in capital of corporations and understand the classifications of paid-in capital other than capital stock.

3. To recognize and differentiate among classes of capital stock and their various value classifications.

4. To record the issuance of both common and preferred stock and to account for stock subscriptions.

5. To understand the nature of retained earnings.

6. To make entries restricting retained earnings for various purposes.

7. To record transactions involving cash dividends and those involving both large and small stock dividends.
8. To understand and account for stock splits.
9. To record treasury stock transactions.
10. To compute book value of a share of stock.
11. To understand the importance of earnings per share.
12. To understand the basic elements of internal control of stockholders' equity items.

The Corporation as a Form of Business Organization

A **corporation** is a legal entity as well as an accounting entity. This means that, in the eyes of the law, a corporation is an artificial being. Hence, it has the powers and rights of and may act as a single individual. Acting through appropriately designated officials, a corporation may enter into contracts, sue or be sued in court, and carry on other activities of an individual in the business world. For this and other reasons, its income is subject to direct federal and state income taxes.

Deciding to Incorporate

When a group of people form a business, they must decide what type of business organization they should choose—corporation or partnership. If they choose the corporate form, they must ascertain that such advantages as limited liability of shareholders (discussed in Chapter 2), ease of transferring shares, continuity of life, and the variety of ways of raising funds are greater than the disadvantages of difficulty and cost of incorporation, and legal restraints.[1] Since there are many corporations, business groups appear to believe that the advantages generally outweigh the disadvantages.

Once a decision is made to incorporate, the incorporators must apply to the secretary of state (or another designated state official) for a **charter**. This legal document is the copy of the articles of incorporation prepared by the incorporators, which is returned by the secretary of state with a certificate of incorporation. Routine and restricting provisions usually specified in a corporate charter are (1) the name of the corporation; (2) the type of business in which it is authorized to engage; (3) the duration of existence (usually perpetual unless specified otherwise); (4) the location of its principal office or

---

[1] At the time of this writing, corporate earnings are taxed twice: once as corporate income tax and again as dividends received by stockholders. The Internal Revenue Code permits the taxation of income of certain closely held corporations as partnerships; the net income is taxed to the stockholders whether it is distributed or not. "Double taxation" is not present in these cases.

place of business; and (5) the classes (or types) of shares of capital stock and the number of shares of each type that the corporation will be authorized to issue.

Preparing the Corporation for Operations

Many corporations start off as small family or closely held corporations (with only a small group of stockholders), hoping to expand as business grows. Once this group receives the charter and certificate of incorporation, the capital stock (of one or more classes, discussed below) is issued. If the business is successful and does expand, it may then offer its stock to the general public.

The stockholders of a corporation elect directors to represent them in setting policies. In a new corporation, directors are stockholders of that corporation. These directors appoint officers—president, one or more vice presidents, secretary, treasurer, and other designated officers—to operate the new business as a corporation in conformity with the articles of incorporation. Often the directors appoint themselves as these officers. As a corporation expands and offers stock to the general public (referred to as "going public"), it seeks individuals other than officers to be elected to its board of directors. These nonofficer directors are called *outside directors*. These directors serve a "watchdog" purpose. They are often asked to serve on committees such as the audit committee that sets policies related to the audit process and reviews the report of the independent auditing firm.

Accounting issues peculiar to a corporation primarily involve the accounting for the stockholders' equity. The stockholders' equity in a corporation comes from a number of sources. It is of the utmost importance that these sources be clearly identified and stated and that the terminology used to designate them be precise and meaningful. In the next section the various sources of stockholders' equity are indicated, followed by a description of the different classes of capital stock and the meaning and significance of terms used to measure capital stock.

Paid-in Capital

Sources of Capital

Operating transactions—revenue and expenses—are recorded in the same manner for all forms of business organization. Since the primary difference in the accounting for a corporation is in stockholders' equity, the chart of accounts for this business form must distinguish between investments by stockholders and the earnings retained (reinvested). This distinction is essential because most state laws normally allow only earnings to be distributed to the stockholders. Both for the protection of corporate creditors and for the continued operation of the business, amounts exceeding cumulative retained earnings usually cannot be legally distributed to the stockholders. Hence, sep-

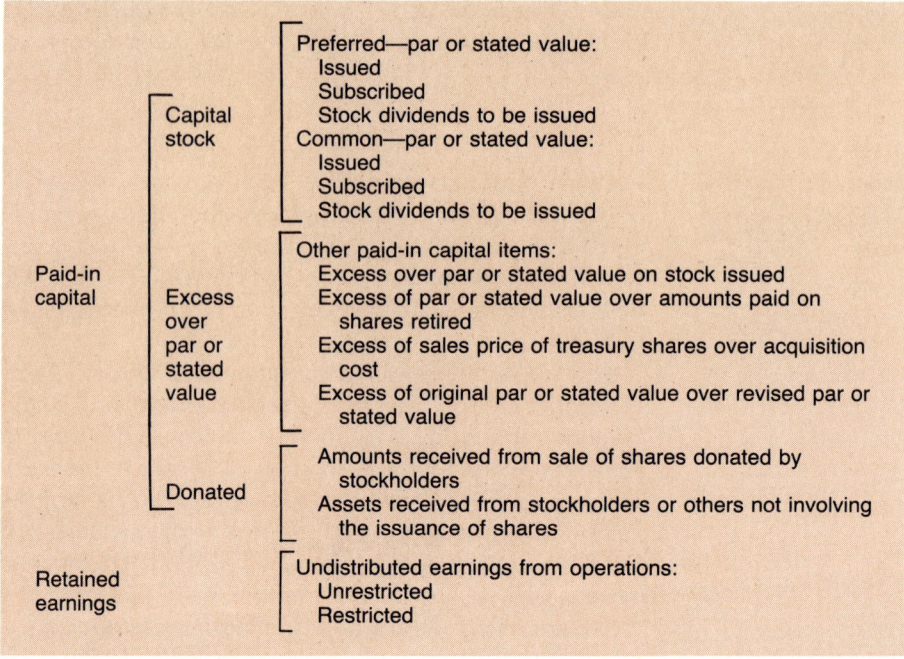

Figure 13–1 Sources of Stockholders' Equity

arate accounts designating the several sources of stockholders' equity should be kept and clearly set forth in the stockholders' equity section of the corporate balance sheet. The various sources of paid-in capital are outlined in Figure 13–1. This section emphasizes the accounts used to record the capital paid in by stockholders. Retained earnings are dealt with more fully in the latter part of this chapter.

Capital Stock

The charter granted by the state of incorporation authorizes the newly formed corporation to issue a designated number of shares of capital stock of one or more classes. The corporation usually secures authorization to issue sufficient shares of each class to allow enough sales in the present to acquire the investment desired and to hold back a substantial number of shares to issue for expansion of the business in the future. The total number of shares of any given class issued cannot exceed the number authorized.[2] Capital stock usually has an arbitrary dollar amount assigned per share called *par value*. Discussed in detail later, this amount is separated in the accounting records from all other invested capital.

---

[2]The owners of shares of stock are called stockholders or shareholders; the two terms mean the same thing.

Detail with respect to the number of shares authorized is customarily included as part of the description in the stockholders' equity section of the balance sheet. The balance sheet presentation after the issuance of common stock may be as shown below:

> Stockholders' equity:
> Paid-in capital:
> Common stock, $10 par value; authorized 10,000 shares, issued
> 5,000 shares. $50,000

Classes of Capital Stock **Capital stock** is usually issued in two classes—preferred and common. A common stock certificate of CBS Inc. is shown in Figure 2–1, page 50. Similar stock certificates representing ownership in a corporation are issued to individuals or organizations who have obtained their shares of capital stock in exchange for funds invested in the company or for services rendered, or who have acquired shares from previous investors.

Preferred Stock **Preferred stock** represents a type of ownership with certain preferences. These preferences usually fall into two groups: (1) preference as to earnings—the dividend preference, and (2) preference as to assets in case of liquidation. The dividend preference may take several different forms depending upon how the preferred **stock indenture** (contract between the corporation and its preferred stockholders) is written. Preferred stock carries a stated dividend rate or amount of annual dividends per share. Most preferred stock is **cumulative**; that is, undeclared dividends accumulate. Accumulated undeclared preferred dividends are called an **arrearage**. Both the arrearage and the current dividend on preferred stock must be declared and paid by the corporation before any dividend payment is made on common stock.[3] Some preferred shares are issued with a stated dividend rate or amount but without this dividend preference. These are called **noncumulative preferred** shares. On this type, if the dividend is not declared in a given period, it is lost to the stockholders.

The recording of dividends is discussed later in this chapter. However, to illustrate the meaning of cumulative preferred stock, the simplified example below shows the division of the *annual* amount available for dividends for both preferred and common shares.

Example: Preferred Stock Is Cumulative. To illustrate this preferred stock characteristic, assume that a corporation has outstanding 15 percent, cumulative preferred stock with a par value totaling $100,000 and common

---

[3] A few types of preferred stock may be *participating* (in part or in full). This preference allows the preferred shareholders to share in the earnings (declared as dividends) in some manner beyond the stated dividend rate or amount. Since fully participating or partially participating preferred stock is a rarity, it is considered to be beyond the scope of this book.

stock with a total par value of $200,000. There is a one year preferred dividend arrearage of $15,000 = (15% × $100,000). The board of directors decided that the *annual* amount available for dividends is $72,000. The calculation of the distribution of this annual amount between the two classes of shareholders is as follows:

Annual amount available for dividends	$72,000
To preferred shareholders:	
In arrears	$15,000
Current year's preference dividend (15% × $100,000)	15,000
Total to preferred shareholders	$30,000
To common shareholders:	
The remainder (being residual owners)	42,000
Total that could be distributed	$72,000

The second type of preference applies to a corporation that is being liquidated. If, for example, a corporation is liquidated and all the creditors are paid in full, then the preferred shareholders who have a preference as to assets in liquidation must be paid before any liquidating payments are made to common shareholders. The manner of the preference application depends on the wording in the stock indenture. The preference may be for the par value of the preferred stock, the par value and accumulated unpaid dividends, or some other stipulated amount. If the preferred stock is not *preferred as to assets,* then the assets are usually distributed to all classes of shareholders on an equal basis proportionate to the respective par values.

Preferred stockholders, on the other hand, are often restricted to a specific dividend rate and do not, therefore, benefit from earnings above that rate. By the inclusion of a provision in the stock indenture, a preferred stockholder is usually denied the right to vote.

One of the reasons for issuing preferred stock is to provide the firm with long-term funds without increasing long-term liabilities or increasing the common stockholders' equity. Another reason is the ability to endow this class of stock with certain features that make it more salable. Thus, the corporation should be able to raise additional funds. A popular form of stock is **convertible preferred**, which gives the holder the right to exchange these shares for a specified number of shares of another security, usually common stock of the same company. If the company grows and common stock values rise, holders of convertible preferred can "convert" and share in the growth.

Common Stock   If a corporation issues only *one* class of stock, then all shares are treated alike and called common stock. If there is more than one class, the class that does not have preferences and that shares only in the residual earnings or assets distribution is known as common stock. **Common stock**, therefore, represents the residual and proportionate ownership that *does* have voting privileges. In other words, common stock represents the part of ownership received in exchange for investment by voting shareholders. Their voting privilege is on the basis of one vote for each share of common stock held. These shareholders are often called residual owners because their dividends cannot be declared until the dividend rights of preferred shareholders are satisfied.

They are the real controlling owners, however. Because they hold the residual ownership stock, the common stockholders elect the members of the board of directors, who appoint the officers of the corporation. The officers execute the policies approved by the board of directors. In effect, the board of directors represents the stockholders in monitoring the activities of corporate management. The accounting for the issuance of both classes of capital stock is illustrated after certain key terms are defined and discussed.

Key Terms

Certain key terms are used to define and measure elements of stockholders' equity. These terms are *authorized capital stock, issued capital stock, treasury stock, outstanding capital stock, par value, no-par value, stated value, market value,* and *legal capital*.

The capital stock of one or more classes in terms of shares or par value granted by the charter is referred to as **authorized capital stock**. **Issued capital stock** refers to the number of shares of capital stock issued to stockholders and still considered to be part of legal capital (defined later). **Treasury stock** refers to the corporation's own capital stock issued and fully paid for, later reacquired by the corporation, but not normally canceled (discussed later in this chapter).

Capital stock is outstanding when it remains in the hands of stockholders. **Outstanding capital stock** is the issued capital stock minus treasury stock. Treasury stock is still considered to be issued stock unless it is formally declared to be canceled by a resolution passed by the board of directors to cause the stock to be changed back to an unissued status.

Par value refers to a specific dollar amount per share, as set forth in the charter of the issuing corporation. It is printed on the stock certificate and generally *represents the minimum amount that must be paid to the issuing corporation* by the original purchaser of the stock. The par value of the common stock of CBS Inc. is $2.50 (see Figure 2–1). Par value may be any amount set forth in the corporation's charter and is rarely an indication of what the stock is actually worth. Used as the basis for crediting the appropriate capital stock account on the corporate books, it is often established at a relatively low value with little or no economic significance.

Because of the various difficulties involved with par value stock, such as a lack of understanding of its meaning at time of issuance and improper valuation of noncash assets received upon issuance, some companies issue stock without any par value written on the stock certificate. This kind of stock is referred to as **no-par value** capital stock. The entire proceeds from the issuance of no-par value stock (*without a stated value*—discussed below) is credited to the appropriate capital stock account. For capital stock without par value, the corporate directors may assign a value, the **stated value**, to each share. This amount, like par value, is the amount that is credited to the appropriate no-par capital stock account. Once assigned, a stated value is accounted for as if it were par value. However, it can be changed by the directors without approval of the chartering state; par value cannot.

The market value of stock is not determined by its par or stated value. The term **market value** indicates the actual price in dollars that a share of stock will bring at the time it is offered for sale. Market prices often change daily and can be determined for many stocks by reference to the stock market quotations in daily newspapers or to a financial magazine or financial service publication. Market value reflects economic and political factors and the feelings, hopes, and expectations of investors about the future growth and earning ability of a corporation.

The term **legal capital** (sometimes referred to as *stated capital*), contained in the laws of a number of states, places certain restrictions on the return of investment to the stockholders in order to protect creditors. The restriction limits the amount of assets that can be withdrawn by stockholders either as dividends or by other means so that sufficient funds should be available for satisfaction of creditors' claims. The creditors of a corporation do not have access to the personal resources of the stockholders; their only protection is in the corporate assets.

Legal capital

***Legal capital** is the amount of capital that a statute requires must be left in the corporation for the protection of creditors because of the limited liability of stockholders. Consequently, creditors are assured that in the event of corporate losses the investors as a group will absorb the losses up to the amount of this capital.*

State laws vary considerably as to the method of determining and applying such restriction provisions. The accountant may require the assistance of an attorney on questions involving legal capital. In most states, legal capital is determined as follows:

1. On par value stock—the par value of all outstanding shares.

2. On no-par, stated value stock—the stated value of all outstanding shares.

3. On no-par, no stated value stock—the total proceeds from the issuance of all outstanding shares.

When, as is often the case, the par value is low in relation to the issue price, the legal capital will be much less than the total paid in by shareholders. In such a situation, legal capital is not a significant constraint on amounts to be distributed to stockholders, and the security of the creditors depends rather on the firm's operating and financial policies and resources.

Recording Capital Stock Transactions

For a small family-type corporation, capital stock is issued only to family members, relatives, and close friends. The *Securities Act of 1933* requires certain large corporations that issue stock to the public in interstate markets to file a registration statement with the SEC. They often use *underwriters* (syndicates of banks or brokerage firms) to help them sell their stock. The corporations—called public corporations—often announce that stock is available through ads similar to the one shown in Figure 13–2. This type of announcement is usually referred to as a *tombstone ad*. The SEC restricts official advertising to a booklet of facts called a *prospectus*. The tombstone ad announces

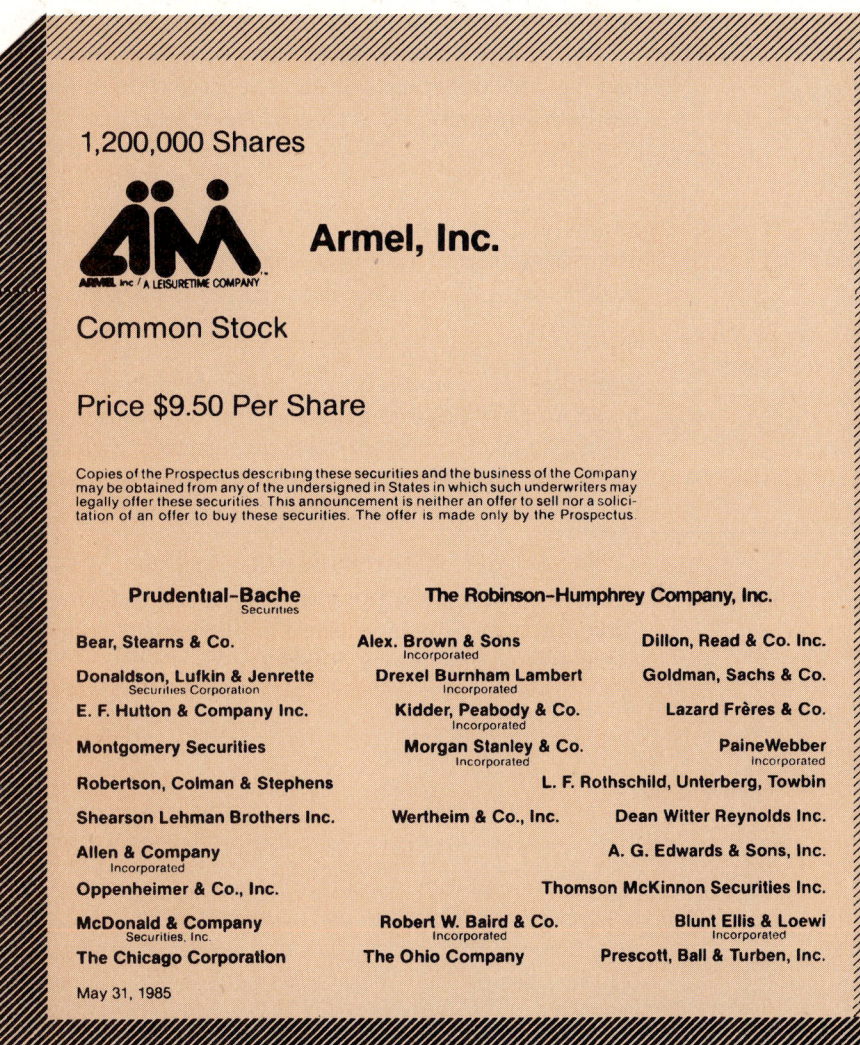

Figure 13–2 Announcement of Stock for Sale

only that the stock is available for sale and states where the prospectus may be obtained. Note particularly the restrictive provision in the middle of the ad. The ad shown in Figure 13–2 announced that 1,200,000 common shares of Armel, Inc. are available for sale at $9.50 per share. It also listed the underwriters from whom a copy of the prospectus could be obtained.

Great care needs to be taken to record stock transactions in strict compliance with the corporate laws of the state of incorporation, keeping in mind the interests of stockholders and creditors and the statutory requirements regarding legal capital. Enough accounts should be created, especially those arising from invested capital, so that the stockholders' equity section shows in adequate detail the sources of corporate capital.

Two groups of illustrations are presented below: first, for a corporation that has only par value common stock authorized; then, for a corporation that has both common and preferred stock authorized.

Illustration Group A

Assume that on February 2, 1987, the Kheel Corporation, which is organized as a marine supply business, received its charter authorizing the issuance of 50,000 shares of common stock carrying a $10 par value.

Memorandum Entry to Record Charter Data

The initial entry on a corporate set of books may be a simple memorandum narrative statement made in the general journal and the capital stock accounts. It notes certain basic data taken from the corporate charter, including the name of the corporation, the date of incorporation, the nature of the business, the classes and the number of shares authorized to be issued.

Example A–1: Common Stock Issued at Par for Cash

On February 2, 1987, Kheel Corporation issued 10,000 shares of common stock at par value for cash. This transaction is recorded as follows (explanations to all of these journal entries are omitted):

1987				
Feb.	2	Cash...	100,000	
		Common Stock		100,000

The Common Stock account represents a part of stockholders' equity. After stock has been issued to an investor, that individual may sell those shares to new owners. *Such resales are not recorded in the accounting records.* These transfers are private transactions between the buyers and sellers, but they are reported to the corporation for record-keeping purposes.[4] This information is

---

[4] Most corporations use the services of agents—usually banks (referred to as *registrars*)—to maintain a current list of names and addresses of stockholders and to issue new certificates (for this latter function, the agent is referred to as a *transfer agent*).

needed by the corporation for determining the individual shareholder's dividend payment and the number of votes allowed at stockholders' meetings.

Example A–2: Common Stock Issued at Par for Cash and Noncash Assets

On February 11, 1987, Kheel Corporation issued 9,000 shares for $40,000 in cash plus land and buildings having a fair cash value of $10,000 and $40,000, respectively. This transaction is recorded as follows:

1987				
Feb.	11	Cash..	40,000	
		Land..	10,000	
		Buildings	40,000	
		Common Stock		90,000

A key issue related to this transaction is that the accountant must make sure that the land and buildings are properly valued at current fair cash value. An error often made in the past was that the noncash assets were sometimes valued at the par amount of the common stock issued without any effort to determine a fair cash value.

Example A–3: Common Stock Issued for Organizing Services

On March 4, 1987, the Kheel Corporation issued 1,000 shares of common stock to the organizers of the corporation in payment for their services billed at $10,000. This transaction is recorded as shown:

1987				
Mar.	4	Organization Costs	10,000	
		Common Stock		10,000

Organization costs are shown in the Kheel Corporation's balance sheet as an intangible asset and written off over future periods.

After the above transactions, the stockholders' equity section of the Kheel Corporation balance sheet shows the following:

Stockholders' equity:
  Paid-in capital:
    Common stock, $10 par value; authorized 50,000 shares,
      issued 20,000 shares................................ $200,000

The asset and liability sections of the balance sheet are essentially the same regardless of the form of business organization. The only difference would be the inclusion of certain assets and liabilities that are peculiar to a particular organizational form. For example, in the foregoing A examples, one new asset account is present—Organization Costs. This account would be shown under the intangible assets section of the corporate balance sheet.

Example A–4: Common Stock Issued at a Premium for Cash

On November 4, 1987, the Kheel Corporation issued 10,000 shares of common stock at $10.80 per share. The market price has changed since it depends on many factors such as the condition and reputation of the corporation and the availability of funds for investments. The entry to record this transaction is:

1987				
Nov.	4	Cash..	108,000	
		Common Stock.............................		100,000
		Paid-in Capital—Excess over Par Value, Common		8,000

The $8,000 **paid-in capital—excess over par value** is recorded in a separate paid-in capital account in order to establish the legal capital amount only in the Common Stock account. An alternative account title for this Paid-in Capital account is **Premium on Common Stock**. Both Common Stock and Paid-in Capital—Excess over Par Value, Common are paid-in capital investment items (see Figure 13–1); both are shown in the balance sheet under a stockholders' equity subsection, paid-in capital.

Immediately following the issuance of the 10,000 shares for $108,000, the stockholders' equity section of the balance sheet now appears as:[5]

Stockholders' equity:		
Paid-in capital:		
Common stock, $10 par value; authorized 50,000		
shares, issued 30,000 shares	$300,000	
Paid-in capital—excess over par value, common	8,000	
Total paid-in capital		$308,000

Example A–5: Common Stock Subscribed

The descriptions of stock issuance transactions in the previous examples were based on the assumption that the full payment for the stock was received and the stock certificates issued at once. Small or closely held corporations and often new banks sometimes sell and issue stock under a **stock subscription** plan. Pledges to buy the stock are taken first, and payment is made later in a lump sum or in installments. The stock certificates are *not* issued until completion of the payment.

---

[5]This method of disclosure of paid-in capital items is referred to as the "source of capital approach." Another variation, called the legal capital approach, is illustrated in Appendix 13.1.

On November 2, 1988, the Kheel Corporation received subscriptions for 10,000 shares of $10 par value common stock at $10.50 a share. Full payment was received on December 2, 1988, and the stock certificates were issued. The entries to record these transactions are:

1988				
Nov.	2	Subscriptions Receivable—Common	105,000	
		Common Stock Subscribed		100,000
		Paid-in Capital—Excess over Par Value, Common		5,000
Dec.	2	Cash	105,000	
		Subscriptions Receivable—Common		105,000
	2	Common Stock Subscribed	100,000	
		Common Stock		100,000

The Subscriptions Receivable—Common account is a current asset and shows the amount due on stock that has been subscribed but has not been fully paid for. The tentative nature of the ownership is indicated by the Common Stock Subscribed account, a temporary stockholders' equity account showing the par or stated value of subscribed stock. Thus if a balance sheet were to be prepared between November 2 and December 2, the common stock subscribed item would be shown in the paid-in capital subsection of the stockholders' equity section immediately below the issued common stock. The excess of the issue price over par is typically credited to the permanent real account, Paid-in Capital—Excess over Par Value, Common, *when the subscription is received.*

Capital Stock Issued at a Discount

In most states, par value stock cannot be issued at a discount. If the state law permits the issuance at less than par value, the amount of the discount (recorded in the Discount on Capital Stock account) becomes a contingent liability to the investor. This contingent liability is passed to future holders of the shares. Since issuance at a discount is extremely rare, it is not illustrated here.

Illustration Group B

On March 1, 1987, the Dexter Corporation, which is authorized to operate a television cable company, received its charter authorizing the issuance of 100,000 no-par value common shares and 30,000, $10 par value, 15 percent preferred shares (15 percent is the annual dividend rate based on par value). Again, the initial entry may be a simple memorandum narrative statement made in the journal and capital stock accounts setting forth the basic data contained in the corporate charter. The following three examples illustrate the accounting in this more complex illustration.

Example B–1: Preferred Stock Issued at a Premium
On March 5, 1987, the Dexter Corporation issued 10,000 shares of preferred stock at $11 per share for cash. The entry to record the issuance is:[6]

1987 Mar.	5	Cash...	110,000	
		Preferred Stock		100,000
		Paid-in Capital—Excess over Par Value, Preferred		10,000

The accounting for the issuance of par value preferred stock is the same as that for common stock, except that the names of the two accounts credited contain the description *preferred*. Both of these items are paid-in capital.

Example B–2: No-par Common Stock Issued for Cash
On March 5, 1987, the Dexter Corporation issued for cash 10,000 shares of its no-par common stock at $6 per share.

Assumption 1. As stated previously, no-par stock may be "pure" no-par, that is, it has no stated value (the entire proceeds in this case become the amount of legal capital), or the board of directors may be authorized to set a stated value per share for the no-par stock. In the latter case, the stock is handled like par value stock. Assume here that the no-par stock has no stated value. Then the entry to record the issuance is:

1987 Mar.	5	Cash...	60,000	
		Common Stock		60,000

Assumption 2. The board of directors of the Dexter Corporation had set a stated value of $5 for each share of no-par common stock. The entry then would be:

1987 Mar.	5	Cash...	60,000	
		Common Stock		50,000
		Paid-in Capital—Excess over Stated Value, Common.........		10,000

---

[6]Technically, a corporation would issue common stock before it would issue preferred stock. In the first two B group illustrations, preferred and common are issued on the same day. The issuance of the preferred stock is discussed first to show the similarity to the accounting for par value common stock.

The stated value amount typically becomes the legal capital and hence is the amount that is credited to Common Stock. Both of the foregoing credit items are shown in the paid-in capital section of stockholders' equity.

Example B–3: No-par Common Stock Subscribed

On April 1, 1987, the Dexter Corporation received subscriptions for 10,000 shares of no-par common stock at $6.50 per share. Full payment was received on May 1, 1987, and the stock certificates were issued.

Assumption 1. If the no-par common stock has no stated value, these transactions are recorded as follows:

1987				
Apr.	1	Subscriptions Receivable—Common	65,000	
		Common Stock Subscribed		65,000
May	1	Cash	65,000	
		Subscriptions Receivable—Common		65,000
	1	Common Stock Subscribed	65,000	
		Common Stock		65,000

Assumption 2. If the no-par common stock has a stated value of $5 per share, the transactions are recorded as follows:

1987				
Apr.	1	Subscriptions Receivable—Common	65,000	
		Common Stock Subscribed		50,000
		Paid-in Capital—Excess over Stated Value, Common		15,000
May	1	Cash	65,000	
		Subscriptions Receivable—Common		65,000
	1	Common Stock Subscribed	50,000	
		Common Stock		50,000

Donations

Cities, towns, and sometimes local organizations may donate land, buildings, and other facilities to entice a corporation to establish itself in the area. Sometimes donations of assets are made by the stockholders of a company in financial difficulty to enable it to raise funds. A gift or donation to a corporation increases the assets and the stockholders' equity and is credited to *Paid-in Capital—Donations*. A contribution of land and buildings by a town to a newly established firm is recorded by the receiving corporation at the fair market value of the assets contributed. To illustrate, assume that on October 4, 1987, East Towne donated land (valued at $30,000) and buildings (valued at $70,000) to the Dexter Corporation for it to locate in East Towne. The entry on the Dexter Corporation books is:

1987 Oct.	4	Land.. Buildings.. Paid-in Capital—Donations .... To record, at fair market value, the land and buildings contributed by East Towne.	30,000 70,000	 100,000

Disclosure of Paid-in Capital on the Balance Sheet

Now that the key elements of paid-in capital have been discussed, the way they are disclosed on the balance sheet is illustrated. The balance sheet prepared on October 5, 1987, would disclose the paid-in capital of the Dexter Corporation as follows (assuming that the no-par common is given a stated value):

DEXTER CORPORATION
Partial Balance Sheet
October 5, 1987

Exhibit C

Stockholders' equity:
Paid-in capital:
  15% Preferred stock, $10 par value; authorized 30,000
    shares, issued 10,000 shares $100,000
  Paid-in capital—excess over par value, preferred 10,000
    Total capital paid in by preferred stockholders $110,000
  Common stock, no-par value, stated value established
    at $5 per share; authorized 100,000 shares, issued
    20,000 shares $100,000
  Paid-in capital—excess over stated value, common. ... 25,000
    Total capital paid in by common stockholders 125,000
Other paid-in capital:
  Paid-in capital—donation of land and building by East
    Towne 100,000
    Total paid-in capital $335,000

This method of disclosing the paid-in capital sources is referred to as the *source of capital approach.* Another variation (the legal capital approach) of disclosure of paid-in capital is discussed in Appendix 13.1, where a complete stockholders' equity section of a balance sheet is illustrated.

Retained Earnings

Undistributed earnings arising from profitable operations are known as **retained earnings**. Retained earnings are total net income of past years minus total net losses and dividends declared during those years. These are sources of stockholders' equity other than paid-in capital. Such terms as *earned surplus, retained income, accumulated earnings,* and *earnings retained for use in the business* are alternative terms for earnings that have not been distributed to the stockholders as dividends. If cumulative losses and dividend distributions exceed earnings, the Retained Earnings account will have a debit balance and will be shown in the balance sheet as a deduction in the stockholders' equity section as a **deficit**.

Retained earnings constitute a significant percentage of total stockholders' equity of many firms. For example, at the end of a recent year, American Can Company showed 69.3 percent = ($633,400,000 ÷ $914,000,000) of total stockholders' equity as retained earnings. For the Times Mirror Company, retained earnings at year-end 1983 showed 92.4 percent = ($1,035,582,000 ÷ $1,120,389,000) of stockholders' equity.

The primary factors that affect the Retained Earnings account are discussed below. They include: (1) net income or net loss, (2) restrictions of retained earnings, (3) prior period adjustments, and (4) dividends. In addition, a parallel item to stock dividends, the stock split, is discussed in this section.

Net Income and Net Loss

It is important to review how the results of operations are recorded in the accounts of a corporation.

Example 1: Net Income For the first example, suppose that all the 1987 revenues and expenses of Spirit Corporation have been closed to Income Summary. This account shows a credit balance of $106,500, which represents a net income for 1987. The entry to close this net income to Retained Earnings is:

1987				
Dec.	31	Income Summary	106,500	
		Retained Earnings		106,500
		To close net income to Retained Earnings.		

The credit to Retained Earnings would increase it by $106,500.

Example 2: Net Loss For the next example, suppose that all the 1987 revenues and expenses of Truro Corporation have been closed to Income Summary. This account now shows a debit balance of $72,400, which represents a net loss for 1987. The entry to close this net loss to Retained Earnings is:

1987				
Dec.	31	Retained Earnings.............................	72,400	
		Income Summary.........................		72,400
		To close net loss to Retained Earnings.		

The debit to Retained Earnings would decrease it by $72,400. This action does not necessarily mean that now there will be a deficit. If a credit balance larger than $72,400 existed in Retained Earnings prior to the foregoing closing entry, there would still be a positive (credit) balance in the account. If a credit balance smaller than $72,400 existed in Retained Earnings prior to the foregoing closing entry, there would be a negative balance in the Retained Earnings account and a deficit on the balance sheet. Stockholders of a corporation cannot withdraw amounts in excess of retained earnings. This concept is explored further in the next section.

Retained Earnings—Restricted or Appropriated

The creation of special **restricted retained earnings** accounts (sometimes called *appropriated*) indicates that a portion of the earnings of the corporation is not available for dividends. This does not mean that a special cash fund has been set up, nor does the restriction provide cash funds. It is an accounting device by which a corporation, following a resolution of the board of directors, intentionally reduces the amount of earnings available for dividend distributions, thus indicating its intention to conserve corporate assets for other purposes. The restriction does not in any way alter the total retained earnings or the total stockholders' equity but merely earmarks a portion of the earnings in an account specifically designated to indicate its purpose. The same information can be communicated in the balance sheet by a footnote or by a parenthetical notation.

Each restricted account, although separated from the parent Retained Earnings account, is nevertheless a part of retained earnings and is so classified in the stockholders' equity section of the balance sheet. When the special account has served its purpose and the requirement for which it was set up no longer exists, the amount in the restricted account is transferred back into the Retained Earnings (unappropriated) account.

Restrictions may be either voluntary or involuntary and typically are made for three broad purposes:

1. To show management's intended use of earnings (voluntary).
2. To provide a buffer against possible future losses (voluntary).
3. To show compliance with legal and contractual arrangements (involuntary).

A restriction for plant expansion, for example, may be set up by voluntary action of the board of directors showing management's intention to retain cash or other assets for use in connection with a projected plant expansion program rather than to distribute them in the form of dividends. When cash dividends are paid, the assets of the corporation are depleted. To the degree, then, that dividend declarations are restricted, assets are retained for other business purposes, such as plant expansion. A restriction of retained earnings required by the indenture to bonds payable (discussed in Chapter 14) is an involuntary action required by a contract. Whether the restriction is voluntary or involuntary, the accounting methodology is the same. To establish the restriction, the Retained Earnings account is debited and Retained Earnings—Restricted for *(name of purpose)* is credited. Once the purpose of the restriction is achieved, the restriction should be removed by reversing the foregoing entry.

Prior Period Adjustments

A company may make an error in the financial statements of one accounting period that is not discovered until a subsequent period. The correction of this error, if material, should be treated as a prior period adjustment of retained earnings.[7] That is, the correction should be disclosed as an adjustment of the opening balance of retained earnings. For a very simple illustration, assume that the Whacker Corporation recorded depreciation of machinery in 1986 of $18,000; the correct amount was $81,000. This means that the depreciation expense for 1986 was understated by $63,000 = ($81,000 − $18,000), and thus net income for 1986 was overstated by $63,000. The Retained Earnings account will likewise then be overstated by $63,000 after closing on December 31, 1986. The error was discovered on March 10, 1987, after the books had been closed for 1986. Ignoring the effect on income taxes, the entry to record this correction is:

1987				
Mar.	10	Retained Earnings...........................	63,000	
		Accumulated Depreciation—Machinery		63,000
		To correct the error in depreciation of machinery in 1986.		

The foregoing prior period adjustment should be reported in the statement of retained earnings, net of any tax effect. While not illustrated here, Whacker Corporation would file amended income tax returns in 1987 (for 1986) for a refund of the overpaid tax, which would increase retained earnings.

---

[7]FASB *Statement of Financial Accounting Standards No. 16* (Stamford, Conn.: FASB, 1977), paragraphs 10–12. This statement also specifically lists as a prior period adjustment the realization of income tax benefits of preacquisition operating loss carry forwards of purchased subsidiaries.

Dividends

Another action of the board of directors resulting in a decrease in retained earnings is the declaration of a dividend. **Dividend** refers to the distribution of cash, stock, or other corporate property to the stockholders. A dividend must be declared formally by the board of directors, a record of which should be entered in the minutes of meetings of the board of directors. The entry should indicate declaration date, date of record, and payment date. For a cash dividend distribution to be made, there must be accumulated and unrestricted retained earnings and assets available for distribution. If there are no accumulated earnings, the dividend becomes a reduction in paid-in capital, which may be illegal. There must also be sufficient cash or other readily distributable type of assets. Only the board of directors has the authority to determine whether a dividend is to be paid, to which classes of stock it is to be paid, and the time, manner, and form of payment. This applies to both classes of stockholders, preferred and common. Once formal action has been taken by the board the declaration immediately becomes a current liability of the corporation. It is customary, particularly for larger corporations with numerous stockholders, to make a public announcement of the dividend declaration in newspapers or magazines.

Cash Dividends

Declaration of a Dividend   The dividend may be stated as a percent of par or as a specified amount per share. Following is a typical dividend notice:

National Ore Company
60 Rockefeller Plaza, New York, N.Y.
Dividend No. 310

The board of Directors has today declared a regular quarterly dividend at the rate of forty-seven and one-half cents (47½¢) per share on the Common Stock of this Company, payable January 15, 1988, to stockholders of record at the close of business December 31, 1987.

J. V. Couches
Secretary

December 14, 1987

The holder of 100 shares of common stock of National Ore Company will be mailed a check for $47.50 on January 15, 1988. An investor who buys the stock in time to be recorded as its owner by December 31, 1987, the record date, will receive the dividend. An investor who buys stock of this company too late to be recorded as owner by the record date is said to buy the stock **ex-dividend**—that is, without the right to receive the latest declared dividend. Stock traded on the stock exchanges is quoted ex-dividend typically three days prior to the record date to allow time for the recording of the transfer securities. During the interval between December 31, 1987, and January 15, 1988, the list of eligible stockholders is prepared and all other tasks incident to the mailing of the dividend checks are performed. Usually these functions are carried out by independent transfer agents—banks or trust companies that also handle the recording and issuance of stock and transfer of stock.

Because of dividend priorities, a separate Dividends account for each class of stock could be established. These Dividends accounts are debited each time a dividend is declared. Assume that the Elmer Corporation had 10,000 shares of common stock outstanding and declared its regular quarterly dividend of 30 cents a share on January 7, 1987, payable on January 28, 1987, to stockholders of record on January 20, 1987. The declaration and payment of this quarterly dividend would be recorded as follows:[8]

1987 Jan.	7	Dividends—Common Stock .... Dividends Payable—Common Stock .... To record the declaration of a 30-cents-a-share cash dividend on 10,000 shares of common stock outstanding.	3,000	3,000
	28	Dividends Payable—Common Stock .... Cash .... To record payment of the dividend declared on January 7.	3,000	3,000

Note that no journal entry is needed nor made on January 20, 1987, the date of record. At the end of the year, if four quarterly dividends of the same amount are declared, the Dividends—Common Stock account would contain a debit balance of $12,000. Since they are temporary accounts that serve the purpose of reducing stockholders' equity, all Dividends accounts are closed into the permanent stockholders' equity account, Retained Earnings, at the end of the year. For the Elmer Corporation, such an entry would be:

1987 Dec.	31	Retained Earnings .... Dividends—Common Stock .... To close the Dividends account.	12,000	12,000

Although some prefer to debit Retained Earnings to record a dividend declaration, the use of Dividends accounts segregates dividends declared during the year; it also keeps Retained Earnings clear of debits that would require

---

[8]*The Tax Equity and Fiscal Responsibility Act of 1982* as amended requires a 20 percent backup withholding from taxpayers who have not provided a taxpayer identification number (usually their social security number). This backup withholding is ignored in this book.

analysis at the end of the year when the statement of retained earnings is prepared. The Dividends accounts, representing a reduction in the stockholders' equity, are then shown on the statement of retained earnings as deductions from the total of the beginning balance of retained earnings plus net income and other increases to retained earnings. Dividends Payable, on either common or preferred stock, is a current liability.

Cash Dividends on Preferred Stock As mentioned previously, preferred stock has certain dividend preferences. The right of a preferred stockholder to a dividend, however, must await a formal declaration by the board of directors. On declaration, a stated amount per share is paid to the preferred stockholders before any dividend distribution is made to holders of common stock.

As indicated earlier in this chapter, if the preferred stock is *cumulative,* undeclared dividends are accumulated, and the accumulated past dividends plus the current dividend on preferred must be paid before any dividend payment is made on common stock. These dividends not declared in past periods on cumulative preferred stock are referred to as a **dividend arrearage** (or *dividends in arrears*). If the preferred stock is *noncumulative,* a dividend not formally declared by the board of directors in any period is lost.

Preferred dividends are typically declared either quarterly or semiannually. To illustrate, assume that on July 1, 1987, the Columbia Corporation has outstanding 1,000 shares of 15 percent, cumulative preferred stock with a par value of $100. Normally preferred dividends are declared semiannually by Columbia Corporation, but no dividends on the preferred stock were declared during 1986. This means that $15,000 = (15% × $100,000) of dividends are in arrears as of July 1, 1987. The preferred dividend to be declared on this date is $22,500, calculated as follows:

Preferred dividends in arrears: 15% × $100,000	$15,000
Current semiannual preferred dividends: ½ × $15,000.	7,500
Total preferred dividend declared.	$22,500

The journal entry to record the declaration of this dividend is:

1987				
Jul.	1	Dividends—Preferred Stock	22,500	
		Dividends Payable—Preferred Stock.		22,500
		To record the declaration of the preferred dividend, which includes the current semiannual dividend plus the dividends in arrears for 1986.		

The payment of the foregoing liability results in a debit to Dividends Payable—Preferred Stock and a credit to Cash.

Stock Dividends

Stock dividend refers to the issuance by a corporation to its existing stockholders of additional shares of its authorized stock without investment of any kind by them. There are various occasions for the declaration of a stock dividend, such as:

☐ A large unappropriated retained earnings balance.
☐ A desire by the directors to reduce the market price of the stock.
☐ A desire to increase the permanent capitalization of the company by converting a portion of the retained earnings into paid-in capital.
☐ A need to conserve available cash.

While a cash dividend decreases both the assets and the stockholders' equity of a corporation, a stock dividend simply transfers a certain amount of retained earnings to paid-in capital accounts and has no effect on either total assets or *total* stockholders' equity. The change is within the stockholders' equity section (retained earnings decrease and paid-in capital increases).

Impact of Stock Dividend Consider that the Peet Corporation, with $500,000 of common stock, $10 par value, issued and outstanding, and retained earnings of $80,000, declares a 10 percent stock dividend. A distribution of 5,000 new shares = [($500,000 ÷ $10) × 10%] is to be divided among existing stockholders in proportion to the number of shares each holds. For a stock dividend of this size, the amount of retained earnings transferred to paid-in capital is measured by the market price of the stock (discussed in the next section). The effect of the declaration on stockholders' equity is shown below. To simplify this illustration, *assume that the market value of the stock is equal to its par value.*

	Stockholders' Equity			Outstanding Shares	
	Immediately before Declaration	Immediately after Declaration	Immediately after Stock Issuance	Before Stock Issuance	After Stock Issuance
Stockholders' equity:					
Common stock, $10 par value .	$500,000	$500,000	$550,000		
Stock dividends to be issued. .		50,000			
Retained earnings	80,000	30,000	30,000		
Total stockholders' equity . .	$580,000	$580,000	$580,000	50,000	55,000

After the declaration of the stock dividend, but before the stock is formally issued, the par value of the 5,000 shares to be issued is carried in an account called Stock Dividends to Be Issued. As the foregoing illustrates, this account is part of the stockholders' equity. It is not a liability because its reduction will result in an increase in common stock, not in a reduction of a current asset. The account should therefore be shown following common stock in the stockholders' equity section of the balance sheet.

Because a stock dividend has no effect on the total stockholders' equity, the relative interest of each stockholder is unchanged. For example, Mary Pele, a stockholder with 1,000 shares before the stock dividend, will have 1,100 shares after the fact. Her proportionate holdings remain unchanged at two percent of the total stock outstanding. Hence, all her rights and privileges compared to other stockholders are unaltered, as shown below:

	Before Declaration and Issuance	After Declaration and Issuance
1. Total stockholders' equity.	$580,000	$580,000
2. Number of shares outstanding.	50,000	55,000
3. Stockholders' equity per share (Line 1 ÷ Line 2).	$11.60	$10.54½
4. Shares owned by Mary Pele.	1,000	1,100
5. Pele's equity (Line 3 × Line 4).	$11,600	$11,600

A stock dividend is significant to the stockholder, even if it does not alter the recipient's equity in the company. If the stock dividend does not cause a significant decline in the price of stock, the stockholder's gain is equal to the market value of the new shares received. If, in addition, the corporation does not reduce the amount of its cash dividends per share, the stockholder gains the dividends on the additional shares in the future. The expectation of greater dividends as well as the availability of more shares for possible ultimate profitable resale creates a favorable reception for a stock dividend. A corporation could, however, continue to pay the same total dividend by simply adjusting the amount per share. In this case, the aggregate market price of the stock would change very little, and the stockholders would gain very little.

A stock dividend provides certain advantages to the corporation. Its earnings are capitalized (that is, retained earnings are transferred to paid-in capital accounts). There is no reduction in assets (other than for the cost of issuing the new stock). The corporation may use its assets for expansion or other purposes. A large stock dividend (say, from 25 percent to 100 percent) allows the corporation to create conditions that reduce the market price of its shares to attract more buyers. Issuance of substantially more shares representing the same total equity will cause the *price per share* to decrease.

Recording Small Stock Dividends

The AICPA has recommended that for **small stock dividends**—those involving less than 20 to 25 percent of the number of shares previously outstanding—the corporation should transfer from retained earnings to capital stock and other paid-in capital accounts "an amount equal to the fair value of the additional shares issued."[9]

---

[9]*Accounting Research Bulletin No. 43*, "Restatement and Revision of Accounting Research Bulletins" (New York: AICPA, 1953), Chapter 7, Section B, paragraphs 10 and 13. The question of whether to use 20 or 25 percent depends upon whether the market price is influenced if a rate higher than 20 percent is used.

Assume that the market value of the stock dividend shares issued by the Peet Corporation in the previous example was $60,000 = (5,000 shares × $12 a share) and that the board of directors, in authorizing the stock dividend, directed that it be recorded at market value. The entries to record the declaration on May 1, 1987, and stock issuance on May 15, 1987, are:

1987				
May	1	Stock Dividends—Common (or Retained Earnings)	60,000	
		Stock Dividends to Be Issued—Common		50,000
		Paid-in Capital—Excess over Par Value on Stock Dividends. . . .		10,000
		To record declaration of stock dividend.		
	15	Stock Dividends to Be Issued—Common	50,000	
		Common Stock		50,000
		To record issuance of stock dividend.		

Should a balance sheet be prepared between May 1 and May 15, the Stock Dividends to Be Issued—Common account would be disclosed in the stockholders' equity section of the balance sheet as a part of paid-in capital by the common shareholders because it represents stock to be issued. It is not a liability because it does not require assets to liquidate it. The Stock Dividends account must be closed to Retained Earnings at the end of the year along with other Dividends accounts.

The rationale with respect to small stock dividends is that the market value of the shares previously held remains substantially unchanged. "Many recipients of stock dividends look upon them as distributions of corporate earnings and usually in an amount equivalent to the fair value of the additional earnings and usually in an amount equivalent to the fair value of the additional shares issued."[10] Therefore, the accounting should show that the amount of retained earnings available for future dividend distribution has been reduced by the market value of the stock dividend.

Recording Large Stock Dividends For **large stock dividends**—those involving the issuance of more than 25 percent of the number of shares previously outstanding—the AICPA recommends that "there is no need to capitalize retained earnings other than to the extent occasioned by legal requirements."[11]

For large stock dividends the amount of retained earnings capitalized (transferred to paid-in capital) is represented by the par or stated value (the legal capital amount) of the shares issued.[12] To illustrate, assume that on May 1, 1987, the Hart Corporation has sufficient retained earnings and declares a

---

[10]Ibid.

[11]Ibid., paragraph 11.

[12] Ibid.

stock dividend of 20,000 shares, or 50 percent of the 40,000 shares of $10 par value common stock previously outstanding. The entry to record the declaration is shown below:

1987 May	1	Stock Dividends—Common (or Retained Earnings) .... Stock Dividends to Be Issued—Common .... To record the declaration of 20,000 shares of additional common stock as a stock dividend.	200,000	200,000

Recall that the par amount that is credited to Stock Dividends to Be Issued—Common is the amount that will be later transferred to Common Stock. The rationale with respect to accounting for large stock dividends is that the effect is to reduce materially the per share market value, and the transaction is "a split-up effected in the form of a dividend."[13] There is, therefore, no need to capitalize retained earnings beyond the legal requirements. Stock splits are discussed in the next section.

Stock Split

A corporation may wish to reduce the par value of its stock, or it may desire to reduce the price at which the stock is being issued to make it more salable. This is accomplished by a **stock split**, whereby the shares outstanding are increased and the par or stated value per share is reduced. The total capitalized value of the outstanding shares remains the same. There is no change in retained earnings. The Common Stock account is noted to show the new par or stated value per share and the subsidiary **stockholders' ledger** (the record of the shares owned by each stockholder) is revised by the registrar to show the new distribution of shares.

Assume, for example, that on December 1, 1987, a corporation has outstanding 500,000 shares of $10 par value common stock. The current market price of the stock is $175 a share. The corporation, wishing to create a condition that will result in a reduction of the high market price to obtain a broader market for a forthcoming additional stock issue, reduces the par value from $10 to $5 and increases the number of shares from 500,000 to 1,000,000.[14] This "two-for-one split" should result in a decrease of the former market price by almost one-half. The split in shares may be accomplished by calling in all the old shares and issuing certificates for new shares on a two-for-one basis or by issuing an additional share for each old share owned.

---

[13]*Accounting Research Bulletin No. 43,* Chapter 7, Section B, paragraph 11.

[14]To be able to take this action, this corporation must have at least 500,000 authorized but unissued shares or must obtain an amendment to the charter.

This action is recorded either by a memorandum notation in the journal and Common Stock account or by the following journal entry:

| 1987 Dec. | 1 | Common Stock ($10 par value) ....
     Common Stock ($5 par value) ....
     To record a 2-for-1 split, increasing the number of outstanding shares from 500,000 to 1,000,000 and reducing par value from $10 to $5. | 5,000,000 | 5,000,000 |

The market price of the shares should now be reduced so as to enhance the marketability of the new issue. A split of no-par stated value stock would be recorded in a similar manner.

Both stock dividends and stock splits change the number of shares outstanding without changing either total stockholders' equity or the pro rata share of ownership of each stockholder. A stock dividend, unlike a stock split, requires a transfer from retained earnings to paid-in capital and increases the Common Stock account by the par or stated value of the dividend shares. A stock split, unlike a stock dividend, changes the par or stated value of the common stock without changing the dollar balances of any account.

Treasury Stock and Other Corporate Capital Concepts

Treasury Stock

A corporation may repurchase some of its own stock, preferred or common, or receive it as a donation or settlement of a debt. Such stock is known as **treasury stock**. Provided that the amount received when the stock was first issued was equal to or greater than par or stated value, the treasury stock may be reissued at a price below par or stated value. There will be no contingent liability to the corporation's creditors by the purchaser of this stock for the amount of this type of discount. Treasury stock does not fall into the category of new issues; it is the corporation's own stock that has been issued and later reacquired. While in the treasury, it has issued but not outstanding status and therefore does not have voting or dividend rights.

A corporation may purchase some of its own stock to bolster a sagging market or to distribute the stock to its employees in place of other compensation. Sometimes the stock is purchased because it is available at a favorable price. Returning assets (the cash) to stockholders by acquisition of treasury stock reduces both the assets and the stockholders' equity. The Treasury Stock account, therefore, is disclosed in the stockholders' equity section as a deduction from total paid-in capital and retained earnings. Since the acquisition of treasury stock results in a distribution of corporate assets to stockholders, some states have enacted restrictive provisions pertaining to this kind of acquisition to protect the corporate creditors. Some require a restriction of retained earnings equal to the cost of the treasury stock as a means of preserving the legal capital.

Recording the Purchase of Treasury Stock

The most commonly used method for recording the purchase of treasury stock is cost; this is the only one used in this book.[15] The Treasury Stock account is debited for the cost of the shares acquired. To illustrate the cost method, assume that on August 5, 1987, the Ell Corporation reacquired 200 shares of its own $5 par value common stock at $5.50 a share. The entry to record this reacquisition is as shown below:

1987				
Aug.	5	Treasury Stock—Common..................................	1,100	
		Cash		1,100
		Purchased 200 shares of own common stock at $5.50 a share.		

The purchase of the 200 shares of stock reduces cash by $1,100 and stockholders' equity by $1,100. It also reduces the number of shares outstanding, but does not legally reduce the amount of *issued* stock. State law or company policy may require the restriction of retained earnings in an amount equal to the cost of treasury stock held. The journal entry is a debit to Retained Earnings and a credit to Retained Earnings—Restricted for Treasury Stock Purchases. Such a restriction should be increased as more treasury stock is acquired and reduced by the cost of shares reissued.

Recording Reissuance of Treasury Stock

Above Cost The reissuance of treasury stock is recorded by a credit to Treasury Stock for the *cost of the shares reissued*. The difference between the cost and the issue price of treasury stock when it is issued above cost is credited to Paid-in Capital from Treasury Stock Transactions. To illustrate, assume that on October 2, 1987, the Ell Corporation reissued 50 shares for $6.50 a share. The entry for reissuance is:

1987				
Oct.	2	Cash..	325	
		Treasury Stock—Common...............................		275
		Paid-in Capital from Treasury Stock Transactions, Common....		50
		Reissued 50 shares of treasury stock at $6.50 a share.		

---

[15]Another method recommended by some accounting theorists is called the par value method—the Treasury Stock account is debited for par value and other stockholders' equity accounts are debited for the excess of cost over par. Later, when the stock is reissued, it is accounted for in a manner similar to the original issue of capital stock.

Below Cost The entry to record the issuance of treasury stock below cost depends on the existence of capital accounts that are not considered to be part of the legal capital. To illustrate, assume that on November 4, 1987, the Ell Corporation reissued another 50 shares of treasury stock (which cost $275) for $225. The difference of $50 is debited to Paid-in Capital from Treasury Stock Transactions, as follows:

1987 Nov.	4	Cash...	225	
		Paid-in Capital from Treasury Stock Transactions, Common.....	50	
		Treasury Stock—Common...........................		275
		Reissued 50 shares of treasury stock at $4.50 each.		

If the excess of the cost of the treasury shares over the reissue price exceeds the amount in Paid-in Capital from Treasury Stock Transactions, the excess may be debited to any other paid-in capital account arising from the same class of stock that is not classified as legal capital. In the absence of such accounts, the difference between the cost and the selling price of the treasury stock is debited to Retained Earnings. To illustrate, assume that on November 29, 1987, the Ell Corporation reissued the remaining 100 shares at $5 per share. Assuming that the paid-in capital—excess over par value, common does not constitute legal capital, the entry to record the transaction is:

1987 Nov.	29	Cash...	500	
		Paid-in Capital—Excess over Par Value, Common...........	50	
		Treasury Stock—Common...........................		550
		Reissued the remaining 100 shares of treasury stock at $5 per share.		

To repeat, if there had not been any paid-in capital in excess over par value (arising from the original issuance of the class of stock involved in the treasury stock transaction), the debit would have been to Retained Earnings.

Recording Treasury Stock Donations

One or more shareholders may donate a portion of their shares to the corporation for reissuance to raise cash. Shares acquired by donation do not affect the total dollar amounts on the balance sheet, as there is no change in the assets, liabilities, or stockholders' equity. On acquisition, a memorandum is made in the journal and Treasury Stock account indicating the date and the number of shares donated. No dollar value is assigned at this point because treasury stock is recorded at cost. The cost of a donation is zero. When the shares are reissued, the proceeds are credited to Paid-in Capital—Donations.

Taxation of Income

As indicated in Chapter 4, because the corporation is treated as a legal entity separate and distinct from its stockholders, it is taxed as a business entity. The tax is based on corporate net income before taxes and is estimated and paid quarterly. Quarterly entries to record the taxes—debiting Income Tax Expense and crediting Income Taxes Payable—are the basis for part of the expense when the corporation issues interim financial statements. *APB Opinion No. 28,* "Interim Financial Reporting," in paragraph 19 requires that a company use its best estimate of its effective tax rate in computing this quarterly expense. Income Taxes Payable is classified as a current liability in the balance sheet.

Managerial Analysis—Book Value and Earnings per Share

Two types of analysis are uniquely applicable to a corporation: book value of common stock and earnings per share. These are discussed in the following section.

Book Value of Common Stock

When Only One Class of Stock Is Outstanding

Book value per common share represents the net assets for each common share outstanding. The book value of a share of common stock (or the stockholders' equity per share), assuming there is only one class of stock outstanding, is computed as follows:

	Amount
1. Total stockholders' equity	$750,000
2. Number of common shares outstanding	60,000
3. Book value per share (Line 1 ÷ Line 2)	$12.50

As shown by this calculation, the book value of a share of stock of any class is derived by dividing the total stockholders' equity applicable to that class by the number of shares of stock of that class issued and outstanding. The stockholders' equity applicable to a given class of stock depends upon respective owners' claims against the assets in liquidation, *not upon the amounts invested by each class* of shareholders. The book value per share is the amount each stockholder could receive for each share held in the event of liquidation if the assets are sold without gain or loss; that is, at book value. Since the valuations on the books—especially for inventories and property, plant, and equipment—do not necessarily reflect asset market values, the book value of a share of stock may be of limited significance as an indicator of the resale value. Even so, many speculators study book value of companies with certain assets that have a reasonably determinable value to make a decision as to whether or not to buy stock in these particular companies.

When More Than One Class of Stock Is Oustanding

When more than one class of stock is outstanding, it becomes necessary to determine the liquidation claims of each class against the assets of the corporation. The stockholders' equity is divided between the two classes on the basis of the preferences accorded to the preferred stock in liquidation. Assume that a corporation has the following capital structure:

Preferred stock, 12%, $100 par value, cumulative; issued 1,000 shares	$100,000
Common stock, $10 par value; issued 10,000 shares	100,000
Paid-in capital—excess over par value, common stock	5,000
Retained earnings—restricted for plant addition	10,000
Retained earnings	45,000
Total stockholders' equity	$260,000

Dividends are in arrears for two years. The indenture usually provides that preferred shareholders have a claim on the assets in liquidation of an amount equal to par value plus any dividends in arrears.

Using the foregoing typical assumption, the book value of a share of preferred stock at the end of the year is $124, computed as follows:

1. Preferred stock ($100 par value × 1,000 shares)	$100,000
2. Dividends in arrears (2 years × $12,000)	24,000
3. Total equity of preferred stockholders	$124,000
4. Number of preferred shares outstanding	1,000
5. Book value per preferred share (Line 3 ÷ Line 4)	$124

The book value of a share of common stock is $13.60, computed as shown:

1. Total stockholders' equity	$260,000
2. Deduct: Equity of preferred stockholders	124,000
3. Total equity of common stockholders	$136,000
4. Number of common shares outstanding	10,000
5. Book value per common share (Line 3 ÷ Line 4)	$13.60

Earnings per Share (EPS)

Earnings per share is introduced in Chapter 3, and now discussed in greater depth. Earnings per common share (EPS) has long been of primary interest to investors, financial analysts, and readers of financial publications. Although this figure is not a satisfactory substitute for a thorough financial analysis, investors consider it a key indicator in investment decision making. Earnings per common share or net loss per share must be shown on the face of the income statements of large corporations for several elements of net income, among which are (1) income before extraordinary items and (2) net income.[16] Earnings per share is calculated and is meaningful only for common shares.

Under *APB Opinion No. 15,* the earnings per share computations and presentation vary with the company's capital structure, whether simple or complex.[17] When the capital structure consists of one class of common stock only, the capital structure is said to be simple. Earnings per share is calculated for a simple capital structure by dividing the net income available to common stockholders for the period by the *weighted average* number of shares of common stock outstanding during the period. For corporations with a capital structure containing common stock and other convertible securities (a complex capital structure), two types of earnings per share amounts may be necessary. The first type, **primary earnings per share**, is calculated by dividing the applicable net income (described later) for the period by the weighted average number of common shares outstanding plus **common stock equivalents** (securities that the holder is entitled to convert to common stock that meet a set of complex criteria in *APB Opinion No. 15*). The second type, **fully diluted earnings per share**, is calculated by dividing the applicable net income for the period by the weighted average number of common shares outstanding, plus common stock equivalents, plus any other securities with conversion privileges that could decrease earnings per share.

To illustrate, assume that a company with net income for the year of $100,000 has a weighted average of 10,000 common shares outstanding. Also, assume that 1,000 shares of 12 percent convertible preferred stock, $100 par, convertible into two common shares for each share of preferred are outstanding. The preferred shares do not meet the specified conditions to qualify as common stock equivalents. The EPS calculation is shown in Figure 13–3.

APB Opinion No. 15 details the procedures for the computation of earnings per share under a variety of conditions. These procedures convert the figure from an historically oriented one to an hypothetical one based on the "as if" assumption of certain securities having been converted into common stock. The many complex problems that may be involved in determining common stock equivalents are beyond the scope of this text and therefore are not illustrated here.

---

[16]*APB Opinion No. 30* and other authoritative statements specify that EPS data must be disclosed on the face of the income statement for other elements of net income.

[17]*APB Opinion No. 15,* "Earnings per Share" (New York: AICPA, 1969).

Calculation of primary EPS:		
Actual net income	$100,000	
Deduct: Dividends on preferred stock, 1,000 shares at $12 a share	12,000	
Adjusted net income	$ 88,000	(A)
Adjusted shares outstanding:		
Actual weighted average shares outstanding	10,000	
Additional shares classified as common stock equivalents (the preferred shares are not specified as common stock equivalents)	0	
Adjusted shares outstanding	10,000	(B)
Primary EPS (A ÷ B)	$8.80	
Calculation of fully diluted EPS:		
Net income applicable to all classes ($88,000 + $12,000)	$100,000	(C)
Adjusted shares outstanding:		
Actual weighted average shares outstanding	10,000	
Additional shares issuable to preferred shareholders (although not common stock equivalents, they are securities with potential to decrease EPS)	2,000	
Adjusted shares outstanding	12,000	(D)
Fully diluted EPS (C ÷ D)	$8.33	

Figure 13–3   **Calculation of EPS**

Internal Control Issues

For a small closely held corporation, the internal control over the stockholders' equity area involves adequate protection of blank stock certificates as well as the recording and documentation of shares issued and dividends declared.

The stock certificate book with stubs is similar to a checkbook. Care should be taken to make sure that the certificates are prenumbered and are unsigned. A carefully documented record of both the shares issued and the ones unissued—those in the stock certificate book—must be maintained. The shares issued should be recorded in a ledger often referred to as the stockholders' ledger. This record must contain the name, address, social security number, and number of shares of each class of stock owned by each stockholder.

Internal control of dividends requires that the resolution of the board of directors declaring the dividends be noted in the minute book of the board. These minutes should be approved and signed by the corporate secretary. A separate bank account should be maintained for dividends. This account would add to the internal control of dividends since it could be reviewed and checked rather rapidly. Also, it could be reconciled very easily.

For a large "public" corporation, the internal control provisions take a different form. These corporations name trust companies, banks, or other entities to be registrars and transfer agents. These organizations handle the issue and transfer of corporate shares. With thousands of cancellations and new issues, it is necessary to maintain computer records. The separation of these activities from the affected corporation adds an element of internal control. The corporation (and its auditors) should make spot checks to ensure that the records of the registrars and transfer agents are accurate. The internal control provisions for a closely held corporation also apply to the large public corporations.

In summary, in each of the preceding situations, a good system of internal control involves the separation of duties of individuals so that the work of one can be checked against another's. Also, adequate protection of corporate property and prenumbered forms must be maintained. Proper authorization of events should exist in the minutes of the board, and proper documentation of shares issued and dividend payments should be maintained.

Appendix 13.1
Two Methods of Illustrating Stockholders' Equity

Introduction

There are two methods of disclosing the various paid-in capital items in stockholders' equity: the source of capital approach and the legal capital approach. The illustrations in this chapter use the **source of capital approach** where all paid-in capital items are arranged under subsections showing the amount of capital paid in by the various classes of stockholders. This type of information is helpful to management and the board of directors in making decisions involving the management and possible return of invested capital. Some corporations, for example, the Grow Group, Inc. and the Goodyear Tire & Rubber Company, use the **legal capital approach**. In this approach the paid-in capital items are arranged to reveal the legal capital subtotals. The remaining stockholders' equity items are shown in appropriately titled subsections. When the legal capital approach is used, the stockholders' equity section usually discloses the par or stated amount of both preferred and common stock in a subsection to establish the legal capital amount; then all other paid-in capital items are shown in a subsection often called additional paid-in capital. The retained earnings subsection is shown in the same manner under both approaches.

Learning Goals

1. To be able to prepare the stockholders' equity section of a balance sheet using the source of capital approach.

2. To be able to prepare the stockholders' equity section of a balance sheet using the legal capital approach.

Stockholders' Equity Illustrated

Figure A13–1 illustrates the source of capital approach for the Bern Corporation using the data described below. The same data are used for the legal capital approach illustrated in Figure A13–2. The data are numbered to trace the information to its method of disclosure in both figures.

BERN CORPORATION
Partial Balance Sheet
December 31, 1987

Exhibit C

Stockholders' equity:			
Paid-in capital:			
[1]	Preferred stock, 14% cumulative, $100 par value; authorized 2,500 shares, issued 2,000 shares	$200,000	
[1]	Paid-in capital—excess over par value, preferred stock	10,000	
	Total paid in by preferred stockholders		$210,000
[2]	Common stock, no-par value, $40 stated value; authorized 7,000 shares, issued 5,000 shares of which 500 shares are held in treasury	$200,000	
[2]	Paid-in capital—excess over stated value, common	50,000	
[2]	Paid-in capital—excess from reduction of stated value of 5,000 shares of common stock from $50 to $40 per share	50,000	
[3]	Paid-in capital from treasury stock transactions, common	2,500	
	Total paid in by common stockholders		302,500
[6]	Other paid-in capital:		
	Donation of land by town of Stowe		50,000
	Total paid-in capital		$562,500
[5]	Retained earnings:		
	Restricted:		
[4]	For treasury stock acquisitions	$ 27,500	
	For anticipated plant expansion	45,000	
	Total restricted	$ 72,500	
	Unrestricted	127,500	
	Total retained earnings		200,000
	Total paid-in capital and retained earnings		$762,500
[4]	Deduct: Cost of treasury stock—common		27,500
	Total stockholders' equity		$735,000

Figure A13–1 Partial Balance Sheet—Stockholders' Equity, Source of Capital Approach

[1] The Bern Corporation has issued 2,000 shares of $100 par value, 14 percent, preferred stock at an average price of $105 per share. The total par value of these shares (2,000 × $100 = $200,000) is labeled preferred stock. This amount represents part of the legal capital. The excess ($5 × 2,000) over the par value of the preferred stock is reported separately as paid-in capital—excess over par value, preferred stock.

[2] The Bern Corporation also issued 5,000 shares of no-par, stated value common stock at $60 per share. The stated value of the shares—originally $50

per share but reduced to $40 per share on December 31—multiplied by the number of shares issued ($40 × 5,000) is shown as common stock. The excess of the issue price ($60) over the original stated value ($50), multiplied by the number of shares issued ($10 × 5,000), not being part of the stated capital, is shown separately as paid-in capital—excess over stated value, common stock. The excess of the original stated value ($50) over the revised stated value ($40) multiplied by the number of shares issued ($10 × 5,000) is also entered separately.[18] As with all other excess paid-in capital, it is clearly labeled to show its source.

[3] On July 10, the Bern Corporation acquired 1,000 shares of its own common stock for $55 per share. On August 3, it sold 500 shares for $60 per share. The paid-in capital—excess of the reissue price over the cost is shown as paid-in capital from treasury stock transactions, common.

[4] The July 10 acquisition of 1,000 shares of its own common stock and reissuance of 500 shares on August 3 leaves 500 shares in the Bern Corporation treasury on December 31, 1987. The laws of the state of incorporation limit the payment of dividends to the extent of the amount in the unrestricted Retained Earnings account. Since both the purchase of treasury stock and the declaration of a cash dividend reduce corporate assets and stockholders' equity, the limitation applies equally to dividend payments and to treasury stock acquisitions. A company with unrestricted retained earnings of $25,000, for example, may either reacquire treasury stock or declare cash dividends or do both, provided the total disbursement is not over $25,000. Such a restriction improves the protection of the corporate creditors. The treasury stock balance of $27,500 ($55,000 from the transaction of July 10 less $27,500 from the transaction of August 3) appears twice in the stockholders' equity section: (a) as a restriction of retained earnings, and (b) as a reduction to the stockholders' equity resulting from a distribution of $27,500 in cash to the stockholders from whom the stock was acquired.

[5] The retained earnings total represents undistributed earnings from current and prior years. Of that amount, $72,500 was restricted for specific purposes; the remainder, $127,500, is unrestricted.

[6] A building site with an estimated cash market value of $50,000 was donated by the town of Stowe as an inducement to the Bern Corporation to establish itself there. This gift increased assets and paid-in capital.

Using the same numbered data, the stockholders' equity section is recast according to the legal capital approach in Figure A13–2.

---

[18]This is not a stock split. The directors have reduced the stated value by $10 without increasing the number of shares outstanding. Accordingly, $10 per share is removed (by journal entry) from the Common Stock account and moved to a Paid-in Capital—Excess from Reduction of Stated Value, Common.

BERN CORPORATION
Partial Balance Sheet
December 31, 1987

Exhibit C

Stockholders' equity:		
Capital stock:		
[1] Preferred stock, 14% cumulative, $100 par value; authorized 2,500 shares, issued 2,000 shares	$200,000	
[2] Common stock, no-par value, $40 stated value; authorized 7,000 shares, issued 5,000 shares of which 500 shares are held in treasury	200,000	
Total capital stock[a]		$400,000
Additional paid-in capital:		
[1] Paid-in capital—excess over par value, preferred stock	$ 10,000	
[2] Paid-in capital—excess over stated value, common stock	50,000	
[2] Paid-in capital—excess from reduction of stated value of 5,000 shares of common stock from $50 to $40 per share	50,000	
[3] Paid-in capital from treasury stock transactions, common	2,500	
[6] Paid-in capital—donation of land by town of Stowe	50,000	
Total additional paid-in capital		162,500
Total capital stock and additional paid-in capital		$562,500
[5] Retained earnings:		
Restricted:		
[4] For treasury stock acquisitions	$ 27,500	
For anticipated plant expansion	45,000	
Total restricted	$ 72,500	
Unrestricted	127,500	
Total retained earnings		200,000
Total paid-in capital and retained earnings		$762,500
[4] Deduct: Cost of treasury stock—common		27,500
Total stockholders' equity		$735,000

[a]This is usually the legal capital amount.

Figure A13–2   Partial Balance Sheet—Stockholders' Equity, Legal Capital Approach

The legal capital approach in Figure A13–2 differs from the source of capital approach in Figure A13–1 as follows:

☐ The total par value and stated value of the preferred stock and common stock are shown in one subsection, entitled capital stock.

☐ The paid-in capital from all sources except that represented by the par value of preferred stock and the stated value of common stock is shown in a separate subsection, entitled additional paid-in capital.

Note that the retained earnings subsection is the same under both approaches.

These two variations do not pose any great theoretical arguments. The authors favor the source of capital approach from a managerial viewpoint because the subsections reveal where the capital has come from. However, because the claims against the assets in liquidation are not the same as the capital sources, this approach may mislead an untrained reader. The legal capital approach also does not disclose the claims against the assets in liquidation, but it does not create a cloud about the issue either, and is used in practice more often than the source of capital approach.

Glossary

Arrearage Accumulated undeclared preferred dividends.

Authorized capital stock Shares of capital stock granted by the charter.

Book value per share The amount that a shareholder would receive on a per share basis in the theoretical event that assets were sold at no gain or loss; the portion of the stockholders' equity assigned to a class of stock divided by the number of shares of that class of stock issued and outstanding.

Capital stock Shares representing fractional elements of ownership of a corporation; usually of two classes, preferred and common.

Charter The legal document issued by a state that includes the articles of incorporation and certificate of incorporation.

Common stock The residual class of ownership if more than one class of stock is issued; if only one class, then all shares are treated alike, and that stock is called common stock.

Common stock equivalents Securities that may be converted by the holder to common stock according to the terms under which they were issued and that have a high probability of conversion.

Convertible preferred stock Stock that gives the right to exchange the preferred shares for a specified number of common shares.

Corporation A form of business that is a legal entity as well as an accounting entity.

Cumulative preferred stock The class of preferred stock on which undeclared dividends are accumulated and must be paid together with the current dividends before any dividend payment can be made on common stock.

Deficit The negative retained earnings caption used in the balance sheet to indicate that the retained earnings balance is negative.

Dividend A distribution of some portion of net income in the form of cash, stock, or other corporate property by a corporation to stockholders.

Dividend arrearage The amount of dividends on cumulative preferred stock not declared or in arrears for any dividend period or periods.

Ex-dividend Stock purchased *without* the right to receive the latest declared but unpaid dividend.

Fully diluted earnings per share The earnings per share amount calculated by dividing the applicable net income for the period by the common stock outstanding, plus common stock equivalents, plus other securities with conversion privileges that could decrease earnings per share.

Issued capital stock The capital stock issued and not reacquired and canceled by the corporation.

Large stock dividend See *Stock dividend*.

Legal capital The minimum amount of capital that state law requires to be left in the corporation for the protection of creditors and which cannot be withdrawn by the stockholders.

Legal capital approach An approach used to prepare a stockholders' equity section with the various subsections arranged to reveal the legal capital, all other paid-in capital, and retained earnings.

Market value The amount that a share of stock will bring the seller if the stock is offered for sale.

Noncumulative preferred stock A class of preferred stock on which a dividend not declared (passed) in any one year is lost.

No-par value stock Stock without an indicated par value.

Outstanding capital stock Capital stock still in the hands of the shareholders and not in the treasury of the corporation; it is issued capital stock minus any treasury stock of a given class.

Paid-in capital—excess over par value That part of capital paid in by stockholders that is not credited to the capital stock accounts and is usually not a part of legal capital.

Paid-in capital—excess over stated value See *Paid-in capital—excess over par value*.

Par value The nominal or face amount printed on a stock certificate, representing the minimum amount to be paid to the issuing corporation by the original purchaser.

Preferred stock A class of capital stock having various preferences, two of which are preference as to dividends and preference as to assets in liquidation.

Premium on common stock Another term for *paid-in capital—excess over par value,* common (a similar premium account could be used for preferred stock).

Primary earnings per share The earnings per share amount calculated by dividing the applicable net income for the period by the common stock plus common stock equivalents.

Restricted retained earnings The portion of retained earnings not available for dividends.

Retained earnings Cumulative earnings minus cumulative dividends.

Small stock dividend See *Stock dividend*.

Source of capital approach An approach used to prepare a stockholders' equity section with the various subsections arranged to reveal the broad sources of capital.

Stated value A value assigned to each share of no-par value stock by the directors of the corporation.

Stock dividend The issuance by a corporation of additional shares of its authorized stock without additional investment by the stockholders. A stock dividend may be classified as *large* (involving the issuance of enough new shares of stock to cause a decrease in the market price of the stock) or *small* (involving the issuance of a sufficiently small number of shares as not to materially affect the market price of the stock). The dividing line between a large and a small stock dividend is approximately 20–25 percent.

Stockholders' ledger A subsidiary ledger to the capital stock controlling accounts in the general ledger. Only those whose names appear in the stockholders' ledger are recognized as share owners.

Stock indenture The corporate contractual agreement setting forth the rights and privileges of the holders of the capital stock; it could be an indenture for preferred or common stock.

Stock split An increase in the number of shares of stock outstanding without a change in the *total* par or *total* stated value of the outstanding shares (usually the par or stated value will be decreased).

Stock subscription A pledge to buy capital stock, with payment to be made later in a single lump sum or in installments.

Treasury stock A corporation's own capital stock issued and fully paid for, and later reacquired by the corporation.

Questions

Q13–1 What factors should a business group consider in determining whether to incorporate or not?

Q13–2 Differentiate among the following terms: common stock and preferred stock; par value and stated value; liquidation value, market value, and book value; cumulative and noncumulative stock; restricted and unrestricted retained earnings; stock dividend and stock split.

Q13–3 What are the meanings of the following terms: earnings per share; limited liability; paid-in capital—excess over par value; paid-in capital—excess over stated value; paid-in capital; treasury stock; stock subscription?

Q13–4 What is the extent of the legal responsibility of the owner of a majority of the shares of stock of a corporation to pay its debts if the corporation gets into financial difficulty?

Q13–5 What is the meaning of the term *legal entity*? How does it differ from that of *accounting entity*?

Q13–6 Does a corporation earn revenue by selling its stock at a figure in excess of par value? Conversely, does a corporation sustain a loss if it sells its stock at a discount?

Q13–7 What is the meaning of no-par value? What are some reasons for a firm to seek authorization to issue no-par stock?

Q13–8 What are the balance sheet classifications of the following accounts: (a) Subscriptions Receivable, (b) Common Stock Subscribed, (c) Organization Costs, and (d) Paid-in Capital—Excess over Par Value, Common?

Q13–9 Since it represents earnings retained for use in the business, is the Retained Earnings account an asset? Explain.

Q13–10 In which form of business organization is ownership most readily transferable? Explain why.

Q13–11 Distinguish between authorized and unissued stock and issued and outstanding stock.

Q13–12 Student A says that if he were buying stock, he would purchase only stock having a par value. Student B takes the opposite viewpoint. Discuss.

Q13–13 What is legal capital? How is it determined? How does it differ from paid-in capital? Retained earnings? Stockholders' equity? Why should the state of incorporation regulate the amount that may be distributed to stockholders in the form of dividends?

Q13–14 The following quotation is adapted from the notes to the financial statements of a large company: "Retained earnings of $28,500,000 are restricted from payment of cash dividends on common stock because of a promissory note agreement. Further restrictions of $1,700,000 are made to cover the cost of the company's own common stock reacquired." What is the significance of this note (a) to a short-term creditor? (b) to a long-term creditor? (c) to a stockholder?

Q13–15 (a) What is a stock dividend? (b) What conditions prompt the declaration of a stock dividend? (c) How does a stock dividend affect (1) the total stockholders' equity, (2) the total assets, (3) the book value per share, (4) the taxable income of the recipient, and (5) the market price per share?

Q13–16 (a) What is treasury stock? (b) Why do corporations buy back their own shares? (c) How does the reacquisition of a company's own shares affect its financial position? (d) Why do some states place certain restrictions on treasury stock acquisitions? (e) How is the purchase of treasury stock recorded? (f) How is the issuance of treasury stock recorded? (g) How does the issuance of treasury stock affect the financial statements?

Q13–17 Student A argues that she would rather buy 100 shares of $50 par value treasury common stock for $49 per share. Student B says that he would rather buy 100 shares of unissued common stock of the same company at a discount and pay $49. With which student do you agree? Why?

Q13–18 Discuss briefly the internal control issues involved with stockholders' equity items.

Q13–19 (Appendix) (a) What are the major subdivisions of the stockholders' equity section of the balance sheet under the source of capital approach? (b) What are the major subdivisions under the legal capital approach? (c) What are the main arguments for each of these approaches?

Exercises

E13–1
Recording common stock transactions

The Slavon Corporation was authorized to issue 10,000 shares of common stock. Record in general journal form the issue of 6,000 shares for cash at $7.25 a share on January 7, 1987, assuming:

a. That the shares have a $5 par value.
b. That the shares have no par and no stated value.
c. That the shares have no par value but have a stated value of $3.

E13–2
Issuing common stock for cash and noncash items

The County Computer Corporation is authorized to issue 500,000 shares of $5 par value common stock. The following transactions occurred in sequence:

a. Issued for cash 6,000 shares at par value.
b. Issued 2,000 shares to the promoters for services valued at $10,000 in organizing the corporation.
c. Issued 2,000 shares to attorneys for services valued at $10,000 in organizing the corporation and securing the corporate charter.
d. Issued 36,000 shares in exchange for a factory building and land valued at $170,400 and $24,000, respectively.
e. Issued for cash 30,000 shares at $5.50 a share.
f. Issued for cash 60,000 shares at $6 a share.

Record the transactions in general journal form using transaction letters instead of dates.

E13–3
Recording common and preferred stock subscriptions

The World Finance Corporation received its charter on September 2, 1987, authorizing the issuance of 10,000 shares of $50 par value, 16 percent preferred stock and 100,000 shares of no-par common stock. No stated value was assigned to the no-par common stock. The following transactions took place in September and October:

1987

Sep. 4 Issued 10,000 shares of the common stock at $12 per share for cash.
6 Issued 2,000 shares of the preferred stock at par for cash.
16 Received subscriptions for 1,000 preferred shares at $52 per share; no down payment was received.
20 Received subscriptions for 5,000 common shares at $12.50 per share; no down payment was received.
Oct. 15 Collected amount due from preferred subscribers and issued the 1,000 preferred shares.
21 Collected amount due from common subscribers and issued the 5,000 common shares.

Record the foregoing transactions in general journal form.

E13-4
Preparing paid-in capital section of balance sheet—source of capital approach

On December 31, 1987, the ledger of the Rex Electronics Company included, among others, the following accounts:

Notes Receivable	$ 24,000
Merchandise Inventory	85,000
Temporary Investments—U.S. Treasury Certificates	18,000
Common Stock ($10 par value)	400,000
Subscriptions Receivable—Common Stock	40,000
Preferred Stock ($100 par value)	300,000
Goodwill	30,000
Common Stock Subscribed	175,000
Organization Costs	20,000
Paid-in Capital—Excess over Par Value, Preferred	12,000
Building	225,000
Paid-in Capital—Excess over Par Value, Common	45,000
Notes Receivable Discounted	7,000
Cash	90,000

Prepare the paid-in capital portion of the stockholders' equity section of the balance sheet as of December 31, 1987, using the source of capital approach.

E13-5
Recording common stock transactions and donation of assets

The Tri-County Sales Corporation received its charter on August 7, 1987, authorizing the issuance of 100,000 shares of $10 par value common stock. The following transactions took place during August:

1987

Aug. 7 Issued 10,000 shares of common stock at $15 per share for cash.
    15 The County of Cork donated land worth $60,000 to the new corporation for locating on its border.
    20 Issued 1,000 shares to incorporators as reimbursement for their expenses of $16,000 to form the corporation.

Record the foregoing transactions in general journal form.

E13-6
Various common and preferred stock issues

The Ruplkin Corporation was authorized to issue 40,000 shares of no-par value common stock and 10,000 shares of $20 par value preferred stock. Organizers of the corporation received 3,000 shares of the no-par common stock for services valued at $15,000. A total of 3,000 shares of the preferred stock was issued for cash at $22 a share, and 3,000 shares of common stock were issued for cash at $6 a share. A total of 5,000 shares of preferred stock was subscribed at $23 a share. Subscriptions to 2,500 preferred shares of stock were paid in full; these shares were issued. The subscribers to the other preferred shares made no payments.

1. Record the transactions in ledger accounts. Designate the transactions as a, b, c, and so on—then use these letters instead of dates.
2. Prepare a balance sheet (assume a date of July 10, 1987).

E13-7
Effect of transactions on retained earnings

Indicate the effect—increase, decrease, no effect—of each of the following transactions on *total* retained earnings of the Fitch Company:

a. The board of directors declared a 5 percent stock dividend to be issued one month from the current date.
b. Issued the stock dividend declared in transaction a.

c. Wrote off accounts receivable against the allowance for doubtful accounts.
d. Paid accounts payable.
e. Collected accounts receivable.
f. Issued $50 par value common stock at $60 a share.
g. Restricted retained earnings for contingencies.
h. Issued $50 par value preferred stock at $58 a share.
i. Purchased machinery on open account.
j. Issued long-term notes and received cash in return.

E13–8
Recording stock and cash dividends and treasury stock

The stockholders' equity section of the Virginia Company's balance sheet shows the following:

Common stock, no-par value; issued 10,500 shares.	$165,000
Retained earnings.	125,000
Total	$290,000

Record each of the following events, occurring in sequence (using letters instead of dates in the journal):

a. The declaration of a 15 percent stock dividend; the market price of the stock is $18 per share.
b. The issuance of the dividend.
c. The acquisition of 200 shares of the company's own stock for $18 a share.
d. The reissuance of the 200 reacquired shares for $20 a share.
e. The declaration of a $1-per-share cash dividend.
f. The payment of the dividend.

E13–9
Recording treasury stock transactions

On July 8, 1987, the Acme Corporation had the following stockholders' equity:

Common stock, $2 par value, authorized; issued and outstanding, 40,000 shares	$ 80,000
Paid-in capital—excess over par value, common stock (not a part of legal capital)	175,000
Retained earnings.	610,500

The following selected transactions took place during July and August 1987:

1987

Jul. 9 Reacquired 500 shares of own common stock at $22 per share. State law requires the restriction of retained earnings for the cost of the treasury shares.
12 Reissued 100 treasury shares for $23 per share.
18 Reissued 100 treasury shares for $21.50 per share.
Aug. 15 Reissued the remaining 300 shares to employees for $18 per share.

Prepare journal entries to record the foregoing transactions.

E13–10
Calculating primary earnings per share

The net income after taxes of the Erno Corporation for 1987 was $212,205. The weighted average number of shares of common stock was 110,000; common stock equivalents amounted to 40,500 shares. There is no preferred stock. Calculate the primary earnings per share for 1987.

E13-11
Calculating book value per share

The condensed balance sheet of the K. Edwards Corporation as of December 31, 1987, contained the following items:

Total assets	$720,000
Liabilities	$200,000
Preferred stock, 12 percent, $50 par value; cumulative	100,000
Common stock, no-par value; stated value $5	300,000
Paid-in capital—excess over par value, preferred	10,000
Paid-in capital—excess over stated value, common	15,000
Retained earnings—restricted for plant expansion	45,000
Retained earnings	50,000
Total liabilities and stockholders' equity	$720,000

The liquidating value of the preferred stock is equal to the par value plus any dividends in arrears.

1. Determine the book value per share of common stock, assuming that there are no dividend arrearages.
2. Calculate the book value per share of common stock, assuming that dividends on the preferred stock are in arrears for the years 1986 and 1987.

E13-12
Preparing stockholders' equity section

(Appendix) The following account balances were taken from the ledger of the Sanderson Company as of December 31, 1987:

Paid-in Capital—Excess over Par Value, Preferred	$ 65,000
Paid-in Capital—Donated by Town of Pamet	144,000
Paid-in Capital from Treasury Stock Transactions—Common	12,000
Preferred Stock (12% cumulative, $100 par value; issued 9,600 shares)	960,000
Retained Earnings—Restricted for Plant Additions	192,000
Retained Earnings—Restricted for Contingencies	24,000
Paid-in Capital—Excess of Original Stated Value over Revised Stated Value of Common Stock	180,000
Common Stock ($5 stated value; issued 48,000 shares)	240,000
Retained Earnings	408,200
Treasury Stock—Common (600 shares)	18,000
Paid-in Capital—Excess over Stated Value, Common	96,000
Estimated Income Taxes Payable	115,000
Organization Costs	24,000

Prepare the stockholders' equity section of the balance sheet as of December 31, 1987, using the legal capital approach.

E13-13
Determining various stockholders' equity amounts

Refer to E13-12. Compute (a) the amount contributed by the preferred stockholders, (b) the amount contributed by the common stockholders, (c) the book value per share of preferred stock, assuming that the current year's preferred dividends are in arrears, and (d) the book value per share of common stock. The liquidation value of the preferred is equal to par value plus any dividends in arrears.

E13-14
Recording quarterly dividends

National Agribusiness Company has 400,000 shares of $25 par value, 12 percent, cumulative preferred stock outstanding. It also has 45,000,000 shares of $1.20 par value common stock outstanding. The following actions occurred in 1987:

1987

Jan.	4	At its monthly meeting, the board of directors reviewed the tentative 1986 financial statements and approved the following: a. The declaration of a total dividend of $8,400,000 as a fourth quarter 1986 dividend on both preferred and common stock payable on February 6 to stockholders of record on January 23, 1987. b. The acceptance of an offer by a stockholder to sell back to the corporation 1,000,000 shares of common stock at $22 a share on January 9.
	9	The acquisition of 1,000,000 shares of common stock was carried out for cash.
Apr.	4	The directors reviewed interim statements for the first quarter of 1987 and approved a first quarter total dividend of $8,220,000 on both preferred and common stock payable on May 10 to stockholders of record on April 25.

No dividends were in arrears and no other stock transactions occurred during the period. Dividends on both common and preferred are declared quarterly. All dividends declared were paid when due. In general journal form, record all events stemming from the directors' actions.

A Problems

P13–1A
Recording capital stock transactions and preparing a paid-in capital portion of balance sheet

The following selected transactions occurred at the newly formed Jordan Corporation:

1987

Jul.	1	Received a charter authorizing the issuance of 10,000 shares of $50 par value preferred stock and 100,000 shares of $5 par value common stock.
	5	Issued for cash 25,000 shares of common stock at $10 per share.
	5	Issued 500 shares of common stock to an incorporator for a patent that he had perfected valued at $5,000.
	8	Received subscriptions from four investors for 260 shares each of preferred stock at $52.50 per share.
	8	Received 60 percent down payments on the subscriptions from all four subscribers.
	19	Received payment in full from three of the preferred subscribers and issued the stock.
	29	Received payment in full from the fourth preferred subscriber and issued the stock.
Aug.	9	Purchased the following assets, shown at their fair market value, from Sanford Jones, who had been operating a single proprietorship in a similar business:

Land	$10,000
Building	40,000
Equipment	25,000

The Jordan Corporation would assume an outstanding $20,000 mortgage note payable on the building in addition to $500 representing two months' accrued interest. Jones agreed to accept common stock at $10 per share as payment for his net equity in the assets.

	30	Issued common stock at $11 per share for equipment valued at $33,000.

Required:

1. Journalize the transactions in general journal form.
2. Post the transactions to appropriate ledger accounts.
3. Prepare the paid-in capital portion of the stockholders' equity section of the Jordan Corporation balance sheet as of August 31, 1987, using the source of capital approach.

P13–2A

Recording various capital stock transactions and preparing a paid-in capital portion of balance sheet

The paid-in capital portion of the stockholders' equity section of the Islands Import Company on July 1, 1987, was as follows:

Stockholders' equity:
Paid-in capital:
Preferred stock, $50 par value	$250,000
Paid-in capital—excess over par value, preferred	40,000
Common stock, no-par value, $10 stated value	300,000
Paid-in capital—excess over stated value, common	25,000
Paid-in capital from warehouse donated by stockholder	50,000
Total paid-in capital	$665,000

The following transactions occurred during the next three months:

1987

Jul. 1 Issued for cash 1,000 shares of preferred stock at $52 a share.
    1 Issued for cash 5,000 shares of common stock at $26 a share.
   19 Issued for cash 8,000 shares of common stock at $27 a share.
Aug. 1 Issued for cash 12,000 shares of preferred stock at $52 a share.
    2 Issued 100 shares of preferred stock in payment for a patent valued at $5,100.
Sep. 16 Issued 2,000 shares of common stock in exchange for land and a building appraised at $23,000 and $33,000, respectively.

Required:

1. Open ledger accounts for the stockholders' equity items; enter the balances from the partial stockholders' equity section.
2. Journalize the foregoing transactions.
3. Post the journal entries to the stockholders' equity accounts only.
4. Prepare the paid-in capital portion of the stockholders' equity section of the balance sheet as of September 30, 1987, using the source of capital approach.
5. Assume that the no-par common stock had no stated value; prepare journal entries to record the issuance of the common stock on July 1, July 19, and September 16.

P13–3A

Recording capital stock transactions with specified subscribers

The following selected transactions occurred at the newly formed Magnet Corporation:

1987

Mar. 1 Received a charter authorizing the issuance of 20,000 shares of $10 par value preferred stock and 1,000,000 shares of $1 par value common stock.
    2 Received subscriptions for preferred stock at $12 per share from the following subscribers:

Samuel Tuten	2,000 shares
James Hassell	4,000

    2 Received subscriptions for common stock at $3 per share from the following subscribers:

Earl Deal	4,000 shares
Eugene Motsinger	6,000
Randolph Owens	3,800
Thomas Peters	8,000

  29 Tuten and Hassell paid 50 percent of their subscriptions.
  29 Deal paid 100 percent of his subscription; Motsinger, Owens, and Peters paid 40 percent. The stock subscribed by Deal was issued.

Apr. 30 Tuten and Hassell paid the remaining amount owed on their stock subscriptions; their subscribed stock was issued.
30 Motsinger and Owens paid the remaining amount owed on their stock subscriptions; their subscribed stock was issued.
30 Peters informed the officials of the corporation that he would be unable to pay the balance of his subscription contract. Both parties agreed that 3,200 common shares would be issued to Peters and that the remaining account balances would be reversed and that the balance of the subscriptions would be cancelled.

Required:

1. Prepare journal entries to record the foregoing transactions.
2. Prepare a paid-in capital portion of the balance sheet of Magnet Corporation using the source of capital approach.

P13–4A
Journalizing various stockholders' equity transactions

The Lindwood Corporation was organized on January 3, 1987, with authority to issue 30,000 shares of no-par value common stock and 7,500 shares of 12 percent cumulative preferred stock, $50 par value. During 1987 and 1988, the following selected transactions occurred, in this sequence:

a. Issued 8,000 shares of common stock for cash at $12 a share. A stated value of $10 a share is set by the board of directors for the common stock.
b. Issued 1,000 shares of preferred stock at $60 a share.
c. Issued 150 shares of common stock, in lieu of a $1,800 fee, to the corporation's attorneys for their services in drafting the articles of incorporation and a set of bylaws.
d. Acquired 325 shares of common stock for $4,225 from the estate of a deceased stockholder.
e. Reissued the 325 shares of the treasury stock at $14 a share.
f. The 1987 end-of-year credit balance in the Income Summary account of $256,000 was closed. (Make the closing entry.)
g. Declared a 12 percent annual dividend on preferred stock and a $0.30-per-share cash dividend plus a 50 percent stock dividend on common stock. The dividends are distributable on February 10, 1988, to stockholders of record on January 31, 1988.
h. In 1988, the board authorized the restriction of retained earnings of $50,000 for plant expansion.

Required: Prepare the journal entries to record the transactions using letters in the place of dates.

P13–5A
Book value and earnings per share

Part I
The condensed balance sheet data of the Cookerville Corporation as of December 31, 1987, were as follows:

Total assets	$825,000
Liabilities	$250,000
Preferred stock, 12 percent, $50 par value; cumulative	100,000
Common stock, no-par value; stated value $5	300,000
Paid-in capital—excess over par value, preferred	10,000
Paid-in capital—excess over stated value, common	15,000
Retained earnings—restricted for plant expansion	50,000
Retained earnings.	100,000
Total liabilities and stockholders' equity	$825,000

(continued on next page)

Required:

1. Determine the book value per share of common stock, assuming that there are no dividend arrearages. The liquidation value of the preferred stock is equal to the par value plus any dividends in arrears.
2. Calculate the book value per share of common stock, assuming that dividends on the preferred stock are in arrears for the years 1985, 1986, and 1987.
3. What is the significance of the book value per share?
4. What is the interrelationship between book value per share and market value per share?

Part 2

Calculating earnings per share

Assume the following information for the Simplex Corporation:

Weighted average shares of common stock outstanding	100,000
12% Convertible preferred shares, Class A, $50 par value (not a common stock equivalent, but convertible to common shares on a 1 preferred share for 2 common shares basis)	20,000
6% Convertible preferred shares, Class B, $100 par value (a common stock equivalent convertible to common shares on a 1 preferred share for 3 common shares basis)	30,000
Net income for 1987	$650,800

Assume that both class A and B were outstanding during the entire year of 1987.

Required: Calculate (a) the primary earnings per share, and (b) the fully diluted earnings per share.

P13–6A
Thought-provoking problem: decision on form of organization

William Triton, a professor of chemistry in a state university, had a hobby of working with engines of automobiles. He invented an automobile engine that he felt would yield about 200 miles to a gallon of gasoline for a small vehicle. He spent six months making a three-wheel automobile into which he inserted his specially built engine. Triton named the automobile the Triton Tricar. Upon testing the vehicle, he found that it in fact did produce slightly over 200 miles to a gallon of gasoline. Triton applied for a patent on his invention and received it. He was undecided whether to sell the patent to one of the "Big Three" automobile makers or whether to go into business for himself. He had about $100,000 he could make available as capital. He considered that he would need $400,000 more to start a limited production of the Triton Tricar. To see whether he might be able to go into business, Triton approached two other professor friends, a professor of marketing and a professor of engineering. They became excited about the potential of the Triton Tricar. These two agreed to put up $300,000 and to help in the management of the new business. Triton said that he would transfer the patent and invest his $100,000 in the business. More capital, at least $100,000, was necessary to organize, to launch an area marketing campaign, and to equip a factory to start production of the Triton Tricar.

The three promoters decided to seek additional capital from borrowing and to hire a professional staff to build and market the Triton Tricar, but they did not agree as to the form of organization for the new business.

Required:

1. Would you recommend that these three people form a partnership or a corporation for this business?
2. Write a report to these three justifying your recommendation. If you recommend a partnership, include in your report techniques for raising capital. If you recommend incorporation, include in your report a discussion of (a) types of stock to be issued, (b) par value, (c) number of shares, and (d) initial issue price.

13 / Accounting for Corporate Equity

P13–7A
Preparing a stockholders' equity section of balance sheet

(Appendix) On December 31, 1987, the ledger of the Cobb Corporation included the following accounts:

Land.	$ 40,000
Notes Receivable.	40,000
Merchandise Inventory.	160,000
Temporary Investments—U.S. Treasury Notes.	34,000
Common Stock, $10 par value.	600,000
Retained Earnings.	200,000
Subscriptions Receivable—Common Stock.	80,000
Preferred Stock, $25 par value.	300,000
Patents.	10,000
Common Stock Subscribed.	225,000
Organization costs.	10,000
Paid-in Capital—Excess over Par Value, Common.	20,000
Building.	300,000
Paid-in Capital—Excess over Par Value, Preferred.	60,000
Paid-in Capital—Donation of Land by Town of Exeter.	40,000

Required: Select the proper items and prepare the stockholders' equity section of the Cobb Corporation balance sheet as of December 31, 1987, using the legal capital approach.

B Problems

P13–1B
Recording capital stock transactions and preparing a paid-in capital portion of balance sheet

The following selected transactions occurred at the newly formed Franko Corporation:

1987

Aug.	1	Received a charter authorizing the issuance of 8,000 shares of $25 par value preferred stock and 100,000 shares of $5 par value common stock.
	5	Issued for cash 30,000 shares of common stock at $8 per share.
	5	Issued 800 shares of common stock to an incorporator for a patent that he had perfected valued at $6,400.
	6	Received subscriptions from four investors for 300 shares each of preferred stock at $30 per share.
	6	Received 50 percent down payments on the subscriptions from all four subscribers.
	20	Received payment in full from three of the preferred subscribers and issued the stock.
	29	Received payment in full from the fourth preferred subscriber and issued the stock.
Sep.	10	Purchased the following assets, shown at their fair market value, from Daisy Fox, who had been operating a single proprietorship in the same business:

Land.	$ 8,100
Building.	45,000
Equipment.	30,000

The Franko Corporation would assume an outstanding $25,000, 12 percent mortgage note payable on the building in addition to two months' accrued interest. Fox agreed to accept common stock at $8 a share as payment for her net equity in the assets.

	30	Issued common stock at $8 a share for equipment valued at $40,000.

Required:

1. Journalize the transactions in general journal form.
2. Post the transactions to appropriate ledger accounts.
3. Prepare the stockholders' equity section of the Franko Corporation's balance sheet as of September 30, 1987, using the source of capital approach.

P13–2B

Recording various stock transactions and preparing a paid-in capital portion of balance sheet

The paid-in capital portion of the stockholders's equity section of the Texarca Import Company on August 1, 1987, was as follows:

Stockholders' equity:
  Paid-in capital:
    Preferred stock, $30 par value. $126,000
    Paid-in capital—excess over par value, preferred. 19,000
    Common stock, no-par value, $10 stated value 150,000
    Paid-in capital—excess over stated value, common 12,500
    Paid-in capital from warehouse donated by stockholder 25,000
      Total paid-in capital. $332,500

The following transactions occurred during the next three months:

1987

Aug. 1 Issued for cash 2,000 shares of preferred stock at $32 a share.
    12 Issued for cash 7,500 shares of common stock at $14 a share.
    20 Issued for cash 10,000 shares of common stock at $16 a share.
Sep. 2 Issued for cash 6,000 shares of preferred stock at $33 a share.
     2 Issued 200 shares of preferred stock in payment for a patent valued at $6,600.
Oct. 15 Issued 3,500 shares of common stock in exchange for land and a building appraised at $18,000 and $41,500, respectively.

Required:

1. Open ledger accounts for the stockholders' equity items; enter the balances from the partial stockholders' equity section.
2. Journalize the foregoing transactions.
3. Post the journal entries to the stockholders' equity accounts only.
4. Prepare the paid-in capital portion of the stockholders' equity section of the balance sheet as of October 31, 1987, using the source of capital approach.
5. Assume that the no-par common stock had no stated value; prepare journal entries to record the issuance of the common stock on August 12, August 20, and October 15.

P13–3B

Recording capital stock transactions with specified subscribers

The following selected transactions occurred at the newly formed Oakley Corporation:

1987

Oct. 1 Received a charter authorizing the issuance of 30,000 shares of $5 par value preferred stock and 750,000 shares of $2 par value common stock.
    2 Received subscriptions for preferred stock at $8 per share from the following subscribers:

        Henry Holton . . . . 5,000 shares
        Philip Bolton. 6,000
        Sampson Dullard 4,000

    2 Received subscriptions for common stock at $4 per share from the following subscribers:

        Burl Davis . . . . 100,000 shares
        Johnson Taylor 150,000

    30 Holton, Bolton, and Dullard paid 60 percent of their subscriptions.
    31 Davis paid 100 percent of his subscription; and Taylor paid 30 percent. The stock subscribed by Davis was issued.
Nov. 29 Holton and Bolton paid the remaining amount due on their stock subscriptions; their subscribed stock was issued.

29 Dullard informed the officials of the corporation that he was unable to pay the balance of his subscription contract. Both parties agreed that 2,400 = (60% × 4,000) preferred shares should be issued to Dullard, and that the remaining account balances would be reversed and the balance of the subscriptions would be cancelled.

29 Taylor paid the remaining amount due on his stock; his subscribed stock was issued.

Required:

1. Prepare journal entries to record the foregoing transactions.
2. Prepare the paid-in capital portion of the balance sheet of Oakley Corporation using the source of capital approach.

P13–4B
Journalizing various stockholders' equity transactions

The Pope Corporation was organized on April 1, 1987, with authority to issue 50,000 shares of no-par value common stock and 15,000 shares of 14 percent cumulative preferred stock, $25 par value. During 1987 and 1988 the following transactions occurred, in this sequence:

a. Issued 16,500 shares of common stock for cash at $15 a share. A stated value of $12 is set by the board of directors for the common stock.
b. Issued 1,500 shares of preferred stock at $28 a share.
c. Issued 200 shares of common stock in lieu of a $3,000 fee to the corporation's attorneys for their services in drafting the articles of incorporation and a set of bylaws.
d. Acquired 600 shares of common stock for $9,600 from the estate of a deceased stockholder.
e. Reissued the 600 shares of the treasury stock at $17 a share.
f. The 1987 end-of-year credit balance in the Income Summary account of $216,800 was closed. (Make the closing entry.)
g. Declared a 14 percent annual dividend on preferred stock and a $0.35-per-share cash dividend plus a 40 percent stock dividend on common stock. The dividends are distributable on February 12, 1988, to stockholders of record on January 31, 1988.
h. The board authorized the restriction of retained earnings of $60,000 for plant expansion.

Required: Prepare the journal entries to record the transactions using letters in the place of dates.

P13–5B
Book value issues and earnings per share

Part 1

The condensed balance sheet data of the Princeville Corporation as of December 31, 1987, were as follows:

Total assets	$745,000
Liabilities	$179,000
Preferred stock, 15 percent, $25 par value; cumulative	100,000
Common stock, no-par value; stated value $6	312,000
Paid-in capital—excess over par value, preferred	15,000
Paid-in capital—excess over stated value, common	24,000
Retained earnings—restricted for plant expansion	75,000
Retained earnings.	40,000
Total liabilities and stockholders' equity	$745,000

Required:

1. Determine the book value per share of common stock, assuming that there are no dividend arrearages. The liquidation value of the preferred stock is equal to the par value plus any dividends in arrears.

2. Determine the book value per share of common stock, assuming that dividends on the preferred stock are in arrears for the years 1985, 1986, and 1987.
3. What is the significance of the book value per share?
4. What is the interrelationship between book value per share and market value per share?

Part 2

Calculating earnings per share

Assume the following data for the Secondo Corporation:

Weighted average shares of common stock outstanding	130,000
14% Convertible preferred shares, preference 1 stock, $25 par value (not a common stock equivalent, but convertible to common shares on a 1 preferred share for 2.5 common shares basis)	28,000
5% Convertible preferred shares, preference 2 stock, $100 par value (a common stock equivalent convertible to common shares on a 1 preferred share for 4 common shares basis)	50,000
Net income for 1987	$1,264,000

Assume that both types of preferred stock were outstanding during the entire year of 1987.

Required: Calculate (a) the primary earnings per share, and (b) the fully diluted earnings per share.

P13–6B

Thought-provoking problem: stock dividends, restricting retained earnings, and other issues

The following is an adaptation of a footnote that appeared in a recent annual report of a United States corporation:

Shareholders' equity:

The Board of Directors on June 3, 1987, declared a 100 percent common stock distribution on common shares, payable July 15, 1987. The per share amounts in the consolidated statement of income have been adjusted retroactively to reflect this July 1987 stock distribution.

The $3.00 preferred is convertible into 3.6 common shares and has liquidating preferences of $100 per share, redeemable beginning in 1995 at $103 per share, and is entitled to one vote per share. The company has been advised by counsel that there are no restrictions on income retained in the business as a result of the excess of liquidating preference over stated value of the preferred stocks.

In January 1988, the company increased the number of authorized shares of common stock from 7,000,000 to 45,000,000 shares. Of the common shares authorized but unissued at December 31, 1988, a total of 15,949,307 were reserved for conversion of preferred stocks and convertible subordinated debentures [bonds] and for exercise of stock options and warrants.

Required:

1. What was achieved by the 100 percent common stock distribution (a) from the corporation's viewpoint? (b) From the stockholders' viewpoint?
2. How did the stock distribution affect the balance sheet?
3. What is the purpose of the conversion privilege attaching to the preferred shares?
4. What is the significance of the advice by counsel regarding retained earnings restrictions?
5. Give some reasons for the large increase in the number of authorized shares of common stock.

P13–7B

Preparing a stockholders' equity section of a balance sheet

(Appendix) On December 31, 1987, the ledger of the Charles River Corporation included the following accounts (in scrambled order):

Accounts Receivable	$ 35,000
Merchandise Inventory	115,000
Temporary Investments—U.S. Treasury Notes	80,000
Land	42,500
Common Stock, $5 par value	800,000
Retained Earnings	165,000
Subscriptions Receivable, Common Stock	75,000
Preferred Stock, $50 par value	250,000
Franchises	25,000
Common Stock Subscribed	200,000
Organization Costs	20,000
Paid-in Capital—Excess over Par Value, Common	85,000
Paid-in Capital—Excess over Par Value, Preferred	90,000
Paid-in Capital—Donation of Land by City of Squares	42,500

Required: Select the proper items and prepare the stockholders' equity section of the Charles River Corporation's balance sheet as of December 31, 1987, using the legal capital approach.

14 Long-Term Liabilities

Introduction

Doing business on credit is a way of life in the United States. It is not unusual for over half of the assets of a business to be financed by creditor sources. For example, on December 31, 1983, 68.5% = ($1,092,899,249 ÷ $1,596,101,462) of the assets of the Fruehauf Corporation came from all creditor sources. Because of the heavy reliance on debt, the accounting for the acquisition of both short-term and long-term creditor funds is extremely important. The short-term creditor source has already been discussed in Chapter 9 and other chapters. For a more complete understanding of borrowing from creditors, this chapter discusses bonds payable in depth and introduces certain other long-term liabilities.

Learning Goals

1. To understand the nature and classification of bonds payable.

2. To understand the reason for issuing bonds instead of capital stock.

3. To record transactions for (a) bond issuance, (b) bond retirement and refunding, and (c) conversion of bonds into capital stock.

4. To understand the nature of and reasons for amortization of premium and discount on bonds payable by both the straight line and the interest methods.

5. To record an early retirement of bonds payable.

6. To make the accounting entries for bond sinking funds.

7. To understand the nature of and account for mortgage notes payable and long-term unsecured notes payable.

8. To be able to calculate the times bond interest earned ratio.

9. To appreciate the internal control measures involved with bonds payable.

Definitions and Types of Long-Term Liabilities

Obligations that have maturity dates beyond the next year or operating cycle are classified on the balance sheet as **long-term liabilities** or long-term debt. The maturity dates of some long-term debt items cover 20 to 30 or more years. Often these obligations are paid off from the proceeds derived from the issuance of other long-term debt instruments. This rollover of the long-term debt makes it similar to certain types of capital stock. This is because no net resources (other than interest payments) are paid out in the process of continuing the liability item for an indefinite period into the future.

Typical long-term liabilities include bonds payable, mortgages payable, unsecured long-term notes payable (discussed in this chapter), and obligation under capital leases (discussed in Chapter 11).

Bonds Payable

One of the means by which businesses and governments borrow funds that will not be repaid for many years is the issuance of bonds. A **bond**, or **bond certificate**, is a written promise under the corporate seal to pay a specific sum of money on a specified or determinable future date to the order of a person named in the certificate or to the order of the bearer. An example of a governmental bond is the 8.8 percent North Carolina Housing Finance Authority, 1985 Series A, Callable Bond, due on March 1, 1994. An example of a commercial bond is the 12.25 percent debentures due on May 15, 2010, issued by the First Interstate Bank Corp. The interest rate on state and local government bonds is usually lower than that of commercial bonds because the interest revenue is not taxable by either the federal or issuing state governments. At the time this is being written, interest rates on commercial bonds are ranging from approximately 10 percent to 16 percent.

Bonds are usually issued in denominations of $100, $500, $1,000, or $5,000 each. This variation enables the issuing company to obtain funds from many different investors or groups of investors. Denominations smaller than $100 have been used by the U.S. government in the past. On the other hand, municipal bonds issued in $5,000 denominations are also common.

Bonds may be issued directly to buyers by the borrowing corporation or marketed through agents such as banks, brokers, or other underwriting syndicates (groups of firms that sell securities for issuing corporations for a fee). These agents, in turn, sell the bonds through their own channels and charge a fee to the issuing company for the sale; or they may in fact buy the whole issue and resell them at a profit. **Bondholders** are creditors of the corporation. Except for currently maturing amounts, the Bonds Payable account is a long-term liability. Bonds contain provisions for interest to be paid at regularly stated intervals. Interest is usually paid semiannually on industrial bonds.

A bond, like a promissory note, represents a corporate debt to the borrower, which must be satisfied from the assets of the corporation in preference to stockholders' equity claims. Bonds, however, may be bought and resold by investors as common and preferred stocks are. The contract or covenant between the corporation and its bondholders is called a **bond indenture**.

Classification of Bonds

A corporation may issue several kinds of bonds that are tailored to meet the particular financial needs of the issuing corporation or to attract a wider variety of investors. Bonds may be registered to an individual or unregistered (bearer). They may be secured by assets or unsecured.

Registered and Coupon Bonds

Registered bonds are issued in the name of the bondholder. They require proper endorsement on the bond certificate to effect a transfer from one owner to another. The debtor corporation or its transfer agent (usually a bank or trust company appointed by the corporation, which acting for the issuer physically makes the transfer of securities bought and records ownership of the securities) maintains complete ownership records. Bonds may be registered as to both principal and interest, in which case interest checks are issued only to bondholders of record. It is possible, however, to register the principal only. One way to do this is to issue coupon bonds. The owner of **coupon bonds** (also called **bearer bonds**) detaches interest coupons from the bond certificate and deposits them at the stated interest dates at the owner's bank or at a designated bank.

In the early 1980s, changes in the federal income tax laws provided for withholding of income tax on interest in certain cases. The effect of these tax laws and other related regulations may serve to restrict the use of coupon bonds by commercial-type corporations.[1]

Secured Bonds

A **secured bond** is one that pledges some part of the corporate assets as security for the bond. The asset pledged may consist of land and buildings (for *real estate mortgage* bonds), machinery (for *chattel mortgage* bonds), negotiable securities (for *collateral trust* bonds), or other corporate assets. Several loans may use the same assets for collateral; this gives rise to *first mortgage* bonds and *second mortgage* bonds. The numbers indicate the order to be followed in satisfying the bondholders' claims if the corporation fails to meet its obligations under the bond indenture. In the event of **default** (failure to pay the bonds by the issuer) the pledged property may be sold and the proceeds used to pay creditors. Second and third mortgage bonds necessarily carry a higher interest rate than first mortgage bonds because of the order of priority of payment in the event of a default. Thus they are not as marketable as first mortgage bonds and are more costly to the borrowing company. It is, therefore, desirable for the borrower to raise the required funds through a single, large first mortgage bond issue.

---

[1] The *Tax Equity and Fiscal Responsibility Act of 1982* as amended requires a 20 percent backup withholding from individual taxpayers who have not provided taxpayer identification numbers (usually their social security number).

Unsecured Bonds

Holders of unsecured bonds rank as general, or ordinary, creditors of the corporation and rely upon the corporation's general credit. These **unsecured bonds** are commonly referred to as **debenture bonds**, or often simply as *debentures*. Sometimes debenture bonds are issued with a provision that interest payments will depend on earnings; these are called **income bonds**.

Other Bonds

Bonds may have other special features; for instance, the bonds may mature serially (**serial bonds**); specified portions of the outstanding bonds will mature in installments and be paid at stated intervals. Sometimes the issuing corporation retains an option to call in the bonds before maturity (**callable bonds**); in other cases the bondholder may be given an option to exchange the bonds for capital stock (**convertible bonds**). The bond indenture may require the issuing corporation to make deposits to a **sinking fund** (a fund created to retire bonds), often in the name of a trustee for the bondholders, at regular intervals. This ensures the availability of adequate funds for the redemption of the bonds at maturity.

Bonds Compared to Capital Stock

A better knowledge of bonds may be gained by referring to Figure 14–1, in which bonds are compared to capital stock.

Bonds	**Capital Stock**
Bondholders are creditors.	Stockholders are owners.
Bonds Payable is a long-term liability account.	Capital Stock is a stockholders' equity account.
Bondholders, along with other creditors, have primary claims on assets in liquidation.	Stockholders have residual claims on assets in liquidation.
Interest is typically a fixed charge; it must be paid or the creditors can institute bankruptcy proceedings against the debtor corporation.	Dividends are not fixed charges; even preferred dividends are at best only *contingent charges;* these are paid if income is sufficient and if declared by the corporate board of directors.
Interest is an expense.	Dividends are not expenses; they are distributions of net income.
Interest is deductible in arriving at both taxable and business income.	Dividends are not deductible in arriving at taxable and business income.
Bonds do not carry voting rights.	All stock carries voting rights unless they are expressly denied by contract, as is usually the case with preferred stock.

Figure 14–1   Comparison of Bonds to Capital Stock

Reasons for Issuing Bonds instead of Capital Stock

It is important for an accountant to understand the variety of factors that cause managers to issue bonds rather than capital stock. One factor influencing this decision is that management, by issuing bonds, has access to an important market source of funds it would not have through a stock issue. Many banks and other financial institutions are restricted by law in the amount of stock they can buy. They then look for an alternative investment—often in bonds.

A second factor, **leverage**, involves **trading on the bondholder's equity**. Leverage can be described simply: If funds borrowed at 14 percent can be used in the business enterprise to earn 23 percent after taxes, additional earnings of 9 percent = (23 percent − 14 percent) accrue to the common stockholders, who have invested no additional money for this return. However, the opposite effect is always possible: the borrowed funds may earn less than the cost of borrowing. This is an instance of unfavorable leverage.

A third reason why corporations decide to issue bonds instead of capital stock is the income tax on corporate net income. Because a corporation pays part of its net income in federal and state income taxes, it naturally considers the issuance of bonds as a means of effecting tax savings.

To illustrate how leverage and heavy income taxes affect the choice of alternative methods of fund raising, assume that the Levirite Corporation, which has $10 par value common stock outstanding in the amount of $1,000,000, needs $500,000 to purchase additional plant assets. Three plans are under consideration: Plan 1 is to issue additional common stock at $10 par value; Plan 2 is to issue 14½ percent cumulative preferred stock at $100 par value; Plan 3 is to issue 13 percent bonds at face. Figure 14–2 shows the calculations which would be helpful in making the decision. All three plans assume

	Plan 1 (Common Stock)	Plan 2 (Preferred Stock)	Plan 3 (Bonds)
Common stock outstanding	$1,000,000.00	$1,000,000.00	$1,000,000.00
Additional funds needed	500,000.00	500,000.00	500,000.00
Total	$1,500,000.00	$1,500,000.00	$1,500,000.00
Net income before bond interest and income taxes	$ 350,000.00	$ 350,000.00	$ 350,000.00
Deduct: Bond interest expense	0	0	65,000.00
Net income after bond interest expense	$ 350,000.00	$ 350,000.00	$ 285,000.00
Deduct: Income taxes (assumed rate of 40%)	140,000.00	140,000.00	114,000.00
Net income after income taxes	$ 210,000.00	$ 210,000.00	$ 171,000.00
Deduct: Dividends on preferred stock	0	72,500.00	0
Available for common stock dividends or reinvestment in Levirite Corporation	$ 210,000.00	$ 137,500.00	$ 171,000.00
Projected earnings per share on common stock (150,000 shares outstanding under Plan 1; 100,000 shares under Plans 2 and 3)	$ 1.40	$ 1.37½	$ 1.71

Figure 14–2   Three Plans for Obtaining Long-Term Funds

that the securities will be issued at face or par value, that annual earnings of $350,000 before bond interest expense is deducted will be maintained, and that an income tax rate of 40 percent will prevail.

Assuming that projected earnings per share on common stock is the best basis for making the decision, Plan 3 is desirable for the common stockholders, particularly if the net income before income taxes exceeds $350,000, because the bond interest rate is fixed. If the annual net income falls below $350,000, one of the other plans may become more advantageous. Since the securities market and corporate net earnings remain uncertain, there is no exact mathematical formula to solve this financial problem. The decision requires sound judgment based on past experience and projected future needs.

A fourth reason for management to issue bonds instead of common stock is that bonds, and to a lesser extent preferred stock, aid in offsetting losses due to shrinkage in the purchasing power of the funds invested in assets. Bonds, for example, carry fixed contract maturity values in terms of the monetary unit at the maturity date. If the value of the dollar decreases due to inflation before the bonds are paid, a gain resulting from the use of the more valuable money received at the time of borrowing accrues to the owners of the business.

A fifth factor is control. The issuance of additional common stock may result in a loss of management control because the ownership of the corporation is distributed over a larger number of stockholders. Bondholders, on the other hand, are creditors and do not participate in managerial decisions, except in the rare instances when this is a specific provision of the bond indenture.

Other reasons may influence the decision of management to issue bonds, but these five factors indicate the scope of the problem.

The Bond Issue

Authorizing the Bond Issue

Even after management decides that bonds should be issued, it is faced with months of preliminary work before the bonds can actually be floated, or sold. For example, the exact amount to be borrowed, the **stated or nominal interest rate** (the rate on the bond certificate that applies to the face value), the maturity date, and the assets, if any, to be pledged must be determined. The provisions of the bond indenture must be chosen with extreme care. For instance, should the bonds be callable, and should they be convertible into some other form of security? Careful long-range financial planning helps to reduce the cost of securing the long-term funds. For example, if there is any chance that the company will need additional funds in the near future, management—by pledging the company's total mortgageable assets—should not close the door on the possibility of marketing additional bonds. Management probably should seek authority for a bond issue large enough to meet all foreseeable needs.

The financial vice-president or the controller, working with other corporate officers, is responsible for answers to these and other questions. This officer prepares a written report for the board of directors, summarizing the proposed features of the bond financing and stating why the funds are needed, how they are to be used, and the means of ultimately retiring the bond issue. Various alternative methods of raising funds, such as those shown in the example of the Levirite Corporation (Figure 14–2), are presented to point up the financial advantage of issuing the bonds.

The board of directors studies this written report and other factors before passing a resolution recommending to the stockholders that bonds be issued. Next, the proposal is presented to the stockholders for their approval. Approval by the stockholders is required because the bondholders will have a preferred position. As creditors, they have a prior claim to the assets of the corporation in the event of liquidation.

Recording Issuance and Interest

No formal journal entry is required to record the authorization of the bond issue by the stockholders, but a memorandum should be made in the Bonds Payable account indicating the total amount authorized. This information is needed when the balance sheet is prepared since a firm should disclose the total authorization as well as the amount issued.

The issue price, usually stated as a percentage of the face value, is affected primarily by the prevailing market interest rate on bonds of the same grade. Bonds are graded by independent investment advisory services; the grade depends on the financial condition of the issuing corporation. The two major investment advisory services in the United States are Moody's and Standard & Poor's. Standard & Poor's highest grade is AAA; the next, AA; and in descending order: A, BBB, and so on, down to a grade that is simply referred to as "unrated."

Example A: Bonds Issued at Face Value   To show the essential similarity between the accounting for notes payable (see Chapter 9) and for bonds payable, Example A is a simple situation in which a corporation issues bonds at **face value** (sometimes called *issuance at par*) on an interest date. Suppose that the Amerson Corporation needs funds and that the best alternative is to issue bonds. The stockholders approve a bond issue of $200,000. Ten-year, 16 percent, first mortgage bonds are to be issued.[2] The interest will be calculated by using the **stated interest rate** (the legally indicated rate applicable to the principal) written in the indenture and will be paid semiannually on April 1 and October 1. Amerson Corporation closes its books each December 31. Assume that the corporation issues to banks and insurance companies all of the authorized bonds on April 1, 1987, at 100 or face value (*100* means 100 percent of face). The entries to record the issue, to pay the

---

[2]When this book was written the interest rate for borrowing money on all types of credit instruments was very erratic, ranging from 10 to 18 percent. The rates used in the illustrations should not be construed as typical 1987 rates.

first interest payment, and to make the adjusting entry on December 31 follow along with the entry for the first 1988 payment:[3]

1987 Apr.	1	Cash..
		    First Mortgage Bonds Payable...................
		        To record the issuance of 16 percent bonds due April 1, 1997.
			200,000	200,000

Oct.	1	Bond Interest Expense..........................
		    Cash...
		        To record the payment of interest on the first mortgage bonds.
			16,000	16,000

Dec.	31	Bond Interest Expense..........................
		    Accrued Bond Interest Payable..................
		        To record the accrual of bond interest for three months.
			8,000	8,000

1988 Apr.	1	Bond Interest Expense..........................
		Accrued Bond Interest Payable....................
		    Cash...
		        To record payment of semiannual interest.
			8,000
			8,000
				16,000

Comments on these entries follow:

1. The First Mortgage Bonds Payable account is a long-term liability since it will not be repaid for 10 years. On the balance sheet, the particular real property that is pledged as security should be disclosed in a footnote.

2. The entries to record the Bond Interest Expense are very similar to those recording Interest Expense on notes payable discussed in Chapter 9.

3. The adjusting entry for accrued bond interest is similar to the recording of accrued interest on notes payable. Accrued bond interest payable is a current liability since it must be liquidated in three months—on April 1, 1988.

4. In computing bond interest to be paid or accrued in this book, each year is assumed to be divided into 12 equal months (30-day month time).

Why Bonds Sell at a Premium or Discount

If the average market interest rate on bonds of a comparable grade is higher than the stated (nominal) interest rate on the bonds being issued, investors will offer less than the face value of the bonds in order to make up the difference between the rates. The difference (**discount**) between the issue price and the maturity value plus receipts of the semiannual interest will give the investors a return on their investments approximating the return on simi-

---
[3] Transactions involving cash are normally recorded in the cash receipts and cash payments journals. They are shown here recorded in general journal form for ease of illustration and teachability.

amounts invested at the prevailing market interest rate. This market rate is called the *effective rate;* it is also called the yield or yield rate. If the stated interest rate is higher than the current market rate, investors will tend to offer a **premium** (an amount greater than the face value) because they know that this premium will be returned to them as a part of the periodic interest payments that exceed the amount that would have been received on other investments made at the current market rate.

Two examples are presented to emphasize the reasons for bonds selling at a premium or a discount. First, assume that the Higho Company has an AAA financial rating and is planning to issue debenture bonds. Assume also that all AAA debenture bonds on the market have an effective average market interest rate of 16 percent. If the Higho Company issues debenture bonds with a 16 percent stated interest rate, it will receive the face value of the bonds. If, however, the Higho Company issues bonds with a 17 percent stated rate, it will receive an amount in excess of the face value; that is, the bonds will sell at a *premium*. On the other hand, even with its excellent credit rating, if the Higho Company issues bonds with a 15 percent stated rate, it will receive an amount less than face value; that is, the bonds will sell at a *discount*.

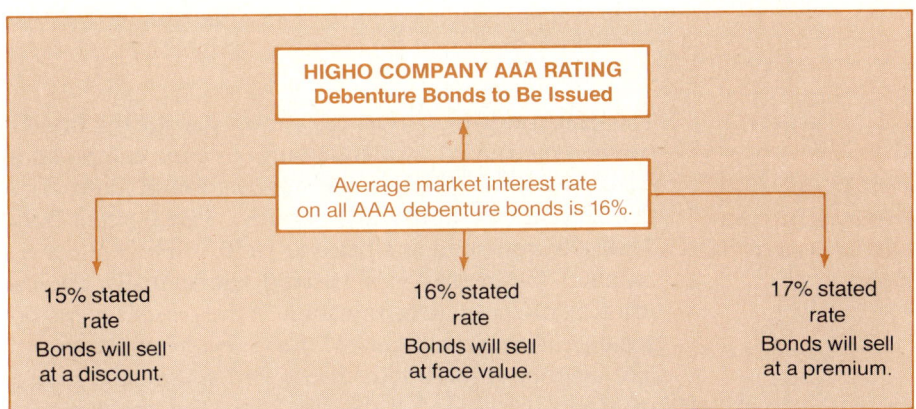

The second example shows that the single basic determinant of the issue price of the company's bonds is the fact that the stated interest rate is different from the going average effective rate on a particular grade of bond. Assume that the Lorat Company, with a BB financial rating, intends to issue first mortgage bonds. Further assume that the average effective market interest rate on BB first mortgage bonds is 17 percent. If the Lorat Company issues its bonds with a 17 percent stated interest rate, it will receive the face value of the bonds. Even with its relatively poor credit rating, if it issues bonds with an 18 percent stated interest rate, the Lorat Company will receive an amount in excess of the face value; but if it issues bonds with a 16 percent stated interest rate, it will receive an amount less than the face value.

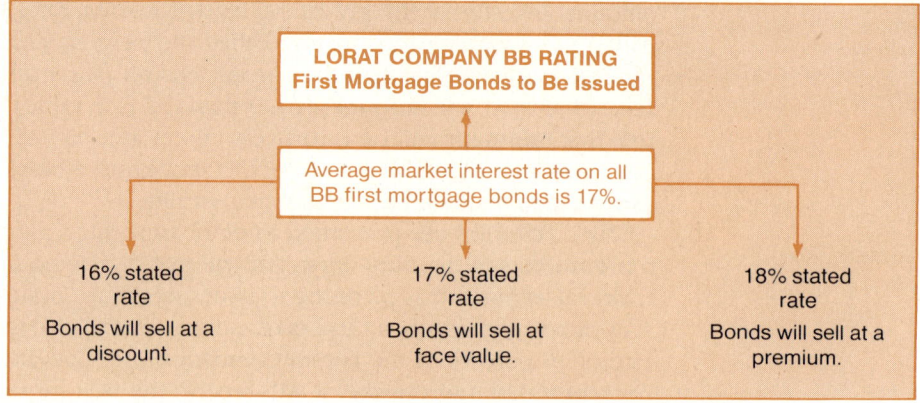

The premium and the discount arise as a result of differences in the average market rate of interest on a comparable grade of bond and the particular stated rate on these bonds. A knowledge of this fact suggests the approach to the accounting for the amortization of the premium and discount elements given in the illustrations which follow.

Calculation of the Exact Price of Bonds to Yield a Given Rate

The exact price that an investor must pay for the bonds to yield a given rate can be determined by a compound interest computation or by reference to a *bond yield table*. To illustrate the compound interest computation, assume that 20-year (40 semiannual periods), 16½ percent bonds with a face of $100,000 are issued at a price to yield 16 percent (or 8 percent every six months); the interest is to be paid semiannually. The calculation of the issue price involves the determination of the *present value* at the issue date of two separate items (see Chapter 7 for a review of present value concepts): (1) the face amount of the bonds discounted at the yield rate, and (2) the interest payments discounted at the yield rate. This calculation is shown below.

Present value of the face amount of $100,000 (a single sum) for 40 periods at yield rate of 8% = ($100,000 × 0.046031) . . . . $ 4,603.10
Add: Present value of 40 interest payments of $8,250 = (½ × 16½% × $100,000) (an ordinary annuity) each at yield rate of 8% = ($8,250 × 11.924613). 98,378.06
Total price to yield 16% annually $102,981.16

The foregoing bonds would be said to sell at approximately 103 percent of face. The price derived in the calculation shows that a premium is expected since the effective interest rate of 16 percent is below the stated or face interest rate of 16½ percent.

Methods of Amortization of Premium and Discount

In developing the accounting for the issuance of bonds, two methods of **amortization of the premium and discount on bonds payable** (the writing off of these items to bond interest expense) are presented: (1) the *straight line method,* and (2) the *interest method.* Theoretically, bond interest expense should be measured by the amount of the effective interest; that is, the yield rate multiplied by the **carrying value** of the bonds (face plus unamortized premium, or face minus unamortized discount) at the beginning of each interest period. This method results in the use of the **interest method of amortization**. The Accounting Principles Board states in its *Opinion 21* that the interest method is the correct one to be used for the amortization of discount or premium on nontrade notes receivable and payable issued at an interest rate that is substantially lower than the current borrowing rate; but it implies that it is equally applicable to discount or premium on bonds payable. The APB states that

> . . . the difference between the present value and the face amount should be treated as discount or premium and amortized as interest expense or income [revenue] over the life of the note in such a way as to result in a constant rate of interest when applied to the amount outstanding at the beginning of any period. This is the "interest" method.' . . . However, other methods of amortization may be used if the results obtained are not materially different from those which result from the interest method.[4]

Practitioners have interpreted the last provision in the foregoing statement as permitting the use of the **straight line method** (recognition of equal interest expense each period over the life of the bonds) in those cases where the results obtained are not materially different from those resulting from the use of the interest method. In many cases, the difference is not material, and thus the simpler straight line method is still extremely popular.

Three examples follow showing the accounting for the issuance of bonds at a price other than face amount. They are first treated using the simpler straight line method of amortization (B set). The interest method of amortization is then used with the same three examples in the C set of illustrations.

Examples Using Straight Line Amortization

Example B–1: Bonds Issued at a Premium on an Interest Date

Assume that on July 1, 1987, the Bonkers Corporation is authorized to issue 16½ percent first mortgage bonds with a face value of $100,000 and a maturity date of June 30, 2007. Interest is paid semiannually on June 30 and December 31. Books are closed each December 31. All the bonds are issued on July 1, 1987, for $102,981.16 (see previous calculation) to yield 16 percent.

---

[4]*Opinions of the Accounting Principles Board, No. 21,* "Interest on Receivables and Payables" (New York: AICPA, August 1971), paragraph 15.

Journal Entry to Record the Issue The issuance of these bonds to banks and insurance companies is recorded as follows:

1987 Jul.	1	Cash.. First Mortgage Bonds Payable..................... Premium on Bonds Payable........................ To record the issuance of 16½ percent first mortgage bonds due June 30, 2007.	102,981.16	100,000.00 2,981.16

Statement Disclosure A balance sheet prepared on July 1, 1987, would show bonds payable and premium on bonds payable as follows:

> Long-term liabilities:
>   16½% first mortgage bonds payable,
>   due June 30, 2007 .... $100,000.00
>   Add: Premium on bonds payable 2,981.16
>   Total long-term liabilities $102,981.16

The assets pledged as security for the bonds payable would be disclosed in the following footnote:

> Land and buildings costing $300,000 (market value $350,000) are pledged as security for the bonds payable.

The method of disclosure of the premium on bonds payable is consistent with the concept that the right-hand side of the balance sheet describes the sources of business funds. The footnote discloses important information that may influence the decision of an investor to buy or not to buy the company's bonds.

Recording Bond Interest Expense and Amortization of Premium
As the premium account is reduced by periodic amortization, it becomes smaller on each subsequent statement. Again, this procedure is consistent with the concept that when bonds are issued at a premium each interest payment contains, in effect, a payment of the interest expense on the debt and also a partial return of the premium element borrowed. If part of the $2,981.16 premium is repaid, a balance sheet prepared at a later date would naturally show a smaller carrying value.

The amount received from the issuance of the bonds is $2,981.16 greater than the amount that must be repaid at maturity. This amount is not a gain, for by definition a gain or revenue cannot result directly from the borrowing process. The premium arose because the *stated rate of interest* on the bonds issued was higher than the prevailing market rate on similar grade bonds. Therefore, it is sound accounting practice to allocate part of the premium on bonds payable to each interest period as a reduction of the periodic bond interest expense. In summary, under the straight line amortization method, equal bond interest expense is recognized each period. This equal expense is the total cash paid for bond interest expense over the life of a bond issue, adjusted—and reduced—by equal periodic amortization of the premium on bonds payable.

The bond interest expense of the Bonkers Corporation is recorded on December 31, 1987, as follows:

1987 Dec.	31	Bond Interest Expense	8,175.47	
		Premium on Bonds Payable	74.53	
		Cash		8,250.00
		To record the semiannual bond interest payment and amortization; the amount of amortization is $2,981.16 ÷ 40 semiannual periods = $74.53.		

If the $2,981.16 premium on the bonds payable represents a reduction in interest over the entire 20-year life of the bonds, it is evident that by the straight line amortization method the reduction in interest for the six months ended December 31, 1987, is $2,981.16 divided by 40 semiannual periods, or $74.53.

This compound entry emphasizes that the $8,250 constitutes the payment of measured bond interest expense of $8,175.47 and a partial return of the premium element borrowed, the $74.53 amortized. (For the problems in this text, premiums or discounts on bonds payable should be amortized each time the bond interest expense is recorded to emphasize that this amortization is an adjustment of the bond interest.) Even though the compound entry is acceptable under the straight line method, two separate entries may be made: (1) an entry to record the payment or accrual of the bond interest, and (2) a separate entry to record the semiannual amortization of the premium.[5]

---

[5]These two entries as of December 31, 1987, for the Bonkers Corporation could be:

In the cash payments journal:

1987 Dec.	31	Bond Interest Expense	8,250.00	
		Cash		8,250.00
		To record cash payment for semiannual interest.		

In the general journal:

1987 Dec.	31	Premium on Bonds Payable	74.53	
		Bond Interest Expense		74.53
		To record amortization of premium for six months.		

Assuming the use of straight line amortization of the premium on bonds payable, the proof of the $8,175.47 semiannual bond interest figure can be calculated by another means, as follows:

Cash payments to be made:	
Face value of bonds at maturity	$100,000.00
Total interest (16½% × 20 years × $100,000)	330,000.00
Total cash payments	$430,000.00
Cash receipts:	
Bonds with face value of $100,000 issued for	102,981.16
Net interest expense for 20 years	$327,018.84
Net semiannual interest expense:	
$327,018.84 / 40 semiannual periods	$ 8,175.47

Retirement of Bonds at Maturity Assume that the 16½ percent first mortgage bonds payable are repaid *(retired)* on June 30, 2007. After the June 30, 2007, semiannual interest payment entry is made, the Premium on Bonds Payable account has a zero balance. The second entry records the retirement of the bonds at maturity.

2007				
Jun.	30	Bond Interest Expense	8,175.51	
		Premium on Bonds Payable	74.49[a]	
		Cash		8,250.00
		To record the last semiannual interest payment on the 16½ percent bonds payable and the last semiannual amortization of bond premium.		
	30	First Mortgage Bonds Payable	100,000.00	
		Cash		100,000.00
		To record the retirement of the 16½% bonds payable at maturity.		

[a]The last amortization debit will be $0.04 less than all the others [$2,981.16 − (39 × $74.53)] due to rounding.

Example B–2: Bonds Issued at a Discount on an Interest Date

Assume that on July 1, 1987, the Davidson Company is authorized to issue 16 percent debenture bonds with a face value of $200,000 and a maturity date of June 30, 1997. Interest is paid semiannually on June 30 and December 31. Books are closed each December 31. All the bonds are issued on July 1, 1987, for $181,742.94. This is a price that will yield 18 percent. The bonds sell at a discount because the **yield rate** (the prevailing market rate on similar grades of debenture bonds) is higher than the stated (or contract) rate of interest on the bonds issued.

Journal Entry to Record the Issue The issuance of the bonds to banks and insurance companies is recorded as follows:

1987 Jul.	1	Cash................................. Discount on Bonds Payable........................ Debenture Bonds Payable......................... To record the issuance of 16 percent debenture bonds due June 30, 1997.	181,742.94 18,257.06	200,000.00

Statement Disclosure A balance sheet prepared on July 1, 1987, would disclose bonds payable and discount on bonds payable as follows:

Long-term liabilities:		
16% Debenture bonds payable, due June 30, 1997 .	$200,000.00	
Deduct: Discount on bonds payable	18,257.06	
Total long-term liabilities		$181,742.94

Note the similarity of this method of disclosure to that of a premium on bonds payable.

Recording Bond Interest Expense and Amortization of Discount

The following compound entry records the first semiannual interest payment by the Davidson Company and semiannual amortization of the Discount on Bonds Payable account by the straight line method.

1987 Dec.	31	Bond Interest Expense .... Cash .... Discount on Bonds Payable .... To record semiannual bond interest payment and amortization; the amount of amortization is $18,257.06 ÷ 20 semiannual periods = $912.85.	16,912.85	16,000.00 912.85

This entry indicates that the measured absolute semiannual interest expense is $16,912.85, not $16,000. Assuming the straight line method of amortization, the measured interest is equal to the cash interest payment plus a pro rata share of the discount—in effect, a part of the total interest cost over the entire life of the bonds. This accounting procedure, therefore, recognizes the reason for the discount on the bonds—that the stated rate of interest was lower than the prevailing market interest rate on similar grades of securities.

The proof of this semiannual bond interest expense can be seen by the following calculation:

Cash payments to be made:	
Face value of bonds at maturity	$200,000.00
Total interest (16% × 10 years × $200,000)	320,000.00
Total cash payments	$520,000.00
Cash receipts:	
Bonds with face value of $200,000 issued for	181,742.94
Net interest expense for 10 years	$338,257.06
Net semiannual interest expense:	
$\dfrac{\$338{,}257.06}{20\text{ semiannual periods}}$	$ 16,912.85

Retirement of Bonds at Maturity On June 30, 1997, the 16 percent debenture bonds payable are retired. After the June 30, 1997, semiannual interest payment entry is made, the Discount on Bonds Payable account has a zero balance. The second entry records the retirement of the bonds at maturity.

1997				
Jun.	30	Bond Interest Expense	16,912.91	
		Cash		16,000.00
		Discount on Bonds Payable		912.91[a]
		To record the last semiannual interest payment and final amortization of bond discount on the 16 percent bonds payable.		
	30	Debenture Bonds Payable	200,000.00	
		Cash		200,000.00
		To record the retirement of 16 percent bonds payable at maturity.		

[a]The last amortization credit will be $0.06 more than all the others [($18,257.06 − (19 × $912.85)] due to rounding.

Example B–3: Bonds Issued at a Discount Requiring Interest to Be Accrued at End of Year

Assume the same facts as stated in Example B–2 except that the Davidson Company issued the 16 percent bonds to banks and insurance companies on March 31, 1987, rather than on July 1, 1987, and that the interest dates are September 30 and March 31.

Journal Entry to Record the Issue Not all the steps in the preceding examples need to be repeated. The journal entry to record the issue is:

1987				
Mar.	31	Cash	181,742.94	
		Discount on Bonds Payable	18,257.06	
		Debenture Bonds Payable		200,000.00
		To record the issuance of 16 percent debenture bonds due March 31, 1997.		

Recording Bond Interest Expense and Amortization of Discount

The entries from September 30, 1987, to March 31, 1988, with the accompanying calculation of straight line amortization included as a part of the explanation to the journal entries, are shown below:

1987				
Sep. 30	Bond Interest Expense		16,912.85	
	Cash			16,000.00
	Discount on Bonds Payable			912.85
	To record semiannual bond interest and amortization; the amount of amortization is $912.85.[a]			
Dec. 31	Bond Interest Expense		8,456.43	
	Accrued Bond Interest Payable			8,000.00
	Discount on Bonds Payable			456.43
	To record the accrual of bond interest and the amortization for three months; the amount of amortization is $456.43.[b]			
1988				
Mar. 31	Bond Interest Expense		8,456.42	
	Accrued Bond Interest Payable		8,000.00	
	Cash			16,000.00
	Discount on Bonds Payable			456.42
	To record payment of semiannual interest and recognition of interest expense for three months in 1988; the amount of amortization is $456.42 (to make six months' total $912.85).			

[a] Calculation: 6/120 × $18,257.06 = $912.85. The fraction used in this calculation is stated in months as a means of establishing an approach that will be useful when interest is recorded for a partial period, such as the accrual at the end of year.
[b] Calculation: 3/120 × $18,257.06 = $456.43.

Another method of calculating the amount of amortization for the period October 1 through December 31, 1987, is to take 3/6 or 1/2 of the semiannual amortization of $912.85 = $456.43.

Examples Using the Interest Method of Amortization

The same three examples are now used with the interest method of amortization. Many of the accounting issues are identical regardless of whether the straight line method or the interest method of amortization is used.

Example C–1: Bond Issued at a Premium on an Interest Date

On July 1, 1987, the Bonkers Corporation is authorized to issue 16½ percent first mortgage bonds with a face value of $100,000 and a maturity date of June 30, 2007. Interest dates are June 30 and December 31. Books are closed each December 31. These bonds are issued on July 1, 1987, for $102,981.16, a price to yield 16 percent.

Journal Entry to Record Issue The issuance of the bonds is recorded as follows:

| 1987
Jul. | 1 | Cash...
    First Mortgage Bonds Payable.....................
    Premium on Bonds Payable........................
        To record the issuance of 16½ percent first mortgage bonds
        due June 30, 2007. | 102,981.16 | 100,000.00
2,981.16 |

Recording Bond Interest Expense and Amortization of Premium

The interest method of amortization, sometimes referred to as the effective yield method, measures the interest expense on the basis of the effective yield rate multiplied by the carrying value of the bonds at the beginning of each interest period. The amount of amortization is *residually determined*; it is the difference between the effective interest computed as described above and the stated interest, calculated by multiplying the stated interest rate by the face value of the bonds.

The effective interest calculation at 16 percent (8 percent each six months) and the attendant amortization by the interest method for December 31, 1987, and June 30, 1988, appear below (calculations are shown in the journal entries):

| 1987
Dec. | 31 | Bond Interest Expense (8% × $102,981.16) ....
Premium on Bonds Payable ($8,250.00 − $8,238.49).........
    Cash (Nominal rate of 8¼% × $100,000) ....
        To record payment of interest and amortization of premium on
        a 16 percent annual yield basis. | 8,238.49
11.51 | 8,250.00 |
| 1988
Jun. | 30 | Bond Interest Expense [8% × ($102,981.16 − $11.51)] ....
Premium on Bonds Payable ($8,250.00 − $8,237.57).........
    Cash ....
        To record payment of interest and amortization of premium on
        a 16 percent annual yield basis. | 8,237.57
12.43 | 8,250.00 |

Comparison of Straight Line and Interest Methods

An important fact is that the *total amount of bond interest expense over the life of the bond* recognized by the interest method is exactly the same as that recognized by the straight line method. The two methods differ in the amount of bond interest expense recognized in each period. The interest method will produce a *constant rate* of expense on the carrying value of the bonds payable (face plus unamortized premium). The straight line method will produce a constant absolute interest expense amount. The diagrams shown in Figure 14–3 reveal this difference.

When the straight line method is used, both the amount of the measured bond interest expense and the amount of premium amortization are uniform over time. If the bond interest expense is divided by the carrying value of the bonds each year, the resulting interest rate would be increasing, a phenomenon contrary in theory to what actually exists. When the interest method is used, the absolute amount of measured bond interest expense decreases over

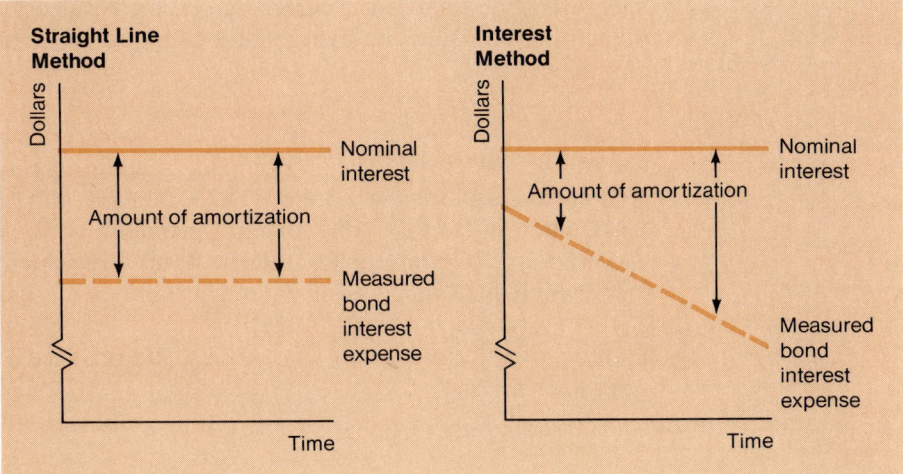

Figure 14-3 **Comparison of Measured Interest by the Straight Line and Interest Methods for Bonds Issued at a Premium**

time with the amount of amortization increasing over time. Under this latter method, the interest rate calculated on the carrying value of the bonds will remain constant since as the bond interest expense declines so does the carrying value. In Figure 14-3, the total amount of amortization is the same under both methods.

The diagram in Figure 14-3 shows an overall view of the entire life of the bond issue. Recall that the total bond interest expense over the entire life of the bond issue is the same under each of the two amortization methods. The difference is in the amount of bond interest expense that is recognized for each period of that life. The difference during the *first year* (the first twelve months) in the results of the two amortization methods is shown in Figure 14-4.

	Method		Difference	
	Interest	Straight Line	Absolute	Percent
Bond interest expense (first 12 months)............	$16,476.06	$16,350.94	$125.12	0.8%
Amortization of premium (first 12 months)	23.94	149.06	125.12	522.6%

Figure 14-4 **Comparison of Interest (Example C-1) and Straight Line (Example B-1) Methods for First Year (16½ Percent, 20-Year Bonds Issued to Yield 16 Percent)**

Although the absolute difference between the bond interest expense and the first year's amortization is $125.12, the percentage in the resulting expense is less than one percent (0.8 percent), a difference that would not be material in this particular case. The large percentage difference between the first year's amortization of the premium is irrelevant to the materiality decision since *APB Opinion No. 21* refers only to the difference arising from the measured bond interest expense—" . . . the results obtained."[6] It is presented here to show the total difference between the two methods during the first year.

Example C–2: Bonds Issued at a Discount on an Interest Date

On July 1, 1987, the Davidson Company is authorized to issue 16 percent debenture bonds with a face value of $200,000 and a maturity date of June 30, 1997. Interest dates are June 30 and December 31. Books are closed each December 31. On July 1, 1987, all the bonds are issued for $181,742.94, a price yielding 18 percent (or 9 percent each six months).

Journal Entry to Record the Issue   The issuance of these bonds is recorded as follows:

1987 Jul.	1	Cash... Discount on Bonds Payable............................. Debenture Bonds Payable............................. To record the issuance of 16 percent debenture bonds due June 30, 1997.	181,742.94 18,257.06	 200,000.00

Recording Bond Interest Expense and Amortization of Discount

The procedure used in applying the interest method in a discount case is exactly the same as it is with a premium case. The effective interest is measured by multiplying the effective semiannual interest rate (9 percent in the Davidson Company case) by the carrying value of the bonds at the beginning of the interest period. The amount of the periodic amortization is always residually determined and is the difference between the measured effective bond interest expense and the stated interest amount. The effective interest calculation and the attendant amortization for the Davidson Company bonds by the interest method for December 31, 1987, and June 30, 1988, follow:

1987 Dec.	31	Bond Interest Expense (9% × $181,742.94)................ Cash (8% × $200,000)................................... Discount on Bonds Payable ($16,356.86 − $16,000)........ To record payment of interest and amortization of discount on an 18 percent annual yield basis.	16,356.86	 16,000.00 356.86
1988 Jun.	30	Bond Interest Expense [9% × ($181,742.94 + $356.86)] ...... Cash (8% × $200,000)................................... Discount on Bonds Payable............................. To record payment of interest and amortization of discount on an 18 percent annual yield basis.	16,388.98	 16,000.00 388.98

---

[6]*APB Opinion No. 21,* "Interest on Receivables and Payables" (New York: AICPA, August 1971), paragraph 15.

The recording of interest expense and the accompanying amortization by the interest method for the remaining interest period follows a pattern similar to that of the first two illustrated above.

Comparison of Straight Line and Interest Methods   The difference between the results obtained from the use of the two amortization methods when amortizing a discount is shown in Figure 14–5. When the straight line method is used both the amount of the measured bond interest expense and the amount of discount amortization are uniform (equal) over time. Yet the interest rate calculated on the carrying value of the bonds will decrease over time, because in subsequent years' calculation of this rate a constant numerator will be divided by an increasing denominator (face of bonds less the remaining unamortized discount). Under the interest method, on the other hand, the absolute amount of the measured bond interest expense increases over time, with the amount of the discount amortization also increasing over time. The interest rate on the carrying value is constant over the life of the bonds. The method of calculating the price to be paid for the bonds guarantees this uniform rate to occur. Again, it should be noted that total bond interest expense and total amortization are not affected by the method of amortization used.

The diagram in Figure 14–5 shows an overall view of the entire life of the bond issue. As indicated with the premium case, the total bond interest expense over the entire life of the bond issue is the same under each of the two amortization methods. The difference is in the amount of bond interest expense that is recognized for each period of that life. The difference during

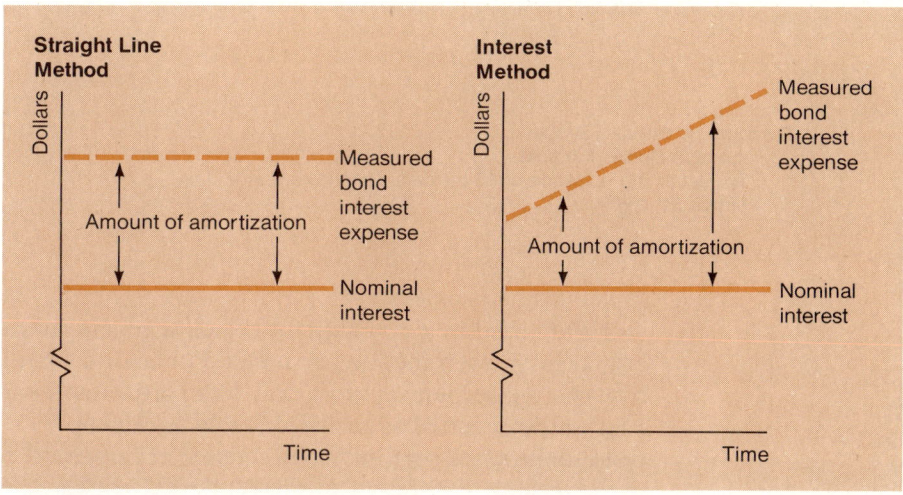

Figure 14–5   **Comparison of Measured Interest by the Straight Line and Interest Methods for Bonds Issued at a Discount**

	Method		Difference	
	Interest	Straight Line	Absolute	Percent
Bond interest expense (first 12 months)	$32,745.84	$33,825.70	$1,079.86	3.3%
Amortization of discount (first 12 months)	745.84	1,825.70	1,079.86	144.8%

Figure 14–6 Comparison of Interest (Example C–2) and Straight Line (Example B–2) Methods for First Year (16 Percent, 10-Year Bonds Issued to Yield 18 Percent)

the first year (first 12 months) in the results of the two amortization methods is shown in Figure 14–6.

Although the absolute difference between the bond interest expense and the first year's amortization is $1,079.86, the percentage in the resulting expense is only 3.3 percent, a difference that would probably not be deemed material in this particular case. The large percentage difference between the first year's amortization of the discount is irrelevant to the materiality guideline set forth by *APB Opinion No. 21*.

Example C–3: Bonds Issued at a Discount Requiring Interest to Be Accrued at End of Year

For this illustration, assume the same facts in Example C–2 except that the Davidson Company issued the 16 percent bonds on March 31, 1987, rather than on July 1, 1987, and the interest dates are September 30 and March 31.

Journal Entry to Record the Issue The journal entry to record the issue is:

1987				
Mar.	31	Cash	181,742.94	
		Discount on Bonds Payable	18,257.06	
		Debenture Bonds Payable		200,000.00
		To record the issuance of 16 percent debenture bonds due March 31, 1997.		

Recording Bond Interest Expense and Amortization of Discount A tool often used in accounting for bonds is an amortization table. It is particularly helpful when the interest method of amortization is used, perhaps more so when the accountant must deal with partial interest period data. Figure 14–7 shows a partial amortization table for Example C–3. The amortization table summarizes periodic bond interest expense and amortization and aids in the making of the regular interest period entries. It is extremely useful in making the accrued bond interest expense adjusting entry.

(1) 6 Months' Interest Period Ending	(2) Carrying Value at Beginning (Face − Discount)	(3) 6 Months' Interest Expense (9% × Col. 2)	(4) 6 Months' Interest Payment (8% × Face)	(5) 6 Months' Discount Amortization (Col. 3 − Col. 4)	(6) Carrying Value at End (Col. 2 + Col. 5)
September 30, 1987	$181,742.94	$16,356.86	$16,000	$356.86	$182,099.80
March 31, 1988	182,099.80	16,388.98	16,000	388.98	182,488.78
September 30, 1988	182,488.78	16,423.99	16,000	423.99	182,912.77

Figure 14–7   **Partial Amortization Table by Interest Method**

The September 30, 1987, entry for the first interest payment is the same as that made for December 31, 1987, under Example C–2:

1987 Sep. 30	Bond Interest Expense (see Col. 3, Figure 14–7)............. Cash .... Discount on Bonds Payable (See Col. 5, Figure 14–7) .... To record the payment of interest and amortization of discount on an 18 percent annual yield basis.	16,356.86	16,000.00 356.86

The adjusting entry for December 31, 1987, is:

1987 Dec. 31	Bond Interest Expense (½ × $16,388.98^a)............... Accrued Bond Interest Payable .... Discount on Bonds Payable (½ × $388.98^b).............. To record the accrual of interest and the amortization of discount by the interest method.	8,194.49	8,000.00 194.49

^{a}Figure taken from Column 3, Figure 14–7.
^{b}Figure taken from Column 5, Figure 14–7.

The entry for payment of interest on March 31, 1988, is:

1988 Mar. 31	Bond Interest Expense (½ × $16,388.98^a)............... Accrued Bond Interest Payable .... Cash .... Discount on Bonds Payable (½ × $388.98^b).............. To record the payment of semiannual interest and the amortization of discount for three months by the interest method.	8,194.49 8,000.00	16,000.00 194.49

^{a}Figure taken from Column 3, Figure 14–7.
^{b}Figure taken from Column 5, Figure 14–7.

Note that the effective interest is only computed on a precise present value basis each six months. The interest for a shorter period is simply the pro rata portion (one-half in the foregoing case) of the six months' measured interest.

The Issuance of Bonds between Interest Dates

The preceding examples emphasized the basic accounting procedures, the reasons for amortizing bond premiums and discounts, and the amortization procedure by both the straight line and interest methods. A more complex problem involving the issuance of bonds between interest dates is presented below. In this illustration and other complex problems, only the straight line amortization method is used. The general principle, however, is the same regardless of which amortization method is used.

Bonds may be authorized by the stockholders but not issued for several months or even years because market conditions are not favorable. Some of the bonds may be issued and the rest held until a specific need for the additional funds arises. Often, the time needed for clerical work delays the issuance past an interest date.

The interest on bonds issued between interest dates will have accrued from the last interest date to the date of issuance. Since the bonds carry an inherent promise to pay not only the face value at maturity but six months' interest at each interest date, it is customary in these cases for the investor to pay the issue price of the bonds *plus an amount equal to the accrued interest. In turn, the first interest payment to the bondholder will be for one full interest period*—six months' interest—thereby returning to the bondholder the accrued interest paid plus the interest earned from the date of purchase to the current interest date. This practice allows corporations to avoid the expense of computing and paying interest for fractional periods.

Example D: Bonds Are Issued between Interest Dates Using Straight Line Amortization

Assume that on October 1, 1985, the Greensboro Company is authorized to issue 18 percent debenture bonds with a face value of $1,000,000 and a maturity date of October 1, 1995. The semiannual interest dates are April 1 and October 1. The bonds are held until *June 1, 1987,* when bonds with a face value of only $400,000 are issued to financial corporations at 105 plus accrued interest. The amount of cash that the Greensboro Company receives is $432,000: $420,000 for the bonds plus $12,000 for accrued interest. Note that the promise to pay six months' interest is not retroactive beyond April 1, 1987, the last interest date preceding the date of issuance. Note also that the stated rate or contract interest rate and face value are used for calculating the accrued interest. On October 1, 1987, the purchaser of the bonds receives an interest payment of $36,000, although the interest on $400,000 at 18 percent from June 1 to October 1 is only $24,000. The payment includes a return of the $12,000 that the investor paid for accrued interest on June 1, as illustrated in Figure 14–8.

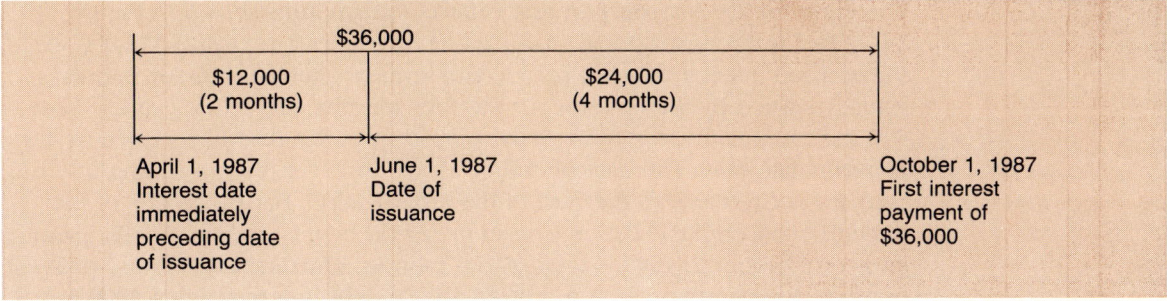

Figure 14–8 Accumulation of Interest

Journal Entry to Record the Issue The Greensboro Company records the bond issuance as shown below:

1987				
Jun.	1	Cash..	432,000	
		Debenture Bonds Payable........................		400,000
		Premium on Bonds Payable......................		20,000
		Accrued Bond Interest Payable..................		12,000
		To record the issuance of bonds at 105 plus accrued interest.		

The accrued interest is credited to a current liability account since it must be repaid on the next interest date.

Recording Bond Interest Expense and Amortization of Premium

In a complex example such as the Greensboro Company one, it is simpler to make two entries to record interest and amortization: (1) to record the cash payment for interest (this would actually be made in the cash payments journal), and (2) to record the amortization of the premium (this would be made in the general journal). These entries for the Greensboro Company, in general journal form, are shown below:

1987				
Oct.	1	Bond Interest Expense...........................	24,000	
		Accrued Bond Interest Payable.................	12,000	
		Cash...		36,000
		To record the payment of semiannual interest at 18 percent on bonds payable.		
	1	Premium on Bonds Payable......................	800	
		Bond Interest Expense...........................		800
		To record the amortization of the bond premium for 4 months [($20,000 ÷ 100 mos.) × 4 = $800].		

The entry for the interest payment reflects the amounts shown in Figure 14–8; that is, the semiannual cash payment includes a return of $12,000 for the accrued interest that was sold to the investor plus $24,000 for interest actually earned by the investor for the four months' use of the money. Note that the **amortization period** is the period from the date of issuance to the maturity date only. The date of authorization and even the preceding interest date are not relevant to the start of the amortization. For the bonds of the Greensboro Company, the amortization period begins on June 1, 1987, and ends on October 1, 1995, a total of 100 months. The amount of bond premium to be amortized each month by the straight line method is $200 = ($20,000 ÷ 100 months); the amount for four months is $800 = ($200 × 4).

Assuming that the Greensboro Company closes its books on a calendar year basis, the following adjusting entries are made on December 31, 1987:

1987				
Dec.	31	Bond Interest Expense	18,000	
		Accrued Bond Interest Payable		18,000
		To record the accrual of bond interest for three months, computed as follows: $400,000 × 0.18 × 3/12 = $18,000.		
	31	Premium on Bonds Payable	600	
		Bond Interest Expense.		600
		To record the amortization of bond premium for three months by the straight line method: 3 × $200 = $600.		

The effect of the end-of-year adjustment is that the Bond Interest Expense account reflects the correct interest expense for 1987 ($40,600) incurred for the seven months during which the bonds were outstanding (June 1 to December 31).

On April 1, 1988, the next regular interest date, the following entries are made to record the payment of interest and the amortization of the bond premium:

1988				
Apr.	1	Bond Interest Expense	18,000	
		Accrued Bond Interest Payable	18,000	
		Cash		36,000
		To record the payment of semiannual bond interest.		
	1	Premium on Bonds Payable	600	
		Bond Interest Expense.		600
		To record the amortization of bond premium for three months (3 × $200 = $600).		

Note that only three months' amortization of the bond premium is recorded; the other three months' was applicable to a 1987 expense and was so recorded in the December 31, 1987, adjusting entry.

If the interest method had been used by the Greensboro Company, its accountant would measure the bond interest expense for the additional three months at the end of the fiscal year by multiplying the yield rate by the carrying value of the bonds as of October 1, 1988. The accountant then would multiply the results by 3/6 (1/2), the fraction of the semiannual period falling in 1987. The remaining procedure would be consistent with that previously described for the interest method.

Retirement of Bonds Payable

The borrowing company may retire its outstanding bonds at the maturity date by paying the contract face value in cash. Even if the bonds were originally issued at a premium or a discount, the entry to record the retirement *at maturity* is a debit to Bonds Payable and a credit to Cash for the face value. Serial bonds are retired in serial installments. Assume, for example, a $500,000, 10-year serial bond issue at face amount with $50,000 to be retired at the end of each year. The annual retirement of principal entry (ignoring any interest payments) is again a debit to Bonds Payable and a credit to Cash for $50,000.[7] The timing of the retirement of serial bonds is a matter of contractual provision. The foregoing example is a *regular serial bond* issue. Another popular variation involves the issuing corporation to provide for annual retirement dates to begin at a fixed number of years after date of issue—these are *deferred serial bonds*.

Other methods of bond **retirement** discussed below include the retirement of all or part of a bond issue by call (the exercise of the issuer's right to redeem) or purchase on the open market before the bonds are actually due; the conversion of bonds payable into capital stock; and the retirement of bonds with sinking fund assets and the attendant problem of accumulating the sinking fund. Another form of retirement is described according to the source of the funds used for the retirement. New bonds with favorable features are issued with the proceeds used to retire old bonds. Since no new accounting principles are introduced by this device, called *refunding*, it is not illustrated here.

Retirement of Bonds before Maturity

Recall or Purchase A corporation that has issued bonds may find itself with more cash than it expects to need for operations, thus permitting it to retire all or part of its outstanding bonded indebtedness prior to maturity date. Management may decide to retire the bonds immediately if the cash is available, if there appears to be no better use now or in the future for the excess cash, and if it wishes to decrease the fixed charges for the bond interest. Bonds may be retired early in different ways—the bonds may contain a

---

[7] The accounting for interest on serial bonds issued at a premium or discount is complex and beyond the scope of this book.

call provision, or they may be purchased on the open market in the way any other investor would purchase them. For bonds to be *callable,* the indenture must contain a provision permitting the issuing corporation to redeem the bonds by paying a specified price, usually slightly above face value.

Retirement of bonds at a price less than the carrying value (face plus unamortized premium or face minus unamortized discount) adjusted to the date of retirement results in a gain; a loss is incurred if the purchase price exceeds the adjusted carrying value. Material gains and losses on the early retirement of bonds payable are classified in the income statement as extraordinary items and are shown in the income statement in a separate section after net income from ordinary operations.

To illustrate the early retirement of bonds payable, suppose that the Greensboro Company (see Example D for information) found itself with excess cash on October 1, 1988. Management decided to retire all of the debenture bonds which had been issued on June 1, 1987. These bonds were retired at 104½ on the October 1, 1988, interest date. The liability accounts as of this date follow:

Debenture Bonds Payable   Acct. No. 251

				1987				
				Jun.	1		CR62	400,000

Premium on Bonds Payable   Acct. No. 252

1987					1987				
Oct.	1		J75[a]	800	Jun.	1	16,800[b]	CR62	20,000
Dec.	31		J79[a]	600					
1988									
Apr.	1		J91[a]	600					
Oct.	1		J98[a]	1,200					

[a]The last four entries to this account are posted from the general journal. If two entries are made for the interest and amortization, this is correct. If a compound entry were made, it would have to be made in the cash payments journal.
[b]The 16,800 figure is the December 31, 1988, balance of the account.

The carrying value of the liability (face plus unamortized premium) is $416,800. Thus if the Greensboro Company pays $418,000 = (1.045 × $400,000) for the bonds, there is a loss on retirement of $1,200 = ($418,000 − $416,800). This information is recorded in the journal as follows:

1988					
Oct.	1	Debenture Bonds Payable	400,000	
		Premium on Bonds Payable	16,800	
		Loss on Retirement of Bonds Payable	1,200	
		Cash		418,000
		To record the retirement of the debenture bonds at 104½.		

Once the foregoing is posted, the two liability accounts will be reduced to zero. Again, the loss on retirement of bonds payable, if material, is shown as an extraordinary loss in the extraordinary items section of the income statement.

Conversion of Bonds into Common Stock

To make bonds more attractive to investors and thus increase their marketability, the bond agreement may give investors the option of exchanging bonds on a given interest date, or dates, for a certain number of shares of stock, usually common, of the issuing company. These securities, referred to as *convertible bonds,* have the advantage of offering the investor an initial fixed return on investment combined with an opportunity to share in profitable operations of the issuing company by later conversion of the bonds to stock. The terms and conditions for conversion are designated in the bond indenture. Conversion is at the option of the bondholder, so that if earnings are unfavorable he or she does not need to exercise the conversion privilege and may retain the fixed return and greater security of the bonds. The conversion of bonds into stock changes the legal and accounting status of the security holder from creditor to owner. When conversion occurs, the most often used accounting procedure is the book value method. It transfers the *carrying value of the convertible bonds payable* to *paid-in capital accounts,* which probably will include both Common Stock and Paid-In Capital—Excess over Par Value, Common.

Bond Sinking Fund

The borrowing corporation may agree in the bond indenture to accumulate cash in a **bond sinking fund** to retire the bonds at maturity. Periodic cash payments are made to a sinking fund trustee, usually a bank or a trust company. These payments are ordinarily invested in revenue-producing securities. When the bonds mature, the sinking fund trustee sells the securities, and the proceeds are used to pay the bondholders. In some instances, the corporation itself may act as trustee, thereby retaining control over the activities of the sinking fund.

To illustrate the operation of a simple sinking fund managed by a trustee, assume that on the authorization date, January 1, 1987, the Rimson Corporation issues 10-year sinking fund bonds with a face value of $600,000.[8] The bond indenture provides that at the end of each year a deposit of $60,000—reduced by any net earnings of the fund from its investments—be made to

---

[8] Many sinking funds are acturially determined with the deposits being of equal amount. These deposits (R) are determined as follows:

$$R = \frac{\text{Future amount needed in sinking fund } (A_O)}{\text{Table factor for } A_{O_{n,i}}}.$$

the trustee. The entry to record the initial deposit with the trustee is shown below:

1987 Dec. 31	Bond Sinking Fund	60,000	
	Cash		60,000
	To record the initial sinking fund deposit with the trustee.		

The Bond Sinking Fund account is a controlling account. The trustee must invest all the available cash in the fund in revenue-producing securities. As a practical matter, it would not always be possible for the trustee to invest odd amounts of cash or to purchase securities immediately on the receipt of cash. Hence, the fund is composed of a number of individual items, such as cash, securities, and accrued interest receivable. Rimson Corporation does not need to maintain a separate general ledger account for each asset contained in the bond sinking fund because the trustee will keep detailed records.

If, at the end of the second year, the trustee reports net earnings (revenue earned minus trustee's fees) of $4,800 from investments in bonds, the following entries record the second deposit:

1988 Dec. 31	Bond Sinking Fund	4,800	
	Bond Interest Earned.............................		4,800
	To record net earnings of the bond sinking fund per report of the trustee.		
31	Bond Sinking Fund	55,200	
	Cash		55,200
	To record the second sinking fund deposit with the trustee; the amount is $60,000 less the earnings of $4,800, or $55,200.		

The following entry is made to record the retirement of the bonds at maturity by the payment of assets in the bond sinking fund (observe that the trustee would have to convert any investments to cash before the sinking fund bonds could be retired):[9]

1997 Jan. 1	Sinking Fund Bonds Payable	600,000	
	Bond Sinking Fund		600,000
	To record the retirement of the bonds at maturity date with the sinking fund.		

---

[9] Any excess assets left in the sinking fund after retirement are returned to the corporation by the trustee.

The bond sinking fund item is classified in the assets section as a long-term investment on each balance sheet except the one prepared at the end of the year preceding the date of the retirement of the bonds. On this statement, the bond sinking fund should be shown as a current asset, and sinking fund bonds payable should be disclosed as a current liability.

Restriction of Retained Earnings for Bond Redemption

In addition to the requirement for sinking fund deposits, the bond indenture may require a restriction of retained earnings up to the amount in the sinking fund. The bondholders thus are provided with twofold protection: the sinking fund ensures the availability of adequate cash for the redemption of the bonds, and the restriction of retained earnings for bond redemption reduces the amount available for distribution as dividends to the stockholders. This restriction tends to improve the company's cash position and its ability to meet its regular needs as well as its requirements for bond interest and bond sinking fund payments. An improved cash position also is advantageous in enabling the company to meet its regular operational cash requirements and to maintain a favorable credit standing. As discussed in Chapter 13, the entry to record this restriction is a debit to Retained Earnings and a credit to Retained Earnings—Restricted for Bond Retirement. After the bonds are retired, this entry is reversed.

Long-Term Notes Payable

Another long-term liability is mortgage notes payable, sometimes called mortgages payable, arising from the purchase on credit of land and buildings in which the purchaser gives to the seller a long-term note with a mortgage attached. A **mortgage note payable** involves the issuance of a long-term note with an assignment of an interest in property to the seller as collateral in case the purchaser defaults on the payment of the long-term obligation.

Money may be borrowed on a long-term basis by the issuance of a **long-term unsecured note payable**. Firms or individuals with a good credit rating are able to borrow significant amounts for longer periods of time and to issue to the credit grantor an unsecured long-term note. The credit grantor will require that annual financial statements be filed with it—usually a balance sheet and income statement.

If interest is payable semiannually, the accounting for the issuance of both items is essentially the same as the accounting for bonds payable issued at face value. The typical transaction would involve a debit to Cash and a credit to Long-Term Unsecured Notes Payable. The accounting for interest payment is exactly the same as for bonds issued at face value.

A special long-term debt disclosure issue is considered next—that of short-term debt expected to be refinanced.

Current Liabilities (Short-Term Debt) Expected to Be Refinanced

In its *Statement No. 6,* the FASB has taken the position that if a company (1) intends to refinance certain current liabilities on a long-term basis and (2) has or can demonstrate the ability to refinance them, it should show these liabilities on its balance sheet as long-term liabilities. *Refinancing* means that the company intends to substitute long-term debt such as bonds payable or ownership securities such as common stock for the short-term debt. *Ability to refinance* on a long-term basis must be demonstrated by one of two acts:

1. Actually having issued bonds or equity securities after the balance sheet date but before the statement is issued.

2. Having signed an agreement that will enable the company to refinance the short-term debt on a long-term basis when it becomes due.

This treatment causes the working capital amount to be more realistic. Thus, the statement is more useful to a user.

Managerial Analysis—Number of Times Bond Interest Earned

A long-run solvency measurement of particular importance to investors and hence to the issuer of bonds is the number of times bond interest expense is earned. Investors look to this ratio as a measure of the safety of their investment; it is an indication of a firm's ability to meet its annual bond interest requirement. Issuers of bonds look to it as meeting a standard that is necessary to be able to attract long-term funds in the future. To illustrate, assume that Afco Corporation has bonds outstanding with a face value of $500,000 and that in 1987 it reports bond interest expense of $40,000, income taxes of $60,000, and net income (after income taxes) of $80,000. Since bond interest expense is deductible in determining taxable income, the following formula seems appropriate:

$$\text{Number of times bond interest expense is earned} = \frac{\text{Net income} + \text{Income tax expense} + \text{Annual bond interest expense}}{\text{Annual bond interest expense}}$$

Substituting the amounts given for the Afco Corporation:

$$\text{Number of times bond interest earned} = \frac{\$80,000 + \$60,000 + \$40,000}{\$40,000} = 4.5 \text{ times.}$$

Although there are no established universal standards of safety, a ratio of 4.5 appears to be relatively safe for investors holding bonds of Afco Corporation.

The safety margin depends in part on the type of collateral used, the type of business in which the firm is engaged, and the liquidity of the firm. Investors in a privately owned public utility with mortgageable plant assets, for example, may feel secure with a ratio of 2.5 times, whereas investors in businesses without mortgageable assets may feel insecure with a ratio smaller than five times.

Internal Control Measures

Internal control over bonds payable is similar to that for capital stock. It involves the adequate protection of the unissued bond certificates and the safeguarding of cash receipts from the issuance and cash payment for semiannual interest.

If a company issues its own bonds, unissued certificates must be protected. Blank certificates should be prenumbered and periodically verified to be intact by unannounced inspections. Separation of duties should provide that the person who records cancellation (when bondholders sell their bonds to another party) not be the same person who issues new bonds to the new bondholders. Cancelled bond certificates should be clearly marked in some way to prevent their reissuance. If they are destroyed, a procedure is needed to verify the certificate numbers of the destroyed certificates and the fact that actual destruction occurred. Procedures for updating the names, addresses, Social Security numbers, and certificate numbers of current individual and institutional bondholders should be designed to prevent anyone putting fictitious names on the list to receive interest checks. If the list of current bondholders is computerized, passwords at various steps in the computer program can help prevent unauthorized access to the files.

If a separate registrar issues the bond certificates, as is usual, that in itself adds an element of internal control—the separation of duties from the involved corporation. The receipt of cash and the periodic outflow of cash for interest payments require the internal control measures discussed in Chapter 8.

Glossary

Amortization of premium or discount on bonds payable The periodic writing off of the premium or discount on bonds payable as a decrease or an increase to interest expense, accomplished by either the straight line method or the interest method.

Amortization period The period for which the premium or discount should be amortized; it spans the period from the date of issuance of the bonds to the maturity date.

Bearer bond A bond issued without the owner's name being registered; the title to this kind of bond is deemed to be vested in the holder of the bond.

Bond A written promise under the corporate seal to pay a specified sum of money on a specified or determinable future date to the order of a person named in the bond certificate or to the order of bearer.

Bond certificate Evidence that a loan has been made to a corporation; it contains the written promise under the corporate seal to pay a specific sum of money on a specified or determinable future date to the order of a person named in the certificate or to the order of bearer.

Bondholder A creditor who has lent money to a corporation or government and has received a bond certificate as evidence of the loan.

Bond indenture A contract between the corporation issuing bonds and the bondholders, containing all privileges, restrictions, covenants, and other provisions of the contract.

Bond sinking fund A special fund in which assets are segregated for the purpose of retiring bonds, usually at maturity.

Callable bond A bond on which the issuing corporation retains an option to retire before maturity at a specified price on specific dates.

Carrying value of bonds payable The face or principal amount of the bonds payable plus the unamortized premium (or face minus the unamortized discount) on bonds payable.

Contract interest rate See *Stated interest rate.*

Convertible bond A bond that contains a provision entitling the bondholder to exchange the bond at predetermined amounts for capital stock at the bondholder's option.

Coupon bond A bond that has the periodic interest coupons attached to the bond certificates.

Debenture bonds Often referred to as debentures; they are unsecured bonds carrying no pledge of collateral; also see *Unsecured bonds.*

Default The failure by the issuer to pay interest and principal on bonds.

Discount on bonds payable The amount by which the face value of bonds exceeds the price received for the bonds on issuance; it arises because the nominal (contract) rate of interest is lower than the going market rate of interest on similar grade bonds.

Face value The principal or par amount of bonds that will be repaid on the maturity date.

Income bond A bond with a provision that interest payments will depend upon earnings.

Interest method of amortization A method of amortization of premium or discount on bonds payable in which periodic amortization is the difference between the effective interest expense determined by multiplying the effective yield rate by the bond carrying value at the beginning of the interest period and the nominal interest calculated on the face of the bonds.

Leverage The practice of trading on the bondholders' equity, that is, of borrowing money at a given rate of interest and utilizing the borrowed funds in the business to earn a higher rate of return than the borrowing rate.

Long-term liabilities Obligations that are due to be paid after the coming year or operating cycle.

Long-term unsecured notes payable Long-term notes issued to grantors of credit without a pledge of collateral; they are long-term liabilities.

Mortgage notes payable Long-term notes issued with a pledge of specified property, plant, and equipment for the loan granted.

Premium on bonds payable The excess of the price received for bonds payable above face value; it arises because the stated (contract) rate of interest is higher than the going market rate of interest on similar grade bonds.

Registered bond A bond whose owner's name is recorded by the issuing corporation; for this bond to be transferred to another individual, it must be endorsed and a request must be filed to have the owner's name changed on the records of the issuing corporation.

Retirement The payment of the principal amount at maturity or at an earlier date.

Secured bond A bond for which the issuing corporation pledges some part of the firm's assets as security.

Serial bonds Bonds that mature in periodic installments and will be paid at stated intervals of time.

Sinking fund A fund created to retire bonds.

Stated interest rate The rate of interest that is written in a bond indenture; it is the rate based on face or principal amount that will be paid on the stated periodic interest dates; this rate is also called the nominal interest rate.

Straight line method A method of amortizing bond premium or discount in equal amounts for each period over the term of the bonds in such a manner that equal interest expense will be recognized during each period.

Trading on the bondholders' equity See *Leverage*.

Unsecured bonds Bonds for which there is no pledge of assets for security; also called debenture bonds or often simply debentures.

Yield rate The rate of interest that, when applied on a discount basis to principal and interest, will yield a present value equal to the selling price of the bonds.

Questions

Q14–1 Distinguish between stated and effective interest rates on bonds.

Q14–2 On January 1, 1987, the Columbia Sales Company issued 10-year, 12 percent bonds having a face value of $1,000,000. The proceeds to the company were $950,000; that is, on January 1, 1987, the bonds had a market price of 95 percent of face value. Explain the nature of the $50,000 difference between the face value and the market value of the bonds on January 1, 1987.

Q14–3 In light of the definition and criteria of liabilities set forth by the FASB, justify the classification of bonds payable and accrued interest payable as liabilities.

Q14–4 What is the difference (a) between a stock certificate and a bond? (b) Between a bond and a promissory note?

Q14–5 Identify the following terms: (a) registered bonds, (b) bearer bonds, (c) secured bonds, (d) unsecured bonds, (e) serial bonds, (f) convertible bonds, (g) coupon bonds, (h) income bonds.

Q14–6 A corporation needs cash for the acquisition of plant assets. It is considering three alternative sources: additional common stock, 14 percent preferred stock, and 13 percent bonds. (a) What are some of the factors involved in this decision? (b) Will the decision affect the present common stockholders? Discuss.

Q14–7 (a) What are the general requirements for the approval of a bond issue? (b) Should the stockholders approve a bond issue? Why or why not?

Q14–8 (a) Why does the buyer of a bond purchased between interest dates pay the seller for accrued interest on the bond? (b) Is the accrued interest included in the stated purchase price of the bond?

Q14–9 List three ways that bonds can be retired.

Q14–10 Does the total amount of premium or discount amortized over the life of a bond differ if the interest method is used instead of the straight line method? What is the difference between the two methods?

Q14–11 The APB in *Opinion 21* stated that the interest method should be used in amortizing premium and discount on certain long-term debt instruments. From a theoretical point of view, state why this method is superior to the straight line method.

Q14–12 What is the significance of collateral? How is an asset which is pledged as collateral disclosed in the financial statements?

Q14–13 Why are bonds not always issued at the prevailing interest rate, thereby eliminating bond discount or bond premium?

Q14–14 (a) What is the difference to the issuing corporation between common stock issued at a premium and bonds issued at a premium? (b) Does revenue directly result from either?

Q14–15 When should short-term debt be excluded from current liabilities? Explain.

Exercises

E14–1
Premium and discount concepts

Fill in the proper response: (1) premium or (2) discount.

a. If the market rate of interest exceeds a bond's stated interest rate, the bonds will sell at a _____.
b. If a bond's stated interest rate exceeds the market rate of interest, the bonds will sell at a _____.
c. In computing the carrying value of a bond, unamortized _____ is subtracted from the face value of the bond.
d. In computing the carrying value of a bond, unamortized _____ is added to the face value of the bond.
e. If a bond sells at a _____, an amount in excess of the face value of the bond is received on the date of issuance.
f. If a bond sells at a _____, an amount less than the face value of the bond is received on the date of issuance.

E14–2
Issuance of bonds payable at face and recording interest

On the date of authorization, January 1, 1987, the McSwain Corporation issued 20-year, 15 percent bonds to financial corporations with a face value of $800,000 at 100. Interest is payable each January 1 and July 1.

1. Record the issuance of the bonds.
2. Record the first interest payment.
3. Record the accrued interest expense on December 31, 1987.
4. Record the payment of semiannual interest on January 1, 1988.
5. Record the last interest payment and the retirement of the bonds on January 1, 2007.

E14–3
Carrying value issues

Compute the carrying value as of October 1, 1987, of each of the following:

a. Ten-year bonds payable issued at 105 on October 1, 1987; face value $300,000, stated interest rate of 16 percent payable on April 1 and October 1 of each year.
b. Twenty-year bonds payable issued at 90 on October 1, 1987; face value $500,000, stated interest rate of 14 percent payable on April 1 and October 1 of each year.
c. Ten-year, 15 percent bonds with a face value of $600,000 issued at 102 on April 1, 1987. Interest is payable each April 1 and October 1. Assume straight line amortization.
d. Twenty-year, 14 percent bonds with a face value of $400,000 issued at 98 on April 1, 1987. Interest is payable each April 1 and October 1. Assume straight line amortization.
e. Ten-year, 13½ percent bonds with a face value of $700,000 issued at 97 on April 1, 1987. Interest is payable each April 1 and October 1. Assume amortization by the interest method and a yield rate of 14 percent.
f. Ten-year, 14 percent bonds with a face value of $200,000 issued at 105½ on April 1, 1987. Interest is payable each April 1 and October 1. Assume amortization by the interest method and a yield rate of 13 percent.

14 / Long-Term Liabilities

E14–4
Issuance of bonds—straight line amortization method

On the date of authorization, January 1, 1987, the Oxford Corporation issued 10-year, 16 percent bonds to financial corporations with a face value of $1,000,000 at 104. Interest is payable each January 1 and July 1.

1. Record the issuance of the bonds.
2. Record the first interest payment and amortization of the premium by the straight line method.
3. Record the accrued interest expense and amortization of the premium on December 31, 1987.
4. Open a Bond Interest Expense account and post the transactions.
5. Prepare a schedule proving the interest cost for 1987 by the straight line amortization method.

E14–5
Issuance of bonds—interest method of amortization

On the date of authorization, July 1, 1987, the Peters Investment Company issued 10-year, 14 percent bonds to financial corporations with a face value of $2,000,000, for $1,803,636.58, which is a price to yield 16 percent. Interest is payable June 30 and December 31.

1. Record the issuance of the bonds on July 1, 1987.
2. Record the December 31, 1987, and June 30, 1988, interest payments with accompanying amortization, using the interest method of amortization.
3. Briefly compare the reasons for using the interest method as compared to the straight line method of amortization.

E14–6
Issuance of bonds—interest method of amortization

On the date of authorization, July 1, 1987, the Owens Corporation issued 20-year, 14½ percent bonds to financial corporations with a face value of $600,000, for $619,997.34, which is a price to yield 14 percent. Interest is payable each June 30 and December 31.

1. Record the issuance of the bonds.
2. Record the interest expense payment and amortization of the premium on December 31, 1987, by the interest method.
3. Record the two interest payments for 1988 and amortization of the premium by the interest method.

E14–7
Issuance of bonds between interest dates

On October 1, 1987, the Elizabeth Corporation issued 16 percent bonds to financial corporations with a face value of $400,000 for $411,960 plus accrued interest. The bonds mature on June 1, 1995, and interest is paid each June 1 and December 1. The straight line amortization of premium is recorded each time bond interest expense is recorded. Prepare all the entries relating to the bond issue during 1987.

E14–8
Issuance of bonds—interest method of amortization (requires familiarity with compound interest techniques)

Dobblestein Corporation issued the following during 1987:

a. Issued on May 1, 1987, 15 percent, 20-year debenture bonds to financial corporations with a face of $300,000 at a price to yield 16 percent. Interest is paid each May 1 and November 1.
b. Issued on May 1, 1987, 14 percent, 10-year debenture bonds to banks with a face of $800,000 at a price to yield 12 percent. Interest is paid each May 1 and November 1.
c. Issued on November 1, 1987, 14 percent, 10-year debenture bonds to insurance companies with a face of $800,000 at a price to yield 16 percent. Interest is paid each May 1 and November 1.
d. Issued on November 1, 1987, 14 percent, 10-year debenture bonds to financial corporations with a face of $500,000 at a price to yield 13 percent. Interest is paid each May 1 and November 1.

(continued on next page)

Prepare journal entires related to the above bond issuances for the period from May 1, 1987, through November 1, 1987, assuming that amortization by the interest method is recorded.

E14–9
Convertible bonds

On July 1, 1985, Holmes Corporation issued $200,000 of 10-year, 15 percent convertible bonds to the Tew Corporation at 102. Each $10,000 bond is convertible into 1,000 shares of Holmes Corporation, $5 par value common stock. It is now July 1, 1987, and Tew Corporation is considering converting its bonds into common stock.

1. Why would a bondholder opt to convert bonds into common stock?
2. Assume that Tew Corporation does convert its bonds into common stock on July 1, 1987. Make the appropriate entry on the Holmes Corporation books, assuming straight line amortization of the premium.
3. Since amounts supplied by creditors and stockholders are both on the same side of the accounting equation, will the conversion of the bonds into stock by the Tew Corporation change the position of Tew's investment in the Holmes Corporation's balance sheet? Explain.

E14–10
Sinking fund

On January 1, 1987, the Beta Corporation issued 10-year sinking fund bonds to banks with a face value of $500,000. The bond indenture provides that at the end of each year, a deposit of $50,000—reduced by any net earnings of the fund from its investments—be made to the trustee. Interest is earned each year in the amount of 10 percent on the fund balance as of the beginning of the year. Beta must also restrict retained earnings for the amount of money in the sinking fund.

Required:

1. Prepare the necessary journal entries on the books of Beta Corporation for the sinking fund and the accompanying restriction on retained earnings for December 31, 1987, through December 31, 1990.
2. Prepare the necessary journal entries on January 1, 1997.

E14–11
Issuance of bonds—straight line amortization method

On the date of authorization, January 1, 1987, the Helen Company issued 10-year, 18 percent bonds to an insurance company. Interest is paid semiannually on January 1 and July 1. On July 1, 1987, the accountant for the Helen Company prepared the following journal entry to record the payment of bond interest and the straight line amortization of the discount:

1987				
Jul.	1	Bond Interest Expense	23,000	
		Cash		22,500
		Discount on Bonds Payable		500
		To record the bond interest expense for the preceding six months.		

From this information, reconstruct the journal entry that was made to record the issuance of the bonds. Show all your calculations.

E14–12
Issuance and early retirement of bonds

On October 1, 1987, the Alpha Psi Corporation issued 10-year, 16 percent bonds to banks with a face of $200,000 at 100. Interest dates are April 1 and October 1. The maturity date is October 1, 1997. Apha Psi Corporation closes its books annually on December 31. On April 1, 1989, the Alpha Psi Corporation, having accumulated some excess cash, purchased its own bonds on the open market at 101½. Prepare all entries (including adjusting entries but excluding closing entries) related to these bonds from October 1, 1987, to April 1, 1989.

A Problems

P14–1A
Issuance of bonds—straight line amortization method

On April 1, 1987, the stockholders of the Tronton Corporation authorized the issuance of 20-year, 16 percent first mortgage bonds with a face value of $800,000. The bonds mature on April 1, 2007, and interest is payable each April 1 and October 1.

Required: Make journal entries to record the following transactions:

1987

Jun.	1	Issued all the bonds to financial corporations at 104 plus accrued interest.
Oct.	1	Paid the semiannual interest. (Assume that premium on bonds payable is amortized by the straight line method each time bond interest expense is recorded.)
Dec. 31		Accrued the bond interest.
	31	Closed the Bond Interest Expense account.

1988

Apr.	1	Paid the semiannual interest.
Oct.	1	Paid the semiannual interest.
Dec. 31		Accrued the bond interest.
	31	Closed the Bond Interest Expense account.

P14–2A
Issuance of bonds—interest method of amortization

On July 1, 1987, the Timberly Corporation issued 10-year, 14 percent bonds to a bank with a face value of $800,000 at $844,073.99, which is a price to yield 13 percent. Interest is payable June 30 and December 31.

Required:

1. Prepare journal entries to record the following transactions, assuming that the interest method of amortization is used:

1987

Jul.	1	Issued all the bonds for cash.
Dec. 31		Paid the semiannual interest and recorded the proper amortization.

1988

Jun. 30		Paid the semiannual interest and recorded the proper amortization.
Dec. 31		Paid the semiannual interest and recorded the proper amortization.

2. Calculate and state what would be the carrying value of the bonds payable after each of the foregoing interest payments.

P14–3A
Issuance of bonds—straight line amortization method; calculation of number of times bond interest is earned

On March 1, 1987, the authorization date, the Tyrrell Company issued 10-year, 15 percent debenture bonds to an insurance company with a face value of $600,000 at 96. Interest is payable each March 1 and September 1. The company closes its books on December 31. The following selected transactions and adjustments were made:

1987

Mar.	1	Issued all the bonds for cash.
Sep.	1	Paid the semiannual interest.
Dec. 31		Accrued the bond interest.

1988

Mar.	1	Paid the semiannual interest.
Sep.	1	Paid the semiannual interest.
Dec. 31		Accrued the bond interest.

(continued on next page)

1992

Mar.	1	Paid the semiannual interest.
Sep.	1	Paid the semiannual interest.
Dec.	31	Accrued the bond interest.

1997

Mar.	1	Paid the semiannual interest.
	1	Paid the bonds outstanding at maturity.

Required:

1. Record the foregoing transactions. (Assume that the discount is amortized by the straight line method each time the bond interest expense is recorded.)

2. Assuming that the Tyrrell Corporation with an income tax rate of 40 percent had a net income of $333,500 in 1992, calculate the number of times bond interest is earned in 1992.

P14–4A
Various bond issue situations

The stockholders of the Ames Corporation authorized a 10-year, $500,000 bond issue with a stated interest rate of 15 percent on April 1, 1987. The maturity date is March 31, 1997. Interest is payable on March 31 and September 30.

Required: Consider the following independent cases:

1. Due to unfavorable market conditions, the bonds are not issued to financial institutions until December 1, 1988, at 103 plus accrued interest. Prepare the journal entries required on December 1, 1988, and December 31, 1988 (year-end). Assume straight line amortization.

2. The Ames Corporation issues the bonds to the Elon Investment Company on April 1, 1987, at 99. The underwriter then sells the bonds at 100. Prepare the journal entry required on April 1, 1987, on Ames's books.

3. The bonds are issued to a bank at 105 on April 1, 1987. On April 1, 1992, the corporation purchases the bonds on the open market at 102. Prepare the journal entry to record the purchase and retirement of the bonds after the March 31, 1992, interest payment has been made and recorded. Assume straight line amortization.

P14–5A
Preparing an amortization table and recording various bond transactions by interest method (requires familiarity with compound interest techniques)

On March 1, 1987, the authorization date, the Franklin Company issued five-year, 14 percent debenture bonds with a face value of $600,000 at a price to yield 12 percent. Interest is payable each March 1 and September 1. The company closes its books on December 31 and uses the interest method of amortization. The following selected transactions and adjustments were made:

1987

Mar.	1	Issued all the bonds for cash.
Sep.	1	Paid the semiannual interest.
Dec.	31	Accrued the bond interest.

1988

Mar.	1	Paid the semiannual interest.
Sep.	1	Paid the semiannual interest.
Dec.	31	Accrued the bond interest.

1992

Mar.	1	Paid the semiannual interest.
	1	Paid the bonds outstanding at maturity.

Required:

1. Determine the issue price and prepare an amortization table.
2. Record the foregoing transactions.

P14–6A
Reconstructing original issue data

The Reliant Company issued 16 percent bonds to an investment corporation on September 1, 1987, at a certain price plus accrued interest. The bonds mature on June 1, 1997. Interest is paid each June 1 and December 1. The accountant for the company recorded the first semiannual bond interest payment as follows:

1987				
Dec.	1	Bond Interest Expense	1,660	
		Accrued Bond Interest Payable	1,600	
		Discount on Bonds Payable		60
		Cash		3,200
		To record the payment of semiannual bond interest and the straight line amortization of the discount for three months.		

Required:

1. Compute the following: (a) face value of bonds issued, and (b) original issue price and discount.
2. Reconstruct the journal entry to record the issuance of the bonds on September 1, 1987.
3. Does the fact that the Reliant Company bonds sell at a discount mean that they have a relatively low rating (such as a B rating)? Discuss.

P14–7A
Thought-provoking problem: deciding on method of acquiring long-term funds

The Fenton Corporation, with 200,000 shares of $10 par value common stock outstanding, needs an additional $2,000,000 for plant expansion. Three plans for raising the funds have been proposed to the board of directors: (a) the issuance of additional common stock at $10 par value; (b) the issuance of 14 percent preferred stock; and (c) the issuance of 20-year, 13½ percent bonds. It is estimated that the corporation will earn $1,600,000 annually before bond interest and will pay income taxes of 42 percent.

Required:

1. Determine the earnings per share of common stock under each plan. Assume that the securities will be issued at *par* or *face* value.
2. Using earnings per share as a basis for your decision, which plan should the Fenton Corporation employ?
3. Discuss factors other than earnings per share that might influence your decision.

B Problems

P14–1B
Issuance of bonds— straight line amortization method

On April 1, 1987, the stockholders of the David Corporation authorized the issuance of 20-year, 16 percent first mortgage bonds with a face value of $900,000. The bonds mature on April 1, 2007, and interest is payable each April 1 and October 1.

Required: Make journal entries to record the following transactions:

1987		
Jun.	1	Issued all the bonds to a bank at 102 plus accrued interest.
Oct.	1	Paid the semiannual interest. (Assume that premium on bonds payable is amortized by the straight line method each time bond interest expense is recorded.)
Dec.	31	Accrued the bond interest.
	31	Closed the Bond Interest Expense account.

(continued on next page)

1988

Apr.	1	Paid the semiannual interest.
Oct.	1	Paid the semiannual interest.
Dec.	31	Accrued the bond interest.
	31	Closed the Bond Interest Expense account.

P14–2B

Issuance of bonds—interest method of amortization

On July 1, 1987, Crumm Corporation issued 10-year, 15 percent bonds to an investment company with a face value of $500,000 for $526,485.03, which is a price to yield 14 percent. Interest is payable June 30 and December 31.

Required:

1. Prepare journal entries to record the following transactions, assuming that the interest method of amortization is used:

1987

Jul.	1	Issued all the bonds for cash.
Dec.	31	Paid the semiannual interest and recorded the proper amortization.

1988

Jun.	30	Paid the semiannual interest and recorded the proper amortization.
Dec.	31	Paid the semiannual interest and recorded the proper amortization.

2. Calculate and state what would be the carrying value of the bonds payable after each of the foregoing interest payments.

P14–3B

Issuance of bonds—straight line amortization method; calculation of number of times bond interest is earned

On March 1, 1987, the authorization date, the Clunny Company issued 10-year, 14 percent debenture bonds to a bank with a face value of $400,000 at 98. Interest is payable each March 1 and September 1. The company closes its books on December 31. The following selected transactions and adjustments were made:

1987

Mar.	1	Issued all the bonds for cash.
Sep.	1	Paid the semiannual interest.
Dec.	31	Accrued the bond interest

1988

Mar.	1	Paid the semiannual interest.
Sep.	1	Paid the semiannual interest.
Dec.	31	Accrued the bond interest.

1992

Mar.	1	Paid the semiannual interest.
Sep.	1	Paid the semiannual interest.
Dec.	31	Accrued the bond interest.

1997

Mar.	1	Paid the semiannual interest.
	1	Paid the bonds outstanding at maturity.

Required:

1. Record the foregoing transactions. (Assume that the discount is amortized by the straight line method each time the bond interest expense is recorded.)

2. Assuming that the Clunny Company with an income tax rate of 40 percent had a net income of $220,000 in 1992, calculate the number of times bond interest is earned in 1992.

P14–4B
Various bond issue situations

The stockholders of the Nisson Corporation authorized a 10-year, $750,000 bond issue with a stated interest rate of 15 percent on April 1, 1987. The maturity date is March 31, 1997. Interest is payable on March 31 and September 30.

Required: Consider the following independent cases:

1. Due to unfavorable market conditions, the bonds are not issued to banks until December 1, 1988, at 103 plus accrued interest. Prepare the journal entries required on December 1, 1988, and December 31, 1988 (year-end). Assume straight line amortization.
2. The Nisson Corporation issues the bonds to the Salmonid Investment Company on April 1, 1987, at 99. The underwriter then sells the bonds at 100. Prepare the journal entry required on April 1, 1987, on Nisson's books.
3. The bonds are issued to an insurance company at 105 on April 1, 1987. On April 1, 1992, the corporation purchases the bonds on the open market at 101. Prepare the journal entry to record the purchase and retirement of the bonds after the March 31, 1992, interest payment has been made and recorded. Assume straight line amortization.

P14–5B
Preparing an amortization table and recording various bond transactions by interest method (requires familiarity with compound interest techniques)

On April 1, 1987, the authorization date, the Person Corporation issued five-year, 12 percent first mortgage bonds with a face value of $400,000 at a price to yield 14 percent. Interest is payable each April 1 and October 1. The company closes its books on December 31 and uses the interest method of amortization. The following selected transactions and adjustments were made:

1987

Apr.	1	Issued all the bonds for cash.
Oct.	1	Paid the semiannual interest.
Dec. 31		Accrued the bond interest

1988

Apr.	1	Paid the semiannual interest.
Oct.	1	Paid the semiannual interest.
Dec. 31		Accrued the bond interest.

1992

Apr.	1	Paid the semiannual interest.
	1	Paid the bonds outstanding at maturity.

Required:

1. Determine the issue price and prepare an amortization table.
2. Journalize the foregoing transactions.

P14–6B
Reconstructing original issue data

The Sanctum Company issued 16 percent bonds to a bank on September 1, 1987, at a certain price plus accrued interest. The bonds mature on June 1, 1997. Interest is paid each June 1 and December 1. The accountant for the company recorded the first semiannual bond interest payment as follows:

(continued on next page)

1987 Dec. 1	Bond Interest Expense	6,610	
	Accrued Bond Interest Payable	6,400	
	Discount on Bonds Payable		210
	Cash		12,800
	To record the payment of semiannual bond interest and the straight line amortization of the discount for three months.		

Required:

1. Compute the following: (a) face value of bonds issued, and (b) original issue price and discount.

2. Reconstruct the journal entry to record the issuance of the bonds on September 1, 1987.

3. Does the fact that Sanctum Company's bonds sell at a discount mean that they have a relatively low rating such as a BB? Discuss.

P14–7B

Thought-provoking problem: determining various bonds payable issues

The board of directors of the Howard Corporation has approved management's recommendation to expand the production facilities. The firm currently manufactures only heavy machinery, but plans are being developed for diversifying the corporation's activities through the production of smaller and more versatile equipment.

The directors have concluded that, whereas a number of factors should influence their choice of the method of financing to be used in obtaining investment funds of $2,000,000 needed, *prime attention should be devoted to observing the expected income effect on the corporate equity of the common stockholders as measured by earnings per share.* They are considering the following methods of providing funds:

a. They can issue 50,000 shares of $35 par value common stock at a net price of $40 a share.

b. They can issue 20,000 shares of $100 par value, 16 percent, cumulative preferred stock at a net price of $100 a share.

c. They can issue 20-year, 15 percent bonds with a $1,980,000 face value at a premium to produce $2,000,000.

d. They can issue 20-year, 14½ percent bonds with a $2,040,000 face value at a discount to produce $2,000,000.

The corporation's liability and stockholders' equity structure is:

Current liabilities.	$ 180,000
14% bonds payable, due in 10 years	300,000
12% preferred stock, cumulative, $100 par value; authorized 100,000 shares, issued 10,000 shares	1,000,000
Common stock, $35 par value; authorized 200,000 shares, issued 40,000 shares	1,400,000
Paid-in capital—excess over par value, common.	150,000
Retained earnings.	600,000

Management expects that the new investment of $2,000,000 will yield a return of 22 percent before interest and income taxes, which will be computed at a 45 percent rate. The corporation is currently realizing a return of 20 percent on all long-term capital before interest and income taxes.

Required:

1. Compare the expected effect of each proposed financial method on the corporate equity of the common stockholders. Use straight line amortization.

2. Applying the single expressed criterion established by the directors, what method of financing should be employed? Why?

3. Discuss other factors that must influence a decision of this type.

15 Temporary and Long-Term Investments

Introduction

Most companies list various kinds of investments among their assets in either a current or noncurrent asset section. The Eaton Corporation reported the following investments in its 1983 *Annual Report:*[1]

	(Thousands of Dollars) December 31	
	1983	1982
Current assets: Short-term investments—at cost (approximates market)...............	$355,028	$43,828
Other assets: Investment in and advances to finance subsidiaries....	37,816	35,215
Investment in associate companies	20,247	46,325

As of December 31, 1983, the total investments made up 18.1 percent = ($413,091,000 ÷ $2,279,084,000) of the total assets of the Eaton Corporation. These amounts represent a material portion of the total assets. As indicated, some of these investments are classified as current and some as noncurrent. Such investments, their differences, similarities, and valuation are the subject of this chapter.

Learning Goals

1. To differentiate between long-term and temporary investments.
2. To understand and record temporary investments.
3. To be acquainted with the process of valuation of investments.

---
[1]Eaton Corporation, *Annual Report,* 1983, p. 20.

4. To be acquainted with the valuation process of temporary and long-term investments in marketable equity securities at lower of cost or market.

5. To record unrealized losses and gains in valuation of marketable equity securities.

6. To be acquainted with the method of disclosure of the unrealized losses and gains arising out of the valuation process.

7. To understand and record transactions using the cost and equity methods of accounting for long-term investments in stock.

8. To record the amortization of premium and discount on long-term investments in bonds by both the straight line and the interest methods.

9. To determine and record appropriate end-of-period adjustments for accrued interest on bond investments.

10. To understand the nature of other long-term investment items.

Temporary Investments

Nature of Temporary Investments

A firm should invest any seasonal excess of cash as it becomes available in order to maximize income by putting idle, nonrevenue-producing funds to work when they are not needed in the operations of the business. If it is expected that the funds will be needed in the near future, a **temporary investment** can be made; that is, they can be temporarily invested in readily salable securities which management intends to hold for a relatively short period of time and then sell when funds are needed. In order to be readily salable, the securities should be listed on a stock exchange or have another accepted medium through which they could be and normally are sold. They should be high-grade bonds, other debt instruments, or **blue-chip stocks** listed on a stock exchange by a financially strong corporation. The primary emphasis with temporary investments is the preservation of the amount originally invested while earning revenue during the holding period.

Because of the low risk involved, this kind of security usually yields a slightly lower rate of return than other securities, a common characteristic of readily salable, high-grade securities. Such temporary investments are classified as current assets because the intent of management is to convert them back into cash as soon as a seasonal shortage of cash is experienced. The accounting examples that follow illustrate the recording of the purchase of bonds and the receipt of interest and the purchase of stock and the receipt of dividends.

Bonds as Temporary Investments

Assume that on July 1, 1987, Bylinski Corporation purchased as a temporary investment 14 percent, AAA bonds of the Williford Company with a face value of $30,000 at 102 (that is, 102 percent of face). Interest is paid on January 1 and July 1. The brokerage fee and other costs incidental to the purchase are $60. This information is recorded as follows:

1987 July	1	Temporary Investments in Bonds—Bonds of Williford Company . . . Cash . . . . To record the purchase of bonds of the Williford Company as temporary investments.	30,660	30,660

Cost of temporary investments

Temporary investments, like all assets, are recorded at full cost. Cost includes the bond price plus the brokerage fee as well as other incidental costs.

The following points deserve emphasis:

1. In accordance with the generally accepted principle of recording all assets at historical cost, bonds purchased as temporary investments are recorded in one account at full cost. Cost includes the bond price including the addition of the premium or the deduction of the discount, the brokerage fee, and other incidental costs. Thus, no separate premium or discount account is used. With assets, this is the traditional approach.

2. The account title, Temporary Investments in Bonds—Bonds of Williford Company, includes the general ledger control account Temporary Investments in Bonds and the name of the individual bond for posting to a subsidiary record, referred to as an *investment register*. All temporary investments are assumed to be marketable securities, and the account used to record them is sometimes called Marketable Securities.

Assuming that books are closed on December 31, 1987, the accountant for the Bylinski Corporation should accrue the semiannual bond interest in a revenue account, **Bond Interest Earned**, and an accrued receivable asset account called *Accrued Bond Interest Receivable*, as follows:

1987 Dec.	31	Accrued Bond Interest Receivable . . . . Bond Interest Earned. . . . . To accrue the semiannual interest on the Williford Company bonds; 14% × ½ × $30,000.	2,100	2,100

In the foregoing entry the premium element of the temporary investments is not amortized. This procedure is generally acceptable because the length of time that the bonds will be held is not known. It is expected that they will not be held until maturity date. Also, since the bonds will be held for a short time, any amortization results, if applied, would likely be immaterial. The revenue amount in this entry is credited to Bond Interest Earned. This revenue item would be shown as other revenue on the income statement.

The receipt of semiannual interest on January 1, 1988, is recorded as follows:[2]

1988 Jan. 1	Cash..	2,100	
	Accrued Bond Interest Receivable...................		2,100
	To record receipt of semiannual bond interest on the Williford Company bonds.		

To complete the cycle, assume that on February 1, 1988, Bylinski Corporation found that it needed cash and decided to sell the bonds of the Williford Company. They were sold at 101¾ (net of brokerage fees and other costs) plus accrued interest; the transaction is recorded as follows:

1988 Feb. 1	Cash..	30,875	
	Realized Loss on Disposal of Temporary Investments........	135	
	Bond Interest Earned...............................		350
	Temporary Investments in Bonds—Bonds of Williford Company..		30,660
	To record sale of temporary investment securities.		

1. The computation of the income statement item **realized loss on disposal of temporary investments** (the loss occasioned by the actual sale) is:

Original full cost of bonds..	$30,660
Deduct: Selling price of bonds ($30,000 × 101¾%)..............	30,525
Realized loss on disposal of temporary investments.............	$ 135

2. The cash received comes from two sources: (a) the sale of the bonds, $30,525, and (b) the sale of the accrued interest, $350 = (14% × 1/12 × $30,000). Interest accrues as time passes. The Bylinski Corporation has held the bonds for one more month, thus earning interest for that period.

3. The Temporary Investments in Bonds account must be credited with cost.

Realized loss on disposal of temporary investments is shown in the income statement under the caption "other expense." Management must consider this loss, along with the bond interest earned, in evaluating the success of its decision to invest in the bonds of the Williford Company.

---

[2] This cash receipt transaction is normally recorded in the cash receipts journal. It is shown here recorded in general journal form for ease of illustration and teachability.

Stocks as Temporary Investments

To illustrate the recording of a purchase of stock as a temporary investment, assume that on April 1, 1987, Bowen Corporation purchases 200 shares of Edwin Corporation preferred stock at 105, which for stocks means $105 per share. (In this example, for the purpose of initial recording, the par value is irrelevant to the accounting). This stock is listed on the New York Stock Exchange and is readily marketable at any time. Brokerage fees are $108. The entry to record the purchase is:

1987 Apr.	1	Temporary Investments in Stocks—Preferred Stock of Edwin Corporation. . . . . Cash . . . . To record the purchase of 200 shares of Edwin Corporation preferred stock at $105 a share.	21,108	21,108

The amount of the debit to the asset is the full cost, including brokerage fees.

Assume that on July 1, 1987, a quarterly dividend of $1.50 per share is received on the 200 shares of the Edwin Corporation stock. The entry to record the cash and the revenue earned is:

1987 Jul.	1	Cash . . . . Dividends Earned . . . . To record the receipt of a quarterly dividend from the Edwin Corporation.	300	300

Dividends Earned is a revenue account; it is classified under other revenue on the income statement.

To meet a seasonal cash shortage, on September 15, 1987, the preferred stock of Edwin Corporation is sold for 106½ (net of brokerage fees and other costs). The sale is recorded as follows:

1987 Sep.	15	Cash . . . . Temporary Investments in Stocks—Preferred Stock of Edwin Corporation . . . . Realized Gain on Disposal of Temporary Investments . . . . To record sale of preferred stock of Edwin Corporation at $106.50 a share.	21,300	21,108 192

The income statement item **realized gain on disposal of temporary investments** is determined as follows:

Selling price of preferred stock (200 × $106.50)	$21,300
Deduct: Original full cost	21,108
Realized gain on disposal of temporary investments	$ 192

Realized gain on disposal of temporary investments is shown on the income statement under other revenue. Management must consider this amount, along with dividends earned, in evaluating the success of its decision to buy the preferred stock as a temporary investment.

Valuation of Temporary Investments

Ideally, all current assets should be shown at current market price on the balance sheet since this statement should reflect the financial position as of a given time. Certain companies, such as insurance companies, disclose their temporary investments at current market price. Most, however, following generally accepted accounting principles (GAAP), value these securities at either *cost* or **lower of cost or market (LCM)**. These two methods of valuation are discussed in the following sections of this chapter.

Valuation of Temporary Investments at Cost

Current GAAP permit temporary investments in bonds or other debt instruments of other entities to be valued at *either* cost or lower of cost of market. Cost is certainly the simplest of all valuation methods to apply to these securities since they are initially recorded at cost. If they are valued at cost, the current market value, obtainable from the financial page of many daily newspapers, should also be disclosed in the balance sheet by a parenthetical notation, such as the following, to enable the reader to evaluate the item for purposes of financial position analysis:

Assets

Current assets:		
Cash		$ 562,000
Temporary investments in bonds; shown at cost (current market price, $175,000)		158,000
Accounts receivable	$200,000	
Deduct: Allowance for doubtful accounts	8,000	192,000
Merchandise inventory		300,000
Prepaid insurance		2,000
Total current assets		$1,214,000

Even though the current market value is disclosed parenthetically, the securities are *still* valued at cost; that is, only the original cost is added into the figures that are totaled. The cost method of valuation is consistent with the fundamental principle of matching expired actual costs with revenues as well as being consistent with income tax requirements. As stated above, temporary investments in bonds could be valued at lower of cost or market. If they are, the procedures described below for temporary investments in marketable equity securities could be followed.

Valuation of Temporary Investments in Marketable Equity Securities at Lower of Cost or Market

Because of the substantial decline in market value of equity or ownership securities during 1973 and 1974, the Financial Accounting Standards Board concluded that both temporary and long-term investments in marketable equity securities should be shown on the balance sheet at lower of cost or market (LCM) value applied on a basis of comparing the total cost of all marketable equity securities with the market value of all marketable equity securities, the aggregate LCM method.[3] In its *Statement No. 12,* the FASB has defined **equity securities** as including ownership shares or the right to acquire or dispose of ownership shares in a company at fixed or determinable prices. The term does not include certain preferred stock that by its terms either must be redeemed by the issuing company or is redeemable at the option of the investor, nor does it include treasury stock or convertible bonds. In other words, equity securities include primarily all common stock and certain preferred stocks that contain only basic ownership characteristics. If these securities are readily marketable and if management intends to sell them when cash is needed, they are called temporary investments in **marketable equity securities**.

FASB Statement No. 12 applies to *all* marketable equity securities, whether they are purchased as temporary investments or for long-term investments. The discussion in this section emphasizes the valuation of temporary investments. The LCM valuation of long-term investments is considered briefly later in this chapter.

FASB Statement No. 12 requires that all temporary investments in marketable equity securities be valued at LCM, but by implication temporary investments in *other types of securities,* such as bonds, may also be valued at LCM. In the discussion that follows, it will be assumed that the temporary investments involve only equity securities—common stock, for the most part.

When temporary investments are sold, the *realized gain or loss* is determined by comparing the selling price with the original cost, regardless of the method of valuation used. When valuation is by the LCM method, an *unrealized loss* or *gain* may be recorded—one that is recognized before the sale of the securities. Unrealized losses and gains arise from change in the asset valuation account **Allowance to Reduce Temporary Investments in Equity Securities to Market**. (This account reveals the amount by which the total

---

[3]*Statement of Financial Accounting Standards No. 12,* "Accounting for Certain Marketable Securities" (Stamford, Conn.: Financial Accounting Standards Board, December 1975), paragraph 7.

cost of the temporary investments exceeds the total market value.) Both realized and unrealized gains and losses on temporary investments are included in the determination of net income of the period in which they occur.

Example: Valuation of Temporary Investment in Marketable Equity Securities To illustrate the method recommended by the FASB, suppose that the Brummet Company purchased three readily marketable common stocks as a temporary investment during 1987. Suppose further that the Brummet Company held these securities through 1988, and then on January 15, 1989, it sold Common Stock A for $9,500. The accounting for the valuation at December 31, 1987, and December 31, 1988, and the sale on January 15, 1989, is presented in the following paragraphs. Value information concerning the portfolio as of December 31, 1987, is presented below:

Common Stock	Cost When Purchased	Market Value as of December 31, 1987
A	$10,000	$12,000
B	5,000	3,000
C	7,000	2,000
Total	$22,000	$17,000

The difference between the *total cost* of $22,000 and the *total market value* of $17,000 is a $5,000 loss, an *unrealized* one since no sale has been made (this is the aggregate LCM method required by *FASB Statement No. 12*). The recommended title of the loss account is **Unrealized Loss on Temporary Investment in Equity Securities**, and, as stated previously, the loss should be shown on the 1987 income statement even though it is called an unrealized one. Thus, it is closed to Income Summary at the end of the period.

The adjusting entry necessary to give recognition to the valuation as of December 31, 1987, is:

1987 Dec. 31	Unrealized Loss on Temporary Investment in Equity Securities . . .	5,000	
	Allowance to Reduce Temporary Investments in Equity Securities to Market.		5,000
	To give recognition to lower of cost or market method of valuation of temporary investments.		

The Allowance to Reduce Temporary Investments in Equity Securities to Market is a valuation offset to Temporary Investments on the balance sheet. This allowance and the accompanying temporary investments are shown on the balance sheet on December 31, 1987, as indicated below:

Assets

Current assets:

Temporary investments in equity securities (at cost)	$22,000	
Deduct: Allowance to reduce temporary investments in equity securities to market	5,000	
Temporary investments in equity securities at lower of cost or market		$17,000

Brummet Company will have to go through the same valuation process again on December 31, 1988. Assume that the price of Common Stock A goes down in 1988 and the price of the other securities goes up. This value information follows:

Common Stock	Cost When Purchased in 1987	Market Value as of December 31, 1987	Market Value as of December 31, 1988
A	$10,000	$12,000	$ 9,000
B	5,000	3,000	6,000
C	7,000	2,000	5,000
Total	$22,000	$17,000	$20,000

There is still an *unrealized loss* of $2,000 between the original total cost and the total market value as of December 31, 1988, but, since there was an unrealized loss recognized during 1987, there has been a *net recovery* of $3,000 of that amount during 1988. Thus, the Allowance to Reduce Temporary Investments in Equity Securities to Market must be decreased, and an *unrealized gain* must be recorded in an income statement account entitled **Unrealized Gain on Temporary Investments in Equity Securities** (sometimes called Unrealized Recovery in Market Value of Temporary Investments in Equity Securities) by the following adjusting entry at December 31, 1988:

1988				
Dec.	31	Allowance to Reduce Temporary Investments in Equity Securities to Market	3,000	
		Unrealized Gain on Temporary Investment in Equity Securities		3,000
		To give recognition to lower of cost or market method of valuation of temporary investments.		

This unrealized gain (or recovery) is recognized *only to the extent that it represents a recovery of an unrealized loss recognized in past years*. If the total market value should increase above the total original cost, no unrealized gain would be recognized for any increase above original cost. The gain is referred to as unrealized since no sale has been made, but it is still closed to the Income Summary and shown on the income statement under other income.

The balance sheet of December 31, 1988, shows an LCM valuation of $20,000 for temporary investments. To illustrate the accounting for a subsequent sale of a security, consider the sale of Common Stock A as of January 15, 1989, for $9,500. Remember that only the original cost of the common stock of $10,000 and the selling price of $9,500 now need to be considered to determine the realized loss or gain. Thus the sales transaction is recorded as follows:

1989				
Jan.	15	Cash..	9,500	
		Realized Loss on Sale of Temporary Investments	500	
		Temporary Investments in Equity Securities—		
		Common Stock A...............................		10,000
		To record sale of equity security A.		

To repeat, the realized loss on sale of temporary investments is calculated in the typical manner by comparing only the original cost with the selling price. The loss is $500 = ($10,000 − $9,500). The loss, shown in the income statement under other expenses, is *realized* since the sale has now taken place.

In the adjusting entry of December 31, 1989, any change in the Allowance to Reduce Temporary Investments in Equity Securities to Market would be recorded as an unrealized loss or gain. However, the amount of the unrealized gain which is recognized *must not and cannot reduce the valuation allowance below zero;* that is, the valuation allowance must never have a debit balance.

Long-Term Investments

Stocks and bonds, two major items in which firms make investments to be held for a long period of time (called **long-term investments**), are emphasized in this discussion. Other long-term investments include such items as: long-term accounts receivable and notes receivable, land held for future use, cash surrender value of life insurance on key officers, and special funds such as sinking funds to retire bonded indebtedness or plant replacement funds to buy property, plant, and equipment items. Some firms make long-term investments in office or apartment buildings. These long-term investments are classified on the balance sheet in a noncurrent caption entitled "long-term investments."

Although a company may buy stock in another company specifically for the dividend revenue, it may also do so in order to influence that company. Buying a substantial percentage of the stock of another company (referred to as the **investee company**) allows expansion and diversification of operations as well as a better competitive position. Unless there are indications to the contrary, ownership by an **investor company** of from 20 percent to 50 percent of voting stock in an investee suggests the ability to exercise significant influence, but not control. Emphasized in this chapter is the purchase by the investor company of less than 50 percent of the stock of an investee company. Discussion of majority control of such a company is deferred to Chapter 16.

Long-Term Investments in Stocks

There are a number of issues involved in the accounting for investments in stocks. In this chapter, the following are discussed: (1) the cost method of recording and valuation, (2) recording and valuation of long-term investments in marketable equity securities at lower of cost or market, and (3) the equity method of accounting for investment in an investee.

The Cost Method of Recording and Valuation

Long-term investments in stocks as well as temporary investments should be initially recorded at full cost, including brokerage fees. Under the cost method of accounting for long-term investments, the investor recognizes dividends as revenue. The APB recognized that the cost method may be appropriate when the investor *cannot exert significant influence* over the policies of an investee and the investment is considered to be permanent. It has stated that ownership of less than 20 percent of the voting stock is presumptive evidence that an investor cannot exercise significant influence over an investee company.[4] If cash is paid for the purchase of stock, there is no problem in establishing the amount of the cost. Where payment is not in cash, problems of valuation may arise. A sound accounting rule is to record the investment asset at the most objective measurement of the *cash equivalent* cost of the securities.

Recording Purchase of Stocks
To illustrate the accounting for investment in stocks, assume that the Phyllis Corporation makes two purchases of stock of David Corporation. First, on July 1, 1987, it purchases 10,000 shares of $10 par value common stock at $10.50 per share with a broker's fee of $440 (total cost, $105,440). Then, on July 15, 1987, it buys 20,000 shares of

---

[4]*APB Opinion No. 18,* "The Equity Method of Accounting for Investments in Common Stock" (New York: AICPA, March 1971), paragraph 17.

this stock at 10⅝ (or $10.625) per share with a broker's fee of $880 (total cost, $213,380). These two entries are made to record the investments:

1987				
Jul.	1	Investment in Stocks—Common Stock of David Corporation	105,440	
		Cash		105,440
		To record the purchase of 10,000 shares of $10 par value common stock of David Corporation; the cost is computed as follows: (10,000 shares × $10.50 = $105,000) + $440 = $105,440.		
	15	Investment in Stocks—Common Stock of David Corporation	213,380	
		Cash		213,380
		To record the purchase of 20,000 shares of $10 par value common stock of David Corporation; the cost is computed as follows: (20,000 shares × $10.625 = $212,500) + $880 = $213,380.		

The asset account, Investment in Stocks, is debited for the *cost,* not the par value, of the stock. The account title shows the general ledger controlling account, Investment in Stocks, and the subsidiary account, Common Stock of David Corporation. The information about the specific stock is transferred to a subsidiary record. In this case, assume that 30,000 shares is less than 20 percent of the common stock of David Corporation, and that Phyllis cannot exert significant influence over David's operating policies.

Receipt of Cash Dividend To illustrate the accounting for receipt of declared dividends, assume that the board of directors of David Corporation declared a quarterly dividend of $0.06 per share at the end of October. As a general rule, for convenience, a cash dividend is not recorded until it is actually received. If Phyllis Corporation receives the dividend check from David Corporation on November 20, 1987, it records this information as follows:

1987				
Nov.	20	Cash	1,800	
		Dividends Earned		1,800
		To record the receipt of a $0.06 per share dividend from the David Corporation.		

A necessary exception to the foregoing cash basis rule is the case of a dividend declared in one year and payable in another year.

Recognizing declared dividends

Sound accrual accounting theory dictates that the dividend revenue be recognized in the year in which the dividend is declared, if paid in a different year.

To record a dividend declared in one year and payable in the next, the accountant should debit Dividends Receivable (a current asset) and credit Dividends Earned (a revenue item) as an adjusting entry at the end of the year of declaration. Then, when the dividend is received, the accountant should debit Cash and credit Dividends Receivable.

Another exception arises when stock is purchased *after a dividend has been declared* but before the ex-dividend date. In all cases of stock purchases, the *one* price (unlike the price of bonds) that an investor company pays includes *all* rights purchased, including the right to receive the declared dividend. Obviously, the dividend is from earnings accumulated before the investment was made. Thus the price paid for the stock under these circumstances should be divided between the investment in stock and the dividends receivable that are in fact purchased. The investment purchase entry would, therefore, include debits to Investment in Stocks and Dividends Receivable and a credit to Cash. Later, when the dividend is received by the investor company, it will debit Cash and credit Dividends Receivable, not Dividends Earned.

Receipt of Stock Dividend or Stock Split   Instead of cash dividends, a corporation may issue additional shares of stock to stockholders as a *stock dividend,* or a *stock split*—see Chapter 13. The additional shares received by an investing company are not revenue to it because its net equity in the investee has not increased. Only a memorandum entry is necessary to record the increase in the number of shares owned. Under the cost method, the unit cost is decreased, however, because of the larger number of shares held after the stock dividend is issued. For example, assume that David Corporation declared a 100 percent stock dividend (a two-for-one split would be treated in the same way). Using a specific identification approach, the receipt of the additional 30,000 shares on December 12, 1987, by Phyllis Corporation is typically noted in the journal as follows (observe that the stock of David Corporation was bought in two lots: the first 10,000 shares have a cost of $105,440; the second 20,000, of $213,380):

1987							
Dec.	12	Memorandum Entry—Today there were received 30,000 additional shares of stock of David Corporation, representing a 100 percent stock dividend. The specific identification cost per share of the stock is recomputed as follows:					
		Lot	Old Number of Shares	New Total Number of Shares			
		1	10,000	20,000			
		2	20,000	40,000			
			Total Cost	New Cost per Share			
		1	$105,440	$5.2720			
		2	213,380	5.3345			

Should there be a future disposal of the David Corporation stock, the realized gain or loss per share is determined by comparing the selling price with the applicable adjusted cost of the particular shares sold. If stock is sold from Lot 1, the cost per share is $5.272; if from Lot 2, $5.3345. Instead of a specific identification assignment of cost, a FIFO approach is considered to be an acceptable alternative to the specific identification approach. Generally accepted accounting theory also permits the use of a weighted average approach. The new unit cost by this approach would be $5.313\frac{2}{3} = [(\$105,440 + \$213,380) \div 60,000$ shares now held].

Financial Statement Disclosure and Valuation at Cost

The Dividends Earned account balance is disclosed in the income statement under other revenue. The Investment in Stocks account is reported in the balance sheet under long-term investments, a noncurrent caption appearing between current assets and property, plant, and equipment. If the investment in stocks is considered to be a permanent, *nonmarketable* item and if the percentage of ownership is less than 20 percent, then cost is the generally accepted amount for balance sheet valuation. As with temporary investments, long-term investments are *initially* recorded at cost; therefore, there would be no immediate valuation problems. These items would be disclosed on the balance sheet at the figures that appear in the ledger accounts. If the long-term investments are in marketable equity securities, they are required by *FASB Statement No. 12* to be valued at lower of cost or market. This procedure is considered next.

Recording and Valuation of Long-Term Investments in Marketable Equity Securities at Lower of Cost or Market

Some long-term investments in equity securities—mostly common stock—are considered marketable. The initial recording and subsequent interim period accounting follow the pattern described above for long-term nonmarketable equity securities. The valuation at the end of a period, however, must be at lower of cost or market. The procedure for valuation of these noncurrent equity securities is exactly the same as that described for temporary investments in marketable equity securities. A major difference, however, arises in the disclosure area: the unrealized loss on investment in noncurrent marketable equity securities is not shown in the income statement and thus is not absorbed into current net income. Rather, it is disclosed as a negative item directly *in the stockholders' equity section* of the balance sheet. For example, suppose the trial balance of the Dorothy Corporation contained the following items:

DOROTHY CORPORATION
Partial Trial Balance
December 31, 1987

Account Title	Debits	Credits
Investment in Noncurrent Marketable Equity Securities	$210,000	
Allowance to Reduce Noncurrent Marketable Equity Investments to Market		$8,000
Unrealized Loss on Investment in Noncurrent Marketable Equity Securities	8,000	

These data are shown on the Dorothy Corporation balance sheet on December 31, 1987, as follows:

DOROTHY CORPORATION
Partial Balance Sheet
December 31, 1987

Assets

Long-term investments:
  Investment in noncurrent marketable equity securities, at cost $210,000
  Deduct: Allowance to reduce noncurrent marketable equity investments to market 8,000
  Investment in noncurrent marketable equity securities, at lower of cost or market $202,000

Stockholders' equity:

  Unrealized loss on investment in noncurrent marketable equity securities[a] .... ($ 8,000)

[a]This item appears in the stockholders' equity section in an unlabeled section between the paid-in capital group and the retained earnings group.

A number of other complex issues discussed in *Statement No. 12* are beyond the scope of this book.

The Equity Method of Accounting for an Investment in Stock

In the illustrations thus far for investments in stock of other corporations, the stock is valued at cost or lower of cost or market. When a corporation's investment in a domestic or foreign investee is large enough *to presume* ability to exercise significant influence over it (evidenced by ownership of 20 percent or more of the voting stock), the equity method should be used to account for the investment.[5]

When the **equity method of accounting for investment in stock** is used, the initial purchase of stock is also recorded at cost. After the initial acquisition, however, as shown by the example presented below, the investment account of the investor company is debited or credited to give recognition to income or losses and dividend declarations of the investee company. In other words, the investment account is increased or decreased to reflect changes in the stockholders' equity of the investee company.

Example: Stock of Investee Corporation Is Purchased at Book Value

The following summary transactions of the Parento and Sunno Corporations are used to illustrate the equity method:

---

[5]*APB Opinion No. 18*, "The Equity Method of Accounting for Investments in Common Stock" (New York: AICPA, March 1971), paragraph 17.

1987

Jan.	2	Parento Corporation purchased 40 percent of the stock of the Sunno Corporation at book value for $400,000.
Aug.	8	Sunno Corporation declared and paid a total dividend of $20,000.
Dec.	31	Sunno Corporation earned a net income of $80,000 in 1987.

1988

Dec.	31	Sunno Corporation suffered a net loss of $3,000 in 1988.

Transactions affecting the Parento Corporation are recorded by the equity method, as follows:

1987					
Jan.	2	Investment in Stocks—Common Stock of Sunno Corporation		400,000	
		Cash			400,000
		To record purchase of 40 percent of the stock of Sunno Corporation.			
Aug.	8	Cash		8,000	
		Investment in Stocks—Common Stock of Sunno Corporation			8,000
		To record receipt of dividend from the Sunno Corporation.			
Dec.	31	Investment in Stocks—Common Stock of Sunno Corporation		32,000	
		Investor's Share of Investee Income			32,000
		To record investor's share of reported net income.			
1988					
Dec.	31	Investor's Share of Investee Loss		1,200	
		Investment in Stocks—Common Stock of Sunno Corporation			1,200
		To record investor's share of reported net loss.			

When the foregoing information is posted, the Investment in Stocks account will appear as presented below (the posting references are not shown, but explanations are indicated).

Investment in Stocks   Acct. No. 152

1987					1987				
Jan.	2	Initial cost of Sunno stock	400,000		Aug.	8	Dividend received		8,000
					1988				
Dec.	31	40% share of income	32,000		Dec.	31	40% share of loss		1,200
		422,800[a]							

[a]Balance.

Using the equity method, an investor corporation recognizes an economic reality: income and losses of the investee are essentially part of the investor corporation's own income and losses since it can influence the investee's operating policies. The **Investor's Share of Investee Income** and **Investor's Share of Investee Loss** accounts are used in this book to indicate the investor's share of net income or net loss of an investee under the equity method of accounting. They are closed to Income Summary and shown on Parento's income statement under other revenues and other expenses. Since the investor's share of the investee's net income is included in revenue by the entry made at the end of the year, the receipt of dividends is considered a return of a portion of previously recorded investor's investment—not revenue.

The equity method of accounting for long-term investment in stock is also a valuation method for the purpose of balance sheet presentation. The Investment in Stock account would be shown at the equity amount (in Parento's case, $422,800) in the balance sheet under the long-term investment caption.

In the foregoing illustration, it is assumed that the Parento Corporation purchased the stock of Sunno Corporation at book value. If the stock had been purchased at a figure above or below book value, additional entries *amortizing* the excess or deficiency would be required under some circumstances. These are discussed in Chapter 16.

In addition to investing in stocks of various companies, an investor often makes long-term investments in bonds. The accounting for this kind of investment is now considered.

Long-Term Investments in Bonds

A number of institutional investors are prohibited by law from buying common stock; others are restricted in the amount of common stock they may buy. Organizations such as banks, insurance companies, some trusts, and pension funds may acquire bonds as investments. Industrial companies also frequently buy bonds, either for the interest revenue to be received or for reasons of business connection. The decision to buy a given kind or grade of bond will depend upon: (1) the security desired (collateral required); (2) the amount of risk that is acceptable (with higher net interest rates as risk increases)—that is, the degree of safety of both principal and interest desired; and (3) other factors.

If, on the issue date, the **stated interest rate** applicable to the face value of the bonds issued—also called the *contract* or *nominal interest rate*—is the same as the prevailing market interest rate for the particular grade of bonds, the investor can buy these bonds at face value. On the other hand, if there is a difference between the stated bond interest rate and the prevailing market rate for the particular grade of bonds, the investor will pay a price for the bonds that is above or below face value; that is, the investor will buy the bonds at a *premium* or a *discount*.

Accounting by the purchaser of long-term bonds is almost the opposite of accounting by the issuer of bonds and notes. This opposite but conceptually similar accounting—the investor's point of view—is emphasized here by assuming that certain bonds issued in Chapter 14 are now purchased by investors at the issue price. This assumption, however, is not always realistic since investors may pay more for bonds than the issuer receives because of transfer taxes and other possible brokers' commissions. The problem data for certain of the examples in Chapter 14 are restated, then the basic accounting is shown, followed by a brief discussion of key issues introduced by the accounting entries.

Example A: Bonds Purchased at Face Value on an Interest Date

Assume that on April 1, 1987, the Global Finance Corporation purchased Amerson Corporation 16 percent first mortgage bonds with a face value of $200,000 and a maturity date of April 1, 1997. Interest is paid each April 1 and October 1. Books are closed each December 31. All of the bonds are purchased at 100, or at face value. (In this and the next three examples, assume that all costs—for bonds, brokerage fees, and any other costs—are the same as the issue cost (for Example A, see page 579 in Chapter 14). The accounting entries related to the investment in the bonds of the Amerson Corporation for the period April 1, 1987, to April 1, 1988, are shown in Figure 15–1.

1987 Apr.	1	Investment in Bonds—Amerson Corporation. . . . . Cash . . . . To record purchase of Amerson Corporation 16 percent first mortgage bonds due April 1, 1997.	200,000	200,000
Oct.	1	Cash. . . . . Bond Interest Earned. . . . . To record the receipt of semiannual interest on the Amerson Corporation bonds.	16,000	16,000
Dec.	31	Accrued Bond Interest Receivable . . . . Bond Interest Earned. . . . . To record the accrual on the Amerson Corporation bonds for three months.	8,000	8,000
1988 Apr.	1	Cash. . . . . Accrued Bond Interest Receivable . . . . Bond Interest Earned. . . . . To record the receipt of semiannual interest on the Amerson Corporation bonds.	16,000	8,000 8,000

Figure 15–1   Example A   Accounting Entries for Investment—Bonds Purchased at Face Amount

Accounting Theory Highlights—Investment in Amerson Corporation Bonds   The following comments highlight the important issues involved in the accounting for the investment in the Amerson Corporation bonds:

1. The accounting is practically the mirror image of the accounting for issuance—see page 580 in Chapter 14.

2. The Investment in Bonds account is a noncurrent asset; it is disclosed in the balance sheet under a caption entitled long-term investments. This caption appears on the balance sheet between current assets and property, plant, and equipment.

3. The adjusting entry for accrued bond interest receivable is similar to the recording of accrued interest on notes receivable; Accrued Bond Interest Receivable is a current asset account.

4. If Amerson retires the bonds at maturity, Global, upon the receipt of this cash, would debit Cash for $200,000 and credit Investment on Bonds—Amerson Corporation for $200,000.

Methods of Amortization

As stated previously, the accounting for the investment in bonds is the opposite of that for the issuance of bonds. This *opposite-type similarity extends to the amortization of the premium and discount elements of the long-term investment in bonds* involving the write-off of these elements to the revenue account Bond Interest Earned. As with the issuance of bonds, there are two methods of amortization of the premium and discount elements of the long-term investments: (1) the interest method, which is preferred, and (2) the straight line method, which may be used if its results are not materially different from those produced by the interest method. It appears that often the straight line method does produce acceptable results, so it is still very popular.

Examples B and C Using Straight Line and Interest Methods of Amortization

In the next series of examples, both methods of amortization are illustrated at the same time, assuming that investors buy the bonds that are issued in Chapter 14 (pages 583–592) at the issue price. The problem data are restated from the investor's point of view. Then the recording issues are presented. Last, the accounting theory highlights are surveyed.

Examples B–1 and C–1: Bonds Purchased at a Premium on an Interest Date

Assume that on July 1, 1987, the Douglass Corporation purchased the 16½ percent, first mortgage bonds of the Bonkers Corporation for $102,981.16, a price to yield 16 percent (8 percent each six months). The bonds have a face value of $100,000 with a maturity date of June 30, 2007. Interest is paid semiannually on June 30 and December 31. The Douglass Corporation's books are closed each December 31. The accounting entries for the period July 1, 1987, to June 30, 1988, related to the investment in the bonds of Bonker Corporation are shown in Figure 15–2. The first journal pair of columns show the accounting for Example B–1 (see corresponding entries for the issuer on pages 584–585 in Chapter 14) using the straight line method of amortization. The second journal pair of columns show the ac-

Date	Debit–Credit–Account Titles: Explanation	F	Example B–1 Straight Line Method		Example C–1 Interest Method	
1987 Jul. 1	Investment in Bonds—Bonkers Corporation . . . Cash . . . . To record purchase of 16½ percent, first mortgage bonds of Bonkers Corporation due June 30, 2007.		102,981.16	102,981.16	102,981.16	102,981.16
Dec. 31	Cash. . . . . Bond Interest Earned. . . . . Investment in Bonds—Bonkers Corporation . . . . To record the receipt of semiannual interest from Bonkers Corporation and to record amortization of the premium element on the investments.		8,250.00	8,175.47[b] 74.53[a]	8,250.00	8,238.49[c] 11.51[d]
1988 Jun. 30	Cash. . . . . Bond Interest Earned. . . . . Investment in Bonds—Bonkers Corporation . . . . To record the receipt of semiannual interest from Bonkers Corporation and to record amortization of the investment.		8,250.00	8,175.47[b] 74.53[a]	8,250.00	8,237.57[e] 12.43[f]

[a] The total premium element is $2,981.16 = ($102,981.16 − $100,000.00). The uniform straight line amortization for each six months is $74.53 = ($2,981.16 ÷ 40 semiannual periods).
[b] The Bond Interest Earned amount by the straight line method is $8,175.47 = ($8,250.00 stated interest − $74.53 amortization).
[c] The Bond Interest Earned amount for the first interest period by the interest method is $8,238.49 = (8% × $102,981.16).
[d] The amount of amortization for the first interest period by the interest method is residually determined; it is for the first six months $11.51 = ($8,250.00 − $8,238.49).
[e] The Bond Interest Earned amount for the second interest period by the interest method is $8,237.57 = [8% × ($102,981.16 − $11.51)].
[f] The amount of amortization for the second interest period by the interest method is $12.43 = ($8,250.00 − $8,237.57).

Figure 15–2   Examples B–1 and C–1   Accounting Entries for Investment—Premium Case

counting for Example C–1 (see corresponding entries for the issuer on page 590) using the interest method of amortization. Key calculations are shown as footnotes to Figure 15–2.

Accounting Theory Highlights—Investment in Bonker Corporation Bonds

The following comments highlight the important issues involved in the accounting for the investment in Bonker Corporation bonds:

1. Following the accounting principle of recording assets at cost, the Investment in Bonds account is debited for the full cost of the bonds including brokerage fees, transfer taxes, and other costs; no separate premium or dis-

count is established. Thus the amount of periodic amortization of the premium element is credited to the Investment in Bonds account (at maturity, the book value is the same as face).

2. The basic concepts of the accounting for the investment are the same as those for the issuer. The reader should turn back to pages 583–592 to compare and to verify this fact.

3. By the straight line method of amortization, Example B–1, the bond interest earned amounts are uniform over time; but the rate of return on book value *increases* over time since the book value of the investment decreases with the amortization.

4. By the interest method of amortization, Example C–1, the bond interest earned amounts *decrease* over time—the June 30, 1988, amount of $8,237.57 is smaller than the December 31, 1987, amount of $8,238.49. Yet the rate of return on book value is uniform over time at the effective annual rate of 16 percent or 8 percent per semiannual period.

5. Current GAAP requires the use of the interest method. The straight line method, however, may be used if the results achieved are not materially different from that of the interest method; i.e., is $8,175.47 (the first interest period's bond interest earned by the straight line method) materially different from $8,238.49 (the first interest period's bond interest earned by the interest method)? The difference of $63.02, or 0.8 percent, is definitely not material.

6. Even though the amounts of the bond interest earned are different for the two methods, the total amount of bond interest earned for the entire life of the bonds must be the same for each of the methods—the total stated interest less the total premium element.

Examples B–2 and C–2: Bonds Purchased at a Discount on an Interest Date

Assume that on July 1, 1987, the date of authorization, the Britton Corporation purchased Davidson Company's 16 percent debenture bonds (see pages 586–592 in Chapter 14) with a face value of $200,000 and a maturity date of June 30, 1997. Britton paid $181,742.94 for these bonds, a price that will yield 18 percent. Interest dates are June 30 and December 31. Britton's books are closed each December 31. The discount is caused by the difference in the existing average market rate on similar grades of debenture bonds and the stated rate of interest on the Davidson bonds being purchased. Davidson's debenture bonds have a stated interest rate lower than the prevailing market rate on similar grade securities. The accounting entries for the period July 1, 1987, to June 30, 1988, related to the investment in bonds of Davidson Company are shown in Figure 15–3. As with the previous set of examples, both the straight line and the interest methods of amortization are illustrated.

Date	Debit–Credit–Account Titles: Explanation	F	Example B–2 Straight Line Method		Example C–2 Interest Method	
1987 Jul. 1	Investment in Bonds—Davidson Company............ Cash.................. To record the purchase of Davidson Company 16 percent debenture bonds, due June 30, 1997.		181,742.94	181,742.94	181,742.94	181,742.94
Dec. 31	Cash.................. Investment in Bonds—Davidson Company............ Bond Interest Earned........ To record the receipt of semiannual interest on the Davidson Company debenture bonds.		16,000.00 912.85[a]	16,912.85[b]	16,000.00 356.86[d]	16,356.86[c]
1988 Jun. 30	Cash.................. Investment in Bonds—Davidson Company............ Bond Interest Earned........ To record the receipt of semiannual interest on the Davidson Company debenture bonds.		16,000.00 912.85[a]	16,912.85[b]	16,000.00 388.98[f]	16,388.98[e]

[a] The total discount element is $18,257.06 = ($200,000.00 − $181,742.94). The uniform straight line amortization for each six months is $912.85 = ($18,257.06 ÷ 20 semiannual periods).
[b] The Bond Interest Earned amount for any six months by the straight line method is $16,912.85 = ($16,000.00 + $912.85).
[c] The Bond Interest Earned amount for the first interest period by the interest method is $16,356.86 = (9% × $181,742.94).
[d] The amount of amortization for the first interest period by the interest method is residually determined; it is $356.86 = ($16,356.86 − $16,000.00).
[e] The Bond Interest Earned amount for the second interest period by the interest method is $16,388.98 = [9% × ($181,742.94 + $356.86)].
[f] The amount of amortization for the second interest period by the interest method is $388.98 = ($16,388.98 − $16,000.00)

Figure 15–3   Examples B–2 and C–2   Accounting Entries for Investment—Discount Case

Accounting Theory Highlights—Investment in Davidson Company Bonds   The following comments highlight the important issues involved in the accounting for the investment in the Davidson Company bonds.

1. Again, the Investment in Bonds account is debited with the full cost of the bonds. Since no separate discount account is established, the amount of periodic amortization of the discount element is *debited* to the Investment in Bonds account, thus increasing it (at maturity the book value is the same as face).

2. By the straight line method of amortization, Example B–2, the bond interest earned amounts are uniform over time; but the rate of return on book

value *decreases* over time since the book value of the investment increases with the amortization.

3. By the interest method of amortization, Example C–2, the bond interest earned amounts increase over time (see Figure 15–3)—yet the rate of return on book value over time is uniform at the annual effective rate (yield) of 18 percent.

4. Since GAAP specifies the use of the interest method, the straight line method could be used only if the results achieved ($16,912.85 bond interest earned for the first interest period) are not materially different from that of the interest method ($16,356.86 for the first interest period). The difference is $555.99, or 3.4 percent, a difference that may not be material.

5. As with the premium case, the amount of bond interest earned for the full life of the investment must be the same regardless of whether the straight line or interest method of amortization is used. That total bond interest earned for the discount case equals the stated interest for the entire life of the bonds plus the amount of the discount element.

Example D: Bonds Purchased between Interest Dates

The preceding sets of examples emphasize basic accounting procedures, reasons for amortizing the premium and discount elements of the Investment in Bonds account, and the amortization procedure by both the straight line and interest methods. A more complex problem involving the purchase of bonds between interest dates, with the required end-of-period adjustments, is presented next using only straight line amortization.

Assume that on June 1, 1987, Dawson Corporation purchased Greensboro Company 18 percent debenture bonds with a face value of $400,000 (see pages 596–598 in Chapter 14) and a maturity date of October 1, 1995. The bonds were authorized on October 1, 1985, but not issued until June 1, 1987. The interest is paid semiannually on April 1 and October 1. Dawson Corporation paid 105 plus accrued interest. The Dawson Corporation paid $432,000 in cash for these bonds: $420,000 for the bonds (including all costs), plus $12,000 for the accrued interest purchased. The promise to pay six months' interest is retroactive only to April 1, 1987, the interest date immediately preceding the date of purchase. On October 1, 1987, the Dawson Corporation receives an interest check in the amount of $36,000, although the interest on $400,000 at 18 percent from June 1 to October 1, the period Dawson held the bonds, is only $24,000. The semiannual interest check includes a return of the $12,000 the Dawson Corporation paid for the accrued bond interest receivable purchased on June 1, as illustrated in Figure 14–8, page 597. The accounting entries for the period June 1, 1987, to April 1, 1988, related to the investment in bonds of Greensboro Company are shown in Figure 15–4. With these more complex examples, only straight line amortization is used.

Date	Debit–Credit–Account Titles: Explanation	F	Example D Straight Line Method	

1987 Jun. 1	Investment in Bonds—Greensboro Company . . . .
	Accrued Bond Interest Receivable . . . .
	    Cash . . . .
	      To record the purchase of Greensboro debenture bonds at 105 plus accrued interest.
			420,000
			12,000
				432,000

Oct. 1	Cash . . . .
	    Accrued Interest Receivable . . . .
	    Bond Interest Earned . . . .
	      To record the receipt of semiannual interest at 18 percent on the Greensboro bonds.
			36,000	12,000
				24,000

1	Bond Interest Earned . . . .
	    Investment in Bonds—Greensboro Company . . . .
	      To record the amortization of the premium element for four months:
	      [($20,000 ÷ 100 months) × 4 = $800]
			800	800

Dec. 31	Accrued Bond Interest Receivable . . . .
	    Bond Interest Earned . . . .
	      To record the accrual of bond interest for three months: 18% × $400,000 × 3/12 = $18,000.
			18,000	18,000

31	Bond Interest Earned . . . .
	    Investment in Bonds—Greensboro Company . . . .
	      To record the amortization of premium element for three months: 3 × $200 = $600.
			600	600

1988 Apr. 1	Cash . . . .
	    Accrued Bond Interest Receivable . . . .
	    Bond Interest Earned . . . .
	      To record the receipt of semiannual interest at 18 percent on the Greensboro bonds.
			36,000	18,000
				18,000

1	Bond Interest Earned . . . .
	    Investment in Bonds—Greensboro Company . . . .
	      To record the amortization of premium element for three months: 3 × $200 = $600.
			600	600

Figure 15–4   Example D Accounting Entries for Investment— Premium Case with Bonds Issued between Interest Dates

Accounting Theory Highlights—Investment in Greensboro Bonds

The following comments highlight the important issues involved in the accounting for the investment in the Greensboro bonds.

1. Two assets are purchased: the bonds at 105 and the accrued interest of $12,000. The Accrued Interest Receivable is a current asset account since it will be collected on October 1, 1987. The Investment in Bonds is a long-term investment (noncurrent) account.

2. Two entries are made on October 1 and December 31, 1987, and on April 1, 1988: (1) to record the unadjusted recognition of bond interest earned and (2) to record the amortization of the premium element. This approach makes it easier to handle complex information one step at a time.

3. The amortization period begins on the *date of purchase,* June 1, 1987, and ends at the *maturity date,* October 1, 1995, a total of 100 months; therefore the *monthly* amortization is $200 = ($20,000 ÷ 100 months).

4. The end of year adjustments follow the typical accrual. It must be accompanied by three months' amortization of the premium element, or $600 = (3 × $200).

5. The receipt of interest on April 1, 1988, represents three months of bond interest earned and the collection of a receivable for three months of interest placed on the books on December 31, 1987. Also, three months of amortization of the premium element ($600) must be recorded.

In this chapter, only the basic topics involving long-term investments in bonds have been presented. Other complex bond investment topics, such as sales and conversion of one type into another type, are covered in intermediate and advanced accounting books.

Other Long-Term Investment Items

Other long-term investment items are briefly discussed beginning with *long-term accounts receivable.* For accounts receivable to be classified as long-term investments, they should be nontrade items resulting, say, from loans to officers or to other employees. Trade installment accounts receivable of three years' length would still be classified as *current assets* since the operating cycle would now be three years, not one year.

Often either *secured or unsecured notes* may be acquired to be held for a long period of time. Much of the accounting for investments in bonds would apply to the accounting for investments in long-term notes.

Only land actually used in operations should be classified as property, plant, and equipment. *Land purchased for a future plant building site* should be classified as a long-term investment.

Many companies will insure the lives of their key officers and take out life insurance policies that, after a certain period of time, have a cash value that can be obtained upon the cancellation of the policies. This cash value, referred to as the *cash surrender value of life insurance,* reduces the effective life insurance expense and should be set up as a long-term investment by the company that has taken out the policies.

Companies create *long-term funds* for various purposes—for example, to retire a long-term debt (sinking fund) or to buy property, plant, and equipment (property, plant, and equipment acquisition fund). Long-term funds are established through segregation of cash, which is then invested. These investments should be accounted for as other investments are, except that the investment account should have as a part of its title the name of the particular fund—for example, Property, Plant, and Equipment Acquisition Fund—Investments in Bonds, or Sinking Fund—Investment in Bonds.

Managerial Analysis

Investors are interested in the profitability and growth potential of their investee firms. They are also interested in the safety of principal and interest in their creditor-type investments. Many of the ratios that an investor would calculate have been presented in earlier chapters, chiefly: earnings-per-share (an earning power and growth potential measurement—Chapter 13); rate of return on total investment and rate of return on stockholders' equity (two earning power measurements—Chapter 3); property, plant, and equipment to long-term liabilities and property, plant, and equipment to stockholders' equity (two long-run solvency measurements—Chapter 11); and the number of times bond interest is earned (another measure of long-run solvency indicating the safety of the bond investment—Chapter 14).

An additional investor-oriented ratio similar to the number of times bond interest is earned is the *number of times preferred dividends is earned*. This ratio is of particular interest to investors in preferred stock as a safety measure for their investment. To illustrate, assume that Raye Corporation has 14 percent preferred stock outstanding with a par value of $1,000,000 and earned a net income of $160,000. Since preferred dividends are *not* deductible in determining taxable income, the following formula is appropriate:

$$\text{Number of times preferred dividends is earned} = \frac{\text{Net income}}{\text{Annual preferred dividends}}.$$

Substituting the amounts given for Raye Corporation,

$$\text{Number of times preferred dividends is earned} = \frac{\$160,000}{\$140,000}$$
$$= 1.14 \text{ times}.$$

The adequacy of this ratio must be interpreted in the same manner as that described for the number of times bond interest is earned (in Chapter 14); that is, the safety margin that is acceptable will depend in part on the type of business in which the investee firm is engaged, the liquidity of the investee, and other factors.

Two other earning power measurements of considerable significance and usefulness to the investor are the ratios of earnings and dividends to the market value of the shares, because it is the cash represented by the market value of the shares that can be put to other uses. Two such ratios are:

$$\text{Earnings yield rate} = \frac{\text{Earnings per share}}{\text{Market value per share}}.$$

$$\text{Dividends yield rate} = \frac{\text{Dividends per share}}{\text{Market value per share}}.$$

A careful analysis of the relationship and trend of these ratios indicates the profitability of the firm as related to the market value of its shares, its growth prospects, and its ability to pay dividends.

Internal Control of Investments

Internal control over investments involves the accurate recording of securities received and the safeguarding of securities and cash receipts from dividends and interest. The recording aspect not only involves journalizing but also the creation of a perpetual-type subsidiary record for recording each lot acquired at a different price. This subsidiary record could be in the form of an investment register containing information about each purchase—cost, shares or face value, dividend or interest rates, dividend or interest dates, location of securities, the names of those assigned responsibility for the securities, and other relevant internal control information. The securities should be kept in a fireproof safe, vault, or independent storage medium such as a safe-deposit box. A periodic inventory of the securities should be taken and checked against the subsidiary record. The plan of internal control over the cash receipts for interest and dividends should put into force the principles discussed in Chapter 8.

Glossary

Allowance to Reduce Temporary Investments in Equity Securities to Market A valuation offset to Temporary Investments in Equity Securities reflecting the excess of total cost of the securities over the total market value of the temporary investments. A similar account could be established for noncurrent marketable equity securities.

Blue-chip stocks High-grade stocks that are listed on one of the stock exchanges.

Bond Interest Earned A revenue account which shows the net interest earned on bonds—the gross amount received adjusted for amortization of premium or discount element of bond investment.

Equity method of accounting for investment in stocks An accounting method that adjusts the cost of the investments by the investor's share of the net income or net loss of the investee and treats receipts of dividends as a return of the investment in stock.

Equity securities Ownership shares in common stock and certain preferred stock with basic ownership characteristics.

Investee company A corporation whose stock is partially or fully owned by another corporation, the investor company.

Investor company A corporation owning stock in another corporation.

Investor's Share of Investee Income As used in this book, a revenue account used to record the investor's share of investee's net income under the equity method.

Investor's Share of Investee Loss As used in this book, an expense or loss account used to record the investor's share of investee's net loss under the equity method.

Long-term investments Investments in stocks, bonds, other securities, and certain other kinds of property that management intends to hold for a long period.

Lower of cost or market (LCM) A method of valuation of investments in marketable equity securities in which the lower of cost or market is chosen as the value to be presented on the balance sheet.

Marketable equity securities Equity securities that can readily be resold, usually on a stock exchange.

Realized gain on disposal of temporary investments The excess of actual selling price at the time of sale over the original cost of the temporary investments.

Realized loss on disposal of temporary investments The excess of original cost of temporary investments over the actual selling price at the time of sale.

Stated interest rate The interest rate that is stated on the bonds themselves; sometimes called *nominal or contract interest rate*.

Temporary investments Investments in high-grade, blue-chip securities that management intends to hold for a relatively short period; these are always classified as current assets on the balance sheet.

Unrealized gain on temporary investments in equity securities An income statement gain item that is considered to be unrealized since the securities have not yet been sold; it arises when securities recover some previously lost market value.

Unrealized loss on temporary investments in equity securities An income statement loss item that is considered to be unrealized since the securities have not yet been sold; it arises out of the lower of cost or market valuation process when the market value is lower than cost.

Questions

Q15–1 Discuss the following statement: Generally speaking, the accounting for investment in bonds is the mirror image of the accounting for the issuance of bonds. In your discussion, state the differences and similarities in the accounting for each. Be specific in regard to the account titles used and the accounting for temporary and long-term investments.

Q15–2 What are temporary investments? How are they classified on the balance sheet?

Q15–3 List four types of investments that may qualify as temporary investments.

Q15–4 Name and discuss the methods of valuation of temporary investments.

Q15–5 Discuss the accounting involved in the lower of cost or market method of valuation of temporary investments in marketable securities. Give journal entries to illustrate your discussion.

Q15–6 Why do firms acquire stock as a long-term investment?

Q15–7 Do dividends legally accrue? Can a firm buy dividends receivable? Explain.

Q15–8 What is a stock split? Discuss the accounting for a stock split from the point of view of the investor. Would there be any difference in the accounting for a stock dividend and for a stock split on the investor's books? Explain.

Q15–9 Name the various groups of investors who typically buy bonds as a long-term investment.

Q15–10 Why is the interest method theoretically preferable to the straight line method of amortization?

Q15–11 Does the straight line amortization method in the first year of an investment in bonds always produce a larger bond interest earned amount than does the interest method? Discuss.

Q15–12 What are the balance sheet classifications of these accounts: (a) Bond Sinking Fund, (b) Accrued Bond Interest Receivable, (c) Accrued Bond Interest Payable, (d) Cash Surrender Value of Life Insurance, and (e) Long-Term Secured Notes Receivable?

Q15–13 When are investments accounted for by the equity method? How is the receipt of dividends treated under this method?

Q15–14 Where would the "Unrealized loss on investment in equity marketable securities" caption appear on the financial statements if it relates to short-term investments? To long-term investments?

Q15–15 By valuing investments in short-term equity securities and long-term marketable securities at lower of cost or market, the financial statements deviate from the historical cost measurement principle. Why, then, does the Financial Accounting Standards Board require valuation at lower of cost or market?

Q15–16 List five key ratios that an investor would likely want to determine before buying stocks and bonds of a given company. Briefly indicate the importance of each ratio.

Exercises

E15–1
Differentiating between temporary and long-term investments

On July 1, 1987, the De Angelis Corporation purchased 13½ percent, AAA, first mortgage bonds of the Taylor Company with a face value of $180,000 at 102½ plus $136 brokerage fees. Interest is payable on July 1 and January 1.

1. If these bonds were purchased as a *temporary investment,* what account title(s) would be debited and for what amount(s)?
2. If these bonds were purchased as a *long-term investment,* what account title(s) would be debited and for what amount(s)?
3. Explain briefly the difference in accounting for the purchase of the bonds and the subsequent treatment of the investment as a temporary investment as compared to a long-term investment.

E15–2
Various transactions in temporary investments

The Wayne Corporation had the following transactions in *temporary* investments during 1987:

1987		
Mar. 1		Purchased 14 percent, AAA bonds of Hydro Company with a face value of $300,000 at 102 plus accrued interest. Interest is paid on January 1 and July 1. Brokerage fees and other costs incident to the purchase were $360. The bonds have a maturity date of July 1, 2007.
Apr. 10		Purchased 900 shares of $100 par value, 15 percent preferred stock of Arnold Company at $105 a share. Dividends are paid semiannually on January 1 and July 1. Brokerage fees and other costs incident to the purchase were $250.
Jul.	1	Received the semiannual interest from the Hydro Company.
	5	Received the semiannual dividends from the Arnold Company.
Aug.	1	Sold the bonds of Hydro Company at 102½ plus accrued interest.

Journalize the transactions on the books of Wayne Corporation.

E15–3
Valuation of temporary investments

The Faison Company had the following *temporary* investments in equity securities for the period 1987 to 1988:

	Cost	Market Price at December 31	
		1987	1988
Common stock of Norris Company	$70,000	$67,600	
Common stock of HiTech Company	40,000	40,300	$40,800

On February 1, 1988, immediately after receiving and recording the semiannual dividend, the Faison Company sold the common stock of Norris Company for $67,000. Assuming the use of a valuation offset account, record the necessary adjusting entry under the lower of cost or market method as of December 31, 1987, and December 31, 1988, and the sale on February 1, 1988.

E15–4
Recording temporary investments with dividends attached

The Cork Corporation had the following transactions in temporary investment in stocks during 1987:

1987

Jan. 5 Purchased 60,000 shares of $10 par value common stock of Birmingham Company at $10.60 per share. The Birmingham Company had declared a $0.10 per share dividend on January 2, 1987, payable on January 20, 1987, to stockholders of record January 10, 1987.
   20 Received the cash dividend from the Birmingham Company.
Mar. 10 Purchased 40,000 shares of $10 par value common stock of Birmingham Company at $11.00 per share.
Jul. 20 Received a $0.12 per share cash dividend from the Birmingham Company.
Dec. 16 The Birmingham Company declared a $0.15 per share cash dividend, payable January 20, 1988, to stockholders of record on December 31, 1987.

Journalize the transactions on the books of Cork Corporation, assuming that all the Birmingham stock was still owned on December 31, 1987.

E15–5
Long-term investment in bonds—straight line amortization of premium

On January 1, 1987, the Cannes Corporation purchased as a *long-term* investment 15 percent bonds of Blough Corporation with a face value of $400,000 at 102. The bonds have a maturity date of January 1, 1997. Interest is payable each January 1 and July 1. Record (a) the purchase of the bonds by the Cannes Corporation, and (b) all the necessary remaining entries for 1987. Use the straight line method of amortization.

E15–6
Long-term investment in bonds—straight line amortization of discount

Assume that the Cannes Corporation (see E15–5) purchased the Blough Corporation bonds at 99 instead of 102. Prepare all the required entries for 1987. Use the straight line method of amortization.

E15–7
Accounting for long-term investment in stocks

On December 31, 1986, the Hackney Corporation made a *long-term* investment in the Sparrow Company by acquiring stock at book value. During 1987, the Sparrow Company paid total dividends of $24,000 and had net income of $84,000. During 1988, it paid total dividends of $12,000 and had a net loss of $20,000.

a. Assuming that Hackney Corporation purchased 12 percent of Sparrow Company's stock, journalize all transactions for 1987 and 1988 that should appear on Hackney Corporation's books. Use the year date only; in the date column use a, b, etc.
b. Assuming that Hackney Corporation purchased 30 percent of Sparrow Company's stock, journalize all transactions for 1987 and 1988 that should appear on Hackney Corporation's books. Use the year date only; in the date column use a, b, etc.

E15–8
Accounting for long-term investment in stock

The Gary Corporation acquired 4,000 of the 16,000 total shares of the Littlefield Company on January 1, 1987, for $480,000, the book value of the stock. During 1987, Littlefield paid total dividends of $40,000 ($10,000 on July 11 and $30,000 on November 14) and had net income of $80,000. Journalize the transactions on Gary Corporation's books, including any necessary end-of-year adjusting entries on December 31, 1987.

E15–9
Reconstructing original issue data

On May 1, 1987, the Lennox Corporation purchased as a *long-term* investment 16 percent bonds of Steeler Company. Interest is paid semiannually on May 1 and November 1. The bonds mature on May 1, 1999. On November 1, 1987, the accountant for the Lennox Company prepared the following entry to record the receipt of bond interest and the amortization of the premium:

1987 Nov.	1	Cash... Investment in Bonds—Steeler Company Bonds .... Bond Interest Earned.............................. To record the receipt of bond interest from the Steeler Company and to amortize the premium for six months by the straight line method.	24,000	750 23,250

From this information, reconstruct the journal entry that was made to record the purchase of the bonds. Show all your calculations.

E15–10
Long-term investment in bonds—interest method of amortization

On July 1, 1987, the Benson Corporation purchased as a *long-term* investment 15 percent, 10-year bonds of McDaniel Company with a face value of $300,000 for $315,891.02, which is a price to yield 14 percent (7 percent each six months). Interest is paid June 30 and December 31. Maturity date of the bonds is June 30, 1997. Record the purchase of the bonds on the books of the Benson Corporation; record the receipt of interest on December 31, 1987, and June 30, 1988, and the amortizing of the premium element by using the interest method.

E15–11
Long-term investment in bonds purchased between the interest dates—straight line amortization

Janzen Corporation acquired as a *long-term* investment on March 1, 1987, Truman Company bonds for $260,730 plus accrued interest. The date of authorization is January 1, 1987. The bonds of the Truman Company have a face value of $300,000 with an interest rate of 12 percent. The maturity date is January 1, 2007. Interest is payable each January 1 and July 1.

1. For 1987, record the acquisition of the bonds; receipt of the interest on July 1, including amortization of the discount by the straight line method; and any necessary adjusting entries on December 31, 1987 (year-end).
2. For 1988, record receipt of the semiannual interest payments, including amortization of the discount by the straight line method.

E15–12
Long-term investment in bonds—interest method of amortization

On February 1, 1987, the date of authorization, Watagua Corporation acquired as a *long-term* investment 10-year, 16 percent bonds of Lincoln Company for $737,639.21, which is a price to yield 12 percent. Interest is payable each February 1 and August 1. The face amount of the bonds is $600,000.

1. For 1987, prepare journal entries to record the acquisition of the bonds; receipt of interest on August 1, including amortization of the premium by the interest method; and any necessary adjusting entries on December 31 (year-end).
2. For 1988, prepare journal entries to record the receipt of semiannual interest, including amortization of the premium by the interest method.

Part Three / Sources and Uses of Capital

E15–13
Valuation of noncurrent marketable equity securities at LCM

The Edwards Corporation had the following *long-term* investments in noncurrent marketable equity securities for the period 1987 to 1988:

	Cost	Market Price at December 31	
		1987	1988
Common stock of Todd Corporation.	$300,000	$299,120	$297,000
Common stock of Hutch Corporation	251,000	250,000	250,200
Common stock of Hank Corporation.	312,000	310,000	310,800

Record the necessary adjusting entries for December 31, 1987, and 1988, for valuation of these long-term investments in noncurrent marketable equity securities.

E15–14
Managerial analysis of a corporation: number of times bond interest and preferred dividends are earned

The Utah Manufacturing Company had the following bonds and preferred stock outstanding as of December 31, 1987:

13% Debenture bonds payable.	$1,000,000
14% Cumulative preferred stock	1,500,000

Net income after deducting a 40 percent income tax was $800,000. Calculate (a) the number of times bond interest is earned, and (b) the number of times preferred dividends are earned; comment on the importance of these two ratios to the investors in Utah's bonds and preferred stock.

A Problems

P15–1A
Recording temporary investments

The Jaimson Corporation had the following selected transactions involving *temporary* investments during 1987:

1987

Jan. 1 Purchased 14 percent, AAA bonds of Kelly Company with a face value of $300,000 at 101 plus accrued interest. Interest is paid each March 1 and September 1. Brokerage fees and other costs incidental to the purchase were $300. The bonds have a maturity date of September 1, 1997.
Mar. 1 Received semiannual interest on the bonds of Kelly Company.
15 Purchased 4,000 shares of $10 par value, 15 percent preferred stock of Brown Company at $12 a share. Dividends are paid semiannually on February 25 and August 25. Brokerage fees and other costs incidental to the purchase were $205.
Aug. 15 Sold 600 shares of preferred stock of Brown Company at $13 a share. On August 10, the board of directors of the Brown Company declared the regular semiannual dividend on this stock, payable on August 25 to stockholders of record on August 20.
25 Received the dividend on the remaining preferred stock of Brown Company.
Sep. 1 Received semiannual interest on the bonds of Kelly Company.
Oct. 1 Sold the bonds of Kelly Company at 102 plus accrued interest.

Required: Journalize the transactions on the books of Jaimson Corporation.

P15–2A
Valuation of temporary investments

The Faber Corporation had the following *temporary* investments in marketable equity securities for the period January 1, 1987, to February 15, 1989:

	Cost	Market Price at December 31	
		1987	1988
Common stock of Kolb Company	$62,500	$63,000	$64,000
Common stock of Scott Company	56,250	55,250	
Common stock of Ford Company	77,500	76,250	79,200

The following transactions involving the investments occurred in 1988 and 1989:

1988

Jan. 15　Sold the common stock of Scott Company for $55,500.

1989

Feb. 15　Sold the common stock of Ford Company for $79,100.

Required:

1. Assuming the use of a valuation offset account, record the necessary adjusting entries for December 31, 1987, and 1988, under the lower of cost or market method.
2. Show how the temporary investments valuation, losses, and gains should be disclosed on the end-of-period financial statements as of December 31, 1987.
3. Record the sales of the temporary investments in 1988 and 1989.

P15–3A
Recording transactions of long-term investments in stock—cost method

The Wright Corporation had the following transactions involving *long-term* investment in stocks in 1987:

1987

Jan. 4　Purchased 2,000 shares of $50 par value common stock of Enchanto Company at 58.
Feb. 10　Purchased 3,000 shares of $50 par value common stock of Enchanto Company at 62.
Mar. 2　Received a cash dividend of $1.20 per share on the stock of Enchanto Company.
　　　3　Purchased 2,000 shares of $50 par value common stock of Enchanto Company at 64.
Sep. 10　The Enchanto Company declared a 100 percent stock dividend. The Wright Company received 7,000 additional shares of $50 par value common stock from the Enchanto Company.
Nov. 1　Sold 2,500 shares of lot number 1 of the common stock of Enchanto Company at 40. Assign cost on a specific identification basis.
Dec. 31　The Enchanto Company declared a $0.72 a share cash dividend payable January 16, 1988, to stockholders of record on December 31, 1987.

Required:

1. Journalize the transactions on the books of the Wright Corporation using the *cost* method.
2. Show how the long-term investment in stock should be shown on the balance sheet of the Wright Corporation as of December 31, 1987.
3. What does the use of the cost method imply about the investment?

P15–4A
Issues involving long-term investments in stock

The Hilton Corporation purchased 12,000 of the total 48,000 outstanding shares of Marko Corporation common stock on January 1, 1987, at the book value price of $40 per share. The following summary of results of operations for Marko Corporation is available:

	Operations of Marko		
	Total Net Income (Net Loss)	Total Cash Dividend	Transactions of Hilton
1987	$16,000	$4,000	
1988	20,000	8,000	
1989	4,000	2,000	Sold 2,000 shares at $44 per share on December 31, 1989
1990	(8,000)	2,000	
1991	8,000	1,000	Received 10 percent stock dividend

(continued on next page)

Required:

1. Which method of accounting should Hilton Corporation use for the investment in Marko Corporation stock? Why?
2. What would be the balance in the investment account at the end of each year, 1987 through 1991?

P15–5A
Long-term investment in bonds—both methods of amortization of premium

On June 30, 1987, the Gnee Corporation purchased as a *long-term* investment 15 percent bonds of the Rouddy Corporation for $395,705.35, which is a price to yield 13 percent. Interest is payable each June 30 and December 31. The bonds mature on June 30, 2002. The face amount of the bonds purchased is $350,000.

Required: Prepare all entries for 1987 and 1988 on the books of the Gnee Corporation except closing entries using the:

1. Straight line method of amortization.
2. Interest method of amortization.

P15–6A
Long-term investment in bonds—interest method of amortization of discount

On February 1, 1987, the date of authorization, Starship Corporation acquired as a *long-term* investment 20-year, 13 percent bonds of CSN Company for $746,672.87, which is a price to yield 14 percent. Interest is payable each February 1 and August 1. The face amount of the bonds is $800,000.

Required: Prepare all entries for 1987, 1988, and 1989, including adjusting entries at December 31 of each year on the books of Starship Corporation. Do not prepare closing entries. Starship Corporation uses the interest method of amortization.

P15–7A
Thought-provoking problem: determining quality of investment in bonds and preferred stock

Certain financial information for the Glazer Company and the Quaid Company as of the end of 1987 are shown below:

	Glazer Company	Quaid Company
Current assets	$ 720,000	$ 660,000
Property, plant, and equipment	3,048,000	2,310,000
Accumulated depreciation	(480,000)	(360,000)
Patents	12,000	0
Goodwill	0	30,000
Total assets	$3,300,000	$2,640,000
Current liabilities	$ 390,000	$ 204,000
Bonds payable, 11%, due in 10 years	600,000	720,000
Preferred stock, 12%, $100 par value	720,000	480,000
Common stock, $25 par value	1,200,000	900,000
Paid-in capital—excess over par value, common	0	156,000
Retained earnings	270,000	180,000
Retained earnings restricted for contingencies	120,000	0
Total liabilities and stockholders' equity	$3,300,000	$2,640,000
Analysis of retained earnings.		
Balance, beginning of year	$ 309,600	$ 172,800
Net income for year	224,400	118,800
Dividends: preferred	(86,400)	(57,600)
Dividends: common	(57,600)	(54,000)
Additions to retained earnings—		
restricted for contingencies	(120,000)	0
Balance, end of year	$ 270,000	$ 180,000
Market price of common stock per share	$ 40	$ 40
Market price of preferred stock per share	110	107

Required: Under the assumption that the two companies are generally comparable, write a brief answer to each of the following questions. Use only the ratios that will most reasonably substantiate your answer and indicate why. Compute the amount of each ratio and percentage indicated (carry your computations to one place beyond the decimal point).

1. Since the market prices of the bonds are not given, what ratios would aid potential investors to determine the rated quality of bonds and thus which one would probably sell at the higher price and which bonds would probably yield the higher return?
2. What ratios would aid potential investors in preferred stock (nonconvertible) to determine which company's preferred stock is the safer investment?
3. To what extent is each company benefiting from the leverage factor inherent in the existence of the bonds? of preferred stock?
4. What is the earnings per share for the common stock of each company? (Only one earnings per share needs to be calculated.)

B Problems

P15–1B
Recording temporary investments

The Roark Corporation had the following selected transactions involving *temporary* investments during 1987:

1987

Jan. 1 Purchased 13 percent, AAA bonds of Cannister Company with a face value of $400,000 at 101 plus accrued interest. Interest is paid each March 1 and September 1. Brokerage fees and other costs incidental to the purchase were $380. The bonds have a maturity date of September 1, 1997.
Mar. 1 Received semiannual interest on the bonds of Cannister Company.
15 Purchased 800 shares of $40 par value, 12 percent preferred stock of Roxboro Company at $50 a share. Dividends are paid semiannually on February 25 and August 25. Brokerage fees and other costs incidental to the purchase were $178.
Aug. 15 Sold 200 shares of preferred stock of Roxboro Company at $55 a share. On August 10, the board of directors of the Roxboro Company declared the regular semiannual dividend on this stock, payable on August 25 to stockholders of record on August 20.
25 Received the dividend on the remaining preferred stock of Roxboro Company.
Sep. 1 Received semiannual interest on the bonds of Cannister Company.
Oct. 1 Sold the bonds of Cannister Company at 102 plus accrued interest.

Required: Journalize the transactions on the books of Roark Corporation.

P15–2B
Valuation of temporary investments

The Tamy Corporation had the following *temporary* investments in marketable equity securities for the period January 1, 1987, to February 15, 1989:

	Cost	Market Price at December 31 1987	1988
Common stock of Albert Company	$53,000	$53,600	$53,360
Common stock of Eddie Company	45,500	44,300	
Common stock of Wayne Company	71,000	69,500	69,440

The following transactions involving the investments occurred in 1988 and 1989:

1988

Jan. 15 Sold the common stock of Eddie Company for $44,600.

1989

Feb. 15 Sold the common stock of Wayne Company for $71,350.

(continued on next page)

Required:

1. Assuming the use of a valuation offset account, record the necessary adjusting entries for December 31, 1987, and 1988, under the lower of cost or market method.
2. Show how the temporary investments valuation, losses, and gains should be disclosed on the end-of-period financial statements as of December 31, 1987.
3. Record the sales of the temporary investments in 1988 and 1989.

P15–3B
Recording transactions of long-term investments at cost

The Morrisville Corporation had the following transactions involving *long-term* investments in stocks in 1987:

1987		
Jan. 4	Purchased 400 shares of $25 par value common stock of Raleigh Company at 28.
Feb. 10	Purchased 600 shares of $25 par value common stock of Raleigh Company at 30.
Mar. 12	Received a cash dividend of $0.60 per share on the stock of Raleigh Company.
14	Purchased 1,000 shares of $25 par value common stock of Raleigh Company at 32.
Sep. 10	The Raleigh Company declared a 100 percent stock dividend. The Morrisville Company received 2,000 additional shares of $25 par value common stock from the Raleigh Company.
Nov. 1	Sold 600 shares of lot number 1 of the common stock of Raleigh Company at 20. Assign cost on a specific identification basis.
Dec. 31	The Raleigh Company declared a $0.30 a share cash dividend payable January 16, 1988, to stockholders of record on December 31, 1987.

Required:

1. Journalize the transactions on the books of Morrisville Corporation using the cost method.
2. Show how the long-term investment in stock should be shown on the balance sheet of the Morrisville Corporation as of December 31, 1987.
3. What does the use of the cost method imply about the securities?

P15–4B
Issues involving long-term investments in stock

The Elm Corporation purchased 3,000 of the total 10,000 outstanding shares of Hickory Corporation common stock on January 1, 1987, at the book value price of $10 per share. The following summary of results of operations for Hickory Corporation is available:

	Operations of Hickory		
	Total Net Income (Net Loss)	Total Cash Dividend	Transactions of Elm
1987	$4,000	$1,000	
1988	5,000	2,000	
1989	1,000	500	Sold 500 shares at $11 per share on December 31, 1989
1990	(2,000)	500	
1991	2,000	250	Received 10 percent stock dividend

Required:

1. Which method of accounting should Elm Corporation use for the investment in Hickory Corporation stock? Why?
2. What amount would be reflected in the investment account at the end of each year, 1987 through 1991?

P15–5B
Long-term investment in bonds—both methods of amortization

On March 31, 1987, the Changeor Corporation purchased as a *long-term* investment 14 percent bonds of the Nelson Corporation for $925,200.56, which is a price to yield 12 percent. Interest is payable March 31 and September 30. The bonds mature on March 31, 1997. The face amount of the bonds purchased is $830,000. Changeor Corporation has a fiscal year that ends on March 31 of each year.

Required: Prepare all entries from March 31, 1987, to March 31, 1989, except closing entries, on the books of the Changeor Corporation using the:

1. Straight line method of amortization.
2. Interest method of amortization.

P15–6B
Long-term investment in bonds—interest method of amortization

As a *long-term* investment, Snuffy Corporation purchased on March 1, 1987, $300,000, 15 percent bonds of Barny Corporation for $285,272.71, which is a price to yield 16 percent. The bonds mature in 10 years, and interest is payable each March 1 and September 1.

Required: Prepare all entries for 1987, 1988, and 1989, including adjusting entries at December 31 of each year on the books of Snuffy Corporation. Do not prepare closing entries. Snuffy Corporation uses the interest method of amortization.

P15–7B
Thought-provoking problem: decision about what investment to make and whether to convert or not

The Ringling Corporation had two situations involving temporary investment over a period of two years as indicated below.

Situation 1
The Ringling Corporation has excess funds that it desires to invest in temporary investments at the present time (January 1, 1987). It narrows down the investment opportunities to two securities:

a. 13½ percent, 10-year AAA first mortgage bonds of the Disco Corporation currently selling at 97.4.
b. 15½ percent, 10-year AAA first mortgage bonds of the Excello Corporation currently selling at 108.

Assume that the average price of all AAA first mortgage bonds is approximately 14 percent.

Required: Assume that you are asked as a consultant to advise the Ringling Corporation which investment appears to be the better choice; what would be your advice and why?

Situation 2
The Ringling Corporation owns as a temporary investment 10,000 shares of Newco Corporation $50 par value, 10 percent preferred stock on January 1, 1988. The Newco stock is callable at $50 per share and convertible at the rate of 1.1 shares of common per share of preferred. Newco has announced its intention of exercising the call privilege simultaneously with payment of the quarterly dividend on January 8, 1988. Newco common stock is currently selling for $55 per share. Newco's common dividends per share for the past three years have been $1.28, $1.70, and $1.95, respectively.

Required: As an accounting consultant to Ringling Corporation, prepare a recommendation as to whether to convert to Newco common before January 8 or to wait and accept the redemption. Show calculations to support your conclusion. If you need additional information, what would it be? Ignore income taxes.

Part Four

Financial Reporting

16 Consolidated Statements and International Accounting

Introduction

Large corporations grow as a result of their own operations; most, however, speed up the growth process by acquiring other companies. Typically, companies combine by:

☐ Purchase of part or all of the voting stock of another company where the purchased company *continues to exist* (an *acquisition*).

☐ Purchase of all the stock of another company where the purchased company *is eliminated* (a *merger*).

☐ Formation of a new corporation to purchase all the voting stock of two companies that are put together under a new name (a *consolidation*).

In this chapter, the concept of consolidated financial statements is described with only enough detail to illustrate the types of eliminations needed in the consolidation process.

Learning Goals

1. To understand the concept of reciprocal accounts.

2. To know why corporations acquire and hold majority or total ownership of other corporations.

3. To recognize the nature and types of affiliations and intercompany transactions.

4. To understand some of the basic concepts of preparation of consolidated financial statements.

5. To understand the need for elimination of certain transactions in preparing consolidated statements.

Reasons for Business Acquisitions

As indicated in the introduction to this chapter, it is typical for large corporations to acquire ownership in other corporations. One reason for acquisition is the *opening of new markets for products*. A major wholesale food distributor reported that " . . . new division is a major IGA supplier and has a strong retail base with the capability and desire to expand. Fleming looks forward to increased contributions from this new operation and is optimistic about the potential for growth in the mid-South area."[1] A related reason for acquisition is the development and establishment of *a fair market share in new products*. Amp, Incorporated, reported that: "Several years ago, we began developing membrane switches and keyboards. Then in May 1981, we acquired the membrane switch and keyboard business of Chomerics, Inc., which was the industry leader with 1980 sales of $11,000,000 in this rapidly growing product area."[2] Amp continues this management philosophy; in 1984, the company reported, "As part of our continuing efforts to logically diversify into related component areas, in July 1983 we acquired 60 percent (with option of full ownership in the future) of small, privately owned Carroll Touch Technology Corporation. . . . Carroll is a pioneeer in infrared touch screen devices for data entry into computer-based systems."[3]

A third reason for acquisition is *to achieve growth*. Knight-Ridder Newspapers, Inc., recounts the history of its growth as two groups—one that started with an Akron, Ohio newspaper in 1933 and another that began with a German-language newspaper in 1892—combined in 1974 to form the present group. By 1984, Knight-Ridder had grown to the point that it owned 65 subsidiaries and divisions incorporated in 17 states.[4] Included are such newspapers as *The Miami Herald, The Philadelphia Inquirer* and *The Philadelphia Daily News,* and *The Charlotte Observer and News*. Also owned in 1984 by Knight-Ridder were five major television stations. Total revenues have grown from $399 million in 1971 to $1.473 billion in 1983—more than tripling in 12 years.[5]

Some companies acquire other companies *to complement existing operations*. For example, "On August 3, 1983, one of Warner Lambert's wholly owned subsidiaries acquired the high-precision microscope business from McBain Instruments, Inc."[6] In the opposite direction, some companies continue *to diversify into nonrelated fields*. The percentage contributions to 1983 net sales and earnings of R. J. Reynolds Industries were: tobacco, 54 percent; foods and beverages, 33 percent; energy, 9 percent; other businesses, 4 percent.[7] Reynolds' projections are that by 1984–1986, capital expenditures will

---

[1] Fleming Companies, Inc., *1983 Annual Report,* p. 3.
[2] Amp, Incorporated, *1981 Annual Report,* p. 3.
[3] Amp, Incorporated, *1983 Annual Report,* p. 3.
[4] Knight-Ridder Newspapers, Inc., *1983 Annual Report,* p. 55.
[5] Ibid., p. 42.
[6] Warner Lambert Company, *1983 Annual Report,* p. 31.
[7] R. J. Reynolds Industries, *1983 Annual Report,* p. 27.

be made as follows: tobacco, 41 percent; foods and beverages, 24 percent; energy, 30 percent; and other businesses, 5 percent.[8]

The one overriding objective in business acquisitions is an attempt to *achieve and improve overall profitability,* especially as reflected in earnings per share. All other reasons support this one. One successful company probably summarizes the goals of many corporations as follows:

> United Technologies' diversification strategy has withstood the test of economic difficulties that have beset America and its trading partners in recent years. Many of our businesses are cyclical, but the cycles have tended to be staggered because of our involvement across a span of industries and our growing involvement in overseas markets. Despite adverse economic conditions, our sales and net income increased again in 1981, rising 11 percent and 16 percent respectively. Fully diluted earnings per share rose 8 percent.[9]

Against this background, it is appropriate to consider the nature of parent-subsidiary relationships in the next section.

Parent-Subsidiary Relationships

The equity method of accounting for long-term investments in stock of another corporation is described in Chapter 15. Ownership of 20 percent or more of the voting stock of another company leads to the presumption that the investor can exercise *significant influence* over the policies of the investee and should account for its investment by the equity method.[10] The term **investor company** is used here to describe the company acquiring some percent of ownership in another company. The term **investee company** describes the company whose voting stock is held by another company.

Exercise of Control

When an investor holds 50 percent or more of the voting stock of a going concern, it has the ability to *control* rather than just exert substantial influence.[11] At this point, the investor is known as a **parent company** and the investee as a **subsidiary company**. When the parent-subsidiary relationship exists or when several subsidiary companies have a common parent, the group is known as **affiliates** or **affiliated companies**. The share of ownership not held by the parent is known as the **minority interest**. Usually, the minority share of ownership is scattered among many shareholders.

---

[8]Ibid., p. 33.

[9]United Technologies Corporation, *1981 Annual Report,* p. 2. Fully diluted earnings per share (explained in Chapter 13) represents the most conservative possible EPS computation.

[10]*Opinions of the Accounting Principles Board No. 18,* "Equity Method for Investments in Common Stock" (AICPA: New York, March 1971), paragraph 17.

[11]Ibid., paragraph 3c.

A subsidiary company that is totally owned by a parent company (holding 100 percent of voting stock) is often left as a legal entity operating under its own name. Such a subsidiary would have its own set of accounting records and prepare its own financial statements for management purposes, although they may not be released publicly. A parent company may choose such an arrangement because the liability of a subsidiary corporation to its creditors is limited to the extent of its own assets.

Some wholly owned corporations operate in one state or foreign country. In such cases, it may be advantageous from the viewpoint of regulations as to legal capital (see Chapter 13) or state or foreign tax laws for the subsidiary to operate as a legal entity.

Federal income taxes are levied at a lower rate on the first $100,000 of taxable income of a corporation. When separate legal entities file separate income tax returns, each can take advantage of the lower rates. Certain federal laws provide incentives and aid to smaller businesses; in some cases, this may be a reason to retain separate corporate identity.

Although the legal status of entities owned by a parent company may not be changed, the economic status is changed. This aspect is discussed next.

Economic versus Legal Entity

Although a group of affiliated corporations may be separate *legal* entities, the nature of their affiliation is often such that they are in substance a single *economic* entity (see Figure 16–1). In these cases, the operating results and financial condition of the economic entity are more meaningful when reported in consolidated financial statements. **Consolidated financial statements** are reports in which the assets, liabilities, revenues, and expenses of subsidiary companies are combined with those of the parent company. The result is a set of statements that represents all the individual corporations as a single economic unit. Consolidated statements do not take the place of individual financial reports for the investee corporations. When consolidated statements are prepared, the individual financial statements are usually not published in

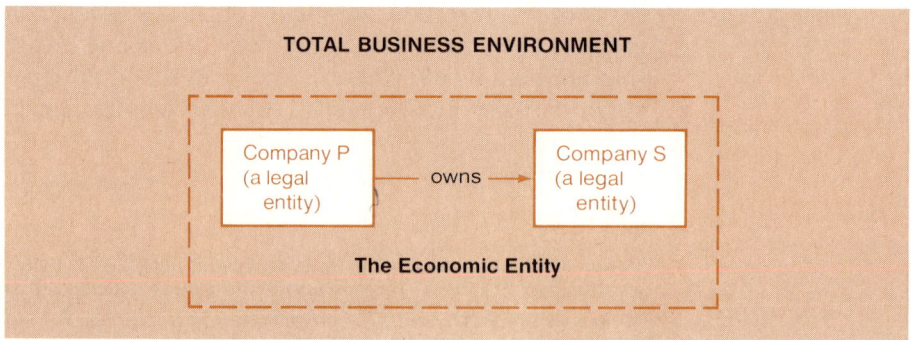

Figure 16–1   **Concept of Economic Entity**

annual reports; the consolidated statements are considered more meaningful.

Figure 16–1 shows the simple situation where one parent company (Company P) owns one subsidiary company (Company S).[12] Company P exercises control over the operating policies of Company S. If S is 100 percent owned by P, all dividends it pays go to P. Although each will have independent transactions with other companies in the business environment, they also have many *controlled* transactions between themselves. There may be loans or sales to each other, for instance. When such events occur between two affiliates, they are called **intercompany transactions** (discussed later). For these reasons, consolidated financial statements for the economic entity as a whole are more useful to the public than the individual statements of P and S.

The AICPA has indicated the existence of " . . . a presumption that consolidated statements are more meaningful than separate statements and that they are usually necessary for a fair presentation when one of the companies in the group directly or indirectly has a *controlling* financial interest in the other companies."[13] Such a presumption had a sound basis in the 1950s when most business combinations tended to enhance concentration in a single line of business. In today's business climate, where combinations have brought forth large diversified firms (called *conglomerates*), a set of consolidated financial statements is probably less useful.

The usual definition of *controlling interest* for purposes of consolidation of financial statements is the ownership of more than 50 percent of the voting stock of the investee company.[14] The AICPA recognized certain exceptions to this general rule. Consolidated financial statements should not be prepared where:

1. Control is temporary.

2. The minority interest is so large that separate statements may be more meaningful and useful.

3. The presentation of separate statements for a subsidiary would be more informative to shareholders and creditors (for example, a subsidiary finance company owned by an industrial corporation).

4. Control does not rest with the majority owners (as may be the case when the organization is in the hands of a trustee for reorganization or bankruptcy).[15]

In a later pronouncement, the AICPA stated that information about the accounting policies of a company is needed by financial statement users. Among significant accounting policies to be disclosed as an integral part of

---

[12] Recall that in the typical situation, one parent company owns many subsidiaries.

[13] *Accounting Research Bulletin No. 51,* "Consolidated Financial Statements" (New York: AICPA, August 1959), paragraph 1 (emphasis added).

[14] Ibid., paragraph 2.

[15] *ARB No. 51,* paragraphs 2 and 3.

the statements is the *basis of consolidation.*[16] Recall from Chapter 15 that investments in other companies may be accounted for by the cost or equity method. This fact is recognized in the consolidation process. The consolidated statements are the same regardless of the method used to account for the investment.

In its 1984 *Annual Report,* Ford Motor Company stated that the consolidated financial statements presented therein included " . . . the accounts of the Company and its majority-owned domestic and foreign subsidiaries except the finance, insurance, real estate, and dealership subsidiaries, which are included on an equity basis."[17] Since the annual reports of practically all large corporations include consolidated financial statements, it is useful to consider some techniques of consolidation. Before this can be done, the nature of certain reciprocal accounts in the books of a parent and subsidiary must be understood. They are discussed in the next section.

Reciprocal Accounts and Their Elimination

Businesses often find an advantage in splitting all or a portion of some accounts out of the general ledger and locating them elsewhere. Manufacturers may find it better to locate in the factory some accounts that are devoted exclusively to the production process. Other businesses open branches and find a need to have a portion of some accounts maintained at the branch. In these split-ledger situations, there must be an account in each portion of the ledger that represents the amount of the common "split-off" elements. Such accounts are known as **reciprocal accounts**. Assume, for example, that San Diego Company opened a branch in Fullerton and transferred $100,000 to begin branch operations. So that the Fullerton Branch manager can be better informed, a set of accounts will be maintained there. When the $100,000 is transferred, San Diego's accountant must credit the Cash account. The account debited at San Diego Company is called Fullerton Branch—a *reciprocal account* that represents the company's net assets carried in the branch accounts. At the same time, the accountant for the branch debits the branch Cash account and credits an account called Home Office—a *reciprocal account* that represents the company's equity in branch net assets.

Accounts in the books of affiliates that have offsetting elements and would duplicate each other if combined are also reciprocal accounts. They can arise from the act of investment or from transactions that occur after an acquisition has been completed. Both circumstances are illustrated in the sections that follow. The similarity between reciprocal accounts in a home office and its branch and in a parent and its subsidiary is illustrated in Figure 16–2. In the branch and home office situation, the reciprocal accounts are in the decentralized accounts of a single company. In the parent-subsidiary situation, they

---

[16]*Opinions of the Accounting Principles Board No. 22,* "Disclosure of Accounting Policies" (New York: AICPA, April, 1972), paragraphs 8 and 13.

[17]Ford Motor Company, *1984 Annual Report,* p. 29.

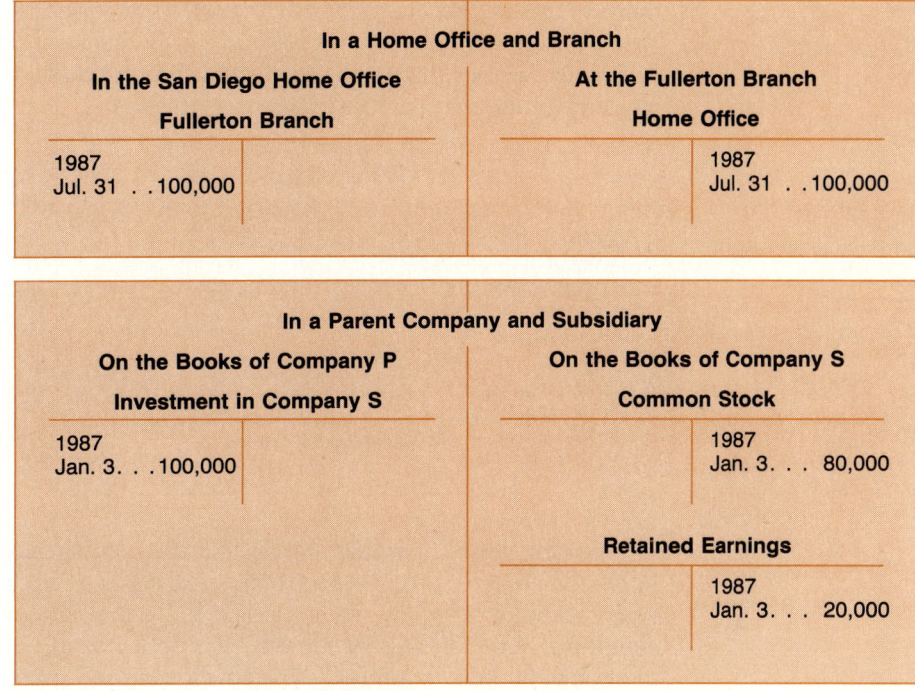

Figure 16–2 **Reciprocal Account Relationships**

are accounts in the books of two separate legal entities. Because of the purpose they serve, they are reciprocal in concept.

Example 1: Arising from Investment Assume that Company P purchased from stockholders 100 percent of the voting stock of Company S at its *book value* of $100,000 on January 3, 1987. The entry on the books of Company P to record the acquisition is:[18]

1987				
Jan.	3	Investment in Company S	100,000	
		Cash		100,000
		To record the purchase of 100 percent of common stock of S.		

There would be no entry on the books of Company S to record this purchase; its stock remains outstanding in the hands of a new stockholder. Com-

---

[18]At the introductory level, the investment at book value of acquired assets is the only example used. Accounting for investments at other than book value raises issues of fair market value of assets and liabilities.

pany S does not receive the cash; it goes to its former stockholders who sold their stock to Company P.

Assume further that immediately after the purchase, the balance sheet amounts of the two companies were as follows:

	Company P	Company S
Cash	$ 50,000	$ 40,000
Investment in Company S	100,000	0
Property, plant, and equipment	150,000	65,000
Total assets	$300,000	$105,000
Liabilities	$ 75,000	$ 5,000
Common stock	175,000	80,000
Retained earnings	50,000	20,000
Total liabilities and stockholders' equity	$300,000	$105,000

From the above, it would appear that the combined assets of the two corporations are $405,000 = ($300,000 + $105,000). The combined liabilities and stockholders' equity would appear to be the same amount. Such an assumption, however, fails to consider the presence of reciprocal accounts in the books of the two affiliates. The Investment in Company S account in the assets of P represents equity in Company S. At the same time, the Common Stock and Retained Earnings accounts on the books of S represent ownership equity held by Company P. These sets of accounts are reciprocal accounts that must be eliminated, often by use of a work sheet, before a consolidated balance sheet *on the date of acquisition* can be prepared. Such a work sheet is shown in Figure 16–3. It is important to note that the elimination entry made in the work sheet would *never be journalized or posted* in the accounting records of either the parent or subsidiary company. It is a work sheet entry only to remove the reciprocal accounts (or reciprocal elements of accounts to be discussed later) before preparing a consolidated financial statement. In Figure 16–3 the work sheet amounts are added horizontally, taking into consideration the amounts in the **Eliminations** (removal of duplicate reciprocal elements) columns. As can be seen from the work sheet, the combined assets of the economic entity are $305,000 (not $405,000). To have failed to eliminate reciprocal elements before combining all amounts would give an inflated picture of its total worth.

In recording corporate acquisitions, there are two types of accounting that apply. One is *purchase* accounting, which involves the recognition of the assets and liabilities of the subsidiary at their fair market value as of the date of acquisition in the consolidated statements. The other is *pooling of interests,* in which assets and liabilities are recognized at book value in the consolidated financial statements. Which method to use depends upon how the acquisition was made and the nature of ownership after the acquisition. Since the accounting issues discussed in the next section apply to both methods

COMPANY P AND SUBSIDIARY S
Work Sheet for Consolidated Statements
January 3, 1987

Account Titles	Company P	Company S	Eliminations Debit	Eliminations Credit	Consolidated Balance Sheet
Debit Accounts					
Cash	50,000	40,000			90,000
Investment in Company S	100,000	0		(a) 100,000	0
Property, Plant, and Equipment	150,000	65,000			215,000
Totals	300,000	105,000			305,000
Credit Accounts					
Liabilities	75,000	5,000			80,000
Common Stock	175,000	80,000	(a) 80,000		175,000
Retained Earnings	50,000	20,000	(a) 20,000		50,000
Totals	300,000	105,000	100,000	100,000	305,000

Figure 16–3 Work Sheet for Consolidated Statements at Date of Acquisition

because of the assumption that cost of the subsidiary is at book value, a detailed discussion of purchase versus pooling of interests is not essential at this point and is, therefore, not covered in this book.

Example 2: Arising after Acquisition Affiliated companies often have transactions with each other. Such transactions introduce both new reciprocal accounts and reciprocal elements into existing accounts. Some typical examples of such transactions are:

- ☐ Intercompany revenue and expense, for example, sales of merchandise that inflate both the Sales and Purchases accounts from the viewpoint of the economic entity.
- ☐ Intercompany receivables and payables that may arise from sales or loans to each other.
- ☐ Intercompany dividends—for example, any dividends paid by Company S would be received by its parent, Company P.

Because of transactions of this nature, it is not possible to convey an accurate picture of the financial position of an *economic entity* by simply combining the balance sheet accounts into a consolidated statement. Neither can the results of operations be correctly portrayed by combining accounts to produce a consolidated income statement and statement of retained earnings. To eliminate the "double counting" of reciprocal accounts or their elements, the accountant prepares a work sheet on which eliminations similar to those in Figure 16–3 are made. To illustrate the concept and techniques of consolidation after acquisition, Example 1 is modified slightly to include intercompany receivables and payables. Assume that Company P loaned $20,000 on a 15 percent 180-day note to its subsidiary on January 4, 1987. The entries to record the loan are below.

On the books of Company P:

| 1987 Jan. | 4 | Notes Receivable from S .... Cash .... To record 180-day loan to subsidiary at 15%. | | 20,000 | 20,000 |

On the books of Company S:

| 1987 Jan. | 4 | Cash .... Notes Payable to P .... To record 180-day loan from parent at 15%. | | 20,000 | 20,000 |

If consolidated statements are to be prepared as of January 4, the eliminations shown in Figure 16–4 would be needed. Since there have been no transactions with the outside business environment, the total assets of the economic entity are still $305,000. The elimination of $120,000 in reciprocal accounts shown in Figure 16–4 prevents the combining of amounts that are generated internally within the economic entity. There is no need to make an elimination to reflect the transfer of cash. Although $20,000 has moved from P to S, the combined amount of $90,000 is still an accurate measure of total cash in the economic entity. By the end of the accounting year, many other transactions would have taken place. Some of them would be intercompany transactions of the type described earlier. Because they affect the operating results as well as the balance sheet, an illustration is given to show the elimination of such an item.

Example 3: Elimination of Income Statement Item—Cost Method

In Example 2, an intercompany loan was made by the parent to the subsidiary. When this loan was repaid the parent would record interest earned and the subsidiary would record interest expense of $1,500 = ($20,000 × 0.15 × 180/360). To include these items in the consolidated income statement would inflate both the interest earned and the interest expense of the economic entity. Thus, they should be eliminated so that the consolidated income statement will reflect only revenue and expense trans-

COMPANY P AND SUBSIDIARY S[a]
Work Sheet for Consolidated Statements
January 4, 1987

Account Titles	Company P	Company S	Eliminations Debit		Eliminations Credit		Consolidated Balance Sheet
Debit Accounts							
Cash	30,000	60,000					90,000
Notes Receivable from S	20,000	0			(b)	20,000	0
Investment in Company S	100,000	0			(a)	100,000	0
Property, Plant, and Equipment	150,000	65,000					215,000
Totals	300,000	125,000					305,000
Credit Accounts							
Liabilities	75,000	5,000					80,000
Notes Payable to P	0	20,000	(b)	20,000			0
Common Stock	175,000	80,000	(a)	80,000			175,000
Retained Earnings	50,000	20,000	(a)	20,000			50,000
Totals	300,000	125,000		120,000		120,000	305,000

[a]This illustration makes the simplifying assumption that no revenue and expense transactions took place between P and S during January 3 to 4. The only intercompany transaction was the loaning of $20,000 on the note.

Figure 16–4   **Work Sheet for Consolidated Statements after Date of Acquisition—Balance Sheet Items**

actions with outsiders. The elimination of this item is shown in Figure 16–5. Other amounts except the Investment account; property, plant, and equipment; and the stockholders' equity in Figure 16–5 are assumed to have arisen from 1987 transactions, and represent the preclosing trial balances of Companies P and S. There were no intercompany sales between these two affiliates. If there had been, the amounts would be reflected in both the Sales and the Cost of Goods Sold (purchases) accounts of the two companies and should be eliminated against each other. In Figure 16–5, elimination (a) (under the cost method) is necessary to avoid double counting the investment, as explained in Example 1. This problem still remains at the end of the year. Elimination (b) removes $1,500 of interest paid by Company S to Company P from the consolidated income statement because this transaction does not extend outside the scope of the economic entity.

With the reciprocal items eliminated, it would be a simple task to extend each item in the Consolidated Trial Balance columns to columns for financial statements. There would be columns added for the consolidated income

COMPANY P AND SUBSIDIARY S
Work Sheet for Consolidated Statements
For the Year Ended December 31, 1987

Account Titles	Company P	Company S	Eliminations Debit	Eliminations Credit	Consolidated Trial Balance
Debit Accounts					
Cash	81,500	71,500			153,000
Investment in Company S	100,000[a]	0		(a) 100,000	0
Property, Plant, and Equipment	150,000	65,000			215,000
Cost of Goods Sold	300,000	200,000			500,000
Interest Expense	0	1,500		(b) 1,500	0
Other Expenses	55,000	40,000			95,000
Totals	686,500	378,000			963,000
Credit Accounts					
Liabilities	60,000	18,000			78,000
Common Stock	175,000	80,000	(a) 80,000		175,000
Retained Earnings	50,000	20,000	(a) 20,000		50,000
Sales	400,000	260,000			660,000
Interest Earned	1,500	0	(b) 1,500		0
Totals	686,500	378,000	101,500	101,500	963,000

[a] In order to keep this illustration simple, it is assumed that the cost method was used to account for the investment. Accordingly, the Investment account balance remains unchanged and there is no Investor's Share of Investee Income (or Loss) account on P's books.

Figure 16–5 Work Sheet for Year-End Consolidated Statements—Income Statement Items: Cost Method

statement, consolidated statement of retained earnings, and consolidated balance sheet. The formal consolidated financial statements would be prepared from the work sheet.

To complete the examples of eliminations for consolidated statements, one more idea is introduced to make them more like actual corporate situations. The next example deals with the elimination of the Investment account when it has been accounted for by the *equity method* of accounting.

Example 4: Elimination of Investment: Equity Method

As shown in Chapter 15, the equity method of accounting for an investment should be used when an investor company owns more than 20 percent of the stock of an investee company. Under this method, the Investment account is reduced to reflect dividends received from the investee and is increased to reflect the investor's share of investee income. When a parent/subsidiary relationship exists, the equity method would normally be used. This means that the Investment account would not have the same balance at the end of the accounting period that it had at the beginning. Thus, the elimination of the investment at cost as shown in the three previous illustrations would not completely eliminate the new end-of-period balance in the Investment account. To correct this situation, elimination entries are first made to reverse the effect of recording subsidiary earnings and dividends during the year. The effect is to restore the Investment account to its beginning-of-the-year balance; then, its elimination on the work sheet can be made as shown in the three previous examples.

Assume the same data as in Example 3 *except that Company S net income of $18,500 in 1987* has been recognized by its parent. Company S declared no dividends. Figure 16–6 shows the work sheet with elimination (a) to re-

COMPANY P AND SUBSIDIARY S
Work Sheet for Consolidated Statements
For the Year Ended December 31, 1987

Account Titles	Company P	Company S	Eliminations Debit	Eliminations Credit	Consolidated Trial Balance
Debit Accounts					
Cash	81,500	71,500			153,000
Investment in Company S	118,500	0		(a) 18,500	
				(b) 100,000	0
Property, Plant, and Equipment	150,000	65,000			215,000
Cost of Goods Sold	300,000	200,000			500,000
Interest Expense	0	1,500		(c) 1,500	0
Other Expenses	55,000	40,000			95,000
Totals	705,000	378,000			963,000
Credit Accounts					
Liabilities	60,000	18,000			78,000
Common Stock	175,000	80,000	(b) 80,000		175,000
Retained Earnings (1/1/87)	50,000	20,000	(b) 20,000		50,000
Sales	400,000	260,000			660,000
Interest Earned	1,500	0	(c) 1,500		0
Investor's Share of Investee Income	18,500	0	(a) 18,500		0
Totals	705,000	378,000	120,000	120,000	963,000

Figure 16–6   Elimination of Investment: Equity Method

verse 100 percent of Company P's share of Company S income. With the Investment account balance now brought back to its beginning balance of $100,000 = ($118,500 − $18,500), entry (b) completes its elimination. Elimination entry (c) is the same as in Example 3—the elimination of intercompany expense and revenue.

As noted earlier, some eliminations are quite complex and will not be illustrated here. Two points should be kept in mind about the techniques of consolidation:

1. The only events that change the status of the economic entity are transactions with the outside business environment. In consolidated statements, therefore, the effects of intercompany transactions must be eliminated.

2. The elimination entries on the work sheet are for the purposes of preparing consolidated statements only. They are never reflected in the records of any of the affiliates or in any affiliate's financial statements.

Acquisition at a Price in Excess of Fair Market Value

When an investor company acquires a portion or all of the stock of an investee company, the price paid is often in excess of the book value of the assets acquired. This difference—sometimes called the differential—is allocated to specific assets of the investee such as land, buildings, or machinery to bring them up to fair market value. Often there is an unallocated balance left in the differential that cannot be allocated to any of the tangible assets acquired. This is an asset called goodwill (see Chapter 11). In preparing consolidated statements of a parent and a subsidiary, the goodwill in the economic entity must be shown on the consolidated statements. When this is done, the goodwill in the economic entity must be amortized. An elimination entry on the work sheet records the reduction of goodwill and the accompanying expense that results in a reduction in consolidated net income. The reverse situation of the price paid being less than the book value of the assets acquired is possible. This case does not occur as frequently as the former and is not considered here.

Minority Interest

In the examples used up to this point, it has been assumed that the parent company owned 100 percent of the voting stock of subsidiary companies. Remember, however, that unless there are indications to the contrary, ownership of more than 50 percent of the voting stock of a subsidiary is sufficient to presume control and thus to present consolidated financial statements. The voting stock held by companies or persons other than the parent company (obviously less than 50 percent) determines the amount of minority interest in all subsidiaries not wholly owned by the parent company. In a consolidated balance sheet, the minority interest represents neither liabilities nor stockholders' equity of the parent. The total amount represented by minority interest is usually presented as a single amount on the total liabilities and stockholders' equity side of a balance sheet *between* the liabilities and the stockholders' equity. For example, Ford Motor Company reported total liabilities and stockholders' equity of $27,485.6 million at December 31, 1984. Of this total, $137.9 million was reported between the liabilities and the stockholders' equity as "Minority interests in net assets of consolidated subsidiaries."[19]

Importance of Acquisition Information

The reader of a set of consolidated financial statements should be alert to acquisitions because they affect the operating results. They are normally disclosed in the "Notes to Financial Statements"—often referred to as **footnote disclosure**. For example, Dow Chemical disclosed in Note G to its 1981 *Annual Report* that "Under the terms of an Agreement and Plan of Reorganization with Richarson-Merrill, Inc. (RMI), the Company acquired the ethical pharmaceutical business of RMI in exchange for approximately 7.3 million shares of Dow common stock having a fair market value of $250 million."[20] The footnote goes on to explain details of the acquisition.

In the *Opinions of the APB,* corporations are required to show the effects of discontinued operations—the opposite of acquisitions—in their income statements.[21] No such requirement exists for acquisitions, yet they can have a significant effect on income and changes in assets and liabilities. The informed reader will look carefully at footnotes to financial statements to determine the effect of acquisitions of all types.

Managerial Analysis: Segment Reporting

As more firms combined and expanded horizontally, forming conglomerates, the data in consolidated statements became less useful to the investing public. In the mid-1960s, various organizations sponsored studies to determine the feasibility of line-of-business segment reporting to provide more information in detail to investors. From 1969 to 1974 the SEC issued requirements for reporting line-of-business information, and in December 1976 the FASB issued *Statement of Financial Accounting Standards No. 14,* providing for specific segment reporting.[22] The statement provides for segment reporting in three ways:[23]

1. The enterprise's operations in different industries.
2. The enterprise's foreign operations and foreign sales.
3. The enterprise's operations by major customers.

---

[19] Ford Motor Company, *1984 Annual Report,* p. 26.

[20] Dow Chemical, *1981 Annual Report,* p. 24.

[21] *Opinions of the Accounting Principles Board No. 30,* "Reporting the Results of Operations" (New York: AICPA, 1973), paragraph 8.

[22] "Financial Reporting for Segments of an Enterprise" (Stamford, Conn.: FASB, December, 1976).

[23] Ibid., paragraph 3.

The major purpose of *FASB Statement No. 14* is to disaggregate the consolidated financial report information to assist financial statement users. The FASB felt that such additional detail would permit better assessment of the enterprise's past performance and future prospects.

Segment information is provided in the Notes to Financial Statements. For example, ITT Corporation (formerly International Telephone and Telegraph Corporation) reported segment information for its consolidated and unconsolidated subsidiaries combined in 1983 as follows:

Segment	Sales and Revenues		Operating Income (Dollars in millions)	
Telecommunications	$ 5,388	(26.6%)	$ 423	(35.2%)
Industrial Technology	4,805	(23.7%)	333	(27.7%)
Natural Resources and Food Products	2,539	(12.5%)	182	(15.2%)
Diversified Services	7,517	(37.2%)	380[a]	(21.9%)[a]
Totals	$20,249	(100.0%)	$1,201	(100.0%)

[a] Includes ($117) of unallocated income that is not in total; all percentages computed by the authors.

ITT Corporation reported several different subcategories under each of these major industry segments. The company also supplied industry segment information on identifiable assets; gross property, plant, and equipment; gross plant additions; and depreciation. In addition to industry segment information, ITT Corporation provided a geographical breakdown of the same data. As is usual in annual reports, the segment information was supplied for the current year and the two previous years.

While the use of consolidated statements is still meaningful to report on the activities of the economic entity as a whole, there is a need for more details about the diverse operations of many giant corporations. Segment reporting helps fill the information gap. It should be noted, however, that comparison of segments among companies is usually misleading. Individual firms may define segments differently; for example, telecommunications for ITT may be quite different from another company. However, it may be safely assumed that a corporation defines telecommunications in the same way for consecutive years so that comparison of segments within a company is feasible.

Foreign Operations

Many large corporations operate internationally. With foreign divisions or foreign subsidiaries, new problems are introduced that require close managerial supervision. A major problem that stems from the international nature of these companies is caused by fluctuations in currencies. The relative values of currencies change constantly so that sales and later collections are made at different exchange rates. The fluctuations cause gains or losses from currency exchange called *transaction gains or losses*.

Financial reports are prepared in terms of a single currency. Companies today typically deal in yen, francs, dollars, and other currencies and prepare financial reports in dollars. The gains and losses from converting from foreign currency figures to dollars are called *translation gains and losses*. These problems are discussed and illustrated in Appendix 16.1.

Appendix 16.1
International Accounting

Introduction

Many corporations today are multinational. For example, a recent Ford Motor Company *Annual Report* indicated that about 54 percent of its total revenues were generated in the United States. Sales in Europe were about 22 percent; in Canada, 10 percent; and in Latin America, 8 percent; with remaining sales in several other countries. Because the values of national currencies fluctuate constantly with respect to each other, international operations create special problems in accounting. The basic issues and related concepts of international accounting are explained in this appendix.

Learning Goals

1. To understand the nature of changes in relative values of national currencies.
2. To understand the concept of a functional currency.
3. To be able to compute and record exchange gains and losses.

Currency Fluctuations

When a seller in the United States makes a sale to a buyer in France, the seller expects to end up with dollars when the collection is made. In a similar manner, the buyer in France expects to pay in francs. If the buyer pays in francs, the seller must use those frances to purchase dollars—a transaction called **foreign currency exchange**. If the relative values of the dollar and the franc remain constant during the period from sale to collection and exchange, there would be no problem. However, currencies don't remain constant; in fact, they consistently fluctuate in value against each other. On June 26, 1984, the French franc's closing value was 11.68 francs per United States dollar. Exactly one year prior to that date it was 13.21 francs. During the year, the value of the franc fell relative to the dollar. Other national currencies rise and fall in a similar manner daily as they are exchanged for each other. This relationship can be expressed in either currency. For example, assume that the franc gained strength against the dollar and rose to an exchange value of 15 cents; it required $0.15 to purchase one franc. A company in France would probably take the opposite view; that is, that the dollar is worth 6⅔ francs = ($1.00 ÷ $0.15) because it would have to exchange 6⅔ francs to obtain one dollar.

Financial Reporting Issues

Two basic financial reporting issues arise when international transactions involve dealings in more than one national currency:

1. Translation for an exchange transaction.

2. Translation for the statement item in preparing combined or consolidated financial statements.

The first issue arises when currencies fluctuate while a transaction is in process. The second issue arises at the end of an accounting period when statements are being prepared. Either may result in a gain or loss from currency exchange.

In December 1981, the Financial Accounting Standards Board issued revised guidelines for transactions in which the currency of one country is exchanged for that of another.[24] In that issuance, the FASB introduced the concept of a functional currency. Basically, the **functional currency** is the currency that is being used to *measure* the assets, liabilities, revenues, or expenses. For example, a United States corporation may have a subsidiary, located in France, that makes sales both in France and Germany. A basic problem is determining whether those sales should be measured in French francs or German marks before being translated into dollars in preparation of a consolidated income statement. The FASB said that the functional currency should be ". . . the currency of the environment in which an entity primarily generates revenues and expends cash."[25] Based on a set of rather complex rules, an entity must decide which country's currency is the functional currency before the translation into dollars can be made. When the functional currency and the reporting currency are not the same, **foreign currency exchange gains and losses** result from translation into the reporting currency.[26] The concept of functional currency is primarily important in translation of foreign financial statement items when consolidated statements are prepared; translation for consolidated statements is briefly considered later. The illustration discussed next covers the problems of translation of a foreign currency into dollars for recording international transactions.

---

[24]*Statement of Financial Accounting Standards No. 52,* "Foreign Currency Translation" (Stamford, Conn.: FASB, December, 1981).

[25]Ibid., paragraph 5.

[26]For example, if demand in the United States for French goods or services increases significantly, there will be a greater dollar demand for French francs. As a result, the price of francs will increase, and it may be said that the franc has risen relative to the dollar.

Translation for Specific Transactions

Assume that Alabama Corporation is a United States company engaged in significant foreign operations. Its basic reporting currency is dollars; it closes the books annually each December 31. On December 16, 1987, it made a sale in France for 2,000,000 francs when the exchange rate was $0.15 per franc. On Alabama Corporation's books, the sale would be recorded as follows:

1987				
Dec.	16	Accounts Receivable	300,000	
		Sales		300,000
		To record a sale for 2,000,000 francs at an exchange rate of $0.15, n/30.		

With a rate of $0.15, the dollar translation on the date of sale is $300,000 = (2,000,000 × $0.15).

When Alabama Corporation closed its books on December 31, 1987, the exchange rate had risen to $0.16⅔ per franc. The franc had gained in respect to the dollar. Since payment is to be measured in francs, the 2,000,000 francs to be collected now have a dollar value of $333,333.33 = (2,000,000 × $0.16⅔). The exchange gain is recognized when the books are closed as follows:

1987				
Dec.	31	Accounts Receivable	33,333.33	
		Foreign Currency Exchange Gain		33,333.33
		To recognize gain from translation of asset receivable in foreign currency.		

The exchange gain is a part of net income of Alabama Corporation in 1987. It is reported in the other revenues section of the income statement.

Assume further that, on the date of collection, the dollar has gained. The new exchange rate is $0.135 per franc. The journal entry for collection of the receivable is as follows:

1988				
Jan.	15	Cash	270,000.00	
		Foreign Currency Exchange Loss	63,333.33	
		Accounts Receivable		333,333.33
		To record collection of 2,000,000 francs at an exchange rate of $0.135.		

The exchange loss is a part of 1988 net income. It is reported in the other expenses section of the income statement.

Translation for Consolidated Statements

When some elements of financial statements are translated from a foreign currency in the process of preparing combined or consolidated financial statements, *FASB Statement No. 52* specifies that a current exchange rate be used. For assets and liabilities, the current exchange rate to be used is the rate in effect at the balance sheet date.[27] A difference between the exchange rate used to record the original items and the current rate results in a gain or loss. Gains and losses in these translations are treated differently from transaction gains and losses. Instead of being included in the determination of net income, they " . . . shall be reported separately and accumulated in a separate component of equity."[28] The commonly accepted method of doing so is to *report the item between paid-in capital and retained earnings* in the stockholders' equity section of the balance sheet.

As an example of such reporting, R. J. Reynolds Industries, Inc. had a negative amount of $51,000,000 accumulated and reported in this manner as "cumulative translation adjustments" at the end of 1982. During 1983, foreign currency translations and other adjustments amounted to an additional $52,000,000, leaving R. J. Reynolds' balance sheet at the end of 1983 with a deduction of $103,000,000 opposite this caption. This figure must be considered, along with $6,000,000 of *transaction exchange gains* in 1983 that were reported in Reynolds' income statement for 1983.

Other problems in accounting arise when international corporations take actions to protect themselves against the effect of translation gains and losses. They do this by buying and selling contracts for future acceptance of foreign currencies. This practice, known as *hedging,* raises complex accounting issues that are treated in more advanced accounting courses.

Glossary

Affiliates (or affiliated companies) Companies between which a parent/subsidiary relationship exists.

Consolidated financial statements Financial reports in which the assets, liabilities, revenues, and expenses of subsidiary companies are combined with those of the parent company.

Eliminations Removal of duplicate items in subsidiary and parent financial statements from the consolidated amount.

Footnote disclosure Information disclosed in notes to financial statements rather than in the bodies of the statements.

Foreign currency exchange A transaction in which one currency is used to purchase another.

Foreign currency exchange gains and losses Gains and losses from translation of a functional currency into a reporting currency.

Functional currency The currency that is being used to *measure* the assets, liabilities, revenues, and expenses.

---

[27]*FASB Statement No. 52,* paragraph 12. Other elements such as revenues and expenses are translated as of the date of occurrence or at a weighted average exchange rate. These specific requirements are complex and not necessary to understand the concept presented here.

[28]Ibid., paragraph 13.

Intercompany transactions Transactions that take place between affiliated companies.

Investee company A corporation whose stock is acquired by another corporation.

Investor company A corporation acquiring the stock of another corporation.

Minority interest The portion of subsidiary corporation ownership held by stockholders other than the parent company.

Parent company A company that owns a controlling interest (more than 50 percent) in voting stock of another company.

Reciprocal accounts Accounts in two locations that offset each other and would cause double counting if combined into a consolidated total.

Subsidiary company A company controlled by another corporation that holds a controlling interest (more than 50 percent) in its voting stock.

Questions

Q16–1 What is the nature and purpose of reciprocal accounts in a single company? In different companies?

Q16–2 What are some reasons that a corporation would make a long-term investment in stock of another corporation? How do these reasons compare with reasons for *temporary* investments in stock of another company?

Q16–3 What is the difference between ability to "exert substantial influence" and ability to "control"? Why do you believe a company making an investment of 33⅓ percent of the stock of another company would not go ahead and buy at least 51 percent, since it is already past the 20 percent area?

Q16–4 In its 1982 *Annual Report*, Gearhart Industries, Inc., reported that it had issued 150,000 shares valued at $4,344,000 to acquire the outstanding minority interest of a consolidated subsidiary. Does this make Gearhart a parent company, or was it already one? Explain your answer.

Q16–5 Some corporations report that they are accounting for investments in other companies by the equity method. What does this tell you about the percent of ownership? Why do you think a company would benefit from having ownership in this proportion?

Q16–6 Is a parent company an investor company? Is an investor company always a parent company? Explain.

Q16–7 What is required for a group of companies to be called "affiliated"? Must each affiliate own a portion of each of the other affiliates? Explain.

Q16–8 What is the minority interest? Do the investors holding the minority interest have voting rights? Do they receive dividends? Explain.

Q16–9 What are consolidated financial statements? When is it appropriate to use them in reporting to stockholders and to the public?

Q16–10 What is an intercompany transaction? Give three examples. How do they fit into consolidated statements? Why?

Q16–11 (Appendix) What is the reason that a company can have a gain or loss from foreign currency fluctuations? Explain fully.

Exercises

E16–1
Review of equity method

On June 1, 1987, Oregon Corporation purchased 36,000 of the 90,000 outstanding shares of voting common stock of Corvallis Company for cash at $22 per share. On June 28, 1987, Oregon received a regular quarterly cash dividend of $0.30 per share, and on June 30, 1987 (the end of the fiscal year), Corvallis reported a net income of $207,000. Record the events in general journal form.

E16–2
Exceptions to consolidated statements

Pensacola Company (a machine manufacturer) owns 100 percent of the voting stock in three other corporations: (a) Gull Point Company, a producer of parts used in Pensacola's assembly operations; (b) Warrington Finance Company, which provides loans to purchasers of Pensacola's products; and (c) Santa Rosa Company, a company in the hands of a trustee during bankruptcy proceedings. Which of these affiliates should be combined in the consolidated financial statements? Give reasons if you decide that any should not.

E16–3
Elimination of investment accounts immediately after acquisition

Immediately after acquisition, the following accounts were in the trial balances of Grandview Corporation and its wholly owned subsidiary, Columbus Company:

Account Title	Grandview	Columbus
Investment in Stocks—Common Stock of Columbus Company	$2,875,000	$ 0
Common Stock, $2 Par value	1,150,000	920,000
Paid-in Capital—Excess over Par Value, Common	5,980,000	1,552,500
Retained Earnings	3,599,500	402,500

What is the amount of each account to be shown in the consolidated balance sheet?

E16–4
Intercompany transactions—eliminations

Parents Company owns 100 percent of the voting stock of Daughter, Inc. Included in the trial balances of the two companies at the end of the accounting year 1987 are the following:

a. A note payable to Downtown Bank on the books of Parents for $50,000.
b. A note payable to Parents from Daughter for $30,000.
c. Sales as follows:
   Parents: $60,000 (10 percent to Daughter).
   Daughter: $180,000 (75 percent to Parents).
d. Accounts receivable as follows:
   Parents: $50,000 (15 percent from Daughter).
   Daughter: $30,000 (90 percent from Parents).

What amounts (if any) should be eliminated when the financial statements are combined into consolidated statements?

E16–5
Intercompany transactions—inventory profits

Mile High Corporation sold 120 hang gliders to Grandfather Mountain Dealers, its 100 percent owned subsidiary, in 1987. The gliders cost $4,800 each and were sold to the dealer for $5,280 each. At the end of 1987, Grandfather Mountain Dealers had sold 107 of these gliders; the remaining 13 were still on hand in ending inventory. Compute the amount of Grandfather Mountain Dealers' inventory to be eliminated from the inventory amount in the consolidated balance sheet.

E16–6
Preparing a partial balance sheet with minority interest

On December 31, 1983, CSX Corporation included the following items in its *Annual Report* (dollars in millions):

Total current liabilities	$1,776.5
Long-term debt	2,354.8
Claims and other long-term liabilities	337.6
Deferred income taxes	1,505.7
Minority interest in subsidiaries	322.7
Redeemable preferred stock	10.9
Common stock	146.0
Other capital	1,571.1
Retained earnings	2,809.3

Treating deferred income taxes as if they were all long-term liabilities, prepare the Liabilities and Stockholders' Equity section of the balance sheet.

E16–7
Work sheet for parent and subsidiary

On December 31, 1987, the accounts of Antelope Corporation and its wholly-owned subsidiary, Eagle Corporation, showed the following balances:

Account Title	Antelope	Eagle
Cash.	$100,000	$ 40,000
Accounts Receivable from Eagle	15,600	0
Accounts Receivable—Other	60,500	32,180
Investment in Eagle Corporation	163,930	0
Property, Plant, and Equipment	182,250	125,600
Accounts Payable to Antelope.	0	15,600
Accounts Payable—Other	31,500	18,250
Common Stock	400,000	125,000
Retained Earnings.	90,780	38,930

Enter the balances on a work sheet to prepare consolidated financial statements, complete the work sheet, and prepare a consolidated balance sheet assuming the investment had been purchased on December 31, 1987.

E16–8
Acquisition at a price greater than book value

On January 1, 1987, Central State Corporation purchased for cash all the assets of Wilberforce Company. The purchase price was $6,200,000. At the time of purchase, Wilberforce's books showed the following assets:

Total current assets.	$ 520,000
Land.	610,000
Buildings (net of depreciation).	2,340,000
Machinery and equipment (net of depreciation).	1,530,000

An immediate appraisal by Central State showed that the following acquired assets had fair market values greater than the above book values by the following amounts:

Land.	236,000
Buildings (net of depreciation).	345,100
Machinery and equipment (net of depreciation).	118,900

Compute the amount of each acquired asset to be shown on the books of Central State Corporation after the merger.

E16–9
Computing and comparing currency exchange rates

(Appendix) As of June 26, 1984, the following exchange rates were reported in *Business Week*:

	Units per U.S. Dollar	
	Today	Year Ago
German mark.	2.79	2.52
Swiss franc	2.32	2.08
Japanese yen.	237.00	238.00
Canadian dollar.	1.31	1.23
Mexican peso.	191.00	148.00

Compute to the nearest four decimal places the cost of one unit of each of these currencies in U.S. dollars on June 26, 1984, and a year prior to that date. Which currency has lost the most strength against the dollar during the year? Which currency maintained the most strength against the dollar?

E16–10
Computing foreign currency exchange gain or loss

(Appendix) On June 26, 1983, Export Sales, Inc. sold a piece of equipment to a Mexican firm for 4,440,000 pesos to be paid in pesos one year later. Believing that the dollar would gain in strength against the peso, Export required a one-year note (payable in pesos) with interest at 20 percent. Using the data in E16–9, compute the foreign currency exchange gain or loss in U.S. dollars on this transaction. Did the interest offset the gain or loss? Show computations to support your answer. If the rate had changed to 120 pesos per U.S. dollar at the time of collection, show computations to indicate how this would change your answers.

A Problems

P16–1A
Elimination of investment

Gardner Corporation and its wholly owned subsidiary, Webb Inc., have the following items in their trial balances on December 2, 1987, immediately after Gardner made the investment at book value:

Account Titles	Gardner	Webb
Investment in Stocks—Common Stock of Webb Inc.	$867,500	$ 0
Common Stock, $1 Par Value	500,000	0
Common Stock, $2 Par Value	0	300,000
Paid-in Capital—Excess over Par Value, Common	623,200	212,500
Retained Earnings	311,520	355,000

Required: Enter the balances on a work sheet for consolidated statements, make the necessary eliminations, and carry the consolidated amounts to the proper column.

P16–2A
Elimination of intercompany payables and receivables

Austin Corporation and its wholly owned subsidiary, Lufkin Inc., have the following items in their trial balances on June 30, 1987, the end of the fiscal year for both companies:

Account Titles	Austin	Lufkin
Accounts Receivable—General Customers	$275,000	$118,000
Accounts Receivable—Affiliate	42,500	15,650
Accounts Payable—General Creditors	186,750	92,670
Accounts Payable—Affiliate	15,650	42,500
Notes Receivable—Affiliate	75,000	0
Notes Payable to Banks	150,000	0
Notes Payable to Affiliate	0	75,000

Required: Enter the balances on a work sheet for consolidated statements, make the necessary eliminations, and carry the consolidated amounts to the proper column.

P16–3A
Using work sheet to prepare consolidated income statement: cost method

The following accounts and balances as of May 31, 1987, appear in the trial balances of Company A and its wholly owned subsidiary, Company B. Company B was acquired on May 1, 1987, so there have been no dividends declared and no earnings reported by either company since acquisition.

Debit Accounts	Company A	Company B
Receivables from A	$ 0	$ 30,000
Receivables from B	50,000	0
Other Current Assets	520,000	182,500
Investment in Stocks—Common Stock of Company B	237,500	0
Property, Plant, and Equipment (Net)	910,000	137,000
Cost of Goods Sold	400,000	250,000
Operating Expenses	35,000	28,000
Total debits	$2,152,500	$627,500

Credit Accounts		
Payables to A	$ 0	$ 50,000
Payables to B	30,000	0
Common Stock, $1 Par	750,000	200,000
Retained Earnings	688,000	37,500
Sales	684,500	340,000
Total credits	$2,152,500	$627,500

None of the receivables or payables is interest-bearing. Included in the sales of Company A are $84,500 of sales to Company B. All of B's sales were made to groups outside the economic entity and include resale of the $84,500 purchased from A.

Required:

1. Enter the account balances on a work sheet, and make the necessary eliminations to obtain a consolidated trial balance.
2. Prepare a consolidated income statement for May.
3. Explain the significance of Company A's sales to its subsidiary and the reason you treated them as you did in requirements 1 and 2.

P16–4A
Elimination of investment: equity method

Saskatoon Company and its wholly owned subsidiary, Moose Jaw Company, had the following account balances at December 31, 1987, the end of their fiscal years:

Debit Accounts	Saskatoon Company	Moose Jaw Company
Cash	$ 73,800	$115,800
Investment in Moose Jaw Company	174,000	0
Property, Plant, and Equipment	180,000	78,000
Cost of Goods Sold	360,000	240,000
Other Expenses	66,000	48,000
Totals	$853,800	$481,800

Credit Accounts		
Liabilities	$ 79,800	$ 19,800
Common Stock	210,000	96,000
Retained Earnings	60,000	54,000
Sales	480,000	312,000
Investor's Share of Investee Income	24,000	0
Totals	$853,800	$481,800

No sales were made to each other and no dividends were declared by either company in 1987.

Required:

1. Enter the above data in a work sheet, make the necessary eliminations, and complete the work sheet with a consolidated trial balance.
2. From the work sheet data, prepare a separate income statement for each company and prepare a consolidated income statement.
3. Explain why consolidated net income is not equal to the sum of the net incomes on the separate income statements.

P16–5A
Thought-provoking problem: use of segment reporting

In its 1983 *Annual Report,* Community Psychiatric Centers and Subsidiaries reported the following information for 1983 (dollars in thousands) among other data:

	Operating Revenues	Operating Profit	Depreciation Expense
Psychiatric hospitals	$ 96,839	$35,700	$2,007
Dialysis services	35,920	11,977	1,142
Home health services	5,427	465	25
Totals	$138,186	$48,142	$3,174[a]

[a] Corporate depreciation expense not identified with any segment was $503.

Required:

1. Show by computations the operating results of the various segments as compared to overall operating results.

(continued on next page)

2. How is this segment information useful to management? To the public?

3. Do you think it would be better for a company with diverse operations not to issue consolidated financial reports, but issue a separate financial report for each legal entity? What are the reasons, pro and con, for your answer? (At the time of this report, Community Psychiatric Centers owned and operated 20 free-standing hospitals in 11 states and London, England. It also owned and operated 44 dialysis centers in 13 states, and a home nursing service business with eight offices in California.)

P16–6A
Recording foreign currency exchange gains and losses

(Appendix) Seattle Company made a sale to Vancouver Corporation on December 27, 1987, for $750,000 (Canadian dollars) when the exchange rate was $1.25 (Canadian) = $1.00 (United States). Terms of the sale were n/30. When Seattle Company closed its books on December 31, 1987, the exchange rate was $1.30 (Canadian) = $1.00 (United States). When the collection was made on January 26, 1988, the exchange rate was $1.22 (Canadian) = $1.00 (United States).

Required: Rounding to the nearest cent where necessary, record in general journal form:

1. The sale in United States dollars.
2. The foreign currency exchange gain or loss upon closing.
3. The collection of the account.

B Problems

P16–1B
Elimination of investment

Boiling Corporation and its wholly owned subsidiary, Springs Inc., have the following items in their trial balances on December 1, 1987, immediately after Boiling made the investment at book value:

Account Titles	Boiling	Springs
Investment in Stocks—Common Stock of Springs Inc.	$433,750	$ 0
Common Stock, $1 Par Value	250,000	0
Common Stock, $2 Par Value	0	150,000
Paid-in Capital—Excess over Par Value, Common	311,600	106,250
Retained Earnings	155,760	177,500

Required: Enter the balances on a work sheet for consolidated statements, make the necessary eliminations, and carry the consolidated amounts to the proper column.

P16–2B
Elimination of intercompany payables and receivables

Loyola Corporation and its wholly owned subsidiary, Bayou Inc., have the following items in their trial balances on June 30, 1987, the end of the fiscal year of both companies:

Account Titles	Loyola	Bayou
Accounts Receivable—General Customers	$137,500	$59,000
Accounts Receivable—Affiliate	21,250	7,825
Accounts Payable—General Creditors	93,375	46,335
Accounts Payable—Affiliate	7,825	21,250
Notes Receivable—Affiliate	37,500	0
Notes Payable to Bank	75,000	0
Notes Payable to Affiliate	0	37,500

Required: Enter the balances on a work sheet for consolidated statements, make the necessary eliminations, and carry the consolidated amounts to the proper column.

P16-3B
Using work sheet to prepare consolidated income statement: cost method

The following accounts and balances as of June 30, 1987, appear in the trial balances of Company P and its wholly owned subsidiary, Company S. Company S was acquired on June 1, 1987, so there have been no dividends declared and no earnings reported by either company since acquisition.

Debit Accounts	Company P	Company S
Receivables from P	$ 0	$ 39,000
Receivables from S	65,000	0
Other Current Assets	676,000	237,250
Investment in Stocks—Common Stock of Company S	308,750	0
Property, Plant, and Equipment (Net)	1,183,000	178,100
Cost of Goods Sold	520,000	325,000
Operating Expenses	45,500	36,400
Total debits	$2,798,250	$815,750

Credit Accounts		
Payables to P	$ 0	$ 65,000
Payables to S	39,000	0
Common Stock, $2 Par	975,000	260,000
Retained Earnings	894,400	48,750
Sales	889,850	442,000
Total credits	$2,798,250	$815,750

None of the receivables or payables is interest-bearing. Included in the sales of Company P are $109,850 of sales to Company S. All of S's sales were made to groups outside the economic entity and include resale of all of the $109,850 purchased from P.

Required:

1. Enter the account balances on a work sheet, and make the necessary eliminations to obtain a consolidated trial balance.
2. Prepare a consolidated income statement for June.
3. Explain the significance of Company P's sales to its subsidiary and the reason you treated them as you did in requirements 1 and 2.

P16-4B
Elimination of investment: equity method

Las Cruces Company and its wholly owned subsidiary, Dona Ana Company, had the following account balances at June 30, 1987, the end of their fiscal year:

Debit Accounts	Las Cruces	Dona Ana
Cash	$ 62,730	$ 98,430
Investment in Dona Ana Company	147,900	0
Property, Plant, and Equipment	153,000	66,300
Cost of Goods Sold	306,000	204,000
Other Expenses	56,100	40,800
Totals	$725,730	$409,530

Credit Accounts		
Liabilities	$ 67,830	$ 16,830
Common Stock	178,500	81,600
Retained Earnings	51,000	45,900
Sales	408,000	265,200
Investor's Share of Investee Income	20,400	0
Totals	$725,730	$409,530

No sales were made to each other and no dividends were declared by either company during the fiscal year.

Required:

1. Enter the above data in a work sheet, make the necessary eliminations, and complete the work sheet with a consolidated trial balance.
2. From the data in the work sheet, prepare a separate income statement for each company and prepare a consolidated income statement.
3. Explain why the consolidated net income is not equal to the sum of the net incomes on the separate statements for each company.

P16–5B
Thought-provoking problem: separate reporting for extraordinary items and discontinued operations

APB Opinion No. 30, "Reporting the Results of Operations," was issued in June 1973. It defined the disposal of a segment of a business as *discontinued operations* and events that are of an unusual nature and would not reasonably be expected to recur in the forseeable future as *extraordinary items.* The opinion stated that such items should be reported separately from operating items on the income statement and be shown net of their income tax effects. The following consolidated income statement for Varlen Corporation and Subsidiaries is reproduced from Varlen's 1984 Annual Report:

Consolidated Statements of Income

Varlen Corporation and Subsidiaries — Years ended January 31, 1984, 1983, and 1982

	1984	1983	1982
Net sales	$110,938,036	$108,442,984	$134,401,219
Cost of sales	83,055,420	81,978,840	100,015,225
Gross profit	27,882,616	26,464,144	34,385,994
Selling, general, and administrative expenses (note 6)	15,174,920	14,848,068	14,758,054
Income from operations	12,707,696	11,616,076	19,627,940
Interest expense	(2,232,462)	(2,263,910)	(3,366,746)
Interest income	83,659	812,343	1,149,310
Income before Federal income taxes	10,558,893	10,164,509	17,410,504
Provision for Federal income taxes (note 6)	4,574,000	4,492,000	8,059,000
Income from continuing operations before extraordinary item	5,984,893	5,672,509	9,351,504
Discontinued operations (less applicable income taxes of $512,000) (note 3)	—	—	(598,682)
Extraordinary item (less applicable income taxes of $398,000) (note 10)	(379,289)	—	—
Net income	$ 5,605,604	$ 5,672,509	$ 8,752,822
Weighted average number of shares outstanding	4,032,736	3,997,946	3,991,232
Earnings per share:			
Continuing operations before extraordinary item	$1.48	$1.42	$2.34
Discontinued operations	—	—	(.15)
Extraordinary item	(.09)	—	—
Earnings per share	$1.39	$1.42	$2.19

16 / **Consolidated Statements and International Accounting**

The 1982 discontinued operation was the sale of " . . . the Union Iron Works subsidiary in view of the fact that there had been a continuing decline in the agriculture-related business in which that subsidiary was engaged." The extraordinary item was the settlement of a legal action brought in 1971 by an individual who claimed the rights to an invention disclosed to a predecessor of the company.

Required:

1. Recognizing that these statements are published to the public, discuss the value of reporting these two items separately in the statements.
2. Why is it desirable to report them net of income tax effect?
3. Are the earnings per share figures more meaningful with this type of reporting? Why or why not?

P16–6B
Recording foreign currency exchange gains and losses

(Appendix) El Paso Company made a sale to Senorita Corporation on December 18, 1987 for 3,625,000 Mexican pesos when the exchange rate was 145 pesos = $1.00 (United States). Terms of the sale were n/30. When El Paso Company closed its books on December 31, 1987, the exchange rate was 140 pesos = $1.00. When the collection was made on January 17, 1988, the exchange rate was 148 pesos = $1.00.

Required: Rounding to the nearest cent where necessary, record in general journal form:

1. The sale in United States dollars.
2. The foreign currency exchange gain or loss on closing.
3. The collection of the account.

17 Statement of Changes in Financial Position

Introduction

With the exception of Chapter 1, only three of the four basic financial statements are emphasized in the preceding chapters. The major objective of a business enterprise is to earn net income. To do so, it must engage in operations to earn revenue. Resources for operations are provided by the earnings process, by financing activities (such as borrowing money and issuing common stock), and by investing activities (such as acquisition of plant assets). The balance sheet shows the status of these resources at a specific moment. The income statement discloses the results of operations, while the statement of retained earnings reconciles the beginning balance of retained earnings to the ending balance.

None of the foregoing statements indicates the *cause of the changes in financial position* that resulted from operating, financing, and investing activities that the company engaged in during the year. It is important to statement readers to know details of the resources provided, such as those from (1) operations, (2) the issuance of bonds, and (3) the issuance of common stock; and the resources used in (1) the purchase of property, plant, and equipment, (2) the purchase of long-term investments, and (3) other similar investing activities. These activities change financial position. A fourth major accounting statement prepared to disclose the causes of changes in resources of a firm is the **statement of changes in financial position**, sometimes called the funds statement. Chapter 17 begins with a description of this statement and its broad objectives and content, considering the two most popular concepts of funds: working capital and cash. First, the single concept of working capital is explored to develop the analytical background steps for the statement of changes in financial position. Then, various techniques are presented that may be used to collect information for the statement based on a working capital concept. Last, the statement is considered as it relates to a

688 Part Four / Financial Reporting

cash basis. In two appendices to this chapter, additional approaches to collecting information for the statement are presented.

Learning Goals

1. To understand and interpret the statement of changes in financial position.
2. To understand the various definitions of funds.
3. To recognize the effect on working capital of increases or decreases in noncurrent items.
4. To prepare a schedule of changes in working capital components that becomes a part of the statement of changes in financial position.
5. To compute the amount of working capital provided by (or used in) operations.
6. To use the simple analytical approach to develop sources and uses of all financial resources on a working capital basis concept of funds.
7. To use the simple analytical approach to develop sources and uses of all financial resources on a cash basis concept of funds.

Broad Objectives and Content of the Statement

Broad Objectives

According to *APB Opinion No. 19,* the statement of changes in financial position has two broad objectives:

1. To summarize the financing and investing activities of the entity, including the extent to which the enterprise has generated funds from operations during the period.

2. To complete the disclosure of changes in financial position during the period.[1]

Figure 17–1 shows how this statement fits in with other financial statements to accomplish these objectives.

The information shown on the statement of changes in financial position is useful to a variety of users of financial statements in making economic decisions regarding the enterprise. For example, when *budgets* (financial plans) for items such as capital equipment are prepared, the accountant looks to past statements of changes in financial position as a reference point. Also, the statement of changes in financial position is the only document, for example, to show why dividends may not be declared when net income has been earned. It shows inflows and outflows of funds and the change in working capital or cash position that may make it unwise to declare a dividend. Before proceeding to a specific study of the statement, its evolution and content is presented in the next section.

---

[1]*Opinions of the Accounting Principles Board No. 19,* "Reporting Changes in Financial Position" (New York: AICPA, March 1971), paragraph 4.

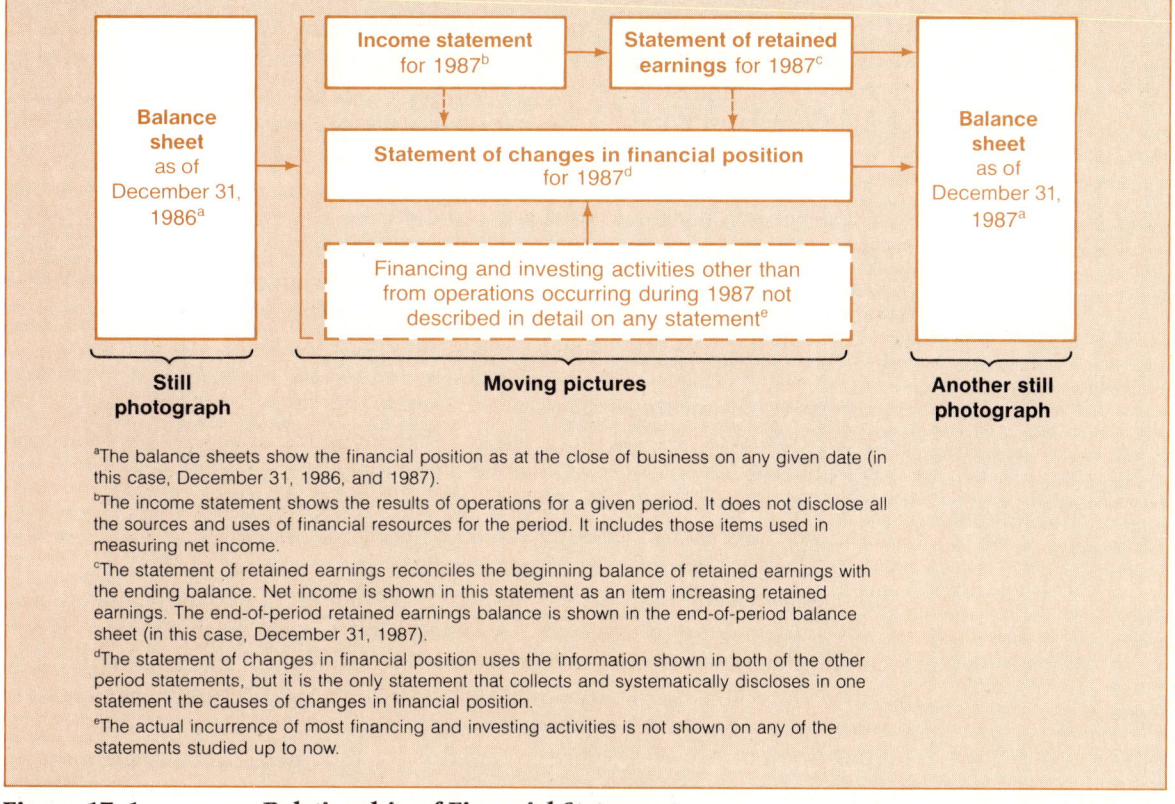

Figure 17–1   **Relationship of Financial Statements**

Evolution and Content of the Statement

Prior to 1971, some annual reports presented various **statements of sources and uses of funds** (the typical name used for the present statement of changes in financial position). These older statements disclosed the operating, financing, and investing activities of a firm during a given period of time, but they defined funds in several different ways: working capital, cash only, cash and temporary investments, current assets, or all financial resources. The most often used definition of funds up to that point had been **working capital**, which is total current assets minus total current liabilities: mathematically, $CA - CL = WC$.

Now, however, a cash basis or cash and near cash (temporary investments) basis for the statement of changes in financial position is receiving emphasis. In a survey of 32 annual reports for 1983, the authors found that 11 used either the cash or cash plus temporary investments, while 21 still used the working capital basis. Many corporate giants, such as Goodyear Tire and Rubber Company and the Eaton Corporation, have adopted a concept of funds of cash and temporary investments (near cash). The Nordson Corporation,

Georgia Pacific Corporation, and IBM, used the cash basis only, but neither of these companies disclosed any temporary investments in their balance sheet. CP National Corporation, Coachmen Industries, Inc., and Community Psychiatric Centers continue to use the working capital basis. Most of the utility companies surveyed still use the working capital basis; for example, Wisconsin Electric Power Company and Public Service Company of Colorado use the working capital basis.

These recent changes to the cash and the cash plus temporary investment (near cash) bases are sufficient to show a definite trend in this direction. The continued use of the working capital basis, however, requires that consideration be given to this concept. Both concepts are discussed in this chapter, starting with the working capital basis as modified by the **all financial resources** concept. This concept, developed in the late 1960s and early 1970s, encompasses all important aspects of a company's "financing and investing activities regardless of whether cash or other elements of working capital are directly affected."[2] In other words, the all financial resources concept includes both the sources and uses of working capital (or cash) and the other sources and uses of nonworking capital or noncash resources.

In 1971, *APB Opinion No. 19* required that this variation of the concept of "all financial resources" be used. It also recommended (1) that the statement be titled *statement of changes in financial position,* and (2) that it be a basic financial statement for each period for which an income statement is presented.[3] This latter requirement elevates the statement of changes in financial position to a major statement status.

APB Opinion No. 19 requires a business to disclose in this statement the **sources of financial resources** and **uses of financial resources**—the inflows and outflows—of all these resources of the business. The *Opinion* specifically permits flexibility in form, content, and terminology but requires that information about sources and uses of funds be presented on either (1) all financial resources on a working capital basis, or (2) all financial resources on a cash basis. The first variation shows sources and uses of *working capital* plus other sources and uses of financial resources not affecting working capital (such as the issuance of bonds payable in exchange for land, the issuance of common stock to acquire property, plant, and equipment items, and the conversion of bonds into common stock). The other variation shows the sources and uses of *cash,* plus other noncash sources and uses of financial resources.

Since both bases specified by *APB Opinion No. 19* require that the sources and uses not affecting working capital or cash be included, the two variations of the all financial resources approaches hereafter are referred to as (1) statement of changes in financial position—working capital basis or (2) statement of changes in financial position—cash basis. Both are illustrated in this chapter.

---

[2]*Opinions of the Accounting Principles Board No. 19,* "Reporting Changes in Financial Position" (New York: AICPA, March 1971), paragraph 8.

[3]Ibid.

17 / Statement of Changes in Financial Position

All Financial Resources on a Working Capital Basis

Sources and Uses of Working Capital The chief sources of working capital are operations, additional investments by owners, long-term borrowing, the sale of noncurrent assets, and conversion of current liabilities into common stock. The chief uses of working capital are purchases of noncurrent assets, payment of long-term debt, reduction of stockholders' equity by declaration of dividends, and purchases of treasury stock. The statement of changes in financial position—working capital basis starts with an emphasis on the interrelationship of the sources (inflows) and uses (outflows) of working capital. A chart of working capital inflows and outflows based on their impact on the two working capital elements—current assets and current liabilities—is shown in Figure 17–2. The specifics involved in the causes of changes in working capital are discussed in the next section.

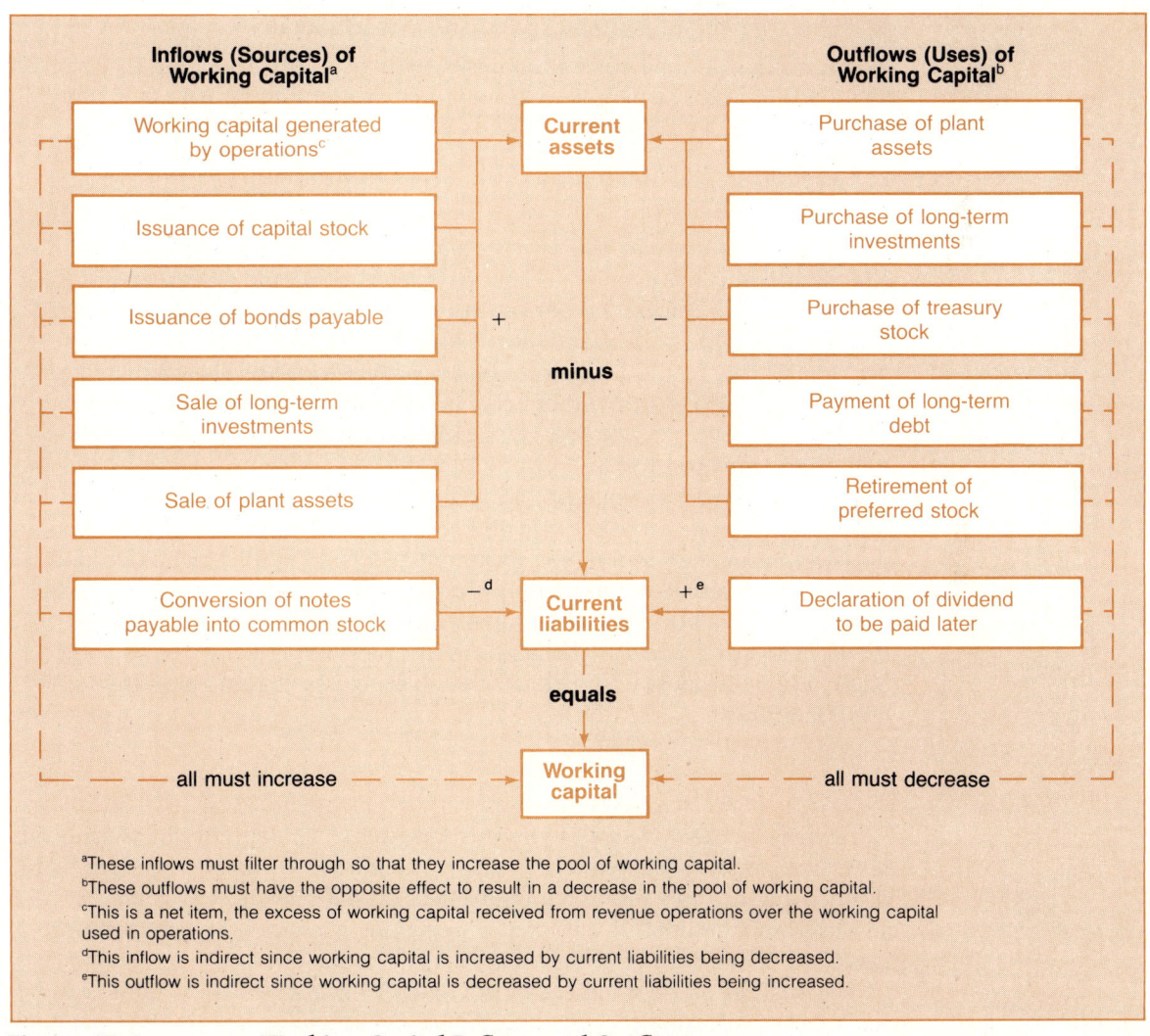

Figure 17–2 **Working Capital Inflows and Outflows**

Causes of Changes in Working Capital   An *increase* in working capital (source of working capital) must result when there is:

1. An increase in total current assets without a corresponding increase in total current liabilities (example: issuance of bonds or common stock).

2. A decrease in total current liabilities without a corresponding decrease in total current assets (example: conversion of a short-term debt to a long-term debt).

A *decrease* in working capital (use of working capital) must result when there is:

1. A decrease in total current assets without a corresponding decrease in total current liabilities (example: purchase of machinery).

2. An increase in total current liabilities without a corresponding increase in total current assets (example: declaration of dividend to be paid at a later date).

Approaches to Determination of Sources and Uses of Working Capital   To determine the sources and uses of working capital for a specific period, say a year or a quarter, the accountant could analyze every transaction occurring during the period that affects a current asset or a current liability—the *current accounts*—to determine the causes of changes in working capital. This method requires considerable effort, because so many transactions exist. Also, some of them change current assets and current liabilities equally and hence *do not* change working capital—for example, the collection of accounts receivable.

A shorter approach would be to analyze in total the transactions occurring during the period that affect *noncurrent accounts*—long-term investments; property, plant, and equipment; intangible assets; long-term liabilities; and stockholders' equity—to determine the causes of change in working capital. Every change in working capital must result in a change in one or more of the *noncurrent accounts*. The application of this approach requires a knowledge of how business transactions affect balance sheet elements—the topic considered next.

Analysis of Business Transactions and Their Effect on Balance Sheet Elements   Since the transactions that enter into the inflow and outflow of financial resources vary greatly, it is helpful to classify transactions in distinctive categories indicating their effect on balance sheet elements. Figure 17–3 shows a number of ways that transactions, identified by letter, may be classified by their effect on specific balance sheet elements.

The analysis of the transactions in Figure 17–3 is essential to understanding the method used to collect the information that appears on the statement

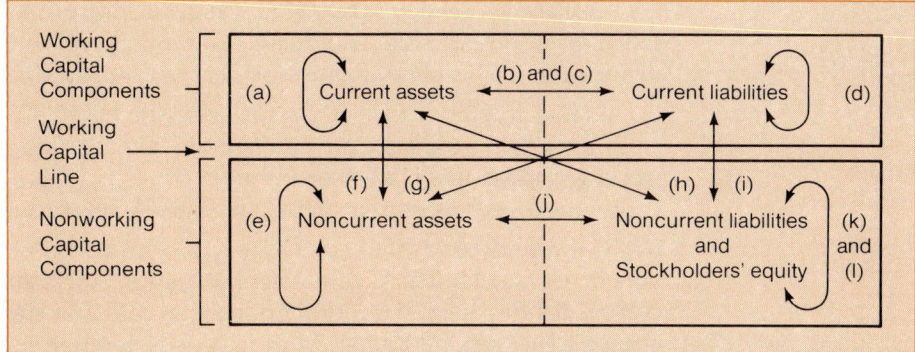

Figure 17–3   **Kinds of Business Transactions That Affect and Do Not Affect Working Capital**

of changes in financial poisiton. Each example of the transactions shown in this figure is analyzed as follows:

(**a**) Collected an account receivable (increased a current asset, cash, and decreased a current asset, accounts receivable, thus not changing the total working capital amount).

(**b**) Purchased merchandise on account (increased a current asset, merchandise inventory, and increased a current liability, accounts payable; this transaction did not change total working capital).

(**c**) Payment of accounts payable (decreased a current liability, accounts payable, and also decreased a current asset, cash, thus not changing the total working capital amount).

(**d**) Issued a note payable to settle an open accounts payable (increased a current liability, notes payable, and decreased a current liability, accounts payable, thus not changing the total working capital amount).

(**e**) Exchanged land for a dissimilar asset, machinery, incurring no gain or loss (increased a noncurrent asset, machinery, and decreased a noncurrent asset, land; this transaction did not change working capital, but it is an example of a special financing transaction that is discussed later as both a source and a use of all financial resources).

(**f**) Purchased land and paid cash (increased a noncurrent asset, land, and decreased a current asset, cash; this transaction is a use or decrease in working capital).

(**g**) Purchased machinery on open charge account (increased a noncurrent asset, machinery, and increased a current liability, accounts payable; this transaction resulted in a use or decrease in working capital).

(**h**) Liquidated bonds payable before they became a current liability (decreased a current asset, cash, and decreased a noncurrent liability, bonds payable; this transaction is another example of a use or decrease in working capital).

(i) Declared a dividend payable in the near future (increased a current liability, dividends payable, and decreased a noncurrent item, retained earnings; this transaction resulted in a use or decrease in working capital).

(j) Issued common stock at par for land (increased a noncurrent asset, land, and increased a stockholders' equity item, common stock, thus not changing working capital; this is another example of a special financing transaction that is discussed later as both a source and a use of all financial resources).

(k) Converted bonds into common stock with no premium (increased a noncurrent stockholders' equity item, common stock, and decreased a noncurrent liability item, convertible bonds payable; this transaction did not change total working capital. As in (j), this is another example of a special financing transaction that is discussed later as both a source and a use.)

(l) Declared and issued a stock dividend on common stock (this increases noncurrent stockholders' equity items, common stock and, possibly, paid-in capital—excess over par value on stock dividends, and decreases a noncurrent stockholders' equity item, retained earnings; this transaction did not change total working capital. According to *APB Opinion No. 19,* this transaction is considered an internal change in capital structure and *not* a source and use of financial resources).

Reviewing the transactions illustrated in Figure 17–3, two important observations can be made:

1. A transaction that causes a change in working capital must cross the working capital line shown in the figure; in other words, one account in the transaction was above the line, and the other account was below the line.

2. Every source and use of working capital affects the nonworking capital components (noncurrent accounts), thus showing pictorially the validity of using the noncurrent accounts method of determining the sources and uses of total resources. Even those special examples of financing and investing that do not affect working capital but that must be shown as both a source and use of financial resources can be determined by an analysis of the noncurrent accounts, since only these are affected by the special types of transactions.

Working Capital Provided by Operations

Chapter 3 suggests that for cross-referencing purposes the income statement be marked Exhibit A; the statement of retained earnings, Exhibit B; and the balance sheet, Exhibit C. The statement of changes in financial position is now marked Exhibit D.

Direct Method of Calculating Working Capital Provided by Operations

An important primary source of working capital is the regular operating activities of the business. The determination of working capital from this source is complicated by the fact that the change in working capital may be greater than, or less than, the net income shown in the income statement. To illustrate what the FASB refers to as the direct method of calculating

Figure 17–4 Income Statement of CHL Company for 1987

CHL COMPANY
Income Statement
For the Year Ended December 31, 1987

Exhibit A

Sales		$250,200
Cost of goods sold		165,000
Gross margin on sales		$ 85,200
Operating expenses:		
Depreciation—machinery	$ 2,100	
Other	81,600	
Total operating expenses		83,700
Net income		$ 1,500

the working capital provided by operations, assume that the CHL Company's income statement for its first year of operation, which ended December 31, 1987, is as shown in Figure 17–4. Figure 17–5 presents an analysis of this statement in terms of the change in working capital resulting from operations. It shows the excess of inflows of working capital over the outflows to be $3,600. Note that the depreciation expense is properly shown on the income statement as reducing net income. Yet in the second column (Figure 17–5), it is shown as not reducing working capital, because the recording of

Figure 17–5 Working Capital Basis Income Statement for CHL Company for 1987

CHL COMPANY
Income Statement
For the Year Ended December 31, 1987
(Converted from Accrual Basis to a Working Capital Basis)

	Income Statement Increase or (Decrease)	Working Capital Increase or (Decrease)	Explanation of Effect on Working Capital
Sales	$250,200	$250,200	Increase in cash or accounts receivable
Cost of goods sold	(165,000)	(165,000)	Decrease in inventories
Gross margin on sales	$ 85,200	$ 85,200	Gross inflows of working capital
Deduct: Operating expenses:			
Depreciation—machinery	$ (2,100)	$ 0	Decrease in net income and the carrying value of machinery; but no change to working capital
Other	(81,600)	(81,600)	Decrease in cash or increase in accounts payable
Total operating expenses	$ (83,700)		
Total outflow of working capital		$ (81,600)	Gross outflows of working capital
Net income	$ 1,500		
Working capital provided by operations		$ 3,600	Gross inflows in excess of outflows

the depreciation expense results in a credit to Accumulated Depreciation (that decreases noncurrent assets) and does not decrease current assets or increase current liabilities.

Indirect Method of Calculating Working Capital Provided by Operations   Another method, most often used in practice, to calculate working capital provided by operations is the indirect method. This method requires a backward-type calculative adjustment to net income to compute working capital provided by operations. The calculation involves the use of **nonworking capital charges to operations** and **nonworking capital credits to operations**—defined more specifically in the diagram on page 697. These two groups of items properly change net income but do not change working capital. For the simple example of the CHL Company (data shown in Figure 17–4), the working capital from operations is determined as shown in Figure 17–6.

Working capital provided by operations:	
Net income	$1,500
Add: Nonworking capital charges to operations:	
Depreciation expense—machinery	2,100
Subtotal	$3,600
Deduct: Nonworking capital credits to operations[a]	0
Working capital provided by operations	$3,600

[a]Although there are no nonworking capital credits to operations in this case, it is shown with a zero value to establish a generalized approach.

Figure 17–6   **Indirect Calculation of Working Capital Provided by Operations for CHL Company**

Had the CHL Company suffered a net loss in 1987, the calculation of working capital provided by operations would start the same as described in Figure 17–6, except that the first item would be a negative figure, net loss. For example, if a net loss of $300 had occurred in 1987, this negative item would have been added to $2,100 to get $1,800 working capital provided by operations.

APB Opinion No. 19 specifies that when the indirect method of calculation is used, it must start with net income before extraordinary items. Since *APB Opinion No. 30,* however, more strictly qualifies **extraordinary items** as being both *unusual* and *infrequent,* it seems that the final net income figure will typically be the net income before extraordinary items. Hence, all the illustrations except one—Figure 17–17—used in this chapter make the assumption that there are no extraordinary items; therefore the starting figure for them is net income.

The indirect method of converting net income to working capital provided by operations is the method in general use. An expanded version of the indirect calculation of working capital provided by operations is as follows:

Working capital provided by operations:	
Net income	$XX
Add: Nonworking capital charges to operations [expenses, losses, adjuncts (additions) to expenses or contra items (offsets) to revenue, which do not affect working capital].	XX
Subtotal.	$XX
Deduct: Nonworking capital credits to operations [revenues, gains, adjuncts (additions) to revenue or contra items to expense, which do not affect working capital].	XX
Working capital provided by operations	$XX

Figure 17–7 illustrates the calculation of working capital provided by operations. All of the additions and deductions included in the computation are reflected in the income statement. They represent costs and expenses or gains and losses that enter into the determination of net income but do not affect working capital in the current period. The expenditures or receipts related to those items were made or received in a prior period, or will be made or received in a future period. The recognition of depreciation, for example, while essential to income measurement, does not change the amount of working capital.

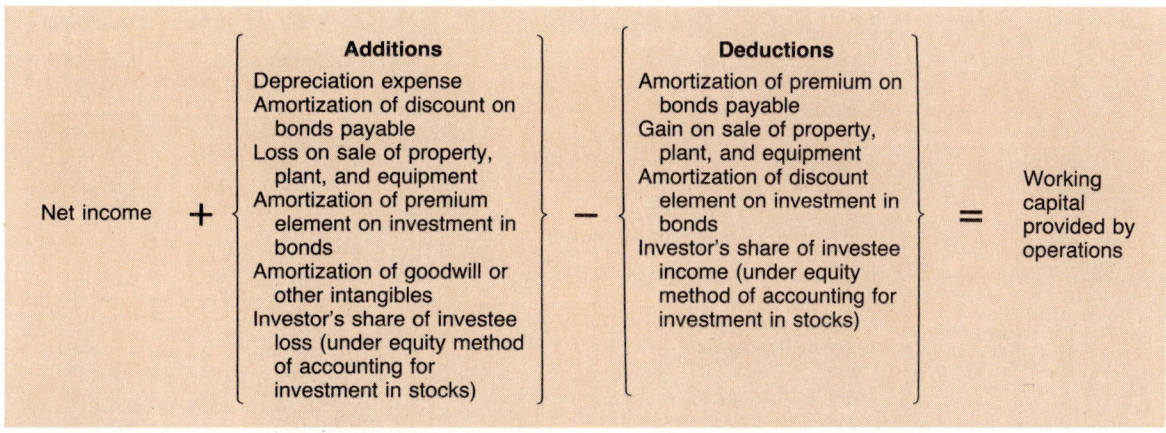

Figure 17–7   **Generalized Approach to Computing Working Capital Provided by Operations**

Preparation of Statements by Simple Analytical Method

Different approaches can be used to obtain the information that appears on the statement of changes in financial position—working capital basis. In many cases, an accountant may determine the sources and uses of financial resources by analyzing the changes that occur in the noncurrent accounts determined from the **comparative balance sheets** (two balance sheets prepared as of the end of two succeeding periods). This is done by the use of a series of computations and schedules, referred to in this book as the

simple analytical approach. In more complex cases, a work sheet or T account approach may be used. These more complex approaches are illustrated in the appendices to this chapter.

Example 1: The Simple Analytical Approach, Year 1987

The statement of changes in financial position includes all financial resources on either a working capital basis or a cash basis. Example 1, however, includes only sources and uses of working capital, omitting those special sources and uses of financial resources that do not affect working capital. These are illustrated in Example 2.

This illustration considers the CHL Company, which received its charter on December 31, 1986, and during the early part of 1987 issued stock, received necessary licenses, and then started operations. Its comparative balance sheets and a note as to the amount of net income earned and dividends declared during 1987 are shown in Figure 17–8.

CHL COMPANY
Comparative Balance Sheet Accounts
December 31, 1987 and 1986

Exhibit C

Debit Accounts	December 31 1987	December 31 1986	Change Increase or (Decrease)
Cash	$25,600	$0	$25,600
Accounts Receivable (net)	10,400	0	10,400
Merchandise Inventory	8,750	0	8,750
Prepaid Insurance	910	0	910
Machinery	21,000	0	21,000
Totals	$66,660	$0	$66,660
Credit Accounts			
Accumulated Depreciation—Machinery	$ 2,100	$0	$ 2,100
Accounts Payable	4,710	0	4,710
Notes Payable—Banks	5,000	0	5,000
Accrued Payables	850	0	850
Common Stock, $10 par	53,500	0	53,500
Retained Earnings	500	0	500
Totals	$66,660	$0	$66,660

Additional information:
   Net income for 1987, $1,500 (see Figure 17–4)
   Dividends declared and paid during 1987, $1,000

Figure 17–8   Comparative Balance Sheet Accounts of CHL Company

Step 1: Preparing the Schedule of Changes in Working Capital Components (Part B)   The first step in preparing the statement of changes in financial position—working capital basis is to determine the net change in working capital and the change in its components. For the CHL

Part B—Schedule of Changes in Working Capital Components

	December 31		Changes in Working Capital	
	1987	1986[a]	Increase	Decrease
Current assets:				
Cash	$25,600	$0	$25,600	
Accounts receivable (net)	10,400	0	10,400	
Merchandise inventory	8,750	0	8,750	
Prepaid insurance	910	0	910	
Total current assets	$45,660	$0		
Current liabilities:				
Accounts payable	$ 4,710	$0		$ 4,710
Notes payable—banks (short-term) . .	5,000	0		5,000
Accrued payables	850	0		850
Total current liabilities	$10,560	$0		
Working capital	$35,100	$0		
Totals			$45,660	$10,560
Net increase in working capital				35,100
Totals			$45,660	$45,660

[a]Obviously there is no balance sheet on December 31, 1986, but one is shown with all items having zero balances so as to establish a basic format.

Figure 17–9   Schedule of Changes in Working Capital Components of CHL Company

Company, these are shown in Figure 17–9. Labeled "Part B," the schedule of changes in working capital components becomes an integral part of the final formal statement of changes in financial position (shown in Figure 17–10). This schedule shows what working capital items changed but not what caused the items to change.

Step 2: Analysis of Changes in Noncurrent Accounts

The next simple analytical step is the analysis of changes in all noncurrent accounts to determine the sources and uses of financial resources—working capital in this example. Throughout this analysis, the abbreviation *EB* is used to mean *ending balance,* and *BB, beginning balance* of accounts.

Analysis of Retained Earnings, Working Capital Provided by Operations, and Related Noncurrent Accounts   The amount of working capital provided by operations is usually determined first. The change in the noncurrent account, Retained Earnings, of $500 = ($500 *EB* − $0 *BB*) is accounted for by the net income for 1987 of $1,500 and the declaration of dividends of $1,000. The net income increases retained earnings, and dividends decrease them, leaving a balance of $500. The change in Accumulated Depreciation of $2,100 = ($2,100 *EB* − $0 *BB*) is caused by the normal depreciation for 1987 (see income statement in Figure 17–4). With this information, the working capital provided by operations can be calculated by the indirect method as follows (the calculation shown in Figure 17–6):

> Working capital provided by operations:
>   Net income..................................... $1,500
>   Add: Nonworking capital charges to operations:
>   Depreciation expense 2,100
>   Working capital provided by operations........................ $3,600

As indicated above, the analysis of the Retained Earnings account shows that the declaration of dividends of $1,000 reduced this account. Therefore, to summarize, the working capital provided by operations as shown above is $3,600 and the only use of financial resources indicated by the analysis in this section is:

> Declaration of dividends, a use of $1,000.

Other Sources and Uses of Working Capital   Two other noncurrent items changed: Machinery has increased, and Common Stock has increased. Machinery has increased by $21,000 = ($21,000 *EB* − $0 *BB*). In the absence of proof to the contrary, it must be assumed that this change was a purchase of machinery using working capital of $21,000. Common stock increased by $53,500. Since this is a new company, the stock was presumably issued for working capital, probably in the form of cash. The preceding analysis indicates the following additional sources (and uses) of financial resources (working capital):

> Purchase of machinery, a use of $21,000.
> Issuance of common stock, a source of $53,500.

It is always necessary *to test to see if the excess of sources of working capital over uses of working capital equals the net increase in working capital* as shown in Part B—the schedule of changes in working capital components. This test should explain the cause of the change in working capital of $35,100, that is, the excess of $57,100 sources over $22,000 uses. Once this test is applied, the solution is virtually complete; all that remains is the preparation of the formal statement of changes in financial position, as illustrated in Step 3.

Step 3: Preparing the Statement of Changes in Financial Position—Working Capital Basis

The information derived from the analysis of the noncurrent accounts (Step 2) is combined with Part B from Figure 17–9 to form a statement of changes in financial position—working capital basis. This statement is shown in Figure 17–10. *APB Opinion No. 19* requires that working capital provided (or used) by operations be shown first on the statement.

CHL COMPANY Exhibit D
Statement of Changes in Financial Position—Working Capital Basis
For the Year Ended December 31, 1987

Part A—Sources and Uses of Financial Resources

Financial resources were provided by:
  Operations:
    Net income .... $ 1,500
    Add: Nonworking capital charges against operations:
      Depreciation of machinery 2,100
    Working capital provided by operations .... $ 3,600
  Issuance of common stock 53,500
    Total financial resources provided $57,100
Financial resources were used for:
  Purchase of machinery $21,000
  Declaration of dividends 1,000
    Total financial resources used 22,000
Net increase in working capital $35,100

Part B—Schedule of Changes in Working Capital Components

	December 31 1987	December 31 1986	Changes in Working Capital Increase	Changes in Working Capital Decrease
Current assets:				
Cash	$25,600	$0	$25,600	
Accounts receivable (net)	10,400	0	10,400	
Merchandise inventory	8,750	0	8,750	
Prepaid insurance	910	0	910	
Total current assets	$45,660	$0		
Current liabilities:				
Accounts payable	$ 4,710	$0		$ 4,710
Notes payable—banks (short-term)	5,000	0		5,000
Accrued payables	850	0		850
Total current liabilities	$10,560	$0		
Working capital	$35,100	$0		
Totals			$45,660	$10,560
Net increase in working capital ...				35,100
Totals			$45,660	$45,660

Figure 17–10   Formal Statement of Changes in Financial Position

***Example 2:
The Simple
Analytical
Approach,
Year 1988***

The preceding example contained no unusual financial activities that are required to be shown in the statement of changes in financial position. Example 2 includes both the sources and uses of working capital and other sources and uses of financial resources, using the simple analytical approach. *APB Opinion No. 19* makes it clear that the all financial resources concept on a working capital basis requires the inclusion of the following:

1. Sources and uses of working capital.

2. Sources and uses of other financial resources not affecting working capital, such as:
    a. Issuance of bonds payable or other long-term debt instruments in exchange for property, plant, and equipment items.
    b. Issuance of capital stock in exchange for property, plant, and equipment items.
    c. Conversion of bonds payable into common stock.
    d. Conversion of preferred stock into common stock.[4]

Each item listed in 2 above would be shown *both* as a source and as a use of financial resources. For example, in the issuance of bonds payable for land, the issuance of bonds payable would be listed as a source and the acquisition of land as a use. It is viewed as essentially being two transactions: the issuance of bonds for cash and the use of the cash received to buy land.

Not all changes in balance sheet items are to be listed as sources and uses of financial resources. *APB Opinion No. 19* excludes (1) stock dividends and stock splits, and (2) restrictions on retained earnings. These items are considered to be primarily changes in accounts that do not alter the basic nature of financial resources.

For Example 2, assume that business picked up rapidly in the latter part of 1987. During 1988, the CHL Company planned an expansion campaign and engaged in financing and investing transactions, some of which affected working capital. Where more complex transactions are involved, a method such as the two illustrated in the appendices to this chapter may be helpful in collecting and analyzing the information to appear on the statement of changes in financial position, but the simple analytical approach may be also used to collect and analyze this information. To illustrate the more complex example, assume that CHL Company has information for 1987 and 1988 as shown in Figure 17–11 and the related data. These data are accumulated from the comparative balance sheets, the income statement and statement of retained earnings for the period, and the journals and ledger accounts.

Step 1: Preparing the Schedule of Changes in Working Capital Components
As with the preceding example, the first step is to prepare the schedule of changes in working capital accounts, Part B to the statement

---

[4]*Opinions of the Accounting Principles Board No. 19,* "Reporting Changes in Financial Position" (New York: AICPA, March 1971), paragraph 14.

of changes in financial position. This is presented first in Figure 17–12, and is incorporated in the formal statement (Figure 17–13).

CHL COMPANY
Comparative Balance Sheet Accounts
December 31, 1988 and 1987

Exhibit C

Debit Accounts	December 31 1988	December 31 1987[a]	Change Increase or (Decrease)
Cash	$197,560	$25,600	$171,960
Accounts Receivable (net)	30,250	10,400	19,850
Merchandise Inventory	89,850	8,750	81,100
Prepaid Insurance	3,750	910	2,840
Land	200,000	0	200,000
Machinery	196,000	21,000	175,000
Totals	$717,410	$66,660	$650,750
Credit Accounts			
Accumulated Depreciation—Machinery	$ 14,200	$ 2,100	$ 12,100
Accounts Payable	16,710	4,710	12,000
Notes Payable—Banks (short-term)	0	5,000	(5,000)
Dividends Payable	40,000	0	40,000
Accrued Payables	1,500	850	650
15% Bonds Payable	300,000	0	300,000
Premium on 15% Bonds Payable	9,000	0	9,000
Convertible Preferred Stock	100,000	0	100,000
Common Stock, $10 Par	153,500	53,500	100,000
Paid-In Capital—Excess over Par, Common	2,000	0	2,000
Retained Earnings	30,500	500	30,000
Retained Earnings—Restricted for Plant Expansion	50,000	0	50,000
Totals	$717,410	$66,660	$650,750

[a]These figures are from Figure 17–8.

Figure 17–11   Comparative Balance Sheet Accounts for CHL Company

Additional 1988 Information for CHL Company   The following additional information is from the files of CHL Company and pertains to activities in 1988:

a. Net income for 1988 was $120,000.

b. A dividend of $40,000 was declared on December 15, 1988, payable on January 12, 1989.

c. During 1988, machinery was purchased for $175,000.

d. The annual depreciation expense on machinery was $12,100.

e. On January 1, 1988, the company issued at 105 for cash 15 percent bonds with a face value of $200,000. The maturity date of the bonds is January 1, 1998.

f. On December 31, 1988, the company issued directly to Jefferson Realty Company 15 percent bonds with a face value of $100,000 at 100 for land valued at $100,000.

g. On December 31, 1988, convertible preferred stock was issued at par to Jefferson Realty Company for an adjoining parcel of land valued at $100,000.

h. An additional 10,000 shares of common stock was issued for cash at $10.20 per share.

i. On December 31, 1988, the board of directors voted to restrict retained earnings in the amount of $50,000 for plant expansion.

j. The annual amortization of premium on 15 percent bonds payable was $1,000.

Part B: Schedule of Changes in Working Capital Components

	December 31		Changes in Working Capital	
	1988	1987	Increase	Decrease
Current assets:				
Cash	$197,560	$25,600	$171,960	
Accounts receivable (net)	30,250	10,400	19,850	
Merchandise inventory	89,850	8,750	81,100	
Prepaid insurance	3,750	910	2,840	
Total current assets	$321,410	$45,660		
Current liabilities:				
Accounts payable	$ 16,710	$ 4,710		$ 12,000
Notes payable—banks (short-term)	0	5,000	5,000	
Dividends payable	40,000	0		40,000
Accrued payables	1,500	850		650
Total current liabilities	$ 58,210	$10,560		
Working capital	$263,200	$35,100		
Totals			$280,750	$ 52,650
Net increase in working capital				228,100
Totals			$280,750	$280,750

Figure 17–12 Schedule of Changes in Working Capital Components of CHL Company

Step 2: Analysis of Changes in Noncurrent Accounts As in Example 1, the next step is the analysis of changes in all noncurrent accounts to determine the sources and uses of financial resources. An excellent starting place within this step is the analysis of retained earnings and the determination of the working capital provided by operations.

Analysis of Retained Earnings, Working Capital Provided by Operations, and Related Noncurrent Accounts   To determine the working capital provided by operations, the accountant must know the amount of net income—a cause of change in retained earnings—and the nonworking capital charges and credits to operations. Retained Earnings increased by $30,000 = ($30,500 *EB* − $500 *BB*). Information for 1988 (items a, b, and i) indicates the following three causes of change in retained earnings:

Increase in retained earnings caused by net income—a part of working capital from operations.	$120,000
Decrease in retained earnings caused by the declaration of dividends—a use of financial resources.	(40,000)
Decrease in the Retained Earnings account caused by the restriction of retained earnings—not listed as either a source or use of financial resources.	(50,000)
Net increase in retained earnings explained.	$ 30,000

The first item (net income of $120,000) in the preceding analysis represents part of the working capital provided by operations. To the figure must be added the nonworking capital charges to operations. The only nonworking capital charge in this example is depreciation expense on machinery of $12,100 (item d of the additional 1988 data). This amount explains the change in another noncurrent account, Accumulated Depreciation—Machinery ($14,200 *EB* − $2,100 *BB*) = $12,100, the amount of the depreciation expense.

To determine the (net) working capital provided by operations, any nonworking capital credits to operations must be subtracted from the subtotal of net income plus nonworking capital charges to operations. Item j of the additional 1988 data is the only nonworking capital credit to operations in this example. The amortization of premium on 15 percent bonds payable of $1,000 explains part of the change (a decrease) in the Premium on 15 Percent Bonds Payable account. The account was increased by $10,000 when the 15 percent bonds payable were issued at 105. Then the amortization reduced the Bond Interest Expense account, *thus causing an increase in net income without producing an increase in working capital.* After amortization, the Premium on 15 Percent Bonds Payable account had a net increase of $9,000 = ($9,000 *EB* − $0 *BB*). Thus financial resources of $210,000 were provided by the issuance of the bonds on January 1, 1988 (item e from the additional 1988 data).

The following two summaries show the impact on financial resources of the preceding analysis up to this point:

Working capital provided by operations:	
Net income	$120,000
Add: Nonworking capital charges to operations:	
Depreciation expense—machinery	12,100
Subtotal	$132,100
Deduct: Nonworking capital credits to operations:	
Amortization of premium on 15 percent bonds payable	1,000
Working capital provided by operations	$131,100
Summary of other sources (and uses) of financial resources:	
Declaration of dividends, a use of $40,000.	
Issuance of 15 percent bonds payable at 105, a source of $210,000.	

These items will be incorporated in the formal statement of changes in financial position (see Figure 17–13). Note, however, that the $210,000 source from the issuance of the bonds represents only part of the source from the issuance of bonds. The remaining $100,000 cause of increase in 15% Bonds Payable is discussed in the next section.

Other Sources and Uses of Financial Resources The accountant in using the simple analytical approach should adopt a systematic approach to complete the problem. Once the analysis shown in the preceding section is accomplished, the preparer should then examine and analyze each remaining noncurrent item in the comparative balance sheet in sequential order to explain the cause of change in any other noncurrent account. In the CHL Company example, the next unexplained noncurrent item shown in the comparative balance sheet is land. It changed by $200,000 = ($200,000 *EB* − $0 *BB*). Items f and g of the additional 1988 data explain this change. Land was purchased for $200,000 and was paid for by the issuance at 100 of 15 percent bonds payable of $100,000 and the issuance at par value of convertible preferred stock of $100,000. Even though this transaction did *not* affect working capital, it is considered to be two sources and one use of financial resources. The use of financial resources is $200,000 for the purchase of land (explaining the cause of the change in the Land account). The two sources are: (1) issuance of bonds payable, $100,000 (explaining the remaining change in bonds payable—$200,000 was explained by the issuance for cash in the preceding section), and (2) issuance of convertible preferred stock of $100,000 (explaining the change in the Convertible Preferred Stock account—$100,000 *EB* − $0 *BB*). The substance of the foregoing transactions is essentially the same as if securities were issued for cash and then the cash were used to acquire land.

The next noncurrent asset to be considered is Machinery. The change in the Machinery account is $175,000 = ($196,000 *EB* − $21,000 *BB*). Item c in the additional 1988 data reveals the cause of this change: purchase of machinery, a use of financial resources of $175,000. The remaining noncurrent

CHL COMPANY   **Exhibit D**
Statement of Changes in Financial Position—Working Capital Basis
For the Year Ended December 31, 1988

Part A—Sources and Uses of Financial Resources

Financial resources were provided by:		
Operations:		
Net income	$120,000	
Add: Nonworking capital charges to operations:		
Depreciation of machinery	12,100	
Subtotal	$132,100	
Deduct: Nonworking capital credits to operations:		
Amortization of premium on 15% bonds payable	1,000	
Working capital provided by operations	$131,100	
Issuance of 15% bonds payable at 105	210,000	
Issuance of 15% bonds payable at 100	100,000	
Issuance of convertible preferred stock at par	100,000	
Issuance of common stock	102,000	
Total financial resources provided		$643,100
Financial resources were used for:		
Declaration of dividends	$ 40,000	
Purchase of machinery	175,000	
Purchase of land (by issuance of bonds and convertible preferred stock)	200,000	
Total financial resources used		415,000
Net increase in working capital		$228,100

Part B—Schedule of Changes in Working Capital Components

	December 31		Changes in Working Capital	
	1988	1987	Increase	Decrease
Current assets:				
Cash	$197,560	$25,600	$171,960	
Accounts receivable (net)	30,250	10,400	19,850	
Merchandise inventory	89,850	8,750	81,100	
Prepaid insurance	3,750	910	2,840	
Total current assets	$321,410	$45,660		
Current liabilities:				
Accounts payable	$ 16,710	$ 4,710		$ 12,000
Notes payable—banks (short-term)	0	5,000	5,000	
Dividends payable	40,000	0		40,000
Accrued payables	1,500	850		650
Total current liabilities	$ 58,210	$10,560		
Working capital	$263,200	$35,100		
Totals			$280,750	$ 52,650
Net increase in working capital				228,100
Totals			$280,750	$280,750

Figure 17–13   **Formal Statement of Changes in Financial Position for CHL Company**

accounts that have not been explained are Common Stock and Paid-in Capital—Excess over Par, Common. The Common Stock account changed (increased) by $100,000 = ($153,500 *EB* − $53,500 *BB*), and Paid-in Capital—Excess over Par, Common changed (increased) by $2,000 = ($2,000 *EB* − $0 *BB*). These two accounts were increased by one transaction, the issuance of 10,000 shares of $10 par value common stock at $10.20 per share (item h of the additional 1988 data). This transaction represents a source of financial resources of $102,000, and it explains the cause of change in these two noncurrent accounts.

All of the changes in the noncurrent accounts are now explained. A summary of the impact on financial resources of the analyses in this section is shown below.

> Summary of sources (and uses) of financial resources:
> Purchase of land, a use of $200,000.
> Issuance of 15 percent bonds payable at 100, a source of $100,000.
> Issuance of convertible preferred stock, a source of $100,000.
> Purchase of machinery, a use of $175,000.
> Issuance of common stock, a source of $102,000.

Step 3: Preparing the Statement of Changes in Financial Position—Working Capital Basis

Now that the noncurrent accounts have been analyzed, Part A of the formal statement of changes in financial position on the working capital basis can be prepared directly from the summaries presented in Step 2. The completed statement showing both Parts A and B is shown in Figure 17–13. Recall that, as stated in Example 1, a test must be made to see if the excess of sources of financial resources over uses of financial resources equals the net increase in working capital. In Example 2, this test shows that the excess of $228,100 shown in Part A of Figure 17–13 equals the net increase in working capital as shown in Part B of this figure. Appendix 17.1 shows the work sheet method, and Appendix 17.2 shows the T account method for preparing the statement of changes in financial position for the CHL Company for 1988. Both use the same data just analyzed. The chapter now turns to the topic of preparing the statement on the cash basis.

All Financial Resources: Cash Basis

As indicated previously, *APB Opinion No. 19* permits the presentation of the all financial resources statement of changes in financial position on either a cash or a working capital basis. Also with the current emphasis on **liquidity** (the nearness of assets and liabilities to cash), the cash basis format appears to be the trend in the near future. The all financial resources statement prepared on a cash basis approach requires the inclusion of the following:

1. Sources and uses of cash, including the calculation of cash provided by (or used in) operations.

2. Sources and uses of other financial resources not affecting cash, such as:
   a. Issuance of bonds payable or other long-term debt instruments in exchange for property, plant, and equipment items.
   b. Issuance of common stock in exchange for property, plant, and equipment items.
   c. Conversion of bonds payable into common stock.
   d. Conversion of preferred stock into common stock.
   e. The exchange of temporary investments for repurchase of treasury stock.

The *Opinion* specifically excludes the declaration of stock dividends and the restriction of retained earnings from being shown in the statement of changes in financial position on a cash basis. As with the working capital basis, these exclusions are required because they are essentially book-type changes. Hence they do not represent financing and investing activities.

Besides the trend toward the cash basis format for external reporting purposes, the cash basis statement often will be more important to an internal user than the working capital basis statement. For example, for many short-run financial purposes, a statement based on cash is useful to management for analysis in budgeting and forecasting cash requirements. When interest rates are extremely high, the administration of cash and the attention accorded the concept of liquidity are of paramount importance.

Generalized Approach to Cash Basis Statement

The logic of the analysis for a cash basis statement of changes in financial position is the same as that for a working capital basis statement: both consider the relationships of the items in the financial statements. The cause of the changes in cash—sources and uses—are determined by analyzing the changes in *all* accounts other than Cash. Figures from the income statement are used to determine the changes in cash as a result of operations, and figures from the balance sheet together with supplementary data reveal the remaining causes for change.

As with working capital provided by operations, determination of the cash generated by operations presents a major problem, which is complicated by the fact that the revenue and expense figures used for income measurement are different from cash receipts and cash disbursements. The time lag in the settlement of accounts with customers and creditors and the prepayment of certain expenses, for example, necessitate the conversion of accrual basis revenue and expense amounts to their cash equivalents.

In the illustration that follows, the *simple analytical approach* is used also to determine the information that appears on the statement of changes in financial position—cash basis.

Example: Cash Basis Statement

Information related to the Athens Corporation is shown in Figure 17–14. The simple analytical method of determining the sources and uses of cash for the Athens Corporation is then used, based on this information.

Comparative Balance Sheet Accounts

Debit Accounts	December 31 1987	December 31 1986	Change Increase or (Decrease)
Cash	$ 78,000	$ 61,000	$ 17,000
Accounts Receivable (net)	270,000	240,000	30,000
Merchandise Inventory	300,000	193,000	107,000
Long-Term Investments	36,000	30,000	6,000
Land	60,000	60,000	0
Buildings (net)[a]	480,000	510,000	(30,000)
Machinery (net)[a]	600,000	370,000	230,000
Totals	$1,824,000	$1,464,000	$360,000
Credit Accounts			
Accounts Payable	$ 225,000	$ 195,000	$ 30,000
Accrued Payables	9,000	12,000	(3,000)
14% Bonds Payable	210,000	174,000	36,000
Common Stock, $10 Par Value	900,000	750,000	150,000
Retained Earnings	480,000	333,000	147,000
Totals	$1,824,000	$1,464,000	$360,000

[a]Buildings and machinery are shown net of the accumulated depreciation; but the depreciation for the year will have to be considered in determining the cause of change.

Abbreviated Income Statement Accounts for 1987

	Debits	Credits
Sales		$2,430,000
Cost of Goods Sold	$1,440,000	
Depreciation Expense—Machinery	60,000	
Depreciation Expense—Building	30,000	
Other Operating Expenses (requiring cash)	663,000	

Additional Data

a. From the above operating data, net income is determined to be $237,000.
b. Dividends declared and paid during 1987, $90,000.
c. The change in the Machinery account is caused by two transactions: (1) depreciation and (2) purchases of machinery for cash.
d. Long-term investments were from purchases for cash.
e. The decrease in buildings (net) was from depreciation expense.
f. Common stock was issued at par value for cash.

Figure 17–14 Information Required for Statement of Changes in Financial Position—Cash Basis Approach for Athens Corporation

Cash Provided by Operations The first step in preparing a statement of changes in financial position on a cash basis is to determine the amount of cash provided by (or used in) operations. As indicated in the foregoing section, this calculation focuses on the operating (income statement) transactions affecting cash. As with determining working capital provided by operations, there are two general approaches: (1) the direct approach where the income statement is in effect converted to a cash basis statement, or (2) the indirect approach where the net cash provided by operations is determined by adding the noncash charges against operations to net income and subtracting from the resulting total the noncash credits to operations. As with working capital, the shorter indirect method is preferred in practice and is the only one illustrated here.

Indirect Method of Calculating Cash Provided by (or Used in) Operations A short-cut method of calculating the net cash provided by (or used in) operations can be developed by the same techniques as used for working capital. This indirect method starts with net income to which is added the *noncash charges against operations.* (This term includes expenses, losses, adjuncts to expenses, contra items to revenues, and changes in current items that decrease net income but *do not decrease cash.*) From the total of net income and noncash charges is subtracted the *noncash credits to operations.* (This term includes revenues, gains, adjuncts to revenues, contra items to expenses, and changes in current items that *increase net income but not cash.*) The difference is net cash provided by (or used in) operations. Figure 17–15 shows that the net cash provided by operations is $217,000.

Increases in most of the current liabilities and decreases in most of the current assets other than cash are noncash charges to operations; that is, they result in decreases in net income without decreasing cash. In a similar but opposing way, decreases in most of the current liabilities and increases in most of the current assets are treated as noncash credits to operations since they result in increases in net income without increasing cash. Exceptions to this generalization are those current items not affecting operations, such as temporary investments (these changes are treated separately). Depreciation expense and other noncash charges and noncash credits are similar to the nonworking capital charges and credits to operations. Again, both the direct and indirect methods will produce the same answer. The indirect method is

Cash provided by operations:		
Net income..		$237,000
Add: Noncash charges against operations:		
Depreciation expense—machinery...............		60,000
Depreciation expense—building.................		30,000
Increase in accounts payable......................		30,000
Subtotal...		$357,000
Deduct: Noncash credits to operations:		
Increase in accounts receivable..................	$ 30,000	
Increase in merchandise inventory...............	107,000	
Decrease in accrued payables.....................	3,000	140,000
Net cash provided by operations......................		$217,000

Figure 17–15   **Indirect Method of Calculating Cash Provided by (or Used in) Operations**

used more often than the direct method because it highlights the differences between net income and the net cash provided by operations. These differences (application of the exception principle) help a manager in making certain decisions affecting the distribution of net income.

Completing the Cash Basis Statement of Changes in Financial Position   The sources and uses of cash other than that resulting from operations can be determined by examining the changes that have occurred in the noncurrent accounts and certain nonoperating current accounts along with any additional information that is given. First, using the additional data (Figure 17–14), item b describes a specific use of cash, the payment (not the declaration) of dividends of $90,000. Retained earnings increased by $147,000 = ($480,000 EB − $333,000 BB). Net income of $237,000 used in calculating net cash provided by operations increased retained earnings; the dividends declared decreased retained earnings by $90,000. The *net increase* is $147,000 = ($237,000 − $90,000); thus the change in retained earnings is explained.

The net increase in machinery (item c) is the result of a purchase of machinery and depreciation. Since there is a decrease caused by depreciation, the increase caused by the purchase of $290,000 is calculated as follows:

End-of-year balance	$600,000
Beginning-of-year balance	370,000
Net increase	$230,000
Add: Depreciation expense	60,000
Machinery purchased during 1987	$290,000

The increase in long-term investments results from purchases of securities (item d). This increase of $6,000 = ($36,000 EB − $30,000 BB) is a use of cash.

The decrease in buildings (net) is caused by depreciation (item e). This amount was used in calculating the net cash provided by operations; hence nothing more is required to be done. The net decrease in the noncash account, Buildings, is explained.

Item f explicitly states that cash is provided by the issuance of common stock at par. This amount is $150,000 = ($900,000 EB − $750,000 BB).

The changes in all accounts have now been explained except the change in the 14% Bonds Payable account. This account increased by $36,000 = ($210,000 EB − $174,000 BB). An assumption must be made as to what produced this increase. A logical one is that additional bonds of $36,000 must have been issued for cash, hence this transaction results in a source of cash. The excess of the total sources of cash over the total uses of cash must produce a figure that equals the net increases in cash of $17,000 = ($78,000 EB − $61,000 BB). The foregoing analysis is summarized in a statement of changes in financial position prepared on a cash basis, shown in Figure 17–16.

ATHENS CORPORATION   Exhibit D
Statement of Changes in Financial Position—Cash Basis
For the Year Ended December 31, 1987

Part A—Sources and Uses of Financial Resources

Financial resources were provided by:[a]		
Operations:[b]		
Net income		$237,000
Add: Noncash charges against operations:		
Depreciation expense—machinery		60,000
Depreciation expense—building		30,000
Increase in accounts payable		30,000
Subtotal		$357,000
Deduct: Noncash credits to operations:		
Increase in accounts receivable	$ 30,000	
Increase in merchandise inventory	107,000	
Decrease in accrued payables	3,000	140,000
Net cash provided by operations		$217,000
Issuance of common stock at par		150,000
Issuance of 14% bonds payable at par		36,000
Total sources of financial resources		$403,000
Financial resources were used for:		
Payment of dividends		$ 90,000
Purchase of long-term investments		6,000
Purchase of machinery		290,000
Total uses of financial resources		386,000
Net increase in cash		$ 17,000

Part B—Schedule of Changes in Cash

Cash, December 31, 1987	$78,000
Cash, December 31, 1986	61,000
Net increase in cash	$17,000

[a] In this example, these are all cash and the item could be called "Cash was provided by."
[b] See Figure 17–15.

Figure 17–16   Statement of Changes in Financial Position—Cash Basis for Athens Corporation

Extraordinary Income Statement Items

In *Opinion No. 19,* the APB specifically states that

> The Statement [of changes in financial position] should prominently disclose working capital or cash provided from or used in operations for the period, and the Board believes that the disclosure is most informative if the effects of extraordinary items (see *APB Opinion No. 9, Reporting the Results of Operations,* paragraphs 21 and 22) are reported separately from the effects of normal items.[5]

---

[5] *APB Opinion No. 19,* paragraph 10.

The *Opinion* goes on to describe two acceptable methods of calculating the "working capital provided from [used in] operations for the period exclusive of extraordinary items." It then says:

> This total should be immediately followed by working capital or cash provided or used by income or loss from extraordinary items, if any; extraordinary income or loss should be similarly adjusted for items recognized that did not provide or use working capital or cash during the period.[6]

To illustrate the authors' interpretation of the foregoing pronouncement, assume that the Extra-Ord Corporation had the following information relating to the changes in its financial position during 1987:

Summary of Financial Information Relating to Extra-Ord Corporation

Net increase in working capital	$ 50,000
Net income	200,000
Sale of long-term investments required by newly enacted legislation (extraordinary gain on this forced sale of $50,000 is included in the above net income; the cost is $70,000)	120,000
Depreciation expense	30,000
Purchased land	250,000

This information is shown in the partial (Part A) statement of changes in financial position—working capital basis presented in Figure 17–17.

EXTRA-ORD CORPORATION — Exhibit D
Statement of Changes in Financial Position—Working Capital Basis
For the Year Ended December 31, 1987

Part A—Sources and Uses of Financial Resources

Financial resources were provided by:		
Operations:		
Net income before extraordinary items	$150,000	
Add: Nonworking capital charges to operations:		
Depreciation expense	30,000	
Working capital provided by operations exclusive of extraordinary items	$180,000	
Extraordinary gain on forced sale of long-term investments	50,000[a]	
Sale of long-term investments (total proceeds, $120,000; the extraordinary gain is shown above)	70,000	
Total sources of financial resources		$300,000
Financial resources were used for:		
Purchase of land		250,000
Net increase in working capital		$ 50,000

[a]Generally accepted accounting principles require that extraordinary items be shown net of the income tax effect. The tax effect is ignored here.

Figure 17–17   Partial Statement of Changes in Financial Position of Extra-Ord Corporation

---

[6]Ibid.

Managerial Analysis of Statement of Changes in Financial Position—Working Capital Basis

The data in the statement of changes in financial position can be analyzed by recasting the statement in common-size form, which requires that the items in the statement be arranged in a slightly different order. The net increase in working capital must be shown as a use of financial resources. The statement then shows the disposition of all sources provided—those going for specific uses, and the remainder to build up the pool of working capital. Part A of the CHL Company's statement of changes in financial position for 1988 is shown in Figure 17–18, which reveals both the absolute amounts and the common-size percentages.

CHL COMPANY   Exhibit D
Statement of Changes in Financial Position—Working Capital Basis
For the Year Ended December 31, 1988

Part A—Sources and Uses of Financial Resources

	Amount	Percent
Financial resources were provided by:		
Operations:		
Net income	$120,000	
Add: Nonworking capital charges to operations:		
Depreciation of machinery	12,100	
Subtotal	$132,100	
Deduct: Nonworking capital credits to operations:		
Amortization of premium on 15% bonds payable	1,000	
Working capital provided by operations	$131,100	20.4%
Issuance of 15% bonds payable at 105	210,000	32.7
Issuance of 15% bonds payable at 100	100,000	15.5
Issuance of convertible preferred stock at par	100,000	15.5
Issuance of common stock	102,000	15.9
Totals	$643,100	100.0%
Financial resources were used for:		
Declaration of dividends	$ 40,000	6.2%
Purchase of machinery	175,000	27.2
Purchase of land (by issuance of bonds and convertible preferred stock)	200,000	31.1
Net increase in working capital	228,100	35.5
Totals	$643,100	100.0%

Figure 17–18   Common-Size Statement of Changes in Financial Position—Working Capital Basis

---

An analysis of the information in Figure 17–18 in question and answer form to indicate how this statement *may be used* by management, investors, and other interested persons follows.

1. What was the net change in working capital? An increase of $228,100.

2. What was the effect of plant asset acquisitions on financial resources? The purchase of machinery and land decreased the available financial resources by $375,000, or 58.3 percent = (27.2% + 31.1%) of available resources.

3. What financial resources were made available from investment by owners? From operations? These sources provided approximately 51.8 percent = (20.4% + 15.5% + 15.9%) of the available financial resources.

4. What financial resources came from outside borrowing? The issuance of 15 percent bonds payable provided 48.2 percent = (32.7% + 15.5%) of the available financial resources.

5. What financial resources came from the sale of noncurrent assets? None.

6. What was the effect of the dividend declaration on financial resources? Dividends declared totaled $40,000, which decreased financial resources. The declaration of dividends represented approximately 33.3 percent = ($40,000 ÷ $120,000) of net income and 6.2 percent of available financial resources.

Appendix 17.1
Illustration Using Work Sheet Method

Introduction

Where more complex transactions are involved, a work sheet (or T accounts shown in Appendix 17.2) may be helpful in collecting and analyzing the information to appear in the statement of changes in financial position. The data for the CHL Company for 1988 are rather complex for the simple analytical method. Situations similar to Example 2 suggest the possible use of an analytical technique similar to the work sheet or the T account method. The application of these two analytical methods to the 1988 CHL Company example is shown in this and the next appendix.

Learning Goals

1. To use a work sheet to develop sources and uses of funds based on the all financial resources on a working capital basis concept of funds.

2. To understand how to use a work sheet to develop sources and uses of funds based on the all financial resources on a cash basis concept of funds.

Work Sheet Illustration—Working Capital Basis

Step 1: Preparing the Schedule of Changes in Working Capital Components The data for the work sheet analysis of the 1988 CHL Company statement are presented in Figure 17–11 and in the additional 1988 data in Example 2 in the body of this chapter. The first step is the preparation of the schedule of changes in working capital accounts, Part B to the statement of changes in financial position; it is the same as the schedule prepared by the simple analytical approach. This schedule is presented in Figure 17–12; it is also incorporated in the formal statement (Figure 17–13).

17 / Statement of Changes in Financial Position

Step 2: Preparing the Work Sheet for the Statement of Changes in Financial Position   A work sheet showing the analysis of changes in noncurrent accounts then may be prepared. This work sheet shows the beginning and ending working capital (summarized into amounts) and the account balances of all noncurrent accounts. Space is provided—two columns' width—between these beginning and ending balances to permit the necessary analysis of the transactions producing the change in the noncurrent accounts. Thus each work sheet line (except working capital) in the top section represents an account and its change. The work sheet ready to begin analysis entries is shown in Figure A17–1. (See page 718 before reading further.)

The analytical work sheet entries involve a reconstruction in summary form of all the transactions that occurred during the period that changed these accounts. Those portions of summary transactions that increase financial resources or decrease financial resources are noted in the work sheet on the bottom part under sections entitled "Sources of financial resources" and "Uses of financial resources." In the work sheet for this more complex example, note that there are some financial activities that do not affect working capital but do affect the sources and uses of financial resources. As required by *APB Opinion No. 19,* these activities must be determined. The completed work sheet is shown in Figure A17–2. The explanations to the work sheet reconstruction entries are keyed to the letters (a), (b), (c), etc. from the additional 1988 data in the main body of the chapter in Example 2.

Explanation of Work Sheet Entries: CHL Company   The work sheet reconstruction entries for this example are explained in more depth.

(**a**)   The Retained Earnings account has increased by a net change of $30,000 = ($30,500 *EB* − $500 *BB*). Entries (a), (b), and (i)—net income increased retained earnings, dividends and the restriction on retained earnings decreased retained earnings—explain this change. To record the impact of net income on financial resources, a debit is made to Sources of financial resources: Operations, $120,000; and a credit to Retained Earnings, $120,000.

(**b**)   Dividends were declared payable in 1989. Financial resources are used in 1988 since working capital is *reduced* in 1988 by the creation of a current liability. The work sheet entry is a debit to Retained Earnings, $40,000; and a credit to Uses of financial resources: Declaration of dividends, $40,000.

(**c**)   The Machinery account has increased by $175,000 = ($196,000 *EB* − $21,000 *BB*). This change was caused by the purchase of machinery. This transaction represents a use of financial resources of $175,000—the acquisition of machinery. The work sheet entry is a *debit* to Machinery, $175,000; and a *credit* to Uses of financial resources: Purchase of machinery, $175,000. This transaction explains the cause of the change in Machinery, $175,000 and a check mark (√) is placed by the ending balance.

(**d**)   The accumulated Depreciation—Machinery account has increased by $12,100 = ($14,200 *EB* − $2,100 *BB*). The depreciation expense on machinery is $12,100 (see Figure 17–12), which explains the change in the

CHL COMPANY
Work Sheet for Statement of Changes in Financial Position
For the Year Ended December 31, 1988

	Balances December 31, 1987	Analysis of Transactions for Current Year		Balances December 31, 1988
		Debit	Credit	
Debit Accounts				
Working Capital	35,100			263,200
Land[a]	0			200,000
Machinery	21,000			196,000
Totals	56,100			659,200
Credit Accounts				
Accumulated Depreciation—Machinery	2,100			14,200
15% Bonds Payable[a]	0			300,000
Premium on 15% Bonds Payable	0			9,000
Convertible Preferred Stock	0			100,000
Common Stock, $10 Par	53,500			153,500
Paid-in Capital—Excess over Par, Common	0			2,000
Retained Earnings[a]	500			30,500
Retained Earnings—Restricted for Plant Expansion	0			50,000
Totals	56,100			659,200
		Sources	Uses	Remarks
Sources of financial resources:				
Operations:				
Uses of financial resources:				

[a] Where more than one debit or credit to an item can be anticipated an extra line should be left blank.

Figure A17–1   Work Sheet Ready for Analysis of Changes in Noncurrent Accounts

CHL COMPANY
Work Sheet for Statement of Changes in Financial Position
For the Year Ended December 31, 1988

	Balances December 31, 1987	Analysis of Transactions for Current Year - Debit		Analysis of Transactions for Current Year - Credit		Balances December 31, 1988
Debit Accounts						
Working Capital	35,100	(z)	228,100			263,200 ✓ c
Land[a]	0	(f)	100,000			200,000 ✓
		(g)	100,000			
Machinery	21,000	(c)	175,000			196,000 ✓
Totals	56,100					659,200 ✓
Credit Accounts						
Accumulated Depreciation—Machinery	2,100			(d)	12,100	14,200 ✓
15% Bonds Payable[a]	0			(e)	200,000	300,000 ✓
				(f)	100,000	
Premium on 15% Bonds Payable	0	(j)	1,000	(e)	10,000	9,000 ✓
Convertible Preferred Stock	0			(g)	100,000	100,000 ✓
Common Stock, $10 Par	53,500			(h)	100,000	153,500 ✓
Paid-in Capital—Excess over Par, Common	0			(h)	2,000	2,000 ✓
Retained Earnings[a]	500	(b)	40,000	(a)	120,000	30,500 ✓
		(i)	50,000			
Retained Earnings—Restricted for Plant Expansion	0			(i)	50,000	50,000
Totals	56,100		694,100		694,100	659,200 ✓

		Sources		Uses		Remarks
Sources of financial resources:						
Operations:						
Net income		(a)	120,000			
Add: Depreciation expense—machinery		(d)	12,100			From operations,
Deduct: Amortization of						131,100
premium on 15% bonds payable				(j)	1,000	
Issuance of bonds payable at 105		(e)	210,000			
Issuance of bonds payable at 100		(f)	100,000			
Issuance of preferred stock		(g)	100,000			
Issuance of common stock		(h)	102,000			
Uses of financial resources:						
Declaration of dividends				(b)	40,000	
Purchase of machinery				(c)	175,000	
Purchase of land				(f)	100,000	
				(g)	100,000	
Total sources and uses of financial resources[b]			644,100		416,000	
Increase in working capital				(z)	228,100	
Totals			644,100		644,100	

[a] Where more than one debit or credit to an item can be anticipated, an extra line should be left blank.
[b] The total sources and uses of financial resources are really $643,100 and $415,000, respectively, when the deduct item, amortization of premium on 15% bonds payable, is deducted from the sum of other operational items. From a work sheet check and balance point of view, it is better to add the debits and credits under the Sources and Uses columns.
[c] A check mark (✓) can be used to show that a line representing an account has been "explained." A line (account) is explained when the debits and credits in the Analysis columns reconcile the difference between beginning and ending balances.

Figure A17–2   **Work Sheet after Analysis of Changes in Noncurrent Accounts**

account. The work sheet entry for this transaction is a debit to Sources of financial resources: Operations (add-back for depreciation of machinery), $12,100; and a credit to Accumulated Depreciation—Machinery, $12,100.

(e) Two noncurrent accounts were affected by transactions involving 15 percent bonds payable: (1) the 15% Bonds Payable account was increased by a total amount of $300,000 = ($300,000 EB − $0 BB); and (2) Premium on 15% Bonds Payable, by $9,000 = ($9,000 EB − $0 BB). These bonds were issued at two different times at different prices. One lot (e) was issued at 105, thus providing financial resources of $210,000. The work sheet reconstruction entry for the first issuance is a debit to Sources of financial resources: Issuance of bonds payable at 105, $210,000; and credits to 15% Bonds Payable, $200,000 and Premium on 15% Bonds Payable, $10,000. This transaction does not fully explain either of the noncurrent accounts. Entries (f) and (j) are required before the two account changes are explained.

(f) Bonds payable were issued at face value directly to a realtor for land, $100,000. This transaction does not affect working capital but represents *both* a source and a use of financial resources under the all financial resources concept of funds. Two separate work sheet entries are needed in the analysis in this transaction: (1) a debit to Sources of financial resources: Issuance of bonds payable at 100, $100,000; and a credit to 15% Bonds Payable, $100,000; (2) a debit to Land, $100,000; and a credit to Uses of financial resources: Purchase of land, $100,000. This transaction now fully explains the remaining change in the 15% Bonds Payable amount.

(g) This reconstruction is similar to (f). Convertible preferred stock was issued at par directly for land, $100,000. This transaction [like (f)] does not affect working capital; but it represents *both* a source and a use of financial resources under the all financial resources concept of funds. Two separate work sheet entries are needed in the analysis in this transaction: (1) a debit to Sources of financial resources: Issuance of preferred stock, $100,000; and a credit to Convertible Preferred Stock, $100,000; and (2) a debit to Land, $100,000; and a credit to Uses of financial resources: Purchase of land, $100,000. This transaction explains the change in Convertible Preferred Stock of $100,000. It also completes the explanation of the change in the Land account: (f) explains $100,000 and (g) explains the remaining $100,000.

(h) An additional 10,000 shares of common stock were issued at $10.20 per share. This transaction provided working capital of $102,000. The work sheet entry to explain two noncurrent accounts, Common Stock and Paid-in Capital—Excess over Par, Common, is a debit to Sources of financial resources: Issuance of common stock, $102,000; and two credits—(1) Common Stock, $10 Par (for par amount), $100,000 and (2) Paid-in Capital—Excess over Par, Common, $2,000. The change in both of the accounts credited is now explained.

(i) The board of directors voted to restrict retained earnings for expansion in the amount of $50,000. This transaction is deemed simply to be a book-type entry to show management's intended use of earnings; hence, the APB indicated that it need not be shown on the statement of changes in financial position. A work sheet entry is *required,* however, to explain the change in Retained Earnings—Restricted for Plant Expansion and to complete the explanation of the change in Retained Earnings. Thus, to keep from drawing a wrong conclusion about what produced this change, it is necessary to make a work sheet entry debiting Retained Earnings for $50,000 and crediting Retained Earnings—Restricted for Plant Expansion for $50,000.

(j) The Premium on 15% Bonds Payable account needs a debit of $1,000 to show that the total change has been explained. The amortization of premium on bonds payable for 1988 was $1,000; this amortization explains what produced the remaining net change in the Premium on 15% Bonds Payable amount. This amortization reduced the Bond Interest Expense account, *thus causing an increase in net income without producing an increase in working capital.* To provide for a subtraction from the working capital provided by operations, a work sheet reconstruction entry must be made debiting Premium on 15% Bonds Payable for $1,000 and crediting Sources of financial resources: Operations (deduct for the nonworking capital credit item, amortization of premium on 15 percent bonds payable) for $1,000. This entry completes the explanation of the changes in all the noncurrent accounts.

(z) The net increase in working capital is $228,100 = ($263,200 *EB* − $35,100 *BB*). The details of this change are shown in Schedule B (see Figure 17–13). An entry, lettered (z) to distinguish it from the regular transaction analysis entries, is made on the work sheet debiting Working Capital and crediting Increase in working capital (shown in the uses section) for $228,100 to provide a balancing figure. If the analysis is accurate and complete, the sum of the sources will equal the sum of the uses plus the increase in working capital. Or, if there had been a decrease in working capital, the sum of the sources plus the net decrease in working capital should equal the sum of the uses. The fact, however, that the Sources and Uses columns are in balance provides only a limited proof of accuracy, a proof that debits equal credits in all the analytical entries. Many errors could still exist within these equal debits and credits, for example, counterbalancing errors, amounts debited or credited to wrong accounts, and various omissions. In like manner, if the work is accurate and complete, all changes in accounts in the upper half of the work sheet will be explained and total debits will equal total credits in the Analysis columns.

Since the work sheet indicated total sources of $644,100 equal the total uses of $416,000 plus the increase in working capital of $228,100, it can be presumed that the work sheet is correct up to this point. Next, the work sheet is completed by determining the net source of working capital from operations by adding to net income the nonworking capital add-backs and subtracting any nonworking capital deductions. The working capital provided by operations can then be summarized and shown as noted in the Remarks column. After the work sheet is completed, the formal statement of changes in financial position—working capital basis is prepared.

Step 3: Preparing the Statement of Changes in Financial Position—Working Capital Basis Now that the work sheet has been completed, Part A of the formal statement of changes in financial position on the working capital basis can be prepared directly from the Sources and Uses section of the work sheet. The debits represent sources of financial resources; the credits, uses of financial resources. Supporting figures for working capital received from operations must be taken from the add-back and deduct items shown under the Sources of financial resources: Operations title. The completed statement showing both Parts A and B is shown in the body of the chapter in Figure 17–13.

Adaptation of the Work Sheet for Cash Basis

The work sheet method could be easily adapted to provide the data for the statement of changes in financial position prepared on a cash basis. Work sheet account items could be opened for all accounts, and various subsections could be created at the bottom of the work sheet for the sources of cash including the sources from operations and for the uses of cash. Then it would be necessary to reconstruct in summary form those transactions affecting the changes in the noncash accounts. Also, to repeat, in addition to the sources and uses of cash, *APB Opinion No. 19* requires that the financing and investing activities other than those affecting cash (such as the issuance of bonds directly for land) be included in the statement of changes in financial position prepared on a cash basis.

Appendix 17.2
Illustration Using T Account Method

Introduction

The **T account method** uses the identical analysis that the work sheet method does. It has one major advantage: it is more flexible than the work sheet method. Where several changes occur in one or more noncurrent accounts (see transaction items e, f, and g in Example 2 of the main body of the chapter), the T account approach is more adaptable in that space is always available in T accounts without having to anticipate the skipping of lines as the user of a work sheet must do. The T account approach is described next, using the CHL Company data for 1988 (see Figure 17–11 and the additional 1988 data in Example 2.)

Learning Goals

1. To use a T account work sheet to develop sources and uses of funds based on the all financial resources on a working capital basis concept of funds.

2. To understand how to use a T account work sheet to develop sources and uses of funds based on the all financial resources on a cash basis concept of funds.

Basic Steps in the T Account Method—Working Capital Basis

Step 1 Starting with a comparative balance sheet, the first step is the preparation of a schedule of changes in working capital components, Part B to the formal statement of changes in financial position.

Step 2 A T account is opened for each noncurrent *balance sheet account*. The amount of the net increase or decrease occurring during the period—obtained from the comparative balance sheet—is entered in each account. Increases in assets and decreases in liabilities and stockholders' equity accounts are debit changes and are entered on the debit side; decreases in assets and increases in liabilities and stockholders' equity accounts are credit changes and are entered on the credit side. A single horizontal line is then drawn under each amount, across the account.

Step 3 Two additional T accounts, Financial Resources Summary and Operating Summary, are opened. The **Financial Resources Summary** T account is used to accumulate sources on the debit side and uses on the credit side. The amount of the net change in working capital as determined in Step 1 is entered in this account: it is a debit if there is a net increase; a credit if there is a net decrease. A single horizontal line is drawn under this figure also. The **Operating Summary** T account is used to determine the amount of working capital provided by operations: no amount is entered in this account at this point. The amounts entered above the horizontal lines in all the T accounts are added to make sure that total debit changes equal total credit changes.

Step 4 The net changes entered above the horizontal lines in the T accounts in Steps 2 and 3 represent, in summary form, all the transactions that occurred during the period. These transactions are now reconstructed by separate entries below the horizontal lines in the appropriate T accounts. (The reconstructed entries are the same as those used in the work sheet method.) The aim is to match or account for each above-the-line balance. An offsetting debit or credit to a noncurrent account may be made to one of the following:

1. *Another noncurrent account.* Although such a transaction may not affect financial resources (for example, a stock dividend), the entry is made so that all changes may be explained. This entry is necessary to prevent a later possible erroneous assumption as to what may have produced a given change in a noncurrent account.

2. *Financial Resources Summary.* This T account is debited or credited for transactions that caused changes in financial resources. Financial resources generated by operations are transferred from Operating Summary as a single figure to the Financial Resources Summary T account.

3. *Operating Summary.* This T account is debited or credited for transactions affecting revenue, expense, nonworking capital charges to operations, and nonworking capital credits to operations. It adjusts the net income figure to one representing working capital provided by operations. Step 4 is completed only when the balance of the amounts below the horizontal line in each account (except the two summary accounts) is equal to the net change entered above the horizontal line in Steps 2 and 3. This ensures that all the transactions affecting financial resources have been accounted for. Each entry should be identified by a letter or number (together with a brief notation in the two summary accounts), giving the source of the entry to facilitate the preparation of the formal statement.

Step 5 The balance of Operating Summary is closed into Financial Resources Summary to show in one figure the net source from operations (or, in some cases, the net use). At this point, net changes above the horizontal lines in *all* accounts are explained and the balance in Operating Summary is zero.

Step 6 The formal statement of changes in financial position is prepared. Operating Summary shows the details of working capital provided by operations. Financial Resources Summary contains details of sources and uses of financial resources; to repeat, the debit entries represent sources, and the credit entries are uses. At this point, the balance below the horizontal line equals the balance above the line.

Applying the T Account Method to the CHL Company for 1988—Working Capital Basis

The comparative balance sheet of the CHL Company and related supplementary data (contained in Figure 17–11 and the additional 1988 data in Example 2) are used to illustrate step-by-step the T account method for the preparation of a statement of changes in financial position—working capital basis for 1988.

Step 1 A schedule of changes in working capital components is prepared. It is necessary to calculate the net change in working capital over the period before Part A of the statement of changes in financial position can be prepared. Since this must be done, Part B should be prepared at this time. This schedule is shown in Figure 17–12.

Step 2 A T account is opened for each noncurrent balance sheet account, and the amount of change during the year is entered. A single horizontal line is drawn under each amount, as shown in Figure A17–3.

Step 3 Two additional T accounts are opened—Financial Resources Summary and Operating Summary. The net change in working capital ($228,100 increase) is entered in the Financial Resources Summary T account, and a line is drawn. These two accounts for the CHL Company with explanatory comments are shown as follows:

Operating Summary		Financial Resources Summary	
Net income	Nonworking capital credits to operations	228,100	
+		Increases in financial resources	Decreases in financial resources
Nonworking capital charges to operations			
		Sources	Uses

Before proceeding to Step 4, the accountant should test the accuracy of the debit and credit changes in the T accounts, including the net change in working capital: *the sum of the debit changes must equal the sum of the credit changes;* these do equal—the sum of the debits and the credits is $603,100.

Step 4 The summarized transactions affecting the noncurrent accounts for the year are analyzed and reconstructed by entries below the double line in the T accounts. They are derived from the income statement, comparative balance sheet, and supplementary data. The starting point is usually net income. These analytical entries are shown on the T account work sheet. A brief explanation to each of these entries is given in the next section. They

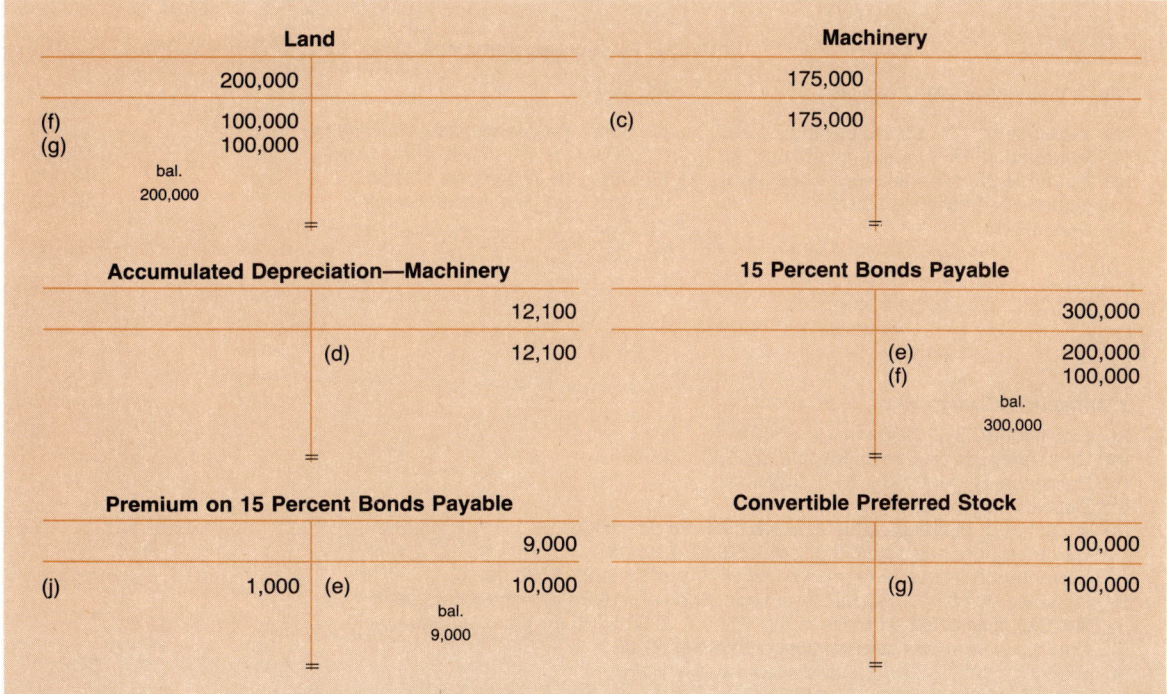

Figure A17–3 T Account Work Sheet for the Statement of Changes in Financial Position for the Year Ended December 31, 1988, CHL Company

(continued on next page)

Figure A17–3 *(continued)*

	Common Stock, $10 Par				Paid-in Capital—Excess over Par, Common	
		100,000				2,000
	(h)	100,000			(h)	2,000

	Retained Earnings				Retained Earnings—Restricted for Plant Expansion	
			30,000			50,000
(b)	40,000	(a)	120,000		(i)	50,000
(i)	50,000					
		bal.	30,000			

Operating Summary

	(Working capital provided by operations)			
(a) Net income	120,000	(j) Amortization of premium of 15% bonds payable		1,000
(d) Depreciation of machinery	12,100	(k) To Financial Resources Summary		131,100
	132,100			132,100

Financial Resources Summary

Net increase in working capital	228,100		
(e) Issuance of 15% bonds payable at 105	210,000	(b) Declaration of dividends	40,000
(f) Issuance of 15% bonds payable at 100	100,000	(c) Purchase of machinery	175,000
(g) Issuance of convertible preferred stock	100,000	(f) Purchase of land	100,000
(h) Issuance of common stock	102,000	(g) Purchase of land	100,000
(k) Operations	131,100		
	643,100		415,000
bal. 228,100			
Sources		Uses	

Transaction Coding Key
(a) Net income, $120,000.
(b) Declaration of dividends payable in 1989, $40,000.
(c) Purchase of machinery, $175,000.
(d) Depreciation of machinery, $12,100.
(e) Issuance of bonds payable at a premium for $210,000.
(f) Issuance of bonds payable at par for land, $100,000.
(g) Issuance of convertible preferred stock at par for land, $100,000.
(h) Issuance of 10,000 shares of common stock at $10.20 per share for cash.
(i) Restricted retained earnings in the amount of $50,000 for plant expansion.
(j) Amortization of premium on bonds payable, $1,000.
(k) Working capital provided by operations, $131,100.

are exactly the same as the reconstructed work sheet entries for the CHL Company (as shown in Figure A17–2). As check marks showed changes explained on the work sheet, the equals signs on the T accounts indicate that the change is explained.

Explanation of T Account Work Sheet Entries The various entries made in the T account work sheet are described below.

Summary Transaction (a). Net income for 1988 was $120,000. The debit is to Operating Summary for $120,000; and the credit is to Retained Earnings for $120,000 to show part of the working capital provided by operations.

Summary Transaction (b). Dividends of $40,000 were declared payable in 1989. Working capital was reduced in 1988, since a current liability was created. Hence the debit is to Retained Earnings for $40,000; and the credit is to Financial Resources Summary for $40,000.

Summary Transaction (c). Machinery was purchased for cash of $175,000. This transaction represents a use of financial resources. The entry in the T accounts is a debit to Machinery for $175,000 and a credit to Financial Resources Summary for $175,000 (use). The debit to Machinery explains the change that occurred in the Machinery account. This is shown by the fact that there is a debit balance under the horizontal line that equals the debit balance above this line. An equals sign or some other symbol is written across the vertical line of the T to indicate that the change has now been explained.

Summary Transaction (d). The depreciation of machinery reduced net income by $12,100. This represents an add-back item to determine working capital provided by operations. The debit is to Operating Summary, $12,100; and the credit is to Accumulated Depreciation—Machinery, $12,100.

Summary Transaction (e). Bonds payable were issued at 105; $210,000 was received. This transaction represents a source of financial resources and is entered by a debit to Financial Resources Summary, $210,000 (the source), with credits to 15 Percent Bonds Payable, $200,000 (face); and Premium on 15 Percent Bonds Payable, $10,000 (premium element).

Summary Transaction (f). Bonds payable were issued at face directly to a realtor for land, $100,000. This transaction does not affect working capital but represents both a source and a use of financial resources under the all financial resources concept of funds. Two separate entries should be made to the T accounts: (1) a debit to Financial Resources Summary, $100,000 (for the source); and a credit to 15 Percent Bonds Payable, $100,000; (2) a debit to Land, $100,000; and a credit to Financial Resources Summary, $100,000 (for the use).

Summary Transaction (g). In the expansion process, convertible preferred stock was also issued at par directly to a realtor for another tract of land, $100,000. This transaction is handled in the same manner as Transaction (f). Since it represents both a source and a use of financial resources, two entries should be made in the T accounts. These are: (1) a debit to Financial Resources Summary, $100,000 (for the source); and a credit to Convertible Preferred Stock, $100,000; (2) a debit to Land, $100,000; and a credit to Financial Resources Summary, $100,000 (for the use).

Summary Transaction (h). The company issued an additional 10,000 shares of common stock for cash at $10.20 per share. This transaction provided financial resources of $102,000 and is recorded in the T accounts by a debit to Financial Resources Summary, $102,000 (for the source), and credits to Common Stock, $100,000 and Paid-in Capital—Excess over Par, Common, $2,000. These entries explain the changes in the latter two accounts.

Summary Transaction (i). Retained earnings are restricted for plant expansion in the amount of $50,000. This action does not affect financial resources; yet an entry should be made debiting Retained Earnings for $50,000 and crediting Retained Earnings—Restricted for Plant Expansion for $50,000 to complete the explanation of the changes in these two accounts. Otherwise, a wrong conclusion may be drawn about what produced the unexplained changes.

Summary Transaction (j). Amortization of premium on bonds payable for 1988 was $1,000. This amortization reduces an expense, thus causing an increase in net income without producing an increase in working capital. To provide for a subtraction from the working capital provided by operations, an entry is made in the T accounts debiting Premium on 15 Percent Bonds Payable, $1,000, and crediting Operating Summary, $1,000 (for the subtraction effect).

Summary Transaction (k). Working capital provided by operations was $131,100. After all the noncurrent accounts are explained, the balance in the Operating Summary account should be the amount of the working capital provided by operations. This is transferred to the Financial Resources Summary account by a debit to Financial Resources Summary, $131,100, and a credit to Operating Summary, $131,100.

All T accounts should now be explained—even the Financial Resources Summary account—and have equals signs written across the vertical line of the T. The results of the foregoing analysis are shown in the T account work sheet for the statement of changes in financial position shown in Figure A17–3.

Step 5 The final step is to prepare the formal statement of changes in financial position. Part B, prepared earlier, is now incorporated into the formal statement. Part A can quickly be prepared from two T accounts—Operating Summary and Financial Resources Summary. Both parts are shown in Figure 17–13.

17 / Statement of Changes in Financial Position

Adaptation of T Account Work Sheet for Cash Basis

The T account method is easily adaptable to any concept of funds. For example, if sources and uses of cash are to be determined, T accounts for all balance sheet accounts must be opened. The Cash Summary account replaces the Financial Resources Summary T account in the T account work sheet. Its opening amount above the line is the change in Cash. Then the changes that occurred in these accounts must be explained in a manner similar to that used for working capital in the CHL Company for 1988.

Glossary

All financial resources A concept of funds that includes the disclosure of not only the sources and uses of working capital or cash but also other financial and investment information that does not affect working capital or cash.

Comparative balance sheets The balance sheet as of a given date compared with one or more immediately preceding balance sheets.

Extraordinary items Gains and losses that are both infrequent and unusual; they are shown on the income statement in a separate section at the bottom.

Financial Resources Summary A work sheet item used to record on the debit side the sources of all financial resources and on the credit side the uses of all financial resources.

Liquidity The nearness to cash of assets and liabilities.

Nonworking capital charges to operations Losses, expenses, adjuncts to losses or contra items to revenue that decrease net income but do not affect working capital.

Nonworking capital credits to operations Gains, revenues, adjuncts to revenues or contra items to expenses that increase net income but do not affect working capital.

Operating Summary A T account in the work sheet used to record the working capital provided by or used in operations.

Schedule of changes in working capital components A schedule of comparative balances in current assets and current liabilities that shows how each account balance change affected working capital; it is usually shown as part of the statement of changes in financial position.

Simple analytical approach for statement of changes in financial position The analysis of noncurrent account changes by the use of a series of computations and schedules to obtain the information for this statement.

Sources of financial resources Inflows of working capital and other financial resources.

Sources of funds See *Sources of financial resources*.

Statement of changes in financial position A statement showing sources and uses of funds prepared on either (1) an all financial resources—working capital basis, or (2) an all financial resources—cash basis.

Statement of sources and uses of funds A title formerly used for the statement of changes in financial position.

T account method A method of determining the sources and uses of financial resources by analyzing changes in noncurrent items in T accounts.

T account work sheet for the statement of changes in financial position The device consisting of noncurrent accounts plus two summary accounts—Financial Resources Summary, and Operating Summary—that provides an orderly means for determining the sources and uses of financial resources.

Uses of financial resources Outflows of working capital and other financial resources.

Uses of funds See *Uses of financial resources*.

Work sheet for statement of changes in financial position A device that provides an orderly means for determining the sources and uses of financial resources.

Working capital Current assets less current liabilities, or amount of current assets not required to liquidate current liabilities.

Questions

Q17–1 What is meant by the term *funds?* Discuss three popular concepts of funds.

Q17–2 In *APB Opinion No. 19*, what concepts of funds are recommended for typical presentation in annual reports?

Q17–3 Student A argues that net income is the same as the amount of working capital provided by operations. Student B says the amount of working capital provided by operations may be more or less than the net income amount. Which student is right? State why.

Q17–4 Why does an analysis of changes in noncurrent accounts reveal the net change in the current accounts?

Q17–5 What is the purpose of the statement of changes in financial position?

Q17–6 How may working capital provided by operations be determined?

Q17–7 What are the major elements that increase working capital from operations? The major elements that decrease working capital from operations?

Q17–8 Certain transactions changing noncurrent balance sheet amounts do not appear in the statement of changes in financial position. Why? Give two examples.

Q17–9 How may the statement of changes in financial position—all financial resources on a working capital basis be used to advantage by management? By investors? By others?

Q17–10 How may the statement of changes in financial position—all financial resources on a cash basis be used to advantage by management? By investors? By others?

Q17–11 What are some of the sources of information for the preparation of the statement of changes in financial position—working capital basis?

Q17–12 What is the effect of a cash dividend declaration on working capital? Of the payment of a dividend?

Q17–13 When interest rates are extremely high, is the statement of changes in financial position more useful on a working capital basis or on a cash basis? Why?

Q17–14 Describe how an accountant would use the simple analytical approach to determine the sources and uses of cash to appear on the statement of changes in financial position prepared on a cash basis.

Q17–15 What is the effect on working capital of a change from straight line to an accelerated method of depreciation? Ignore income taxes.

Q17–16 In arriving at working capital provided by operations, certain items are added to net income and other items are deducted. Illustrate and explain.

Q17–17 Payment on a noncurrent note payable affects working capital, whereas payment on a current note payable does not. Why? If the exchange of stock for land does not affect working capital, why is it included on the statement of changes in financial position?

Q17–18 A distinguished professor has stated, "A statement of changes in financial position is like a motion picture, explaining the difference between two photographs, the balance sheet as of the end of the current year and the balance sheet as of the end of the preceding year." Do you agree with this analogy? Justify your response.

Exercises

E17–1
Determining effect on working capital

For each of the following transactions, state whether (a) it was a source of working capital (strictly interpreted), (b) it was a use of working capital, or (c) it had no effect on working capital.

1. Purchased U.S. Treasury bills maturing in 6 months.
2. Declared and issued a stock dividend to common stockholders.
3. Restricted retained earnings for anticipated contingencies.
4. Issued common stock in exchange for land.
5. Acquired machinery for $75,000; paid $30,000 in cash and issued a long-term note for the balance.
6. Reacquired some outstanding preferred stock for retirement.
7. Issued additional common stock at a premium for cash.
8. Issued bonds directly to preferred shareholders to retire preferred stock.
9. Purchased treasury stock for cash.

E17–2
Financing sources and uses not affecting working capital

Refer to E17–1 and state which of the transactions are a source or use of total financial resources yet are *not* a source or use of working capital.

E17–3
Explaining decrease in working capital

Comparative financial statements of the Burris Corporation showed the following balances:

	December 31 1987	December 31 1986
Cash	$ 75,000	$ 78,000
Other current assets	165,000	172,500
Property, plant, and equipment (net)	210,000	165,000
Current liabilities	165,000	172,500
Stockholders' equity	285,000	243,000

There were no disposals of property, plant, and equipment during the year. Dividend payments totaled $15,000; depreciation expense was $16,500. Prepare a schedule explaining the cause of the decrease in working capital in spite of reported net income of $57,000.

E17–4
Partial statement of changes in financial position—working capital basis

The property, plant, and equipment section of the Johns Company's comparative balance sheet shows the following amounts:

	December 31 1987	December 31 1986
Property, plant, and equipment:		
Machinery	$412,500	$375,000
Deduct: Accumulated depreciation	187,500	180,000
Total property, plant, and equipment	$225,000	$195,000

Acquisitions of new machinery during the year totaled $107,500. The income statement shows depreciation expense of $50,000 for the year and a loss from machinery disposals of $18,000.

a. Determine the original cost and accumulated depreciation of machinery sold during the year and the proceeds of the sale.
b. Prepare a partial statement of changes in financial position—working capital basis.

E17-5
Working capital provided by or used in operations

For each of the following cases, compute the working capital generated by (or used in) operations:

	a	b	c	d	e
Net income (loss) per income statement	$45,000	$(46,000)	$165,000	$140,000	$(58,000)
Depreciation of property, plant, and equipment	5,000	6,000	13,000	8,000	4,000
Gain (loss) on sale of long-term investments			(4,000)	6,000	(1,500)
Periodic amortization of discount on bonds payable			3,000	1,500	750
Periodic amortization of patents				1,500	900

E17-6
Explaining reason for change in noncurrent accounts

Analyze the following changes in noncurrent accounts to determine the possible cause of each change; describe each cause of change.

a. Abandoned fully depreciated equipment costing $62,000. No other dispositions of equipment. Equipment account increased $8,000.
b. The Accumulated Depreciation—Equipment account decreased $4,000 (consider in conjunction with a).
c. The Patents account decreased $2,000 (10-year life).
d. The Mortgage Payable account decreased $20,000.
e. The Retained Earnings balance on January 1, $76,000. Dividends declared and paid during year, $6,000. No other dividends declared or paid. Balance of Retained Earnings on December 31 (year-end), $74,000.
f. Investments costing $14,000 were sold for $26,000; balance of the Investments account increased $8,000. There were no additional dispositions of investments.
g. One hundred shares of $10 par value common stock were issued. No other stock transactions occurred. What was the dollar amount of the increase to this account if the stock was issued for $14 per share? What other account would be affected if the stock were issued at $14 per share?

E17-7
Statement of changes in financial position—working capital basis by the simple analytical approach

During the year 1987, the changes in the accounts of the Wiggins Company were as follows:

	Increases	Decreases
Cash		$10,000
Accounts Receivable	$ 9,000	
Merchandise Inventory	30,000	
Long-Term Investments	9,000	
Property, Plant, and Equipment	87,000	
Accumulated Depreciation	6,000	
Accounts Payable	11,250	
Taxes Payable		750
Mortgage Payable		9,000
Common Stock	74,000	
Retained Earnings	43,500	

Additional information:

a. Net income per statement, $57,975.
b. Dividends declared, $14,475.
c. There were no disposals of property, plant, or equipment during the year.

Prepare a statement of changes in financial position—working capital basis concept for the year 1987. Use the simple analytical approach.

E17–8

Statement of changes in financial position—working capital basis by the simple analytical, work sheet, or T account method

The following information regarding the changes in financial position is indicated for the year 1987 for The Sandra Company:

THE SANDRA COMPANY
Comparative Balance Sheet Accounts
December 31, 1987 and 1986

Debit Accounts	December 31, 1987	December 31, 1986	Change Increase or (Decrease)
Cash	$206,875	$165,625	$ 41,250
Accounts Receivable (net)	33,750	30,000	3,750
Merchandise Inventory	222,375	150,000	72,375
Prepaid Insurance	2,250	1,875	375
Land	37,500	0	37,500
Machinery	168,750	150,000	18,750
Totals	$671,500	$497,500	$174,000

Credit Accounts			
Accumulated Depreciation—Machinery	$ 11,250	$ 7,500	$ 3,750
Accounts Payable	9,375	7,500	1,875
Dividends Payable	18,750	3,750	15,000
14% Bonds Payable	112,500	0	112,500
Premium on 14% Bonds Payable	3,375	0	3,375
Convertible Preferred Stock	0	66,250	(66,250)
Common Stock, $10 Par Value	347,500	300,000	47,500
Paid-in-Capital—Excess over Par, Common	18,750	0	18,750
Retained Earnings	150,000	112,500	37,500
Totals	$671,500	$497,500	$174,000

Additional information:

a. Net income for 1987 was $56,250.
b. A dividend of $18,750 was declared on December 16, 1987, payable on January 14, 1988.
c. On December 27, 1987, the company sold a machine that cost $37,500 and had an accumulated depreciation of $3,750 for $30,000 cash. The loss of $3,750 was an ordinary loss.
d. The company purchased new machinery for $56,250.
e. The annual depreciation expense on machinery was $7,500.
f. On January 1, 1987, the company issued 14 percent bonds with a face value of $75,000 at 105 for cash. The maturity date of the bonds is January 1, 1997.
g. On December 31, 1987, the company issued directly to Cates Realty Company 14 percent bonds with a face value of $37,500 at 100 for land valued at $37,500.
h. The convertible preferred stock was converted during 1987 into 4,750 shares of $10 par value common stock.
i. The annual amortization of premium on 14 percent bonds payable was $375.

1. Prepare a separate Part B (schedule of changes in working capital components).
2. Prepare Part A of a statement of changes in financial position—working capital basis concept for 1987. Use either the simple analytical, work sheet, or T account method as directed by your instructor.

Part Four / Financial Reporting

E17–9
Calculating cash received from customers

The accounts receivable of a business totaled $36,000 at the beginning of the year and $30,000 at the end of the year. Accounts receivable written off as uncollectible during the year amounted to $2,800, and cash discounts allowed to customers amounted to $1,100. The sales for the year were $80,000. What were the cash receipts during the year from sales of the current and prior periods?

E17–10
Calculating cash paid to suppliers of merchandise

The purchases of merchandise of a business amounted to $150,000 during 1987. Accounts payable at the beginning and end of the year were $43,000 and $39,600, respectively; notes payable given to trade creditors in settlement of open accounts were $9,000 at the beginning of the year and $9,800 at year-end. Returns and allowances on purchases were $1,020. What were the cash payments during 1987 for purchases of 1987 and prior periods?

E17–11
Calculating cash generated by operations

The financial statement information of Propst Company is given below:

PROPST COMPANY   **Exhibit A**
Income Statement
For the Year Ended December 31, 1987

Net sales.		$98,500
Cost of goods sold		70,950
Gross margin on sales		$27,550
Expenses:		
Salaries expense	$13,800	
Depreciation expense	2,250	
Rent expense	3,600	
Supplies expense	1,500	21,150
Net income		$ 6,400

PROPST COMPANY
Comparative Balance Sheet Accounts
December 31, 1987 and 1986

Debit Accounts	December 31, 1987	December 31, 1986
Cash	$25,075	$17,040
Accounts Receivable	9,165	10,830
Merchandise Inventory	12,150	12,150
Supplies on Hand	450	1,050
Equipment	22,680	18,000
Totals	$69,520	$59,070

Credit Accounts		
Accounts Payable	$ 5,850	$ 4,650
Accrued Rent Payable	600	300
Accrued Salaries Payable	450	150
Accumulated Depreciation	9,450	7,200
Common Stock	37,500	37,500
Retained Earnings	15,670	9,270
Totals	$69,520	$59,070

Prepare a schedule of net cash generated by operations for 1987.

E17–12
Statement of changes in financial position—cash basis by the simple analytical method

The data of Ralston Company follow:

RALSTON COMPANY
Comparative Balance Sheet Accounts
December 31, 1987 and 1986

Debit Accounts	December 31, 1987	December 31, 1986
Cash	$ 164,000	$ 51,000
Accounts Receivable (net)	270,000	288,000
Merchandise Inventory	300,000	240,000
Land	60,000	45,000
Buildings (net)	480,000	300,000
Machinery (net)	600,000	450,000
Totals	$1,874,000	$1,374,000

Credit Accounts		
Accounts Payable	$ 225,000	$ 195,000
Accrued Payables	9,000	12,000
Mortgage Payable	210,000	174,000
Common Stock, $1 par value	950,000	750,000
Retained Earnings	480,000	243,000
Totals	$1,874,000	$1,374,000

RALSTON COMPANY — Exhibit A
Income Statement
For the Year Ended December 31, 1987

Sales		$2,430,000
Cost of goods sold		1,440,000
Gross margin on sales		$ 990,000
Operating expenses:		
Depreciation—machinery	$ 60,000	
Depreciation—buildings	30,000	
Other operating expenses	663,000	753,000
Net income		$ 237,000

Additional data:

a. No dividends were declared during the year.
b. The increase in machinery, buildings, and land were from purchases for cash.
c. 200,000 additional shares of common stock were issued for cash at par value.

Prepare a statement of changes in financial position—cash basis for 1987, using the simple analytical approach.

A Problems

P17-1A
Statement of changes in financial position—working capital basis by the simple analytical approach

The comparative balance sheet accounts of Wilfong Company, as of December 31, 1987 and 1986, disclosed the following:

WILFONG COMPANY
Comparative Balance Sheet Accounts
December 31, 1987 and 1986

Debit Accounts	December 31, 1987	December 31, 1986
Cash	$ 82,000	$ 194,500
Accounts Receivable (net)	88,200	74,700
Merchandise Inventory	127,500	97,500
Long-Term Investments	102,000	90,000
Machinery	525,000	450,000
Buildings	405,000	337,500
Land	75,000	75,000
Patents	27,000	30,000
Totals	$1,431,700	$1,349,200

Credit Accounts		
Accumulated Depreciation—Machinery	$ 60,000	$ 45,000
Accumulated Depreciation—Buildings	52,500	30,000
Accounts Payable—Trade	82,500	75,000
Notes Payable—Trade	12,000	15,000
Mortgage Payable	75,000	190,000
Common Stock	825,000	750,000
Retained Earnings	324,700	244,200
Totals	$1,431,700	$1,349,200

Additional data:

a. Net income for the year was $80,500.
b. There were no sales or disposals of property, plant, and equipment during the year.

Required: Prepare a statement of changes in financial position—working capital basis concept for 1987. Use the simple analytical approach.

P17-2A
Statement of changes in financial position—working capital basis by the simple analytical, work sheet, or T account method

Following is the comparative postclosing trial balance of the Werley Company:

WERLEY COMPANY
Comparative Postclosing Trial Balance
December 31, 1987 and 1986

Debit Accounts	December 31, 1987	December 31, 1986
Cash	$ 152,500	$ 125,000
Temporary Investments	0	165,000
Accounts Receivable (net)	102,500	110,000
Merchandise Inventory	380,000	302,500
Prepaid Expenses	6,000	3,750
Property, Plant, and Equipment	750,000	450,000
Patents	96,000	102,000
Totals	$1,487,000	$1,258,250

Credit Accounts

Accumulated Depreciation—Property, Plant, and Equipment	$ 202,500	$ 150,000
Accounts Payable	150,000	90,000
Common Stock	800,000	800,000
Retained Earnings	334,500	218,250
Totals	$1,487,000	$1,258,250

Additional data:

a. Net income for the period was $187,500.
b. Dividends declared were $71,250.
c. The temporary investments were sold at a gain (included in Item a) of $22,500.
d. Equipment with an original cost of $30,000 and accumulated depreciation of $15,000 was sold at an ordinary loss (included in Item a) of $3,000.
e. Patents are being amortized over their legal life of 17 years.

Required: Prepare a statement of changes in financial position—working capital basis concept for 1987. Use either the simple analytical, work sheet, or T account method as directed by your instructor.

P17–3A

Statement of changes in financial position—working capital basis by the simple analytical, work sheet, or T account method

Data of Westerhoff, Inc., are given below.

WESTERHOFF, INC.
Comparative Balance Sheet Accounts
December 31, 1987 and 1986

	December 31	
Debit Accounts	**1987**	**1986**
Cash	$ 95,000	$ 72,500
Accounts Receivable	136,000	121,000
Merchandise Inventory	60,000	48,000
Investments (Long-Term)	45,000	75,000
Machinery	60,000	37,500
Buildings	135,000	112,500
Land	15,000	15,000
Totals	$546,000	$481,500

Credit Accounts		
Allowance for Doubtful Accounts	$ 5,500	$ 4,000
Accumulated Depreciation—Machinery	11,250	4,500
Accumulated Depreciation—Buildings	27,000	18,000
Accounts Payable	65,000	54,500
Accrued Payables	6,750	5,250
Mortgage Payable	52,500	60,000
Common Stock, $2 par value	300,000	300,000
Retained Earnings	78,000	35,250
Totals	$546,000	$481,500

Additional data:

a. Net income for the year was $90,000.
b. Dividends declared during the year were $47,250.

(continued on next page)

c. Investments that cost $30,000 were sold during the year for $37,500. The gain is an ordinary one and is included in Item a.

d. Machinery that cost $7,500, on which $1,500 in depreciation had accumulated, was sold for $9,000. The gain is ordinary and is included in Item a.

Required: Prepare a statement of changes in financial position—working capital basis for 1987. Use either the simple analytical, work sheet, or T account method as directed by your instructor.

P17–4A
Statement of changes in financial position—working capital basis by the simple analytical, work sheet, or T account method

You are given the following information from the books of the Murrell Corporation:

MURRELL CORPORATION
Balance Sheet Accounts
December 31, 1987 and 1986

Debit Accounts	December 31, 1987	December 31, 1986	Change Increase or (Decrease)
Cash	$ 29,800	$ 28,400	$ 1,400
Accounts Receivable	81,400	53,600	27,800
Merchandise Inventory	33,000	42,000	(9,000)
Machinery	123,600	131,100	(7,500)
Sinking Fund Cash[a]	25,000	0	25,000
Totals	$292,800	$255,100	$37,700

Credit Accounts			
Allowance for Doubtful Accounts	$ 4,200	$ 3,750	$ 450
Accumulated Depreciation—Machinery	34,300	37,300	(3,000)
Accounts Payable	31,500	26,300	5,200
Dividends Payable	3,000	0	3,000
Bonds Payable	30,000	0	30,000
Premium on Bonds Payable	1,425	0	1,425
Common Stock	150,000	150,000	0
Retained Earnings	13,375	37,750	(24,375)
Retained Earnings—Restricted for Sinking Fund[b]	25,000	0	25,000
Totals	$292,800	$255,100	$37,700

[a]The original entry to create the sinking fund was a debit to Sinking Fund Cash and a credit to Cash.
[b]The original entry to restrict retained earnings for the sinking fund was a debit to Retained Earnings and a credit to Retained Earnings—Restricted for Sinking Fund.

MURRELL CORPORATION   **Exhibit B**
Statement of Retained Earnings
For the Year Ended December 31, 1987

Retained earnings, December 31, 1986		$37,750
Add: Net income for year ended December 31, 1987		11,125
Subtotal		$48,875
Deduct: Dividends declared and paid in cash	$ 7,500	
Dividend declared in 1987, payable January 15, 1988	3,000	
Restriction for sinking fund	25,000	35,500
Retained earnings, December 31, 1987		$13,375

MURRELL CORPORATION
Income Statement
For the Year Ended December 31, 1987

Exhibit A

Sales		$138,175
Cost of goods sold		97,500
Gross margin on sales		$ 40,675
Operating expenses:		
Salaries expense	$22,050	
Bad debts expense	450	
Depreciation of machinery	5,250	
Taxes expense	600	
Insurance expense	450	28,800
Net income from operations		$ 11,875
Other ordinary expenses:		
Bond interest expense	$ 1,575	
Deduct: Amortization of bond premium	75	
Net bond interest expense	$ 1,500	
Other ordinary revenue:		
Gain on sale of machinery	750	750
Net income to retained earnings		$ 11,125

Additional data:

a. Bonds payable in the amount of $30,000 were issued on April 30, 1987, at 105.
b. Machinery that cost $10,500 and had accumulated depreciation of $8,250 was sold for $3,000 in cash.

Required: Prepare a statement of changes in financial position—working capital basis for 1987. Submit all supporting computations. Use either the simple analytical, work sheet, or T account method as directed by your instructor.

P17–5A
Statement of changes in financial position—cash basis by the simple analytical method

The data of the Bello Company follow:

BELLO COMPANY
Comparative Balance Sheet Accounts
December 31, 1987 and 1986

	December 31	
Debit Accounts	**1987**	**1986**
Cash	$ 49,000	$ 65,500
Accounts Receivable (net)	145,000	154,000
Merchandise Inventory	160,000	130,000
Investments (Long-Term)	18,000	15,000
Land	30,000	22,500
Buildings (net)	240,000	150,000
Machinery (net)	300,000	225,000
Totals	$942,000	$762,000
Credit Accounts		
Accounts Payable	$132,500	$117,500
Accrued Payables	14,500	16,000
Mortgage Payable	105,000	87,000
Common Stock, $1 Par Value	450,000	375,000
Retained Earnings	240,000	166,500
Totals	$942,000	$762,000

(continued on next page)

BELLO COMPANY
Income Statement
For the Year Ended December 31, 1987

Exhibit A

Sales		$1,215,000
Cost of goods sold		720,000
Gross margin on sales		$ 495,000
Operating expenses:		
Depreciation—machinery	$ 30,000	
Depreciation—buildings	15,000	
Other operating expenses	331,500	376,500
Net income		$ 118,500

Additional data:

a. Dividends paid during the year were $45,000.

b. The increase in long-term investments, machinery, buildings, and land were from cash purchases.

c. Issued 75,000 shares of common stock at par value for cash.

Required: Prepare a statement of changes in financial position—cash basis for 1987, using the simple analytical approach.

P17–6A
Thought-provoking problem: justifying decision not to declare a cash dividend

The following information is presented in the annual report of the Woodbury Corporation.

WOODBURY CORPORATION
Income Statement
For the Year Ended December 31, 1987

Exhibit A

Sales		$3,550,000
Cost of goods sold		2,110,000
Gross margin on sales		$1,440,000
Operating expenses:		
Depreciation—property, plant, and equipment	$ 55,000	
Other expenses	110,000	165,000
Net income before taxes		$1,275,000
Income taxes @ 40%		510,000
Net income		$ 765,000

WOODBURY CORPORATION
Statement of Changes in Financial Position—Working Capital Basis
For the Year Ended December 31, 1987

Exhibit D

Part A—Sources and Uses of Financial Resources

Financial resources were provided by:		
Operations:		
Net income		$765,000
Add: Nonworking capital charges to operations:		
Depreciation of property, plant, and equipment		55,000
Working capital provided by operations		$820,000
Financial resources were used for:		
Purchase of equipment	$550,000	
Early retirement of bonds payable in current year	300,000	
Total working capital used		850,000
Net increase (decrease) in working capital		$ (30,000)

(continued on next page)

Part B—Schedule of Changes in Working Capital Components

	December 31		Changes in Working Capital	
	1987	1986	Increase	Decrease
Current assets:				
Cash	$ 30,000	$ 35,000		$ 5,000
Accounts receivable (net)	65,000	50,000	$15,000	
Merchandise inventory	100,000	95,000	5,000	
Prepaid insurance	2,000	3,000		1,000
Total current assets	$197,000	$183,000		
Current liabilities:				
Accounts payable	$110,000	$ 87,000		23,000
Bank loans payable (short-term)	48,000	30,000		18,000
Accrued payables	8,000	5,000		3,000
Total current liabilities	$166,000	$122,000		
Working capital	$ 31,000	$ 61,000		
Totals			$20,000	$50,000
Net decrease in working capital			30,000	
Totals			$50,000	$50,000

Walter Davis and his wife own 10,000 shares of stock in Woodbury Corporation and would like to know why no dividends were declared in 1987, even though net income for the year was $765,000.

Required: Using the information given above, justify to Mr. and Mrs. Walter Davis the corporation's decision not to declare a dividend.

B Problems

P17–1B
Statement of changes in financial position—working capital basis by the simple analytical approach

The comparative balance sheet accounts of the Post Company, as of December 31, 1987 and 1986, disclosed the following:

POST COMPANY
Comparative Balance Sheet Accounts
December 31, 1987 and 1986

	December 31	
Debit Accounts	1987	1986
Cash	$ 144,500	$ 189,500
Accounts Receivable (net)	176,900	149,900
Merchandise Inventory	256,000	196,000
Long-Term Investments	204,000	180,000
Machinery	1,050,000	900,000
Buildings	810,000	675,000
Land	150,000	150,000
Patents	54,000	60,000
Totals	$2,845,400	$2,500,400

(continued on next page)

Credit Accounts

Accumulated Depreciation—Machinery	$ 120,000	$ 90,000
Accumulated Depreciation—Buildings	105,000	60,000
Accounts Payable—Trade	167,000	152,000
Notes Payable—Trade	24,000	30,000
Mortgage Payable	150,000	180,000
Common Stock	1,650,000	1,500,000
Retained Earnings	629,400	488,400
Totals	$2,845,400	$2,500,400

Additional information:

a. Net income for the year was $141,000.
b. There were no sales or disposals of property, plant, and equipment during the year.

Required: Prepare a statement of changes in financial position—working capital basis concept for 1987. Use the simple analytical approach.

P17–2B
Statement of changes in financial position—working capital basis by the simple analytical, work sheet, or T account method

Following is the comparative postclosing trial balance of the Davis Company:

DAVIS COMPANY
Comparative Postclosing Trial Balance
December 31, 1987 and 1986

	December 31	
Debit Accounts	**1987**	**1986**
Cash	$ 26,500	$ 37,750
Temporary Investments	0	82,500
Accounts Receivable (net)	71,500	60,250
Merchandise Inventory	195,000	146,250
Prepaid Expenses	3,000	1,875
Property, Plant, and Equipment	375,000	225,000
Patents	48,000	51,000
Totals	$719,000	$604,625
Credit Accounts		
Accumulated Depreciation—Property, Plant, and Equipment	$101,250	$ 75,000
Accounts Payable	75,500	45,500
Common Stock	375,000	375,000
Retained Earnings	167,250	109,125
Totals	$719,000	$604,625

Additional data:

a. Net income for the period was $93,750.
b. Dividends declared were $35,625.
c. The temporary investments were sold at a gain (included in Item a) of $11,250.
d. Equipment with an original cost of $15,000 and accumulated depreciation of $7,500 was sold at an ordinary loss (included in Item a) of $1,500.
e. Patents are being amortized over their legal life of 17 years.

Required: Prepare a statement of changes in financial position—working capital basis concept for 1987. Use either the simple analytical, work sheet, or T account method as directed by your instructor.

P17–3B
Statement of changes in financial position—working capital basis by the simple analytical, work sheet, or T account method

Data of Efland Corporation are given below.

EFLAND CORPORATION
Comparative Balance Sheet Accounts
December 31, 1987 and 1986

Debit Accounts	December 31, 1987	December 31, 1986
Cash	$ 45,500	$ 34,250
Accounts Receivable	68,000	60,500
Merchandise Inventory	31,000	25,000
Investments (Long-Term)	22,500	37,500
Machinery	30,000	18,750
Buildings	67,500	56,250
Land	7,500	7,500
Totals	$272,000	$239,750

Credit Accounts	1987	1986
Allowance for Doubtful Accounts	$ 2,250	$ 1,500
Accumulated Depreciation—Machinery	5,625	2,250
Accumulated Depreciation—Buildings	13,500	9,000
Accounts Payable	31,000	25,750
Accrued Payables	4,375	3,625
Mortgage Payable	26,250	30,000
Common Stock, $1 Par Value	150,000	150,000
Retained Earnings	39,000	17,625
Totals	$272,000	$239,750

Additional data:

a. Net income for the year was $45,000.
b. Dividends declared during the year were $23,625.
c. Investments that cost $15,000 were sold during the year for $18,750. The gain is an ordinary one and is included in Item a.
d. Machinery that cost $3,750, on which $750 in depreciation had accumulated, was sold for $4,500. The gain is ordinary and is included in Item a.

Required: Prepare a statement of changes in financial position—working capital basis concept for 1987. Use either the simple analytical, work sheet, or T account method as directed by your instructor.

P17–4B
Statement of changes in financial position—working capital basis by the simple analytical, work sheet, or T account method

You are given the following information from the books of the Hunt Corporation:

HUNT CORPORATION
Balance Sheet Accounts
December 31, 1987 and 1986

Debit Accounts	December 31, 1987	December 31, 1986	Change Increase or (Decrease)
Cash	$ 40,600	$ 47,800	$ (7,200)
Accounts Receivable	142,800	97,200	45,600
Merchandise Inventory	66,000	104,000	(38,000)
Machinery	247,200	262,200	(15,000)
Sinking Fund Cash[a]	50,000	0	50,000
Totals	$546,600	$511,200	$ 35,400

(continued on next page)

Credit Accounts

Allowance for Doubtful Accounts	$ 8,400	$ 7,500	$ 900
Accumulated Depreciation—Machinery	48,600	54,600	(6,000)
Accounts Payable	64,000	73,600	(9,600)
Dividends Payable	6,000	0	6,000
Bonds Payable	60,000	0	60,000
Premium on Bonds Payable	2,850	0	2,850
Common Stock	300,000	300,000	0
Retained Earnings	6,750	75,500	(68,750)
Retained Earnings—Restricted for Sinking Fund[b] . .	50,000	0	50,000
Totals.	$546,600	$511,200	$35,400

[a]The original entry to create the sinking fund was a debit to Sinking Fund Cash and a credit to Cash.
[b]The original entry to restrict retained earnings for the sinking fund was a debit to Retained Earnings and a credit to Retained Earnings—Restricted for Sinking Fund.

HUNT CORPORATION Exhibit B
Statement of Retained Earnings
For the Year Ended December 31, 1987

Retained earnings, December 31, 1986		$75,500
Add: Net income for year ended December 31, 1987.		2,250
Subtotal		$77,750
Deduct: Dividends declared and paid in cash	$15,000	
Dividend declared in 1987, payable January 15, 1988	6,000	
Restriction for sinking fund	50,000	71,000
Retained earnings, December 31, 1987		$ 6,750

HUNT CORPORATION Exhibit A
Income Statement
For the Year Ended December 31, 1987

Sales		$256,350
Cost of goods sold		195,000
Gross margin on sales		$ 61,350
Operating expenses:		
Salaries expense	$44,100	
Bad debts expense	900	
Depreciation of machinery	10,500	
Taxes expense	1,200	
Insurance expense	900	57,600
Net income from operations		$ 3,750
Other ordinary expenses:		
Bond interest expense	$ 3,150	
Deduct: Amortization of bond premium	150	
Net bond interest expense	$ 3,000	
Other ordinary revenue:		
Gain on sale of machinery	1,500	1,500
Net income to retained earnings		$ 2,250

Additional data:

a. Bonds payable in the amount of $60,000 were issued on April 30, 1987, at 105.
b. Machinery that cost $21,000 and had accumulated depreciation of $16,500 was sold for $6,000 in cash.

17 / Statement of Changes in Financial Position

Required: Prepare a statement of changes in financial position—working capital basis concept for 1987. Submit all supporting computations. Use either the simple analytical, work sheet, or T account method as directed by your instructor.

P17–5B
Statement of changes in financial position—cash basis by the simple analytical method

The data of Kathey Company follow:

KATHEY COMPANY
Comparative Balance Sheet Accounts
December 31, 1987 and 1986

Debit Accounts	December 31, 1987	December 31, 1986
Cash	$ 78,500	$ 111,500
Accounts Receivable (net)	270,500	288,500
Merchandise Inventory	301,000	241,000
Investments (Long-Term)	36,000	30,000
Land	60,000	45,000
Buildings (net)	480,000	300,000
Machinery (net)	600,000	450,000
Totals	$1,826,000	$1,466,000

Credit Accounts		
Accounts Payable	$ 226,000	$ 196,000
Accrued Payables	10,000	13,000
Mortgage Payable	210,000	174,000
Common Stock, $1 Par Value	900,000	750,000
Retained Earnings	480,000	333,000
Totals	$1,826,000	$1,466,000

KATHEY COMPANY Exhibit A
Income Statement
For the Year Ended December 31, 1987

Sales		$2,435,000
Cost of goods sold		1,445,000
Gross margin on sales		$ 990,000
Operating expenses:		
Depreciation—machinery	$ 60,000	
Depreciation—buildings	30,000	
Other operating expenses	663,000	753,000
Net income		$ 237,000

Additional data:

a. Dividends paid during the year were $90,000.
b. The increase in long-term investments, machinery, buildings, and land was from cash purchases.
c. There were 150,000 shares of common stock issued at par value for cash.

Required: Prepare a statement of changes in financial position for 1987, using the all financial resources—cash basis concept. Use the simple analytical approach.

P17–6B
Thought-provoking problem: various funds and liquidity issues

You have been assigned by the acquisitions committee of Control Group, Inc., to examine a potential acquisition, Retailers, Inc. This company is a merchandising firm that appears to be available because of the death of its founder and principal shareholder. Recent statements of Retailers, Inc., are shown below.

RETAILERS, INC.
Comparative Balance Sheets
As of January 31

	1987	1986	1985
Cash	$ 130,000	$ 120,000	$ 100,000
Accounts receivable	430,000	370,000	300,000
Merchandise inventory	400,000	400,000	200,000
Property, plant, and equipment	900,000	800,000	700,000
Deduct: Accumulated depreciation	(325,000)	(250,000)	(200,000)
Total assets	$1,535,000	$1,440,000	$1,100,000
Accounts payable	$ 300,000	$ 260,000	$ 220,000
8% Notes payable due 1/31/92	280,000	280,000	0
Common stock outstanding	690,000	690,000	690,000
Retained earnings	265,000	210,000	190,000
Total equity	$1,535,000	$1,440,000	$1,100,000

RETAILERS, INC.
Comparative Income Statements
For the Years Ended January 31, 1987 and 1986

	1987	1986
Sales	$2,943,000	$2,629,000
Operating expense:		
Cost of goods sold	$2,200,000	$2,000,000
Wages expense	350,000	300,000
Supplies expense	42,600	36,600
Depreciation expense	100,000	75,000
Interest expense	22,400	22,400
Loss on sale of property, plant, and equipment	75,000	105,000
Total deductions	$2,790,000	$2,539,000
Net income before taxes	$ 153,000	$ 90,000
Income taxes	68,000	40,000
Net income	$ 85,000	$ 50,000

RETAILERS, INC.
Statement of Changes in Financial Position
For the Years Ended January 31

	1987	1986
Financial resources were provided by:		
Net income	$ 85,000	$ 50,000
Add: Depreciation	100,000	75,000
Loss	75,000	105,000
Notes payable	0	280,000
Total	$260,000	$510,000
Financial resources were used for:		
Net plant assets purchased	$200,000	$230,000
Dividends paid	30,000	30,000
Total	$230,000	$260,000
Increase (decrease) in net working capital	$ 30,000	$250,000

Required:

1. Calculate the inventory turnover for 1987 and for 1986. Is the turnover better or worse in 1987 than in 1986?
2. Calculate the current ratio for 1987.
3. Calculate a rate of return on the stockholders' equity for 1987.
4. Describe the cash flow for 1987 by redrawing the statement of changes in financial position to explain the changes in cash position instead of net working capital.
5. Does the amount shown for net plant assets purchased equal the funds spent for newly acquired assets? Explain your answer.
6. The statement of changes in financial position is required in published financial reports. What reasons are given to support the requirement that this statement be included in published financial reports?

A Use of Computers in Accounting

Introduction

Computerized accounting is all around us today. We do our banking by computer. Our paychecks are prepared by computers, as are the bills that we receive for using credit cards. Computers enable businesses to maintain optimum amounts of inventory so that we are able to buy what we want, when we want. In today's business world, computers maintain almost all the accounting data that managers rely on. In fact, financial survival of a business may depend on the quality and timeliness of the information that computerized accounting systems can provide. This appendix presents an introduction to the computerization of the general record keeping and production of decision making information from accounting data.

Learning Goals

1. To become familiar with the parts of a basic computerized accounting system.

2. To understand the functions of each part of a computerized accounting system.

3. To understand how electronic spreadsheet programs can assist in areas such as managing cash or accounting for long-term bonds.

4. To understand the part that graphics play in communicating accounting information.

5. To understand how data base management software can be useful in the maintenance of information.

6. To understand the benefits of a computerized accounting system.

Computerization of the General Accounting Function

Functional Parts of a Computerized Accounting System

A computerized accounting system is composed of two principal segments; the computer equipment, referred to as **computer hardware**, and the computer programs, referred to as **computer software**.

The computer hardware used in the accounting application varies in size and makeup depending on the accounting task and the size of the business. Large businesses computerizing their general accounting function would use large scale computer systems, referred to as mainframes. These computers are capable of processing thousands of transactions a day, storing millions of transactions, and meeting the information needs of managers who may be located all around the world. Small businesses that need to process only a few dozen transactions a day and provide the information to a couple of managers might use a microcomputer. With the development of the microcomputer, businesses of almost any size are able to computerize their accounting systems.

The chief functions of computer hardware, whether a mainframe or a microcomputer, are input, output, processing, secondary storage, and data communications. Each function requires specific hardware. Data today are commonly input using a keyboard connected to a video display terminal. The terminal's display screen provides one form of output capability. The other primary form of output, called hard copy, is produced by a printer attached to the system. Processing utilizes the other components to manipulate the input data under control of the program to produce the output. Secondary storage, the storage of programs and data for future retrieval and use, is accomplished primarily with disk or diskette. Using a computer, the manager is able to communicate with other computers at remote locations. This function, called data communications, is important to the manager in today's business environment.

In addition to the computer hardware, a computerized accounting system requires software designed to perform the accounting procedures that you have learned. The software for an accounting system is made up of many different computer programs. Each **computer program** directs the hardware to perform the operations necessary to accomplish one of the accounting tasks. All of the programs that perform the accounting procedures associated with one area of accounting, for example accounts receivable, are termed a **module**. All of the modules that are a part of the computerized accounting system make up the **accounting software package**. In many modern accounting packages, the modules are tied together in what is termed an **integrated accounting system**. This means that all of the functional modules are connected with one another so that an entry made in one module will update affected data in other modules. For example, when a sale on account is entered, the system not only will create the journal entry and post it to the general ledger, it will also make the necessary postings to the accounts receivable subsidiary ledger and the detailed inventory records.

The Basic Computerized Accounting System

In its simplest form, a computerized accounting system may consist of programs to make entries and prepare financial statements. A typical computerized accounting system consists of four basic modules: general ledger, accounts receivable, accounts payable, and payroll. As a computerized accounting system is expanded, modules such as order entry/inventory control, purchase order preparation, sales analysis, and property, plant, and equipment accounting can be added.

The general ledger module is used to tie together all of the other accounting modules and for entering nonroutine events, such as adjusting entries. It is also the portion of the computerized system that produces financial reports for management and external users. The general ledger module of the accounting package also completes the closing process and sets up the accounts for the new accounting period. In addition, this module enables the user to maintain the chart of accounts.

The accounts receivable module permits a user to enter sales data and maintain information on how much is owed to the firm by each customer and when the customer should pay. This module can also be used to prepare invoices and statements, as well as to analyze periodically the accounts receivable to disclose slow paying accounts. Many accounts receivable modules provide the ability to maintain detailed data about customers—such as their product preferences and buying patterns. Also, because the module has captured all of the sales data, it can be used to analyze sales trends.

The accounts payable module will perform similar functions for the amounts owed by a business. Through this module, managers can keep track of how much is owed to each vendor by due dates. This knowledge allows better planning of the cash requirements of the firm. The accounts payable function can also be used to schedule payments to take advantage of cash discounts and, at the appropriate time, to prepare the actual checks.

The payroll module performs all of the calculations associated with the determination of pay and various withholdings. It also automates the preparation of the payroll checks. In addition, payroll packages keep track of the information necessary to file the various payroll tax returns required of an employer.

Many other modules can be added to a computerized accounting system. These expand the types of information that can be produced by the system and thus help management with its decision making.

One module commonly added is the inventory module. This module adds the ability to enter purchase orders, sales orders, receipts of merchandise, and shipments of merchandise. With these transactions entered as they occur, the system maintains an up-to-date perpetual inventory (the cost flow assumption is an election on the part of the user). Also, by entering purchase orders, management knows exactly what is on order, from whom, and how long an order has been outstanding—and can judge when receipt of the order is expected. Having sales orders entered gives managers information on commitments against inventory, which can be used to judge the need to place orders for new merchandise.

A / Use of Computers in Accounting

Another benefit of computerization of the inventory system is a detailed sales analysis. With a product code (stock number) assigned to each product item in inventory, very detailed sales histories and analyses can be produced by most computerized inventory systems. The types of information available include: quantities sold by period, by sales location, and by sales representative; the sales prices charged; the gross margin earned; and inventory turnover by product line. With this information, management should be more able to maintain the necessary inventory levels and to reduce any overinvestment in inventory items. Since investment in inventory makes up a significant part of working capital, control of inventory levels is critical to a profitable operation. For many businesses, the savings associated with the control of investment in inventory contributes significantly to the financial return generated by computerization.

Functioning of a Computerized Accounting System

Today's computerized accounting systems require accounting expertise but not computer expertise on the part of the user. Accounting software packages are now designed to be **user friendly**. This means that the user of accounting software does not require knowledge of computer programming and needs very limited knowledge of computer operations. When the user calls up the accounting package from storage, a menu appears on the screen of the terminal. A **menu** is a list of options available to the user at that point in the program. The user selects from the menu the function he or she wants to

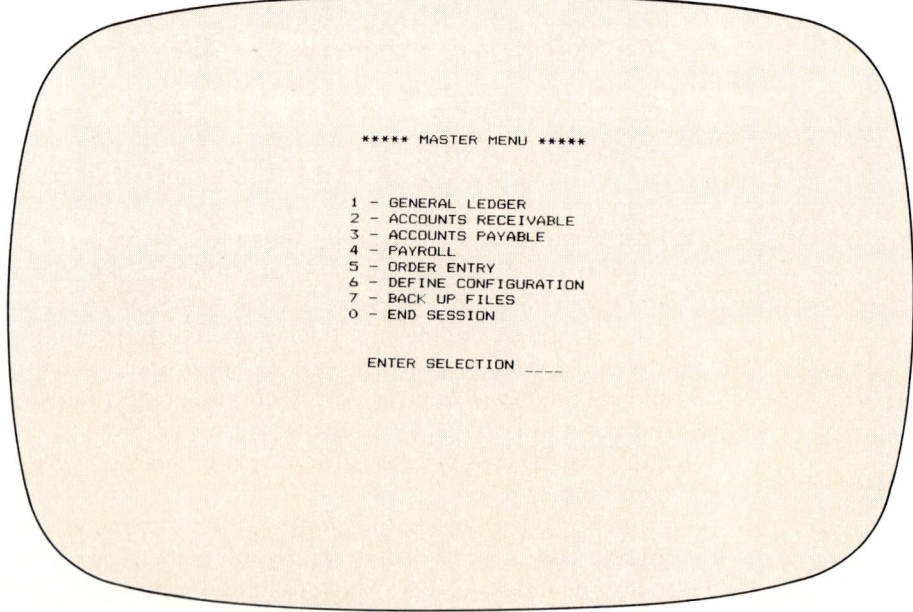

Figure A–1 **Accounting System Master Menu**

perform by keying in a number at the keyboard. Figure A–1 shows what a master menu might look like for a small accounting system.

The user works through the package using a series of menus. For example, if the user wants to access the general ledger module, he or she selects option 1 of the master menu in Figure A–1. In many systems, to gain access to further parts of the system the user is asked to enter a password. A **password** is a unique group of characters—for example DH82Y—assigned to each user.

This type of protection is a part of the internal control of computerization. The requirement for a password may be repeated at several places to prevent unauthorized users from gaining access to portions of the accounting system that are outside their areas of responsibility. Thus, different users will be given different passwords depending on the types of information they may have access to and the types of entries they may make. If the password entered is acceptable, the system will proceed to the next step. If the password is unacceptable, the user will be prevented from using that portion of the system, and a record will be made of the unauthorized attempt to use it.

In this illustrative system, the next step is a detailed menu for the general ledger system, such as that shown in Figure A–2. After selecting the desired option, the system may again ask for a password; certain individuals may, for example, be allowed to enter transactions but may be prevented from changing the chart of accounts. If option 1 is selected and the proper password entered, a journal entry menu might appear that would give the user options such as entering transactions, printing the journal, or correcting journal entries.

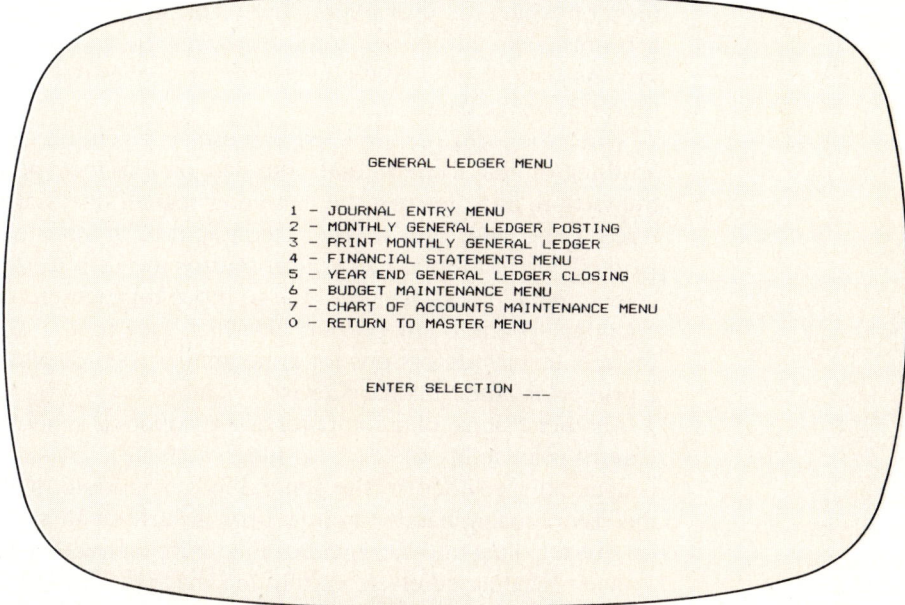

Figure A–2   **General Ledger Module Master Menu**

```
                    ENTER JOURNAL DATA

         DATE:                 .. / .. / ..
         DESCRIPTION:          ..............................
         ACCOUNT NO:           .........
         AMOUNT:
                    DEBIT:     .........
                    CREDIT:    .........

                    **************************
                       IS THE ENTRY CORRECT? .
         (Y TO ENTER; N TO CORRECT; <ESC> WHEN ALL ENTRIES ARE MADE)
```

Figure A–3   **Journal Entry Screen Display**

If the user selects the option to journalize transactions, a display appears, such as that illustrated in Figure A–3, that allows the actual entry of data into the system to journalize transactions. The system has in essence displayed a form on which the user keys in the blanks from the top down. The chart of accounts is already stored in the files; only the account numbers are necessary. As each blank is filled in, the system moves the user to the next required piece of data.

When the form is completed, the user is given the opportunity to correct anything on that form, to enter the data on that form and proceed to the next transaction, or to instruct the computer that all necessary data have been entered. If the latter option is selected, the user is returned to the last menu worked. On each menu an option returns the user to the immediately preceding menu. Users are thus able to move through the computerized accounting system to any portion for which they have a valid password. Many of the menus include options for generating screen displays or reports through a printer or other auxiliary device.

Another feature of a computerized accounting system important to internal control is an ability to **back-up** files, or create copies, of files. This capability is generally provided by the general ledger module. With a manual system the risk of losing handwritten records is fairly small and is minimized by careful handling and storage. But in a computerized system, where all of the data are maintained electronically and magnetically, the risk of loss is much higher. This risk is minimized by storing copies of both the program files and data files in a separate location. Should the working copies of the files accidentally be destroyed, new working copies can be made from the back-ups. Data files can be rebuilt using the back-up copies and records of recent transactions.

Managers require information in addition to the traditional financial statements. The remainder of this appendix presents some of the methods used by accountants in producing that information.

Managerial Information with Personal Computing

The microcomputer has made possible the personal computer for the manager. The **personal computer** is a complete computer system designed for individual use. It contains all of the components of the central computer system enabling the manager to maintain data and produce information for decision making in the form that is needed when it is needed.

Electronic Spreadsheet Software

One of the most significant software developments for the accountant is the **electronic spreadsheet** program for personal computers. This program is in essence electronic sheets of columnar paper that permit the user to enter labels, numbers, and formulas at each position on the work sheet. By using these capabilities any type of report or work sheet that can be developed on paper can also be developed on the computer. Benefits are that the computations are all done by the computer, and when any single number is changed, all of the numbers based upon that number are automatically recomputed. The results are displayed on the screen and can be printed out when desired. Many types of accounting information are especially suited for processing with an electronic spreadsheet. The cash forecast and bond amortization table are illustrated.

Cash Forecast

The cash forecast shows the beginning cash balance, plus the projected cash receipts for the period, minus the projected cash disbursements for the period. The usefulness of such a forecast is covered in Chapter 8. Figure A–4 is an example of the screen display of a cash forecast prepared with an electronic spreadsheet program.

In Figure A–4, using the Lotus 1-2-3™ software package, each column is identified by a letter and each row by a number. The intersection of a row and a column forms a **cell**. Each cell is referred to with its column and row designation. For example, A1 refers to the cell formed by the intersection of the first column, A, and the first row, 1. Each cell may contain a label, such as in cell A3, or a number, such as in cell B3.

The power of the spreadsheet comes from the fact that a **formula** (a computation algorithm) can also be entered into a cell. In this spreadsheet, a very

```
C3: (C2) +B20                                                          READY

              A                   B            C           D           E
     1                                   CASH FORECAST
     2                            1st Quarter 2nd Quarter 3rd Quarter 4th Quarter
     3   Beginning cash balance    $1,200.00   $8,300.00  $5,400.00    $700.00
     4   Add: Collections
     5   Cash sales                $4,000.00   $3,500.00  $5,000.00  $7,000.00
     6   Sales on account -
     7     Current period           8,000.00    6,000.00   7,000.00   8,600.00
     8     Prior period            15,000.00   12,000.00   8,000.00   9,000.00
     9     2nd prior period         2,000.00    1,000.00   2,300.00   1,800.00
    10   Total collections        $29,000.00  $22,500.00 $22,300.00 $26,400.00
    11   Cash available           $30,200.00  $30,800.00 $27,700.00 $27,100.00
    12   Deduct: Cash payments
    13   Purchases -
    14     Current period          $9,000.00  $10,000.00  $9,800.00  $5,900.00
    15     Prior period             3,000.00    4,600.00   6,800.00   5,700.00
    16   Payroll                    6,500.00    6,800.00   8,000.00   8,200.00
    17   Other                      3,400.00    4,000.00   2,400.00   4,000.00
    18   Total disbursements      $21,900.00  $25,400.00 $27,000.00 $23,800.00
    19
    20   Cash balance forward      $8,300.00   $5,400.00    $700.00  $3,300.00
```

Figure A–4 **Cash Forecast**

simple formula, +B20, has been entered into cell C3. The contents of a cell can be verified by moving the screen cursor to that cell and referring to the upper left corner of the display. Here are displayed C3: (C2) +B20. The C3 indicates that the content of cell C3 is being shown. (C2) indicates that the format is currency with two decimal places, and +B20 is the formula entered into that cell. The simple formula +B20 means that C3 should be set equal to +B20 or that the contents of cell B20 are to be copied in cell C3. In a cash budget, the beginning balance for one period is the same as the ending balance for the prior period. Use of this simple formula has caused this to happen without the number being reentered.

If the cursor were moved to cell B10, the upper left corner would show B10: (C2) @SUM(B5..B9) the formula stored in cell B10. Since cell B10 is to contain the total of cash receipts for the period, the sum of cells B5 through B9, the formula for this computation has been entered into the cell instead of manually adding up the numbers and then inserting the answer. By using the formula, if any one of the projected cash receipts is changed, the total is automatically recalculated.

Once all of the formulas for the first quarter have been entered into column B, they can be copied, using the appropriate command, from column B into columns C, D, and E for the second through fourth quarter budgets. These capabilities allow the creation of a very useful cash forecast that is accurate and can be readily changed for managerial planning.

The real benefit of electronic spreadsheets to management is the ability to answer "what if" questions. For example, in Figure A–4, what if the disbursements for purchases made in the current period were $12,000 and not

A / Use of Computers in Accounting

$9,000? The accountant could simply change the number stored in cell B14, and all of the other numbers on the spreadsheet that are affected by this number (all of the ending balances, for example) would automatically be recalculated. This feature gives the accountant a better understanding of what might happen to the cash position under varying circumstances.

Bond Amortization Table

When long-term bonds are issued at either a premium or a discount, accounting for the interest expense requires the amortization of the premium or discount. Most businesses prepare a bond amortization table similar to the one illustrated in Figure 14–7 as an aid in making the interest expense and amortization entries. Since the amortization schedule is simply a columnar work sheet containing calculations, it is an excellent application for the electronic spreadsheet.

If the business had several different long-term bond issuances, the user can construct a template and store it as a disk file for future use. A **template** is in essence a spreadsheet with all of the labels and formulas entered but with no values inserted. The template is loaded into the computer memory, and the pertinent values are entered into the appropriate cells. Since the formulas are a part of the template, all of the calculations are automatically performed when the values are entered.

Figure A–5 shows the amortization schedule completed with the data from Example C–2 in Chapter 14 illustrating a bond issued at a discount. After the

```
C11:  (C2) +B11*$E$4*0.5 a                                           READY

         A           B             C              D           E           F
1                              BOND AMORTIZATION SCHEDULE
2
3     Face Amount:            $200,000.00   Issue Price:  $181,742.91
4     Stated Rate:                 16.00%   Yield Rate:        18.00%
5     Date Issued:               7/1/87     Maturity Date    6/30/97
6     Interest Paid:           semi-annual
7                  Carrying                                         Carrying
8                  Value      Interest       Interest                Value
9     Period      Beginning   Expense        Payment    Amortization  Ending
10        0                                                         $181,742.91
11        1     $181,742.91   $16,356.86    $16,000.00   $356.86   $182,099.77
12        2     $182,099.77   $16,388.98    $16,000.00   $388.98   $182,488.75
13        3     $182,488.75   $16,423.99    $16,000.00   $423.99   $182,912.74
14        4     $182,912.74   $16,462.15    $16,000.00   $462.15   $183,374.89
15        5     $183,374.89   $16,503.74    $16,000.00   $503.74   $183,878.63
16        6     $183,878.63   $16,549.08    $16,000.00   $549.08   $184,427.70
17        7     $184,427.70   $16,598.49    $16,000.00   $598.49   $185,026.19
18        8     $185,026.19   $16,652.36    $16,000.00   $652.36   $185,678.55
19        9     $185,678.55   $16,711.07    $16,000.00   $711.07   $186,389.62
20       10     $186,389.62   $16,775.07    $16,000.00   $775.07   $187,164.69
```

[a]This is the formula to multiply the carrying value by one-half the yield rate (effective interest rate).

Figure A–5   **Bond Amortization Schedule—View 1**

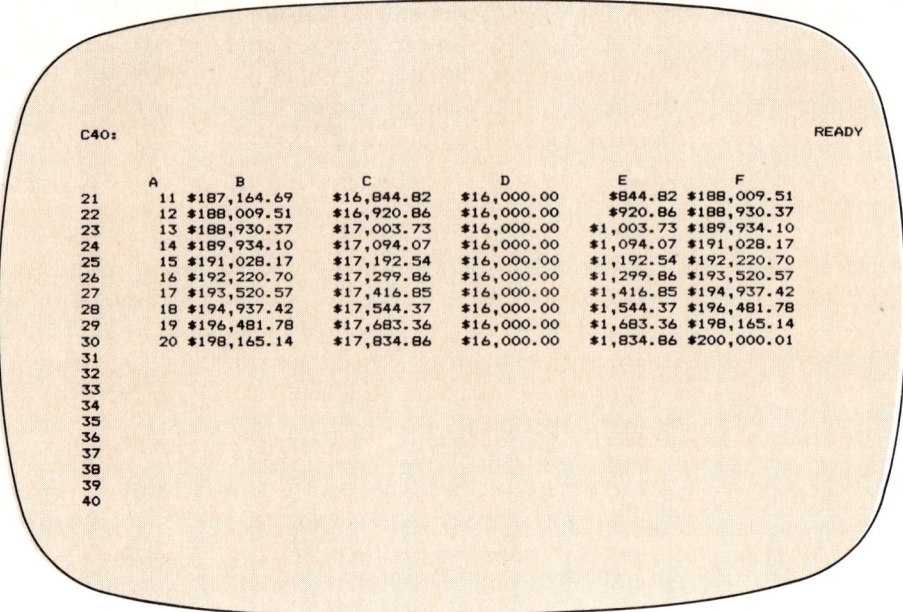

Figure A-6   **Bond Amortization Schedule—View 2**

template is loaded, the bond issue data are entered at the top of the spreadsheet, all of the computations are performed by the computer, and the schedule is completed. In this case the relevant numbers for the bond issued at a discount are entered in the top portion of the spreadsheet. No numbers have to be entered into the bottom portion of the spreadsheet because the template contains the appropriate formulas to complete the bottom portion using the data entered into the top.

This application illustrates another feature of the electronic spreadsheet. The display screen is actually a window through which the user views the spreadsheet. In Figure A-5, only the first 10 periods of the bond amortization schedule are shown. The remainder of the bond amortization schedule has been calculated and is in the memory of the computer but is not presently visible on the screen. By moving the window across or up and down the spreadsheet, the user can view other portions. Figure A-6 shows the window moved down to reveal rows 21 through 40 of the spreadsheet and the rest of the bond amortization schedule.

Generation of Graphs for Accounting Information

Graphics are increasingly being used to communicate accounting information. Research has shown that greater amounts of numeric information can be rapidly communicated through graphics. Many of the electronic spreadsheet packages available contain graphics capabilities.

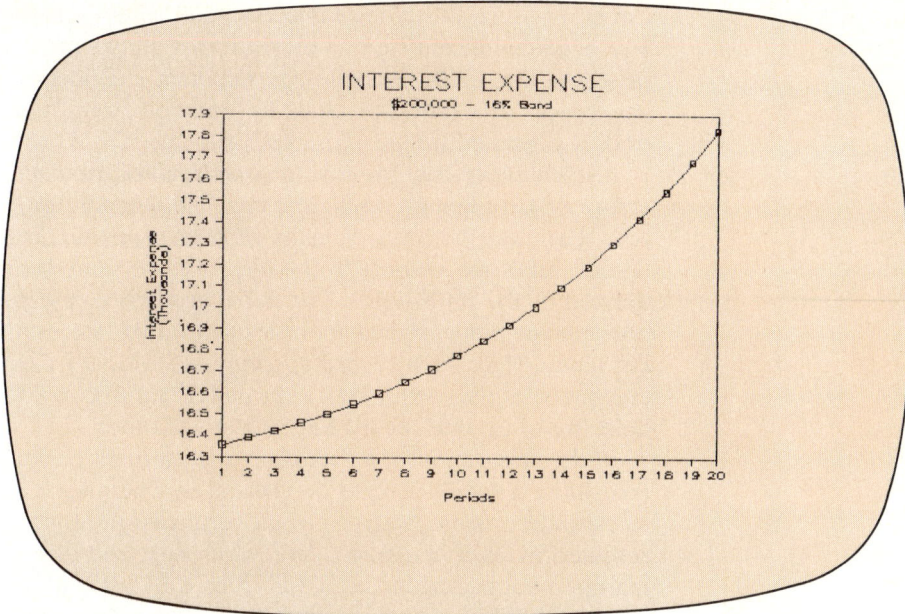

Figure A–7 Graph Generated by the Electronic Spreadsheet Package for Interest Expense

The data generated in the bond amortization spreadsheet can be used to draw a graph of the interest expense by period. Utilizing commands available in the spreadsheet package, the user specifies the type of graph to be produced and the data to be used for the X axis and the Y axis. In this case, a line graph is selected; the time periods in cells A11 through A30 of Figures A–5 and A–6 are selected for the X axis; and interest expense cells C11 through C30 are selected for the data on the Y axis. Once these choices are made, the user tells the computer to draw the graph, and a display similar to that in Figure A–7 appears on the screen. Hard copy of the graph can be prepared with a graphics plotter or dot matrix printer.

Application of Data Base Management Software

Many data gathering and information production situations in accounting and business require the accumulation, updating, and use of large volumes of financial and nonfinancial data. An example is data regarding the stockholders of a corporation. A corporation must maintain data about who owns stock and how much stock is owned. Most often, the business employs another organization known as a transfer agent to do this. Regardless of who does it, the data must be maintained.

This type of data gathering and maintenance task can be performed using specialized software written specifically for stockholder records. Today there is a general type of software, known as data base management software, that can be used for this type of processing. A **data base management package** is a generalized type of software that allows the user, who may not have programming skills, to create and maintain a collection of data pertaining to any topical area and to produce information from these data. This collection of data is termed a **data base** or **data file**.

A stockholder data file would contain all of the data pertaining to the ownership of a company's stock. The data file is made up of individual data records. Each **data record** contains all of the specific data about one stockholder. All of the records in the file have the same format. This format is defined by the **data fields** that make up each data record. A field contains one specific piece of data about a stockholder, for example, the stockholder's last name. Thus, each record is composed of many fields, one for each specific piece of data required for an individual stockholder. In the file these fields make up one record for each stockholder.

In the application of a data base management package to stockholder information, a data file might be created in which each record contains the stockholder's name, address, stock certificate numbers, number of shares represented by each certificate, date purchased, and date sold. In most data base management packages, the file is created by making selections from menus presented on the display screen. The user answers questions regarding the number of fields in the record, the name (title) to be given to each field, the type of data to be stored in each field (alphanumeric or numeric), and the number of characters. The program then uses this information to set up a file.

After this has been done, the user can enter, or **input**, data into records in the file by selecting the appropriate option from a menu. After selecting the "Enter Data" option, the user is presented with a display which is a form to be completed, as in the data input for journal entries shown earlier. The user then fills in the blanks.

Reports are designed by selecting a "Create Report" option from the menu. The user answers a series of questions in the same manner as when the file was designed. The user may be asked which fields are to be included in the output, and where on the page they are to be printed. After designing the report, the user receives the **output** by selecting a "Print Report" option on the menu.

The data stored in the file can be maintained by **editing** the data file. The user selects that option from the menu, and the package asks which record is to be edited. When the user enters the value identifying that record, the current contents of the record are displayed on the screen. The user enters new data for any field that has changed, and the data base management package updates the data file.

Data base management packages are commonly available software packages for computers of all sizes, mainframe to microcomputer. The important features of the data base management package include:

☐ The ability of the nonprogrammer to use the computer for maintenance of data files.

- The ability to use the same software package to maintain data files for many different types of applications—customer lists, stockholder lists, and plant asset records are examples.

Data base management packages are becoming more powerful, easier to use, and less costly as computer technology improves.

Benefits of Computerization in Accounting

The computerized accounting system is like any other asset in which a business invests; the asset must generate a satisfactory return on the investment. This means that the financial benefits derived from the system must be sufficiently greater than the costs incurred so that a contribution is made towards the profitability of the business.

Costs of computerization are relatively easy to measure. They include the cost of the initial computer hardware, the cost of expanding the hardware as the business grows and the number of accounting functions performed on the system increases, and the cost of the initial accounting software and software expansions. The cost of personnel training and labor to convert a manual accounting system to a computerized system must be considered, as well as normal operating costs such as wages and salaries (sometimes higher due to the more specialized personnel involved), paper, and utilities. Computer system costs also include hardware and software maintenance.

Computerization of the accounting system offers many benefits to a business. The primary benefits are the quality of information available to the decision maker, the timeliness of the information, and the variety of information available. Many types of information based upon data in the accounting system—for example a list of customers with zip code 50625—would not be prepared manually. The time and cost required to prepare the information would not be justified. But once the data are captured in the computer system, it is a much less costly process to extract the data from the computerized records and process them into the needed form of information.

In order to be beneficial in decision making, accounting information must be available to the user as needed. When manual accounting systems handled information for larger businesses, many users of information received the information too late for use. Computerization helps to accumulate data and prepare reports with much greater speed and accuracy. If managers receive information in time to affect their decisions, the potential exists for better decision making.

The economic impact of benefits is hard to measure. The major economic benefits of computerization come from decreasing the firm's investment in working capital for any given level of operations. For example, the firm may increase its accounts receivable turnover and inventory turnover. Without an increase in sales volume, this action requires a decrease in the level of accounts receivable and inventory. Also, more closely managing its cash flow permits the business to pay its bills on time and to control its short-term borrowing. The computer is one tool that the manager can use to get more appropriate, accurate, and timely information, and thus better manage the firm's assets.

Summary

This appendix introduces the impact made by computers on the practice of accounting. Managerial use of computers in decision making is advancing constantly as tremendous changes occur in computer hardware and software technology. A successful accountant and business manager must stay up-to-date and be ready and able to apply the computer to decision-making responsibilities.

Glossary

Accounting software package A set of computer programs designed to perform accounting functions.

Back-up A copy of the files that can be used to recreate the working copies of the files if the latter are destroyed. This is a part of the internal control system.

Cell The intersection of a row and a column in an electronic spreadsheet where data or formulas can be stored.

Computer hardware The equipment items in a computer system.

Computer program A set of instructions that direct the operation of the computer hardware.

Computer software The computer programs that control the operation of the computer hardware.

Data base A collection of data pertaining to a given subject.

Data base management package Computer software packages for design, maintenance, and output of information from data files.

Data field The smallest logical unit of data, consisting of the characters that make up that unit of data.

Data file See *Data base*.

Data record All of the related data fields that are treated as a single unit.

Editing The process of updating data stored in a data base.

Electronic spreadsheet A computer program that permits the construction of a work sheet.

Formula A computation algorithm that can be entered into a spreadsheet cell that automatically computes the value to be displayed in that cell.

Input The process of entering data into computer files, or the data entered.

Integrated accounting system A computerized accounting system that updates all affected data items with one entry.

Menu A screen display in a computerized accounting system that allows the user to choose the next operation.

Module The set of computer programs that perform all of the operations associated with one area of accounting.

Output The process of printing out data or information from computer files, or the information printed out.

Password A code that permits access to the various parts of the computerized accounting system. Different users are given different passwords as an internal control measure.

Personal computer A complete computer system designed for individual use, with all of the computing resources of a larger system but smaller in scale.

Template An electronic spreadsheet with formulas and data common to all situations entered but with data specific to a situation left to be entered for that situation.

User friendly A method of designing a computerized accounting system to permit a person with little or no computer expertise to use the programs.

Discussion Questions

QA–1 Define a computerized accounting system. Why is the computerization of the accounting function important?

QA–2 What are the four modules of a basic computerized accounting system? Discuss the functions performed by each of the modules.

QA–3 What types of reports will be prepared by the accounts receivable system that will aid in managing accounts receivable? How will they be of assistance?

QA–4 What is meant by backing up the files? Why is this important to a computerized accounting system?

QA–5 What is a software package? What is its significance to accounting?

QA–6 What is meant by the term *menu*? How do menus play a role in the user friendly nature of a computerized accounting system?

QA–7 What is an electronic spreadsheet? How does it operate? What is a template? Where does the primary benefit come from in using electronic spreadsheets?

QA–8 In an electronic spreadsheet, what is a cell? What is a label? What is a value? What is a formula?

QA–9 How does a formula strengthen the power of the spreadsheet?

QA–10 How can electronic spreadsheets be used to manage cash better?

QA–11 Describe the preparation of a bond amortization schedule with an electronic spreadsheet.

QA–12 What is a data base management package? How can it be used in maintaining accounting information?

QA–13 Define the terms *data file*, *data record*, and *data field*.

QA–14 What are the types of benefits that can reasonably be expected as a result of computerizing an accounting system?

Note: Due to the nature of the material in Appendix A, exercises and problems are not appropriate.

B Price-Level Accounting

Introduction

Accountants use historical cost as the primary basis for asset valuation. Because of the effects of inflation, great concern has been expressed by many accountants and other people in the financial community as to the information value of traditional, historical cost financial statements. In 1983, General Motors Corporation reported a net income of $3,730,200,000 on its historical cost income statement. If the same operating results had been restated in terms of dollars of 1967 purchasing power, the net income would have been $1,199,200,000, a 68 percent decrease.

In the decade ending in 1980, profits reported by the 500 companies making up the Standard & Poor's Composite Index nearly tripled. Had these profits been adjusted for the effects of changes in the purchasing power of the dollar, there would have been no increase in profits reported. In fact, a small decline would have been shown.

These facts indicate that there is a need to provide the users of financial information, both managers and external users, with measurements of the effects of inflation on the financial statements. This appendix introduces some of the issues involved in the accounting for changing prices.

Learning Goals

1. To understand both the advantages and shortcomings of historical cost financial reporting.

2. To understand the purpose and effect of the financial reporting alternatives to historical cost accounting and their advantages and disadvantages.

3. To distinguish between nominal dollar accounting and constant dollar accounting.

4. To become acquainted with purchasing power gain or loss.

5. To become acquainted with the reporting requirements of *FASB Statements No. 33* and *No. 82*.

Historical Cost Reporting

The methods of accounting presented in this text are based on **historical cost** reporting. Each asset acquired or expense incurred is recorded at cost when the asset was purchased or the expense incurred. This recording will cause no problem with the reported results if the value of the measuring unit does not change. But, if the value of the measuring unit is changing, misleading results may be reported.

The accountant is faced with two types of changes in the value of the measuring unit. One is called a *specific price-level change,* which occurs when the value of a specific good or service changes. For example, the cost of an automobile may go up by 15 percent, while the cost of a computer system may go down by 10 percent.

The problem with specific price-level changes can be seen in another illustration. If, for example, a company purchased a milling machine in 1975 for $10,000, the purchase would be recorded at $10,000 in the accounting records. If a second identical milling machine were purchased in 1983, it would be recorded at the amount paid, say $18,500. Under the stable dollar assumption, each of the recorded costs is assumed to represent dollars of equal purchasing power and are added together to arrive at a total for plant assets. Also, since the dollars are assumed to have equal purchasing power, the second machine is assumed to have 85 percent more revenue-generating capability, because it has an 85 percent higher cost. This assumption is implied by the costs recorded even though the machine is identical. If straight line depreciation were used, this would result in 85 percent more depreciation expense each year for the same productive capabilities.

The second type of change in the value of the measuring unit is termed *general price-level changes.* This change is a result of the change in the price of all goods and services, each of which has had a specific price-level change. As the general level of prices of goods and services rises, the ability of each dollar to purchase goods and services declines—a change known as **inflation**. The opposite condition is known as **deflation**. Because of inflation, when older assets, purchased at a lower price level, are used in generating revenues, the expense is recorded at an amount less than it would be if the assets had been acquired recently. This in turn means that the net income and stockholders' equity reported would be higher than if newer assets were used, leading to a problem with the maintenance of the company's capital.

In order for a company to continue in business, it must replace assets as they are consumed. In a period of inflation, therefore, each replacement of assets costs more than the previous one. But since the depreciation expense on the older, lower cost assets was lower, and net income higher, the company will have to use some of the capital generated by earnings to replace the assets. This problem can be avoided only if the method of accounting reports no income until sufficient expense has been reflected to permit the replacement of the assets at the new, higher prices when they are consumed.

To overcome problems such as these, which stem from historical cost financial reporting in a period of changing prices, and to avoid mixing dollars of different values, several alternative reporting methods have been suggested.

B / Price-Level Accounting

Alternative Methods to Historical Cost

Since 1965, considerable research and discussion has centered on reporting methods which would report the effects of inflation. In 1979, the FASB issued a comprehensive statement requiring the reporting of the effects of price-level changes in annual reports to stockholders. *FASB Statement No. 33* requires large qualifying companies—and encourages smaller companies—to present in their published annual reports the following as a supplement to the conventional historical cost financial statements:

1. Income adjusted for the effects of general inflation and the effects of changes in specific prices of resources used by the business.
2. The purchasing power gain or loss on net monetary items.
3. The current cost amounts of inventory and property, plant, and equipment.
4. Increases or decreases in current cost amounts of inventory and property, plant, and equipment, net of inflation.
5. A five-year summary of selected financial data, with inventory and property, plant, and equipment adjusted for the effects of changing prices.

Thus, *Statement No 33* calls for two supplemental income computations. One deals with the effects of general inflation; the other deals with the effects of changes in the specific prices of resources used by the enterprise. The board believed both types of information were likely to be useful.[1] The FASB thus provided for three accounting bases to be used in financial statement reporting in the annual report to stockholders for certain large companies.[2]

1. Historical cost, still the generally accepted accounting principle, required for the audited financial statements, often referred to as the primary statements.
2. Historical cost adjusted for general price-level changes.
3. Current cost based on price-level changes of specific items.

The latter two items are in an unaudited section of the financial statements.

After a five-year trial period, the FASB concluded that the use of two different methods of reporting the effects of changing prices might detract from the usefulness of inflation adjusted information. In December 1984, the Board published *Statement of Financial Accounting Standards No. 82,* amending *Statement No. 33.* For fiscal years ending on or after December 15, 1984, if current cost information is disclosed, companies would not be required to disclose historical cost adjusted for general price-level changes. The amend-

---

[1] Financial Accounting Standards Board, *Statement of Financial Accounting Standards No. 33,* "Financial Reporting and Changing Prices" (Stamford, Conn.: September 1979), p. iii.

[2] The disclosure requirements apply to public companies that have inventories and property, plant, and equipment (before deducting accumulated depreciation and amortization) greater than $125 million or total assets net of accumulated depreciation and amortization of $1 billion or more.

ment, however, does require that companies affected by *Statement 33* continue to report current cost.[3]

Although the general price-level accounting is no longer required for external reporting, a user of financial information, whether internal manager or external user, must understand the different effects the two indicators of inflation have on financial information. This appendix therefore presents an introduction to both general price-level adjusted accounting and current cost accounting.

General Price-Level Adjusted Accounting

The purpose of using price-level adjusted cost figures in accounting is to restate historical costs in terms of dollars of common purchasing power **(constant dollar accounting)**. The restated dollars then show the number of dollars now required to match the amount of general purchasing power invested when an item was acquired **(general price-level adjusted cost)**. An expenditure of $10,000 for a tract of land, for example, represents a commitment of $10,000 of current purchasing power. The subsequent reporting of that item in financial statements should be in terms of dollars of purchasing power as of the respective statement date. If, a year later, prices in general have increased by 10 percent, the land should be reported at an amount 10 percent higher than the historical cost, or $11,000. Thus, the land will be stated in dollars of uniform size, or in common dollars—that is, the land will be stated in dollars with a purchasing power size prevailing at the statement date. The cost in the accounting records remains at $10,000, but it has been restated in more units (dollars) of lesser purchasing power for purposes of financial statement presentation.

The $1,000 increase is a recognition of the change in the value of the measuring unit, the dollar. This recognizes the fact that there has been a 10 percent increase in the general level of prices, so that $11,000 is now required to buy the goods and services that could have been bought for $10,000 a year before. The $1,000 increase is not a gain. It simply means that recorded assets and paid-in capital will have been increased by an amount sufficient to equal the general purchasing power of the paid-in capital at its original amount.

The actual number of dollars needed to replace the *specific* tract of land may be greater or less than $11,000, depending on the current prevailing market conditions for that specific asset. If the tract of land has a current market value of $15,000, it will still be restated at $11,000 under general price-level accounting. The additional $4,000 = ($15,000 − $11,000) is due to a specific price change and is not recognized in statements adjusted for general price-level changes. It is recognized, however, in statements showing current cost or current value, the topic discussed in the next section.

---

[3]Financial Accounting Standards Board, *Statement of Financial Accounting Standards No. 82,* "Financial Reporting and Changing Prices: Elimination of Certain Disclosures" (Stamford, Conn.: December 1984).

Current Cost Accounting

The alternative to general price-level accounting is current cost accounting. Statements based on current cost (or current value) accounting measure the changes in price levels of *specific* items used in the business. They measure changes in specific purchasing power of the dollar and are influenced by factors not common to all goods and services.

The difference between general price-level accounting and current cost accounting is significant. General price-level accounting adjusts historical cost to a common purchasing power measuring unit. **Current cost accounting**, on the other hand, revalues assets at the cost to replace them at the current time, assuming that they could be replaced in kind **(replacement cost)**. If these assets cannot be replaced in kind, the current cost is measured by the cost to provide an equivalent productive capacity.

Basic Concepts

Several basic concepts related to general price-level accounting need to be discussed in introducing general price-level accounting.

Use of Index Numbers to Adjust Costs

The financial reporting process should measure and report purchasing power. Therefore, the items being compared must be expressed in terms of a *comparable purchasing power yardstick*, or price index. A **price index** is a statistical average of prices expressed as a percentage of a base period.

The **Consumer Price Index for All Urban Consumers (CPI–U)** suggested by the FASB uses the *average* of 1967 prices as the base. Accordingly, the index for 1967 is 100. A year later the price index would be 100 plus the percent average prices have increased over 1967. CPI–U is measured monthly by the U.S. Department of Labor; at the end of each year, an average-for-the-year index is also determined. Since the index for the last month of each year is available (end-of-year index), historical dollar amounts may be adjusted by either set of index numbers (average-for-the-year or end-of-year).

A general formula to convert historical costs of items into constant dollars of a uniform purchasing power is as follows:

$$\text{Cost measured in current year's constant dollars} = \text{Historical Cost} \times \frac{\text{Index on date converted TO}}{\text{Index on date converted FROM}}$$

If the index number used in the numerator of this formula is an end-of-year index number, the amounts are said to be stated in **end-of-year constant dollars**. An alternative method is to use average-for-the-year index numbers in the numerator of the formula. In this case, the amounts are restated in **average-for-the-year constant dollars**. *FASB Statement No. 33* allows the use of either method, but most of its examples are shown using average-for-the-year constant dollars.

Monetary vs. Nonmonetary Items

Monetary items are those items in which the dollar amount exchanged or to be exchanged is fixed, typically by contractual agreement. Monetary items include cash, notes and accounts receivable, notes and accounts payable, and bonds and mortgages payable. These items are fixed in terms of the total number of dollars that will be collected on the assets and the number of dollars that must be paid to creditors on the liabilities, regardless of changes in the price level.

This monetary position is significant in adjusting for the effects of inflation. Since cash or claims to cash will buy fewer goods during periods of rising prices, holding or acquiring these will cause the firm to lose purchasing power. Conversely, in periods of falling prices, they are worth more and will buy more and produce a gain. In a similar manner, the burden of paying off debt during periods of rising prices is eased by payment in current, cheaper dollars. Therefore, the firm experiences a gain by holding or incurring debt during rising prices. The opposite is true if prices are falling. These gains and losses are called **purchasing power gains and losses**. Observe that:

1. During a period of rising prices
   a. A purchasing power loss arises from holding monetary assets.
   b. A purchasing power gain arises from holding monetary liabilities.
2. Conversely, during a period of declining prices
   a. A purchasing power gain arises from holding monetary assets.
   b. A purchasing power loss arises from holding monetary liabilities.

A different effect is experienced from holding the other balance sheet items called **nonmonetary items**. Examples of nonmonetary items are merchandise inventory; land; property, plant, and equipment; and common stockholder's equity. Since these are not claims to specific amounts of cash, the purchasing power represented by their dollar amounts is not fixed contractually. Their balance in the historical cost accounting records is not stated in terms of current dollars. Rather, as price levels change, the purchasing power of their dollar amounts fluctuates. Therefore, nonmonetary items must be converted or restated by applying the general formula shown in the previous section.

The specifics of converting historical cost financial statements to general price-level adjusted statements are not presented in this appendix. A real life example showing the application of these concepts and the FASB requirements is included next.

Illustration of Price-Level Information in an Annual Report

FASB Statement No. 33 as amended by *Statement No. 82* requires that management of certain large corporations shall provide price-level information and explanations of its significance on the operating success of the business. The statement applies to companies with more than $1 billion in net assets or more than $125 million in inventory and gross property, plant, and equipment.[4]

---

[4]*FASB Statement No. 33,* paragraph 37.

Shown below is an example of the reporting from the 1984 Annual Report of Martin Marietta Corporation. As required by *FASB Statement No. 33*, the company has provided a discussion and explanation of the information disclosed.

Supplementary Information on Changing Prices
(Unaudited)

The supplementary information that follows has been prepared in accordance with the requirements of the Financial Accounting Standards Board. The Board's experimental Standard requires the Corporation to present data intended to estimate the effects of specific price changes on inventories, property, plant, and equipment and earnings from continuing operations.

Since the use of arbitrary assumptions, approximations, and estimates is required, the resulting measurements should be viewed in that context and not as complete or precise indicators of the effects of inflation. For these reasons and due to the experimental nature of the Standard, management does not endorse the current cost method or the manner of presentation, since they may be misinterpreted. The following information supplements the Corporation's primary financial statements on pages 14 through 17, which are prepared on the historical cost basis in accordance with generally accepted accounting principles.

Supplementary Statement of Earnings from Continuing Operations
for the year ended December 31, 1984 (millions)

	As Reported In Primary Statements	Adjusted For Specific Prices (Current Cost)
Net sales	$3,920	$3,920
Cost of sales, other costs, and expenses	3,634	3,715
	286	205
Other income	55	55
Interest expense on debt	(32)	(32)
Taxes on income	(133)	(133)
Earnings from continuing operations	$ 176	$ 95

(continued on next page)

Selected Financial Data Comparisons (millions of average 1984 dollars, except per share and price index)

	1984	1983	1982	1981	1980
Net sales	$3,920	$3,366	$3,263	$3,062	$2,432
Dividends per common share	1.34	1.35	1.38	1.37	1.30
Year-end market price per common share in average 1984 constant dollars	44	37	31	27	39
Current cost information:					
Earnings (losses) from continuing operations	95	64	(5)	96	95
Earnings (losses) per share, assuming no dilution, from continuing operations	2.41	2.08	(.11)	1.73	1.70
Nets assets at year-end	960	1,841	1,859	2,895	2,726
Increase in the general price level in excess of (less than) increase in specific prices of inventories and properties	27	288	41	6	(38)
Gain from decline in purchasing power of net amounts owed	39	55	31	44	29
Average consumer price index	311.1	298.4	289.2	272.3	246.9

Current Cost The current cost method is intended to estimate what it would cost in 1984 dollars to replace the Corporation's inventories and to reconstruct its existing facilities. Depreciation expense and cost of sales are stated at the estimated current cost of their replacement rather than the amounts originally expended to acquire or produce them.

Adjustments are not made to reflect the significant efficiencies or cost savings that would be gained by the replacement of existing facilities with new facilities that incorporate technological advances. Further, in accordance with the Standard, income taxes have not been adjusted.

The Corporation's primary financial statements are prepared using inventory methods which generally result in cost-of-sales amounts approximating current costs other than current cost depreciation.

The current cost of property, plant, and equipment was determined on the basis of actual and estimated construction or acquisition costs restated using appropriate price indices. Depreciation has been computed by the same methods and applying the same service lives used in the primary financial statements.

The current cost of inventory was $279 million, and the current cost of property, plant, and equipment, net of accumulated depreciation,

(*continued on next page*)

was $1.3 billion at December 31, 1984. On the current cost basis, 1984 depreciation, depletion, and amortization expense was $195 million, which was $81 million higher than the amount reflected in the primary financial statements.

Purchasing Power Increase Inflation also affects monetary assets such as cash and claims to cash (notes and accounts receivable). Holding a monetary asset during periods of inflation results in a decline in the value of the asset since the dollar loses purchasing power when it is held. Conversely, debtors benefit during inflationary periods because less purchasing power is required to satisfy obligations in the future when they can be paid with less valuable dollars. The Corporation was a net monetary borrower throughout 1984 and 1983.

Significance of the Information Earnings from continuing operations shown in the supplementary statement are less than in the primary financial statements because of increased depreciation expense.

The Corporation's investment in property, plant, and equipment is included in the primary statements at the actual cost of acquisition or construction. As a result of inflation and other factors, the current cost to replace these facilities would be substantially higher than their historical cost. In the past, when the Corporation incurred higher costs to replace productive facilities, the increased depreciation generally has been offset by increased productivity, efficiencies, increased selling prices, and other factors; and the Corporation, on an overall basis, has been able to ameliorate the effects of higher replacement costs.

Source: From Martin Marietta Corporation's, 1984 Annual Report.

Glossary

Average-for-the-year constant dollars Financial statement amounts restated to average-for-the-year purchasing power equivalents.

Constant dollar accounting A method of reporting assets, liabilities, revenues, and expenses in dollars having the same purchasing power.

Consumer Price Index for All Urban Consumers (CPI–U) The index used to compute information on a constant dollar basis, published monthly by the Bureau of Labor Statistics of the U.S. Department of Labor.

Current cost accounting A method of measuring and reporting assets and expenses associated with the use or sale of assets at current cost on the balance sheet date or on the date of use or sale.

Deflation A downward change in the general price level resulting in an increase in the purchasing power of the dollar.

End-of-year constant dollars Financial statement amounts restated to end-of-year purchasing power equivalents.

General price-level adjusted cost The number of general purchasing power dollars currently required for the amount of purchasing power invested when the item was acquired.

Historical cost The principle that an asset should be recorded at the actual cost required to attain it.

Inflation An upward change in the general price level resulting in a decrease in the purchasing power of the monetary unit.

Monetary items Assets and liabilities with a dollar value that would not be expected to change with changes in price levels (cash, accounts and notes receivable, accounts and notes payable, bonds payable).

Nonmonetary items Assets with a dollar value that would be expected to change with changes in price levels (inventories, property, plant, and equipment, intangible assets).

Price index Statistical averages of prices expressed as percentages of a base period.

Purchasing power gains and losses Gains and losses arising out of holding monetary items during periods of inflation and deflation; the difference between the monetary items based on historical cost and the same items adjusted for changes in price levels.

Replacement cost The current cost of replacing one specific asset with another asset of equivalent capacity.

Questions

QB-1 What are the major reasons to consider changing price levels in financial reports?

QB-2 What is inflation? Deflation? What are their effects on financial statements?

QB-3 What is the difference between historical cost accounting, general price-level adjusted accounting, and current cost accounting?

QB-4 What is meant by a price index? What is the major index used for adjusting financial statements and what does it measure?

QB-5 What is the equation for restating historical cost items into (a) end-of-year constant dollars? (b) average-for-the-year constant dollars?

QB-6 What is the difference between a monetary item and a nonmonetary item?

QB-7 Define the term *purchasing power gain or loss*. Under what circumstances could either occur?

QB-8 Give three illustrations of distortions or inaccuracies in conventional financial statements resulting from changes in the purchasing power of the dollar.

QB-9 Zuber Company constructed a plant in 1975 at a cost of $2 million and a second, similar plant in 1987 at a cost of $5 million. What will be that gross plant cost in conventional financial statements? Is this a fair report? Why?

QB-10 Why is the effect of adjusting depreciation expense for changes in prices so often much more pronounced than adjusting other expenses?

QB-11 On January 1, 1980, a company borrowed $200,000, which was payable on December 31, 1999. Ignoring interest, what is the relative position December 31, 1987, of (a) the company that borrowed the sum? (b) the lender?

Exercises

Note: Because the actual CPI-U index numbers are more difficult to use in calculations, assumed even-number indexes are used in the exercises.

EB–1
Adjusting sales

Newport Inc. reports the following data:

	1987	1986
Sales	$600,000	$500,000
January 1 price index	175	150
Average for the year price index	190	160
December 31 price index	210	175

Assuming no seasonal fluctuation in sales, what conclusions may be drawn about the two years' sales?

EB–2
Real growth in sales

The sales manager and the financial vice-president of the Byon Company disagree on the significance of the company's sales increases during the last three years. Gross sales were as follows:

1985	$3,000,000
1986	4,250,000
1987	5,000,000

Relevant average price indexes were, respectively, 100, 150, and 180. The sales manager is satisfied with the level of "growth" in sales during the three-year period. The financial vice-president argues that there has been a decline in sales. Who is correct? Why?

EB–3
Income adjusted for current cost

The Yam Company reported a net income for 1987 of $500,000. The owner observed that although physical levels of inventory had been nearly the same, the income statement showed merchandise inventory with an increase of $20,000. She also noted that the balance sheet reported property, plant, and equipment at $2,000,000 whereas it would require $5,000,000 to replace it. Depreciation expense was 10 percent of property, plant, and equipment. The owner questioned the accuracy of reported income. Comment.

EB–4
Monetary vs. nonmonetary assets

You have been asked by a fellow student for advice concerning the investment of some excess cash. He says that he has two alternatives. One is to buy a high grade corporate bond with a purchase price of $4,000 and a maturity value in five years of $5,000; no specific interest is paid. The other is to buy a small parcel of land for $4,000 in a growing neighborhood. Assuming that you expect the rate of inflation to be 10 percent per year, compare the impact of inflation on these two items as it affects the decision.

EB–5
Asset adjustment with index

The Luff Sales Company purchased a piece of equipment on January 2, 1980, for $250,000. The estimated useful life of the equipment was eight years with no salvage value. The company uses the straight line method, and price indexes were as follows:

January 1, 1980	160
December 31, 1987	220

1. Calculate the depreciation expense for 1987 using (a) historical cost, and (b) historical cost/constant dollar.
2. Comment on the usefulness of each amount.

EB–6
General price-level adjustments—assets

Tew Company had the following merchandise items in ending inventory (specific identification method):

Date Purchased	Cost	Price Index
October 1, 1987	$ 300	180
November 1, 1987	500	185
December 1, 1987	2,000	190

Assuming the December 31, 1987, price index was 195, calculate the dollar amount for inventory on a general price-level adjusted balance sheet for December 31, 1987.

EB–7
Price-level adjustments—cost of goods sold

The Lunt Corporation began business on July 1, 1987, by acquiring merchandise that cost $400,000. On July 31, 1987, 60 percent of the merchandise was sold. The price indexes on July 1, 1987, and July 31, 1987, were 150 and 170, respectively. Compute the adjusted cost of goods sold in end-of-month constant dollars.

A Problems

PB–1A
Thought-provoking problem: is a withdrawal in order?

Assume that you are the chief accountant for Successful Supply Company. The company reported income for 1987 of $350,000. The president, who is also the owner and founder of the business, has asked your advice regarding his withdrawal of $300,000 for 1987, saying that the retention of $50,000 in the business should be sufficient for the planned growth he has in mind.

The business was founded in 1970 when substantially all of the property, plant, and equipment was purchased. Since that time the average rate of inflation has been 10 percent per year. During the past year it dropped to 8 percent and is expected to stay there for the near future.

Required: Prepare a memo to Mr. Success, the president, in which you either support his position or attempt to convince him of any error he may have made in his reasoning. Include any computation that you believe necessary, and create figures for the computations.

B Problems

PB–1B
Thought-provoking problem: effect of inflation

The 1983 *Annual Report* of the Martin Marietta Corporation showed the following information (rounded to the nearest $1,000,000):

	1983	1982	1981
Net sales	$3,899	$3,639	$3,610
Year-end market price per common share in average 1983 constant dollars	35	30	25
Net earnings (loss)—constant dollars	51	(19)	114
Net earnings (loss)—current cost	14	(51)	75
Gain from decline in purchasing power of net amounts owed	53	30	42

Required: Discuss the effects of inflation on Martin Marietta's financial disclosures in its statements.

C Compound Interest Tables

Table C–1 Future Amount of a Single Sum of 1

n	1½%	2½%	4%	4½%	5%	5½%	6%	6½%
1	1.015000	1.025000	1.040000	1.045000	1.050000	1.055000	1.060000	1.065000
2	1.030225	1.050625	1.081600	1.092025	1.102500	1.113025	1.123600	1.134225
3	1.045678	1.076891	1.124864	1.141166	1.157625	1.174241	1.191016	1.207950
4	1.061364	1.103813	1.169859	1.192519	1.215506	1.238825	1.262477	1.286466
5	1.077284	1.131408	1.216653	1.246182	1.276282	1.306960	1.338226	1.370087
6	1.093443	1.159693	1.265319	1.302260	1.340096	1.378843	1.418519	1.459142
7	1.109845	1.188686	1.315932	1.360862	1.407100	1.454679	1.503987	1.553987
8	1.126493	1.218403	1.368569	1.422101	1.477455	1.534687	1.593848	1.654996
9	1.143390	1.248863	1.423312	1.486095	1.551328	1.619094	1.689479	1.762570
10	1.160541	1.280085	1.480244	1.552969	1.628895	1.708144	1.790848	1.877137
11	1.177949	1.312087	1.539454	1.622853	1.710339	1.802092	1.898299	1.999151
12	1.195618	1.344889	1.601032	1.695881	1.795856	1.901207	2.012196	2.129096
13	1.213552	1.378511	1.665074	1.772196	1.885649	2.005774	2.132928	2.267487
14	1.231756	1.412974	1.731676	1.851945	1.979932	2.116091	2.260904	2.414874
15	1.250232	1.448298	1.800944	1.935282	2.078928	2.232476	2.396558	2.571841
16	1.268986	1.484506	1.872981	2.022370	2.182875	2.355263	2.540352	2.739011
17	1.288020	1.521618	1.947900	2.113377	2.292018	2.484802	2.692773	2.917046
18	1.307341	1.559659	2.025817	2.208479	2.406619	2.621466	2.854339	3.106654
19	1.326951	1.598650	2.106849	2.307860	2.526950	2.765647	3.025600	3.308587
20	1.346855	1.638616	2.191123	2.411714	2.653298	2.917757	3.207135	3.523645
21	1.367058	1.679582	2.278768	2.520241	2.785963	3.078234	3.399564	3.752682
22	1.387564	1.721571	2.369919	2.633652	2.925261	3.247537	3.603537	3.996606
23	1.408377	1.764611	2.464716	2.752166	3.071524	3.426152	3.819750	4.256386
24	1.429503	1.808726	2.563304	2.876014	3.225100	3.614590	4.048935	4.533051
25	1.450945	1.853944	2.665836	3.005434	3.386355	3.813392	4.291871	4.827699
26	1.472710	1.900293	2.772470	3.140679	3.555673	4.023129	4.549383	5.141500
27	1.494800	1.947800	2.883369	3.282010	3.733456	4.244401	4.822346	5.475697
28	1.517222	1.996495	2.998703	3.429700	3.920129	4.477843	5.111687	5.831617
29	1.539981	2.046407	3.118651	3.584036	4.116136	4.724124	5.418388	6.210672
30	1.563080	2.097568	3.243398	3.745318	4.321942	4.983951	5.743491	6.614366
31	1.586526	2.150007	3.373133	3.913857	4.538039	5.258069	6.088101	7.044300
32	1.610324	2.203757	3.508059	4.089981	4.764941	5.547262	6.453387	7.502179
33	1.634479	2.258851	3.648381	4.274030	5.003189	5.852362	6.840590	7.989821
34	1.658996	2.315322	3.794316	4.466362	5.253348	6.174242	7.251025	8.509159
35	1.683881	2.373205	3.946089	4.667348	5.516015	6.513825	7.686087	9.062255
36	1.709140	2.432535	4.103933	4.877378	5.791816	6.872085	8.147252	9.651301
37	1.734777	2.493349	4.268090	5.096860	6.081407	7.250050	8.636087	10.278636
38	1.760798	2.555682	4.438813	5.326219	6.385477	7.648803	9.154252	10.946747
39	1.787210	2.619574	4.616366	5.565899	6.704751	8.069487	9.703507	11.658286
40	1.814018	2.685064	4.801021	5.816365	7.039989	8.513309	10.285718	12.416075

Table C-1 Future Amount of a Single Sum of 1 (continued)

n	7%	8%	9%	10%	12%	14%	16%	20%
1	1.070000	1.080000	1.090000	1.100000	1.120000	1.140000	1.160000	1.200000
2	1.144900	1.166400	1.188100	1.210000	1.254400	1.299600	1.345600	1.440000
3	1.225043	1.259712	1.295029	1.331000	1.404928	1.481544	1.560896	1.728000
4	1.310796	1.360489	1.411582	1.464100	1.573519	1.688960	1.810639	2.073600
5	1.402552	1.469328	1.538624	1.610510	1.762342	1.925415	2.100342	2.488320
6	1.500730	1.586874	1.677100	1.771561	1.973823	2.194973	2.436396	2.985984
7	1.605781	1.713824	1.828039	1.948717	2.210681	2.502269	2.826220	3.583181
8	1.718186	1.850930	1.992563	2.143589	2.475963	2.852586	3.278415	4.299817
9	1.838459	1.999005	2.171893	2.357948	2.773079	3.251949	3.802961	5.159780
10	1.967151	2.158925	2.367364	2.593742	3.105848	3.707221	4.411435	6.191736
11	2.104852	2.331639	2.580426	2.853117	3.478550	4.226232	5.117265	7.430084
12	2.252192	2.518170	2.812665	3.138428	3.895976	4.817905	5.936027	8.916100
13	2.409845	2.719624	3.065805	3.452271	4.363493	5.492411	6.885791	10.699321
14	2.578534	2.937194	3.341727	3.797498	4.887112	6.261349	7.987518	12.839185
15	2.759032	3.172169	3.642482	4.177248	5.473566	7.137938	9.265521	15.407022
16	2.952164	3.425943	3.970306	4.594973	6.130394	8.137249	10.748004	18.488426
17	3.158815	3.700018	4.327633	5.054470	6.866041	9.276464	12.467685	22.186111
18	3.379932	3.996019	4.717120	5.559917	7.689966	10.575169	14.462514	26.623333
19	3.616528	4.315701	5.141661	6.115909	8.612762	12.055693	16.776517	31.948000
20	3.869684	4.660957	5.604411	6.727500	9.646293	13.743490	19.460759	38.337600
21	4.140562	5.033834	6.108808	7.400250	10.803848	15.667578	22.574481	46.005120
22	4.430402	5.436540	6.658600	8.140275	12.100310	17.861039	26.186398	55.206144
23	4.740530	5.871464	7.257874	8.954302	13.552347	20.361585	30.376222	66.247373
24	5.072367	6.341181	7.911083	9.849733	15.178629	23.212207	35.236417	79.496847
25	5.427433	6.848475	8.623081	10.834706	17.000064	26.461916	40.874244	95.396217
26	5.807353	7.396353	9.399158	11.918177	19.040072	30.166584	47.414123	114.475460
27	6.213868	7.988061	10.245082	13.109994	21.324881	34.389906	55.000382	137.370552
28	6.648838	8.627106	11.167140	14.420994	23.883866	39.204493	63.800444	164.844662
29	7.114257	9.317275	12.172182	15.863093	26.749930	44.693122	74.008515	197.813595
30	7.612255	10.062657	13.267678	17.449402	29.959922	50.950159	85.849877	237.376314
31	8.145113	10.867669	14.461770	19.194342	33.555113	58.083181	99.585857	284.851577
32	8.715271	11.737083	15.763329	21.113777	37.581726	66.214826	115.519594	341.821892
33	9.325340	12.676050	17.182028	23.225154	42.091533	75.484902	134.002729	410.186270
34	9.978114	13.690134	18.728411	25.547670	47.142517	86.052788	155.443166	492.223524
35	10.676581	14.785344	20.413968	28.102437	52.799620	98.100178	180.314073	590.668229
36	11.423942	15.968172	22.251225	30.912681	59.135574	111.834203	209.164324	708.801875
37	12.223618	17.245626	24.253835	34.003949	66.231843	127.490992	242.630616	850.562250
38	13.079271	18.625276	26.436680	37.404343	74.179664	145.339731	281.451515	1020.674700
39	13.994820	20.115298	28.815982	41.144778	83.081224	165.687293	326.483757	1224.809640
40	14.974458	21.724521	31.409420	45.259256	93.050970	188.883514	378.721158	1469.771568

Table C–2 Present Value of a Single Sum of 1

n	1½%	2½%	4%	4½%	5%	5½%	6%	6½%
1	0.985222	0.975610	0.961538	0.956938	0.952381	0.947867	0.943396	0.938967
2	0.970662	0.951814	0.924556	0.915730	0.907029	0.898452	0.889996	0.881659
3	0.956317	0.928599	0.888996	0.876297	0.863838	0.851614	0.839619	0.827849
4	0.942184	0.905951	0.854804	0.838561	0.822702	0.807217	0.792094	0.777323
5	0.928260	0.883854	0.821927	0.802451	0.783526	0.765134	0.747258	0.729881
6	0.914542	0.862297	0.790315	0.767896	0.746215	0.725246	0.704961	0.685334
7	0.901027	0.841265	0.759918	0.734828	0.710681	0.687437	0.665057	0.643506
8	0.887711	0.820747	0.730690	0.703185	0.676839	0.651599	0.627412	0.604231
9	0.874592	0.800728	0.702587	0.672904	0.644609	0.617629	0.591898	0.567353
10	0.861667	0.781198	0.675564	0.643928	0.613913	0.585431	0.558395	0.532726
11	0.848933	0.762145	0.649581	0.616199	0.584679	0.554911	0.526788	0.500212
12	0.836387	0.743556	0.624597	0.589664	0.556837	0.525982	0.496969	0.469683
13	0.824027	0.725420	0.600574	0.564272	0.530321	0.498561	0.468839	0.441017
14	0.811849	0.707727	0.577475	0.539973	0.505068	0.472569	0.442301	0.414100
15	0.799852	0.690466	0.555265	0.516720	0.481017	0.447933	0.417265	0.388827
16	0.788031	0.673625	0.533908	0.494469	0.458112	0.424581	0.393646	0.365095
17	0.776385	0.657195	0.513373	0.473176	0.436297	0.402447	0.371364	0.342813
18	0.764912	0.641166	0.493628	0.452800	0.415521	0.381466	0.350344	0.321890
19	0.753607	0.625528	0.474642	0.433302	0.395734	0.361579	0.330513	0.302244
20	0.742470	0.610271	0.456387	0.414643	0.376889	0.342729	0.311805	0.283797
21	0.731498	0.595386	0.438834	0.396787	0.358942	0.324862	0.294155	0.266476
22	0.720688	0.580865	0.421955	0.379701	0.341850	0.307926	0.277505	0.250212
23	0.710037	0.566697	0.405726	0.363350	0.325571	0.291873	0.261797	0.234941
24	0.699544	0.552875	0.390121	0.347703	0.310068	0.276657	0.246979	0.220602
25	0.689206	0.539391	0.375117	0.332731	0.295303	0.262234	0.232999	0.207138
26	0.679021	0.526235	0.360689	0.318402	0.281241	0.248563	0.219810	0.194496
27	0.668986	0.513400	0.346817	0.304691	0.267848	0.235605	0.207368	0.182625
28	0.659099	0.500878	0.333477	0.291571	0.255094	0.223322	0.195630	0.171479
29	0.649359	0.488661	0.320651	0.279015	0.242946	0.211679	0.184557	0.161013
30	0.639762	0.476743	0.308319	0.267000	0.231377	0.200644	0.174110	0.151186
31	0.630308	0.465115	0.296460	0.255502	0.220359	0.190184	0.164255	0.141959
32	0.620993	0.453771	0.285058	0.244500	0.209866	0.180269	0.154957	0.133295
33	0.611816	0.442703	0.274094	0.233971	0.199873	0.170871	0.146186	0.125159
34	0.602774	0.431905	0.263552	0.223896	0.190355	0.161963	0.137912	0.117520
35	0.593866	0.421371	0.253415	0.214254	0.181290	0.153520	0.130105	0.110348
36	0.585090	0.411094	0.243669	0.205028	0.172657	0.145516	0.122741	0.103613
37	0.576443	0.401067	0.234297	0.196199	0.164436	0.137930	0.115793	0.097289
38	0.567924	0.391285	0.225285	0.187750	0.156605	0.130739	0.109239	0.091351
39	0.559531	0.381741	0.216621	0.179665	0.149148	0.123924	0.103056	0.085776
40	0.551262	0.372431	0.208289	0.171929	0.142046	0.117463	0.097222	0.080541

Table C-2 Present Value of a Single Sum of 1 (*continued*)

n	7%	8%	9%	10%	12%	14%	16%	20%
1	0.934579	0.925926	0.917431	0.909091	0.892857	0.877193	0.862069	0.833333
2	0.873439	0.857339	0.841680	0.826446	0.797194	0.769468	0.743163	0.694444
3	0.816298	0.793832	0.772183	0.751315	0.711780	0.674972	0.640658	0.578704
4	0.762895	0.735030	0.708425	0.683013	0.635518	0.592080	0.552291	0.482253
5	0.712986	0.680583	0.649931	0.620921	0.567427	0.519369	0.476113	0.401878
6	0.666342	0.630170	0.596267	0.564474	0.506631	0.455587	0.410442	0.334898
7	0.622750	0.583490	0.547034	0.513158	0.452349	0.399637	0.353830	0.279082
8	0.582009	0.540269	0.501866	0.466507	0.403883	0.350559	0.305025	0.232568
9	0.543934	0.500249	0.460428	0.424098	0.360610	0.307508	0.262953	0.193807
10	0.508349	0.463193	0.422411	0.385543	0.321973	0.269744	0.226684	0.161506
11	0.475093	0.428883	0.387533	0.350494	0.287476	0.236617	0.195417	0.134588
12	0.444012	0.397114	0.355535	0.318631	0.256675	0.207559	0.168463	0.112157
13	0.414964	0.367698	0.326179	0.289664	0.229174	0.182069	0.145227	0.093464
14	0.387817	0.340461	0.299246	0.263331	0.204620	0.159710	0.125195	0.077887
15	0.362446	0.315242	0.274538	0.239392	0.182696	0.140096	0.107927	0.064905
16	0.338735	0.291890	0.251870	0.217629	0.163122	0.122892	0.093041	0.054088
17	0.316574	0.270269	0.231073	0.197845	0.145644	0.107800	0.080207	0.045073
18	0.295864	0.250249	0.211994	0.179859	0.130040	0.094561	0.069144	0.037561
19	0.276508	0.231712	0.194490	0.163508	0.116107	0.082948	0.059607	0.031301
20	0.258419	0.214548	0.178431	0.148644	0.103667	0.072762	0.051385	0.026084
21	0.241513	0.198656	0.163698	0.135131	0.092560	0.063826	0.044298	0.021737
22	0.225713	0.183941	0.150182	0.122846	0.082643	0.055988	0.038188	0.018114
23	0.210947	0.170315	0.137781	0.111678	0.073788	0.049112	0.032920	0.015095
24	0.197147	0.157699	0.126405	0.101526	0.065882	0.043081	0.028380	0.012579
25	0.184249	0.146018	0.115968	0.092296	0.058823	0.037790	0.024465	0.010483
26	0.172195	0.135202	0.106393	0.083905	0.052521	0.033149	0.021091	0.008735
27	0.160930	0.125187	0.097608	0.076278	0.046894	0.029078	0.018182	0.007280
28	0.150402	0.115914	0.089548	0.069343	0.041869	0.025507	0.015674	0.006066
29	0.140563	0.107328	0.082155	0.063039	0.037383	0.022375	0.013512	0.005055
30	0.131367	0.099377	0.075371	0.057309	0.033378	0.019627	0.011648	0.004213
31	0.122773	0.092016	0.069148	0.052099	0.029802	0.017217	0.010042	0.003511
32	0.114741	0.085200	0.063438	0.047362	0.026609	0.015102	0.008657	0.002926
33	0.107235	0.078889	0.058200	0.043057	0.023758	0.013248	0.007463	0.002438
34	0.100219	0.073045	0.053395	0.039143	0.021212	0.011621	0.006433	0.002032
35	0.093663	0.067635	0.048986	0.035584	0.018940	0.010194	0.005546	0.001693
36	0.087535	0.062625	0.044941	0.032349	0.016910	0.008942	0.004781	0.001411
37	0.081809	0.057986	0.041231	0.029408	0.015098	0.007844	0.004121	0.001176
38	0.076457	0.053690	0.037826	0.026735	0.013481	0.006880	0.003553	0.000980
39	0.071455	0.049713	0.034703	0.024304	0.012036	0.006035	0.003063	0.000816
40	0.066780	0.046031	0.031838	0.022095	0.010747	0.005294	0.002640	0.000680

Table C–3 Future Amount of an Ordinary Annuity of 1

n	1½%	2½%	4%	4½%	5%	5½%	6%	6½%
1	1.000000	1.000000	1.000000	1.000000	1.000000	1.000000	1.000000	1.000000
2	2.015000	2.025000	2.040000	2.045000	2.050000	2.055000	2.060000	2.065000
3	3.045225	3.075625	3.121600	3.137025	3.152500	3.168025	3.183600	3.199225
4	4.090903	4.152516	4.246464	4.278191	4.310125	4.342266	4.374616	4.407175
5	5.152267	5.256329	5.416323	5.470710	5.525631	5.581091	5.637093	5.693641
6	6.229551	6.387737	6.632975	6.716892	6.801913	6.888051	6.975319	7.063728
7	7.322994	7.547430	7.898294	8.019152	8.142008	8.266894	8.393838	8.522870
8	8.432839	8.736116	9.214226	9.380014	9.549109	9.721573	9.897468	10.076856
9	9.559332	9.954519	10.582795	10.802114	11.026564	11.256260	11.491316	11.731852
10	10.702722	11.203382	12.006107	12.288209	12.577893	12.875354	13.180795	13.494423
11	11.863262	12.483466	13.486351	13.841179	14.206787	14.583498	14.971643	15.371560
12	13.041211	13.795553	15.025805	15.464032	15.917127	16.385591	16.869941	17.370711
13	14.236830	15.140442	16.626838	17.159913	17.712983	18.286798	18.882138	19.499808
14	15.450382	16.518953	18.291911	18.932109	19.598632	20.292572	21.015066	21.767295
15	16.682138	17.931927	20.023588	20.784054	21.578564	22.408663	23.275970	24.182169
16	17.932370	19.380225	21.824531	22.719337	23.657492	24.641140	25.672528	26.754010
17	19.201355	20.864730	23.697512	24.741707	25.840366	26.996403	28.212880	29.493021
18	20.489376	22.386349	25.645413	26.855084	28.132385	29.481205	30.905653	32.410067
19	21.796716	23.946007	27.671229	29.063562	30.539004	32.102671	33.759992	35.516722
20	23.123667	25.544658	29.778079	31.371423	33.065954	34.868318	36.785591	38.825309
21	24.470522	27.183274	31.969202	33.783137	35.719252	37.786076	39.992727	42.348954
22	25.837580	28.862856	34.247970	36.303378	38.505214	40.864310	43.392290	46.101636
23	27.225144	30.584427	36.617889	38.937030	41.430475	44.111847	46.995828	50.098242
24	28.633521	32.349038	39.082604	41.689196	44.501999	47.537998	50.815577	54.354628
25	30.063024	34.157764	41.645908	44.565210	47.727099	51.152588	54.864512	58.887679
26	31.513969	36.011708	44.311745	47.570645	51.113454	54.965981	59.156383	63.715378
27	32.986678	37.912001	47.084214	50.711324	54.669126	58.989109	63.705766	68.856877
28	34.481479	39.859801	49.967583	53.993333	58.402583	63.233510	68.528112	74.332574
29	35.998701	41.856296	52.966286	57.423033	62.322712	67.711354	73.639798	80.164192
30	37.538681	43.902703	56.084938	61.007070	66.438848	72.435478	79.058186	86.374864
31	39.101762	46.000271	59.328335	64.752388	70.760790	77.419429	84.801677	92.989230
32	40.688288	48.150278	62.701469	68.666245	75.298829	82.677498	90.889778	100.033530
33	42.298612	50.354034	66.209527	72.756226	80.063771	88.224760	97.343165	107.535710
34	43.933092	52.612885	69.857909	77.030256	85.066959	94.077122	104.183755	115.525531
35	45.592088	54.928207	73.652225	81.496618	90.320307	100.251364	111.434780	124.034690
36	47.275969	57.301413	77.598314	86.163966	95.836323	106.765189	119.120867	133.096945
37	48.985109	59.733948	81.702246	91.041344	101.628139	113.637274	127.268119	142.748247
38	50.719885	62.227297	85.970336	96.138205	107.709546	120.887324	135.904206	153.026883
39	52.480684	64.782979	90.409150	101.464424	114.095023	128.536127	145.058458	163.973630
40	54.267894	67.402554	95.025516	107.030323	120.799774	136.605614	154.761966	175.631916

Table C–3 Future Amount of an Ordinary Annuity of 1 (*continued*)

n	7%	8%	9%	10%	12%	14%	16%	20%
1	1.000000	1.000000	1.000000	1.000000	1.000000	1.000000	1.000000	1.000000
2	2.070000	2.080000	2.090000	2.100000	2.120000	2.140000	2.160000	2.200000
3	3.214900	3.246400	3.278100	3.310000	3.374400	3.439600	3.505600	3.640000
4	4.439943	4.506112	4.573129	4.641000	4.779328	4.921144	5.066496	5.368000
5	5.750739	5.866601	5.984711	6.105100	6.352847	6.610104	6.877135	7.441600
6	7.153291	7.335929	7.523335	7.715610	8.115189	8.535519	8.977477	9.929920
7	8.654021	8.922803	9.200435	9.487171	10.089012	10.730491	11.413873	12.915904
8	10.259803	10.636628	11.028474	11.435888	12.299693	13.232760	14.240093	16.499085
9	11.977989	12.487558	13.021036	13.579477	14.775656	16.085347	17.518508	20.798902
10	13.816448	14.486562	15.192930	15.937425	17.548735	19.337295	21.321469	25.958682
11	15.783599	16.645487	17.560293	18.531167	20.654583	23.044516	25.732904	32.150419
12	17.888451	18.977126	20.140720	21.384284	24.133133	27.270749	30.850169	39.580502
13	20.140643	21.495297	22.953385	24.522712	28.029109	32.088654	36.786196	48.496603
14	22.550488	24.214920	26.019189	27.974983	32.392602	37.581065	43.671987	59.195923
15	25.129022	27.152114	29.360916	31.772482	37.279715	43.842414	51.659505	72.035108
16	27.888054	30.324283	33.003399	35.949730	42.753280	50.980352	60.925026	87.442129
17	30.840217	33.750226	36.973705	40.544703	48.883674	59.117601	71.673030	105.930555
18	33.999033	37.450244	41.301338	45.599173	55.749715	68.394066	84.140715	128.116666
19	37.378965	41.446263	46.018458	51.159090	63.439681	78.969235	98.603230	154.740000
20	40.995492	45.761964	51.160120	57.274999	72.052442	91.024928	115.379747	186.688000
21	44.865177	50.422921	56.764530	64.002499	81.698736	104.768418	134.840506	225.025600
22	49.005739	55.456755	62.873338	71.402749	92.502584	120.435996	157.414987	271.030719
23	53.436141	60.893296	69.531939	79.543024	104.602894	138.297035	183.601385	326.236863
24	58.176671	66.764759	76.789813	88.497327	118.155241	158.658620	213.977607	392.484236
25	63.249038	73.105940	84.700896	98.347059	133.333870	181.870827	249.214024	471.981083
26	68.676470	79.954415	93.323977	109.181765	150.333934	208.332743	290.088267	567.377300
27	74.483823	87.350768	102.723135	121.099942	169.374007	238.499327	337.502390	681.852760
28	80.697691	95.338830	112.968217	134.209936	190.698887	272.889233	392.502773	819.223312
29	87.346529	103.965936	124.135356	148.630930	214.582754	312.093725	456.303216	984.067974
30	94.460786	113.283211	136.307539	164.494023	241.332684	356.786847	530.311731	1181.881569
31	102.073041	123.345868	149.575217	181.943425	271.292606	407.737006	616.161608	1419.257883
32	110.218154	134.213537	164.036987	201.137767	304.847719	465.820186	715.747465	1704.109459
33	118.933425	145.950620	179.800315	222.251544	342.429446	532.035012	831.267059	2045.931351
34	128.258765	158.626670	196.982344	245.476699	384.520979	607.519914	965.269789	2456.117621
35	138.236878	172.316804	215.710755	271.024368	431.663496	693.572702	1120.712955	2948.341146
36	148.913460	187.102148	236.124723	299.126805	484.463116	791.672881	1301.027028	3539.009375
37	160.337402	203.070320	258.375948	330.039486	543.598690	903.507084	1510.191352	4247.811250
38	172.561020	220.315945	282.629783	364.043434	609.830533	1030.998076	1752.821968	5098.373500
39	185.640292	238.941221	309.066463	401.447778	684.010197	1176.337806	2034.273483	6119.048200
40	199.635112	259.056519	337.882445	442.592556	767.091420	1342.025099	2360.757241	7343.857840

Table C–4 Present Value of an Ordinary Annuity of 1

n	1½%	2½%	4%	4½%	5%	5½%	6%	6½%
1	0.985222	0.975610	0.961538	0.956938	0.952381	0.947867	0.943396	0.938967
2	1.955883	1.927424	1.886095	1.872668	1.859410	1.846320	1.833393	1.820626
3	2.912200	2.856024	2.775091	2.748964	2.723248	2.697933	2.673012	2.648476
4	3.854385	3.761974	3.629895	3.587526	3.545951	3.505150	3.465106	3.425799
5	4.782645	4.645828	4.451822	4.389977	4.329477	4.270284	4.212364	4.155679
6	5.697187	5.508125	5.242137	5.157872	5.075692	4.995530	4.917324	4.841014
7	6.598214	6.349391	6.002055	5.892701	5.786373	5.682967	5.582381	5.484520
8	7.485925	7.170137	6.732745	6.595886	6.463213	6.334566	6.209794	6.088751
9	8.360517	7.970866	7.435332	7.268790	7.107822	6.952195	6.801692	6.656104
10	9.222185	8.752064	8.110896	7.912718	7.721735	7.537626	7.360087	7.188830
11	10.071118	9.514209	8.760477	8.528917	8.306414	8.092536	7.886875	7.689042
12	10.907505	10.257765	9.385074	9.118581	8.863252	8.618518	8.383844	8.158725
13	11.731532	10.983185	9.985648	9.682852	9.393573	9.117079	8.852683	8.599742
14	12.543382	11.690912	10.563123	10.222825	9.898641	9.589648	9.294984	9.013842
15	13.343233	12.381378	11.118387	10.739546	10.379658	10.037581	9.712249	9.402669
16	14.131264	13.055003	11.652296	11.234015	10.837770	10.462162	10.105895	9.767764
17	14.907649	13.712198	12.165669	11.707191	11.274066	10.864609	10.477260	10.110577
18	15.672561	14.353364	12.659297	12.159992	11.689587	11.246074	10.827603	10.432466
19	16.426168	14.978891	13.133939	12.593294	12.085321	11.607654	11.158116	10.734710
20	17.168639	15.589162	13.590326	13.007936	12.462210	11.950382	11.469921	11.018507
21	17.900137	16.184549	14.029160	13.404724	12.821153	12.275244	11.764077	11.284983
22	18.620824	16.765413	14.451115	13.784425	13.163003	12.583170	12.041582	11.535196
23	19.330861	17.332110	14.856842	14.147775	13.488574	12.875042	12.303379	11.770137
24	20.030405	17.884986	15.246963	14.495478	13.798642	13.151699	12.550358	11.990739
25	20.719611	18.424376	15.622080	14.828209	14.093945	13.413933	12.783356	12.197877
26	21.398632	18.950611	15.982769	15.146611	14.375185	13.662495	13.003166	12.392373
27	22.067617	19.464011	16.329586	15.451303	14.643034	13.898100	13.210534	12.574998
28	22.726717	19.964889	16.663063	15.742874	14.898127	14.121422	13.406164	12.746477
29	23.376076	20.453550	16.983715	16.021889	15.141074	14.333101	13.590721	12.907490
30	24.015838	20.930293	17.292033	16.288889	15.372451	14.533745	13.764831	13.058676
31	24.646146	21.395407	17.588494	16.544391	15.592811	14.723929	13.929086	13.200635
32	25.267139	21.849178	17.873551	16.788891	15.802677	14.904198	14.084043	13.333929
33	25.878954	22.291881	18.147646	17.022862	16.002549	15.075069	14.230230	13.459088
34	26.481728	22.723786	18.411198	17.246758	16.192904	15.237033	14.368141	13.576609
35	27.075595	23.145157	18.664613	17.461012	16.374194	15.390552	14.498246	13.686957
36	27.660684	23.556251	18.908282	17.666041	16.546852	15.536068	14.620987	13.790570
37	28.237127	23.957318	19.142579	17.862240	16.711287	15.673999	14.736780	13.887859
38	28.805052	24.348603	19.367864	18.049990	16.867893	15.804738	14.846019	13.979210
39	29.364583	24.730344	19.584485	18.229656	17.017041	15.928662	14.949075	14.064986
40	29.915845	25.102775	19.792774	18.401584	17.159086	16.046125	15.046297	14.145527

Table C–4 Present Value of an Ordinary Annuity of 1 (*continued*)

n	7%	8%	9%	10%	12%	14%	16%	20%
1	0.934579	0.925926	0.917431	0.909091	0.892857	0.877193	0.862069	0.833333
2	1.808018	1.783265	1.759111	1.735537	1.690051	1.646661	1.605232	1.527778
3	2.624316	2.577097	2.531295	2.486852	2.401831	2.321632	2.245890	2.106481
4	3.387211	3.312127	3.239720	3.169865	3.037349	2.913712	2.798181	2.588735
5	4.100197	3.992710	3.889651	3.790787	3.604776	3.433081	3.274294	2.990612
6	4.766540	4.622880	4.485919	4.355261	4.111407	3.888668	3.684736	3.325510
7	5.389289	5.206370	5.032953	4.868419	4.563757	4.288305	4.038565	3.604592
8	5.971299	5.746639	5.534819	5.334926	4.967640	4.638864	4.343591	3.837160
9	6.515232	6.246888	5.995247	5.759024	5.328250	4.946372	4.606544	4.030967
10	7.023582	6.710081	6.417658	6.144567	5.650223	5.216116	4.833227	4.192472
11	7.498674	7.138964	6.805191	6.495061	5.937699	5.452733	5.028644	4.327060
12	7.942686	7.536078	7.160725	6.813692	6.194374	5.660292	5.197107	4.439217
13	8.357651	7.903776	7.486904	7.103356	6.423548	5.842362	5.342334	4.532681
14	8.745468	8.244237	7.786150	7.366687	6.628168	6.002072	5.467529	4.610567
15	9.107914	8.559479	8.060688	7.606080	6.810864	6.142168	5.575456	4.675473
16	9.446649	8.851369	8.312558	7.823709	6.973986	6.265060	5.668497	4.729561
17	9.763223	9.121638	8.543631	8.021553	7.119630	6.372859	5.748704	4.774634
18	10.059087	9.371887	8.755625	8.201412	7.249670	6.467420	5.817848	4.812195
19	10.335595	9.603599	8.950115	8.364920	7.365777	6.550369	5.877455	4.843496
20	10.594014	9.818147	9.128546	8.513564	7.469444	6.623131	5.928841	4.869580
21	10.835527	10.016803	9.292244	8.648694	7.562003	6.686957	5.973139	4.891316
22	11.061240	10.200744	9.442425	8.771540	7.644646	6.742944	6.011326	4.909430
23	11.272187	10.371059	9.580207	8.883218	7.718434	6.792056	6.044247	4.924525
24	11.469334	10.528758	9.706612	8.984744	7.784316	6.835137	6.072627	4.937104
25	11.653583	10.674776	9.822580	9.077040	7.843139	6.872927	6.097092	4.947587
26	11.825779	10.809978	9.928972	9.160945	7.895660	6.906077	6.118183	4.956323
27	11.986709	10.935165	10.026580	9.237223	7.942554	6.935155	6.136364	4.963602
28	12.137111	11.051078	10.116128	9.306567	7.984423	6.960662	6.152038	4.969668
29	12.277674	11.158406	10.198283	9.369606	8.021806	6.983037	6.165550	4.974724
30	12.409041	11.257783	10.273654	9.426914	8.055184	7.002664	6.177198	4.978936
31	12.531814	11.349799	10.342802	9.479013	8.084986	7.019881	6.187240	4.982447
32	12.646555	11.434999	10.406240	9.526376	8.111594	7.034983	6.195897	4.985372
33	12.753790	11.513888	10.464441	9.569432	8.135352	7.048231	6.203359	4.987810
34	12.854009	11.586934	10.517835	9.608575	8.156564	7.059852	6.209792	4.989842
35	12.947672	11.654568	10.566821	9.644159	8.175504	7.070045	6.215338	4.991535
36	13.035208	11.717193	10.611763	9.676508	8.192414	7.078987	6.220119	4.992946
37	13.117017	11.775179	10.652993	9.705917	8.207513	7.086831	6.224241	4.994122
38	13.193473	11.828869	10.690820	9.732651	8.220993	7.093711	6.227794	4.995101
39	13.264928	11.878582	10.725523	9.756956	8.233030	7.099747	6.230857	4.995918
40	13.331709	11.924613	10.757360	9.779051	8.243777	7.105041	6.233497	4.996598

Index

Absences, compensated, 341–342
Accelerated cost recovery system (ACRS), 458–459
Accelerated depreciation methods, 454–456
  declining balance, 454–455
  sum-of-the-years'-digits, 455–456
Account(s), 67, 71
  chart of, 113–114
  contingent liability, 393
  contra, 166
  controlling, 106
  creation of, 67–69
  current, 692
  formal, 71–72
  nominal, 147–150, 209
  noncurrent, 692, 699–700, 704–708
  open, 55, 384, 390
  real, 147, 150
  reciprocal, 662–670
  receivable subsidiary ledger, 106
  T, 70, 71, 722–729
  three-amount-column-form of, 72
  uncollectible, 367–368
  valuation, 367, 377
Accountants, 8–9
Account form of balance sheet, 52–53, 60, 97, 98
Accounting, 4–10
  accrual basis of, 155–156
  cash basis of, 154–156
  constant dollar, 767
  current cost, 768
  double-entry, 95
  entity, 9, **48**
  history of, 5–6
  human resources, 48n
  international, 673–676
  price-level, 767–772
  reasons for studying, 6–7
  software package, 750
  tools of, 70–72
Accounting bases, 154–156
Accounting cycle, 214–215
Accounting entity, 9–10, 27, 48, 52
Accounting equation, 52, 63–65, 105
Accounting information, users of, 7–8
Accounting period, 199n, 457–458
Accounting Principles Board. (APB), 26
Accounting process, 197–199
Accounting Research Bulletins **(ARBs),** 25
  no. 43, 414n, 427n, 542n, 543n, 544n
  no. 51, 661n
Accounting sequence, 109–112
Accounting software package, 750, 752–753, 755–761
Accounting standards, 27
  See also Generally accepted accounting principles
Accounting system, 146–147, 215, **265**
  computerized, 751–755
  developing, 58–74
  integrated, 750
Accounts payable, 56–57, 381
  net price method for recording, 257–258
  payment of, 60–61, 62, 66
  schedule of, 121
Accounts payable subsidiary ledger, 108, 120, 349
Accounts receivable, 55, 364, 365
  aging of, 370–372
  collection of, 63, 66
  credit cards, 364, 365, 377–380
  internal control of, 380–381
  as long-term investment, 641
  schedule of, 120–121

  turnover, 380
  See also Bad debts expense
Accounts receivable subsidiary ledger, 106–108, 119
Accrual(s), 157
  summary, of, 175
Accrual basis of accounting, 155–156
Accrue, 57, 157
Accrued expense, 157, 171–174
Accrued interest receivable, 212–213, 365
Accrued liabilities, 57, **173**
Accrued revenue, 157, 169–171
Accrued wages payable, 213–214
Accumulated depreciation, 168–169
Accumulated earnings. *See* Retained earnings
Accurate interest, 382
Acid-test ratio, 22, 508
Acquisition, 658–659, 670
  See also Affiliate; Subsidiary company
Acquisition information, 671
ACRS. *See* Accelerated cost recovery system
Adjusted cash balance, 329
Adjusted trial balance, 203–204
Adjusting entries, 117, 156
  for bad debt expense, 366
  for interest on notes payable, 388
  for interest on notes receivable, 391
  result of, 209
  reversal of, 177–179
Adjustments, 154–179
  accruals, 157, 169–174
  accrued expenses, 157, 171–174
  accrued revenues, 157, 169–171
  bad debts, 366
  classification of, 156–157
  deferrals, 157, 159–169, 176–177
  for depreciation, 165–169
  for income tax expense, 173–174
  keying of, 203
  long-term cost apportionment, 165–169
  materiality concept and, 175–176
  in merchandising, 252
  of office supplies, 162–163
  of prepaid insurance, 161–162
  of prepaid rent, 159–161
  prior period, 537
  recording in general journal, 207–209
  short-term cost apportionment, 156, 159–163
  short-term revenue apportionment, 156, 163–165
  summary of, 174–175
  of unearned rent, 163–165
  for unrecorded interest expense, 172–173
  for unrecorded interest revenue, 169–171
  for unrecorded wages expense, 171–172
Affiliate, 659–673
  consolidated financial statements, 660
  control of, 659–660
  foreign, 672–673
  intercompany transactions, 661–670
Agent, 528n, 551–552
Aging, Accounts Receivable, 370–372
Aging schedule, 370
All financial resources, 690
Allowance for Doubtful Accounts, 367, 369–375
Allowance to reduce temporary Investments in equity Securities to Market, 623
American Institute of Certified Public Accountants (AICPA), 25
Amortization, 470, 480–481, **583**–599
  of discount on bonds, 586–589, 592–596, 637–639
  interest method of, 583, 589–596, 635–639
  of premium on bonds, 583–586, 589–592, 635–637

  straight line, 583–589, 590–592, 593–594, 596–599, 635–639
Amortization period, 598
Amortization table, 594, 595, 757–758
Annual effective interest rate, 387–388
Annual report, 435, 436
Annuity
  future amount of, 309–311
  ordinary, 309–315
  present value of, 312–315
APB (Accounting Principles Board), 26
APB Opinons, 26, 476
  no. 9, 713
  no. 15, 550
  no. 17, 470n, 471n
  no. 18, 627n, 631n, 659n
  no. 19, 688, 690, 696, 701–702, 708, 709, 713–714, 717
  no. 20, 431n, 454n, 462n
  no. 21, 383n, 583n, 591–592
  no. 22, 435, 662n
  no. 28, 548
  no. 29, 465n, 467n
  no. 30, 550n, 671n
Apportionment, 156–157
  long-term cost, 165–169
  short-term cost, 156, 159–163
  short-term revenue, 156, 163–165
Appropriated retained earnings, 536–537
Arrearage, 523, 524
  dividend, 540
Assets, 12, **48**
  classification of, 55–56
  current, 12, 55–56
  depreciation of, 165–169, 451–462
  estimated salvage value of, 452
  estimated useful life of, 452
  intangible, 447, 448, 469–472
  internal control over, 472–473
  leases, 472, 476–481
  net, 13n, 52
  sale of, 462–464
  tangible plant, 447, 448–468
  trade-in of, 464–468
  wasting, 447, 468–469
  See also Long-lived assets
Auditing, 7
  internal, 396
Auditors' opinion, 30, 321
  qualified, 321
Authorized capital stock, 525
Average costing, 414
Average-for-the-year constant dollars, 768

Back-up files, 754–755
Bad debts expense, 157n, **365**–377
  allowance method, 365–375, 377
  direct write-off method, 375–377
  estimating, 368–373
  recording, 366–367
  recovery of, 374–375, 376
  writing off, 367–368, 374
Balance, 67
Balance sheet, 12–13, 52–54
  account form of, 52–53, 60, 97, 98
  common-size, 73–74
  comparative, 697, 702–704
  consolidated, 436, 474–475, 666, 667
  illustrated, 17, 64–65, 207
  inventory on, 436
  lease on, 481
  in merchandising, 255
  notes receivable on, 393–394
  paid-in capital on, 534
  preparing from trial balance, 123–124
  property, plant, and equipment on, 474–475

Index

Balance Sheet (*continued*)
  report form of, 53–54
  significance of, 22
  transactions and, 59–63, 692–694
Balance sheet approach (to estimating bad debts expense), 368, 369–373
Bank discount, 385
Bank loans, notes for, 384–388
Bank reconciliation, 329–333
Bank statement, 327–334
  letter codes on, 328–329
  reconciliation of, 329–333
Bargain purchase option, 477
Bearer bonds, 575
Blank endorsement, 395
Blanket percentage method for obtaining allowance for doubtful accounts, 372–373
Blue-chip stocks, 618
Bond(s), 57, 574–603
  amortization of discount on, 586–589, 592–596
  amortization of premium on, 583–586, 589–592
  callable, 576, 600
  capital stock vs., 576–578
  control and, 578
  convertible, 576, 601
  coupon, 575
  debenture, 576, 586–588
  default on, 575
  discounted, 580–581
  income, 576
  internal control of, 605
  investment in, 365
  leverage and, 577–578
  as long-term investment, 633–641
  mortgage, 575, 583–586
  premium on sale of, 581–582
  purchase of, 599–601
  recall of, 599–600
  registered, 575
  retirement of, 588, 599–603
  secured, 575
  serial, 576, 599
  stated interest rate on, 578, 579, 633
  taxes and, 577–578
  as temporary investment, 618–620
  unsecured, 576
  yield on, 581, 582, 586
Bond amortization table, 757–758
Bond certificate, 574, 605
Bondholders, 574
  corporate control and, 578
  protection of, 603
Bondholders' equity, 577
Bond indenture, 574, 603
Bond Interest Earned, 604–605, **619**
Bond interest expense, 584–586, 587–588, 589, 590, 592–593, 594–596, 597–599
Bond issues, 578–580
  at a discount on an interest date, 586–588, 592–594
  at a discount requiring interest to be accrued at end of year, 588–589, 594–596
  at face value, 579–580
  at a premium on an interest date, 583–586, 589–592
  between interest dates, 596–599
Bond purchases:
  at a discount on an interest date, 637–639
  at face value on an interest date, 634–635
  at a premium on an interest date, 635–637
  between interest dates, 639–641
Bond sinking fund, 576, 601–603
Bond yield table, 582
Bonus method of admitting partner, 507
Book value, 166, 167
  of common stock, 548–549
  of preferred stock, 549
  sale of assets and, 463–464

stock of investee corporation purchased at, 631–633
  trade-in of assets and, 465–467
Boot, 467
Budget, 8, 688
Buildings, 56
  purchase of, 60, 61, 66
  See also Property, plant, and equipment
Business acquisition, 658–659, 670
  See also Affiliate; Subsidiary company
Business document, 59
Business organization, forms of, 49–52
  See also Corporation; Partnership; Single proprietorship

Callable bonds, 576, 600
Call provision, 600
Capital:
  paid-in, 521–534
  raising of, 497
  sources of, 521–522
  See also Legal capital; Working capital
Capital expenditures, 460–461
  initial, 448
Capitalization, 448
Capital leases, 476–481
  accounting for, 478–481
  definition, 476
  identifying, 476–478
  on balance sheet, 481
  terminology, 477
Capital stock, 522–535
  authorized, 525
  bonds vs. 576–578
  issued, 525
  issued at a discount, 531
  issued at a premium, 530–532
  no-par value, 525–526
  outstanding, 525, 548–549
  par value of, 522, 525
  recording transactions of, 527–534
  sale of, 527–528
  started value, 526
  subscribed, 530–531, 533
  See also Common stock; Preferred stock
Capital structure (partnership), changes in, 506–508
Carrying value, 454, 583
  See also Book value
Cash, 55, 321–349
  analysis of needs for, 324–325
  checks, 327–334
  forecast, 324, 361, 755–757
  internal control of, 322–323
  payrolls, 337–343
  petty, 325–327
  provided by operations, 710–712
  vouchers, 335–337, 343–349
Cash balance, adjusted, 329
Cash basis for statement of changes in financial position, 690, 708–713, 722, 729
Cash basis of accounting, 154–156
Cashbook 281
Cash discount, 240–241
Cash dividend, 538–540
  accounting for, 539–540
  declaration of, 538–539
  on preferred stock, 540
  receipt of, 628–629
Cash flows, 323
Cash forecast, 324–325, 755–757
Cash management systems, 322–334
Cash over and short, 327
Cash payments journal, 276–280, 281, 333
Cash proceeds from discounted notes, 391–393
Cash receipts journal, 271–276, 281, 333
Cell, (electronic spreadsheet), 755–757
Certified check, 329
Certified Internal Auditor (CIA), 9
Certified Management Accountant (CMA), 9
Certified Public Accountant (CPA), 8–9

Chain discount, 259
Charter, 49, **520,** 522, 528
Chart of accounts, 113–114
Chattel mortgage bonds, 575
Check(s), 327–334
  certified, 329
  for deposit only, 322
  outstanding, 330
Check register, 336, 346–347, 348, 349
Check request, 335
  See also Voucher
Classification, 54–58
  of assets, 55–56
  of liabilities, 56–57
  need for, 54
  of ownership claims, 57–58
Closing entries, 148–149, **209**–210, 256–257
Closing the books, 148–149
Collateral trust bonds, 575
Collection method (of revenue recognition), 29
Common-size balance sheet, 73–74
Common-size income statement, 124–125
Common-size statement, 216
Common-size statement of changes in financial position, 715
Common stock, 50, **57,** 524–525
  book value of, 548–549
  conversion of bonds into, 601
  issuance of, 60, 66
  issued at par for cash, 528–529
  issued at a premium for cash, 530
  issued for organizing services, 529–530
  no par, 532–533
  sale of, 527–528
  subscribed, 530–531, 533
  voting privileges and, 525
Common stock equivalents, 550
Comparative balance sheets, 697, 702–704
Compensated absences, 341–**342**
Compound discount, 307
Compound entry, 95
Compound interest, 302–315
  simple vs., 302–303
  tables for, 777–784
Compound interest techniques, 303–315
  future amount of an ordinary annuity, 309–311
  future amount of a single sum at compound interest, 303–307
  present value of an ordinary annuity, 312–315
  present value of single given sum, 307–309
Computer(s) in accounting, 264, 323, 343, 472, 749–762
Computer hardware, 750
Computer program, 750
Computer software, 750, 752–753, 755–761
Conglomerate, 661
Conservatism, 27
Consistency, 27, 431
Consolidated financial statements, 660–670
  balance sheet, 436, 474–475, 666, 667
  for foreign operations, 676
  work sheets for, 665, 667, 668, 679
Constant dollar(s):
  average-for-the-year, 768
  end-of-year, 768
Constant dollar accounting, 767
Consumer Price Index for All Urban Consumers (CPI–U), 768
Contingency, 23–24
Contingent liability, 391, 394
Contingent liability account, 393
Contra account, 166
Contract interest rate. *See* Stated interest rate
Control. *See* Internal control
Controlling, 8
Controlling account, 106
Controlling interest, 661
Convertible bonds, 576, 601
Convertible preferred stock, 524
Copyright, 471

Corporation, 49–51, 520–522
  acquisitions, 658–672
  advantages of, 50
  bond issues and, 576–578
  charter of, 49, 520, 522, 528
  creation of, 49, 520–521
  directors of, 521, 524
  dividends of (see Dividend)
  foreign operations of, 672–673 (see also International accounting)
  liability in, 50, 520
  parent-subsidiary relationships, 659–672
  sources of capital for, 521–522
  taxation of, 520n, 548, 577–578
  voting privileges in, 525
  See also Capital stock
Cost, 102
  current, 768, 771–772
  depreciable, 452
  executory, 477
  historical, 29, 48, 765
  inventoriable, 469
  of goods sold, 245
  organization, 529
  replacement, 427, 768
  undepreciated, 167
Cost apportionment adjustment:
  long-term, 165–169
  short-term, 156
Costing:
  FIFO, 414, 418–419, 421–422, 433
  LIFO, 414, 419–420, 422–423, 433
  moving average, 422–423
  specific identification, 414–415, 417–418
  weighted average, 414, 420
Cost method of accounting:
  consolidated financial statements and, 666–668
  for recording and valuation of stocks, 627–630
  for recording purchase of treasury stock, 546
Cost of an inventory item, 414
Cost of goods sold accounts, 241–245
Cost principle, 48
Cost recovery basis (of revenue recognition), **29**
Coupon bonds, 575
CPA. See Certified Public Accountant
Credit, 55, **70**–71, 104–105
Credit balances in customer accounts, 379
Credit card receivables, 364, 365, 377–380
Credit card sales slips, 378
Credit entry, 70
Credit memo, 329
Credit memorandum, 240
Creditors, 7, 49
Cumulative preferred stock, 523, 540
Currency, functional, 674
Currency exchange, 672–675
Current account, 692
Current assets, 12, 55–56
Current cost, 768, 771–772
Current cost accounting, 768
Current liabilities, 12, 56–57
Current ratio, 22, 508

Data base, 706
Data base management software, 759–761
Data fields, 760
Data file, 760
Data record, 760
DDB. See Double-declining balance method of depreciation
Debenture bonds, 576, 586–588
Debit, 70–71, 104–105
Debit entry, 70
Debit memo, 328–329
Debt-equity ratios, 72–73
Declared dividends, recognizing, 628
Declining balance method of depreciation, 454–455
Default, 390, 575
Deferral(s), 157, 159–169
  alternative adjustment methods for, 176–177
  long-term cost apportionment, 165–169

short-term cost apportionment, 159–163
short-term revenue apportionment, 163–165
summary of, 175
Deferred serial bonds, 599
Deficit, 535
Deflation, 765
Delivery equipment, 56
Depletion, 468–469
Deposit(s):
  refundable, 365
  in transit, 330
Depreciable cost, 452
Depreciation, 165–169, 451–462
  accelerated cost recovery system and, 458–459
  accumulated, 168–169
  of automobiles, 167–169
  changing of, 461–462
  estimated salvage value and, 452
  estimated useful life and, 452
  of office equipment, 165–167, 451–462
  for partial accounting periods, 457–458
  recording, 459–460
  purpose of, 451
Depreciation expense, 165
Depreciation methods, 452–457
  accelerated, 454–456
  comparison of, 456–457
  declining balance, 454–455, 457, 458
  guidelines for, 459
  production unit, 453–454
  straight line, 165, 452–453, 457
  sum-of-the-years'-digits, 455–456, 457
  working hours, 453
Directors, corporate, 521, 524
Direct write-off method for bad debts expense, 375–377
Disbursement, 102
Disclosure:
  in financial statements, 435, 473–475
  footnote, 671
  full, 28, 393
Discount(s), 243
  amortization of, 586–589, 592–596
  bank, 385
  on bonds, 580–582
  capital stock issued at, 531
  chain, 259
  compound, 307
  purchases, 243, 248, 257–258
  sales, 240–241, 246
  trade, 258–259
Discounting, 55, 391–395
Dishonored note, 390–391
Dissolution, 506
Dividend(s), 13, 51, 103–104, **538**–545
  cash, 538–540, 628–629
  declaration of, 538–539, 628–629
  ex-, 538–539
  internal control of, 551
  on preferred stock, 540
  stock, 541–544, 629–630
Dividend arrearage, 540
Dividends yield rate, 643
Donations, 533–534
  treasury stock, 547
Double-declining balance (DDB) method of depreciation, 454–455, 457, 458n
Double-entry accounting, 95

Earned revenue, 155
Earned surplus. See Retained earnings
Earnings per share (EPS), 122, 125–126, 550–551
  calculation of, 551
  fully diluted, 550
  primary, 550
Earnings retained for use in the business. See Retained earnings
Earnings yield rate, 643
Economic Recovery Tax Act of 1981, 458
Editing (computer), **760**

Effective interest rate, 387–388, 581
Electronic spreadsheet, 755–759
Eliminations, 664
End-of-period process, 147–179, 197–216
  accruals, 155–159, 169–174
  adjustments, 154–179
  closing nominal accounts, 147–149
  deferrals, 157, 159–169, 176–177
  interrelationship of financial statements, 152–154
  postclosing trial balance, 151
  ruling nominal accounts, 149–150
  statement of retained earnings, 151–152
End-of-year constant dollars, 768
Endorsements, 395
Entity concept, 9–10, **27,** 48, 52
Entry. See Journal entry
EPS. See Earnings per share
Equipment, 56
  depreciation of, 165–169, 451–462
  notes for, 383
  See also Property, plant, and equipment
Equipment record, 450, 451
Equities, 12
Equity, 12–13
  See also Owners' equity; Stockholders' equity
Equity method of accounting:
  consolidated financial statements, 668–670
  for investment in stock, 631–633
Equity securities, 623–626
  marketable, 623
  unrealized gain on temporary investment in, 625
  unrealized loss on temporary investment in, 624
  See also Stock
Estimated salvage value, 452
Estimated useful life (EUL) of asset, 452, 470
Exception, management by, 257–258
Ex-dividend, 538–539
Executory costs, 477
Expense, 11, 100–101, **102,** 105
  accrued, 157, 171–174
  bad debts, 157n, 365–377
  depreciation, 165
  general and administrative, 250
  matching with revenue, 155
  operating, 21, 250
  other, 251
  selling, 250
Extraordinary income statement items, 713–714
Extraordinary items, 696

Face value, 384, 385–388, **579**
  bonds issued at, 579–580
Fair market value, 450, 465, 466, 467, 670
FASB (Financial Accounting Standards Board), 26
FASB Statements of Financial Accounting Concepts, 26
  no. 1, 6n
  no. 3, 11n, 48n, 49n, 98n, 100n, 101n, 103n
FASB Statements of Financial Accounting Standards, **26**
  no. 2, 470n
  no. 5, 366n
  no. 12, 623, 624, 630
  no. 13, 476–478, 479n, 480n
  no. 14, 671–672
  no. 16, 537n
  no. 33, 766, 768, 769, 770
  no. 43, 341
  no. 52, 674n
  no. 82, 475, 767, 769
Federal Insurance Contributions Act (FICA), 339
Federal Unemployment Tax Act (FUTA), 339, 340
FICA (Federal Insurance Contributions Act), 339
FIFO (first-in, first-out) costing, 414
  with periodic inventory system, 418–419
  with perpetual inventory system, 421–422
  turnover rate and, 432–433

Index

Financial Accounting Standards Board. *See* FASB
Financial resources:
  sources of, 690
  uses of, 690
Financial Resources Summary, 723, 724, 726
Financial statement, 10–24
  classification in, 54–58
  common-size, 73–74, 124–125, 216, 715
  consolidated, 660–670, 676
  disclosure in, 435, 473–475
  illustrated and explained, 15–21
  interim, 215
  interrelationship of, 15, 152–154
  inventory in, 435
  in merchandising, 253–255
  notes to, 18–20, 23–24, 474, 672
  for partnership, 505–506
  preparing from trial balance, 121–124
  preparing from work sheet, 205–207, 253–255
  property, plant, and equipment in, 473–475
  relationship of, 689
  significance of, 21–24
  for single proprietorship, 500
  See also names of specific financial statements
Financing, short-term, 381–382
Financing transactions, 323
First-in, first-out. *See* FIFO costing
First mortgage bonds, 575
F.O.B. destination, 242–243
F.O.B shipping point, 242
Folio column, 71
Footed, 68
Footnote disclosure, 671
Foreign currency exchange, 673–675
Foreign currency exchange gains and losses, 674
Foreign operations, 672–676
Formula (in computer spreadsheet cell), 755–756
Franchise, 471
Full disclosure, 28, 393
Full endorsement, 395
Fully diluted earnings per share, 550
Functional currency, 674
Funds, long-term, 641–642
Furniture:
  purchase of, 60, 61, 66
  sale of, 61–63, 66
FUTA (Federal Unemployment Tax Act), 339, 340
Future amount of an ordinary annuity, 309–311
Future amount of a single sum at compound interest, 303–307

Gains, 100
General and administrative expenses, 250
General journal, 90
  cash in, 334
  closing entries in, 149, 210, 256–257
  correcting entries in, 281–282
  expansion of, 264–265
  illustrated, 95, 115–116
  journalizing and posting in, 91–97, 115–116
  in merchandising, 256–257
  recording adjustments in, 207–209
  recording expenses in, 101
  recording revenue in, 99
  unusual current transactions in, 281
General ledger, 106
  closing process and, 211
  illustrated, 96, 107, 211
  posting to, 108–109, 117–119
  See also Split ledger
General partner, 496
Generally accepted accounting principles (GAAP), 27–31
George, Claude S., 5n
Going concern, 27
"Going public," 521
Goodwill, 471, 507

Gross margin method (of inventory estimating), **428**–429, 431
Gross margin on sales, 21, **245**
Gross pay, 337–338
Gross price method, 257

Historical cost, 28–29, 48, 766
Human resources accounting, 48n

Imprest petty cash system, 326–327
Income, net, 12, 102, 103, 535
Income bonds, 576
Income statement, 10–12, **103**
  common-size, 124–125
  consolidated, 666–668
  illustrated, 16, 206, 249
  preparing from trial balance, 122
  significance of, 21
  working capital basis, 695
Income statement approach (to estimating bad debts expense), **368**–369
Income Summary account, 500
Income tax:
  adjustment for expense, 173–174
  bonds and, 577–578
  corporate, 520n, 548, 577–578
  depreciation method and, 459
  in merchandising, 251
  of unincorporated business, 497
  See also Taxes
Incorporation, 520–521
  See also Corporation
Incremental interest rate, 477
Index, 769
Individual compensation record, yearly, 340
Individual Retirement Arrangements (IRAs), 338n
Inflation, 24, 766
Initial capital expenditures, 448
Input (computer), 760
Installment basis (of revenue recognition), **29**
Institute of Chartered Accountants, 25
Insurance:
  as long-term investment, 641
  prepaid, 55–56, 161–162
Intangible assets, 447, 448, 469–472
  amortization, 470
  copyright, 471
  franchise, 471
  goodwill, 471
  internal control over, 472–473
  leasehold improvements, 472
  leases, 472, 476–481
  patents, 470–471
Integrated accounting system, 750
Intercompany transactions, 661–670
Interest:
  accurate, 382
  on bank statement, 329
  compound, 301–315, 776–783
  on notes, 385–388
  ordinary at exact time, 382
  simple vs. compound, 302–303
  unrecorded expense, 172–173
  unrecorded revenue, 169–171
  See also Compound interest
Interest formula, 170
Interest method of amortization, 583, 589–596
  bonds issued at a discount on an interest date, 592–594
  bonds issued at a discount requiring interest to be accrued at end of year, 594–596
  bonds issued at a premium on an interest date, 589–592
  bonds purchased at a discount on an interest date, 637–639
  bonds purchased at a premium on an interest date, 635–637
  straight line method vs., 590–592, 593–594
Interest rate:
  on bonds, 578
  effective, 387–388, 581
  incremental, 477

  stated, 578, 579, 633
Interest receivable, accrued, 212–213, 365
Interim statements, 215
Internal auditing, 396
Internal control, 74
  of accounts receivable, 380–381
  over bonds payable, 605
  of cash, 322–323
  of dividends, 551
  over inventory, 259–260, 431–435
  of investments, 643
  of notes receivable, 395–396
  over plant and intangible assets, 472–473
  over stockholders' equity, 551–552
  of unincorporated business, 508
International accounting, 673–676
Inventoriable costs, 469
Inventory, 413–436
  in annual report, 436
  internal control over, 259–260, 431–435
  merchandise, 55, 244–245, 246–248
  turnover, 260, 432
  working capital and, 433–434
Inventory cost, 414–415, 416–417
Inventory estimating, 428–431
  evaluation of methods, 431
  gross margin method of, 428–429, 431
  retail method of, 429–430, 431
Inventory item, cost of, 414
Inventory systems:
  comparison of, 415–416, 424–426
  periodic, 238, 417–420
  perpetual, 238, 420–424
Inventory turnover, 260, 432–433
Inventory valuation, 414–415
  consistency in, 431
  estimation of, 428–430
  FIFO, 414, 418–419, 421–422, 433
  LIFO, 414, 419–420, 422–423, 433
  lower of cost or market, 426–428
  moving average, 422–423
  weighted average, 414, 420
Investee company, 627, 659
Investee corporations, 23
Investment, rate of return on total, 126–127
  See also Long-term investments; Temporary investment
Investment register, 619
Investor, 7
Investor company, 627, 659
Invoice, 239
Issuance at par, 579
Issued capital stock, 525

Journal. *See* General journal; Special journals
Journal entry, 91
  for cash, 333–334
  closing, 148–149, 209–210, 256–257
  compound, 95
  correcting, 281–282
  reversing, 177–179
  unusual current transactions, 281
  See also Adjusting entries; Adjustments
Journalizing, 91–97, 115–116

Keying of adjustments, 203

Land, 56
  as long-term investment, 641
  purchase of, 60, 61, 66
  See also Property, plant, and equipment
Large stock dividend, 543–544
Last-in, first-out. *See* LIFO costing
LCM. *See* Lower of cost or market
Lease, 472
  amortization of, 480–481
  capital, 476–481
  inception of, 477
  operating, 476
  recording, 479
Leasehold improvements, 472

788 Index

Lease payments:
  minimum, 477
  recording, 479–480
Ledger, 72, 91
  accounts payable subsidiary, 108, 120, 349
  accounts receivable subsidiary, 106–108, 119
  cash balance in, 333
  posting to, 108–109, 117–120, 282–283
  stockholders', 544
  See also General ledger; Split ledger
Legal capital, 526
Legal capital approach to stockholders' equity, 530n, **552**–556
Legal liability, 496–497
  contingent, 391, 393, 394
  corporations, 50, 520
  limited, 50, 496, 520
  in partnerships, 51, 496–497
  in single proprietorships, 51, 496–497
  unlimited, 51
Lessee, 476
Lessor, 476
Leverage, 577–578
Liabilities, 12–13, 49
  accrued, 57, 173
  classification of, 56–57
  current, 12, 56–57
Liability. *See* Legal liability
Life insurance, 641
LIFO (last-in, first-out) costing, 414
  with periodic inventory system, 419–420
  with perpetual inventory system, 422–423
  turnover rate and, 433
Limited liability, 50, 496, 520
Limited partner, 496
Liquidation, 508
Liquidity, 708
Long-lived assests, 12, 56, 447–481
  depreciation of, 165–169, 451–462
  intangible, 447, 448, 469–472
  internal control over, 472–473
  leases as, 472, 476–481
  sale of, 462–464
  tangible plant, 447, 448–468
  trade-in of, 464–468
  valuation of, 448–450
  wasting, 447, 468–469
Long-term cost apportionment, 165–169
Long-term funds, 641–642
Long-term investments, 12, 626–643
  in accounts receivable, 641
  in bonds, 633–641
  in funds, 641
  internal control of, 643
  in land, 641
  in life insurance, 641
  in notes, 641
  in stocks, 627–633
Long-term liabilites, 13, 57, 573–605
  defined, 574
  refinancing and, 604
Long-term notes payable, 603–604
  mortgage, 603
  unsecured, 603
Loss, 101
  See also Net loss
Lotus 1-2-3, 755
Lower of cost or market (LCM), 426–428
  recording and valuation of long-term investments, 630
  valuation of temporary investments, 622, 623

Management by exception, 257–258
Markdowns, 430
Marketable equity securities, 623–626
Market value, 526, 541
Markons, 429, 430
Markups, 430
Matching concept, 30, 103, 365
Matching revenues and expenses, 155
Materiality concept, 28, 175–176
Maturity (bonds)
  retirement at, 588

retirement before, 599–601
Maturity date (note), 382
Maturity value (note), 385
Menu (computer), 752–753
Merchandise, notes for, 384
Merchandise inventory, 55, **244**–245, 246–248
Merchandising, 238–260
  closing entries, 256–257
  cost of goods sold accounts, 241–245
  financial statements, 253–255
  gross margin on sales, 245
  income tax expense, 251
  internal control over inventory, 259–260
  management by exception, 257–258
  merchandise inventory accounts, 244–245, 246–248
  net operating margin, 250
  operating expense accounts, 250
  sales revenue accounts, 239–241
  sales taxes, 260
  trade discounts, 258–259
  work sheet, 251–253, 254
Minimum lease payments, 477
Minority interest, 659, 670–671
Module (computer software), 750
Monetary items, 768–769
Mortgage, 57
Mortgage bonds, 575, 583–586
Mortgage note payable, 603
Moving average costing, 422–**423**
Mutual agency, 497

Natural resources, 468–469
Negotiable instrument, 395
Net assets, 13n, 52
Net cost of purchases, 242, **243**–244
Net income, 12, 103, 535
Net loss, 12, 103, 535–536
Net operating margin, 250
Net pay, 338
Net price method, 257–258
Net realizable value, 365
Nominal accounts, 147–150
  closing, 148–149, 209
  ruling, 149–150
Nominal interest rate. *See* Stated interest rate
Noncumulative preferred stock, 523
Nonmonetary items, 769
Nontrade receivables, 364, 365
No-par value capital stock, 50, **525**–526, 532–533
Note(s), 381–396
  dishonored, 390–391
  as long-term investment, 641
  maturity dates of, 382
  promissory, 382
Notes to financial statements, 18–20, 23–24, 474, 672
Notes payable, 57, 382–388
  discounted on face value, 385–388
  interest on, 385–388
  long-term, 603–604
  maturity dates of, 382
  mortgage, 603
  recording procedures for, 383–388
  refinancing and, 604
  unsecured, 603, 641
Notes receivable, 55, 364, 365, **388**–396
  discounting, 391–395
  dishonored, 390–391
  interest on, 391
  internal control of, 395–396
  recording procedures for, 388–390
"Not sufficient funds" (NSF), 332

Objective evidence, 28, 58–59
Office equipment:
  depreciation of, 165–167, 451–462
  notes for, 383
  See also Equipment; Property, plant, and equipment
Office supplies:
  adjustment of, 162–163

  classification of, 56
Open accounts, 55
  notes for, 384, 390
Operating expenses, 21, **250**
Operating lease, 476
Operating Summary, 723, 724, 726
Operating transactions, 323
Opinions of the Accounting Principles Board. *See* APB Opinions
Ordinary annuity, 309–315
Organization cost, 529
Other expenses, 251
Other revenue, 251
Output (computer), 760
Outside directors, 521
Outstanding capital stock, 525, 548–549
Outstanding checks, 330
Owners' equity, 13, 49
  statement of, 500
  See also Partners' equity, Stockholders' equity
Owners' equity accounts, 497–498

Paid-in capital, 521–534
Par value, 525
  issuance at, 528–529
Parent company, 659
Parent-subsidiary relationships, 659–670
  consolidated financial statements, 660–670
  control, 659–660
  eliminations in, 664
  foreign operations, 672–676
  intercompany transactions, 661–670
Participating preferred stock, 523n
Partner(s):
  admission of, 506–507
  death or retirement of, 507
  general, 496–497
  limited, 496
  withdrawals by, 501–502
Partner's drawing account, 502
Partners' equity, statement of, 505–506
Partnership, 51–52, 496–498, 501–508
  changes in capital structure of, 506–508
  characteristics of, 496–497
  division of profits and losses in, 503–505
  financial statements for, 505–506
  formation of, 496, 501
  internal control in, 508
  legal liability of, 496–497
  liquidation of, 508
  mutual agency and, 497
  owners' equity account for, 497–498
  raising capital for, 497
  size of, 496
  taxation of, 497
  withdrawals by partners, 501–502
Partnership property, 497
Par value, 50, 57n, 522, **525,** 528–531, 541
Par value method for recording purchase of treasury stock, 546
Parent company, 659
Password (computer), 753
Patents, 470–471
Pay:
  gross, 337–338
  net, 338
  See also Wages
Payables, 363
  See also Accounts payable; Notes payable
Payment allocations, table of, 479
Payroll deductions, 338–339
Payroll register, 340
Payroll systems, 337–343
Payroll taxes, 338–341
Percentage of completion method of revenue recognition, 29–30
Percentage of receivables (trade) approach. *See* Balance sheet approach to estimating bad debts expense
Percentage of sales approach. *See* Income statement approach to estimating bad debts expense

Index

Periodic inventory system, **238**, 417–420
   FIFO costing, 418–419
   LIFO costing, 419–420
   perpetual vs., 415–416, 424–426
   specific identification costing, 417–418
   weighted average costing, 420
Periodicity, 28
Perpetual inventory system, 238, 420–424
   periodic vs., 415–416, 424–426
Personal computer, 755
Personal computing, 755–761
Petty cash fund, 325–327
Petty cash voucher, 325
Phantom profits, 426n
Planning, 8
Plant. *See* Property, plant, and equipment
Plant assets. *See* Tangible plant assets
Plant expansion, restriction for, 537
Point of sale, 29
Pooling of interests, 664–665
Postclosing trial balance, 151, 210, 212
Posting, 91–97, 108–109, 280–281
   from cash payments journal, 278–280
   from cash receipts journal, 274–275
   from check register, 349
   flow chart for, 93
   illustrated, 94–97, 117–120
   from purchases journal, 270–271
   from sales journal, 268–269
   from voucher register, 349
   to subsidiary ledgers, 282–283
Posting reference (P.R.), 71n
Preferred dividends earned (times), 642
Preferred stock, 523–524
   book value of, 549
   cash dividends on, 540
   convertible, 524
   cumulative, 523, 540
   issued at a premium, 532
   noncumulative, 523, 540
   participating, 523n
   par value of, 522, 525
Premium:
   amortization of, 583–586, 589–592
   on bonds, 581–582
   on common stock, 530
   on preferred stock, 532
Prepaid insurance, 55–56, 161–162
Prepaid items, 55–56
Prepaid rent, 159–161
Present value, 582
Present value of an ordinary annuity, 312–315
Present value of single given sum, 307–309
Price changes, 24, 770–772
Price-earnings ratio, 126
Price index, 768
Price-level accounting, 767–772
Primary earnings per share, 550
Prior period adjustments, 537
Processing, 263
Production unit method of depreciation, 453–454
Profit, 4
   phantom, 426n
   See also Net income
Promissory note, 382
   See also Notes payable
Property, plant, and equipment, 12, **56**
   defined, **448**
   depreciation of, 451–462
   in financial statements, 473–475
   internal control over, 472
   as long-term investment, 641
   notes for, 383
   ratios for investment in, 473
   sale of, 462–464
   trade-in of, 465–468
   valuation of, 448–450
Proprietor:
   equity of, 497–498, 500
   withdrawals by, 499–500
Proprietorship. *See* Single proprietorship
Prospectus, 527–528

Protest fee, 393
Public corporation. *See* Corporation
Purchase accounting, 664
Purchase option, bargain, 477
Purchases account, 242, 247
Purchases Discounts account, 243, 248
Purchases discounts lost method, 257–258
Purchases journal, 269–271
Purchases Returns and Allowances account, 243, 247
Purchasing power gains and losses, 769

Qualified auditors' opinion, 321
Qualified endorsement, 395

Rate of return on stockholders' equity, 127
Rate of return on total investment, 126–127
Ratio, 22
   acid-test, 22, 508
   current, 22, 508
   debt-equity, 72–73
   dividends yield rate, 643
   earnings yield rate, 643
   inventory to working capital, 433–434
   net sales to property, plant, and equipment, 473
   number of times bond interest is earned, 604–605
   number of times preferred dividends is earned, 642
   price-earnings, 126
   property, plant, and equipment to long-term liabilities, 473
   property, plant, and equipment to stockholders' equity, 473
   turnover, 260, 380
Ratio analysis, 508
Real account, 147, 150
Real estate mortgage bonds, 575
Realization, 508
Realized gain on disposal of temporary investments, 621–622
Realized loss on disposal of temporary investments, 620
Receivables, 363
   nontrade, 364, 365
   trade, 364
   See also Accounts receivable; Bad debts expense; Notes receivable
Receivables turnover, 380
Reciprocal accounts, 662–670
Reconciliation (bank), **329**–333
Record system, design of, 261–264
Refinancing, 604
Refundable Deposits, 365
Refunding, 599
Registered bonds, 575
Registrar, 528n, 551–552
Rent, 309
   prepaid, 159–161
   unearned, 163–165
Rents (in annuities), 309
Replacement cost, 427, 769
Report form of balance sheet, 53–54
Report of independent accountants, 20
Residual value, 165
Restricted retained earnings, 536–537
Retail method (of inventory estimating), **429**–430, 431
Retained earnings, 13, 51, 57, 535–545
Retained income. *See* Retained earnings
Retirement (bonds):
   at maturity, 558
   before maturity, **599**–601
Returns and allowances, 377
Revenue, 11, 98–99
   accrued, 157, 169–171
   earned, 155
   matching with expenses, 155
   other, 251
   unrecorded interest, 169–171
Revenue apportionment, short-term, 156, 163–165

Revenue-dollar statement, 215–216
Revenue expenditures, 461
Revenue realization methods, 29–30
Reversing entries, 177–179
Ruling closed nominal accounts, 149–150

Salary, accrual of, 341
   See also Payroll systems; Wages; Wages payable
Sales, gross margin on, 21, 245
Sales account, 239, 246
Sales Discounts account, 240–241, 246
Sales invoice, 239
Sales journal, 267–269
Sales Returns and Allowances account, 240, 246
Sales revenue accounts, 239–241
Sales taxes, 260
Salvage value, 165
   estimated, 452
Schedule of accounts payable, 121
Schedule of accounts receivable, 120–121
Second mortgage bonds, 575
Secured bonds, 575
Securities Act of 1933, 572
Securities and Exchange Commission (SEC), 26
Securities Exchange Act of 1934, 26
Segment reporting, 671–672
Selling expenses, 250
Serial bonds, 576
   deferred, 599
   regular, 599
Service charge, 328
Shareholders. *See* Stockholders
Short-term cost apportionment adjustment, 156, 159–163
Short-term financing, 381–382
Short-term revenue apportionment, 156, 163–165
Simple analytical approach to preparing statement of changes in financial position, 697–708
Single proprietorship, 51, 496–500
   characteristics of, 496–497
   closing of income summary account, 500
   formation of, 498–499
   internal control in, 508
   legal liability of, 496–497
   owner's equity accounts for, 497, 498
   raising capital for, 497
   size of, 496
   statement of owner's equity, 500
   taxation of, 497
   withdrawals by proprietor of, 499–500
Sinking fund, 576, **601**–603
Small stock dividend, 542–543
Software, 750, 752–753, 755–761
Source documents, 261–263
Source of capital approach to stockholders' equity, 530n, 534, **552**–553
Special journals, 265–283
   cashbook, 281
   cash payments, 276–280, 281
   cash receipts, 271–276, 281
   purchases, 269–271
   sales, 267–269
Specific identification method (of inventory valuation), **414**–415, 417–418
Split ledger, 662
Stable dollar concept, 29
Stated capital. *See* Legal capital
Stated interest rate, 578, 579, **633**
Stated value, 526
Statement classification, 55
   See also Classification
Statement of changes in financial position, 14–15, **687**–729
   cash basis, 690, 708–713, 722, 729
   content of, 689–690
   evolution of, 689–690
   objectives of, 688
   significance of, 22–23
   simple analytical method for preparing, 697–708

Index

Statement of changes in financial position (*continued*)
   T account method for, 722–729
   working capital basis, 690, 691–708, 715–728
   work sheet, for, 716–722
Statement of changes in stockholders' equity, 21
Statement of owner's equity, 500
Statement of partners' equity, 505–506
Statement of retained earnings, 13–14, 123
   with beginning balance, 151–152
   illustrated, 16, 206
   in merchandising, 255
   preparing from trial balance, 123
   significance of, 21
Statements of Financial Accounting Concepts. *See* FASB Statements of Financial Accounting Concepts
Statements of Financial Accounting Standards (SFAS). *See* FASB Statements of Financial Accounting Standards
Statements of sources and uses of funds, 689
State unemployment compensation tax, 339
Stock:
   blue-chip, 618
   convertible, 524
   cost method of recording and valuation of investment in, 627–630
   cumulative preferred, 523, 540
   equity method of accounting for investment in, 631–633
   issuance of, 60, 63, 521
   as long-term investment, 627–633
   noncumulative preferred, 523, 540
   participating, 523n
   price per share of, 542
   purchase of, 627–628
   recording and valuation at lower of cost or market, 630–631
   sale of, 527–528
   subscribed, 530–531, 533
   as temporary investment, 621–626
   See also Capital stock; Common stock; Preferred stock; Treasury stock
Stock certificate, 50
Stock certificate book, 551
Stock dividend, 541–544
   advantages of, 542
   impact of, 541–542
   large, 543–544
   receipt of, 629–630
   small, 542–543
Stockholders, 49, 522n
Stockholders' equity, 13, 17, 49
   classifications, 57
   expenses and, 105
   issuance of common stock and, 60, 66
   legal capital approach to, 530n, 552–556
   rate of return on, 127–128
   recording changes in, 98–105
   source of capital approach to, 530n, 534, 552, 553
   sources of, 13, 521–522
   statement of changes in, 21
Stockholders' ledger, 544
Stock indenture, 523
Stock split, 544–545, 629–630
Stock subscription, 530–531, 533
Store equipment, 56
Store supplies, 56
Straight line method of amortization, 583–589
   bonds issued at a discount on an interest date, 586–588, 593–594
   bonds issued at a discount requiring interest to be accrued at end of year, 588–589
   bonds issued at a premium on an interest date, 583–586, 590–592
   bonds issued between interest dates, 596–599
   bonds purchased at a discount on an interest date, 635–639
   bonds purchased at a premium on an interest date, 635–637
   interest method vs., 590–592, 593–594

Straight line method of depreciation, 165, 452–453, 457
Subscribed stock, 530–531
Subsidiary company:
   acquisition of, 658–**659**
   consolidated financial statements, 660–670
   control of, 659–660
   foreign, 672–673
   intercompany transactions, 661–670
Subsidiary ledger, 106–109
   accounts payable, 108, 120
   accounts receivable, 106–108, 119
   posting to, 108–109, 119–120, 282–283
   stockholders', 544
Sum-of-the-years'-digits (SYD) method of depreciation, 455–456, 457
SYD. *See* Sum-of-the-years'-digits method of depreciation

Table of payment allocations, 479
T account, 70, 71
T account method for preparing statement of changes in financial position, 722–729
T account work sheet, 725–726, 727–728
Tangible plant assets, 447, 448–468
   depreciation of, 451–462
   sale of, 462–464
   trade-in of, 465–468
   valuation of, 448–450
Taxable wage base, 339
Tax Equity and Fiscal Responsibility Act of 1982, 539n, 575n
Taxes:
   accounting information and, 7–8
   payroll, 338–340, 341
   sales, 260
   unemployment, 339
   See also Income tax
Tax rate, 339–340
Template (electronic spreadsheet), 757
Temporary investment(s), 55, 618–626
   bonds as, 618–620
   cost of, 619
   realized gain on disposal of, 621–622
   realized loss on disposal of, 620
   stocks as, 621–626
   valuation of, 622–626
Temporary investment cost, 619
Time period zero, 307
Times earnings, 126
Tombstone ad, 527–528
Trade discounts, 258–259
Trade-ins, 464–468
Trade receivables, 364
Trading on the bondholders' equity, 577
Transaction(s), 58–67
   accumulating data on, 65–67
   analyzing, 114–115
   balance sheet and, 59–63, 692–694
   journalizing, 115–116
Transaction gains or losses, 673
Transfer agent, 528n, 551–552
Translation gains and losses, 673, 674–676
Transportation In account, 242, 247
Treasury stock, 525, 545–548
   purchase of, 546
   reissuance of, 546–547
   stock donations, 547
Trial balance, 68, 70
   adjusted, 203–204, 253
   in merchandising, 252, 253
   postclosing, 151, 210, 212
   preparing, 95–97, 120
   preparing financial statements from, 121–124
Truth in Lending Law, 388n
Turnover rate, 260, 380, 432–433
Turnover ratio, 508

Uncollectible accounts, 367–368
   See also Bad debts expense
Undepreciated cost, 167
Underwriters, 527
Unearned rent, 163–165

Unemployment taxes, 339
Uniform Partnership Act, 51n, 496, 503n
Unlimited liability, 51
Unrealized gain on temporary investments in equity securities, 625
Unrealized loss on temporary investment in equity securities, 624
Unsecured bonds, 576
User friendly software, 752

Valuation:
   of inventory, 414
   of long-term investments, 630, 633
   of stock, 630, 633
   of temporary investments, 622–626
Valuation accounts, 367, 377
Value:
   book, 454n
   carrying, 454, 583
   face, 384, 385–388, 579–580
   fair market, 450, 465, 466, 467, 670
   market, 526, 541
   net realizable, 365
   no-par, 50, 525–526, 532–533
   present, 582
   residual, 165
   salvage, 165
   stated, 526
   See also Book value
Voucher, 335–337, 343–349
   advantages of, 377
   cancelling, 348–349
   limitations of, 337
   paying, 347
   petty cash, 325
   recording, 347–348
   replacing, 348–349
   system, 335
   unpaid, 347
Voucher register, 336, 344–346, 347, 349
Vouchers Payable, 345–346

Wage base, 339–340
Wages, unrecorded, 171–172
   See also Payroll systems
Wages payable, accrued, 213–214, 341
Wasting assets, 447, 468–469
Weighted average costing, 414, **420**
Weighted average shares, 21
"Without recourse" endorsement, 395
Working capital, 22, 433, 689
   business transactions affecting, 692–694
   calculation of, 22
   decrease in, 692
   funds as, 689
   increase in, 692
   inflows and outflows, 691
   provided by operations, 694–697
   ratio of inventory to, 433–434
   schedule of changes in, 698–699
   sources of, 691, 692, 700
   uses of, 691, 692, 700
Working capital basis for statement of changes in financial position, 690, 691–708, 715–728
Working hours method of depreciation, 453
Work sheet, 199–210
   completion of, 204–205
   for consolidated statements, 665, 667, 668, 669
   illustrated, 200, 202, 254
   for merchandising business, 251–253, 254
   overview of, 200–201
   preparation of, 201–204
   preparation of financial statements from, 205–207, 253–255, 716–722
   recording closing entries from, 209–210
   T account, 725–726, 727–728
Write off:
   direct method, 375–377
   of uncollectible accounts, 367–368, 374

Yearly individual compensation record, 340
Yield, 581, 582, 586

Check List of Key Figures for Exercises and Problems

Chapter 1
E1–5	Net income understated by $95,000 = ($125,000 − $30,000)
E1–6	$792,000
E1–7	609,000 shares
E1–8	Total to Julia Klein, $1,170
E1–9	(1) 1983, 1.906 to 1; 1982, 2.264 to 1
E1–10	$431,277,000
E1–12	$1,095,000
P1–1A	Net income, $144,462,000
P1–2A	Current ratios, 1983, 1.05 to 1; 1982, 0.84 to 1
P1–3A	(1) 1987, 28.28%; 1986, 33.45%
P1–4A	(1) 62.8%
P1–6A	Net income, $124,401
P1–7A	(1) Ford; (2) General Motors; (3) Republic Airlines
P1–1B	Net income, $133,443,000
P1–2B	Current ratios, 1983, 1.40 to 1; 1982, 1.13 to 1
P1–3B	(1) 1987, 28.28%; 1986, 33.44%
P1–4B	(2) 37.2%
P1–6B	Net income, $273,682
P1–7B	Delta Air Lines: current ratio, 0.61 to 1

Chapter 2
E2–2	Total current liabilities, $69,500
E2–3	Total current assets, $55,600
E2–4	Total property, plant, and equipment, $360,000
E2–5	Total current liabilities, $17,500
E2–7	Property, plant, and equipment, $304,000
E2–8	(1) Total assets, $644,500
E2–10	(2) Trial balance totals, $471,600
E2–13	(2) Long-term liabilities, $122,000 (4) Common stock, $137,000
P2–1A	(1) Amount of notes payable, $42,000
P2–2A	(1) Total assets, $530,400
P2–3A	(1) Total assets, $96,950 (3) Total current assets, 44.3%
P2–4A	(2) Trial balance totals, $166,000
P2–5A	(2) Trial balance totals, $329,000
P2–1B	(1) Amount of notes payable, $7,000
P2–2B	(1) Total assets, $387,920
P2–3B	(2) Total assets, $184,200 (3) Total current assets, 46.8%
P2–4B	(2) Trial balance totals, $306,500
P2–5B	(2) Trial balance totals, $268,050
P2–6B	(1) Trial balance totals, $310,000

Chapter 3
E3–1	Step 4—preparing a trial balance
E3–4	(3) Trial balance totals, $471,600
E3–9	(3) Total accounts receivable, $70
E3–10	(1) Net income, $30,390
E3–11	Retained earnings, February 28, 1987, $3,030
E3–12	(1) Net income, $88,800 Total assets, $335,050
E3–13	Jul. 1, 1987 balance, $20,200
P3–1A	(3) Trial balance totals, $216,000
P3–2A	(3) Trial balance totals, $390,220
P3–3A	(3) Total accounts payable $6,800
P3–4A	(6) Trial balance totals, $28,875
P3–5A	(1) Net income, $14,857
P3–1B	(3) Trial balance totals, $331,500
P3–2B	(3) Trial balance totals, $706,800
P3–3B	(3) Total accounts receivable, $150
P3–4B	(6) Trial balance totals, $65,240
P3–5B	(1) Net income, $29,714

Chapter 4
E4–1	Income Summary credit, $130,000
E4–2	Income Summary debit, $8,000
E4–3	Net income, $35,390
E4–4	Income Summary credit, $25,000
E4–5	(e) Debit Wages Expense, $10,560
E4–6	$1,730
E4–7	(e) Depreciation expense, $500
E4–8	Credit Unearned Subscriptions, $54,000
E4–9	Income tax expense, $116,900
E4–10	(2) Interest expense, $900
E4–11	Debit Insurance Expense, $4,300
E4–12	(a) Credit Office Supplies Expense, $680
E4–13	September 30: Accrued interest receivable, $5.25; Accrued interest payable, $15.56
E4–14	Insurance expense understated by $800
E4–15	Accrued wages payable, $600
E4–16	(1) Debit Insurance Expense, $8,000; (2) No reversing entry
P4–1A	(2) Net income, $73,200
P4–2A	(2) Depreciation expense, $3,750
P4–3A	(b) Accumulated Depreciation—Automobiles, Contra-asset; balance, $9,000
P4–4A	(c) Insurance expense, $1,920
P4–5A	(2d) Credit Advertising Expense, $2,380
P4–6A	Net income, $7,050; Common-size percent, 26%
P4–1B	(2) Net income, $44,600
P4–2B	(2) Depreciation expense, $1,700
P4–3B	(b) Accumulated Depreciation—Vans, Contra-asset; balance, $10,800
P4–4B	(c) Insurance expense, $2,955.75
P4–5B	(2d) Credit Advertising Expense, $600
P4–6B	(3) Revised net income, $43,500

Chapter 5
E5–1	Revised net income, $27,952.50
E5–2	Net income, $20,000
E5–3	Accrued interest receivable, $213.33; payable, $31.25
E5–4	(1)Debit Insurance Expense, $1,800; (2)credit Rent Expense, $3,000
E5–5	(3) Net income, $582
E5–6	Net income, $13,650
E5–7	Net income, $12,600
E5–8	Net income, $4,460
P5–1A	Net income, $8,999
P5–2A	Net income, $27,909
P5–3A	Net income, $14,299
P5–4A	Net income, $12,357; total assets, $236,560
P5–5A	Net income, $22,844
P5–6A	Net income, $5,485.50; accounts receivable, $1,464.00; payable, $600.00
P5–7A	Retained earnings, December 31, 1987, $35,624
P5–1B	Net income, $12,187
P5–2B	Net income, $13,940
P5–3B	Net income, $17,482
P5–4B	Net income, $15,082; total assets, $283,072
P5–5B	Net income, $9,857
P5–6B	Net income, $10,941.28; accounts receivable, $2,928.00; payable, $1,200.00
P5–7B	Retained earnings, December 31, 1987, $13,500

Chapter 6
E6–2	Net sales, $12,570
E6–3	Gross sales, $52,000
E6–4	Net income, $30,105
E6–5	(1) Cash, $8,839; (3) Cash, $9,114
E6–8	June 20 Accounts Receivable credit, $10,204.08
E6–9	Purchases debit, $8,208
E6–10	Cash debit, $18,928
E6–11	Total journalized, $500
E6–12	Amounts journalized, $2,275 and $9,345
E6–13	Cash total, $20,462
E6–14	Cash total, $26,270
P6–1A	Cash account balance, $8,114.60
P6–2A	Net income, $11,466
P6–3A	Net income, $175,901; total assets, $1,115,021
P6–4A	(1b) Cost of goods sold, $695; (2b) Cost of goods sold, $691.25
P6–5A	Sales journal total, $11,500
P6–6A	Purchases journal total, $11,900
P6–7A	Sales increase, $20,794 = 4.2%
P6–1B	Cash account balance, $10,652.60
P6–2B	Net income, $15,463
P6–3B	Net income, $177,312; total assets, $1,022,518
P6–4B	(1b) Cost of goods sold, $1,430; (2b) Cost of goods sold, $1,421
P6–5B	Sales journal total, $19,550
P6–6B	Purchases journal total, $19,040
P6–7B	Sales increase, $1,210,164 = 32.8%

Chapter 7
E7–1	(3) a; (4) b
E7–2	(1) $18,903.08; (2) $9,034.82; (3) $14,618.38
E7–3	(1) $9,784.12; (2) $1,507.56; (3) $1,615.06
E7–4	$6,548.59
E7–5	$2,767.41
E7–6	$33,438.87
E7–7	$11,911.23
E7–8	$34,182.80
E7–9	$7,270.47
E7–10	$627.03
E7–11	Annual payments, $8,771.59
E7–12	One year: $251.08
E7–13	(2) $2,466.57
P7–1A	$52,880.83
P7–2A	Rents = $30,360.07
P7–3A	Rents = $7,791
P7–4A	Rents = $1,401.80
P7–5A	Rents = $14,299.55
P7–1B	$99,680.65
P7–2B	Rents = $21,200.32
P7–3B	Rents = $12,078.88
P7–4B	Rents = $1,991.41
P7–53	Rents = $10,117.67

Chapter 8
E8–2	Cash credit, $901.90
E8–3	Cash shortage, $1.62
E8–4	(1) d; (2) a; (9) a; (10) c
E8–5	Adjusted cash balance, $21,999.17
E8–6	Cash debit, $108.39; Cash credit, $78.60
E8–7	Adjusted cash balance, $8,222.60
E8–8	Gross pay, $661.50; net pay, $464.05
E8–9	Payroll tax expense, $723.85
E8–10	Vacation pay expense, $2,800
E8–11	Vouchers Payable credits, $8,625; debits, $6,150
E8–12	Vouchers Payable credits, $5,352; debits, $5,352
E8–13	Vouchers Payable, $6,450 gross
P8–1A	(2) Cash credit, $981.35
P8–2A	Adjusted cash balance, $7,321.20
P8–3A	Adjusted cash balance, $10,871.56
P8–4A	Vouchers Payable balance, $6,600
P8–1B	(2) Cash credit, $1,278.65
P8–2B	Adjusted cash balance, $3,660.60
P8–3B	Adjusted cash balance, $21,743.12
P8–4B	Vouchers Payable balance, $11,430
P8–5B	Cash balance, March 31, $10,130

Chapter 9
E9–1	Long-term investments, $52,000 and $18,500
E9–3	(1) Bad debts expense, $3,612
E9–4	(1) Bad debts expense, $4,148.40
E9–5	Cash received, $560,900
E9–6	S, $54,400; CP, $39,500
E9–8	Cash debit, $20,246
E9–9	March 1 note due July 29, 1987; maturity value, $3,200
E9–10	Accrued interest receivable, $229.75
E9–11	(2) December 31 notes payable, $15,000 minus discount of $375
E9–12	(2) Notes payable, $12,000; Accrued interest payable, $170
E9–13	December 31 accrued interest receivable, $69
E9–14	Cash proceeds, $1,231.36
E9–15	Cash proceeds, $5,510.70

Check List of Key Figures for Exercises and Problems

P9–1A	(2) Account balance, December 31, 1988, $13,025	E11–12 (a) for 1987, 1.26; for 1986, 1.10	E13–12 Total stockholders' equity, $2,303,200
P9–2A	(3) Total accounts receivable, December 8, $27,600	E11–14 January 1, $125,186.78; December 31, $12,518.68	E13–13 (c) Book value per preferred share, $112
P9–3A	(3) Bad debts expense, $3,086.55	P11–1A (1) Building, $35,000; Production Equipment, $120,000; Cleaning Equipment, $80,000	(d) Book value per common share, $25.91
P9–4A	Interest expense recognized December 31, $190	P11–2A 1985 depreciation, $3,750; 1988 depreciation, $7,700	E13–14 Jan. 4 (a) transaction, dividends payable to preferred, $300,000
P9–5A	Proceeds February 28, $4,014.41; Cash paid for dishonored note, $4,065.67	P11–3A Gain on sale, $12,000	P13–1A (3) Total paid-in capital, $397,100
P9–6A	Effective rates: At prime +1 = 14%; for discount = 13.86%	P11–4A (1) Cost assigned to new press, $88,875	P13–2A (4) Total paid-in capital, $1,748,100
P9–7A	Average collection periods: 1983, 76.29 days; 1982, 79.58 days	P11–5A (1) $3,900,000	P13–3A (2) Total paid-in capital, $123,000
P9–1B	(2) Account balance, December 31, 1988, $28,600	P11–6A (2) 1984, 1.79; 1983, 1.98	P13–4A (g) Dividends payable to common stockholders, $2,445
P9–2B	(3) Total accounts receivable, December 10, $60,720	P11–7A (1) January 1 debit, $31,592.35	P13–5A Part I (1) Book value per share of common, $7.92
P9–3B	(3) Bad debts expense, $3,852.98	P11–1B (2) Building, $4,500; Production equipment, $160,000; Cleaning equipment, $50,400	(2) Book value per share of common, $7.32
P9–4B	Interest expense recognized on December 31, $1,424	P11–2B 1985 depreciation, $7,500; 1988 depreciation, $15,400	Part II (1) Primary EPS, $279
P9–5B	Proceeds April 30, $10,023.75; Cash paid for dishonored note, $10,137	P11–3B Loss on sale, $6,250	(2) Fully diluted EPS, $2.83 (would not disclose because it is larger than primary EPS)
P9–6B	Effective rates: At prime + 1 = 13%; for discount = 12.69%	P11–4B (1) Cost assigned to new press, $171,750	P13–7A Total stockholders' equity, $1,445,000
P9–7B	1983, 2.83%; 1982, 3.23%	P11–5B (1) $3,937,500	P13–1B (3) Total paid-in capital, $380,000
Chapter 10		P11–6B (2) 1983, 4.89; 1984, 3.93	P13–2B (4) Total paid-in capital, $925,600
E10–1	Gross margin on sales, $26,000	P11–7B (1) January 1 debit, $109,359.06	P13–3B (2) Total paid-in capital, $1,107,200
E10–2	Inventory valuation, $525; Cost of goods sold, $486	**Chapter 12**	P13–4B (g) Dividends payable to common stockholders, $5,845
E10–3	Inventory valuation, $331.50; Cost of goods sold, $754.50	E12–1 Total assets, $63,000; J. Rockford, Capital, $62,000	P13–5B Part I (1) Book value per share of common, $8.96
E10–4	Ending inventory FIFO, $19,500; LIFO, $17,550	E12–2 Ending capital, $66,000	(2) Book value per share of common, $8.10
E10–5	Inventory valuation, $489.90; Cost of goods sold, $930.10	E12–3 Credit to: Barnes, Capital, $164,320; Strong, Capital, $42,000	Part II (1) Primary EPS, $3.53
E10–6	Inventory valuation, $612	E12–4 Credit to: David, Capital, $39,500; Hills, Capital, $34,100	(2) Fully diluted EPS, $3.16
E10–7	Estimated loss, $115,176	E12–5 Jan. 1, 1987—credit to: Wang, Capital, $31,000; Ding, Capital, $43,080	P13–7B Total stockholders' equity, $1,632,500
E10–8	Estimated inventory valuations: (a) $665,340; (b) $660,300	E12–6 Capital balances: Ormand, $67,000; Peters $59,000; Queens, $65,000	**Chapter 14**
E10–9	Unit, $3,950; class, $4,200, total, $4,250	E12–7 Dec. 31, 1987 capital balances: Hickson, $11,650; Sipps, $100	E14–1 (a) Discount
E10–10	Loss from inventory shrinkage, $2,721.25	E12–8 Credit to: Lloyd, Capital, $88,000; Minton, Capital, $20,000	(b) Premium
E10–11	Turnover: 1987, 6.0; 1986, 4.0	E12–9 Debit to Leuter, Capital; credit to Melson, Capital	E14–2 Bond Interest Expense for 1987 has a balance of $120,000
P10–1A	Net income, $47,224	E12–10 Dec. 31, 1987 balance in Petrocelli, Capital, $202,340	E14–3 (a) $315,000
P10–2A	Ending inventory: FIFO, $687.50; LIFO, $500.00; average, $587.50	P12–1A Paul, Capital, Dec. 31, 1987, $20,740	(c) $611,400
P10–3A	Cost of goods sold: FIFO, $3,124.00; LIFO, $3,121.00; average, $3,123.40	P12–2A Credit to Condon, Capital, $77,372	(f) $210,715
P10–4A	LCM by item, $23,235; by category, $24,090; by inventory total, $24,610	P12–3A Credit to Turner, Capital (1) $12,000; (2) $15,000; (3) $46,000; (4) $24,700	E14–4 (4) Balance of Bond Interest Expense account, $156,000
P10–5A	(1) $173,058; (2) $43,807.50; (3) $44,025	P12–4A Capital balances Dec. 31, 1987: Walters, $82,760; Winston, $72,240	E14–5 (2) On June 30, 1988, Discount on Bonds Payable is credited for $4,634.20
P10–6A	(1) 3.6 times; (2) 1983, 79.8%; 1982, 66.9%	P12–5A Net income to: Gleem, $8,280; Hooter, $15,720	E14–6 (3) On July 1, 1988, Bond Interest Expense is debited for $43,392.80
P10–7A	Net income: FIFO, $55,264; LIFO, $53,344; average, $54,658	P12–6A Income distribution to each partner, $18,000	E14–7 On Dec. 31, 1988, Premium on Bonds Payable is debited for $130
P10–1B	Net income, $145,350	P12–1B Hawk, Capital, Dec. 31, 1987, $15,560	E14–8 (a) Cash received, $282,113.09
P10–2B	Ending inventory: FIFO, $16,087.50; LIFO, $13,000.00; average, $14,769.06	P12–2B Credit to Song, Capital, $74,483	(b) Cash received, $891,759.58
		P12–3B Credit to Barnard, Capital (1) $9,200; (2) $10,800; (3) $57,500; (4) $35,300	(c) Cash received, $721,454.63
P10–3B	Cost of goods sold: FIFO, $2,910.00; LIFO, $2,925.00; average, $2,913.00	P12–4B Capital balances December 31, 1987; Barbara, $119,015; Merton, $85,735	(d) Cash received, $527,546.25
P10–4B	LCM by item, $11,955.00; by category, $12,404.40; by inventory total, $12,767.40	P12–5B Net income to: Glenn, $27,200; Greer, $32,800	E14–9 (2) 20,000 shares of common stock are issued
P10–5B	(1) $86,697; (2) $87,615; (3) $87,824	P12–6B Loss distribution to each partner, $40,000	E14–10 (2) On Jan. 1, 1997, Bond Sinking Fund is credited for $500,000
P10–6B	(1) 4.1 times; (2) 1983, 78.3%; 1982, 108.8%	**Chapter 13**	E14–11 Original proceeds of bond issue, $240,000
P10–7B	(1) 1987 net income understated by $120,000	E13–1 (c) Credit to Paid-in Capital—Excess over Stated Value, Common $25,500	E14–12 Loss on retirement of bonds, $3,000
Chapter 11		E13–2 For transaction d, credit to Paid-in Capital—Excess over Par Value, Common, $14,400	P14–1A At end of 1987, the Bond Interest Expense account had a balance of $73,725.49
E11–2	$23,150	E13–3 For Sept. 16, 1987, credit to Paid-in Capital—Excess over Par Value, Preferred, $2,000	P14–2A (2) Carrying value on Dec. 31, 1987, $842,938.80; Carrying value on June 30, 1986, $841,729.82
E11–3	Debit to Factory Building, $278,000	E13–4 Total paid-in capital, $932,000	P14–3A The Bond Interest Expense account at the end of 1987 is $77,000
E11–4	(a) $170,000; (b) $375,000; (c) $320,000; (d) $163,200	E13–5 Aug. 20 transaction, debit to Organization Costs, $16,000	P14–4A (1) Bond Interest Expense for 1988, $6,100
E11–5	1988 expense: (a) $24,500; (b) $42,166.66; (c) $51,763.33	E13–6 (2) Total stockholders' equity, $214,000	(2) Cash proceeds, $495,000
E11–6	Revised rate, $4,375 per year	E13–7 (a) Decrease	(3) Gain on retirement of bonds payable, $2,500
E11–7	Gain on sale, $6,500	(b) No effect	P14–5A (1) Issue price, $644,160.65
E11–8	(2a) Cost price of new truck, $19,000; (2b) Loss on disposal, $1,500	E13–8 (e) Amount of dividends, $12,075	P14–6A (1b) Original issue price, $37,660
E11–9	$572,250	E13–10 Primary EPS, $1.41	P14–1B At end of 1987, the Bond Interest Expense account had a balance of $83,470.59
E11–10	1987, $2,000; 1988, $3,000	E13–11 (1) Book value per common share, $7.00	P14–2B (2) Carrying value on Dec. 31, 1987, $525,838.98 Carrying value on June 30, 1988, $525,147.71
E11–11	1987, $2,400; 1988, $4,800	(2) Book value per common share, $6.60	P14–3B The Bond Interest Expense balance at end of 1987 is $47,333.34
			P14–4B (1) Bond Interest Expense for 1988, $9,150

Check List of Key Figures for Exercises and Problems

	(2)	Cash proceeds, $742,500
	(3)	Gain on retirement of bonds payable, $11,250
P14–5B	(1)	Issue price, $371,905.57
P14–6B	(1b)	Original issue price, $151,810

Chapter 15

E15–1	(2) Investments in Bonds-Taylor Company, $184,636
E15–2	Realized gain on disposal, $1,140
E15–3	The Dec. 31, 1988 debit to Allowance to Reduce Temporary Investments in Equity Securities to Market is $26,437.50
E15–4	Balance in Dividends Earned account at end of year, $27,000
E15–5	Dec. 31, 1987, balance in Bond Interest Earned, $59,200
E15–6	Dec. 31, 1987, balance in Bond Interest Earned, $60,400
E15–7	(1) Total dividends earned for *two* years, $4,320 (2) In 1987 a credit is made to Investor's Share of Investee Income for $25,200
E15–8	In 1987 a credit is made to Investor's Share of Investee Income for $20,000
E15–9	Cost of original investment, $318,000
E15–10	The amortization of premium element for period ending June 30, 1988 is $414.76
E15–11	On Dec. 31, 1987, a debit is made to Investment in Bonds for $990
E15–12	(1) A credit made to Investment in Bonds on Dec. 31, 1987, for $3,305.12
E15–13	On Dec. 31, 1988, the Allowance to Reduce Noncurrent Marketable Equity Investments to Market is credited for $1,120
E15–14	(a) Number of times bond interest is earned, 11.26
P15–1A	On Aug. 15, 1987, the realized gain is $119.25
P15–2A	(1) On Dec. 31, 1988, Allowance to Reduce Temporary Investments in Equity Securities to Market is debited for $1,750
P15–3A	On December 31, 1987, the 11,500 remaining shares had a cost of $357,500
P15–4A	Balance in Investment account at end of 1991, $404,791.67
P15–5A	(1) Interest revenue for 1987 is $24,726.49
P15–6A	(2) Interest revenue for 1987 is $25,720.85
	Bond interest earned for 1987 is $95,838.60
P15–1B	On Aug. 15, 1987, the realized gain is $475.50
P15–2B	(1) On Dec. 31, 1988, Allowance to Reduce Temporary Investments in Equity Securities to Market is debited for $900
P15–3B	On Dec. 31, 1987, the 3,400 remaining shares had a cost of $52,800
P15–4B	Balance in Investment account at end of 1991, $26,437.50
P15–5B	(1) Interest revenue for fiscal year ending March 31, 1988 is 106,679.94 (2) Interest revenue for fiscal year ending March 31, 1988, is $110,868.79
P15–6B	Bond interest earned for 1987 is $38,053.53

Chapter 16

E16–1	Investor's share of investee income, $82,800
E16–3	Common stock, $1,150,000
E16–4	Eliminate item b and corresponding receivable, $141,000 of intercompany sales and purchases, and $34,500 of intercompany accounts receivable and payable
E16–5	$6,240
E16–7	Consolidated total assets, $540,530
E16–8	Amount assigned to goodwill, $500,000
E16–9	German mark today, $0.3584; year ago, 0.3968
E16–10	Translation loss, $6,753.93
P16–1A	Consolidated amounts: Common stock, $500,000; Paid-in excess, $623,200; Retained earnings, $311,520
P16–2A	Elimination debits, $58,150 and $75,000
P16–3A	Consolidated net income, $311,500
P16–4A	Consolidated net income, $78,000
P16–5A	Operating revenues as percent of total: hospitals, 70.0%; dialysis, 26.0%; home health services, 4.0%
P16–6A	(2) Loss, $23,076.93
P16–1B	Consolidated amounts: Common stock, $250,000; Paid-in excess, $311,600; Retained earnings, $155,760
P16–2B	Elimination debits, $29,075 and $37,500
P16–3B	Consolidated net income, $404,950
P16–4B	Consolidated net income, $66,300
P16–5B	1982 loss from discontinued segment was about 6.8% of final net income; 1984 extraordinary item about 6.7% of net income
P16–6B	(2) Gain, $892.86

Chapter 17

E17–2	4, Part of 5, and 8
E17–3	Working capital provided by operations, $73,500
E17–4	(1) Original cost of machinery sold, $70,000; proceeds from sale, $9,500
E17–5	(c) Source, $185,000 (e) Use, $50,850
E17–6	(a) New equipment purchased, $70,000 (e) Net income for year, $4,000 (g) Dollar amount increase to Common Stock, $1,000
E17–7	Total sources of financial resources, $137,975; total uses, $119,475
E17–8	Total sources of financial resources, $279,625; total uses, $178,750
E17–9	Cash received, $82,100
E17–10	Cash paid, $151,580
E17–11	Cash generated by operations, $12,715
E17–12	Sources of cash, $548,000; uses, $435,000
P17–1A	Sources of financial resources, $196,000; uses, $269,500
P17–2A	Sources of financial resources, $276,000; uses, $401,250
P17–3A	Sources of financial resources, $143,250; uses, $107,250.
P17–4A	Sources of financial resources, $50,050; uses, $38,500
P17–5A	Sources of cash, $249,000; uses, $265,500
P17–1B	Sources of financial resources, $372,000; uses, $339,000
P17–2B	Sources of financial resources, $138,000; uses, $200,625
P17–3B	Sources of financial resources, $71,625; uses, $53,625
P17–4B	Sources of financial resources, $80,100; uses, $77,000
P17–5B	Sources of cash, $498,000; uses, $531,000

INTERNAL CONTROL PRINCIPLES AND TECHNIQUES

Definition
A self-policing interaction of the organizational structure of a business with the accounting system that helps prevent errors, helps prevent misappropriation of assets, and establishes responsibility for business actions.

Principles

☐ Employees should be carefully selected and adequately trained, and their duties, responsibilities, and authority should be clearly defined.

☐ Separation of duties should exist so that no one person is in complete charge of any single business transaction.

☐ The flow of documents and recording of transactions should be organized so that, wherever possible, the work of one employee is subject to automatic verification by another.

☐ All documents used should be prenumbered.

☐ All transactions should be properly authorized.

☐ Periodic inspections should be made to verify that the prescribed accounting system and internal control procedures are operating effectively.

TECHNIQUES

Cash (Chapter 8)

☐ Receipts should be deposited intact daily and all payments should be made by check.

☐ Management must properly authorize disbursements.

☐ The bank statement should be reconciled monthly.

Receivables (Chapter 9)

☐ Statements of account should be checked and mailed by persons who do not make entries into the subsidiary ledger.

☐ Delinquent accounts should be reviewed periodically.

☐ Recording of returns and allowances and bad debt write-offs should be authorized by a supervisor.

☐ Written procedures should exist for the receipt, recording, storage, and endorsement of notes.

☐ Unannounced examinations of notes receivable records and comparison with the actual file of notes should be made.